Crime Prevention and Justice in 2030

Helmut Kury • Sławomir Redo
Editors

Crime Prevention and Justice in 2030

The UN and the Universal Declaration of Human Rights

Springer

Editors
Helmut Kury
Max Planck-Institute for Foreign
and International Penal Law
Freiburg, Germany

Sławomir Redo
Wien, Austria

ISBN 978-3-030-56226-7 ISBN 978-3-030-56227-4 (eBook)
https://doi.org/10.1007/978-3-030-56227-4

This Springer imprint is published by the registered company Springer Nature Switzerland AG.
The registered company address is: Gewerbestrasse 11, 6330 Cham, Switzerland

Ho-o Raigi (The Holy Birds)
Photo/Jolanta Redo
"*The Holy Birds will only descend to earth when there is peace and justice in the world.*" Sagenji Yoshida (1925–1999).

The painting is based on one of the five sacred scriptures of ancient Chinese Reiki philosophy. This painting was donated in 1996 to the United Nations Office at Vienna (Austria) by the Asia Crime Prevention Foundation whose Chairman Minoru Shikita was earlier the Chief of the United Nations Crime Prevention and Criminal Justice Branch (1982–1986). The painting invites the visitors to the Vienna International Center to participate in the goal that is at the heart of all the United Nations' striving: Peace.

In Honour of the United Nations

Foreword

The year 2020 marks the seventy-fifth anniversary of the founding of the United Nations and the fifth year of the implementation of the 2030 Sustainable Development Agenda.

This book is a timely contribution to the United Nations–related literature regarding three major issues: overcoming grinding poverty; healing and securing our planet; and establishing human rights, the rule-of-law, and universal peace and freedoms. The academic perspectives presented in this book celebrate the accomplishments of the United Nations and point to the future challenges it must address. The authors explore new ideas and potential solutions to the challenges of our troubled world.

I would recommend this collection of essays to anyone interested in international approaches to contemporary political, legal, and social discourses.

Brigitte Bierlein
Former Chancellor of Austria (2019–2020)
Former President of the Austrian Constitutional Court (2018–2019)

Vienna, Austria — Brigitte Bierlein

Austrian Constitutional Court, Vienna,
Austria

Foreword

Solidarity is a necessary word to implement the United Nations 2030 Agenda through global partnership for sustainable development. It facilitates an intensive global engagement in support of implementation of all its goals and targets, bringing together governments, the private sector, civil society, the United Nations System and other actors, and mobilizing all available resources. Solidarity is a holy word for me. In its spirit I desire its global strengthening. Solidarity is especially needed with the poorest and with people in vulnerable situations. It requires the participation of all countries, all stakeholders and all people. Solidarity is also the guarantee of peace and justice in the world. This book about human rights in the light of the 2030 Agenda, whose valours I appreciate highly, is a contribution to the effort for larger freedom for the succeeding generations pledged by the United Nations Charter.

Lech Wałęsa
Co-founder and First Chairman of "Solidarność" Independent Self-Governing Trade Union
President of the Republic of Poland (1990–1995)
Laurate of the Nobel Peace Prize (1983)

Lech Wałęsa

Contents

Editors and Contributors

About the Editors

Helmut Kury Prof. h.c. mult., Dr., Dipl.-Psych., studied Psychology at the University of Freiburg (Freiburg im Brsg., Germany), diploma, Dr. in Psychology and Habilitation at the University of Freiburg. Between 1970 and 1973, he was an assistant teacher at the University of Freiburg, Institute for Psychology, between 1973 and 1980 and from 1989 to 2006, senior researcher at the Max-Planck-Institute for Foreign and International Penal Law in Freiburg im Brsg., Department of Criminology; 1980–1988 first and founding director of the Criminological Research Institute of Lower Saxony – KFN. His research areas include offender rehabilitation, crime prevention, attitudes to punishment, fear of crime, punitiveness, alternatives to punishment, diversion, methodological problems of empirical social science research, international comparison of crime and punishment. He cooperated with many universities and research institutes internationally, especially with countries of the former Soviet Union. His most recent publications in English are: Kury, H., Ferdinand, T.N. (Eds.) (2008). *International Perspectives on Punitivity.* Bochum: Universitätsverlag Dr. Brockmeyer; Kury, H. (Ed.) (2008). *Fear of Crime – Punitivity. New Developments in Theory and Research.* Bochum: Universitätsverlag Dr. Brockmeyer; Kury, H., Shea, E. (Eds.) (2011). *Punitivity – International Developments.* 3 Vols., Bochum: Universitätsverlag Dr. Brockmeyer; Kury, H., Redo, S., Shea, E. (Eds.)

(2016). *Women and Children as Victims and Offenders: Background, Prevention, Reintegration. Suggestions for Succeeding Generations.* 2 Vols., International Publishing Switzerland: Springer; Kury, H., Kuhlmann, A. (2016). *Mediation in Germany and Other Western Countries*. Kriminolgijos Studijos 4, 2016, 5–46; Kury, H. (2017). *Harsh Punishment or Alternatives: Which Is the Better Crime Prevention*. Juricia international, University of Tartu, 15, 91–99; Kury, H., Glonti, G. (2017). *Migration in Germany and Georgia (Comparative Analyses)*. Davit Aghmashnenebeli University of Georgia Academic Journal 1, 6–13; Kury, H. (2018). *Rehabilitation in Prison. German Experiences and What Can Be Done Better*. Rom. Journ. of Sociological Studies, New Series, Bucharest, No. 1, 19–36; Kury, H. (2018). *Integration of Refugees in Germany – Has the Criminal Burden Increased. Criminology: Yesterday, Today, Tomorrow - The Journal of St. Petersburg International Criminology Club* 1, 48, 37–45; Kury, H., Redo, S. (Eds.) (2018). *Refugees and Migrants in Law and Policy. Challenges and Opportunities for Global Civic Education*. International Publishing Switzerland: Springer; Kuhlmann, A., Kury, H. (2018). *Some Considerations of Restorative Justice Before and Outside of Contemporary Western States*. Kriminologijos studijos – Criminological Studies, Vilniaus Universitetas, 5, 5–42; Kury, H. (2019). *Refugees: Post Traumatic Stress, and Crime – Experiences from Germany*. Kultura i Edukacja – Culture and Education 124, 73–90; Kury, H., Kuhlmann, A., Quintas, J. (2019). *On the Preventative Effect of Sanctions for Drug Crime: The United States, Germany and Portugal*. Archiwum Kryminologii, Polska Akademia Nauk, Instytut Nauk Prawnych, 41, 261–295. E-mail: helmut.kury@web.de.

Sławomir Redo Dr. hab. (Law/Criminology) is a Visiting Professor of United Nations Law. He is a member of the United Nations Studies Association. Former United Nations Senior Crime Prevention and Criminal Justice Expert and staff of the UN Office on Drugs and Crime (ret.). He had been involved in numerous projects implementing the UN standards and norms in crime prevention and criminal justice. In other capacities, he assisted in the implementation of the United Nations Convention against Transnational Organized Crime, and on-line international crime prevention and criminal justice education. He published four books, co-edited four others, including *Women and Children as Victims and Offenders: Background, Prevention, Reintegration. Suggestions for Succeeding Generations* (Springer 2016), and *Refugees and Migrants in Law and Policy – Challenges and Opportunities for Global Civic Education* (Springer 2018) plus about 80 articles—mostly on the UN law and practice of crime prevention and criminal justice. University course lecturer on "The United Nations and Crime Prevention" & "The United Nations and War Crime Prevention" (Austria, China, Poland); Promoter of crime prevention & criminal justice training and education for meeting the goals of the 2030 UN Sustainable Development Agenda. Co-editor of the first criminological UN Agenda-based textbook *KRYMINOLOGIA. Stan i perspektywy rozwoju z uwzględnieniem założeń Agendy ONZ na rzecz zrównoważonego rozwoju 2030* (Wolters Kluwer, Warsaw 2020). E-mail: s@redo.net.

Contributors

Shankar Prakash Alagesan University of Madras, Department of Criminology, Chennai, India

Mehrdad Rayejian Asli Department of Law, Research Center for Study and Development of Humanities, Tehran, Islamic Republic of Iran

Tina L. Bertrand McMurry University, Department of Political Science, Abeline, TX, USA

Aneta Breczko University of Białystok, Faculty of Law, Department of Theory and Philosophy of Law, Białystok, Poland

Anastasia Chalkia National and Kapodistrian University of Athens, Athens, Greece

Yvon Dandurand University of the Fraser Valley, School of Criminology and Criminal Justice, Abbotsford, BC, Canada
International Centre for Criminal Law Reform and Criminal Justice Policy, Vancouver, BC, Canada

Pedro R. David Argentine John F. Kennedy University, Law School, Buenos Aires, Argentina

Maciej Duda University of Warmia and Mazury in Olsztyn, Faculty of Law and Administration, Department of Criminology and Forensic Science, Olsztyn, Poland

Maximilian Edelbacher Vienna University Department of Sociology, Vienna, Austria

Alistair D. Edgar Wilfrid Laurier University, Balsillie School of International Affairs, School of International Policy and Governance, Waterloo, ON, Canada

Wojciech Filipkowski University of Białystok, Faculty of Law, Department of Criminal Law and Criminology, Forensic Laboratory, Białystok, Poland

Friedrich Forsthuber Regional Criminal Court of Vienna, Vienna, Austria

Ewa M. Guzik-Makaruk University of Białystok, Faculty of Law, Department of Criminal Law, Białystok, Poland

Romy Heße Remchingen, Germany

Christopher Inkpen RTI International, Division for Applied Justice Research, Durham, NC, USA

Jessica Jahn International Centre for Criminal Law Reform and Criminal Justice Policy, Vancouver, BC, Canada

J. Maria Agnes Sasitha Department of Sociology and the Gender Centre, Stella Maris College, Chennai, India

Emilia Jurgielewicz-Delegacz University of Białystok, Faculty of Law, Department of Criminal Law and Criminology, Białystok, Poland

Susanne Karstedt Griffith University, School of Criminology and Criminal Justice, Mt Gravatt, QLD, Australia

Izabela Kraśnicka University of Białystok, Faculty of Law, Department of Public International and European Law, Białystok, Poland

Peter C. Kratcoski Kent State University, Kent, OH, USA

Manu Krishan Global Campus of Human Rights, Venice, Italy

Helmut Kury Max Planck-Institute for Foreign and International Penal Law, Freiburg, Germany

Pamela Lattimore RTI International, Division for Applied Justice Research, Durham, NC, USA

Chris E. Marshall University of Nebraska-Omaha, Omaha, NE, USA

Ineke Haen Marshall Northeastern University, Boston, MA, USA

Srinivasan Murugesan University of Madras, Department of Criminology, Chennai, India

Joanna Narodowska University of Warmia and Mazury in Olsztyn, Faculty of Law and Administration, Department of Criminology and Forensic Science, Olsztyn, Poland

Manfred Nowak Global Campus of Human Rights, Venice, Italy
Vienna University, Vienna, Austria

Wayne Pitts RTI International, Division for Applied Justice Research, Durham, NC, USA

Michael Platzer Coalition of Faith-Based Organizations for Crime Prevention and Criminal Justice, Vienna, Austria

Emil W. Pływaczewski University of Białystok, Faculty of Law, Department of Criminal Law and Criminology, Białystok, Poland

Wiesław Pływaczewski University of Warmia and Mazury in Olsztyn, Faculty of Law and Administration, Department of Criminology and Forensic Science, Olsztyn, Poland

Jeff Readman Innovation Consultant, Brighton, UK

Sławomir Redo United Nations Studies Association, Wien, Austria

Karol Rutkowski Institute of Justology, Warsaw, Poland

Krzysztof Sawicki University of Białystok, Faculty of Education, Białystok, Poland

Toine Spapens Tilburg University, Tilburg, The Netherlands

Julia Stepnowska University of Gdańsk, Gdańsk, Poland

Riaz Tejani University of Redlands, School of Business, Redlands, CA, USA

Jebamalai Vinanchiarachi Knowledge Management Associates, Vienna, Austria

Irvin Waller University of Ottawa, Ottawa, ON, Canada

Thomas G. Walsh Universal Peace Federation, New York, NY, USA

Rob White University of Tasmania, School of Social Sciences, Hobart, TAS, Australia

Inez Wijngaarde UNIDO Consultant, Vienna, Austria

Candence Wills Northeastern University, Boston, MA, USA

Hanming Xu Zhongnan University of Economics and Law, Research Center for Rule of Law Development and Judicial Reform, Wuhan, China

Kamil Zeidler University of Gdańsk, Faculty of Law and Administration, Department of Theory and Philosophy of State and Law, Gdańsk, Poland

Ying-Jun Zhang South-Central University for Nationalities, Law Faculty, Wuhan, China

Ling Zhou Zhongnan University of Economics and Law, Criminal Justice School, Wuhan, China

Abbreviations

AHTA	Anti-Human Trafficking Act
AI	Artificial Intelligence
AML/CFT	Anti-Money Laundering/Counter-Terrrorism Financing
AoC	Alliance of Civilizations
BBNJ	Marine Biodiversity of Areas Beyond National Jurisdiction
BIM	The Ludwig Bolzman Institute of Human Rights
CITES	Convention on International Trade in Endangered Species of Wild Fauna and Flora
COVID-19	Coronavirus disease 2019
CRPD	Convention on the Rights of Persons with Disabilities
DELC	Division of International Law and Conventions
DNA	Deoxyribonucleic Acid
E4J	Education for Justice
EC	European Commission
ECHR	European Court of Human Rights
ECOSOC	Economic and Social Council
EIUC	European Inter University Centre for Human Rights and Democratization
EU	European Union
FATF	Financial Action Task Force
FBI	Federal Bureau of Investigation
FBO	Faith-based Organizations
FDA	Fight against Drugs
GA	General Assembly
HCHR	High Commissioner for Human Rights
HRC	Human Rights Committee
ICCPR	International Covenant on Civil and Political Rights
ICCWC	International Consortium Combating Wildlife Crime
IOM	International Organisation for Migration
IPC	Islamic Penal Code

ISRD	International Self-Report Delinquency Study
IUCN	The International Union for Conservation of Nature
LAPOP	Latin American Public Opinion Project
MDGs	Millennium Development Goals
MEA	Multilateral Environmental Agreements
MSWM	Municipal Solid Waste Management
NGO	Non-governmental Organization
NHRI	National Human Rights Institutions
NPM	National Preventive Mechanism
OECD	Organization for Economic Cooperation and Development
OHCHR	Office of High Commissioner for Human Rights
R2P	Responsibility to Protect
RCT	Random Controlled Trials
RJ	Restorative Justice
SARS-CoV-2	Severe acute respiratory syndrome coronavirus 2
SD	Sustainable Development
SDGs	Sustainable Development Goals
SHERLOCK	Sharing Electronic Resources on Laws and Crime
UDHR	Universal Declaration of Human Rights
UN	United Nations
UNDP	United Nations Development Programme
UNEP	United Nations Environmental Programme
UNESCO	United Nations Scientific, Educational and Cultural Organization
UNFPA	United Nations Fund for Population Activities
UNHCHR	United Nations High Commissioner for Human Rights
UNICEF	United Nations Children's Emergency Fund
UNICRI	Interregional Crime and Justice Research Institute
UNIDO	United Nations Industrial Development Organization
UNODC	United Nations Office on Drugs and Crime
UNSDGs	United Nations Sustainable Development Goals
UNTS	United Nations Treaty Series
WHO	World Health Organization
WVS	World Values Survey

Prologue

Helmut Kury and Sławomir Redo

Abstract This introductory part of the book addresses the post-Second World War developments in democracy whose instrumental background emerged in 1945 with the United Nations Charter in 2020—the year of the 75th anniversary of the establishment of the United Nations—two United Nations declarations are particularly symbolic: the 1948 The Universal Declaration of Human Rights and the 2030 United Nations Sustainable Development Agenda. Within this frame, in the Prologue we first look into dynamics of democratic developments across the world and find that available data and the accounts of these developments are at best mixed, if not ambiguous or disconcerting.

Against this background, we then introduce the contributions to this book. Its essence may rectify the ambiguities and help to chart the way to make in the United Nations academic terms the human rights, crime prevention and criminal justice a springboard for meeting the challenges prompted by a powerful populistic counter-democratic trend. However strong it may be, of universal significance is not it, but the global aging of humankind, climate change, environmental degradation and migration. It is this broader framework, confounded by the coronavirus pandemic, in which the texts in this book should be read, contemplated and inspire the readership for joint action to attain the goals of the 2030 Agenda.

Keywords Children · Crime prevention · Criminal justice · Climate change · Democracy · Education · Elderly · Exclusion · Human rights · Inclusive societies · Migration · Nationalism · Poverty · Populism · Rule of law · Sustainable development · Victims · Violence · War · United Nations

H. Kury (✉)
Max Planck-Institute for Foreign and International Penal Law, Freiburg, Germany

Criminological Research Institute of Lower Saxony, Hannover, Germany
e-mail: helmut.kury@web.de

S. Redo
United Nations Studies Association, Wien, Austria
e-mail: s@redo.net

H. Kury, S. Redo (eds.), *Crime Prevention and Justice in 2030*,
https://doi.org/10.1007/978-3-030-56227-4_1

In 2020—the year of the 75th anniversary of the establishment of the United Nations—two United Nations declarations are particularly symbolic: the 1948 Universal Declaration of Human Rights (UDHR)—of which the *travaux préparatoires* (Schabas 2013) and academic accounts of the legislative background (Morsink 1999, 2009, 2017) offer an incisive and painstaking effort of its drafters to overcome essential hurdles in crafting and adopting it—and the 2030 United Nations Sustainable Development Agenda (A/RES/70/1). Within this frame, the book conspicuously follows Sir Winston Churchill's (1874–1965) maxim: "The farther backward you can look, the farther in the future you are likely to see." He also should be credited for the following statement: "Contemplate that if Hitler falls into our hands we shall certainly put him to death... This man is the mainspring of evil. Instrument – electric chair, for gangsters" (CAB 1951).

In the above context, this book presents secular and non-secular aspects of crime prevention and justice until 2030 and beyond. This book was developed in full awareness of dramatic population shifts (migration/aging), climate change, impressive technology information developments, including artificial intelligence, but also mass digital surveillance. In one way or another, they call into question universal ethics and morality—"conscience of humankind" and "larger freedom"—both of which have emerged from the ashes of the Second World War. They still prompt identity crisis in societies undergoing change in their ethnic make-up, including xenophobia and hate crime. But they should also prompt pangs of conscience because such manifestations counter the spirit and letter with which the United Nations adopted the United Nations Charter, the UDHR, and the 2030 Agenda.

The United Nations is uniquely predisposed to revive the essential messages originally communicated through its Charter and other foundational instruments, thus show why do we need the Organization nowadays to have a better world, rather than to hear from politicians that it will come only when and if someone will be re-elected. The book through its authors, topics, and arguments advanced through empirical findings, documents what the Organization did and still should do to change the world that has been in the twenty-first century so critically globalized that feels more insecure than two-three decades ago. Reverberated identity factors, such as ethnicity, linguistic community, cultural roots, communitarian aspirations, religion, and general desire among many for a community of solidarity show that globalism and regionalism have failed to produce and retain one greater commitment, except, perhaps, for however fragile remains the post-Second World War commitment to peace. A fig-leaf role of the United Nations nowadays with its perfunctory input into the genuine implementation of the 2030 Agenda and collateral to it human rights, crime prevention, and criminal justice standards and norms is a major problem for multilateral governance in the years to come.

Whether this prognosis is right or not, victimization, crime, terrorism including, has played its role in it, for fear has a quick ear. Reported rampant corruption alone, at times of staggering proportions, gives rise to a grave concern about world's ability to successfully pursue the rule of law work, especially in the Global South countries. Their hopeless residents "vote by feet" migrating to Global North and invite there xenophobic resilience. Those who stay and are left behind, may give up their ethical standards and pursue sustainable living with crime. How secular and non-secular authorities should react to this evident discontent with the conditions of life in the South and North is in the focus of this book.

In 2019, when the UDHR still remains a huge and unfinished agenda, anxiety emerged that the world backtracks on its provisions by populist claims and actions; civil conflicts are on the rise, genocide continues, UDHR's role subsides. With some success, though, in the years 2000–2015 UDHR had been supported by the Millennium Development Goals, and in the years 2016–2030 by the United Nations Sustainable Development Agenda whose present impact remains ambiguous. Moreover, much to be desired leaves the related implementation of the United Nations crime prevention and criminal justice standards and norms-a corpus of altogether more than 2000 substantive provisions contained in ca. 60 legal instruments (UNODC 2016) that should contribute to the achievement of the Agenda's cross-cutting goal 16 "Promote peaceful and inclusive societies for sustainable development, provide access to justice for all and build effective, accountable and inclusive institutions at all levels."

The best evidence of this weakness is that since 2007, the United Nations Commission on Crime Prevention and Criminal Justice has effectively abandoned their monitoring (Redo and Platzer 2014; Redo 2012, pp. 197–198, 216). In 2018, the United States has withdrawn its membership in the Human Rights Council—another UN intergovernmental body monitoring these standards and norms. The United States and several other Member States have also withdrawn their support for the 2018 Global Compact for Safe, Orderly and Regular Migration (A/RES/73/195). Only the UN expert treaty bodies now are unreservedly and incisively seized with the selective implementation of such human rights-relevant legal instruments—the remnant of the hopeful past human rights role of the entire United Nations. Outside it, there is an exceptionally large disparity of opinions concerning human rights, criminal justice, crime prevention, and about the erosion of the rule of law.

With these disappointing facts do not coincide other available facts and figures from 1948 to 2014 on democratic developments—perhaps only because the undemocratic impact of the most recent developments could not have been more incisively assessed. Available statistical studies from that period of study, document that while in 1948 more than 763 million people lived in "democracy," in 2014 there were almost 4 billion, i.e., five times more. In 1948, there were 23 democratic countries, but 87 in 2009 (Roser 2019).[1] Moreover, since 1820 the share of people living in extreme poverty considerably dropped. More than 80% lived then in poverty, in 1948 about 70%, and 24% in 1992. Regarding the extent of extreme poverty in 1981–2010, as measured by the share of the world population living with less than 1.25 US $ per day, the respective figures were even more pronounced: 52% and 21%. Considering these figures, there is no reason for complacency. It is clear that

[1]"A democracy is a political system with institutions that allows citizens to express their political preferences, has constraints on the power of the executive, and a guarantee of civil liberties" (Roser 2014).

the trajectory of change is pointing in the right direction and the world is changing very fast right now (Roser 2014).

More recent findings seem to be more incisive. According to the authoritative World Values Surveys, from 1900 until 2016, high levels of democracy remain a distinctive feature of nations in which emancipative values have grown strong over the generations (Brunkert et al. 2019). The last survey's analysts write that, by the same token, backsliding and autocratization are limited to cultures with underdeveloped emancipative values. In line with this finding, these authors conclude that public support for democracy neither favors democratization, nor does it prevent autocratization in disjunction from emancipative values. On the contrary, public support for democracy shows such pro-democratic effects if—and only if—it co-exists in close association with emancipative values. The reason is that—in disconnect from emancipative values—support for democracy frequently reverts its meaning, indicating the exact opposite of what intuition suggests: namely, support for autocracy. In conclusion, the prospects for democracy are bleak where emancipative values remain weak. To put it more pragmatically and less contemplatively: where civil society and global civic education is underdeveloped or discouraged.

An even more incisive WVS' analysis of the implementation of SDG 16 allowed its authors to observe, that:

> [O]bstacles remain in efforts to reach many of the goal 16 targets. Crucially, when it comes to many aspects of governance, the world has experienced an overall deterioration in recent years, including: Declines in participatory engagement, related to citizen engagement in formal political processes and more informal processes. For instance, countries from every region apart from North America had declining scores on civil society participation in the last three to four years.
>
> Declines in checks on government and representative government have also occurred during the last 3–4 years. This is partly driven by recent developments in Americas and Euroasia, in countries such as Brazil, India, Hungary, Poland, Turkey, and the United States.
>
> There are particularly discouraging trends in the areas covered by target 16.10, related to public access to information and the protection of fundamental freedoms. Although many countries (125 out of 193 UN Member States) have now adopted laws guaranteeing access to information, the current data do not adequately monitor the extent to which these laws are implemented. At the same time, there is widespread evidence suggesting a growing hostility towards the media and journalists, including violence and abusive treatment. Fifty-four killings of journalists, directly attributable to their profession, were reported in 2018. Most of these remain unprosecuted.
>
> Developing countries make up 71% of intergovernmental organizations' membership, but have only 47% of the voting rights, reflecting a lack of representation and inclusive decision-making within the global community.
>
> For the second year in a row, more countries are declining than improving in overall rule of law performance.
>
> Despite some progress, most countries are failing to make serious inroads against corruption (WVS 2019).

The two latter findings look disconcerting in the time of growing populism, with corruption as its Achilles' heel. Earlier empirical findings from this recurrent project suggest that building institutional trust in civil society is pivotal to counter corruption. More specifically, anti-corruption organizations which cultivate trust not only in fellow members but the wider society in general are the successful ones. They create broader identities, democratic values, and an interest in the common good. They are more effective than civil society organizations composed of mistrusting members whose narratives about common good are narrow (Griesshaber 2013, p. 12).

It follows that the liberal part of civil society should make the Rule of Law and anti-corruption an urgent priority at the domestic level in countries undergoing populism. But "it is a pious hope for liberals to think that all they have to do is expose corruption to discredit populists. They also have to show that for the vast majority, populist corruption yields no benefits, and that a lack of democratic accountability, a dysfunctional bureaucracy, and a decline in the rule of law will in the long run hurt the people - all of them" (Műller 2017, pp. 52–53).

Save the above finding, there are two others about the changing rule-of-law picture.

First, investigations into the progress of democracy in 2006–2016 showed that some of the highly democratic countries including the USA gradually converted to moderate democratic countries. It was also observed that there exists a strong negative relation between democracy index and nonreligious population fractions for most of these countries. That is an increase of non-religious population fraction of a country may decrease the democracy index of that country (Rahman and Nahar 2017).

Second, despite that, growing economic inequality since 1992 is another troubling finding. According to the same study, the world returns to high levels of inequality of the early twentieth century (Rahman and Nahar 2017).

Many other findings suggest that while democracy continues to expand its global reach, there is a significant decline in its quality across the board, as far as checks and balances are concerned. Such ones like an independent judiciary, a free press, the ability of legislatures to apply oversight, and more are in a short supply. Their global review carried out under the umbrella of the World Justice Project (WJP) with its 2019 Rule of Law Index revealed rising authoritarianism in more countries than any other factor worldwide in comparison with 2018 (61 countries declined, 23 stayed the same, 29 improved). Over the past 4 years, Poland, Bosnia and Herzegovina, and Serbia have lost the most ground in this dimension of the rule of law (WJP 2019).

This is separately confirmed by the most recent report of the Freedom House (2020). This non-governmental organization in consultative status with the United Nations Economic and Social Council annually scores the implementation of the UDHR across the world. In these terms was assessed the group of 29 Central European and Central Asian countries stretching from Germany to China. Over the 2010–2020 period, Bosnia and Herzegovina has further lowered its standing as a "transitional hybrid regime" (the lowest tier) with Serbia and Hungary in the same tier, previously and respectively in higher tiers, i.e., "semi-consolidated democracy" and "consolidated democracy." At the same time, Poland (previously a "consolidated democracy") has just joined the group of "semi-democratic" countries. In sum, on this three-tier scale there are fewer democracies in Eurasia today than at any point since the annual report was launched in 1995. "The erosion has left citizens especially vulnerable to further rights abuses and power grabs associated with the coronavirus pandemic" (Freedom House 2020, p. 1). The Sustainable Development Goals Report (2019) adds an interregional observation regarding the enlargement of freedom:

> The pace of progress in establishing national human rights institutions [NHRIs] that are in compliance with the principles relating to the status of national institutions (the Paris Principles) must be accelerated. In 2018, only 39 per cent of all countries had successfully achieved compliance; an increase of 3 per cent (7 countries) from 2015. If growth continues at the same rate by 2030 only around half of all countries will have compliant NHRIs to ensure that States deliver on their human rights obligations (p. 55).

How many in fact will resort to them for their effective protection and enhancement in the spirit of social justice, progress for larger freedom may be seen after 2030. Clearer than ever before in contemporary time becomes difference between "thick" (expansive) and "thin" (reductionist) understanding of the rule of law (Godson 2000). The "thick" sense is less diplomatically and more opportunistically turned into a "thin" one under the guise of democratic legal reform. If one considers the important difference between "thick" and "thin" democracy, then—as of this writing—the number of "democratic" countries with its genuine observance shrinks. The so-called "illiberal democracy" with "thinner" freedom (of speech, assembly, media, the independence of judiciary, etc.) is nowadays the most prominent case in point with the rhetoric of "democracy," however contrary to "larger freedom" proclaimed in the United Nations Charter.

As if these findings and outcomes were not enough action-compelling, discussions ensued concerning whether amid the bleak prospects for genuine democracy it will be overshadowed by "liberal fascism," "illiberal democracy," "soft despotism," or some other kind of essential detour from the idea of "larger freedom." In our opinion to a sobering interpretation of the current de-constitutionalization of democracy contributes the following quote:

> The truth is that today's threats to democracy don't parallel 20th-century experiences. Fascism – as distinct from authoritarianism or racism – is not being revived: the mass mobilisation and militarisation of entire societies is not taking place; and while the hatred of vulnerable minorities is being fanned, a systemic cult of violence which glorifies mortal combat as the apotheosis of human existence is not being instituted. Nor are states being thoroughly remade on the basis of racism – which is not to deny that racial (and religious) animus, in Hungary, Brazil and the US, gets its legitimacy from the very top (Műller 2019, p. 36).

He adds: "However, even if some analogies may be in place [...] we have become extremely skilful at teaching the lessons of history, but quite bad at teaching actual history" (Műller 2019, p. 36).

The UN 2030 Agenda's draws on the tragic history of humankind in the twentieth century. It is a case in point for "thick" democracy. It should be anyone's concerned guidance in the next 10 years of its implementation. Its crosscutting goal 16, together with the Global Compact's numerous objectives, both set out the parameters according to which poverty and crime in the age of migration may and can be countered, larger freedom in sending and host countries can be pursued to help the UDHR to continue its democratizing mission.

Although goal 16 is so crosscutting, it does not address the non-secular aspects of countering crime and poverty. Neither does the entire Agenda, nor the Global Compact. Therefore, the UDHR with a number of less known than its UN follow-up legal instruments and arrangements has a particularly challenging role to settle the question of the freedom of religion within the rule of law, the latter already prioritized by the UDHR in its preamble. For in a democratic society there cannot be freedom of religion without the rule of law over it. It is this preambular arrangement that enables to pursue under the Organization's auspices social justice and equity work through the interfaith dialogue.

It is this context in which the Editors note the statement of the UN Secretary-General "I firmly believe in the power of faith leaders to shape our world for good" (UNSG 2017). Their role is growing immensely in "God's Century," because in some "Nations under God" (Toft et al. 2011; Morsink 2017) churches use moral authority to influence policy. However, in other dimensions of human development powered by biotechnology a contrasting vision of "*Homo deus*" emerges—likewise powerful.

As of this writing, the above developments are in the shadow of the coronavirus (COVID-19) pandemic which within 3 months spread to 180 countries. About 80 countries have declared some form of emergency, including at least 20 where the allegations of human rights violations were deemed most troubling (OHCHR 2020).

The Secretary-General assessed the impact of pandemic on human rights in the following words:

> The COVID-19 pandemic is a public health emergency — but it is far more. It is an economic crisis. A social crisis. And a human crisis that is fast becoming a human rights crisis [. . .] [H]uman rights cannot be an afterthought in times of crisis — and we now face the biggest international crisis in generations [. . .] The message is clear: People — and their rights — must be front and centre. A human rights lens puts everyone in the picture and ensures that no one is left behind. Human rights responses can help beat the pandemic, putting a focus on the imperative of healthcare for everyone. But they also serve as an essential warning system — highlighting who is suffering most, why, and what can be done about it. We have seen how the virus does not discriminate, but its impacts do — exposing deep weaknesses in the delivery of public services and structural inequalities that impede access to them. We must make sure they are properly addressed in the response. We see the disproportionate effects on certain communities, the rise of hate speech, the targeting of vulnerable groups, and the risks of heavy-handed security responses undermining the health response. Against the background of rising ethno-nationalism, populism, authoritarianism and a pushback against human rights in some countries, the crisis can provide a pretext to adopt repressive measures for purposes unrelated to the pandemic (UNSG 2020).

If this risk were not enough for upholding the Rule of Law globally, a growing number of the UN Member States (as of 30 April 2020 up to 69[2]) limited exports of personal protective equipment, medicines, and other medical goods. This figure

[2]See: Gonzalez (2020); CEPR (2020), p. 103.

includes 24 Member States of the European Union—nowadays a bedrock of universal values,[3] but also a region with its own cultural circle.

It would be therefore not enough here to admit the opinion of Charles Louis Baron de Secondat Montesquieu (1689–1755) who said, that "[o]ne nation should never exclude another from trading with it, except for very great reasons. . .for it is competition which sets a just value on merchandise, and establishes the relation between them" (Montesquieu 2001/The Spirit of Laws/SL XX.9) or that "[t]he spirit of trade produces in the mind of a man a certain sense of exact justice, opposite. . . to robbery" (SL XX.2).

Nowadays, one must also admit that the art of a just living by standards of the UDHR and the 2030 Agenda in this new world is more complex because of by far greater than three centuries ago global interdependence and the globalization of crime and justice issues. They are in the focus of this book in honor of the United Nations.

Rightly credited for its forming, Churchill is also credited for the saying "Never let a good crisis go to waste" (Gruère 2019). Whether the latter credit is legitimate or not, many contributions to this book convey a similar message to its readership: turn the disadvantage into advantage.

We realize that this is easier said than done. Neither the UDHR or the 2030 Agenda can revert the world in favor of fairer economy nor less invasive digital surveillance, or make people more spiritually committed to make their earthly living more sustainable and freer at the time of climate change. Whereas they complimentarily offer an entirely new paradigm to counter poverty and exclusion at the structural, interstate, state, community, and individual level, it is really up to the reader of this book in whatever capacity, to take an incisive look around themselves and see to applying these two important United Nations larger freedom tools in their native or host country, community, and family.

In this book honored by the introductions of H.E. Lech Wałęsa, Nobel Prize laurate, and H. E. Brigitte Bierlein, former President of the Constitutional Court of Austria, we may comment on the vagaries of progress in the present world, i.e., social and justice progress for larger freedom. **First**, while it is true that social progress is even decreed by the United Nations Charter in its Preamble and Art. 55, neither this progress has been or can be linear, nor it should exclusively be credited to the Organization. **Second**, while such a hopeful linear vision had indeed successfully been pursued in terms of normative developments enabling judicial review across federalist states since its 1789 US constitutional founding, it has had its upshot in the Austrian constitution of 1920, wherefrom after the Second World

[3]Although with its own cracks. This is because governmental reactions to pandemic in the European Union suggest that there are authoritarian and authoritative methods of countering it. This may be exemplified by the Swedish and Hungarian responses to pandemic—both constitutionally warranted. While in Hungary, its Prime Minister received for an unlimited time the prerogative to counter pandemic by decrees, in Sweden, detached expert guidance rather than governmental reaction yields the eventual response.

War it encouraged judicial reviews in the Federal Republic of Germany, Italy, Portugal, and Spain (Ginsburg 2008, pp. 84–85).

The tragedy of the Second World War had also motivated other formerly belligerent countries to pursue judicial reviews. In some of them, however, the ensuing from them subordination of judges to the will of parliament have later been contested. Originally it was believed, that "[d]esignated constitutional courts make a good deal of sense in new democracies where the ordinary judiciary has low status or capacity, as in post-fascist and later in post-Communist contexts" (Ginsburg 2008, p. 85). Poland and Hungary were then in the vanguard of the constitutional democratization in Europe. Both had followed the Austrian model of judicial review (Lustig and Weiler 2018, p. 320). Much later, when the autonomy of ordinary and supreme court judges has found itself under anti-liberal scrutiny and impact of newly elected parliaments of those two countries, it has become clear that judicial review and autonomy—whether in constitutional or other court matters—may as long exist as the justices meet the priorities of power holders.

This is *not* the idea which in 1789 enlightened the drafters of the US Constitution and the French Declaration of the Rights of the Man and of the Citizen, both of which prompted developments toward a tri-partite division of powers—the bedrock of democracy and the instrument of larger freedom. It was the Frenchmen Alexis de Tocqueville (1805–1859). In his "Democracy in America" (1917, Book I, ch. XV), when confronted with the argument for populist justice he said, that if the judicial independence fails under its pressure, his own solution would be to refuse to obey an unjust law: "I do not contest the right of the majority to command, but I simply appeal from the sovereignty of the people to the sovereignty of mankind."

Kermit Roosevelt's somewhat similar view suggests that "The constitution does not belong to judges, as a mystery intelligible only to a priestly caste, and it does not belong to political activists, as a set of incendiary talking points. It belongs to the people. It is our responsibility to judge the Court, and it is our judgment that must be decisive in the end" (Roosevelt 2008, p. 7). However, whether indeed both views are akin depends on two answers: **first**, whether the invoked people's sovereignty is equal to that of mankind's or is only tribal/partisan; **second**, by what kind of sovereignty ("democratic" or "republican") is guided an individual decisive judgement *vis à vis* the Rule of Law.

This book takes the reader under the narrative surface of such statements. It seeks to offer an intellectual adventure to those who may want to know more about their United Nations aspects.

In **Part I,** "Rule of Law and Realities of Life in the Context of the 2030 Justice and Crime Prevention," including three chapters, this book opens with the text by *Friedrich Forsthuber* about "Democracy – Human Rights – Rule of Law: European Developments and the Importance of an Independent Judiciary." He emphasizes that the independence of the judiciary is a major pillar of any constitutional state based on the separation of powers. "Only in a state based on the rule of law can there be a guarantee of democracy as well as an effective protection of human rights," he writes. Effective guarantees for the preservation of democracy and the rule of law can only be achieved through a broad societal consensus on the value of rule-of-law principles. Political education is not just a task for politics and the school system, but for civil society as a whole. This means political participation with free elections, free press, and independent courts. The author discusses challenges in a contemporary democratic state. In history it happened that democracy and the rule of law are trampled on, so in Germany in 1933 and the following years during the Nazi regime. *Forsthuber* differentiates between professional and personal judicial independence. "People who tend to feel left out are susceptible to manipulation by ideologies and populists, who promise simple solutions, thus reinforcing fear and xenophobia."

J. Maria Agnes Sashita presents the chapter: "Youth Perception on Hate Crimes, Hate Speeches and Nationalism in Contemporary India." Against the background of an increasing number of hate crimes in India, particularly against minority groups such as Dalits and Muslims, the author presents data about youth perceptions of hate crimes, hate speech, and ideas of nationalism. How can education impact their point of view? Sasitha argues that a new form of nationalism founded based on religious resentment among different religious groups is slowly emerging in present-day India. In this process, communalism has come to be conflated with nationalism. Results of the qualitative study show that "young people are lacking in a thorough understanding of these issues, although they do not appear to be altogether evasive of contemporary realities. This points towards the need for increased public awareness and education delivered through a critical lens, and alerts us to the dangers of overestimating the reach and influence of mass media to convey the magnitude of certain crucial issues." The UN points out clearly that hate speech signifies an attack on tolerance, inclusion, and diversity, it erodes values, and can lay the foundation for violence. Nationalism in India is now being built through arousing religious sentiments and instigating animosity against followers of various other beliefs, the author points out. In India, the concept of nationalism came about during the independence struggle. India as the second most populous country in the world after China, more than 50% of its population is below the age of 25, is characterized by more ethnic and religious groups than most other countries of the world. The author presents an overview about important literature about the topic, and the results of a survey carried out on the question of hate speech in India.

Mehrdad Rayejian Asli has written the chapter "Incorporating the United Nations Norms into Iranian Post-Revolution Criminal Policy: A Criminological-Victimological Approach." The author emphasizes that Iran has had a "diverse attitude to international norms and standards inter alia the concrete norms within the United Nations system at the domestic Post-Revolution criminal justice policy." Also today, certain concrete norms of the United Nations "have not even half a chance to draw the attention of the Islamic Republic of Iran/IRI for incorporating into its domestic legal system." IRI welcomes primarily those international standards and norms that seem to be in a lesser degree of conflict with *Shari'a*—the law of the land. Like many other countries, Iran through the history has been organized by a social system of patriarchy. The standards and norms concerned with non-discrimination and non-violence against women have not been welcomed by IRI. IRI is willing to cooperate with UN to combat narcotic drugs. Iran has not joined the Convention on the Elimination of All Forms of Discrimination Against Women.

Internationally agreed norms against violence against women seem to be opposed by IRI because of their contradiction with the recognized Islamic rules and practices on women's issues.

Part II "Leaving No One Behind: Intergenerational Vulnerability and Educating for Justice" includes seven chapters. It opens with the text from *Peter C. Kratcoski* and *Maximilian Edelbacher* on the "Perspectives on Elderly Crime and Victimization in the Future." Elderly people are an increasing part of the population worldwide. The authors discuss the current trends in criminality and victimization of the elderly. The increase in crime by the elderly "as well as the increases in the amount of criminal victimization of the elderly, are the result of both an aging population and social, economic, political, and communication changes in the world community that affect the lives of people." The authors discuss why the amount of crime committed by the elderly will continue to grow, the types of crimes committed by this part of population, and the criminal justice response to the perpetrators. Special programs help elderly victims of crime. Today, older people have more opportunities to commit crimes, they work longer before retirement. Most older people who engage in criminal activities are situational criminals. ". . . the profile of the older criminal in the year 2030 is likely to be an offender who has engaged in minor crimes, such as various forms of theft, who is poor, sometimes homeless, does not have a great number of social support groups, and may have some form of physical disability, substance abuse problem, or a psychological disability. The criminal justice response of arresting these law violators and sending them to jail for a short period has not been effective. A public health response is required."

Inez Wijgaarde, Jebamalai Vinanchiarachi, and *Jeff Readman* discuss in their chapter the topic "Universal Basic Income (UBI) for Reducing Inequalities and Increasing Socio-Economic Inclusion: A Proposal for a New *Sustained* Policy Perspective." Article 25 of the Universal Declaration of Human Rights states that "everyone has the right to a standard of living adequate for the health and well-being of himself and of his family." This provision alludes to a universal basic income. But it "has never been implemented globally through appropriate government interventions and redistributive measures." The authors point out that we are too often confronted with "fragmentary interventions that rely on market-oriented solutions to rekindle socio economic transformation without empowering the poor in the development process." The authors provide an overview of UBI with evidence of an emerging policy practice. "UBI could be a foundation policy programme to which all other interventions can build upon." The authors point out that a universal basic income's simplicity would make it an attractive alternative to welfare programs. The authors discuss evidence from country experiences and present examples from different continents. The intention of UBI is to ensure that no one will be left behind. However, UBI transfers can allow improvements in health and education levels, lower crime, and other social objectives. Poverty cannot be alleviated by charity but wealth creation. To this effect is this UBI chapter.

Helmut Kury discusses in his chapter the topic "Prisoners and their Families – The Effects of Imprisonment on the Family." The public and political debate on criminals and crime usually deals primarily and very often exclusively with the crime and the perpetrator at the time of the crime, but hardly with his development and, above all, little with his family and the impact of detention, especially imprisonment, on them. If the perpetrator still has young children, their psychological development can be significantly negatively affected by the detention of a parent, usually the father. In Germany during the last years, more and more institutions have been created to take care of the families of the detainees, but there is still a lot of work to be done. The author provides a brief overview of the national and international discussion of the topic. The empirical research clearly shows the negative effects of separating (young) children from their parents. In the case of the detention of a parent, the stigmatization of the related, especially the children, still plays an essential role. Much more should be done here, for example, through large-scale regulations on the visits of prisoners by relatives.

Helmut Kury and *Romy Heße* add in their chapter information from empirical research about "Dealing with Mental Illness and Violence in the (Youth-)Prison." The authors cite Nelson Mandela who emphasized: "It is said that no one truly knows a nation until one has been inside its jails. A nation should not be judged by how it treats its highest citizens, but its lowest ones." While there are relatively many reports and research projects on violence in prisons, the issue of mental illness of prisoners has so far played only a relatively minor role in criminology, also in public reports. Overall, the public is uninformed about the prison system, especially through the media, which usually report very selectively, especially about problems but rarely about the every-day-living-situation. In recent years, in Western countries public punitiveness has increased. People with mental health problems are significantly over-represented in prisons compared to the normal population. In particular, the suicide rate among prisoners significantly increased in this context. Due to the unfavorable living conditions and the multiplicity of inmates' problems, violence among them is also relatively high. In this context, it is difficult for the institutions to implement their real resocialization task. In many cases, incarceration contributes to a deterioration rather than an improvement in the social behavior of prisoners. The chapter discusses the background of a development of violence in prison and possibilities of prevention.

Sławomir Redo and *Krzysztof Sawicki* discuss in the text "On Nelson Mandela Rule 63, Prisoner's Moral Vulnerability and Development in the Context of the 2030 United Nations Sustainable World" the experience of prison administration across the world with the implementation of the Standard Minimum Rules for the Treatment of Prisoners Rules' provision on offenders' "wireless" (i.e., mass media) communication with the outside world (Rule 63). First, they review the *in situ* experience of prison administration. Second, they recast that experience in the context of the 2030 United Nations Sustainable Development Goals (UN SDGs) relevant to increasing crime prevention returns through civic education. The text calls on the prison administration and non-governmental organizations authorized in assisting in the rehabilitation and reintegration of ex-prisoners to pursue through training, periodicals, and special institutional publications the related SDGs' action-oriented prophylactic content, with due regard to the group-oriented and individual respective resilience or vulnerability of inmates and ex-prisoners. Throughout the chapter, its authors seek to demonstrate the interconnectedness and universality of the SDGs which altogether aspire to transform the world so "no one will be left behind," even if they stay behind prison bars, or behind others as one of the other kind of minority in an open multicultural society.

Ineke Haen Marshall, Candence Wills, and *Chris E. Marshall* present a chapter about "Parents Who Hit. Troubled Families and Children's Happiness: Do Gender and National Context Make a Difference?" They discuss the correlation of gender and national context with the happiness of children in troubled families. The 2030 UN Sustainable Development Goal 16, Target 16.2 aims at the elimination of corporal punishment of children. Violent forms of discipline against children are widespread. In 69 countries (mostly low and middle-income countries) with data from 2012 to 2019, nearly eight in ten children aged one to 14 were subjected to some form of psychological aggression and/or physical punishment at home in the previous month (E/2020, para. 24). An open question is whether girls are more or less affected by the violent family context than boys, and if the ban of corporal punishment reduced the violent family context. The authors analyzed data from Belgium, Denmark, Italy, and the USA collected among 10,000 12–16-year old adolescents, as part of the third sweep of the International Self-Report Delinquency survey (ISRD3). The survey aimed to answer the question, whether the association between troubled family life, use of violence by parents, attachment to parents, and subjective wellbeing (happiness) is different for girls than for boys, and whether it is contingent on national context. The findings suggest that gender and national context indeed do matter. The authors conclude with an expression of two concerns: about the universal implementation of Article 19 of the Convention on the Rights of the Child across different national contexts, and, likewise, about the challenge of promoting a culture of lawfulness so the children of the next generation will be happier than the present one.

Manfred Nowak and *Manu Krishan* write about "The UN Global Study on Children Deprived of Liberty – The Role of Academia in "Making the Invisible and Forgotten Visible." The authors summarize the study's findings. Although the Global Study was prepared through a concerted effort of states, non-governmental organizations, professional bodies, UN agencies, treaty bodies, special procedures and children, each research group was led by a research institute and close collaboration with academia. The chapter exemplifies the significant leading role of academia in 'making the invisible and forgotten visible' throughout the world. The Study addressed the conditions of detention by considering the personal views and experiences of children and it assessed justifications for and limits of deprivation of liberty of children in light of all relevant provisions of international law, above all, the Convention on the Rights of the Child (CRC). Finally, the study exemplified how the close cooperation between the United Nations, civil society, and academia is needed more than ever, and it confirmed the spirit of the famous opening words of the UN Charter, namely "the Peoples of the United Nations," which founded the world organization 75 years ago.

Part III is entitled "Living in Harmony with Nature: Mother Earth's Criminol ogy." It includes four texts, first a chapter by *Rob White* about the "United Nations

Initiatives in Preventing Environmental Crime." This chapter reviews the nature and dynamics of environmental crime, broad approaches to preventing crimes such as illegal fishing, and the role of United Nations agencies in responding to environmental crime. These UN responses range from collaborative interventions involving government and non-government bodies, through knowledge provision and educational initiatives. The scale of present environmental catastrophes, particularly related to the effects of climate change and the extinction of species, presents considerable institutional challenges in addressing global environmental harms. These are compounded by the political obstacles stemming from the actions and/or inactions of nation-states that impede measures needed to prevent environmental harm.

Wiesław Pływaczewski, Joanna Narodowska, and *Maciej Duda* wrote the second chapter about "Assessing the Viability of Environmental Projects for a Crime Prevention-Inspired Culture of Lawfulness." The 2030 United Nations Sustainable Development Agenda emphasizes the importance of green spaces for urban safety (SDG 11.7), sets the goal of living in harmony with nature (SDG 12.8), and pursuing sustainable lifestyles (4.7). While in the Global North countries urban planning and (pre)school education such goals are autonomously pursued by relevant local (non)-secular actors, whether in city or in countryside, hardly there is any criminological analysis, let alone reflection, which could show how this is all relevant to the Agenda's crosscutting goal 16 about promoting peaceful and inclusive societies for sustainable development. With a view to connecting these two attitudes, this chapter reviews such green city, forest, and other environmental/land projects, in terms of their assumptions, objectives, and accomplishments. Consequently, it offers a comprehensive criminological advice to local actors that may enhance those projects' effectiveness in terms of their environmental-friendly, integrative crime prevention potential, especially between native and immigrant populations.

The chapter written by *Murugesan Srinivasan* and *Alagesan Shankar Prakash* focuses on the "Actualising the Right to Adequate Standard of Living: A Critical Examination of Green Criminology from an Indian Perspective." During the last 70 years, several international instruments have been emphasizing the importance of the right to adequate standard of living. However, many of the provisions of such international instruments, particularly the right to adequate standard of living, is too far from becoming a reality. The authors of this chapter have substantiated their arguments by presenting a few case studies conducted in the city of Chennai (formerly Madras, India). The disjuncture between the provisions of the international instruments and the reality of the contemporary quality of the environment is also to some extent exposed in this contribution. It is also argued why the scope of green criminology should be widened to study the various forms of environmental crime, environmental harm, and connected issues. The authors strongly believe that understanding such issues from the perspective of green criminology would provide several benefits, including sensitizing the stakeholders.

Pedro R. David's text is entitled "Notes on the Case of Orangutan Sandra, the Non-Human Subject of Rights." The author notes that depending on religion or legal philosophy, an animal may be considered a "non-human person" whose welfare rights should be acknowledged and protected by people. Law enforcement authorities and courts address cases of treatment of animals by people, including shared by them natural habitat—"Mother Earth," to use the term of the 2030 United Nations Sustainable Development Agenda. This chapter discusses the philosophical and legal underpinnings for welfare rights of animals, prompted by the case of the retired orangutan Sandra. She became the first non-human subject of such rights, granted by a ground-breaking Argentinian jurisprudence with the first-ever court-backed her transfer to an animal sanctuary in the United States, where her relative welfare and freedom has been secured.

Part IV comprises four texts. It opens with a chapter written by *Toine Spapens* about the topic "Surveillance and the Impossible Search for Ideal Behaviour." He writes that information and communication technology and the Internet created unprecedented opportunities for collecting "big data" and apply it to surveillance and influence the behavior of citizens, for instance in their roles of voters, customers, partners, and workers. There is a growing risk that data on these different roles is exchanged and combined for purposes for which it was not collected. Surveillance may be defended from the perspective of law and order, protection of safety and health, and economic development, but it may also impact negatively on several United Nations (UN) sustainable development goals (SDGs) to be attained by 2030. Being one of the crucial issues in the world today, it comes as no surprise that the topic of surveillance is being studied by lawyers, urbanists, sociologists, computer scientists, political scientists, and others. However, criminologists have until now mainly looked at surveillance in the context of preventing and detecting crime and terrorism from a "what happens and what works" angle. *Spapens'* chapter applies a broad perspective by taking the social construction of deviance as a starting point and addressing the consequences of the definition for those who do not live up to the ideal, in terms of criminalization, social exclusion, and other potential effects, keeping in mind the context of the UN's development goals.

Aneta Breczko, Wojciech Filipkowski, and *Izabela Kraśnicka* discuss "Ethics and the Development of Artificial Intelligence – Challenges and Dilemmas in the Context of the 2030 United Nations Agenda for Sustainable Development." The chapter aims to introduce both the threats and chances involved in the artificial intelligence (AI) in the context of crime prevention as one of the elements of the Goal 16 of the 2030 Agenda for Sustainable Development: to promote peaceful and inclusive societies for sustainable development, provide access to justice for all and build effective, accountable, and inclusive institutions at all levels. Authors argue that the ethical approach toward artificial intelligence should be crucial and serve as point of departure for any further developments of AI. Analysis of the essence of the artificial intelligence, the scope of its influence on human lives and potential for the future use bring definite conclusion: technological codes and legal codes are not enough for the secured and controlled progress in the most advanced intelligence field. Ethical codes must be introduced to guarantee eliminations of threats and enjoyment of benefits provided by constantly developing artificial intelligence.

Emil W. Pływaczewski, Ewa M. Guzik Makaruk, Wojciech Filipkowski, and *Emilia Jurgielewicz-Delegacz* in the chapter "From Wonders as Crime to Forensics in Service of the 2030 United Nations Agenda" emphasize the role of Forensic Sciences in fighting crime, especially the use of genetic and polygraph tests. They point out, that "if one intends to combat … threats to sustainable development effectively, this cannot happen without supporting the development of Forensic Science." The authors present selected methods of detection, securing, and analysis of forensic traces, namely genetic tests and polygraph tests. They illustrate the development of forensic techniques and, at the same time, outline the legal problems associated with their use by the judiciary to make them more effective. The chapter points out the dilemmas we face that need to be resolved to achieve the UN 2030 Agenda goals.

Alistair D. Edgar discusses the topic of "The Rule of Law, Peacebuilding, and Agenda 2030: Lessons from the Western Balkans." He points out that "in the countries of the Western Balkans, Rule of Law deficits remain a significant obstacle to achieving the Agenda and its sustainable development goal (SDG) 16 in particular, as well as standing in the way of countries' ambitions for the EU accession." The double nature—the legal and the political dimensions—can make rule of law initiatives problematic, "since as a political project it can challenge the deeply entrenched and often closely intertwined or interdependent interests of political-economic elites and organized crime." The author points out that "rule by law can be little more than a framework used by totalitarian governments for enforcing social control, engaging in the active repression or denial of human rights, and even committing mass atrocities." As illustrated in the chapter, "in the countries of the Western Balkans, rule of law deficits remain a significant obstacle to achieving the 2030 Agenda, and SDG 16 in particular, as well as standing in the way of countries' ambitions for EU accession." This chapter briefly reviews the nature and content of rule of law in both understandings; frames rule of law within SDG16 and Agenda 2030; highlights the interconnected problems of weak rule of law, lack of political will, and organized crime in the Western Balkans; and identifies examples of good practices or paths of action to foster or strengthen rule of law as a contribution to achieving the 2030 Agenda. The situation and development in the different states are presented and discussed. A roadmap for policy and practice is finally discussed to show the way forward. Necessary actions to bring the countries forward are presented.

Part V includes five chapters on "Research & the Promotion of Peaceful and Inclusive Societies." It starts with the text from *Christopher S. Inkpen, Wayne J. Pitts,* and *Pamela Lattimore* entitled "Crime, Victimization, and Intentions to Migrate in the Northern Triangle," that is Guatemala, El Salvador, and Honduras. In this migration context, the authors discuss important topics of the Universal Declaration of Human Rights relevant to violence. The authors present and discuss empirical evidence "to measure the relationship between expressing intentions to migrate and crime, violence, and perceptions of insecurity for residents of the Northern Triangle countries of Guatemala, El Salvador, and Honduras." They point out, that the decision to migrate is complex, "with motivating factors operating at the individual, familial, community, and country level." Their study aims to examine how measures of crime and victimization relate with expressing a desire to leave one's country in the Northern Triangle, by using data from cross-sectional national surveys collected biennially from 2006 to 2016. The study examines the relationship between personal and familial victimization, opinions of security, and other factors linked to expressing the motivation to migrate. The results show that victimization in the Northern Triangle is consistently associated with a desire to migrate. "The 1948 Universal Declaration of Human Rights and the more recent, but related, 2030 Agenda for Sustainable Development provide an important opportunity to reflect on global migration from a human rights point of view."

Anastasia Chalkia writes about "Criminal Violence and its Prevention in Context. Specific Challenges for the Integration of Refugees and Migrants in the Twenty-First Century." The chapter stresses the role of refugee and migrant integration towards crime prevention. Issues such as migration and integration are central in public debate, internationally and in Europe. As for the EU, most Member States face significant integration challenges regarding the integration of refugees and migrants, including the new Member States which have just recently called upon to manage the phenomenon of migration as well as those which for decades, but not always satisfactorily, have addressed the challenges of migration and integration. In this context, the chapter explores the specific ways under which criminal violence, either from the part of victimization or from the part of criminal behavior, in conjunction with the characteristic of the above populations as well as the circumstances they live in, can be prevented.

Riaz Tejani discuss the topic of "Legal Education for Profit and the United Nations Call for "Quality Education" and "Strong Institutions" in the 2030 Sustainable Development Agenda." The author emphasizes that this call by the UN "underscores the supreme importance of the rule of law in global perspective by construing law as both constitutive of social institutions and a fundamental institution in its own right." Especially law schools where new lawyers and especially judges are trained, "have been a particularly sensitive kind of institution." The rise of "for-profit" law schools in the 2000s in the West is presented critically, what will be the effect on democratic ideals, implications for criminal justice in the twenty-first century, like access to justice, business ethics, and market fundamentalism are discussed. "The consideration of for-profit law schools in the context of the UN call for "sustainable institutions" is especially instructive here. Many of our key institutions are established on the bedrock of law."

Ling Zhou and *Hanming Xu* present a chapter about "Money Laundering: China and its Evolving Criminal Policy Response." The problem of money laundering is huge and has seriously affected the operation of world economy. Money laundering activities globally is estimated to be as high as approximately 1 trillion euros, allegedly taking up almost 5% of the global GDP. This chapter looks into the legal shortcomings and effectiveness issues for countering money laundering, in line with the United Nations Agenda's Sustainable Development Goals 16.4. "By 2030, significantly reduce illicit financial and arms flows, strengthen the recovery and return of stolen assets and combat all forms of organized crime," and 16.a "Strengthen relevant national institutions, including through international cooperation, for building capacity at all levels, in particular in developing countries, to prevent violence and combat terrorism and crime." While in the above context China has a strong understanding of the money laundering and terrorist financing risks it faces, its criminal policy is fundamentally short of counter measures for laundering of proceeds of crime and sources used for its national risk assessment. Moreover, financial institutions including the People's Bank of China and non-financial institutions have an insufficient understanding of the risks they face and how their services could be abused by criminals and terrorists. This deficiency also notably affects efforts to address corruption. The authors review the legal foundation, functioning, and operational effectiveness of China's Anti-Money Laundering and Counter-Terrorism Financing (AML/CFT) law enforcement, and make recommendations to improve the use of criminal policy to counter money laundering more effectively.

The chapter written by *Susanne Karstedt* addresses "The Policy Relevance of Comparative Criminology: On Evidence-Based Policies, Policy Learning and the Scales of the Discipline." The author points out that Comparative Criminology is increasingly important for national as well international crime and justice policies. Karstedt discusses the question: "Can comparative and macro-level criminological research provide an evidence base for global crime and justice policies akin to and equivalent to the 'gold standard' of experimental methods on national and local levels?" Other disciplines, in particular comparative political science, or development studies have produced exemplary research demonstrating the usage and usefulness of comparative studies for policy making, evaluation, transfer and policy learning. This chapter discusses the potential of comparative criminological research for enhancing the pool of evidence-based crime and justice policies, and recommends strategies in harnessing them for policymaking and transfer on a global scale.

Part VI has the title "Countering Art Crime & Violence." It includes two chapters. *Kamil Zeidler* and *Julia Stepnowska* write about the "United Nations Perspective on Preventing Transnational Organised Crime against Cultural Property in the Era of Sustainable Development and Restitution Arguments." The protection of the world's cultural heritage is one of the goals of the UN 2030 Agenda. Combating transnational organized crime against cultural property, including the illicit trade in art and antiquities, requires fostering international cooperation and drawing conclusions from past and future restitution cases. This chapter discusses the endeavors of the UN and other major stakeholders in protecting cultural property and presents a set of arguments that can serve as a toolkit in restitution disputes.

Irwin Waller's chapter deals with the topic "Reducing Violent Crime by 50 % Before 2030: Decisive Action Now to Achieve These SDGs." Globally each year, half a million persons are victims of homicide, 25 million women are raped, and one billion children are victims of violence. "Governments are reluctant to go forward to reduce violent crime effectively." This chapter proposes ways to get actions to dramatically reduce violence by 2030. It explains solutions that violence prevention science shows are effective and cost effective and how to find out more. It shows how to implement these solutions by learning from city successes and government difficulties in following the essentials agreed in the UN legal instruments. It identifies how to foster sustainable and smarter investments by policymakers. It calls on faith-based organizations, civil society, and cities to spearhead decisive action, in partnership with UN agencies and pathfinder governments, by five initiatives: (1) get to know the science, the essentials for success, and how to get by; (2) raise awareness among politicians and the public of effective solutions and strategies, using modern communication tools; (3) foster the human talent to implement effective strategies successfully; (4) act locally to deliver effective solutions; and (5) work collaboratively to convince policymakers to invest now, including policy proposals based on effective solutions and strategies.

Part VII has the title "Philosophies of Law & New Legal Realities in the Context of the 2030 Justice and Crime." It includes five texts, starting with the chapter by *Yvon Dandurand* and *Jessica Jahn* about "The Erosion of Justice Symbolism." The authors point out that "the symbolism that has long embodied our justice images has gradually eroded." Whereas our justice symbols may have once reminded us of the spiritual nature of our longing for justice, they have been replaced by those meant to evoke secrecy and detachment. Lady Justice has become the emblem for our resignation to settle for predictability in laws, even when we might have wished to stay true to our aspirations for justice and dared to dream of cooperation and harmony. In recent time, Lady Justice herself is increasingly replaced by a simple scale as the prevailing image of justice, signifying that human intervention in justice may no longer be required since the system for which we have settled has acquired a life of its own. Such an erosion is both a threat to the authority structures that such symbols depict and a promise for renewal. This chapter considers the symbolism of our justice images and the ways in which it may constrain our collective imagination. It suggests that our justice mythology, of which our human rights discourse is part, must be renewed and put at the service of another vision for our future together, particularly one that is less legalistic and less nationalistic.

Sławomir Redo addresses "The Relevance of Philosophical and Religious Ideas to the United Nations Quest for Universalizing Criminal Justice." In this context, he ventures into the UN Charter, the Universal Declaration of Human Rights, and the 2030 Sustainable Development Agenda with their many calls for universal justice. The chapter selectively reviews the UN-relevant roots of "justice" and goals of criminal punishment from the perspective of universalistic philosophers with their own views on justice *vis-à-vis* natural and positive law. In conclusion, the author points out that the UN work has its own "Reason" whose ecumenism originated from the tragic Nazi Holocaust. With this "Reason" the Organization continues going its own way over the conceptual divides between the world of Member States and of religious and philosophical values.

Ying-Jun Zhang's chapter is about "The Universal Declaration of Human Rights: Public International Law and the Confucian Legal Culture for 2030 and Beyond." Based on *travaux préparatoires* (official records) for the Universal Declaration of Human Rights, the author analyses the Chinese contribution to it. This document engages the wisdom of Chinese culture, she writes. Chinese Confucian legal culture not only addresses human rights thoughts but also the political governance. "The core ideas of that culture may be put in concert with the United Nations, the new goals of sustainable development, whose progress and impact depend on Member

States commitment to the Organization's objective." After more than 70 years since the adoption of the Declaration, the fundamental human rights and freedoms it stated have become the standard of human rights principles. The Chinese representation to the United Nations brought in the discussion of Human Rights Chinese ideas, breaking religious and cultural barriers that initially thwarted the drafting process.

Sławomir Redo adds the chapter about "Is Socrates Mortal? On the Impact of Socratic Logic on Teaching and Learning the United Nations Crime Prevention Law." He describes and comments on canons of action-oriented formal logic credited to Socrates by his student Plato. Socratic Method is particularly popular in the Western world. Since 2007, that method enjoys a worldwide imprimatur of the United Nations Scientific, Educational and Cultural Organization. The author presents and discusses his own experience in logistical and substantive issues involved in altogether five Socratic workshops with regard to their preparation, implementation, and evaluation, in the comparative context of Socratic and Confucian logic. *Redo* concludes that progressive Socratic logic and United Nations law blend well with the Western and Confucian legal cultures. The application of this logic to any other material law is likewise possible and may be beneficial for legal education worldwide.

Karol Rutkowski presents in his chapter "Reflections on the 'Right to Justice' – Now and in the Future." He discusses the topic that there is only one justice, "but it may be and should be analysed in various ways and, for classification purposes, divided and named in numerous ways." The author points out that the United Nations finds itself confronted with two concepts of justice: natural and that created in cyberspace, recently through artificial intelligence (AI). The right to justice is the basis for the entire system of human rights in the world. "These rights have been and are being developed by the United Nations, most recently via the implementation of the 2030 United Nations Sustainable Development Agenda." "The United Nations human rights and the 2030 Agenda form an ordered system that determines whether humanity will survive and will not rest on the way to knowing and understanding its existence and its condition." But the 2030 Agenda does not explicitly mention the threats associated with the development of AI and cyberspace. The author emphasizes that justice will increasingly play the role of a regulator of social development as the best fit for this function among the fundamental values of the human civilization. "Owing to the United Nations position on the crossroads, the Organization may be ecumenical in its own terms." Rutkowski comes to the conclusion that "the post 2030 UN Agenda for sustainable development, with the horizon reaching mid-twenty-first century, must face the threats associated with the development of artificial intelligence and cyberspace, considering the emerging opportunities for humanity. The role and importance of the UN in this context cannot be overestimated. After all, it is the only global organization capable of carrying out coordinated actions that can stop bad and support positive trends." He emphasizes that we need science related to justice. "Such science was, is, and will be needed. If it has not emerged until now, then it is necessary to create it and name it. I would name it 'justology'."

Part VIII, as the last one, is about "Faith and Crime Prevention." It has four texts, including the Epilogue of the Editors. *Michael Platzer* presents the text "The Faith-Based Organizations and the United Nations." The author emphasizes that the United Nations has had an ambiguous relationship with faith-based organizations (FBOs) since its founding in 1945. Only with the arrival of Kofi Annan did the UN see the need to work with civil society, which included religious and local community institutions. The major conferences held in the 1990s provided sufficient space for non-governmental organizations (NGOs) to be taken seriously. The UN 2000 Millennium Development Goals (MDGs) and the 2016 Sustainable Development Goals (SDGs) gave NGOs an importance equal to government and international agencies. An Inter-Agency Task Force for engaging with FBOs was established and various fora were created to develop concrete collaborative initiatives. It is estimated that there have been ten times more FBO projects in the last 5 years than at the millennium. Each of the UN Agencies is supposed to supply a report to the General Assembly describing its activities. While many professionals in the Agencies are still skeptical about the effectiveness of FBOs, the mutual respect and active cooperation in development and humanitarian assistance has steadily increased since 1945, particularly in this millennium.

Tina L. Bertrand writes about "Turning the Tables on the War on Terror: The Alliance of Civilization as a United Nations Response to It." The author discusses the topic "how states limit or prevent the United Nations [. . .] from fulfilling its mission, especially when great powers have a vested interest in influencing outcomes themselves." A violation of the UN's mission was the 2003 invasion of Iraq by the United States and its allies. After the invasion, the UN Secretary-General created the Alliance of Civilizations (AoC). It concentrates on bridging the cultural and religious divides between Islam and the West to reduce prospects for violence. The AoC has five specific focus areas in this regard: education, youth, migration, the media, and women. The number of countries experiencing violent extremism and terrorism has steadily risen the last years. The author discusses the role played by the UN Secretary-General in reframing the international response to terrorism via the AoC. *Bertrand* takes up "two factors that seem to have significantly impacted the AoC's competency in carrying out its agenda: requisite support of key actors to adopt and promote norms. . ., and the ability to graft a new norm dimension onto a broader, pre-established one. . . ." The author comes to the conclusion that the AoC can "boast of successes, as well as bemoan failures. It has widespread membership, but its donor base, which is critical to its survival, remains small."

Thomas Walsh writes about "Spirituality, Crime Prevention and Criminal Justice: The Ongoing Significance of Faith-Based Organizations to the Work of the United Nations." The author discusses the capacities of religion to bring value to the efforts of governments and international organizations, including the United Nations, in their effort to mitigate or solve social problems and secure peace and prosperity. Religion continues to be a social force that impacts our world, with capacities at times problematic and at other times socially redemptive. "This social fact stands out independently of one's personal views about religion: believer, non believer, atheist, disinterested, or advocate." This does not mean that religion is incorruptible, on the contrary. The author discusses the significance and relevance of religion and faith-based organizations to the mission and goals of the United Nations, and particularly the UN Office of Drugs and Crime. Walsh points out that populism and nationalism are on the rise in the early twenty-first century. FBOs and interfaith activists are increasingly engaged with many UN agencies and this may help to counter these developments.

The volume finishes with an "Epilogue" from *Sławomir Redo* and *Helmut Kury* which emphasizes main threads of this book.

The Editors would like to thank very much, foremost, all the contributors for bearing with us through the long editorial process and attending to our many queries on points of detail. Without their excellent cooperation, it would have been impossible to edit this collective work on a particularly important event, the 75th Anniversary of the United Nations. We have been honored by the introductions provided to this book by the eminent personalities: H. E. Brigitte Bierlein and H. E. Lech Wałęsa. We also thank very much the publisher, Springer, and especially Ms. Anke Seyfried for the excellent advice, cooperation, and other logistical support in bringing the manuscripts into fruition through this publication.

Heuweiler, Germany Helmut Kury
Wien, Austria Sławomir Redo

16 May 2020, International Day of Living Together in Peace

References[4]

A/RES/2017 (A) III The Universal Declaration of Human Rights, 10 December 1948.

A/RES/70/1 Transforming our world: the 2030 Agenda for sustainable development, 25 September 2015.

A/RES/73/195 Global Compact for Safe, Orderly and Regular Migration, 19 December 2018.

Brunkert, L., Kruse, S., & Welzel, C. (2019). A tale of culture-bound regime evolution: the centennial democratic trend and its recent reversal. *Democratization, 26*(3), 422–443

CAB 195/1, War Cabinet Minutes, W.M.(42) 47th Meeting – W.M.(42) 155th Meeting: 67-68. http://www.nationalarchives.gov.uk/documents/cab_195_1_transcript.pdf

CEPR/Centre for Economic Policy Research. (2020). *COVID-19 and trade policy: Why turning inward won't work.* London: CEPR Press.

de Tocqueville, A. (1917). *Democracy in America* (H. Reeve, Trans.). The Library of the world's best literature. An anthology in thirty volumes. Toronto-Glasgow: Warner Library Company/ Brook and Company.

E/2020. Progress towards the Sustainable Development Goals. Report of the Secretary-General. Economic and Social Council. United Nations: New York. https://bit.ly/3bN8007

Freedom House. (2020). *Nations in transit 2020.* Washington, D. C.: Dropping the Democratic Façade.

[4] All United Nations parliamentary documentation, retrieved May 15, 2020 from the United Nations website http://www.un.org.

Ginsburg, T. (2008). The global spread of constitutional review. In K. Whittington, R. D. Kelemen, & G. A. Caldeira (Eds.), *The Oxford handbook of law and politics* (pp. 81–95). Oxford: Oxford University Press.

Godson, R. (2000). Guide to developing a culture of lawfulness. *Trends in Organized Crime, 5*(3), 91–102.

Gonzalez, A. (2020). *A memo to trade ministers on how trade policy can help fight COVID-19.* Washington, D.C.: Peterson Institute for International Economics. https://bit.ly/2KQCumU

Griesshaber, N. (2013). *Forms of civic engagement and corruption: Disentangling the roles of voluntary associations, elite challenging mass movements and the type of trust within social networks.* https://bit.ly/3doF5Ro

Gruère, G. (2019). *Never let a good water crisis go to waste.* https://bit.ly/3exv0SN

Lustig, D., & Weiler, J. H. H. (2018). Judicial review in the contemporary world - Retrospective and prospective. *ICON, 16*(2), 315–372.

Montesquieu, Ch. (2001). *The spirit of laws* (T. Nugent & Kitchener, Trans.). ON: Batoche Books.

Morsink, J. (1999). *The Universal Declaration of Human Rights. origins, drafting of intent.* Philadelphia: University of Pennsylvania Press.

Morsink, J. (2009). *Inherent human rights: Philosophical roots of the Universal Declaration.* Philadelphia: University of Pennsylvania Press.

Morsink, J. (2017). *The Universal Declaration of Human Rights and the challenge of religion.* Columbia: University of Missouri Press.

Műller, J.-W. (2017). *What is populism?* London: Penguin.

Műller, J.-W. (2019). Populism and the people. *London Review of Books, 41*(10), 35–37.

OHCHR/Office of the High Commissioner for Human Rights. (2020). 'Toxic lockdown culture' of repressive coronavirus measures hits most vulnerable. Retrieved from https://bit.ly/2KREs6z

Rahman, M. S., & Nahar, S. (2017). Variance and time series analysis of democracy index. *Journal of Education, Society and Behavioural Science, 23*(4), 1–12.

Redo, S. (2012). *Blue criminology. The power of United Nations ideas to counter crime globally.* Helsinki: European Institute for Crime Prevention and Control, affiliated with the United Nations.

Redo, S., & Platzer, M. (2014). The United Nations role in crime control and prevention: from "what?" to "how?". In P. Reichel & J. Albanese (Eds.), *Handbook of transnational crime and justice* (2nd ed., pp. 291–299). Thousand Oaks: Sage.

Roosevelt, K. (2008). *The myth of judicial Activism. Making sense of Supreme Court Decisions.* New Heaven: Yale University Press.

Roser, M. (2014). *OurWorldInData.org – a new web publication by INET Oxford shows how the world is changing.* https://bit.ly/386i4zx

Roser, M. (2019). *Democracy.* https://bit.ly/2I1oUeX

Schabas, W. A. (2013). *The Universal Declaration of Human Rights. The travaux préparatoires* (Vol. I. https://bit.ly/2I1oUeX&II). Cambridge: Cambridge University Press.

The Sustainable Development Goals Report. (2019). New York: United Nations.

Toft, M. D., Philpott, D., & Shah, T. S. (2011). *God's century: Resurgent religion and global politics.* New York: W.W. Norton & Company.

UNODC. (2016). *Compendium of United Nations standards and norms in crime prevention and criminal justice.* Vienna: United Nations.

UNSG. (2017). *António Guterres secretary general's remarks on the launch of the Fez plan of action*, 14 July 2017. https://bit.ly/2VrGnW1

UNSG. (2020). *António Guterres. We are all in this together: Human rights and COVID-19 rsponse and recovery*, 23 April 2020. https://bit.ly/2Gn7nR2

World Values Survey/WVS. (2019). *The SDG16 Data Initiative 2019 Global Report.* https://bit.ly/2uINApO

WJP. (2019). World Justice Project Rule of Law Index. https://bit.ly/3bhvSKT

Helmut Kury Professor Dr. h.c. mult. Dipl.-Psych., Former Member of the Psychological Institute of the University of Freiburg (1970–1973), Member of the Research Group of the Max Planck-Institute for Foreign and International Penal Law in Freiburg/Germany (1973–1980 and 1988–2006; meanwhile retired), First Director of the Criminological Research Institute of Lower Saxony in Germany (1980–1988). His research areas include offender rehabilitation, crime prevention, attitudes to punishment, fear of crime, punitiveness, alternatives to punishment, diversion, methodological problems of empirical social science research, international comparison of crime and punishment. He cooperated with many universities and research institutes internationally, especially with countries of the former Soviet Union. His most recent publications in English are: Kury, H., Ferdinand, T.N. (Eds.) (2008). *International Perspectives on Punitivity.* Bochum: Universitätsverlag Dr. Brockmeyer; Kury, H. (Ed.)(2008). *Fear of Crime – Punitivity. New Developments in Theory and Research.* Bochum: Universitätsverlag Dr. Brockmeyer; Kury, H., Shea, E. (Eds.) (2011). *Punitivity – International Developments.* 3 Vols., Bochum: Universitätsverlag Dr. Brockmeyer; Kury, H., Redo, S., Shea, E. (Eds.) (2016). *Women and Children as Victims and Offenders: Background, Prevention, Reintegration. Suggestions for Succeeding Generations.* 2 Vols., International Publishing Switzerland: Springer; Kury, H., Kuhlmann, A. (2016). Mediation in Germany and Other Western Countries. Kriminolgijos Studijos 4, 2016, 5-46; Kury, H. (2017). Harsh Punishment or Alternatives: Which Is the Better Crime Prevention. Juricia international, University of Tartu, 15, 91–99; Kury, H., Glonti, G. (2017). Migration in Germany and Georgia (Comparative Analyses). Davit Aghmashnenebeli University of Georgia Academic Journal 1, 6-13; Kury, H. (2018). Rehabilitation in Prison. German Experiences and what can be done better. Rom. Journ. Of Sociological Studies, New Series, Bucharest, No. 1, 19-36; Kury, H. (2018). Integration of refugees in Germany – Has the criminal burden increased" Criminology: Yesterday, Today, Tomorrow - The Journal of St. Petersburg International Criminology Club 1, 48, 37-45; Kury, H., Redo, S. (Eds.) (2018). Refugees and Migrants in Law and Policy. Challenges and Opportunities for Global Civic Education. International Publishing Switzerland: Springer; Kuhlmann, A., Kury, H. (2018). Some Considerations of Restorative Justice Before and Outside of Contemporary Western States. Kriminologijos studijos – Criminological Studies, Vilniaus Universitetas, 5, 5–42; Kury, H. (2019). Refugees: Post Traumatic Stress, and Crime – Experiences from Germany. Kultura i Edukacja – Culture and Education 124, 73–90; Kury, H., Kuhlmann, A., Quintas, J. (2019). On the Preventative Effect of Sanctions for Drug Crime: The United States, Germany and Portugal. Archiwum Kryminologii, Polska Akademia Nauk, Instytut Nauk Prawnych, 41, 261–295. E-mail: helmut.kury@web.de.

Slawomir Redo Dr. hab. (Law/Criminology) is Visiting Professor of United Nations Law. He is a member of the United Nations Studies Association. F. United Nations Senior Crime Prevention and Criminal Justice Expert and staff of the UN Office on Drugs and Crime (ret.); He had been involved in numerous projects implementing the UN standards and norms in crime prevention and criminal justice. In other capacities he assisted in the implementation of the United Nations Convention against Transnational Organized Crime, and on-line international crime prevention and criminal justice education. He published 4 books, co-edited 4 others, including "Women and Children as Victims and offenders: Background, Prevention, Reintegration. Suggestions for Succeeding Generations" (Springer 2016), and "Refugees and Migrants in Law and Policy – Challenges and Opportunities for Global Civic Education" (Springer 2018) plus about 80 articles – mostly on the UN law and practice of crime prevention and criminal justice. University course lecturer on "The United Nations and Crime Prevention" & "The United Nations and War Crime Prevention" (Austria, China, Poland); Promoter of crime prevention & criminal justice training and education for meeting the goals of the 2030 UN Sustainable Development Agenda. Co-Editor of the first criminological UN Agenda-based textbook *KRYMINOLOGIA. Stan i perspektywy rozwoju z uwzględnieniem założeń Agendy ONZ na rzecz zrównoważonego rozwoju 2030* (Wolters Kluwer, Warsaw 2020). E-mail: s@redo.net.

Part I
Rule of Law and Realities of Life in the Context of the 2030 Justice and Crime Prevention

Democracy–Human Rights–Rule of Law: European Developments and the Importance of an Independent Judiciary

Friedrich Forsthuber

Abstract Only in a state based on the rule of law can there be a guarantee of democracy as well as an effective protection of human rights. The independence of the judiciary is a major pillar of any constitutional state based—within the framework of the separation of powers—on a balanced system of separation and control of powers. Effective guarantees for the preservation of democracy and the rule of law can only be achieved through a broad societal consensus on the value of rule-of-law principles. Political education is not just a task for politics and the school system, but for civil society as a whole.

Keywords Democracy · Dictatorship · European Convention of Human Rights · European Union · Human rights · Independence of judiciary · Political education · Rule of law · Verein Justizgeschichte und Rechtsstaat

1 Introduction

In an ideal world, democracy and the rule of law are typically "Siamese twins". Only in a state based on the rule of law can there be a guarantee of democracy, that is, political participation through free elections, freedom of opinion, association, and the press, as well as an effective protection of human rights by independent courts. The opposite of a democratic state is dictatorship, tyranny, intolerance, despotism, torture, and killing. This text addresses current challenges in a contemporary democratic state confronting the rule-of-law crisis.

F. Forsthuber (✉)
Regional Criminal Court of Vienna, Vienna, Austria
e-mail: friedrich.forsthuber@justiz.gv.at

H. Kury, S. Redo (eds.), *Crime Prevention and Justice in 2030*,
https://doi.org/10.1007/978-3-030-56227-4_2

2 Democracy and the Rule of Law

In the nineteenth century, *the rule of law* was seen as a stance against absolute monarchy: it called for limitation of the omnipotence of the monarch, an administration and adjudication based on legal rules, and the supremacy of a constitution guaranteeing separation of powers, fundamental rights, and individual freedoms.

For Immanuel Kant (1724–1804), the aim of the state was to establish the widest possible consensus based on legal principles. The substantive concept of the rule of law is that every state works toward the realization of supranational values. It is thus inherently tied to a higher order of values.

The failure of the 1848 Revolution put a temporary end to the hope for political participation. The apolitical concept of the rule of law was limited to formal legal protection in justice and administration. This was what all political parties could agree to, given that a solid legal basis has a stabilizing effect on society. The rule of law is the "state of well-ordered administrative law," as formulated by the German jurist Otto Mayer (1924, p. 58) but, nevertheless, its aims and content remained open.

The emergence of national socialism led to the end of both the substantive and the formal concept of the rule of law. Institutions providing legal protection were sidelined, the adherence to laws was weakened, and basic rights were suspended. In a dictatorship, there is no place for ideas and institutions based on the rule of law, as these restrict and control the activities of a state and its scope of political action.

To prevent totalitarian regimes in the future, a substantive understanding of the state based on the rule of law emerged after 1945. The German Basic Law (*Grundgesetz*) signed in Bonn in 1949 provided a constitutional framework for the Federal Republic of Germany, designed to correspond to the "principles of a republican, democratic, and social constitutional state" (Basic Law 1949, Art. 28 (1)).

The concept of the democratic constitutional state is based on a balanced division of control and power, that is, *checks and balances*—constitutionally binding legislation, binding administrative and case law, separation of powers, immediately effective human rights, and the guarantee of legal protection by independent courts. International agreements were concluded for the protection of democracy, human rights, and the rule of law; these provided for judicial control as well as reactions and sanctions in the event of violations by member states.

3 Independence of the Judiciary

The independence of the judiciary is a major pillar of the rule of law regarding the right to a fair trial according to Article 6, para 1 of the European Convention of Human Rights (ECHR): *"In the determination of his civil rights and obligations or of any criminal charge against him, everyone is entitled to a fair and public hearing within a reasonable time by an independent and impartial tribunal established by law."*

We basically differentiate between professional and personal judicial independence. Professional independence means that, in exercising their judicial duties, judges are exclusively guided by the law and are not bound by any directives. Any executive or legislative intervention in pending court proceedings must be excluded. The personal judicial independence guarantees that a judge cannot be dismissed or transferred against their will, except upon the decision of a court.

In his speech at a Convention of Jurists in Leipzig (Germany), the President of the German Federal Constitutional Court, Andreas Voßkuhle, said:

> Although we are very familiar with the concept of democracy based on the rule of law, this cannot be taken for granted. The rule of law and democracy have not developed simultaneously in Germany and are in a state of mutual tension and complementarity. But both principles converge in the service of freedom. Democracy ensures the self-determination of the people by organizing the formation, legitimation, and control of those organs that exercise state authority over the citizen. The rule of law, on the other hand, answers questions about the content, scope, and procedure of government activity. It aims to limit and bind state power in the interests of securing individual freedom, in particular by recognizing fundamental rights, the legality of administration and the protection of individual rights by independent courts (DIE ZEIT 27 September 2018).

The European Court of Justice (ECJ—Grand Chamber) stressed in its decision of 19 November 2019 (a case in which three Polish judges of the Supreme Administrative Court and the Supreme Court contested their premature retirement) that a court is not independent if "the objective circumstances in which such a court was formed, its characteristics and the means by which its members have been appointed are capable of giving rise to legitimate doubts, in the minds of subjects of the law, as to the imperviousness of that court to external factors, in particular, as to the direct or indirect influence of the legislature and the executive and its neutrality with respect to the interests before it" (Doc. 62018CJ0585).

4 European Conventions on the Protection of Democracy, Human Rights, and the Rule of Law

On 10 December 1948, the United Nations adopted in Paris the Universal Declaration of Human Rights (RES 217 III A), which, however, did not provide for legal enforceability of the rights. The Statute of the Council of Europe was signed in London in 1949. In the Treaty of London the governments:

> reaffirm their devotion to the spiritual and moral values which are the common heritage of their peoples and the true source of individual freedom, political liberty and the rule of law, principles which form the basis of all genuine democracy - believing that, for the maintenance and further realization of these ideals and in the interests of economic and social progress, there is a need of a closer unity between all like-minded countries of Europe (ETS No. 1).

In 1950 the Council of Europe drew up the European Convention on Human Rights, which was signed by Austria in 1958, and in 1964 included in the Austrian Constitution.

The European Convention on Human Rights enables individual citizens to submit individual complaints to the European Court of Human Rights in Strasbourg in the event of violations of their guaranteed human rights (after having exhausted recourse to national courts). In addition, each contracting state has the right to bring another contracting state before the ECHR in the event of a systematic violation of human rights, such as the right to a fair trial.

In 1990 the Ministerial Committee of the Council of Europe founded the European Commission for Democracy through Law ("Venice Commission") to provide opinions on constitutional issues and the rule of law for members of the Council of Europe, "*guided by the three basic principles of the European constitutional heritage, namely, democracy, human rights and the rule of law*" (CDL-AD (2016)007).

The Council of Europe includes all European countries with the exception of Belarus, which is the only European country that still has the death penalty.

In 2000 the Charter of Fundamental Rights of the European Union was proclaimed in Nice, and entered into force on 1 December 2009 simultaneously with the Treaty of Lisbon. The fundamental rights guaranteed in this treaty are the basic guidelines for the European Court of Justice in Luxembourg.

In Article 2 of the Treaty of Lisbon, the European Union lists 13 basic values: respect for human dignity, freedom, democracy, equality, rule of law, protection of human rights, protection of minorities, pluralism, non-discrimination, tolerance, justice, solidarity, and equality of women and men (TL 2007).

The main progress achieved by the democratic states since 1945 was, in form and content, the protection of democracy, human rights, and the rule of law by communities of states (e.g., UN, Council of Europe, EU), as well as by multilateral agreements. The adherence to the basic values defined by these agreements is a legal guarantee, particularly for courts such as the European Court of Human Rights in Strasbourg, and the European Court of Justice in Luxembourg.

5 Endangering and Undermining Democracy and the Rule of Law

A functioning democracy and the rule of law cannot be taken for granted. If the rule of law is questioned, authoritarian leadership and dictatorship soon follow, in which universal human rights are trampled on. Such developments have happened at a dizzying pace countless times in history, for example, in Germany in 1933, when the parliament, a compromised judiciary, the press, and large parts of the manipulated population were ready to abandon political participation, separation of powers, and ultimately their own rights to liberty.

Undermining the independence of the judiciary, freedom of press, protection of minorities, and human rights by instrumentalizing a crisis under the pretense of an alleged state of emergency is invariably rationalized by the statement that "this is what the people want." In this way we paradoxically experience the elimination of the rule of law by a perverted understanding of democracy.

In Feodor Dostoevsky's famous chapter in *The Brothers Karamazov* (1880, translated, e.g., 2003, p. 19) a Grand Inquisitor reproaches Christ for having made the biggest mistake by giving man his free will, whereas the inquisition decides everything, and the people will gladly accept these decisions: "And men rejoiced at finding themselves led once more like a herd of cattle, and at finding their hearts at last delivered of the terrible burden (of the free will) laid upon them by Thee, which caused them so much suffering."

There are probably several reasons to prefer a "strong leader" over a state based on the rule of law, for example, lack of political education, loss of the trust in the institutions of the democratic state, loss of perspective, namely, the feeling of belonging to the losers of society, and the fear of missing out on values and security, such as a family, a home, and a job. People who tend to feel left out are susceptible to manipulation by ideologies and populists, who promise simple solutions, thus reinforcing fear and xenophobia.

At present we are also confronted with such developments, as, for example, in Turkey, where President Erdoğan and the Justice and Development Party (AKP), after the attempted coup on 15 July 2016 abolished freedom of the press and the independence of the judiciary by emergency laws.

For the first time the European Union initiated sanction procedures against Poland (2018) and Hungary (2018) according to Article 7 of the Treaty of Lisbon, as a reaction to the measures taken by these countries to undermine the independence of the judiciary because of the risk of a serious violation of the basic values mentioned in Article 2.

6 An Example of the Undermining of the Rule of Law: Turkey

After the attempted coup of 15 July 2016 there was a wave of dismissals and arrests based on previously established "black lists" encompassing approximately one quarter of the Turkish judiciary. The declaration of the state of emergency and its repeated prolongation was the starting point of the final abolition of the independence of the judiciary whose council had already been politically infiltrated by the AKP. At the same time, the judges and public prosecutors remaining in office were threatened with imprisonment and confiscation of property if they did not act in accordance with the political directives. The majority of the lawyers, journalists, and academics detained in Turkey are political prisoners.

In many cases the reasons for arrest are not given for a long time, and then evidence is desperately sought to support allegations of membership in a terrorist organization. Many of the accusations are downright copy-and-paste jobs, based on the fact that a witness (frequently anonymous) stated that the accused might belong to a prohibited organization and used the ByLock messenger app, which is generally attributed to the Gülenists.

Prejudiced court proceedings, as well as the equal phrasing of the indictments and judgments, are clear indicators of the "alignment" of the Turkish judiciary. Individual court decisions resulting in a different verdict are not implemented, as, for example, the verdict of the constitutional court, which decided in the case of the two journalists, Alpay and Altan, in mid-January 2018 that detention pending trial of more than a year was a violation of the right of personal freedom and security of the accused and an infringement of the freedom of speech and press, as guaranteed by the constitution. Following political objections, the judgment was not implemented by the courts, and the journalists remained in detention.

The Venice Commission entrusted by the Council of Europe with the examination of the draft amendment of the Turkish constitution came to the following discouraging result concerning the Turkish judiciary:

> The enhanced executive control over the judiciary and prosecutors which the constitutional amendments would bring about, would be even more problematic. In the context in which there have already been longstanding concerns regarding the lack of independence of the Turkish judiciary the amendments would weaken an already inadequate system of judicial oversight of the executive (CDL-AD (2017) 005, § 129).

President Erdoğan was not impressed and changed the constitution by means of the referendum of 16 April 2017. Appeals by the Parliamentary Assembly of the Council of Europe and the Commissioner for Human Rights of the Council of Europe to the institutions of the Council of Europe and the European Union to urge Turkey to respect the minimum standards of the rule of law were unsuccessful. In 2019 there seemed to be a glimmer of democratic hope, when the opposition was able to win the mayoral elections in Ankara and Istanbul. Erdoğan, however, again urged national unity through the military intervention in Syria.

7 The Independence of the Judiciary As a Constitutional Concept and Its Realization: The Example of Austria

At the time of absolute monarchy, rulers had arbitrary power to remove civil servants and judges from office. This was based on the perception that there was a contractual relationship between the ruler and the civil servants—judges were seen as the extended arm of the ruler. There are only a few exceptions to this situation, as, for example, the Rules of the Imperial Chamber Court (*Reichskammergericht*) of 1495 and 1555, which guaranteed professional and personal independence to the judges of the Imperial Chamber Court.

Inspired by the developments in England, where the independence of the judge from the king had been implemented, Montesquieu developed his theory of three separate powers of state:

> There would be an end of everything, were the same man or the same body, whether of the nobles or of the people, to exercise those three powers, that of enacting laws, that of executing the public resolutions, and of trying the causes of individuals (Montesquieu 1748, Book XI, 6).

In 1817 Anselm von Feuerbach, in his inaugural address as the President of the Court of Ansbach/Bavaria, vigorously objected to any interference in judicial proceedings by the monarch, asserting that: "The judge receives his office from the king's hand, but an office which has the duty to serve no other master other than justice, to obey no will other than the will of the law" (Quoted after Wolf 1949, p. 281).

Judicial independence as a guaranteed fundamental right was laid down in the Frankfurt Constitution (Constitution of St. Paul's Church [*Paulskirchenverfassung*]) of 1848/49 in the chapter on "Fundamental Rights of the German People" (§§ 174–183), making a clear statement of the right of defense against the state (Die Paulskirchenverfassung 1848).

In Austria, even after the outbreak of revolution in 1848, Emperor Ferdinand I still insisted that, according to the so-called "Pillersdorf Constitution" of 25 April 1848, all administration of justice emanated from the emperor and was carried out in his name; however, in the chapter on citizens' rights he acknowledged the right to a statutory judge, and conceded that judges could only be dismissed or transferred upon the decision of a court. The ministerial decree of 21 August 1848 announced that the judicial authorities must administer the judicial office in all relations completely independently of the Ministry of Justice according to existing laws.

In the Constitution of December 1867, the judiciary was established as an independent and autonomous power of the state by the constitutional law on the judiciary of 22 December 1867. The Federal Constitutional Law—the great constitutional document of the First Republic—was passed by the National Parliament on 1 October 1920. Article 87, para 1, of the Austrian Federal Constitutional Law (Bundes-Verfassungsgesetz) states that judges are independent in the execution of their judicial duties.

Today, in contrast with the First Republic, where women were excluded from judicial office and judges were mainly recruited from conservative and German nationalist circles, the female and male judges of the ordinary courts (civil and criminal courts) represent a wide spectrum of the population; since 1947 women have been admitted and constitute at present about 50% of Austrian judges.

Professional and personal independence are guaranteed by the constitution. The more strongly the institutional guarantees for protection of judicial independence are anchored in the constitution, the greater the inherent independence of the judges.

Dr. Rudolf Wassermann, former President of the Higher Regional Court of Braunschweig, noted that:

> On the one hand, there are various, mainly unconscious influences arising from the social circumstances in which the judge is embedded on the basis of origin, education, professional socialization, and exposure to social developments. On the other hand, there are targeted influences from the social environment that judges are exposed to (Die richterliche Gewalt: Macht und Verantwortung des Richters in der modernen Gesellschaft, 1985).

The Austrian Association of Judges, which consists of almost all judges of the ordinary courts—and an increasing number of judges of the administrative courts active since 2014—issued the Wels Declaration of Ethics (*Welser Erklärung*) as a basic statement of ethical principles. Apart from Articles I and II, special emphasis is given to the personal independence of judges in Article IX of the Wels Declaration by the Association of Austrian Judges (*Vereinigung der österreichischen Richterinnen und Richter*):

> "*Art. I. Fundamental Rights:*
>
> Human rights and fundamental freedoms form the basis of our democratic constitutional state. As guarantors of the rule of law, we allow our behavior and our decisions to be guided by these fundamental rights. We decisively oppose every attempt to question the democratic and constitutional order of our Republic.
>
> *Art. II. Independence:*
>
> We decide exclusively on the basis of statutory law and our free inner conviction. We reject any form of unlawful exertion of influence, invitations and gifts, and disclose all attempts to intervene. Judicial independence serves the protection of people seeking justice, and may never be abused as a pretext for arbitrariness or for behavior that is intellectually or socially detached from reality.
>
> In selecting and evaluating fellow judges, we are guided according to the criteria of the Austrian Judicial Services Act (*Richterdienstgesetz*) by their professional and social abilities, and reject any patronage.
>
> *Art. IX. Private Behavior:*
>
> We scrutinize carefully and critically whether our actions or statements might make us dependent on someone, or might even only give the appearance thereof. This also applies to our off-duty activities, in so far as we can expect this to compromise our credibility as judges or cause our credibility to be questioned. We are convinced that being a member of a political party or being politically active within such a party can be detrimental to the credibility of an independent judiciary that cannot be swayed by political parties and is not bound to any interest groups and lobbies" (Wels Declaration of Ethics, 2007).

8 Associations of Judges for the Defense of Independence and the Rule of Law

The International Association of Judges (IAJ) with its present seat in Rome was founded on 6 September 1953 in Salzburg, Austria, as an apolitical international professional association. As of this writing, its members are associations of judges from 92 countries in all five continents.

The main aim of the International Association of Judges is the protection of judicial independence as an essential condition for the execution of judicial functions and the guarantee of human rights and fundamental freedoms. An important sub-organization is the European Association of Judges (EAJ) with currently 44 member associations.

The International as well as the European Association of Judges are repeatedly called upon to disclose attacks on judicial independence and the rule of law. These have not always been successfully defended.

In the following paragraphs will be presented some problem areas on which the Associations have had to act during the last 10 years, as well as the resulting resolutions with their *calendārium*.[1]

Dismissal of judges:

E.g., interference with the duration of employment, dismissals, new vacancy announcement with revised service criteria.

Serbia 7.5.2010 and 10.11.2010 EAJ and 8.9.2011 IAJ, Slovakia 04.06.2014 EAJ, Ukraine 8.10.2015 IAJ, Poland 26.12.2017 IAJ and 15.9.2019 EAJ

Forced transfer of judges:

Turkey 11.11.2012, EAJ as well as 13.11.2014 and 8.10.2015 IAJ, Argentina 7.7.2015 IAJ, Serbia 25.5.2018 EAJ

Influence of ministers on disciplinary action:

Slovakia 4.9.2011 EAJ, Poland 17.10.2018 and 10.5.2019 EAJ

Abuse of disciplinary action against judicial representatives:

South Africa 11.11.2014 IAJ, Ukraine 08.10.2015 IAJ, Poland 10.5.2019 and 15.9.2019 EAJ

Imprisonment, arrest, and criminal proceedings against judges:

Turkey 25.5.2018 EAJ

Prosecution of individual judges based on court decisions:

[1]For this information regarding the activities of the IAJ and EAJ, I would like to thank their former President, Gerhard Reissner.

Venezuela 10.12.2014 IAJ (Judge Maria Lourdes Afiuni Mora), Turkey 16.5.2015 IAJ (Imprisonment of two judges), Turkey Oct. 2016 IAJ (Murat Arslan)

Attempts to counteract the principle of division of powers:

Turkey 11.11.2012 EAJ, Serbia 25.5.2018 EAJ, Poland 25.5.2018 IAJ and 17.10.2018 EAJ, Spain spring 2018, Poland 10.5.2019 and 15.9.2019 EAJ

Propaganda (Bashing) against court decisions and non-execution by the Executive:

Bolivia 15.10.2009 IAJ, Slovakia 4.9.2011 EAJ, Panama 9.11.2014 IAJ, Peru 11.11.14 IAJ, Uruguay 13.11.2014 IAJ, Greece 19.5.2017 EAJ, Poland 10.5.2019 EAJ

Salary Problems:

Judges were repeatedly confronted with salary cuts, unfair salaries, the absence of inflation adjustment, or severe cuts in income upon retirement—a matter needing resolutions, as the financial security of a judge is a major component of judicial independence.

Slovakia 4.9.2011 EAJ, Lithuania 11.11.2012 EAJ, Greece 15.11.2012 IAJ and 25.5.2013 EAJ, Peru 11.11.2014 IAJ, Uruguay 13.11.2014 IAJ, Puerto Rico Oct 2018 IAJ (income cuts upon retirement).

9 Austria's Path Toward the Democratic Rule of Law

In 1848 Austria's citizens, students, and workers went on to the streets for the first time to protest against censorship and Metternich's police state, demanding political participation, a constitution, and fundamental rights. The revolution was also an essential catalyst for fairer criminal procedures in Austria. The "Provisional Regulation on procedures in press matters and against misuse of the press" of 18 May 1848 (Provisorische Verordnung 1848) provided for trial by jury as a counterbalance to the professional judges of ordinary and municipal courts who were dependent on the powerful, as well as for indictments as opposed to inquisition (without public prosecutors), and for oral public proceedings. Despite the suppression of the revolution and neo-absolutism, the present organization of the judiciary, with district courts, regional courts, higher regional courts, and a supreme court, including the establishment of public prosecution authorities, was introduced on 1 July 1850.

In 1867 Austria became a constitutional monarchy. As the position of Emperor Franz Joseph I had weakened after losing wars, he had to surrender power and accept a constitution, a parliament—however with voting according to tax class—and, based on the constitution, fundamental rights, and the independence of judges. In

1907 universal and equal suffrage for men was introduced, a right that was granted to women only after the proclamation of the Republic on 12 November 1918.

The Austrian Federal Constitution (Bundes-Verfassung 1920), authored by Hans Kelsen, granted the right to the Constitutional Court to review (and repeal) laws regarding their constitutionality, a worldwide unprecedented event.

A special mechanism was provided to protect the fundamental principles of the Austrian Constitution (democratic, republican, federal, and rule of law), setting forth that any restriction of these principles would be considered to present a modification of the constitution as a whole, for which it was not only necessary to obtain a two-thirds majority in parliament, but also a referendum.

As the principles and institutions of the democratic state had not yet been fully assimilated by the politicians and the population, social problems increased. In March 1933 Austria—as well as other European countries—started to drift into dictatorship despite its sound constitution.

First this led to Austrofascism (the "*Ständestaat*" of the Christian Socialist Party) and after the Annexation (*Anschluss*) from 1938 to 1945 to the German National Socialist regime.

Constitutional democracy was restored after 1945, and was furthermore strengthened by Austria's entry into the Council of Europe, the European Convention on Human Rights, and the European Union (1995). In 1950 the death penalty was abolished, and this was anchored in the Constitution in 1968. Finally, in 1975 a modern criminal code was introduced, aiming for resocialization of offenders instead of retribution.

As of 1 January 2014 legal protection was reinforced in the Austrian administrative process by the establishment of administrative courts; the Federal Administrative Court, the Federal Financial Court, and nine Regional Administrative Courts have since been integrated into administrative procedures as a second instance, with the Federal Administrative Court acting as supreme court.

10 Austria in the Ranking of Constitutional Democracies and the Necessity of Political Education

Political systems are annually ranked by various institutions, taking political and social developments into consideration.

The Democracy Index, published by the British weekly *The Economist* evaluates 167 countries and distinguishes between *Full democracy* with 8–10 points (2019: 22 countries), *Flawed democracy* with 6–8 points (2019: 54 countries), *Hybrid regime* (a mixture of autocracy and democracy) with 4–6 points (2019: 37 countries), and *Authoritarian regime* with 0–4 points (2019: 54 countries).

The criteria underlying the Democracy Index are *Electoral process and pluralism*, *Functioning of government*, *Political participation*, *Political culture*, and *Civil liberties*.

Austria is placed in 2019 at number 16 (and at number 8 within the 27 EU countries) with 8.29 points. Out of a total of 22 countries labeled *Full democracy,* only Austria and France obtained such a low rating on *Political culture* with 6.88 points. For comparison, Norway, Iceland, Sweden, and Ireland have the highest ranking with 10 points. This underlines the need for a better political education, also by establishing it as a compulsory school subject to promote a broad understanding and acceptance of the principles of democracy and the rule of law.

Opinion formation is increasingly shaped by the tabloids and social media, which, as "echo chambers", confirm existing fears and prejudices and devalue other views. It is important to prevent people who are amenable to rational argument from "caving in". This is all the more urgent in view of threatening international developments affecting institutions such as the independence of the judiciary, freedom of the press, and protection of fundamental rights and freedoms. Effective guarantees for the preservation of democracy and the rule of law can only be achieved through political education and a broad societal consensus on the value of rule-of-law principles.

11 Conclusions

Only those who know their rights and recognize "fake news" and populist agitation can think differently, act independently, and protect their fundamental and freedom rights guaranteed by the constitution and the European Convention on Human Rights. In 2018 the Association of Judicial History and Rule of Law (*Verein Justizgeschichte und Rechtsstaat*) was founded. Its aim is to familiarize all age groups and social classes with the nature and the significance of the democratic rule of law and the common values of the European Union. To enhance the knowledge of these values and the historical development of democratic institutions, the Association uses the website www.justizgeschichte-rechtsstaat.at/ and organizes exhibitions, events, as well as educational material which can be downloaded from the organization's website.

References

CDL-AD. (2016). 007. Council of Europe. European Commission for Democracy through Law Rule of Law Checklist, 11–12 March 2016. https://bit.ly/37EBnjd

CDL-AD. (2017). 005. Council of Europe. Opinion No. 875/2017 Turkey. Opinion on the Amendments to the Constitution adopted by the Grand National Assembly on 21 January 2017 and to be submitted to a national referendum on 16 April 2017. https://bit.ly/38JFnjY

Die Paulskirchenverfassung. (1848). https://bit.ly/37GfHU3

Doc. 62018CJ0585, ECJ/European Court of Justice Judgment of the Court (Grand Chamber) of 19 November 2019, A. K. and Others v Sąd Najwyższy. https://bit.ly/2PaSKlk

Dostoevsky, F. (1880). *The Brothers Karamazov* (H. P. Blavatsky, Trans.). (2003). Aegitas Publishing House.
European Treaty Series ETS No. 001. Statute of the Council of Europe. London, 1949. https://bit.ly/2V4cavP
European Treaty Series ETS No. 005. European Convention on Human Rights/ECHR. Rome, 1950. The Convention for the Protection of Human Rights and Fundamental Freedoms. https://bit.ly/2SY2G2M
Mayer, O. (1924). *Deutsches Verwaltungsrecht* (Vol. I, 3rd ed.). Leipzig: Duncker & Humblot.
Montesquieu, Ch. L. (1748). The Spirit of Laws (*De l'esprit des lois*). https://bit.ly/38RYdWd
Provisorische Verordnung über das Verfahren in Preßsachen, 18. Mai 1848. https://bit.ly/3bPz7cj
RES/217 III A The Universal Declaration of Human Rights, 10 December 1948. https://bit.ly/2T0CGDV
The Austrian Federal Constitutional Law/Bundes-Verfassungsgesetz. (1920). https://bit.ly/2Pak7vY
The Economist. (2019). Democracy index. http://www.eiu.com/topic/democracy-index
The German Basic Law/Grundgesetz. (1949). https://bit.ly/2SGCbQv
The Treaty of Lisbon. (2007). https://bit.ly/2wuN7YN
Vereinigung der österreichischen Richterinnen und Richter. (2007). Welser Erklärung. https://bit.ly/2HDace1
Voßkuhle, A. (2018). Rechtsstaat unter Druck. Die Zeit. https://bit.ly/2V5NqU0
Wassermann, R. (1985). *Die richterliche Gewalt: Macht und Verantwortung des Richters in der modernen Gesellschaft*. Heidelberg: Wassermann.
Wolf, N. E. (1949). *Quellenbuch zur Geschichte der deutschen Rechtswissenschaft*. Frankfurt am Main: Vittorio Klostermann.

Friedrich Forsthuber since 2010 has been the President of the Regional Criminal Court of Vienna (Austria). Chairman of the Expert Group on Criminal Law of the Austrian Association of Judges. From 1981 to 1985 he studied Law at the University of Vienna (Master of Law). In 1990 he was appointed judge. Since 2018 he has also been active as Chairman of the Association of Judicial History and Rule of Law, www.justizgeschichte-rechtsstaat.at. E-mail: friedrich.forsthuber@justiz.gv.at.

Youth Perception on Hate Crimes, Hate Speeches and Nationalism in Contemporary India

J. Maria Agnes Sasitha

Abstract In view of the recent surge in the number of hate crimes in India, particularly against minority groups such as Dalits and Muslims, this chapter aims to explore youth perceptions about hate crimes, hate speech, and ideas of nationalism, and examine the ways in which education has impacted their point of view. Through a critical examination of the reasons behind this sudden rise in hate crimes and hate speech, this chapter argues that a new form of nationalism founded based on religious sentiments and animosity among different religious groups is slowly emerging in present-day India. In the process, communalism has come to be conflated with nationalism. Results of this qualitative inquiry suggest that young people are lacking in a thorough understanding of these issues, although they do not appear to be altogether evasive of contemporary realities. This points towards the need for increased public awareness and education delivered through a critical lens, and alerts us to the dangers of overestimating the reach and influence of mass media to convey the magnitude of certain crucial issues.

Keywords *Bharat Mata ki Jai* · Conflict · Communalism · Diversity · Hate · Nationalism · Religion · Youth perceptions

1 Introduction

On 25 July 2019, the General Assembly of the United Nations passed a resolution to counter hate speech by promoting interreligious and intercultural dialogue and tolerance (A/RES/73/328) (United Nations 2019b). Before this, at the launch of the United Nations Strategy and Plan of Action on Hate Speech in New York on 18 June 2019, the UN Secretary-General António Guterres remarked that hate speech signifies "an attack on tolerance, inclusion, diversity and the very essence of our human rights norms and principles. More broadly, it undermines social

J. Maria Agnes Sasitha (✉)
Department of Sociology and the Gender Centre, Stella Maris College, Chennai, India

H. Kury, S. Redo (eds.), *Crime Prevention and Justice in 2030*,
https://doi.org/10.1007/978-3-030-56227-4_3

cohesion, erodes shared values, and can lay the foundation for violence, setting back the cause of peace, stability, sustainable development and the fulfilment of human rights for all"(UNIS/INF/545) (United Nations 2019a). He added that over the past 75 years, hate speech has resulted in a number of atrocity crimes, including genocide, and it has been strongly linked with violence and killings in several regions of the world. A manifestation of these tendencies can be seen in India as well. In 2018, Amnesty International's India chapter noted a staggeringly increasing number of hate crimes against Muslims and Dalits.

This chapter aims to critically examine the reasons behind the prevalence of hate speech and hate crimes in the name of religion in India. It is crucial to uncover why our country, once known for its secularist values, is now subordinating politics to religion. This has led to a new process of nationalism. Nationalism is now being built through arousing religious sentiments and instigating animosity against followers of various other beliefs.

"Nationalism" is not a tangible but rather an abstract concept. Over time its definitions have remained fluid as well as static. According to Gellner (1983, p. 5), it permitted the growth of an impersonal society where individuals were bonded through defining a shared culture and learning about a shared history. Within India, owing to its mixed plurality and multiplicity of cultures, nationalism has taken on many forms. According to Hobsbawm (1990), what began as a limited idea among the elite of colonial India, was soon converted to a mass movement during the twentieth century.

As India changed over time, so did its nationalistic identity. Pseudo-nationalists started to exaggerate the importance of a single history of one religious community as being the pre-eminent history of the nation, as well as to denigrate and distort the history of other communities. It was soon realised that no one identity could represent what was built on the backs of many. This resulted in multiple identities competing for visibility and inevitable conflict and inequality.

Owing to its long and rich history, much of what affects India today was due to nationalism as an ideology which arose to fight against the foreign imperialism but today it is affecting its own people. As Thapar et al. (1987) opined, wherever national consciousness failed, communalism developed. Even as children, our history books have indoctrinated in our minds that our national leaders fought vehemently against various alien enemies, beginning with the Muslim rulers. This has unconsciously led to the belief that there has always been a Hindu nation constantly fighting against certain evil powers. In time this has created a blatant culture of animosity, clearly estranging the Muslim population. This communal approach has injured and fractured our society deeply. As a wave of nationalism is now making its way across the globe, much of it has affected India's own democratic process. For India, the concept of nationalism came about during the Independence struggle.

Today the idea of nationalism has been influenced by conservative right-leaning political policies. Instead of focusing on cultural diversity, the election mandate of the current ruling party has chosen to foreground religious and cultural divisiveness. This has contributed to an increase in pro-Hindu and anti-Muslim rhetoric. Hate crimes are a reality of the disintegration of our religious diversity and peaceful coexistence. A discussion of the apparent changes in the national rhetoric is important.

2 Religious Diversity and Conflict in India

India is characterised by more ethnic and religious groups than most other countries of the world. India is the second most populous country in the world after China, with over 1.3 billion people. India has more than 50% of its population below the age of 25. It has more than 2000 ethnic groups and every major religion finds representation here. Hinduism comprises of 79.80% of the country's total population, Islam 14.23%, Christianity 2.30% and Sikhism 1.72%.

In the recent past, highlighting the contradictions between various religious faiths has led not only to a divisive society on religious grounds but has also instilled fear in the minds of the minorities and the marginalised. According to Fact Checker 2019, an analyst of Hate Crime Watch in India, a database organisation violence has increased, leading to incidents such as the murder of rationalists, mob lynching following rumors of beef-eating and cow slaughter, honour killings, "*gharwapsi*" (*home coming*) campaigns and similar other disturbing social trends. The rising trend of religious hatred and the ensuing violence have been posing a major threat towards the integrity of the nation.

3 The Trend of *Bhakthi* Tradition

The *Bhakthi* movement that originated in South India in the ninth century B.C. is famous for two schools of thought: *Nirguna* (worship of God as a formless divine) and *Saguna* (worship of God in a physical form). Nevertheless, both carry the message of love, devotion, compassion and humanity to all. Today, India is experiencing a *Bhakthi* fad, but of a different kind, *Bhakthi* or devotion for the country. Unfortunately, this has united people on communal grounds which, in turn, is being posited as nationalism. Those opposed to this ideology are viewed as anti-nationals.

4 Meaning of Nationalism

There is no one understanding of the term nationalism, as it is an abstract concept. According to Carlton J. H. Hayes, "Loyalty and attachment to the interior of the group (namely the nation and homeland) are the basis of nationalism" (Hayes 1960). In fact, "it is attachment to nationality that gives direction to one's individual and social postures, not attachment to religion and ideology. A human being takes pride in his national achievements and feels dependent on its cultural heritage, not on the history of religion and his faith" (Hayes 1960, p. 56).

He further adds, "What distinguishes one human being from another are not their beliefs, but their birth-place, homeland, language and race. Those who are within the four walls of the homeland and nation belong to it, and those who are outside it, are aliens. It is on the basis of these factors that the people have a feeling of sharing a single destiny and a common past" (Hayes 1960).

According to scholar Anderson, nationalism is when "a new emerging nation imagines itself to be antique" (Benedict 1991, p. 68). Benedict Anderson, political scientist and historian, referred to this in his influential book *Imagined Communities: Reflections on the Origin and Spread of Nationalism.*

In *Nations and Nationalism*, Gellner (1983), the British social anthropologist and a leading thinker on the subject of nationalism, linked it more closely to a new kind of society that grew out of an earlier society. The former permitted the growth of an impersonal society where individuals were bonded through defining a shared culture and learning a shared history.

Gellner E further argues that nationalism has become a necessity in the modern world and an interdisciplinary view including sociology becomes imperative.

Eric J. Hobsbawm, British thinker and historian, made a connection in *Nations and Nationalism since 1780* (1990) between history and nationalism and explained how history is reconstructed in a way that suits the ideology of nationalism, and how this enterprise is crucial to the construction of nationalism. In the initial stages, anti-colonial Indian nationalism had a more limited role as compared to when it eventually evolved into a mass movement during the twentieth century. History played a crucial role in both creating the basis of the unity and for sustaining it.

Historian Breuilly (1993) defends a more modern theory of nationalism, similar to Benedict Anderson's. According to Breuilly (1993, p. 401), one can understand nationalism as that class of political movement, in this perspective nationalism is a form of politics.

According to Thapar et al. (2016), the evolution of nationalist ideas in India was coupled with colonialism. She states "All of us in the Indian subcontinent, not to mention other ex-colonies, have faced the same questions of how to define ourselves as citizens of a new nation." This relates to the question of identity or identities. We in India thought the answer was simple—it was the single identity of being Indian (Thapar et al. 2016, p. 7).

Nationalism was built by coalescing many identities and aspiring to be inclusive of the entire society. It inevitably opposed the contemporary tendency to rest the conception of a nation on the idea of a single identity being superior to the rest. Interestingly, according to Thapar et al. (2016), for such claims of superiority to take hold, an imagined history is put forth that endorses the dominance of the supposedly superior group.

I believe it is worth noting here, that the erudite scholar Thapar in recent times has become a target of hate crimes and hate speeches for her stand. This also becomes a fitting proof for a study of this nature.

According to the Stanford Encyclopedia of Philosophy (2002), the term "nationalism" is generally used to describe two phenomena: (1) the attitude that the members of a nation have when they care about their national identity, and (2) the actions that the members of a nation take when seeking to achieve (or sustain) self-determination.

For this chapter, we shall define nationalism as an emotional attachment to the nation, the manifestations of which can be observed in the form of citizens who take pride in national achievements and who share a common cultural heritage, irrespective of caste, creed, sex, and race.

5 Meaning of Hate Speech and Hate Crime

The term "hostility" encompasses ill-will, ill-feeling, spite, contempt, prejudice, unfriendliness, antagonism, and resentment that sometimes culminate as malicious propaganda.

5.1 Hate Speech

The term "hate speech" was coined by a group of legal scholars in the late 1980s in the United States in response to what they saw as the ways in which different legal systems tackled certain sorts of harmful racist speech. Matsuda et al. (2018) first used the term "hate speech" in her article from 1989, "*Public Response to Racist Speech: Considering the Victim's Story*". Her central purpose in using the term "hate speech" was to highlight the lacunae in the US legal system to address harmful racist speech. Undoubtedly, due to the work of legal scholars like Matsuda, the term "hate speech" has now been taken up by legislators and legal professionals. However, today, its usage is commonplace even among the media and the public, and consequently, the term has come to assume a plurality of meanings. However, given that the right to freedom of expression is one of the core freedoms to be incorporated in the Bill of Human Rights, defining the limits of what counts as hate speech has become a difficult task laden with innumerable ambiguities.

UN Strategy and Plan of Action on Hate Speech (2019c) defines hate speech as any kind of communication in speech, writing or behaviour, that attacks or uses pejorative or discriminatory language with reference to a person or a group based on who they are, in other words, based on their religion, ethnicity, nationality, race, colour, descent, gender or other identity factor. This is often rooted in, and generates intolerance and hatred and, in certain contexts, can be demeaning and divisive.

Hate speech has not been defined in any law in India. However, legal provisions provided by certain legislations prohibit select forms of speech as an exception to freedom of speech.

For this chapter, hate speech can be defined as the vilification of a community or social group, whose stereotyping based on some specific religious characteristics is accompanied by hostility and discrimination against them.

5.2 Hate Crimes

A sociological understanding of hate crime is that which occur when a perpetrator targets a victim because of his or her perceived membership in a certain social group, usually defined by racial group, religion, sexual orientation, disability, class, ethnicity, nationality, age, sex, or gender identity.

The Office for Democratic Institutions and Human Rights (OSCE ODHIR 2018, p. 16) defines hate crimes as criminal acts committed with a bias motive. A hate crime is any act which is prohibited under criminal law. This act is usually motivated by prejudice towards a specific characteristic of the person or social group. The offence can be directed towards one or more persons or property. The bias motivation is the offender's prejudice towards the victim based on a characteristic that represents a shared group identity, such as race, language, religion, ethnicity, nationality, gender or other characteristics.

5.3 Literature Review

This section offers an overview of a few works that can help enhance our understanding of nationalism and its changing contours, and the ways in which nationalist sentiments often result in hate crimes.

Arvind Rajagopal in "*Politics after Television: Hindu Nationalism and the Reshaping of the Public in India*" (2004) examines how a larger historical context was woven into and eventually changed the character of Hindu Nationalism. In 1987, the Indian State run television began broadcasting a Hindu epic in serial form, the Ramayana. This resulted in the largest political campaign during the post-Independence period around the symbol of Lord Ram led by the Hindu Nationalists. "Indian Politics irrevocably changed," writes Rajagopal (2004, p. 1). While the audiences were harking back to an epic of the golden age, Hindu Nationalists leaders were embracing the prospects of neo-liberalism and globalisation.

Dibyesh Anand's work, "*Hindu Nationalism in India and the Politics of Fear*" (2011) argues that Hindutva in India is chauvinist, majoritarian and nationalistic which, in turn, creates the image of a peaceful Hindu vis-à-vis a threatening minority other. Anand asserts that Hindu Nationalism normalises the politics of fear as a defensive reaction to the imagined threats posed by Muslims to the Hindu collective.

Radha Krishnan in his article, "*Religion Under Globalization*" (2004) analyses the interface of religion and globalisation. He writes that the major consequences of globalisation have been: the trans-magnification of traditional religions and belief systems, the beginning of the disintegration of traditional social fabrics and shared norms by consumerism, cyber culture, newfangled religions and changing work. His work asserts that there is fast spreading anomie, making individuals dependent on religion. This, in turn, has resulted in a scenario where religion is being deployed to give rise to extremist and terrorist tendencies in third world countries.

Rajeev Bhargava argues in *"State and Religious Diversity: Can Something be Learnt from the Indian Model of Secularism?"* (2014) that secularism must be viewed differently: as a critical, ethical and moral perspective, and not against religion but against religious homogenisation and institutionalised domination. This helps to shed a different light on social issues related to religion.

Romila Thapar et al., in *"On Nationalism"* (2016), contemplates on why it is important to understand what nationalism is, given that certain people with ulterior motives are seeking to create exclusive tendencies by segregating Indians into superior and second class Indians.

Thapar et al. (2016) criticise the communal approach to Indian history and point out the obstructions which its communal interpretation places to the holistic understanding of our history and the concept of nationalism.

Jack Levin and Mc Devitt in their study *"Hate Crime: The Rising Tide of Bigotry and Bloodshed"* (1993), analyse how hate crimes have become a growing threat to the well-being of our society. Hate offences, the authors claim, can be regarded as acts of domestic terrorism. They conclude by stating that all hate crimes are motivated by bias or bigotry and impact the broader continuity. And these arise not out of the rare or few deviant types of individual in society but of the very mainstream society.

William Gould explores a controversial theme in *"20th Century Indian History and Politics: The Nature of Hindu Nationalism as an Ideology and Political Language"* (2004). He analyses how Hindu Nationalism affected the Congress, supposed to be a secular political party, particularly in the state of Uttar Pradesh. The work is a historical analysis of the Partition and Independence in 1947. Gould portrays how language and ideologies transformed the relations between the Congress and North Indian Muslims.

5.4 "Historical" Construction of Communalism in India

Bipin Chandra in his article, *"Historians of Modern India and Communalism"* (1987) writes that it is widely accepted today that the teaching of Indian history has a great deal to do with the spread of communalism in the last 100 years.

Thapar, in her book, *"Communalism and the Writing of Indian History"* (Thapar et al. 1987) says that historical interpretation can be a product of contemporary ideology since it is integrally connected to a people's notion of their culture and nationality. Naturally, this impacts political ideologies and nationalism. For example, she states that attempts are being made to highlight the importance of Aryan culture by trying to prove that the Harappan culture was also Aryan despite the fact that extant archeological evidence contradicts this theory. This boosting up of the Aryan culture is directly proportional to the propagation of the Hindu interpretation of Indian History. What makes it even worse is that the entire enterprise rests on giving an incorrect description of the Aryan way of life. For instance, to deny that the Aryans ate beef and consumed alcohol is to deny the evidence presented by both literary and archeological sources.

The absence of any critical analyses is further evident in the widespread assumption that only Muslim rulers vandalised idols and temples out of their opposition to idol worship. Thapar substantiates her claim through an example of Harsha, the eleventh century king of Kashmir, who appointed a special officer to plunder temples for their wealth. Further, history is replete with examples of destruction of places of worship by Buddhist, Hindu and Muslim rulers. It is recorded that Aurangzeb destroyed a masjid when he attacked a ruler in Lahore (Azgar Ali 1995).

Regarding conversion, Thapar et al. (1987) writes that conversions, mostly at mass level, were voluntary in nature. Although Emperor Ashoka popularised Buddhism and converted people using the state machinery, he is projected as a great emperor. On the contrary, in medieval India, although the state was not interested in proselytising, it stands condemned. For generations, history books have taught us that the State was an agency in converting people to Islam. This type of convoluted and inauthentic interpretation has given rise to pejorative attitudes against certain communities which, in turn, have resulted in the contemporary conflicting situation in India. Mukhia writes that the state in medieval India was not a perfectly secular state. Rather, the medieval Indian state was negatively secular, that is, it subordinated religion to politics rather than politics to religion.

Thapar et al. (1987) further opines that even during the seventeenth century when great popular uprisings (like the Maratha, Sikh and Jat uprisings) took place and led to enormous conflict between the state and others, communal riots at the social level were absent. The causes of these uprisings could be more appropriately attributed to economic and political reasons rather than religious, and religion did not have any role to play in aggravating them further.

6 Growth of Communalism As Nationalism

Thapar et al. (1987) refers to the creation of "national – heroes" in the second half of the nineteenth century as the product of an emotional attraction to the spread of a national consciousness, the chief aim of which was to counter the British view that Indians lacked the capacity for self-government. Rana Pratap, Sivaji and Guru Gobind Singh emerged as national heroes, as opposed to those who had fought against the British for purely political reasons. The creation of these heroic figures was meant to arouse nationalism, although in reality, they did not fight against the British, as they belonged to medieval India, when the principal aim was to fight against the Moghul authority. This clearly establishes the communal approach.

Mukhia asserts that hero myths are political creations and not a product of genuine historical writing.

The culture of estranging Muslims continues in our society until today. This communal approach has injured and fragmented the society deeply. Muslims are unable to express their nationalist sentiments with the same enthusiasm as the majoritarian groups, as they are continually projected as the common foreign enemy against whom our national heroes fought. Under such circumstances, for assimilation to take place, both groups should cooperate. As long as one group is made to feel foreign, true integration and nationalism is hard to develop.

6.1 Communal Approach and the Present Scenario

The question of how to define ourselves as citizens of a new nation was perceived to be an uncomplicated one by our leaders during the rise of Independent India. Thus, they envisioned a common identity for everyone– that of an Indian.

Today, the reality is different, and the answer to the question of a common identity is no longer as simple as it was originally imagined. It necessitates the adoption of a pluralistic approach to the understanding of India's history, both before and after Independence. The Congress's support for minority fundamentalism has produced a sharp divide among Hindu-Muslim groups. The campaigns leading up to the 2014 general elections witnessed multiple clashes between the two major political parties –the Congress and the BJP–each with its own distinct ideology. BJP's political campaign had undertones suggesting that the Hindu population was being marginalised for the progress of the minorities. This "otherisation" was way more overtly and vigorously expressed during the campaigns for the 2019 elections when open hate speeches became the order of the day. For instance, the BJP leader Maneka Gandhi during a political rally remarked that she would not give jobs to Muslims if they did not vote for her (Economic Times, April 15, PTI 2019a).

The communal riots that took place in Calcutta and Bombay in 1992 saw Indian Muslims desperate to escape from their own birthplace and homeland to seek refuge in another state. The identity of being Indian became a travesty. Clearly, they had become entrenched in this "otherisation".

Two important events that took place in modern India can be linked to this ever-increasing trend of hate crimes and hate speeches in India, and the resultant identity politics. The destruction of the Babri-Mosque in Ayodhya on December 6, 1992 and the communal riots that took place in Gujarat in the year 2002 are two significant events that have redefined nationalism and led to a major political transformation in India.

Following these two events, religion came to occupy the center stage in the country's public life. This is conspicuous in identity-based nationalism. Hate speeches have become a tool to rekindle Hindu sentiments, resulting in huge electoral victories for communal political parties.

The BJP White paper states: "The Ayodhya movement also clears the confusion as to what is nationalism and what constitutes the ideal basis for inter religious harmony. It asserts that it is not the spiritually bankrupt Western concept of secularism, but the assimilative Hindu cultural nationhood that is the basis for religious harmony" (BJP 1993, p. 15).

7 Magnitude of the Problem

The government of India does not register religion-based hate crimes as a separate offence, and therefore, statistics on communally motivated crimes in India is not available. Hence, this analysis relies on statistics produced by media reports.

According to Fact Checker 2019, an analyst of Hate Crime Watch in India, a database organisation, 91% of religiously motivated hate crimes have taken place in the last 5 years in India. An analysis of hate crime records reveals that in the past 10 years, 262 of 287 (91%) of religion biased crimes have taken place in the recent past only.

Further, surveys reveal that, from 2014 to 2019, 99 persons were killed and at least 703 were injured in hate crimes motivated by some form of religious bias across 23 of 36 states and Union Territories (UTs) in India. Even states (particularly those in the southern part of India) which did not experience religiously motivated crimes in the past, reported such crimes in 2014.

7.1 Hate Speeches

At the time of writing this chapter, the most debated and controversial issue concerned Nathuram Godse, who assassinated Mahatma Gandhi, one of the founders of the Indian nation. An actor turned politician made a statement in the recent election campaign that Godse was the first Hindu terrorist. What followed was despicable hurtling of abuses by political leaders, all in the name of religion. In all these, the attempt was to project the idea that to be a nationalist, one has to be a Hindu. The argument was that all Hindus are patriots; Godse is a Hindu, and therefore, Godse is a patriot. These fallacious inferences ignited the emotions of the public and creates false labels such as "patriot" for some and "alien" for others.

According to a national news channel, NDTV, the use of hateful and divisive language by high-ranking politicians has increased almost 500% in the past 4 years (NDTV April 19, Jaiswal et al. 2018).

7.2 *Media Reports on the Trends of Hate Crimes and Hate Speech in the Recent Past*

Alimuddin Ansari, a Muslim beef smuggler, was killed by a crowd of angry Hindu extremists in June 2017 in India. Ansari's killing played out in almost real time on WhatsApp, a messaging platform that is widely used in India, which has progressively become a vehicle for the spread of hate speech. Harsh Mander, Director of the Center for Equity Studies in New Delhi, observes that perpetrators often film these lynchings and post videos online to threaten victims who are often minorities (Washington Post, Oct 31, Gowen and Sharma 2018).

Pew Research Center, a US-based think tank, in its 2017 analysis ranked India among the worst in the world for religious intolerance. The nation of 1.3 billion trailed behind Syria, Nigeria and Iraq. It is clear that India has been witnessing the rise of religion-based hate speeches and resultant crimes at an alarming rate (PEW, Majumdar 2018, fact tank on religions in India).

7.3 *Hate Crimes and Hate Speech Trends in the Year 2018*

According to India Spend that tracks reports of violence in English language media, since the BJP has come to power in 2014, an overwhelming number of Muslims have been victimised in crimes largely perpetrated by Hindus (Scrollin, Oct 14, Mander 2018).

India's Prime Minister, Narendra Modi (Washington Post, Oct 31, Gowen and Sharma 2018) has said that the onus of punishing the perpetrators largely lies with the state governments, and that his administration is committed to upholding the law. However, critics opine that his party has emboldened Hindu extremists across the country.

In fact, data collected by India Spend (Scroll in Oct 14, Mander 2018) supports this claim: more than half of the cases of hate crimes reported in 2018 through October came from three states in northern India—Uttar Pradesh, Bihar and Jharkhand—where Modi's Bharatiya Janata Party, or BJP, enjoys strong support (Scrollin, Oct 14, Mander 2018).

In 2018, 30 deaths were recorded as religious bias crimes. Of that, 60% of the victims were Muslim, 33% Hindus and 7% of the victims were Christians (Scrollin, Oct 14, Mander 2018).

The year 2018 witnessed 63 religiously-motivated attacks, of which 71% of the perpetrators belonged to the Hindu religion followed by 27% who claimed to profess Islam (NDTV, Trends of Hate crime and Hate speech, Hate Crime Watch Jaiswal et al. 2018).

7.4 *Trends of Hate Crime and Hate Speeches in 2019*

As of April 2, 2019, Hate Crime Watch has recorded 282 attacks which have resulted in 100 deaths. Muslims, who constitute 14% of India's population, were victims in 57% of the incidents, Christians–2% of the population–were victims in 15% of the cases. Hindus, constituting the majority or 80% of the population, were victims in 13% of the cases. In 12% or 30 incidents, the religion of the victim was not reported (NDTV, Trends of Hate crime and Hate speech, Hate Crime Watch Jaiswal et al. 2018).

Considering only the 252 incidents where the religion of the victims was known, Muslims were victimised in 64% of the total number of attacks, Christians in 16% of the incidents, and Hindus in 16% of the total number of cases. Overall, Hindus were alleged perpetrators in 56% cases, while Muslims in 12% cases. In 85 cases, the religious identity of the perpetrator was not known (NDTV, Trends of Hate crime and Hate speech, Hate Crime Watch Jaiswal et al. 2018).

Nearly 91% (262 of 287) of hate crimes motivated by religious-bias recorded in the decade between January 2009 and April 30, 2019 took place in the last 5 years, after Prime Minister Narendra Modi and the Bharatiya Janata Party (BJP) came to power, according to Hate Crime Watch, a Fact Checker database that tracks such crimes (NDTV, Trends of Hate crime and Hate speech, Hate Crime Watch Jaiswal et al. 2018).

Between May 2014 and April 2019, 99 persons were killed and at least 703 were injured in hate crimes motivated by religious bias, across 23 of 36 states and Union Territories (UTs) in India (NDTV, Trends of Hate crime and Hate speech, Hate Crime Watch Jaiswal et al. 2018).

7.5 *Five Hundred Percent (500%) Increase in Hate Speech According to National Television News Channel Report*

NDTV (Jaiswal et al. 2018) scanned nearly 1,300 articles and cross-referenced this with existing databases on hate speech. It analysed 1000 recent tweets of politicians and public figures, and cross-referenced this information with databases such as the Documentation of the Oppressed and Amnesty International's Halt the Hate Tracker. The use of hateful and divisive language by high-ranking politicians has increased by almost 500% in the past 4 years, according to NDTV. Ninety percent (90%) of hateful comments made during the 2014–2018 period were by BJP politicians. For example, Anant Kumar Hegde a BJP Member of Parliament from Karnataka, in March 2016, stated, "As long as we have Islam in the world, there will be no end to terrorism. If we are unable to end Islam, we won't be able to end terrorism" (The Economic Times, March 31, Aji 2016).

As a reward, in September 2017, he was promoted to the position of Union Minister of Skill Development. Since 2014, Hegde has made seven such hate speeches. In 2017, he declared that the party would remove the term "secular" from the Constitution. He gave a new connotation to the term "secularist" as those people without parentage/lineage. (The Economic Times, Dec 26, PTI 2017).

8 Reasons for Hate Speeches by Political Leaders

In at least two cases, hate speech appears to have profited the politicians making them. In September 2014, Yogi Adityanath, the current Chief Minister of Uttar Pradesh ascribed the rise in riots in Western Uttar Pradesh to the population growth of a minority community (India Today Aug 31, 2014).

As further proof that such divisive speech has no negative consequence on the careers of political leaders, it was found that at least 21 political leaders (or 48%) had recorded more than one instance of hate speech (NDTV, Jaiswal et al. 2018). They were not reprimanded for their hateful comments, nor did they issue any apologies. A BJP MLA, T. Raja Singh, has repeatedly made public speeches inciting violence. In November last year, he threatened to burn down theatres screening a movie called "Padmavat". He publicly stated that every Hindu should carry weapons and attack other communities (The News Minute Jan 20, 2018).

Other prominent repeat offenders include former BJP Member of Parliament Vinay Katiyar, and the Governor of Tripura Tathagata Roy. Katiyar, in February this year, issued statements to the effect that Muslims have no business being in India, and should go to Pakistan or Bangladesh, and that the cremation ground inside the Taj Mahal will be destroyed since the Taj Mahal was originally a temple (The Economic Times Feb 7, PTI 2018).

9 *Ghau Rakshak* (Cow Protectors)

A significant number of instances of hate speech invoke the rhetoric of cow protection, a subject that has gained currency under this government. Elected leaders, including MPs, MLAs and even Chief Ministers, have used the language of vigilantes while calling for violence against those who kill cows. "There is no such thing (cow slaughter) happening in the state. It hasn't happened in the state in the last 15 years. Has it? We will hang those who kill cows," said Raman Singh, the Chief Minister of Chattisgarh, in April 2017. "I had promised that I will break the hands and legs of those who do not consider cows their mother and kill them," proclaimed Vikram Saini, a BJP MLA from Uttar Pradesh, last year (The Economic Times Feb 7, PTI 2018).

The rise in political vitriol over cow protection in the past 4 years appears to correlate with a rise in cow-related vigilantism. The fact-checking site India Spend reported that 97% of *gauraksha* attacks since 2010 occurred under the current government. They counted 76 attacks from May 2014 to December 2017, compared to only two instances during the earlier period (from 2010 to May 2014) (India Spend June 27, 2017) (Human Right Watch 2019).

According to India Spend (2016), there have been 63 cows or beef related attacks from 2010 to 2017. During the period of 2014–2017, 96.8% of the attacks occurred. The data clearly indicates that 51% of the attacks were targeted towards Muslims and confirms the trend of rising religious intolerance in India.

10 Retaliatory Hate Speeches

In instances of hate speech by prominent leaders of the opposition during the past 4 years, threats of violence against Prime Minister Modi feature more than once. In October 2017, Bihar MLA and Rashtriya Janata Dal leader TejPratap Yadav said, "A conspiracy is being hatched to kill Lalu-*ji*. We will not stay silent. We will skin Narendra Modi." Just a week before this threat, Rabri Devi, TejPratap's mother and a former Chief Minister of the state, reacted to a comment by BJP MP Nityanand Rai saying he would cut off any fingers or any hand raised against PM Modi. "I dare them to cut (hands), there are many people who can cut the hands and neck of PM Modi," she said (The Economic Times April 21, PTI 2019b).

10.1 Non-BJP Hate Speeches

Under the previous government, there were at least 21 instances of hate speech recorded across party lines. Amongst prominent instances, Rahul Gandhi in 2014, then a member of parliament, said, "If the BJP comes to power, 22,000 people will be killed" (NDTV May 10, 2014, Jaiswal et al. 2018). Also in the run-up to the general elections, Congress candidate, Imran Masood said, "If Modi tries to turn Uttar Pradesh into Gujarat, then we will chop him into tiny pieces" (The Hindu March 29, 2014, Chandramohan 2014).

Akbaruddin Owaisi, leader of the All India Majlis-e-Ittehadul Muslimeen and then an MLA in Andhra Pradesh, had issued a violent threat against Hindus in December 2012. "Remove the police for 15 mins, we will finish off 100 crore Hindus," he had said during a speech. He spent 40 days in jail on charges of hate speech before getting bail (Times of India Dec 28, 2012).

Political parties consider religion as means to appease their vote banks. In July 2016, Maharashtra Hindu National Shiv Sena Party leader, Uddav Thackeray called for action to declare the country a Hindu state. He affirmed that this would prevent attacks on Hindus (IANS, 2016).

In December 2015, the then Uttar Pradesh minister, Azam Khan was quoted as saying that many leaders of RSS are unmarried as they are homosexuals (Times of India Dec1, Tiwari 2015). This led to objectionable comments against prophet Mohammed resulting in the Kalichak riots. In July 2016, Gujarat Police used batons and fired 24 gas shells against Muslim agitators who were seeking legal remedy against people responsible for a viral video accusing Muslims of "love jihad"- a term used to describe an alleged strategy used by Muslim men to marry women from other religions for the purpose of converting them to Islam (PTI 2017).

11 The Significance of the Study

In the present study, the investigator attempts to understand the perception of the public on this topic of concern by undertaking an empirical study entitled, "A Study on Youth Perception of Hate crimes, Hate Speeches, and Nationalism in Contemporary India".

11.1 Objective

The Universal Declaration of Human Rights turned 70 in 2018. But the continuous onslaught on the fundamental values underpinning the Declaration has assumed dangerous proportions in India and elsewhere. Political leaders in India are using social and economic issues to perpetuate fear and hatred against religious minorities and various ethnic groups. Although outrage and protest against such vilification have been taking place, the costs of protesting against injustice these days is also steep. Today, the Government which has the duty of protecting its people from violence and terrorism are indirectly and sometimes directly, through hate speeches, involved in such acts. In this scenario, an understanding of the struggle for the values of human dignity which are slipping away in the name of religion is important to resist repression and violence, and create harmony and love- the real understanding of religion.

Given the background of the present Indian society, it becomes imperative to understand the perception of young adults on nationalism, hate crimes and hate speech to assess effectiveness of Sustainable Development Goals 16 (SDGs 16) in such a situation. SDGs 16 work towards promoting peaceful and inclusive societies for sustainable development, providing access to justice for all and building effective, accountable, and inclusive institutions at all levels.

11.2 Research Questions

- Given the present scenario what is the perception of the youth on hate crimes, hate speeches and on nationalism?
- Has education impacted their view and raised social consciousness to bring about peace, justice and building strong institutions?

11.3 Methodology

11.3.1 Research Design

Keeping in view the objectives of the study and the issues mentioned at the outset, an appropriate logic of inquiry was applied. The qualitative study is descriptive in nature. It attempts to delve into the various definitions of hate speeches, hate crimes and nationalism formulated by the religiously diverse college students of Chennai city in Tamil Nadu. Through the adoption of an inductive strategy, the researcher collected data related to the aforementioned concepts and produced limited generalisation. The study was conducted in three prestigious city colleges of Chennai, Tamil Nadu, India. The random sampling technique was used to select the sample. The reason for this being that the researcher's ability to conduct this study was contingent upon whether she received permission from the respective colleges as well as the availability of the students. Considering the sensitive nature of the issue, not many institutions were forthcoming in involving their students in this survey.

A very small group of the general public, across age groups, was also interviewed to shed light on a different dimension to the study.

11.3.2 Sources of Data

The current study is empirical and analytical in nature, and the analysis was carried out on primary data collected by the researcher.

11.3.3 Tools of Data Collection

This sample survey was conducted using a semi-structured questionnaire developed specifically for this study by the investigator. The respondents were asked to provide qualitative definitions of the following concepts: hate speech, hate crime and nationalism, to determine their attitude towards these concepts.

11.3.4 Limitations of the Study

The tool used, although it gave scope for free expression, had its own advantages and disadvantages. As the questions were all open-ended, the responses were highly subjective. Consequently, most of the questions had multiple answers. Hence, aggregation was difficult.

12 Analysis

The questionnaire used in this study was designed keeping in mind the current political climate of the country, specifically with respect to hate speeches, hate crimes, and nationalism. On social media platforms, many youths not only actively participate in perpetuating hate speech, but also fall prey to hate crimes. This automatically raises the question as to what nationalism means to the younger generation. This question assumes further importance as this generation is going to set the course for future India and assess the possibility of fulfilling the SDGs.

12.1 Demographic Details of the Respondents

Data was collected from a total of 92 respondents. Of the respondents 83% belonged to the 15–24 years age group, and 17% belonged to a higher age group, ranging from 25 to 29 years. The rationale behind this strategy was to see if there are any differences of opinion among the two age groups.

The results showed that respondents from the higher age group had a greater clarity with respect to their understanding of the issues discussed, and there were fewer questions that were left unanswered by them. For example, to the question on the reasons for hate speeches, only 66% of the younger age respondents even replied, whereas all the respondents in the higher age group gave a definite answer. Likewise, for the other questions, the respondents in the higher age group gave responses which reflected their experience and understanding of the issues at hand, whereas the younger respondents exhibited a certain degree of apathy, which can also be construed as fear. This will be discussed at the relevant places.

12.2 Sex-Wise Distribution

The sample comprised of 51% males and 49% females.

12.3 Religion-Wise Distribution

The respondents in this study were 52% Hindus, followed by 24% Christians while 20% belonged to the Islam faith. A small number of respondents (3%) were followers of Jainism. One respondent refrained from revealing his religious affiliation.

12.4 State-Wise Distribution

A vast majority of the respondents (91%) belonged to the Southern state of Tamil Nadu, where the study took place. The survey had one respondent each from Karnataka and Manipur.

13 Results of the Study: Hate Speech

13.1 On the Interpretation of Hate Speech

For the question on what hate speeches involve, 74% of the respondents said that it involves discrimination, whereas one person stated that it involved politics. The responses resonated with the view that hate speech creates an atmosphere of distrust and conflict.

13.2 On the Targets of Hate Speeches

Seventy-two percent (72%) of the respondents identified religious and ethnic minorities as the targets of hate speeches. Some of them even mentioned that Muslims are being targeted. The next highest category of response (33%) was that the marginalised and the poor were being targeted. Most of the respondents opined that it is usually the powerless who are the easy targets in society. Politicians were the targets according to 17% of the respondents which was also apparent in the election campaign speeches. Some respondents (3%) stated that the secular nature of the country's democracy was being targeted in hate speeches. The rhetoric of secularism being a western concept often resorted to by the political leaders was acknowledged in the responses in this section.

13.3 On Reasons for Increase in Hate Speech

Intolerance as the main reason behind hate speeches was mentioned by 60% of the respondents while 23% said that the reason was politics. As mentioned earlier, this question was left unanswered by 34% of the younger respondents. This inability to provide their views could be attributed to fear. Hate speeches have paved the way for a climate of suspicion and fear and that might have prevented many of the respondents from expressing their views out of the apprehension that their opinions on this issue might jeopardise their future prospects. A recent incident from 2019 offers insights into what might be perpetuating such a climate of fear. An Indian student traveling with a political leader had told the politician that BJP is a fascist party. Complaints of threats to life were registered against the student who then had to face arrest and other legal consequences. This news became widespread and created an outrage among the public.

Among the older respondents in the sample, 56% opined that the reason for hate speeches was intolerance. The remaining 44% felt that politics was the reason. Comparatively, among the younger respondents, 14% felt that politics was the reason for hate speech while 86% was of the view that it was intolerance which resulted in hate speeches.

13.4 On the Reason for Hate Speeches by Political Leaders

More than 55% of the respondents felt that politicians indulged in hate speeches to appease their vote banks. Only one person mentioned it was for nationalism. Around 37% felt that politicians wanted to instigate differences among people and hence, they used hate speeches. Here again, the cases of Yogi Adithyanath and Hegde, as mentioned earlier, bear testimony to the fact that hate speeches delivered by them have translated into political gains for them despite creating discord among the people.

13.5 On the Repercussion of Hate Speeches by Politicians

The consequences of political hate speech made by politicians could be many but the consequence mentioned by 35% of the respondents was appeasement of their own political party, followers of their own religion, and members of their own caste and community. Some of the respondents (20%) felt that attacking and threatening other religious groups, especially the minorities and the powerless, were the consequences of political hate speech.

14 Results of the Study: Hate Crimes

14.1 What Does Hate Crime Involve?

All the respondents, who had given relevant answers, converged on the point that hate crimes involve violence. The types of violence mentioned by the respondents were varied ranging from mob lynching, honour killing, acid attacks, murder, mass killing, rape, etc. The Ram Janma Bhoomi and Godhra incidents, which brought about major transformations in India's politics as mentioned earlier, lend support to this finding from the study. Parallels can also be drawn with the genocides that have taken place in history because of hate crimes.

14.2 Who Are the Victims of Hate Crimes?

Forty-nine percent (49%) of the respondents felt that hate crimes are largely committed against the marginalised, especially the poor and the powerless. The next highest percentage (45%) of respondents felt that religious, linguistic, and racial minorities are the victims of hate crimes. Women as victims of hate crimes such as rape, acid attacks and honour killings was mentioned by 26% of the respondents and 9% said that children also become victims of hate crimes. This resonates with the fact that almost every incident of hate crime in the recent past has involved the rape, killing, burning, and mutilation of children. For example, the rape case of 8-year old Asifa in Kashmir.

14.3 What Is the Motive for Hate Crimes?

Thirty-eight percent (38%) of the respondents named the desire for power as the main reason behind hate crimes. Other motives mentioned included factors such as the need to maintain the status quo, for instance, in the case of honour killing and mob lynching, or to launch an attack on a particular race, as in genocide. Dress was mentioned by two respondents as the reason for hate crimes. This is because certain symbolic gestures as well as attire do embody the potential to turn an individual into an easy target for hate crime. This response clearly shows that certain communities do hold views about the superiority of their own communities and tend to treat others with contempt. Additionally, a complete lack of fear of any kind of repercussions as their party is in power gives them the clout and audacity to commit such crimes openly.

14.4 How Can the Victims of Hate Crimes Be Described?

There was consensus among the respondents on the fact that all victims of hate crimes are innocent and they are not responsible in any way for their victimisation.

14.5 How Can Perpetrators of Hate Crimes Be Described?

Many a time, the perpetrators of hate crime are projected as patriots by those who instigate and support them. However, the respondents, in unison, agreed that hate crime perpetrators cannot be considered as patriots and should be punished under the law.

15 Results of the Study: Nationalism

15.1 What Is the Meaning of Nationalism?

There were varied responses to this question. Seventy-five percent (75%) of the respondents felt that nationalism means respect for one's own nation as opposed to limiting oneself to upholding one's own ethnic group which was mentioned by 8% of the respondents. This finding corroborates the view of Thapar on nationalism (Thapar et al. 2016) that in India, nationalism is a confusing concept laden with ambiguities.

15.2 How Do You Interpret Bharat Mata ki Jai?

"Bharat Mata ki Jai" is a Hindu nationalist slogan meaning "Hail Mother India" and is chanted across the country. Can there be one mother, in a country of religious and linguistic pluralities like India? This slogan, often heard in contemporary times, is opposed by the Muslims as it goes against their belief which is monotheism. All these led to numerous controversies when the new BJP government came to power in 2019. BJP leaders shouted slogans such as Bharat Mata ki Jai and Jai Shri Ram (Hail Lord Rama). On the other hand, Muslims raised slogans such as Allahuakbar. Such a frenzied atmosphere prevailed in the parliament as well this year. Given this context, it is crucial to gain an understanding of the respondents' views and understanding of nationalism.

In this study, 59% of the respondents felt that the chant has a religious undertone to it, whereas only 26% said that it is an attribute of patriotism. However, the fact that the majority of the respondents stated that the chant does not indicate patriotism could also be attributed to their lack of knowledge of Hindi, the language in which the chant is composed. This is because most individuals residing in the southern part of India are not familiar with Hindi, mostly spoken in the northern and central parts.

15.3 What Is Your Identity When in India?

The question of how one would identify himself or herself within and outside India elicited interesting responses. Majority of the respondents (91%) stated that they identify themselves as Tamil (linguistic identity) as they hail from the state of Tamil Nadu. Religious identity was mentioned by four respondents who specified that they would identify themselves as Muslims in India. When in another country, majority (77%) of them responded that they will identify themselves as Indians. This could be seen as an outcome of pseudo-nationalist attempts at promoting a singular, monolithic history rather than emphasising the multiple pluralities that form an intrinsic part of India's cultural fabric. In this study, respondents' linguistic identity emerged stronger than other aspects of their self-identification.

15.4 Who Is an Anti-national?

In recent times, any criticism against the current government's policies or programmes has been labeled as anti-national. Many academics, journalists, and social activists have been jailed for pointing out the lacunae in various government policies. Any view against Hinduism is being labeled as anti-Indian. In such a scenario, the responses to the question of who counts as an anti-national are of immense significance. Eighty-seven percent (87%) of the respondents labeled those who work against the country or harm the country as anti-nationals. Only 2% of the respondents said that those who are against the major religion are anti-nationals. Respondents were clear about the fact that anti-nationalism and expressing one's opinion against something are two very distinct practices and should not be conflated. Among the respondents, there was agreement regarding the importance of public opinion in a democratic society.

15.5 What Do You Think Is the Identity of an Indian?

The question about the identity of an Indian elicited responses that appeared apparently irrelevant, but were thought provoking. Among those who defined the Indian identity, 40% said that it entails a feeling of pride to be a citizen of India, 18% felt that being an Indian involves being a secularist, and 4% felt that to be an Indian is to defend the country and to stand for it. One respondent appeared cynical about answering the question. The respondent said that singing the National Anthem in the theatre before a movie has the potential to strengthen one's identity as an Indian. Thirty-eight percent (38%) of the respondents emphasised the importance of identification documents to establishing one's identity as an Indian.

This tendency to assert one's identity and citizenship, and in effect, one's legitimacy as a citizen, through the possession of appropriate documents could be interpreted in two ways. First, the fact that identity is thought to be so intrinsically tied to the possession of documents that establishes one's citizenship within a nation state implies that, to a large extent, one's attachment to one's nation is something that is superficially constructed and reinforced. Contributing to such nationalistic fervor are things such as the highly contentious National Registry of Citizens being undertaken by the government of Assam. Second, at some levels, this tendency also appears to stand in opposition to the premium place on linguistic identity over nationalist identity by some people. In the second instance, one's sense of identification derives not from the country one has been born into and/or resides in, but the language one speaks, and the linguistic groups that one belongs to.

16 Discussion and Recommendations

Through an analysis of the issues of hate speech, hate crime and nationalism, this study was an attempt to delve into the extent to which the aims of the SDGs 16, which are to promote peaceful and inclusive societies for sustainable development, provide access to justice for all and build effective, accountable and inclusive institutions at all levels, are being fulfilled.

India, today, is facing a lot of discrimination based on religion, caste, class, ethnicity, language, state, race, gender, etc. It is doubtful whether the idea of a peaceful and inclusive society is at all being promoted in India. Hate speeches, hate crimes, and misrepresenting nationalism– all for political gains– have become the order of the day.

Every day there are media reports about the increasing rates of hate crimes and hate speeches. It is important to understand not only why this form of intolerance is currently widespread but also the historical and cultural contexts that have paved the way for a scenario such as this. Nationalism appears to be a highly misunderstood term, misconstrued further by erroneous interpretations and political ideologies inspired by ulterior motives.

Under such circumstances, this study was undertaken to explore whether the youth recognise and understand these processes that are currently underway in the country. Broadly, the conclusions can be categorised as follows:

16.1 Targets and Victims of Hate Crimes

Hate speeches are made against minorities and the marginalised.

Hate crimes target the marginalised and the minorities.

The victims of hate crimes are innocent people.

16.2 Perpetrators and Their Motives

The youth understand that hate speeches involve discrimination.

Intolerance is the reason for hate speeches.

Appeasement is the major motivation behind hate speeches.

Political hate speeches are made to expand vote banks.

All hate crimes involve violence.

The greed for power and status are the motives behind hate crimes.

The perpetrators of hate crime are all offenders and hence should be punished.

16.3 Communal Nationalism As a Trigger for Hate Crimes

Nationalism refers to respect for one's country. Linguistic identity can assume prime importance as well.

Slogans such as *Bharat Mata Ki Jai* ("Hail Mother India") are not an attribute of patriotism but have religious undertones to them.

Ethnic identity (such as the Tamil identity) can emerge as more powerful as compared to that of the Indian identity.

An anti-national is one who works against the country or harms the country, and not merely anyone who questions a particular religion.

The identity of an Indian can be defined by the pride one feels to be an Indian.

The present analysis and findings shed light on the subjective interpretations that young adults have of phenomena such as hate crime, hate speech and nationalism. Participants' perceptions of hate crimes, and hate speeches, and why they occur, reveal a shallow understanding of these issues, although they do not appear altogether evasive of the current realities.

The reason behind adopting a semi-structured questionnaire in this study was to elicit responses that are detailed and uninhibited. However, contrary to expectations, the responses received were not as informative as anticipated. In all probability, this could stem from an apathy on issues that did not concern the respondents directly. An alternative interpretation is that the views expressed by the respondents of this study are largely symptomatic of a high degree of regional orientation. Given that majority of the respondents in this study are from Tamil Nadu where issues such as lynching or *gharwapsi* (reconversion) are not as apparent as in the northern parts of the country where communally divisive politics operates with a much greater force, it is highly probable that the respondents are not fully aware of how hate speeches and hate crimes can pave the way for a certain kind of nationalistic fervor that rests on the perpetuation of hatred, divisiveness, and exclusionary tendencies. This could also imply that the power of mass media to convey the magnitude of certain issues to the general public has been largely overestimated.

All these, in turn, point towards the need for increased public awareness and education. Historians and academics are faced with the tall task of presenting historical facts in an unbiased, objective manner. Academics need to debunk the myth that Muslim invasion marked the end of a golden age in India. This becomes crucial, given that it is ingrained in the minds of many that India will revert to its golden era once it has managed to successfully eliminate the aliens residing within its boundaries.

Further research is necessary to gain an understanding of what other factors exist that might influence the formation of individual perceptions on issues such as hate speech, hate crimes, and nationalism. Research is also needed to shed light on the constraints that may inhibit people from expressing their opinions on issues such as these. This study, in an attempt to offer a comparative framework, also involved collecting data from an older population to ascertain how their perceptions on these topics might be different from a younger generation. The findings reveal that although the older generation had a greater degree of clarity, they were either unable or unwilling to provide deeper insights into the issues at hand, in all likelihood, owing to the fear that has been instilled in their minds. All these also highlight the tremendous power that mass media and social media tend to exert over individual minds, pointing towards their ability to control mass psychology and influence personal interpretation and understanding, to the point that very few people, in fact, venture to unearth facts beyond what they are being offered via media messages. In this context, focus group discussions could be a useful strategy to gain deeper insights into these sensitive issues. Additionally, face-to-face interviews can help to affirm whether young adults are merely confused about their identity and therefore cannot affirm their loyalty, or whether their understanding of nationalism is indeed superfluous.

17 Conclusion

The latest announcement (September 2019) from Amit Shah, President of the BJP and the Home Minister of India, is that India needs One Language, One Culture to be One Nation (The Telegraph online, Sept 17, Editorial Board 2019).

A statement of this magnitude from a person occupying one of the most powerful positions within the government is intimidating. This statement alone justifies the purpose of this chapter, and highlights the pressing need for research on issues of hate speech, hate crime, and nationalism in today's context.

Is it even practical to aspire for a common culture and one language in a culturally diverse, multi-linguistic country such as India? Speeches like that of Shah's only serve to perpetuate hatred and fear and contribute to disharmony in society. While they are clearly in line with BJP's vision of creating a Hindu nation which is being projected as paving the way for religious harmony (BJP White Paper 1993), provocative speeches such as this and the crimes they instigate are also, without a doubt, a violation of the principles laid down by the Universal Declaration of Human Rights. Promoting substantive equality among human beings, including freedom from discrimination, is a foundational idea in human rights, and this is reflected in the very first article of the Universal Declaration on Human Rights (UDHR), adopted by the UN General Assembly in 1948. Additionally, Article 19 of UDHR guarantees the right to freedom of expression, including to "seek, receive and impart information and ideas through any media and regardless of frontiers." The right to freedom of expression is a fundamental human right which sets the context for the protection of all other rights. At the same time, it is not an absolute human right in the sense that it cannot override considerations of equality and public order. International law contains a number of provisions which provide a framework for balancing hate speech.

Currently, the COVID-19 which has had an unprecedented impact on the world has not been spared of political agendas. Even in a dire situation of a global pandemic, political agencies prioritise the agenda of polarisation aiming to create conflict and animosity. As economies and health care systems struggle to cope with COVID-19, we are witnessing how the coronavirus pandemic is shaping political agendas across the world.

The term China Virus as coined by the US leadership is an attempt to segregate nations by creating prejudice and animosity by drawing attention to the world that China is the cause of the health crises. In this context, global agencies such as the UN's WHO—which were designed to help tackle such crises—have had their purpose and credibility questioned, and their role reduced. Even in the middle of the crisis, Trump announced in April 2020 that he would halt US funding (the world's largest) for the World Health Organization.

The Indian social media's usage of emerging terms such as Corona *Jihad* cast shadows of discrimination against certain religious communities. How do we separate politics of religion and formulate a globally viable culture of harmony and coexistence? This paper on the whole expresses social concerns on hate politics which aggressively creates conflict and divisiveness. Arguably, although we have entered by the phenomenon of globalisation into an era of global integration through global connectivity, I would argue that we are threatened by the dark forces of political and religious polarisation and would strongly advocate achieving a status of global communal integration and coexistence.

As stated earlier, attempting to re-construct history in a way that overemphasises the role of one religious community in contributing to the glory of the nation, while at the same time denigrating and distorting the history and contribution of all other communities, produces hatred and divisiveness. The strength of India lies in its diversity. Only the acceptance of multiple identities can pave the way for a harmonious coexistence of all communities. This has to start through education and the creation of varied platforms that facilitate the free expression of thoughts and promote the uniqueness of every culture without bias and fear.

In the quest for our identity as a nation, it is important that we do not lose out on our respect for humanity which is the essence of peaceful and inclusive collective living.

References

Aji, S. (2016). BJP MP AnantkumarHegde booked for hate speech. *Economic Times Politics and Nation*. https://bit.ly/2yiuc4R

Anand, D. (2011). *Hindu Nationalism in India and the politics of fear*. New York: Palgrave Macmillan.

Azgar Ali Engineer. (1995). *Communalism in India-A historical and empirical study*. New Delhi: Vikas Publishing House. pg 31.

Benedict, A. (1991). *Imagined communities*. New York: VERSO.

Bhargava, R. (2014). *State and religious diversity: Can something be learnt from the Indian model of Secularism?* Fiesole: European University Institute.

BJP White Paper. (1993). *Ayodhya and the Rama Temple Movement*. https://bit.ly/35wcuql

Breuilly, J. (1993). *Nation and the State*. Manchester: Manchester University Press.

Chandramohan, C. K. (2014). Congress candidate arrested. *The Hindu*. https://bit.ly/2YxRnmm

Editorial Board. (2019). One India one language why is Amit Shaw inviting trouble? *Telegraph India*. https://bit.ly/3c3pXbQ

Gellner, E. (1983). *Nation and nationalism*. New York: Cornell University Press.

Gould, W. (2004). *Hindu nationalism and the language of politics in late Colonial India*. New York: Cambridge University Press.

Gowen, A., & Sharma, M. (2018). Rising hate in India. *Washington Post*. https://wapo.st/2L13wbf

Hayes, C. J. H. (1960). *Nationalism: A religion*. New York: Macmillan Company.

Hobsbawm, E. J. (1990). *Nations and nationalism since 1780: Progress myth and reality*. Cambridge: Cambridge University Press.

Human Right Watch. (2019). *Violent cow protection. International Dalit Solidarity Network*. https://bit.ly/3aYCewN

IANS. (2016). Enough of being a secular declare India 'a hindu rashtra' says Uddav Thackeray. *Firstpost*. https://www.firstpost.com/india/enough-of-being-secular-declare-india-a-hindu-rashtra-says-uddhav-thackeray-2913432.html

India Today. (2014). *A bizarre analysis of riots, by Yogi Adityanath*. https://bit.ly/3c3Avrx

Jaiswal Nimisha., Sreenivasan Jain., Pratap Singh. (2018). Under Modi Government VIP Hate speech skyrockets. *NDTV*. https://bit.ly/2SzmNov

Levin, J., & Devitt, J. (1993). *Hate crimes: The rising tide of bigotry and bloodshed*. New York: Springer and Business Media LLC.

Majumdar, S. (2018). *5 facts about religion in India*. PEW Research Center. https://pewrsr.ch/2SwxbgA

Mander, H. (2018). Victims are predominantly muslims, perpetrators Hindus. *Scroll.in*. https://bit.ly/2WkRH54

Mari J. Matsuda., Charles R.Lawrence., Richard delgado., Kimberle Williams Crenshaw. (2018). *Words that wound: Critical race theory, assaultive speech and the first amendment*. Abingdon: Routledge.

OSCE ODHIR. (2018). *Hate crime reporting*. https://bit.ly/3b0CsDQ

PTI. (2017). Union Minister Hegde hints at removing "secular" from Constitution. *Economic Times Politics and Nation*. https://bit.ly/35rABqo

PTI. (2018). Muslims have no business to be in India: BJP MP Katiyar. *The Economic Times*. https://economictimes.indiatimes.com/news/politics-and-nation/muslims-have-no-business-to-be-in-india-bjp-mp-katiyar/articleshow/62823901.cms

PTI. (2019a). Vote for me you will need me once elections are over: Maneka to Muslims. *The Economic Times*. https://bit.ly/2YvMPNh

PTI. (2019b). BJP wants to Poison Lalu. *The Economic Times*. https://bit.ly/3drg0W7

Radhakrishnan, P. (2004). Religion under globalization. *Economic and Political Weekly, 39*(13), 1403–1411.

Rajagopal, A. (2004). *Politics after television: Hindu nationalism and the reshaping of the public in India*. Cambridge: Cambridge University Press.

Stanford Encyclopedia of Philosophy. (2002). *The metaphysics research lab*. Stanford: Stanford University.
Thapar Romila., Harbhans Mukhia., Bipin Chandra. (1987). *Communalism and the writing of Indian history*. New Delhi: Peoples Publishing House.
Thapar Romila., Noorani.A.G., Sadanand Menon. (2016). *On Nationalism*. New Delhi: Aleph Book Company.
The News Minute. (2018). *Burn and Vandalize theatres screening Padmaavat: Raja Singh*. https://bit.ly/2W1kigF
The Times of India. (2012). *Akbaruddin in trouble*. https://bit.ly/2zdKbkr
Tiwari, M. (2015). RSS workers are homosexuals says Aza Khan. *The Times of India*. https://bit.ly/2SQ3doj
United Nations. (2019a). *Strategy and plan of action on Hate Speech*, UNIS/INF/545. https://bit.ly/3dg5O2p
United Nations. (2019b). *Promoting interreligious and intercultural dialogue and tolerance in countering hate speech A/RES/73/328*. https://bit.ly/2zcWwFu
United Nations. (2019c). *Strategy and plan of action on hate speech*. https://bit.ly/35sy27x

J. Maria Agnes Sasitha Dr. heads the Department of Sociology and the Gender Centre at the Stella Maris College (Chennai, India). With more than a decade of teaching experience to her credit her interests also lie in sociological research, development and activism. Her areas of expertise are Gender and Sociology of Religion. She has published papers and presented papers in International programs. She is also specialized in the field of disaster rehabilitation and has grappled with issues related to disaster management in the Philippines in 2013. An active participation in an International academic program on Social leadership in Trinity Western University (Langley, Canada, 2017), has stimulated her interest in women's leadership development in India. Additionaly, Dr. Sasitha's rigorous activism is on promoting awareness on environmental issues, specifically in the much needed and restorative practice of green rehabilitation in the cities. E-mail: jsasitha@gmail.com.

Incorporating the United Nations Norms into Iranian Post-Revolution Criminal Policy: A Criminological-Victimological Approach

Mehrdad Rayejian Asli

Abstract In the aftermath of World War II, the international community has started to elaborate internationally protected individual rights by the creation of many legal instruments containing concrete standards and norms, particularly legitimized by the United Nations/UN system. Since the 1979 Revolution, the Islamic Republic of Iran at the domestic level has demonstrated a diverse attitude to these international standards and norms. This divergence took two forms: positive and reluctant towards incorporating the UN standards and norms into domestic Post-Revolution policy-making. This chapter specifically examines the rights of offenders and victims of crime from a criminological-victimological perspective. Throughout 40 years since the 1979 Revolution, Islamic Republic of Iran, as the first modernistic Islamic government in Persian's history, has sought to balance these two forms. Some UN standards and norms have been incorporated into the Islamic Republic of Iran's criminal policy. Conversely, certain UN standards and norms have not even half a chance to be incorporated into Islamic Republic of Iran's domestic legal system. Issues relating to children and juveniles, persons with disabilities, narcotic drugs, and human trafficking are the examples of positive attitude that the present chapter explores. The women's issues in relation to discrimination and violence are the negative example. Finally, the chapter concludes that the Islamic Republic of Iran's positive attitude regarding the implementation of the UN standards and norms helps to reinforce peaceful relations in the international community.

Keywords Criminal justice policy · Criminology · Discrimination · Victimology · Violence · United Nations

---

M. R. Asli (✉)
Department of Law, Research Center for Study and Development of Humanities, Tehran, Islamic Republic of Iran

H. Kury, S. Redo (eds.), *Crime Prevention and Justice in 2030*,
https://doi.org/10.1007/978-3-030-56227-4_4

1 Introduction

The establishment of the UN opened a new era. Numerous international legal instruments have been adopted under the Organizations' aegis. Among them are the Universal Declaration of Human Rights (the 1948 Declaration, RES/217 A III) and the Agenda for Sustainable Development (the 2030 Agenda, A/RES/70/1). These instruments not only provide specific rights and protections for individuals,[1] but also require Member States to enact and adopt domestic legislation and policies for guaranteeing the recognized rights and protections.

The UN has always sought to play a key role in policy-making and codifying essential standards and norms to control to counter crime and victimization worldwide. This function is significant to the extent that some authors discussed resultant criminal policy within the UN system (e.g., Nadjafi Abrand Abadi 1995, pp. 287–356). Others, more recently, have described the UN standards and norms as one of their kind in criminal matters, deserving to be specially addressed by "blue criminology" (Redo 2012) and "blue victimology" (Dussich 2016, pp. 47–65).

Among all UN Member States, Islamic Republic of Iran has demonstrated contrasting attitudes to the international standards and norms, particularly those adopted by the UN since the country's Post-Revolution period. After 1979, Islamic Republic of Iran has fundamentally changed its legislation and practices within the domestic legal system to such a degree that Article 4 of the 1979 Constitution stipulated the requirement of absolute conformity of all laws and provisions with Islamic rules and norms ("*Shari'a*").[2] Thus, a number of statutes were enacted among which Islamic Penal Code/IPC is the significant example.[3]

Regardless of these new laws, Islamic Republic of Iran has sought to rebalance its criminal justice system with international developments in the field of countering crime and protecting victims based upon the criminological and victimological recommendations. This shift has been evident in the second half of Post-Revolution period, specifically, since 1988, after the Iran-Iraq War. One of the most important consequences was to incorporate some international standards and norms, above all

[1]For example, Article 3 of the 1948 Declaration enunciates the rights to life, liberty, and personal security. In the Preamble of the 2030 Agenda, all people are determined to ensure the fulfillment of their human rights based upon dignity and equality.

[2]According to Article 4: "All civil, penal, financial, economic, administrative, cultural, military, political, and other laws and regulations must be based on Islamic criteria. This principle applies absolutely and generally to all articles of the Constitution as well as to all other laws and regulations and the wise persons of the Guardian Council are judges in this matter" (Islamic Parliament Research Center of the Islamic Republic of IRAN 2004).

[3]The first IPC was enacted in 1982 composing four parts (General Provisions, "*Hodud*", "*Qisas*", and "*Diyat*"). Its fifth part ("*Ta'zirat*") was passed in 1983. Subsequently, IPC 1982 was replaced by a new code in 1991 (with its fifth part in 1996). Finally, the newest IPC, consisting of four sections was enacted in 2014. Consequently, the fifth section of the new IPC is still the 1996 provisions ("*Ta'zirat*").

the UN concrete norms, into the Iranian criminal justice policy. The Islamic Republic of Iran's position on such an incorporation has fluctuated. Two attitudes emerged.

On the one hand, Islamic Republic of Iran welcomes those international standards and norms that seem to be in a lesser degree of conflict with its recognized "*Shari'a*". Therefore, Iranian provisions on the control of drugs and narcotics, and provisions of protecting the particular vulnerable groups (especially children, juveniles, and disabled persons) are among those positively interacting with the UN standards and norms.

On the other hand, Islamic Republic of Iran has been reluctant to admit that certain international standards and norms appeared to be in a serious conflict with "*Shari'a*". The adopted norms of the UN system relating to women's issues, particularly with the internationally recognized standards and norms concerning non-discrimination and non-violence against women are among those, which are not domestically acceptable.

Considering the above-mentioned points and in the light of two instruments, i.e., the 1948 Declaration and the 2030 Agenda, the present chapter consists of two main parts. In the first part, it demonstrates the Islamic Republic of Iran's positive attitude towards the UN standards and norms on certain vulnerable groups relevant to the Iranian criminal justice policy. The second part discusses the reluctant attitude of Islamic Republic of Iran towards specific international standards and norms, particularly on women's issues. These provisions face serious obstacles in domestic implementation.

2 Attitudes

2.1 *Positive Attitude*

The provisions on the control of narcotics drugs and the protection of particular groups of persons (esp. children, juveniles, and persons with disabilities) are the most significant examples of those concrete rules incorporating the UN standards and norms into the Iranian criminal justice system.

2.1.1 Islamic Republic of Iran's Commitment to the UN Standards and Norms for Combating Narcotic Drugs

The Single-Article of joining Islamic Republic of Iran to the UN Convention against Illicit Traffic in Narcotic Drugs and Psychotropic Substances (the 1988 Convention, 1582 UNTS 95) passed by the Iranian Parliament (Islamic Consultative Assembly) is one example of such a positive attitude. It resulted in establishing Iran Drug Control Headquarters after the Fight against Drugs Act in 1988 (the 1988 FDA) approved by the Expediency Council of Islamic Republic of Iran. As some Iranian scholars have pointed out (Koosha and Shaygan 2011, p. 189), Islamic Republic of Iran regards the fight against narcotics drugs as its fundamental domestic priority. Meeting it is obvious. Iran has long common borders with Afghanistan and Pakistan to the East and with Turkey to the West—in either case major drug trafficking routes to Europe and beyond.[4]

Notwithstanding the Islamic Republic of Iran's policy, there are conflicting issues within country's domestic legislation. The Act of Accession to the 1988 Convention (1991/09/03) stipulates criminalizing acts or activities such as production, manufacture, supply, sale, and distribution, which are punishable with criminal sanctions in domestic jurisdiction. However, the 1988 FDA, with its amendments as yet, has expanded the scope of criminalization and penalization mechanisms to other individuals including drug users, abusers, and the addict.

Such a strategy could be criticized from the perspective of a differential criminal policy vis-à-vis narcotic drugs, sometimes referred to in criminology as "bifurcation" (McLaughlin and Muncie 2019, p. 79)—a reaction to theoretical and practical forces within transnational criminal justice systems (McLaughlin and Muncie 2019, p. 79). Its theoretical force is based on the just deserts theory, which assumes differentiated treatment of offenders according to their dangerousness. Thus, those who pose a higher risk to the society deserve incarceration, whilst the rest with a lower risk deserves community-based measures. The practical force of bifurcation concerns the expansion of incarceration policy in some Western countries (e.g., USA) in the late decades of twentieth century that compelled their criminal policymakers to reform by reducing the imprisonment rates through penal mechanisms such as alternative criminal sanctions (McLaughlin and Muncie 2019, p. 80).

Regardless of the philosophy of bifurcation, Islamic Republic of Iran adopted another criminal policy against drug offenses. According to it, perpetrators of drug offenses are treated with a tough policy leading to severe penalties (Akbari 2014, pp. 7–34[5]). In the meanwhile, the 1988 FDA (with its later amendments) has provided a range of penalties from fines, seizure and forfeiture to the corporal punishment (whipping) and death penalty.[6] However, Islamic Republic of Iran, perhaps not necessarily by international pressure,[7] has in 2017 reviewed its penal

---

[4]According to statements of the Islamic Republic of Iran's commander of Police Forces ("NAJA"), the organ has lost over 4000 peoples in fight against trafficking of illicit drugs and narcotics after the establishment of NAJA in the late of 1980s (TASNIM 2019).

[5]This article concludes that Iranian criminal policy on narcotic drugs mainly bases upon un-proportional and severe penalties. However, some amendments on treatment of the addicted persons are excluded in which the rehabilitation policy has been influenced by international standards, including those contained in the 1988 Convention.

[6]For example, not only acts or activities such as production, manufacture, supply, sale, and distribution, which are criminalized by the 1988 Convention, but also other behaviors including drug use and abuse (other than for medicine purposes) may lead to the corporal punishments mentioned before. (See, e.g., Arts 2, 3, 4, 5, 6, 8, and 19 of the 1988 FDA (Islamic Parliament Research Center of the Islamic Republic of IRAN 1988)).

[7]The argument could be referred to the decarceration measures in Islamic Republic of Iran's sentencing policy to reduce the penal population of the Prisons and Security and Corrective Measures Organization. For example, the new Head of the Judiciary passed new regulations on

policy. It introduced a new amendment in Article 45 of the 1988 FDA[8] upon which the use of death penalty is reduced. Consequently, as the new amendment would limit the number of death sentences, it could be construed in a partial correspondence with the international norms and standards relating to human rights.[9]

2.1.2 Islamic Republic of Iran's Commitment to the UN Standards and Norms Relating to Children and Juveniles As Victims of Crime

Another example of Islamic Republic of Iran's commitment to the UN standards and norms involves two acts relating on children and juveniles as victims of crime. The Protection of Children and Juveniles Act (PCJA) 2002[10] is the first statute in Iran that criminalizes child abuse and recognizes children and juveniles as victim alongside the UN Convention on the Rights of the Child (the 1989 Convention, 1577 UNTS 3) which Islamic Republic of Iran joined in 1993. "Child abuse" or "child maltreatment" is one of the most significant topics in the literature of criminal sciences. Criminologists define it as all forms of acts or behaviors not only resulting in actual victimization of the child but also providing for potential delinquency and criminality in their future life (McLaughlin and Muncie 2019, op cit., p. 114.). Such a definition has been reflected in the international norms relating to the child, particularly in the 1989 Convention.[11]

---

the decarceration. The Directive of Online Information of Entry to the Prison System to the Competence Judicial Authorities of August 2019 is a major instance directing the prosecutors and judges to avoid the decisions, which may result to jail or prison. (Rayejian Asli 2019a, p. 10).

[8] According to the amended provision, the penalty for offenders sentenced to death or life imprisonment, under some circumstances (e.g., not engaging in armed trafficking in narcotic drugs), may be mitigated to monetary or financial penalties as fines and/or confiscation.

[9] As a notable instance, in its 2018 Report, Amnesty International recorded 253 cases of death penalty in Iran that is the lowest rate of executions in this country since 2010. According to the Amnesty International's report, the falling numbers of death penalty sentences were the result of amending the 1988 FDA and suspending or deferring some executions for drug-related offenders (Amnesty International 2019, p. 16).

[10] It should be pointed out that a distinction between two terms "child" and "juvenile" could be construed from the laws and provisions of Islamic Republic of Iran. In the country's legal system, the term "child" is often seen in those legislations derived from Islamic jurisprudence (called "*fiqih*"), where its Arabic equivalent "*tifil*" (pl. "*atfaal*") is used in certain legislation as the Civil Code and the IPC. The term "juvenile', conversely, is found in those legislations influenced by the academic literature, particularly the criminological one, through which the Persian word (Farsi) "*nojavaan*" referred to as the equivalent of English term "juvenile".

[11] For example, Articles 34 and 36 of the 1989 Convention emphasize on the prevention of all forms of sexual exploitation and sexual abuse as well as on the protection of the child against all other forms of exploitation prejudicial to any aspects of the child's welfare. It seems obvious that focusing on sexual forms of child abuse or ill-treatment is indicating its distinctive feature at the international level.

Furthermore, the 2007 Act of Accession of Islamic Republic of Iran to the Optional Protocol of the Convention on the Rights of the Child on the Sale of Children, Child Prostitution and Child Pornography 2000 (2171 UNTS 227) is another example of incorporation into Iranian criminal policy of the UN standards and norms. The Protocol criminalizes acts or activities, which are defined as "transnational organized crime". As Siegel (2018, p. 485), US criminologist, says, one feature of organized crime is to set up a structural system of trade and enterprise for supplying services such as prostitution, pornography, gambling, and narcotics. It is clear that children are among the suitable targets for such criminal organizations. For this reason, victimologists categorize the children as particular groups of victims eligible to enjoy special support and protection. Accordingly, Article 8-1 of the Protocol requires State Parties to provide such protections including recognition of victims, information to child victims, and granting compensation to them as the main components of a victims' rights system. Thus, in the light of accession of Islamic Republic of Iran to the Protocol, these measures are considered as the national law of Iran upon which specific legislations and practices must be adopted and promoted by the government within the community as a whole.

2.1.3 The Islamic Republic of Iran's Commitment to the UN Standards and Norms Relating to Countering Human Trafficking

One of the most significant legislation in this regard is the Anti-Human Trafficking Act 2004 (the AHTA 2004). It expands the protective measures to all peoples who are victimized for the purpose of forced labor, sexual slavery, or commercial sexual exploitation. The AHTA 2004 also relates to the international standards reflected in the UN Protocol to Prevent, Suppress, and Punish Trafficking in Persons, Especially Women and Children (Protocol I,[12] 2237 UNTS 319). Enacting the AHTA 2004 parallel with the Palermo Convention and the Protocol I thereto indicates the importance of human trafficking not only as a domestic issue for the Iran's society but also as a global concern for international community in the beginning of the Third Millennium. The AHTA 2004 seems to be adequate because it criminalizes the acts defined in the Palermo Convention.[13]

[12]It is the Protocol I of the United Nations Convention against Transnational Organized Crime 2000 (the Palermo Convention, 2225 UNTS 209).

[13]It should be noted that the Bill of Islamic Republic of Iran's Accession to the Palermo Convention was initially passed by Islamic Consultative Assembly in 2017, but the Guardian Council as a filtering organ to realize conformity all laws and provisions with "*Shari'a*" (Islam) rejected it. According to Guardian Council's statement, Islamic Consultative Assembly revised some provisions contained in the Bill in 2018, but then it could not convince the Guardian Council. Nevertheless, the Bill could still have a chance to pass if the Expediency Council, as the organ to resolve the dispute between the Islamic Consultative Assembly and the Guardian Council, approved the Islamic Consultative Assembly's requirements (TASNIM News 2018). Despite of the chance, the Expediency Council, in its session on January 2019, failed to resolve the current problem (IRNA 2019a, 83336157).

Although there is no official statistics of trafficking in persons in Iran, some reports (MEHR News 2019b, 4511202) show that it is a current issue for Islamic Republic of Iran. For example, as some news agencies have reported, Iran wrestles with human trafficking in its eastern borders where citizens and residents of Afghanistan and Pakistan are trafficked to Iran for economic purposes, inter alia, to find a job that is usually considered as illegitimate. In the meanwhile, the Islamic Republic of Iran's Customs Administration reported three cases of human trafficking in which 250 illegals were detected in 2019 (MEHR News 2019a, 4510565). These facts prompted President Rouhani to submit a bill for amending the AHTA 2004 to the Islamic Consultative Assembly in April 2019 (MEHR News 2019c, 4587500). The bill will be effective to control and reduce human trafficking, if drafted in parallel to the Protocol I.[14]

2.1.4 Islamic Republic of Iran's Commitment to the UN Standards and Norms on the Protection of Disabled Persons

Joining Islamic Republic of Iran to the Convention on the Rights of Persons with Disabilities (the CRPD) and its Optional Protocol (2215 UNTS 3) is another demonstration of the country's positive attitude to the international legal regime.[15] Islamic Consultative Assembly enacted the Act of Ratifying CRPD in 2009 while it had already passed a special statute entitled the Comprehensive Act for Protection of the Rights of Persons with Disabilities 2004 (The Comprehensive Act 2004). The latter was recently substituted by a new legislation named the Act of Protecting the Rights of Persons with Disabilities 2018 (the 2018 Act) that not only places in parallel with CRPD but also seeks to frame a model for protecting disabled victims in Iranian criminal justice system.[16] Despite not signing the Optional Protocol to the CRPD by Islamic Republic of Iran, the mentioned developments have been

[14]President Rouhani also submitted "the Bill of Accession of Islamic Republic of Iran to the Palermo Convention" to Islamic Consultative Assembly in 2013. Its justification informs that Islamic Republic of Iran has been victim of transnational organized crime (such as trafficking in persons particularly women and children) in some cases. Moreover, the economic and social security of country requires to prevent activities of criminal organizations (*Mafia*). Thus, it is appropriate that Islamic Republic of Iran passes the Palermo Convention through which the State would able to enjoy facilities and aids of, and cooperation with other States against transnational organized crime (The Presidential Office 2013, p. 1).

[15]It should be recalled that Islamic Republic of Iran has not ratified the Optional Protocol of CRPD.

[16]From a victimological perspective, Article 1 of the Optional Protocol of CRPD is a sample that denotes the term "victim" in the context of victimization aspects in the CRPD. Considering the duty contained in this Article upon which State Parties of CRPD recognize the competence of a Committee on the rights of persons with disabilities, it may be inferred why the State Parties like Islamic Republic of Iran have not accepted the Optional Protocol of CRPD. Under the provision, any individual or groups of individuals who claim to be victimized by their respective State would be able to declare or report a violation of the provisions of the Convention by that State Party to the Committee concerned (Rayejian Asli 2013, p. 59).

interpreted as positive and effective within Iran's legal system (Tabatabaei and Nouri 2009, p. 105[17]).

According to the Director-General of Documents and Publications of the Foundation of Martyrs and Veterans Affairs (Young Journalists Club 2019), in Iran there are 583,064 persons with disabilities as a result of the Iran-Iraq War, and of terrorist activities in its Post-Revolution period. To these persons must be added the handicapped persons, in particular those covered under the State Welfare Organization of Iran. Unfortunately, in this area there is no official statistics (IRNA 2019b, 661478). It may bring to light the difficulties for the group of disabled persons, especially deprivation of enjoying support and protections measures recognized in domestic legislations such as the 2018 Act as well as at international level.

2.2 *Reluctant Attitude*

The second main part of the present chapter appertains to explore the reluctant attitude of Islamic Republic of Iran to some particular international norms that face with serious obstacles to incorporate into Iranian criminal policy from a critical perspective based upon the criminology-victimology literature. Two major examples in this area are the UN standards and norms relating to non-discrimination against women, and those concerning violence against women.

2.2.1 Islamic Republic of Iran's Reluctance to Implement the UN Standards and Norms Relating to Non-discrimination Against Women

The Convention on the Elimination of All Forms of Discrimination against Women (the Convention 1979, 1249 UNTS 13) is the most important instrument within the UN system containing the principle of non-discrimination against women. The non-discrimination principle has been addressed in the 2030 Agenda that reaffirms respecting, protecting, and promoting the human rights for all humankind without any kind of distinction such as race, color, sex, etc. (Introduction of the Declaration, Item 19). Furthermore, the 2030 Agenda emphasizes gender equality of women and girls, including by equal accessibility and opportunities with men and boys (the Declaration, Item 20, Goal 5).

Although the 1979 Convention recognizes the principle as an internationally concrete norm, Islamic Republic of Iran is among certain Member States of UN

[17] The article explores cultural rights composing the right to education, to participate in cultural life of the society, and to have access to information. The authors conclude that the Comprehensive Act 2004 provided a series of more privileged rights including some aspects of education for the disabled persons in comparison with the CRPD.

which have not signed or joined this instrument.[18] From a historical viewpoint, the 1979 Convention was adopted by the UN General Assembly in the same period of the 1979 Islamic Revolution in Iran, perhaps for the reason it was initially influenced as a revolutionary negative attitude. The revolutionary approach to such an international concrete norm also deteriorated due to serious disputes within the domestic organs. For instance, despite the Supreme Council of Cultural Revolution opposed joining Islamic Republic of Iran to the 1979 Convention in 1998, the Iranian Cabinet indeed approved the Islamic Republic of Iran's accession by stipulating some conditions in 2001. According to the Cabinet's Approval, Islamic Republic of Iran would join the 1979 Convention provided the reservations contained in this convention and certain conditions are established. The first condition requires that Islamic Republic of Iran considers provisions of the 1979 Convention to be applicable in cases that do not conflict with the sacred "*Shari'a*". The second condition necessitates that Islamic Republic of Iran does not obliged to implement Article 29-1 of the 1979 Convention with respect to resolving disputes by arbitration and/or to refer to International Court of Justice/ICJ (Ayatollahi 2002, p. 97).

Notwithstanding the Cabinet's Approval, Islamic Consultative Assembly has not yet succeeded at enacting a statute for Islamic Republic of Iran's accession to the 1979 Convention. As some Iranian scholars argue (Ghamat and Saberi Ghomi 2012, p. 179), the Islamic Republic of Iran's accession to the 1979 Convention would be a rational decision at the policy-making level since some signs of abating the debates between opponents and supporters appeared.

2.2.2 Islamic Republic of Iran's Reluctance to Implement the UN Standards and Norms Relating to Violence Against Women

There are a number of UN norms and standards concerning countering of violence against women. The Declaration on the Elimination of Violence against Women (the 1993 Declaration, A/RES/48/104) is one of the most important.[19] Islamic Republic of Iran has always resisted such internationally agreed instruments because of their contradiction with the recognized Islamic rules and practices on women's issues. Although the 1993 Declaration is a soft law and thus does not constitute an international obligation, like a convention, the Islamic Republic of Iran has been reluctant to implement it.

[18]Somalia, Sudan and Tonga, Paula, and USA are another Member States, which have not signed or joined the Convention 1979 (1249 UNTS 13).

[19]The UN has adopted several measures relating to end the violence against women. Although the Convention 1979 may imply the inclusion of discrimination to the concept of violence against women, other measures like conferences and resolutions adopted by the UN assert violence against women as a global issue to be addressed. For example, The General Assembly's 2012 bi-annual resolutions have asserted eliminating all forms of violence against women and trafficking in women and girls (A/RES/67/144; A/RES/76/145). The phrase "violence against women and girls" comes from the 2030 Agenda (A/RES/70/1).

Yakin Ertürk, the UN Special Rapporteur on Violence against Women, after her visit to Iran in 2005, requested some Iranian officials, lawyers of Bar Association, and journalists to encourage the Government to join the 1979 Convention (E/CN.4/2006/61/Add.3; Gharachoorloo 2006, p. 234). She concluded that the judicial and social systems need a comprehensive reform to recognize basic protections and support for promoting the women's rights (E/CN.4/2006/61/Add. 3, paras. 62–75).

Violence against women in Iran has its own historical and socio-cultural factors placing the issue beyond the mere structure of Islamic Republic of Iran. Although the report of the UN Special Rapporteur on violence against women in Islamic Republic of Iran considers the issue as a form of gender inequality relating to masculinities (E/CN.4/2006/61/Add. 3, paras. 62–75), other circumstances concerning the socio-cultural contexts of Iranian society precipitate the issue in question. Iran has been influenced by a social system of patriarchy throughout history. After converting to Islam, the patriarchal approach intensified for centuries in Iranian beliefs, because Islam rose within Arabian culture that has been formed by the patriarchy based on male supremacy. This socio-cultural feature was officially established when Islamic Republic of Iran came to power in the 1979 Revolution. Consequently, the Post-Revolutionary's State structure has required a gender-orientation derived from a strict interpretation of "*Shari'a*". It also resulted in a reluctance to certain international standards and norms that Islamic Republic of Iran deems in contradiction with "*Shari'a*".

From a criminological-victimological perspective, it must not be ignored that the phenomenon of violence against women overlaps with domestic violence.[20] Accordingly, the UN report (A/HRC/11/6/Add.5, paras. 28–61, 30–36) defines domestic violence as a key area of legal focus. There are some cases in which domestic violence seems precipitated through the current reluctance to concrete norms relating to violence against women. Two major examples are murder in the marriage bed, and forced marriage.

In the first instance, Article 630 of IPC 1996 permits a husband to kill his wife and her lover when the husband sees they are committing adultery ("*zina*"). The provision is recognized in the new IPC 2014 (Art 302) that exempts the murder of one's wife and the alien by her husband from the retaliation according to the Islamic rule. That provision existed in the Pre-Revolutionary period (General Penal Code 1925). It has a long history in the Islamic jurisprudence known as "*fiqih*" (Rostami Nadjaf Abadi and Haghshenas 2016, pp. 176, 194) and in some other legal systems.[21] Nonetheless, it is a form of violence against women sometimes referred to as "femicide", as well as a form of domestic violence sometimes called as "spousal killing" (Rayejian Asli 2013, op cit., p. 53).

---

[20]For criminological and victimological perspectives, see, respectively: McLaughlin and Muncie (2019), op cit., pp. 298–301; also Rayejian Asli (2013), op cit., p. 58.

[21]For example, the old Penal Code of France (1810) provided such a murder as an exemption for the husband. However, there is not a similar provision in the new Penal Code (1992): Rostami Nadjaf-Abadi and Haghshenas (2016), p. 195.

In the second instance, notwithstanding Articles 1041 of Civil Code and 50 of Family Protection Act 2012 (Islamic Parliament Research Center of the Islamic Republic of IRAN 2012) that respectively provide some conditions for marriage of under-age girls and criminal sanction for all men who marry with these girls contrary to the Civil Code,[22] statistics demonstrate that forced marriage still occurred in some areas of Iran.[23]

It is obvious that in both cases the commitment of Islamic Republic of Iran to accept the international concrete norms could play a significant role to adopt appropriate policies for controlling and preventing these forms of violence against women. As some Iranian scholars already mentioned (Rayejian Asli and Amrollahi Byouki 2016, pp. 748, 750), one of the ways to eradicate these types of violence is to fulfil its international obligation by Islamic Republic of Iran in terms of appropriate legislations and practices such as raising public awareness. Nevertheless, accession of Islamic Republic of Iran to the 1989 Convention, as a major example of the government's commitment to the UN norms, at least in the field of children's and juvenile's issue, appears to have failed in formulating such a criminal justice policy in practice.[24]

3 Conclusion

Considering the importance of the 1948 Declaration and the 2030 Agenda, all UN Member States should be responsible for respecting standards and norms contained in these global instruments. However, Islamic Republic of Iran shows an ambiguous approach to policy-making in respect of its international obligations and commitments. This equivocal attitude in turn obscures the criminal justice policies that could be major criteria to measure the legitimacy of governments in itself. Although Islamic Republic of Iran demonstrates a positive attitude to the United Nations standards and norms, including the 1989 Convention in the field of children's rights, adopting policies such as the reservation clause may be in conflict with the philosophy of concrete norms contained in such international instruments. In other words, reservation is a strategy to maintain the identity of treaties and conventions as well as to preserve the international order based on the peaceful relations between states in the international community. Otherwise, taking a measure as reservation clause in accession to the international instruments not only fails their appropriate function but also contradicts the spirit of norms and rules they contained. Consequently,

[22]In addition to these domestic legislations, from an international perspective, the 1948 Declaration recognizes the right to marry providing full age of men and women (Art 16-1) as well as the free and full consent of the intending spouses (Art 16-2).

[23]For example, The Yearbook of Statistics of Iran 2005 reported that 750,000 girls under 18 married (Rayejian Asli 2019b, p. 101, foot page 1). According to recent reports, 17% of marriages in Iran included girls under 18 in 2016 (ISNA 2016. also see: Rayejian Asli 2019b, op cit., p. 101).

[24]For further study, see Rayejian Asli (2013), op cit., p. 58: foot page 1.

incorporating the internationally recognized norms into domestic legal systems would enhance the efficacy of criminal justice policies, particularly with respect to the satisfaction of victims of crime, criminals, and the public as a whole.

References[25]

A/HRC/11/6/Add.5 Report of the Special Rapporteur on violence against women, its causes and consequences, Yakin Ertürk. *15 Years of The United Nations Special Rapporteur On Violence Against Women, Its Causes And Consequences (1994-2009) - A Critical Review*. 27 May 2009.

A/RES/48/104. The Declaration on the Elimination of Violence against Women, 20 December 1993, at.

A/RES/67/144. Intensification of efforts to eliminate all forms of violence against women. 27 February 2013.

A/RES/76/145. Trafficking in women and girls. General Assembly Resolution, 20 December 2012.

Akbari, A.-A. (2014). Analyzing criminal policy on narcotic drugs in Iran. *Criminal Law Research, 2*, 7–34.

Amnesty International. (2019). *Global report of death penalty: Year 2018* (p. 16), at https://www.amnesty.org

Ayatollahi, Z. (2002). A critique to the convention on the elimination of all forms of discrimination against women. *Sci-Res Qr Women's Strategic Studies, 15*, 97–113.

Convention on the Elimination of All Forms of Discrimination against Women, 1249 13 UNTS 13.

Convention on the Rights of Persons with Disabilities, 2215 UNTS 3.

Convention on the Rights of the Child, 1577 UNTS 3.

Dussich, J. P. (2016). Blue victimology and femicide: The United Nations' response to victims and female victims of gender killings. In H. Kury, S. Redo, & E. Shea (Eds.), *Women and children as victims and offenders: Background, prevention, reintegration, suggestions for succeeding generations* (Vol. 1, pp. 47–65). Cham: Springer.

E/CN.4/2006/61/Add.3. (2006). Economic and Social Council. *Integration of the human rights of women and a gender perspective: Violence against Women*. Report of the Special Rapporteur on violence against women, its causes and consequences: Takin Ertürk, Addendum, Mission to the Islamic Republic of Iran (29 January to 6 February 2005).

Ghamat, J., & Saberi Ghomi, P. (2012). Iran's accession to the convention on the elimination of discrimination against women: Opportunities and threats. *The Quarterly of Studies on International Relations, IAUCB, 5*(18), 179–212.

Gharachoorloo, R. (2006). A study on the violence against women and the Report of Dr. Yakin Ertürk, the UN Special Rapporteur. *J Association Bar, 192–193*, 30–39.

IRNA. (2019a). at https://plus.irna.ir/news/83336157

IRNA. (2019b). at https://www.irinn.ir/fa/news/661478/

Islamic Parliament Research Center of the Islamic Republic of IRAN. (1988). at https://rc.majlis.ir/fa

Islamic Parliament Research Center of the Islamic Republic of IRAN. (2004). at https://rc.majlis.ir/fa/law/show/133730

Islamic Parliament Research Center of the Islamic Republic of IRAN. (2012). at https://rc.majlis.ir/fa/law/show/840814

ISNA. (2016). at http://www.isna.ir/news/95092112286

[25]All United Nations parliamentary documentation starting with "A" and "E" symbols from the United Nations website http://www.un.org.

Koosha, J., & Shaygan, F. (2011). An attitude to traffic in narcotic drugs and smuggling migrants in international treaties. *Lgl Res Qu: Shahid Beheshti University, Faculty of Law, 55*, 165–211.
McLaughlin, E., & Muncie, J. (Eds.). (2019). *The SAGE dictionary of criminology*. London: SAGE.
MEHR NEWS. (2019a). at https://www.mehrnews.com/news/4510565
MEHR NEWS. (2019b). at https://www.mehrnews.com/news/4511202
MEHR NEWS. (2019c). at https://www.mehrnews.com/news/4587500
Nadjafi Abrand Abadi, A.-H. (1995). The criminal policy of the United Nations. *Lgl Res Qu: Shahid Beheshti University, Faculty of Law, 18*(Special Issue), 288–355.
Optional Protocol to the Convention on the Rights of the Child on the sale of children, child prostitution and child pornography, 2171 UNTS 227.
Protocol to Prevent, Suppress and Punish Trafficking in Persons, Especially Women and Children, supplementing the United Nations Convention against Transnational Organized Crime, 2237 UNTS 319.
Rayejian Asli, M. (2013). Introducing a general theory of victimology in criminal sciences. *International Journal of Humanities, 20*(3), 53–79.
Rayejian Asli, M. (2019a). *Criminology: An introduction & overview*. Tehran: SAMT.
Rayejian Asli, M. (2019b). *Victimology* (Vol. I. Authorial Syllabuses). Tehran: S.D.I.L.
Rayejian Asli, M., & Amrollahi Byouki, M. (2016). Forced marriage in Islamic countries: The role of violence in family relationships. In H. Kury, S. Redo, & E. Shea (Eds.), *Women and children as victims and offenders: Background, prevention, reintegration, suggestions for succeeding generations* (Vol. II, pp. 729–753). Cham: Springer.
Redo, S. (2012). *Blue criminology: The power of United Nations ideas to counter crime globally, A monographic study. HEUNI Publication Series 72*. Helsinki: The European Institute for Crime Prevention and Control, affiliated with the United Nations.
RES/217 III A. The Universal Declaration of Human Rights, General Assembly Resolution, 10 December 1948, at https://www.un.org/en/universal-declaration-human-rights
Rostami Nadjaf Abadi, H., & Haghshenas, M. (2016). A new approach to the nature of murder in the marriage bed in jurisprudence and penal law. *Journal of Studies on Jurisprudence and Islamic Law, 15*(8), 175–200.
Siegel, L. J. (2018). *Criminology: Theories, patterns, and typologies*. Boston: CENGAGE Learning.
Tabatabaei, S.-A., & Nouri, N. S. (2009). Obligations of the Islamic Republic of Iran regarding cultural rights of persons with disabilities, private law. *Sci-Res Bi-Quarterly of Tehran University (Farabi Campus), 15*(6), 105–131.
TASNIM NEWS. at https://www.tasnimnews.com/fa/news/1397/07/03/1836665/
TASNIM NEWS. at https://www.tasnimnews.com/fa/news/1398/02/10/2000775
The Presidential Office. (2013). *The bill of accession IRI to the UN convention against transnational organized crime*. Chicago: IRI.
United Nations Convention against Illicit Traffic in Narcotic Drugs and Psychotropic Substances, 1582 UNTS 95.
United Nations Convention against Transnational Organized Crime, 2225 UNTS 209.
Young Journalists Club. (2019). at https://www.yjc.ir/fa/news/6941122

Mehrdad Rayejian Asli is an Iranian criminologist and victimologist. In 2006 He received a PhD in Criminal Law and Criminology from Shahid Beheshti University, Tehran, Iran. Between 2010 and 2014, he was Assistant Professor of Tarbiat Modares University; and now he is Faculty Member and Director-General of Research Department of Law in Research Center for Study and Development of Humanities (SAMT Organization); Deputy of Research of UNESCO Chair for Human Rights, Peace and Democracy; and Adjunct Professor of Allame Tabatabaei University, all in Tehran, Islamic Republic of Iran. Rayejian's international career began as a Visiting Scholar in Leiden University (the Netherlands) in 2002 and in 2005 at the Max-Planck Institute for Foreign and Comparative Criminal Law (Freiburg im Brsg., Germany). Rayejian is amongst the highly-cited authors at the *ResearchGate* and *GoogleScholar*. His foreign publications include "Theory of victimology in criminal sciences" (2013) and "Forced marriage in Islamic countries" (2016). His latest books in Persian include: CRIMINOLOGY: An Introduction and Overview (2019); 3rd Pub.: 2019 (1st & 2nd Pubs 2019), SAMT, Tehran, Iran. VICTIMOLOGY: Vol. I, Authorial Syllabuses, 2nd Edition: 2019, S.D.I.L., Tehran, Iran. E-mail: mehrdad.rayejian@gmail.com.

Part II
Leaving No One Behind: Intergenerational Vulnerability and Educating for Justice

Perspectives on Elderly Crime and Victimization in the Future

Peter C. Kratcoski and Maximilian Edelbacher

Abstract The proportion of the population for most developed countries of the world, particularly the United States and countries of Europe, composed of elderly persons is expected to continue to increase significantly. This trend toward an older population has many repercussions, including the availability of health care and housing, a drain on entitlement funds, and the ability of service agencies to meet the greater demand for the services they provide. In this chapter, we have focused on the current trends in the criminality and victimization of the elderly that are expected to continue into the year 2030, when the United Nations Sustainable Development Agenda will have its end. The increases in the amount of crime committed by the elderly (operationally defined as 65 years old and older), as well as the increases in the amount of criminal victimization of the elderly, are the result of both an aging population and social, economic, political, and communication changes in the world community that affect the lives of people. In addition to discussing the reasons why the amount of crime committed by the elderly will continue to increase, the types of crimes committed by the elderly and the criminal justice response to the elderly criminal are included in the chapter. Legal, law enforcement, and community efforts to prevent crime by the elderly and to protect the elderly from harm are included in the chapter.

Keywords Elderly · Criminal victimization · Opportunity theory · Socially isolated · Poverty · Universal Declaration of Human Rights · UN Sustainable Development Agenda

---

P. C. Kratcoski (✉)
Kent State University, Kent, OH, USA

M. Edelbacher
Vienna University Department of Sociology, Vienna, Austria

H. Kury, S. Redo (eds.), *Crime Prevention and Justice in 2030*,
https://doi.org/10.1007/978-3-030-56227-4_5

1 Introduction

The criminal behavior of older persons has generally been neglected by those engaged in research on the amount of crime and the causes of criminal behavior. Although reports on sensational crimes, such as child sexual abuse, mass murders, or white collar crimes committed by an older person gain attention in the mass media for a short period, the interest in the elderly criminal quickly disappears as what seems to be more important topics gain attention.

There are a number of reasons for the lack of interest in the older criminal. In addition to the fact that the elderly are responsible for only a small proportion of the total crime of a country, it is difficult to determine the amount of crime committed by the elderly. A large number of crimes, particularly property crimes, are never solved, and the perpetrator of the crime is not known. In addition, some victims of crime will not report that they were victimized although they know the identity of the offender. The reasons for this include the fact that the offender is a family member, as in the case of theft or domestic violence, a close friend or relative, or the victims fear retaliation, as in instances when an older person's home is being vandalized by "teen-age" gang members. Or in other cases, the victims are disillusioned with the justice system because when they were previously victimized and reported the crime nothing was done about it by the officials.

Efforts by global organizations, such as the United Nations' Sustainable Development Agenda for 2030, include the prevention of victimization by crime for all persons by focusing on striving for universal human rights, and such factors as poverty, migration, rights of refugees, discrimination, opportunities to obtain an education, corruption in government, and other factors that have been shown to relate to crime causation. However, these agendas do not specifically focus in on older crime and victimization.

Serious crimes against person are reported more frequently than minor crimes, and a larger proportion of such crimes end with an arrest of the offender. As a result, a more accurate count of the crimes against persons involving older individuals can be obtained from official statistical report such as the Uniform Crime Reports published by the U.S. Federal Bureau of Investigation (FBI). Edelbacher (2018) projects that white collar crimes such as fraud, Internet thefts, and other financial crimes by the elderly are likely to increase in Europe in the future, while some property crimes and violent crimes are likely to decline.

Statistics on the proportion of arrests for crimes committed by older persons in the United States (generally the accepted age for a definition of elderly [older] is 65 years of age and above) consistently reveal that less than 1% of all arrests are of persons age 65 and above. Kratcoski (2018a, p. 15) notes, "A report on violent crime trends completed by the Bureau of Justice Statistics (2014) reveals that the violent crime by those aged 60–65 has remained consistently low when 1980, 1994, and 2012 are compared."

2 The Greying of the World's Population

The older population of the economically developed countries of the world has increased significantly during the latter part of the twentieth century, and this trend in the growth of the populations by older persons is likely to continue through the twenty-first century. For example, Thought (2019, p. 2) lists 14 countries in which it is predicted that there will be a negative population growth between 2006 and 2050. The European countries with a negative population growth include both small and large countries. The populations of Germany, Hungary, Romania, and Russia are predicted to have significant declines by the year 2050. Himes and Kilduff (2019) note that, according to the U.S. Census Bureau's 2018 population estimates, 52 million Americans will be aged 65 or older in that year. Mather and Kilduff (2019, p. 1) state that, "the United Nations projects that there will be 366 million older Chinese adults by 2050, which is substantially larger than the current total U.S. population of 331 million." They observe that the large older population of China will result in significant health and standard of living problems.

The prediction of a future negative population growth for a country is based on the fact that the country will have more deaths than births during the years covered in the prediction. Even if the residents have a longer life span and there is substantial immigration, these factors will not be sufficient to offset the declining birth rate currently being experienced in most of the developed countries. The longer life span of the residents, coupled with a declining birth rate will result in some major changes in the characteristics of the population. For example, by 2030 it is predicted that the number of residents in the United States who are age 65 and older will exceed the number of residents who are under 18 years of age (U.S. Bureau of the Census 2018).

The same trend exists in Europe and several of the countries in Asia. In Europe, the older population (age 65 and older) was 17.8% in 2012 and is predicted to exceed 25% by 2030 (AGE Platform Europe 2012). However, it was predicted (Eurostat 2012) that the population of the European Union would decrease by 16% from 2010 to 2050, and the older population would increase by more than 75%. In Japan, Yokoyama (2018, p. 142) stated that the older population constituted more than 25% of the total population. Much of this shift in the age distribution of the population can be attributed to the fact that a sizable proportion of the younger age population is not getting married, or getting married later in life, planning when to have children, if any, and deciding how many children they desire. Immigration policies that restrict the number of people entering the countries has also influenced the size and distribution of the population.

The reasons for people to leave their country of origin and immigrate to another country are complex. Edelbacher and Kratcoski (2010, p. 86; Kratcoski and Edelbacher 2016) cite the "Push-Pull" theory pertaining to immigration. The theory suggests some people are being pushed out of a country as a result of internal political conflict, discrimination, or economic conditions. They are being "pulled" toward a country because of economic opportunity, political freedom, or a desire for a better quality of life. This theory applies to the European situation during the present period since peoples of various European countries have opportunities to move across national borders. The large majority of those who want to immigrate tend to be poor, and to have a large number of children. For the pull factors, the industrial leaders and other establishments of the Western European nations were eager to have a source of workers coming from the east who were ready to leave their country of birth and willing to work at some of the more menial and lower paying jobs. However, the immigration from the Eastern Countries has slowed down. The population size and age distribution of the populations of Europe and in other parts of the world will continue to move toward a "greying" population.

These changes in the growth and age distribution of the population have not gone unnoticed by demographers, economists, and futurists. Many programs have already been implemented in anticipation of filling the increased health, housing, recreation, economic, and social relations needs of older persons. For example, universities have developed new areas of study in gerontology, hospitals have developed special units for geriatric patients, and numerous housing units admit only older persons. Communities provide special concessions in public transportation to older persons and have developed recreational programs and educational programs designed to keep the elderly socially involved in the life of the community. The European Union Agency for Fundamental Rights was organized in 2007. A coordination of social protection at the EU level was implemented. It does not replace national systems, but only provides common rules to protect the social security rights of citizens who move within the European Union.

To address the consequences of the free movement of workers from country to country regarding occupational pensions, the European Pension Forum was established. An advisory committee recommended that older people's organizations should contact and try to convince their national and the European Union policymakers to enlarge the scope of the European Pension Forum and to apply a holistic approach to pension reforms to cover all pension schemes and assess relevant policies that have an impact on the adequacy of pensions.

3 Trends in Crime and Victimization of the Elderly

In the United States, the federal government and state, and local governments and private organizations have been involved in crime prevention programs and in assisting the victims of crime. The legislation, funds, and personal assistance provided by such programs are beneficial to the elderly victims of crime, but may not take into consideration the special needs of older persons who have experienced physical and/or property victimization.

A special report on the prediction of the size of the older population (aged 65 and above) is that by 2030 it will be more than the population under the age of 18 (U.-S. Bureau of the Census 2018, p. 1). On criminal behavior, assuming the older population does not change its behavior patterns pertaining to crime, one would expect that the increase in the size of the older population would result in the elderly being responsible for a larger proportion of crime than in the past.

Most self-report surveys on crime are not focused on the older offender, but one study (Ghossoub and Khoury 2018), using data from the U.S. National Survey on Drug Use and Health from 2008 through 2014, focused on the crimes of older non-institutionalized (aged 65 and above) persons. Questions included in the survey pertained to the criminal activity of the older persons during the past year, and whether the criminal activity was detected. The sample of more than 17,000 respondents aged 65 and older persons, included slightly more than 50% female respondents, and more than 75% non-Hispanic white respondents. Ghossoub and Khoury (2018, p. 31) found that, "slightly more than 5% of the older respondents reported that they had committed one or more of the following offenses during the past 12 months:" drove under the influence of alcohol, sold illegal drugs, stole something ($50.00 of value or more), attacked someone with intent, or drove under the influence of drugs." The researchers found that, "Only 0.4% of the older population surveyed reported being arrested in the past year; around half of those arrested reported being arrested only once, and close to 45% of those arrested reported being arrested twice."

In addition to the fact that a large proportion of the elderly respondents who admitted committing crimes was not detected or arrested for their offenses, the researchers found that some of the elderly offenders had a long history of offending, dating back to their offenses as juvenile delinquents, and many of the offenders had committed serious felony offenses. Ghossoub and Khoury (2018, p. 31) noted, "Elderly lawbreakers in our sample were more likely to have a history of juvenile substance abuse, and past-year diagnoses of psychiatric, alcohol, and drug use disorders." They concluded, "Although elderly crime is rare, it is not negligible. Elderly law breakers seem to have distinct characteristics that separate them from non-lawbreakers and possibly from younger lawbreakers."

4 Statistics on Elderly Crime

Self-report surveys on crimes by the elderly provide a source of information on the amount of crime and to some extent the types of crimes committed by the elderly. Official data sources such as the Uniform Crime Report, published yearly, provide the characteristics of those arrested for various types of offenses in the United States. The existence of yearly reports, with the information categories being the same each year, provides an opportunity for researchers to establish trends in the criminal behavior of selected categories of offenders. In addition to official reports, researchers have used the case files of those arrested, convicted, or incarcerated to draw out information on the characteristics of the offenders as well as their criminal histories. Biermann et al. (2011), using police arrests data, found that slightly more than 2% of the arrests were of persons age 65 or older.

Kratcoski (2018a, p. 15) completed an analysis of the elderly (aged 65 and above) who were arrested for one or more crimes in 2000 and the elderly who were arrested for one or more crimes in 2013. The information used to make the comparison was abstracted from the Crime in America reports complied by the Federal Bureau of Investigation for the years 2000 and 2013. The data for the two periods revealed that the proportion of all felony crimes committed by the elderly increased significantly from 2000 and 2013, except for robbery and fraud. Several types of felony level crimes, such as forgery, theft, and embezzlement increased significantly, as did some types of misdemeanor level crimes, such as drug and alcohol offenses, assault, and receiving stolen property.

A report by the U.S. Bureau of Justice Statistics (2014) reveals that the arrests of older offenders (aged 60 and above) for violent crimes remained consistently low (less than 2%) and the proportions of arrests of the elderly for property crimes and public order crimes were less than 5% for the years 1980, 1994, and 2012. Of the total number of arrests reported for the year 2017, the arrests of the elderly (aged 65 and above) ranged from less than 1% for public order crimes, less than 2% for crimes against persons, and less than 5% for property crimes. The proportion of those arrested of those considered elderly remains consistently low when compared with that of previous years, although there were increases in most of the crime categories. As was the case in the previous periods mentioned, the arrests for the older offenders in 2017 were predominately male (more than 70%), as was the case for all other age groups (Uniform Crime Report 2018, tables 38,39).

5 Theories of Elderly Crimes Causation

Kratcoski (2019, p. 1003) contends that, "as a result of improvements in health care, communications, and education, changes in life styles (including types of employment), and changes in social relationships, the life span of the populations of most countries has increased. People are living longer, working longer before retirement, and have more formal and informal contacts with people outside their primary social relationships." Consequently, older people have more opportunities to commit crimes. To engage in a criminal act, a person must be motivated (to make a gain, to hurt someone, or destroy something), have the opportunity, and have the means (tools, resources) to complete the act. Depending on the situation and circumstances, older people who have continued to be employed, particularly those in the financial and corporate enterprises, may be motivated to make a larger profit by engaging in some type of scam to cheat the consumers, or to engage in theft. They also have the opportunity and the means to complete the crime. Contrary to what was the situation in the past, the large majority of those who are victimized by those engaged in financial crimes are complete strangers rather than people of their primary group, such as family members, relatives, and residents of their community. These offenders may never meet their victim face to face, since the communications between offender and victims are made through the Internet.

6 Older Career Criminals and Situational Criminals

Those defined as career criminals have engaged in some form of criminal behavior most of their lives. They may have started their criminal careers as youths, after being socialized into delinquent behavior. As adults, they may have had opportunities to follow several different paths, but were motivated to engage in criminal behavior and continued to follow that path. For other individuals, the opportunity for committing criminal acts came after they assumed a position in an organization, became a political official, or after they created an opportunity to engage in criminal behavior, found the easy targets, and were assured that the risks were low. They would be likely to continue their behavior as long as the opportunity existed and the chances of being caught and punished for their behavior were low. Such theories as differential association (Sutherland 1949) and social learning (Akers 1988) explain how the causes of all types of deviant behavior can be understood, including property crimes, violent crimes, and sex related crimes. These theories emphasize how a person learns to become a criminal, that is, the process involved, but also how to rationalize the behavior as being appropriate. Convenience and opportunity theories (Cohen et al. 1980) emphasize the fact that many people may want to commit crimes, that is, they are motivated and know the techniques, but do not have the opportunity. Opportunity theory has been used to explain various forms of white collar crime (Gottschalk 2016). Gottschalk (2018, p. 54), in a discussion on white collar crime, emphases the point that although a person within an organization may develop the desire to commit a crime, learns the techniques on how to commit the crime from others within the organization, and develops the rationale for committing the crime (everyone is doing it, you need to engage in this behavior to get ahead), nevertheless the crime committed is an individual act. He describes white collar criminals in the following way: "White collar criminals are often effortless both before and after they have committed financial crime. They feel no discomfort at their crime, and they may live well with their crime. This lack of guilt feeling and lack of bad conscience can be explained by a number of behavioral theories, such as neutralization theory and self-control theory. Neutralization techniques help reduce potential guilt feelings both before and after an offense, while a lack of self control causes the threshold for committing an offense to decline."

How does the notion of a "career" criminal pertain to the elderly? In many instances it is not the age of the person, but the person's position within an organization, agency, family, government, or within a community that will determine if an opportunity for the older person who is motivated to commit criminal behavior will exist. For example, as previously mentioned, a large proportion of individuals are continuing their employment well beyond the customary retirement age of 65. Those who had the opportunity to engage in crime will continue to have this opportunity as long as they hold the position, regardless of their ages. Many political figures who are well into their senior years still will have the same opportunities to engage in such crimes as corruption, fraud, or graft as they did when they were younger. This may also be true for the head of a private organization, such as a labor union, if there is no mandatory retirement age. On the other hand, if a person who held a position in an organization is required to retire at a certain age, as is the case for many types of public officials, such as the police, the opportunity to engage in crimes often associated with public officials such as those related to fraud and corruption, as well as the opportunity to steal from the organization are likely to disappear.

One should not assume that all of the crimes committed by career criminals originate from an organization. Criminal behavior is an individual act. Many criminal acts committed by persons of all age groups are the result having the motivation to commit the act, and either having an opportunity, or creating an opportunity to engage in the act. This may be true of some property crimes, sex related crimes, such as pedophilia, and other crimes such as drug trafficking. Kratcoski and Walker (1988) in a study of older inmates, found a large proportion of older men in prison who were convicted of child molestation offenses had long histories of child molesting. In most cases, the victims were either their own children, grandchildren, or the children of a close relative.

Based on the trends in the population distribution of various countries of the world, one would assume that the crime rates for these countries will continue to decline and the proportion of the crimes committed by older offenders will continue to increase. In addition, since the largest number of arrests for violent crimes are of younger persons (between the ages of 18 to 40), the crime rates for homicide, robbery, rape, and aggravated assault are likely to decrease more than the rate for property crimes. Following the reasoning in opportunity theory, the older person is not as likely to have either the opportunity, motivation, resources, or accessible targets to engage in crimes against persons as might have been the case when of a younger age. For example, the career criminal who specialized in street crimes, such as robbery and hold-ups of small business establishments, may not feel quite as capable of continuing this line of behavior, especially when the victims are likely to be younger persons who are capable of resisting. However, Kratcoski (2018a, p. 12) contends that, "Opportunity theory, convenience theory, and routine activities theory are helpful in explaining the trend in increases in crime among the elderly as well as why some types of crimes are more frequently committed by the elderly than other types. The advances in communication systems, particularly the Internet, provide opportunities to persons to commit sex-related crimes, fraud, extortion, hate crimes, sale of stolen property, and other crimes without having personal contact with a victim. Thus, any person who is mentally component, regardless of their age, can partake in most types of criminal acts."

One should not assume that older persons will not engage in such crimes against persons as homicide, manslaughter, rape, and assault in the future. Research reveals that many of these offenses are spontaneous, not planned, not motivated by a desire for monetary gain, but out of anger, revenge, fear, and in some cases the older person not being mentally component. If the person has access to a weapon such as a firearm, the fear of being physically harmed is lowered.

Edelbacher (2018, p. 35) notes that, although the victimization of elderly persons is still a major concern of the police, since the elderly are the targets of many types of crimes, "The police now must also respond to a significant number of situations in which the criminal offenders are older persons, often in their twilight years. Although the crimes of older persons are predominately concentrated in property crimes, such as fraud, receiving stolen property, drug, and alcohol offenses, older persons have been arrested for all types of crimes against person, including murder, rape, and robbery."

Although the opportunities to engage in occupational crimes may decline as the person reaches the "elderly" age, other opportunities may emerge for those who are motivated to engage in some form of criminal activity. For example, in the United States (FBI, Crime in the U.S. 2017, table 38) more than 15% of all of the arrests of those age 60 and above were for forgery, counterfeiting, fraud, embezzlement, and receiving, buying, or possessing stolen property. The typical cases of fraud and forgery are generally related to fraudulently obtaining entitlements which the person is not eligible to receive, such as those connected to insurance fraud involving the amount of damage to an auto involved in a wreck, or the damage to one's home resulting from a natural disaster. Other fraud may involve receiving health or social security benefits for a person who had been dead for a considerable amount of time, and forging signatures on documents, checks, and forms for bank account withdrawals.

Some older persons who may have been "law abiding" their entire lives may nevertheless be enticed to engage in some type of fraud. Many older persons who have skills to offer are known to engage in the "informal or shadow economy." The difference between the formal and informal economy is not always clear. Perhaps the main distinction is that in the formal economy, employers pay taxes on the products obtained from the work of their employees and the employees pay taxes on the money received for their work, while in the informal economy the taxes are either not paid at all or only a portion of the taxes are paid to the agencies having the authority to collect the taxes. On the informal economy, Edelbacher et al. (2016, p. 1) state, "An analysis of the definitions (informal economy) shows that there are attempts to merge these concepts and blur the distinctions between the *white* (legal, formal economic activity, not protected from paying taxes), the *gray* (legal, informal economic activity, with the services completed off the record) and *black* (illegal, informal economic activity) economics." Perhaps the majority of older workers who continue to perform some service for which they are paid, but do not report their income to the tax bureau, would fall into the *gray* economy. Many workers, both young and old, find temporary employment in the areas of hospitality, farm work, construction, and recreation. Generally, the employer will pay the required taxes, but the workers will not declare either all of their earnings or only a part of the amount earned, an example of the *gray* market. Trafficking in human beings is a good example of the *black market*, an illegal activity that involves its victims in different forms of undeclared work.

The large majority of older persons who engage in criminal activities are situational criminals. Persons who are employed, have a steady source of income, have benefits connected to the employment such as health insurance, and feel that they are contributing something of value to society through their work, may experience considerable anxiety when they become retirees. Most individuals make the transition without a great deal of difficulty, but others find the transition overwhelming. Crossman (2017) emphasizes the emotional strain that many of the elderly experience if they are forced to retire. Kratcoski (2018a, p. 11) notes, "The poor economic situations of a large proportion of the elderly may be related to the increase in cases of theft, shoplifting, and even fraud involving the elderly. An increase in mental health problems such as depression, psychosis, and radical expressions of anger and aggressiveness could help to explain the increased rate of violent crimes among the elderly." In addition, an older person may have one or several severe health problems that require the use of expensive drugs. A large number of the elderly live alone after the death of their spouses. The loneliness they experience often leads to engagement in drug or alcohol abuse [United Nations Office of Drug Control (UNODC), 2019].

In summary, the profile of the older criminal in the year 2030 is likely to be an offender who has engaged in minor crimes, such as various forms of theft, who is poor, sometimes homeless, does not have a great number of social support groups, and may have some form of physical disability, substance abuse problem, or a psychological disability. The criminal justice response of arresting these law violators and sending them to jail for a short period has not been effective. A public health response is required.

7 Responses to Older Criminal Offenders (Diversion, Public Health, Special Facilities and Programs)

Kratcoski (2018b, p. 198) noted that criminal justice functionaries who respond to the criminal activity of older offenders must first consider their prior criminal histories making decisions on how to process them. "Other factors, such as the severity of the crime, the circumstances surrounding the criminal act, the laws pertaining to the crime existing in the jurisdiction in which the crime occurred, the likelihood of the desistance of the criminal activity if the older offender is diverted, and the special needs of the offender, such as mental health treatment, must be taken into account in the disposition of cases of older offenders."

The criminal codes of most countries of the world do not make distinctions in how the justice process will be employed based on age, with the exception of cases involving juveniles. Conviction on some offenses, such as murder, usually requires a mandatory life imprisonment and even a death sentence. However, judges generally have wide discretion in the sentencing of those convicted of other types of offenses, such as theft, drug and/or alcohol offenses, fraud, disturbing the peace, and other public order offenses. If the community resources are available, older offenders with drug, alcohol, or mental health issues can be diverted to residential community treatment centers, rather than given the more traditional sentence to a short stint in the local jail. A number of older criminal offenders may have several problems that in some way relate to their deviant behavior. Bratina (2017, p. 55) states, "In fact, a significant proportion of offenders are frequently 'cross-over' clients in multiple systems of care (including criminal justice, mental health, public welfare, and substance abuse)".

To improve the systematic response to this population, there is a need for the development of a conceptualized model of diversion. An example of an innovative program used to divert offenders suspected of having mental health problems is The Los Angeles Police Department's Special Problems Unit. These officers have special training and experience in recognizing behavior characteristic of those with mental illness. "These officers help police officers on the scene evaluate and deal with people who may be dealing with a mental health crisis. The mental evaluation unit officer stationed at the triage desk asks the officer on the scene to report on the person's behavior in regard to acting disorganized, speaking incoherently, or being aggressive or uncooperative. In those cases in which the person shows definite signs of mental illness, low grade misdemeanor cases will generally be diverted from jail" (O'Neill 2015, pp. 1–3).

8 Community Treatment Centers

Although the large majority of older criminal offenders can be either diverted from the justice system or given community based sanctions, the seriousness of their offenses requires that those convicted of more serious offenses be formally supervised, either in the community or in a secure correctional facility.

It is difficult to describe the characteristics of community residential facilities, since there is no common model that adequately portrays such facilities. In the United States:

- Community residential centers and treatment facilities are both private and public;
- Some of them are open facilities and others are secure facilities;
- Rarely will a facility, either private or public, be structured for or have programming specifically for older offenders;
- Some facilities only accept residents who are under community supervision by a court and who were ordered to reside in the facility as part of their sentence or offenders who have been released from jail or prison and are under state supervision, while others accept direct referrals from both justice agencies and social service agencies; Some of the facilities may accept only a special type of offender, such as a substance abuser, and structure the treatment program to treat that specific offender, while others have a more open admission policy and offer a variety of treatment programs designed to serve the special needs of the residents; and
- Some community residential facilities are profit making organizations, although the majority are non-profit organizations.

Oriana House, Inc. provides a good example of a multi-functional community based program serving a variety of offenders. It consists of 34 residential and non-residential facilities located in several parts of the state of Ohio, U.S.A. Several of the facilities are secure and others are open facilities. The programs are designed to serve the needs of residents by providing counseling and treatment pertaining to their problems with physical and sexual abuse, control of anger, substance abuse, and mental health matters. A survey of the older offenders housed in the Oriana House residential facilities (Kratcoski 2018c, p. 214) revealed that older residents (aged 65 and above) constituted less than 1% of the total residency population, more than 90% of the older residents were male, and the large majority of the older residents had one or several problems relating to substance abuse or mental health matters.

9 Older Offenders Committed to Secure Correctional Facilities

Although the prison populations have declined in recent years in most countries throughout the world as a result of efforts to divert non-dangerous offenders from prison, the proportion of elderly offenders in prisons and correctional facilities has been on a continuous increase.

Since most secure correctional facilities were designed to house younger offenders, the increase in the number of older inmates, who generally have special needs, often creates considerable administrative problems. Field (2018, p. 69), noting that older inmates are the fastest growing group in the prisons of England and Wales, states, "There are many unique challenges relating to the enforcement of sentences given to the elderly convicted of crimes. The elderly may have mental, physical, or mobility problems which make them ill-suited for imprisonment, particularly given that the infrastructure of many outdated prisons in England and Wales is not constructed to provide the type of living quarters and other facilities they need in their daily functioning."

Bezuidenhout and Booyens (2018, p. 83), citing the results of a report completed by the South Africa Department of Correctional Services, note, "Elderly offenders are considered a vulnerable group due to physical and mental health issues, victimization, the physical environment, and issues concerning release, reintegration, and dying inside a correctional facility." Bratina (2018, p. 232), commenting on the unique challenges the geriatric inmate presents to correctional administrators and staff, states, "These challenges include providing adequate care during confinement, including mental health treatment and medication; providing programs for older inmates with histories of trauma/substance abuse; providing structural or environmental accommodations/needs (e.g., housing for persons with disabilities); offending and victimization among inmates and staff; and terminal illness, stressors related to death and dying, and related policy decision-making (e.g., compassionate release)."

Some correctional administrators and policymakers have tried to make changes in the corrections system needed to accommodate the elderly offender, either through legislation or through making improvements in the correctional facilities housing older inmates. In the United States, The U.S. Federal Bureau of Prisons (FOB) and the corrections administrations of some states have designated facilities specifically designed to house inmates with physical health and mental health problems. Although these facilities accommodate inmates of all age groups, the programming and housing units are beneficial to the elderly inmate, who is likely to have multiple physical and mental health problems.

Some countries have changed their criminal codes in ways that prove beneficial to the older offender. In China, Li (2018, p. 56) notes, "The crime code takes age as a consideration." Using the age 75 and above, older offenders are given special consideration on eligibility for a sentence of probation, the length of a prison sentence imposed, and exclusion from the death penalty, except in cases in which the older offenders used exceptionally cruel methods when they murdered someone.

10 Elderly Victims of Crime

The concept *victimization* is very broad and, depending on the way it is defined, could range from being denied a position of employment solely based on one's age, to an encounter of an elderly person who is suffering from dementia with another individual during which the older person is publicly ridiculed. These examples may or may not be criminal acts, depending on the laws in effect in the country in which the incidents occurred.

The laws and customs of a country may tolerate forms of elderly victimization that would definitely be defined as criminal in another country. Platzer (2018, p. 181) discussed the fact that custom and traditions in some countries allow older women to be victimized by violence and loss of property. He noted, "In some societies, widows are stigmatized, becoming "nonpersons," and are the most vulnerable and destitute. Urbanization and the breakup of multigenerational support systems have also destroyed the traditional respect and feelings of obligation toward the widowed grandmother in all parts of the world."

11 Types of Elderly Victimization

Similar to the categories used to indicate types of criminal offenses, the victims of crime can be categorized based on being a victim of a personal crime, such as murder, assault, robbery, rape, and other forms of abuse such as caregivers not providing a sufficient standard of living in terms of food, clothing, and shelter. The large majority of victimization of the elderly is related to property crimes, including various forms of theft, destruction of property, breaking and entering, and various fraud and scams. At times the elderly person may be the victim of both property and personal offenses, as in the case of having one's dwelling broken into and in the attempts to subdue the assailant the elderly victim is physically beaten.

In Japan, Yokoyama (2018), citing national statistics on the criminal victimization of the elderly, noted that the total number of elderly persons victimized by crime declined in recent years as did the total number of crimes. However, since the population of Japan has become older, the elderly constitute a larger portion of the victims of criminal acts. The major types of victimization older people fall into are property crime categories such as theft of property and loss of funds through scams. Bezuidenhout and Booyens (2018, p. 93) claim, "Although South Africa has specialized legislation to protect the aged, many still fall prey to unscrupulous family members or caregivers who treat them in a rough, indifferent and undignified manner. Many elders live a life of isolation and bear the brunt of abuse on their own. Some are sexually abused, while others are emotionally, psychologically or physically abused and neglected."

Kratcoski and Edelbacher (2016, p. 61) reported on a case of a number of elderly persons being murdered while under hospital care in a hospital in Austria. Edelbacher, as Head of the Major Crime Bureau in Vienna, investigated the case. It was determined that, "In a hospital in Vienna, four nurses killed more than thirty elderly patients who were very ill and weak, rather than providing these patients with the support and treatment they needed." When investigating these murders, the Major Crime Bureau in Vienna found 383 reports of suspicious death cases. The case received worldwide attention in the media during the trial. The four nurses were convicted of multiple murders of elderly persons under their care and this incident resulted in the passage of new legislation to protect the elderly.

Victimization surveys (Kratcoski 2018c, p. 252) identified the most frequent forms of criminal victimization of the elderly. They are:

- property crimes, such as theft, property destruction, and vandalism;
- frauds and scams, such as insurance fraud, homeowner repair frauds, and Internet scams of all types; and
- physical violence, such as assault, robbery, and physical abuse.

The National Council on Aging (2015, pp. 1–3) lists some of the most frequently employed frauds and scams perpetrated on the elderly. They include health care and health insurance fraud, counterfeiting prescription drugs, telemarketing scams of all types; investment schemes, homeowner reverse mortgage scams, charity scams, home repair scams, anti-aging scams, and scams in which a relative is in trouble and needs money immediately. In the United States, older persons, may be the victims of hate crimes, mass murders and other types of violent crimes if they happen to be in the crowd, building, or public area where the victimization occurred.

12 Elder Abuse

Joseph and Gonzalez (2018, p. 126), acknowledging the fact that there is no "universally accepted legal or social definition of elder abuse," stated, "Elder abuse can be defined as the intentional infliction of harm on an older adult. It can also take the form of intentional or unintentional neglect of an older adult by the caregiver." Using the American Psychological Association (2017) categorization of elderly abuse, Joseph and Gonzalez (2018, p. 126), note that elder abuse consists of:

- physical abuse;
- verbal, emotional, or psychological abuse;
- sexual abuse;
- financial abuse and exploitation; and
- caretaker neglect.

Pillemer et al. (2016) conducted research on the abuse and neglect of the elderly by an analysis of the research completed on elderly abuse and neglect in countries throughout the world. Specifically, they focused on the factors that were associated with a strong risk of being abused, those factors that reduced the risk of abuse, and the strategies used for the prevention of elderly abuse and neglect. Pillemer et al. (2016, p. 5) found that, when summarizing the rates of elderly abuse from the research studied, Canada, the United States, and Europe, in the order given, had the lowest rates of elderly abuse. Data was not available for the large majority of countries in Asia and Africa. However, two research studies from China revealed that its elderly abuse rate was somewhat higher than that of Europe.

In an attempt to identify the important risk factors for elder abuse, Pillemer et al. (2016, p. 9) assigned factors that have been found to be associated with "substantial evidence" as being a *strong risk*, a *potential risk*, or a *contested risk* for abuse. In addition, they identified those factors that served as protective factors, that is, reduced the risk of being abused. They found that individual factors of the victim associated with a strong risk of being abused included functional dependence/disability, poor physical health, cognitive impairment, poor mental health, and a low income. The factors associated with the perpetrator that increased the risk of being victimized were mental illness, substance abuse, and the dependency level in cases in which the elderly victim and offender are members of a family, or closely related.

On prevention, Pillemer et al. (2016, p. 17) contend, "Helplines facilitate early intervention that can prevent or forestall mistreatment. Such helplines are typically staffed by trained volunteers or professionals." Other prevention strategies include the establishment of emergency shelters for abused elderly persons. Pillemer et al. (2016, p. 17) conclude, "In all counties, effective elder abuse prevention requires the coordination of available services. The responses required for elder mistreatment cut across many systems, including criminal justice health care, mental health care, victim services, civil legal services, adult protective services, financial services, long-term care, and proxy decision making."

13 Preventing Elderly Victimization: United Nations Sustainable Goals

The prevention of crime and victimization of the elderly requires a united effort on the global, national, state, community, and individual levels. Such organizations as the United Nations can be instrumental in establishing goals, developing standards, recommending policies, and commissioning research to determine what types of laws and programs are effective in preventing elderly crime and the victimization of the elderly. Wilson (2009) noted that the United Nation adopted the Declaration of Basic Principles of Justice for Victims of Crime and Abuse of Power in 1985, with the goal of recognizing the extent of criminal victimization throughout the world and the need to support those who were victimized by corrupt leaders of nations.

National and state legislation has been enacted to protect the elderly from being victimized. Morton (2016, p. 1) noted that, in the United States, "Thirty-three states, the District of Columbia and Puerto Rico addressed financial exploitation of the elderly and vulnerable adults in the 2016 legislative session." Legislative changes made to protect the elderly included educational programs, having more control over financial advisors, and increasing civil and criminal penalties for those perpetrating scams on older persons.

14 European Union Flagship Initiatives: 2020

With the European population getting older, as people live longer and have fewer children, European Union Member States face the challenge of ensuring the long term sustainability of public finances needed to provide services to the population. The impact of demographic change, a larger older, non-employed population, and a smaller younger employed population has led to many of the EU Member States facing considerable challenges to assure that the national pension schemes employed in their country can meet the demands of having a larger older population drawing on the pension funds, while the younger working age population that is paying into the pension plan is declining (European Commission 2012).

One of the major goals of the EU Flagship initiatives (Stability and Growth Pact 2012a) is to reduce the level of poverty and social exclusion by at least 20 million people, and another is to assure the employment of 75% of the eligible population between the ages of 20 and 64. Both of these goals pertain to the elderly as well as to the problem of assuring that the elderly will have an adequate standard of living, and have the health care needed.

AGE Platform Europe (2019), a network of European non-profit organizations for European Union citizens, has a goal of protecting the dignity and standard of living of older citizens by combatting discrimination in employment, pension reform, health, and neglect, and abuse. Austria, the Czech-Republic, and France have implemented action programs directed toward preventing the commission of property crimes and neglect of the elderly. Others countries that initiated action programs to protect the elderly include Ireland, Portugal, Slovakia, and Sweden (AGE Platform Europe 2012). Using the opportunity offered by the European Innovation Partnership on Active Health and Ageing (EFORT 2019), a virtual network on age-friendly environment mobilizing various stakeholders, including local and regional authorities was implemented. This network is built on the work done by the World Health Organization (WHO). Its guidelines on age-friendly environments were adapted to the European Union context and facilitated the exchange of information on relevant EU policy dossiers and instruments. AGE has also addressed the problem of poverty among older person within the European Union Member States by promoting older people's social inclusion and participation in society and in working toward ending the discrimination in employment for older persons who wish to continue their employment beyond the age of retirement, as well as promoting policies to establish adequate living standards for the elderly who are poor (Active Senior Citizens for Europe 2012; European Union 2012b).

On the community level, Kratcoski (2019, p. 1004) lists several strategies that have been employed to prevent the victimization of the elderly. They include:

- developing a communications network to keep the elderly informed on potential scams and other criminal activity;
- providing information and training on how to report crime; and
- establishing victim services for the elderly victims who may suffer from the impact of being physically, emotionally, and financially victimized; and providing access to products, training, and other services to prevent victimization.

Some elderly leaders in government, education, communities, corporate organizations, and civic organizations have assisted in the prevention of the victimization of the elderly by demonstrating that perhaps the large majority of older persons are capable of functioning in today's social and economic environment and in fact are making major contributions to the welfare of the society. They are in good health, economically secure, socially engaged, contribute to the economy either through employment, or volunteer contributions, and often use their knowledge and experiences to guide younger persons who are troubled with economic or emotional problems.

The elderly who are poor, do not have strong support systems to rely on, and who have some physical and mental dysfunction are the most vulnerable for both being physically victimized and being victimized by property crimes, especially scams of all types such as home repair, health insurance, and financial investments. Mass communications, especially the Internet, have reduced the need for face to face communication in the victim-victimizers relationship. However, in many cases the victim and victimizer are closely related or close associates.

Research on the extent of abuse and neglect of the elderly is not conclusive as a result of the different methodologies used in the research designs, and often a failure of the researchers to follow the scientific method. However, in general the findings of the research reveal that there are higher rates of elder abuse in those countries that have a large proportion of the population that is poor, and lower rates for the wealthier countries. The individual characteristics of the elderly that have been found to be related to a strong risk of abuse are being poor, having a weak social and family support system, being never married, widowed, or a divorced woman in some cultures, and having a physical or mental problem. Elderly persons living in a family household in which the members are not supportive have a higher risk of being abused than those who live in a single person household. The risks of being abused and neglected are much lower for those elderly persons who are economically stable, have a strong family and community support system, and do not suffer from a severe physical or mental health problem.

The World Health Organization (2019) has targeted the prevention of elder abuse and the assisting of the abused as a major United Nations sustainable goal for 2030 (SDG 3). Several strategies must be followed to reach this goal. These include legislation that provides more protection of the elderly against being victimized, increasing funding to develop more programs for the elderly victims of abuse and neglect, and the coordination of all available resources, including the activity of those professionals working in service agencies and community volunteers.

15 Conclusion

Goal 16 of the 2030 United Nations Sustainable Development Agendas (United Nations Sustainable Goals Agenda 2015) pertains to "Peace, Justice, and Strong Institutions." Underlying the notion of justice for the elderly (broadly defined as persons aged 65 and above) is that those who are affected by crime, either as perpetrators of crime or as victims of crime, should be treated fairly. The older offender should receive a punishment in line with the degree of liability for the offense and the harm created for the victim and the community. The victims of crime should also be treated fairly by being provided the financial compensation and mental health assistance needed.

Perhaps the only characteristic shared by all older criminals is age. They have been convicted of all types of offenses, from the most serious, such as murder, to the trivial, such as loitering, disturbing the peace, and public intoxication. Some of the older offenders are career criminals, such as those who are involved in organized crime, and some are white collar criminals who have engaged in corrupt practices throughout their entire work span. Some started their criminal activity early in life, were caught, convicted, and became old while serving long prison sentences.

Some older offenders have obtained considerable wealth from their criminal activities. However, the large majority of older offenders became involved in criminal activity during the later years of their lives. Their crimes are in some way related to their attempts to make adjustments to the changes that occurred in their lives after "becoming old." This large majority of older offenders, often referred to as "situational" criminals, share some common characteristics, such as being forced to lower their standard of living as a result of having a decreased income, poor health, and increased costs of health care. Anxiety, fear of the future, loneliness, and depression are related to the use of adjustment mechanisms such as the misuse of alcohol and drugs.

In line with the United Nations sustainable goals of preventing crime and achieving justice in the 2030 world, government agencies and justice agencies have made changes in laws, policies, and practices that attempt to provide more equitable treatment for the elder offender, as well as to prevent much of the crime committed by elderly persons by addressing the causes of their criminal behavior. Reflecting the notion that much of the crime of the elderly should be treated as a public health problem rather than a criminal justice problem, governments have adopted laws that have decriminalized some minor criminal offenses, allow diversion from official processing, and give special consideration for those older offenders convicted of minor crimes. Changes in justice system practices has resulted in the creation of specialty courts, such as drug, domestic violence, and mental health courts, as well as placement of some types of offenders in community based treatment facilities rather than being sentenced to jail or prison. These changes reflect the awareness that a large majority of older offenders have problems that cannot be solved by punishment. By addressing the sources of the problem through appropriate treatment, the older person as well as the community benefit.

Since the proportion of the elderly in the entire population of most societies is increasing, it is expected that the amount of crime by the elderly will also increase during the coming years of the twenty-first century. However, this trend can be disrupted if the causes of crime by the elderly, such as poverty, mental health issues, substance abuse, and lacking a network of social support are addressed through community programs that offer help to those elderly persons who need assistance.

References

AGE Platform Europe. (2012). *Active senior citizens for Europe: A guide for the EU, European year for active aging and solidarity between generations*. Vienna: AGE Platform.

AGE Platform Europe. (2019). *About AGE* (pp. 1–4). http://www.age.platform.eu/about-age

Akers, R. (1988). *Deviant behavior: A social learning approach* (3rd ed.). Belmont, CA: Wadsworth.

American Psychological Association. (2017). *Elder abuse and neglect: In search of solutions*. https://bit.ly/2KTJYph

Bezuidenhout, C., & Booyens, K. (2018). The elderly offender and the elderly victim of crime: A South African overview. In P. Kratcoski & M. Edelbacher (Eds.), *Perspectives on elderly crime and victimization* (pp. 79–97). Cham, Switzerland: Springer.

Biermann, T., Dippel, O., & Bergner, M. (2011). Assaults in the elderly-A population based study with victims and perpetrator characteristics. *Journal of Forensic Science, 56*(3), 669–673.

Bratina, M. (2017). Forensic mental health: Framing integrated solutions. In *Perspectives on crime and victimization of the elderly*. New York: Routledge/Taylor &Francis Group.

Bratina, M. (2018). Management and care of older offenders with mental illness (OOMI). In P. Kratcoski & M. Edelbacher (Eds.), *Perspectives on elderly crime and victimization* (pp. 225–245). Cham, Switzerland: Springer.

Cohen, L., Felson, M., & Gand, K. (1980). Property crime rates in the United States: A macrodynamic analysis. *American Journal of Sociology, 86*, 90–113.

Crossman, S. (2017). *Disengagement theory: An overview and critique thoughtco* (pp. 1–9). https://bit.ly/2VXUiCX

Edelbacher, M. (2018). Trends in types and amounts of crimes committed by the elderly in Europe. In P. Kratcoski & M. Edelbacher (Eds.), *Perspectives on elderly crime and victimization* (pp. 25–40). Cham, Switzerland: Springer.

Edelbacher, M., Dobovsek, B., & Kratcoski, P. (2016). The relationship of the informal economy to corruption, fraud, and organized crime. In M. Edelbacher, P. Kratcoski, & B. Dobovsek (Eds.), *Corruption, fraud, organized crime, and the shadow economy* (pp. 1–17). Boca Raton: FL CRC Press/Taylor & Francis Group.

Edelbacher, M., & Kratcoski, P. (2010). Protecting the borders in a global society: An Austrian and American perspective. In J. Winterdyk & K. Sundbergs (Eds.), *Border security in the Al-Qaeda era* (pp. 77–119). Boca Raton, FL: CRC Press/Taylor & Francis Group.

EFORT. (2019). *European innovation partnership on active and healthy ageing program.* https://www.efort.org/eu-initiatives/active-health/ageing/

European Commission. (2012). *White paper: An agenda for adequate, safe and sustainable pensions*. https://bit.ly/3aSiNG0

European Union. (2012a). *Stability and growth pact*. https://bit.ly/2YsouYA

European Union. (2012b). *White paper on adequate, safe, and sustainable pensions*. https://bit.ly/2VWn7zN

Eurostat. (2012). *Population projections*. European Commission.

Federal Bureau of Investigation. (2018). *2017 Crime in the United States*. https://bit.ly/3aSiNG0

Field, R. (2018). The elderly and crime in England and Wales. In P. Kratcoski & M. Edelbacher (Eds.), *Perspectives on elderly crime and victimization* (pp. 61–77). Cham, Switzerland: Springer.

Ghossoub, E., & Khoury, R. (2018). Prevalence and correlates of criminal behavior among non-institutionalized elderly: Results from the National Survey on Drug Use and health. *Journal of Geriatric Psychiatry and Neurology, 31*(4), 211–222.

Gottschalk, P. (2016). *Convenience theory in explaining white-collar crime 9* (pp. 5–310). Springer. Retrieved February 9, 2017, from https://bit.ly/2WncFAo

Gottschalk, P. (2018). Convenience theory on crime in the corporate sector. In P. Kratcoski & M. Edelbacher (Eds.), *Fraud and corruption; Major types, prevention and control* (pp. 43–60). Cham, Switzerland: Springer.

Himes, C., & Kilduff, L. (2019). *One quarter of older Americans live in California, Florida and Texas*. www.ptborg2017-worldpopulation-data-sheet

Joseph, J., & Gonzalez, A. (2018). Elderly abuse in communities of color in the United States: A literature review. In P. Kratcoski & M. Edelbacher (Eds.), *Perspectives on elderly crime and victimization* (pp. 125–139). Cham, Switzerland: Springer.

Kratcoski, P. (2018a). Trends in types of crime committed by the elderly in the United States. In P. Kratcoski & M. Edelbacher (Eds.), *Perspectives on elderly crime and victimization* (pp. 5–24). Cham, Switzerland: Springer.

Kratcoski, P. (2018b). Justice system response to elderly criminality. In P. Kratcoski & M. Edelbacher (Eds.), *Perspectives on elderly crime and victimization* (pp. 197–224). Cham, Switzerland: Springer.

Kratcoski, P. (2018c). Summary: Older criminals and victims. In P. Kratcoski & M. Edelbacher (Eds.), *Perspectives on elderly crime and victimization* (pp. 245–261). Cham, Switzerland: Springer.

Kratcoski, P. (2019). Older victims of crime. In R. Morgan (Ed.), *The Sage encyclopedia of criminal psychology* (pp. 1003–1005). Santa Barbara, CA.

Kratcoski, P., & Edelbacher, M. (2016). Trends in the criminality and victimization of the elderly. *Federal Probation, 80*(1), 58–67.

Kratcoski, P., & Walker, D. (1988). Homicide among the elderly: Analysis of the victim/assailant relationship in older offenders. In B. McCarthy & R. Langworthy (Eds.), *Older offender perspectives in criminology and criminal justice* (pp. 62–75). New York: Praeger.

Li, X. (2018). Trends in types and amounts of crimes committed by the elderly in China. In P. Kratcoski & M. Edelbacher (Eds.), *Perspectives on elderly crime and victimization* (pp. 41–60). Cham, Switzerland: Springer.
Mather, M., & Kilduff, L. (2019). *Aging and health in China: What can we learn from the world's largest population of older people*. https://bit.ly/3fgBiaD
Morton, H. (2016). *Financial crimes against the elderly 2016, legislation* (pp. 1–22). https://bit.ly/3feBWp6
National Council on Aging. (2015). *Top 10 scams targeting seniors* (pp. 1–9). https://bit.ly/35xC9PB
O'Neill, S. (2015). *LA police unit intervenes to get mentally ill treatment, not jail time*. R6 https://n.pr/3aXJI3f
Pillemer, K., Burnes, D., Riffin, C., & Lachs, M. (2016). Elder abuse: Global situation, risk factors, and prevention strategies. *The Gerontologist, 56*(Suppl. 2), 194–205. Retrieved 8/24/2019 from https://bit.ly/2z7Glt3
Platzer, M. (2018). Victimization of elderly women, "witches," and widow. In P. Kratcoski & M. Edelbacher (Eds.), *Perspectives on elderly crime and victimization* (pp. 191–193). Cham, Switzerland: Springer.
Sutherland, E. (1949). *White collar crime*. New York: Dryden Press.
Thought, B. (2019). *Countries with a negative population growth* (pp. 1–7). https://bit.ly/2YqbHpD
United Nations. (2015). *2030 sustainable development agenda: Goal 16: Peace, justice and strong institutions*. https://bit.ly/2VX7Rm3
United Nations Office of Drug Control (UNODC). (2019). *Outcome of the yearly four to six meetings at the UNO in Vienna between 2016 and 2019.*
United States Bureau of Justice Statistics. (2014). *Age specific arrest rate trends* (p. 1). OJJDP statistical briefing book. https://bit.ly/2StGgH4
United States Bureau of the Census. (2018). *Older people projected to outnumber children for the first time in U.S. history*. pio@census.gov
Wilson, J. (2009). Chronology of selected victimology events. In J. Wilson (Ed.), *The Praeger handbook of victimology* (pp. ix–xii). Santa Barbara, CA: Praeger.
World Health Organization. (2019). *Ageing*. Retrieved August 30, 2019, from https://www.who.int/ageing/sdes/en/
Yokoyama, M. (2018). Elderly victimization in aging Japan. In P. Kratcoski & Edelbacher (Eds.), *Perspectives on elderly crime and victimization* (pp. 141–160). Cham, Switzerland.

Peter C. Kratcoski earned a PhD in sociology from Pennsylvania State University, University Park (Pennsylvania, USA); an MA in sociology from the University of Notre Dame, Notre Dame (Indiana, USA), and a BA in sociology from King's College (Wilkes-Barre, Pennsylvania, USA). Throughout the USA he taught at the College of St. Thomas, St Paul, Minnesota, and at the Pennsylvania State University before he assumed the position of Assistant Professor of Sociology at Kent State University, Kent, Ohio (USA) in 1969. He retired as Professor of Criminal Justice Studies and Chair of the Department of Criminal Justice Studies at Kent State University, where he is currently a Professor Emeritus and adjunct professor. He has published many books, chapters in books, and journal articles in the areas of juvenile delinquency, juvenile justice, international policing, crime prevention, corrections, and victimology. His most recent writing and research focuses on juvenile justice, collaborative policing, correctional counselling, financial crimes, corruption and fraud, and victimization of the elderly. The sixth edition of his book on *Juvenile Delinquency, Theory, Research, and the Juvenile Justice Process* was published in 2020. E-mail: petekrat@aol.com.

Maximilian Edelbacher was born in 1944 in Vienna, Austria. He graduated from Vienna University, Mag. Jur., and as *Hofrat* of the Federal Police of Austria. He served as the Chief of the Major Crime Bureau, as International Expert for the Council of Europe, the Organization for

Security and Cooperation in Europe, and the United Nations. He chaired the Austrian Antifraud Insurance Bureau, lectured at several universities in Austria, USA and Finland. In 2011, Edelbacher was appointed as Director of the International Police Executive Symposium, in 2015 as chair of the Vienna Liaison Office of the Academic Council on the United Nations System, and as chair of the Arbitration Court of the Austrian Association of Criminal Investigators (*Vereinigung Kriminaldienst Österreich*). He authored more than 60 book-chapters and books in different languages and more than 150 journal articles. He served as adjunct professor of the Vienna University Department of Sociology, Vienna, Austria. E-mail: edelmax@aon.at.

Universal Basic Income (UBI) for Reducing Inequalities and Increasing Socio-Economic Inclusion: A Proposal for a New *Sustained* Policy Perspective

Inez Wijngaarde, Jebamalai Vinanchiarachi, and Jeff Readman

Abstract The consequences of poverty, current technological innovation (the change of the nature of work) for the labour market and overall societal transformation strengthened the interest of governments, intergovernmental policy-making bodies and international experts in Article 25 of the Universal Declaration of Human Rights. This Declaration states that "Everyone has the right to a standard of living adequate for the health and well-being of himself and of his family, including food, clothing, housing and medical care and necessary social services, and the right to security in the event of unemployment, sickness, disability, widowhood, old age or other lack of livelihood in circumstances beyond his control". The article alludes to a universal basic income/unconditional basic income (UBI)—a kind of cash welfare programme in which all citizens (or permanent residents) of a country receive a regular, liveable and unconditional amount of money from the government. Governments recommitted themselves to ensuring decent work and social protection for all through the 2030 Agenda for Sustainable Development. Article 25 has never been implemented globally through appropriate government interventions and redistributive measures. Such measures are and have been pursued on a trial basis as evidenced by country experiences contained in this chapter. This could eventually open the door to a global basic income elsewhere in the world, framed on the specific needs and conditions of countries. The United Nations Industrial Development Organization (UNIDO) likewise could explore whether such an unconditional income yields returns in terms of Inclusive Sustainable Industrial Development (ISID) within the framework of possible income and employment effects of UBI triggered by technical assistance and business support services. Such an endeavour would take UBI beyond its monetary threshold and make it a potential source of sustainable livelihoods for social wellbeing and income

I. Wijngaarde (✉)
UNIDO Consultant, Vienna, Austria

J. Vinanchiarachi
Knowledge Management Associates, Vienna, Austria

J. Readman
Innovation Consultant, Brighton, UK

H. Kury, S. Redo (eds.), *Crime Prevention and Justice in 2030*,
https://doi.org/10.1007/978-3-030-56227-4_6

creation. In these unprecedented times, citizens in almost every country will face an uphill battle to address their socio-economic basic needs. The insecurity and great uncertainties caused by COVID-19 in 2020 and beyond, especially among the poor and small-scale businesses and subsistence farmers, will compel governments and UN agencies to develop new strategies. UBI, with all its variations, should be accepted as a universal condition and safety net for everyone.

Keywords Universal basic income · Human rights and justice · Poverty alleviation · Socio-economic needs · Development goals · Sustainability

1 Introduction

National priorities underpinned by compelling social obligations are increasingly factored in economic development goals. In less industrialised countries, and in countries recovering from war and natural disaster, large sections of the population face insurmountable challenges that cannot be overcome by traditional policy prescriptions. Policy interventions aiming at ushering in a system that meets basic needs ought to go beyond economic reasoning when social concerns are critical to ensure human justice. Too often we see fragmentary interventions that rely on market-oriented solutions to rekindle socio-economic transformation without empowering the poor in the development process.

Agencies continue to support business development mostly through extensive training programmes. Upgrading skills, while a critical element in business development, is not sufficient to alleviate the challenges faced by the extremely poor. People that cannot meet their subsistence needs cannot be expected to devote resources to riskier ventures such as a business start-up, nor can everyone who received training be expected to become an entrepreneur as the success rate for business start-ups are very low. Moreover, business development training programmes fail to address the complex social and economic problems facing countries dealing with post-conflict reconstruction or in countries with high levels of one-parent or female-headed households. A different mind-set of states is required if we are serious about tackling long-term structural poverty. One alternative path is to provide people with a base income, regardless of any preconceived qualifying criteria or set conditions. A universal basic income (UBI) is a government guarantee that each citizen receives a minimum income. This scheme is also called a citizen's income, guaranteed minimum income, or basic income.

This chapter provides a strategic overview of UBI with evidence of an emerging policy practice. The objective is to alert donor agencies, financial institutions, banks and development assistance agencies that supporting UBI can complement other developmental interventions. The authors justify the importance of UBI schemes, which can be framed differently, not only to support economic opportunities, but also as a mechanism to widen social inclusion for sustained development. It is a human right for all people to live above a subsistence level and strive to use their potential for self-realisation. UBI could be a foundation policy programme to which all other interventions can build upon. The issues related to mainstreaming basic income has entered the policy agenda in many countries with networks built up, including in the European Union (EU). The questions to be raised within this context is can UBI contribute to build more resilience in communities undergoing transformation to reduce the worst effects of poverty, unemployment and social exclusion.

2 What Is Universal Basic Income?

At its most fundamental level, basic income or universal basic income is the provision of some level of income to all members of a community, region or country. These regular payments do not require further means testing or work requirements (Van Parijs 2004). UBI would be provided to all participants without (or minimal) conditions (Francese and Prady 2018). This unconditionally differentiates other payment programmes that often target specific population groups to meet social or economic objectives. UBI is informed by values of human rights and individual freedom (Lacey 2017; Van Parijs 2004). This commitment can also be directed to wider poverty alleviation (Lacey 2017; Ravallion 2019). The intention behind the payment is to provide enough monies to cover the basic cost of living and provide financial security.

The universal basic income's simplicity makes it an attractive alternative to welfare programmes. Traditional welfare programmes target specific disadvantaged groups, often using means testing criteria, in order to provide health, economic and other much needed assistance. These programmes can incur high administrative costs. Targeted income schemes, on the other hand, whereby groups in society such as small-scale farmers and low income families would receive a basic income, could replace bureaucratically administered welfare programmes. However, such targeting, usually justified by funding limitations or meeting a specific need, sets limits that dilute universality and therefore the underpinning human rights values (Van Parijs 2004). From a policy perspective, providing UBI to all citizens of the community (country) can ensure that the programme will be protected from future political interference. UBI should not be viewed only through the lens of economic efficiency.

The introduction of UBI can encourage labour market participation (for example, by removing welfare traps where a beneficiary loses the entitlement at around the same rate as their income increases), reduce poverty and curb government expenditure by removing unnecessary red-tape and administration costs related to multiple benefit programmes (Standing 2019). A review of ten UBI programmes by the University of Glasgow revealed that, although the evaluated UBI programmes differed in scope and time frames, UBI did not impair labour market participation (Gibson et al. 2018). All the reviewed interventions provided regular payments unconditionally.

3 Emerging Good Practices in UBI Programmes: Evidence from Country Experiences

Evidence on the economic benefits from UBI programmes remain inconclusive. However, some pilot projects are on-going and full evaluations have not materialised while other projects ended prematurely before a thorough cost/benefit analysis could be undertaken. Where evaluations have taken place, it is difficult to compare the different results because different UBI approaches and frameworks with a range of objectives were pursued. Some programmes include qualitative or quantitative results, while other programmes have not been reviewed systematically. While costs can be counted, specifically by the monies injected into the system, causal results are difficult to measure, particularly as most results will include latent outcomes. Nonetheless, pertinent policy lessons have emerged from a variety of UBI pilot schemes. The following UBI programmes illuminate several critical issues.[1]

- From 2008 to 2009, a pilot basic income project was implemented in the Namibian villages of Otjievero and Omitara. The project was organised by the Namibian Basic Income Grant Coalition (Bregman 2017; Haarmann and Haarmann 2014). The amount paid out per head was N$100 (approximately US $12). Positive social benefits included reduced child malnutrition and increased school attendance. The community's income rose significantly above the actual amount from the grants as it allowed citizens to partake in more productive economic activities. Another outcome was that, after the introduction of the pilot, overall crime rates fell by 42%. These conclusions are derived from two internal empirical studies conducted by the Basic Income Grant Coalition (Haarmann and Haarmann 2014).
- Alaska has had a guaranteed income programme since 1982, with much success. The Alaska Permanent Fund pays each resident an average of US$1200 a year out of oil revenues. Almost three-fourths of recipients save it for emergencies.
- Stockton, California introduced a private sector-initiated income support programme in 2018, for its poorest residents. It would provide US$500 a month to 100 local families (randomly selected). However, an adult resident earning above US$46,033 is still be eligible to participate. The objective of the programme is to keep families together, and to keep them away from payday lenders, pawn shops, and gangs (SEED 2019).
- Finland provided from 2017 to 2018 to 2000 unemployed people an amount of €560 per month for 2 years (age group 25 to 58 years—selected nationwide). The monthly stipend continued even if they found work. According to preliminary reviews, recipients indicated that their basic income reduced stress and fear related to financial struggles, increased the feeling of wellbeing and health. The

[1] Kimberly Amadeo provides examples of UBI programmes in the USA, Africa and Asia (Amadeo 2019).

basic income also provided a psychological feeling of security as well an incentive to find a good job or start a business. Some showed more engagement in their communities. The un-conditionality was most relevant for recipients. This experiment was however not extended after the 2 years. A final evaluation was expected to be completed in 2019 (Demos Helsinki 2019).

- The Netherlands has been exploring the concept of UBI for some years within the context of government assistance to develop more equality. The Dutch city of Utrecht began an experiment in basic income at the beginning of 2017 by providing 250 citizens receiving unemployment assistance with a guaranteed monthly income of €960 per month. Other groups of people will be given more money if they volunteer in a study comparing the effects of different basic income programmes. The experiment is part of a project called "Weten Wat Werkt", or "Know What Works", aimed at comparing the possibilities of a universal basic income approach with the Dutch welfare system that is currently in place. Three other Dutch cities have launched similar experiments in basic income, and more are scheduled to participate, should political support be provided (BIEN 2019).
- India launched a pilot UBI programme in 2010 in the State of Madhya Pradesh. An 18-month basic income trial took place in 2010 in this central Indian state, home to 73 million people. The trial provided more than 6000 individuals in eight villages with unconditional cash transfers that ranged from 100 to 300 rupees per month (US$1.5 to US$4.5). UBI in India is restricted and targeted to individuals below the poverty line and linked to family planning. One qualification criterion is that families should not have more than two children. Equivalent to less than a month's pay at the minimum wage in a city, it is well short of what anyone might need to lead a life of leisure. But it is estimated that the programme could cut absolute poverty from 22% to less than 0.5% in the State.
- Kenya's southwest region initiated in 2017 a 12-year pilot to benefit 6000 villagers. Local residents receive a US$22 monthly payment on their smart phone. It is expected that this stipend will double most residents' income. To qualify, a person must remain in the region and their local town (Bregman 2017)
- Poland initiated in 2016 a programme named "500+", satisfying the conditions of the basic income. The allowance amount was set for 500 PLN monthly (about €120). The "500+" Programme was launched on April 1, 2016. However, it currently includes only the parents or the legal guardians of all the second and subsequent children. The allowance on the first child is dependent on the income of the family (Chancellery of the Prime Minister 2019).

Several countries have researched the possibility of launching some form of UBI. Scotland and New Zealand, particularly, have explored the potential of UBI:

- Scotland is funding research into a programme that pays every citizen for life. Retirees would receive £150 a week. Working adults would get £100 and children under 16 would be paid £50 a week.
- New Zealand's UBI scheme has attracted growing interest in recent years. The New Zealand Treasury produced a paper on the topic in 2010. In 2016 its Labour Party commissioned the discussion paper and considered a monthly basic income

of NZ$ 211. Among the key debates that mark basic income initiatives are the budgetary consequences and impacts on poverty and labour market participation (Harris and Bierema 2016).

Gibson et al. (2018) suggest that further pilot schemes may not provide more revelations. Pilot and test programmes are limited by definition and ramping up UBI across an entire region or country will require different approaches and face vastly different implementation challenges (Gibson et al. 2018).

3.1 UBI and Social Outcomes

Discussions on UBI tend to focus on the direct economic outcomes such as, are the benefits of UBI, as measured by income or other monetary metrics, greater than the costs? Other concerns focus on the possible indirect or unintended consequences of UBI, particularly if people receiving UBI transfers will be less inclined to participate in the labour market. While economic wellbeing is paramount, many UBI schemes also focus on non-monetary objectives. According to a 2018 scoping review of NHS Health Scotland, in groups where reductions in labour market activity occurred, time seems to have been channelled into other productive activities.

UBI transfers can affect directly or indirectly improvements in health and education levels, lower crime and substance rates and other social objectives. Studies that collected data on criminal behaviour reported reductions (Gibson et al. 2018). The challenges of attributing social effects (as with economic impact) to UBI solely is noted and moderating and mediating factors cannot always be considered, nor can we ignore latency issues. Nonetheless, there remains instances of notable success.

The following examples reveal some important lessons that cannot be ignored when understanding the wider impact UBI can have in communities:

- The Great Smoky Mountains Study programme (North Carolina, USA)—mental health improved in those children that participated the longest in the programme. It was also noted that the relationships between children and their parents improved, children remained in the school system longer and there were lower rates of offending and substance abuse (Costello et al. 2010).
- The Manitoba Basic Annual Income Experiment (Dauphin Manitoba, Canada)—there was a reduction in the overall use of health service for accidents and mental health. This may result from the indirect effects on non-recipients of the reductions in poverty-related stress, alcohol abuse and violence. There is also some evidence that, for youth, decisions to remain in school for another year were influenced by their friends' choices, which were influenced by the availability of the income supplement (Forget 2013). These effects may have also led to lower crime rates, but no data are available.
- Families participating in the New Jersey Graduated Work Incentive Experiment (NJ, USA), which was a negative income tax programme in the 1970s,

Table 1 Advantages and disadvantages to UBI

Advantages	Disadvantages
People in their productive age could afford to wait for a better job or better wages.	UBI is costly to administer.
People will have the freedom to return to schools or further studies to upgrade their skills and knowledge.	UBI does not focus on causes of poverty and could have a neutral or negative impact on poverty alleviation.
The "poverty trap" would be removed from traditional welfare programmes. The structural inequality and polarity prevent the poor from investing in long-term goals.	Higher prices would make the basics unaffordable to those at the bottom of the income pyramid.
Citizens could have simple, straightforward financial assistance and cash payments that minimises bureaucracy.	Free income may discourage employment and make work seem optional. If people receive a free income, it could remove the incentive to work hard.
The government would spend less time and cost to administer the programme than with traditional welfare.	It could be difficult to get legislation passed by politicians because of stiff opposition to so-called "hand-outs" for the unemployed.
Payments would help young couples start families in countries with low birth rates. A guaranteed income would give young couples the confidence they need to start a family.	In several countries, citizens and politicians are opposed to handouts to those who do not work. Many oppose welfare and unemployment benefits and UBI would fall under this banner.
The payments could help stabilise the economy during recessionary periods.	Inflation could be triggered due to a sudden increase in demand for goods and services.
A basic income for poor population groups can contribute to the prevention of emigration and brain drain.	People will spend the extra money on consumption goods and not for productive uses.

Source: Amadeo (2019), Bregman (2017), Demos Helsinki (2019) and Harris and Bierema (2016)

experienced a 25–30% increase in high school completion for teen age youths (Mallar 1977).

- Crime rates were noted to fall in populations that participated in several UBI schemes. The Seattle/Denver Income Maintenance Experiment (Washington, Colorado, USA) saw a small decrease in reported teen crime (Groeneveld et al. 1979). In the Rural Income Maintenance Experiment in North Carolina, crime rates fell with the group that received the most generous benefits (although it should be noted that there was a small increase for those on less generous plans; Hannan 1978).

3.2 *Advantages and Disadvantages of UBI Schemes*

While UBI programmes differ in their approach and intended objectives, a pattern of policy practice demonstrated has emerged. The advantages and disadvantages of UBI are presented in Table 1.

4 Addressing Human Integrity and Human Justice

A system that guarantees basic income should not be interpreted as an act of charity. Instead, UBI systems can complement human rights. The United Nations Sustainable Development Goals (SDGs) address policies to reduce inequalities and increase inclusiveness. UBI could be a possible answer for countries to be developed. We need a paradigm shift with sharing knowledge and experiences for fresh ideas and inspire new thinking in a time of transformation, which is required by the international community, including the UN and one of its specialised agencies, i.e. UNIDO, to use UBI as a potential source of wealth creation and societal empowerment.

The following questions arise when aligning UBI with policies supporting full socio-economic inclusion.

1. How could UBI assist countries to make their population groups in crisis more resilient and to prepare them for societal and socio-economic changes, including poverty reduction and employability?
2. Who could be considered eligible for UBI, to ensure fairer and equal distribution of societal resources?
3. What could be the overall challenges for governance, societies and financing for a long-term vision when UBI is introduced in a time of transformation, especially motivated by Artificial Intelligence (AI), and the erosion of industrial employment patterns?
4. Considering that by 2030 our societies and quality of life will have to look different, how does UBI, as a public good, fit into policies ensuring that "no one is left behind" with relevance to the UN SDGs set for 2030 and the UNIDO Inclusive Sustainable Industrial Development (ISID) goals? How can we advance poverty eradication and inclusiveness, build productive capacities, and provide more opportunities for men and women across social groups and partnerships with stakeholders involved in innovation for industrialisation and value-added processes?
5. How could we get the beneficiaries of UBI schemes empowered in the development process which is being increasingly triggered by rapidly changing facets of producing, digitalisation, robotics, processing and marketing?

4.1 A Human Rights and Crime Prevention Issue

Although UBI differs in its implementation across countries and regions, a basic justification can be derived from the UN Universal Declaration of Human Rights. The Charter reaffirmed their faith in fundamental human rights, in the dignity and worth of the human person and in the equal rights of men and women. These were determined to promote social progress and better standards of life in larger freedom. In particular, reference is to be made to the following:

> Article 22: Everyone, as a member of society, has the right to social security and is entitled to realization, through national effort and international co-operation and in accordance with the organization and resources of each State, of the economic, social and cultural rights indispensable for his dignity and the free development of his personality.
>
> Article 25 Everyone has the right to a standard of living adequate for the health and well-being of himself and of his family, including food, clothing, housing and medical care and necessary social services, and the right to security in the event of unemployment, sickness, disability, widowhood, old age or other lack of livelihood in circumstances beyond his control.

Moreover, recalling the Resolution of the Human Rights Council (22 June 2017, 35th Session) the concept of UBI can be considered within the context of the call to address Extreme Poverty and Human Rights. In particular, we need to recall that, in its Resolution 70/1 of 25 September 2015, the General Assembly adopted the 2030 Agenda for Sustainable Development and resolved to end poverty in all its forms and dimensions by 2030, recognising that eradicating poverty is the greatest global challenge and an indispensable requirement for countries' sustainable development.

The Council expressed its deep concern that extreme poverty persists in all countries of the world, regardless of their economic, social and cultural situation, and that its extent and manifestations are particularly severe in developing countries. The Council reaffirmed that the existence of widespread extreme poverty inhibits the full and effective enjoyment of human rights and that its immediate alleviation and eventual eradication must remain a high priority for the international community. It stressed that respect for all human rights—civil, political, economic, social and cultural rights—which are universal, indivisible and interdependent and interrelated, is of crucial importance for all policies and programmes to effectively fight extreme poverty at the local and national levels. It has called upon all governments and invited relevant UN agencies and the private sector to continue to give high priority to extreme poverty and human rights, to undertake all efforts towards the achievement of this goal and to cooperate (with the Council's Special Rapporteur) to supply all necessary information requested by the mandate holder. UBI can be reviewed as a useful tool for states in the formulation and implementation of poverty reduction and eradication policies. Moreover, UBI would give people basic security in an era of chronic economic insecurity and societal transformation. It would improve lives, enhance freedom and security and is a matter of social justice (Standing 2019).

5 Can UBI Support UN Sustainable Development Goals: A Key Precondition for Policy Interventions

Considering that the UN General Assembly adopted in 2015 the 2030 Agenda for Sustainable Development that includes 17 Sustainable Development Goals (SDGs) universally set for each country, there is an obvious link to be made to UBI to build a sustainable basis for inclusiveness. Building on the principle of "leaving no one behind", the new Agenda emphasises a holistic approach in achieving sustainable development for all. All forms of poverty linked to all the 17 Goals with its targets set for each one separately would provide societies to develop broad based programmes and projects. However, for this process to take root in society and how to get there, countries will have *"to put their money where their mouth is*" and to bring its citizens back to the realities of their daily lives! New thinking is required to generate solutions in support of achieving the SDGs. The questions posed by UBI must be urgently addressed with a focus on countries' related development constraints, which are all intertwined, and which will impact us all. Although we could see many variations of UBI framed by countries, it does have a notion of universality cutting across economies.

Considering that SDG 9 is set as a basis to "build resilient infrastructure, promote inclusive and sustainable industrialization and foster innovation for creating a sustainable future", UNIDO's Inclusive Sustainable Industrial Development (ISID) is the related strategy and call for implementing SDG 9. These should be focusing on socio-economic inclusion targeting sustainable entrepreneurship development, innovation and digitalisation processes.

Overall, UNIDO's technical cooperation programmes for sustainable development related to quality infrastructure are linked to Food and Agriculture; Good health and Well-Being; Affordable and Clean Energy; Clean Water and Sanitation; Decent Work and Economic Growth; Responsible Consumption and Production; Life on Land and Water; and Climate Action. A compelling concept such as the UBI to support related policies and (sub-)sectors to be prioritised by member countries can be conducive for societal pressing needs and transformation.

5.1 Policy Space and UNIDO's Institutional Direction

To promote sustainable transformations, institutional support will be crucial in the following targeted areas:

- Develop quality, reliable, sustainable and resilient infrastructure, including regional and trans-border infrastructure to support economic development and human wellbeing, with a focus on affordable and equitable access for all.
- Promote inclusive and sustainable industrialisation and, by 2030, significantly raise industry's share of employment and gross domestic product, in line with national circumstances, and double its share in least developed countries.
- Increase the access of small-scale industrial and other enterprises, in particular in developing countries, to financial services, including affordable credit, and their integration into value chains and markets.
- By 2030, upgrade infrastructure and retrofit industries to make them sustainable, with increased resource-use efficiency and greater adoption of clean and environmentally sound technologies.
- Enhance scientific research, upgrade the technological capabilities of industrial sectors in all countries, in particular developing countries, including, by 2030,

encouraging innovation and substantially increasing the number of research and development workers per 1 million people and public and private research and development spending.
- Facilitate sustainable and resilient infrastructure development in developing countries through enhanced financial, technological and technical support to African countries, least developed countries, landlocked developing countries and small island developing states.
- Support domestic technology development, research and innovation in developing countries, including by ensuring a conducive policy environment for, inter alia, industrial diversification and value addition to commodities.
- Significantly increase access to information and communications technology and strive to provide universal and affordable access to the Internet in least developed countries by 2020.

The UBI concept can be used in conjunction with the targeted areas to be developed. It can be seen as an enlightened way to develop a basis to address poverty reduction strategies and equal opportunities for women, youth and rural communities in especially developing economies, economies in transition and countries with post-conflict reconstruction programmes. Collective action and universality are essential within the context of the targets set by UNIDO's ISID.

5.2 *Going Beyond the Monetary Threshold of UBI*

The definitional challenges related to UBI stems from the fact that it seems to hinge entirely on the monetary threshold of absolute minimum income needed to subsist without being deprived of necessities in terms of food, shelter and clothing. When one does not have enough to command basic necessities of life, they live below the poverty line and identify themselves economically a distant citizen of a given country, having less than others in a society underpinned by inequality of income. Income being used as an absolute measure of extreme poverty necessarily creates the need for eradicating non-income poverty, such as health, education and individuals' basic infrastructure which constitute the preconditions for earning income. Those non-income parameters are factored in the multi-dimensional poverty exercise. Just sufficient in terms of income is not sufficient to make the poor development catalysts. As human needs are subject to change, development imperatives also change. Specific country-context and the basic needs of a given country's poor entail the UBI definition cannot be generalised to all. The scope and operational modalities differ from country to country as evidenced by the country experiences furnished in this chapter. Rolling out UBI programmes will have to be framed in such a way that it can effectively respond to the specific conditions and challenges of individual countries and regions.

Reflecting on the preconditions in achieving income targets of the Millennium Development Goals (MDGs), UNIDO in 2004 estimated the growth to be generated by non-income indicators, such as basic health, education and infrastructural needs. According to UNIDO research findings, achieving the income poverty goal depends on trade and development, but a part of the required growth needs to stem from the achievement of non-income targets. UNIDO reckons that in Sub-Saharan Africa, where poverty is still widespread, an effective GDP growth impulse of about 1.5% per year would need to be generated apart from growth generated by trade and development. This had to be generated from the achievement of non-income targets. UNIDO research findings lend credence to the fact that meeting universal basic needs are critical for ushering in universal basic income on a sustainable basis.

The challenge is to make the target beneficiaries of UBI development catalysts, empowered in the development process and thereby adding practical meaning to UNIDO's inclusive sustainable industrial development (ISID). Notwithstanding the fact that UBI is not functioning as microcredit, it is important that the target beneficiaries of UBI graduate from subsistence to commercial and from commercial to active actors of sustainable sources of livelihoods development. The political system should not use UBI as pure charity and welfare with conditions posed to enable the poor to subsist. Instead, we need a shift in mind-sets and "societal" thinking, and UBI will need to be used to strengthen the preconditions for generating income on a sustainable source of livelihoods enhancement, complying with the contours and tenets of famous approach "Aid to end Aid".[2] In technical cooperation projects, UBI should be destined for a given period along with the provision of technical assistance, support services and incentive systems to rekindle the potential of its beneficiaries to development agents in the sphere of inclusive sustainable industrial development.

There are certainly compelling reasons for the political system to guarantee UBI, as a positive change, without any strings attached to it, and to take the debate to another level. It is equally crucial to think beyond the traditional welfare paradigm. UBI should be used as a buffer for the poor to adjust and advance in an increasingly complex world which is being rapidly exposed to creative destruction triggered by pandemics, and disruptive technologies with an increasing role being played by robotics, Artificial Intelligence (AI) and machine learning. These sophisticated technologies may exasperate work redundancy and unemployment. Only persons imbued with enhanced skills and capabilities to use modern technologies and commercialise new knowledge survive. Others will be left behind. The positive intention of UBI is to ensure that no one will be left behind. People should not be bystanders by the ever-increasing technological marvels. Enhancing the relevance of the poor in the new course of prosperity and transition is relevant and inclusive.

---

[2] With the exception of a few countries, Bangladesh in particular, micro finance failed to create expected results in many countries because of the fact that the NGOs involved in channelling microcredit did not possess the required knowledge and technical expertise to train the recipients of microfinance in acquiring the required skills and capabilities to emerge as micro entrepreneurs, nor did they learn to make optimal use of business support services offered by governments as free public goods.

6 Conclusion

In a time of uncertainty and transformation, UBI has figured prominently on the development policy agenda in many countries. At a macro level, governments and their respective stakeholders, including the private sector, have broaden the discussions to include socio-economic considerations. Mainstreaming UBI can contribute to inclusive development and make societies more resilient to bring about poverty alleviation. Also, in times of pandemics such as COVID-19, different and expansive approaches will be required to stimulate economic growth for all.

"Give a man a fish, and you feed him for a day. Teach a man to fish, and you feed him for a lifetime". Teach him better methods of fishing and you can ensure sustainability of livelihoods for generations. This often-quoted saying has been used by development agencies to support technical training programmes and away from direct hand-outs. This laudable assessment was an important step-change in the arena of poverty alleviation, and while this perspective remains valid, experience from the training arena suggests that more could be done. Training activities are often established with a one-size fits all approach. Even with all the good instruments and intentions, training programmes require resources and planning in advance, which often do not align with the reality on the ground. UBI could provide an important strategic element in developing (training) programmes. It can be viewed as a safety net programme alongside other developmental goals *but should have a sustainability focus in line with the SDGs and the ISID.* Instead of teaching men and women *only* "to fish" with better methods, people can decide for themselves the type of activities they would like to pursue. UBI can facilitate people to move beyond day-to-day subsistence, giving them the full responsibility to develop their potential and creativity.

The relevance and effectiveness of UBI will not be realised unless it is included as a complementary component to programmes that support economic growth. As we have indicated, UBI programmes have a long history and good practices have evolved. Many UBI programme leaders have shared their experiences, and these lessons could be used to formulate instrumental and focused interventions. The linkages with the wider international UBI networks such as the Basic Income Earth Network (BIEN) and Unconditional Basic Income Europe (UBIE) are crucial. The experiences gained from these activities can be linked to wider development programmes in line with the targets set by the UN/SDGs and UNIDO/ISID.

The outcomes from any UBI policy will depend on the particular characteristics of the implemented UBI programme. Most professionals envision an UBI programme that is truly universal. UBI should provide enough income for people to live on, and beyond a subsistence-level. Furthermore, UBI programmes should complement other social programmes that provide good health care, infrastructure and other social benefits. This vision would be truly transformative when good governance is also in place.

It is imperative that we find strategies for poverty alleviation in a sustainable manner. One way is to transform national tax systems and income compensations programmes to free up funding for UBI to address poverty alleviation. Providing a basic income is to recognise that economic security and freedom is a priority for everyone, especially in difficult times. This is perhaps more an ethical debate on human justice than only an economic issue. UBI is a necessity in all countries irrespective of their level of development and degree of industrialisation. However, being poor without basic income should not be a life-style choice as societies transform. UBI can alleviate the negative effects of economic downturns and technological change, and it can even be a springboard to long-term wellbeing.

The real test of UBI is to implement a programme that even the most vulnerable groups in all countries can bank on. Any country could conceivably implement their own version of UBI. It is a matter of honest support and political will. UBI could have an indelible impact on communities with reduced crime and increased justice by 2030. Inclusive and just societies are preconditions for peace and prosperity. The appealing idea of UBI is that it provides hope for the "hopeless", eventually serving as a potential source of creating jobs for the "jobless" to reduce poverty, and inequality on a sustainable basis and thereby adding practical meaning to inclusiveness.

This chapter has offered a brief overview of the various UBI schemes launched in the past 30 years. The critics of UBI focus on two arguments, namely: first, the costs of any UBI programmes that moved beyond the pilot stage will be extortionately high. The direct costs and economic benefits of UBI are not obvious given the limited time to assess the pilot programmes, although The Joseph Rowntree Foundation argues that UBI will have a net negative economic benefit (Goulden 2018). The second criticism focuses on the possibility that UBI may encourage opportunistic behaviour to avoid work by giving some members of society 'free' money. As we have tried to argue, the objective of improving the wellbeing of the economically-disadvantaged should consider both social and economic outcomes. While the evidence has not been overwhelming, the advantages, specifically those social benefits availed to the less fortunate communities, outweigh the disadvantages. UBI may indeed contribute to some altered behaviour although the evidence from past pilot programmes suggests otherwise. Researchers have found examples of positive—but difficult to measure—social outcomes such as lower crime rates, improved health and greater family unity (Marinescu 2017).

But no policy will receive support unless attention is given to costs and management of possible negative consequences. Concerns raised by UBI critics can be mitigated by policymakers during the implementation phase. Robert Jameson suggests that UBI could be deployed either through an incremental approach or a radical (D-Day) approach (Jameson 2019). The incremental approach would envision UBI gradually take the place of existing welfare schemes. Incrementalism has the advantage of not upsetting the status-quo while ensuring that policy learning takes place in real time. The radical approach and other unexpected developments, on the other hand, will upend the existing social welfare system. Contingencies and possible outcomes will have to be considered before the launch of the UBI programmes. However, this will mean that UBI will become the central social welfare policy, for good or bad. Regardless of the approach, implementation is the next step in the evolution of UBI.

In these unprecedented times, citizens in almost every country will face an uphill battle to address their socio-economic basic needs. The insecurity and great uncertainties caused by COVID-19, especially among the poor and small-scale businesses and subsistence farmers, will compel governments and UN agencies to develop new strategies. UBI, with all its variations, should be accepted as a universal condition and safety net for everyone. The need is there; what is required is the will.

References

Amadeo, K. (2019). *Universal basic income, its pros and cons with examples* [Online]. The Balance. Available: https://www.thebalance.com/universal-basic-income-4160668

Basic Income European Network (BIEN). (2019). *The Netherlands: Social assistance experiments under review* [Online]. Louvain-la-Neuve, Belgium: Basic Income European Network. Available: https://basicincome.org

Bregman, R. (2017). *Utopia for realists and how we can get there*. London: Bloomsbury.

Chancellery of the Prime Minister. (2019). *Rodzina 500+* [Online]. Warsaw: The Chancellery of the Prime Minister. Available: https://www.premier.gov.pl/

Costello, E., Erkanli, J., Copeland, W., & Angold, A. (2010). Association of family income supplements in adolescence with development of psychiatric and substance use disorders in adulthood among an American Indian population. *JAMA, 202*, 1954–1960.

Demos Helsinki. (2019). *We work towards fair and sustainable societies* [Online]. Demos Helsinki. Available: https://www.demoshelsinki.fi/en/

Forget, E. L. (2013). New questions, new data, old interventions: The health effects of a guaranteed annual income. *Preventive Medicine, 57*, 925–928.

Francese, M., & Prady, D. (2018). What is universal basic income? Finance and development. *Finance & Development, 55*, 38.

Gibson, M., Hearty, W., & Craig, P. (2018). Potential effects of universal basic income: A scoping review of evidence on impacts and study characteristics. *The Lancet, 392*, S36.

Goulden, C. (2018). *Universal basic income - not the answer to poverty* [Online]. The Joseph Rowntree Foundation. Available: https://www.jrf.org.uk/blog/universal-basic-income-not-answer-poverty

Groeneveld, L. P., Short, J. F., & Tholts, P. (1979). *Design of a study to assess the impact of income maintenance on delinquency*. SRI International.

Haarmann, C., & Haarmann, D. (2014). *BIG Coalition Namibia* [Online]. Windhoek, Namibia. Available: http://www.bignam.org/

Hannan, M. T. (1978). Noneconomic outcomes. In J. Palmer & J. Pechman (Eds.), *Welfare in rural areas: The North Carolina-Iowa income maintenance experiment*. Washington D.C.: Brookings Institution.

Harris, M., & Bierema, S. (2016). *A universal basic income for New Zealand* [Online]. The Future of Work. Available: www.futureofwork.nz/background_papers

Human Rights Council, Thirty-fifth session 6–23 June 2017, Agenda item 3. Resolution adapted by the Human Rights Council on 22 June 2017, 35/19, Extreme Poverty and human rights, A/HRC/RES/35/19, 36th Meeting.

Jameson, R. (2019). *The big choice about how to implement basic income* [Online]. Basic Income. Available: https://medium.com/basic-income/the-big-choice-about-how-to-implement-basic-income-f1559369f2f7

Lacey, A. (2017). Universal basic income as development solution? *Global Social Policy, 17*, 93–97.
Mallar, C. D. (1977). The educational and labor-supply responses of young adults in 89 experimental families. In H. W. Watts & A. Rees (Eds.), *New-Jersey income-maintenance experiment 2. Labor-supply responses*. New York: Academic Press Inc.
Marinescu, I. (2017). *No strings attached: The behavioral effects of U.S. unconditional cash transfer programs*. The Roosevelt Institute.
Ravallion, M. (2019). Guaranteed employment or guaranteed income? *World Development, 115*, 209–221.
SEED. (2019). *Our vision for SEED: A discussion paper* [Online]. Stockton: Stockton Economic Empowerment Demonstration. Available: www.stocktondemonstration.org
Standing, G. (2019). *Basic income as common dividends: Piloting a transformative policy*. London.
Van Parijs, P. (2004). Basic income: A simple and powerful idea for the twenty-first century. *Politics & Society, 32*, 7–39.

Inez Wijngaarde Drs. (Suriname/Austria) is an entrepreneurship development and management specialist, with 25 years international professional experience in programme and policy development with United Nations agencies, including ILO, UNODC and UNIDO. After several field postings in Asia and the Pacific, she managed at UNIDO HQ in Vienna, Austria, EU/multi-bilateral development cooperation projects in developing economies to empower women, youth, migrants and other population groups in severe disadvantage positions, e.g. internally displaced persons and refugees in agri-businesses and technical training. She is currently an international consultant with academia and UNIDO, the UN specialized agency that promotes inclusive industrial development (ISID) for poverty reduction, inclusive globalization and environmental sustainability. She has forged professional networks with agencies such as the UNCTAD Creative Industries Programme, the European Union, the European Forum Alpbach and Slow Food International. She has received awards from the International Professional Women's Network (USA) and co-authored several articles related to unleashing human potential through sustainable entrepreneurship and fair migration policies for job creation; demand oriented industrial training; and creative industries of unemployed youth. E-mail: wijngaarde.inez@gmail.com.

Jebamalai Vinanchiarachi Dr. (India) is a sustainable development expert, with over 30 years of professional experience in the United Nations Industrial Development Organization (UNIDO), Vienna, Austria, where he served in various capacities. He eventually retired as the Principal Adviser to the Director General of UNIDO. He has to his credit several degrees and awards with distinctions. As an economist, he has authored several journal articles, books and reports, highlighting the changing patterns of sustainable development, with a focus on economic efficiency, ecological compliance and social inclusion. Recent books include *Myths and Realities of East Asian Model of Development, India's Time, Rethinking Development Realities, Intervene to Industrialise,* and *The Poverty of Economic Thinking.* A book on his personal life, penned by him, is entitled *In Joy and Sorrow.* Forthcoming books co-authored by him include *Positioning Africa in the Context of the New Industrial Revolution,* and *Myths and Realities of Indian Economy.* Using his outstanding performance with professional excellence, he is working as the Principal Adviser to the Knowledge Management Associates, Vienna, Austria. E-mail: vinanchiarachi@yahoo.com.

Jeff Readman Dr., (Canada/United Kingdom) as an economist, political science specialist researcher, and senior lecturer, he has over 20 years of outstanding professional experience specializing in technology and innovation management, digital transformation, value chain development, small and medium enterprises start-ups, business education services and applied industry research. He has worked in EU/UN international development projects supporting business skills development and innovation. He managed the MBA Innovation Programme for the University of Brighton (2011–2018). He led research projects globally as project leader with substantive training, coaching and workshop facilitation know-how. Research interests, apart from the theme Universal Basic Income (UBI), include machine learning programmes changing innovation landscapes and management practices; exploring changing boundaries of firms and outcomes arising from outsourcing & SMEs upgrading/global value chains; vocational training and policy interventions to develop SME capabilities in less industrialised countries. Publications include: Readman, J., Bessant, J., Neely, A. & Twigg, D. 2018. Positioning UK research and technology organizations as outward-facing technology-bases. Legacy standards and innovation: the Kyrgyz construction materials value chain. Conference Exploring Technology Upgrading in Emerging and Transition Economies: "Shifting Wealth I" to "Shifting Wealth II." Readman, J. (2017). E-mail: jeff.readman@btinternet.com.

Prisoners and Their Families: The Effects of Imprisonment on the Family

Helmut Kury

Abstract The public debate regarding criminals and crime usually deals primarily with the crime and the perpetrator at the time of the crime, but hardly with its development and, above all, little with his family and the impact of detention on them. Especially if the perpetrator still has young children, their development can be significantly negatively affected by the detention of a parent, usually the father. In the last few years, more and more institutions have been created in Germany to take care of the families of the detainees, but there is still a lot of work to be done. In many cases, NGOs are also active in this field. The chapter provides a brief overview of the national and international discussion of the topic. The empirical research clearly shows the negative effects of separating (small) children from their parents. In the case of the detention of a parent, the stigmatisation of the related, especially the children, still plays an essential role. The detention of the mother usually has even more serious negative effects on the children than when the father is in custody. According to German legal provisions on prison sentences, negative effects of a prison sentence should be avoided as far as possible. Much more should be done here, for example through large-scale regulations on the visits of prisoners by relatives.

Keywords Prisoners and their families · Negative side effects of a prison sentence · Negative effects on children · Task of the resocialisation of detainees · Crime prevention · Visiting opportunities in prison for relatives · Stigmatisation

1 Introduction

Under Article 9, paragraph 3 of the 1989 UN Convention on the Rights of the Child (CRC/1577 UNTS 3), children have the right to have contacts with both parents. This right also applies if, for example, the detention of a parent makes it difficult to

H. Kury (✉)
Max Planck-Institute for Foreign and International Penal Law, Freiburg, Germany

H. Kury, S. Redo (eds.), *Crime Prevention and Justice in 2030*,
https://doi.org/10.1007/978-3-030-56227-4_7

implement the maintenance of contacts. The best interests of the child must be taken into account as a matter of priority (Article 3 of the CRC), the Contracting States are obliged to pay particular attention to the rules governing the treatment of detained parents with their minor children (Feige 2019a). Heberling (2012, p. 8) emphasises: "Internationally and nationally, a number of conventions and legal provisions refer very clearly to the necessity and also the right of family members to contact each other even in the event of (temporary) separation." In addition to the UN Convention on the Rights of the Child, he also refers to several corresponding German legal regulations, such as the Constitution ("Grundgesetz"), the Civil Code ("Bürgerliches Gesetzbuch – BGB") or the Social Code ("Sozialgesetzbuch – SGB").

There is therefore less lack of legal regulations and more in their consistent implementation. In its judgment of 31 May 2006, the Federal Constitutional Court ("Bundesverfassungsgericht") also expressly emphasises the importance of visiting prisoners to maintain family contacts (2 BvR 1673/04; 2 BvR 2402/04). In a new judgment of January 2020, the German Federal Constitutional Court ("Bundesverfassungsgericht") once again stressed that admission to the freedom of release for the preservation of the viability of detainees belongs above all in the case of long prison sentences. The resocialisation of detainees is in the foreground (Westdeutscher Rundfunk – WDR 2020).

Mittermaier (1954, p. 109) emphasised decades ago: "Today the prisoner should not be so strictly closed by the outside world, because for his later life it is necessary that he has other relations. In particular, the connection with the family is of the utmost importance and is often the only means of upholding the prisoner, in him strengthening courage and the will for later life. Maintaining or re-connecting this link is an important task for prison care."

The Freiburg "*Verein für systemische Therapie von straffällig gewordenen Menschen, deren Angehörigen sowie Menschen in schwierigen Lebensituationen*" (Association for Systemic Therapy of Persons Who Have Become a Criminal, Their Relatives and People in Difficult Life Situations) (Cocon e.V. Freiburg 2020, p. 2) quotes in its annual report 2018/2019 against the background of many years of experience in the care of relatives of detainees from a conversation between mother and child regarding the imprisoned man or father: "Why is my father not allowed to come home? - Because he has to work. - Not even for a day? - No, that is not possible. Why? Because his boss doesn't allow it."

It is emphasised (Cocon e.V. Freiburg 2020, p. 2) that these "'questions about questions' (be) that children ask again and again and a mother who is psychologically overwhelmed with the detention of the father. Emergency lies in almost unsustainable extreme situations serve to protect one's own emotional worlds and, in the case of incarceration, also to protect children from reactions from their environment. Emergency lies that at the same time, on a non-verbal level, send a different message to the children, which irritate and disturb the children and thus silence their voices too quickly. Children's souls who cannot understand the frameworks and rules of a legal world at all; Children who urgently need safety, support, reliability in their development in order to be able to grow and who are very injured in this context".

This succinctly describes the essential problems of the detention of a family member, especially the father of children, for the rest of the family. The public discussion on crime focuses mainly on individual (serious) crimes and the perpetrator's holding at the time of the crime, the final sentence imposed. Here, very selective reports are made about "public" crimes, especially sexual offences and those involving children as victims. For example, Hestermann (2016) emphasises "Violence Against Children Sells Very Well." The media are (understandably) particularly interested in reading or being seen in their reporting against the background of economic interests. This essentially determines the choice and type of reporting. At the same time, however, this also contributes to a very distorted information to the public about the 'crime scene'.

For example, relatively little is reported about the background of criminality, why individuals become criminals, the situation in the penitentiary and hardly any collateral damage to detention, for example among the families concerned. Too much such reporting, for example on the living conditions of offenders, could direct responsibility to society as such and thus ultimately to each individual, and thus also to call into question the specific attribution of guilt to the "evil" perpetrator. Thus, the problem of the relatives of detainees is largely unknown in public, "even in scientific research relatives are still marginalized today" (Heberling 2012, p. 9).

From the criminal policy side, too, one concentrates almost exclusively on the perpetrator at the time of the crime. There is no examination of the central question, why the perpetrator has become the perpetrator, thus withdraws from the responsibility for his usually pronounced bad conditions of socialisation in childhood, suggests against this background, a "solution" to the problem primarily in a tightening of criminal sanctions, knowing from polls that this is a major public vote. Politicians are primarily interested in obtaining public approval so that they can be re-elected. Criminal policy is an "easy" policy in that, against the background of punitive attitudes, one receives applause from a large part of the public at a general demand for a tightening of penalties. In many cases, politicians in this complex area are also little informed about research results. Populist politics generally receives a great deal of public support, but it does not solve the problems in any way, incurs more costs than a rational approach based on modern research.

In recent years, the punitive reaction of the population has increased. Apparently, this is due to the increase in the number of immigrants but also because of the increasing complexity of the way in which life is created in modern society (Kury and Shea 2011; Kury and Redo 2018). This has been helped by, for example, the increasing digitalisation, the expansion of information exchange via the Internet and smartphones, the growing international coverage and the resulting feelings of overdemand and Unpredictability. For example, Streng (2014, p. 60) found a clear affirmation of the death penalty "for some crimes" in his latest assessment of law students. While this most severe sanction was approved by 11.5% in 1977, it was 31.9% in 2010. It should be noted that in Germany the death penalty was abolished in 1949.

The CSU ("Christlich Soziale Union") in the German Bundestag (2020, p. 4) at its closing ceremony at the beginning of January 2020 called for a lowering of the age of criminal liability for under-14s for serious crimes. Suliak (2020) quotes the Cologne criminal lawyer Frank Neubacher in a critical contribution to this decision, according to which there are "good reasons" for the legislator's decision of the 1953 Youth Court Act to change the minimal age for criminal sanctions from 12 to 14 years. The National Socialists reduced it to 12 years. "Why should the behaviour of under-14s be prosecuted? I do not see what criminal law could achieve, which could not be achieved by other means, for example through family courts and youth welfare – apart perhaps from a 'deterrent effect' that far too many wrongly believe in."

For decades, criminological research has convincingly shown that a reduction in crime in a society can hardly be achieved by tightening criminal sanctions. Thus, Dölling et al. (2011, p. 374) conclude based on their extremely comprehensive and meaningful meta-analysis on the effect of sanctions: "the severity of punishment clearly has a lower deterrent effect than the probability of punishment [...] the theory of negative general prevention is unsuitable as a basis of legitimising all sanctions...". The authors (Hermann and Dölling 2016, p. 19) explicitly emphasise: "the deterrent effect of severe punishment should be considered with scepticism."

It should also be borne in mind that, when assessing the effect of sentences, collateral damage to the families of the detainees and the costs and ancillary costs of detention are generally disregarded. Light (1993, p. 324f.) points out in this context: "The victims of crime include not only those who have committed offences against them, but also families and dependents of those convicted offences, especially if the offender is sentenced to a period in prison. The more serious the crime the greater all round is the suffering."

Politicians are unwilling to take further decisions, often against the background of their own ignorance of relevant criminological research results, but above all to retain the support of the general public and to be (re-)elected (Kury and Schüßler 2019). For example, Hagan and Dinovitzer (1999, p. 130) emphasise that some large US states are now spending the same amount or more of money, "to incarcerate young adults than to educate their college-age citizens." California, for example, has built a new prison per year for the past two decades, but at the same time in the two decades only one new university (Ambrosio and Schiraldi 1997).

The negative effects of detention on the perpetrators in a generally unfavourable environment for resocialisation (Kury 2020a, b), in the light of the attitude that deterrence helps reduce crime is hardly seen. It is precisely the harmful effect of a parent's detention on existing children, which often leads to long-term problems and often to their own subsequent criminal behaviour, that is generally not seen in the context of custodial sentences of parents.

Although the family rightly plays an important role in our society, Article 6 of the German Basic Law ("Grundgesetz - GG") emphasises the responsibility of the state for the protection of the family. In penal proceedings, however, "and here especially in the execution of the long-term custodial sentence, the state is now obviously acting precisely in a marriage-disruptive, if not marriage-destroying manner" (Neibecker 1984, p. 335). According to Ebbers (1993, p. 49), "the special protection for marriage and family enshrined in the Basic Law (GG, Art. 6) is subordinated to the perpetrator-oriented premises of legal and enforcement practice." Family members of detainees, especially their children and the impact of a guardian's detention on them, have long been overseen in criminological research and is little noticed. As Heberling (2012, p. 8) emphasises: "The group of relatives of detainees are still marginalised in both prison and scientific research and are hardly noticed as a serious target group. The same time Relatives also bear the consequences of detention."

In 2012, the German journal *Forum Strafvollzug—Zeitschrift für Strafvollzug und Straffälligenhilfe* devoted a 2012 issue to the topic "Co-punished third parties" ("*Mitbestrafte Dritte*") with significant contributions to the topic. Pfalzer et al. (2012, p. 7) emphasise in their introductory chapter that the "detention of a family member ... is always a massive intervention in existing family structures, if they exist." In view of the fact that it was estimated at the time that in Germany about 50,000 children are affected by the detention of a parent, especially fathers, this has negative consequences for a significant proportion of children, such as financial disadvantages or stigmatisation in the environment, which can lead to a withdrawal from social references. "The remaining contact options, such as letters, parcels and telephone conversations, which are proposed in the Penal Enforcement Act as well as in the youth detention laws of the Länder, cannot replace the personal contact, although they are signalizing relations at least symbolically." Visits to prisons are often discouraging and stressful.

In her article, Heberling (2012, p. 8ff.) discusses the "situation of the relatives of detainees" in a differentiated way. The author emphasises that the group of relatives is marginalised in prison and scientific research and is "hardly noticed as a target group to be taken seriously."

Goll et al. (2012, pp. 15–18) discuss the "Parent-Child Project Chance", a model project carried out since 2010 in Baden-Württemberg, a part of Germany, that was designed for 3 years. The project is particularly concerned also with the training of the employees, with the children of the detainees at the centre. About 60% of detainees with children were interested in working together in the project. Due to the detention, "the emotional availability of the bondpersons is threatened", this is to be counteracted, it is about bonding promotion and relationship work (p. 16). The project is part of the EUROPEAN Union-funded COPING project, which is being supervised in Germany by the Technical University of Dresden.

The existence of other, especially more resocialisation and family-friendly forms of imprisonment can be seen in examples from Scandinavia (Larson 2013), where prisons are partly located on islands, such as Suomenlinna Island, in Helsinki's South Harbor.

The Island hosts an "open" prison since 1971. Here prisoners can spend time with electronic monitoring with their families in Helsinki. In Scandinavia prisoners wear their own clothes. Larson (2013) points out, that not all Scandinavian prisons are open prisons. "But the most profound difference is that correctional officers fill both rehabilitative and security roles. Each prisoner has a "contact officer" who monitors and helps advance progress toward return to the world outside—a practice introduced to help *officers* avoid to damage experienced by performing purely punitive functions: stress, hypertension, alcoholism, suicide, and other job-related hazards that today plague American corrections officers, who have an average life expectancy of 59. This is all possible because, throughout Scandinavia, criminal justice policy rarely enters political debate. Decisions about best practices are left to professionals in the field, who are often published criminologists and consult closely with academics" (Larson 2013, p. 4). Contacts with families are particularly maintained. "Whatever other differences may exist between law-abiding families and people convicted of crimes, the prison system itself does not seek to widen the social distance between them" (Larson 2013, p. 14).

In the meantime, the number of studies, especially in the international sector, the USA, and the United Kingdom, has increased significantly in some cases (Besemer et al. 2019, p. 65). In the following, key research results on the topic in the German and international field are to be presented.

2 Investigations So Far

2.1 Discussion and Investigation in Germany

It will first briefly present the discussion in Germany and give a summarising report on research results before referring to international studies. Clephas and Althoff (2003, p. 279) emphasised years ago: "For a long time, the group of detainees and prisoners after release was neglected. It is only in recent years that the Criminal Assistance has recognised this as an independent target group in so far as different counselling and support aids are offered" (see Kanisch and Asprion 1997).

Römer (1967) was able to show in his study that a large part of the children concerned suffered from hostility, which was met by neighbours, especially other children. According to the author (p. 37), the own criminality of the children studied can be attributed to a significant extent to the stigmatisation by the environment, a problem which is regularly raised in this context (see Condry 2003, 2007; Fontaine et al. 2015). The paternal role model is no longer valid, stigma through the environment often leads to an overburden and a withdrawal from social references (Pfalzer et al. 2012). Wildeman et al. (2017, p. 8) found that the detention of a parent even had a negative effect on the behaviour of teachers on the pupils concerned (see also Dallaire et al. 2010).

Carlson and Cervera (1992, pp. 140–144) also examined the coping mechanisms of the women of detained men. Support from the family, faith and religion, children, communication and visits to the detainees, involvement with school or work were important. Support from the family, faith and religion, children, communication and visits to the detainees, involvement with school or work were important. Almost half of all women did not inform the children (father is on assembly, hospital, to cure). The situation was also often not disclosed to kindergarten or school. Almost half of the children showed school reading and difficulty concentrating after the detention of a parent (Busch et al. 1987). In assessing the assessment of the previous situation compared to the current pair situation among the detainees and their partners showed only minor discrepancies, indicating that the incarceration itself had only a minor impact on the couple's cohesion (Busch 1989).

According to Heberling (2012, p. 11), 81% of women and 23% of men in a marriage and family seminar wanted more intensive follow-up after release from prison (Busch 1989). Unprocessed and undiscussed loss of trust on the part of the partners, is seen as the greatest danger to the existence of a partnership (Koepsel 1989, p. 152; Kern 2007, p. 89f.). Children of detainees are "the weakest and most dependent members of the family [. . .] confronted with a situation that is incomprehensible to them, often with traumatic effects. Unfortunately, they are overseen mostly by both the prison system as well as from criminology" (Heberling 2012, p. 10). The detained parent was also missing as an identification figure (Mohme and Dellbrügge 2010, p. 1).

The earlier the children were separated from their father, "the more serious the current burdens and late consequences in the further course of development" (Busch et al. 1987, p. 487). The children process the trauma of separation, for example through depressive moods, aggressive behaviour or social withdrawal (Ebbers 1993, p. 49ff.). Hagan and Dinovitzer (1999, p. 21ff.) describe three core areas of separation: economic deprivation, lack of a socialising parent, which also has an impact on the role behaviour of the rest of the family and loss of social recognition by Stigmatisation. The prison system "too easily categorises the concern of the relatives into the category of remote marginal problems."

As Heberling (2012, p. 12) points out, the whole family is very quickly in danger of being prejudged by society as the "delinquent family" (Ebbers 1993, p. 50), especially families who suffer damage because the penitentiary need special attention and accompaniment (Götte 2000, p. 24). The relationship between the partners, which should be maintained during incarceration, is an important factor in the Continuity of the father-child relationship (Wolleb et al. 2009a, b). More than three quarters of male detainees rate their need for contact very highly, especially concerning visits of the family, letter and telephone contacts. The most important persons outside of the prison include members of the family of origin, as well as partners and children. In the event of a separation of the partners, a separation support is extremely important.

Heberling (2012, p. 12) gives examples of support projects. An extraordinary project of family-friendly prisons was launched in 2005 with the "Family House Engelsborg" in Copenhagen/Denmark. The "Pension Engelsborg" has existed there since 1979, in which the detainees are prepared for everyday life in freedom. Inmates are specifically supported just before release. Detainees are also accepted who can spend their custodial sentence together with their family in one of the five dwellings inside the house. In the meantime, the family house has moved into the standard offer has been accepted.

Compared to a very low recidivism rate in Denmark at 30%, this project showed significantly fewer detainees relapsed after release (Heberling 2012, p. 13). Special therapy offers for children are also mentioned (Roggenthin 2011, p. 10ff.). These examples clearly show that it is possible to deal with the "problem" in a more constructive and, above all, cheaper way. If the public is informed in a valid manner, the majority are generally also behind such alternative projects (see, for example, Allen 2016; Kury 2016).

Heberling (2012, p. 13) rightly emphasises: "In addition to deprivation of liberty, the threat of loss of social and family ties can also jeopardize the desired rehabilitation of the detainees." It is important to have imprisonment close to home and an increase in the number of visitors and a family-friendly visiting atmosphere. "The relatives of detainees must be perceived and recognised as a target group with their own specific need for help." The relatives play a major part in shaping the rehabilitation efforts of the detainees through their contacts (Bakemeier 2010, p. 45ff.). It would be desirable "if family work were to be given a higher priority in the daily life of the penitentiary than has been the case so far." Employees of external counselling centres should be included in this. Relatives must feel that they are not only tolerated but recognised, valued and welcome.

According to Beichner and Hagemann (2016, p. 85), the detention of the mother has significantly more negative effects on children or adolescents, they speak of "detrimental effects of mothers' incarceration on children" (p. 85). Mothers are more the main reference for children than fathers. "In terms of the magnitude of the effects on children, there is compelling evidence to suggest that women's incarceration is much more disruptive for children than men's" (p. 93; see also Murray and Farrington 2008). Beichner and Hagemann (2016) also deplore the low level of support for the children and families concerned.

Allen (2016, p. 194) also emphasises the particularly negative effects of maternal incarceration on children. The author emphasises (2016, p. 197): "In many cases, diversion away from prosecution and punishment offers a better prospect of reducing recidivism than does formal processing by the courts. The use of imprisonment can have particularly damaging consequences" (see also Allen 2016; Kury 2016). Corston (2007, p. 1) emphasises in this context:

> In trying to break the inter-generational transmission of offending, related at least in part to inconsistent parenting and family breakdown it is recognised as important to divert women who do not present a risk to the public away from custody.

Busch et al. (1987) interviewed imprisoned men and their partners about the situation of their own children. For these authors, too, "it is astonishing to what extent this subject has been neglected so far" (p. 131). The authors estimate that in the 1980s, about 50,000 children and adolescents in Germany were affected by the detention of a parent (Pfalzer et al. 2012).

More than half of the detainees' partners were completely surprised by the crime and imprisonment. The detention of the man had led to the collapse of the previous world among the women.

There are numerous problems of a financial nature, loneliness and overuse. Visits are often very limited in time, the atmosphere is often stressful, there is a danger of alienation of the partners, and against this background a "displacement and gentle attitude" creeps in. The education of the children would be significantly burdened to avoid stigma, the women would often break off contacts, which could lead to further isolation (Heberling 2012, p. 10; Geisler and Jung 1989, p. 144ff.).

Condry (2003, p. 249) also found in his investigation that the discovery of the crime was a shock to the relatives. The sudden separation was a personal crisis for most. These authors estimate that around 40,000 children are affected by the detention of a parent. A financial disadvantage of the families usually is resulting in a social loss (Busch 1989, p. 134). It should be noted that detention in the first place largely affects parents from poorly off-the-top families (Besemer and Dennison 2019). A research project of the social background of detained young people and adolescents was able to clearly show the significant socialisation deficits of those affected in generally poor family circumstances (Kury 1979; but see also: Craig et al. 2020). Robertson et al. (2016, p. 206), which give an overview of the situation of children in troubled families, believe that the problem is now seen more, including by international aid organisations, such as the EU or UNICEF. The research shows "that most children suffer following parental imprisonment."

In special cases it can also be a reduction of problems for some children if a parent, such as a father who is extremely violent and stressful in the family climate, is removed from the family. Violence in the family of origin of children and adolescents, against the background of a history of suffering that has often been a long-term, often causes violent problems or psychological problems, but not necessarily (see Thiel 2020). Results from northern European countries, such as Sweden, show how important independent research is. These countries are often presented as positive examples in dealing with social problems, that this is to be verified show recent studies (see Wemrell et al. 2019).

Hermes (2011) points out that ties to the family also play a major role in the re-entry of released prisoners, family members are largely overlooked in connection with detention.

In the meantime, further programmes have also been set up in Germany to support relatives of detainees in detention and after release, although there are still considerable gaps, in many cases also an adequate secured financial support (see, for example, Cocon e.V. Freiburg 2020). This is despite the fact that the problem has been repeatedly pointed out here for decades (see Meyer 1983; Busch et al. 1987; Busch 1989, Geisler and Jung 1989; Preusker 1989).

In Germany, despite the importance of the problem, there is still a lack of empirical studies on the subject. It is not known exactly how many children in Germany are affected by the detention of a parent, it can only be estimated, official statistics are not available. According to estimates by the German Institute for Human Rights (2017, p. 80), about 100,000 children are affected daily in Germany from the detention of a parent (see also Bieganski et al. 2013, p. 4). The fact that no precise statistics on the subject exist can be interpreted as a lack of interest on the subject by the state. The lack of publicity of the topic easily puts it in the background.

"The possibilities for children to visit or contact their imprisoned parents are very different throughout Germany." The duration of visits varies in different prisons in Germany between 1 and 4 h per month (Feige 2019b, p. 9). A survey of 83 German prisons showed significant deficiencies in child-friendly conditions regarding visits of children to the detained parents (Feige 2019b, p. 22). Pfalzer et al. (2012, p. 7) emphasise: "Visits to the prison are stressful and unencouraging, not least in the context of the prison atmosphere and the necessary monitoring." In many cases, the rooms for children are unsuitable. It became clear that "offers and sensitivity to the rights and needs of children exist within the prisons in many ways, but by no means as a reliable structure for all children in every prison" (International Committee of the Red Cross - ICRC 2018; Feige 2019b, p. 34). "Existing offers appear to be less part of the resocialisation plan of the individual detainee than depending on the commitment and engagement of (volunteer) persons" (p. 35).

As the German Institute for Human Rights (2017, p. 81) points out, studies on the impact of a parent's detention on the children concerned in Europe have been increasingly the subject of research since 2001 (Cunningham 2001). An international EU-funded study on the impact of a parent's detention on children in 2012 (COPING study, see Jones 2013) first collected comparable data for Germany. The 145 children between the ages of 7 and 17 interviewed, clearly expressed a massive burden due to the detention of a parent, and an increased risk of mental illness was found (Jones 2013).

Döbber (2020) summarises the main results of the COPING study:

- There are around 800,000 children in the EU where at least one parent is detained 25% of the children affected are conspicuously mentally stressed.
- Children often react distraught and confused, especially during the arrest, proceedings and at the beginning of detention.
- Older children and adolescents are more likely to suffer from eating disorders, drug addiction and are more likely to also become offenders.
- Many of the affected children after the parent's detention lose learned skills such as falling asleep alone and being clean.
- Good contact with the detained parent is essential for resilience of the children.

"The biggest problem for children when a parent is in custody is the limited access and contact options," according to the study authors. Women who have become criminals can live together with their babies in a "mother-child execution", but this possibility will only be offered in 13 German prisons in 2018. In Schleswig-Holstein, inmates can now skype with relatives, "in Bavaria this would be unthinkable." Each federal state has its own Law for the execution of the custodial sentence in Germany—"and also takes children into consideration to varying degrees."

The monitoring centre UN Convention on the Rights of the Child at the German Institute for Human Rights ("*Monitoringstelle UN-Kinderrechtskonvention beim Deutschen Institut für Menschenrechte*") states that "the awareness is slowly changing that children are also affected when people are imprisoned".[1] At least once a week, children should be allowed to visit their imprisoned parents, and young children even more often, the agency is required to do, also following a recommendation from the Council of Europe. "Longer visits or the possibility of long-term visits for families, however, require more prison staff – and cause higher costs.

[1] See https://www.institut-fuer-menschenrechte.de/suche/.

Given the negative impact on 100,000 children, politicians should consider investments in child-friendly prisons. And: For imprisoned parents, it should not be a lottery whether they can continue to keep in touch with their children – depending on the state in which they are imprisoned."

In Germany, none of the *Länder* systematically collected data on children of inmates, only Bavaria, Bremen, Hesse and Schleswig-Holstein collected information in the reception process with the detainees (Zwönitzer et al. 2013, p. 236). The children mentioned as helpful in their stressful situation above all contact with the detained parent (Bieganski et al. 2013, p. 9; Bocknek et al. 2009). Heberling (2012, p. 8) also emphasises that there are no systematic statistical surveys on marriages and partnerships and children of detainees. According to their estimates, about two-thirds of male inquests are family fathers. Children of imprisoned mothers often come to homes, which is sometimes shocking for those affected.

In an exploratory study, Kern (2002) interviewed women of incarcerated male partners with problem-centred interviews on the impact on them and existing children (see Kury and Kern 2003a, b). The average age of women was 40. More than half of the women had no idea about the criminal activities of their partners, so they were completely surprised by his imprisonment. Especially for these, the living conditions changed suddenly and seriously.

Some of the men were arrested outside the house and the family, who were left behind, were not informed by the police, or very late. A central question for the mothers of especially smaller children was how much they should be informed about the detention of the father.

For the children concerned, the situation of life changes considerably with the detention of the father, who are much more helpless than the adult women. The women, whose husbands were first detained, usually lacked any information about the prison and judicial system at the beginning. The situation during visits in prison is experienced by most women, especially at the beginning, as exhausting and unpleasant. One often feels unappreciated, exposing arbitrary actions and regulations, sometimes treated unkindly. According to Turney (2014, p. 1628), the detention of the father also influences the relationship of the mother to the child, for example her parenting behaviour, very often in a negative way.

In its final report on "Children of Detainees", the Open Working Group of the German Federal Criminal Prison Law Committee (2019) notes, among other things, that, according to estimates, almost one million children in the EU and 100,000 in Germany are affected by the detention of a parent, thus more children than prisoners (p. 2). "Children of detained parents are highly likely to be convicted or imprisoned even in the course of their lives," children of detained parents are a high-risk group. "Children of incarcerated parents have an increased lifetime prevalence for the genesis of psychiatric diseases, especially personality disorders. Internalising behavioural disorders and the likelihood of addiction to addictive substances are also directly related to the detention of a parent" (Bailey et al. 2006, 2009).

In particular, the Council of Ministers of the Council of Europe on 4 April 2018 strengthened the rights of children of detained parents. It made it clear that "children of imprisoned parents have the same rights as other children." In particular, it is stressed that "children with detained parents have not committed a criminal offence and should not be treated as if they were in conflict with the law as a result of their parents' actions or alleged acts" (p. 4).

In the light of the Council of Europe's recommendations, the Ministers of Justice of the countries addressed the situation of children of detained parents at the 2018 Spring Conference. They decided that it was necessary to deal with the situation of the children of detained parents in relation to the implementation of the UN Convention on the Rights of the Child and the "Recommendation CM/Rec(2018)5 of the Committee of Ministers to Member States concerning children with imprisoned parents." The National Penitentiary Committee of the Länders is invited to submit proposals for the implementation of the recommendations. An open-country working group was set up to examine the individual recommendations and discuss ways of implementing them.

Fifty-six "summary guidelines" were formulated, which emphasise, among other things, that "in all measures, regulations and the organisation of the prison system . . . the well-being, rights and needs of children with a detained parent must be duly taken into account." The "personal interaction between children and their imprisoned parents (should) be promoted as a matter of priority. Children have the right to regular, direct and personal contact with their detained parent" (p. 8f.). "In order to maintain and strengthen contact with the children and to facilitate the transition from detention to freedom, the legal provisions on measures to an open prison system must be exhausted" (p. 9).

The recommendations in detail highlight, inter alia, that when a parent is detained, particular attention should be paid to instructing him to a facility close to his or her children (p. 11). Children should normally be allowed to visit a detained parent within 1 week of their detention and then regularly and frequently (p. 17). Particular emphasis is also placed on the constructive treatment of prison staff with the children of detainees. They must uphold the rights and dignity of detained parents and their children. Special training measures are required. Groups of experts should review practice and propose improvements. Accompanying research should be financially supported.

"The implementation of child-friendly practices and concepts, including international standards with regard to children of detained parents, must be regularly reviewed and evaluated" (p. 39). Media coverage should be "child-friendly." "The media, professionals and the general public should be provided with reliable and up-to-date data and examples of good practice in order to raise awareness of the number of children affected and the impact of parental detention, and to avoid the negative stereotyping and stigmatisation of children of imprisoned parents" (p. 40).

2.2 International Studies

Penal Reform International (2018)[2] discusses the topic "The rehabilitation and reintegration of offenders in the era of sustainable development" in the report on "Global Prison Trends." In this context, contacts with relatives play an essential role here too, and due to the increase in prisoners, which has often been noted, a much greater role. It provides information on the general development of imprisonment and, above all, it is stressed that the "trend of over-incarceration and punishment of people who use drugs is seen on every continent" (p. 4). It is rightly emphasised (p. 7): "Accurately measuring levels of crime is not possible, although general trends suggest that crime rates have continued downwards in recent years for homicide and other violent crimes, as well as for property crimes. Prosecutions for drug possession offences, on the other hand, increased between 2003 and 2013, while drug trafficking prosecutions remained stable. Cybercrime, such as internet-based theft, fraud and exploitation, is increasingly recognised as a major concern.... The growth of the world prison population has exceeded the rate of general population growth since 2000, and, in many countries, this increase has led to more overcrowded prisons. Data suggests that the number of prisoners exceeds official prison capacity in at least 120 countries."

The sometimes catastrophic overcrowding of prisons with generally far too few staff significantly hinders resocialisation measures, especially the organisation of contacts of prisoners to relatives. Against this background, the recommendations are rightly pronounced, which also have a special significance in this context (Penal Reform International 2018, p. 8): "States should introduce a range of law and policy changes to reduce rates of imprisonment, such as crime prevention measures, the expansion of alternative measures, and a renewed focus on rehabilitation in both prisons and community settings. ... Strategies to address prison overcrowding should focus on crime prevention, expanding the use of alternatives to imprisonment and social interventions that promote sustainable development and reduce poverty and inequality." Alternatives to incarceration, such as diversion measures (Kury and Lerchenmüller 1981), serve above all to maintain good contacts with one's own families.

Above all, the punitive treatment of drug offenders is also the topic, which has led to a considerable increase in the number of detainees, especially in the USA, without producing the expected positive effect (Penal Reform International 2018, p. 14): "The enforcement of punitive drug laws continues to have significant implications for the use and practice of imprisonment. Harsh criminal justice responses to drugs are a major contributor to prison overcrowding, and the 'war on drugs' persists in some countries with disastrous consequences." In this context, it is recommended that (p. 15): "States should review their drug policies in order to adopt evidence-based policies that include decriminalisation of minor offences, proportionality of

[2]See also: https://cdn.penalreform.org/wp-content/uploads/2018/04/PRI_Global-Prison-Trends-2018_EN_WEB.pdf.

sentencing, and non-custodial alternatives to imprisonment. Treatment as an alternative to imprisonment must be voluntary and human-rights compliant. Metrics to measure the outcomes of drug policies should include their impact on human rights, health and development."

On the detention of women, for whom the negative impact on existing children is even more serious, it is stressed that (Penal Reform International 2018, p. 17): "New data published showed that there are now more than 714,000 women and girls in prison globally." In this context, the recommendation is made: "The UN Bangkok Rules should guide states in criminal justice reform to ensure systems meet the needs of women. Sentencing of women should take account of any victimisation, caretaking responsibilities and context of the criminal conduct, giving preference to non-custodial sanctions."

As far as children are concerned, emphasis is placed on (Penal Reform International 2018, p. 18): "The total number of children in detention – those under 18 years of age – was estimated to be about a million in 2010. . . . Detention of children should be used as a very last resort, and the death penalty and life imprisonment should be prohibited for children. States should adopt child friendly justice systems and protect children from violence and ill-treatment" (p. 19).

Particularly harsh detention conditions with little contact with the outside world often do not lead to the expected success; it only cause additional damage to the affected persons and rather lead to further prisonisation damage. It is rightly emphasised in this context that (Penal Reform International 2018, p. 26): "Solitary confinement – often also labelled 'segregation', 'isolation', 'lockdown' or 'supermax' – is defined by the Nelson Mandela Rules as the 'confinement of prisoners for 22 h or more a day without meaningful human contact'. With some notable exceptions, it continues to be used across the globe – including for vulnerable groups such as prisoners with disabilities and children – in contravention of international standards. This is despite increasing recognition of its detrimental psychological and physiological effects, and of the economic costs . . ."

In this context, states are rightly called upon to (p. 7): "States should develop criminal justice and prison policies with full consideration of their relevance and importance for achieving the Sustainable Development Goals of the 2030 Agenda, so that 'no one is left behind' and criminal justice systems play their part to contribute to a just, equitable, tolerant, open and socially inclusive world, in which the needs of the most vulnerable are met."

Particularly harsh and usually harmful measures of detention should be avoided as far as possible, as they are counterproductive (Penal Reform International 2018, p. 27): "In line with the Nelson Mandela Rules and the Bangkok Rules, states should prohibit both indefinite and prolonged solitary confinement, as well as for certain groups, as stipulated in international standards. It should only be used as a last resort in exceptional cases, and then should only be applied for the shortest time possible and be subject to regular, independent review."

In the light of the conditions observed in prisons, which are still frequently found, measures to open up the institutions to the outside world are becoming particularly important, also to keep the prisoners' contact with the world outside. Ultimately, the aim of the prison sentence must be to enable the prisoner to live a life without criminal offences after being released to freedom, which is also particularly emphasised in the German Prison Code ("Strafvollzugsgesetz").

"Contact with the outside world" is rightly emphasised in this context: "The availability and forms of contact with the outside world by prisoners varies greatly from country to country. Evidence has shown that prison visits and contact with family and friends helps reduce recidivism. For example, a 2017 review by the UK's Ministry of Justice found that prisoners who receive visits from families or partners have a 39 per cent lower reoffending rate than those who have no visits" (Penal Reform International 2018, p. 27; see also Farmer 2017; May et al. 2008).

The importance of family visits to detainees becomes clearer when one considers that the children of detainees are at increased risk of becoming criminals themselves, such as studies related to intergenerational transmission of criminal behaviour has shown. As Besemer (2017) emphasises intergenerational transmission of violence means "that children of violent offenders are more likely to become violent. Some of the prominent theories include social learning, genetics, official bias, and the transmission of risk factors.... The available studies suggest that both biological as well as environmental factors are important in explaining the transmission" (Rowe and Farrington 1997; Van de Rakt et al. 2008; Capaldi et al. 2012; Hjalmarsson and Linquist 2012). Obviously the common idiom "the apple does not fall far from the tree" "illustrates the common assumption in society and popular press that children and parents share similarities" (van de Weijer et al. 2017, p. 279; Thornberry 2009; Besemer and Farrington 2012). For example, Farrington et al. (1996) found that 63% of the sons of detainees were also convicted.

Tzoumakis et al. (2019) report a study in which over 21,000 Australian children and their parents were examined for the extent to which there is a link between the prevalence of criminal behaviour of parents and conduct problems in the Children aged 11 years. "The study found that parental offending increases a child's likelihood of conduct problems, and the offending most strongly associated with child conduct problems is maternal violent offending. It also found that the intergenerational transmission of antisocial behaviour begins early, highlighting the importance of intervention for at-risk children and programs targeted at mothers as well as fathers" (p. 1).

van de Weijer et al. (2017, p. 279) in their empirical study on intergenerational transmission of crime, in which they considered data from international studies, note that: "this work empirically demonstrates that a link between parental offending and child offending exists. More so, this work also demonstrates that the relationship between parental crime and child crime is conditioned by the timing of the parental offending" (see also Eichelsheim and van de Weijer 2018; Thornberry et al. 2018).

As the authors point out, the first scientific studies on the subject were carried out as early as the nineteenth century, such as by Dugdale (1877) or later by Goddard (1912). Recent studies, for example in England (Farrington et al. 1996; Rowe and Farrington 1997) and the USA (e.g. Thornberry et al. 2003; Thornberry 2009) or the Netherlands (e.g. Bijleveld and Wijkman 2009; Van de Weijer et al. 2014) were able to confirm the results. van de Weijer et al. (2017, p. 294) finally conclude that: "...

the results of this study show that crime is transmitted across generations within three different countries. … Intergenerational transmission of offending is … an international phenomena, at least in Western countries". Knusden (2016) points out, it is important to help families achieve the goal that detention is supposed to serve resocialisation. He stresses that families must also not be instrumentalised or used to fill the goals of the criminal justice system and gaps created by professionals. Children of prisoners are often convicted themselves (Ministry of Justice 2017, p. 19; Murphey and Mae 2015).

Augustyn et al. (2019) discuss the extent to which labeling plays a role in the Intergenerational Transmission of Criminal Behaviour. The results are based on an analysis of 312 parent-child dyads from the Rochester Youth Development Study and the Rochester Intergeneratio-nal Study. The results confirm the labelling theory and show that parental detention influences deviant behaviour of children. A contact "with the police on subsequent offending is greater when the focal parent has an arrest history, regardless of when the most recent arrest occurs in the life course of the child" (p. 137; see also Augustyn et al. 2017).

The Penal Reform International (2018) report also sets out in particular international results that show progress in supporting contacts with family members and, above all, show that in the case of openness to the problem, favourable results can be achieved, in particular costs incurred by criminal behaviour can be reduced (see e.g. Federal Interagency Working Group for Children of Incarcerated Parents 2013). Some prisons now also allow Skype to support contact with family members, especially when the distance between the prison and relatives is large. New technical possibilities can help.

> The European Court of Human Rights delivered a verdict that imprisoning prisoners thousands of miles away from their relatives in Russia violated their right to family life. The Court held that the distance between the penal facilities and the homes of the prisoners' families – ranging from 2,000 to 8,000 kilometres – was so great that it had inflicted hardship. Technology is increasingly used to facilitate contact with family and friends (Penal Reform International 2018, p. 27).

The costs of telephone contacts between prisoners and their relatives are sometimes so high that they cannot be provided, so contacts are made more difficult. In some cases, ceilings have been set for telephone charges, especially if they are not justifiable. In Germany, for example, the "Constitutional Court ruled against the overpricing of phone calls made by prisoners, saying that disregarding the economic interests of prisoners violates their constitutional right to rehabilitation and that private providers must offer phone services at fair market prices" (Penal Reform International 2018, p. 27).

In the international field, especially in the USA and the United Kingdom, meanwhile there are significantly more studies about women and children of detainees. One of the first studies examined the difficult financial problems of the families of detainees (Bloodgood 1928; see also Sacks 1938). Only 20 years ago, however, Hagan and Dinovitzer (1999, p. 145) complained that there were few studies on the families of detainees and their children.

As far as the current debate in the United States is concerned, it must also be seen in the context of the enormously high incarceration rate there, which until recently stood at 716 and has declined only slightly in recent years. According to Banach (2016, p. 1), the "lobby of private prison companies ... regularly advocates a tightening of the criminal law in order to ensure the constant influx of prisoners and profit." The private prison industry is "one of the fastest growing industries in the USA," he said. According to Hagan and Dinovitzer (1999, p. 137), this development attracted little public attention in the USA. The consequences of the detention of a family member on the rest of the family are not well received by the population.

Numerous studies show that the detention of the father significantly increases the likelihood that children and adolescents will also become criminals and be detained later (see Thornberry 1997, for example). Murray (2007, p. 55) speaks in this context of a "cycle of punishment."

According to RT-Deutsch – Reuters (2016, p. 1), more than five million children and adolescents in the United States have one parent in custody, with some "terrifying effects of detention" on the children, which is usually hardly noticed by the public. Over a period of 40 years, the number of children who had to give up their father while growing up because he is in custody has increased by around 500%. For the children, this means above all increased instability, also because of financial problems. Sixty-five per cent of families, one of whom is in custody, cannot meet their basic needs, leading to an increased risk of homelessness. The proportion of children with a detained parent differs significantly between the states, which is linked to a different policy of sanctions.

Hoffmann et al. (2010, p. 397) emphasise: "Parental incarceration increases the risk that children will experience later behavioural and emotional problems, have troubles in school, and become involved in the juvenile and criminal justice systems." The detention of a parent, which is significantly higher especially among blacks than among whites, generally makes the bad situation for the children even worse, also increases the existing racial disparity in law enforcement and sanctions (Wakefield and Wildeman 2013; Wildeman 2014).

Several studies have shown positive effects of visits to detainees by family members, but also on family members, for example on children and adolescents. Ditchfield (1990, p. 8) concludes based on his literary analysis that: "The result of both detailed social research and large scale statistical studies strongly indicate that family ties and responsibilities may help reduce further offending, partly in themselves (because of the support they offer), and partly because they tend to be associated with other factors which help offenders to desist."

Besemer et al. (2019) rightly emphasise, however, against the background of their international comparison of studies on the subject: "By comparing results across countries, we consider which effects of parental imprisonment on children are internationally generalizable. We find that with the current evidence available, it is difficult to disentangle cross-national differences in the effects of parental imprisonment on children from differences in sample selection, time of data collection, and other differences in research design".

The U.S. Minnesota Department of Corrections (2011) investigated the "effects of prison visitation on offender recidivism" among 16,420 prisoners released between 2003 and 2007. The results show that detainees who received visits during detention had a significantly lower recidivism rate after release than the comparison group without visits (see Bales and Mears 2008). The behaviour of prisoners in custody has also been improved by visits, and aggressive behaviour went backwards. However, almost 40% of the prisoners did not receive any visits. Visits by siblings, in-laws, the father or clergymen showed the most positive effects. The results show simultaneously (p. 1): "For those who are married, visits with either spouses or children may be difficult because they create more stress and are often reminders of how their incarceration is preventing them from raising their children or helping provide for their families." In contrast, visits from former spouses increased the risk of recidivism.

Frequent visits by different persons and those at the end of detention significantly reduced the likelihood of recidivism. The authors stress that supporting visits to detainees is also a cost-effective method of crime prevention. Against this background, the National Advisory Commission on Criminal Justice Standards and Goals (1973, p. 7) recommended "that prisons develop policies more conducive to visitation." It requires the facilitation of visits, the reduction of bureaucratic obstacles, and above all the imprisonment as close as possible to the place of residence of relatives.

Holt and Miller (1972) also demonstrated a positive effect of visits to prisoners on their recidivism rate. Only 2% of prisoners who had three or more visits in the previous year before release were relapsed within a year, compared to 12% of those who did not receive visits. Mitchell et al. (2016) found in their meta-analysis on the recidivism-preventive effect of prisoner visits, which considered 16 studies, that prisoners with visits showed 26% fewer recidivisms after release than the comparison group without visits. In particular, visits about a year before release from prison had a positive effect here too, where the recidivism rate decreased by 53% within 1 year after release (see also Besemer et al. 2017).

The negative effects of a parent's incarceration on families, especially children, have been clearly demonstrated in international studies around the world, for example in the United Kingdom (Murray 2007; Murray and Farrington 2008; Murray et al. 2014), the Netherlands (Van de Rakt et al. 2012), Denmark (Wildeman and Andersen 2017) or Australia (Besemer et al. 2018; Dawson et al. 2012).

3 Discussion

In Germany, custodial sentences are primarily used to resocialise detainees, according to the legal regulations. Thus, the German Prison Law Act of 1977 ("Strafvollzugsgesetz") clearly defines in Paragraph 2 as "Tasks of Imprisonment" ("Aufgaben des Vollzuges") and as the aim of imprisonment ("Vollzugsziel") to enable the prisoner to "lead a life without criminal offences in the future under social responsibility." Furthermore, the custodial sentence "also serves to protect the general public from further offences." Paragraph 3 of the German Law for the execution of the custodial sentence ("Deutsches Strafvollzugsgesetz") emphasises: "Practice of imprisonment." (1) Life in prison should be brought into line with general living conditions as far as possible. (2) Harmful consequences of deprivation of liberty shall be counteracted. (3) Imprisonment shall be designed to assist the prisoner in his incorporation into life in freedom. This includes, in particular, the granting of relaxation of enforcement of imprisonment.

Walter (1999, p. 366) emphasises in this context: "The conditions of detention tend to contribute to endangering a future life without criminal offences" (cf. also Götte 2000, p. 220). Heberling (2012, p. 8) emphasises that the resocialisation goal is primarily focused on the person of the detainee "for which the prison is responsible. At the same time, the protection of marriage and family should also guarantee the appropriate treatment of the enforcement authorities to the (marriage) partners and the children involved" (Götte 2000, p. 216). This means that "the living conditions of the prisoners should be 'family-friendly' and child-friendly" (Götte 2000, p. 217).

Social isolation on the one hand and de-individualisation on the other lead to undesirable personality changes, making it more difficult to live independently and in a legal way after imprisonment (Ebbers 1993, p. 52). The detention complicates the relationship with the family, and often leads to frustration and mistrust (Mohme and Dellbrügge 2010, p. 20). "Maintaining family relationships during the period of imprisonment and the associated feeling of family affiliation are an important criterion for resocialisation."

In the public debate and accordingly on the political side, on the other hand, aspects of sanctions and the injustice committed are brought to the fore. A lack of information about the background of criminal behaviour and, above all, the negative side effects of incarceration play an essential role here. Treatment programs in custody often involve no or insufficient preparation for release and, above all, follow-up after release from prison. For example, Walkenhorst and Koop (2019, p. 249) rightly emphasise: "Not least aftercare and, if necessary, long-term follow-up, decide on the success of the enforcement efforts during the imprisonment period."

Some countries in Germany have made progress in this area in recent years. As of January 1, 2019, Hamburg has put into effect a Resocialization and Victims' Assistance Act ("Hamburger Resozialisierungs- und Opferhilfegesetz - HmbResOG") to assist prisoners in their transition from prison to freedom (Justizbehörde Hamburg 2020). Prisoners then have a right to draw up an integration plan within the framework of integrated transitional management. Support will be provided in particular concerning search for work and housing, the application for social benefits or the continuation of therapy. The offer to join the transitional management regularly begins 6 months before release from prison.

Even in freedom, the released prisoners will then have specialists in transitional management at their disposal for a further 6 months as contact persons. "The aim of the Resocialisation Act is to avoid re-criminality by identifying at an early stage the specific need for assistance and by taking appropriate measures to support them in the final months of imprisonment, for example by: debtor advice or qualification measures" (Justizbehörde Hamburg 2020). In integration conferences, enforcement staff sit down with case managers, including independent carriers and the respective prisoners, and develop an individual concrete "roadmap" for the first 6 months after release.

In the debate on custodial sentences, the general negative effects on the environment of the detainees, especially existing families with children, are largely overlooked. In many cases, these families belong to the lower social classes and are now slipping further into their social status due to the elimination of a parent. Families are often blamed for criminal behaviour, children are often stigmatised, sometimes even by teachers in schools. Rudolf and Windfuhr (2017, p. 4) emphasise: "Children of detainees also belong to a group of persons in need of protection, which is largely invisible to the public and politicians."

State institutions often provide insufficient assistance, and access is often made much more difficult by bureaucratic hurdles. Condry (2003, p. 262) emphasises in this connection:.".. if relatives do take on these responsibilities and have an important role to reduce recidivism as the literature suggests, it is important that they are supported in doing so." Busch et al. (1987, p. 88) refer to families affected by the detention of the man as "co-punished third parties" (see, among others, Pfalzer et al. 2012). The exclusion of the detainee creates a "Two-World Reality" of indoors and outdoors (Ebbers 1993).

In recent decades, private aid agencies have often been established, which can provide significant support to the families who are under pressure. Cocon e.V. Freiburg (2020, p. 5), for example, states that in 2019 there was a "significant increase in affected children in infancy and up to 5 years of age." Heberling (2012, p. 8) rightly emphasises: "The discrepancy between claim and reality is still blatant in prison practice by the exclusion of the 'perpetrators' and the punishment also of the relatives, security and punishment are often in the foreground and make it more difficult to establish family-friendly measures."

The debate on custodial sentences often pays too little attention to the collateral damage of detention to the families of the detainees, which is also due to the fact that these are underclass groups, to which the public as a whole has little regard for the attention, to which the causes of your situation itself are often attributed. Alternative sanctions, such as victim-offender-mediation or a wider use of diversion, have a hard time attracting attention in this context, although research clearly shows that this often results better than through a incarceration, and above all cheaper (Kury and Lerchenmüller 1981; Allen 2016; Kury 2016).

4 Conclusion

The high incarceration rate in some countries, especially in the USA, rightly points out the disadvantages of a criminal strategy. Incarceration serves not only the objectives set out in the laws, but also political interests. The public should be as fully informed as possible about scientific research results on the effect of custodial sentences, especially the negative side effect. A relatively small group of dangerous perpetrators may require custodial sentences, but minimum standards, as formulated by the UNODC, should be respected. For example, United Nations Office on Drugs and Crime – UNODC (2015) rightly emphasises:

Rule 1: "All prisoners shall be treated with the respect due to their inherent dignity and value as human beings. No prisoner shall be subjected to, and all prisoners shall be protected from, torture and other cruel, inhuman or degrading treatment or punishment, for which no circumstances whatsoever may be invoked as a justification. The safety and security of prisoners, staff, service providers and visitors shall be ensured at all times" (p. 2). Contact with the outside world is very important, especially the family (p. 18). Against this background, it is particularly important:

Rule 58: 1. "Prisoners shall be allowed, under necessary supervision, to communicate with their family and friends at regular intervals: (a) By corresponding in writing and using, where available, telecommunication, electronic, digital and other means; and (b) By receiving visits. 2. Where conjugal visits are allowed, this right shall be applied without discrimination, and women prisoners shall be able to exercise this right on an equal basis with men. Procedures shall be in place and premises shall be made available to ensure fair and equal access with due regard to safety and dignity."

Rule 59: "Prisoners shall be allocated, to the extent possible, to prisons close to their homes or their places of social rehabilitation." Very important are social relations and aftercare" (p. 31). Rule 106: "Special attention shall be paid to the maintenance and improvement of such relations between a prisoner and his or her family as are desirable in the best interests of both."

Rule 107: "From the beginning of a prisoner's sentence, consideration shall be given to his or her future after release and he or she shall be encouraged and provided assistance to maintain or establish such relations with persons or agencies outside the prison as may promote the prisoner's rehabilitation and the best interests of his or her family."

Penal Reform International (2018, p. 8) stresses in this context: "States should introduce a range of law and policy changes to reduce rates of imprisonment, such as crime prevention measures, the expansion of alternative measures, and a renewed focus on rehabilitation in both prisons and community settings. … Strategies to address prison overcrowding should focus on crime prevention, expanding the use of alternatives to imprisonment and social interventions that promote sustainable development and reduce poverty and inequality." Particular attention is paid to the special situation of women and children (see above).

Where a custodial sentence is considered and imposed for security reasons, it should always be observed that "Imprisonment is associated with a range of unavoidable harms such as the rupturing of community and family ties. . .the goal for the prison system must be to anticipate these harms and soften their impact while not adding to them" (O'Donnell 2016, p. 45; see also: Codd 2008; Brunton-Smith and McCarthy 2016; Markson et al. 2015; Spjeldnes et al. 2012; Knusden 2016).

Incarceration also serves above all the wishes of the population for sanctions, the reduction of often vague feelings of insecurity, which have only partly to do with crime (see Klimke et al. 2019). Since offenders, as usually members of the lower social classes, often have little opportunity to enforce their rights, they are placed in the particular danger of being excluded from society in the event of criminality. This has a particularly negative effect on relatives, especially children, a forgotten group in connection with crime and law enforcement. Criminology should focus more on the problems arising here, including by educating the population, through more research in this area.

References

Allen, C. R. (2016). The impact of sanctions on child and female offenders. In H. Kury, S. Redo, & E. Shea (Eds.), *Women and children as victims and offenders: Background, prevention, reintegration. Vol. 2: Suggestions for succeeding generations* (pp. 173–202). Cham: Springer.

Ambrosio, T.-J., & Schiraldi, V. (1997). *From classrooms to cell blocks: A national perspective.* Washington, D.C.: Justice Policy Institute.

Augustyn, M. B., Ward, J. T., & Krohn, M. D. (2017). Exploring intergenerational continuity in gang membership. *Journal of Crime and Justice, 40*(3), 252–274.

Augustyn, M. B., Ward, J. T., Krohn, M. D., & Dong, B. (2019). Criminal justice contact across generations: Assessing the intergenerational labeling hypothesis. *Journal of Developmental and Life-Course Criminology, 5*, 137–175.

Bailey, J. A., Hill, K. G., Oesterle, S., & Hawkins, J. D. (2006). Linking substance use and problem behavior across three generations. *Journal of Abnormal Child Psychology, 34*, 273–292.

Bailey, J. A., Hill, K. G., Oesterle, S., & Hawkins, J. D. (2009). Parenting practices and problem behavior across three generations: monitoring, harsh discipline and drug use in the intergenerational transmission of externalizing behavior. *Developmental Psychology, 45*, 1214–1226.

Bakemeier, C. (2010). *BAG-S, Arbeit mit Angehörigen Inhaftierter*. Bonn: Orientierungshilfe für die Praxis.

Bales, W. D., & Mears, D. P. (2008). Inmate social ties and the transition to society: Does visitation reduce recidivism? *Journal of Research in Crime and Delinquency, 45*, 287–321.

Banach, O. (2016). *Das Ende der Menschlichkeit: In den USA dürfen Gefangene oft nur noch per Chat mit Familie sprechen*. Berlin: RT-Deutsch. https://deutsch.rt.com/gesellschaft/38472-ende-menschlichkeit/

Beichner, D., & Hagemann, O. (2016). Incarcerated women: Their situation, their needs and measures for sustainable reintegration. In H. Kury, S. Redo, & E. Shea (Eds.), *Women and children as victims and offenders: Background, prevention, reintegration. Vol. 2: Suggestions for succeeding generations* (pp. 85–116). Cham: Springer.

Besemer, K. L., & Dennison, S. (2019). Intergenerational social exclusion in prisoners' families. In M. Hutton & D. Boran (Eds.), *The Palgrave handbook of prison and the family. Palgrave studies in prisons and penology* (pp. 479–501). Cham: Palgrave Macmillan.

Besemer, K. L., Dennison, S. M., Bijleveld, C. C. J. H., & Murray, J. (2019). Effects of parental incarceration on children: Lessons from international research. In J. M. Eddy & J. Poehlmann-Tynan (Eds.), *Handbook on children with incarcerated parents* (pp. 65–81). Cham: Springer.

Besemer, K. L., van de Weijer, S. G. A., & Dennison, S. M. (2018). Risk marker or risk mechanism? The effect of family, household, and parental imprisonment on children and adults' social support and mental health. *Criminal Justice and Behaviour, 45*(8), 1154–1173.

Besemer, S. (2017). Intergenerational transmission of violence. In *The Encyclopedia of Juvenile Delinquency and Justice*. Wiley Online Library. https://onlinelibrary.wiley.com/doi/book/10.1002/9781118524275

Besemer, S., Ahmad, S. I., Hinshaw, S. P., & Farrington, D. P. (2017). A systematic review and meta-analysis of the intergenerational transmission of criminal behavior. *Aggression and Violent Behavior, 37*, 161–178.

Besemer, S., & Farrington, D. (2012). Intergenerational transmission of criminal behaviour: Conviction trajectories of fathers and their children. *European Journal of Criminology, 9*(2), 120–141. https://doi.org/10.1177/1477370811422801

Bieganski, J., Starke, S., & Urban, M. (2013). *Informationsbroschüre. Kinder von Inhaftierten. Ergebnisse und Empfehlungen der COPING-Studie*. Dresden: TU Dresden.

Bijleveld, C. C. J. H., & Wijkman, M. (2009). Intergenerational continuity in convictions: A five-generation study. *Criminal Behaviour and Mental Health, 19*, 142–155.

Bloodgood, R. (1928). *Welfare of Prisoners' families in Kentucky. Publication No. 182*. Washington, D.C.: U.S. Department of Labor, Children's Bureau.

Bocknek, E., Sanderson, J., & Britner, P. A. (2009). Ambiguous loss and posttraumatic stress in school-age children of prisoners. *Journal of Child and Family Studies, 18*, 323–333.

Brunton-Smith, I., & McCarthy, D. J. (2016). *The effects of prisoner attachment to family on re-entry outcomes: A longitudinal assessment.*

Busch, M. (1989). Kinder inhaftierter Väter. *Zeitschrift für Strafvollzug und Straffälligenhilfe, 38*, 131–138.

Busch, M., Fülbier, P., & Meyer, F. W. (1987). *Zur Situation der Frauen von Inhaftierten. Analyse und Hilfeplanung. Schriftenreihe der Bundesminister für Jugend, Familie, Frauen und Gesundheit. Band 194/1-3*. Stuttgart: Kohlhammer.

Capaldi, D. M., Pears, K. C., Kerr, D. C. R., Owen, L. D., & Kim, H. K. (2012). Growth in externalizing and internalizing problems in childhood: A prospective study of psychopathology across three generations. *Child Development, 833*, 1945–1959.

Carlson, B. E., & Cervera, N. (1992). *Inmates and their wives: Incarceration and family life*. London: Greenwood.

Clephas, H., & Althoff, H. (2003). Angehörigenarbeit in der Straffälligenhilfe. *Zeitschrift für Strafvollzug und Straffälligenhilfe, 52*, 279–283.

Cocon e.V. Freiburg. (2020). *Jahresbericht 2018/2019. Freiburger Verein für systemische Therapie von straffällig gewordenen Menschen, deren Angehörigen sowie Menschen in schwierigen Lebenssituationen. Freiburg*.

Codd, H. (2008). *In the shadow of prison: Families, imprisonment and criminal justice*. Cullompton: Willan.

Condry, R. (2007). *Families shamed: The consequences of crime for relatives of serious offenders*. Oxford: Routledge.

Condry, R. F. (2003). *After the offence: The construction of crime and its consequences by families of serious offenders*. Dissertation, University of London.

Corston, J. (2007). *A report by Baroness Jean Corston of a review of women with particular vulnerabilities in the criminal justice system*. London: Home Office.

Craig, J. M., Trulson, C. R., DeLisi, M., & Caudill, J. W. (2020). Toward an understanding of the impact of adverse childhood experiences on the recidivism of serious juvenile offenders. *American Journal of Criminal Justice, 45*, 245–270.

CSU-Landesgruppe im Deutschen Bundestag. (2020). *Unsere Politik für einen starken Staat und eine wehrhafte Demokratie – für ein neues Jahrzehnt der Souveränität. 44. Klausurtagung der*

CSU im Bundestag. https://www.csu-landesgruppe.de/sites/default/files/2020-01/BESCHLUSS_%23seeon20_Sicherheit_Migration.pdf
Cunningham, A. (2001). Forgotten families – The impact of imprisonment. *Family Matters, 59*, 35–38.
Dallaire, D. H., Ciccone, A., & Wilson, L. C. (2010). Teachers' experiences with and expectations of children with incarcerated parents. *Journal of Applied Development Psychology, 31*, 281–290.
Dawson, A., Jackson, D., & Nyamathi, A. (2012). Children of incarcerated parents: Insights to addressing a growing public health concern in Australia. *Children and Youth Services Review, 34*, 2433–2441.
Deutsches Institut für Menschenrechte. (2017). *Entwicklung der Menschenrechtssituation in Deutschland. Juli 2016 – Juni 2017. Berlin.*
Ditchfield, J. (1990). *Control in prisons: A review of the literature*. London: Home Office Research Study 118.
Döbber, C. (2020). *100.000 Kinder sehen Eltern nur im Gefängnis: Was das mit ihnen macht - und was hilft. FOCUS-Online vom 14. 02. 2020.*
Dölling, D., Entorf, H., Hermann, D., & Rupp, T. (2011). Meta-analysis of empirical studies on deterrence. In H. Kury & E. Shea (Eds.), *Punitivity – International developments. Vol. 3: Punitiveness and punishment* (pp. 315–378). Bochum: Universitätsverlag Dr. Brockmeyer.
Dugdale, R. L. (1877). *The Jukes: A study in crime, pauperism, and heredity*. New York: Putnam.
Ebbers, F. (1993). Wenn ein Elternteil inhaftiert ist. In P. Kaiser (Ed.), *Psycho-Logik helfender Institutionen. Beiträge zu einer besseren Nutzerfreundlichkeit der Organisationen im Sozial- und Gesundheitswesen* (pp. 49–78). Heidelberg: Asanger.
Eichelsheim, V. I., & van de Weijer, S. G. A. (Eds.). (2018). *Intergenerational continuity of criminal and antisocial behavior: An international overview of studies*. New York: Routledge.
Farmer, M. (2017). *The importance of strengthening prisoners' family ties to prevent reoffending and reduce intergenerational crime*. London: Ministry of Justice. https://assets.publishing.service.gov.uk/government/uploads/system/uploads/attachment_data/file/642244/farmer-review-report.pdf
Farrington, D. P., Barnes, G., & Lambert, S. (1996). The concentration of offending in families. *Legal and Criminological Psychology, 1*(1), 47–63.
Federal Interagency Working Group for Children of Incarcerated Parents. (2013). *Promoting social and emotional well-being for children of incarcerated parents a product of the federal interagency working group for children of incarcerated parents*. Washington DC: National Institute of Corrections.
Feige, J. (2019a). *Kinder von Inhaftierten*. Berlin: Deutsches Institut für Menschenrechte.
Feige, J. (2019b). *Kontakt von Kindern zu ihren inhaftierten Eltern: Einblicke in den deutschen Justizvollzug*. Berlin: Deutsches Institut für Menschenrechte, Monitoring-Stelle UN-Kinderrechtskonvention.
Fontaine, J., Taxy, S., Peterson, B., Breaux, J., & Rossman, S. B. (2015). *Safer return demonstration: Impact findings from the research-based community reentry initiative*. Washington, DC: Urban Institute.
Geisler, B., & Jung, H. (1989). Ehe, Partnerschaft und Strafvollzug. Zur Situation der Frauen von Inhaftierten. *Zeitschrift für Strafvollzug und Straffälligenhilfe, 38*, 143–147.
Goddard, H. H. (1912). *The Kallikak family: A study in the heredity of feeble-mindedness*. New York: Macmillan.
Goll, U., Egerer, H., & Wulf, R. (2012). Eltern-Kind-Projekt chance. *Forum Strafvollzug, 61*, 15–18.
Götte, S. (2000). *Die Mitbetroffenheit der Kinder und Ehepartner von Strafgefangenen: eine Analyse aus der Sicht unterhaltsrechtlicher Interessen*. Berlin: Duncker und Humblot.
Hagan, J., & Dinovitzer, R. (1999). Collateral consequences of imprisonment for children, communities, and prisoners. *Crime and Justice, 26*, 121–162.

Heberling, A. (2012). Die Situation der Angehörigen Inhaftierter. Forum Strafvollzug. *Zeitschrift für Strafvollzug und Straffälligenhilfe, 61*, 8–14.

Hermann, D., & Dölling, D. (2016). General prevention: Does it work? In H. Kury, S. Redo, & E. Shea (Eds.), *Women and children as victims and offenders: Background, prevention, reintegration. Suggestions for succeeding generations* (Vol. 2, pp. 3–22). Cham: Springer.

Hermes, P. A. M. (2011). *Zur Lebensrealität der Angehörigen von Inhaftierten*. München: GRIN Verlag.

Hestermann, T. (2016). "Violence against children sells very well." Reporting crime in the media and attitudes to punishment. In H. Kury, S. Redo, & E. Shea (Eds.), *Women and children as victims and offenders: Background, prevention, reintegration. Suggestions for succeeding generations* (Vol. 1, pp. 923–947). Cham: Springer.

Hjalmarsson, R., & Linquist, M. J. (2012). Like godfather, like son: Exploring the intergenerational nature of crime. *Journal of Human Resources, 47*, 550–582.

Hoffmann, H. C., Byrd, A. L., & Kightlinger, A. M. (2010). Prison programs and services for incarcerated parents and their underage children: Results from a national survey of correctional facilities. *The Prison Journal, 90*(4), 397–416.

Holt, N., & Miller, D. (1972). *Explorations in inmate-family relationships. Research Report No. 46*. Sacramento: California Department of Corrections: Research Division.

International Committee of the Red Cross - ICRC. (2018). *Towards humane prisons. A principled and participatory approach to prison planning and design*. Geneva: ICRC.

Jones, A. (2013). *Children of prisoners: Interventions and mitigations to strengthen mental health*. Huddersfield: University of Huddersfield. http://eprints.hud.ac.uk/18019/1/childrenofPrisonersReport-final.pdf

Justizbehörde Hamburg. (2020). *Hamburg erzielt weitere Fortschritte bei Resozialisierung*. https://www.hamburg.de/pressearchiv-fhh/13508756/2020-01-20-jb-hamburg-erzielt-weitere-fortschritte-bei-resozialisierung/

Kanisch, B., & Asprion, P. (1997). Zehn Jahre "Familienseminar mit Inhaftierten und ihren Partnerinnen.". *Zeitschrift für Strafvollzug und Straffälligenhilfe, 3*, 152–154.

Kern, J. (2002). *Die Situation der Frauen und Partnerinnen von Inhaftierten*. Freiburg: Institut für Psychologie, Diplomarbeit.

Kern, J. (2007). *Frauen und Partnerinnen von Inhaftierten. Theorie und Praxis*. Saarbrücken: VDM Verlag Dr. Müller.

Klimke, D., Oelkers, N., & Schweer, M. K. W. (Eds.). (2019). *Sicherheitsmentalitäten im ländlichen Raum*. Wiesbaden: Springer VS.

Knusden, E. M. (2016). Avoiding the pathologizing of children of prisoners. *Probation Journal, 63*, 362–370.

Koepsel, K. (1989). Besondere Probleme verheirateter Strafgefangener. *Zeitschrift für Strafvollzug und Straffälligenhilfe, 37*, 152–158.

Kury, H. (1979). *Sozialstatistik der Zugänge im Jugendvollzug Baden-Württemberg für das Jahr 1978*. Freiburg: Berichte aus dem Max-Planck-Institut für ausländisches und internationales Strafrecht, Nr. 8.

Kury, H. (2016). Mediation, restorative justice and social reintegration of offenders: The effects of alternative sanctions on punishment. In H. Kury, S. Redo, & E. Shea (Eds.), *Women and children as victims and offenders: Background, prevention, reintegration. suggestions for succeeding generations* (Vol. 2, pp. 249–282). Cham: Springer.

Kury, H. (2020a). Umgang mit psychischen Erkrankungen im (Jugend-)Strafvollzug. *Zeitschrift für Jugendkriminalrecht und Jugendhilfe – ZJJ, 31*, 36–43.

Kury, H. (2020b). Frauen und Kinder von Inhaftierten. Eine internationale Perspektive. Forum Strafvollzug. *Zeitschrift für Strafvollzug und Straffälligenhilfe, 69*, 31–36.

Kury, H., & Kern, J. (2003a). Frauen und Kinder von Inhaftierten. Eine vergessene Gruppe. *Kriminologisches Journal, 35*, 97–110.

Kury, H., & Kern, J. (2003b). Angehörige von Inhaftierten. *Zeitschrift für Strafvollzug und Straffälligenhilfe, 52*, 269–278.

Kury, H., & Lerchenmüller, H. (1981). *Diversion. Alternativen zu klassischen Sanktionsformen*. Bochum: Studienverlag Dr. N. Brockmeyer.

Kury, H., & Redo, S. (Eds.). (2018). *Refugees and migrants in law and policy. Challenges and opportunities for global civic education*. Cham: Springer.

Kury, H., & Schüßler, J. (2019). Der Umgang mit Kriminalität auf parteipolitischer Ebene. Eine Auswertung von Wahlprogrammen. *Kriminologisches Journal, 51*, 87–106.

Kury, H., & Shea, E. (Eds.). (2011). *Punitivity – International developments. 3 Vols*. Bochum: Universitätsverlag Dr. Brockmeyer.

Länderoffene Arbeitsgruppe des Strafvollzugsausschusses. (2019). *Abschlussbericht Kinder von Inhaftierten*. Berlin.

Larson, D. (2013). Why Scandinavian Prisons Are Superior. "Open" prisons, in which detainees are allowed to live like regular citizens, should be a model for the U.S. *The Atlantic*, 24. September 2013. https://www.theatlantic.com/international/archive/2013/09/why-scandinavian-prisons-are-superior/279949/

Light, R. (1993). Why support prisoners' family-tie groups? *The Howard Journal, 32*, 322–329.

Markson, L., Lösel, F., Souza, K., & Lanskey, C. (2015). Male prisoners' family relationships and resilience in resettlement. *Criminology and Criminal Justice, 15*(4), 423–441.

May, C., Sharma, N., & Stewart, D. (2008). *Factors linked to reoffending: A one-year follow-up of prisoners who took part in the Resettlement Surveys 2001, 2003 and 2004*. London: Ministry of Justice.

Meyer, F. W. (1983). Angehörige von Inhaftierten – oder wie man eine Problemgruppe übersieht. In Institut für Soziale Arbeit (Ed.), *Familienarbeit und Strafvollzug* (pp. 17–31). Münster: Eigenverlag.

Minnesota Department of Corrections. (2011). *The effects of prison visitation on offender recidivism*. Minnesota: St. Paul. https://mn.gov/doc/assets/11-11PrisonVisitationResearchinBrief-Final_tcm1089-272782.pdf

Mitchell, M. M., Spooner, K., Jia, D., & Zhang, Y. (2016). The effect of prison visitation on reentry success: A meta-analysis. *Journal of Criminal Justice, 47*, 74–83.

Mittermaier, W. (1954). *Gefängniskunde. Ein Lehrbuch für Studium und Praxis*. München: Vahlen.

Mohme, M., & Dellbrügge, V. (2010). *Kinder nicht mitbestrafen! Wie "Freiräume" Kilndern helfen, mit der Inhaftierung eines Elternteils umzugehen. Freiräume des Ev. Gemeindedienstes Bielefeld e.V.* Bielefeld: Evangelisches Johanneswerk e.V.

Murphey, D., & Mae Cooper, P. (2015). *Parents behind bars: What happens to their Children?* Available online: http://www.childtrends.org/wp-content/uploads/2015/10/2015-42ParentsBehindBars.pdf

Murray, J. (2007). The cycle of punishment: Social exclusion of prisoners and their children. *Criminology and Criminal Justice, 7*, 55–81.

Murray, J., Bijleveld, C. C., Farrington, D. P., & Loeber, R. (2014). *Effects of parental incarceration on children: Cross-national comparative studies*. Washington, DC: American Psychological Association.

Murray, J., & Farrington, D. P. (2008). The effects of parental imprisonment on children. In M. Tonry (Ed.), *Crime and justice: A review of research* (Vol. 37, pp. 133–206). Chicago: University of Chicago Press.

National Advisory Commission on Criminal Justice Standards and Goals. (1973). *Corrections*. Washington, D.C.: U.S. Government Printing Office.

Neibecker, B. (1984). Strafvollzug und institutionelle Garantie von Ehe und Familie. *Zeitschrift für Strafvollzug und Straffälligenhilfe, 33*, 335–343.

O'Donnell, I. (2016). The aims of imprisonment. In Y. Jewkes, J. Bennett, & B. Crewe (Eds.), *Handbook on prisons* (p. 45). Oxford: Routledge.

Penal Reform International. (2018). *Global prison trends 2018*. Bangkok: Thailand Institute of Justice. https://cdn.penalreform.org/wp-content/uploads/2018/04/PRI_Global-Prison-Trends-2018_EN_WEB.pdf

Pfalzer, S., Schroven, G., & Walkenhorst, P. (2012). Mitbestrafte Dritte. Forum Strafvollzug. *Zeitschrift für Strafvollzug und Straffälligenhilfe, 61*, 7.

Preusker, H. (1989). Erfahrungen mit der "Ehe- und familienfreundlichen Besuchsregelung" in der JVA Bruchsal. *Zeitschrift für Strafvollzug und Straffälligenhilfe, 38*, 147–150.

Robertson, O., Christmann, K., Sharratt, K., Berman, A. H., Manby, M., Ayre, E., et al. (2016). Children of prisoners: Their situation and role in long-term crime prevention. In H. Kury, S. Redo, & E. Shea (Eds.), *Women and children as victims and offenders: Background, prevention, reintegration. Vol. 2: Suggestions for succeeding generations* (pp. 203–232). Cham: Springer.

Roggenthin, K. (2011). Perspektiven eines familiensensiblen Strafvollzugs – das Familienhaus in Kopenhagen. *BAG-S Informationsdienst Straffälligenhilfe Bonn, 19*, 9–13.

Römer, W. (1967). *Die Nebenfolgen der Freiheitsstrafen auf die Kinder der Delinquenten*. Hamburg: Kriminalistik Verlag.

Rowe, D. C., & Farrington, D. P. (1997). The familial transmission of criminal convictions. *Criminology, 36*, 177–202.

RT-Deutsch – Reuters. (2016). *Neue Studie: Generation Knast – Bei über 5 Millionen Kindern in den USA sitzen Eltern im Gefängnis*. https://deutsch.rt.com/nordamerika/38042-5-millionen-kinder-betroffen-/

Rudolf, B., & Windfuhr, M. (2017). Vorwort. In *Deutsches Institut für Menschenrechte. Entwicklung der Menschenrechtssituation in Deutschland*. Juli 2016 – Juni 2017. Berlin.

Sacks, J. (1938). *The social and economic adjustments of the families of a selected group of imprisoned felons*. Master's Thesis, American Catholic University, School of Social Work.

Spjeldnes, S., Jung, H., Maguire, L., & Yamatani, H. (2012). Positive family social support: Counteracting negative effects of mental illness and substance abuse to reduce jail Ex-inmate recidivism rates. *Journal of Human Behavior in the Social Environment, 22*(2), 130–147.

Streng, F. (2014). *Kriminalitätswahrnehmung und Punitivität im Wandel. Kriminalitäts- und berufsbezogene Einstellungen junger Juristen – Befragungen von 1989 bis 2012*. Heidelberg: Kriminalistik.

Suliak, H. (2020). *Kinder unter 14 Jahren ins Gefängnis?*. LTO Legal Tribune Online. https://www.lto.de/recht/hintergruende/h/strafrecht-strafmuendigkeit-alter-14-sanktionen-csu-cdu-kinder-jugendliche/

Thiel, J. (2020). *KEIN Pausenbrot, KEINE Kindheit, KEINE Chance. Wie sich Armut in Deutschland anfühlt und was sich ändern muss*. München: Piper.

Thornberry, T. P. (Ed.). (1997). *Developmental theories of crime and delinquency*. New Brunswick: Transaction.

Thornberry, T. P. (2009). The apple doesn't fall far from the tree (or does it?): Intergenerational patterns of antisocial behaviour – the American Society of Criminology 2008 Sutherland Address. *Criminology, 47*, 297–325.

Thornberry, T. P., Freeman-Gallant, A., Lizotte, A. J., Krohn, M. D., & Smith, C. (2003). Linked lives: The intergenerational transmission of antisocial behaviour. *Journal of Abnormal and Child Psychology, 31*, 171–184.

Thornberry, T. P., Henry, K. L., Krohn, M. D., Lizotte, A. J., & Nadel, E. L. (2018). Key findings from the Rochester intergenerational study. In *Intergenerational continuity of criminal and antisocial behavior: an international overview of current studies*. London: Routledge.

Turney, K. (2014). The consequences of paternal incarceration for maternal neglect and harsh parenting. *Social Forces, 92*(4), 1607–1636.

Tzoumakis, S., Burton, M., Carr, V. J., Dean, K., Laurens, K. R., & Green, M. J. (2019). *Parental offending and children's conduct problems. Trans and Issues in Crime and Criminal Justice 571*. Canberra: Australian Institute of Criminology.

United Nations Office on Drugs and Crime – UNODC. (2015). *The United Nations standard minimum rules for the treatment of prisoners (the Nelson Mandela Rules)*. Vienna: UN International Centre. https://www.unodc.org/documents/justice-and-prison-reform/GA-RESOLUTION/E_ebook.pdf

Van de Rakt, M., Murray, J., & Nieuwbeerta, P. (2012). The long-term effects of paternal imprisonment on criminal trajectories of children. *Journal of Research in Crime and Delinquency, 49*(1), 81–108.
Van de Rakt, M., Nieuwbeerta, P., & De Graaf, N. D. (2008). Like father, like son? The relationships between conviction trajectories of father and their sons and their daughters. *British Journal of Criminology, 48*, 538–556.
Van de Weijer, D., Bijleveld, C. C., & Blokland, A. A. (2014). The intergenerational transmission of violent offending. *Journal of Family Violence, 29*, 109–118.
van de Weijer, S., Augustyn, M. B., & Besemer, S. (2017). Intergenerational transmission of crime. An international, empirical assessment. In A. Blokland & V. van der Geest (Eds.), *The Routledge international handbook of life-course criminology* (pp. 279–297). London: Routledge.
Wakefield, S., & Wildeman, C. (2013). *Children of the prison boom: Mass incarceration and the future of American inequality*. Oxford: Oxford University Press.
Walkenhorst, P., & Koop, G. (2019). Was bleibt HAFTen? Über die Bedeutung von Nachsorge, Entlassungsvorbereitung und Übergangsgestaltung. *Forum Strafvollzug, 68*, 249.
Walter, M. (1999). *Strafvollzug*. Stuttgart: Boorberg.
Wemrell, M., Stjernlöf, S., Aenishänslin, J., Lila, M., Gracia, E., & Ivert, A.-K. (2019). Towards understanding the Nordic paradox: A review of qualitative interview studies on intimate partner violence against women (IPVAW) in Sweden. *Sociology Compass, 13*, 1–23.
Westdeutscher Rundfunk – WDR. (2020). *Bielefelder Häftling erstreitet Recht auf bewachten Freigang*. https://www1.wdr.de/nachrichten/westfalen-lippe/bielefelder-haeftling-erstreitet-am-bundesverfassungsgericht-recht-auf-freigang-100.html
Wildeman, C. (2014). *Parental incarceration and child wellbeing: An annotated bibliography*. Marshfield: The Sills Family Foundation.
Wildeman, C., & Andersen, S. H. (2017). Paternal incarceration and children's risk of being charged by early adulthood: Evidence from a Danish policy shock. *Criminology, 55*(1), 32–58.
Wildeman, C., Scardamalia, K., Walsh, E. G., O'Brien, R. L., & Brew, B. (2017). Paternal incarceration and teachers' expectations of students. *Socius: Sociological Research for a Dynamic World, 3*, 1–14.
Wolfe, S., McLean, K., & Pratt, T. (2017). I learned it by watching you: legal socialization and the intergenerational transmission of legitimacy attitudes. *British Journal of Criminology, 57*(5), 1123–1143. https://doi.org/10.1093/bjc/azw038
Wolleb, A., Spycher, M., Blaser, R., & Felder, W. (2009a). Eingewiesene und ihre familiären Kontakte. Eine explorative Studie. *Zeitschrift für Vormundschaftswesen, 3*, 177–191.
Wolleb, A., Spycher, M., Blaser, R., Znoj, H., & Felder, W. (2009b). Eingewiesene und ihre familiären Kontakte im Zusammenhang mit dem Wohlbefinden. *Schweizerische Zeitschrift für Kriminologie, 2*, 3–13.
Zwönitzer, A., Pillhofer, M., & Ziegenhain, U. (2013). Die Situation von Kindern mit einem inhaftierten Elternteil. Eine Bestandsaufnahme in baden-württembergischen Justizvollzugsanstalten. *Monatsschrift für Kriminologie und Strafrechtsreform, 96*, 325–333.

Helmut Kury Prof. h.c. mult., Dr., Dipl.-Psych., studied Psychology at the University of Freiburg (Freiburg im Brsg., Germany), diploma, Dr. in Psychology and Habilitation at the University of Freiburg. Between 1970 and 1973, he was an assistant teacher at the University of Freiburg, Institut for Psychology, between 1973 and 1980 and from 1989 to 2006, senior researcher at the Max-Planck-Institute for Foreign and International Penal Law in Freiburg im Brsg., Department of Criminology; 1980–1988 first and founding director of the Criminological Research Institute of Lower Saxony—KFN. His research areas include offender rehabilitation, crime prevention, attitudes to punishment, fear of crime, punitiveness, alternatives to punishment, diversion, methodological problems of empirical social science research, international comparison of crime and punishment. He cooperated with many universities and research institutes internationally, especially with countries of the former Soviet Union. His most recent publications in English are: Kury, H., Ferdinand, T.N. (Eds.) (2008). *International Perspectives on Punitivity.* Bochum: Universitätsverlag Dr. Brockmeyer; Kury, H. (Ed.)(2008). *Fear of Crime – Punitivity. New Developments in Theory and Research.* Bochum: Universitätsverlag Dr. Brockmeyer; Kury, H., Shea, E. (Eds.) (2011). *Punitivity – International Developments.* 3 Vols., Bochum: Universitätsverlag Dr. Brockmeyer; Kury, H., Redo, S., Shea, E. (Eds.) (2016). *Women and Children as Victims and Offenders: Background, Prevention, Reintegration. Suggestions for Succeeding Generations.* 2 Vols., International Publishing Switzerland: Springer; Kury, H., Kuhlmann, A. (2016). Mediation in Germany and Other Western Countries. Kriminolgijos Studijos 4, 2016, 5–46; Kury, H. (2017). Harsh Punishment or Alternatives: Which Is the Better Crime Prevention. Juricia international, University of Tartu, 15, 91–99; Kury, H., Glonti, G. (2017). Migration in Germany and Georgia (Comparative Analyses). Davit Aghmashnenebeli University of Georgia Academic Journal 1, 6–13; Kury, H. (2018). Rehabilitation in Prison. German Experiences and what can be done better. Rom. Journ. of Sociological Studies, New Series, Bucharest, No. 1, 19–36; Kury, H. (2018). Integration of refugees in Germany – Has the criminal burden increased" Criminology: Yesterday, Today, Tomorrow - The Journal of St. Petersburg International Criminology Club 1, 48, 37–45; Kury, H., Redo, S. (Eds.) (2018). Refugees and Migrants in Law and Policy. Challenges and Opportunities for Global Civic Education. International Publishing Switzerland: Springer; Kuhlmann, A., Kury, H. (2018). Some Considerations of Restorative Justice Before and Outside of Contemporary Western States. Kriminologijos studijos – Criminological Studies, Vilniaus Universitetas, 5, 5–42; Kury, H. (2019). Refugees: Post Traumatic Stress, and Crime – Experiences from Germany. Kultura i Edukacja – Culture and Education 124, 73–90; Kury, H., Kuhlmann, A., Quintas, J. (2019). On the Preventative Effect of Sanctions for Drug Crime: The United States, Germany and Portugal. Archiwum Kryminologii, Polska Akademia Nauk, Instytut Nauk Prawnych, 41, 261–295. E-mail: helmut.kury@web.de.

Dealing with Mental Illness and Violence in the (Youth-)Prison

Helmut Kury and Romy Heße

Abstract While there are relatively many reports and research projects on violence in prison, the issue of mental illness of prisoners has so far played only a relatively minor role in criminology. Overall, the public is uninformed about the prison system, especially through the media, which usually report very selectively, especially about problems. In recent years, public punitiveness has increased on the background of growing problems in society. People with mental health problems are significantly over-represented in prison compared to the normal population. In particular, the suicide rate among prisoners is also significantly increased in this context. This is confirmed by international data from many countries. Due to the unfavourable living conditions and the multiple problems of the prisoners, it is not surprising that the violence among the prisoners is also relatively high. This is especially true for juvenile male detainees. On prison violence, living conditions and, in particular, contact between prisoners and staff and their quality play a major role. In this context, it is difficult for prisons to realise their real task of resocialising the prisoners. Prisons are very unfavourable places to achieve the statutory resocialisation task. In many cases, incarceration contributes to a deterioration rather than an improvement in the social behaviour of prisoners.

Keywords Prisoners · Juvenile detention · Mental health problems in offenders · Suicide rate of prisoners · Social atmosphere in prisons · Contact between prisoners and staff · Resocialisation · Prisonisation · Contact with relatives

H. Kury (✉)
Max Planck-Institute for Foreign and International Penal Law, Freiburg, Germany

R. Heße
Remchingen, Germany

H. Kury, S. Redo (eds.), *Crime Prevention and Justice in 2030*,
https://doi.org/10.1007/978-3-030-56227-4_8

1 Introduction

The public, and in some cases experts, are often only poorly informed about individual aspects of crime and in particular the prison system. This applies especially to the extent of mental disorders in (juvenile) prisoners. In the meantime, there have been extensive studies on the problem, but the results differ considerably, which is mainly due to different definitions of mental illness and delimitation of individual aspects as well as different survey methods and the composition of the examined samples (Kury 2008).

As a rule, citizens receive information on crime only through the media. The media report on the background of their own interests, if possible, to attract attention, ultimately, above all, to be bought or seen, usually selectively and imprecise (Hestermann 2016). Primarily, information is provided about the offence and the behaviour of the offender, but hardly on the crucial question why the offender has become the perpetrator.

For effective crime prevention, one of the central questions is why a perpetrator has become the perpetrator in the context of his social development, how he has developed and what needs to be done to prevent such a development. In examining this issue, socio-political aspects are addressed which take criminal policy as a whole into account, and thus also the public. A sole attribution of criminal behaviour to the perpetrators usually falls short. Crime, as international comparisons show, is clearly dependent on social conditions in a country. A social policy, for example, which supports disadvantaged groups, particularly regarding the education of children, can contribute significantly to greater social peace, thus also to a reduction in social and criminal conspicuousness.

Internationally, the majority of the general population sees a tightening of criminal sanctions as the best and most adequate means of reducing the crime rate in a country. Punitive attitudes have also increased in connection with an increasingly complex lifestyle process in recent years, but also with an expanding number of immigrants and growing uncertainty. Criminals are made more responsible for their deviant behaviour alone. The treatment of offenders and the conditions of detention vary widely worldwide and often have little or no impact on security in a country (see de Cock 2005).

For example, against the background of his long-term survey of young lawyers, Streng (2014, p. 60) reports an increase in support for the death penalty abolished in Germany in 1949 for "some crimes." In 1977, 11.5% of the respondents agreed to this most severe sanction; in 2010, it was 31.9%. Support values for the death penalty of 50% are sometimes reported for Great Britain, and significantly higher values for countries where the death penalty is still practiced, such as Japan or China (Oberwittler and Qi 2009). Attitudes to harsh sanctions generally decrease significantly when respondents are informed about the lack of effectiveness of strict criminal sentences and their disadvantages (Roberts and Hough 2005; Sato 2014).

There is also a punitive stance on public perceptions of (mental) illnesses in prisoners and the care of those affected. For example, "poorer health care for prisoners as part of the punishment... is largely recognized and unanimously approved" (Stöver 2008, p. 238). As Foerster (2005, p. 144) reports in connection with the reference to "dramatic undersupply" of mentally ill people in prisons (cf. Witzel et al. 2004), there are considerable prejudices and reservations even among experts: "General clinical psychiatry has no interest in the problem of mentally ill prisoners. These patients are primarily seen as 'criminals' and not also as mentally ill people, for whom psychiatry is *also* responsible. The aversion of some relevant specialist representatives currently goes so far that forensic psychiatry has already been denied the right to still belong to psychiatry. Unfortunately, it has still not been recognized that caring for mentally ill offenders is... also a form of applied social psychiatry."

Against the background of the fact that the mental stress among the population has increased overall in the past few decades, it is not surprising that this also applies to prisoners. For example, the Federal Agency for Civic Education (Bundeszentrale für Politische Bildung 2018) emphasises that social inequalities are growing in many advanced societies. For example, the low-skilled have become increasingly difficult to find employment, the integration of immigrants becomes more difficult, the unemployed lack money, self-respect and recognition, and more and more people are considered poor. "The once leading and politically stabilizing middle classes are shrinking... The social and political significance of social inequality can be... hardly overestimate" (see Chassé 2010). In children and adolescents in particular, mental disorders increased years ago, but according to Brünger and Weissbeck (2008) they often go undetected in everyday practice. The stress factors would often also be related to an increased risk of delinquency.

In the following, data on the prevalence of mental illnesses in prisoners, especially in the prison system for young people, will be presented and discussed in connection with international development (see also Kury 2020). What can be seen as the causes of an ever-higher burden of mental illness among criminals? In another section, the treatment situation for the affected group of detainees is to be presented and any deficiencies are pointed out, especially against the background of international guidelines, such as those of the United Nations or the European Union. In the final chapter approaches and possibilities for an improvement of the situation are discussed.

2 Prevalence of Mental Illness in (Juvenile) Offenders

There is agreement in the international literature that the prevalence of mental disorders among detainees is higher than that of the general population. However, the information on the proportion of mentally disturbed among all prisoners then clearly differ in connection with different sample compositions, definitions of mental illness/disorder and, above all, different measurement methods. For example, the differences in the understanding and definition of mental illness, the excerpt of the recorded aspects, are considerable. For example, Schröder (2005, p. 10) reports that the term mental disorder encompasses a wide and complex spectrum of numerous individual diagnoses, which are described in the most common diagnostic and classification systems, such as the DSM-IV and the ICD-10. The Ministry of Justice of Baden-Württemberg (2015) set up an expert commission in December 2014 to seek advice on how to deal with mentally abnormal prisoners.

Given the complexity of mental disorders/illnesses, the varying clinical pictures and facets of different disorders and the often excessive demands placed on the prison system when dealing with this group of detainees, it is not surprising that the results on the prevalence of individual disorders in prisoners are extremely different. The studies consistently show significantly higher exposure figures among detainees than among the general population.

The expert commission of the Ministry of Justice Baden-Württemberg/Germany (2015, p. 17) emphasises that an increase in the proportion of mental disorders in the population has been observed, especially in recent years. The total annual prevalence for mental disorders in Germany is estimated at 27.7% of the total population (Jacobi et al. 2014, p. 77ff.). Anxiety disorders were the most common mental illness at 15.3%, followed by depressive illnesses (7.7%) and substance abuse/dependence (5.7%). For the EU, an almost identical overall prevalence for Axis-I-Diseases was determined at 27% (Wittchen et al. 2011, pp. 655ff.).

As for detainees, on the other hand, Dudeck et al. (2009) found for short-term prisoners of up to 3 years in prison, a lifetime prevalence for an Axis-I-Disorder of 83.3%. Of those examined, 80% had at least one personality disorder. The authors emphasise (p. 219): "Short-term prisoners represent a psychologically highly stressed population and require a wide range of therapeutic offers." Almost one in six prisoners reported suicidal thoughts, almost as many reported self-harm. The test subjects showed the most restriction through depression, anxiety, paranoid thinking and compulsiveness (p. 223).

Suicide rates are significantly higher among prisoners than among the general population (Missonie and Konrad 2008). Blocher et al. (2001) found that more than half of the prisoners reported moderate or severe psychological problems, especially depression and anxiety. More than 10% would show a suicide risk. The exposure levels were significantly increased, especially for prisoners on remand and younger detainees. John (2010, pp. 37f.) found a mental disorder in 67% of the prisoners at the JVA Neumünster in Germany. Forty-four percent (44%) had an alcohol syndrome, 33% had a major depression and 17% had an anxiety disorder, almost 20% had thoughts of suicide, in the group of juvenile convicts it was even a third.

A study by the Central Institute for Mental Health (*Zentralinstitut für Seelische Gesundheit*) in Mannheim was able to show that prison inmates in Europe with a prevalence of Axis-I-Disorders of over 90% represent a significantly psychologically/psychiatrically stressed population (Salize et al. 2007). Schöch (2008, pp. 5ff.) estimates that the proportion of prisoners with a dissocial personality disorder alone is at least 30%, and sees this high proportion as one of the greatest problems of health care in prisons.

The results from German studies are confirmed by international results. Graf (2008, p. 40) reports for Switzerland that the prevalence rate of mental disorders in imprisoned people is between 37% and 65%, compared to 22% in the general population. Gunn et al. (1991) found a 37% prevalence rate of psychiatric disorders among male prisoners in England and Wales (U.K.), 23% of whom showed substance abuse and 10% had personality disorders. Stringer (2019) reports for the United States that major depression was found in more than 24% of prisoners, in 17% a bipolar disorder and in 13% a personality disorder. Teplin (1994) found severe psychological or substance-related disorder in 30.7% of US prisoners, and approximately 50% showed signs of an anti-social personality disorder.

According to Anderson (2004), the prevalence of mental disorders among offenders in prisons in Europe is lower than in the USA. In an Australian study, Herrman et al. (1991) found a lifetime prevalence of mental illness in prisoners of 82%, while 69% suffered from a substance problem. Fazel and Danesh (2002) summarised 62 studies from 12 countries with a total of 22,790 detainees and found that 65% of the inmates studied had a personality disorder, including 47% an antisocial disorder. A study on detainees in Iran can also confirm the international results.

Sepehrmanesh et al. (2014) examined a random sample of 180 prisoners aged 31.9 years on average. Psychiatric disorders were found in 43.4%, 27.9% had major depression and 17.4% had PTSD or substance abuse. Personality disorders were found in 28.3% of prisoners, 62.2% had an antisocial disorder and 44.6% had suicidal thoughts. The authors emphasise (p. 6): "About half of all prisoners suffered from psychiatric disorders; therefore treatment of psychiatric disorder in this group is essential for prevention of crime."

As far as juvenile detainees are concerned, there is less specific research on the mental illnesses of prisoners in this group, although the studies on the subject often do not differentiate according to the age of the prisoners (Klatt et al. 2016, p. 1). It is rightly pointed out by several authors that the diagnostics used to record mental disorders, for example during initial examinations in youth prisons, are often extremely superficial, so that existing problems are not recognised (Brünger and Weissbeck 2008; Frädrich and Pfäfflin 2000). Accordingly, the Ministry of Justice of Baden-Württemberg/Germany (2015, p. 29) calls for an improvement in diagnostics, especially at an interdisciplinary level.

Against this background, a significant proportion of prisoners with serious mental disorders are housed in the regular prison system, although they actually belong in a special prison for treatment, which is also true for juvenile detainees (Brünger and Weissbeck 2008). von Schönfeld et al. (2006, p. 830) emphasise based on their investigation that the number of mentally disturbed prisoners is much higher than that of the detainees in special facilities. According to Ukere (2012), the allocation to regular prisons or treatment institutions is more or less dependent on chance in the context of a lack of valid diagnostic examinations (see also Orlob 2017). The author emphasises (p. 51): "In accordance with most of the available literature, the assumption is confirmed that the prevalence of personality disorders in regular prisons is not much smaller than in prisons for treatment" (cf. also Schröder 2005).

Also, according to Brünger and Weissbeck (2008), mental disorders in children and adolescents has significantly increased and, in this context, delinquent behaviour, whereby the increase in crimes by female juveniles and adolescents is particularly worrying. In particular, mentally ill criminals in adolescence are at risk of falling out of the social network, and this in the important phase of developing school, professional and social progress and relations. Of children and adolescents with low socio-economic status, 23.2% would show evidence of psychological problems. Above all, the authors also call for better diagnostics to identify mental disorders.

Kopp et al. (2009) found increased rates of traumatisation in childhood and adolescence among prisoners. John (2010, p. 37f.) found in his study in the JVA Neumünster/Germany that the risk of suicide among juvenile prisoners was higher than among adults (one-third compared to almost 20% for adults; see also Ministry of Justice Baden-Württemberg 2015, p. 14). Boxberg et al. (2016, p. 428) stress that juvenile offenders would represent a highly polluted population.

The United Nations Office on Drugs and Crime published a handbook years ago, "designed to be used by all actors involved in the criminal justice system, including policymakers, legislators, prison managers, prison staff, members of non-governmental organizations and other individuals interested or active in the field of criminal justice and prison reform" (UNODC - United Nations Office on Drugs and Crime 2009, p. 1). The handbook "covers the special needs of eight groups of prisoners, which have a particularly vulnerable status in prisons: Prisoners with mental health care needs; Prisoners with disabilities; Ethnic and racial minorities and indigenous peoples; Foreign national prisoners; Lesbian, gay, bisexual, and transgender (LGBT) prisoners; Older prisoners; Prisoners with terminal illness and Prisoners under sentence of death" (p. 1).

"The focus on the handbook is prisoners: However, it must be emphasized that the social reintegration of most offenders with special needs is much better served in the community, rather than in prisons, where their requirements can rarely be met and where their situation is likely to deteriorate" (p. 2). "All prisoners are vulnerable to a certain degree. When the liberty of a group of individuals is restricted and they are placed under the authority of another group of people, and when this takes place in an environment which is to a large extent closed to public scrutiny, the abuse of power has proven to be widespread. Even where no abuse exists, prisons conditions themselves in a large majority of countries worldwide are harmful to the physical and mental well-being of prisoners, due to overcrowding, violence, poor physical conditions, isolation from the community, inadequate prison activities and health care" (p. 4).

When it comes to prisoners with mental health care, emphasis is placed on (p. 10): "In most countries there is a need to address problems relating to adequate health care in the general population and to improve access to health care services by the poor, homeless, unemployed and people with mental disabilities, as a first step towards reducing the unnecessary and harmful imprisonment of individuals with mental health care needs, thereby relieving pressure on the scarce resources of prison health services. Punitive sentencing policies, which lead to the increasing imprisonment of disadvantaged groups, such as offenders with mental disabilities, need to be reassessed to reverse the dramatic increase of prisoners with mental disabilities in institutions which were not designed to cater for the health care and social reintegration needs of this vulnerable group. The large majority of prison systems worldwide fail to provide an environment which does not harm the mental well-being of its inhabitants. Isolation from society, poor prison conditions, overcrowding and lack of safety induce distress, depression and anxiety in most prisoners, which may develop into more serious mental disabilities. The promotion of mental health in prisons should be a key element of prison management and health care policies. The development of comprehensive policies and strategies aiming to protect the mental well-being of all prisoners and to ensure that those with mental disabilities have timely access to suitable and individualized treatment, provided on the basis of informed consent, equivalent to that in the community, is essential to ensure the effective management of mental health care in prisons."

The report continues (p. 16): "International studies indicate that suicide rates in prisons significantly exceed those in the general population and have been increasing within the last decades in some countries. Long-term sentences, single-cell use, mental disabilities, substance abuse and a history of suicidal tendencies are associated with an increased suicide risk" (see for example: Matschnig et al. 2006; Shaw et al. 2005, p. 75). The immense challenges relating to the provision of equitable health care, including mental health care, in prisons, cannot be resolved by prison administrations and prison health care services alone, are rightly pointed out: (p. 22): Offenders with mental disabilities require a comprehensive community-based treatment approach that provides essential services, ensure public safety and reduces re-offending."

Rightly, social responsibility is pointed out (p. 22): "The immense challenges relating to the provision of equitable health care, including mental health care, in prisons, cannot be resolved by prison administrations and prison health care services alone. Offenders with mental disabilities require a comprehensive community-based treatment approach that provides essential services, ensures public safety and reduces re-offending."

For the USA, it is reported that 2002 "suicide rates among prisoners with mental disabilities who had made previous suicide attempts were more than 100 times higher than the rate in the general population. Over 50 per cent of jail suicides were committed within the first 24 h in jail. More than 95 per cent of those who committed suicide in prisons had a treatable psychiatric disability" (p. 17). For Australia, it is reported that the rate of suicide in prisons "is estimated to be between 2.5 and 15 times that of the general population. It has been estimated that for every suicide there are 60 incidents of self harming behaviour" (see also Borrill et al. 2003; McArthur et al. 1999; Penal Reform International 2007).

The importance of alternatives, as diversion measures are rightly emphasised (see also Kury and Lerchenmüller 1981): "Principles for the protection of persons with mental illness and the improvement of mental health care (Mental Illness Principles) make clear that person with mental disabilities should have the right to be treated and cared for, as far as possible, in the community in which they live. WHO recommends that mental health services be based in the community and integrated as far as possible to general health services, in accordance with the vital principle of the least restrictive environment" (p. 23).

3 Prison Violence

In their own investigation, Boxberg et al. (2016) found that 80–90% of young male prisoners said they had been victims or offenders of psychological violence in custody in the past 3 months, 62–68% of physical violence. According to Kury and Smartt (2002a, b), 34.9% of the detained adolescents experienced physical violence, 53.3% were threatened (see also Kury and Brandenstein 2002).

Klatt and Baier (2016, p. 256) found in their research project in five juvenile detention centres that 34.1% were victims of violence at least once in the 4 weeks before the interview, while 33.0% used violence themselves at least once in the period. Previous victim impacts at school correlated positively with victimisation in prison (p. 257). In addition to the personality characteristics of the perpetrators, conditions of the prisons, such as the relationship between staff and detainees, also had an influence on the level of violence (p. 258; see also the overview of internationally comparative studies on violence in the Youth penal system of Häufle et al. 2013).

Heße (2019, pp. 41ff.) interviewed former prison inmates and have found that the probability of being confronted with violence in prison was highly regarded as a matter of course. The prisoner subculture, its own understanding of violence and power and respect played a major role. Even according to Stelly (2015, p. 327) "Violence . . . an everyday phenomenon in juvenile detention and encounters one in different forms."

Heße (2019) emphasises that published experience reports of (former) prisoners, national and international research results as well as documented incidents of violence among detainees show that violence exists and also has a significant impact on the everyday life of prisoners (Wirth 2006; Hartenstein and Hinz 2014; Heinrich 2002; Ernst 2008; Cunningham et al. 2005; Kury and Smartt 2002a, b; Ireland 1999). However, since the prison system is characterised by its secretiveness and secrecy, the meaningfulness of the depiction of internal prison conditions remains uncertain.

Influenced by new impressions that differ from the outside world, violence within a correctional facility can be explained by various theoretical approaches. Violence results from learned structures, attribution processes, subcultural conditions and is to be understood as a form of situation management or as the result of rational decisions. A wide variety of individual and external factors also affect experiences of violence and making them difficult to classify. In everyday prison life, special circumstances complicate the everyday life of detained people, so that they resort to coping strategies that seem atypical for non-detained people. Self-experienced or perceived violence result in new dimensions of meaning that are subjectively assigned to violence within the prisoner society.

Studies dealing with the life of criminals in detention have already shown that rigid hierarchical structures within the subculture shape the lives of prisoners (cf. Sykes 1958; Harbordt 1972; Goffman 1977). The code of conduct for a prisoner subculture puts enormous pressure on the individual and forces them to perform unwanted acts—including violent situations that serve to defend or protect other people that they would not have gotten outside of the institution.

Different approaches deal with changed behaviour patterns and the handling of new experiences in detention. In addition to classic attempts to explain criminal behaviour, which violence remains in custody, it seems interesting to look at the construction of one's own reality.

3.1 Construction of One's Own Reality

Berger and Luckmann (1969) state that the perception of reality and the importance it is given depend on individual actions within a society. Individual behaviour is linked to subjective perception and it can therefore be assumed that the understanding of violence differs in different societies. These thoughts can be transferred in their entirety to the prisoner subculture and its actors. The particular focus of this approach is the concept of *institutionalisation*. This describes the process-based takeover of already existing, habitual activities of a society and the existing system of values and norms (Berger and Luckmann 1969, pp. 24–28).

According to Durkheim, the integration of the individual into society is process-based. Actions arise that become habits and ultimately manifest as rules of conduct. At the end of the chain is the creation of a generally valid system of standards for society (cf. Abels 2009, p. 33f.). Sykes (2007) and Goffman (1977) dealt extensively with the subject of prisoner subculture and the existing systems of values and norms. In the context of this, violence is legitimised, among other things, as a means of inducing one's ability to act (cf. Goffman 1977, pp. 58–60; Sykes 2007, pp. 80–82).

These thoughts can be completed with Weber's theory of action. According to him, both actively and passively performed actions have a personal meaning and always refer to the behaviour of others (cf. Weber 1967, p. 653). Characterised by the fact that reality can only be filled with meaning and considered meaningful by people, Berger and Luckmann (1969) shape the concept of *the reality of everyday life*. In addition, they developed the concept of two successive socialisation processes. In the primary process, people accept the values and norms of society, live with them and act accordingly. The second socialisation process is characterised by the change and adaptation of new values and norms, which in turn arise from the acquisition of new knowledge (cf. Berger and Luckmann 1969, pp. 148f.).

In the context of detention, this means that new patterns of action, such as the use of violence, are accepted and (further) developed within a socialisation process. Berger and Luckmann formulate the secondary adaptation as an overlay of primary reality and refer to Goffman's thoughts regarding the role distance within total institutions (Goffman 1977). These are characterised, among other things, by the intervention in the socialisation of an individual, through which a new subjective reality must be developed (cf. Abels 2009, pp. 127–130).

Due to the forced context of a correctional facility, detainees are forced to form a subjective understanding of violence. The factors that determine this differ from the constraint context of the community and many other factors that entail detention. It can therefore be assumed that, regardless of socialisation before detention, the subjective understanding of violence differs from detained people to non-detained people and that violence is assessed differently within these two groups.

3.2 Significance for Judicial Practice

Following these assumptions, prisoners learn from the moments and people around them. To create a non-violent reality in custody for the people living in it, it is important to treat each other with respect. Concepts such as the implementation of residential groups transfer responsibility for a successful everyday life in the community to the detainees and thus also transfer the responsibility of having to protect something that the group has determined to be worth protecting (see Heße 2019, p. 69).

However, the judicial practice of deprivation of liberty provides for an older and more isolated form of detention more often than the execution of residential group enforcement. In this context, power relationships and subcultural hierarchies are evidently predominant, especially in large prisons, which increase the risk of becoming a victim of violence (cf. Kury and Smartt 2002a, p. 328).

Violence in prison is a common problem. In particular, the trade in illegal goods, subcultural hierarchies, conflicts brought from outside, institutional harmful effects that detention can bring and the problematic relationship between employees and detainees due to the balance of power make everyday prison life difficult. Individual skills to deal with new challenges and own interests also play an important role. A weighting of these factors can hardly take place due to the individuality of each detainee. A distinction can be made between the assumption that violent behaviour due to socialisation would be brought before the detention by the prisoners, and the approach that violence occurs due to institutional circumstances of a prison system.

The thesis of a "production of violence" by the prison system that is shaped by subcultural acts, the lack of autonomy and own decision-making options, a deprivation in a confined space, a foreign determination in the existential areas of life and the constant control of the subjective action is in the context of the deprivation thesis of Sykes (1958) represented (see Suhling and Rabold 2013, p. 72). Because of these negative effects of imprisonment or "pains of imprisonment" (Sykes 1958), the prisoners are forced to develop new values and norms.

According to this assumption, violence can be seen as a coping strategy. This deviant behaviour can serve to create a capacity to act to escape a feeling of powerlessness caused by the detention (cf. Böhnisch 1999, pp. 179f.; Goffman 1977, pp. 58–60; Sykes 2007, pp. 80–82). Due to the prison conditions and the resulting subculture with their inherent hierarchies and the massive deprivation in prison, Kury and Smartt (2002a, p. 328) consider new victimisation experiences to be "[. . .] obvious and downright to be expected."

The theoretical assumptions of the *import hypothesis* by Irwin and Cressey (1962) stand in the way of the deprivation thesis. These focus on the personal behaviours and values that were in place before being detained. Violence within prisons is explained based on the transfer of these personality traits and strategies of action, which can be classified as criminal, into everyday prison life.

However, both approaches are mutually dependent. To explain violence in detention, the interaction of both approaches must be considered. Because no prison can be thought of without the society that lives in it, which can have a wide range of criminal skills. Furthermore, it cannot be denied that, due to the institutional circumstances already mentioned, this society in particular is forced to adopt alternative maxims for action. Prisoners react to deprived conditions within a correctional facility with inappropriate behaviour. This is perceived by staff as disturbing. The result of this is stricter monitoring and control, which in turn creates more stressful prison conditions (see Boxberg and Bögelein 2015, p. 242).

The feeling of unjust treatment, which can result from the reaction of increased control and surveillance, also has a negative impact on violent behaviour.

A special role in dealing with violence can be attributed to the contact between prison staff and detained persons. This is often described as untrustworthy (see Heße 2019, p. 74). Therefore, experiences of violence can hardly be worked up constructively together. Even employees of the social services within the prisons are faced with the challenge of a double mandate (Böhnisch and Lösch 1973), between official reporting and documentation of everyday prison life for possible detention relief (control) and the support of the detainees (help).

In addition, prisons have difficulty dealing with inter-prisoner violence due to a lack of options. Appropriate handling seems problematic because the isolation of the victim of an act of violence is characterised by distrust of the prisoner subculture of having a traitor among them and the victims themselves often reject such a solution. Only a common manner seems effective. Commonality can be created through respectful treatment and participation. For the practical implementation of new, conceptual proposals for dealing with violence among prisoners, it would be desirable to publish the violence profiles of the individual prisons. However, this is often not possible due to the confidentiality and impenetrability of prison structures.

It can be said that the importance assigned to violence from an individual point of view appears to depend on characteristics of detention. In addition, it must be emphasised that this is difficult to grasp due to the countless factors influencing violence. The subjective perception and reality of the detainees remains just as individual.

Overall, no causal connection can be seen between imprisonment and the use of violence. However, the likelihood of experiencing violence in custody is high (see Heße 2019, p. 70f.). Therefore, within a correctional facility, a conceptual adjustment to these factors that promote violence is necessary to exemplify and realise a non-violent day in prison. This should be characterised by respect, looking and clarity (see Neubacher and Boxberg 2018, pp. 210–211; Endres and Breuer 2018, pp. 594–595; Wirth 2013, p. 132). The resulting improvement in the prison climate can ultimately make a significant contribution to creating a non-violent setting within prisons.

In this context, it should also be noted that violence by and against employees is an "empirical wasteland" (Stelly 2015, p. 328). The attempt to record the attacks on employees of the Bundes der Strafvollzugsbediensteten Deutschlands e. V. (Confederation of Prison Staff in Germany) is "almost impossible" (Selle 2019, p. 1). In 2019, for example, the media again noticed the subject of violence against prison staff and consistently pointed to an increase. The *Badische Zeitung* (December 28, 2019, p. 6) emphasised that over the past 10 years the number of serious attacks on prison officers had tripled in Baden-Württemberg prisons. There is a high dark field, as the correctional facilities would not report to prevent a deterioration of their reputation (see for example also *Kleine Zeitung* from May 9, 2017; Märkische Allgemeine from August 5, 2019).

Grübler (2019) reports that there is now an inpatient psychiatry in the Hameln juvenile facility, the largest youth prison in Germany. The number of juvenile prisoners is decreasing, but the proportion of mentally ill is increasing. The prisoners usually come from difficult social backgrounds and regularly have disturbances in the social ties. Again and again, the considerable social damages and problems that (juvenile) prisoners have is rightly pointed out.

A survey of young prisoners in Baden-Württemberg with an average age of 19.5 years (Kury 1979) shows a lot of stress factors, including that—24.2% had no permanent residence,—only 13.2% were in custody for the first time,—42.1% committed the offences only in groups,—75.5% were criminals among the friends,—59.2% committed the offence(s) under the influence of alcohol,—46% had already used drugs,—15.4% regularly,—30.0% of the fathers showed alcohol problems,—48.2% of the inmates were unemployed at the time of the crime,—52.4% reported that their family of origin had frequent disputes, temporary or permanent separation of the parents,—48.4% grew at least temporarily in an incomplete family before the age of 14,—42.8% were at least temporarily in a home,—37.6% had at least once fled from home before the age of 14,—79.5% skipped school several times,—54.7% had no school leaving certificate,—79.1% had no vocational training,—88.6% were unemployed before detention,—93.7% belonged to the lower social classes,—65.3% had debts after being released. Against this background, Bonta et al. emphasise (1998, p. 138): "Early childhood environment and social position provide the contexts in which criminal activities are modeled and reinforced. Delinquent behavior… is likely to be tolerated in dysfunctional families that fail to provide adequate supervision" (cf. also Rowe and Farrington 1997; Kopp et al. 2009).

Against this background, psychological difficulties and conspicuous behaviour in prisons are regarded as problems within the framework of the importation theory that the detainees bring with them into custody (Irwin and Cressey 1962). However, the deprivation theory rightly points out the additional importance of unfavourable prison conditions that favour violence in custody (Boxberg et al. 2016, p. 428).

4 Treatment of (Juvenile) Delinquents in Prisons

According to §2 of the German Prison Law (*Strafvollzugsgesetz—StVollzG*), which came into force in 1977, it is primarily the task of imprisonment and the "goal of imprisonment" to enable prisoners to "live a life without criminal offenses in future in a socially responsible manner." Only in second place is stated: "The execution of the prison sentence also serves to protect the general public from further crimes", whereby a re-socialisation of the detainees also serves above all to ensure the security of the population.

The social rehabilitation task of the penal system, including the juvenile sentence and imprisonment, is particularly expressed in a criminal judgement by the Federal Constitutional Court (Bundesverfassungsgericht) in 2006 (cf. guideline on the criminal judgement of the Second Senate of the Federal Constitutional Court on May 31, 2006, paras. 51ff.): "The execution the prison sentence must be geared towards the goal of enabling the detainee to live a life free of punishment in the future (. . .). This - often also referred to as a rehabilitation goal - the goal of social integration (. . .), which is simply stipulated in §2 sentence 1 *StVollzG*[1] for adult penal system, is anchored in the applicable juvenile justice law as an educational goal (§91 (1) JGG - Jugendgerichtsgesetz). The constitutional status of this goal of enforcement is based on the one hand on the fact that only a penal system geared towards social integration complies with the obligation to respect the human rights of every individual (. . .) and the principle of proportionality of punishment by the state (. . .). With the commandment from Art. 1 Para. 1 GG - *Grundgesetz*, never to treat people as a mere means for social purposes, but always as a purpose - as a subject with their own rights and their own concerns to be taken into account (. . .), and with the principle of proportionality means that the prison sentence can only be reconciled as a particularly far-reaching encroachment on fundamental rights if, taking into account its social protective function, it is consistently aimed at a future free of punishment for the person concerned. At the same time, the need to align the penal system with the goal of re-socialization also follows from the state's duty to protect the security of all citizens. In this respect, there is no contradiction between the goal of integration in the execution and the concern to protect the public from further crimes.

The goal of empowering people to live free from punishment is of particular importance for the execution of juvenile justice. This is evident from the fact that the state's obligation to minimize the negative effects of the punishment on the prisoner's ability to live as far as possible a positive life is particularly pronounced here. The imprisonment affects the adolescent in a phase of life that, even if the course is not delinquent, still serves to develop a personality that is able to lead a righteous life in full independence. By intervening in this phase of life by the state through

[1]StVollzG = Gesetz über den Vollzug der Freiheitsstrafe und der freiheitsentziehenden Maßregeln der Besserung und Sicherung = Strafvollzugsgesetz; German Law on the execution of custodial sentences and detention measures of improvement and security.

deprivation of freedom, it assumes a special responsibility for the further development of those affected. The state can only live up to this increased responsibility by designing a prison system that is particularly geared towards promotion - especially social learning, as well as the training of skills and knowledge that will help future professional integration." Paragraph 54 also emphasises once again: "Prison sentences have a particularly drastic effect on young people."

Now, considering the conditions outlined above, the prison system is not a favourable environment for the re-socialisation of the detainees; on the contrary, it often contributes to further harm to those affected, especially if they are brought in with (serious) mental illnesses. Considering the shortage of personnel, which is mostly prevalent in the law enforcement system, especially concerning specialists such as psychologists, social workers or medical doctors, the prisoners are often left alone, especially in the initial phase after being admitted, which is particularly stressful.

The World Health Organization – WHO (2019a) emphasises in its report on prisoner health and the health system in 39 European countries, which is based on extensive data collection: "The report reveals that the general state of monitoring and surveillance systems for health in prisons is poor." Although detainees should have the same health care standard as the general population, the results show, "that we have indicate an enormous difference in the general health of people in prison compared to those in the outside world." Significantly, Germany is not one of the countries considered in the analyses because no comparable national data are available.

The Council of Europe also pointed out the need for adequate psychiatric care for prison inmates years ago (cf. Dudeck et al. 2009, pp. 219, 223). In the recommendations of the Ministerial Committee No. (98) 7 of April 8, 1998 (Council of Europe 1998): "The health policy in detention should be part of and compatible with national health policy. The health service in a correctional facility should be able to provide general medical, psychiatric and dental treatment under conditions comparable to those outside the institution and to carry out programs in the field of hygiene and preventive medicine" (see also Stöver 2008, p. 238).

In its report, the WHO (2019a) also emphasises the importance of good care in the often stressful first days after release from prison, in which the risk of suicide and the risk of self-harm would increase. Aid was particularly important during the transition to freedom. "Gaps in care during this period have significant negative public health implications and can constrain a country's ability to address inequalities. . . A prison sentence takes away a person's liberty; it should not also take away their health and their right to health." Of the European countries considered, 14% would not check if there were (serious) mental disorders when the prisoners were admitted to the prison. A supplementary report (World Health Organization 2019b, p. VII) emphasises: ". . . the prison service is often the least known and understood of all public services, despite its importance for keeping society safe... Governments are expected to give a degree of priority to health in prisons to meet their duty of care for those deprived of their liberty, as mandated by the United Nations Nelson Mandel and Bangkok Rules."

5 Final Discussion

According to Stöver (2008, p. 238), the first approaches to health promotion of prisoners can be discovered as early as the eighteenth century. John Howard (1777) commented on the English "Act for Preserving the Health of Prisoners" about 240 years ago and emphasised that the care of the detainees should be provided by specialists. Foerster (2005, p. 144) emphasises that, for example, the dramatic undersupply of specialist staff in prisons and thus the poor conditions for treating mentally ill inmates in prisons had already been described over 20 years ago, "without a fundamental change to date would have raised" (cf. Binswanger 1979).

Against the background of the available uniform research results, there can be no doubt that prisoners have a significantly higher rate of psychological stress than the general population, which is also reflected in the higher suicide rate. The background to this can be seen in the much worse socialisation conditions and the situation in detention. The initial phase of detention is particularly stressful, especially among young people (Anderson 2004). Due to missing or inadequate diagnostic examinations, psychological stress is often not recognised (Widmann 2006; Brünger and Weissbeck 2008; Iglehart 2016), if they are then obvious, the specialist staff for adequate treatment are often missing.

Against the background of rather punitive attitudes in public, which can be seen above all in connection with little specific knowledge about delinquency and its background, the "solution" of the crime problem is seen above all in the tightening of sentences. Politics has been following this increasingly in recent decades, also in connection with experiencing greater uncertainties and problematic problems in public (Kury and Schüßler 2019). A similar development can be seen in judicial practice. Demands for a tightening of the prison conditions in response to violent attacks among inmates show this development as an example and, in addition to creating security, also serve to protect against the criticism of inadequate and irresponsible handling of the problem.

In this context, Hassemer (2009, p. 12) emphasises: "Changes that are made to criminal law almost always follow society's changing assessments of just and effective punishments." The author further emphasises (p. 285f.): "Criminal law, like other areas of our life, has been moving towards the pole of security for some time now, in the tension between security and freedom. In this movement, criminal law is tightened, it does not improve. It extends through more and more complicated bans, through higher threats of punishment and punishments, by tightening the investigative tools, by removing guarantees that serve the goals of protection and sparement, but can delay the procedure. It thus responds to the growing fear of modern societies about unmanageable risks, to widespread control needs, to processes of normative disorientation in which certainties fade that we previously relied on blindly."

Increased penalties may bring votes to politicians, but they can hardly contribute to reducing the problem. For example, Dölling et al. (2011) in a comprehensive international analysis of criminal sentences clearly demonstrate their limited effectiveness that "the severity of punishment clearly has a lower deterrent effect than the probability of punishment" (p. 374). If one also considers the enormously high dark field, which some authors estimate up to 90% (Kürzinger 1996, p. 181), these statements are confirmed. Social Rehabilitation programs in prisons can sometimes significantly reduce the relapse rate (Kury 1987), whereby research shows that "the most effective programs for reducing recidivism are those that target needs closely related to criminality, for example, procriminal attitudes, criminal associates, and unstable lifestyle" (Bonta et al. 1998, p. 138).

At the same time, empirical studies have shown that mental disorders do not generally result in a higher relapse rate among detainees (Steadman and Cocozza 1974; Thornberry and Jacoby 1979). Bonta et al. (1998, p. 137) against the background of their literature analysis even come to the conclusion that "... mentally disordered offenders, on average, showed lower recidivism rates compared with general offenders." The importance of intensive preparation before release and aftercare is rightly pointed out (Justizministerium Baden-Württemberg 2015).

Considering the high cost of imprisonment, which is estimated in Germany at around € 130 per detainee per day in prison (Miniserium der Justiz NRW – Nordrhein Westfalen 2018), as well as the negative effects of detention on those affected, especially young people, as well as their families and the social environment (Kury and Kern 2003), understand the criminological demands for expanding alternatives and diversion (Kury and Lerchenmüller 1981; World Health Organization 2005, p. 80). Bland et al. (1998, p. 278) rightly emphasise about the penal system: "Society bears the costs but derives little benefit."

According to Henham (2014), the time has come for a "paradigm shift" on criminal sanctions. However, this requires the support of the population to persuade politicians to rethink. The more the public is informed about crime and its background as well as about effective measures to integrate criminals, the less punitive it is (Kury and Obergfell-Fuchs 2011). A task of criminology can also be seen here to come closer to the over 100-year-old insight of Liszt (1905, pp. 338f.): "If an adolescent or an adult commits a crime and we let him go, the likelihood that he will commit another crime is less than if we punish him." Criminological research has meanwhile convincingly confirmed his thesis: "A good social policy is the best crime policy."

References

Abels, H. (2009). Einführung in die Soziologie. In *Band 1: Der Blick auf die Gesellschaft*. Berlin: Springer.

Anderson, H. S. (2004). Mental health in prison populations. A review – with special emphasis on a study of Danish prisoners on remand. *Acta Psychiatrica Scandinavica, 424*, 5–59.

Badische Zeitung. (2019, December 28). Mehr Angriffe auf Vollzugsbedienstete. Badische Zeitung vom 28. 12. 2019, S. 6.

Berger, P., & Luckmann, T. (1969). *Die gesellschaftliche Konstruktion der Wirklichkeit. Eine Theorie der Wissenssoziologie*. Frankfurt/M.: Fischer.

Binswanger, R. (1979). Probleme der Gefängnispsychiatrie. *Nervenarzt, 50*, 360–365.
Bland, R. C., Newman, S. C., Thompson, A. H., & Dyck, R. J. (1998). Psychiatric disorders in the population and in prisoners. *International Journal of Law and Psychiatry, 21*, 273–279.
Blocher, D., Henkel, K., Ziegler, M., & Rösler, M. (2001). Prevalence of psychopathological distress in a male prison population. *Recht und Psychiatrie, 19*, 136–140.
Böhnisch, L. (1999). *Abweichendes Verhalten. Eine pädagogische soziologische Einführung*. Weinheim: Juventa Verlag.
Böhnisch, L., & Lösch, H. (1973). Das Handlungsverständnis des Sozialarbeiters und seine institutionelle Determination. In H.-U. Otto & S. Schneider (Eds.), *Gesellschaftliche Perspektiven der Sozialarbeit* (Vol. 2). Neuwied: Luchterhand.
Bonta, J., Law, M., & Hanson, K. (1998). The prediction of criminal and violent recidivism among mentally disordered offenders: A meta-analysis. *Psychological Bulletin, 123*, 123–142.
Borrill, J., Burnett, R., Miller, S., Briggs, D., Weaver, T., & Maden, A. (2003). Patterns of self-harm and attempted suicide among white and black/mixed race female prisoners. *Criminal Behaviour and Mental Health, 13*, 229–2040.
Boxberg, V., & Bögelein, N. (2015). Junge Inhaftierte als Täter und Opfer von Gewalt. Subkulturelle Bedingungsfaktoren. *Zeitschrift für Jugendkriminalrecht und Jugendhilfe, 26*, 241–247.
Boxberg, V., Fehrmann, S. E., Häufle, J., Neubacher, F., & Schmidt, H. (2016). Gewalt als Anpassungsstrategie? Zum Umgang mit Belastungen im Jugendstrafvollzug. *Monatsschrift für Kriminologie und Strafrechtsreform, 99*, 428–449.
Brünger, M., & Weissbeck, W. (2008). Psychisch kranke Straftäter im Jugendalter – eine interdisziplinäre Herausforderung. In M. Brünger & W. Weissbeck (Eds.), *Psychisch kranke Straftäter im Jugendalter* (pp. 3–14). Berlin: Medizinisch Wissenschaftliche Verlagsgesellschaft – MWV.
Bundesverfassungsgericht. (2006). *Leitsatz zum Urteil des Zweiten Senats vom 31. Mai 2006 (2 BvR 1673/04, 2 BvR 2402/04)*. Berlin: Bundesverfassungsgericht.
Bundeszentrale für Politische Bildung (Federal Agency for Civic Education). (2018). *Soziale Ungleichheit – Eine Gesellschaft rückt auseinander*. https://www.bpb.de/politik/grundfragen/deutsche-verhaeltnisse-eine-sozialkunde/138379/soziale-ungleichheit
Chassé, K. A. (2010). *Unterschichten in Deutschland*. Wiesbaden: VS.
Council of Europe. (1998). Recommendation Nr. (98) 7, in Kurzform Zeitschrift für Strafvollzug 1999, S. 104.
Cunningham, M., Sorensen, J., & Reidy, T. (2005). An actuarial model for assessment of prison violence risk among maximum security inmates. *Assessment, 12*, 40–49.
de Cock, J. (2005). *Hotel hinter Gittern. Von Knast zu Knast. Tagebuch einer außergewöhnlichen Weltreise*. München: Kunth.
Dölling, D., Entorf, H., Hermann, D., & Rupp, T. (2011). Meta-analysis of empirical studies on deterrence. In H. Kury & E. Shea (Eds.), *Punitivity – International developments. Vol. 3: Punitiveness and punishment* (pp. 315–378). Bochum: Universitätsverlag Dr. Brockmeyer.
Dudeck, M., Kopp, D., Kuwert, P., Drenkhahn, K., Orlob, S., Lüth, H. J., et al. (2009). Die Prävalenz psychischer Erkrankungen bei Gefängnisinsassen mit Kurzzeitstrafe. Ergebnisse aus einer norddeutschen Haftanstalt. *Psychiatrische Praxix, 36*, 219–224.
Endres, J., & Breuer, M. (2018). Übergriffe gegen Bedienstete im Justizvollzug. *Forum Strafvollzug, 67*, 107–112.
Ernst, S. (2008). *Gewalt unter erwachsenen männlichen Inhaftierten in Deutschen Justizvollzugsanstalten*. Hamburg: Kovač.
Fazel, S., & Danesh, J. (2002). Serious mental disorders in 23000 prisoners: A systematic review of 62 surveys. *The Lancet, 359*, 545–550.
Foerster, K. (2005). Psychisch Kranke im Strafvollzug. In T. Hillenkamp & B. Tag (Eds.), *Intramurale Medizin – Gesundheitsfürsorge zwischen Heilauftrag und Strafvollzug* (pp. 143–157). Berlin: Springer.

Frädrich, S., & Pfäfflin, F. (2000). Zur Prävalenz von Persönlichkeitsstörungen bei Strafgefangenen. *Recht & Psychiatrie, 18*, 95–104.

Goffman, E. (1977). *Asyle. Über die soziale Situation psychiatrischer Patienten und anderer Insassen*. Frankfurt/M: Suhrkamp.

Graf, M. (2008). Psychisch Kranke im schweizerischen Strafvollzug. In B. Tag & T. Hillenkamp (Eds.), *Intramurale Medizin im internationalen Vergleich. Gesundheitsfürsorge zwischen Heilauftrag und Strafvollzug im Schweizerischen und internationalen Diskurs* (pp. 39–47). Heidelberg: Springer.

Grübler, B. (2019). Psychisch kranke junge Männer im Gefängnis: "Wenn ich verzweifelt bin, finde ich hier einen Ansprechpartner.". *Deutsches Ärzteblatt, 116*, 190–193.

Gunn, J., Maden, A., & Swinton, M. (1991). Treatment needs of prisoners with psychiatric disorders. *British Medical Journal, 303*, 338–341.

Harbordt, S. (1972). *Die Subkultur des Gefängnisses. Eine soziologische Studie zur Resozialisierung*. Stuttgart: Enke.

Hartenstein, S., & Hinz, S. (2014). Evaluation des Jugendstrafvollzuges in Sachsen – Erste Ergebnisse einer Befragung von Inhaftierten. *Forum Strafvollzug, 63*, 124–127.

Hassemer, W. (2009). *Warum Strafe sein muss. Ein Plädoyer*. Berlin: Ullstein.

Häufle, J., Schmidt, H., & Neubacher, F. (2013). Gewaltopfer im Jugendstrafvollzug – Zu Viktimisierungs- und Tätererfahrungen junger Strafgefangener. *Bewährungshilfe – Soziales Strafrecht, Kriminalpolitik, 60*, 20–38.

Heinrich, W. (2002). Gewalt im Gefängnis – eine Untersuchung der Entwicklung von Gewalt im hessischen Justizvollzug (1989 – 1998). *Bewährungshilfe, 4*, 369–383.

Henham, R. (2014). *Sentencing. Time for a paradigm shift*. London: Routledge.

Herrman, H., McGorry, P., Mills, J., & Singh, B. (1991). Hidden psychiatric Morbidity in Sentenced Prisoners: An Australian Study. *American Journal of Psychiatry, 148*, 236–239.

Heße, R. M. (2019). *Bedeutungsdimensionen und Handlungsmaximen von Gefangenen im Umgang mit Gewalt – aus der Perspektive ehemals inhaftierter Personen*. Masterthesis Universität Hamburg, Fakultät für Wirtschafts- und Sozialwissenschaften, Weiterbildender Masterstudiengang Kriminologie.

Hestermann, T. (2016). "Violence Against Children Sells Very Well." Reporting crime in the media and attitudes to punishment. In H. Kury, S. Redo, & E. Shea (Eds.), *Women and children as victims and offenders: Background, prevention, reintegration. Vol. 1: Suggestions for succeeding generations* (pp. 923–947). Cham: Springer.

Howard, J. (1777). *The State of the Prisons in England and Wales with preliminary observations, and an account of some foreign prisons and hospitals*. Warrington: Eyres.

Iglehart, J. K. (2016). Decriminalizing mental illness – The Miami model. *The New England Journal of Medicine, 374*, 1701–1703.

Ireland, J. (1999). Bullying behaviors among male and female prisoners: A study of adult and young offenders. *Aggressive Behaviour, 25*, 161–178.

Irwin, J., & Cressey, D. R. (1962). Thieves, convicts and the inmate culture. *Social Problems, 10*, 142–155.

Jacobi, F., Höfler, M., Strehle, J., Mack, S., Gerschler, A., Scholl, L., et al. (2014). Psychische Störungen in der Allgemeinbevölkerung. Studie zur Gesundheit Erwachsener in Deutschland und ihr Zusatzmodul Psychische Gesundheit (DEGS1-MH). *Der Nervenarzt, 85*, 77–87.

John, L. (2010). Screeninguntersuchung zur Prävalenz psychischer Störungen bei Gefangenen der Justizvollzugsanstalt Neumünster. Diss - Uni Kiel.

Justizministerium Baden-Württemberg. (2015). *Umgang mit psychisch auffälligen Gefangenen*. Stuttgart: Abschlussbericht der Expertenkommission.

Klatt, T., & Baier, D. (2016). Gewalt im Jugendstrafvollzug: Einflussfaktoren der Opfer- und Täterschaft. *Zeitschrift für Jugendkriminalrecht und Jugendhilfe - ZJJ, 3*, 253–259.

Klatt, T., Hagl, S., Bergmann, M. C., & Baier, D. (2016). Violence in youth custody: Risk factors of violent misconduct among inmates of German young offender institutions. *European Journal of Criminology, 13*, 1–17.

Kleine Zeitung. (2017, May 9). *Gewalt in Justizanstalten – 500 strafrechtliche relevante Vorfälle unter Häftlingen 2016*. https://www.kleinezeitung.at/oesterreich/5215000/Gewalt-in-Justizanstalten_500-strafrechtliche-relevante-Vorfaelle

Kopp, D., Spitzer, C., Kuwert, P., Barnow, S., Orlob, S., & Lüth, H. (2009). Psychische Störungen und Kindheitstraumata bei Strafgefangenen mit antisozialer Persönlichkeitsstörung. *Fortschritte der Neurologie – Psychiatrie, 77*, 152–159.

Kury, H. (1979). *Sozialstatistik der Zugänge im Jugendstrafvollzug Baden-Württemberg*. Freiburg: Bericht aus dem Max-Planck-Institut für ausländisches und internationales Strafrecht Nr. 8.

Kury, H. (1987). *Die Behandlung Straffälliger. 2 Bde*. Berlin: Duncker & Humblot.

Kury, H. (2008). Zu Punitivität und der Validität der Erfassung von Sanktionseinstellungen. In T. Görgen, K. Hoffmann-Holland, H. Schneider, & J. Stock (Eds.), *Interdisziplinäre Kriminologie. Festschrift für Arthur Kreuzer zum 70. Geburtstag* (pp. 395–415). Frankfurt: Verlag für Polizeiwissenschaft, Erster Band.

Kury, H. (2020). Umgang mit psychischen Erkrankungen im (Jugend-)Strafvollzug. *Zeitschrift für Jugendkriminalrecht und Jugendhilfe – ZJJ, 31*, 36–43.

Kury, H., & Brandenstein, M. (2002). Zur Viktimisierung (jugendlicher) Strafgefangener. *Zeitschrift für Strafvollzug und Straffälligenhilfe, 51*, 22–33.

Kury, H., & Kern, J. (2003). Frauen und Kinder von Inhaftierten. Eine vergessene Gruppe. *Kriminologisches Journal, 35*, 97–110.

Kury, H., & Lerchenmüller, H. (Eds.). (1981). *Diversion. Alternativen zu klassischen Sanktionsformen*. Bochum: Studienverlag Dr. N. Brockmeyer.

Kury, H., & Obergfell-Fuchs, J. (2011). Punitiveness- impacts and measurement. In H. Kury & E. Shea (Eds.), *Punitivity. International developments. Vol. 2: Insecurity and punitiveness* (pp. 165–209). Bochum: Universitätsverlag Dr. Brockmeyer.

Kury, H., & Schüßler, J. (2019). Der Umgang mit Kriminalität auf parteipolitischer Ebene. Eine Auswertung von Wahlprogrammen. *Kriminologisches Journal, 51*, 87–106.

Kury, H., & Smartt, U. (2002a). Prisoner-on-prisoner violence: Victimization of young offenders in prison. Some German findings. *Criminology and Criminal Justice, 2*, 411–437.

Kury, H., & Smartt, U. (2002b). Gewalt an Strafgefangenen: Ergebnisse aus dem anglo-amerikanischen und deutschen Strafvollzug. *Zeitschrift für Strafvollzug und Straffälligenhilfe, 51*, 323–337.

Kürzinger, J. (1996). *Kriminologie. Eine Einführung in die Lehre vom Verbrechen*. Stuttgart ua: R. Boorberg Verlag.

Liszt, F. V. (1905). Die Kriminalität der Jugendlichen. Strafrechtliche Aufsätze und Vortrage, Band 2 Berlin.

Märkische Allgemeine. (2019, August 5). *Mehr Gewalt gegen Justizbedienstete in Brandenburger Gefängnissen*. https://www.maz-online.de/Brandenburg/Mehr-Gewalt-gegen-Justizbedienstete-in-Brandenburger-Gefaengnissen

Matschnig, T., Frühwald, S., & Frottier, P. (2006). Suizide hinter Gittern im internationalen Vergleich – Suicide behind bars – An international review. *Psychiatrische Praxis, 33*, 6–13.

McArthur, M., Camilleri, P., & Webb, H. (1999). *Strategies for managing suicide and self-harm in prisons* (p. 1). Canberra: Australian Institute of Criminology.

Ministerium der Justiz NRW. (2018). Kosten des Vollzuges. Justizministerium NRW, Abteilung IV.

Missonie, I., & Konrad, N. (2008). Beurteilung der Suizidgefährdung in Untersuchungshaft. Ergebnis einer Studie in der JVA Berlin Moabit. *Recht Psychiatrie, 26*, 3–14.

Neubacher, F., & Boxberg, V. (2018). Gewalt und Subkultur. In B. Maelicke & S. Suhling (Eds.), *Das Gefängnis auf dem Prüfstand*. Wiesbaden: Springer.

Oberwittler, D., & Qi, S. (2009). *Public opinion on the death penalty in China. Results from a general population survey conducted in three provinces in 2007/08*. Freiburg: Max-Planck-Institut für ausl. und internat. Strafrecht, Research in Brief 41.
Orlob, S. (2017). *Unsichtbar im Knast. Behandlungskonzepte für Menschen mit Psychose hinter Gittern. Ohne Ort*. http://www2.medizin.uni-greifswald.de/psych/fileadmin/user_upload/veranstaltungen/2017/15.-17.02.2017__Die_Subjektive_Seite_der_Schizophrenie_/Vortraege/Vortraege_16.02.2017/Orlob_Unsichtbar_im_Knast.pdf
Penal Reform International. (2007). Health in prisons: realising the right to health. Penal Reform Briefing No. 2, p. 4.
Roberts, J. V., & Hough, M. (2005). *Understanding public attitudes to criminal justice*. Maidenhead: Open University Press.
Rowe, D. C., & Farrington, D. P. (1997). The familial transmission of criminal convictions. *Criminology, 35*, 177–201.
Salize, H. J., Dreßing, H., & Kief, C. (2007). *Mentally disordered persons in European Prison Systems – Needs, Programmes and Outcome (EUPRIS)*. Mannheim: European Commission – Central Institute of Mental Health.
Sato, M. (2014). *The death penalty in Japan. Will the public tolerate abolition?* Wiesbaden: Springer VS.
Schöch, H. (2008). Psychisch kranke Gefangene im Strafvollzug. *Forensische Psychiatrie und Psychotherapie, 15*, 5–18.
Schröder, T. (2005). Psychische Erkrankungen bei männlichen Gefangenen im geschlossenen Vollzug. Diss. Uni Lübeck.
Selle, R. (2019). Datenerhebung des BSBD Bund zur "Gewalt gegen Justizvollzugsbedienstete." Fachzeitschrift für Bedienstete des Justizvollzuges. Der Vollzugsdienst. 4-5/2019. 1.
Sepehrmanesh, Z., Ahmadvand, A., Akasheh, G., & Saei, R. (2014). Prevalence of psychiatric disorders and related factors in male prisoners. *Iranian Red Crescent Medical Journal, 16*, 1–7.
Shaw, J., Appleby, L., & Baker, D. (2005). Safer prisons: A national study of prison suicides 1999–2000. The National confidential inquiry into suicides and homicides by people with mental illness. In D. Richford & K. Edgar (Eds.), *Troubled inside: Responding to the mental health needs of men in prison* (p. 75). London: Prison Reform Trust.
Steadman, H. J., & Cocozza, J. J. (1974). *Careers of the criminally insane: Excessive social control of deviance*. Lexington/MA: Lexington Books.
Stelly, W. (2015). Gewalt im Jugendstrafvollzug. In W. Melzer, D. Hermann, U. Sandfuchs, M. Schäfer, W. Schubarth, & P. Daschner (Eds.), *Handbuch Aggression, Gewalt und Kriminalität bei Kindern und Jugendlichen* (pp. 327–331). Bad Heilbronn: Verlag Julius Klinkhardt.
Stöver, H. (2008). Healthy Prisons – Eine innovative und umfassende Strategie zur Reduktion gesundheitlicher Ungleichheiten in Haft. In B. Tag & T. Hillenkamp (Eds.), *Intramurale Medizin im internationalen Vergleich. Gesundheitsfürsorge zwischen Heilauftrag und Strafvollzug im Schweizerischen und internationalen Diskurs* (pp. 235–264). Heidelberg: Springer.
Streng, F. (2014). *Kriminalitätswahrnehmung und Punitivität im Wandel. Kriminalitäts- und berufsbezogene Einstellungen junger Juristen – Befragungen von 1989 bis 2012*. Heidelberg: Kriminalistik Verlag.
Stringer, H. (2019). *Improving mental health for inmates. Using a variety of new strategies, psychologists in correctional settings are transforming care for people in prisons and jails*. Washington, D.C.: American Psychological Association.
Suhling, S., & Rabold, S. (2013). Gewalt im Gefängnis. Normative, empirische und theoretische Grundlagen. *Forum Strafvollzug, 62*, 70–76.
Sykes, G. (1958). *The Society of Captives: A Study of a Maximum Security Prison*. Princeton, NJ: Princeton University Press.
Sykes, G. (2007). *The Society of Captives: A Study of a Maximum Security Prison*. Princeton, NJ: Princeton University Press.

Teplin, L. A. (1994). Psychiatric and substance abuse disorders among male urban jail detainees. *American Journal of Public Health, 84*, 290–293.
Thornberry, T. P., & Jacoby, J. E. (1979). *The criminally insane: A community follow-up of mentally ill offenders*. Chicago: University of Chicago Press.
The Ministry of Justice of Baden-Württemberg (2015). Umgang mit psychisch auffälligen Gefangenen. Abschlussbericht der Expertenkommission. Stuttgart: Ministry of Justice
UNODC - United Nations Office on Drugs and Crime. (2009). *Handbook on Prisoners with special needs. Criminal Justice Handbook Series*. New York: United Nations.
Ukere, A. (2012). Zur Pravalenz von Personlichkeitsstorungen bei Strafgefangenen. Universität Ulm: Dissertation Medicine.
von Schönfeld, C.-E., Schneider, F., Schröder, T., Widmann, B., Botthof, U., & Driessen, M. (2006). Prävalenz psychischer Störungen, Psychopathologie und Behandlungsbedarf bei weiblichen und männlichen Gefangenen. *Der Nervenarzt, 77*, 830–841.
Weber, M. (1967). *Wirtschaft und Gesellschaft. Grundriss der verstehenden Soziologie*. Wiesbaden: Westdeutscher Verlag.
Widmann, B. (2006). Die Prävalenz psychischer Störungen bei Frauen in Haft. Diss. Med. Uni Aachen
Wirth, (2006).Please change in: Wirth, W. (2013). Gewaltprävention im Strafvollzug: Ein neuer Handlungsansatz. In: Dessecker, A., Egg, R. (Eds.), Justizvollzug in Bewegung. Vol. 64. Wiesbaden: Kriminologische Zentralstelle, 127-143.
Wirth, W. (2013). Gewaltprävention im Strafvollzug: Ein neuer Handlungsansatz. In A. Dessecker & R. Egg (Eds.), *Justizvollzug in Bewegung* (Vol. 64, pp. 127–143). Wiesbaden: Kriminologische Zentralstelle.
Wittchen, H. U., Jacobi, F., Rehm, J., Gustavsson, A., Svensson, M., Jönsson, B., et al. (2011). The size and burden of mental disorders of the brain in Europe 2010. *European Neuropsychopharmacology, 21*, 655–679.
Witzel, J. G., Bausch-Hölterhoff, J., & Skril, M. (2004). Zur Situation des psychisch Kranken in Haft in Nordrhein-Westfalen. *Forensische Psychiatrie und Psychotherapie, 11*, 53–67.
World Health Organization - WHO. (2005). *Resource book on mental health, human rights and legislation*. Geneva: WHO.
World Health Organization – WHO. (2019a). *New WHO report: Ignoring the health of people in prisons now comes at a high cost for society later*. Copenhagen: WHO. http://www.euro.who.int/en/media-centre/sections/press-releases/2019/new-who-report-ignoring-the-health-of-people-in-prisons-now-comes-at-a-high-cost-for-society-later
World Health Organization – WHO. (2019b). *Status report on prison health in the WHO European Region*. Copenhagen: WHO. https://apps.who.int/iris/bitstream/handle/10665/329943/9789289054584-eng.pdf

Helmut Kury Prof. h.c. mult., Dr., Dipl.-Psych., studied Psychology at the University of Freiburg (Freiburg im Brsg., Germany), diploma, Dr. in Psychology and Habilitation at the University of Freiburg. Between 1970 and 1973, he was an assistant teacher at the University of Freiburg, Institut for Psychology, between 1973 and 1980 and from 1989 to 2006, senior researcher at the Max-Planck-Institute for Foreign and International Penal Law in Freiburg im Brsg., Department of Criminology; 1980–1988 first and founding director of the Criminological Research Institute of Lower Saxony—KFN. His research areas include offender rehabilitation, crime prevention, attitudes to punishment, fear of crime, punitiveness, alternatives to punishment, diversion, methodological problems of empirical social science research, international comparison of crime and punishment. He cooperated with many universities and research institutes internationally, especially with countries of the former Soviet Union. His most recent publications in English are: Kury, H., Ferdinand, T.N. (Eds.) (2008). *International Perspectives on Punitivity*. Bochum: Universitätsverlag Dr. Brockmeyer; Kury, H. (Ed.) (2008). *Fear of Crime – Punitivity. New Developments in Theory and Research*. Bochum: Universitätsverlag Dr. Brockmeyer; Kury, H.,

Shea, E. (Eds.) (2011). *Punitivity – International Developments.* 3 Vols., Bochum: Universitätsverlag Dr. Brockmeyer; Kury, H., Redo, S., Shea, E. (Eds.) (2016). *Women and Children as Victims and Offenders: Background, Prevention, Reintegration. Suggestions for Succeeding Generations.* 2 Vols., International Publishing Switzerland: Springer; Kury, H., Kuhlmann, A. (2016). Mediation in Germany and Other Western Countries. Kriminolgijos Studijos 4, 2016, 5–46; Kury, H. (2017). Harsh Punishment or Alternatives: Which Is the Better Crime Prevention. Juricia international, University of Tartu, 15, 91–99; Kury, H., Glonti, G. (2017). Migration in Germany and Georgia (Comparative Analyses). Davit Aghmashnenebeli University of Georgia Academic Journal 1, 6–13; Kury, H. (2018). Rehabilitation in Prison. German Experiences and what can be done better. Rom. Journ. of Sociological Studies, New Series, Bucharest, No. 1, 19–36; Kury, H. (2018). Integration of refugees in Germany – Has the criminal burden increased" Criminology: Yesterday, Today, Tomorrow - The Journal of St. Petersburg International Criminology Club 1, 48, 37–45; Kury, H., Redo, S. (Eds.) (2018). Refugees and Migrants in Law and Policy. Challenges and Opportunities for Global Civic Education. International Publishing Switzerland: Springer; Kuhlmann, A., Kury, H. (2018). Some Considerations of Restorative Justice Before and Outside of Contemporary Western States. Kriminologijos studijos – Criminological Studies, Vilniaus Universitetas, 5, 5–42; Kury, H. (2019). Refugees: Post Traumatic Stress, and Crime – Experiences from Germany. Kultura i Edukacja – Culture and Education 124, 73–90; Kury, H., Kuhlmann, A., Quintas, J. (2019). On the Preventative Effect of Sanctions for Drug Crime: The United States, Germany and Portugal. Archiwum Kryminologii, Polska Akademia Nauk, Instytut Nauk Prawnych, 41, 261–295. E-mail: helmut.kury@web.de.

Romy Heße grew up in southern Germany. After completing her education as a state-recognized Preschool Teacher, she completed a Bachelor of Social Work and a Master of Social Research/ Social Work at Esslingen University of Applied Sciences. Even during her studies, she dealt intensively with the everyday life of detained people. Interest in this topic increased through volunteer work at the Prison Stuttgart-Stammheim and the probation service in Karlsruhe (Germany). During her employment in a care center for German and refugee young people in Karlsruhe and in a communication center for undocumented migrants in Amsterdam, she gained further experience that shaped her. Her subsequent employment as a social worker in the prison *Die Justizvollzugsanstalt* Moabit (Berlin, Germany) aroused further interest in wanting to investigate the lives of imprisoned people from a scientific perspective. Most recently, she therefore studied part-time the Master Criminology at the University of Hamburg (Hamburg, Germany). E-mail: romymaria.hesse@gmail.com.

On Nelson Mandela Rule 63: Prisoner's Moral Vulnerability and Development in the Context of the 2030 United Nations Sustainable World

Sławomir Redo and Krzysztof Sawicki

In memory of Paweł Adamowicz, the Mayor of the City of Gdańsk (Poland), killed by a mentally ill offender

Abstract This public policy chapter analyses and discusses the provision of prison inmates with "wireless" communication with the outside world (Rule 63 of the United Nations Standard Minimum Rules for the Treatment of Prisoners (Nelson Mandela Rules). In the context of the 2030 United Nations Sustainable Development Goal (SDG) 16 to promote peaceful, just and inclusive societies, the chapter calls on the prison administration and non-governmental organisations authorised to assist in the rehabilitation and reintegration of inmates and ex-prisoners to jointly pursue through training, periodicals and special institutional publications the related SDGs' action-oriented preventive content, with due regard to the group-oriented and individual respective resilience or vulnerability of inmates. Throughout the chapter, the authors seek to demonstrate the importance of the 2030 United Nations SDGs which aspire to transform the world so "no one will be left behind," even if they stay behind prison bars, or behind others as one of the other kind of minority in an open multicultural society.

Keywords Inclusiveness · Information and communication technologies · Mentally disabled prisoners · Nelson Mandela Rules · Rehabilitation · Schizophrenia · Sustainable development goals · United Nations

S. Redo
United Nations Studies Association, Wien, Austria
e-mail: s@redo.net

K. Sawicki (✉)
University of Białystok, Faculty of Education, Białystok, Poland
e-mail: k.sawicki@uwb.edu.pl

H. Kury, S. Redo (eds.), *Crime Prevention and Justice in 2030*,
https://doi.org/10.1007/978-3-030-56227-4_9

1 Legislative Background

In 2015, the United Nations General Assembly adopted the revised text of the Standard Minimum Rules for the Treatment of Prisoners (A/RES/70/175). They were named after Nelson Mandela—the legendary President of the Republic of South Africa. Before assuming office, he had for long been imprisoned by the previously apartheid regime of that country.

In the Nelson Mandela Rules, there are 5 provisions on "prisoner file management" and 24 amended provisions on rehabilitation/aftercare programmes, including medical screening, work and other meaningful activities (present Rules 4, 23, 30, 34, 64–66, 89, 91–94, 96–108).

According to the Rule 107, the core of prison rehabilitation should involve incarceration and reentry activities. This is compatible with the contemporary concept or rehabilitation. Contact with the outside world is a special factor supporting the efficiency of rehabilitation and reentry treatments. However, both new and the amended texts of the Rules have word-by-word same provisions on contacts with the outside world insofar as it involves inmates' access to mass media information.

> The respective 2 rules read:
>
> Rule 63 (old 39):
>
> Prisoners shall be kept informed regularly of the more important items of news by the reading of newspapers, periodicals or special institutional publications, by hearing wireless transmissions, by lectures or by any similar means as authorized or controlled by the prison administration.
>
> Rule 64 (old 40):
>
> Every prison shall have a library for the use of all categories of prisoners, adequately stocked with both recreational and instructional books, and prisoners shall be encouraged to make full use of it.

Save the above provisions advancing "prison file management," there has been nothing in the Rules which otherwise be relevant to the role and use of television or/and technologies ("digital technologies") in the rehabilitation and reintegration of offenders, but many direct and indirect rules regarding the "analogue" treatment of offenders, numbered above. It goes without saying that new media in prison is not only a way to counter inmates' boredom but also a source of information about the outside world, close family and personal legal status. Additionally, it is also the way to avoid digital exclusion and even the chance for the online employment. In general, it is an important element supporting prison rehabilitation.

2 On the Experience of Prison Administration and the United Nations Anticipation Regarding the Implementation of Standard Minimum Rules 63 and 64

In the 2018 Global Prison Trends Report by the Penal Reform International, a non-governmental organisation in consultative status with the UN Economic and Social Council (ECOSOC) especially focused on "the rehabilitation and reintegration of offenders in the era of sustainable development." From there comes the following excerpt involving the role and use of technologies in rehabilitation and reintegration:

> Prisoner survey and usage data suggested that prisoners felt more in control of their lives and more confident in coping with technology in the outside world. Combating prisoners' digital exclusion is important, but concerns expressed included the fact that placing computers in cells can transform the dynamic of prisons, leading to more isolation and fewer opportunities to build constructive relationships with prison staff... In Malawi, an NGO introduced an application for smartphones and tablets called 'Open Trial' that has information about fair trial and detention rights, a checklist that people can use to determine whether their friends, family members or detainees have been detained legally, and a reporting function to notify the NGO of violations or concerns (PRI 2018, p. 35).

The report concludes with the following recommendation: "States should leverage technology to improve prisoners' opportunities for education, skill-building and communication, and to promote the efficiency of criminal justice systems. However, such initiatives should not reduce or replace face-to-face interaction for prisoners (SDGs 4, 10 and 16)" (PRI 2018, p. 35).

Prisoners have a great need for knowledge which corresponds to the above-mentioned goals. For example, from the research of prisoners in Nigeria, it appears that they concern medical, education and security information, life after prison, spiritual and moral contexts, financial and legal issues (Sambo and Ojei 2018). They are universal and, for example, gender factors have a slight impact on their diversity (Eze 2016).

Prison libraries are a typical treatment available for the inmates throughout the world. The *"Guidelines for Library Services to Prisoners"* published by The International Federation of Library Associations and Institutions/IFLA (Lehmann and Locke 2005) states that "The prison library should provide the offenders with the opportunity to develop literacy skills, pursue personal and cultural interests, as well as life-long learning. The library should provide resources for all these activities" (p. 4), and... "the prison library can be the vital information resource that makes the difference of whether or not a newly released ex-offender fails or succeeds on the outside" (p. 6).

The analysis of reports of the Polish Commissioner for Human Rights (2008–2016) shows a typical form of organising access to the library and other resources during incarceration. The country's implementation is consistent with global trends (Knight 2016). Prison libraries book collections are relatively numerous, but usually there are no new publications, or they form only a small fraction.

As a part of access to information, current legal regulations are an important source of knowledge. The above reports document that they were not always available. The problem also concerns providing access to knowledge for foreign prisoners. They did not always have the opportunity to get acquainted with information about their legal status in the language they use. This also concerned with information about the decisions of, e.g. the European Court of Human Rights on the legal situation of persons deprived of liberty.

Access to the press in prisons is organised in several ways. Penal institutions subscribe nationwide journals, allow prisoners to order magazines or deliver printed media by their families. Occasionally, old magazines are available. The issuing of own newspapers by prisoners has especially significant rehabilitation value, motivating personal development. This is an opportunity to ensure contact with the outside world in a form compatible with the rehabilitation, especially important not only for the majority of inmates, but also for those coming from minorities or who are mentally impaired.

Prison broadcasting center is a common form used in penal institutions. It broadcasts selected nationwide or regional radio stations. Radio programmes prepared and aired by prisoners are particularly noteworthy as a recommended way of transferring information from outside world, implemented in agreement between prisoners with prison staff. Additionally, they inspire inmates to creativity, development and personal endeavour according to the acceptable social rules and norms.

Watching selected movies or TV programmes are typical forms of using television in cell blocks. It is possible to use prisoners or institutional television sets. According to the commonly accepted rules, it is allowed to use one TV set in one cell block.

Fixed telephone devices are a relatively new way of prisoners' contact with the outside world. They can use them according to the rules of procedure at the appointed time. It should be emphasised that due to the popularisation of smartphones this is technically a bit archaic form of contact and fit into a special area of challenges for prison management in worldwide perspective.

3 On the ICT As the Two-Edged Sword

New media are a special challenge for prison staff. Unfortunately, the Mandela Rules did not notice their role in contemporary social relations. Despite the prohibitions, smartphones are commonly used behind prison walls. It makes contacts with the outside world completely out of control of the prison administration, at times with its acquiescence.

Social media in prison reality is a double-edged sword. On the one hand, the lack of regulation in this area is an opportunity for abuses by prisoners. This is an opportunity to contact outside the prison against the rules set out in the regulations and even intimidate victims or witnesses. As Ian Acheson (a former prison governor) said: "It's a problem because uncontrolled access to mobile phones and other technology assists criminality inside prisons, particularly organized crime and the drugs market. This drives the misery, violence and despair we are seeing broadcast almost nightly on our TV screens" (Marsh and Waterson 2018). The inmates send messages to Facebook, tweet, download photos and videos, despite the rigors and prohibitions. This is not only an example of sharing prison work in social media but also a problem with enforcing prison bans by prison staff.".

A case in point is a videoclip made by inmates in the South Carolina (USA) penal institution in 2014 and posted on the Youtube. This is the first example of illegal online transmission from the prison.[1] In this case, video sharing was treated as a sign of breaking the rules, indicating that if prisoners want to communicate with the outside world, they should do it in a traditional way (writing letters, talking to visitors) (Wiltz 2017). This situation raises question about how to effectively integrate new media into the prison realities, caring for the public safety and successful rehabilitation.

Prison staff tries to counteract such situations by limiting the possibility of contact with the non-prison environment. For example, Scottish (UK) prisons test the ways to track and block individual handsets (BBC 2017a). The evaluators postulated to limit the trading of tiny, plastic phones in the size of lipstick—impossible to detect using metal detectors (BBC 2017b).

On the other hand, the ban on using social media increases isolation and social exclusion, making reentry process more complicated. As David Fathi of the American Civil Liberties Union (ACLU) representative said: "Banning the use of social media is counterproductive in terms of rehabilitation" (Wiltz 2017). Social media allow to maintain contact with family or relatives and build social support. This is important in a situation when the closest relatives can wait to see an incarcerated family member for up to several months (Kusic 2008).

Undoubtedly, the use of social media during incarceration positively motivates and decreases risk of recidivism. The importance of new technologies in building social relations during rehabilitation is described by Chandra Bozelko (ex-prisoner who has been released in 2014 after 6 years in prison):

> The years 2008 to 2014 might have been the worst time to live outside of society from a technological perspective. During that time the smartphone became ubiquitous. Twitter, Instagram, and Facebook all reached critical mass. I hadn't used Facebook before I was incarcerated but I learned about the platform by reading *Facebook for Dummies*, which is like learning to swim on dry land. Dealing with the device was hard enough - I tapped when I should have swiped, swiped when I should have stopped - but not knowing the hierarchy of platforms and chat/messaging abbreviations branded me an outsider more brightly than felony convictions. I was so lost I couldn't find my app with both hands. FML. That's the one to use, right? (Bozelko 2017).

[1]https://www.youtube.com/watch?v=8wbqiSVLUq8&t=9s.

Recidivism is indirectly generated by the fact that a former inmate goes into the realities radically different from those in which they functioned before isolation. In this context, new technologies are an added barrier that they must face in interacting in a digital world. This problem also concerns shaping inmates' competences in using new technologies. This coincides with the civic participation in open society after release, including challenges but also threats. Referring to this problem, journalist Mia Armstrong (2018) asks: "How can we expect former inmates to be able to identify fake news without any experience on the platforms that spread?."

Additionally, new media in prison can give an opportunity to evaluate the transparency of the penitentiary systems. The US nationwide strike in penal institutions as a protest during the "Modern-Day Slavery" (due to inappropriate isolation conditions) is an example how the social media for information share may be used (Brown 2018). The strike was organised using social media to which prisoners (according to staff) should not have access.

4 On Being Wireless and "Hearing Voices"

On 15 January 2019 in the city of Gdańsk (Poland), the ex-prisoner apparently suffering from paranoid schizophrenia murdered its liberal Mayor Paweł Adamowicz (Easton 2019; Wojciechowski and Włodkowska 2019a, b; Woźnicki and Wojciechowska 2019; Goraj 2019). The offender stabbed the Mayor to death during his on-stage statement applauding all-Poland volunteer largest annual charity event, which raises money for hospital equipment to treat children. Before the offender's on-stage apprehension, he grabbed the microphone and told the crowd that he blamed the Mayor's former party for sending him to prison.

The offender was released in the previous month from an open prison after serving five and a half years of depravation of liberty for four bank armed robberies. Altogether, he was consulted 20 times by psychiatrists who made recommendations to prison administration regarding his treatment. While in detention, he was classified as "dangerous." He spent almost 2 years in a solitary confinement. There, initially, he could only listen to the prison broadcasts, then watch television. He started the in-prison treatment in the second year of his term, when he complained that he was "hearing the voices." "One day he said that heads come out from the screen" (Wojciechowski and Włodkowska 2019b). He took medicines and had "psycho-correctional talks," but did not take part in any therapeutic programmes, e.g. Aggression Replacement Training.

During the last two talks before the prisoner was released, he declared to corrections officer that he may kill the Mayor because "his" party [in fact, the Mayor was not a party-member] stands in the way to dictatorial power and position of the Head of the ruling party. The officer reported this information to his superiors and then to the police. Had the offender been referred to an outpatient medical treatment, his whereabouts would have been monitored, including the referred visits. Had his imprisonment term been suspended to allow for a psychiatric hospital treatment, it might have not immediately followed his temporary release in lieu of a legal loophole preventing it. However, legal loopholes in the referral procedure had prevented the relevant authorities to act to that end.

Eight days before the offender's eventual release, his mother, a major in prison rehabilitation, informed the prison administration and police precinct that her son's illness may entail dangerous consequences. After the release, her son had discontinued taking medicines.

Adamowicz was one of 11 Polish mayors targeted in 2017 with fake death certificates by a far-right group called All-Polish Youth, after signing a declaration to welcome refugees in opposition to government policy. Two weeks before the homicide, the Procuracy had discontinued the criminal proceedings against that group. The Procuracy held that the group exercised its permittable critique. Some of the mayors filed their objection and requested to resume the proceedings.

Critics reportedly argue that Poland's politicians crank up hate speech in public life (Raport 2018, pp. 3–18). This begs the question whether indeed the above murder case is here in point.

To understand this problem, several factors should be considered. Mental disorder is a special challenge for rehabilitation practice in every penal and rehabilitation system. According to the Mandela Rule 109:

> Persons who are found to be not criminally responsible, or who are later diagnosed with severe mental disabilities and/or health conditions, for whom staying in prison would mean an exacerbation of their condition, shall not be detained in prisons, and arrangements shall be made to transfer them to mental health facilities as soon as possible.

This means a different perception of typical and mentally disordered prisoners. It indicates the need to apply of special forms of interactions (alternative to imprisonment). It requires demarcation between typical and mentally disordered prisoners. It points to the necessity of applying alternative to imprisonment specialised treatments.

Rule 109 § 2 specifies that "prisoners with mental disabilities and/or health conditions can be observed and treated in specialized facilities under the supervision of qualified health-care professionals." The above recommendation is relevant to quite a part of the entire prison population in the world. For example, the proportion of inmates with mental disorders (depending on the diagnostic criteria) ranged from 38% (Poland, the UK) to 65% (the USA) of the prison population, whereas severe psychiatric disorders are found in about 15% of the US prison population (Niewiadomska 2007). Mental diseases are diagnosed in 10-12% of prisoners, a low level of mental development is found in 20% of inmates (ibidem). Threat of mental disorder increases when people fall into conflict with the law during adolescence and in recidivism (Niewiadomska 2007). The analysis of data from around the world shows that mentally disabled persons (Craig et al. 2006) (mostly diagnosed as schizophrenics and with manic-depressive psychosis) are three to four times more often convicted of violent crimes than the general prison population (Fisher et al. 2006).

In the above picture, several, almost self-explanatory, factors are in the background. First, the personality traits of people placed in prisons. They are characterised by a higher than average percentage of people with low social competences, delayed development, emotional and behavioural disorders (Gaes 2008). Prisoners are a group of people with a low level of education. This causes them to cope with everyday challenges below average level (Whitehead et al. 2007).

Second, prison isolation stimulates individual tendencies to mental disorders, intensifies criminogenic needs and (in effect) disintegrates personality (Mann et al. 2004). These are the side effects of deprivation of liberty experienced during the imprisonment: lack of security and typical stimulus, overcrowding, limited access to data or restrictions on social contacts. Incarceration is also a condition leading to sensory deprivation, which results in mental disorders (Mears 2013). This problem concerns especially prisoners incarcerated in supermax, especially since they are a place for unjustified placing for mentally ill persons (King et al. 2008; Mears 2013). It should be emphasised that treatment for the mentally disordered prisoners is usually carried out through pharmacotherapy. Unfortunately, many prisoners (especially those with schizophrenia) refuse to take medication, and the compulsory use of pharmacotherapy is possible by a decision of a special committee. In effect, medicines are used rarely and with a long delay due to procedural restrictions (Torrey et al. 2014).

Third, a positive change of highly demoralised prisoners (and mentally disordered inmates are very often defined in such way) during incarceration may be impossible. This argument reduces a priori the success of any rehabilitation treatments due to the assumed low effectiveness.

A therapeutic diagnosis (which is used to identify mental problems) lead to locate such prisoners in the therapeutic system. Unfortunately, this assumption is hard to put in place. According to the reports of the Polish Commissioner on Human Rights, the use of both individualised diagnoses and the therapeutic system of serving sentences is difficult due to the small number of psychologists and therapists in penitentiary institutions. The situation from prison in Strzelce Opolskie (South-Western Poland) is a spectacular example: one psychologist per 500 and one corrections officer per 100 inmates.

Fourth, the effectiveness of rehabilitation depends on the prison staff and their attitudes to inmates and everyday duties. Studies show that they are characterised by a high level of insecurity, they feel threatened by detainees, they perceive their profession as dangerous (Guzik-Makaruk 2011, pp. 103–104). Almost half of prison staff (45%) are afraid of violence and aggression, every fifth loss of life or health. Every third prison staff member declares the experience of a threat situation. In addition, the implementation of programmes based on contemporary social rehabilitation assumptions is also troublesome due to their prison staff perception. More than 60% believe that the tightening of penalties is a way to improve security, because it deters people from committing crimes. Every eighth prison staff member follows the restoration of the death penalty. The lack of specialised solutions that can be used by prison staff is an added problem during rehabilitation of prisoners with mental disorders. Seclusion is a typical measure for violent prisoners. Unfortunately, such measures increase prisoners' disorders and (as a result) intensify their mental problems (Torrey et al. 2014).

Fifth, the intellectual and mentally disordered inmates are rarely treated in the Polish judicial and penitentiary system according to the Mandela Rules. The case of inmate named Radosław convicted for multiple thefts is a spectacular example and starting point for research reported a few years ago in cooperation with the Polish Commissioner on Human Rights (Dawidziuk and Mazur 2017). The man earned money collecting scrap metal, stealing other metal objects or bicycles. During the court proceedings, the proficient psychiatrist stated his diminished responsibility but he was still imprisoned. Second diagnosis during imprisonment showed that his mental and moral development is at the child level so he behaviour cannot be judged in the category of good and evil. In this situation, imprisonment was without merit.

According to the report (Dawidziuk and Mazur 2017), there are many people in penitentiary institutions who were imprisoned without considering their specific status. Some of these people should not be in prison, while some of the others should be placed in the therapeutic system. It was found that during court proceedings, mental and intellectual disabilities are not treated as important factors, which is reflected in the rare appointment of proficient psychiatrists. The prison staff do not provide information about inmates' mental problems to prosecutors or judges because they are not educated and trained in such issues.

The above-mentioned problems of the Polish penal and prison system affect the functioning of inmates with tendencies to schizophrenia. Scientific findings show that schizophrenic personalities in comparison with healthy people ("nonclinical controls") are overly sensitive to mass media influence. They suffer from social cognitive deficit (Brown 2011), hence are socially difficult learners less predisposed to law abiding. Therefore, schizophrenics victimise others less discriminatively than healthy people.

Criminological evidence on the link between schizophrenia and criminal/delinquent acts overwhelmingly supports the above. Schizophrenics in comparison with non-schizophrenics more often throughout their childhood, adolescence and adulthood commit such acts (Ellis et al. 2009, pp. 165–167). Schizophrenic acts are less rational than those of healthy perpetrators, are rather happenstance and undertaken impulsively.

Analytical and meta-analytical reviews document that: (a) mental disorders like schizophrenia is more prevalent in the underprivileged social strata, including marginalised groups (Brown 2011), and (b) generally, people from this or that kind of minority are more frequently than others clients of the criminal justice system, and, eventually, prison inmates (Ellis et al. 2009). This pattern of inequality is global.

The following two quotes reflect the conduct of schizophrenics, and their control limits, with somewhat conflicting accounts:

> Schizophrenics tend to create their own pictures of reality and people. Common is idealizing oneself. Often comes to the situations when even a person realizing his/her sickness is not able to function correctly because of fear, phobia and illusions. Third persons may take advantage of this to profit financially or acquire property rights. On the other hand,

schizophrenics may commit acts contrary to the law, not realizing what they are doing (Tanajewska 2019, p. 67).

In the family home, this can create a stressful environment that erodes the quality of life for parents and siblings. It can be very difficult to manage in many living situations leading to altercations with other residents. On the street, in hospitals and in jails, the risk of escalation is great... A focus on criminal records substantially underestimates the prevalence of aggressive behaviour in schizophrenia, and the burden of caring/coping with aggression, threats of violence, and violent acts falls on family members, clinical care staff, those who share housing, police, and staffs of emergency rooms and jails (Wehring and Carpenter 2011, p. 877).

In jails (prisons), the prevalence of schizophrenic inmates is higher than in a general population (e.g. in the USA that was 2-6.5% vs. 1%) (Prins 2014). During imprisonment, such schizophrenic symptoms accentuate, and this process is a serious challenge for prison staff. Accusing mentally disordered prisoners of simulating mental illness is one of the pathological mechanisms associated with this problem.

The Polish Commissioner on Human Rights in his report gives the description of a prisoner named Mirosław. During the court proceedings, it was found that he simulates mental disorder. From the first days of the incarceration his behaviour disturbed the prison staff. Prison psychiatrist identified schizophrenia symptoms and indicated the need of therapy (forced psychiatric treatment). According to the Polish Commissioner on Human Rights report, in spite of submitting an application by prison management it was stated that Mirosław had been waiting for the court's decision staying for about 5 months in conditions unfavourable for his mental health from submission (Brzostymowska 2017, p. 201).

The story of a prisoner named Paweł may be another example pointed out by the Polish Commissioner on Human Rights. In 2000 Paweł committed a crime but after this incident he broke off his relationship with the criminal environment. From 2008 he was treated psychiatrically (pharmacotherapy, outpatient psychiatric care) due to the observed paranoid schizophrenia. The criminal trial began in 2010 and the sentence was passed in 2013 (5 years in prison). Despite the health condition he was placed in the therapeutic prison treatment 2 years later. Based on the Polish Commissioner on Human Rights case study, it was found that Paweł has a progressive personality disorder. Considering the above facts, he applied for a furlough in the Paweł's imprisonment. Imprisonment in the light of the facts was inadequate: he was not fully aware of his responsibility, and the applied measures could aggravate his mental illness (Brzostymowska 2017, pp. 207–208).

The above indicated dysfunctional mechanisms of the penitentiary system play into the "Nothing Works" strategy: static and ineffective, in the case of prisoners with mental disorder increasing the likelihood of risk behaviour. They jeopardise the safety of fellow prisoners, prison staff and the society. As stated by one of the staff of the Polish Commissioner on Human Rights:

In case of prisoner's mental illness (acute psychosis), his prison term should be limited to the minimum, followed by his immediate placement in a psychiatric hospital. Only such an arrangement can provide the sick person with due and necessary care without risking loss of

> life or health. Leaving a mentally ill person. . .in a prison or detention center without round-the clock supervision and immediate psychiatric care may amount to inhuman and degrading treatment and thus violate applicable legal regulations (Brzostymowska 2017, p. 193).

5 On "The Sound of Silence"

After the tragic death of the Mayor of Gdańsk, the above titled song by Simon & Garfunkel had been aired as an a capella interpretation of David Dreiman of the group "Disturbed." The song, full of dramatic expressions of concern about the silent people impervious to encroaching populism, was heard by the "motionless" crowd "with tears running down people's faces . . . The music has been switched off at the Red Light pub in the heart of the picturesque old town of Gdańsk. A single candle adorned with a black ribbon rests on the bar. The city is in mourning" (Davies 2019).

6 On the Outside and Inner World

Notwithstanding this truly deep mourning eulogised in the above press account, criminological ramifications of the above facts and figures suggest that rather little can be done to control for the victimising schizophrenic behaviour. This should not imply the inevitability of violence insofar as its place and time are concerned. The so-called "environmental" factors affecting schizophrenic behaviour have a substantial impact on it (van Os et al. 2010; Brown 2011). However complex this impact is, the share of mass media cannot be overlooked, especially in closed institutions, like psychiatric hospitals and prisons.

Consequently, this chapter's major focus is on a much broader question involving the functioning of Rule 63 in the rehabilitation and reintegration of all inmates. It should be read in connection with Rule 3:

> Imprisonment and other measures that result in cutting off persons from the outside world are afflictive by the very fact of taking from these persons the right of self-determination by depriving them of their liberty. Therefore the prison system shall not, except as incidental to justifiable separation or the maintenance of discipline, aggravate the suffering inherent in such a situation.

7 On Freedom of the Press in the Outside and Inner World

Since 1980 "Freedom House," a non-governmental organisation in consultative status with the UN Economic and Social Council[2] publishes global reports on freedom of the press.[3] Over these years (1980/1990/2015/2017), Poland has evolved in its classification from "not free" (1980), to "partly free" (1990), "free" (2015) and, again, to "partly free" (2017).[4] Regarding the lowered country's classification, the 2017 Freedom House Report informed that since 2016, several legal changes have narrowed the public access to some media outlets.[5]

There is no evidence that the narrowing of public access to the mass media market could have commensurate influence on prisoners' worldview. Only a conjuncture could suggest that their worldview may have become more vulnerable to regressive thinking and volatile behaviour. And this conjuncture was made by the Polish Commissioner on Human Rights. Specifically, he publicly did not "exclude" the thesis that the violent motivation of the killer of the Mayor of Gdańsk was prompted by a state-run information channel criticised for the biased provision of news on political opponents. However, the Commissioner's thesis proved wrong, for the local prison administrator informed that in his facility no such news channel was available to the inmates (Kublik 2019). As a matter of fact, in the Polish prison administration there is no centrally managed list of media outlets accessible to inmates. An inmate may subscribe at their own cost any dailies, save those with pornographic or nationalistic content.

[2]Established in 1941, first co-chaired by Eleanor Roosevelt, the wife of the US President Franklin Delano Roosevelt who proclaimed the "Four Freedoms."

[3]Countries are given a total score from 0 (most free) to 100 (least free) based on a set of 23 methodology questions and 109 indicators divided into three broad categories covering the legal, political, and economic environment. Based on the scores, the countries are then classified as "Free" (0–30), "Partly Free" (31–60), or "Not Free" (61–100).

[4]Regarding the lowered country's classification, the 2017 Freedom House Report informs that in 2016 the following legal changes took effect:

[5]A media law that took effect in January empowered the treasury minister, rather than an independent body, to appoint the managers of Poland's public television and radio broadcasters. "By April, over 140 public media employees had resigned or been fired. In December, the governing Law and Justice … party attempted to limit reporters' access to lawmakers inside the parliament, but abandoned the initiative following resistance by the opposition and the public. Government offices cancelled subscriptions to opposition-friendly media, while state-owned companies redirected advertising money to progovernment outlets" (Freedom House 2017).

8 On Prisoner's Information Needs

Prisoners have three basic information needs: unactivated (requiring identification and activation by prison staff, or fellow prisoners or family members), unexpressed (inmates declaring information and education needs were met, but the prison staff did not succeed in satisfying them) and expressed (needs précised by inmates, and successfully identified by staff). This division indicates the need to diversify work with each prisoner, regardless of the social, ethnic, religious or cultural context. Their efficiency depends on flexible adaptation of methods to working conditions with isolated persons.

The use of the "classical" methods based (for example) on the library resources gives effects even in rehabilitation work with radical inmates. Angell and Guanaratna (2012) describe their experience from the detention centers for Muslim terrorists. Thanks to cooperation of isolated persons they can use (except access to selected radio stations or pre-recorded television programmes) the typical library service; except of Qur'an they were read in Arabic "The Da Vinci Code" and numerous romantic novels (Angell and Guanaratna 2012, p. 164).

Readership is still important tool for rehabilitation, especially for the contact with the world outside the prison walls. For example, it allows to maintain and even rebuild relationships between incarcerated fathers and their children. Prisoners record the stories they read, and recordings are sent (with colouring books) to children. Coloured books are returned to prisoners and become a material factor motivating to positive "good" change (Greenway 2007).

Prison libraries are gradually digitised. The implementation of the tablet-based library programme implemented in South Dakota (the USA) can be an example of this change. Such solutions not only increase the use of library resources. In addition, they will familiarise prisoners with the new media, technologies, possibility of using a tablet and texts in an e-book format (Finkel and Bertram 2019). Additionally, such solutions minimise cultural jet lag as the typical incarceration side effect.

Other technological solutions are an important part of this trend. Trust Fund Limited The Inmate Computer System (TRULINCS) is a way to use the Internet by prisoners in secure manner. This is an alternative solution for typical contact with outside world by writing letters. TRULINCS allows prisoners controlled and secure online contact by emails with family or court. Such solution reinforces reentry into community and (in effect) reduces risk of recidivism (Steele 2016). JOLT (an acronym for the first letter of each of the last of inmates who created the software) is another secure internet tool available in San Quentin. This secure search engine allows to analyse uploaded textbooks or offline Wikipedia content (Lapowski 2018). The above-mentioned solutions not only minimise prisoners' cyber exclusion but also enhance their relations with family members.

The use of new technologies during rehabilitation allows to build proper interpersonal relationships, strengthens positive behaviours and has educational values. In addition, it allows to find a job giving "the new sort of imagined future" (Wells 2014). Last Mile is the organisation preparing inmates to reentry through

"Code.7370"—first computer coding curriculum, allowing for inmates to learn HTML, JavaScript or Python languages. Prisoners from San Quentin (CA, the USA) who completed the course work online for a rate several times higher than the average inmates' salaries (Armstrong 2018).

Prisoners' participation in the education programmes (including ICT) increases chance for successful rehabilitation especially among juveniles (Vacca 2008). Inmates who participated in such forms of activities during incarceration were rarely noted as recidivists. It should be emphasised that new technologies support rehabilitation process, constitute an important factor shaping the proper habitus during incarceration. This is particularly important in rehabilitation of prisoners with mental and emotional disorders. It is an indispensable but also insufficiently used tool in prison rehabilitation treatments and reentry programmes (Vandebosch 2005).

9 On Imprisonment and Inclusiveness

From the perspective of the above-mentioned affairs, incidents and penitentiary treatments, it should be stated that the deep rethinking on contemporary understanding of inclusion is required. It results not only from a radical, technological change (which dominated access to information in the analysis of the Mandela Rules above) but above all from the understanding and perception of imprisonment in the contemporary times, in particular the role of punishment, the sense of prison isolation, the vision of reentry and—in effect—social inclusion. In their current meaning, they are very often archaic and inadequate to the requirements of societies or to the application of the subsidiarity principle.

Analysing the fossilised manifestations of the impact of the penitentiary system, it should be stated that they require a radical redefinition under SDG 16. In this respect, experience from the Nordic countries in the implementation of penitentiary policy is especially valuable, because of the few advanced and enlightened features, i.e. restricted use of post-conviction indefinite detention in Denmark and Finland, abolished preventive detention following criminal conviction in Sweden or abolished life imprisonment in Norway. In general, this is an area for observation of the human rights well balancing between crime and punishment (van Zyl Smit and Appleton 2019, p. 18).

The starting point for the analysis is the understanding of inclusive practice according to rehabilitation theory. According to T. Ward and S. Maruna:

> Rehabilitation theory, therefore, is essentially a hybrid theory comprised of values, core principles, etiological assumptions and practice guidelines. In effect, it contains elements of normative, etiological and practice/treatment theories within it while being somewhat broader than just the sum of these parts. It contains multiple levels and enables correctional workers to intervene in diverse but coherent ways. Without a rehabilitation theory, practitioners and clients will be unaware of the broad aims of an intervention and their relationship to the causes of offending (2007, p. 33).

The authors indicate the basic contexts (metaphysical, epistemological, ethical and normative) which can be used to reflect on the essence and meaning of rehabilitation (pp. 33–36). In this context, they are also useful framework for reflection on the inclusion in the prison systems.

Metaphysical assumptions boil down to determining the essence of entities involved in the inclusion process. They are the answer to the question how the human beings (prisoners) are perceived: as evil, sinful, prone to crime, or (despite their isolation) as members of society with the right to coexist. It is also a question about the perception of prisoners with such mental disorders which are defined as immutable.

Analysis of prison policy in the Nordic countries shows that in these penal systems incarcerated people are perceived primarily as citizens and members of the larger society (Warner 2011, p. 94). For example, in the Finnish prison system they are defined as "our principal customers." Moreover, "*Vankeinhoito*" is the term used in describing penitentiary practice, which means "care of prisoners" (Ibidem).

Metaphysical assumptions are also a question about the scope of basic conceptual categories, such as support, reentry, treatment, but also risk of reoffending, which is a threat to society. As Ward and Maruna ask: "Does risk reside within the person or in the situation?" (2007, p. 35). According to these authors, it is also a question about the essence of rehabilitation. Inclusive practice should include not only medical, correctional treatment but also based on the social network, leading to self-control and self-realisation.

The idea of "humane containment" is a starting point for thinking about work preparing prisoners for life outside the prison walls in Scandinavia. It is thinking about incarceration with the diminishing role of culture of control and leading to the normalisation of prison life (Garland 2001). In this context, Scandinavian researchers emphasise that time spent in prison serves to reduce the chances of living a conventional life—with a legitimate income—and thus contributes to marginalisation and social exclusion (Nilsson 2003; Skardhamar 2003). In prison strategy in Nordic countries, it is therefore pointed out that prison isolation minimises the chances of positive, good inclusion and it should take a form similar to the above-mentioned normal life. Danish Storstrøm Prison (called as the world's most humane maximum security penal institution) is a material example for contemporary understanding of imprisonment in the Nordic countries (Parsi 2018). As Claus Dalsgaard Nielsen (project manager) said: "We wanted to develop a prison that supports the prisoners' physical and mental well-being while helping them re-enter society" (Parsi 2018, p. 65).

Doing research on the incarnated persons and knowledge development about rehabilitation are crucial points for epistemology of the penal systems and for inclusion. There are the core elements in making decisions about incarceration. It should relate not only to the significance or superiority of the quantitative or qualitative approach but to their usefulness in minimising false (negative or positive) data about incarcerated persons. They are the basis for the decision on the therapeutical treatment or reentry process.

Such decisions depend on the proper recognition of factors strengthening inclusion process. In addition to standardised tools supporting the diagnosis of prisoners, it is also necessary to identify factors limiting inclusion. Research on the needs of prisoners covered by reentry procedures in Sweden may be an interesting example (Nilsson 2003). They concern the basic problems experienced by incarcerated persons, such as employment, education, housing after leaving prison and financial security.

These are the main factors that carry over recidivism. On the epistemological assumptions, mentally disordered prisoners are a special category of incarnated persons. In their case, false data lead especially to inadequate decisions, improper procedures and (as a result) to pathological reentry mechanisms and tragedies, such as the assassination of Mayor Adamowicz.

Ethical principles play a special role in identifying inclusion in contemporary penal systems. As Ward and Maruna state:

> they represent foundational or core standards used to construct ways of living and behaving. They bestow a sense of meaning, significance and purpose on human lives and are at the heart of the rehabilitation process. A value judgment asserts that specific types of quality, which are evaluated as positive or negative, characterize aspects of the world or people (2007, p. 36).

The statement of the prison staff members brings the way of thinking about incarcerated persons in the Nordic system: "paedophile can be moral in other respects; a thief can be a good parent" (Warner 2011, p. 98). This indicates a holistic, multidimensional perception of prisoners, which aims to identify and empower socially desirable traits and values. Additionally, ethical principles lead to identifying areas that are ethically crucial as the goal of human action. An analysis of inclusive practices in the Nordic countries shows that work with prisoners takes place in three areas (or even values): housing, income and something meaningful to do (like education, training or work) (Warner 2011, pp. 98–99).

Normative principles are practical indicators and guidelines for the inclusion of the rehabilitated inmates. To paraphrase the thought of Ward and Maruna (2007, p. 37), they are the answers to the questions about who, when and how undertakes actions for incarnated persons, considering potential restrictions. Prisoners' activation is one of the crucial features. For example, *Toverikunta* is a form of prisoners' association functioning in Finnish prisons and leads in the prisoners' inclusion. Cormac Behan describes this solution as follows: "Elections are held for prisoner representatives and in one prison, Kerala, issues discussed included extended family visits at weekends, longer time to telephone and more materials for the prison library" (Behan 2014, pp. 195–196). This is a special example of Nordic thinking about prison system, alternative to prison culture, implementing incarcerated persons into a sense of shared responsibility, leading to successful inclusion.

Normative principles of inclusion can also be seen in a wider social context and SGDs are an important clue (Goal 4b/4c). Educational staff and teachers' training (especially in developing countries) should be seen not only as providing the skills necessary to work with students of all ages (including adults and incarnated ones) but also as carrying out tasks leading to respect for rights of individuals, minimising stereotypes. Such strategies have added value, they increase the chances of successful inclusion. As Werner writes (analysing The White paper), school curriculum should pay attention to the fact that prisoners can be quite ordinary people (Warner 2011, p. 105). This is an important starting point for minimising social prejudices and stigma and is crucial background for inclusive practice.

10 On the Impact of the 2030 UN Agenda on Rule 63

Theoretically, the above elucidations hardly make a case for the relevance of Rule 63, but they all provide substantive arguments to connect an inmate with outside world and make them ready to re-entry. Practically, the limited PRI accounts of rather perfunctory implementation of Rule 63, and no less perfunctory commensurate activity in the Polish prison administration, invite now the question, are there any comprehensive initiatives to use Rule 63 for communicating the SDGs to inmates?

We are not talking about the bare minimum, i.e. no provision of pornographic and nationalistic media content (SDG 4.7; 5; 10.2, 10.3; 16.b), but also not about a rhetorical mention of the entire UN 2030 Agenda. This public policy chapter attempts to sensitise to possible concrete efforts of mass media and the United Nations to create *glocal* content partnerships with and about the UN SDGs, so the Rule 63 stakeholders could share high-value media content with inclusiveness potential.

Of course, it would be premature to find any answer now in the United Nations handbooks and manuals on prisoners' rehabilitation and social reintegration, exactly as per Rule 63. But, as a matter of fact, there are already good recommendations regarding, e.g. trafficking and use of mobile phones, as a part of intelligence-led anti-corruption measures in prisons (UNODC 2017). However, the United Nations Office on Drugs and Crime is not only the custodian of Nelson Mandela Rules (among other 60+ standards and norms instruments), but also a caretaker of the SDG related concept of "culture of lawfulness," and the implementer of a global programme of "Education for Justice" (Pływaczewski and Redo 2019). On the strength of these mandates, the UNODC should be able to advise how within Rule 63 the relevant stakeholders may engage prison inmates in the realm of SDGs.

Finally, since the UN Open-Ended Intergovernmental Expert Working Group on the indicators for the SDGs has concluded its work, only for the post-2030 realm (and in case a new long-term Agenda is adopted), this article leaves for its record to consider the viability of idea of establishing an indicator on the number of convicted offenders with mental disorders. As for now, there is too much ambiguity to determine how salient is their situation, and even more when one considers Goal 3.4 ("promote mental health and wellbeing").

11 Conclusion

The conduct of the mentally ill offender who took the life of Paweł Adamowicz, the Mayor of Gdańsk, certainly has nothing to do with limiting the access to public media but rather with the resonance of the public news inside prisons amongst inmates. If in the case in question there exists any tawny line between prisons and the outside world, then all those concerned with the violent effect of hatred should now be alerted to the instigation made through the Polish public media regarding the successor of the late Mayor of Gdańsk. Reportedly, her alleged "filoHiterism" gives her opponents "a moral right" to threats to kill her (UZ 2019). Interestingly, the Commissioner for Human Rights queried the constitutionally recognised media authority—the National Broadcasting Council—if some public broadcasters, especially the television, indeed incited such hatred. The Council composed of most members from the ruling political elite, gave a negative reply to the Commissioner's query (Kublik 2020).

Such very tawny cases are important for discussion about the impact of media on the inmates. The challenge for prison staff is to eliminate the illegal access and use of smartphones and other ICT tools by prisoners but also to apply solutions that minimise digital exclusion, enable and facilitate the proper use of contemporary communication tools and stimulate individual development

To meet the UN paradigm of inclusiveness, journalists, political decision-makers, rehabilitation theorists, prison administrators and non-governmental organisations need to engage seriously with SDGs issues in terms of their normative relevance to prisoners' rehabilitation and reintegration, including the unintended consequences. They need to answer the question what particular elements of rehabilitation would interplay with the idea of promoting inclusiveness via Rule 63. This should not be a vehicle for a mindless routinised application which makes inmates even more morally vulnerable than in the pre-SDGs era—absent of smart phones, Facebook, computer games, etc.

The SDGs' paradigm is a new code of ethical conduct for inclusiveness. With its ambitious, progressive and constructive action-oriented content it should become a part of the programmed relationship between the prison administrator and the inmate, not a mere technique for risk management and public protection. In this paradigm, important are mentally disordered inmates. Left alone with their problems, flooded by information from the world outside the prison walls and unable to detach to their interpretation they become a threat to society. Killing of the Mayor of Gdańsk is a tragic example of this risk.

We note with satisfaction that the United Nations has embarked on the SDG Media Compact (2018) whose aim is to develop with media companies high-value media content and newsworthy opportunities relating to the SDGs. We hope that this effort will be multi-pronged and driven by the crosscutting goal of promoting peaceful, just and inclusive societies whereby some of its less fortunate than other members will be adequately informed about culture of lawfulness, the lifestyles, choices and mental problems, and their prison past will not be a source of harassment or social stigma.

References

A/RES/70/175 The Standard Minimum Rules for the Treatment of Prisoners (the Nelson Mandela Rules) 17 December 2015.

Angell, A., & Guanaratna, R. (2012). *Terrorist rehabilitation. The U.S. experience in Iraq*. London: CRC Press.

Armstrong, M. (2018). *How prisons can use tech to slow their ever-revolving doors*. https://slate.com/technology/2018/06/how-prisons-can-use-tech-to-help-reduce-recidivism.html

BBC. (2017a, November 14). *New tech to block mobile phones in Scottish jails*. https://www.bbc.com/news/uk-scotland-41971718

BBC. (2017b, December 17). *Ban sale of mini mobile phones, justice secretary says*. https://www.bbc.com/news/uk-42383351

Behan, C. (2014). *Citizen convicts: Prisoners, politics and the vote*. Manchester: Manchester University Press.

Bozelko, C. (2017). *Inmates need social media. Take it from a former prisoner*. https://www.wired.com/story/inmates-need-social-media-take-it-from-a-former-prisoner/

Brown, A. S. (2011). The environment and susceptibility to schizophrenia. *Progress in Neurobiology, 93*(1), 23–58.

Brown, D. (2018). Prisoners nationwide go on strike to protest 'modern-day slavery'. *USA Today*. https://eu.usatoday.com/story/news/2018/08/21/prisoners-strike-protest-attica-lee-correctional/1045008002

Brzostymowska, E. (2017). Osoby pozbawione wolności z niepełnosprawnością psychiczną. In E. Dawidziuk & M. Mazur (Eds.), *Osoby z niepełnosprawnością intelektualną lub psychiczną osadzone w jednostkach penitencjarnych (z uwzględnieniem wyników badań przeprowadzonych przez pracowników Biura Rzecznika Praw Obywatelskich)*. Warszawa: Biuro Rzecznika Praw Obywatelskich.

Craig, L. A., Beech, A., & Browne, K. D. (2006). Cross-validation of the risk matrix 2000 sexual and violent scales. *Journal of Interpersonal Violence, 21*(5), 612–633.

Davies, Ch. (2019). 'Hatred is becoming more visible': shocked Gdańsk mourns slain Mayor. Residents take part in vigils after stabbing of Paweł Adamowicz on stage at charity concert, *The Guardian*, 15 January 2019. https://www.theguardian.com/world/2019/jan/15/gdansk-polish-city-mourning-mayor-pawel-adamowicz-stabbing

Dawidziuk, E., & Mazur, M. (Eds.). (2017). *Osoby z niepełnosprawnością intelektualną lub psychiczną osadzone w jednostkach penitencjarnych (z uwzględnieniem wyników badań przeprowadzonych przez pracowników Biura Rzecznika Praw Obywatelskich)*. Warszawa: Biuro Rzecznika Praw Obywatelskich.

Easton, A. (2019). *Pawel Adamowicz: Murder on stage stuns a divided Poland*. https://www.bbc.com/news/world-europe-46878325

Ellis, L., Beaver, K., & Wright, J. (2009). *Handbook of crime correlates*. Oxford: Elsevier/Academic Press.

Eze, J. (2016). Information needs of prisoners in Southeast Nigerian prisons. *Information Development, 32*(3), 243–253.

Finkel, M., & Bertram, W (2019, March 7). *More states are signing harmful "free prison tablet" contracts*. https://www.prisonpolicy.org/blog/2019/03/07/free-tablets/

Fisher, W., Roy-Bujnowski, K., Grudzinska, A., Clayfield, J., & Wolf, N. (2006). Patterns and prevalence of arrest in a statewide cohort of mental care consumers. *Psychiatric Services, 57*, 1623–1628.

Freedom House. (2017). https://freedomhouse.org/report/freedom-world/freedom-world-2017

Gaes, G. (2008, February 18) *The impact of prison education programs on post-release outcomes*. http://www.antoniocasella.eu/nume/Gaes_2008.pdf

Garland, D. (2001). *The culture of control crime and social order in contemporary society*. Chicago: University of Chicago Press.

Goraj, P. (2019). *Thousands walk with coffin of murdered Polish Mayor*, 18 January 2019. https://www.reuters.com/article/us-poland-stabbing-procession/thousands-walk-with-coffin-of-murdered-polish-mayor-idUSKCN1PC28R

Greenway, S. A. (2007). Library services behind bars. *Bookmobile and Outreach Services, 10*(2), 43–63.

Guzik-Makaruk, E. (2011). Poczucie bezpieczeństwa i zagrożenia w związku z wykonywaniem obowiązków służbowych. (The feeling of security and thread in connection with the implementation of official duties). In E. Guzik-Makaruk (Ed.), *Poczucie bezpieczeństwa obywateli w Polsce. Identyfikacja i przeciwdziałanie współczesnym zagrożeniom*. Warszawa: Wolters Kluwer.

King, K., Steiner, B., & Breach, S. R. (2008). Violence in the supermax: A self-fulfilling prophecy. *Prison Journal, 88*(1), 144–168.

Knight, V. (2016). *Remote control. Television in prison*. London: Palgrave Macmillan.

Kublik, A. (2019, February 12). *TVP pozywa Adama Bodnara. Chce przeprosin za wiązanie jej ze śmiercią Pawła Adamowicza (TVP sues Adam Bodnar. They want apology for their connecting with the death of Paweł Adamowicz)*. http://wyborcza.pl/7,75398,24450250,tvp-pozywa-adama-bodnara-chce-przeprosin-za-wiazanie-jej-ze.html

Kublik, A. (2020, January 3). *KRRiT do Bodnara: TVP słusznie donosi o "proniemieckiej polityce" władz Gdańska (KRRiT to Bodnar: TVP correctly denounces the "pro-German policy" of the authorities of Gdańsk)*. https://wyborcza.pl/7,75398,25565371,krrit-odpowiada-bodnarowi-tvp-polska-slusznie-donosi-o-proniemieckiej.html

Kusic, G. (2008). *Lack of media access in prison is a crime*. http://www.oocities.org/three_strikes_legal/media_access.html

Lapowski, I. (2018). *How San Quentin inmates built a search engine for prison*. https://www.wired.com/story/san-quentin-inmates-jolt-the-last-mile/

Lehmann, V., & Locke, J. (2005). *Guidelines for library services to prisoners* (3rd ed.). Hague: International Federation of Library Associations and Institutions IFLA.

Mann, R. E., Webster, S. D., Schofield, C., & Marshall, W. L. (2004). Approach versus avoidance goals in relapse prevention with sexual offenders. *Sexual Abuse: A Journal of Research and Treatment, 16*(1), 65–75.

Marsh, S., & Waterson, J. (2018). Tweeting jailbirds: Social media use by prisoners triples. *The Guardian*. Retrieved from https://www.theguardian.com/society/2018/jul/09/tweeting-jailbirds-social-media-use-by-prisoners-triples

Mears, D. P. (2013). Supermax prisons: The policy and the evidence. *Criminology & Public Policy, 12*(4), 681–719.

Niewiadomska, I. (2007). *Osobowościowe uwarunkowania skuteczności kary pozbawienia wolności. (Personal conditions of effectiveness of serving the penalty of deprivation of liberty)*. Lublin: Wydawnictwo KUL.

Nilsson, A. (2003). Living conditions, social exclusion and recidivism among prison inmates. *Journal of Scandinavian Studies in Criminology and Crime Prevention, 4*, 57–83.

Parsi, N. (2018). Beyond bars. *PM Network, 32*(6), 64–69.

Pływaczewski, E. W., & Redo, S. (2019). Advancing culture of lawfulness: Towards the achievement of the 2030 agenda. *Białostockie Studia Prawnicze, 23*(3), 1–125.

PRI/Prison Reform International. (2018). *Global prison trends 2018*. London: Prison Reform International.

Prins, S. J. (2014). Prevalence of mental illnesses in U.S. State prisons: A systematic review. *Psychiatric Service, 65*(7), 862–872.

Raport. (2018). Polska: Reagowanie na mowę nienawiści (*Poland: Reaction to the hatred*]. 2018 Raport *[Poland: Reaction to hate speech. 2018 Report*]. https://www.article19.org/wp-content/uploads/2018/04/Poland-Hate-Speech-report%E2%80%94-Polish.pdf

Sambo, A. S., & Ojei, N. L. (2018). Women in prison and their information needs: South—South prison libraries perspective. *Library Philosophy & Practice*, 1–14.

SDG Media Compact. (2018). https://www.un.org/sustainabledevelopment/sdg-media-compact-about/

Skardhamar, T. (2003). Inmates social background and living conditions. *Journal of Scandinavian Studies in Criminology and Crime Prevention, 4*, 39–56.

Steele, G. R. (2016). You've got legal mail. Applying constitutional protections to attorney-inmate e-mail communications. *Georgia Law Review, 50*(3), 947–984.

Tanajewska, R. (2019). Prawne aspekty zdolności do czynności prawnych osób chorych na schizofrenię. In M. Guzik-Makaruk, N. Waszkiewicz, S. Chojnowska, & S. D. Szajda (Eds.), *Wybrane prawne i medyczne aspekty zaburzeń psychicznych i ich profilaktyki [Selected aspects of capacity for legal action of persons sick on schizophrenia]* (pp. 65–78). Białystok: Temida 2.

Torrey, E., Zdanowicz, M., Kennard, A., Lamb, R., Eslinger, D., & Biasotti, M. (2014). *The treatment of persons with mental illness in prisons and jails: A state survey*. http://tacreports.org/storage/documents/treatment-behindbars/treatment-behind-bars.pdf

UNODC. (2017). *Handbook on anti-corruption measures in prisons*. New York: United Nations.

UZ. (2019, August 7). Andrzej Gwiazda usprawiediwia groźby pod adresem prezydent Gdańska, "Maja do tego moralne prawo" (Andrzej Gwiazda justifies threats addressed to the Mayor of Gdańsk. "They have a moral right." Gazeta Wyborcza, 7 August 2019.

Vacca, J. S. (2008). Crime can be prevented if schools teach juvenile offenders to read. *Children and Youth Review, 30*(9), 1055–1062.

van Os, J., Kenis, G., & Rutten, P. F. (2010). The environment and schizophrenia. *Nature, 468*, 203–212.

van Zyl Smit, D., & Appleton, C. (2019). *Life imprisonment. A global human rights analysis*. Cambridge: Harvard University Press.

Vandebosch, H. (2005). The perceived role of mass media use during incarceration in the light of prisoners' re-entry into society. *Journal of Criminal Justice & Popular Culture, 12*(2), 96–115.

Ward, T., & Maruna, S. (2007). *Rehabilitation. Beyond the risk paradigm*. London: Routledge.

Warner, K. (2011). Valued members of society'? Social inclusiveness in the characterisation of prisoners in Ireland, Denmark, Finland and Norway. *Administration, 59*(1), 87–109.

Wehring, H. J., & Carpenter, W. T. (2011). Editorial: Violence and schizophrenia. *Schizophrenia Bulletin, 37*(5), 877–878.

Wells, D. (2014). *Training and preparing inmates for post-prison employment*. https://www.ncjrs.gov/pdffiles1/nij/248574.pdf

Whitehead, P. R., Ward, T., & Collie, R. M. (2007). Time for a change: Applying the good lives model of rehabilitation to a high-risk violent offender. *International Journal of Offender Therapy and Comparative Criminology, 51*(5), 578–598.

Wiltz, T. (2017). *Should social media be banned in prison?* https://www.pewtrusts.org/en/research-and-analysis/blogs/stateline/2017/01/13/should-social-media-be-banned-in-prison

Wojciechowski, P., & Włodkowska, K. (2019a, January 17). *Zabójca Adamowicza planował "spektakularny zamach" już w grudniu. Jego matka ostrzegała policję (The Assassin of Adamowicz planned a „spectacular attack" already in December. His mother warned the Police, Gazeta Wybrocza)*. http://trojmiasto.wyborcza.pl/trojmiasto/7,35612,24371285,matka-zabojcy-ostrzegala-policje.html

Wojciechowski, P., & Włodkowska, K. (2019b). Wywiad z matką Stefana W. "Przepraszam za syna i proszę o wybaczenie" [*Interview with the mother of Stefan W. "I apologize for my son and ask for forgiveness*"], Gazeta Wyborcza. 21 January 2019. http://wyborcza.pl/duzyformat/7,127290,24377564,wywiad-z-matka-stefana-w-przepraszam-za-syna-i-prosze-o.html

Woźnicki, Ł., & Wojciechowski, P. (2019). *Co się działo ze Stefanem W., zanim zaatakował prezydenta Pawła Adamowicza (What happened with Stefan W. before he attacked Mayor Adamowicz)*, 18 January 2019. http://trojmiasto.wyborcza.pl/trojmiasto/7,35612,24375391,co-sie-dzialo-ze-stefanem-w-zanim-zaatakowal-prezydenta-pawla.html

Sławomir Redo Dr. hab. (Law/Criminology) is Visiting Professor of United Nations Law. He is a member of the United Nations Studies Association. F. United Nations Senior Crime Prevention and Criminal Justice Expert and staff of the UN Office on Drugs and Crime (ret.); He had been involved in numerous projects implementing the UN standards and norms in crime prevention and criminal justice. In other capacities he assisted in the implementation of the United Nations Convention against Transnational Organized Crime, and on-line international crime prevention and criminal justice education. He published four books, co-edited four others, including "Women and Children as Victims and offenders: Background, Prevention, Reintegration. Suggestions for Succeeding Generations" (Springer 2016), and "Refugees and Migrants in Law and Policy – Challenges and Opportunities for Global Civic Education" (Springer 2018) plus about 80 articles – mostly on the UN law and practice of crime prevention and criminal justice. University course lecturer on "The United Nations and Crime Prevention" & "The United Nations and War Crime Prevention" (Austria, China, Poland); Promoter of crime prevention and criminal justice training and education for meeting the goals of the 2030 UN Sustainable Development Agenda. Co-Editor of the first criminological UN Agenda-based textbook *KRYMINOLOGIA. Stan i perspektywy rozwoju z uwzględnieniem założeń Agendy ONZ na rzecz zrównoważonego rozwoju 2030* (Wolters Kluwer, Warsaw 2020). E-mail: s@redo.net.

Krzysztof Sawicki Dr. hab. is Associate Professor at the Faculty of Education, University of Białystok (Białystok, Poland), member of the Academic Council on the United Nations System; Expert in the Social Rehabilitation Unit and Youth Studies Unit of the Committee of Pedagogical Sciences of the Polish Academy of Sciences. His books, manuscripts and research projects cover youth at risk and juvenile offenders (particularly youth subcultures, youth work, peer groups, environmental contexts of juvenile delinquency and rehabilitation). In his last work "Dyads, cliques, gangs. Juvenile offenders from the perspective of the contemporary social rehabilitation" (ISBN 978-83- 8095-337-6) he paid attention on dialectic relationship between the individual and the environment (identification of criminogenic needs, risk and protective factors). He cooperates with universities and high schools from Belgium, Netherlands, Sweden, Finland, Germany, Lithuania and Russia as a visiting professor or projects team member.E-mail: k.sawicki@uwb.edu.pl

Parents Who Hit, Troubled Families, and Children's Happiness: Do Gender and National Context Make a Difference?

Ineke Haen Marshall, Candence Wills, and Chris E. Marshall

Abstract According to the Convention on the Rights of the Child, Article 19, "children have the right to be protected from being hurt and mistreated, physically or mentally." The 2030 UN Sustainable Development Goal 16 target 16.2 ("end abuse and violence against children") aims toward the elimination of corporal punishment of children. Physical punishment by parents (and others) is banned by law in a growing number of countries. This chapter explores if girls are more affected by the violent family context than boys, and if countries where corporal punishment is banned do have lower level of parental maltreatment of children. We analyze data from Belgium, Denmark, Italy, and the USA collected among 12–16 year-old adolescents ($n = 10{,}216$) as part of the third sweep of the International Self-Report Delinquency survey (ISRD3) to answer the question of whether the association between troubled family life, use of violence by parents, attachment to parents, and subjective wellbeing (happiness) is different for girls than for boys, and whether it is contingent on national context. The findings suggest that gender and national context indeed do matter. We conclude the chapter with an expression of two concerns: about the universal implementation of Article 19 of the Convention on the Rights of the Child across different national contexts, and, likewise, about the challenge of promoting a Culture of Lawfulness so the children of the next generation will be happier than the present one.

Keywords Children's subjective wellbeing · Corporal punishment · Parental violence · Gender · Convention on the Rights of the Child

I. H. Marshall (✉) · C. Wills
Northeastern University, Boston, MA, USA
e-mail: i.marshall@northeastern.edu; c.wills@northeastern.edu

C. E. Marshall
University of Nebraska Omaha, Omaha, NE, USA
e-mail: cmarshall@unomaha.edu

H. Kury, S. Redo (eds.), *Crime Prevention and Justice in 2030*,
https://doi.org/10.1007/978-3-030-56227-4_10

1 Introduction

Among academic criminologists, there is an increasing recognition of the need to include human rights violations as an urgent and important area of study (Hagan et al. 2006; Karstedt 2012; Savelsberg 2010), which of course includes the rights of children. Interestingly (and not surprisingly), much of the empirical research on child abuse and use of violence against children produced by researchers located in the USA tends to focus primarily on the *negative outcomes* of parental use of violence, rather than on the *intrinsic wrongness* of violating children's rights.

In this chapter, we aim to contribute to both perspectives through analysis of responses to a questionnaire from the third sweep of the International Self-Report Delinquency survey (ISRD3) among youth approximately 12–16 years old (Enzmann et al. 2018). Although the total ISRD3 sample covers 35 countries (and over 70,000 cases), for the current chapter we decided to focus on a subsample of 10,216 cases collected in four western countries (Belgium, Denmark, Italy, and the USA) to allow a more in-depth investigation of the national and cultural contexts of physical violence by parents.

We start with a brief description of the legal frameworks related to corporal punishment of children—internationally as well as in the Belgium, Italy, and the USA. This section also includes reference to data on national cultural attitudes towards parental use of violence towards children in Belgium, Denmark, Italy, and the USA.

The second section highlights gender differences in the experience of parental use of violence. Violence against women and girls is one of the most systematic and widespread human rights violations. Girls and women have been particularly vulnerable to victimization and violation of human rights (e.g., UN Declaration on the Elimination of Violence against Women).[1] Corporal punishment, the most common form of violence against girls, is rarely included in the global movement to eliminate violence against women and girls (Global Initiative to End All Corporal Punishment of Children 2015). We are particularly interested to see whether any gender differences in experiencing corporal punishment reveal themselves in our school-based self-report survey of 12–16 year olds in four countries.

The third section briefly introduces the right to happiness as a univeral right—for children and adults alike, and presents evidence that physical maltreatment by parents may negatively affect a child's sense of wellbeing (happiness). Indeed, a UN resolution adopted in 2012 identifies the pursuit of happiness as "a fundamental human goal"—one that recognizes happiness and wellbeing as important pieces of sustainable and equitable development.[2] From a human rights perspective, children

[1]For a comprehensive overview of the norms and standards and other intergovernmental work on violence against women, see https://www.unwomen.org/en/what-we-do/ending-violence-against-women/global-norms-and-standards.

[2]https://unstats.un.org/unsd/broaderprogress/pdf/Happiness%20towards%20a%20holistic%20approach%20to%20development%20(A-67-697).pdf.

are not only protected from abuse and neglect, but they also have the right to a healthy development. The World Health Organization defines physical, mental, and social wellbeing as major components of health (WHO 1946). Happiness, defined as subjective wellbeing, squarely fits under the broader WHO definition of health. The main outcome or dependent variable in our study is the self-reported level of subjective wellbeing or happiness of the 10,216 children in the four country samples.

After briefly describing the ISRD3 methodology, as well as the used measurements, we present our findings. We first describe the extent to which parental violence against children is reported by the children in the samples from Belgium, Denmark, Italy, and the USA—countries that vary in the legislative prohibition against corporal punishment of children. We selected these four countries because they represent different levels of criminalization of this behavior; we expect that children in countries with a legal prohibition on corporal punishment would report lower levels of parental maltreatment. Second, using the same data from the Belgium, Denmark, Italy, and the USA, we test a multivariate model with the child's subjective wellbeing (happiness) as the dependent/outcome variable, and indicators of quality of family life as predictors (including of course corporal punishment/parental violence, but also troubled family life, and the child's attachment to parents). Specifically, we want to answer two research questions: (a) Is the association between use of violence by parents, troubled family life, attachment to parents, and subjective wellbeing (happiness) *different for girls than for boys?* And (b) Is the association between use of violence by parents, troubled family life, attachment to parents, and subjective wellbeing (happiness) *different for children in the Belgium, Denmark, Italy, and the USA?*

1.1 Brief Comment on Terminology

Much of the literature in the human rights and legislative fields uses 'corporal punishment', while empirical writings by criminologists, social psychologists, and welfare workers tend to use 'physical child abuse', 'child maltreatment,' 'parental violence,' or 'domestic violence'. Choice of terms reflect severity of injuries, intent and motivation, as well as academic discipline and professional training.[3] In this chapter we use the terms 'corporal punishment' and 'parental violence' interchangeably.

[3]Physical discipline, also known as corporal punishment, refers to "any punishment in which physical force is used and intended to cause some degree of pain or discomfort, however light."

It includes acts such as kicking, pinching, spanking, shaking or throwing children, hitting them with a hand or implement (such as a whip, stick, belt, shoe or wooden spoon) or forcing them to ingest something. Violent psychological discipline involves the use of verbal aggression, threats, intimidation, denigration, ridicule, guilt, humiliation, withdrawal of love or emotional manipulation to control children.

2 Corporal Punishment: Laws and Culture

International governing institutions such as the United Nations and the European Union discourage the use of corporal punishment and promote national policies banning the practice in public spaces and privately in the home (Keyes et al. 2015). We refer you to the website maintained by the Global Initiative to End All Corporal Punishment of Children (www.endcorporalpunishment.org) which provides extensive documentation on the relevant national and international conventions, laws, rules, and regulations.

Reflecting "broadly shared values" and norms of society, policies derive from the consensus of behavioral expectations and the punishment for violations as explained in consensus theory (Romney et al. 1986; Tankebe and Liebling 2013). Policies regarding corporal punishment arguably reflect the cultural acceptance of parental use of force as a form of punishment and physical discipline. European countries which retain the lawful use of corporal punishment report parents resorting to corporal punishment as 1.7 times higher compared to countries where corporal punishment is banned (Keyes et al. 2015), showing that policies may reflect societal views on parental use of force and violence while also potentially reinforcing norms and reducing use of violence as punishment. Although corporal punishment is legally permitted and culturally acceptable in many countries, the practice is facing scrutiny with several studies finding limited efficacy beyond short-term behavioral changes and adverse outcomes of corporal punishment, including negative mental health, anti-social behavior, aggression, and dating violence (Afifi et al. 2006; Gershoff 2010, 2018; Gershoff and Font 2016; Lansford et al. 2014).

Research highlighting the adverse effects of corporal punishment and the international movement recognizing corporal punishment as a violation of human rights may be influencing a global cultural shift in attitude towards parental use of physical discipline. Between 1979 and 2010, 29 countries have reflected the growing disapproval of physical punishment by adopting national legislation banning corporal punishment publicly in schools and privately by parents and other adults (Gershoff 2010). The Global Initiative to End All Corporal Punishment of Children reports that in 2018, 54 countries have prohibited all corporal punishment of children, while another 56 countries have committed to prohibiting all corporal punishment (Global Initiative to End All Corporal Punishment of Children 2019c). Importantly, the 2030 UN Sustainable Development Goal 16 ("Promote peaceful and inclusive societies for sustainable development, provide access to justice for all and build effective, accountable and inclusive institutions at all levels"), target 16.2 (end abuse and violence against children) aims toward the elimination of corporal punishment of children.

Belgium Belgium faces continued scrutiny regarding the country's policies and societal tolerance of corporal punishment. In a study of 2000 10–18 year-old children carried out in 2010–2011 in Flanders, nearly half of the participants reported experiencing physical punishment in the form of pinching, ear pulling, kicking, pushing, slapping, or grabbing by parents, while 25% experienced "extreme violence" as punishment by parents (Global Initiative to End All Corporal Punishment of Children 2019a). Youth further experience physical punishment in schools and youth clubs. Belgium policies do not ban physical punishment by parents or in academic and social settings. Most recently in 2016, the Belgium government accepted a recommendation to prohibit corporal punishment but later stated that the recommendation could not be implemented due to current legislation already punishing violence towards children. Later, in April 2016 a bill was introduced to amend a civil code which provided children the "right to care, safety, and a good education" without being subjected to physical and psychological violence; however in November 2018 Belgium Parliament determined that current legislation already applied to corporal punishment of children and no further changes have been determined (Global Initiative to End All Corporal Punishment of Children 2019a).

Denmark The situation in Denmark is a sharp contrast with Belgium. Denmark in 1985 adopted the Custody and Care Act dictating the responsibility of the parents to protect children from both physical and psychological violence and achieved full prohibition all forms of corporal punishment of children in 1997 (Global Initiative to End All Corporal Punishment of Children 2017). Corporal punishment is unlawful, in all settings, including the home. Students further reflect the state values of eliminating physical punishment with 81.8% believing that a child should *never* be corporally punished and 89% agreeing that children should be protected from violence (UNICEF 2011).

Italy In 1996, the Italian Supreme Court ruled that a law defending parental rights to correct their child cannot be used to defend the use of corporal punishment; however, the ruling has yet to be codified in law. Physical punishment is technically lawful in the home by parents and is apparent in society with half of parents reporting in a study that they smack their children in "exceptional circumstances" (Ipsos Public Affairs 2012) while over 60% of youth ages 7–10 reported "mild" corporal punishment by parents (Lansford et al. 2010). Although corporal punishment is lawful in the home, it is banned from schools, care settings, penal institutions, and as a punishment or sentence for committing a crime (Global Initiative to End All Corporal Punishment of Children 2019b).

United States Although many studies revealing the adverse outcomes of corporal punishment derive from US institutions, the United States federally does not have legislation banning the use of corporal punishment in the home, in schools, or in care settings. A U.S. Supreme Court case *Ingraham v. Wright (1977)* determined that corporal punishment does not violate the Eighth Amendment due process of students, thereby deciding that corporal punishment of children is indeed constitutional. With strong emphasis on state rights in the USA, each state determines the extent and prohibition of violence as a tool for child correction by parents, caregivers, and those in school settings through state specific laws and regulations.

The current study gathered participants from three distinct states, Florida, Colorado, and Massachusetts, with differing population demographics, politics, and cultural values that shape state laws pertaining to corporal punishment. For instance,

Florida is a predominantly socially conservative state with a large Latinx immigrant population holding traditional Catholic values, while Colorado is comparably socially conservative but has a racially homogenous population with 84% identifying as Caucasian (World Population Review 2019). On the other hand, Massachusetts is very socially liberal and 71% of the population identifies as white, non-Hispanic (U.S. Census Bureau 2019).

Differences in demographics and social values shape the state legislation. Permissible in Colorado, corporal punishment involves reasonable discipline considering the child's age, misbehavior, and physical harm (Colorado Revised Statutes §18.6.401). A Bill introduced in 2017 signaled changing views towards corporal punishment. Currently, parents or guardians, teachers, and other school officials, may all use physical force as punishment for children (Colorado Statutes §18.1.703). The Bill introduced legislation that would prohibit anyone in public schools, childcare centers, family care homes, and specialized group facilities from inflicting physical pain on a child and specifically included corporal punishment in the legislative language, but the Bill was postponed indefinitely by the state Senate in March 2017 (Prohibit Corporal Punishment of Children. (2017) Colorado General Assembly HB17-1038).

In Florida, corporal punishment does not constitute child abuse and is permissible by parents and the legal custodial guardian. Child abuse is defined specifically as "inappropriate or excessively harsh" discipline that results in physical, mental, or emotional injury including sprains, fractures, brain or spinal damage, use of a deadly weapon, disfigurement, and significant bruises or welts to name a few (Florida Statutes (2011) Title V. Judicial Branch §39.01). Most recently in May 2019, a Bill was introduced to the Florida House and Senate to remove corporal punishment in public schools. The Bill died in the Senate Judiciary and House Subcommittee allowing the teachers and principals the authority to utilize physical punishment as a means to regulate student; however, as of 2009, schools have to review their punishment rules every 3 years during a school board meeting allowing public statements and rebuttals behavior (Florida Statutes (2011), Title XLVIII. K-20 Education Code §1003.32).

Massachusetts also allows corporal punishment by parents as was decided in *Commonwealth of Massachusetts v. Jean G. Dorvil (2015)*. The court case determined that spanking or reasonable force used against a minor that does not cause substantial risk of physical harm, degradation, or severe mental distress is permissible to prevent or punish misbehavior. Diverging from the policies in both Colorado and Florida, corporal punishment and physical restraint is banned in public schools (Massachusetts General Laws Title XII §71.37G) and is also prohibited for disabled persons (Massachusetts General Laws §16.6A). It appears that the more socially liberal state of Massachusetts has the strictest policies regarding corporal punishment, reflecting societal and cultural disapproval.

3 Corporal Punishment and Gender

One would expect that the experience of parental violence—as most other forms of violence—are gendered. This view is reflected in the statement by the Global Initiative to End all Corporal Punishment of Children in their 2015 paper submitted to the UN working Group on discrimination against women in law and in practice for its research on discrimination against women in relation to their right to health and safety (page 2).

> This experience is often gendered – girls may suffer different types of punishment than boys and may be punished for different reasons, typically reinforcing stereotypic ideas of what it means to be a woman. Corporal punishment is used to control and regulate girls' behaviour, including their social and sexual behaviour, and to encourage deference, submission and timidity. For too many girls, childhood experience of corporal punishment is the beginning of a life of violent victimisation by authority figures and family members that repeatedly violates their right to health and safety. While children are physically punished in their homes by both mothers and fathers, the physical assault of girls, in the guise of (lawful) discipline, by their fathers and other male relatives, strongly reinforces the inequitable relations between men and women which underpin discrimination in all areas of life (Global Initiative to End All Corporal Punishment of Children 2015).

The most readily available evidence regarding gender pertains to the *frequency* of use of physical punishment, rather than the motivations for such behavior. The results of research provide rather mixed evidence on that assertion. Data on physical violence against boys are less prevalent than those against girls (United Nations Children's Fund 2014). A 2010 study conducted in nine countries (China, Columbia, Italy, Jordan, Keya, the Philippines, Sweden, Thailand, and the USA) found that overall, boys were more frequently punished corporally than were girls, but the differences were fairly small (Lansford et al. 2010). The 2014 UNICEF report Hidden in Plain Sight cites research that has shown that boys tend to experience violent discipline to a greater extent than girls, and their own analysis partially supports that claim (United Nations Children's Fund 2014). In just over one-third of the countries with data, boys are slightly more likely to be subjected to violent discipline (including psychological aggression), including in Bosnia and Herzegovina, Costa Rica, Kazakhstan, Kyrgyzstan, and Ukraine. The prevalence of corporal punishment for boys and girls is also quite similar, although "more pronounced sex differences in the experience of this form of violent discipline show up in a few countries or areas, including both Costa Rica and Ukraine, where boys are about one and a half times more likely to be subjected to any form of physical punishment than girls" (United Nations Children's Fund 2014, p. 102).

Recent research in the USA based on a 2014 cross-sectional, telephone survey of a nationally representative sample of US households with children suggests that rates of spanking were lower for girls compared to boys (Finkelhor et al. 2019). On the other hand, Endendijk et al. (2016) report on the results of their meta-analysis of 126 observational studies (15,034 families) to conclude that "in general the differences between parenting of boys versus girls are minimal" (Endendijk et al. 2016).

Although the use of physical discipline by parents on their daughters or sons is not as strongly gendered as expected, it stands to reason that the subjective experience of being physically disciplined may be different for girls than for boys—as well as the behavioral, emotional and psychological outcomes of this experience.

4 Corporal Punishment and Happiness

The research evidence is abundantly clear—corporal punishment of children has a wide range of negative health, developmental and other outcomes (Afifi et al. 2006; Gershoff 2010, 2018; Gershoff and Font 2016; Lansford et al. 2014). The effects of corporal punishment of children include direct physical harm; mental harm and indirect physical harm; impaired cognitive development, and negative behavioral and other outcomes (Global Initiative to End All Corporal Punishment of Children 2015). Criminologists have focused mostly on negative behavioral outcomes, such as increased delinquent, violent and anti-social behavior and have found support for the harmful impact of child exposure to parental violence (Steketee et al. 2019; Widom and Wilson 2015). Social psychologists, mental health researchers, and public health studies study the links of physical punishment to poor mental health and problems such as depression, low self-esteem, anxiety disorders, hostility, and emotional instability. The evidence on the negative effects on mental health is robust; and there is no evidence of any positive outcomes. However, health is not merely the absence of disease, but it also includes positive health—and happiness. Research should also consider the factors that contribute to human flourishing (Holder 2012).

Happiness is a term that is hard to define, it is often defined as a "state of well-being and contentment" (Wexler 2018, p. 3). Happiness is an affective state that is comprised of more positive emotions than negative ones (Hofmann et al. 2013) and most people agree that societies should attempt to promote happiness in their population (Sachs 2012, cited on page 3 in Wexler 2018). No wonder therefore that the UN Secretary-General periodically reports to the General Assembly about happiness (United Nations 2013).

There is a large volume of empirical research on happiness, and an exhaustive review of this topic goes beyond the scope of the current chapter. Happiness is a positive affective state, usually referred to in the literature as subjective wellbeing. Subjective wellbeing can be defined as "the level of well-being experienced by people according to their own subjective evaluations of their lives" (Diener et al. 2013). Subjective wellbeing is also defined as a "state comprising of frequent positive moods, low negative moods, and high overall life satisfaction" (Wexler 2018, p. 8). Wexler (2018, p. 8) argues that, for adolescents—the target group of the current chapter—subjective wellbeing is an indicator of positive youth development and promotes and preserves peak mental health. In the present chapter, we explore whether children whose parents hit or spank them are less happy than their counterparts whose parents do not employ physical discipline.

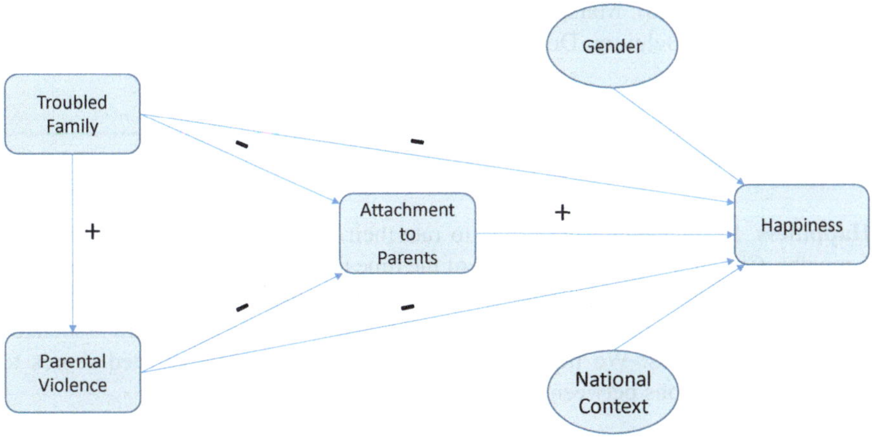

Fig. 1 Conceptual model of correlates of happiness

5 Conceptual Model

The conceptual model is presented in Fig. 1. It is meant as a heuristic aid, rather than as a causal model to be tested in this chapter. The arrows between the three family variables (parental violence, troubled family, and family bonding), and between these indicators of quality of family life and happiness are based on an abundance of existing empirical evidence; and we expect that our data (presented below) will not produce very different results. We are particularly interested in examining the effect of gender and national context on the correlations between family life and children's happiness, using data drawn from the International Self-Report Delinquency study (ISRD3).

6 Methodology

We use data from the International Self-Report Delinquency Study (ISRD3). ISRD3 is an ongoing, major international research collaboration on juvenile victimization and offending that now covers 35 countries.[4] For most of these countries, the samples are drawn from two major cities.[5] It surveys youths from grades 7, 8 and 9 in schools asking about their experiences of crime, both as offenders and as victims, and about their attitudes about crime and justice as well as their home and school life. For detailed information on the methodology of the ISRD project, see

[4]ISRD1 was carried out in 1991–1992 and ISRD2 in 2006–2008.

[5]For more information, see www.northeastern.edu/isrd/.

Enzmann et al. (2018); Marshall and Enzmann (2012). For the current chapter, we use the data from Belgium, Denmark, Italy, and USA only ($n = 10{,}216$).[6]

6.1 Measurements

Happiness Respondents were asked to rate their level of happiness over the past 6 months. Children were asked if most of the time they felt "very happy, happy, a bit more happy than unhappy, a bit more unhappy than happy, unhappy, or very unhappy." This variable had scores between 1 and 6. Higher values are associated with more happiness. We transformed the scores into POMP-adjusted scores to facilitate comparisons between variables.[7]

Parental Violence This is measured by combining the responses to two questions (Enzmann et al. 2018, p. 71). The first question asks, "Has your mother or father (or your stepmother or stepfather) ever hit, slapped, or shoved you?" (Include also times when this was punishment for something you had done). A positive response indicates a mild form of parental violence. The second question measures the harsher use of violence by asking, "Has your mother or father (or your stepmother or stepfather) ever hit you with an object, punched or kicked you forcefully, or beat you up? (Include also times when this was punishment for something you have done). We constructed an ordinal measure of seriousness of parental violence: 0 (none, with a "no" answer to both questions); 1 (mild, with a yes response to the first question and a no response to the second); and 2 (severe, with a yes response to the second question). See Appendix for the question.

Troubled Family Children were asked about serious life events that may impact the quality of their family life. The question asks: "Have you ever experienced any of the following serious events?" (a) One of your parents having problems with alcohol or drugs, (b) physical fights between your parents; (c) repeated serious conflicts between your parents, (d) divorce or separation of your parents. Scores range from 0 (none of these events happened) to 4 (positive answer to all four events). A high score reflects a more troubled family life.

Family Bonding To measure the children's attachment to their parents, a four-item Likert-type question was used. The answers ranged from totally agree, rather agree, neither/nor, rather disagree, totally disagree when asked "How well do you get along with your parents? (a) I get along just fine with my father (stepfather), (b) I get along just fine with my mother (stepmother), (c) I can easily get emotional support and care from my parents; and (d) I would feel very bad disappointing my parents. We

---

[6]There is one exception: in Table 3, we make use of findings for the 27 countries for which full data are currently available and the total sample approaches 63,000 young people.

[7]Transforming the original scale into POMPs (Percentage of Maximum Possible Scores) ranging from 0 to 100, makes it easier to compare between differently-scaled variables (Cohen et al. 1999).

Table 1 Descriptive statistics of key variables

	United States	Belgium	Italy	Denmark	Total sample
Happiness	71.62	71.80	69.34	78.12	71.95
Family bond	85.09	82.83	83.69	89.66	84.65
Family trouble	0.79	0.70	0.47	0.58	0.63
Parental violence	0.46	0.38	0.44	0.16	0.38
Gender					
Female	53.26	50.08	47.28	51.87	50.15
Male	46.74	49.92	52.72	48.13	49.85
Grade in school					
Grade 7	33.23	30.74	30.81	33.16	31.68
Grade 8	35.27	31.95	31.45	34.88	32.96
Grade 9	31.50	37.31	37.74	31.96	35.37
Overall *N* for the samples	2206	3155	3278	1577	10,216

transformed the scores into POMP-adjusted scores to facilitate comparisons between variables.

National Context We used the country where the data were collected as our indicator for national context [Belgium ($n = 3155$), Italy ($n = 3278$), Denmark ($n = 1577$), US ($n = 2206$)]. For our analysis, we dummy-coded the counties, using the USA as our reference category.

Gender We coded 1 for male students and 0 for female students (see Table 1).

Grade We used grade as a proxy for age, for youths who are in grades 7, 8, and 9.

6.2 *Analytic Strategy*

We start the statistical analysis with a rather detailed description of the four sub-samples. This part of the analysis also refers to data on the larger international sample ($n = 27$ countries), as a context to interpret the scores of the Belgian, Danish, Italian and US samples on the key variable of parental violence.

The dependent variable (Happiness) is an ordinal level variable, ranging from 1 to 6. The multivariate approach taken in our chapter is ordinary least squares regression (OLS).[8] It was the most efficient approach for our theoretical goals. The key issues of our chapter concern the relationship between gender and parental violence as well as country and parental violence, and the *interactions* between gender, country, and parental violence.

[8]Ordinary least squares (OLS) regression is a statistical method of analysis that estimates the relationship between one or more independent variables and a dependent variable. We follow the common recommendation that in terms of providing the clearest interpretation of interaction terms and reliable/stable coefficients, OLS is the currently best way to analyze interactions.

To examine the differences between the male and female models as well as the Belgian, Italian, Danish, and US models, we have used the Paternoster (Paternoster et al. 1998) recommendation for the most correct calculation of the regression coefficient equality. The particular test which we have used is $Z = \frac{b_1 - b_2}{\sqrt{\text{SE}b_1^2 + SEb_2^2}}$ (Paternoster et al. 1998).

7 Findings

Table 1 provides the descriptive information of the key study variables, for the total sample and by country. The overall sample is about equally divided between males and females, but there is some variation in the country samples, with the USA having a slight overrepresentation of females (53%), and Italy an overrepresentation of males (53%). The sample is roughly equally divided among 7th, 8th, and 9th graders, with Belgium and Italy having a slight overrepresentation of 9th graders (37%).

Because of our interest in differences between country samples, Table 2 presents the pairwise means *t*-tests by country, for the key variables: Parental violence, happiness, family bonding, and family trouble.

Table 2 Pairwise mean *t*-tests for key study variables by country

	USA	Belgium	Italy
Happiness			
Belgium	−0.18		
Italy	2.28***	2.46***	
Denmark	−6.50***	−6.32***	−8.78***
Family bond			
Belgium	2.27***		
Italy	1.40***	−0.86**	
Denmark	−4.56***	−6.83***	−5.97***
Family trouble			
Belgium	0.09***		
Italy	0.32***	0.23***	
Denmark	0.21***	0.12***	−0.11***
Parental violence			
Belgium	0.08***		
Italy	0.02	−0.07***	
Denmark	0.30***	0.22***	0.28***

Note: In reading this table, consider the difference as the columns MINUS the row means; for example, the US mean happiness is 71.62 and the Belgian mean happiness is 71.80. Thus, 71.62 MINUS 71.80 is −0.18 or the cell entry at the USA-Belgian intersection
* $p < 0.10$; ** $p < 0.05$; *** $p < 0.01$

7.1 Do Children in US, Italy, Belgium, and Denmark Report Comparable Levels of Parental Violence?

In an earlier publication (Enzmann et al. 2018), we presented results on the prevalence of parental violence in the 27 countries for which data were available at that time (Enzmann et al. 2018, Table 4.9 and Table 4.11). About one in five students in the large sample ($n = 61{,}854$) reports that they had experienced mild physical violence in the last year (prevalence 20%). Not surprisingly, we noted substantial variation in the use of force in the countries represented, ranging from a high in the Czech Republic (39%), Indonesia (31%), France and Italy (27%), Serbia (26%), and the USA (24%), to a low in Denmark (4%)—for the milder forms of parental violence (Enzmann et al. 2018, pp. 56–57). The figures for the more serious forms of parental violence are, of course, lower: for the entire sample, about 5% reports that they had been hit with an object, kicked or beaten up by parents, on average four times over the last year (Enzmann et al. 2018, pp. 57–58). The highest rates were reported in the USA and Indonesia (11%), Cape Verde and Venezuela (10%), and India (8%). The lowest rates (for serious parental violence) are reported by children in Denmark (0.4%), Kosovo (1%), and Armenia (2%) (Enzmann et al. 2018, p. 58). In the 2018 analysis, we did some exploratory analysis of the country-level association between the Human Development Index (HDI—a measure of poverty/deprivation combining indicators of life expectancy, education, and per capita income) and severe parental use of violence, and we did not find a systematic correlation. However, we did note two outliers: the USA with a high HDI and a relatively high level of child maltreatment, and Denmark with a high HDI and a very low level of child maltreatment.

This finding challenged us to include the USA and Denmark in the current analysis, together with Italy and Belgium (also high HDI countries). As discussed in the section on law and culture above, these four countries do vary with respect to the attitudes towards use of corporal punishment, as well as the laws in place to ban this practice. Table 3 presents the data for USA, Belgium, Italy and Denmark – for mild as well as for more serious forms of parental use of violence.

Table 3 includes the 95% confidence intervals, so we can determine if the noted differences between countries are statistically significant. First, regarding prevalence of *mild* parental violence, Italy appears to have the highest rate (26.6%), followed by the USA (23.9). However, the confidence intervals of both countries overlap (USA 20.4–27.8; Italy 24.6–28.6), implying that this difference lacks statistical significance. Likewise, Belgium's rate (21.4) is not statistically significant different from the USA, judged by the confidence intervals that overlap. There is no doubt that Denmark's prevalence rate (3.5) is significantly lower than that of the USA, Italy and Belgium. Focusing on the prevalence rates of the *more serious* forms of parental maltreatment, the differences are more pronounced. The USA (11.2%) has a significantly higher level of reported victimization than the three other countries. Denmark is at the bottom of the reports (0.4%). Italy has a higher rate (6.6) than Belgium (5.1), but their confidence intervals show some overlap (Italy 5.6–7.7 and Belgium

Table 3 Parental use of force, prevalence, and incidence, by country

	Mild violence				Serious violence			
	Prevalence rates last year							
Country	%	95% CI		Valid *N*	%	95% CI		Valid *N*
USA	23.9	20.4	27.8	1880	11.2	9.0	13.8	1884
Italy	26.6	24.6	28.6	3305	6.6	5.6	7.7	3407
Belgium	21.4	19.9	22.9	3292	5.1	4.4	5.9	3397
Denmark	3.5	2.7	4.5	1652	0.4	0.2	0.8	1654
	Incidence rates last year							
Country	Incidents	95% CI		Valid *N*	Incidents	95% CI		Valid *N*
USA	5.3	4.2	6.6	450	3.8	2.5	5.9	172
Italy	4.3	3.9	4.7	872	4.6	3.8	5.7	220
Belgium	3.8	3.4	4.3	695	4.0	3.2	4.9	166
Denmark	3.4	2.4	4.9	47	14.6	4.1	52.1	5

Note: Figures are from Enzmann et al. (2018), Tables 4.9 and 4.11 and deviate slightly from sample sizes used in the remainder of our analysis

4.4–5.9). The mean scores for parental violence shown in Table 1 confirm the general picture (USA 0.46; Italy 0.44; Belgium 0.38; Denmark 0.16).

It is difficult to discern any clear pattern when looking at the *incidence* (frequency) of parental use of force over the last year (bottom half of Table 3). This measure is limited to those students who report that their parents used force on them over the last year, and then responded to the follow-up question about how often this has happened. Focusing on the frequency of being punished mildly by their parents, the USA appears to report the highest frequency (5.3 incidents on average for the 450 students who report such experience), and Denmark the lowest frequency (3.4 incidents on average for the 47 students who report such experience), but the confidence intervals of the four countries are overlapping. A similar pattern of overlapping confidence intervals is shown for the more serious forms of parental punishment (but note that there are only five cases in Denmark that report on this variable).

Table 2 provides a slightly different picture because it uses the ordinal level measurement of no-mild-serious parental violence (the measure we use in our multivariate analysis) when calculating the pairwise mean t-tests for parental violence by country. The US sample mean level of reported parental violence is higher (0.08***) than the Belgian sample, slightly higher than Italian sample (0.02 NS), and considerably higher than the Danish sample (0.30***). Comparing mean levels of parental violence between the Belgian and Italian samples shows that the Belgian sample experienced less parental violence than their Italian counterparts (−0.07***), but considerably more than the Danish sample (0.22***). Finally, the Italian sample reported higher levels of parental violence (0.28***) than the Danish.

In sum, it appears that Denmark—without a doubt—has the lowest level of reported use of corporal punishment—both mild and serious—among the four countries. The data suggest further that the use of *serious* corporal punishment may be somewhat more prevalent in the USA than in Belgium or Italy, countries that both show somewhat lower rates of parental maltreatment than the USA (but higher rates than Denmark). However, the differences between the USA, Belgium, and Italy with respect to the *milder* forms of parental use of violence may be statistically negligible. And, of course, as we will discuss in the final section of the chapter, we need to use caution when drawing general conclusions about estimates of victimization between subsamples, because of possible methodological confounds (Enzmann et al. 2018).

7.2 Do Children in the USA, Italy, Belgium, and Denmark Report Comparable Levels of Happiness?

On average, children in the Danish subsample report the highest mean level of happiness (78.12), and the Italian children the lowest level (69.34), with the USA (71.62) and Belgium (71.80) slightly higher (Table 1). Pairwise comparisons of differences in mean happiness (Table 2) suggest that children in the Danish subsample are statistically significant happier than children from the US sample (6.50***), Belgium (6.32***), and Italy (8.78***). US and Belgian children are more happy than Italian children (2.28*** and 2.46***). And there is virtually no difference in mean level of reported happiness between Belgian and US children (−0.18). To further illustrate the country-level differences, we also calculated a ratio happy-to-not-happy measure (Fig. 2 below), which shows very clearly that—proportionally—about twice as many Danish children report that they are either very

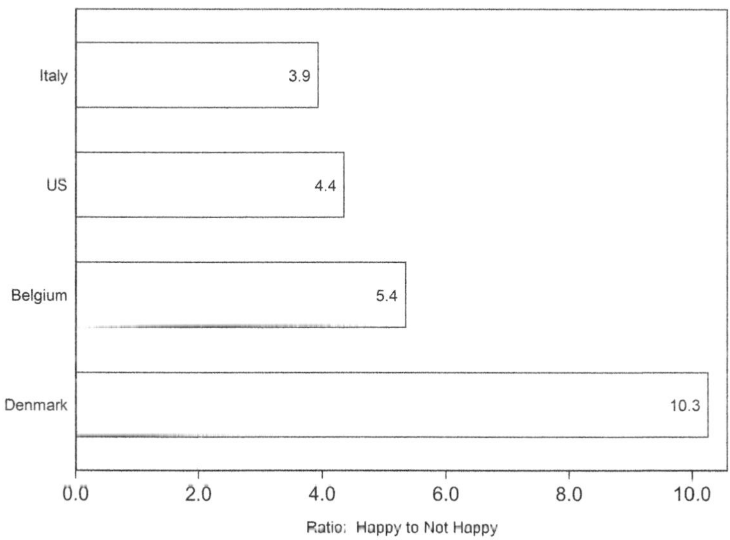

Fig. 2 Ratio of happy-to-not happy respondents by country

happy, pretty happy, more happy than not happy compared to the Belgium sample (10.2 for Danish sample vs. 5.3 for the Belgium sample).

It would be tempting to conclude that the lower level of parental violence in the Danish sample is the reason for the higher level of happiness reported among these children. The plausibility of this interpretation will be tested in the multivariate analysis.

7.3 Do Children in the USA, Italy, Belgium, and Denmark Report Comparable Levels of Family Bonding and Living in a Troubled Family?

Table 1 suggests that the Danish children show the highest level of parental bonding (89.66), followed by the US sample (85.09), Italy (83.69), and Belgium (82.83). Table 2 shows that mean level of family bonding in the Danish sample is significantly higher than the USA (4.56***), Belgium (6.83***), and Italy (5.97***). The mean level of family bonding in the US sample is significantly higher than the Belgian sample (2.27***) and the Italian sample (1.40***). And there is a small, but statistically significant difference in mean level of family bonding between the Belgian and Italian sample (−0.86**).

With regard to living in a troubled family environment, the Danish sample reports statistically significant lower levels of family trouble (0.58) than the US sample (0.79) and the Belgium sample (0.70), but higher than the Italian sample (0.47). The USA and Belgium samples report on average higher levels of family trouble than Italy (mean differences are respectively 0.32*** and 0.23***) and Denmark (0.21*** and 0.12***).

7.4 Bivariate Analysis

Figure 3 is the correlation matrix, which visually shows the relative magnitude of the coefficients. All coefficients are statistically significant, with one important exception: gender and parental violence, which implies a prima facie rejection of the expectation that males will experience higher levels of parental violence than females. There is a correlation between happiness and gender: females report lower levels of happiness than males (r = 0.147***). The highest correlations exist among the three family-related variables: family bonding, living in a troubled family, and exposure to parental violence. Children who report living in a troubled family, tend to report lower bonds with parents and higher exposure to parental violence.

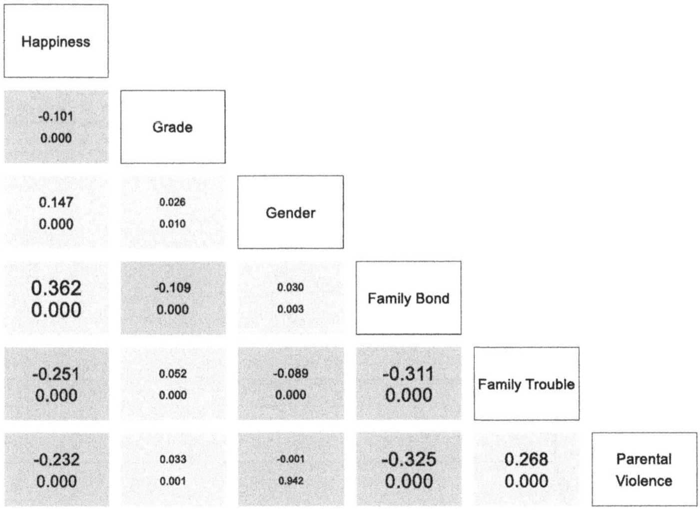

Fig. 3 Correlation matrix of key variables

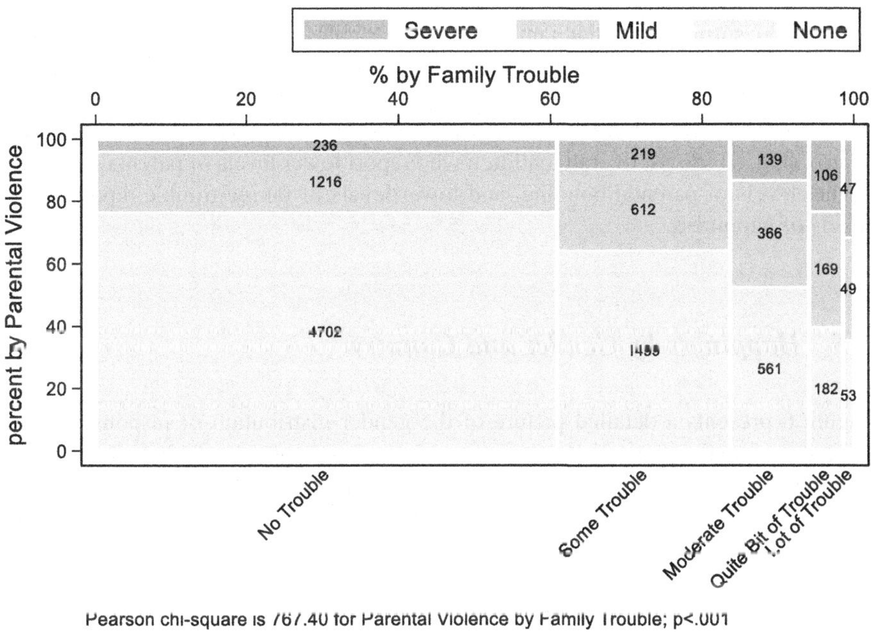

Fig. 4 Cross counts of parental violence and family trouble

Figure 4 is a visual representation of the degree to which children who are on the receiving end of parental physical force also tend to report that they live in a troubled family environment.

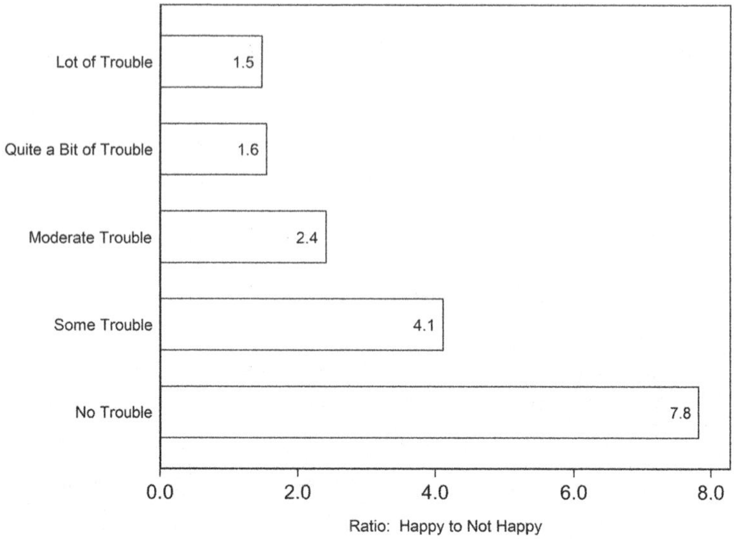

Fig. 5 Ratio of happy-to-not happy respondents to troubled family

Not too surprisingly, the family-related variables all show a correlation with happiness, the main dependent variable. For instance, Fig. 5 shows that for children who report lots of trouble in their family the ratio of happy-to-not-happy (1.5) is much lower than for children who report no family trouble (7.8). As the correlation matrix (Fig. 3) shows, overall, children who report lower levels of parental violence, higher levels of parental bonding, and lower levels of family trouble report higher levels of happiness.

7.5 Happiness by Gender and Country

Figure 6 presents a detailed picture of the gender distribution of responses to the happiness question (very unhappy, unhappy, more unhappy than happy, more happy than unhappy, happy, very happy) by country. This picture shows how, on average, girls are less happy than males in our sample; the Danish sample overall is most happy, with the USA, Italy, and Belgium showing higher levels of unhappiness.

7.6 Multivariate Analysis

We conduct multivariate analysis to test the conceptual model represented in Fig. 1. For current purposes, we have limited the variables included in our models, to three family-related variables (*parental violence*, family trouble, family bonding),

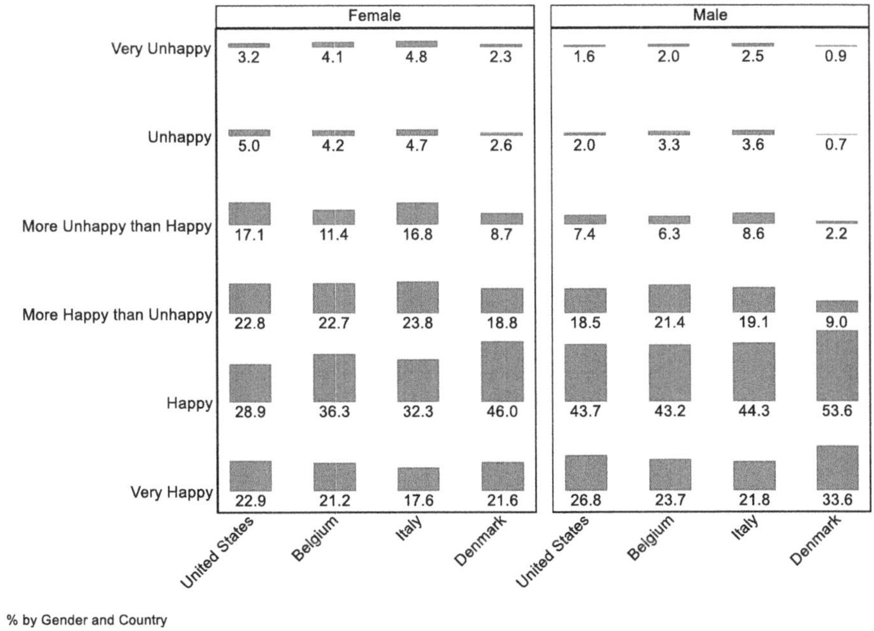

Fig. 6 Percentages of happiness levels by gender and country

national context (Belgium, Denmark, Italy, and USA), and *gender* [Grade is included as a control variable]. Our analysis includes selected interaction terms for respectively gender and parental violence, and national context and parental violence.

Step 1 As a first step, we ran a model including the family-related variables (parental violence, family trouble, family bonding), gender, country, as well as three interaction terms between country and parental violence (using the USA as the reference category), and interaction term gender-parental violence (Table 4).

The strongest predictor of happiness is family bonding (0.271***), which has about twice the effect of living in a troubled family (−0.131***) or parental violence (−0.129***). Not surprisingly, we see that significant effects of gender (0.10***) and the interaction term gender-parental violence (0.073***) on reported happiness. The effects of national context are considerably less strong. Living in Belgium has no effect (compared to the USA), living in Italy (−0.046) significantly reduces happiness, and living in Denmark increases happiness (0.047). However, none of the country-parental violence interaction terms are significant. The model explains 19% of the variance in reported happiness.

Step 2 To further explore the possibility that parental violence may have a different effect on girls' happiness compared to males, as suggested by interaction term

Table 4 Regression model including family-related variables, national context, and interaction terms

Grade in school	−0.063***
Family bond	0.271***
Family trouble	−0.131***
Parental violence	−0.129***
Gender	0.102***
*Gender * Parental Violence*	0.073***
Belgium	0.009
*Belgium * Parental Violence*	0.001
Italy	−0.046**
*Italy * Parental Violence*	−0.025
Denmark	0.047***
*Denmark * Parental Violence*	−0.007
Observations	10,216
R^2	0.191
R^2 adj	0.190
F Value	200.741
F-prob	0.000
AIC	91,944.769
BIC	92,038.781

Note: Standardized beta coefficients
The USA is the reference category for the country variables
* $p < 0.05$, ** $p < 0.01$, *** $p < 0.001$

gender-parental violence (Table 4) (0.073***) we constructed the interaction graph for gender with parental violence (Fig. 7).[9]

The graph shows support for the noted interaction effect of gender and parental violence for females. The axis for the boys is nearly parallel with the x-axis, but for girls, as you move from none to mild to severe, there is a clear dropoff of mean happiness predictions. The effect of parental violence (on happiness) is strongest for girls whose parents treat them severely. At all levels of parental violence, boys and girls have different predicted happiness.

Step 3 The noted interaction between gender and parental violence provides only a partial answer to the larger question of whether the association between use of violence by parents, troubled family life, attachment to parents, and subjective wellbeing (happiness) is *different for girls than for boys? And does national context makes a difference?* To answer that question, we ran the models separately for boys

[9]The interaction graph presents the mean predicted scores at the three levels of parental violence and for the boys and the girls resulting from a regression. We plug in the parental violence (1, 2, or 3) and the gender values (1 or 0) to get the predicted happiness value. For example, you "select" the cases of 1 in for the male variable and 2-say-for parental violence and calculate the mean predictions of those cases; then the same thing for the next: 0 for the male variable and 2 for the parental violence and calculate the mean predictions of those cases, and so on for the other four situations. The six points in the graph are the means of those predictions.

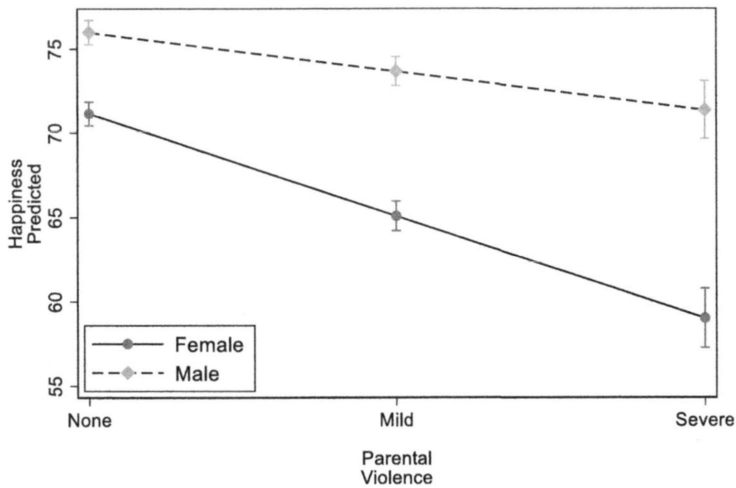

Fig. 7 Interaction graph with gender and parental violence

Table 5 Happiness models separately by gender

	Male	Female
Grade in school	−0.055***	−0.073***
Family bond	0.232***	0.310***
Family trouble	−0.128***	−0.130***
Parental violence	−0.081**	−0.085***
Belgium	−0.038	0.045*
*Belgium * Parental Violence*	0.024	−0.017
Italy	−0.081***	−0.022
*Italy * Parental Violence*	0.005	−0.047*
Denmark	0.065***	0.030
*Denmark * Parental Violence*	0.006	−0.014
Observations	5093	5123
R^2	0.129	0.213
R^2 adj	0.127	0.211
F Value	75.096	138.269
F-prob	0.000	0.000
AIC	45,252.554	46,600.768
BIC	45,324.445	46,672.725

Note: Standardized beta coefficients
The USA is the reference category for the country variables
* $p < 0.05$, ** $p < 0.01$, *** $p < 0.001$

and girls (Table 5). Table 6 presents the pairwise gender model comparisons of the statistical significance of differences in the standardized coefficients.

The higher R^2 for the female model (0.211) compared to the male model (0.127) suggests that this particular collection of variables in the female model is better than

Table 6 Pairwise gender model comparisons

	Male-Female	
	Z-score	prob
Grade in School	0.4644	0.6424
Family Bond	-0.0041	0.9967
Family Trouble	0.0339	0.9729
Parental Violence	0.8696	0.3845
Belgium	-6.1717	0.0000
*Belgium * Parental Violence*	4.6639	0.0000
Italy	-3.6856	0.0002
*Italy * Parental Violence*	5.8460	0.0000
Denmark	3.1066	0.0019
*Denmark * Parental Violence*	8.1312	0.0000
Constant	65.4021	0.0000

in the male model. The comparison of z-scores (Table 6) further shows that the male-female differences for the family-related variables are not significant, but that the country and country-parental violence interactions *are* all significantly different for boys and girls.

Looking at the male model, we find support for the hypothesized relationships between happiness and family bonding(0.232***), family trouble (−0.128***), and parental violence (−0.081**). The effect of parental bonding is twice as high as that of living in a troubled family; the effect of experiencing parental violence (controlling for the other variables) is one-third that of parental bonding. For the males, national context has an independent effect on level of happiness: using the USA as the reference category, living in Italy (compared to living in the USA) significantly reduces reported happiness (−0.081***), and living in Denmark (rather than living in the USA) significantly increases the level of reported happiness (0.065***). The three country/parental violence interaction terms are not significant for the boys. The explanatory power of the model is modest (R^2 0.12).

The results for the female model are comparable to the male model with regard to the family-related variables. There is support for the hypothesized relationships between happiness and family bonding(0.310***), family trouble (−0.130***), and parental violence (−0.085**). From among the three family-related variables, parental violence (−0.85***) has relatively the smallest efffect. For the Belgian females, national context has an independent effect on happiness: using the USA as reference category, for girls, living in Belgium (rather than the USA) slighly increases reported happiness (0.045*), no significant effect was found for the Italian or Danish girls. The explanatory power of the model (R^2 0.21) is greater for the females than the males. For the females, the interaction term Italy*parental violence (−0.047*) suggest that girls who experience parental violence and live in Italy are less happy than girls experiencing parental violence in the USA (holding the other variables constant).

Table 7 Happiness models separately by country

	Belgium	Italy	Denmark	USA
Grade in school	−0.085***	−0.073	−0.025	−0.043*
Family bond	0.253***	0.252***	0.296***	0.301***
Family trouble	−0.156***	−0.106***	−0.086***	−0.150***
Parental violence	−0.145***	−0.181***	−0.134***	−0.103***
Gender	0.052**	0.086***	0.200***	0.129***
*Gender * Parental Violence*	0.092***	0.099***	0.072*	0.035
Observations	3155	3278	1577	2206
R^2	0.176	0.167	0.195	0.210
R^2 adj	0.175	0.166	0.192	0.208
F Value	112.206	109.368	63.252	97.390
F-prob	0.000	0.000	0.000	0.000
AIC	28,460.467	29,848.265	13,660.248	19,866.125
BIC	28,502.864	29,890.930	13,697.791	19,906.017

Note: Standardized beta coefficients
* $p < 0.05$, ** $p < 0.01$, *** $p < 0.001$

Thus, in the third step of the multivariate analysis we find that—although the coefficients of family-related variables (including parental violence) are somewhat lower for boys than for girls—these gender differences are not statistically significant. However, the effect of national context (on happiness) does appear to show significant differences between boys and girls. We will explore this further in the next steps.

Step 4 We saw in step 3 of our multivariate analysis that national context (although showing fairly modest coefficients) does have an impact on happiness, and that the effect of country (and its interaction with parental violence) differs between boys and girls. To further explore the importance of national context, Table 7 shows regression results for Belgium, Italy, Denmark, and the USA. We present the results for Belgium, Italy, Denmark, and the USA separately, to see if the association between the family-related variables, gender and interaction gender-parental violence differs among national contexts. We present the standardized beta coefficients. Table 8 presents pair-wise country comparisons of differences in z-scores.

First, looking at the Belgian model, we find support for the hypothesized relationships between happiness and family bonding (0.253***), family trouble (−0.156***), and parental violence (−0.145**). The effect of parental bonding is about 1.6 times higher than that of living in a troubled family and 1.7 times higher than experiencing parental violence. The effect of gender (0.052**) on happiness is as expected: boys are happier than girls, holding other variables constant. In the Belgian sample, the effect of experiencing parental violence on happiness is related to gender (0.092***). The explanatory power of the model is modest (R^2 0.17).

Examination of the models for Italy, Denmark, and the USA provides largely comparable results to the Belgian model. All coefficients are significant (in the expected direction), with the exception of grade in school for Denmark, and

Table 8 Pairwise country comparisons

	Belgium-Italy		Belgium-Denmark		Belgium-US		Italy-Denmark		Italy-US		Denmark-US	
	Z	prob	Z	prob	Z	prob	Z	prob	Z	prob	Z	prob
Grade in School	-0.1920	0.8478	-1.3851	0.1660	-0.8983	0.3690	-1.1898	0.2341	-0.6957	0.4866	0.5394	0.5896
Family Bond	-0.0017	0.9986	-0.0050	0.9960	-0.0034	0.9973	-0.0030	0.9976	-0.0017	0.9987	0.0012	0.9991
Family Trouble	-0.2901	0.7718	-1.2200	0.2225	-0.1758	0.8604	-1.0071	0.3139	0.1095	0.9128	1.0782	0.2809
Parental Violence	1.8643	0.0623	1.2905	0.1969	-2.7222	0.0065	-1.1994	0.2304	-4.5995	0.0000	-4.8949	0.0000
Gender	-2.4545	0.0141	-7.6616	0.0000	-5.6146	0.0000	-5.3519	0.0000	-3.0290	0.0025	2.7337	0.0063
*Gender*Par Violence*	-0.3610	0.7181	-1.1142	0.2652	5.6846	0.0000	-0.5961	0.5511	6.0248	0.0000	9.0406	0.0000
Constant	70.4441	0.0000	193.8407	0.0000	140.9774	0.0000	119.4809	0.0000	69.0272	0.0000	-49.1589	0.0000

Note: Highlighted cells are p<.05.

interaction gender*parental violence for the US model. The four models do differ in explanatory power (R^2): Belgium (0.17), Italy (0.16), Denmark (0.19), and the USA (0.21).

The pairwise country model comparisons show that the country differences between the impact of family trouble and family bond on happiness are statistically not significant. However, the effect of parental violence (on happiness)—while not statistically significant when comparing Belgium, Italy and Denmark—is statistically significant when comparing the USA with respectively Belgium, Denmark, and Italy. This is also the case with regard to the interaction parental violence*gender for the USA. On the other hand, the noted impact of gender (on happiness) does appear to significantly differ among and between all four countries: Belgium (0.052**), Italy (0.086***), USA (0.129***), and Denmark (0.200***).

Step 5 Although our full regression model (Table 3) did not show a significant coefficient for the country*parental violence interaction terms, our research question—focusing on the effect of parental violence on happiness, and the role of gender and national context—as well as our findings thusfar, require further exploration of this issue. Therefore, we created separate interaction graphs for parental violence, happiness, and country—for boys and girls (Fig. 8—for boys; Fig. 9—for girls); and for parental violence, happiness, and gender—for US (Fig. 10), Belgium (Fig. 11), Italy (Fig. 12) and Denmark (Fig. 13).

7.7 *Interaction Parental Violence, Happiness, Country: For Boys and Girls*

Comparing the slopes in Fig. 8, it appears that the slopes for the impact of physical violence on reported happiness for the USA, Italian and Danish boys are roughly

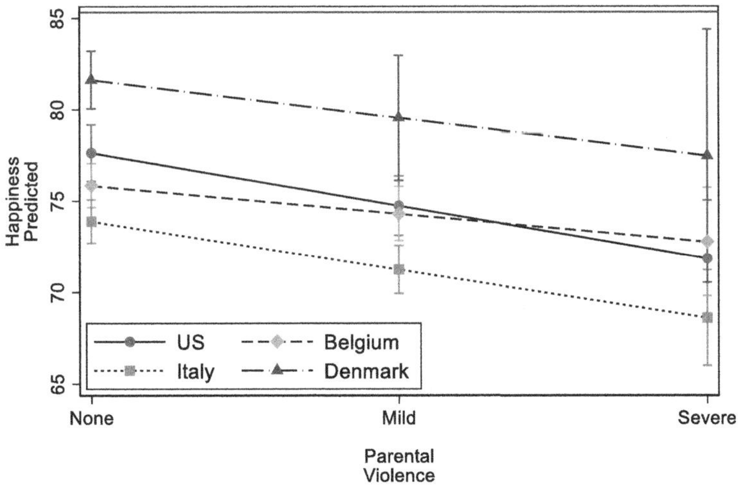

Fig. 8 Interaction graph country, parental violence and happiness—boys

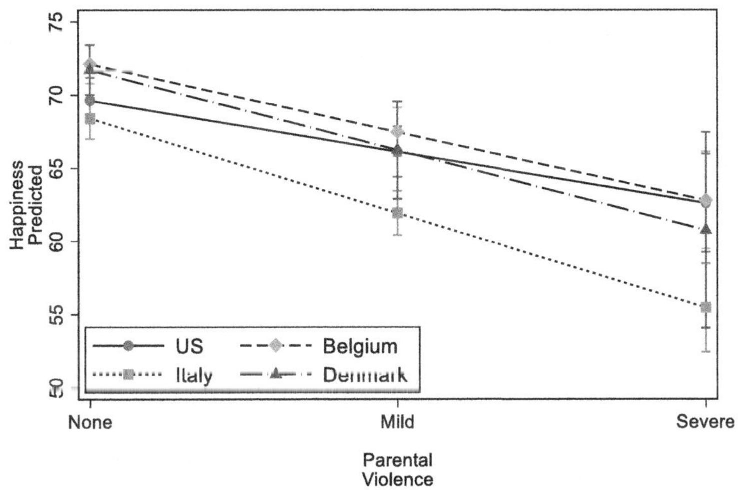

Fig. 9 Interaction graph country, parental violence and happiness—girls

comparable (albeit that the levels of reported happiness differ), but not so for the Belgium boys, whose slope is almost parallel to the x-axis. The impact of country on the effect of parental violence on reported happiness is different for girls (Fig. 9). Among the girls, it is the US context that appears to be irrelevant, whereas the effect of parental violence on reported happiness appears to be comparable among Belgian, Italian and Danish girls.

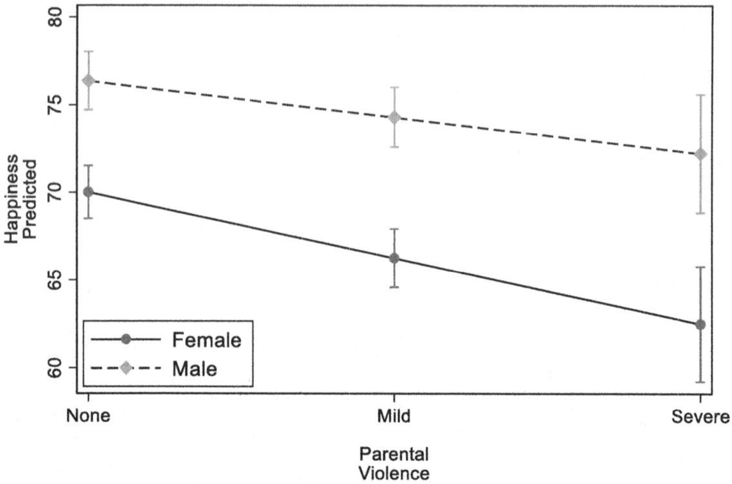

Fig. 10 Interaction parental violence, happiness, gender—USA

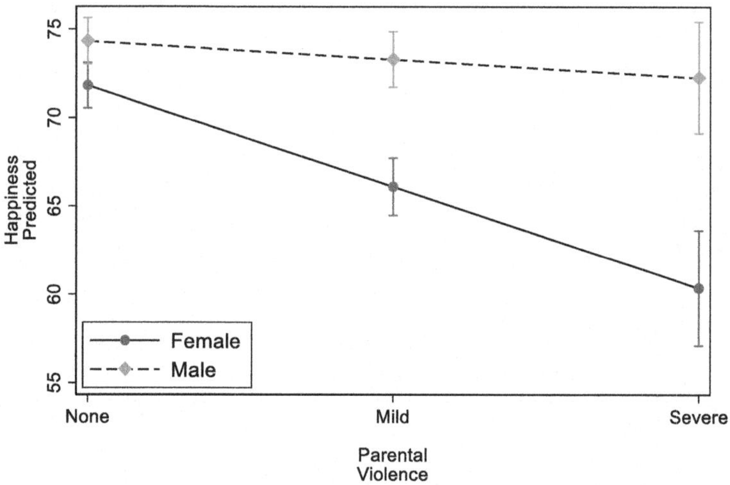

Fig. 11 Interaction parental violence, happiness, gender—Belgium

7.8 Interaction Parental Violence, Happiness, Gender: By National Context

For the US sample, the graph (Fig. 10) shows a slight divergence of slopes, suggesting that the impact of parental violence on happiness is somewhat stronger for girls than for boys. A more marked difference is noted for Belgian girls (Fig. 11), where the impact of parental violence on happiness increases by levels of severity, which is not the case for Belgian boys. The picture (Fig. 12) for the Italian sample is

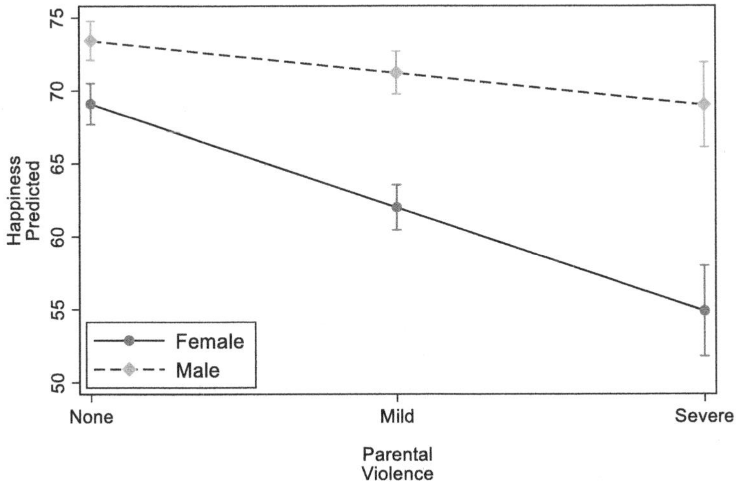

Fig. 12 Interaction parental violence, happiness, gender—Italy

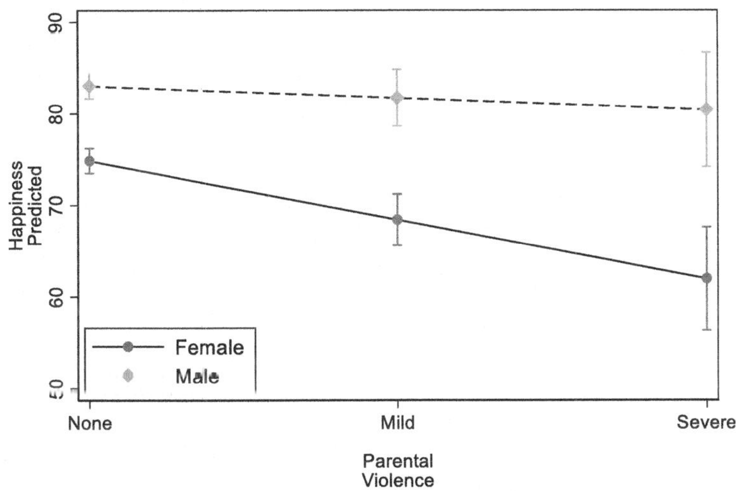

Fig. 13 Interaction parental violence, happiness, gender—Denmark

comparable to the Belgian sample: Italian girls' happiness is more seriously impacted by parental violence than Italian boys' sense of wellbeing. This is also true for the Danish sample (Fig. 13). Thus, here we conclude that (except perhaps for the USA), the effect of parental violence is more pronounced for girls than for boys.

8 Summary

It is not easy to provide a simple summary of our findings, but a number of patterns appear to emerge. First, there is no doubt that Denmark—the country with the most stringent laws banning corporal punishment of children—has the lowest levels of parental use of violence (Tables 1 and 3). The USA, Italy, and Belgium share a lower level of legal prohibitions against corporal punishment, and these countries do report higher levels of corporal punishment of children, with some evidence suggesting the US reporting a somewhat higher level of serious parental violence compared to Italy and Belgium. Second, the findings suggest that there are no clear gender differences in being the victim of the *use* of parental violence, consistent with the bulk of existing research evidence (Fig. 3). Third, our data do suggest that there may be gender differences in the *impact of physical punishment on happiness* (Tables 4 and 6). With the possible exception of the US sample, girls' happiness is much more impacted by the experience of parental violence (in particular the more serious forms) than the happiness of boys (Figs. 3, 7, 11, 12, 13, and Tables 6 and 7).[10] Fourth, although the explanatory power of the model for girls is significantly higher than for boys, there still appears to be a relatively comparable impact of the three family-related variables (i.e., family bonding has the strongest effect on both boys' and girls' happiness, followed by living in a troubled family, with parental violence showing the relatively most modest effect on happiness among both boys and girls) (Table 5 and 6).[11] Fifth, national context (although showing smaller coefficients than the family-related variables) does have an impact on happiness, and the effect of country (and its interaction with parental violence) differs between boys and girls (Tables 5 and 7, Figs. 7, 8, 9, 10, 11, 12 and 13). The impact of gender (on happiness) does appear to significantly differ among and between all four countries: Boys are significantly more happy than girls in Belgium (0.052**), Italy (0.086***), USA (0.129***), and Denmark (0.200***) (Tables 7 and 8).

The USA appears to be a somewhat deviant case. That is, the effect of parental violence as well as the interaction parental violence*gender—while not statistically significant when comparing Belgium, Italy and Denmark—is significantly different when comparing the USA with respectively Belgium, Denmark, and Italy. In Denmark, Belgium, and Italy, the effect of parental violence on happiness is more pronounced for girls than for boys—and this does not seem to be so clearly the case for the USA.

[10]Please note that the interaction graphs do not include the larger number of variables of the OLS models. However, the beta coefficient of 0.73*** for the interaction parental violence*gender in the full model (Table 4) provides additional evidence for the differential gender impact of parental violence on happiness.

[11]It should be noted that the interpretation of the magnitude of the effect of parental violence needs to be approached with caution, since the OLS models do include interaction terms involving parental violence. In the view of some, the interpretation of lower order terms in the presence of an interaction term is complex and is generally avoided (Braumoeller 2004).

Denmark is the country with undisputably the lowest level of reported parental violence, (and the strictest legislation banning corporal punishment) among the four countries, and yet, we find roughly comparable effects of parental violence, troubled family and family bonds on reported level of happiness among the four countries. This finding challenges the notion that the harmful effects of corporal punishment are more pronounced in contexts where such behavior is more universally condemned.

9 Concluding Comments

The data draw from the International Self-Report Delinquency study (ISRD3), a large collaborative international study using standardized research design (sampling, questionnaires, data entry). The findings reported here may be biased, reflecting the multitude of methodological challenges facing comparative survey research among young people (Enzmann et al. 2018). We have to be particularly cautious when comparing estimates of offending and victimization across countries (Enzmann et al. 2018; Marshall and Enzmann 2012). Yet, the findings are robust enough to suggest that our conceptual model is supported across genders and countries: living in a troubled family, low family bonds, and experiencing parental violence tend to decrease reported levels of happiness in boys and girls, in Italy, Belgium, the USA and Denmark. However, there remain country- and gender-based differences in the interrelationship between parental violence and happiness that warrant continued further exploration, moving beyond comparing only four western prosperous countries.

Admittedly, the model of the link between physical violence and happiness used in this chapter is overly simplistic. Although quality of family life is very important for most children, their happiness depends on many factors unrelated to family (see, for example, the World Happiness Report https://worldhappiness.report/ed/2019/). Yet, the current study adds to the mounting and irrefutable evidence that parents who hit, slap or beat their children are likely to have less happy children than their counterparts who refrain from using physical violence. Our data show that parental use of force is still not uncommon, even in prosperous western countries. Encouraging is the evidence that prohibition of corporal punishment of children may eventually change the culture as well as the behavior (e.g., Denmark). On the other hand, legal prohibition is a tool that probably will have little immediate effect in countries that are steeped in a culture of violence, such as the USA.[12] Considering

[12]Considering that the USA is known as an exceptionally violent country (compared to most European countries) with a high level of gun-related violence including mass shootings, suicides, and gang-related violence), it is actually surprising that the level of parental violence in the current study was only marginally higher in the US sample than in the other three samples. This likely reflects the composition of the sample and the method of data collection (school-based self-report surveys).

that the data show that in prosperous western countries like Belgium, Italy, the USA, and even Denmark children are still being hit, slapped, and beaten by their caretakers, we have to conclude that we are still far removed from the universal implementation of Article 19 of the Convention on the Rights of the Child in countries across the globe.

We have a little over a decade (until 2030) to work towards target 16.2 (to end abuse and violence against children) of 2030 UN Sustainable Development Goal 16. Cultural change tends to happen at a glacial pace, and 10 years is over in a blink of an eye. The Thirteenth United Nations Congress on Crime Prevention and Criminal Justice (United Nations 2015) emphasized that education for all children and youth, including the eradication of illiteracy, is fundamental to the prevention of crime and corruption and to the promotion of a culture of lawfulness that supports the rule of law and human rights while respecting cultural identities (para. 7, A/RES/70/174). What about a culture of lawfulness educating parents?

We are inspired and encouraged by the commendable work of the Global Initiative to End all Corporal Punishment of Children. It is through such efforts that we can hope to achieve the global diffusion of norms protecting the physical and mental wellbeing of our children in the future, if not by 2030.

References

Afifi, T. O., Brownridge, D. A., Cox, B. J., & Sareen, J. (2006). Physical punishment, childhood abuse and psychiatric disorders. *Child Abuse and Neglect, 30*(10), 1093–1103.

Braumoeller, B. (2004). Hypothesis testing and multiplicative interaction terms. *International Organization, 58*(4), 807–820.

Cohen, P., Cohen, J., Aiken, L. S., & West, S. G. (1999). The problem of units and the circumstance for POMP. *Multivariate Behavioral Research, 34*, 315–346.

Diener, E., Oishi, S., & Ryan, K. (2013). Universal and cultural differences in the causes and structure of "happiness" – A multilevel review. In C. Keyes (Ed.), *Mental well-being: International contributions to the study of positive mental healths* (pp. 153–176). Dordrecht: Springer.

Endendijk, J. J., Groeneveld, M. G., Bakermans-Kranenburg, M. J., & Mesman, J. (2016). Gender-differentiated parenting revisited: Meta-analysis reveals very few differences in parental control of boys and girls. *PloS one, 11*(7), e0159193. https://doi.org/10.1371/journal.pone.0159193

Enzmann, D., Kivivuori, J., Marshall, I. H., Steketee, M., Hough, M., & Killias, M. (2018). *A global perspective on young people as offenders and victims: First results from the ISRD3 Study*. New York: Springer.

Finkelhor, D., Turner, H., Ormrod, R., Hamby, S., & Kracke, K. (2019). Children's exposure to violence: A comprehensive Natiopnal survey. *Juvenile Justice Bulletin, October 2009.*

Gershoff, E. T. (2010). More harm than good: A summary of scientific research on the intended and unintended effects of corporal punishment on children. *Law and Contemporary Problems, 73*, 31.

Gershoff, E. T. (2018). Corporal punishment associated with dating violence. *Journal of Pediatrics, 198*, 322–325.

Gershoff, E. T., & Font, S. A. (2016). Corporal punishment in US public schools: Prevalence, disparities in use, and status in state and federal policy. *Social Policy Report, 30*, 1–26.

Global Initiative to End All Corporal Punishment of Children. (2015). *Prohibiting and eliminating violent punishment of girls: A key element in guaranteeing the health and safety of women and girls worldwide*. London: Global Initiative to End All Coprporal Punishment of Children.
Global Initiative to End All Corporal Punishment of Children. (2017). *Corporal punishment of children in Denmark*. London: Global Initiative to End All Corporal Punishment of Children.
Global Initiative to End All Corporal Punishment of Children. (2019a). *Corporal punishment of children in Belgium*. London: Global Initiative to End All Corporal Punishment of Children.
Global Initiative to End All Corporal Punishment of Children. (2019b). *Corporal punishment of children in Italy*. London: Global Initiative to End All Corporal Punishment of Children.
Global Initiative to End All Corporal Punishment of Children. (2019c). *Global Report 2018: Progress towards ending corporal punishment of children*. London: Global Initiative to End All Corporal Punishment of Children.
Hagan, J., Schoenfeld, H., & Palloni, A. (2006). The science of human rights, war crimes, and humanitarian emergencies. *Annual Review of Sociology, 32*(1), 329–349. https://doi.org/10.1146/annurev.soc.32.061604.123125
Hofmann, W., Luhmann, M., Fisher, R. R., Vohs, K. D., & Baumeister, R. F. (2013). Yes, but are they happy? Effects of trait self-control on affective well-being and life satisfaction. *Journal of Personality and Social Psychology, 82*, 265–277.
Holder, M. D. (2012). *Happiness in children. Measurement, correlates and enhancement of positive subjective well-being*. New York: Springer.
Ipsos Public Affairs. (2012). *I metodi educative e il ricorso a punizioni fisiche*. Paris: Ipsos Public Affairs.
Karstedt, S. (2012). Mass Atrocities. *Annual Review of Law and Social Science*. https://doi.org/10.1146/annurev-lawsocsci-102612-134016
Keyes, K., Leray, E., Pez, O., Bitfoi, A., Koç, C., Goelitz, D., et al. (2015). Parental use of corporal punishment in Europe: Intersection between public health and policy. *PloS one, 10*(2), e0118059.
Lansford, J. E., Alampay, L. P., Al-Hassan, S., Bacchini, D., Bombi, A. S., Bornstein, M. H., et al. (2010). Corporal punishment of children in nine countries as a function of child gender and parent gender. *International Journal of Pediatrics, 2010*, 1–12.
Lansford, J. E., Sharma, C., Malone, P. S., Woodlief, D., Dodge, K. A., Oburu, P., et al. (2014). Corporal punishment, maternal warmth, and child adjustment: A longitudinal study in eight countries. *Journal of Clinical Child Adolescent Psychology, 43*(4), 670–685.
Marshall, I. H., & Enzmann, D. (2012). Methodology and design of the ISRD-2 study. In J. Junger-Tas, I. H. Marshall, D. Enzmann, M. Killias, M. Steketee, & B. Gruszczynska (Eds.), *The many faces of youth crime. Contrasting theoretical perspectives on Juvenile Delinquency across Countries and cultures* (pp. 21–65). New York: Springer.
Paternoster, R., Brame, R., Mazerolle, P., & Piquero, A. (1998). Using the correct statistical test for the equality of regression coefficients. *Criminology, 36*(4), 859–866.
Romney, A. K., Weller, S. C., & Batchelder, W. H. (1986). Culture as consensus: A theory of culture and informant accuracy. *American Anthropologist, 88*(2), 313–338.
Sachs, J. (2012). Introduction. In J. Helliwell, R. Layard, & J. Sachs (Eds.), *World happiness report*. New York: Sustainable Development Solutions Network.
Savelsberg, J. (2010). *Crime and human rights: Criminology of genocide and atrocities*. Thousand Oaks: Sage.
Steketee, M., Aussems, C., & Marshall, I. (2019). Exploring the impact of child maltreatment and interparental violence on violent delinquency in an international sample. *Journal of Interpersonal Violence*, 088626051882329-undefined. https://doi.org/10.1177/0886260518823291
Tankebe, J., & Liebling, A. (2013). *Legitimacy and criminal justice: An international exploration*. Oxford: Oxford University Press.
U.S. Census Bureau. (2019). *Quick facts Massachusetts* (2019 ed.). Washington, DC: U.S. Census Bureau

UNICEF. (2011). Nordic study on child rights to participate 2009–2010. *UNICEF: Innolink Research.*

United Nations. (2013). Happiness: towards a holistic approach to development. Note by the Secretary-General. (Vol. A/67/697).

United Nations. (2015). Resolution adopted by the General Assembly on 17 December 2015. Doha declaration on integrating crime prevention and criminal justice into the wider United Nations agenda to address social and economic challenges and to promote the rule of law at the national and international levels, and public participation A/RES/70/74.

United Nations Children's Fund. (2014). *Hidden in plain sight: A statistical analysis of violence against children*. New York: eSocialSciences.

Wexler, A. (2018). *Don't worry, be happy! The importance of furthering the study of happiness in the field of criminal justice*. Boston: Northeastern University.

Widom, C. S., & Wilson, H. W. (2015). Intergenerational transmission of violence. In *Violence and mental health* (pp. 27–45). New York: Springer.

World Health Organization (WHO). (1946). *Constitution of the World Health Organization. Basic documents*. Geneva: World Health Organization.

World Population Review. (2019). *Colorado Population*. http://worldpopulationreview.com/states/colorado/.

Ineke Haen Marshall is Professor of Sociology, Criminology and Criminal Justice at North Eastern University in Boston. She received her MA in Sociology from Tilburg University, the Netherlands and her PhD in Sociology from Bowling Green State University (USA). She has published in the areas of comparative criminology, drug policy, criminal careers, minorities and crime, and cross-national methodology. She is the chair of the International Self-Report Delinquency Study (ISRD) and co-author of *A Global Perspective on Young People as Offenders and Victims* (Springer, 2018). E-mail: i.marshall@neu.edu.

Candence Wills M.I.D. is currently completing her doctorate in Criminology and Justice Policy at Northeastern University in the School of Criminology and Criminal Justice (Boston, Mass. USA). She earned a Bachelor of Arts from the University of Pittsburgh and a Master of International Development from Graduate School of Public and International Affairs at the University of Pittsburgh. She focuses her research on both global and domestic institutional responses to victimization, human trafficking, and marginalized populations. Recently, she was awarded a research fellowship to serve at the United Nations Office of Drug and Crime (UNODC) in Vienna, Austria to work on the bi-annual UNODC Global Trafficking in Human Report. E-mail: wills.c@husky.neu.edu; c.wills@northeastern.edu.

Chris E. Marshall is Associate Professor in the School of Criminology and Criminal Justice at the University of Nebraska-Omaha (USA). He received his PhD in Sociology from Iowa State University (USA), and throughout his career, his main areas of interest have been theory construction, juvenile delinquency and quantitative methods. His work on comparative criminology and cross-national methodology, including sophisticated analyses of data from the International-Self Report Delinquency Study (ISRD), has been published in US and international peer-reviewed publications. E-mail: cmarshall@unomaha.edu.

The UN Global Study on Children Deprived of Liberty: The Role of Academia in 'Making the Invisible and Forgotten Visible'

Manfred Nowak and Manu Krishan

Abstract This chapter summarises the detailed findings of the United Nations Global Study on Children Deprived of Liberty and exemplifies the significant leading role of academia in 'making the invisible and forgotten visible' throughout the world. The main objectives of the study were to assess, based on scientific data, the magnitude of the global number of children deprived of liberty in six different situations, including in institutions, for migration related reasons and in the context of the administration of criminal justice. Another goal was to comprehend the root causes and pathways leading to deprivation of liberty as well as to gather best practices of states that have applied non-custodial solutions. The Study also addressed the conditions of detention by considering the personal views and experiences of children and it assessed justifications for and limits of deprivation of liberty of children in light of all relevant provisions of international law, above all the Convention on the Rights of the Child (CRC). Although the Global Study was prepared through a concerted effort of states, non-governmental organisations, professional bodies, UN agencies, treaty bodies, special procedures and children, each research group was led by a research institute and close collaboration with academia. The study exemplified how the close cooperation between the United Nations, civil society and academia is needed more than ever and it confirmed the spirit of the famous opening words of the UN Charter, namely that "the Peoples of the United Nations", which founded the world organisation 75 years ago.

Keywords Children · Deprived · Liberty · Detention · Institutions · Migration · Juvenile · Justice · Security · Conflict · Non-custodial

M. Nowak
Global Campus of Human Rights, Venice, Italy

Vienna University, Vienna, Austria
e-mail: manfrad.nowak@gchumanrights.org

M. Krishan (✉)
Global Campus of Human Rights, Venice, Italy
e-mail: manu.krishan@gchumanrights.org

H. Kury, S. Redo (eds.), *Crime Prevention and Justice in 2030*,
https://doi.org/10.1007/978-3-030-56227-4_11

1 Background

The emergent recognition of the injustices of children's situation, prompted by greater knowledge and understanding of the developmental needs of children, led to a pathway in the twentieth century realising the need to establish and recognise the rights of the child within international law. In 1924, the League of Nations adopted the Geneva Declaration on the Rights of the Child. The Declaration articulates that all people owe children the right to: means for their development; special help in times of need; priority for relief; economic freedom and protection from exploitation; and an upbringing that instils social consciousness and duty. In 1946, the United Nations established the International Children's Emergency Fund, UNICEF, with an emphasis of improving the lives of millions of children around the world. This followed by the adoption of the Declaration of the Rights of the Child in 1959 (A/RES/1386(XIV)), which recognises, among other rights, children's right to play, education, a supportive environment and healthcare. In 1966, with the International Covenants on Civil and Political Rights and on Economic, Social and Cultural Rights, Member States promise to uphold equal rights—including education and protection—for all children (ICCPR and ICESCR). In 1989, the Convention on the Rights of the Child was adopted by the United Nations General Assembly and widely acclaimed as a landmark achievement for human rights, recognising the roles of children as social, economic, political, civil and cultural actors. Children are no longer viewed primarily as vulnerable individuals in need of protection, but as independent rights-holders. In particular, they have the right not to be discriminated against and to participate in all matters directly affecting them (CRC, Art. 2, Art. 12). In all actions concerning children, Article 3 requires that "the best interests of the child shall be a primary consideration". The Convention recognises that children "should grow up in a family environment, in an atmosphere of happiness, love and understanding", and that children shall only in exceptional circumstances be separated from their parents against their will (CRC, preamble, Art. 9). In principle, children shall enjoy the same rights as adults, but in certain contexts, the Convention provides higher standards for children. This applies, in particular, to the administration of criminal justice in Article 40 and to the rights to personal liberty and dignity in Article 37.

In 2000, the United Nations General Assembly adopted two Optional Protocols to the Convention (A/RES/54/263 and A/RES/54/263), obligating State Parties to take key actions to prevent children from partaking in hostilities during armed conflict and to end the sale, sexual exploitation and abuse of children. A third Optional Protocol on a communications procedure where the Committee on the Rights of the Child can receive complaints of child rights violations and undertake investigations was adopted in 2011 (A/HRC/RES/17/18). In 2019, the Convention celebrated its 30th anniversary as the most widely ratified international instrument with 196 States Parties. It is evident that international standards on child rights have advanced dramatically over the past century and despite the improvements that have occurred, states and the international community still have to do a great deal more to meet and ensure these ideals.

One of the most overlooked violations of children's rights which leads to enormous injustices and suffering of children throughout the world concerns their deprivation of liberty (OPCAT, Art. 4(2) and Res 45/113, Art. 11(b)). Children deprived of liberty remain an invisible and forgotten group in society notwithstanding the increasing evidence of these children being in fact victims of many further human rights violations. Childhood is when children develop their personality, their emotional relationships with others, their social and educational skills and their talents. The personal cost to these children is immeasurable in terms of the destructive impact on their physical and mental development, and on their ability to lead healthy and constructive lives in society. Many children may find themselves in a vicious cycle of different situations of deprivation of liberty throughout their childhood, which might start in an 'orphanage', followed by various institutions for educational supervision and drug rehabilitation until culminating in imprisonment and re offending. Deprivation of liberty means deprivation of rights, agency, visibility, opportunities and love. Depriving children of their liberty is depriving them of their childhood.

More than seven million children worldwide are in fact deprived of liberty per year (Nowak 2019). They are detained in settings such as prisons, pre-trial detention centres, police custody, migration detention centres and institutions of all kinds, including institutions for children with disabilities. Still a conservative estimate, this figure stands in direct contrast and is difficult to reconcile with the Convention on the Rights of the Child (CRC). Article 37(b) of the Convention clearly states that deprivation of liberty of children shall be used only as a measure of last resort and for the shortest appropriate period of time. Although there has been progress, it is evident that much more needs to be done in terms of deinstitutionalisation, diversion, ending migration-related detention and other measures to comply with the Convention. Deprivation of liberty of children is a form of structural violence in violation of Goal 16.2 of the Sustainable Development Goals (SDGs) (A/RES/70/1). The Global Study on Children Deprived of Liberty has been preceded by two earlier UN global studies related to the rights of children. In 1996, Graca Machel published the UN Report on the Impact of Armed Conflict on Children (A/51/306), which led to the appointment of a Special Representative of the Secretary-General on Children in Armed Conflict. In 2006, Paulo Sérgio Pinheiro published the UN Study on Violence against Children (A/61/299), which led to the appointment of a Special Representative of the Secretary-General on Violence against Children. Both these studies had a considerable impact on the lives of millions of children around the globe. Shortly after the publication of the Global Study on Violence against Children, NGOs started to campaign for another Global Study on Children Deprived of Liberty, which was also considered as a follow-up to the Pinheiro Study. In May 2014, the Committee on the Rights of the Child sent a formal letter to the UN Secretary-General supporting this initiative, and in December 2014, the UN General Assembly invited the Secretary–General to commission an in-depth Global Study on Children Deprived of Liberty. In 2015, a UN Inter-Agency Task Force, composed of the most relevant UN agencies and offices, was established under the chair of the UN Special Representative on Violence against Children which selected Manfred Nowak as Independent Expert to lead this complex process.

The main objectives of the Global Study on Children Deprived of Liberty were to assess the magnitude of this phenomenon, including the total number of children deprived of liberty (disaggregated by age and gender), as well as the reasons, the root causes, the length and types of deprivation of liberty and conditions. The General Assembly also requested to document good practices of states who managed to reduce the number of children deprived of liberty as well as the views and experiences of children. Like earlier studies, this Global Study also aims at raising awareness and promoting a change in the stigmatising attitudes and behaviour towards children at risk of arrest or detention. Finally, it should provide recommendations for law, policy and practice to safeguard the rights of children concerned, prevent the detention of children through effective non-custodial solutions guided by the best interests of the child. The ultimate aim of the Global Study was not so much to document conditions of detention with the aim of improving such conditions, but to address the root causes with the aim of significantly reducing the number of children deprived of liberty and preventing their arrest and detention.

The Global Study covers the following six situations:

- Children deprived of liberty within the administration of justice;
- Children living in prisons with their primary caregivers, usually mothers;
- Children deprived of liberty for migration-related reasons;
- Children deprived of liberty in institutions;
- Children deprived of liberty in the context of armed conflict;
- Children deprived of liberty on national security grounds.

For each of these situations research groups were established led by a research institute and supported by Advisory Board members, respective UN agencies and NGOs. During the process of preparing the Global Study, further research groups were set up for four cross-cutting themes with the aim of contextualising children's deprivation of liberty:

- Views and perspectives of children deprived of liberty;
- Impacts on health of children deprived of liberty;
- Children with disabilities deprived of liberty;
- Gender dimension.

The United Nations Global Study on Children Deprived of Liberty provides an interesting example of how the United Nations system can benefit from a close cooperation with academic institutions to achieve its aims and objectives. From the very beginning, the process of drafting the Global Study benefitted from the input of its Advisory Board, which consists of 22 of the most well-known international experts in the fields of children's rights and deprivation of liberty. In addition, the Independent Expert could draw on the expertise of two academic institutions to which he has very close ties.

The Ludwig Boltzmann Institute of Human Rights (BIM) at Vienna University is one of the leading academic institutions specialised in applied human rights. Founded by the Independent Expert in 1992, this institute played a major role in the coordination of the input of more than 1500 NGOs to the Vienna World Conference of Human Rights in 1993. During his expert UN functions relating to enforced disappearances, in tracing missing persons in the former Yugoslavia during the 1990s and as Special Rapporteur on Torture between 2004 and 2010, the Independent Expert was actively supported in various ways by the Ludwig Boltzmann Institute of Human Rights. With respect to the Global Study on Children Deprived of Liberty, the support of this institute became even more essential, as the Global Study suffered from the very beginning from a severe lack of funds and thus also from a lack of institutional support by the Office of the UN High Commissioner for Human Rights (OHCHR). In addition to taking the lead in preparing the chapter on the administration of justice, the Boltzmann Institute was forced to assume the final responsibility of coordinating all research groups and academic inputs, of hosting the data base, compiling and assessing the statistical data gathered from various sources, and of editing the Global Study.

The second academic institution which played and still plays a decisive role in the preparation and dissemination of the Global Study is the Global Campus of Human Rights (GC). With roughly 100 member universities, which jointly organise seven master programmes in human rights and democratisation in all world regions, the Global Campus is the largest network of universities dedicated to human rights. As the successor of the European Inter-University Centre for Human Rights and Democratization (EIUC), its Headquarters are based in Venice, with regional hubs in Buenos Aires, Pretoria, Bangkok, Beirut, Sarajevo and Yerevan. In his function as Secretary-General of the Global Campus, the Independent Expert had the privilege of actively involving many member universities, individual scholars and Master students in the preparation of the Global Study. The University of Pretoria, e.g. took the lead in preparing the chapter on institutions, and the research team in Venice was responsible for the drafting of the chapter on children living with their primary caregivers in prison. In addition, two expert workshops involving UN agencies, NGOs, the Advisory Board and other stakeholders were organised in Venice in 2017 and 2019. Thanks to a long-term cooperation with and funding by the Right Livelihood Foundation (RLF), the Global Campus also assumed the primary responsibility for the dissemination of the Global Study and for initiating a follow-up process until the United Nations will be in a position to assume this responsibility.

2 Key Findings of the United Nations Global Study on Children Deprived of Liberty

For all the situations of deprivation of liberty, there was a need to collect reliable empirical data from a variety of sources. Most importantly, a detailed questionnaire was designed and distributed in all UN languages to all UN Member States, National

Human Rights Institutions (NHRIs), National Preventive Mechanisms (NPMs), ombudspersons, UN agencies as well as NGOs. One hundred eighteen (118) replies were received in relation to 92 countries in various languages covering quantitative as well as qualitative areas. With respect to quantitative data, annual data was requested on the number of children deprived of liberty in the six situations, disaggregated by age and gender, for the last 10 years as well as snapshot data on the number of children deprived of liberty at one specific date, namely 26 June 2018.

While the responses to the questionnaire constitute the core of data stored in our database, these responses only covered less than half of UN Member States and were often incomplete. Therefore, there was a need to supplement these original data by a multitude of other reliable data from official government statistics, UN documents and statistics, state reports to the CRC Committee, regional, national and thematic consultations, commissioned studies as well as extraction of relevant data from peer-reviewed literature and other desk research. It must, however, be noted that the data is far from complete, that the findings and conclusions are based on very conservative estimates and extrapolations, and that the figures presented in the Global Study should only be treated as minimum estimates.

3 Children Deprived of Liberty in Institutions

Research for the study and the Independent Expert's first-hand experience, as a former Special Rapporteur on torture, clearly show that children should not be institutionalised to receive care, protection, education, rehabilitation or treatment, as it cannot substitute for the benefits of growing up in a family or in a family –type setting within the community. This need for deinstitutionalisation has already been expressed by states, when adopting the Guidelines for the Alternative Care of Children. In 2009 the Guidelines seem to have had a positive impact on the de-institutionalisation practices of states (A/RES/64/142). While in the Global Study on Violence against Children of 2006, the total number of children living in institutions was estimated as eight million, research conducted for the current Global Study indicates that this number may have dropped to 5.4 million.

The separation of children from their family environment should occur only where children cannot be allowed to remain there based on the best interest's determination, and any separation should be for the shortest possible duration. However, large numbers of children are separated from their families, and the majority of states are failing in their obligation to provide equal access to preventive, protective and supportive mechanisms to families. Due to this, many children in institutions, in particular in privately run institutions which are not state-regulated, 'drop off the radar'. The pathways that unnecessarily lead children to be separated from families include socioeconomic conditions, discrimination, family violence and lack of access to essential services (e.g. health, education, rehabilitation, treatment). Some children end up in institutions owing to the incorrect application of the best interests principle. Many states lack gatekeeping systems and institutions are sometimes characterised by profit motives or commodification of the care of children. The phenomenon of 'voluntourism' still exists in many states (Nowak 2019, p. 526).

The vast majority of children deprived of liberty live in institutions of all kinds which are characterised by a common "institutional culture": Children are isolated from the broader community, are compelled to live together, and do not have sufficient control over their lives and decisions which affect them. The requirements of institutions tend to take precedence over the children's individual needs, lead to fixed routines and are enforced by strict discipline, often amounting to solitary confinement, physical restraints and corporal punishment. In general, institutions can be characterised by de-personalisation, lack of individual care and love, instability of caregiver relationships and lack of caregiver responsiveness. As many recent inquiries into abuse of children show, institutions are often characterised by a high level of violence, sexual abuse and neglect, which amounts to inhuman or degrading treatment in violation of international law. Although much has been achieved in recent years by means of de-institutionalisation, much more remains to be done to ensure that all children, including children with physical and mental disabilities, can enjoy their right to grow up in a family environment and in community based non-custodial settings.

4 Children Deprived of Liberty in the Administration of Justice

A wide-ranging and comprehensive set of international human rights standards is testimony to a strong commitment by the international community to prevent deprivation of liberty of children in the administration of justice. Many states have introduced child justice legislation and established corresponding specialised procedures, including special courts for children, which have led to the effective diversion from the criminal justice system (Nowak 2019, pp. 302–309). These developments seem to have contributed to a certain decrease in the number of children detained in prisons and pre-trial detention centres. While UNICEF in 2007 has estimated the total number worldwide as over one million children, research for the Global Study indicates that this number may have dropped to less than half. There are still at least 410,000 children held in detention every year in remand centres and prisons.

If one counts an estimated number of one million children in police custody, more than 1.4 million children are currently detained per year in the context of the administration of criminal justice, i.e. in police custody, pre-trial detention facilities and prisons. Detaining children in conflict with the law is not per se a violation of the CRC. However, the principle of a "measure of last resort" in Article 37(b) CRC requires all law enforcement agencies, including the police, prosecutors, judges and prison administrators, to examine in each individual case whether proper non-custodial solutions are available and should in fact be applied. Article 40 (4) CRC provides in this respect: “A variety of dispositions, such as care, guidance and supervision orders; counselling; probation; foster care; education and vocational training programmes and other alternatives to institutional care shall be available to ensure that children are dealt with in a manner appropriate to their well-being and proportionate both to their circumstances and the offence.” This means that diversion measures shall be applied at every stage of the criminal procedure: as alternatives to the arrest by the police; to a court decision leading to pre-trial detention; to a decision of a prosecutor to charge a child for a criminal offence; to a court judgment finding a child guilty of a criminal offence and a judgment sentencing a child to imprisonment; and finally to a decision of the prison administration when enforcing such judgments. At each of these stages, the competent authorities shall consider to transfer children from the criminal justice system to the child welfare system. This requires sophisticated instruments for structured inter-agency cooperation between the child welfare system, social protection, education and health systems on the one hand and law enforcement and justice systems on the other hand. The goal of such inter-agency cooperation is to build comprehensive child protection systems and implement prevention and early intervention policies. Above all, there is a strong need to support families, communities, schools and child welfare systems to deal with children in conflict with the law.

There are a number of root causes and pathways leading to such a large number of children deprived of liberty in the context of the administration of justice (Nowak 2019, p. 274). First, many states retain an excessively low age of minimum criminal responsibility. While the Committee on the Rights of the Child advocates that this age shall be raised to at least 14 years of age (CRC/C/GC/24*, para. 22), more than 120 states maintain the minimum age at below 14 (Nowak 2019, p. 280). Second, instead of prevention, states often rely on repressive and punitive policies that lead to excessive criminalisation of children. Behaviours that are typical for children are criminalised as so-called “status offences”: children are charged and detained for truancy, running away from home, disobedience, underage drinking, consensual sexual activity between teenagers, “disruptive” behaviours and practices against tradition and morality. Despite the fact that Article 37(b) CRC allows deprivation of liberty of children only for the “shortest appropriate period of time”, life sentences for children remain legal in 67 states, specifically in Africa, Asia, Oceania, the Caribbean and North America (Nowak 2019, p. 291). Third, many states still lack a functional child justice system with special child courts and specially trained police officers, prosecutors and judges, as required by Article 40(3) CRC.

Discrimination is another important reason for the large number of children deprived of liberty in the administration of justice. Children from poor and socio-economically disadvantaged backgrounds, migrant and indigenous communities, ethnic and religious minorities, the LGBTI community and children with disabilities are largely overrepresented in detention and throughout the judicial proceedings. While boys are committing roughly two-thirds of all criminal offences of children, they account for 94% of all children detained in prisons and pre-trial detention centres (Nowak 2019, p. 225). This significant gender gap can be explained in part by the fact that girls often receive more lenient and non-custodial sentences and benefit much more than boys from diversion and non-custodial solutions during the different phases of the criminal justice system.

The Global Study also revealed significant regional disparities in the detention rate of children in prisons and pre-trial detention centres. While Sub-Saharan Africa has the lowest detention rate (less than 4 children detained out of 100,000 children), the American hemisphere scores highest. With a detention rate of 60, the United States is the country with the largest number of children in detention, followed by South America (19), Central America and Caribbean (16) and Oceania (8). Western Europe (5) as well as Central and Eastern Europe (5.8) show a comparably low detention rate.

In the 110 countries/territories for which data could be obtained and that do not have life imprisonment for children, the maximum sentence for children ranges from 3 to 50 years. The average maximum sentence is 13.3 years. The median average maximum in turn lies at 12 years (Nowak 2019, p. 290). In its recently adopted General Comment No. 24 relating to the administration of child justice, the CRC-Committee has specified certain time limits. For instance, it recommends to States Parties that police custody should never be longer than 24 h and pre-trial detention should not last longer than 30 days. However, the Committee has not yet specified a maximum duration of imprisonment of children after conviction by a criminal court (Nowak 2019, p. 72).

Children consulted for the Study expressed concerns about the lack of access to information, lack of child-sensitive procedures, insufficient contact with family and the outside world and poor detention conditions. This confirmed the Independent Expert's own fact-finding experiences, as a former Special Rapporteur on Torture that conditions of detention often amount to inhuman or degrading treatment in violation of international law.

5 Children Deprived of Liberty in Migration Related Detention

Research for the Global Study finds that at a minimum, 330,000 children are currently detained worldwide for migration-related reasons. This is likely to be a significant under-estimation of the true figure, due to limitations regarding the quality, consistency and coverage of data available (Nowak 2019, p. 465). This figure covers unaccompanied and separated children as well as children migrating with their parents or other family members. Both from a legal and policy oriented point of view, migration-related detention of children raises a number of highly controversial issues. Responses to the Global Study questionnaire indicate that 24 countries, above all in Latin America and Southern Africa, do no longer detain children (Nowak 2019, p. 463). On the other hand, at least 80 states around the world are known to detain children for migration related reasons (Nowak 2019, p. 455).

From a legal point of view, migration-related detention can never meet the high threshold of a "measure of last resort" in Article 37(b) CRC and is never in the best interests of the child, as required by Article 3 CRC. In other words, the Global Study confirms the legal interpretation of the CRC-Committee, the UN Working Group on Arbitrary Detention, the Special Rapporteur on the Human Rights of Migrants, the UN Secretary-General and various other UN bodies and agencies, such as the International Organization for Migration (IOM), the United Nations Children's Fund (UNICEF) and the United Nations High Commissioner for Refugees (UNHCR) as well as regional bodies: Every single case of a child in migration related detention constitutes a violation of the CRC. This applies to unaccompanied and separated children, as well as to children with their families. Detaining children for their "protection", or to "keep families together" where alternative non-custodial solutions are lacking, can never be a justification.

States that do detain children based on their migration status offer multiple justifications, such as illegal entry, identity verification, age assessment, health and security screening or the facilitation of deportation. Children are detained in various facilities, including prisons, closed reception centres, offshore locations, transit shelters and institutional settings. Immigration detention of children and families is often decided under a procedure that does not respect basic procedural rights, and the conditions of detention are often appalling. Research conducted for the Study indicated that immigration detention is particularly harmful to a child's mental and physical health and exposes the child to the risk of sexual abuse and exploitation. Furthermore, it both aggravates existing health conditions and causes new ones to arise (Nowak 2019, pp. 146–152).

6 Children Living with Their Primary Caregivers in Prison

Research for the Global Study shows that approximately 19,000 infants and young children live with their primary caregivers, usually their mothers, in prison. Although they are not legally deprived of liberty, they are so de facto. The possibility for children to live in prison with an imprisoned caregiver, which is allowed in most jurisdictions until a certain age, is tense with difficult considerations, beginning with the question of whether to permit the practice at all. This question can only be decided on a case-by-case basis by adopting a child-rights based approach and considering the best interest of the child, as both the exposure of the child to detention and the separation of the child from a primary caregiver/mother have adverse consequences for the child.

The Global Study follows the approach of the African Charter and the South African Constitutional Court insofar as a situation in which children live with their imprisoned mothers should be avoided as far as possible. This means that every court, when sentencing a mother who is a primary caregiver of dependent children, has the responsibility to assess the possible impact of her imprisonment on child development, taking the best interests of the children as a separate consideration into account. In such cases, alternatives to imprisonment, including house arrest, and non-custodial sentences should always be considered first, when the children cannot stay with the father or another close family member. If neither solution is possible, states have an obligation to establish special alternative institutions for holding such mothers. In the absence of such special institutions, mothers may be allowed to take their children into prison, under the condition that states establish child-friendly "Mother-Child Units" (Nowak 2019, p. 427).

State responses to the questionnaire show that most national laws establish specific age limits for a child's admission into a place of detention (typically between two and six years of age) and place restrictions on the length of permissible stay. In many states, caregivers need to make a specific request and obtain, either separately or jointly, authorisation by judicial, social and/or prison authorities to allow the child to live in prison with them. Some states refer to further indicators such as: breastfeeding needs; lack of alternative child-care solutions; suitability of prison accommodation for the child's development; health of the child; protection of the child's safety; full parental responsibility and ability to exercise parenthood; length of the sentence; and the caregiver-child relationship before entering the prison.

7 Children Deprived of Liberty in Armed Conflict

Children detained in the context of armed conflict often find themselves in a cycle of violence. First, armed groups illegally recruit them, usually through force, coercion or deception. Second, government authorities then detain them for suspected association with those very groups, often subjecting them to torture and other forms of ill-treatment, most often for intelligence gathering purposes or confessions of involvement with armed groups. Many children are detained simply because they appear to be of fighting age or come from communities perceived to be sympathetic to opposition forces, or because their family members are suspected of involvement with such forces. International law prohibits the use of children in direct hostilities, and any recruitment of children by non-state armed groups. States parties shall, when necessary, accord to such persons all appropriate assistance for their physical and psychological recovery and their social reintegration. Yet in at least 16 countries where conflict pertains, children are detained by the government or by non-state armed groups.

Research for the Global Study found that, at a minimum, 35,000 children are currently deprived of liberty in the context of armed conflict. That figure includes an estimated 29,000 foreign children related to alleged ISIS fighters detained in 2019 in camps in Iraq and the north-east of the Syrian Arab Republic. In conflicts involving non-state armed groups designated as terrorist, governments are more likely to detain children than to provide rehabilitation and reintegration, as required under international law. In Nigeria, roughly 1900 children have been detained on suspected Boko Haram affiliation. Hundreds of detained children have also been reported from

Israel, the Democratic Republic of Congo, Somalia and Afghanistan (Nowak 2019, p. 581).

Children are often subjected to torture and ill -treatment, most often for intelligence gathering purposes or confessions of involvement with armed groups. Conditions are often extremely poor, with severe overcrowding and grossly inadequate sanitation, food, and health care. Children are commonly detained with adults and have no access to education, recreation or rehabilitation programmes, and are often tried in military or adult courts without adequate procedural rights. The UN Security Council in 2018 called on all parties to such conflicts to cease unlawful or arbitrary detention of children and encouraged states to establish "standard operating procedures for the rapid handover of the children concerned to relevant civilian child protection actors" (S/RES/2427, paras 19–21). This has already had a positive impact on state practice, as some African states, including Chad, Mali, Niger and Somalia, have signed such handover protocols with the United Nations, transferring children associated with armed groups to child welfare centres, with the aim of ensuring their rehabilitation and reintegration into society (Nowak 2019, p. 607).

8 Children Deprived of Liberty Due to National Security

The Global Study only covers a number of countries where relevant data are available and estimates that at least 1500 children are detained in these countries on national security grounds. Research conducted for the Global Study identified at least 31 conflict and non-conflict countries where children have been detained in the context of national security grounds. The vast majority of these children are detained in conflict countries, such as Syria, Iraq and Afghanistan, as was described above. In countries without an armed conflict on their territories, the number of children detained for reasons of national security is difficult to assess, as many states do not provide relevant data.

In recent years, armed groups designated as terrorist or armed groups termed violent extremist have recruited thousands of children, in some cases across borders, to carry out suicide and other attacks, and for various support roles. Some are recruited through force, coercion or deception, while others are influenced by family members and peer networks, poverty, physical insecurity, social exclusion, financial incentives, or a search for identity and status. The Internet has also provided such groups with new avenues to recruit children, who are often particularly susceptible to propaganda and online exploitation due to their age and relative immaturity.

Thousands of children from more than 80 countries travelled to Iraq or Syria, either alone or with their families, to join ISIS both before and after the declaration of the caliphate" in June 2014. Many of these children originated from either Western or Eastern Europe (Nowak 2019, p. 591). Over 1000 children associated with ISIS are believed to have returned to their home countries, while others were killed in Iraq or Syria or are detained there. A small number of children have been detained and prosecuted after their return home. A number of European countries have passed legislation to revoke citizenship for individuals who travelled abroad to join non-state armed groups designated as terrorist to prevent them from returning.

In response to heightened concerns about threats to their national security and counter-terrorism resolutions adopted by the UN Security Council, the majority of states have adopted new counter-terrorism legislation or amended existing national laws since 2001, often expanding the scope thereof in ways that negatively affect children. Such measures place children at heightened risk of detention for alleged national security offences. These laws often fail to distinguish between adults and children, include overly broad definitions of terrorism, provide fewer procedural guarantees, and impose harsher penalties. Some states criminalise mere association with non-state armed groups designated as terrorist, thereby increasing the number of children detained and prosecuted for association with such groups (Nowak 2019, p. 647). Such laws are also used to detain children for a broad range of activities outside of national security concerns, such as posting political opinions online, participating in peaceful protests, involvement in banned political groups or alleged gang activity.

9 Key Recommendations of the Global Study on Children Deprived of Liberty

For every situation of children's deprivation of liberty and the respective cross-cutting issues such as the views of children, the impact on health, children with disabilities and the gender dimension, there are multiple findings and recommendations which are conveyed in the comprehensive Global Study on Children Deprived of Liberty. The overarching recommendations of the Global Study follow directly from its findings and conclusions as well as from the analysis of best practices. They are inspired by the high legal standards of the CRC regarding the rights to personal liberty, personal integrity and dignity of children and aim at reducing the huge implementation gap between these standards and the reality of children deprived of liberty worldwide in all six focus areas covered by the Global Study.

10 The Overarching Recommendations

Significantly **reduce the number** of children held in places of detention and apply non-custodial solutions and to make all efforts in addressing the **root causes** as well as to invest resources to reduce inequalities and **support families.** Furthermore, it is essential to **address the pathways** leading to the deprivation of liberty in a **systemic and holistic manner.** Invest and **empower families** to foster the physical, mental, spiritual, moral and social development of their children, including children with disabilities. **Repeal all laws and policies** that permit the deprivation of liberty of children based on an actual, or perceived, impairment or based on their sexual orientation and/or gender identity.

In all decisions that may lead to the detention of children, states should **most rigorously apply the requirement of Article 37(b)** of the Convention on the Rights of the Child that deprivation of liberty shall be applied only as a measure of last resort. This means that children may only be detained in truly exceptional cases. If detention is unavoidable under the particular circumstances of a case, it shall be applied only for the shortest appropriate period of time. States have an obligation to apply **child-friendly and gender-sensitive conditions, without any discrimination.** Children shall not be exposed to neglect, violence, sexual abuse or exploitation, ill- treatment, torture and inhuman conditions of detention. States should ensure that children have **access to essential services** aimed at their rehabilitation and reintegration into society, including education, vocational training, family contacts, sports and recreation, adequate nutrition, housing and health care. **Health services** in detention shall be of a standard equivalent to that available in the community at large.

Article 12 of the Convention on the Rights of the Child provides that children have the **right to be heard and actively participate** in all matters directly affecting their lives. Therefore, they should be empowered to influence decisions relating to their treatment and enjoyment of such essential services and have the **right to effective remedies,** as well as to **lodge complaints to an independent and impartial authority** on any grievances and human rights violations during detention. States are strongly encouraged to **ratify the Optional Protocol to the Convention against Torture (OPCAT)** and to establish independent and effective National Preventive Mechanisms with a particular expertise to conduct visits to places where children are, or may be, deprived of liberty. States are strongly encouraged to **ratify the third Optional Protocol to the Convention on the Rights of the Child on a communications procedure,** enabling children to further seek redress for violations of their rights.

It is strongly encouraged that states invest in **awareness-raising, education and training of all professionals** who work with and for children in decisions leading to their deprivation of liberty, and those who are responsible for their well-being while in detention. This applies to the police, judges, prosecutors, prison guards, medical personnel, psychiatrists, psychologists, educators, social workers, probation officers, child protection and welfare officers, asylum and migration personnel and any other individuals in contact with children at risk of deprivation, or deprived, of liberty. States should also **invest significant resources in the child welfare system**. They should ensure a close **inter-agency cooperation** between the child welfare, social protection, education, health and justice systems, the law enforcement as well as the administration of migration and refugee policies. In this way, states are urged to build comprehensive child protection systems and early intervention policies aimed at preventing detention of children.

States should establish an appropriate system of **data collection** at the national level, involving all relevant ministries and other state agencies, coordinated by a focal point. States should further ensure the development and maintenance of an

international database containing all relevant data on children's deprivation of liberty. In developing such a database, a common methodology, based on the Global Study, needs to be applied to enhance comparative research. States should regularly collect data, disaggregated by age, gender and nationality, on the number of children deprived of liberty in all situations covered by the Global Study per year and on a 'snapshot' date. As deprivation of liberty constitutes a form of structural violence against children, it is further recommended that the **detention rate** of children in all situations covered by the Global Study be considered in the implementation of target 16.2 of the Sustainable Development Goals.

To achieve all these goals, states are urged to **develop national action plans** with clear targets and benchmarks indicating how to reduce progressively and significantly the number of children in the various situations and how to replace detention of children by non-custodial solutions. With respect to the follow-up of the United Nations Global Study on Children Deprived of Liberty, the Independent Expert strongly recommended that deprivation of liberty, as one of the most neglected violations of the CRC, remains on the agenda of the General Assembly, the Security Council and the Human Rights Council.

For the six situations of deprivation of liberty covered by the Global Study, the key recommendations are to:

- **Stop all forms of immigration detention of children,** whether unaccompanied or migrating with their families, and replace it by appropriate non-custodial solutions.
- **Adopt a comprehensive deinstitutionalisation policy** by developing appropriate family-type settings, since children should not grow up in institutions, which are characterised by strict discipline, neglect, abuse and lack of love.
- Establish **special child justice systems,** apply diversion at all stages of the criminal justice process and transfer children from the justice to the child welfare system. **Diversion measures** should be equally applied to boys and girls and be appropriate to their age, level of maturity, as well as the situation in the community. Furthermore, states should increase the **minimum age of criminal responsibility** to at least 14 years, **shorten the length of detention** and decriminalise perceived "immoral" or "disruptive" behaviour of children, consensual sexual activities between teenagers as well as behaviour typical of children (status offences).
- **Avoid the imprisonment of mothers** as primary caregivers of young children
- Treat children recruited by armed forces or groups designated as terrorist as **victims rather than as perpetrators.**

11 Follow-Up Initiation and Dissemination of the Global Study

While all UN agencies and mechanisms should play an active role in monitoring and facilitating the implementation of these recommendations, the Independent Expert called upon the General Assembly to consider, as soon as possible, a specific and effective follow-up mechanism and process aimed at disseminating the Study findings, at promoting its recommendations, monitoring progress and ensuring the development and maintenance of an international database, containing all relevant data on children's deprivation of liberty in all UN Member States.

Following the presentation of the report on the Global Study on Children Deprived of Liberty to the UN General Assembly in New York on 8 October 2019, and the presentation of the comprehensive version of the Global Study to the UN in Geneva on 19 November 2019, an expectation was created to widely disseminate the findings and recommendations of the Study and to start a well-coordinated follow-up process. The Independent Expert was invited by several states, national human rights institutions, academic institutions, international and non-governmental organisations to present the Global Study and to advise governments in designing a national action plan aimed at implementing the Study's recommendations. Between October 2019 and the outbreak of the Covid-19 pandemic in late February 2020, the Independent Expert presented and discussed the Study with many representatives of governments and other stakeholders in Australia, Japan, Austria, South Africa, Scotland, Thailand and the European Union. Further launches in Switzerland, Belgium, the Netherlands, the European Parliament, Morocco, Argentina and Uruguay had to be cancelled or postponed.

The UN General Assembly Resolution on the rights of the child of 18 December 2019, however, only took note of the Global Study without deciding on any follow-up (A/RES/74/133, preamble and para. 39). As with earlier global studies on children's rights, it is expected that the General Assembly will take stronger action in December 2020 leading to a more active involvement of the United Nations in follow-up activities as from 2021.

In the meantime, the Global Campus of Human Rights consisting of 100 universities worldwide has taken the main initiative to keep the Global Study on the international agenda and support its dissemination activities. The cooperation between the Global Campus of Human Rights (GC) and the Right Livelihood Foundation (RLF) has taken a pivotal role in supporting the process of the Study to be presented in the different regions of the world. These efforts have been supported by the NGO Panel of 170 NGOs and other stakeholders. For the time being, the further involvement of the Global Campus is essential for the overall success of the Global Study. In the long run, a closer cooperation on the follow-up between the United Nations, the NGO Panel, the Global Campus of Human Rights and regional organisations would create a positive synergy by bringing international organisations, civil society and academia together in facilitating the domestic implementation of the Global Study recommendations.

12 The Objectives and Activities of the Follow-Up Initiation and Dissemination Are to:

- First, to present the Global Study findings, recommendations and to develop the most effective short, mid and long-term follow-up strategies with international, regional and national key-stakeholders by means of trainings, workshops and consultations. In this regard, a number of regional and national launches have taken place throughout the world to raise awareness and create action plans to implement the recommendations as well as use this momentum to support the initiation of a follow-up process to the Study
- Second, to coordinate and support the development and facilitation of further Global Study related research and advocacy activities and outputs such as the creation of thematic toolkits, an executive summary and its translations into all UN languages, an animated child friendly version, multiple e-learning massive open online courses (MOOCs) and further projects related to the implementation of the recommendations through the Global Campus network and its universities
- Third, to maintain and strengthen the Global Study network consisting of research institutes and universities, Advisory Board members and other experts, the NGO Panel of 170 NGOs, UN agencies and other international as well as regional organisations, National Human Rights Institutions, National Preventive Mechanisms and Children's Ombudspersons. This is to be done by a variety of communication channels, by creating a website and a database as well as by a regular newsletter and other advocacy and communication tools.

13 Conclusions

The UN Global Study on Children Deprived of Liberty provided an important occasion to draw the attention of the international community to one of the most overlooked violations of children's rights. In contrast to the clear legal requirement of the CRC, namely that the detention of children shall be used only as a measure of last resort and for the shortest appropriate period of time, the Global Study found that more than seven million children are in fact deprived of liberty in a broad variety of institutions, police lock-ups, prisons, immigration and other detention centres in all world regions. The research conducted for the Global Study also shows the enormous suffering of children who are exposed to inhuman conditions of detention, and the particular harmful effects of deprivation of liberty on the health and development of children. As a form of structural violence, it deprives children of their childhood. The Global Study calls on all states to take urgent action to drastically reduce the number of children deprived of liberty and requests the United Nations to put this gross and systematic violation of children's rights high on its agenda.

Owing to a severe lack of funds made available exclusively through voluntary contributions, the Independent Expert leading the Global Study could only to a limited extent rely on the services of the OHCHR and other UN agencies in the preparation and dissemination of the Global Study. At the same time, he was most actively supported by an NGO Panel of 170 NGOs, led by Human Rights Watch and Defence for Children International, by an Advisory Board of 22 highly renowned experts on children's rights, and by the academic community. The Ludwig Boltzmann Institute of Human Rights at Vienna University assumed the function of coordinating the academic research and editing the Global Study, while the Global Campus of Human Rights took up the function of disseminating the Global Study and of initiating an urgently needed follow-up process. Both academic institutions are financially supported by two private foundations, which together contributed more funds to the UN Global Study than Member States and international organisations.

In our opinion, this close cooperation between the United Nations, civil society and academia confirms the spirit of the famous opening words of the UN Charter, namely that the Peoples of the United Nations, which founded the world organisation 75 years ago, go beyond states and governments. At a time of multiple crises, when the United Nations and multilateralism are increasingly challenged by nationalistic and populist movements, it is essential that the global civil society and global academic networks take up their responsibility as part of the Peoples of the United Nations" to ensure that the main aims and objectives of the world organisation, namely human security, human development and human rights, are not abandoned but further strengthened. In line with the spirit of the CRC, children are increasingly assuming their own responsibility for addressing the global challenges of the twenty-first century, such as urging governments in global Fridays for Future strikes to save our planet from the current climate crisis. We have a particular responsibility to empower children and to protect the rights of children and future generations. In the Agenda 2030, states solemnly promised to leave no one behind. By urging states to leave no child behind bars, a broad range of civil society representatives, who jointly prepared this Global Study, wish to make a small, but distinctive, contribution to this overarching goal for the next decade.

References

A/51/306, Graça M.,*"Impact of armed conflict on children"*, 26 August 1996.

A/61/299, Paulo Sérgio P., *Report of the independent expert for the United Nations study on violence against children*, 29 August 2006.

A/HRC/RES/17/18, UN Human Rights Council, *Optional Protocol to the Convention on the Rights of the Child on a Communications Procedure: resolution / adopted by the Human Rights Council*, 14 July 2011.

A/RES/1386(XIV), UN General Assembly, *Declaration of the Rights of the Child*, 20 November 1959.

A/RES/45/113, United Nations, *Rules for the Protection of Juveniles Deprived of their Liberty* (Havana Rules) of 14 December 1990.

A/RES/54/263, UN General Assembly, *Optional Protocol to the Convention on the Rights of the Child on the Involvement of Children in Armed Conflict*, 25 May 2000.

A/RES/54/263*, UN General Assembly, *Optional Protocol to the Convention on the Rights of the Child on the Sale of Children, Child Prostitution and Child Pornography*, 16 March 2001.

A/RES/57/199, Optional Protocol to the Convention against Torture and other Cruel, Inhuman or Degrading Treatment or Punishment, 9 January 2003.

A/RES/64/142, UNGA Resolution 64/142 on *Guidelines for the Alternative Care of Children*, 18 December 2009.

A/RES/70/1, UNGA Resolution 70/1, *Transforming our world: the 2030 Agenda for Sustainable Development*, 21 October 2015.

A/RES/74/133, *UNGA Resolution on the Rights of the Child*, 18 December 2019, preamble and para 39.

CRC/C/GC/24*, CRC-Committee, *General Comment No. 24*, 18 September 2019, § 22.

E/CN.4/RES/1990/74, UN General Assembly, *Convention on the Rights of the Child*, 20 November 1989.

League of Nations 'Geneva Declaration of the Rights of the Child', Adopted 26 September, 1924. Available at http://www.un-documents.net/gdrc1924.htm

Nowak, M. (2019). The United Nations Global Study on Children Deprived of Liberty, Geneva, November 2019. Available at http://omnibook.com/view/e0623280-5656-42f8-9edf-5872f8f08562

Resolution 2200A (XXI), UN General Assembly, *International Covenant on Civil and Political Rights*, 16 December 1966; United Nations, Treaty Series, vol. 999, p. 171.

Resolution 2200A (XXI), UN General Assembly, *International Covenant on Economic, Social and Cultural Rights, 16 December 1966,* United Nations, Treaty Series, vol. 993, p. 3.

S/RES/2427, 9 July 2018, paras 19–21.

Manfred Nowak is a Professor of Human Rights and Scientific Director of the Vienna Master of Arts in Human Rights at the Vienna University as well as Secretary-General of the Global Campus of Human Rights (Venice, Italy). In 2016, he was appointed as Independent Expert leading the UN Global Study on Children Deprived of Liberty, which he presented to the United Nations General Assembly in 2019. He carried out various expert functions for the UN, the Council of Europe and the EU, including as judge at the Human Rights Chamber for Bosnia and Herzegovina in Sarajevo, as Vice-Chair of the EU Fundamental Rights Agency in Vienna, as UN Expert on Enforced Disappearances and UN Special Rapporteur on Torture. He held professorships at the Universities of Utrecht (the Netherlands), Lund (Sweden), Stanford (Ca., USA) and the Graduate Institute in Geneva (Switzerland), and is author of more than 600 publications, including many books, such as his well-known *CCPR Commentary* (three editions), a joint *CAT-Commentary* (two editions), his *Introduction to the International Human Rights Regime* and his books on *Human Rights or Global Capitalism*, *Torture - An Expert's Confrontation With an Everyday Evil* and *Human Rights: An Answer to Growing Economic Inequality*. E-mail: manfred.nowak@univie.ac.at, manfred.nowak@gchumanrights.org.

Manu Krishan was the Coordinator and the Assistant to the Independent Expert leading the United Nations Global Study on Children Deprived of Liberty (2019). He studied Philosophy before graduating from the Vienna Master of Arts in Human Rights at the University of Vienna. He is a human rights researcher and project manager with proficiency in children's rights, particularly on ethical considerations when researching with and for children. Email: manu.krishan@gchumanrights.org, manukrishan@univie.ac.at.

Part III
Living in Harmony with Nature: Mother Earth's Criminology

United Nations Initiatives in Preventing Environmental Crime

Rob White

Abstract This chapter reviews the nature and dynamics of environmental crime, broad approaches to preventing crimes such as illegal fishing, and the role of United Nations agencies in responding to environmental crime. These UN responses range from collaborative interventions involving government and non-government bodies, to knowledge provision and educational initiatives. The scale of present environmental catastrophes, particularly related to the effects of climate change and the extinction of species, presents considerable institutional challenges to addressing global environmental harms. These are compounded by the political obstacles stemming from the actions and/or inactions of nation-states that impede measures needed to prevent environmental harm.

Keywords Biodiversity · Climate change · Crime prevention · Environmental crime · United Nations

1 Introduction

Environmental crime is typically defined on a continuum ranging from strict legal definitions through incorporation into broader harm-based perspectives. It includes specific types of crime such as air, water and land pollution, illegal disposal of electronic waste, wildlife trafficking, illegal fishing and illegal deforestation. It also includes harms that have yet to be officially criminalised, such as activities that diminish biodiversity and that contribute to global warming. Thus, there is a distinction between environmental crimes defined by illegality, and serious harms that hitherto have been unrecognised under law as illegal, but which nonetheless are of great interest to criminologists and others working in this area.

R. White (✉)
University of Tasmania, School of Social Sciences, Hobart, TAS, Australia
e-mail: r.d.white@utas.edu.au

H. Kury, S. Redo (eds.), *Crime Prevention and Justice in 2030*,
https://doi.org/10.1007/978-3-030-56227-4_12

There are various ways to categorise environmental crime. For example, one can focus on the four elements or building blocks of life—air, water, land and sun—and undertake analyses of crimes related to air, water and land and crimes in the energy industries (e.g. from pollution to fraud). Or we could analyse environmental crime in terms of basic social processes which are institutionalised and generalised in specific ways: taking from nature (e.g. natural resource extraction involving fishing, wildlife, and logging); adding to nature (e.g. pollution, contamination and poisoning); and altering nature (e.g. reducing biodiversity through the use of 'flex crops' such as soy or maize; extensive use of genetic modification technologies). How acts and omissions are described or conceptualised shapes the gaze of the observer and informs how they respond to environmental crimes and harms.

The complexities of environmental crime and harm are mirrored in the sheer number of interventions, agencies and institutions involved in their regulation, prosecution, adjudication and prevention. From the perspective of the United Nations, there are myriad bodies engaged in some aspect of environmental crime analysis and intervention—ranging from the UN Environment Programme (UNEP) to the UN Office on Drugs and Crime (UNODC). Added to this is the significance of the Social Development Goals (SDGs) as applied to both distinct environmental issues and specific criminal justice matters.

This chapter provides a survey of various UN initiative in regards environmental crime prevention. Many of these are not described as 'crime prevention' as such, although they do have a bearing on the prevention of environmental crimes and harms. The chapter begins by outlining some key features of transnational environmental crime before briefly considering specific crime prevention measures. This is followed by discussion of collaboration and capacity building; NGO engagement in environmental law enforcement; and education and community activism, as each demonstrates specific types of United Nations involvement. The chapter concludes by reciting recent information about the 'state of the planet'—a summation that highlights the urgency and need for greater efforts in environmental crime prevention now and into the future.

2 Transnational Environmental Crime

Most environmental harm is intrinsically transnational since it is by nature mobile and easily subject to transference. The classic case of this is air pollution. For example, 2015 saw the worst ever smoke haze over Indonesia, Malaysia and Singapore, extending to Thailand and the Philippines. This was caused by illegal fires started in peatland and forest on Indonesia's Sumatra Island and the Indonesian part of Borneo. The fires were started to cheaply clear land for palm oil and pulp and paper plantations. Analysis of transnational environmental crime therefore requires a sense of scale, and of the essential interconnectedness of issues, events, people and places.

Transnational environmental crime, as defined in conventional legal terms, includes unauthorised acts or omissions that are *against the law* and therefore subject to criminal prosecution and criminal sanctions; crimes that involve some kind of *cross-border transference* and an international or *global dimension*; and crimes related to *pollution* (of air, water and land) and *crimes against wildlife* (including illegal trade in ivory as well as live animals).

The transboundary nature of environmental harm is evident in a variety of international protocols and conventions that deal with such matters as the illegal trade in ozone-depleting substances, the dumping and illegal transport of hazardous waste, illegal trade in chemicals such as persistent organic pollutants, and illegal dumping of oil and other wastes in oceans (White 2011). Together, these are the key focus of national and international laws relating to environmental matters and are the main task areas of agencies such as the UN Office on Drugs and Crime, and Interpol, which has four working groups that focus on fisheries crime, forestry crime, pollution crime and wildlife crime. The UN Sustainable Development Goals likewise have relevance when it comes to conserving, preserving and protecting oceans and seas, providing for sustainable and equitable use of water, forests and other natural resources, and tackling issues such as climate change (UN General Assembly Resolution 70/1).

Complexity of environmental crime is related to geography, ecology and political governance. The laws and rules guiding action on environmental crime vary greatly at the local, regional, and national levels, and there are overarching conventions and laws that likewise have different legal purchase depending upon how they are translated into action in each specific local jurisdiction. In part, differences in law-in-practice and conceptions of what is an environmental crime stem from the shifting nature of what is deemed harmful or not.

There is a myriad of different types of environmental harms, some of which are common across the surface of the planet, others which are specific to particular locales, regions and countries. Moreover, while some environmental crimes can be determined by investigating ecological trends that involve degradation and destruction of place-specific environments (such as clearfelling of forests), others require a mapping of movements from place of origin to place of destination (such as illegal international trade in plants and non-human animals). Thus, the production of global environmental harm is partly determined through complex processes of transference. The global trade in toxic waste (often under the cover of recycling), the illegal dumping of radioactive waste, carbon emission trading and the shifting of dirty industries to developing countries are exemplars of this. The result is the movement of environmentally harmful products, processes and wastes to the most vulnerable places and most exploitable peoples of the world.

At the global level, issues such as plastics pollution in the oceans and climate change are matters that affects us all, regardless of where we live, regardless of skin colour, income, ethnicity, religion and gender. Climate change continues to present as the most significant and urgent matter of our time, with huge implications for peace and social order. The scramble for what's left of the natural environment, in the context of climate-related scarcity and the accelerating limits to ecology, is heightening the sense of foreboding and insecurity in many countries and communities. For example, there has been a dramatic rise in the number of environmental and land activists who are being killed as the competition for access to natural resources intensifies (witness the killing of farmers and Indigenous people in Brazil in 2019). These pressures also mean that unscrupulous methods may be used to satisfy immediate (rather than long-term) self-interests—as in the case of illegal fishing and the use of horsemeat as a substitute for beef for human consumption. Environmental crimes such as these are, in effect, generated by global systemic pressures on the world's ecology.

Climate change and the gross exploitation and contamination of nature are leading to the general demise of the ecological status quo—hence increasing the need for a new type of crime—the crime of *ecocide* (Higgins 2012). Ecocide refers to significant destruction, degradation and diminishment of the environment, in whole or in part, as a result of human acts or omissions. The concept is increasingly being applied at the planetary level, particularly in the light of both widescale environmental destruction (such as the burning of forests in the Amazon) and the effects of global climate change (evident in the prolonged droughts and extreme weather events in many regions of the world) (White 2018).

The global situation is one marked by varying types and levels of criminality, ranging from corporate illegality in shipping contaminated products to the role of organised criminals in disposing of toxic waste, illegal fishing and trafficking of persons. It may well be that 'security' (for some) is built upon a platform of state-level wrongdoing (plundering of other people's lands and resources), corporate wrongdoing (cutting corners to ensure product delivery at affordable costs), and organised criminal wrongdoing (that still guarantees a 'result' for those who sub-contract out or who purchase the fruits of the criminal endeavour) (White 2014). Study of environmental crime cannot be extricated from wider social, economic and political processes and structures.

3 Preventing Environmental Crimes

Environmental crime prevention encompasses a range of substantive considerations. It must deal with acts and omissions that are already criminalised and prohibited, such as illegal fishing or illegal dumping of toxic waste. It must also come to grips with events that have yet to be designated officially as 'harmful' but that show evidence of exhibiting potentially negative consequences. Environmental crime prevention likewise has to negotiate different kinds of harms, as these affect humans, local and global environments, and non-human animals.

There is now an extensive body of work that deals with preventing environmental crime in different geographical locations (see for examples, Cao 2017; Lemieux 2014; Moreto 2018; Sollund 2019; Sollund et al. 2017; Wong 2019). One of the key lessons from the environmental crime prevention literature is that intervention ought to be based on a problem-solving approach. Specific problems demand particular responses. That is, general pronouncements about the nature of harm need to be accompanied by particular site or harm analysis. To illustrate this, we can consider the issue of illegal fishing.

3.1 Crime Prevention and Illegal Fishing

There are major variations in the specific nature of this type of criminal activity. Consider, for example, the following types of illegal fishing (White 2008):

- commercial fishing that involves catches in excess of quota, false declarations, destruction of by-catch linked to marine pollution;
- recreational fishing that involves unlicensed fishing and fishing above allocated quotas;
- Indigenous fishing in traditional but foreign waters, and fishing without a permit;
- large-scale illegal fishing, which also involves the overfishing of particular species, such as sharks;
- specialist illegal fishing that is designed to exploit endangered species specifically for private fish collections or for medicinal purposes.

Illegal fishing differs depending upon location, and studies of illegal fishing (e.g. abalone, lobster and toothfish) show great variation in motives, techniques, local cultures and scale of operation. Environmental crime prevention thus has to address the specific nature of the phenomenon in question if it is to be appropriate to the circumstances. The making of such decisions can be guided by various crime prevention strategies.

In terms of *social crime prevention* methods, for example, children in schools can be exposed to programmes that reshape their concepts of 'the environment', 'fish' and 'fishing'. This could include discussions of 'catch and release' as an imperative for recreational fishing, to doing assignments on the effects of climate change on fish species.

In terms of *environmental prevention*, boating enthusiasts and fishers generally can be advised how best to minimise their impact on fisheries, through measures such as knowledge of marine park boundaries, to the use of suitable receptacles for waste products while at sea. Regular patrols of coastlines, and use of satellites, could facilitate surveillance and monitoring of fishing 'hot spots' and areas where environmental transgressions occur on a frequent basis.

A wide range of crime prevention approaches can in fact be drawn upon in relation to illegal fishing—that incorporate social developmental and communal-oriented measures as well as those that are situational and techniques oriented (see Petrossian and Clarke 2014; Petrossian and Pezzella 2018; Petrossian et al. 2016; Schneider 2008, 2012). These include traditional approaches such as situational crime prevention (focusing on target hardening, for example) to deployment of DNA testing schemes (for species such as salmon and abalone).

The CRAVED Theft Model refers to characteristics of the commodity—**C**oncealable [size, overall catch load]; **R**emovable [easy to catch]; **A**bundant/**A**ccessible/**A**vailable [hot spots]; **V**aluable [larger, scarce]; **E**njoyable [found in recipes]; and **D**isposable [highly commercial]. Researchers and law enforcement practitioners can apply this model to multiple illegally caught species, make comparison across species and locations; focus on methods, perpetrators, and consumers; and draw upon the notion of 'suitable targets of crime'.

In a similar vein, Crime Script Analysis is used to tailor crime prevention to the variety of motives, different sets of skills and knowledge, and different modus operandi involved in illegal fishing. In this framework, crime is viewed as a process, with the actual criminal event only one of the 'events' in this process. Accordingly, the task is to lay out a 'script' and carefully scrutinise the sequential steps. For example, Illegal Unregulated and Unreported (IUU) Fishing Scripts involve analysis of Stage 1: Removal & landing of illegally caught fish; and Stage 2: Processing & distribution of fish. Key elements of the crime script include *Preparation* (e.g. licenses, registrations); *Entry* (e.g. enter into fishery, check equipment); *Target selection* (e.g. activate machinery); *Doing* (e.g. catch fish, discard by-catch, primary and secondary processing); and *Exit* (trans-shipment, mix illegal with legal, distribution to restaurants). A crime prevention response involves 'reading' the script based upon the responses and information provided in each stage of the investigation.

Other approaches concentrate on community crime prevention measures. For instance, these include working at the local level to encourage citizen engagement as guardians of nature and having local tourism and other commercial interests as natural resource managers (through initiatives such as 'Fish Watch' and hot lines), as well as the use of relevant technology such as WildScan (a mobile app) and GPS-linked photos which allow members of the public to report likely illegally sourced or poached animals in both natural settings and commercial markets.

A holistic approach to crime prevention acknowledges that multiple interests need to be accommodated as part of the crime prevention problem-solving process. Such an approach attempts to foster community-level compliance and engagement in guardianship, the tackling of economic and cultural factors that legitimate illegal fishing, uses the full suite of techniques and technologies to monitor and address issues, and situates fish (and the protection of fish) within the context of both ecological and social environments. Many of these principles and values are evident in United Nations efforts to prevent environmental crime.

4 United Nations Initiatives and Interventions

The impact and consequences of environmental crimes and harms on a planetary scale are growing and they are becoming ever more devastating. A big challenge for those responding to environmental crime, therefore, is to extend the scope of analyses—illegal fishing is a global problem; deforestation is a global problem;

air, land and water pollution is a global problem—and to respond accordingly. The transnational character of environmental crime is fundamental to the harms with which it is associated. Global institutional responses are therefore needed.

This is acknowledged in the rationale for and framing of key United Nations agreements. For example, environmental sustainability lies at the heart of the Sustainable Development Goals and this is apparent in targets such as those that focus on species protection and biodiversity.

SDG 14.6.1 Progress by countries in the degree of implementation of international instruments aiming to combat illegal, unreported and unregulated fishing

SDG 15.7 Take urgent action to end poaching and trafficking of protected species of flora and fauna and address both demand and supply of illegal wildlife products

SDG 15.C Enhance global support for efforts to combat poaching and trafficking of protected species, including by increasing the capacity of local communities to pursue sustainable livelihood opportunities

In addressing these targets, UN agencies are themselves playing an important and leading role.

4.1 Collaboration and Capacity Building

In legal terms, transnational environmental crime involves 'the trading and smuggling of plants, animals, resources and pollutants in violation of prohibition or regulation regimes established by multilateral environmental agreements and/or in contravention of domestic law' (Forni 2010, p. 34). Responding to transnational environmental crime requires not only the right kinds of laws and regulatory mechanisms, but the right kinds of environmental law enforcement practices and procedures. Many different international instruments deal with matters pertaining to the protection of biodiversity, pollution and transfer of hazardous waste (Boister and Currie 2014).

According to the Division of Environmental Law and Conventions (DELC), United Nations Environment Programme (2013a), however, the transnational nature of illegal environmental activity makes it distinctive and difficult to combat. Accordingly, part of the role of the DELC is to help build capacity among Member States in fighting environmental crime and in defining international environmental norms. In the specific area of transnational environmental crime, the DELC works with partners towards:

- A better understanding of the global problems and existing gaps on transnational or cross-border environmental crime;
- Common approaches to more efficiently and effectively tackle the problem of transnational environmental crime from a legal standpoint;

- Strengthening and reinforcing current international and national legal and institutional arrangements and law enforcement mechanisms to combat transnational environmental crime;
- Strengthening and reinforcing national environmental laws to counter environmental crime;
- Fostering and enhancing cross-border cooperation in the field of environmental crime;
- Strengthening and developing partnerships, coordination and cooperation between stakeholders.

These activities build upon existing partnerships and initiatives such as the Green Customs Initiative and the DELC capacity building programme for judges that aims to better equip legal practitioners, judges and jurists in their roles in interpreting and applying environmental laws.

The United Nations Interregional Crime and Justice Research Institute—UNICRI (2013) has observed that there has been a considerable expansion of transnational environmental crimes in recent years due to the involvement of organised criminal groups acting across borders. Organisations such as the United Nations Office on Drugs and Crime (UNOCD), the European Union, and Interpol, have likewise each signalled the cross-connections between environmental crime and other crimes such as corruption, money laundering, human trafficking and murder (see for example, UNOCD 2011, 2013; Interpol 2013; Interpol and UNEP 2016).

Responding to these kinds of players demands robust action across the various dimensions of the enforcement chain. Greater attention, therefore, is now being given to the United Nations Convention Against Transnational Organised Crime, since this offers the promise of concerted action and harsher penalties against environmental criminals. The link to the UNTOC Convention, however, depends upon whether the conduct in question meets the definition of transnational organised crime including the requirement that the crime is 'serious' (an offence punishable by a maximum deprivation of liberty of at least four years or a more serious penalty). Yet, the majority of States that are party to legal instruments such as the Convention on International Trade in Endangered Species (CITES) do not impose this level of penalty on wildlife criminals.

Addressing shortfalls or technical difficulties in environmental crime prevention and law enforcement has led to closer connections between international bodies, government and non-government organisations, and national governments. A range of international collaborations have emerged around specific types of commodity, and in relation to specific enforcement and regulatory bodies. For example, the International Consortium Combatting Wildlife Crime (ICCWC) is comprised of 5 inter-governmental organisations: CITES, Interpol, UNODC, World Bank and World Customs Organisation. More broadly, the International Network for Environmental Compliance and Enforcement (INECE) brings together approximately 4000 individual members from more than 150 countries with a view to improving policy and practice in this area.

On another front, Project Leaf (Law Enforcement Assistance for Forests) is an Interpol and United Nations Environment Programme (UNEP) climate initiative consortium that is directed against illegal logging and related crimes. The objectives of this Project are to:

- Form National Environmental Security Task Forces (NESTs) to ensure institutionalised cooperation between national agencies, Interpol NCBs [National Central Bureau], and international partners;
- Conduct operations to suppress criminality, disrupt trafficking routes, and ensure the enforcement of international and national legislations on sustainable forestry;
- Expand the project through awareness raising making a real contribution to global emissions goals, the protection of biodiversity, and preventing environmental destruction (Interpol 2012a, b).

A NEST is a task force of a firmly established team of experts who work together to address specific issues (Higgins and White 2016). They are comprised of senior criminal investigators, criminal analysts, training officers, prosecutors, financial specialists, forensic experts and others, drawn from police, customs, environmental and other specialised enforcement agencies, and also involving non-government and regional organisations as appropriate.

There are also various Multilateral Environment Agreement (MEA) secretariats that coordinate the work and efforts of their member countries and cover themes and commodities (e.g. whaling, migratory birds, Antarctic). For example, the United Nations Environment Programme hosts a number of Multilateral Environmental Agreements Secretariats, including: Convention on Biological Diversity (CBD); Convention on International Trade in Endangered Species of Wild Fauna and Flora (CITES); Convention on the Conservation of Migratory Species of Wild Animals (CMS); Basel Convention on the Control of Transboundary Movements of Hazardous Wastes and Their Disposal (Basel Convention); Stockholm Convention on Persistent Organic Pollutants (POPS); Rotterdam Convention Prior Informed Consent Procedure for Certain Hazardous Chemicals and Pesticides in International Trade (PIC); Vienna Convention for the Protection of the Ozone layer & Montreal Protocol on Substances that Deplete the Ozone Layer (Ozone Convention & Protocol); and the Multilateral Fund Secretariat for the Implementation of the Montreal Protocol (Funding Secretariat).

The World Customs Organisation, amongst others, is involved in the Green Customs Initiative. Customs and border protection personnel constitute the first line of defence of every country's efforts to deal with transboundary illegal trade. They are frequently the first link in the compliance and enforcement chain. The objective of the Green Customs initiative is to enhance the capacity of customs and other relevant enforcement personnel to monitor and facilitate the legal trade and to detect and prevent illegal trade in environmentally-sensitive commodities covered by the relevant conventions and multilateral environmental agreements (MEAs). The initiative provides coordinated training, a green customs guide, workshops and relevant website and materials. The partners comprise the secretariats of the relevant multilateral environmental agreements (Basel, Cartagena, CITES, Montreal,

Rotterdam, Stockholm), Interpol, the Organisation for the Prohibition of Chemical Weapons, UNEP, UNODC and the World Customs Organisation. It also works closely with other regional and international organisations.

Reflecting concern over environmental issues, a summit of International Chiefs of Environmental Compliance and Enforcement was held in March 2012. This forum provided an opportunity for national leaders of environment, biodiversity and natural resources agencies to meet and discuss action around issues such as investigative assistance and operational support, information management, capacity building standards and effective networks, as well as commodity specific side-meetings covering fisheries, forestry, pollution and wildlife. A summary of the event pointed out that:

Particular concern was expressed by many delegates on the scale of environmental crime and the connection with organised transnational crime, including issues of smuggling, corruption, fraud, tax evasion, money laundering, and murder:

- The interconnectivity of environmental crime with other forms of criminal activity requires cooperation and collaboration across all levels of law enforcement to combat and prevent the illegal activities;
- The current scale of environmental crime involves very similar approaches, means and severity as other forms of crime, but is aggravated and exacerbated further by the direct serious implications it has on the development goals of many countries;
- Particular concern is raised on the sheer scale of environmental crime including, but not limited to, illegal logging and deforestation, illegal fisheries and smuggling of toxic waste, and the severe implications of this not only on the environment, but also on human security and economic development (Interpol and UNEP 2012).

It is not only issues which have been highlighted in such summits, but operational policies and practices as well. This is reflected in efforts to link up agencies and personnel across jurisdictions and across substantive enforcement areas, such as illegal logging, fisheries crime, pollution crime, the illegal poaching and trade in Asian "big cats", and the conservation of elephants and rhinoceros (see Interpol website 2019). In a similar vein, the UNODC has the mandate and expertise to assist Member States in strengthening their preventive and law enforcement capacities. In regards environmental crime, for example, it has recently produced guides on drafting legislation to combat wildlife crime and addressing corruption in the fisheries sector (UNODC 2019a, b). As part of its 'Global Programme for Combatting Wildlife and Forest Crime', the UNODC is working to enhance capacity-building and wildlife law enforcement networks. Its work also includes the delivery of specific technical assistance activities, such as coordinating the implementation of the *Wildlife and Forest Crime Analytic Toolkit* (UNODC 2012).

In the end, to be effective, agencies need to be able to harness the cooperation and expertise of many different contributors and to liaise with relevant partners at the local to the international levels. A 'joined up' approach also means that links can be made between different forms of crime as well as between different agencies, and different parts of the world. For instance, illegal fishing has been tied to trafficking of persons, smuggling of migrants and the illicit traffic in drugs. This is due to the influence of transnational organised crime in the fishing industry worldwide (UNODC 2011).

4.2 NGO Engagement in Environmental Law Enforcement

The United Nations has for many years recognised the need to collaborate with non-government organisations (NGOs). In practice, an international organisation can give NGOs an opportunity to participate in ongoing policy development, as was the case for example with the Convention on International Trade in Endangered Species. The same has occurred in regards NGO participation in preparatory committees for an international conference (e.g. Rio Earth Summit in 1992, Johannesburg Summit on Sustainable Development in 2002). NGOs can also send representatives to participate in the negotiations of semi-public international conferences. The International Union for Conservation of Nature (IUCN), for instance, has a membership that includes around 700 NGOs as well as state and government agencies.

It can be difficult to determine the degree of an NGO's impact or significance in influencing global policy, however their involvement is now deemed fundamental to regimes of environmental governance (McCormick 2010). While drawing correlations between NGO actions and negotiation outcomes may be difficult, there are a few instances where particular NGO strategies have clearly contributed to successful environmental policy negotiations. For instance, the outcomes of the working group mandated by the United Nations General Assembly to investigate issues related to the conservation and sustainable use of biodiversity in marine areas beyond national jurisdiction (BBNJ Working Group) is a case in point. The negotiations went on over a decade and included over 1500 individuals representing governments and NGOs. The end result was the building of consensus for the need to negotiate an international binding instrument on BBNJ—a considerable feat in global environmental governance. The government delegations involved in the BBNJ Working Group approached the negotiations with a level of openness and willingness to consider NGOs' perspectives and recommendations to collaborate and reach an agreement. Likewise, the NGOs approached the negotiations with the recognition of the need to work with the political system to achieve compromise on a policy.

When it comes to environmental crime enforcement and prevention, this also includes a wide range of NGOs that operate in various official and unofficial capacities. For instance, in Australia, animal welfare may be deemed to be the official responsibility of organisations such as the Royal Society for the Prevention of Cruelty to Animals (RSPCA) who then investigate and prosecute cases of animal abuse. Other NGOs, such as Greenpeace Amazon, may not have an 'official' role per se, but nonetheless gather evidence of activities such as illegal logging which can then be passed on to relevant police and judicial authorities. Very often it is transnational environmental activists who expose instances of ecological and species harm, providing details of poor regulation and enforcement practices, and contributing both formally and informally to crime reduction and prosecution processes. As increasingly important players in the world of environmental protection, conservation and management, environmental activists frequently have both to confront powerful social, economic and political interests, and to work with and alongside powerful groups, organisations and state apparatus.

The role of 'third parties' is vital when it comes to environmental crime. This is because of the complex nature of environmental harms covering many different issues relating to air, land and water use, biodiversity, the transport and use of hazardous waste, and carbon emissions, and which, in turn, demand expertise across a wide range of areas and extensive networks of surveillance. It is also due to the generally poor level of resources, meagre budgets and low staff numbers devoted to environmental protection and law enforcement activities by governments, especially given the scope and scale of the problems.

There are many ways in which transnational environmental activist groups can work with official agencies and personnel to achieve similar goals, including sharing of intelligence and joint efforts to gather evidence against wrongdoers. On the other hand, in countries and regions where legal and illegal logging is built into the fabric of state-corporate collusion, it may well be the policing of anti-logging activists that predominates. The specific status and role of NGOs will thus vary depending upon immediate social and political circumstances.

There are a number of issues, problems and dilemmas that shape the precise role and contribution of NGOs to environmental law enforcement. Acknowledgement of these by both sides, plus a willingness to engage in dialogue with various stakeholders, provides space in which to build upon the positive aspects of NGO engagement, and to minimise the potential conflicts between NGO and official agencies in their pursuit of social and ecological justice.

4.3 Education and Community Activism

In addition to interagency and NGO collaborations, knowledge provision and education are important areas in which United Nations agencies have made a contribution. In some cases, this is directly tied to contemporary environmental issues such as climate change, and interventions by citizens and community groups. In other instances, initiatives have been established that provide across-the-board educational resources. One example of this is the 'Education for Justice' programme.

The 'Education for Justice' [E4J] initiative seeks to prevent crime and promote a culture of lawfulness through education activities designed for primary, secondary and tertiary levels. The intention is that these activities will help educators teach the next generation to better understand and address problems, including actively engaging in their communities and future professions to do so. In the Doha Declaration, adopted by the 13th United Nations Congress on Crime Prevention and

Criminal Justice in 2015 and subsequently endorsed by the General Assembly in its resolution 70/174, Member States emphasised that education is fundamental for the prevention of crime and for the promotion of the rule of law and human rights.

In operational terms, the Doha Declaration provided the foundation for the development of the E4J initiative, a component of the UN Office on Drugs and Crime 'Global Programme for the Implementation of the Doha Declaration'. The UNODC has coordinated the preparation of E4J tertiary level materials, consisting of a nine peer-reviewed university module series. Modules in the series include topic areas such as integrity and ethics, anti-corruption, crime prevention and criminal justice, organised crime, cybercrime, firearms trafficking, trafficking in persons and smuggling of migrants, and counter-terrorism.

In the specific area of environmental crime, the tertiary modules include three modules on *wildlife, fisheries and forestry crime*. Module 1 provides learning and teaching materials, including lecture content and student exercises, on 'Illicit Markets for Wildlife Products'. Module 2 deals with 'International Frameworks', and Module 3 focuses on 'Criminal Justice Responses to Wildlife and Forest Crime'. These resources are 'open access' and thus not subject to copyright restrictions. They are intended for use by university lecturers and students worldwide. They are supported by SHERLOC—Sharing Electronic Resources and Laws on Crime—an open-access database that is relevant across 15 crime types, including wildlife crimes. Modules such as these are intended to raise consciousness about issues in the same moment as broadening understanding and facilitating the taking of preventive measures.

Another area in which UN agencies have provided useful background materials is climate change. This includes documentation of the gravity of the problem and the role of governments. For example, the UN Environment Programme (2019) *Emissions Gap Report* said that even if all current unconditional commitments under the Paris Agreement are implemented, temperatures are expected to rise by 3.2 °C, bringing even wider-ranging and more destructive climate impacts. It pointed out that collective ambition must increase more than fivefold over current levels to deliver the cuts needed over the next decade for the 1.5 °C goal. The lack of action on the part of nation-states in regards climate change has simultaneously heightened awareness of the need for community action.

The attainment of climate justice will necessarily involve mass political and social movements. These are presently directed against the forces, discourses and policies that stymy needed mitigation and adaptation measures. Many are informed by values, language and tactics that reflect a vision of hope, resilience and equality in regards the future. Student strikes initiated by Swedish activist Greta Thunberg have taken the world by storm, culminating in millions of people taking to the streets in 2019, and her subsequent naming as 'Person of the Year' by *Time Magazine*.

Another important component of citizen engagement is legal action taken in support of climate justice. Climate change litigation involves cases being brought before administrative and judicial bodies that raise issues of law or fact regarding the science of climate change and climate change mitigation and adaption efforts (see

Table 1 Trends in climate change litigation

Legal trend	Substantive issues
Holding governments to their legislative and policy commitments	Hold governments accountable for climate-related commitments, including those made through international climate agreements
Linking the impacts of resource extraction to climate change and resilience	Attempts to compel alternative approaches to natural resource management to those which involve emissions due to combustion of extracted fossil fuels or that impair resiliency and adaptive capacity
Establishing that particular emissions are the proximate cause of particular adverse climate change impacts	Seeks to establish liabilities that generate emissions with full knowledge of those emission's effects on global climate
Establishing liability for failures (or efforts) to adapt to climate change	In the light of improvements in technical understandings of climate science, seeks to assign responsibility where failures to adapt result in foreseeable, material harms
Applying the public trust doctrine to climate change	The state has a responsibility for the integrity of a nation's public trust resources for future generations, and thus to principles of intergenerational equity

Source: drawing upon Burger et al. (2017)

Table 1). While UN agencies are not directly involved in such litigation, they nonetheless provide important documentation of where and how this is occurring. For example, over the past few years several key trends have been identified in climate change litigation and these have been recorded by agencies such as the United Nations Environment Programme (Burger et al. 2017). While most of these cases are civil and rarely criminal, they nonetheless are directed at addressing the ecocidal tendencies associated with climate change. To that end, they deal with matters of fundamental ecological and social harm—key considerations in preventing environmental crime.

Climate change litigation may have implications for national policies and practice relating to mitigation or be directed to addressing issues pertaining to specific projects such as expansion of airports and coal mines. In most instances, the defendant has been governments.

5 The Looming Environmental Collapse

Global warming is transforming the world in ways that are radically and rapidly re-shaping social and ecological futures. The Intergovernmental Panel on Climate Change (IPCC) (2014) has reported that:

- Warming of the climate system is unequivocal, and since the 1950s, many of the observed changes are unprecedented over decades to millennia. The atmosphere and ocean have warmed, the amounts of snow and ice have diminished, sea level has risen, and the concentrations of greenhouse gases have increased (p. 3);

- Each of the last three decades has been successively warmer at the Earth's surface than any preceding decade since 1850 (p. 3);
- Ocean warming dominates the increase in energy stored in the climate system, accounting for more than 90% of the energy accumulated between 1971 and 2010 (p. 4);
- Over the last two decades, the Greenland and Antarctic ice sheets have been losing mass, glaciers have continued to shrink almost worldwide, and Arctic sea ice and Northern Hemisphere spring snow cover have continued to decrease in extent (p. 4);
- The rate of sea level rise since the mid-nineteenth century has been larger than the mean rate during the previous two millennia (p. 4).

Scientific data continues to demonstrate the depth and scale of the problem. The damage caused by global warming is being felt in the form of extreme weather events, increased competition for dwindling natural resources, outbreaks of disease and viral infections, further extinctions of species, continued pressure to trade off food for fuel, intense social conflict and much criminality.

Climate disruption is a term that has been used to emphasise the fact that increases in global average temperature 'does not simply translate into modest, uniform warming but rather triggers surprisingly sharp changes in extreme weather and disrupts longer-term weather and climate patterns' (Steffen 2018). Heavy snow in the United Kingdom and parts of Western Europe in 2018, and record spring and early summer temperatures in Australia in 2019, are symptomatic of changes to what were considered to be the normal air circulation patterns. Disruption of these normal patterns is one of the manifestations of climate change as a biophysical phenomenon.

The point is that climate change disrupts normal weather patterns in various and unexpected ways. Consider the findings of the Australian Climate Council report titled *Weather Gone Wild* that outlines the link between climate change and extreme weather (Steffen et al. 2019).

- *Extreme Temperatures*—hot extremes, heatwaves lasting longer and more frequently;
- *Intense Precipitation*—rain, snow or hail, over various time periods are increasing across most of the world;
- *Cyclones, Storms and Hurricanes*—increase frequency of severe tropical cyclones and decrease of weaker ones, intensity of storms increasing, higher rainfall associated with these events;
- *Droughts;*
- *Bushfires*—increase in extreme fire weather, as measured by the Forest Fire Danger Index that estimates fire danger on a given day based on observations of temperature, rainfall, humidity and wind speed.

The Climate Council report observes that the number of climate-related natural catastrophes has been rising steeply since the 1980s and the most damaging are often

Table 2 Major extreme weather events globally 2018

Place	Event	Example
USA	Wildfires, hurricanes, storms	California—Camp Fire claims 86 civilian lives and burns 153,336 acres
South America	Drought	Crop production decline
Europe	Severe storms	Storm Friederike struck Germany, the Netherlands and Belgium, and include casualties and huge economic losses
Middle East	Flash floods affecting Bahrain, Jordan and Israel	Bahrain airport records wettest October since 1902
Africa	Drought, below average precipitation, floods	Cape Town water crisis
Asia	Extraordinarily heavy rainfall, flash floods, heatwaves, typhoons, extreme monsoon rains	Kerala floods in India with a higher death toll than any other extreme weather event worldwide during 2018
Oceania	Tropical cyclones	'Gina' is worst storm recorded in Tonga in 60 years
Northern Hemisphere	Extreme heat event	Norway experienced a record temperature of 33.5 °C

Source: derived from Steffen et al. (2019), pp. 26–34

the result of combinations of variables, which are called compound extremes. These include geophysical events such as landslides to weather phenomenon like storms.

The number of extreme weather events is rising and are especially impactful in conjunction with each other. Many specific examples can be given from around the world in 2018 alone (see Table 2).

These events have major health implications (for human and non-human alike). The *Lancet* Countdown tracks progress on the health impacts of climate hazards as well as other indicators for a global overview of health and climate change (Watts et al. 2017). The health and social consequences of events resulting from climate change—such as rising temperatures, heat waves, and increases in the frequency of complex extreme weather events—are far reaching and include heat-related deaths to the spread of infectious diseases. The trends and issues arising from climate disruption are very perplexing and worrying.

Meanwhile, the loss of biodiversity likewise continues at a rapid pace today and the principal pressures directly driving biodiversity loss are either constant or increasing in intensity (Secretariat of the Convention on Biological Diversity 2010). Biodiversity is generally defined as the variety of all species on earth. It refers to the different plants, animals and micro-organisms, and their genes, that together make up life on the planet. It also includes reference to the terrestrial (land), marine (ocean) and freshwater (inland water systems) ecosystems of which they are a part.

Changes to an ecosystem by human intervention occurs through manipulation, contamination or destruction of these components (for example, through mining or land clearance or use of pesticides). According to the United Nations there are five principle threats to biodiversity (UNEP 2013b). These are:

1. the unsustainable harvesting of natural resources, including plants, animals and marine species;
2. the loss, degradation or fragmentation of ecosystems through land conversion for agriculture, forest clearing, etc.;
3. invasive non-native or 'alien' species being introduced to ecosystems to which they are not adapted, i.e. where they have no, or not enough, predators, to maintain an ecological balance;
4. pollution; and
5. climate change.

There are complex reasons why these threats emerge as they do, and they are interlinked in a variety of ways. Reduction in species includes both animals and plants. This is significant insofar as complex ecosystems depend upon the interaction between all species, and any change will impact upon overall functioning.

In regards specifically to trees and species that inhabit forests, thirteen per cent of the world's total forest area is under formal protection and almost 75 per cent of forests are covered by a national forest programme. Yet, despite progress in the regulatory sphere, and net gains in forest areas in Europe and Asia, total loss of forest cover during the last decade still averaged around 13 million hectares per year. Most deforestation is occurring in tropical forests, with substantial biodiversity impacts: 'Although the global rate of net forest cover loss has slowed, partly due to the expansion of plantations and to natural forest restoration, forest biodiversity loss continues to occur disproportionately since the highest levels of deforestation and of forest degradation are reported for biodiversity-rich natural forests in developing countries' (UNEP 2011, p. 48). Net losses are especially significant in South America and Africa. Recent events in the Amazon, featuring widespread fires, many of which were deliberately lit, makes the situation even more worrying.

In 2019, it was reported that around 1 million animal and plant species are now threatened with extinction, many within decades, more than ever before in human history (IPBES 2019). The ramifications are catastrophic. Yet, as Greta Thunberg tweeted at the time of the report's release:

Where are the breaking news?
The extra news broadcasts?
The front pages?
Where are the emerging meetings?
The crisis summits?
What could be more important?
We are failing but we have not failed.
We can still fix this.
But not if we continue like today.
Not a chance.
(Greta Thunberg – Twitter, 8 May 2019).

The outlook does not look good. And that is without even considering the extent and geographical reach of water, air and land pollution that is devastating the planet. The impact of plastics in oceans is only the tip of the rapidly melting iceberg. Environmental collapse is occurring across many different fronts, and time is rapidly running out to prevent ecocide on a grand scale.

6 Where to From Here?

Environmental harm on this scale demands responses, large and small, that address the key underlying issues contributing to eco-injustice. Preventing ecocide means resisting and transforming the status quo. Time and space for business as usual must be diminished if social and ecological justice is to be achieved—and basic survival ensured.

For the United Nations, this points to a key conundrum. The main perpetrators of environmental crimes and harms are in fact nation-states themselves, in conjunction with transnational corporations. While specific criminal networks and individuals engage in environmental crimes such as wildlife trafficking, the larger issue really has to do with the lack of political will to combat the world's most ecologically destructive activities. This is especially the case with global warming and the continued rise of carbon emissions even in the face of decades of scientific evidence that says this is destroying our home Planet Earth.

The fact that we are facing extinction of one million species is evidence enough that much more needs to be done to preserve and protect the earth's ecological wellbeing. Similarly, the failure of the Madrid talks on climate change in 2019 merely continues the longstanding lack of consensus about what to do about global warming, to the world's detriment.

On the other hand, arguably it is the actions of UN agencies which have helped to slow the destruction of habitat, the denuding of landscapes, the demise of fishing grounds and the exploitation of vulnerable species. Without the UN Environmental Programme, the UN Office on Drugs and Crime, and other relevant agencies, the situation could be much worse than otherwise. Moreover, educational initiatives such as 'Education for Justice' offer hope that rising generations will seize the day and change the world for the better.

But, ultimately, we are faced with two key dilemmas. First, important powerbrokers of world governance such as the United States, along with countries such as Australia and Brazil, are actively undermining the objectives of climate justice at domestic and international levels. How to overcome the impasse created by stubborn climate change contrarianism is a major problem. We will return to this difficulty shortly.

Second, we are running out of time. Every delay in stopping and reversing carbon emissions puts us into greater peril. Each approval of destructive industries, and endorsement of policies that destroy ecological systems and species habitat, entrenches the so called sixth mass extinction.

Environmental crime prevention matters nought—if there is nothing left to protect and preserve. The challenges facing United Nations agencies and the organisation as a whole are manifest and dire. We know this precisely because of the information and educational resources provided by the UN. But is it too little, too late? That is a key question of the moment, as is the question 'what is to be done?'

There is no shortage of prescriptive answers to the calamities now upon us. For example, SDG 13 says that we must 'Take urgent action to combat climate change and its impacts'. What follows are a series of general statements, such as improving education, awareness-raising and human and institutional capacity on climate change mitigation, adaptation, impact reduction and early warning. Similar measures are advocated by civil society organisations. The key demands of the Climate Justice network, for instance, include:

1. Fight for the transformation of energy systems;
2. Fight for food sovereignty, for peoples' rights to sufficient, healthy and appropriate food and sustainable food systems;
3. Fight for peoples' rights to sufficient, affordable, clean, quality water;
4. Fight for just transitions for all workers beginning with those in the dirty and harmful energy industries;
5. Fight for people's safety and security of homes and livelihoods from climate disasters;
6. Fight for the social, political, economic, cultural and reproductive rights and empowerment of all our people and communities;
7. Fight for mobilisation and delivery of climate finance by all states;
8. Fight for reparations for climate debt owed by those most responsible for climate change;
9. Fight for an end to deception and false solutions in mitigation and adaptation;
10. Fight for an end to policies, decisions and measures by governments, elites, institutions and corporations (domestic, regional and global) that increase the vulnerabilities of people and planet to impacts of climate change;
11. Fight to stop the commodification and financialisation of nature and nature's functions;
12. Fight for an international climate agreement that is rooted in science, equity and justice.

(Global Campaign to Demand Climate Justice 2018).

There is knowledge of what needs to be done—starting with the immediate diminishment and eventual stopping of carbon emissions, especially those emanating from the fossil fuel industries.

However, as the UN Human Rights Council recently pointed out, while the problems are epic and urgent, the response has been lukewarm. In its summary statement for the *Climate Change and Poverty* report (A/HRC/41/39-17 July 2019), the Council asserts that:

> Governments and too many in the human rights community have failed to seriously address climate change for decades. Sombre speeches by government officials have not led to

meaningful action and too many countries continue taking short-sighted steps in the wrong direction.

Much the same can be said about preventing environmental crime more generally. For example, this is most obviously manifest in the administration of President Donald Trump who, upon election, systematically appointed pro-industry officials to key environment and natural resource portfolios (such as Scott Pruitt, who had filed lawsuits against the EPA in support of business while Oklahoma Attorney-General, to head up the US EPA). There has been a generic push to deregulate the natural resource sector, trade groups representing business have had open doors to government officials across government departments, and political appointments have been made into agencies such as the EPA involving people from the industries ostensibly meant to be regulated by the EPA. For example, Nancy B. Beck, after spending the five previous years as an executive at the American Chemistry Council, the chemical industry's main trade association, was appointed a top deputy in the EPA's toxic chemical unit (see Lipton 2017). The nett result has been a broad shift in government administration away from the public interest and in favour of specific private industry and firm interests.

This goes to the heart of the problem. Environmental harm is more often than not associated with exploitation of natural resources that bring profit to powerful companies (both privately-owned and state-owned). The science of biodiversity, of climate change, of pollution and contamination tells us that the environment cannot bear the weight of these exploitations any longer. The problem is not the science. Nor is it simply about 'belief' (as if global warming is simply a matter of opinion). Rather, as the planet burns, it is sectional self-interest which is preventing the application of the fire hose. Ultimately, preventing environmental crime, therefore, is about politics. And it is here that the United Nations agencies walk the peculiar tightrope of speaking about and engaging in emergency action to save the planet but being constrained in doing so by their political masters. It is pressure on our political leaders globally—lead by the young and those whose futures are most in jeopardy—that will have most purchase, and that provides modest hope that positive change is still possible, in a rapidly shortening timeframe.

References

Boister, N., & Currie, R. (Eds.). (2014). *Routledge handbook of transnational criminal law*. London: Routledge.

Burger, M., Gundlach, J., Kreilhuber, A., Ognibene, L., Kariuki, A., & Gachie, A. (2017). *The status of climate change litigation: A global review*. New York: United Nations Environment Programme.

Cao, N. (2017). *Timber trafficking in Vietnam*. London: Palgrave Macmillan.

Forni, O. (2010). Mapping environmental crimes. In *Freedom from fear magazine, March*. Turin: United Nations Interregional Crime and Justice Research Institute.

General Assembly resolution 55/2, United Nations Millennium Declaration, A/55/L.2 (8 September 2000). Available at: https://bit.ly/2VZ8DyZ

General Assembly resolution 70/1, Transforming our world: The 2030 Agenda for Sustainable Development, A/RES/70/1 (25 September 2015). Available at: https://bit.ly/2KRen7E

Global Campaign to Demand Climate Justice. (2018). 'Fight for Climate Justice!' https://bit.ly/3dfpVO3

Higgins, D., & White, R. (2016). Collaboration at the front line: INTERPOL and NGOs in the same NEST. In G. Pink & R. White (Eds.), *Environmental crime and collaborative state intervention*. Basingstoke: Palgrave Macmillan.

Higgins, P. (2012). *Earth is our business: Changing the rules of the game*. London: Shepheard-Walwyn Publishers Ltd..

Intergovernmental Panel on Climate Change (IPCC). (2014). Climate Change 2014 Synthesis Report, Approved Summary for Policymakers. https://bit.ly/2YpN1h3

Intergovernmental Science-Policy Platform on Biodiversity and Ecosystem Services (IPBES). (2019). *The IPBES global assessment report on biodiversity and ecosystem services*. Paris: IPBES.

Interpol. (2012a). *National environmental security task force: Bringing compliance and enforcement agencies together to maintain environmental security*. Lyon: Interpol.

Interpol. (2012b). Environmental Crime Programme: Project LEAF. Lyon, France: Interpol [see environmentalcrime@interpol.int].

Interpol. (2013). *'INTERPOL meeting aims to strengthen cooperation on environmental crime activities' (media release)*. Lyon: Interpol.

Interpol & United Nations Environment Programme. (2012). *Summit report: International chiefs of environmental compliance and enforcement*. Lyon, France: Interpol and UNEP.

Interpol & United Nations Environment Programme. (2016). *Strategic report: Environment, peace and security – A convergence of threats*. Lyon: Interpol.

Lemieux, A. (Ed.). (2014). *Situational prevention of poaching*. London: Routledge.

Lipton, E. (2017). Why has the E.P.A. shifted on toxic chemicals? An industry insider helps call the shots. *The New York Times*, 21 October 2017. https://nyti.ms/2z1h9Vp

McCormick, J. (2010). The role of environmental NGOs in international regimes. In R. Axelrod & S. Vandeveer (Eds.), *The global environment: Institutions, law and policy*. London: Sage.

Moreto, W. (Ed.). (2018). *Wildlife crime: From theory to practice*. Philadelphia: Temple University Press.

Petrossian, G., & Clarke, R. (2014). Explaining and controlling illegal commercial fishing: An application of the CRAVED Theft Model. *British Journal of Criminology, 54*(1), 73–90.

Petrossian, G., & Pezzella, F. (2018). IUU fishing and seafood fraud: Using crime script analysis to inform intervention. *The Annals of the American Academy, AAPSS, 679*, 121–139.

Petrossian, G., Pires, S., & van Uhm, D. (2016). An overview of seized illegal wildlife entering the United States. *Global Crime*. https://doi.org/10.1080/17440572.2016.1152548

Schneider, J. (2008). Reducing the illicit trade in endangered wildlife: The market reduction approach. *Journal of Contemporary Criminal Justice, 24*(3), 274–295.

Schneider, J. (2012). *Sold into extinction: The global trade in endangered species*. Santa Barbara: Praeger.

Secretariat of the Convention on Biological Diversity. (2010). *Global Biodiversity Outlook 3*. Montreal: SCBD.

Sollund, R. (2019). *The crimes of wildlife trafficking: Issues of justice, legality and morality*. London: Routledge.

Sollund, R., Stefes, C., & Germani, A. (Eds.). (2017). *Fighting environmental crime in Europe and beyond: The role of the EU and its Member States*. London: Palgrave Macmillan.

Steffen, W. (2018). Why it's sweltering in Penrith while Florida is in deep freeze. *The Sydney Morning Herald*, 9 January (p. 21).

Steffen, W., Dean, A., & Rice, M. (2019). *Weather gone wild: Climate change-fuelled extreme weather in 2018*. Sydney: Climate Council of Australia.

United Nations. (2015, 31 March). Draft Doha Declaration on integrating crime prevention and criminal justice into the wider United Nations Agenda to address social and economic

challenges and to promote the rule of law at the national and international levels, and public participation. A/CONF.222/L.6. Available at: https://bit.ly/2Ws6sDo
United Nations Environment Programme. (2011). *UNEP year book: Emerging issues in our global environment 2011*. Nairobi, Kenya: UNEP.
United Nations Environment Programme. (2013a). *Division of Environmental Law and Conventions*. https://bit.ly/2z3SjnO
United Nations Environment Programme. (2013b). *Threats to biodiversity*. https://bit.ly/2Swgm5u
United Nations Environment Programme. (2019). *Emissions Gap Report*. Geneva: UNEP.
United Nations Environmental Programme – One World South Asia. (2013). *Theft of natural resources is a new challenge: UNEP*. https://bit.ly/2yo5Kib
United Nations, Human Rights Council. (2019). Climate Change and Poverty: Report of the Special Rapporteur on extreme poverty and human rights, A/HRC/41/39-24 June-12 July 2019, Agenda item 3 (pp. 1–19).
United Nations Interregional Crime and Justice Research Institute. (2013). *Environmental Crimes, 2013*. https://bit.ly/35pGbcK
United Nations Office on Drugs and Crime. (2011). *Transnational organized crime in the fishing industry*. Vienna: United Nations.
United Nations Office on Drugs and Crime. (2012). *Wildlife and Forest Crime Analytic Toolkit*. Geneva: ONODC.
United Nations Office on Drugs and Crime. (2013). *Transnational organized crime in East Asia and the Pacific: A threat assessment*. Vienna: UNODC.
United Nations Office on Drugs and Crime. (2019a). *Guide on drafting legislation to combat wildlife crime*. Vienna: UNODC.
United Nations Office on Drugs and Crime. (2019b). *Rotten fish: A guide on addressing corruption in the fisheries sector*. Vienna: UNODC.
Watts, N., Adger, W. N., Ayeb-Karlsson, S., Bai, Y., Byass, P., Campbell-Lendrum, D., et al. (2017). The Lancet countdown: Tracking progress on health and climate change. *The Lancet, 389*, 1151–1164.
White, R. (2008). *Crimes against nature*. London: Routledge.
White, R. (2011). *Transnational environmental crime: Toward an eco-global criminology*. London: Routledge.
White, R. (2014). Environmental insecurity and fortress mentality. *International Affairs, 90*(4), 835–852.
White, R. (2018). *Climate change criminology*. Bristol: Policy Press.
Wong, R. (2019). *The illegal wildlife trade in China*. London: Palgrave Macmillan.

Rob White is a Distinguished Professor of Criminology in the School of Social Sciences at the University of Tasmania, Australia. He has published extensively in the areas of criminology, youth studies and offender rehabilitation. Among his substantive book contributions are *Crimes Against Nature* (2008), *Transnational Environmental Crime: Toward an Eco-Global Criminology* (2011), *Environmental Harm: An Eco-Justice Perspective* (2013), *Youth Gangs, Violence and Social Respect* (2013), *Green Criminology* (2014, with Diane Heckenberg), *Innovative Justice* (2015, with Hannah Graham), and *Climate Change Criminology* (2018). He has also written textbooks for Australian criminology in areas such as criminological theory, criminal justice institutions, crime prevention, crime and the media, working with offenders, and juvenile justice. E-mail: r.d.white@utas.edu.au.

Assessing the Viability of Environmental Projects for a Crime Prevention-Inspired Culture of Lawfulness

Wiesław Pływaczewski, Joanna Narodowska, and Maciej Duda

Abstract The chapter discusses the issue of counteracting crime against the environment in the context of the concept of a culture of lawfulness initiated by the Doha Declaration of the Thirteenth United Nations Congress on Crime Prevention and Criminal Justice. Demonstrating selected environmental problems, the authors present how crime against the environment negatively affects implementation of the United Nations 2030 Agenda for Sustainable Development. The authors also indicate the cultural determinants that play an important role in the origins of crime against natural heritage. Based on selected examples, including the United Nations Education for Justice (E4J) initiative and other educational programmes aimed at youth, the authors emphasise the importance of promoting a culture of lawfulness in terms of preventing crime against the environment.

Keywords Criminology · Crime prevention · Criminal justice · Culture of lawfulness · Education for Justice (E4J)

1 Introduction

The United Nations 2030 Agenda for Sustainable Development, adopted in 2015 by 193 Member States of the United Nations (UN), has defined a model for responsible development at the global level (A/RES/70/1). From a criminological perspective, of particular importance is Goal 16 on promoting peaceful just and inclusive societies for all and creating effective public institutions, at all levels of state administration. The implementation of Goal 16 requires simultaneous undertaking actions for the benefit of nature protection and elimination of threats occurring in this area. These include, for example, the problem of the protection of marine resources (Goal 14) relevant to countering organised crime. This form of national and international

W. Pływaczewski · J. Narodowska · M. Duda (✉)
University of Warmia and Mazury in Olsztyn, Faculty of Law and Administration, Department of Criminology and Forensic Science, Olsztyn, Poland
e-mail: joanna.narodowska@uwm.edu.pl; maciej.duda@uwm.edu.pl

H. Kury, S. Redo (eds.), *Crime Prevention and Justice in 2030*,
https://doi.org/10.1007/978-3-030-56227-4_13

criminal activity is one of the main challenges for law enforcement and justice authorities across the world, also in the terms of protection of terrestrial ecosystems. It is obvious that attention should be paid to crime against the world's natural heritage. This is evidenced by establishing in 2010 the International Consortium on Combating Wildlife Crime (ICCWC), which operates under the UN aegis.[1] Although the consortium is a quite young initiative, its attainments in implementing programmes on combating poaching, illegal trade and smuggling of wild animal species are noticeable (ICCWC 2010; Pływaczewski 2016, p. 220; Aslaug Sollund 2019, p. 58).

The implementation of the 2030 Agenda requires undertaking actions in different areas. The effective means of combating crime might be the idea of promoting the culture of lawfulness. This initiative has been started by the Doha Declaration of the Thirteenth United Nations Congress on Crime Prevention and Criminal Justice (A/RES/70/174, Annex). Within this concept, an important role plays initiative called "Education for Justice (E4J)." It includes activities aimed at teaching the next generation about crime prevention, and to better understand and address problems that can undermine the rule of law. At the same time, this initiative encourages youth to become actively engaged in initiatives which are performed by their communities.[2]

2 Review of Environmental Crime Prevention Programmes and Projects

The new vision of world development outlined in the 2030 Agenda focuses on five priorities, known as the 5P principle—People, Planet, Prosperity, Peace, Partnership (A/RES/70/1). The implementation of these priorities is only possible if the local communities are involved in its performance. On environmental protection, it has been clearly proven that the strongest and most lasting interpersonal bonds are established at the lowest level of social organisation. This assessment has been confirmed not only by sociologists but also by criminologists, environmentalists and representatives of law enforcement agencies implementing pro-social prevention programmes (Redo 2017).

An example of law enforcement cooperation with the local community is the well-known New York City (USA) programme called "zero tolerance." The very name of the programme, from which even the authors of the strategy distance

[1]The other entities taking part in this international initiative, either organisationally or financially, are: CITES Secretariat, International Criminal Police Organization (INTERPOL), the World Bank and the World Customs Organisation (WCO).

[2]Such activities are undertaken not only by international institutions or state authorities but also by non-governmental organisations operating within local communities. Acting according to the slogan "act locally - think globally" is often the best guarantee of achieving the Doha Declaration (Galli et al. 2018, pp. 159–169).

themselves, may be misleading and communicate counteracting mostly trivial violations of municipal regulations (Greene 1999, pp. 171–187). In fact, this programme refers to the "broken windows theory" (J.Q. Wilson, G.L. Kelling) and its implementation was largely possible thanks to support of the inhabitants of particular boroughs of the New York City (representatives of local authorities, seniors, schools, veterans, social organisations) (Burke 1998, pp. 666–682). An equally interesting police strategy, known as "community policing," has a similar, eminently social character. This strategy, which in many aspects also concerns the protection of the broadly understood environment and the quality of life of people, is a strong local component because its goals assume that the police can only operate effectively with the support of the social environment. Thus, local communities have become not only a strategic partner of the police, but (which should be strongly emphasised) they are also, from the perspective of this prevention strategy, the most important entity verifying the effectiveness of prevention programmes implemented by the police. As an example of this type of relationship, one should mention the programme implemented by the police in many countries, referred to collectively as "safe cities" (Czapska and Kury 2002, p. 231). Such programmes have the strong consent and support from local communities and are in line with 2030 Agenda. Their aim is to eliminate the inconveniences of daily life, often of a pathological nature, reduce crime, prevent violence and provide a safe environment.

Another strategy which draws attention to the role of society in creating a safe public space, including protection of the natural environment, is the theory of "defensible space" created by Oscar Newman (Schmalleger 2004, p. 210). The manifestations of this concept are, among others, the protests of the inhabitants of large global agglomerations against the "appropriation" of green urban spaces for investment purposes. For example, the attempt to take over the Gezi Park in Istanbul (Turkey) by investors, resulted in clashes between nature defenders and the police (Letsch 2014). The spontaneous protest of the inhabitants of Khimki (city located close to Moscow, Russia), who opposed the construction of the Moscow-Petersburg motorway at the expense of the surrounding forests, was also widely publicised worldwide.

The examples show that the effectiveness of the implemented projects aimed at preventing crime in the area of environmental protection depends to a large extent on public support.

In relation to the discussion on the effectiveness of environmental protection initiatives, an interesting, educational experiment on the protection of wild birds can be quoted. Its initiators, pedagogues from a small town of Zbojna (Poland, Podlaskie Voivodeship), prepared, as part of the Earth Day celebrations, a scenario of an original project on the "Ornithological Court." The pupils involved in this project played the role of trial parties (judges, prosecutors and defenders). They presented different standpoints on benefits or damage associated with birds. The views of young participants were characterised by exceptional maturity and knowledge of bird issues (Pływaczewski 2019, pp. 74–76).

After hearing the arguments of both parties (defenders and prosecutors), the "Ornithological Court" pronounced, that "birds are innocent." In the opinion of the "judges," the degree of harmfulness of birds was negligible in comparison with the benefits they bring. It should be emphasised that the court in its judgment referred, among others, to the provisions of the Universal Declaration of Animal Rights proclaimed in Paris on 15 October 1978 at the UNESCO headquarters. According to Article 1 of this non-governmental bill "all animals are born with an equal claim on life and the same rights to existence." Article 2 states that "all animals are entitled to respect; man as an animal species shall not arrogate to himself the right to exterminate or inhumanely exploit other animals. It is his duty to use his knowledge for the welfare of animals; all animals have a right to the attention, care and protection of man" (Neumann 2012, pp. 91–109).

The local experiment in Zbojna had an educational and ecological dimension. In the discussion on the relationship between two worlds: human and birds, members of the new generation took part, which in the future will be responsible for the Earth and its inhabitants. Another example of engagement in environmental protection might be the spectacular protest of young people against the effects of global warming, initiated by the Swedish schoolgirl Greta Thunberg. In August 2019, this young climate activist took part in a sea journey to New York. The expedition was a part of the environmental campaign to reduce the use of air transport—a significant source of greenhouse gas emissions to the atmosphere.

The initiatives to raise legal awareness among children and youth are also taken by academic centres in Poland. For instance, since 2018 the Department of Criminology and Criminal Policy of the University of Warmia and Mazury in Olsztyn (Poland) has been implementing the educational project "University of a Young Explorer",[3] as a part of the Olsztyn School of Ecocriminology (OSE). The targets of the project are closely related to the 16 Goals of the 2030 Agenda (Department of Criminology and Criminal Policy 2019).

This initiative is carried out by researchers, students as well as by practitioners (judges, prosecutors, police officers and customs officers). The classes involve over 500 students of communal primary schools from the region of Warmia and Mazury.[4] The priority of the project is to achieve such goals as: equalisation of social differences and intercultural integration. The lectures are based on an innovative form of education, so-called "eduentertainment/eduplay."

The key objectives of the project are to familiarise pupils with the principles of law, functioning and access to institutions of the justice system. During the project, the scientists conduct research on its effectiveness. The preliminary results showed that the level of knowledge, skills and competencies of children participating in classes has significantly increased. The evaluation of educational results was carried out with the use of questionnaires. The children filled out the questionnaires before they joined the programme and at the end of the project. Comparison of the results of

[3]Financed by a leading institution of scientific support in Poland—the National Centre for Research and Development (NCBiR).

[4]This area is one of the poorest regions of Poland and is inhabited by many national and ethnic minorities.

the above surveys showed the progress of almost half of the project participants (about 40–50%). It confirms that learning through "fun" brings exceptionally good results.[5]

The project is in line with the Education for Justice (E4J) initiative and 2030 Agenda: Goal 4 (Quality Education), Goal 10 (Reduce Inequalities) and Goal 16 (Peace, Justice and Strong Institutions). This project was carried out at the lowest level of education, *id. est* primary level. Attention was paid to environmental issues and the importance of green criminology in identifying threats and counteracting pathologies directed against natural heritage. The classes were part of the crime prevention strategy (in criminological sense) addressed to youth consisting in changing negative social attitudes and promoting a culture of lawfulness.

Another equally interesting initiative carried out by criminologists from Olsztyn is the implementation of grant titled "European Cultural Heritage – Protection of the Polish-German Cultural Heritage of the Borderland".[6] The research activities are performed in the region of North-Eastern Poland (Warmian-Mazurian Voivodeship and Podlaskie Voivodeship), where the borders of four countries meet (Belarus, Lithuania, Poland, Russia). Over the centuries, due to wars and other turbulences, this region was within the borders of different countries. Even today, it is a place of lively intercultural contacts. Simultaneously, the borders are a conducive place for the organised smuggling of cigarettes and alcohol, cars, amber, works of art, protected specimens of wild fauna and flora. Therefore, the criminological diagnosis of pathological phenomena in the border region may be an interesting comparative material used in the construction of prevention strategies by police and customs services of border countries (Pływaczewski 2009, pp. 206–208).

The initiative conducted by the OSE aims, among others, at promoting the culture of lawfulness among local communities on the need to protect the natural and cultural heritage. In this region, the areas of high natural value are located on the border of countries operating within different legal systems. The effective protection of a common legacy requires respect for the rights of each nation to use natural resources while considering the principles of the 2030 Agenda, particularly Goal 15 "Live on land." An example is the Białowieża Forest, which is a famous, primeval forest located on the border of Poland and Belarus. Since 1979 it has been protected by the common Polish-Belarusian inscription on the UNESCO World Heritage List. A similar transboundary conservation designation has been guaranteed to the transborder Polish-German Park Mużakowski/Muskauer Park.

The problems connected with the protection of intercultural (natural and cultural) heritage are also noticeable in the aforementioned ornithological issues, especially those related to the protection of wild avifauna. They concern, among others, the

---

[5]It should be added that the main assumptions and results of the project were also presented at several international scientific conferences and met with great interest from representatives of criminology and pedagogical sciences (e.g. Congress of the European Society of Criminology, Ghent, 18–21 September 2019).

[6]Financed by the Polish-German Science Foundation (Deutsch-Polnische Wissenschaftsstiftung). The implementation period of the project is 2018–2020.

efforts of NGOs to reduce the practice of killing migratory birds which happen in many Mediterranean countries, particularly in Egypt, Greece, Italy, Lebanon and Malta. Because of bird migration across many national jurisdiction boundaries, the effective crime prevention requires collaboration between law enforcement agencies from different legal traditions (e.g. civil law, common law, countries of East Asia and Islamic countries). Hence, the diversity of legal traditions must be considered when creating crime prevention strategies. It is important to think in the term of legal traditions, which place legal systems in a cultural context. In the words of Ambassador Ali bin Jassmim Al-Thani from the State of Qatar, respect for the diversity of culture must always be kept in mind when combating a crime (Reichel 2012, pp. 76–80).

In 2013, the problem of killing birds for entertainment or the so-called exercise (an improvement of shooting accuracy) has appeared in the Polish media with regard to the mass shooting of migrating storks (*Ciconia ciconia*) by Lebanese hunters. In Poland, these birds are an important element of cultural and natural heritage and enjoy a strict legal protection. Acts of aggression against storks are met with widespread condemnation and reaction of law enforcement agencies. Therefore, the Polish Government has taken diplomatic action. The Polish Ambassador to Lebanon conveyed to the Lebanese authorities the concern of his country on maltreatment of birds.

This concern was echoed by pro-ecological organisations. They prepared special educational material for use by Lebanese public agencies, including schools. The results of the campaign for the protection of storks undertaken by both state authorities and the organisations of bird defenders ("EcoLogical Group," "Polish Society for the Protection of Birds – PTOP") were significant.

In 2014, the Lebanese Government adopted a document establishing a nature conservation service. The Government promised to establish a national register of infringements of nature protection, including the perpetrators and rendered sentences. The Lebanese President also took a part in the discussion on shooting at storks, appealing to citizens to limit the customary right to shoot at migratory birds. He stated that "It is a shame to turn Lebanon into a wasteland without plants, trees, birds and sea animals, and cutting down trees to erect buildings is a major crime (...). There should be a peace treaty between Man and the tree as well as Man and birds, because we continue to transgress upon them" (Bonaccorsi 2017, p. 1).

To make the Lebanese society aware of the problem of killing storks and other migratory birds, the "EcoLogical Group" prepared a short, educational fairy tale entitled "Rex and stork." It tells the story of a stork who could not fly away to Africa because of wing injury. The stork was taken care of by dog Rex, who fed his sick friend, protected him from various dangers, and in the spring helped him to build a nest. This touching short animation is addressed not only to the young, but also makes us aware of the need to take care of our winged friends and, at the same time, is a protest against the bloody practices deep-rooted in the tradition of the Middle East. In thousand copies this movie was distributed to Lebanese schools (Pływaczewski 2019, p. 185). The young Lebanese seem to be the best addressees of the film to reveal the truth about the inhumane practices of killing birds, which do not conform to contemporary ethical standards.

Another interesting initiative related to the protection of birds was the project initiated by the Earth Conservation Corps in the USA. It was based on the involvement of youth coming from pathological environments in the programme of the reintroduction of the white-tailed eagle (*Haliaeetus albicilla*). The children took part in this initiative as part of the Washington D.C. police program called "Youth Creating Change." According to Cathy Lanier, a former Washington police chief, children who get into trouble do so because they lack something in life. In her opinion, in most cases, engaging them in the life of birds might be an effective rehabilitation programme (Robbins 2017, p. 385).

No less interesting and at the same time effective in terms of the implementation of rehabilitation objectives are pro-environmental programmes addressed to convicts, facilitating their close relations with nature. Such "green" rehabilitation programmes were implemented by Finnish penitentiary service. They covered criminals who were sentenced to long terms of imprisonment. Among them there were people convicted of robbery, serious bodily harm, rape and even murder. These inmates were placed in the Suomenlinna detention centre located on an island. What is interesting is that the prison does not resemble a classic penitentiary and the prisoners take part in the programme live in typical Finnish houses with standard equipment (kitchen, toilets, showers, sauna, widescreen TV).

The observations so far have shown that detainees are willing to engage in mandatory activities. They can freely move around the island, of following the internal regulations and under discreet supervision of security guards. This means that the residents of this unusual settlement have permanent contact with unspoilt nature. The research carried out on this group of people confirmed that the convicts, apart from minor incidents, did not commit any crimes that could be assessed as particularly dangerous. It should be stressed that over 30% of Finnish prisoners serve their sentences in open prisons. The system of open prisons has contributed to a decrease of recidivism (20% less committed re-offences).

The researchers compared Finnish results with the results obtained in US prisons. These results were found to be extremely unfavourable for the overseas prison service. In the same period, American convicts repeatedly committed dangerous crimes against both other prisoners and prison officers (Larson 2013).

A global challenge which also has local aspects is the illegal market for wild animals (mainly poaching and wildlife smuggling). In particular, the killing of elephants for their ivory tusks or rhinoceroses for horns, which are sought after on illegal international markets, has resulted in a dramatic decline in their populations (Zimmerman 2003, pp. 1657–1689; Commission on Crime Prevention and Criminal Justice 2011). This diagnosis is confirmed, *inter alia*, by the International Criminal Police Organisation—INTERPOL. It identified the intensive activity of organised criminal groups in this area (INTERPOL 2009). These groups are involved in the mass killing of so-called flagship animal species, such as elephants, rhinoceroses, tigers and great apes. According to the reports of the United Nations Office on Drugs and Crime (UNODC), illegal trade in protected species of fauna and flora has been growing at an unprecedented rate, providing international gangs with an income of about 10–20 billion dollars a year. These profits have placed activities related to wildlife market at the forefront of illegal markets, alongside trafficking in drugs, human beings and weapons (UNODC 2006, pp. 149–169; Beirne and South 2007, p. 230; White 2008, p. 186; Clark 2004, p. 161; Hewman 2010, p. 262).

A criminal justice response to wildlife and forest crime is one of the priority areas of activity of the United Nations. One of its manifestations is the UNODC's "Wildlife and Forest Crime Analytic Toolkit." It offers feedback and framework designed to assist government officials in wildlife and forestry administration. The system for preventing this type of crime consists of legislation, law enforcement, judiciary and prosecution, prevention and data analysis (UNODC 2012, pp. 11–12).

It is also worthwhile to discuss some interesting national solutions, particularly from African countries struggling with the problem of illegal hunting (poaching). Due to the problem's huge scale some countries have undertaken unusual and ethically controversial measures. One of the forms of breaking down the solidarity of criminal groups in Kenya and the conspiracy of silence is to ensure impunity for former poachers and to employ them as employees of nature conservation services (Karanja 2012, pp. 74–80). The members of former poaching tribes undergo a rehabilitation process and professional training and then become the guards of national parks. It should be noted that accepting the position of guard often causes social ostracism and exclusion from the local community. However, these officers generally fulfil their statutory obligations. Thus, this innovative method seems to be a perfect tool for overcoming social consent to the killing of protected species of wild animals (Pływaczewski 2011, pp. 51–58).

An equally interesting is "Akashinga" project, implemented and financed by a non-governmental organisation, with the approval of the Government of Zimbabwe. Within its framework, a special team, composed of women, was established to combat poaching. It is the first armed female formation of this kind in Africa appointed to fight directly against poachers. It should be added that women are involved in this structure were victims of crime (domestic violence, rape, abduction, slave labour). This experiment has a double meaning, on the one hand, women-commandoes protect valuable animals from poachers. On the other hand, they undergo a kind of therapy after traumatic experiences they have suffered in their lives. So far, the project has been highly evaluated by both donors and government services. It is enough to note that only in one year, 2018, Zimbabwean nature defenders captured as many as 80 poachers (Thomas 2019).

Programmes addressed to representatives of local tribes or minority groups living the boundaries of national parks (landscape parks) are also noteworthy. Frequent conflicts associated with the destruction of various types of crops by wild animals cause desperate farmers to take actions against animals on their own. In practice, it often results in the elimination of rare species of animals. Penalties and other criminal measures, even the most severe, are ineffective against the perpetrators of such acts. Therefore, programmes implemented by African nature conservation services, including the Kenya Wildlife Service (KWS), are aimed at alleviating tensions and providing natives with compensation for the damage caused by wild animals. Moreover, within the framework of educational activities, the authorities try to raise social awareness of the importance of wildlife in their lives, pointing to new perspectives offered by the dynamically developing ecotourism industry in Africa. However, environmental programmes aimed at indigenous peoples living in areas with valuable species of fauna and flora shall also consider the cultural context of their lives (Kenya Wildlife Service 2019). Otherwise, their efforts will be doomed to failure. The Maasai and other populations living in the savannah have repeatedly felt the negative effects of projects implemented by the authorities. Hence, they are particularly sensitive to issues referring to their natural and cultural heritage. In the new formula, Kenyan and Tanzanian authorities guaranteed the rights of the Maasai people deriving from their rich culture. An important element of the programme for the protection of Kenyan wildlife resources, addressed, among others, to nomadic peoples, is an initiative known as the Community Wildlife Programme. As part of the programme, the Kenyan Nature Conservation Service encourages the inhabitants of parks and nature reserves to take part in the conservation of natural heritage. This protection is implemented, among others, by supporting various forms of professional activity, for example, related to tourism (Wearing and Neil 1999, pp. 21–39; Mihalič 2003, p. 99; Ceballos-Lascurain 1996, pp. 19–55). The aim is to support folk art in all its forms, such as painting, sculpture, singing, dancing, etc. The programme also favours initiatives aimed at developing small businesses in the tourism sector—accommodation, souvenir shops, small gastronomy, tourist offices, etc. (Pływaczewski 2011, p. 49). Additionally, the local authorities with the support of international organisations, promote alternative forms of activity addressed primarily to the Maasai youth. It should also be noted that representatives of peoples living in areas covered by strict natural protection are numerously represented in the Kenya Wildlife Service (mainly Maasai people). Their special features, such as courage and knowledge of the characteristics of bush life, are extremely useful in the performance of duties (Amin et al. 2005, p. 122).

For many African nations and nomadic tribes, wild species of fauna and flora are still the basic source of food, regardless of their uniqueness, nature conservation status or restrictions applied by public services. For instance, the Maasai people believe that the animal world occupies a central place, often constituting the basis for the lifestyle of tribes. An example is the cult of the lion. According to their beliefs, killing a lion is confirmation of strength and courage and gives a growing Maasai the right to be a full-fledged warrior. Criminal sanctions resulting from absolute prohibitions on killing wild animals undermine the foundations of the traditions of many African tribes which, in consequence, may lead to the disintegration of their social structures and to the creation of areas of social pathology.

One can see the results of this kind of destructive processes occurring in many African countries. These include increasing armed conflicts, intertribal wars and progressive demoralisation among the natives (crime, alcohol, drugs). According to Émile Durkheim, the decay of ethical norms and traditional values always leads to the disruption of existing social structures, i.e. to a state of anomie (Barkan 2006, pp. 181–182).

The theory of anomie refers, among others, to the situation of so-called "fragile states." These are countries whose governments are so weak that they are unable to control their territory and to provide public services. Furthermore, there are phenomena such as corruption, crime, exile and economic collapse (Grimm et al. 2014, pp. 197–209). According to the Fragile State Index of the American NGO Fund for Peace, the most unstable countries in the world are: Yemen, Somalia, South Sudan, Syria and the Democratic Republic of Congo (Fund for Peace 2019, p. 7). In such countries, it is practically impossible to implement any crime prevention projects and the observance of Human Rights and Rule of Law is seriously threatened.

Undoubtedly, a symptom of such processes is also the growing phenomenon of poaching. The origin of the phenomenon lies in the historically shaped structure of tribes, thanks to which it is possible to practice criminal activity in conditions involving and accepted by the community members. The conspiracy of silence which accompanies this type of activity ensures impunity for poachers, as police services have difficulties in penetrating criminal environments. One of the forms of breaking down criminal solidarity, which is not accepted by everyone and is controversial from the ethical approach, is employing formerly engaged in illegal poaching tribal people in the nature protection services. As confirmed by the experience of many African countries, this experiment has so far passed the exam, as the former poachers who became the guards of national parks fulfil their professional obligations. Despite intensive educational activities undertaken by the nature conservation services of individual African countries, the consent for killing wild animals among the natives is still high (Robbins 2017).

Regrettably, another global programme for the protection of the Ecuadorian part of the Amazon is seriously threatened. Hoping to gain income from oil production, the Ecuadorian authorities withdrew from international agreements protecting valuable forest areas from industrial exploitation. Local and foreign oil extraction companies have started entering the Amazon region. This may lead to the destruction of the Yasuni National Park—one of the most attractive natural areas of Amazon jungle located in the East of Ecuador. Within its borders still live native inhabitants of these lands, including members of the Huaorani and Zaparo tribes. This is also home to numerous species of amphibians, reptiles, birds and mammals (10–15% of all species on the planet live there). Humberto Cholango, chairman of the organisation that represents the Ecuadorian Indian tribes, criticised decisions made by authorities. He said that every Ecuadorian has a right to defend the reserve and its inhabitants, for whom this place is home (Vidal 2013). Many forms of the ensuing environmental crime can be explained by the so-called resource scarcity thesis. The examples are logging, "Illegal, Unreported and Unregulated"/IUU fishing, various wildlife crimes and illegal land appropriation (Matthew 2008).

As in Ecuador, the current condition of the Amazon primary forests in Brazil is also a source of international concern. Country's President has abandoned the concept of the Amazon Region Protected Areas Program and has maximally expanded in that region its industrial exploitation. At the same time, the authorities have significantly curtailed the mandate and operations of the Brazilian nature conservation service. In 2019, these actions met with strong reaction of the world's public opinion and individual countries. As a result, the German government suspended financing of the Amazon aid scheme (La Organización del Tratado de Cooperación Amazónica 2018).

In contrast, a positive example of the protection of primeval forest in the Amazon basin is private initiative of a conservationist Victoria Da Riva Cristalino. Thanks to her efforts and determination many of animals, including unique bird species has been saved from poachers and illegal lumberjacks. The environmentalist bought several thousand hectares of rainforest and created an ecotourism facility called the "Cristalino Private National Reserve." This complex consists of professional bird watching towers and a research centre where the scientists from all over the world, including ornithologists, can carry out their scientific projects on the Amazon fauna and flora. In 2013, the National Gerographic Society recognized this place as the best ecotourism facility in the world, awarding it the "World's Best Ecolodges 2013" (National Geographic Traveler Magazine 2013). This competition promotes the best practices in the field of nature conservation and responsible tourism. The facility uses renewable energy sources. Furthermore, its owner has initiated several educational projects related to the protection of tropical forests, addressed to youths (Cristalino Lodge 2019).

According to the INTERPOL estimates, the phenomenon of the plundering of the world's natural resources may increase. This will be a major challenge for many countries, especially those facing serious social and economic problems (White and Heckenberg 2014, p. 221). Some countries enter into the so-called "shameful agreements" concerning the exploitation of valuable and protected natural resources by international industrial corporations. This phenomenon is described as "land grabbing" (Coalition Against Land Grabbing 2019). As per the UNODC report (2006, p. 157), funds ensuing from such practices are used to support armed conflicts or to keep authoritarian leaders in power. This is conducive to victimisation of the natural heritage, both in its local and global dimension (White and Heckenberg 2014, p. 175).

The initiatives concerning changing existing customs directed against natural heritage have been undertaken by various non-governmental organisations all over Africa. In the case of the Maasai, the ritual killing of lions was a contentious issue in relations with the official authorities. A similar problem occurred in the case of the Zulus—members of the Baptist Church of Nazareth, also known as the Shembe Church. This sect has incorporated elements of the Zulu tradition into its rituals, in which leopard skin plays an extremely important role. Nowadays, the faithful of the Shembe Church believe that this ritual brings them closer to God and their ancestors. These skins are exhibited during numerous religious ceremonies. Because of their rapid wear, they are replaced every few years. It is not difficult to note that this custom has a direct impact on the number of leopards, whose population in South Africa has fallen to an alarming 7000 specimens. To prevent the extinction of leopards, it was necessary to reduce poaching and illegal trade in their skins. To end such practices, the "Panther" organisation supported a project consisting of the production of artificial leather based on polyvinyl chloride and plush fabric with colours and patterns similar to real leopard skin. With the support of local authorities, a factory produces, under the brand name "Furs for Life," artificial garments for the members of this religious group. The initiators of the project estimate that thanks to the experiment, the number of natural leopard skins has decreased at the Shembe celebration by 30–40%. This is an unquestionable success of ecologists because, until recently at such celebrations leopard skins constituted almost 90% (Conniff 2016).

Individuals with moral authority can also have an impact on changing the customs and preferences related to the protection of natural heritage. An example is the Dalai Lama, the spiritual leader of the Tibetans. In 2006, during "Kalachakra"—one of the most important Buddhist celebrations, he made a dramatic appeal to abandon the custom of decorating traditional costumes with wild animal furs. Reportedly, this spiritual leader was "ashamed" to see photos of Tibetans in tiger fur. He commanded his followers: "When you return to your homes, remember what I told you and never sell or buy wild animals and their products" (Mitra 2006, p. 3). The response of the Tibetans was almost instantaneous—they began to burn clothes made of animal fur. This example confirms the important role of contemporary moral authorities in creating pro-ecological attitudes.

The projects addressed to the fur industry and large fashion salons involve well-known personalities from the worlds of politics, business and film. The French actress Brigitte Bardot, who has devoted a significant part of her life to saving wild animals, is an example of such an attitude. The actress has been a strong opponent of the use of natural leather in the fur industry. Thanks to her efforts, France became the first country in Europe which introduced regulations prohibiting the import of ivory. She was also engaged in several pro-ecological initiatives, among others, campaigns against the killing of seals in Canada and protests against the sale and consumption of horse meat. She opposed the killing of rhinos and tigers to attract aphrodisiacs and defended the wolves killed in Poland (Pływaczewski 2016, p. 243).

The 2030 Agenda also includes the targets for the conservation and sustainable use of oceans and marine resources (Goal 14). However, the efforts made so far by the world community to protect marine and oceanic waters and their resources meet with the incomprehensible resistance of some countries. An example is the attitude of the Japanese government to the capture of dolphins and whales. The unethical practices of marine mammals by Japanese fishermen were stigmatised after broadcasting a film "The Gulf of Dolphins" prepared by environmental organisations. The film triggered many protests and started a worldwide discussion on the ban on capturing these animals. Despite the stigmatisation of the controversial catches by the global public opinion, the Japanese government refused to impose a ban on fishing. The authority invoked regulations allowing fishing for scientific purposes and consistently supported its fishermen. In their opinion, the support was based on a need to cultivate the national culinary heritage.[7] Moreover, in 2019, Japan withdrew

[7]Dolphin meat, recognised in Japan as a delicacy, is used, among others, for the preparation of sushi.

from the International Whaling Commission (IWC) and lifted the ban on commercial whaling in its territorial waters (Pływaczewski 2016, p. 190).

The attention should also be paid to the methods of catching fish and other marine organisms by fleets of particular countries. The international environmental organisations, including the Deep Sea Conservation Coalition, have been pointing to the massive use of controversial fishing techniques. It should be emphasised that the International Council for the Exploration of the Sea (ICES), which is the main scientific body monitoring deep-sea fisheries, has recognised that almost all deep-sea fish species are "outside the safe biological limits" (Deep Sea Conservation Coalition 2019).

3 Conclusion

The idea of sustainable development of the world under the auspices of the United Nations contradicts chaotic and, at the same time, greedy progress which is, above all, subordinated to the economic principle of maximising profit. An extreme example of behaviour that disregards universally accepted moral and legal norms is undoubtedly organised crime. Nowadays, it is increasingly often directed against the natural environment (Liddick 2011, p. 41). The task of criminology is to identify emerging threats (criminal aetiology), describe symptomatic forms (criminal phenomenology), as well as to propose new, innovative and effective preventive solutions (criminological prevention). It is obvious that the existing forms and techniques used to fight against crime need to be complemented by new and more effective solutions. It appears that the projects presented in this chapter (local, regional, global) correspond not only to the goals set out in Agenda 2030, but also constitute a valuable alternative to the existing methods of counteracting pathological phenomena.

The initiatives described in this chapter, including especially these addressed to children and youth, are a part of an emerging culture of lawfulness, which was initiated by the Doha Declaration of the Thirteenth United Nations Congress on Crime Prevention and Criminal Justice (United Nations Office on Drugs and Crime 2015). The declaration highlights the role of education of the youngest in the process of preventing crime and promoting a culture of lawfulness that supports the rule of law and human rights while respecting cultural identities (par. 7 of the Declaration). It is necessary to integrate crime prevention and criminal justice strategies into all relevant social and economic policies and programmes, particularly those affecting youth, with a special emphasis on programmes focused on increasing educational and employment opportunities for youth and young adults.

Promoting the culture of lawfulness is possible through education activities designed for primary, secondary and tertiary levels. In this way, legal attitudes are shaped. The aim of this endeavour is to engage the next generations in the life of their communities. Globalisation and digitisation require the adaptation of teaching methods to changing realities (Platzer 2008). Criminal justice education has a huge impact on the socio-political and economic situation of communities and nations. Changing social attitudes towards the law is particularly important in developing countries. A significant role in promoting Education for Justice is played by academic departments of criminology and criminal justice within the higher education systems.[8]

The Catholic Church also noted the need to prevent crime, particularly crimes against the environment. During the Synod for the Pan Amazon Region (20th International Congress of Penal Law), Pope Francis spoke about "ecological sin" understood as act or omission against God, against one's neighbour, the community and the environment. Examples of such behaviour are acts of the massive pollution of air, land and water resources, large-scale destruction of flora and fauna and any action capable of producing an ecological disaster or destroying an ecosystem. As a result, they lead to hunger, misery, forced migration and death from avoidable diseases, environmental disaster and ethnocide of indigenous peoples. Thus, crimes against the environment become crimes against humanity and should be regarded as "ecocidal." As the Holy Father pointed out, such behaviours cannot go unpunished. This task is to be performed by persons and institutions responsible for creating criminal law and crime prevention strategies (The Holly See 2019, pp. 3–4). This clearly shows the importance of the new field of criminology called "green criminology."

According to forecasts of criminologists gathered in the Green Criminology Working Group (GCWG), the list of offences against the environment may cover an increasingly wide range of new pathological phenomena. These include: crimes related to climate change (criminal climatology), air traffic, plundering of natural resources, threats related to plastic, smog, invasive species, access to water and other natural resources, as well as criminal terror directed against environmentalists, etc. (Pływaczewski and Duda 2017, pp. 43–68; Narodowska 2016).

To ensure effective tools to fight against environmental crime, the individual countries and their agencies should consider new strategies for action. The programmes and projects reviewed in the chapter may motivate to develop strategies for combating environmental crimes. Nevertheless, as it was stressed in the introduction, to implement targets of the United Nations 2030 Sustainable Development Agenda, it is necessary to engage the world community (governments, international organisations and civic initiatives) in programmes promoting a culture of lawfulness, particularly those relating to nature conservation.

[8]The representatives of criminology noted the need to introduce such projects even before the beginning of the E4J initiative (Eskridge 2003).

References

A/RES/70/1 *Transforming our world: the 2030 agenda for sustainable development*. 25 September 2015.

A/RES/70/174 *Doha declaration on integrating crime prevention and criminal justice into the wider United Nations agenda to address social and economic challenges and to promote the rule of law at the national and international levels, and public participation*. 17 December 2015.

Amin, M., Willetts, D., & Eames, J. (2005). *The last of the Maasai*. Nairobi: Camerapix Publishers International.

Aslaug Sollund, R. (2019). *The crimes of wildlife trafficking. Issues of justice, legality and morality*. New York: Routledge.

Barkan, S. E. (2006). *Criminology. A sociological understanding*. Upper Saddle River, NJ: Pearson.

Beirne, P., & South, N. (Eds.). (2007). *Issues in Green Criminology*. Portland: Willan Publishing.

Bonaccorsi, L. (2017). *"Stop the Killing." Lebanese President speaks out for migratory birds*. https://www.birdlife.org/worldwide/news/%E2%80%9Cstop-killing%E2%80%9D-lebanese-president-speaks-out-migratory-birds/

Burke, R. H. (1998). Socio-political context of zero tolerance policing strategy. *Policing: An International Journal, 21*(4), 666–682.

Ceballos-Lascurain, H. (1996). *Tourism, ecotourism and protected areas*. Gland: International Union for Conservation of Nature and Natural Resources.

Clark, R. S. (2004). The United Nations Convention against transnational organized crime. *Wayne Law Review, 50*, 161–175.

Coalition Against Land Grabbing (2019). *About us*. https://www.coalitionagainstlandgrabbing.org

Commission on Crime Prevention and Criminal Justice (2011). *Crime prevention and criminal justice responses against illicit trafficking crime species of wild Fauna and Flora*. Vienna: United Nations, E/CN.15/2011/L.5.

Conniff, R. (2016). *Why Fur Is Back in Fashion*. https://www.nationalgeographic.com/magazine/2016/09/skin-trade-fur-fashion/

Cristalino Lodge (2019). *The Concept*. http://cristalinolodge.com.br/en/about/concept/.

Czapska, J., & Kury, H. (2002). *Mit represyjności albo o znaczeniu prewencji kryminalnej (The Myth of Repression or the Importance of Crime Prevention)*. Kraków: Zakamycze.

Deep Sea Conservation Coalition (2019). *About us*. www.savethehighseas.org.

Department of Criminology and Criminal Policy (2019). *About us*. http://www.uwm.edu.pl/kryminologia/.

Eskridge, C. (2003). Criminal justice education and its potential impact on the sociopolitical-economic climate of Central European nations: A short essay. *Journal of Criminal Justice Education, 14*(1), 105–118.

Fund for Peace (2019), *Fragile State Iddex Annual Report 2019*. https://fundforpeace.org/wpcontent/uploads/2019/04/9511904-fragilestatesindex.pdf

Galli, A., Durovic, G., Hanscom, L., & Knežević, J. (2018). Think globally, act locally. Implementing the sustainable development goals in Montenegro. *Environmental Science and Policy, 84*, 159–169.

Greene, J. A. (1999). Zero Tolerance: A case study of police policies and practices in New York City. *Crime and Delinquency, 45*(2), 171–187.

Grimm, S., Lemay-Hébert, N., & Nay, O. (2014). 'Fragile States', Introducing a political concept. *Third World Quarterly, 35*(2), 197–209.

Hewman, G. R. (Ed.). (2010). *Crime and punishment around the world*. Santa Barbara: ABC-CLIO.

International Consortium on Combating Wildlife Crime (2010). *What is ICCWC?* https://www.cites.org/eng/prog/iccwc.php

International Criminal Police Organization. (2009). *Environmental crime programme. Strategic Plan 2009–2010*. Lyon: INTERPOL.
Karanja, D. (2012). The role of the Kenya Wildlife service in protecting Kenya's Wildlife. *The George Wright Forum, 39*(1), 74–80.
Kenya Wildlife Service (2019). *About us*. http://www.kws.go.ke
La Organización del Tratado de Cooperación Amazónica (2018). *Proyecto Amazonas*. http://www.otca-oficial.info/projects/details/23
Larson, D. (2013). *Why Scandinavian prisons are superior. 'Open' prisons, in which detainees are allowed to live like regular citizens, should be a model for the U.S.* https://www.theatlantic.com/international/archive/2013/09/why-scandinavian-prisons-are-superior/279949/
Letsch, C. (2014). *A Year after the Protests. Gezi Park Nurtures the Seeds of a New Turkey*. https://www.theguardian.com/world/2014/may/29/gezi-park-year-after-protests-seeds-new-turkey
Liddick, D. R. (2011). *Crimes against nature. Illegal industries and the global environmental*. Santa Barbara: Praeger.
Matthew, R. A. (2008). *Resource Scarsity: Responding to the security challenge*. Vienna: International Peace Institute.
Mihalič, T. (2003). Economic instruments of environmental tourism policy derived from environmental theories. In D. A. Fennell & R. K. Dowling (Eds.), *Ecotourism policy and planning* (pp. 99–120). Wallingford: CABI Publishing.
Mitra, B. (2006). Saving the Tiger. China and India move in radically different directions. *PERC Reports. The Magazine of Free Market Environmentalism, 24*(3), 3–6.
Narodowska, J. (2016). *Przestępstwa kłusownictwa rybackiego na wodach śródlądowych. Studium prawnokarne i kryminologiczne (Crimes of Poaching in Inland Waters. Criminal Law and Criminological Study)*. Olsztyn: University of Warmia and Mazury.
National Geographic Traveler Magazine. (2013). *Best Eco-Lodges in the World*. https://www.basecampexplorer.com/awards/best-eco-lodges-in-the-world/
Neumann, J.-M. (2012). The Universal Declaration of animal rights or the creation of a new equilibrium between species. *Animal Law, 19*(1), 91–109.
Platzer, M. (2008). New ways of teaching students about international criminal justice. In K. Aromaa & S. Redo (Eds.), *For the rule of law: Criminal justice teaching and training across the world* (pp. 116–130). Helsinki-Seoul: European Institute on Crime Prevention and Control/HEUNI – Korean Institute of Criminal Justice Policy/KICJP.
Pływaczewski, W. (2009). Niszczenie dziedzictwa kulturowego – między imperatywem ekonomii i ekologii. Kryminologiczne ujęcie problemu z perspektywy województwa warmińsko-mazurskiego (Destruction of Cultural Heritage – Between Economic and Ecological Imperatives. Criminological Approach to the Problem from the Perspective of the Warmian-Mazurian Voivodeship). *Białostockie Studia Prawnicze (Białystok Law Studies), 6*, 196–211.
Pływaczewski, W. (2011). Combating organized poaching in Africa. Activities of the Kenya Wildlife Service. In W. Pływaczewski (Ed.), *Organized crime and terrorism. Reasons. Manifestations. Counteractions* (pp. 49–64). Olsztyn: University of Warmia and Mazury.
Pływaczewski, W. (2016). *Nielegalny rynek chronionych gatunków dzikiej fauny i flory. Geneza. przejawy, przeciwdziałanie (Illegal Market of Protected Wildlife Species. Genesis. Manifestations, Counteractions)*. Szczytno: Wydawnictwo Wyższej Szkoły Policji.
Pływaczewski, W. (2019). *Ornitologia kryminalna (Criminal ornithology)*. Warszawa: Difin.
Pływaczewski, W., & Duda, M. (2017). Dlaczego zginęła Dian Fossey? Prawne oraz wiktymologiczne aspekty zwalczania przestępczości wymierzonej w obrońców przyrody (Why did Dian Fossey Die? Legal and victimological aspects of combating crime against nature defenders). In M. Adamczyk, J. Karaźniewicz, & K. Pruszkiewicz-Słowińska (Eds.), *Karnoprawne aspekty ochrony środowiska – wyzwania dla teorii i praktyki (Criminal law aspects of environmental protection – challenges for theory and practice)* (pp. 43–68). Olsztyn: University of Warmia and Mazury.

Redo, S. (2017). New instruments and approaches for countering social exclusion. A criminological contribution to the United Nations post-2015 educational Agenda. In E. W. Pływaczewski & E. M. Guzik-Makaruk (Eds.), *Current problems of the penal law and criminology* (pp. 723–737). Warszawa: C.H. Beck.

Reichel, P. L. (2012). Promoting the culture of lawfulness by teaching about transnational organized crime. *Białostockie Studia Prawnicze (Bialystok Law Studies), 23*(3), 75–84.

Robbins, J. (2017). *The wonder of birds. What they tell us about ourselves, the world, and a better future*. New York: Spiegel & Grau.

Schmalleger, F. (2004). *Criminology today. An integrative introduction*. Upper Saddle River, NJ: Pearson.

The Holly See. (2019). *Address of His Holiness Pope Francis to Participants at the World Congress of the International Association of Penal Law*. http://www.vatican.va/content/francesco/en/speeches/2019/november/documents/papa-francesco_20191115_diritto-penale.pdf

Thomas, K. (2019). *Akashinga. Protecting the Lower Zambezi with All-female Anti-Poaching Units*. https://www.leonardodicaprio.org/akashinga-protecting-the-lower-zambezi-with-all-female-anti-poaching-units/

United Nations Office on Drugs and Crime. (2006). *The globalisation of crime. A transnational organized crime threat assessment*. Vienna: United Nations.

United Nations Office on Drugs and Crime. (2012). *Wildlife and forest crime analytic toolkit*. Vienna: United Nations.

United Nations Office on Drugs and Crime. (2015). *The Doha Declaration. Promoting the Culture of Lawfulness. Education for Justice*. https://www.unodc.org/e4j/en/index.html

Vidal, J. (2013). *Race to Save Ecuador's Yasuní National Park from Oil Lobby*. https://www.theguardian.com/environment/2013/aug/23/ecuador-yasuni-national-park.

Wearing, S., & Neil, J. (1999). *Ecotourism. Impacts, potentials, and possibilities*. Oxford: Butterworth-Heinemann.

White, R. (2008). *Crimes against nature. Environmental criminology and ecological justice*. Portland: William Publishing.

White, R., & Heckenberg, D. (2014). *Green criminology. In introduction to the study of environmental harm*. London-New York: Routledge.

Zimmerman, M. E. (2003). The black market for wildlife. Combating transnational organized crime in the illegal wildlife trade. *Vanderbilt Journal of Transnational Law, 36*(5), 1657–1689.

Wiesław Pływaczewski is a Professor and graduate of the Nicolaus Copernicus University in Toruń (Poland, 1980). Doctoral degree in law obtained at the University of Łódź (Poland, 1989) based on the thesis entitled "Legal protection of cultural assets in Poland." Habilitation in law at the University of Łódź (1998) based on the thesis titled "Theft of cars. Criminological study." The title of Professor of Legal Sciences awarded in 2017 by the President of the Republic of Poland. Head of the Department of Criminology and Forensic Science at the University of Warmia and Mazury in Olsztyn. Founder of the Olsztyn School of Ecocriminology. Member of the European Society of Criminology, American Society of Criminology, International Police Executive Symposium, Polish Society of Criminology and Polish Society of Forensic Science. Participant in 10 research projects. Author of over 300 publications in the field of criminology, green criminology, and criminal policy. E-mail: wieslaw.plywaczewski@wp.pl.

Dr. Joanna Narodowska was a graduate of the University of Warmia and Mazury in Olsztyn (Olsztyn, Poland, 2009). Her doctoral degree in law was obtained at the University of Warmia and Mazury in Olsztyn (2015) based on the thesis titled "Illegal fishing in inland waters. Criminal and criminological aspects." Assistant Professor at the Department of Criminology and Criminal Policy at the University of Warmia and Mazury in Olsztyn. Member of the European Society of Criminology, Green Criminology Working Group, and the Polish Society of Criminology. Expert at the

International Union for Conservation of Nature, European Union Crime Prevention Network, and Institute for European Environmental Policy. Participant in four research projects. Author of over 50 publications in the field of criminology, green criminology, and criminal law. E-mail: joanna.narodowska@uwm.edu.pl.

Dr. Maciej Duda was a graduate of the Nicolaus Copernicus University in Toruń, Poland (2009). Doctoral degree in law obtained at the University of Warmia and Mazury in Olsztyn, Poland (2015) based on the thesis titled "Hate crimes. Penal and criminological study." Assistant Professor at the Department of Criminology and Criminal Policy at the University of Warmia and Mazury in Olsztyn. Member of the European Society of Criminology, Green Criminology Working Group, and the Polish Society of Criminology. Expert at the International Union for Conservation of Nature, European Union Crime Prevention Network, and Institute for European Environmental Policy. Participant in six research projects. Author of over 70 publications in the field of criminology, green criminology, and victimology. E-mail: maciej.duda@uwm.edu.pl.

Actualising the Right to Adequate Standard of Living: A Critical Examination of Green Criminology from an Indian Perspective

Srinivasan Murugesan and Shankar Prakash Alagesan

Abstract During the last 70 years, several international instruments have been emphasising the importance of the right to adequate standard of living (Article 25, Universal Declaration of Human Rights (UDHR)) and to make cities and human settlements inclusive, safe, resilient and sustainable (Sustainable Development Goal (SDG) 11). However, many of the provisions of such international instruments, particularly the right to adequate standard of living, is too far from becoming a reality. The authors of this chapter have substantiated their arguments by presenting a few case studies conducted in the city of Chennai (formerly Madras, India). The disjuncture between the provisions of the international instruments and the reality of the contemporary quality of the environment is also to some extent exposed in this chapter. It is also argued why the scope of green criminology should be widened to study the various forms of environmental crime, environmental harm and connected issues. The authors strongly believe that understanding such issues from the perspective of green criminology would provide several benefits, including sensitising the stakeholders.

Keywords UDHR · SDG · Green criminology · Environmental crime · Environmental harm · Standard of living · Human settlement · Municipal solid waste · Waste management

1 Introduction

Right to adequate standard of living is directly connected with the quality of the environment in which an individual lives. Over a period of 70 years, a host of international instruments including the UDHR and United Nations SDGs have been emphasising the importance of protecting the right to adequate standard of living and make the cities and human settlements, inclusive, safe, resilient and sustainable.

S. Murugesan · S. P. Alagesan (✉)
Department of Criminology, University of Madras, Chennai, India

H. Kury, S. Redo (eds.), *Crime Prevention and Justice in 2030*,
https://doi.org/10.1007/978-3-030-56227-4_14

Despite these international initiatives, the right to adequate standard of living could not be actualised by a vast section of the population, particularly in countries like India. People in India encounter a host of environmental issues which undermine their quality of life, particularly the standard of living of the disadvantaged sections of the society (Chandra 2015).

Criminologists and criminal justice practitioners have a responsibility to scientifically study a variety of environmental problems, which will expand the scope of criminology in general and green criminology in particular. Such endeavours would certainly contribute to protecting the environment and the various species that thrive in the environmental ecological system. There are several unexplored, untapped and untouched issues to which green criminology can be applied—by redirecting emphasis to omitted forms of environmental harms and methods to control those harms to improve the environmental quality, which can contribute significantly to both criminology and green criminology. For example, how the green approach can integrate environmental policy and crime control policy is demonstrated by examining the eco-city perspective and its design principles (Lynch 2012). Further, the existing criminological research by and large has not paid attention to various environmental issues, crimes against the environment, victims of environmental crime and various laws and the mechanisms to prevent and detect these offences (Lynch et al. 2015; Nurse 2017; Hall 2014; White 2003). Given this background, the authors of the present chapter have attempted to explain certain environmental problems and argue how explaining those environmental problems from the perspective of green criminology would provide an understanding of the problem holistically and sensitise the stakeholders. The authors of this chapter argue the need for and significance of widening the scope of green criminology, particularly in the Indian context, to address various environmental issues including solid waste management. Green criminology would thus help empirically analyse the issues and generate evidence-based literature. Further, the authors argue that the right to adequate standard of living (as mandated by Article 25 of the Universal Declaration of Human Rights and Sustainable Development Goal 11) could be actualised through the efforts of policymakers as well as the local administration. The literature generated through empirical studies would be essential in this respect.

2 The Universal Declaration of Human Rights

The UDHR was adopted by the United Nations General Assembly in 1948 (GA/RES/217A (III)). This document still remains relevant in the contemporary world. That this declaration has been translated into more than 500 languages speaks of its significance in the current scenario (United Nations). All the Member States have committed to implement the provisions of the declaration. Broadly, the UDHR promises to all the human beings a life that ensures their economic, social, political, cultural and civic rights and that is free from fear and bond. These rights are universal in nature and timeless, and do not just apply to a country, or a particular social group or a particular period. The rights promised in the declaration are the inalienable rights of all people at all times and in all places (Al Hussein 2015). The preamble of the UDHR has also clearly spelt out that the recognition of the inherent dignity and the equal and inalienable rights of every member of the human family is a basis of freedom, justice and peace in the world. Article 1 of the UDHR states that all human beings are born free and are equal in dignity and rights. Also, all human beings have an inherent quality to reason and are endowed with conscience. Therefore, the article clearly stipulates that all human beings should act towards one another in a spirit of brotherhood. According to Article 25(1) of the declaration, all human beings have the right to have a standard of living adequate for their health and their family members. The right to adequate standard of living includes access to food, clothing, housing and medical care and the required social services. Everyone has the right to security in the event of unemployment, during sickness, if they are disabled, in the event of their widowhood, in old age or any other lack of livelihood in circumstances beyond their control (United Nations 2015).

All the Member States therefore should take steps to ensure that all her citizens enjoy an adequate standard of living. However, it would be difficult to define "adequate standard of living" because different Member States have different economic and social histories and capacities and also varied understanding of what is meant by adequate standard of living (Almeida et al. 2003). Some international instruments have also emphasised the importance of standard of living but in a different language. According to Article 12(1) of the International Covenant on Economic, Social and Cultural Rights (ICESCR), the state parties should recognise the right of everyone to enjoy the highest attainable standard of both physical and mental health (GA/RES/2200A (XXI)).

This covenant has also recommended certain steps to be taken by the states to achieve the full realisation of the right to the enjoyment of higher attainable standard of physical and mental health. Article 12(2) states that steps should also aim at the improvement of all aspects of environmental and industrial hygiene (GA/RES/2200A (XXI)).

2.1 *The UDHR Vis-à-Vis Environmental Protection*

Though the UDHR does not explicitly mention about the protection of environment, it indirectly indicates that adequate standard of living can be ensured through providing proper environment, which was not a major concern when the UDHR was adopted. It should also be noted that the attention of the international community with regard to the need for appropriate management and protection of the environment gained momentum in the 1960s. Only in the early 1970s, the environmental concepts were crystallised, particularly at the United Nations Conference on the Human Environment (UNCHE) held at Stockholm in 1972. This conference considered the need for both common approach and for common principles to inspire and guide the people of the world in the preservation and improvement of the environment. At the end of the conference, a declaration, popularly called the Stockholm Declaration, was adopted by the participating nations (A/CONF.48/14/Rev.1). According to the declaration, most of the environmental problems in developing countries are caused by under-development. Millions of people continue to live far below the minimum levels needed for a decent human existence. They are deprived of adequate food, clothing, shelter, education, health and sanitation. The declaration, therefore, called on developing countries to direct their efforts to development, keeping in mind their priorities and the need to preserve and enhance the environment.

Particularly, principle 1 of the Stockholm Declaration recognises the right to a healthy environment. This principle has also expressed the link between human rights and the environment since it declared that man has the fundamental right to freedom, equality and adequate conditions of life of dignity and well-being. It also declares that man bears a sincere responsibility to both protect and improve the environment for the present as well as future generations. The above principle also has introduced another dimension, namely, inter-generational equity. Following the Stockholm Declaration, there have been several international initiatives such as the Hague Declaration on the Environment (1989), the United Nations General Assembly Resolution 45/94 (14 December 1990), the Rio Declaration on Environment and Development (1992), the Experts Group of the World Commission on Environment and Development (1996) and so on (A/CONF.48/14/Rev.1; Emeseh 2012).

Apart from the initiatives listed before, the right to a clean and healthy environment is emerging as a part of international law. Though this rights perspective is an emerging component, its origin can be traced to the 1970s. A non-profit public interest law firm called Earth Justice was founded in 1971, which is dedicated to protecting the natural resources, the wildlife of the earth and also to defend the right of all citizens on the earth to a healthy environment. This organisation has consultative status with the United Nations Economic and Social Council (O'Gara et al. 2007). In May 1994, an international group of experts on human rights and environmental protection drafted the Declaration of Principles on Human Rights and the Environment (Ksentini Report). The Draft Declaration, considered as the first international instrument, comprehensively addressed the link between human rights and the environment. The Draft Declaration also demonstrates that the accepted environmental and human rights principles illustrate the right of everyone to secure a healthy and ecologically sound environment. It further describes the environmental dimensions of established human rights including the right to life, the right to health and the right to culture. The procedural rights (the right to participation) necessary for the realisation of substantial rights are also mentioned in the declaration. The corresponding duties apply to individuals, governments, international organisations and transnational corporations to respect this right (E/CN.4/Sub.2/1994/9). In September 2007, the United Nations General Assembly adopted the United Nations Declaration on the Rights of the Indigenous Peoples, which recognised the urgent need to respect and promote the inherent rights of indigenous peoples which derive from both political and socio-economic structures and also from their cultures, spiritual traditions, histories and philosophies, particularly their rights to their lands, territories and resources (A/RES/61/295). The various United Nations organs and agencies, including the United Nations Economic and Social Council (ECOSOC), United Nations Human Rights Council (formerly UN Commission on Human Rights (UNCHR)) and UN Environment Programme (UNEP), have not only established the link between environmental protection and human rights but also recognised the human right to a clean and healthy environment. Unfortunately, all international instruments mentioned earlier are considered as soft laws since they don't possess a binding legal force. However, such laws can be hardened if adopted in practice by the states and thus over time transform into norms of customary international law, in which case they would be binding and legally enforceable. Several regional human rights instruments (for example, African Charter on Human and Peoples' Rights) have recognised the right to a healthy environment. Some state constitutions in the United States (e.g. the Constitution of Montana) also provides for such rights (Emeseh 2012). In this context, it is also worthwhile to mention the Aarhus Convention (United Nations Economic Commission for Europe 1998). This relates to the United Nations Economic Commission of Europe (UNEC) Convention on Access to Information, Public Participation in Decision-Making and Access to Justice in Environmental Matters, which was adopted at the Fourth Ministerial Conference as part of the 'Environment for Europe' process in June 1998 in the city of Aarhus (Denmark). The procedural aspect of the right to healthy environment, articulated in principle 10 of the Rio Declaration is also enshrined in the Aarhus Convention. The Convention has established a number of rights for the public with regard to the environment. The World Development Report published by the World Bank in 2006 has also recognised the importance of procedural rights spelt out in the Aarhus Convention (Emeseh 2012).

3 2030 Agenda for Sustainable Development and the Right to Adequate Standard of Living

In September 2015, the United Nations General Assembly in its 70th session adopted the 2030 Agenda for sustainable development. As spelt out in the preamble of the agenda, it is not only a plan of action for people, planet and prosperity but also seeks to strengthen universal peace and larger freedom. There are 17 SDGs and 169 targets announced in the agenda. All the 17 SDGs and 169 targets seek to build on the Millennium Development Goals. They also seek to realise the human rights of all and to achieve gender equality and empowerment of all women and girls. All the goals and targets are integrated and indivisible and also balance the three dimensions of sustainable development, namely, the economic, the social and the environmental. The 2030 Agenda is guided by various international instruments. The principles of the charter of the United Nations has guided the agenda. It is also grounded in the international human rights treaties, including the Universal Declaration of Human Rights, the Millennium Declaration and the 2005 World Summit outcome. The 2030

Agenda is further informed by other international instruments such as Declaration on the Right to Development. The outcomes of all the major United Nations conferences and summits not only laid a strong foundation for sustainable development but also shaped the new agenda. Some of the conferences and summits which have direct relevance to sustainable development includes Rio Declaration on Environment and Development, the World Summit on Sustainable Development and the United Nations Conference on Sustainable Development. These conferences and summits have identified both the challenges and commitments which are interrelated and requires integrated solutions. To address these challenges and commitments, a new approach is needed. Sustainable development recognises that eradicating poverty, combatting inequality, preserving the planet and creating a sustained, inclusive and sustainable economic growth are linked to one another and are also interdependent. One of the goals of the SDG (SDG 11) is to make cities and human settlements inclusive, safe, resilient and sustainable. According to SDG 11, by 2030 all the countries and all stakeholders will take efforts to enhance 'inclusive and sustainable urbanisation and capacity for participatory, integrated and sustainable human settlement planning and management in all countries'. The goal also is set to 'reduce per capita environmental impact of cities including by paying attention to quality of air and municipal and other waste management' (A/RES/70/1). While this is the goal set to be achieved by 2030, the findings of the Sustainable Development Goals Report 2019 provided shocking data. Based on the data collected between 2010 and 2018, it was found that two billion people were without waste collection services and three billion people did not have access to controlled waste disposal facilities. In 2016, the total amount of waste generated globally was two billion metric tons and is expected to double (to about four billion metric tons) by 2050. Between 2001 and 2010, the proportion of municipal solid waste collected regularly was 76%, which increased to 81% between 2010 and 2018. The report has also revealed that in low- and middle-income countries, many municipal solid waste disposal facilities are open dumping sites. This improper form of solid waste disposal contributes significantly to air, water and soil pollution. The report went on to suggest that investment in waste management infrastructure is urgently needed to improve the solid waste management across most of the countries in the world (United Nations 2019). This disconnect between the goal set in the 2030 agenda and reality in the contemporary world is a matter of serious concern. This should become the subject matter of criminology in general and green criminology in particular. Some authors have discussed at length why criminologists should contribute to the 2030 agenda and how the knowledge of criminologists and their experience would benefit the international development community (Blaustein et al. 2018). The role of criminologists also assumes significance since the SDGs address issues relating to crime, justice and security. For instance, Blaustein et al. (2018) suggest that the criminologists can support the 2030 agenda mainly in two ways. One way is that criminologists can help with the design, implementation, evaluation of projects which would support safe, just and environmentally sustainable societies. This does not mean that criminological knowledge alone is sufficient for bringing about these outcomes. It should be combined with the expertise of development actors and aligned with stakeholder interest and knowledge.

The second way is that criminologists can assume a critical role by lending their expertise to the members of development community and local stakeholders. Specifically, criminologists with expertise on environmental crime can significantly contribute to the 2030 agenda since environmental sustainability lies at the heart of the SDGs. Blaustein et al. (2018) have also highlighted how criminologists can contribute to the realisation of various SDGs including SDG 11.7. This particular goal aims to provide universal access to safe, inclusive and accessible, green and public spaces particularly for women and children, persons with disabilities and older person.

4 Municipal Solid Waste Management in Chennai

Municipal solid waste management (MSWM) is a critical task in metropolitan cities. MSWM is the responsibility of urban local bodies, which in metropolitan cities in India are called corporations. MSWM comprises segregation, collection, storage, transportation, processing and disposal of solid waste to reduce its unfavourable impact on the environment. Poorly managed municipal solid waste (MSW) is one of the causes of innumerable urban disorders (Kumar et al. 2009).

MSWM is governed by Solid Waste Management Rules, 2016 under the Environment (Protection) Act, 1986. However, majority of urban local bodies do not have pertinent action plans for the execution and enactment of MSWM. It is unfortunate that no city in India can claim 100% segregation of MSW. The waste produced in India consists of approximately 40–60% compostable, 30–50% inert and 10–30% recyclable. Out of the total waste collected, only 12.45% is scientifically managed and the rest is disposed in open dumping grounds (Central Pollution Control Board 2013; Joshi and Ahmed 2016). There is also no organised and scientifically managed segregation of MSW either at the household or community level. Waste producers are seldom involved in the process of segregation. This lack of segregation at source means scientific disposal of waste does not happen (Kaushal et al. 2012; Singhal and Pandey 2001). Waste produced by households and street sweepings are usually transferred into community bins. Some commercial complexes and industrial units engage local bodies for the transfer of their waste to open dumping grounds. Uncontrolled open dumping is a common scenario in almost all cities (Kumar et al. 2009; Pujara et al. 2019). Dumping grounds and landfilling would continue to be a widely accepted practice in India. Metropolitan cities like Delhi, Chennai, Kolkata and Mumbai have limited availability of land for dumping grounds, which often exceed their carrying capacity (Sharholy et al. 2008).

In this background, a case study was conducted in Chennai, the capital city of the southern Indian state of Tamil Nadu. According to Indian Census 2011, the city had 4.54 million residents, living in 1.15 million households. The present estimated population of Chennai is about 8.9 million, making it the fourth most populous city in India. The Greater Chennai Corporation (GCC) is responsible for managing solid waste produced in the city. The jurisdiction of the city was extended in 2011 by increasing its area from 174 to 426 km^2. Now the jurisdiction of GCC covers three revenue districts, namely, Chennai, part of Kanchipuram and part of Thiruvallur. On a daily basis, around 5400 metric tons of MSW is collected from the city. The city generates wastes in the following categories: (a) residential (68%); (b) commercial (16%); (c) halls, schools and institutions (14%); (d) industrial (2%) and hospitals and clinics (separately disposed by hospitals/clinics by the supervision of Tamil Nadu Pollution Control Board). At present, MSW generated in Chennai city is dumped at two dumping grounds: Kodungaiyur Dumping Ground (KDG) and Perungudi Dumping Ground (PDG) (Greater Chennai Corporation; Greater Chennai Corporation 2018; Chennai District Administration 2020; Office of the Registrar General & Census Commissioner 2011). KDG is located in the northern part of Chennai and has been in operation since 1980, now extending to about 5 km^2. At the time of its inception, households were already present at the site. Now people are living within a 500-metre distance from the KDG, whereas PDG began its operation from the southern part of Chennai in 1987. During that time, there were no households in its vicinity. But due to rapid expansion of the Chennai city, now the households are within a 500-metre distance from PDG (Greater Chennai Corporation; Parameswari and Mudgal 2014; Eshanthini and Padmini 2015; Ammasi Krishnan et al. 2019).

4.1 Case 1: Kodungaiyur Dumping Ground

The local community informs that till the 1960s, the KDG site was a marshy wetland dominated by grasses, which served as a fodder farm for cattle. Initially there were around 15 huts. As it was a marshy wetland, people used to fill the land with the wastes generated from the Kothavalchavadi Market. Filling the land with construction and demolition waste was costlier compared to market wastes. Hence, the residents who occupied the lands used the site to discard wastes generated from Kothavalchavadi. In the early 1980s, municipal waste from the Chennai city started to be dumped here, which continues even today. The dumping ground receives all types of waste from MSW to hazardous industrial wastes to medical wastes. There are around 100 recyclers (80 of them are women) who depend on this dump yard for their livelihood. They will collect polyethylene (PET) bottles, glass bottles, surgical gloves, rubber slippers, cardboards, metals etc. Since the government failed to segregate wastes at source, the recyclers segregate the waste in the dumping ground. As the dumping ground receives medical waste and some hazardous chemicals, frequently they are inundated with syringes, surgical equipment and exposure to toxic chemicals.

During the rainy season, an unbearable stench emanates from the dump site. Regarding health conditions, the residents around the site are afflicted with a skin infection due to groundwater contamination. The residents are vulnerable to respiratory and skeletal disorders. Previously solid wastes from lorries used to be discarded during daytime and hence the foul smell would not be felt as much. But nowadays, the wastes are dumped in during the night with continuous trips of lorries with the wastes stocked for two or three days in various collection centres. So the stench from the waste has become unbearable. Further, feral dogs cause nuisance at the dumps.

4.2 *Case 2: Perungudi Dumping Ground*

The community members say that around 1987 or 1988, the present Perungudi site was chosen by the Chennai Corporation for dumping MSW. Perungudi dumping ground lies on the Pallikaranai marshland. And around 35% of the marshland is occupied by the dumping ground and it is still expanding beyond its carrying capacity. The residential areas such as Vinayaga Nagar, Sai Nagar and Sri Kumaran Nagar are very close to the dumping ground. Some years back, to increase the longevity of the dumping ground, there was a continuous burning of garbage. It had a negative impact on people living nearby, as it caused various respiratory problems such as chronic cough and asthma.

Ground water in the locality is contaminated because of the dumping ground. As the dumping ground is also a breeding place for mosquitoes, diseases like malaria and dengue are common among the residents. House flies are also a major problem in the neighbourhood, as it is responsible for spreading a range of diseases and infections like cholera, conjunctivitis, dysentery and gastroenteritis. Though the GCC is insisting on segregation of waste at source, the people and conservancy workers are not following it anymore. The GCC has been making announcements regarding plans for a scientific remediation of the dump yard for the past 8 years. But so far, none of those plans have been executed.

A recycler aged 37 years from the PDG narrated that

> Usually the day for me starts at six in the morning and lasts up to seven in the evening. I am very proud that as I could contribute to the waste management by segregating recyclable items from the municipal solid wastes. Collecting recyclable items such as plastic, cardboard, glass bottles etc. is the only source income for our sustenance. We will sell those collected items to the scrap merchants. A daily segregation of the waste may range from 5 kilograms to 30 kilograms. I am into this work by knowing it will definitely cause health risks. As I am handling garbage without any protective gears, I am very susceptible to develop worms, anaemia, respiratory problems etc. Moreover, very often, while segregating waste I am exposed to maggots. It causes a discomfort while having food. As the dumping ground receives all the types of wastes, very often injuries will occur due to cuts and falls. The presence of feral dogs sometimes gives rise to the threat of bites. Very often municipal waste contains disposable syringes and most of the recyclers are afraid of it may cause AIDS if we are injured with such syringes. Apart from the above said health hazards, most of the recyclers are affected with skin diseases. If anything happens, I need to visit the nearby government hospital as costs at private hospitals are higher.

It is therefore clear that improper MSWM can have negative impacts on both environment and public health. Lack of scientifically sound handling and disposal activity could result in soil, water and air pollution. Any deficiency in waste disposal or dumping untreated waste may cause serious health problems for populations surrounding the area of dumping grounds. Leaks from the dumped waste may contaminate soil, ground water and water streams. The presence of heavy metals and persistent organic pollutants will produce air pollution, which ultimately creates health hazards (World Health Organization 2016). In line with World Health Organization (2016) several literature suggest that a direct landfill disposal (without any pre-treatment) of MSW causes considerable geo-environmental problems such as emission of greenhouse gases (GHGs), hazardous volatile organic compounds, groundwater contamination due to seepage and leaching and noxious odours. With regard to human health, studies employing geographic or spatial approaches have suggested that there is an association between household proximity to dumping grounds and health-related effects (Gouveia and do Prado 2010; Fernández-Nava et al. 2014; Patil et al. 2017). Shaddick et al. (2018) opined that higher risk of low birth weight, congenital anomalies (inherited medical condition that occurs at or before birth), respiratory diseases and annoyance from stench were reported among people who live closer to such dumps. Some studies (Bergersen and Haarstad 2014; Lillycrop et al. 2015) showed a significant association between hydrogen sulphide (major odorant at municipal landfills) exposure and deaths caused by lung cancer. Symptoms of respiratory diseases are visible in people who reside near the dumping grounds. The residents were exposed to endotoxin, aerosols and microorganisms from the dumping grounds. Apart from the physical health problems, there is evidence for psychological and emotional impact among the residents living close to dump sites. In several instances, solid waste has been reported to contain human body parts and aborted foetuses, which may affect mental well-being of the residents who stay closer to dump sites. Scavenging animals and birds may also create nuisance to the people (Vrijheid 2000; Brinkel et al. 2009; Ziraba et al. 2016).

Specifically with regard to the health impact of residents near KDG, Deivanayagam et al. (2007) identified that air pollution from the dump critically affected the residents and significantly children. Many of the children reported to have perennial cough and cold, skin diseases, growth retardation, fevers and few other chronic ailments. This results in high absenteeism among school going children. Apart from the above, the residents are exposed to carcinogens such as acrylonitrile, 1,4-dichlorobenzene and chloromethane. Eventually, it will show up as cancerous growth in skin, lungs, throats, urinary bladder and any of the internal organs. Although one of the findings of the study (Deivanayagam et al. 2007) indicate that a serious health problem affects the school attendance rate of children, the research has not examined high absenteeism (truancy) as an indication of deviant behaviour. In other words, if the same study was carried out from a green criminological point of view, it would have brought to light a few other criminological issues, including deviance among children.

As it is obvious from what is happening to people living near dump sites, what is clear is that it is impossible to enjoy one's life without the protection and preservation of the environment. Also, an equilibrium between living organisms free from pollution of air, water, soil and sanitation will ensure one's healthy being. Hence, environmental degradation or ecological abuse is considered to be serious than any type of physical abuse of humans. Environmental degradation and ecological abuse that is state-sponsored are often connected with inequitable distribution of environmental hazards (Adeola 2001). In India, most of the dumping grounds are managed by respective state's civic bodies. The management of solid waste and dumping grounds is the primary responsibility of civic bodies. There are specific provisions given in the Solid Waste Management Rules, 2016, under the Environment (Protection) Act, 1986, to manage solid waste, and whoever fails to comply with or contravenes any of the provisions of this Act will be prosecuted. This may be considered as a preventive strategy. Besides, civic bodies occasionally create awareness among the general public on the appropriate methods of solid waste segregation. Although it is an element that prevents people from not violating the provisions of Environment (Protection) Act, 1986, it cannot *per se* be called as crime prevention by the civic bodies. There is a wide network of Non-Governmental Organisations (NGOs) involved in environmental protection including aiding in creating awareness among people in protecting their environment. However, all the efforts have not culminated in the form of movement for green spaces or safe environment.

The above description of the hard reality demands the attention of academics, administrators, policy-makers and also those who are concerned with environmental sustainability to focus on the ways and methods of addressing or improving MSWM to realise SDG 11. Currently the situation is very grim because of the impact of the improper solid waste management on the people in general and on the marginalised communities in particular, on whom it is greater. This cannot be approached simply as an administrative or management issue but rather it should be addressed through a multi-disciplinary approach. The role of criminologists in general and green criminologists in particular would also be greatly required to address a more complex issue such the impact of improper MSWM on the people.

5 Understanding Green Criminology

The term 'Green Criminology' was introduced in the criminological literature by Lynch (1990). He is currently a professor in the Department of Criminology and an associate faculty member in the Patel College of Global Sustainability, University of South Florida, USA. In the 1990s, some authors (for example South 1998) used the term green issues to include the environment, animal rights and the relationship between human societies and ecological systems. South (1998), in his article, focused on the natural environment and its relationship with criminological concerns. In the field of criminology, such a relationship was considered as underdeveloped and hence the term 'environmental' was still chiefly employed in studies of place and spatial patterning of crime (Bottoms as cited in South 1998). Given this status, South (1998) advocated the enhancement of environmental consciousness in the field of criminology and also for the development of a green perspective. Though he emphasises the importance of "thinking green" as a sensitising perspective, he did not put forward a 'theory' for or of 'a green criminology'. He argued further that such a sensitising perspective should find a prominent place in the criminological agenda. He further expressed his intention explicitly that a green perspective could be reasonably placed alongside other source of change and critique in fields such as feminism, postmodernism, minority representation etc. Some authors have criticised the field of criminology as a fragmented discipline. For example, Ericson and Carriere, as cited in South (1998), observed that criminology is a fragmented field of enquiry and a part of broader process of fragmentation in the academy, and in other social institutions and also in the risk society. Ulrich Beck and Anthony Giddens initially developed the risk society hypothesis, which gained acceptance in the field of sociology and created a debate about risk in postmodern society (Etkin 2016). Due to this fragmented nature of criminology, particularly in the study of the environmental issues of risk society, a green perspective is suggested.

Several other authors over a period of time have attempted to define green criminology. In the late 1990s, some authors engaged in defining the term green. Groombridge (1998) was of the opinion that it is not simply possible to adopt a "green" approach without bringing with it the other issues such as theoretical and methodological. During the same period, South (1998) stated that it would be valuable to describe what the green criminological theories may look like. Therefore, it is necessary to define the meaning of the term green in the process of designing a green criminology. According to Lynch and Stretesky (2003), defining green criminology requires embracing an array of various conceptions and not simply on what green criminology is, but also on conceptions such as what does green criminology seek to achieve; what approach should or should not be included; and contradictory perspectives on what it means to be green.

Lynch and Stretesky (2003) took the view that like other crimes, green crimes are also social constructions influenced by both social locations and power relations in the society. With regard to power issues, they wanted to examine the meaning of the term green since they considered that the meaning of the term green is influenced by two distinct groups, namely, corporate activists and environmental justice activists/movements. That is, they wanted to sketch the main issues connecting points required to construct a definition of green criminology that would recognise the influence of corporate power structures and also the achievements of environmental justice activists/movements.

Green criminology is described as a research area focusing on environmental crime, environmental harm, environmental laws, environmental justice, environmental regulation, victimisation due to environmental crime and so on. The subject matter of green criminology also included moral and philosophical issues relating to environment as such issues relate to human beings, animals, plants and ecosystems and its components (White 2008).

While tracing the origin and evolution of green criminology, White (2013) commented that though there have been a number of scholars working on issues relating to environmental crime, they were not necessarily exploring the green criminology perspective. The author made a reference to various bodies of work on environmental issues that are informed by literature on corporate and organised crime. For example, environmental harm and crime are linked to both the activities of corporations and to organised criminal syndicates. The above issues are not analysed through a green criminology perspective but through the lens of sociology of deviance and political economy. The focus of such studies were on the control and manipulation of waste disposal processes and protection and distribution of toxic chemicals and so on (Ruggiero 1996; Massari and Monzini 2004; Pearce and Tombs 2019).

Few other authors have specifically looked at environmental crime but within the conventional framework. The focus of such analysis has been on traditional illegal activities linked with the environment such as illegal fishing etc. However, such an analysis has been done within the traditional criminological approaches. Broadly the focus of the works of such authors has been based upon the legal concepts of environmental crime, existing legislations and the regulations relating to environmental crime, the nature of environmental law enforcement agencies etc. (Situ and Emmons 2000; O'Connor Shelley and Crow 2009; Fyfe and Reeves 2010). The above criminological works, to some extent, overlap with the traditional legal studies (violation of criminal law and civil statutes) in the area of environmental crime. The key concepts and concerns of these studies lie in the area of substantive law including concepts such as vicarious liability, public interest etc. These studies have also attempted to place a legal or monetary value of environmental harm (Brickey 2008; Mehta 2009; Bell et al. 2017).

Another group of studies has also applied sociological analysis to questions pertaining to environmental justice. The main focus of such studies was to explore the empirical links between toxic environments and some categories of people such as the poor and the dispossessed and also to wage a struggle against issues such as discrimination and racism that underpin such ecological injustice. The issues such as distribution of environmental advantage and disadvantage instead of crime *per se* are the key concepts and concerns emphasised by the above group of studies (Bullard 2005; Pellow 2007).

In the 1990s when the sub-discipline of green criminology emerged, the writings were about the need for criminology to take environmental crimes seriously and to do so in ways that would force the discipline criminology to rethink on the question such as how it does, what it does and also how to conceptualise the issue. The idea of green criminology itself was one of the key concepts and concerns that was the subject matter of analysis during the early period. The other concepts and concerns included the idea that green criminology is not a theory but only a perspective and also the social and ecological significance of studying environmental crime and harm (Lynch 1990; Clifford 1998; South 1998). During the current decade, broadly the term green criminology is used to refer to the study by criminologists of environmental harms, environmental laws and environmental regulation.

In 2014, Lynch and Stretesky in their book titled *Exploring Green Criminology: Towards a Green Criminological Revolution* have dealt in detail both the definition and scope of green criminology. According to them, green criminology is a means for studying various problems relating to environmental harm and crime, environmental law, environmental regulation, environmental justice and victimisation due to environmental crime, moral/philosophical issues since such issues are relating to humans, non-human animals, plant species and so on. The subject matter of green criminology also includes the study of ecosystems and its components. The authors have also attempted to build a green criminological typology by examining the types of research recognised as falling under the green sciences. For a long time, natural scientists have taken up environmental issues and their attention to green studies precedes the emergence of green criminology. Therefore, the concepts employed by natural scientists to organise their green research initiatives are useful for developing a seminal approach within green criminology. One of the reasons for taking this approach to developing a green criminological typology is that the orientation can be adopted to demonstrate inter-connections and intersections between green criminology and green science.

The advantage of focusing on the overlap between green criminology and green science is to encourage green criminologists to draw on the related scientific literature to support their views and ideas. Further, these authors are of the view that green criminology cannot make a substantial contribution to the study of crime and justice without making its connection to science. To demonstrate such a connection and make them more obvious, these authors reviewed the overlap between green criminology and green science in three primary areas: (a) eco approaches: research that addresses environmental issues in relation to non-human species and also their intersections with natural ecology; (b) enviro approaches: research that addresses issues relating to pollution that will have impact on human species and their interaction with environment; (c) green policy approach: research that addresses solutions to environmental harms and their prevention.

However, the above three approaches do not exhaust all types of green criminological research. Still there is a significant quantum of research not covered by these three primary areas of intersections. That is there are various issues addressed by the green criminologists but not included within the green natural science approaches. Green contextual approach is a unique green criminological contribution that stems from research connecting environmental issues to various theories including economic, social, political and philosophical theories (Lynch and Stretesky 2014).

6 Green Criminology: A Tool to Implement SDG 11

As discussed above, the right to adequate standard of living for an individual is directly related to the quality of the environment. Article 25(1) of the UDHR and SDG 11 provide for adequate standard of living and detail ways to make human settlements inclusive, safe, resilient, and sustainable. To achieve these ideals, there is a need to strengthen the MSWM capabilities of various countries. The authors of this chapter strongly believe that the nature and scope of green criminology has to be expanded so as to provide a holistic approach to the study of environmental problems and various environmental issues, including MSWM. In this direction, earnest effort has been made by the authors in the form of a case study conducted in the city of Chennai, which can serve as a prelude for future studies from a green criminological perspective.

Globally, the scope of green criminology has been expanding, through both research and practice. However, in Indian context, literature in the field of green criminology is sparse. While acknowledging the fact that various problems relating to environmental harm, environmental law, environmental regulation and so on are studied independently, a comprehensive approach to environmental sustainability is not a common approach in India. For instance, the improper MSWM is not an issue to be studied from a management perspective but from the perspective of criminologists and victimologists. Independent researchers and governmental agencies have estimated that nearly 80% of MSW is disposed in open dumping grounds. The impact of improper solid waste has also been studied extensively. The health hazards of the people living closer to open dumping grounds is examined and found that such people experience high risk of low birth weight, respiratory disorders and annoyance from stench. All these studies, however, were not done from a green criminological perspective. Green criminology broadly includes the study by criminologists of environmental harms, environmental laws and environmental regulations. Academics in the field of criminology should, therefore, endeavour to study the environmental harms due to improper MSWM and also to study the laws and regulations relating to MSWM. Such a holistic approach would help understand specific environmental issues and outcome of such studies would also help the stakeholders concerned to ensure the right of citizens to adequate standard of living. As argued by several authors, green criminology is not an independent discipline or sub-discipline of criminology, rather it is a perspective to study any environment related issues. By including within its scope the issues such as impact of improper MSWM, green criminologists would contribute to a safe, just and environmentally sustainable community.

Taking forward the domain of green criminology may be one of the several ways to achieve the SDG 11. The right to adequate standard of living has been not only a subject of discussion in several national and international conferences, summits and other platforms for a very long time, it has been incorporated as one of the important SDG in the 2030 agenda. Expanding the scope of green criminology, thereby studying various environmental issues, would certainly enrich the existing literature. Also, the outcome of such intensive research from the green criminological perspective would form the knowledge base and would sensitise all the stakeholders.

References

A/CONF.48/14/Rev.1 Report of the United Nations Conference on the Human Environment. 5-16 June 1972.

A/RES/61/295 Declaration of the Rights of Indigenous Peoples. 2 October 2007.

A/RES/70/1 Transforming our world: the 2030 Agenda for Sustainable Development. 21 October 2015.

Adeola, F. O. (2001). Environmental injustice and human rights abuse: The states, MNCs, and repression of minority groups in the world system. *Human Ecology Review, 8*, 39–59. https://www.jstor.org/stable/24707236
Al Hussein, Z. R. (2015). *Introduction. Illustrated edition of the Universal Declaration of Human Rights*. https://www.un.org/en/udhrbook/pdf/udhr_booklet_en_web.pdf
Almeida, D., Berlin, R., Allison, K., Deinard, A., Dowd, B., Flowers, N., Harrison, I., Maretzki, A., Rudelius-Palmer, K., & Weissbrodt, D. (2003). *Study guide: The right to means for adequate health*. University of Minnesota Human Rights Library. http://hrlibrary.umn.edu/edumat/studyguides/righttohealth.html
Ammasi Krishnan, M., Jawahar, K., Perumal, V., Devaraj, T., Thanarasu, A., Kubendran, D., & Sivanesan, S. (2019). Effects of ambient air pollution on respiratory and eye illness in population living in Kodungaiyur, Chennai. *Atmospheric Environment, 203*, 166–171. https://doi.org/10.1016/j.atmosenv.2019.02.013
Bell, S., McGillivray, D., Pedersen, O., Lees, E., & Stokes, E. (2017). *Environmental law*. London: Oxford University Press.
Bergersen, O., & Haarstad, K. (2014). Treating landfill gas hydrogen sulphide with mineral wool waste (MWW) and rod mill waste (RMW). *Waste Management, 34*, 141–147. https://doi.org/10.1016/j.wasman.2013.09.012
Blaustein, J., Pino, N. W., Fitz-Gibbon, K., & White, R. (2018). Criminology and the UN sustainable development goals: The need for support and critique. *British Journal of Criminology, 58*, 767–786. https://doi.org/10.1093/bjc/azx061
Brickey, K. F. (2008). *Environmental crime: Law, policy, prosecution*. New York: Aspen Publishers.
Brinkel, J., Khan, M. H., & Kraemer, A. (2009). A systematic review of arsenic exposure and its social and mental health effects with special reference to Bangladesh. *International Journal of Environmental Research and Public Health, 6*, 1609–1619. https://doi.org/10.3390/ijerph6051609
Bullard, R. D. (2005). *The quest for environmental justice: Human rights and the politics of pollution* (1st ed.). San Francisco: Counterpoint.
Central Pollution Control Board. (2013). *Status Report on Municipal Solid Waste Management*. https://silo.tips/downloadFile/status-report-municipal-solid-waste-management
Chandra, M. (2015). Environmental concerns in India: Problems and solutions. *The Journal of International Business and Law, 15*, 1–14. https://scholarlycommons.law.hofstra.edu/cgi/viewcontent.cgi?article=1278&context=jibl
Chennai District Administration. (2020). *Chennai district profile 2017*. https://cdn.s3waas.gov.in/s313f3cf8c531952d72e5847c4183e6910/uploads/2018/06/2018062956.pdf
Clifford, M. (1998). *Environmental crime: Enforcement, policy, and social responsiblity* (1st ed.). Gaithersburg, MD: Aspen Publishers.
Deivanayagam, C. ., Geeta, R., Coelho, K., Suchitra, R., Thangaraj, M., & Nazir, M. (2007). *Violations of environmental, labour & human rights due to garbage dumping & burning at Kodungaiyur*. Community Environmental Monitoring: Chennai. http://www.sipcotcuddalore.com/downloads/Kodungaiyur_factfinding.pdf
E/CN.4/Sub.2/1994/9 Human Rights and the Environment. 6 July 1994.
Emeseh, E. (2012). Human rights dimensions of contemporary environmental protection. In M. Odello & S. Cavandoli (Eds.), *Emerging areas of human rights in the 21st century: The role of the universal declaration of human rights* (pp. 66–86). Oxon: Routledge.
Eshanthini, P., & Padmini, T. K. (2015). Impact of leachate on ground water quality near Kodungaiyur Dumping Site, Chennai, Tamil Nadu, India. *International Journal of PharmTech Research, 8*, 171–179. http://sphinxsai.com/2015/ph_vol8_no10/1/(171-179)V8N10PT.pdf
Etkin, D. (2016). *Disaster risk*. Waltham: Butterworth-Heinemann.
Fernández-Nava, Y., Del Río, J., Rodríguez-Iglesias, J., Castrillón, L., & Marañón, E. (2014). Life cycle assessment of different municipal solid waste management options: A case study of Asturias (Spain). *Journal of Cleaner Production, 81*, 178–189. https://doi.org/10.1016/j.jclepro.2014.06.008

Fyfe, N., & Reeves, A. (2010). The thin green line? Police perceptions of the challenges of policing wildlife crime in Scotland. In R. I. Mawby (Ed.), *Rural policing and policing the rural: A constable countryside?* (1st ed.). London: Routledge.

GA/RES/217A (III) Universal Declaration of Human Rights. 10 December 1948.

GA/RES/2200A (XXI) International Covenant on Economic, Social and Cultural Rights. 16 December 1966.

Gouveia, N., & do Prado, R. R. (2010). Health risks in areas close to urban solid waste landfill sites. *Revista de Saude Publica, 44*, 859–866. https://doi.org/10.1590/S0034-89102010005000029

Greater Chennai Corporation. (2018). *City Disaster Management Plan 2018*. Greater Chennai Corporation. https://chennaicorporation.gov.in/images/CDMP%20Book%20Wrapper%20Full%20Book%20(%20English).pdf

Greater Chennai Corporation. Soild Waste Management. https://chennaicorporation.gov.in/departments/solid-waste-management/index.htm

Groombridge, N. (1998). Masculinities and crimes against the environment. *Theoretical Criminology, 2*, 249–267. https://doi.org/10.1177/1362480698002002006

Hall, M. (2014). Environmental harm and environmental victims: Scoping out a "green victimology". *International Review of Victimology, 20*, 129–143. https://doi.org/10.1177/0269758013508682

Joshi, R., & Ahmed, S. (2016). Status and challenges of municipal solid waste management in India: A review. *Cogent Environmental Science, 2*, 1–18. https://doi.org/10.1080/23311843.2016.1139434

Kaushal, R. K., Varghese, G. K., & Chabukdhara, M. (2012). Municipal solid waste management in India-current state and future challenges: A review. *International Journal of Engineering, Science and Technology, 4*, 1473–1489. https://www.researchgate.net/profile/Rajendra_Kaushal/publication/233894305_Municipal_Solid_Waste_Management_in_India-Current_State_and_Future_Challenges_A_Review/links/02bfe50c9adce7b35f000000/Municipal-Solid-Waste-Management-in-India-Current-State-and-Future-Challenges-A-Review.pdf

Kumar, S., Bhattacharyya, J. K., Vaidya, A. N., Chakrabarti, T., Devotta, S., & Akolkar, A. B. (2009). Assessment of the status of municipal solid waste management in metro cities, state capitals, class I cities, and class II towns in India: An insight. *Waste Management, 29*, 883–895. https://doi.org/10.1016/j.wasman.2008.04.011

Lillycrop, K. A., Costello, P. M., Teh, A. L., Murray, R. J., Clarke-Harris, R., Barton, S. J., Garratt, E. S., Ngo, S., Sheppard, A. M., Wong, J., Dogra, S., Burdge, G. C., Cooper, C., Inskip, H. M., Gale, C. R., Gluckman, P. D., Harvey, N. C., Chong, Y. S., Yap, F., Meaney, M. J., Rifkin-Graboi, A., Holbrook, J. D., The Epigen Global Research Consortium., & Godfrey, K. M. (2015). Association between perinatal methylation of the neuronal differentiation regulator HES1 and later childhood neurocognitive function and behaviour. *International Journal of Epidemiology, 44*, 1263–1276. https://doi.org/10.1093/ije/dyv052

Lynch, M. J. (1990). The greening of criminology: A perspective for the 1990s. *The Critical Criminologist, 2*, 11–12.

Lynch, M. J. (2012). Reflections on green criminology and its boundaries. In N. South & A. Brisman (Eds.), *Routledge international handbook of green criminology*. Oxon: Routledge.

Lynch, M. J., & Stretesky, P. B. (2003). The meaning of green: Contrasting criminological perspectives. *Theoretical Criminology, 7*, 217–238. https://doi.org/10.1177/1362480603007002414

Lynch, M. J., & Stretesky, P. B. (2014). *Exploring green criminology: Toward a green criminological revolution*. Surrey: Aspen Publishing Limited.

Lynch, M. J., Stretesky, P. B., & Long, M. A. (2015). Environmental justice: A criminological perspective. *Environmental Research Letters, 10*. https://doi.org/10.1088/1748-9326/10/8/085008

Massari, M., & Monzini, P. (2004). Dirty businesses in Italy: A case-study of illegal trafficking in hazardous waste. *Global Crime, 6*, 285–304. https://doi.org/10.1080/17440570500273416

Mehta, M. C. (2009). *In the Public Interest: Landmark Judgement and Orders of the Supreme Court of India on Environment and Human Rights*. New Delhi: Prakriti Publications.

Nurse, A. (2017). Green criminology: Shining a critical lens on environmental harm. *Palgrave Communications, 3*, 1–3. https://doi.org/10.1057/s41599-017-0007-2

O'Connor Shelley, T., & Crow, M. S. (2009). The nature and extent of conservation policing: Law enforcement generalists or conservation specialists? *American Journal of Criminal Justice, 34*, 9–27. https://doi.org/10.1007/s12103-008-9057-8

O'Gara, R., Mollo, M., Wagner, J. M., Popovic, N., Lador, Y., Osofsky, H., Reddy, S., Ganahl, E., Kastenberg, R., Peters, S. A., & Takacs, D. (2007). *Environmental rights Report 2007*. Oakland: Earth Justice. https://earthjustice.org/sites/default/files/library/references/2007-environmental-rights-report.pdf

Office of the Registrar General & Census Commissioner. (2011). *Census Data*. Office of the Registrar General & Census Commissioner, Ministry of Home Affairs, Government of India. http://www.censusindia.gov.in/pca/SearchDetails.aspx?Id=720012

Parameswari, K., & Mudgal, B. V. (2014). Geochemical investigation of groundwater contamination in Perungudi dumpsite, South India. *Arabian Journal of Geosciences, 7*, 1363–1371. https://doi.org/10.1007/s12517-013-0832-6

Patil, B. S., Agnes Anto, C., & Singh, D. N. (2017). Simulation of municipal solid waste degradation in aerobic and anaerobic bioreactor landfills. *Waste Management & Research, 35*, 301–312. https://doi.org/10.1177/0734242X16679258

Pearce, F., & Tombs, S. (2019). *Toxic capitalism: Corporate crime and the chemical industry* (1st ed.). London: Routledge.

Pellow, D. N. (2007). *Resisting global toxics: Transnational movements for environmental justice*. Cambridge: MIT Press.

Pujara, Y., Pathak, P., Sharma, A., & Govani, J. (2019). Review on Indian municipal solid waste management practices for reduction of environmental impacts to achieve sustainable development goals. *Journal of Environmental Management, 248*, 1–14. https://doi.org/10.1016/j.jenvman.2019.07.009

Ruggiero, V. (1996). *Organized and corporate crime in Europe: Offers that can't be refused*. Hampshire, UK: Dartmouth Publishing Co Limited.

Shaddick, G., Ranzi, A., Thomas, M. L., Aguirre-Perez, R., Dunbar, M. B. N., Parmagnani, F., & Martuzzi, M. (2018). Towards an assessment of the health impact of industrially contaminated sites: Waste landfills in Europe. *Epidemiologia e Prevenzione, 42*, 69–75. https://doi.org/10.19191/EP18.5-6.S1.P069.089

Sharholy, M., Ahmad, K., Mahmood, G., & Trivedi, R. C. (2008). Municipal solid waste management in Indian cities - A review. *Waste Management, 28*, 459–467. https://doi.org/10.1016/j.wasman.2007.02.008

Singhal, S., & Pandey, S. (2001). Solid waste management in India: Status and future directions. *TERI Information Monitor on Environmental Science, 6*, 1–4. https://www.researchgate.net/profile/Shaleen_Singhal/publication/285893254_Solid_waste_management_in_India_Status_and_future_directions/links/5f228492299bf13404927bf5/Solid-waste-management-in-India-Status-and-future-directions.pdf

Situ, Y., & Emmons, D. (2000). *Environmental crime: The criminal justice system's role in protecting the environment*. California: SAGE Publications, Inc..

South, N. (1998). A green field for criminology? *Theoretical Criminology, 2*, 211–233. https://doi.org/10.1177/1362480698002002004

United Nations. (2015). *Illustrated edition of the Universal Declaration of Human Rights*. https://www.un.org/en/udhrbook/pdf/udhr_booklet_en_web.pdf

United Nations. (2019). *The sustainable development goals report 2019*. 44–45. https://unstats.un.org/sdgs/report/2019/The-Sustainable-Development-Goals-Report-2019.pdf

United Nations. *The universal declaration of human rights*. https://www.un.org/en/universal-declaration-human-rights/index.html

United Nations Economic Commission for Europe. (1998). *Convention on Access to Information, Public Participation in Decision-Making and Access to Justice in Environmental Matters*. https://www.unece.org/fileadmin/DAM/env/pp/documents/cep43e.pdf

Vrijheid, M. (2000). Health effects of residence near hazardous waste landfill sites: A review of epidemiologic literature. *Environmental Health Perspectives, 108*, 101–112. https://doi.org/10.1289/ehp.00108s1101

White, R. (2003). Environmental issues and the criminological imagination. *Theoretical Criminology, 7*, 483–506. https://doi.org/10.1177/13624806030074005

White, R. (2008). *Crimes against nature: Environmental criminology and ecological justice*. Devon, UK: Willan Publishing.

White, R. (2013). The conceptual contours of green criminology. In R. Walters, D. S. Westerhuis, & T. Wyatt (Eds.), *Emerging issues in green criminology: Exploring power, justice and harm* (pp. 17–33). London: Palgrave Macmillan.

World Health Organization. (2016). *Waste and human health: Evidence and needs*. http://www.euro.who.int/__data/assets/pdf_file/0003/317226/Waste-human-health-Evidence-needs-mtg-report.pdf

Ziraba, A. K., Haregu, T. N., & Mberu, B. (2016). A review and framework for understanding the potential impact of poor solid waste management on health in developing countries. *Archives of Public Health, 74*, 1–11. https://doi.org/10.1186/s13690-016-0166-4

Srinivasan Murugesan is a Professor and the Head of the Department of Criminology, University of Madras (Chennai, India). He has extensive knowledge and experience in teaching and research in the field of criminology and victimology. He has published nearly 55 articles in regional, national, and international journals. He has conducted 18 research projects sponsored by both national and international funding agencies/institutions such as the United Nations Children's Fund (UNICEF), India's University Grants Commission, Bureau of Police Research & Development, and so on. He has completed two research projects in collaboration with the Tokiwa International Victimology Institute (TIVI), Tokiwa University, Japan, and one research project with the Department of Criminal Justice Sciences, Illinois State University, Normal, Illinois, USA. He has given nearly 70 presentations at national and international workshops, seminars, and conferences. He was previously the General Secretary of the Indian Society of Criminology and, until recently, he was the General Secretary of the Indian Society of Victimology. He has been invited as an expert to the first and third Closed Experts Group Meeting (EGM) on Collaboration between Civil Society Organisations and National Authorities on Victims of Terrorism in Asia-Pacific, organised by the United Nations Counter-Terrorism Centre (UNCCT). He was awarded the Max Planck Society Fellowship twice for research into the areas of money laundering at the Max Planck Institute for Foreign & International Criminal Law, Freiburg, Germany. He is currently involved in a project funded by UNICEF for the training of judicial officers and police officers on juvenile justice and juvenile psychology. He is guiding more than 10 Ph.D. research scholars, and 13 scholars have already successfully completed their Ph.D. research. E-mail: murugesan.srinivasan2013@gmail.com.

Shankar Prakash Alagesan is currently a doctoral candidate at the Department of Criminology, University of Madras. His research is focused on environmental crime in general and wildlife crime in particular. He was awarded the UGC-Senior Research Fellowship for pursuing his doctoral research. He completed his post-graduate in Criminology and Criminal Justice Administration from the University of Madras. Later, he worked as a research assistant in a project conducted at the Department of Criminology and sponsored by Transparency International. He successfully completed an "International Post-graduate course on Victimology, Victim Assistance and Criminal Justice" co-hosted by the World Society of Victimology (WSV) and Inter-University Centre (IUC), Dubrovnik, Croatia. He has also participated in the "Winter School on Environmental Crime" organised by the United Nations Interregional Crime and Justice Research Institute (UNICRI) and the Italian Society for International Organisation (SIOI), Rome, Italy. Recently, he was selected as a United Nations Volunteer for the 14th United Nations Congress on Crime Prevention and Criminal Justice to be held at Kyoto, Japan. E-mail: shankarprakash@live.com.

Notes on the Case of Orangutan Sandra, the Non-Human Subject of Rights

Pedro R. David

Abstract Depending on religion or legal philosophy, an animal may be considered a "non-human person" whose welfare rights should be acknowledged and protected by people. Law enforcement authorities and courts address cases of treatment of animals by people, including shared by them natural habitat—"Mother Earth," to use the term of the 2030 United Nations Sustainable Development Agenda. This chapter discusses the philosophical and legal underpinnings for welfare rights of animals, prompted by the case of the retired orangutan Sandra. She became the first non-human subject of such rights, granted by a ground-breaking Argentinian jurisprudence with the first-ever court-backed her transfer to an animal sanctuary in the United States, where her relative welfare and freedom has been secured.

Keywords Animal rights · Non-human subject · Trialism

1 Introduction

Since the time of the Sixth United Nations Congress on the Prevention of Crime and the Treatment of Offenders (Caracas, Venezuela, 1980), there has been a growing recognition of the postulate that the concept of sustainable development should be reinterpreted. The unanimously adopted Caracas Declaration recognized, inter alia, that "It is. . .essential to review the traditional crime prevention strategies based exclusively on legal criteria." It also stated that "The prevention of crime and penal justice should be considered in the context of economic development, of political systems, of social and cultural values and of social change" (A/RES/35/71, Annex, paras. 1 & 2).

The perspective of the Sixth United Nations Congress radically moved away from the formalism espoused by legal theorists Hans Kelsen and John Austin. The perspective emerged instead from integrative or integral approaches linked to

P. R. David (✉)
Argentine John F. Kennedy University, Law School, Buenos Aires, Argentina

H. Kury, S. Redo (eds.), *Crime Prevention and Justice in 2030*,
https://doi.org/10.1007/978-3-030-56227-4_15

different group contexts in a setting of fluid historical transformation. Drawing on this comprehensive outlook, in 2014, I developed a legal doctrine for a sentence dictated by the Second Chamber of the Cassation Court of the Argentine Republic—which I shared with the other judges of the Second Chamber, Dr. Angela Ledesma and Alejandro Slokar—and we discuss here some notes on the particular case of Sandra, a non-human subject.

2 Roman Law and the Person

A renowned scholar of Roman law, Eugene Petit, reminds us that the word "persona" originally indicated the mask worn by Roman actors in theater performances. These masks allowed them to amplify their voices (*pre-sonare*) (Eugene 1913, paras. 62 & 63). This original meaning was broadened to designate a being with rights and obligations. The first differentiation was one of free persons in contrast to slaves.

More than two thousand years later, the broadening of the "persona" in law comprises the new subjects of law, among them animals—our eternal companions in this life, recognizing the limits that impede their full legitimacy. That original meaning "does not mean to equalize all living beings and take from the human that special value that implies at the same time, a tremendous responsibility. It also does not suppose a "divinizing" of the earth that would deprive us of the call to collaborate with it and protect its fragility. These conceptions will end up creating new imbalances to escape the reality that questions us." (Carta Enciclica Laudato Si 2015, para. 90).

In this story of two thousand years, the protection of fundamental legal values of the person was broadened in scope to eliminate, foremost, the barriers of slavery affecting hundreds of millions of people who live today with fewer limits to their freedom. Discrimination and hate persist in the treatment of social groups marginalized by gender, race, national identity, language and religion.

In this historical global dynamic, the new legislation (juridical normativism) expands when faced with the pressure of unprecedented cultural, scientific and technological changes, including the acute phenomena of globalization.

With this "evolution-revolution" humans are learning that the protection of human life is synonymous with the protection of the earth—including its waters and the non-human life that is at risk of extinction at an alarming scale. The fight for the reform of the law is also tied to the effort to reach social equality in all countries. As we shall see many times in this chapter, the aforementioned *Carta Enciclica Laudato Si* is fundamental for this legal recognition.

3 The Story of Sandra

The story of Sandra begins in 2014 in Buenos Aires (Argentina), when a non-governmental organization (NGO) called the Association of Authorities and Lawyers for the Rights of Animals petitioned for a *habeas corpus* for an orangutan named Sandra which lived in the Buenos Aries City Zoo. The NGO wished to have the orangutan relocate to a sanctuary called the "*Santuario de Sorocaba*" where it could have greater freedom. My Federal Chamber in the Cassation Court where my colleagues Dr. Angela Ledesma and Dr. Alejandro Slokar also voted, gave the right to act jurisdictionally to the misdemeanor of the City of Buenos Aires, which had already intervened in this case.[1]

The resolution said succinctly that Sandra was a non-human subject of rights (*sujeto de derecho no humano*) and opened up the legal protection to include primates.[2] The news of this resolution was widely divulged in Argentina and the world.[3] In 2019, nearly five years later, the 33-year old Sandra left her site in the zoo, which closed in 2016 following reports of animal cruelty. She arrived at the USA to become the new resident of the Center for Great Apes in Florida, a sanctuary much better suited to her needs. Judge Elena Liberatori, who ruled over the landmark decision, said Sandra will now be able to spend the rest of her life "in a more dignified situation" (Cockroft 2019).

The concept of subject of rights, according to the scholar in his quote of *Legaz Lacambre*, is based on the dignity of the person, distinguishing it from all that is an object. The person is treated with dignity when he or she is allowed to operate with freedom (Legaz y Lacambra 1976, pp. 17–22). In the words of *Legaz*, the subjective

[1]Judge Elena Libertori in the *Contencioso Administrativo y Tributario* of the City of Buenos Aires, accepted the *habeas corpus* advanced by the Association of Officers and Lawyers for the Rights of Animals (AFADA) and the Constitutional Lawyer Andrés Gil Domínguez to recognize the right of the orangutan named Sandra (in captivity in the Buenos Aires Zoo) to not be considered an object or thing susceptible to property, and the right not to suffer physical or psychological damage. The examination of this case exceeds the reach of this chapter.

[2]The Orangutan Sandra Case came to the competence of the Court of Cassation upon the brief filed by a non-governmental organization "The Association of Officers and Lawyers for Animal Rights' against the decision rendered by the Appeals Chamber which upheld the denial of the petition of a writ of *habeas corpus* to protect the orangutan Sandra. On 18 December 2014, our chamber in the Court of Cassation ruled that according to a dynamic and not static legal interpretation, it was imperative to acknowledge the animal as a subject of law since 'non-human subjects' (i.e., animals) are still right holders. Therefore, since the case was already under investigation by the misdemeanor court, we ruled to transfer the case to the misdemeanor jurisdiction of the City of Buenos Aires (case N°CCC68831/2014/CFCI, Register N° 2603/14, free translation).

[3]Court in Argentina grants rights to Orangutan, http://www.bbc.com/news/world-latin-america 30571577. Sandra-the-orangutan-limited-human-rights, http://www.telegraph.co.uk/news/world/ Americas Sandra the Orangutan Inside Argentina Zoo granted human rights in landmark ruling, http://www.independent.co.uk9940202.html Habeas corpus conceded to Orangutan of Buenos Aires City Zoo, La Nación.com.ar 1754353 Gorilla Ethic.

law is a legal situation. The action is the way of validating a situation (Legaz y Lacambra 1951, p. 620).

In a similar vein, the so-called persons would not exist without a physical platform and specifically a biological and neural network—no one can be called person if they are not also a bio-neural organism. Not all organic bodies are or can become persons, but they would not exist without the former. Moreover, they could someday become organic bodies that do not strictly coincide with humans. The philosopher Ferrater Mora puts forth a distinction historically made in philosophy: an organic body that has a complex neural network structure can be the platform of what we call person, if he or she makes use of an articulate language. The language does not necessarily have to be a natural or common type of human language. This agent must nevertheless have advanced cognitive abilities and be capable of taking on responsibility for her or his own actions. The person is thus not a being given from the outset, but constitutes herself or himself based on necessary and sufficient bio-neural network conditions, all the while evolving in a natural and cultural context.

Furthermore, we often perceive, particularly when faced with moral conflicts, that one can be more or less of a person (Ferrater Mora 1985, p. 129). With relation to the non-human subject, we do not oppose subject to object. Both inhabit the world, in the 'Dasein' of Martin Heidegger, or in the "*mi vivir*" of José Ortega y Gasset, or in the "*être-pour-soi*" of Jean-Paul Sartre (Ferrater Mora 1985, p. 129).

Similarly, the distinguished legal philosopher of the University of Mérida (Mexico) B. Mantilla Pineda argues that "Just as chlorophyll is a step between the inorganic and organic, the connection between humans and culture is also such a step" (Mantilla Pineda 1947, p. 453). Mantilla Pineda also points out that the word person is not a synonym of individual, while the philosopher Ferrater Mora believes that the person is the oneness of spiritual acts (Ferrater Mora 1985, p. 129).

At present, humans have never before come across such a crossroads in their history, where their way of life in the most advanced societies is destroying the planet, placing at risk not only human life but also the life of all species, added to the adverse effects of climate change and contaminated water resources. Nevertheless, through the values of solidarity and care for the planet, humans are extending greater legal protection to species such as different species of primates or cetacean such as dolphins. These need to be protected from the start as having rights of personhood—not in the wholeness of a legal protection but rather in the most effective means for their care and survival. It is not a question of slapping on protection that is not substantial, when we are facing the dilapidation of the planet, and this calamity continues to be tolerated by the legislation of countries. The future reform of the Argentine Civil Code should therefore include formulations allowing for greater integral protection of some of the most evolved species.

We know at present through important scientific works of contemporary etiology and contributions of legal philosophy and religious philosophy that some major religions granted animals both protection and a privileged status. Through creativity and legal innovation at a national and international level, a broadening of the protection of animals has been fostered through graduate programs in International

Penal Law of Animals as well as through organizations protecting the environment and the rights of non-human animals.

This development of greater equality has relied on scientific research on the sentient, cognitive and behavioral structures of primates such as bonobos, in research centers of great scientific advancement, as well as through the contributions of academics and lawyers in exemplary legislation and academic bibliography.

4 Zen Buddhism and Christianity: Dogen and Saint Francis

The unity of all existence is exemplified in both Zen Buddhism and Christianity. A distinguished friend, Celestino Cavagna, wrote an article comparing the works of Saint Frances of Assisi (1181–1228) and Zen Master Dōgen (1200–1253) with a master ("Roshi") of Zen Buddhism Philip Kapleau. Cavagna writes:

> "Animals in Buddhism are integral to the life cycle as humans themselves." "The high status accorded animals in Buddhism is attested to as well in Jataka stories, parables about the Buddha's previous animal and human existences" (Cavagna in Kapleau 2001, p. 21). He continues by saying: "What strikes us most directly about the Jatakas is the focus on compassion, the self-sacrifice that flows from compassion, and identification of oneself with all living and suffering beings." Likewise: "the Jakarta tales are dramatic presentations of the most fundamental aspects of the Buddhist vision. They express the essential unity of all life" (Cavagna in Kapleau 2001, p. 5). In the same way, "All things, animate and inanimate, are temporary transformations of the one Buddha – or essential Mind-names for the ever 'it' that cannot be named, the substratum of Emptiness (perfection) underlying all existences" (Cavagna in Kapleau 2001, p. 6).

Cavagna concludes that some of the works of Buddhism and Christianity put forward an essential spirit of humans interconnected with all living beings including the sun and moon. He refers to Dogen, who in his work *Kana Shōbōgenzō* (正法眼蔵, lit. "Treasury of the True Dharma Eye") states: "I know with certainty that my heart is in the mountains, the river, the earth, I am sun, moon and star" (Cavagna in Kapleau 2001, p. 4).

Cavagna reveals that when he read these words, he recalled the words of St. Francis singing about God's creatures. In the hymn, Francis famously calls the Sun, Brother and the Sister, Moon. Cavagna writes:

> He (St. Francis) does not say in his expression that he is one with the sun and with the moon. Had he said this, it would not be meaningless in the philosophy and mentality of the West. St. Francis called all creatures Brother and Sister, synthesizing a spiritual union with them although he felt his being as one thing that lived in intimate communion with nature and all creatures of the universe (Cavagna in Kapleau 2001, p. 63).

This is for Cavagna, the representation of the love of the universe: "It is not coincidental that in that hymn where St. Francis praises God for all creatures," he says: "Praise be you, my Lord, for those who give pardon for your love." Everything is interconnected. That is why concern for the environment and its connection with sincere love for human beings, is needed along with commitment when confronting the problems of society" (Cavagna in Kapleau 2001, p. 7).

Cavagna explains that "when the heart is sufficiently open to a universal communion, no one and nothing is excluded from that fraternity. As a result, it is also true that indifference or cruelty towards the creatures of the world always translates into the same treatment towards other human beings. The heart is only one, and the same misery that leads to abusing an animal also manifests in the relationship of one human with another. All viciousness with any creature is "contrary to human dignity" (Cavagna in Kapleau 2001, p. 15).

Let us note that the words of St. Francis are based on the book of Genesis, when God tells Noah and his children (Bible, Genesis 9, 8–15): "Behold, I now establish my Covenant with you and your descendants after you, and with every living creature that was with you – the birds, the livestock, and every beast of the earth – every living being that came out of the ark."

Cavagna (2001, p. 21) acknowledges that although Dōgen and St. Francis are part of different worlds and cultures, they begin from the same concept and their words are similar to the position of the Buddhist meditation known as Sartori. For Cavagna, what Sartori suggests is the clear understanding of everything. This is generally translated as "*iluminación*" in Spanish or "enlightenment" in English (Cavagna in Kapleau, p. 16).

Similarly, we can mention that in Ancient Egypt there were no dichotomies between religion and science, church and state, clergy and lay people. "The gods were everywhere. The king was the essential priest and all the acts were judged against fundamental divine criteria. Gods, men, animals, plants and physical phenomena belonged to the same great order. There were no different dimensions of existence" (Rundle 1960, p. 26).

5 The Unity of Humans, Nature, and the Universe of Native Cultures from the Americas

Three decades ago, in one of my books entitled "*Social Structure and Criminology*," published by the University of Zulia, I observed how the original civilizations of the Americas, facing the arrival of the Spanish, perceived themselves as interconnected with the landscape, nature and even society (David 1979).

I would like to highlight a central concern of human rights in countries of Latin America, which I have discussed in my writings in relation to the law and juridical values. Separation and conflict still exist between norms of Spanish colonial law formulated in the law of Cervantes and his heirs, and on the other hand, the language, values and traditions of original Native Americans of the so-called America named after Américo Vespucci.

The law is language, and this language is the dwelling place, the shelter of all humans within society. In language we find the word, the life, the feelings and the birth of the world. When legislation imposes rights and obligations in a language that is not understood and does not live because it is not its own language, as in the example of native American native societies that were colonized, this legislation leaves whole nations unprotected from a debilitating anomic condition marked by spiritual, social, political and juridical chaos. One cannot know a right imposed by the dominant culture if one doesn't know its phonetic and semantic meanings, its rituals and customs.

Today, when the word is increasingly substituted by web icons, perhaps the ideal of Pierce, the philosopher of North American pragmatism, could be the right opportunity to incorporate official legal language such as the expressions and meanings most alive in Native American law. Some countries have already done this, such as in Guatemala or other countries of Central and South America. But one must continue invigorating this understanding of inclusion; this would help cultures centered on legal norms and litigious states, to move towards instances of meditation and accords that strengthen peace in the community.

A paradigmatic example of this affirmation is the culture of the Mayans. The civilization has been described as upholding "the protection of the neighbor, animals, plants, and whole mountains is the task of men – formerly artisans and guilds - but fundamentally of supernatural beings that must be respected and remembered to be able to live in harmony" (Dary 1997, pp. 299–300).

Likewise, this vision of the cosmos is based on the belief that "no other species is superior to another. We don't say that we exist, we say that we co-exist, that we cohabitate. We are complementary elements despite being different; we are always within a network of relations comparable to a spider's web of exchanges and interdependent relationships. Nothing remains isolated from biological diversity, of plants, animals and human beings; it is a unity within the diversity of all lives in harmony, it is a scene where all species find their relation to water, air, earth and all that surrounds them" (Defensoría Indígena Wajxaqib'noj 2003, p. 151).

This vision is also communicated in the poems of distinguished writers of Guatemala. "In the voices/of old trees/I recognize those of my grandparents/watchmen of centuries/its dream is in the roots" (Ak'Abal 2001, p. 146).

The Native cultures in Central and South America also believe in and affirm the interdependence of all living beings. For reasons of brevity we cannot discuss this in greater depth here. We can nevertheless mention the Pueblos of New Mexico and Arizona, in particular the Zunis, the Hopis and the Taos Pueblos. For them "in the Universe of the Pueblos, there is harmony with everything. For the Zunis, the world is animated. The wind, trees and clouds not only have personhood, but also elements such as human dwellings, their clothes; everything is alive and sentient" (Hamilton 1964, pp. 250–251).

The psychiatrist and writer Carl Jung, in 1924, at the age of 49, visited the Taos Pueblo in Montaña Lagos in Taos, New Mexico (USA). The head of the Taos Pueblo told him:

> "The white appear so cruel. Their lips are thin, their hands are sharp, their faces are full of crevices and distorted by wrinkles. Their eyes have the expression of looking surprised; they are always searching for something. What are they looking for? The whites always want

> something; they are always uncomfortable and restless. We don't know what they want. We don't understand. We think they're crazy. Everyone says they think with their head." Surprised by the answer, Jung asked "With what do you think with?" The head of the Pueblo pointed to his heart (Rosen 1996, p. 248).

The original cultures of North America have been ravaged by the dominant white culture, causing calamities such as high rates of suicide and alcoholism among Native Americans. These world views allow us to replace 'thing' with 'subject of rights' when referring to the more evolved animals in danger of extinction (e.g., primates such as bonobos, chimpanzees, and orangutans). Following this line of analysis, we firmly uphold the replacement of the concept of 'thing' with the concept of 'subject with rights', to allude to those animals that are more evolved and in danger of extinction.

A greater and more effective protection of non-human animals is possible when these offer the characteristics of bio-neural networks and a marked sociability similar to human life. The word "thing" trivializes the more evolved life of primates; it goes along with the great lack of protection of animals in some ancient civilizations. This does not imply that the passion for destruction of humans is tempered or placed in parentheses, or that a linguistic, semantic or legal term is slapped on without corresponding environmental change. For our conception of law as behavior, the only valid changes are the actions of concrete humans and their communities. We thus establish strong bonds between the I then *you* and *we* that also apply to the most evolved animal life.

6 Ethology

Many decades ago, Karl Jaspers discussed in his chapter entitled "Philosophy and Science" that nothing is indifferent to science (Jaspers 1953, pp. 136–148). The smallest and ugliest, the furthest and strangest, that which exists in any place—it already is important to science solely because it exists. The sciences have become absolutely universal. Nothing subtracts from them. Nothing must be hidden or silenced or left as a mystery. The modern sciences are in principle, inconclusive because they ceaselessly advance, while ancient science on the other hand was complete unto itself, without realizing the meaning that this effective evolution suggested, although always near completion. The modern world is thus not a closed system, in contrast to the cosmic vision of the ancient Greeks.

Alternatively, the modern sciences do not value greatly the possibilities of thinking. For them, thinking is only given credit in certain concrete knowledge when it is founded on scientific discoveries, and by this means, continually modified. Modern science is inspired by the ethos of wanting to know with guarantees based on free research and critical thinking. The purity of science demands the purity of philosophy. "Philosophy can call itself a science in so far as the sciences are its building blocks. Scientific truth is 'one for all', philosophical truth is multiple" (Jaspers 1953, p. 140).

An eminent ethologist, Frans de Wall, in his work "The Bonobo and the Atheist," traces a continuity of morality extending between bonobo primates and humans (De Waal 2013). Both species share emotions such as empathy, sympathy, gratitude—loving feelings inspired by fraternity and solidarity. Ethical principles do not emerge from the skies or by drawing on mere reasoning but instead persist over centuries in values of all living beings.

This moral continuity has been well documented in thousands of experimental observations throughout human history. In chapter 10, De Waal cites for example, the solidarity shared among bonobos when they are hurt or become ill. Loving feelings (such as those connected to the neurotransmitter oxytocin), and the instinctual perception of the species work together, including during the moments when they are in contact with humans. De Wall relates the story of a bonobo mother that climbs a tree to feed her disabled daughter and the rest of the group follows suit. Bonobos are happy when a new infant is born, and the other female bonobos comfort the mother by scratching her skin and shrieking. We can summarize this explosion of related research as "the great psychological fiesta."

De Wall also points out that since the time of Aristotle, humans are recognized exclusively as rational animals, and this concept has denied animals from being conceived as similar to humans in their use of reason. De Waal tells us:

> The Moral Law is not imposed from above or derived well from well reasoned principles; rather it arises from ingrained values that have been there since the beginning of time (De Waal 2013, p. 150).

Steven Wise, an eminent legal scholar and animal rights activist, argues that "there is no reason for a corporation a ship, a society or a legal incompetent to have juridical identity and not a chimpanzee. In New Zealand, even a river has juridical personhood. In India, a deity and a mosque. Animals as identities must be protected with fundamental rights. It is a central question of the inalienable value of freedom and equality for conscious and autonomous beings. And the reason is the same for what we have learned to not exploit or mistreat other human beings (Wise 2015).

7 Man: Animal of Realities

In line with this reasoning, we can recall the theologist Xavier Zubirí, who already in the last century defined man as "an animal of realities." Within his virtue, the character of reality of man is a defining moment of his action: man acts in real terms, because it is "his" reality. Here lies the formal reason of this mode of reality that is his own—to be a person. As a form of reality, the animal of realities, is personal animal. Thus, one thing is clear: human reality, to the degree that it belongs to itself, is constituted as itself "in the face of all that is real." In this sense, as a reality, human reality is "absolute," unconstrained from another real condition. It is however a mode that is relative—it is relatively absolute (Zubirí 1974, p. 12).

For the philosopher Xavier Zubirí, what gives genuine meaning to the word intelligence in reference to humans, is a second term: sentient. The intelligence of humans is "sentient." It is that same intelligence in so far as it is sentient. This is why one can invert the terms and define the radical habit of the human as intelligent sentient or intelligent sensitivity. This does not involve that in humans there is a type of intellectual function mounted on a sensitive function. The intellect and sensitivity are two aspects of a single reality. The reducible and absolute difference between animals and humans lies here: Humans, because of a sensitive intelligence, sees things not as stimuli but rather realities. The version of reality is valid for external things and the same human beings. For Zubirí, according to the philosopher Javier Conde, "man is not only sentient but knows he is sentient," and this could be the distinctive feature of the sentient animal (Conde 1953, p. 101). Zubirí also unifies emotion, the sentient, in animals and humans with the reservations this may introduce. "There is a coexistence just with others in so far as they are realities. It is what is missing from domestic or domesticated animals: these animals do not live together with humans as far as this is reality, but humans incorporate them into their lives, to the extent that they are real. In short, the coexistence of a human with other humans in so far as they are realities, is what formally constitutes human society (Zubirí 1984, pp. 65–66).

The Holy Father Francis also reveals a vision of man and creation conceptualized in his *Carta Enciclica Laudato Si* made known on the 24th of May 2015 after the original presentation of this work during the Thirteenth United Nations Congress on Crime Prevention and Criminal Justice (Doha, Qatar). Pope Francis says:

> All of nature, as well as manifesting God is the place of His presence. In each living creature there is a life-giving Spirit that calls us into a relationship with it. The discovery of that presence fosters in us the development of 'ecological virtues'. But when we say this, let us not forget that there is also an infinite distance, that the things of this world do not possess the fullness of God. On the other hand, we would not be something good for the creatures, because we would not recognize their proper and true place, and we would end up demanding unduly what in their smallness they cannot give (Holy Father Francis, 2015, para. 88).

The Spanish philosopher Juan D. García Baca, in his work "Introduction to Philosophizing" (1939, pp. 8–15) asserts: "The Aristotelian definition of man '*zoon, logon, éjon*', an animal that has logos, does not admit the classic translation of 'rational animal', if one does not exactly understand the force of the Greek *logos*."

"In the study on questioning, I have given the following interpretation: man is the living amplified voice of things."

"In contrast and faced with things one cannot know through words, in the universe there is an animal with a cosmic mission added to the essence of things, through which it says (logos) in a high and melodious voice, what is otherwise silent. The aphonia entity of the world remains cured by means of the metaphysical phonetics of man."

To be rational is certainly the characteristic of humans, but it is not an exclusive nor even a primary property of them: rational simply designates its cosmic function, its destiny in the world: to speak in the service of things, the metaphysical amplified voice of the cosmos. Nothing is thus more distant, more contrary to this sense of reason, of cogitation united without dissolution to the word and things in the sense of the *cogitation* (cogent) in Descartes or Leibnitz (Baca Garcia 1939).

In this line of Aristotelian thought we can affirm that: "Theoretical understanding exhibits another perfection"; "Intelligence can think itself occupying the place of the intelligible; it thus becomes intelligible to itself in the act of understanding its object. Intelligence and intelligible are the same thing."

With affirmations and precision, Aristotle defines self-awareness as the reflexive attitude of intelligence, the self-consciousness of the certainty of one's own existence.

"Who perceives that he sees, and who hears perceives that he hears, and who walks perceives that he walks, and analogously, with other acts there is something (in us) that perceives that we carry out acts, so that we perceive perceiving and think thinking. Now the fact that we perceive, and think is that we exist, since existing is to feel and think."

"And since every act of understanding ends in contemplation, it produces pleasure. Thanks to this we find gratifying: vigil, feeling, thinking, and through them hope and remembering" (De Azcarate quoted after Pro 1971, p. 125).

Christian theology echoes Aristotle when it is argued that "The nature that surrounds us, to which we belong, proclaims the existence of a highly noble Creator who has imbued us with mind and discursive reasoning. By means of which we prefer: the living to the inanimate, the being with sensitivity to the insensitive one, the intelligent beings to the irrational ones, the immortal to the transient, the powerful to the impotent, justice to injustice, the beautiful to deformed, the immutable to transitory, good to evil, the incorruptible to the corruptible, the immaterial to the corporeal, happiness to misery" (Przywara 1984, p. 164).

From another perspective, but with similar meaning, Oliver Sacks argues that: "Humans share much with other animals – the basic needs of food and drink or sleep for example – but there are additional mental and emotional needs and desires which are perhaps unique to us. To live on a day-to-day basis is insufficient for human beings; we need to transcend, transport, escape; we need meaning, understanding and explanation; we need to see overall patterns in our lives. We need hope, the sense of a future. And we need freedom (or at least the illusion of freedom) to get beyond ourselves, whether with telescopes and microscopes and our ever-burgeoning technology or in states of mind which allow us to travel to other worlds, to transcend our immediate surroundings. We need detachment of this sort as much as we need engagement in our lives" (Sacks 2012, p. 90).

It is necessary to highlight that both Adam Smith and later Charles Darwin, believed that the normative capacity for self-government is essential in the development of morality, since it is part of the understanding described by Darwin as "this brief but imperious word, so full of meaning: *duty*" (De Waal 2007, para. 150).

"Darwin theorized that the capacity for normative self-government arose from the difference between how our social instincts and our appetites are affected" (De Waal 2007).

Meanwhile, "in an essay entitled Conjectures on the Beginnings of the History of Humanity," Kant theorized the form of self-consciousness that subsists under our autonomy could also play a role in the explanation of some other distinctively human features, including culture, romantic love, and the capacity for self-interested action. Other philosophers have observed the interconnection between this form of self-consciousness and the capacity for language (De Waal).

Underscoring a conceptualization of peace, Erich Fromm tells us that "the prophetic concept of peace transcends the sphere of human relations; the harmony is a harmony between man and nature. Peace between man and nature is harmony between man and nature. Man is not then threatened by nature and ceases his attempts to dominate it; man becomes natural and nature becomes humanized. Both cease to be opposites and become one thing. Man is in the natural world as in his home, and nature becomes part of the human world; this is peace in the prophetic sense (the Hebrew word "*Shalom*," for example can be translated as "plenitude," and expresses the same orientation) (Fromm 1981, p. 150).

8 Norms and Values in Ancient Greece

We live in a time and era where the soil is crushed under our feet, where the answers of today soon become incongruent and far from the reality constructed in the manner of a continually turning kaleidoscope.

In this era of uncertainty, insecurity and anxiety, we have only one anchor: the existence of a 'we' characterized by solidarity, with a 'you' that transcends the practice of individualism, and is guided by values of love, fraternity, charity and solidarity—all adding up to the search for justice and equality. From Ancient Greece onwards, we see a clear relationship between law as system of legislation and fundamental values. Legislation and the establishment of a political order, according to Plato, are the most perfect means of the world to approximate virtue.

Plato therefore avoided decisively deducing laws from the existing constitution, as these laws often manifest a concrete relationship of political rule and subjection. Plato does not admit this class legislation. He insists that he would not recognize them as laws, in the meaning of a just law, none which have been adopted for the welfare of the community. A legislation that would only be useful to the interests of the party in power is for Plato a mere question of convenience and detracts from its quality as a true law.

In these reflections that allude to natural law, Plato finds a basis for affirming that the government is only a servant of the law. Only in a state where the law governs those who govern (laws 715)—only a state in which the government is subject to laws, can be expected to guarantee the good which the gods have destined for genuine communities, that is to say, guaranteeing the true happiness of citizens (Friedrich 1964, paras. 35–37). "Because the laws are the means by which we assure not only that men live, but also live well (in Zen) and become as virtuous as possible."

These reflections are also discussed in the works of Saint Augustine, who speaks of the community of charity or love, in contrast to the legal community. And he also points out that the State today (el regnum in its concepts), if justice is missing from it, is similar to a large band of thieves (Friedrich 1964, para. 60).

9 The Philosophy of Law, Trialism, and Animals

Trialism is a theoretical position of distinguished jurists and philosophers, who have passed it down through their disciples to this day. Surpassing the positivist legal theory that came before it, trialism has paid special attention to the values and factual circumstances of law.

The legal philosopher of the sociology of law, Jerome Hall, argues that "in regards to the integration of norm, value and fact, in the root of human behavior, both object and subject are tied to organic planes, on the one hand, and on the other, the major structures, collectives, specific subsystems of interaction, and the empirical and cultural structure" (David 1970, p. 91).

In summary, "the juridical norm is only one norm: the social norm, the moral norm, the religious norm, the ethical norm—all these can have the same or even greater relevance. What matters is the measure of their influence on the behavior of society. The fact (the behavior) is the reality of law, and it is not comprised in the juridical norm: there is a coexistence among formal, informal, and written law. These may be more relevant, internalized, and effective than the former that is externalized in social behavior (Saucedo and David 2001, p. 802).

The trialism introduced by the philosopher Miguel Herrera Figueroa consisted of a triad of interconnected dimensions: vital-endotimic (vital-*endotímica*), normative-cognoscitive (normative-cognoscitiva) and spiritual-valuational (spiritual-*valorativa*). This is comparable to Hall's norm, value and fact, and is found in the prolific works of Miguel Reale, Luis Recaséns Siches, Werner Goldschmitt, Michele Pallotini and many others.

From this perspective, the great mutations of the three pillars of law make more plausible the extension of protective legislation to include animals and the planet, both at the local and international level. These norms are rooted in scientific evidence, values of dignity of treatment for humans and animals. It translates to a broader vision of cooperation, solidarity, equity and equality that adds up to more justice.

The Convention on Biological Diversity (1760 UNTS 79) in Art. 8 establishes that each party to the contract in so far as possible and subsequently "adapted to its national legislation, will respect, preserve and maintain the knowledge, innovation and practices of indigenous and local communities that hold viscerally traditional styles of biological diversity and will endorse its broader application, with the approval and participation of those who have this knowledge, innovation and practices and will foster the benefits derived from the use of equitably shared knowledge, innovation and practices."[4]

10 The Advancement of Interdisciplinary Studies Centered on the Legal Protection of Animals

The higher learning studies of animals is an important advancement assisting in their legal protection at a global level.

In the United States, at the University of Oregon, through the Center for Animal Studies, offers a Master's in Animals with a curricula including seminars and courses such as: Advanced Seminar in Animal Rights, Animal Rights and Jurisprudence, Domestic Animals, International Comparative Law, Rights of Animals, Law of Animals: Political Influences of Legislation, Jurisprudence, Lobby Pressures and Litigation.

In Japan, the Primate Research Institute of the University of Kyoto carries out rigorous scientific research in the area of advancement of the law.

Meanwhile in Zurich, in the Center of Animal Law, has established a focal point for studies of animal rights (TIR—*Stiftung für das Tier im Recht*).

At present, there is extensive bibliography which is available also on the web site of the University of Idaho, United States.

We can also mention the research journal *Global Journal of Animal Law*, of the Abo Akademy University, Department of Law, in Finland.[5]

11 The Legal Protection of the Environment at a Regional and Global Level

In contrast to conventional criminology, we have developed a new criminology often referred to as "Green Criminology." Similarly, the contributions of the United Nations to "Blue Criminology" (Redo 2012) have emerged from the original section of Social Defense, directed by Manuel López Rey y Arrojo, an acclaimed Criminologist who I honored in a tribute in 1985 (David 1985). The notion of justice which originally included only humans is being transformed to include the rights

[4]See also Convention on International Trade in Endangered Species of Wild Fauna and Flora (993 UNTS 243) and resolutions of the United Nations Economic and Social Council (ECOSOC) 2001/12, 2003/27, 2005/25 2001/36; also the United Nations Convention against Transnational Organized Crime (2225 UNTS 209). All these legal instruments are accessible via the United Nations e-address: http://www.un.org.

[5]Primate Research Institute, Kyoto University, Japan. See Guidelines for Care and Use of nose Human Primates Ch.5, Consideration of the Behavior and Psychological Condition of NHP, June 2010.

animals and those of the environment. Some even propose that since the notion of genocide is the capital crime of conventional criminology, a globalized criminology might be considered as an "Ecocide." This leads us to a philosophy centered on the preservation of ecosystems, on the value of living and non-living entities, as these are synonymous with the viability of human life.[6]

The way has been paved for distinguishing better or worse environmental policies and also for detecting central themes of measures that harm ecosystems.

Ever since the 1970s, the legal protection of the environment has enjoyed a privileged status in multilateral juridical instruments. These have nonetheless multilateral environmental in an integrated manner, the problem of environmental crime.[7]

For example, the Montreal Protocol (A/RES/49/114) specifically takes up the problem of the substances that produce a loss of atmospheric ozone; the Convention on the Control of Transboundary Movement of Hazardous Wastes and Their Disposal ("the Basel Convention," 1673 UNTS 126) meanwhile seeks to prevent the illegal trade of toxic substances.

The environment problems of illegal deforestation and illegal fishing are even more problematic. No agreement exists on forests (there is only a series of agreements on tropical wood). To all of this we can add the diversity of juridical perspectives. At present, these center on environmental crime rooted in concepts of the protection and conservation of the environment. These perspectives originated in 1972 in the Stockholm Conference of the United Nations, where the program of the United Nations for the Environment (UNEP) was established. The 1973 Declaration of Stockholm (A/CONF.48/14/Rev.1) also developed fundamental legal concepts of international environmental law. Its preamble affirms the need to protect nature because it is the environment of humans and the right to life of humans in their most fundamental right. In other words, the protection of nature in all of its manifestations is essential and synonymous with the viability of human life.

The Declaration of Stockholm also interrelates two challenges: the protection of the environment and economic development. In this way the environment becomes essential for humanity, with the emphasis placed on the future generations of humanity. The "Ramsar" Convention on Wetlands of International Importance (996 UNTS 245) of the same period, foreshadows the concept of sustainable development.

The first type of measure to protect the environment consists of establishing systems that monitor, identify and investigate issues of environmental conservation. An example of this is the Convention of Migratory Species of Wild Animals (1651 UNTS 333). Other measures are in their original place, such as the Convention on Biological Diversity (1760 UNTS 79), which focuses on the conservation of ecosystems and natural environments, and the maintenance and recovery of viable species in their natural settings. A clear example of this is the establishment of

[6]In this sense, see White (2008).

[7]See Faber (2009).

protected areas and natural reserves. The Ramsar Convention locates protected areas and includes at least one area of humid land.

For the Convention on Biological Diversity, the sustainable use and the administration of natural resources is essential to protecting environmental development. The protection bestowed by laws against environmental crime, must also be sustained with commercial law acting as a mode of illegal transaction.

The Convention on International Trade in Endangered Species of Wild Fauna and Flora (CITES, 993 UNTS 243) regulates the international trade of animal and plant species listed in the appendix of this international agreement. The trade is regulated according to the level of danger faced by the species that is threatened with loss or extinction.

With respect to the 3% of the species listed in the first Appendix, the trade of these species is highly restricted. The other 97% of the species listed interrelate in a viable manner the right to common conservation and the sustainability of international trade. As a result of the CITES agreement, there are new measures for the protection of the environment, but the reach of CITES is limited when faced with transnational organized crime.

Used as last resort by countries, penal law has been the privileged arena for certain international conventions. The Basel Convention, for example, along with other regional agreements such as the Council of Europe, that in 1988 adopted the Convention on the Protection of the Environment through Criminal Law (COE Conventions; ETS172), were not implemented for lack of sufficient ratification by Member States. This situation did not impede the Council of Europe from adopting in the year 2008, the Directive on the Protection of the Environment through Criminal Law. All these international agreements aim to make Member States work together in combatting environmental crimes and transnational organized crime at a regional and global level.

Finally, the international community has endorsed the Regional Plan of Action for the conservation of Gorillas of the Low Western Lands of Africa and the Chimpanzees of the Central Zone of Africa spanning the decade between 2015 and 2025. In this plan of action, the areas where the gorillas and chimpanzees live are identified; the majority of gorillas and a third of the chimpanzees live in the tropical jungle of Central Africa. The population of large animals in this region has suffered a dramatic decline since the 1960s, largely owing to three factors; hunting, illness and loss of habitat (IUCN 2015).

12 Some Foreign Precedents

In 2016, the French Parliament passed a law recognizing animals as "living and sensitive beings."[8] Before this they were considered a mere property by civil codes dating from Napoleonic times. The government of India in 2013 prohibited dolphins from being used in captivity for commercial exhibition.[9] The Indian Minister defending the decision explained that: "the Cetacean are, in general lines, very intelligent and sensitive. The scientists who have studied the behavior of dolphins have suggested that their unusually high intelligence, in comparison with other animals, means that they must be considered non-human persons and as such they must have specific rights. It is morally unacceptable to keep them in captivity for the purpose of entertainment."

In matters of animal protection, we can mention the legislation of countries such as Costa Rica, Hungary, Chile and Germany. These laws defend the rights of animals to be legally protected as part of the priorities of the government agendas.

13 Building the Juridical Scaffolding

In this globalized era where the State in its role as police and support of society is disappearing, the rule of law (which José Ortega y Gasset referred to as a "skin") has been usurped by the orthopedic State. I would add to this list of negative and harmful features, the factious and criminal State. Today we must include the state as a protagonist of unilateral actions against peace, global security, independence and the welfare of nations.

All of this takes place in a globalized world that excludes individuals and groups and diminishes social equity. The great evils of our time include the alarming and growing social inequality, the diverse forms of transnational organized crime such as the trafficking of persons or the abuse, consumption and trafficking of illegal drugs, and finally terrorism and the financing of terror. Each one of our world citizens faces difficult circumstances of personal, family and work-related problems, within a context of increasing social exclusion and marginality.

This era opens up a new and valid space of reflection for instilling a spirit of solidarity, love and charity, in the context of transformative action of the other in 'you' and 'we' that is essential for returning to a vigorous humanism. It is the same spirit that expands the conceptualization of humanitarian and respectful treatment of animals in nature and society. Pope Francis in his *Carta Enciclica* explains:

---

[8] Ley en Francia reconoce a los animales como "seres vivos y sensibles" (2015), from https://www.bbc.com/mundo/ultimas_noticias/2015/01/150129_ultnot_francia_ley_animales_seres_vivos_ng

[9] India Bans Captive Dolphin Shows as 'Morally Unacceptable', News Editor, 2013, from https://ens-newswire.com/2013/05/20/india-bans-captive-dolphin-shows-as-morally-unacceptable/.

> A feeling of intimate union with other natural beings cannot be real if at the same time in one's heart there is no tenderness, compassion and preoccupation for human beings. There is an incoherence evident when someone fights against the trafficking of animals threatened with extinction, but remains completely indifferent towards the trafficking in persons, or feels no connection to the poor or tries to destroy another human being that is found to be disagreeable. This puts at risk the meaning of the struggle for the environment (Holy Father Francis 2015, para. 91).

The juridical culture needs to be renewed. Not changed with instrumental aims of how best to legislate, but rather by improving the horizons of human dignity and harmonizing the life of all beings on the planet.

We can conclude that "man has a nature that places him beyond his nature," he is a "limited being that constantly tends to overcome his own limits; he is a being organized in time and in space and his intentional consciousness captures and transcends. He is a historical being. In history, man continually makes and remakes himself. Human history on the other hand is intertwined with the world. The realization of man is through the transformation of the world. Values must thus be reconsidered, society must be reformed each moment: the ceaseless search continues for the purpose of liberation, humanization, of greater being. The historical condition of man makes his education serve as a means for conquering the human form presented to us, far beyond the present facts. The 'learning to be' in education will thus be a continual process of human liberation, that will lead to re-creation and world transformation" (Cabrerizo et al. 1991, p. 170). In this intelligence, both a juridical education and teaching in the field of law area are important.

"The social function of education attaches itself to this process. Education must not become an agent of conformity, it should not assist men in their insertion within already established boundaries, if he does this, and he betrays man and his continual process of liberation. The person is denied the right to forge his own future" (Cabrerizo et al. 1991, p. 155).

The challenge of the juridical dimension is important, but: "Roman law offers us a perfect example of an organ destined to adapt legislation: the figure of the Praetor (Cabrerizo et al. 1991, p. 156). The praetor is an important illustration of adaptable legislation as he had the central function in the creation of a new law. This new law was in contrast to the old, formal and solemn Roman law that did not address with justice the socio-economic and cultural conditions of those people emigrating to Rome: the clients, the foreigners, who could not repeat the sacramental formulas and as a result lost during transactions. The Romans found a solution in the role of the praetor as the creator of law, who articulated the lived-out norm, the practices and uses for each concrete, individual case" (Cabrerizo et al. 1991, p. 158).

When one studies what a judge really does in a given moment in many countries today, it is evident that although it may not be desired, the protagonist of the sentence is nevertheless the judge. In some manner, when s/he sentences, s/he is doing the history of himself/herself and also of the person he is judging, although the judge may claim to be interpreting. When a person creates and decides upon an action, s/he has many alternatives open: s/he can follow the tradition of other historical periods and say that the sentence is based on one that thirty years ago established a fruitful relationship. In other words, a sentence that reveres a past based on judicial precedents although the historical conditions may be diverse. That is the possibility—to forget the present historical reality and its pressures and to enter by adhering to a ruling—that negates the historical social responsibility of a judge as well as the possibility of innovation which the law opens up (David 2005, p. 37).

Nevertheless, "the jurisdictional creation does not imply that the legal order must be annihilated to give way to the arbitrary individual decision, but rather within the alternatives open to all judges, he can critique former sentences instead of adhering to them, innovating on values that only he could see and which other judges did not detect (David 2005, p. 37).

The need to explore the limits of the law—and unveil the intelligence of the laws—is a question that has frequently surfaced in juridical history. If we examine the situation of children and adolescents, in a brief overview, we find that Roman law granted parents, the *pater familias* absolute and total powers over the life and death of their children. This included selling them, mutilating them, killing them and disinheriting them. But these rights did not end with the majority of age, but rather the death of the father or when he lost Roman citizenship: "Not even age or ranks, neither honors of the Consular Office, nor any triumph can exempt the most illustrious citizens of the bonds of filial subjection" (Bossard and Stocher Boll 1968, pp. 494–495).

Ancient Greece offers us an ideal of "education for excellence" (*arête*). Nothing better for guiding the proper action than the example and the model, says Jaeger in his studies on education in classical Greece. In all the crimes the minor was granted an attenuated condition or prerogative with the exception of cases of homicide. Theft was not punished if the minor was caught in the act by surprise.

Attenuating the situation of children and adolescents as objects in Roman law, the medieval Christian perspective obtained the Justinian Code. This Code established that children are neither property of the parents that abandoned them nor property of those who found them (Solis Quiroga 2005, p. 47).

The Code also contained a prevision by which a father forced to sell his son, for reasons of extreme poverty, could recover the son later when his situation had changed. In the law of the XII Tables there was a distinction between pubers (*pubescents*) and impubers (*pre-pubescents*)—one could punish an impuber with a diminished sentence. In the beginning of the Roman Empire, the legal distinction was through infants, pubers and minors: infancy lasted until the child could speak well. The impuber was until about the age of procreation, nine and a half years of age, in the case of the woman, and until ten and a half in the case of the male puber. The children with ages close to infancy did not have penal responsibility; the lack of penal responsibility for those who were close to puberty depended on discernment. If one acted with discernment, a diminished penalty was applied. Discernment was the existence of ideas formed on good and bad, the licit and illicit. The death penalty was possible from the age of 12 for women and 14 for men, although this sentence was never applied.

In Medieval Europe, the situation of children and adolescents was greatly marked by unprecedented severity. In England, children could be apprehended from the age of 9 onwards. Children of 6 to 14 years of age could be hanged for theft or less serious crimes, giving way to the probation of today.

Meanwhile, the crimes against children in England were punished with light sentences. For example, Anne Martin (alias Chapburry) was sentenced to two years in prison for taking out the eyes of children to beg with them, inspire pity (Bossard and Stocher Boll 1968, pp. 494–495), and improve her own economic condition.

In the colonial era of the United States, the harshness of the laws continued with respect to children. A law in New York ordered the death penalty for children who insulted their parents unless it was to avoid being killed or mutilated (David 1980, pp. 45–46).

In sixteenth century England, the lack of absolute penal responsibility was established for children until 7 years of age. The origin of the Courts of Minors can be found in the 'Chancery Court' of Equity. These were established by Henry VII, since the State was the final parent of the child in need of protection.

The notion of adolescence in the West was an "invention" and a historically conditioned phenomenon. Starting from the eighteenth century, particularly in Europe, it acquires legitimacy through the widely read novel "Émile" of Jean Jacob Rousseau.

In the "The Laws of the Indies" (*Leyes de las Indias*, 1680)—the entire body of laws issued by the Spanish Crown for the American and Philippine possessions—and following the Castilian statutory code of the *Siete Partidas* ("Seven Divisions") of Alfonso X of Castile, minors below the age of ten and a half were not deemed responsible for any reason and sense. Immunity was extended until 12 and 14 years of age, for crimes of insults and other wrongs.

According to the legal theorist Bruner (2003, p. 130), all of these approaches to law make up a "factory of stories"; the law is culture, narrative and through it we construct, reconstruct, in some sense, until we reinvent our yesterday and our tomorrow. Memory and imagination join in this process. Even when we create the possible worlds of fiction, we do not abandon the familiar, but rather we 'subjectivize', transforming both what could have been and what could be. The human mind, however the memory might be used or its system of registration may be refined, will never be able to completely and faithfully recover the past. But we can also not escape it. Memory and imagination are providers and consumers of the same merchandise.

14 Conclusion

Law is fascinating because it aspires to search in the past and in memory to determine if a present case is a model or not, a resource of what was prescribed in the past. But often in its evolving dialectic a culture is impeded from falling victim to the impossible mnemonic ideal. The system of 'separate-but-equal' of yesterday becomes a discourse of oppression today. And the past is also redefined, as in the *Brown vs. Board of Education* case where the judges cited with approval a decision of the British Royal Court of 1772 in the *Somerset vs. Stewart* case. This case involved an African American slave named James Somerset who was taken by force to England and escaped. After being captured, imprisoned and deported to the United States on a ship to Jamaica, his slave owner demanded his return to slavery. Nevertheless, the ruling of common law in the case of Somerset concluded that slavery was not supported in England. Somerset could not be returned to slavery on English soil because in this country there were no 'municipal statutes' that expressly authorize slavery: the natural condition of this man was freedom. One can only admire the Supreme Court Judge Warren, in the historical opinion pronounced on the *Brown vs. Board of Education* case. I particularly admire the fantasy and intuition upon appraising the affinity of this case with the case of "separate but equal" schools that violated the clause of equal protection of the Constitution of the United States, a document drawn up 17 years after Lord Mansfield, the Lord High Chancellor, had returned to liberate Somerset. Narrative fiction creates possible worlds, but it is extrapolated from the world we know, no matter how much higher one can extend one world over the other. The art of the possible is a dangerous art. It must consider life as we know it and also, alienate us sufficiently so as to tempt us with possible alternatives that transcend. It is something comforting, yet a challenge. Ultimately, it has the power to modify our habits upon conceiving what is real, what is canonic. It can even undermine the decisions of the law regarding what constitutes a canonic reality. To illustrate, the novel "*The Grapes of Wrath*" of John Steinbeck modified the legitimacy of a neglected, semi-deserted region of the United States, while "*Uncle Tom's Cabin*" and the works of Harriet Beecher Stowe incited public indignation against racism and slavery in North America. The novel of Steinbeck and those of Harriet Beecher Stowe, promoted debate as to whether life had to be in a certain given way. And here we locate the beginnings of subversion in a social setting (Bruner 2003).

The challenge of the law explored in this chapter is complex and multi-faceted. Many suppositions in the social sciences exist in relation to animal behavior, some of these are correct but others are not. This situation will not change while research on human behavior continues to be disconnected from research on other animals. Those who like so much to explore the natural world to extract examples when these appear convenient, should nevertheless understand that there are no simple lessons. Just as our species is both noble and cruel, selfish, and generous, a slave or master of instincts, the world of non-human animals presents the same contradictions. Academic researchers will continue comparing and contrasting the behavior of non human animals and that of humans. But let us hope that they do this not so much with the intention of supporting preconceived notions, but instead to discover a reality of nature that is more complex, diverse and multi-layered (De Waal 2002).

I would like to conclude this chapter with the words of a renowned scientist and friend, the late Juan Cuatrecasas, who in the preface of one of his major works (Cuatrecasas 1965, p. 50), quotes P. Teilhard de Chardin:

> Man had finally understood the essential message murmured by the ruins, fossils, the ashes: nothing is worth being found if not that which does not exist. The only discovery worth our effort is the one of constructing our future.

References[10]

A/CONF.48/14/Rev.1 Report of the United Nations Conference on the Human Environment (Stockholm, 1972).

A/RES/35/71 Report of the Sixth United Nations Congress on the Prevention of Crime and the Treatment of Offenders, 15 December 1980.

A/RES/49/114, International Day for the Preservation of the Ozone Layer, 19 December 1994.

A/RES/70/1 Transforming our world: the 2030 Agenda for Sustainable Development 25 September 2015.

Ak'Abal, H. (2001). *Aqajtzij Palabramiel*. Chalsamaj Ed.: Guatemala.

Baca Garcia, J. (1939). *Introducción al filosofar Tucumán*. Argentine: Universidad Nacional de Tucumán.

Bible, Genesis 9, 8-15.

Bossard, J. S., & Stocher Boll, E. (1968). *The sociology of child development*. New York: Harper Row.

Bruner, J. (2003). *La Fábrica de historias. Derecho, literatura, vida.*: Buenos Aires, Argentine: Fondo de Cultura Económica.

Cabrerizo, R., Baroja, A. Caro, J., & Beristáin, A. (Eds.), (1991). *Desde Ignacio de Loyola a Una Educación Liberadora* (pp. 1528–1535). Ignacio de Loyola, magister artium en París. In Libro homenaje de las Universidades del País Vasco y de la Sorbonne a Ignacio de Loyola en el V centenario de su nacimiento. https://ecommons.luc.edu/ignatianpedagogy/

Carta Enciclica Laudato Si. (2015). *Holy Father Francis. On the care of the common house. Argentine Episcopal Conference*. Buenos Aires, Argentina: Office of the Book.

Cavagna, C. (2001). *Zen e Cristianesimo, Attraverso un confronto fra il Maestro Dogan a Francesco d' Assisi*. Tokyo: Universita Kamazawa.

Cockroft, S. (2019). *Orangutan who was granted human rights in landmark legal case flies to US for more 'dignified' life*. The Evening Standard, 28 September 2019, from https://bit.ly/2wW5lTe

Conde, F. X. (1953). *Introducción a la antropología de Xavier Zubiri, Homenaje a Xavier Zubirí*. Revista Alcalá. https://bit.ly/2T7ijWH

Convention of Migratory Species of Wild Animals (1651 UNTS 333).

Convention on Biological Diversity (1760 UNTS 79).

Convention on International Trade in Endangered Species of Wild Fauna and Flora (993 UNTS 243).

Convention on the Control of Transboundary Movement of Hazardous Wastes and Their Disposal (1673 UNTS 126).

Convention on Wetlands of International Importance (996 UNTS 245).

Cuatrecasas, J. (1965). *El hombre, animal óptico*. Buenos Aires, Argentine: Eudeba.

Dary, C. F. (1997). *El derecho internacional humanitario y el orden jurídico maya*. Guatemala: El Comité Internacional de la Cruz Roja: Facultad Latinoamericana de Ciencias Sociales.

David, P. R. (1970). *Conducta, integrativismo y sociología del Derecho*. Buenos Aires, Argentine: Zavalia.

David, P. R. (1979). *Estructura Social y Criminología*. Venezuela: Universidad de Zulia. Instituto de Criminología.

David, P. R. (1980). *Juvenile criminal sociology*. Buenos Aires, Argentine: Depalma.

David, P. R. (1985). *Crime and Criminal Policy*. Papers in Honor of Manuel Lopez Rey y Arrojo. Franco Angeli: Rome UNSDRI.

David, P. R. (2005). *Criminología y Sociedad*. D.F. Mexico: Instituto Nacional de Ciencias Penales.

[10]All United Nations parliamentary documentation starting with "A" symbol are retrieved from the United Nations website http://www.un.org.

De Azcarate, P. (1874). *Obras de Aristóteles, puestas en lengua castellana*. Madrid: Biblioteca Filosófica.

De Waal, F. (2002). *El simio y el aprendiz de sushi. Reflexiones de un primatólogo sobre la cultura*. Madrid, Spain: Paidós.

De Waal, F. (2007 Paidós). *Primates y Filósofos*. La evolución de la moral del simio al hombre. Madrid, Spain: Paidós.

De Waal, F. (2013). *The Bonobo and the Atheist: in search of Humanism among the Primates*. New York and London: Norton.

Defensoría Indígena Wajxaqib'noj. (2003). *A global vision of the Mayan juridical system*. Guatemala.

Faber, D. (2009). Capitalizing on Environmental Crime: A case study of polluter-industrial complex in the age of globalization, ch 5. In K. Kangaspunta & I. H. Marshall (Eds.), *Ecocrimes and justice, essays on environmental crime*. UNICRI: Turin.

Ferrater, M. J. (1985). *Fundamentos de Filosofía*. Madrid, Spain: Alianza Universidad.

Friedrich, C. J. (1964). *Filosofía del Derecho*. D.F. México: Fondo de Cultura Económica.

Fromm, E. (1981). *Y seréis como dioses*. Madrid, Spain: Paidós.

Hamilton, A. T. (1964). *Pueblo Gods and Myths*. Norman, OK: University of Oklahoma Press.

IUCN. (2015). *Regional Action Plan for the Conservation of Western Lowland Gorillas and Central Chimpanzees 2015–2025*.

Jaspers, K. (1953). Origen y meta de la historia. *Revista de Occidente 3*, 136–148. Madrid, Spain.

Kapleau, P. (2001). *Awakening to Zen: The Teachings of Roshi Philip Kapleau*. Boston: Shambala.

Legaz y Lacambra, L. (1951). *Filosofía del Derecho*. Barcelona, Spain: ed. Bosch.

Legaz y Lacambra, L. (1976). Consideraciones sobre la dignidad de la persona y la vida humana. *Annals of the Royal Academy of Moral and Political Sciences, 53*, 17–22.

Mantilla, P. (1947). *Axiología o teoría de los valores*. D.F. México: Casa Unidad de Publicaciones. Grafos.

Petit, E. (1913). *Traite Élémaintaire de Droit Romain*. Paris, France: Arthur Rousseau Ed.

Pro, D. F. (1971). *Temas y Motivos del Pensamiento Griego*. Buenos Aires, Argentine: Amancay.

Przywara, E. (1984). *San Agustín. Perfil humano y religioso*. Madrid, Spain: Ed. Cristiandad.

Redo, S. (2012). *Blue criminology. The power of United Nations ideas to counter crime globally*. Helsinki: European Institute for Crime Prevention and Control.

Rosen, D. H. (1996). *The Tao of Jung*. Buenos Aires, Argentine: Paidós.

Rundle, C. R. T. (1960). *Myth and Symbol in Ancient Egypt*. Great Britain: Thames and Hudson.

Sacks, O. (2012). *Hallucinations*. Toronto, New York: Alfred A. Knopf.

Saucedo, G. H., & David, P. (2001). *Política Criminal, derechos humanos y sistemas jurídicos en el siglo XXI*. Argentine: De Palma

Solis Quiroga, H. (2005). *Justicia de menores*. Mexico: Instituto Nacional de Ciencias Penales.

St. Francisco de Assisi. (2012). So con certezza: il mio cuore sono i monti/i fiumi e la tierra; Sono il sole, la luna e le stelle," en Francis of Assisi, *The Little Flowers* (Fioretti), London.

United Nations Convention against Transnational Organized Crime, 2225 UNTS 209.

White, R. (2008). *The criminalization of environmental harm, criminal justice matters*. London: London Center for Justice Studies, King's College.

Wise, St. (2015). *Conversations*, texto Loreley Gaffoglio. Buenos Aires, Argentine: La Nación.

Zubirí, X. (1974). *Realitas*, Seminario, Sociedad de Estudios y Publicaciones: Madrid, Spain.

Zubirí, X. (1984). *El Hombre y Dios*. Alianza Editorial: Madrid: Spain.

Pedro R. David was a former Judge *ad litem* of The International Criminal Tribunal for the former Yugoslavia (ICTY), The Hague, the Netherlands (2005–2011). Judge of the Argentine Federal Cassation Court (Buenos Aires, Argentina) and twice its President (1993–2017). United Nations Interregional Adviser on Crime Prevention and Criminal Justice (1981–1992), Chairman and Full Professor of Sociology and Criminology of the University of New Mexico (UNM), 1971–1982. Member of the Government Counsel of the United Nations Interregional Crime and Justice Institute/UNICRI, Turin, Italy (2002–2014). Honorary Professor of the Law School of the University of Buenos Aires; the University of Hull, UK; the Autonomous University of Juarez, Mexico; and the University of Moron, Buenos Aires. With more than 20 books and 140 articles on Philosophy of Law, Penal Law, International Criminal Law, Juridical Sociology, Criminology, in Spanish, English, Italian, French, Portuguese, Chinese, etc. At present, the Dean of the Law School of the Argentine John F. Kennedy University. E-mail: pedrordavid@yahoo.com.ar.

Part IV
Ethics and Science in the Service of Countering Crime

Surveillance and the Impossible Search for Ideal Behaviour

Toine Spapens

Abstract Information and communication technology and the internet created unprecedented opportunities for collecting "big data" and apply it to surveillance and influence the behaviour of citizens, for instance in their roles of voters, customers, partners and workers. There is a growing risk that data on these different roles is exchanged and combined for which it was not collected. Surveillance may be defended from the perspective of law and order, protection of safety and health, and economic development, but it may also impact negatively on several United Nations (UN) Sustainable Development Goals (SDGs) to be attained by 2030. Being one of the crucial issues in the world today, it comes as no surprise that the topic is being studied by lawyers, urbanists, sociologists, computer scientists, political scientists and others. However, criminologists have until now mainly looked at surveillance in the context of preventing and detecting crime and terrorism from a "what happens and what works" angle. This chapter will apply a broad perspective by taking the social construction of deviance as a starting point and addressing the consequences of the definition for those who do not live up to the ideal, in terms of criminalisation, social exclusion and other potential effects, keeping in mind the context of the UN's development goals.

Keywords Big data · Mass surveillance · Social construction · Sustainable development goals · Crime prevention · Risks

1 Introduction

Today, we undoubtedly live in an era of mass surveillance, defined as the ability of State and private actors to monitor citizens' and customers' whereabouts, interests and behaviour. In this chapter, I will address this development from a criminological

T. Spapens (✉)
Tilburg University, Tilburg, The Netherlands
e-mail: a.c.spapens@tilburguniversity.edu

H. Kury, S. Redo (eds.), *Crime Prevention and Justice in 2030*,
https://doi.org/10.1007/978-3-030-56227-4_16

perspective. State actors foremost legitimise the gathering of such information by the fact that it helps to solve and prevent crimes, and terrorism in particular, and more recently since the COVID-19 crisis, to reduce the risk of infection. Dictators may use surveillance as an instrument to stay in power. Commercial operators primarily legitimise the gathering of customer data by stating that it helps them to improve their products and services. However, such data may also serve to prevent commercial risks, for instance by denying access to customers who are suspected of jeopardising a company's profits or reputation.

From a broader sociological viewpoint, we may see surveillance as a form of social control and necessary for communities to function. Even the smallest social groups set and monitor norms and will correct or exclude deviants who are unwilling or unable to adhere to them. Norms are not determined objectively but result from a definition process. Although philosophers such as John Stuart Mill and Joel Feinberg have tried to formulate universal liberty limiting principles, these in the end all depend on how social groups define concepts such as harm, paternalism or offense. Of course, some norms, such as not killing other members of the group, are universal. Most, however, are not and differ substantially between social groups. We have no way to objectively determine which norms are "better." Therefore, we are left with two options: either allowing socially, economically and politically dominant powers to set the rules, or accept a certain level of deviance. Democratic societies will generally choose the latter option, not in the least because diverting from existing norms is often essential for scientific, economic and cultural progress, and for the general well-being of large societal groups: nobody can be non-deviant at all times.

When instruments of surveillance are applied in a targeted way, for instance to investigate crimes or to improve a product, in compliance with the Code of Criminal Procedure and data protection laws in general, there is no essential reason to be opposed against it. However, fundamental problems occur when instruments of mass surveillance are applied to search for deviance preventatively. No matter how sophisticated big data analysis will become, without an exact understanding of what constitutes deviant behaviour, such analysis will always be flawed and bound to produce large amounts of errors, particularly false positives, as well as undesired societal outcomes which may put several United Nations' Sustainable Development Goals at risk.

Next, in Sect. 2, I will briefly outline the main drivers of mass-surveillance. Section 3 then addresses surveillance from a criminological viewpoint in more detail. Section 4 delves deeper into the question how social groups define deviance. Section 5 describes the problems of profiling and false positives. Section 6 concludes this chapter by looking at the impact of mass surveillance in the context of the UN's sustainability goals.

2 The Growth of Surveillance

Scholars have identified different and sometimes mutually reinforcing explanations for the increase of the need of surveillance. First, it has been associated with economic structures and modernisations. Others have emphasised the impact of shocking events, particularly the attacks on the World Trade Centre and the Pentagon on 9 September 2001, and the calls for protection that followed from it. Third, developments in information and communication technology have made mass surveillance much easier and encompassing.

Michel Foucault pointed at the transitions caused by industrialisation and emphasised the need of disciplining the workforce for the emerging factory system (Foucault 1977). This required keeping the working classes under surveillance, which did not just involve enforcement and prisons, but an entire array of corrections of deviant behaviour, for instance in schools, the workplace itself, hospitals, and the military. However, in the early 1990s, the concept of discipline seemed to have lost relevance, as societies became ever more diversified and complex. The factory model no longer dominates modern societies and disciplining citizens into this mould is now less necessary. In addition, because of individualisation and migration, the number of subcultures has massively increased. Therefore, in his essay "Post-script on the Societies of Control" French philosopher Gilles Deleuze argued that the need for control has replaced the need for discipline (Deleuze 1992).

Ulrich Beck has argued that the process of technical modernisation itself caused dramatic changes to western culture and has resulted in a wide range of humanly produced risks (Beck 1992). This "risk society" too revolves around the need to control social, political, ecological and individual risks. More importantly, since in the early eighties the economic paradigm of neoliberalism became dominant in the Western world, policies based on it have vastly increased feelings of uncertainty regarding vital human needs such as a sustained source of income; affordable housing; that education will produce better chances in life; and a safe and unpolluted environment in general. Such uncertainties are reflected in a desire to minimise the risk of any sort of harm imaginable, either real or perceived (Ericson 2007). Although advocates of neoliberalism have continuously called for deregulation, in fact the opposite has occurred (Ayres and Braithwaite 1992; Power 2004). Indeed, the free market ideology calls for all sorts of control to keep markets fair and competitive, and to facilitate safety measures (Ericson 2007). Boutellier (2003) defined this inherent paradox as a 'safety utopia': individuals and corporations at the same time wish to enjoy maximum freedom and maximum governmental protection against any potential harm that may result from it.

Shocking events may accelerate this process. Societies have always responded to these with collective moral outrage and a passionate desire for vengeance (Garland 1991). For enforcement agencies, their ability to catch and punish the offenders was for a long time sufficient to restore faith in the protective function of the government. In modern society however, emphasis has increasingly shifted to prevention and protection. Particularly acts of terrorism result in calls for better surveillance of those who might be a threat. Already in the 1970s, the German authorities replied to attacks by the *Rote Armee Fraktion* and other contemporary terrorists with *Rasterfahndung*, a concept to take data automatically from different databases to search for persons with specific risk profiles (Muller and Petit 2008). However, Al Qaida's attacks on the United States in 2001, truly stimulated, and perhaps even more importantly, legitimated, the acceleration and expansion of surveillance trends (Ball and Webster 2003). From Edward Snowden's revelations we first learned of the extent that domestic surveillance by the U.S. National Security Agency had grown into (Sherer et al. 2018).

In recent decades, rapid development of digital techniques has enabled to collect, store and analyse personal data on an unprecedented scale (Ball and Webster 2003). Furthermore, the Internet promoted globalised surveillance (Ball and Murakami Wood 2013). Digitalisation did not just widen the opportunities of States to collect data on their citizens. More importantly, it enabled private actors to gather massive amounts of personal and behavioural information on customers. Particularly "Big tech" corporations such as Google, Facebook and Amazon have become notorious in this respect, but nowadays almost every company that offers products and services which connect to the Internet will gather such data, and may apply it for other commercial purposes than "improving customer experience." Corporations that once started with missions to connect people or to provide the best web search engine, quickly discovered that their most valuable asset was the information that they collected from those who used their services (Zuboff 2019). Big tech companies have increasingly expanded their operations by buying up other platforms and combining different streams of data. Their ambitions do not stop there, which is illustrated by Amazon's plans to engage in for instance food distribution and healthcare, and Facebook led plans to launch the "Libra" as its own cryptocurrency (Rawnsley 2018; Paul 2019).

For a long time, corporations have done so in what is called 'ungoverned space' (Clunan and Trinkunas 2010). This refers to a context in which few regulations exist, and when they do, for example, in the shape of data protection laws, enforcement is highly problematic (Zuboff 2019). Shoshanna Zuboff introduced the term 'surveillance capitalism' to describe the effects of these developments, which she defined in a number of ways. At best it represents a new economic order that claims human experience as free raw material for hidden commercial practices of extraction, prediction, and sales. However, it can also be defined as a movement that aims to impose a new collective order based on total certainty. At its worst, surveillance capitalism will fundamentally change societies and the behaviour of people.

Surveillance researchers particularly worry about the blurring of the boundaries between public and private sector organisations (Haggerty and Ericson 2000; Ball et al. 2012). Indeed, personal and behavioural data collected by private companies, has become increasingly important for intelligence and enforcement agencies, not just for solving crimes, but also for profiling and prevention.

3 Surveillance from a Criminological Perspective

From a criminological perspective, we may look at surveillance in several ways. Mainstream criminologists may be interested in the motives and activities of persons and legal entities who are involved in illegal surveillance practices. "Critical" criminologists may also want to include behaviour that is as such lawful, but does cause blameworthy harm ('lawful but awful'). Criminologists also look at the process of surveillance, which data is collected, where it ends up, whether surveillance is an effective tool to curb crime, and at enforcement of regulations. Finally, criminologists may want to explore structural drivers of illicit and harmful surveillance practices, such as protecting the interests of economically and politically powerful actors. Here, I will look at how surveillance data may be used for specific purposes. This section addresses five main categories, although these may overlap to some extent. The first is the use of surveillance data to commit crimes or cause harm; second is its use to solve crimes; third its use to prevent crimes, including acts of terrorism; fourth, to protect the interests of the powerful; fifth for private actors to gain corporate economic advantages.

To begin with, criminals and terrorists may acquire access to surveillance data and use it to facilitate illegal or otherwise harmful activities. Burglars might for instance gain access to data that 'smart' devices send to their manufacturer, and learn the times when nobody is present at specific addresses. Groups of car thieves would for instance be able to better target their operations if they can track vehicles of specific models and types. They may be able to hack into these data streams, but perhaps these are also for sale on the "Dark net" or from legitimate companies. Indeed, third parties may, in violation of contracts, use data for other purposes than for which it was originally made available, for instance not to provide specific commercial services, but for influencing the outcome of elections. In some cases, surveillance data which is potentially useful for criminals or terrorists, may be openly available. One example was fitness tracking app Strava, which collected GPS data to allow runners to monitor their exercises, and unintentionally gave away the locations of secret U.S. military bases after tracking data had been published online (Hern 2018). The newest technological developments known as "deep fake" are particularly disturbing. These allow for instance to mimic someone else's voice if one possesses just a few minutes of audio and to manipulate videos. Recently, criminals already used it to have a manager of a UK-based energy company transfer € 220,000 to their account, because he thought it was the German chief executive of the parent company who gave him the order by telephone (Stupp 2019).

Surveillance data may, second, be used to solve crimes after these have been committed, or to gather evidence in situations in which illegal activities are ongoing. This for instance refers to the use of listening devices in cars and private homes, interception of telephone conversations or tapping of IP-addresses, physical surveillance of suspects, installing of cameras to monitor specific premises, and controlled deliveries of shipments of for example narcotic drugs. Modern criminal law enforcement agencies will possess the necessary training and certified equipment to use these methods in confirmation with the Code of Criminal Procedure. However, law enforcement agencies also and increasingly rely on information gathered by private actors. An obvious example is the use of recordings of CCTV-cameras citizens and companies have installed to protect against burglary and theft. When some 25 years ago the use of mobile telephones started to become widespread, telephone operator's traffic and location data quickly became an important source of information for investigative authorities (Spapens 2006). Since then, criminals have continuously sought for 'safe' means of communication, but usually without long-term success. For instance, Dutch criminals for a number of years sent text messages via Pretty Good Privacy (PGP) software installed on mobile phones. This worked until Dutch police seized and cracked the servers on which millions of messages were stored. Since then the information helped to solve a variety of cases, including underworld liquidations (Meeus 2017). More recently, normal people's smartphones, combined with the data gathered by tech companies through installed apps and stored on their servers, have become an important tool to help solving crimes. In a recent murder case, a location app allowed the Dutch police to exactly reconstruct the victim's as well as the suspect's whereabouts and thereby solve the case. Finally, financial information kept by banks and other financial service providers has become hugely important for investigation agencies.

The third main purpose of surveillance is to prevent crime. To begin with, the fact that a person is aware of the chance of being watched, this may as such have a direct preventative effect because it increases the threshold for potential offenders. When CCTV-cameras in public areas were first introduced in the 1990s, it was expected that these would contribute to crime prevention. Analysis does indeed show a positive albeit modest effect, depending on the type of crime. CCTV-surveillance does reduce for instance vehicle crime, but has no effect on violence and assault (Bowers and Johnson 2016). More indirectly, surveillance data may be used to identify potential criminals and terrorists. Intelligence agencies, such as the General Communication Headquarters (GCHQ) in the United Kingdom and the National Security Agency have collected signals intelligence for decades, although their focus was not on preventing ordinary crime. After the fall of the Iron Curtain in 1989, western intelligence agencies were starting to partly shift attention to organised crime, mainly because of the perceived emergence of 'organised crime multinationals' such as the Italian Mafia and Russian 'Mafiya' (Andreas and Nadelmann 2006). However, organised crime researchers soon debunked the assumption that such syndicates were systematically setting up shop all over the world (van Dijk and Spapens 2013). In the mid-1990s, intelligence agencies changed focus to terrorism, and particularly after the attacks on the World Trade Centre in 2001 crime largely dropped from their agendas.

In the early 1990s, the police became aware of the potential added value of Intelligence Led Policing (ILP). Although the concept is not defined exactly, it generally reflects a shift from reactive to proactive ways of addressing crime problems. It involves collecting and analysing information about crime patterns to create intelligence products to assess potential problems (e.g. offenders, victims, contexts) and target resources to disrupt the most serious offenses and offenders

(Carter 2009; Ratcliffe 2008; Gibbs 2016). Although the concept is as such broader, it does encompass identifying unknown criminals and threats, based on personal and behavioural profiles. However, experiences in the Netherlands show that it is extremely difficult to draw up such profiles (see below).

Fourth, surveillance may be conducted to serve the interests of the powerful. Traditionally, rulers, particularly of non-democratic states, have had a keen interest in spotting all sorts of suspicious behaviour that might pose a threat to their reign. There are many historical examples, such as Napoleon's France in the eighteenth century and Stalin's Soviet Union in the 1930s.

Classical methods of information gathering such as the use of secret agents, informers and *agents provocateurs*, have over the years been supplemented with technical surveillance systems. Here too, recent developments in digitalisation have further expanded the toolbox of control. The use of facial recognition software and 'smart' cameras in public places, which may be further combined with all sorts of private sector data, illustrates this (Kobie 2019). Surveillance is increasingly globalised and thus also allows foreign states to scrutinise citizens in other countries. For example, the Eritrean government allegedly keeps a close watch on nationals who have fled the country, to prevent them from engaging in activities which might pose a threat to the regime (Opas and McMurray 2015). Criminologically, we may approach such use of surveillance data from the perspective of State crime (Chambliss 1989). This approach refers to acts by actors within the state that results in violations of domestic and international law, human rights, or systematic or institutionalised harm of its or another state's population (Green 2004).

Fifth, surveillance serves corporate economic purposes. Here, I will focus on activities that cause blameworthy harm. To begin with, the data may result in social exclusion if it is used to detect potential risks, to the extent that it may become impossible for anyone with even the slightest perceived flaw to find a job, a house or a partner. Next, corporations may, like totalitarian states, engage in targeted surveillance of people they perceive as a threat. Recently it was revealed that agrochemical corporation Monsanto operated an intelligence center to monitor and discredit journalists and activists. Monsanto for instance targeted journalist Carey Gillam, who wrote a critical book on the company, and singer Neil Young, who released a critical album. The company allegedly paid Google to promote search results for 'Monsanto Glyphosate Carey Gillam' that criticised her work (Levin 2019). Finally, we may question whether data gathering for improving customer experience is necessary to the extent applied. Is it really essential that modern cars' systems collect and send information on your driving style and locations history to the manufacturer, as well as to third parties (Markey 2015)? Do smart TVs constantly need to track what their owners are watching and relay it back to the TV maker and/or its business partners, to improve the product (Popken 2018)?

This section has illustrated the different criminologically relevant issues of surveillance. The techniques may be helpful to commit different types of cybercrime, either by mainstream criminals or corporate offenders, to which enforcement agencies must respond. Conversely, surveillance data may also help to solve crimes, and the examples shown above underline the increased importance of data collected by private actors for targeted investigative purposes. Of course, private as well as state actors must safeguard against the leaking of surveillance data to criminals and terrorists, and in criminal investigations surveillance data must be gathered and used in accordance with adequate requirements set in the Code of Criminal Procedure. However, from a criminological viewpoint, problems with surveillance become fundamental when it is applied for predictive policing, in other words to identify and prevent potential threats, and from a broader perspective, deviance. In the next sections, I will address these problems.

4 The Problem of Defining Deviance

If one wants to scrutinise people to detect deviant behaviour, the premise is that one knows how to define it. For harnessed mainstream criminologists this would not be a topic of much debate: deviance is simply behaviour in violation of what is adopted in the nation's penal code. However, this narrow definition of the object of study of criminology poses problems when we look at modern day surveillance, because it goes far beyond of what is criminalised and also encompasses perceived violations of unwritten social norms. Deviance as such is roughly defined as behaviour that differs from a wide range of societal norms and rules. This raises the question how such norms are determined, and by whom.

The first approach, known as absolutist, assumes that the basic norms of a society are clear and obvious to all members of society in all situations. At the end of the nineteenth century, Emile Durkheim introduced the term collective conscience to refer to widely held social values and beliefs (Durkheim 1964). He reasoned that all behaviour which offends basic normative standards could be considered deviant, and thus be criminalised. Of course, general norms and values exist which are common to all societies, but these cover only a small part of what communities consider deviant behaviour. If we assume that a collective conscience exists, the norms which follow from it will reflect the moral values of the middle class and disregard the complexity of modern societies and the differences between a wide range of subcultures.

This is illustrated by early attempts to survey people's opinions on what constitutes deviant behaviour. Theoretically, such an approach would render an objective picture, but in practice the results are very difficult to interpret. In a classic study, Simmons (1965) asked 180 people what they considered deviant behaviour. It resulted in 1100 different answers, falling into 250 categories. Of course, murder and theft were considered deviant behaviour, but also pacifists and working females. The problem is that almost all human behaviour will be considered deviant by someone and counting does not answer the question whether these opinions are morally defendable.

Howard Becker posed that acts become deviant if others respond to them as such (Becker 1963). However, there cannot be a proper response if deviant behaviour remains unknown. Furthermore, massive expression of public disapproval of deviant behaviour is usually limited to shocking events, which are not necessarily the most harmful if we include long-term effects, for example, pollution. Another problem is that if communities do not respond to behaviour which is essentially deviant from a moral perspective, it will become normalised. In practice however, social groups will largely ignore what other subcultures consider deviant, as long as their behaviour does not harm or restrict them.

These examples underline that deviance has no ontological reality, but is instead socially constructed. The idea of social construction is rooted in symbolic interactionism, an approach which focuses on the way language and other types of interaction structures how people experience, interpret and attribute meaning to everyday reality (Blumer 1969). Communities thus also construct social norms. A social norm is 'any standard rule that states what human beings should or should not think, say or do under given circumstances' (Blake and Davis 1964). These norms are continuously defined and redefined by the members of a given group.

In larger communities it is impossible to constantly discuss and define norms in personal interactions, simply because not every member of a large social group can maintain contact with all the others. Instead, norms are "informally codified" in culture. Culture can be seen as norms that are commonly accepted without need of debate. Religion may also be viewed as a way of codifying cultural norms, in this case in the shape of religious texts and their interpretation, and rituals in which religious norms are learned and explained. Finally, laws can be viewed as formal codifications of societal norms.

Norms are necessarily simplified representations of the complexities of everyday life. In specific situations, there may be many reasons why general norms would perhaps not apply. These are, in other words, the product of a process of simplification known as framing. Frames themselves are the result of a definition process, in which individuals, interest groups, institutions, political parties, religious actors, the media—increasingly also social media—as well as science, interact. The process takes place at different levels: local, national and international. Because the process is continuous, notions about deviance are not static, but change over time. Furthermore, they differ across and within societies. A fundamental problem is that the ability to engage in definition setting is spread unevenly. Economically powerful actors are inherently better placed to influence the process, for instance through the lobbying of politicians, funding of research, and feeding the media.

Paradoxically, the Internet did make it easier for individuals to exert definition power. Think for instance about influencers with large followings on Facebook or YouTube. Another example is Greta Thunberg, a now 16-year old who was catapulted from being a schoolgirl who sat down in August 2018 in front of the Swedish parliament with a cardboard sign telling she was on strike because of the climate, to addressing the United Nations about the subject little more than a year later. The Internet, however, also further complicated the process of definition setting because the number of specialised communication channels has exploded, and 'bubbles' occur that distort the interactive process. Furthermore, the boundaries between the local and global have faded, and actors from all over the world may now try to influence local definition setting.

As I have noted above, surveillance is an instrument of social control: communities use it to detect deviant behaviour and thus to uphold social norms. However, if we cannot objectively determine what deviant behaviour is, we are also unable to define what should become the target of surveillance.

5 The Problem of False Positives

A fundamental question of assessing deviance and thereby the objectives of surveillance is how to avoid false positives. In this context false positives can be defined as behaviour which is not malicious, whereas this cannot be established correctly based on comparative data analysis.

Of course, for totalitarian regimes false positives are not much of a concern: even the slightest sign of discontent may be enough reason to be marked as a threat and carted off to prison or to an 'education and training centre' (Allen-Ebrahimian 2009). For example, how many of the millions who were sent to the Gulag or killed by the Stalinist regime in the 1930s, represented a real danger to communism?

For economic actors the problem of false positives is more ambiguous. On the one hand, better predictions allow for better sales. On the other, advertising companies may be less concerned if they spam someone who is not interested. People may indeed be annoyed about being false positives when they receive adds for paracetamol after tapping in 'headache' in a search engine, or maybe worse, an offer to get insurance for your funeral, but will usually not complain. However, false positives do become problematic when the result is denial of access to specific services.

By comparison, for democratic state actors, avoiding false positives is a key issue when it comes to preventing crime. Criminologists have addressed the errors problem extensively in the context of predicting recidivism. Although prediction methods were able to identify certain groups of offenders having a higher-than-average statistical probability of recidivism, these methods showed a disturbing incidence of false positives: for violent crimes, at least two false positives for every true positive (Monahan 1981). Such mistaken forecasts could be gravely damaging to the individuals involved, for they could lead to their prolonged incarceration (Von Hirsch 1998).

More recently, researchers have for instance looked at surveillance measures intended to prevent terrorist attacks. One example is the No Fly Lists, with thousands of names of people who should be denied to board flights into and out of the USA. A large number of false positives have mistakenly been denied access and missed their flights (Bjørgo 2016). Another example is programs to encourage the public to report suspicious behaviour. It will not come as a surprise that citizens consider a wide range of behaviour 'suspicious', especially when it concerns minorities. In 2006, for example, six Muslim imams were removed from a US Airways flight because passengers thought they were a threat to their safety (Larsen and Piché 2009). The problem is not just confined to serious threats such as terrorism, as anyone who takes part in a neighbourhood WhatsApp group to report suspicious behaviour, will be able to confirm.

From a technical point of view, one might argue that the problem of false positives can be solved by developing better profiles to base surveillance on. Indeed, personal and behavioural data is often lacking in government databases. In 2012, I was involved in a project in which a profile was composed based on the characteristics of the most notorious criminals in the city of Amsterdam. It took a massive effort to integrate the different databases from which we took this information and be able to run the profiles. Government databases had mainly been developed further from mid-1990s software, and had not been set up with the aim of interchangeability. When we finally were able to run the parameters through the integrated database, a substantial number of persons matched the profile, but were hitherto unknown to the authorities. Were they indeed very smart criminals who had so far managed to completely stay under the radar? Of course not: all 'hits' turned out to be false positives.

Critics may argue that the attempt was primitive, considered the amount of information which private entities currently have available, such as search histories, financial transactions, movements, social networks, and postings on social media platforms. Using this information would indeed allow construction of highly detailed profiles, but we still would not know which variables would be relevant from the perspective of detecting deviance. The range of potentially deviant behaviour is simply far too wide to apply general profiles. However, narrowing down the profiles to very specific behaviour will inevitably be perceived as discriminatory and stigmatising to specific population groups (Bjørgo 2016).

More importantly, because the persons who build the profiles of deviance cannot refer to an objective list of what to include as 'suspicious' they have only three options, or combinations of these. The first is simply to follow Durkheim in his assumption that a collective conscience exists and draw up a list of deviant behaviour based on one's perception of it. The problem is that this will result in profiles which are highly biased to the perceptions of the persons who construct them. The second is to use 'self-learning' software which searches for inappropriate content which is similar to what was previously considered deviant, or characteristics of criminals. However, this too requires labelling specific behaviour as deviant before you can find something similar, or to be able to determine what constitutes a criminal, and therefore does not solve our problem. The third option is to search for anomalies. Unfortunately, this also requires that we must know which anomalies are to be considered risky or suspicious.

For all sorts of reasons, public and private surveillance operators have successfully created the impression that their profiling systems are infallible, objective, reliable and accurate in the assessments that they produce (Yeung 2018). They are not. Indeed, *Netflix* may have little difficulty in offering you content similar to what you watched before. This does not require much sophistication, and as argued above, getting it wrong does not cause much harm. And of course, it does not point you to what you are really interested in: something challenging and new that you did not think of before. Accurately predicting the threat someone represents to societal order, based on personal and behavioural characteristics is another matter. If we allow powerful economic or state actors to define what is deviance, this will inevitably result in biased and inaccurate profiles that generate large amounts of errors (Korff and Browne 2013). The impact on society cannot be underestimated. In the next section, I will sum up the issues in the context of the United Nations' sustainability goals.

6 Conclusion: The Impact of Mass Surveillance and the UN's Sustainability Goals

Researchers in the field of surveillance studies have often referred to the negative impact of mass surveillance from the perspective of its panopticon effect (Haggerty and Ericson 2000). The idea of the panopticon was originally defined by nineteenth century philosopher Jeremy Bentham as a prison design which would theoretically allow a single guard to keep all prisoners under surveillance, who at the same time were unable to either see each other, or know when they were watched. The intended effect was to discipline: the fact that one could be watched at any given time but not necessarily all the time, would be enough to encourage inmates to behave correctly. Although the panopticon prison was never built, the idea did exert substantial influence on prison design. In the 1970s, Michel Foucault transposed the panopticon idea to society as a whole (see above, Foucault 1977). Whether or not one wants to use the panopticon metaphor, the impact of living in a society where everybody is kept under constant surveillance is substantial, particularly when it is hard to tell what will be considered deviant behaviour now or in the future, and by whom.

The risk is a "chilling effect" in which citizens will be afraid to speak out or display any behaviour which might be considered inappropriate (Haggerty and Ericson 2000). This may result in mistrust, and people hiding their true selves. Some of my students for instance explained that they maintain two accounts at Instagram: one in which they pose as virtue itself that they may present when a prospective employer or landlord demands access, and another where they post their real life.

Not risking to be deviant will eventually also affect economical, scientific and cultural progress. Throughout history, many crucial innovations have been considered deviant at first, such as Copernicus's idea that the earth and the other planets revolve around the sun, instead of earth being the centre of our solar system. Large numbers of writers, painters and other artists we hold in high esteem today, have in their time been confronted with disapproval of their work, and may have even been prosecuted for it. The fact that democratic societies are able to allow a certain level of deviance, helps to explain their success, and why they attract so many people from nations which do not allow the same levels of freedom. In conclusion, the 'chilling effect' of mass surveillance may put at risk sustainable development goals related to ensuring good health and—mental—well-being (SDG 3) decent work and economic growth (SDG 8); and industry, innovation and infrastructure (SDG 9).

The second problem I identified also follows from the fact that we cannot objectively define deviance, and causes that any attempt at profiling and finding threats through mass surveillance will result in large numbers of false positives. In practice, this problem is aggravated by the fact that powerful private actors increasingly determine what is to be considered deviant. This will inevitably result in bias and social inequalities. An employer may for instance impose surveillance on workers to find out whether they use drugs or regularly drink alcohol, to prevent safety hazards, but the company management will itself be undoubtedly exempt from such requirements although their decisions are potentially far more harmful to people's lives. As we have seen above, it is usually minorities and other less-powerful groups in society who are considered to be a threat when it comes to for instance crime and terrorism. However, criminologists have underlined time and again that corporate deviance causes much more injury, death and financial harm, although it is often not seen as shocking criminal behaviour. Mass surveillance impacts unevenly on societal groups, and threatens the development goals of reducing inequalities (SDG 10) and promoting peace, justice and strong institutions (SDG 16).

Although the public has become increasingly aware of the fact that mass surveillance exists, and because of hit series such as "Black Mirror," so far not much seems to be changing in their daily practices. Perhaps the main reason is submission to the notion that being under constant surveillance cannot be avoided (Romele et al. 2017). But maybe we do see some gradual changes. The big Tech companies are increasingly the object of governmental scrutiny, for instance because of misuse of their monopoly positions, problems with data protection, and tax avoidance. In 2017, the European Commission imposed a fine of €2.4 Billion on Google for unfairly favouring some of its own services over those of rivals (Scott 2017). In September 2019, 50 U.S. states and territories announced to investigate Google's alleged monopolistic practices (Romm 2019). So far, big Tech has been quite successful at fencing off effective regulation of its harvesting of user data (Zuboff 2019). Whether this situation will continue remains to be seen. For the good of the global community, an approach similar to how the early twentieth century 'robber barons' were contained, through breaking up monopolies on the one hand and effective regulation on the other, should perhaps now be applied to the modern 'robbers of personal data', if we aspire to fulfil the UN's Sustainable Development Goals.

References

Allen-Ebrahimian, B. (2009, November 24). Exposed: China's operating manuals for mass internment and arrest by algorithm. *International Consortium of Investigative Journalists*.

Andreas, P., & Nadelmann, E. (2006). *Policing the globe: Criminalization and crime control in international relations*. New York: Oxford University Press.

Ayres, I., & Braithwaite, J. (1992). *Responsive regulation: Transcending the deregulation debate*. New York: Oxford University Press.
Ball, K., Haggerty, K., & Lyon, D. (Eds.). (2012). *Routledge handbook of surveillance studies*. London and New York: Routledge.
Ball, K., & Murakami Wood, D. (2013). Editorial. The political economy of surveillance. *Surveillance & Society, 11*(1/2), 1–3.
Ball, K., & Webster, F. (2003). The intensification of surveillance. In K. Ball & F. Webster (Eds.), *The intensification of surveillance. Crime, terrorism and surveillance in the information age* (pp. 1–15). London: Pluto Press.
Beck, U. (1992). *Risk society: Towards a new modernity*. London: Sage.
Becker, H. (1963). *Outsiders: Studies in the sociology of deviance*. New York: The Free Press.
Bjørgo, T. (2016). *Preventing crime. A holistic approach*. Basingstoke: Palgrave Macmillan.
Blake, J., & Davis, K. (1964). Norms, values, and sanctions. In R. Faris (Ed.), *Handbook of modern sociology* (pp. 456–484). Chicago, IL: Rand McNally & Company.
Blumer, H. (1969). *Symbolic interactionism: Perspective and method*. Englewood Cliffs: Prentice-Hall.
Boutellier, H. (2003). *De veiligheidsutopie*. The Hague: Boom Juridische uitgevers.
Bowers, K., & Johnson, S. (2016). Situational prevention. In D. Weisburd, D. Farrington, & C. Gill (Eds.), *What works in crime prevention and rehabilitation* (pp. 111–135). New York: Springer.
Carter, D. (2009). *Law enforcement intelligence: A guide for state, local, and tribal law enforcement agencies* (2nd ed.). Office of Community Oriented Policing Services, U.S. Department of Justice: http://fas.org/irp/agency/doj/lei.pdf
Chambliss, W. (1989). State-organized crime. *Criminology, 27*(2), 183–208.
Clunan, A., & Trinkunas, H. (2010). *Ungoverned spaces*. Stanford, CA: Stanford University Press.
Deleuze, G. (1992). Postscript on the societies of control. *October, 59*(Winter), 3–7.
Durkheim, E. (1964). *The division of labor in society*. New York: Free Press.
Ericson, R. (2007). *Crime in an insecure world*. Cambridge: Polity Press.
Foucault, M. (1977). *Discipline and punish: The birth of the prison*. New York: Vintage.
Garland, J. (1991). Sociological perspectives on punishment. *Crime and Justice, 14*, 115–165.
Gibbs, C. (2016). Addressing transnational environmental crime: The role of intelligence led policing. In T. Spapens, R. White, & W. Huisman (Eds.), *Environmental crime in transnational context* (pp. 85–100). London and New York: Routledge.
Green, P. (2004). *State crime: Governments, violence and corruption*. London: Pluto Press.
Haggerty, K., & Ericson, R. (2000). The surveillant assemblage. *British Journal of Sociology, 51* (4), 605–622.
Hern, A. (2018, January 28). Fitness tracking app Strava gives away location of secret US army bases. *The Guardian*.
Kobie, N. (2019, June 7). The complicated truth about China's social credit system. *Wired*.
Korff, D., & Browne, I. (2013). *The use of the Internet & related services, private life & data protection: Trends, technologies, threats and implications*. Council of Europe, T-PD (2013)07.
Larsen, M., & Piché, J. (2009). Public vigilance campaigns and participatory surveillance after 11 September 2001. In S. Hier & J. Greenberg (Eds.), *Surveillance: Power, problems, and politics* (pp. 187–202). Vancouver: UBC Press.
Levin, S. (2019, August 8). Revealed: How Monsanto's 'intelligence center' targeted journalists and activists. *The Guardian*.
Markey, E. (2015). *Tracking & hacking: Security & privacy gaps put American drivers at risk*. Published online at: markey.senate.gov
Meeus, J. (2017, June 6). Hoe justitie 3,6 miljoen versleutelde berichten van criminelen ontcijfert, *nrc.nl*.
Monahan, J. (1981). *Predicting violent behavior: An assessment of clinical techniques*. Thousand Oaks, CA: Sage.

Muller, E., & Petit, G. (2008). Strategieën tegen Terrorisme. In E. Muller, U. Rosenthal, & R. de Wijk (Eds.), *Terrorisme: Studies over Terrorisme en terrorismebestrijding* (pp. 271–308). Deventer: Kluwer.
Opas, M., & McMurray, D. (2015). Under the gaze of the state: ICT use and state surveillance of Eritrean refugees in Italy. *Refugee Survey Quarterly, 34*(4), 105–125.
Paul, K. (2019, June 18). Libra: Facebook launches cryptocurrency in bid to shake up global finance. *The Guardian*.
Popken, B. (2018, February 7). Your smart TV is watching you watching TV, Consumer Reports finds, *Nbcnews.com*
Power, M. (2004). *The risk management of everything: Rethinking the politics of uncertainty*. London: Demos.
Ratcliffe, J. (2008). *Intelligence-led policing*. Portland, OR: Willan.
Rawnsley, A. (2018, March 25). Politicians can't control the digital giants with rules drawn up in the analogue era. *The Guardian*.
Romele, A., Gallino, F., Emmenegger, C., & Gorgone, D. (2017). Panopticism is not enough: Social media as technologies of voluntary servitude. *Surveillance & Society, 15*(2), 204–221.
Romm, T. (2019, September 10). Google target of antitrust investigation led by 50 U.S. states and territories. *Nationalpost.com*
Scott, M. (2017, June 27). Google Fined Record $2.7 Billion in E.U. Antitrust Ruling. *The New York Times*.
Sherer, J., Sterling, N., Burger, L., Banaschik, M., & Taal, A. (2018). An Investigator's Christmas Carol: Past, present, and future law enforcement agency data mining practices. In H. Jahankhani (Ed.), *Cyber criminology, advanced sciences and technologies for security applications* (pp. 251–273). Switzerland: Springer.
Simmons, J. (1965). Public stereotypes of deviants. *Social Problems, 13*(2), 223–232.
Spapens, T. (2006). *Interactie tussen criminaliteit en opsporing*. Antwerp and Oxford: Intersentia.
Stupp, C. (2019, August 30). Fraudsters used AI to mimic CEO's voice in unusual cybercrime case. *The Wall Street Journal*.
van Dijk, J., & Spapens, T. (2013). Transnational organized crime networks across the world. In J. Albanese & P. Reichel (Eds.), *Transnational organized crime. An overview from six continents* (pp. 7–27). Thousand Oaks, CA: Sage.
von Hirsch, A. (1998). Penal theories. In M. Tonry (Ed.), *The handbook of crime and punishment* (pp. 659–682). Oxford University Press.
Yeung, K. (2018). *A study of the implications of advanced digital technologies (including AI systems) for the concept of responsibility within a human rights framework*. Council of Europe. MSI-AUT(2018)05.
Zuboff, S. (2019). *The age of surveillance capitalism*. New York: PublicAffairs.

Toine Spapens is a Full Professor of Criminology at Tilburg University, the Netherlands. He received his PhD in criminology in 2006. Since the early 1990s, Spapens has made extensive empirical research on (organized) crime and its containment, international law enforcement cooperation, and environmental crime. His empirical work includes trafficking in illicit firearms, synthetic drug production, large-scale cannabis cultivation, illegal gambling and match fixing, and waste and wildlife trafficking. His PhD focused on the question how criminals adapt to special investigative techniques used by enforcement agencies, such as surveillance and interception of communication. His recent projects concerned the use of administrative law, and powers to maintain public order, for the prevention and disruption of crime (2015); prevention of intergenerational transmission of delinquent behavior in families involved in organized crime (2017, 2020); and criminals who engage in philanthropic activities, through sponsoring of sports clubs and good causes (2018, 2019). In the context of environmental crimes and harms, Spapens co-edited the books *Environmental Crime and Its Victims* (2014); *Environmental Crimes in Transnational Context* (2016) and *Green Crimes and Dirty Money* (2018). E-mail: A.C. Spapens@tilburguniversity.edu.

Ethics and the Development of Artificial Intelligence: Challenges and Dilemmas in the Context of the 2030 United Nations Agenda for Sustainable Development

Aneta Breczko, Wojciech Filipkowski, and Izabela Kraśnicka

Abstract This chapter aims to introduce both the threats and chances involved in the Artificial Intelligence (AI) in the context of crime prevention as one of the elements of the Goal 16 of the 2030 Agenda for Sustainable Development: to promote peaceful and inclusive societies for sustainable development, provide access to justice for all and build effective, accountable, and inclusive institutions at all levels. Authors argue that the ethical approach toward artificial intelligence should be crucial and serve as point of departure for any further developments of AI. Analysis of the essence of the artificial intelligence, the scope of its influence on human lives and potential for the future use bring definite conclusion: technological codes and legal codes are not enough for the secured and controlled progress in the most advanced intelligence field. Ethical codes must be introduced to guarantee eliminations of threats and enjoyment of benefits provided by constantly developing artificial intelligence.

Keywords Artificial intelligence · Ethical codes · Philosophical approach · 2030 Agenda for Sustainable Development

---

A. Breczko
University of Białystok, Faculty of Law, Department of Theory and Philosophy of Law, Białystok, Poland
e-mail: breczko@uwb.edu.pl

W. Filipkowski
University of Białystok, Faculty of Law, Department of Criminal Law and Criminology, Forensic Laboratory, Białystok, Poland
e-mail: w.filipkowski@uwb.edu.pl

I. Kraśnicka (✉)
University of Białystok, Faculty of Law, Department of Public International and European Law, Białystok, Poland
e-mail: krasnicka@uwb.edu.pl

H. Kury, S. Redo (eds.), *Crime Prevention and Justice in 2030*,
https://doi.org/10.1007/978-3-030-56227-4_17

1 Introduction

Artificial Intelligence (AI) belongs to the fastest developing and most significant technologies in the modern world. The scientific progress in the informatics, cybernetics, and robotics in the twenty-first century rises an understandable enthusiasm. Revolutionary changes bring enormous benefits, reaching beyond the economic sphere (Brynjolfsson and McAfee 2015, p. 20). Artificial intelligence may take over human work that is characterized by the repeatability, requires high precision and the same time, it may increase the work's effectiveness, especially if connected with collecting and processing of large amounts of data. One can assume, AI will accompany people in their everyday life, improving its safety, comfort and upgrading the quality of work or entertainment. It will relieve people in dangerous ventures. It can be generally expected that as a result, the AI it will also contribute to the more effective achievement of the goals designed in the 2030 Agenda for Sustainable Development.

Numerous facilities allowed due to the use of AI intertwine however with just as many threats. They result from the unpredictability and possibility of the loss of control over the technological tools. The problems of risk and responsibility for future generations are among those mostly emphasized. It is also underlined that the current state of knowledge is insufficient to prognose actual effects linked to the development of the artificial intelligence. It is still fully unknown how the modern technology tools should be used so that they benefit to the individuals and the society.

Therefore, it is important to look at the AI from the philosophical perspective. The ontological, phenomenological, epistemological, and axiological considerations become crucial in the ethical discourse. The findings of cognitive science, neurobiology as well as psychology as the basic sciences for AI research also come helpful.

2 Artificial Intelligence as a Study Subject for Philosophy and Ethics

Although it is said that technologies are morally neutral and only the use of the technological tools and their results may be subject of moral evaluations, it is difficult to agree with such thesis. The scientific development is not an automatic process. It is a result of human actions which should serve goals, values, and needs (Kass 2002, pp. 4, 35). According to the key visionary in the Microsoft—Sam Shead, artificial intelligence will change not only the general human approach to technology, but also the attitude to another human being and the essence of humanity (Shead 2016). Modern technologies show the ontological and ethical dimension. They actively influence the way people shape their ethics, the way they understand the concepts of "good" and "evil" which are essential from the axiological perspective. The technologies generate new categories and obligations. They condition human decisions dealing with moral problems (Verbeek 2011, p. 5). They impact the human perception and the man's self-understanding (own identity, relations with others, experience, rights, and obligations). As such, they implicate the moral condition of the individual as well as of the entire society.

It can be noted that "old" principles of humanistic ethics are still applicable to post-humanistic technologies. Currently existing ethical concepts become inadequate and outdated. That is why the traditional ethics should be reviewed, updated, and adjusted to the technological opportunities. Such ethics should indicate the moral (and as a result also legal) limits of activities, activities that are technically possible, yet unacceptable from the ethical and legal standpoints. Ability to foresee the directions of the information technologies' progress and artificial intelligence's development seem immensely important, especially in such critical field as providing for the right functioning of the justice administration and consequently—criminal prevention.

Before the technological solutions connected to AI will become applicable, it is worth to consider what goals and values are to be achieved with their usage. It requires the necessity to create hypothetical visions of the world that we want future generations to live in. It is equally important to realize the accountability for the practical consequences following the achievement of one of the visions (Soniewicka 2018, pp. 327–328). The findings of the philosophical and ethical discourse may become quite helpful in this matter.

3 What Is AI and What Can It Do?

The term "artificial intelligence" is difficult to define, at least considering the lack of clear and precise definition "intelligence" itself. The term "artificial intelligence" was first used in 1955 by John McCarthy. Nowadays, artificial intelligence is most often defined as a domain of informatics aiming at developing the computers which will be able to perform operations so far reserved to humans (especially operations requiring intelligence). It should be, however, clear that now we are mostly dealing with the high level of automatization of data and information collecting and processing to describe the reality, to search for interactions among various phenomena. Although the birth of artificial intelligence (in its more pronounced "strong" version) is still ahead of us, it is coming soon and we should already work on the ethical fundaments of the AI functioning.

Zygmunt Vetulani provided an interesting, original definition. He uses "artificial intelligence" in two ways. First, artificial intelligence is a discipline aiming to create artefacts equipped in functionalities and intellectual powers known as typical for human beings (and more generally for beings endowed with intelligence). Second, AI is a collection of tools (programs, data bases, computer models, interfaces, etc.) serving to realize those artefacts. The phrase "robot endowed with artificial intelligence" is a synonym for such understood artificial intelligence (Vetulani 2018a).

With this understanding we will consider the ethical challenges relating to artificial intelligence in the presented chapter.

At the beginning it should be clarified, however, that the subject of artificial intelligence (treated as engineering discipline) is the examination and determination of the rules governing intelligent behaviors of a man as well as their usage in the algorithms and programs (Stylec-Szromek 2018, p. 502). It deals with designing of the technical and programing solutions for the artificial systems created by humans, so they—as precisely as possible—imitate activity of a human brain (Łupkowski 2005). Researchers aim not only at construing machines helpful for people or even taking over people's actions. They also aim to explore the mechanisms of thought and intelligence. Some of them, like M. Minsky claim that the applied methods (modeling and stimulation) can lead to the development of authentic and autonomous states of mind, that is so called "strong" artificial intelligence (Minsky 1982, p. 3). Others, like J. Searle say that those will always remain just the simulations of mental states (Searle 1984, pp. 28–32; Searle 1992, p. 53).

While defining artificial intelligence two approaches can be observed. The above-mentioned "strong" (general) AI, the one that is still to come and the "weak" (narrow) AI which is already present and intensively developed and applied in various technological tools. It is the strong AI that awakes most ethical controversies. The perspective of intelligent machines that would be able to think on their own and take autonomous decisions provides for the biggest fear of philosophers and ethicists (Good 1965, pp. 31–88; Vinge 1993, pp. 11–22; Różanowski 2007, pp. 109–135).

Artificial intelligence in the "weak" version is understood as a system which in the intelligence requiring task will equal or exceed the human abilities. Currently existing beginnings of "weak" artificial intelligence are based mainly on the creation of "deep neural networks" modeled partly on neurons and brain neural networks. In these networks the researchers trigger the process called "machine learning," and in particular "deep learning." Their complexity is however several levels lower than the complexity of human brain. Researchers provide the networks with large amounts of data such as millions of photos or conversations and the AI program learns to find their similarities, differences, hidden patterns, and regularities.

The "weak" artificial intelligence will keep developing in the nearest future. AI in the "strong" version is a self-aware system, system with its own mind. Specialists in the AI field claim that the creation of the artificial intelligence equaling human level will happen before the 2100 (Muehlhauser and Salomon 2012, pp. 15–42). These are however only prognoses which may accelerate with the new technological solutions. What will come even later is the superintelligence understood as "intellect much better than the human brain in every field, including scientific creativity, general knowledge and social skills" (Bostrom 2016). Such intelligence is to significantly surpass the human intelligence (Lindenberg 2018, pp. 67–69). The dominating concept in science is that ultimately the artificial intelligence will gain both—the awareness and self-awareness. Such moment is described as "technological singularity" (Vinge 1993). However, before this happens, the "weak" artificial intelligence will serve people to extend their perception of reality, support the decision-making processes or self-resolving of the minor, standard or repeating problems.

Let us take selected examples to look at the skills of the "weak" artificial intelligence and to see how much it became human-like:

- Machines win in games with people:
  - In 1997 the Deep Blue computer for the first time won the chess match with the grand master in chess—Gary Kasparov;
  - Intelligent machines also win in Go—an extremely difficult old Chinese game which is based on intuition strategy and requires a remarkably high level of creativity due to the number of possible combinations in the game. In 2016 the computer program Alpha Go won the battle with the game grand master Lee Sedol.
- Artificial intelligence has already positively passed the famous "Turing test." In 2014 as much as 33% of qualified questioners considered the Eugene Goostman chatbot as human being;[1]
- Chatbot imitating a 19-year old girl was to learn, acknowledge, talk, analyze the Twits, and to become more efficient and more human every day. It had to be turned off several hours after it had begun working because it started to publish offensive posts touching the politically incorrect, racist, or sexual issues;
- Several other works are the effects of the robot creativity: musical works (the popular Daddy's Car song for example), pieces of literature (poetry of bot Ractor), paintings (Portrait of Edmond De Belamy), film scenarios (Impossible Things or Sunspring), trailers (horror film Morgan), or commercials (Driven by Intuition commercial of Lexus). The disputable question then is whether the artificial intelligence can be only a tool to create art or can it become an artist itself?

The above examples prove that artificial intelligence can create culture, which so far has been regarded as one of the undisputable differentiators of humanity (Szyszkowska 2017, p. 27). Soon we may be dealing with the issues of authorship, copy rights to the works created by the intelligent machines. These issues will undoubtedly have an axiological note in it.

With the expanding autonomy of the artificial intelligence comes the possible expansion of "self-deciding" in the undertaken actions. Such autonomy may bring limitation or—further down the road—even elimination of the human being from the "decision-making processes" of the artificial intelligence system. As a result, it is already now necessary to address the philosophical and ethical reflections which will build the axiological and legal frames for the AI functioning. The Authors believe that the justice administration sphere, and especially the criminal prevention part of it

[1]In the test, people (questioners) conduct computer conversation with other participants of the study. If the computer program is capable of convincing at 30% of questioners that it is a human being, it passes the test.

is unique, because its peculiar "dehumanization" can cause significant negative consequences for numerous aspects of life for particular people as well as social groups or entire societies.

4 Artificial Intelligence as a Philosophical and Legal Project

Artificial intelligence is considered as one of the most relevant philosophical projects of the turn of the twentieth and the twenty-first century. The research on AI bring the postulate to revise way we think about the nature of humanity. It becomes crucial when facing the possibility of the "strong" artificial intelligence entering the scene. Such intelligence will generate real challenges for philosophical and religious doctrines spreading the uniqueness of a man and his/her privileged position in the universe. As Kaplan notes "Intelligent machines may put some objective light on the fundamental questions concerning the nature of our minds, existence of free will as well as the crucial issue whether non-biological subjects may be regarded as alive" (Kaplan 2019, pp. 89–90).

The fundamental philosophical question is whether we can say that a computer machine or any other thing that bears no natural origin—possesses mind and (or) thinks. Alan M. Turing, known as the father of artificial intelligence, considered this matter already back in 1950 (Turing 1950). He rightfully foresaw that at the end of twentieth century the term "to think" will expand enough to reasonably apply it to the machines or programs with proper capabilities (Feigenbaum and Feldman 1997, pp. 24–47). In the twenty-first century, after the machine positively passed the Turing test and along with the further development of the artificial intelligence, the philosophical questions no longer deal only with whether the machine can think, but also whether it can possess free will, awareness and whether it has any feelings (Kaplan 2019, pp. 91–112).

The references to posthumanism and transhumanism are visible. These two philosophical trends provide that modern abilities of a human organism are not unique, and they only constitute one of the evolution stages. The main assumption of posthumanism states that the new philosophical metaphysics will become a foundation for the practical ethics encompassing not only the human but also other beings, including the "virtual creatures" (robots or even avatars) (Przegalińska 2017; Kasperski 2003, pp. 23–40). Transhumanism on the other hand assumes a gradual merger of humans and technology. By overcoming further barriers surrounding people, such merger is to lead to the human perfection. Various technological tools serve to achieve this goal by improving the intellectual, physical, and social possibilities (so called human enhancement). The goal however is the realization of a metaphysical postulate to transform a human being into machine. The transformation may occur due to the above-mentioned possible enhancement of the mechanical devices with biological beings (so called "cyborgization"), as well as to the brain-computer interface. Philosophers deliberate whether thank to the technological advancement the current, imperfect world will be replaced by the "better" ("more perfect") one? They try to answer the core question in metaphysics and ontology: who is a man and where are the boundaries of humanity?

However, before the "strong" artificial intelligence arrives and before the foreseeable threats to the idea of humanity begin to appear, the philosophical discourse focuses on the need to establish the ontological and ethical status for the outcomes of the already functioning "weak" artificial intelligence. Influenced by the findings of cognitive science, a new standpoint arose in ethics known as "infocentrism" (Torrance 2013, p. 404). One of its assumptions is that the brain processes are the cognizable procedures of information processing and all the recognized information processing systems can be recreated in computers. As a result, one can "declare that every respectively complicated information processing system will show enough features to allow considering it an ethical subject" (Michalczak 2016, p. 116). If such assumption serves as a point of departure, another problem arises—whether the potential simulation of the entire human brain that the scientists work on will not contribute to the birth of ephemeral person? (Thiel 2015). As indicated in the above example, some computer experiments may bring along an ethical dimension unnoticeable so far.

The philosophical debate provides room for the considerations on treating artificial intelligence as a subject in the ethical and moral understanding (DeBaets 2014, pp. 76–86). They emphasize that the rapid development of highly intelligent autonomous robots may—in further perspective—question the present classification of persons in accordance with their moral status in the same or even in a deeper way that it happened with animals. The current perception of the human moral status will change. Robots, just like people, will be perceived as integral persons, evaluative, judgmental, self-improving beings (Stylec-Szromek 2018, p. 507). As a result, they should be granted legal personality, and this will become a tremendous challenge for the societies and legal orders of all countries.

The origins of the systematic and philosophically grounded reflection on such legal personality traces back to the article published in 1992 by Lawrence B. Solum titled "Legal Personhood for Artificial Intelligences" (Solum 1992, pp. 1231–1287). For the first time the question was voiced whether artificial intelligence can possess legal personality at all? The Author did not however notice any arguments supporting the logical impossibility of granting such personality to the machine. Other philosophers try to indicate the conditions necessary for the robot to be considered a subject. The autonomy of artificial intelligence becomes the main criterion as it results in unpredictability of particular activities. AI is also characterized by the fact that it deals with problems which until recently only people could handle. Unpredictability of the AI operations is associated with the possibility of mistake making. Fallibility is a price which the AI pays for obtaining the more and more "human" intelligence. Thomas Hellström points out that it is the autonomous power (the number and level of actions, interactions and decisions which the program is capable of self-taking) that differentiates the artificial intelligence from machines which do not possess it (Hellström 2013, p. 99). The existence of the "inter-navigability" feature is significant. It affirms that the actions taken by the machines are navigated by its own experience, not the external, forced algorithms. It is connected to "learning" and "experiencing" by some programs (Russell and Norvig 2009, p. 35). Added attention is given to the requirement to show social skills, that is, ability to communicate with other autonomous machines, refusal to act, ability to propose a different solution. Proactivity is equally important and allows recognition of the user's preferences (Michalczak 2016, pp. 96–97).[2]

The above described philosophical discussion may turn out especially useful during the analysis of the theoretical and legal standpoints which forward look to the extend to postulate constitutional rights and obligations for the "strong" intelligence treated in a way comparable to treating human beings. It should be realized that if the artificial intelligence is assigned with status of a moral subject and legal subject (person), then the question of the rights deriving from such subjectivity will have to be considered. Even if now the problem seems quite futuristic, when the "strong" intelligence comes into being, it will become another challenge, not only for philosophers and ethicists but also for lawyers.

Taking an ontological perspective, one cannot exclude the possibility that intelligent machines (or hybrids of a robot and human being) with intelligence level higher than the human one, will become beings "in itself and for itself", or even a kind of new species—*robo spapiens* (Menzel and D'Aluisio 2001). If such happens, will the immoral act against a man be considered equally immoral against robot?

Stepping away from purely philosophical discussions, some simply pragmatic arguments stand in favor of legal subjectivity of some kinds of intelligent machines and programs. It is especially relevant in terms of autonomous cars, autonomous weapons (to be discussed in greater detail in the further parts of the chapter), stock exchange programs and algorithms referring to data mining. Detailed analysis of the possible models for the legal personality of machines goes beyond the scope of this chapter and requires a separate publishing adventure (see, for example, Michalczak 2016, pp. 115–144).

There is a need to recognize the legal subjectivity of artificial intelligence. One of the signs is the proposal to introduce term "electronic person" (in reference to the most advanced autonomous robots) into the legal language brought up in the European Parliament Resolution of 16 November 2017 with recommendations to the Commission on Civil Law Rules on Robotics (2015/2103 (INL)). Introduction of such term to the language of law will have to be accompanied by the answers to many detailed questions: will the "electronic person" be capable of legal liability?, will the status of the "electronic person" be assigned to the programs without physical presence?, will the currently used notions of "damage", "guilt", "intent", "negligence" be adequate when addressing "electronic persons"?, will the

[2]As a side note, it is worthy to mention that some philosophers believe the artificial intelligence is not capable of reaching a high level of autonomy or intelligence because it operates based on the program designed by someone and as such it is programed from outside. Even if the programs provide for some behaviors which could be considered autonomous, they only operate by following some predefined instructions. Thus, a machine cannot "think." It cannot possess "free will." It only simulates the autonomy (acts as if it was autonomous), at the same time it does not replicate the autonomy (it is not autonomous in its essence) (Searle 1984, p. 29; Searle 1992, p. 53).

institutions such as "self-defense", "necessity" or "mistake" be applied to this kind of subjects? Finally, will the "electronic person" be guaranteed rights of the accused (convicted) in the possible criminal procedure, such as "the right to remain silent" or "right to defense" in the formal sense?

Assuming we will grant artificial intelligence legal personality, it will also become crucial to establish the consequences that the "electronic person" can bear as a result of its "wrongful" actions. The necessity to establish the liability rules for robots was advocated already in 1992 by Leon E. Wein. This creator of cybernetics warned that "these computerized systems may make correct decisions where a human specialist would not, and vice versa." (Wein 1992, p. 114). In addition, the intelligent machine is no longer only a medium for information processing, it became for example an active member of the market processes (Allen and Widdison 1996, p. 26). The cognitive skills of the AI allow for taking individual decisions which also supports the necessity to grant it the legal status. AI can recreate (or at least simulate to recreate) the actions which—if conducted by humans—would be considered as the proof of their "free will" (Allen and Widdison 1996, p. 27).

If robots are assumed to be able to act outside of the designed algorithm, it leads to serious consequences such as redefinition of "perpetration." Some authors consider the need to apply punishments for the robots which cross the norms established for them. They note that machines in the early stage of their development will be in a position equal to those of children where responsibility for their actions is borne the parents. However, the childhood stage passes, and moment comes where you take responsibility for your own actions (Matthias 2008).

The establishment of legal responsibility rules become even more significant when one realizes that machines evolve to be not only more intelligent but also more and more accessible. The establishment must be completed before the robots start to make their own autonomous, legally important decisions about "life" and "death," that is, before they acquire their agency (Braidotti 2014, p. 112).

One cannot forget about an essential issue of liability of scientists who deal with artificial intelligence (Jonas 1996). Technological progress demands creation of macro ethics of co-responsibility that reaches far beyond the conventional morality. Modern technology brought to a much brighter light new activities, objects, and consequences that the traditional ethics frames can no longer comprehend (Jonas 1996, p. 30). Dissemination of the "heuristics of fear" postulated by Hans Jonas may come useful. It orders, in a first place, to consider the worst possible consequences of the planned actions, even if the best intentions are hidden behind them. Heuristics of fear should lead to the situation where the decisions taken are directed by the responsibility for future generations, including those who are not born yet (Jonas 1996, pp. 71 and 76).

5 On the Influence of Artificial Intelligence on Various Social Life Spheres

The relations between humans and machines became interesting for the social sciences (especially psychology and sociology) in the second half of the twentieth century, where together with computers came the era of "intelligent machines." This happened less than decade before the IBM introduced the world to the personal computer. It was back then when the fear firstly appeared that computer-based technologies are not socially neutral because they re-define information, knowledge and culture and they create new social relations patterns (Zuboff 1984). Computer was the first smart machine which prolonged or empowered some brain functions (such as calculations, processing, outside auxiliary storage etc.) (Krzysztofek 2011, p. 76).

Personal computer (as a desktop, then laptop, notebook, palmtop and recently smartphone or tablet) has gained human dimensions and became *amicus familiae*, who "knows" everything, does not fail and creates the feeling that the surrounding world can be understood (Krzysztofek 2011, p. 76). Computer became the tool making it possible to even "free" people (Naisbitt 1984, p. 26). It contributed to the establishment and development of the school of social thought known as Actor-Network Theory which fully explains relations between humans and technologies, including the relations between a man and a machine (Krzysztofek 2011, p. 77).

The humans-machines social relations get even more complicated with the development of "weak" artificial intelligence and the progress in designing the "strong" one, as well as with the inevitably approaching moment of "technological singularity."

Modern computer technologies already have a great impact on individual as well as economic, political, and cultural lives of local and global societies. They bring up questions about the future of democracy and humanity. MIT and Harvard University announced the initiative called "Ethics and Governance of AI Initiative" (https://aiethicsinitiative.org/) which deals directly with the influence of artificial intelligence on the individual and collective lives (Barabas et al. 2017). The above-mentioned Actor-Network Theory adopted a revolutionary assumption of subjectivity (agency) of so-called non-humans including computers and machines and it examines the humans-machines relations in their network.

In deliberations on the influence of artificial intelligence on the human future, special concerns address the perspective of the AI merger with the human nerve system. Scientists warn that it can lead to the end of democracy and to the concentration and domination of one authority over the global society. Special chips placed in human body will not only monitor the mental and physical state of the person, but they will also be able to influence this state. "If every human being will be properly chipped and their nerve system or even their brain will be included into some global network, it can be easily predicted that sooner or later someone will want to take control over it". In this way it will be possible to gain direct access to the power over individuals and entire societies. "These are threats that take us to the universe of

'1984', that is the Orwell universe where one can possess very strong instruments of control over everything" (Vetulani 2018b).

However, before it happens, artificial intelligence in modern democracies should be also considered in the light of election campaigns threats. It should be clear that technological tools in the fake news era can be used to manipulate the opinions and emotions of the voters through the image and sound. Such manipulation supports the antidemocratic movements in their march for power. These movements will be given tools to track and compromise political opponents (Lindenberg 2018, p. 133).

The influence of artificial intelligence on the social life is obvious not only in the world of politics. Technology enters into every other sphere of human activity, including the spiritual one. In turn, it again impacts the politics (through electoral manipulation addressed above). In the debates on the condition of humanism and in relation to the omnipresent technology, philosophical pessimism prevails. We live in times which Neil Postman describes as "technopole," when technology starts thinking for the humans. "Technopole deprives us of social, political, historical, metaphysical, logical or spiritual attitude enabling the recognition of information and statements completely unreliable" (Postman 2004, p. 76). We should notice that artificial intelligence today can already create not only untrue information but also fake photos or films (the Nvidia program). It can be said that the era of "post-truth" has only just begun. Excess of information, mostly trivial and sensational contribute to the "information chaos." It induces the state of internal dispersion. It leads to the ethical loss. People lose the ability to distinguish important information for the unimportant one and they no longer feel the need for a deepen reflection upon them (Sztalt 2017, pp. 279–280). According to Postman, technology does not only begin to "think" but also to "feel" and "live" for people (Postman 2004, p. 68). The current state of human mind but also the current state of culture relies on "deification of technology which means that culture seeks instruments in technology, finds satisfaction in technology and takes orders from it" (Postman 2004, p. 91). Modern relation between people and technology deals with crossing the borders of what is "human" in the broad social and cultural context.

Some believe that gradual transformation of technology occurs—from the role of a supporting element in human life to the role of impersonal manager of this life (Wadowski 2018, pp. 23–39). There comes a risk that in the technocratic social order people will eventually lose their intellectual and spiritual attributes and as a result, they will become part of the impersonal reality of the "mega machine" predicted already half a century ago by Lewis Mumford (Mumford 2011, 2014).

The massive artificial intelligence so far functions in accordance with the rules introduced by humans, rules such as need for the diminished physical and mental effort. The limitless success in the field of quantity progress cause socially negative consequences. The mechanical view of the world puts pressure mainly on the quantity as if the quantity criterion could influence any choice made (Bostrom 2016, p. 504). The reality is perceived through other measurable parameters such as speed, strength, endurance. At the same time, the reality becomes shallow. The main aim of life is the cult of everything that is external (the way that people and their technological gadgets look like) (Wadowski 2018, pp. 33–34). An impersonal society is born where individuals no longer feel the need for direct, inter-personal relations and for individual experience of truth, good and beauty. The visual culture is to weaken the imagination by suggesting prepared patterns to be copied in all spheres. The higher values and ideas are being replaced by what is useful, practical, serves to satisfy interests and comes helpful in the competitions, rivalry that contributes to the success. The value of wisdom expressed in the desire for the recognition of essence of essences is no longer adequately appreciated (Szyszkowska 2014, pp. 18–20).

The moral sensitivity seems to vanish as well. This can lead to "the introduction of practical cynicism and to radical, antidemocratic division of society into those who possess particular 'powers' including financial ones and those who willingly or unwillingly have to become slaves of the techno system of the human exploitation" (Wadowski 2018, p. 37).

Modern technologies already provide possibility of precise control over society by its government. The entire western world is equipped with cameras, microphones and digital methods for tracing information and individual lives partly becoming an emanation of the Bentham's "Panopticon" idea (Bentham 1791). In the ethical discourse attention is drawn to the threats to the individual and social political freedoms associated with artificial intelligence. It is underlined that soon total invigilation will be possible, invigilation that is far more perfect that the one designed by Orwell in "1984".

The beginnings of such tracing power over society can already be observed. For instance, in China, where the Smart Eye system is being implemented, by 2020 it may align views transmitted from millions of cameras equipped with AI technology creating highly sophisticated video surveillance system (Denyer 2018; Velghe 2019). This system already enables precise tracing of each Chinese citizen. A smartphone informs about the localization of a person. Then the AI's ability to identify people by biometric features (e.g., the appearance, face, walking manner, etc.) or analyzing human emotions may prove its high efficiency. When connected with the capacity of eavesdropping and analysis of the conversations (including phone ones), reading of the Internet posts, emails, and messages—it provides an opportunity to know everything about everybody.

Another system known as "Social Credit System" is concurrently tested in China. It allows to gratify or reprimand people depending on their behaviors (Lindenberg 2018, p. 134). It is to come into full operation by 2020. According to the "The Guardian" by the end of 2018 some 23 million citizens were punished, 17.5 million were banned from buying airplane tickets, another 5.5 million were not allowed to buy train tickets. Even the lightest violation of law (such as occupying reserved seats on a train) causes penalties (Kuo 2019). In other words, as Larry Backer argues, the controlling system creates comprehensive data-driven structures for management by algorithms that can produce real time reward-punishment structures for social-legal-economic and other behaviors (Backer 2018, p. 127).

The Social Credit System as any other program in the artificial intelligence sphere will most probably cross Chinese border. However, other arguments should be considered pointing that the Social Credit System may serve as a reference system for the scientists in other countries. It may bring valuable observations for the evolutions of such systems in the Western countries (Sithigh and Siems 2019, pp. 1–2). Full picture is also complete when considering the arguments voiced by Chinese experts advocating for example that that "system has been designed to promote open and inclusive social governance, to involve more actors in the process of social governance, and to boost social governance efficiency while promoting healthy competition in Chinese market economy" (Zhengjie and Bei 2019) or that it "comprises disciplinary technology that rewards those who are honest, trustworthy and virtuous, while punishing those who display signs of dishonesty, corruption and deception is alleged by the Chinese government to be a necessity in fixing moral decay and bringing about a virtuous state of social harmony in China" (Wong and Dobson 2019, p. 221). As in any debate, but especially in the debates concerning sensitive, yet fundamental issues, the pursuit for the truth encompassing both sides' arguments should result in a more balanced view (Ahmed 2019, p. 54).

There is no doubt that China is a major driver of AI surveillance technology in the world, but its leading role should not totally eclipse the developments undertaken by other governments. As the Steven Feldstein report on "The Global Expansion of AI Surveillance" shows, American technology in the field is present and used in thirty-two countries worldwide (Feldstein 2019, p. 8). Liberal democracies are major users of the AI surveillance and their governments are deploying a range of surveillance technology such as city platforms but also facial recognition cameras. Western democracies are not free from scandals and evidences of the human rights abuses. The Echelon or Pegasus eavesdropping systems controversies, the revelations resulting from the Snowden affair can serve as widely known examples. The necessity to guarantee people's safety (for instance from the terrorists) is commonly present. It serves as the excuse for implementation of AI instruments which may violate fundamental human rights. Potential threats are then highly speculative and impossible to verify. Thus, the essential price for the "increased level of safety" is high and the proportionality principle between the protected and sacrificed goods is not always applied. At all times however, it is associated with the resignation from some rights and freedoms (Mamak 2017, p. 192). The key element determining the purpose and rationale behind the use of AI technologies is the quality of governance provided by the country that implements them. The autocratic states, as shown in the quoted above Feldstein's report, will be prone to abuse the technology and apply it for the mass surveillance purposes (Feldstein 2019, p. 2).

Other flagship issues taking us from the science fiction world to the real one, are the already appearing practical ethical dilemmas dealing with the introduction of autonomous cars and possible use of autonomous weapons in the battle fields (Sharkey 2007).

In his technological prognosis, Toby Walsh announces that soon infrastructure oriented to the needs of individual driver will disappear. With time, the nowadays common ability to drive a vehicle will also vanish, just as during fifty years of the twentieth century the ability to ride a horse vanished almost completely. Already today, in big agglomerations citizens give up driving and possessing own cars. Walsh states that in the end, due to safety requirements in traffic, individual driving will be prohibited, and the global communication infrastructure will provide for the people's commuting. It will aim to reduce the number of accidents in ground communication. Gradually, new autonomous wheel vehicles "drive out from the labs." Legislations are tested to manage the traffic, for the time being, in the regions carefully selected for the experiments (Ford 2016, pp. 191–201).

Numerous axiological arguments stand in favor of the autonomous vehicles to be introduced into the traffic. It could not only increase the comfort of those in the traffic. Full automatization would lead to the increased safety on the roads and in general. Autopilots have already proved it right by making the air flights much safer. Although computer programs may also make mistakes, they make them more rarely that human drivers (Simonite 2013).

Next to the safety argument there is the economic effectiveness argument also showing some axiological color. Elimination of the salary payment for the drivers would provide enormous savings for the business (Michalczak 2016, p. 118). Due to the traffic automatization the property problems will no longer exist as cars will be subscribed. There will be less of them in the streets and the positive effects for the environment are certain.

The key moral problem in the car automatization deal with responsibility question. Who and based on what rules will bear it if the cars driven by automatic programs will make mistakes? So far it has been agreed that the software developer will take responsibility for the potential failure as he/she provides for the set of rules to be applied in the driving. Everything changes however with the presence of "machine learning" where the program learns to solve the problems of achieving many goals of safe driving, through the perception of the surrounding, risk calculation, probability of the arrival to destination and the consequences of the undertaken decisions. With time, the machine gains "experience" and its source code changes comparing to the one written by a person in the first place. In such situation it is difficult to decide who is guilty. Other problems arise concerning the following question: in what way should the automatic vehicles be programed to make sure they make morally proper choices when deciding about the scope of collision on the road, or even about saving one man's life over the other.

This is the moment to refer to the famous philosophical dilemma known as the "trolley problem" (Cathcart 2014). Hannah Fry describes the experiment in the new version with the driverless car: "Imagine some years into the future, you are a passenger in an autonomous vehicle, happily driving along a city street. Ahead of you a traffic light turns red, but a mechanical failure in your car means you're unable to stop. A collision is inevitable, but your car has a choice: should it swerve off the road into a concrete wall, causing certain death to anyone inside the vehicle? Or should it carry on going, saving the lives of anyone inside but killing the pedestrians now crossing this road?" (Fry 2018, p. 164). With reference to the moral dilemmas of the trolley driver one can ask: who should the autonomous vehicle hit if the collision is inevitable—two kids or three older ladies? The essential question is whether autonomous cars should have the option of killing their passengers to save the pedestrians? (Mamak 2017, p. 94). Those are of course examples that could occur in the thinking speculations. From the philosophical and ethical perspective, potential consent to take away one life at the cost of saving another can be found in the ethics of utilitarianism and consequentialism. It will certainly not be found in the sanctity of life ethics. Ethics of religious provenance do not allow the possibility to valuate human life as each life is saint and inviolable (Breczko and Breczko 2018, pp. 1–24).

Another problem widely discussed among ethicists is the problem of using the autonomous weapons in the armed conflicts. The fundamental question here is whether the use of war robots to deprive human lives can be morally justified at all? In modern discussions we come across strong resistance to any use of autonomous lethal technologies. Their critics say that the attacks by pilotless aircraft have no moral legitimization under any circumstances. They argue that the autonomous weapons may become instrument of terror and the despots and terrorists will be able to use it against innocent civilians without any ethical limits. Once opened, the "Pandora box" will be difficult to close. It cannot be allowed to happen. That is why, in 2012 a group of engineers, philosophers and activists established the International Committee for Robot Arm Control (ICRAC) headquartered in Berlin (Germany). It calls for the total prohibition for the use of autonomous weapons and for the need of human supervision over artificial intelligence. Similar works in the field are carried out in the United Nations (Autonomous weapons that kill must be banned, insists UN Chief 2019), and NATO (Tonin 2019).

Some ethicists voice out arguments pointing to the positive sides of the prospective use of autonomous military technologies. They consider the kinds of conditions that must be met for such use to be morally justified. The issue of subjectivity and liability already discussed in this chapter would also be of key importance here (Arkin 2009; Sharkey 2010; Kopeć 2017). Equally important is the question of the moral norms that the machines would have to be implemented with.

Ethical dilemmas referring to the potential admission of artificial intelligence to the military actions can be found in many detailed problems. One of them deals with the question whether autonomous weapons will not make war killing too easy? It will be done without direct human involvement. Some armies already possess remote-controlled autonomous instruments of armed conflicts. They aim by using the sensors and can function without human intervention (for example Samson Remote Controlled Weapon Station used by the Israeli army). Most of the military technologies that are in the creation process are to wage war from maximum distance (without direct participation of people). Will this type of distance killing not turn out to be easier during regular traditional war?

Most of the drone operators claim it is impossible. They try to convince that the "distance killing" requires a different, more demanding level of rigor and perfection than during traditional war. More sophisticated equipment is also necessary. A complicated, multitask structure of this type of military actions is supervised by many specialists and controllers: officers, intelligence analysts, military law experts (Braidotti 2014, pp. 246–247). There is however reasonable doubt whether these assumptions are correct. Psychological research and practice indicate that the further the distance from the aim of the attack, the easier decision to launch it. The "blurry" concept of responsibility and feeling of impunity are not without significance.

Some are convinced that wars with the use of autonomous robots will eventually become a fact anyway. They try to find ethical arguments favoring the rationale for the use of autonomous means of warfare. The basic axiological justification comes from the reflection that there will be robot soldiers, not human soldiers killed in the war. In addition, the machines will in practice cause less evil than people. They will precisely locate the target. They will not rape women, torture prisoners, kill civilians or take wrong decisions under pressure (Braidotti 2014, pp. 246–247). Those machines will sometimes have to make very difficult choices, for example if to cannonade the targeted building when there are civilians inside? To take morally right decision they must have the moral system implemented into their algorithms. Since 2007, the U.S. Department of Defense has been working on such system. It also designed the "road map" for the development of the autonomous military combat systems. According to the map, until 2032 the Department will proceed to extend the systems' capabilities to take autonomous actions to accomplish complex missions in the dynamic circumstances. General Paul J. Selvy was quoted in 2016 saying that it will take at least ten years to create a fully autonomous robot that will independently take decisions on who and when to kill (Braidotti 2014, p. 137). Along with the development of autonomization, artificial intelligence will be able to decide not only about the defense actions (this is already happening), but also about offensive measures. Departure from classical war toward the war waged by artificial intelligences will cause threats not only in reference to the judgment of necessity and proportionality of operations. The learning machines nowadays beat masters of the given game and try to achieve the goal (win the game) at any cost, they seek total annihilation of the opponent playing by the "winner takes it all" rule. If such mechanism is used during the "new" war by the AI, it will become a danger to people who can be treated as ethical limitation hindering or preventing from winning.

Another level of the AI modern engagement in the military actions is its use in the new battlefield—cyberspace. Such cybernetic war may lead to the complete paralysis of the opponent's infrastructure, information gathering (the Stuxnet virus) or propaganda conducting.

Common implementation of the intelligent weapon systems has become real and close enough that in July 2018 over 2000 specialists and 10 AI firms signed an agreement that they will not participate in the development of the autonomous weapons, nor will they support its production or trade because the control power over human life cannot be left to the machine (Braidotti 2014, p. 137). The establishment of the "Stop Killer Robots" movement reflects social concerns in this sphere (Sharkey 2010).

Some research centers however decide to actively participate in the global arms race concerning autonomous weapons using artificial intelligence. The Korea Advanced Institute of Science & Technology (KAIST) located in the Republic of Korea may serve as an example. KIST together with the Hanwha Group (one of the largest military industries in South Korea) established the Research Center for the Convergence of National Defense and Artificial Intelligence. The aim of the Center is to develop AI technologies to be used in military armament and to join the global competition in the field of autonomous weapons production. In reaction, fifty-seven scientists from thirty countries in the world where advanced AI research is carried out, addressed a letter calling for a total boycott of all forms of cooperation with KAIST (Vetulani 2018a).

Moving to the economic aspects of the artificial intelligence functioning, it should be underlined that AI can be a threat to the consumer freedom. Using the machine learning and data mining technology companies are already able to profile groups of clients and prepare perfectly fitting marketing campaigns. AI is also a big and growing field for remarkably profitable business. In such business, just like in any other, some unethical operations occur, the grey sphere is there. It may happen that under the guise of rationality, quality of life improvement and "unquestionable" technological standards, the technology is spread without confrontation with the actual good-making for people. Unimaginable financial profits are hidden there which may encourage pathological actions. There is also a risk that the governance being at the disposal of private corporations, will try to impose its own interpretation of the AI directions upon the society and this interpretation will not fully comply with the currently binding human rights standards.

Martin Ford, entrepreneur from the Silicon Valley draws attention to the morally important issue connected with the development of information-based technology. Its success was possible because of engagement of masses of people and organizations. Most research facilitating the progress was financed by the US taxpayers. According to Ford, the key moral question now is this: should access to profits generated by innovation be available to the public or only to the selected elite of those who work on the development of AI? Who should keep the moral right to take over the power over the capital gathered by the entire society? Ford points out that further progress in AI field depends on future innovations. Relevant division of funds is necessary to achieve them. The reflection on the big disproportions in earnings seems essential (Ford 2016, pp. 91–92). Reaching deeper in these considerations, another question may be asked: how will this influence the accomplishment of the sustainable development?

While discussing the economic problems relying to AI, the possibility of the massive loss of jobs by people should be noted as machines will take over the employment where the work is based on the automatic, repeatable acts. Social consequences should be considered as well. Prognosis state that 2050 perspective is the time when almost everything that is done by humans at work now will be done by the robots. The McKinsey Global Institute (consulting firm) evaluates that with the currently existing technology one third of all the works connected to professional activities could automatized (Lindenberg 2018, p. 112). Several arguments support this evaluation: robots are perfectly carrying out the assigned tasks, they are cheaper, they are not paid salaries, there are no additional costs relating to their work such as holidays, benefits, or trainings. The findings of the Institute suggest that in the predictable scenario of slower changes—by 2030 every fourth worker will lose his/her job in the United States, Japan, and Germany. We can assume that in Poland in the next dozen or so years every fifth working person will be replaced by the artificial intelligence.

Martin Ford claims that our "judgment about automatization which according to majority is a threat to poorly educated and low qualified workers" will also change soon (Ford 2016, p. 12). We should be prepared that a lot of jobs will simply disappear. Those will be not only jobs with routines (that is in manufacturing, trade, services, or transportation). It concerns most of the works falling within the paradigm of zero-ones, rules, schemes, and strict guidelines. Information-based technology is already pushing the lawyers, journalists, or pharmacists off the job market (Ford 2016, p. 13). In the future these will be professions only a few will be privileged to have. Upcoming perspective of common automatization of work will inevitably relate to radical change in the job market and social relations (Vetulani 2018b).

In the visions effused by economists, full automatization of work would probably result in the minimal guarantee income paid to non-working people from the public budget. There would be much more free time that could be spent on things that entertain us, please us, interest us. Such change seems quite tempting, but it would require a total reorganization of social life and reconfiguration of culture based on professional achievements. Psychologists are concerned that most of us would not deal well in such situation. Instead of taking up creative activities, intellectual pleasures or physical exercises, people would spend their free time in front of the computer or with a smartphone in their hand sunk in the virtual reality. It can be easily imagined what kind of psychological and psychical destruction would follow the change. Certainly, the number of people suffering from addictions, depressions and other civilization diseases would increase. The suicide statistics would go up. It can be predicted that the need of education would vanish. Education would be unnecessary to make money. The current school system—as a transmission path from "child" to "worker" would be useless. The vision of "common idleness" caused by systematic use of AI for any work can be intriguing and frightening at the same time. One thing is certain. Possible scenarios connected with the development of artificial intelligence and robots demand deep analysis focused on the prognosed social effects, also from the ethical perspective.

The above introduced examples of the AI influence on the social life show that robots become not only "new slaves," gadgets, play partners but also workers or even to some extend—members of the human society. As a result, one must consider what does it mean for the future of not just politics, economy, private life, human work, or social education but for the future of humanity itself?

The benefits-costs balance of the technological expansion in every life dimension may prove to be disadvantageous from the perspective of human moral sensitivity. Human functioning in the reality designed by highly advanced technology can lead to changes in the hierarchy of values, violations of human rights, equality, dignity, autonomy, justice, right to privacy etc. Advantages deriving from the use of innovative solutions may paradoxically become threats to the existence of entire society as much as to the human being in individual dimension. Therefore, the ethical reflection on the artificial intelligence is of such significance not only in general terms but in terms of establishment of ethical codes filled with values that machines are to serve for.

6 On the Need for Artificial Intelligence Ethical Codes

There is no doubt that only societies with proper level of ethical development can use artificial intelligence in the responsible manner. Humans created AI and they cannot allow it to turn against them. The need to comply with ethical codes by persons engaged in the processes of designing and improving AI seems essential along with the establishment of ethical standards to be followed by the intelligent machines. Cooperation among engineers, philosophers, ethicists, lawyers, and political decision-makers is crucial (Braidotti 2014, p. 113).

Deliberations on the AI ethics were initiated during the 2017 Conference of AI Researchers organized in Asilomar, California. Basic rules were discussed there to be used by the creators of the new information-based technologies. It was established that the aim of the research should not be the creation of "undirected" intelligence but of the intelligence which will be useful to humans. Safety would become the main value. It is important for the artificial intelligence systems to be properly secured throughout their operational time so if a failure occurs, the origins of it can be traced. The designers and constructors of the advanced systems are morally responsible for their use, abuse, and the consequences because they are the ones with possibility to shape those consequences. The compatibility of the AI tasks and functions with human values articulated for instance in the Universal Declaration of Human Rights is crucial. The systems should be designed and used in accordance with principles of respect for human dignity, rights, freedoms, and cultural diversity. They are to respect privacy allowing individuals to access, edit and mine their data. Using artificial intelligence to control private information cannot limit human freedom in any unjustified way. The AI technologies should be used for the good and support of possibly biggest number of people. Economic welfare produced thank to AI should be distributed so to bring benefits to all humanity. People should have control over artificial intelligence, they should not let social processes to be undermined and they should contribute to the improvement of society's functioning. Superintelligence should be developed exclusively to serve the shared ethical ideals and with benefits to entire humanity (Lindenberg 2018, pp. 193–198).

The 2030 Agenda for Sustainable Development with its goals should be another guideline source for the progress in AI technology. The AI for Good platform is an important UN initiative to become the place for meetings and discussions involving organizations, entrepreneurs and decision-makers who contribute to formulate global strategies to ensure trusted, safe and inclusive development of AI technologies and equitable access to their benefits (United Nations Activities on Artificial Intelligence 2018, p. VII).

UNESCO focuses, among other things, on elaboration of ethical norms and standards concerning AI with participation of various stakeholders. One particular goal is to achieve "fairness, accountability, transparency, gender equality, cultural diversity in AI, to ensure that AI-driven decisions respect human dignity and protect fundamental human rights" (United Nations Activities on Artificial Intelligence 2018, p. 28) and further to reflect it in the normative solutions.

Another organization is the United Nations Interregional Crime and Justice Research Institute. Based on the support provided in 2017 by the Municipality of The Hague and the Ministry of Foreign Affairs of the Netherlands the Institute established Centre for Artificial Intelligence and Robotics (CAIR). The CAIR seeks to advance knowledge and understanding of the potential implications of AI and robotics for crime prevention, criminal justice, as well as law enforcement and national security, focusing on both possible risks and benefits (United Nations Activities on Artificial Intelligence 2018, p. 39). This will become the basis for the discussions and proposal of the policies or legal frameworks that may be required to address the potential associated risks. The above actions comply with the Sustainable Development Goal No. 16. (that is peace, justice, and strong institutions).

There is a common consent in Europe as to the need of ethical conduct code in robotics. Such postulate derives from the already mentioned European Parliament Resolution including recommendations for the European Commission on civil law rules on robotics (2015/2103(INL)). The code is to become basics for the obedience of fundamental ethical rules beginning in the phase of programming, construction, testing and finally to the phase of robots' development.

In the works on the ethical codes addressed to artificial intelligence key role is played by the research carried out in the framework of so called "machine ethics." In the research the main feature is to equip robots in the ability to distinguish good from evil and to decide on responsibility principles in case of their failure. It should also be established who is at fault if the machine makes wrong decision: the designer, the programmer, the operator or maybe the machine itself? Assigning responsibility requires to run a precise log system that would allow tracing the thought-process connected with the decision making as one of the elements of so-called white boxes. It has been agreed (and it seems very legitimate) that ethical systems created for robots must consider solutions that would be most appropriate for people.

In the research on machine ethics the techniques used in experimental philosophy become useful and indicate the way people deal with ethical dilemmas. The "moral machine" project is realized on the grounds of machine ethics and it attempts to test whether it is at all possible to abstract universal ethics based on the number of particular persons' choices. The aim is to examine what is it that directs people's moral choices, what are their moral preferences and hidden stereotypes. The project is to help in searching answer to the question about the particular way of programming for example autonomous vehicles. Although the machine cannot be "taught" universal ethics, it can be equipped with knowledge on tendencies typical in the solutions of moral dilemmas chosen by human individuals. Such tendencies deal with preferring human life over animal life, life of young people over life of elderly and declared desire to save more (rather than less) number of human beings. Machine learning systems each time take decisions based on an overly complex information processing based on this data. It seems that the algorithms typical for supervised or reinforced machine learning (with significant participation of a person as an expert for example) would be helpful.

Implementation of the machine with particular rules of conduct (of the moral norms, international law norms or EU law norms) is the point of departure. It is also necessary to establish in what way people can control artificial intelligence's actions and if the currently existing proposals provide for enough protection against "unauthorized" decisions made by machines. It should be examined if the advantages of autonomous robots (such as higher speed, precision, fast analysis of big amounts of data, lack of subjectivism burden) allow for their actual control.

It turns out that the "laws of robots" formulated by Isaac Asimov in 1942, prohibiting machines to hurt people and humanity and demanding subordination to human orders are not enough when met by the modern level of AI development and its autonomy (Asimov 1993, 2014). They did not take under consideration fundamental rules of coexistence based on the "principle of mutual respect." Today artificial intelligence should be explicitly subordinated to people and their rights, considering the increasing interest in the possibility to use thinking machines in wars.

Nevertheless, the recommendations addressed by the European Parliament to the European Commission reflect Asimov's laws in the "harmfulness principles" stating for priority meaning of the protection of human health and life. The resolution refers to the imperative interest of human being, its autonomy and justice. Protection of human rights relates to the necessity to respect human dignity, protection of private and family life, safety guarantee, protection of personal data, intellectual property, freedom of speech and information, solidarity, civil rights, and justice administration. It is to provide the individual and humanity rights to self-determination. Research on robotics should be carried out according to principle of caution. Potential consequences should be foreseen for safety and proper caution measures should be applied proportionally to the required level.

7 Conclusions

From the axiological perspective, artificial intelligence that does not threat people should follow the law, be ethical and solid. Artificial intelligence "worth of trust" should meet some conditions. The "human supervision" is the basis. Artificial intelligence systems are to support people and promote fundamental human rights. Algorithms are to be safe and reliable enough to deal with failures or inconsistencies during all stages of life cycle of the AI systems. Individuals (citizens) should have full control over their own data and be assured that they will not be used to harm them or discriminate them. They should be granted transparency. People must be aware that they come into interactions with artificial intelligence systems (Kuchta 2019).

In addition, artificial intelligence should not only be trustworthy but also "nice" ("friendly") to people and other live beings. It is to make choices in the interest of everybody and operate without increasing any harm, it is to self-educate and to transfer its system of value to the next generations (Yudkowsky 2001). For the artificial intelligence to be "trustworthy" and "friendly" it is above all crucial to design ethical guidelines dealing with its development and use.

As the final comment, a promising perspective coming from the European Union should be brought into light.

In 2018 the European Commission established High-Level Expert Group on AI which began working on such kind of guidelines. They are to build trust toward artificial intelligence. Only when the trust is built will the society be able to fully use the new technology. Ethical dimension of artificial intelligence is not an addition, it is the fundament. Ethical artificial intelligence can be used for everybody and be directed toward human rights. The European Union values constitute its axiological foundations. Ethical artificial intelligence will most of all act in accordance with law and provide for: the leading and supervisory role of people, stability and safety, protection of privacy and data, transparency, diversity, non-discrimination and justice, social and environmental welfare, responsibility. The Commission aims to take this approach while addressing artificial intelligence ethics on the global level. It is legitimate as technologies and algorithms have no limits, nor barriers. In April 2018 the Group presented Ethics Guidelines for Trustworthy Artificial Intelligence (https://bit.ly/3fN7cvn). According to the Guidelines, the trustworthy AI should be lawful (respecting all applicable laws and regulations), ethical (respecting ethical principles and values) and robust (both from a technical perspective while considering its social level).

In 2018 the UN Secretary General introduced a special Strategy on New Technologies to "define how the United Nations system will support the use of new technologies like artificial intelligence, biotechnology, blockchain, and robotics to accelerate the achievement of the 2030 Sustainable Development Agenda and to facilitate their alignment with the values enshrined in the UN Charter, the Universal Declaration of Human Rights, and the norms and standards of international law".

Creation and fostering of the collaborative, transparent networks for essential international dialogs laid the ground for the establishment of the AI and Global Governance Platform by the Centre for Policy Research and the United Nations University (Kong et al. 2019).

The United Nations is a natural forum for the global discussions concerning global problems. The discussions may and do turn into more substantive tools available based on the powers given to the UN by its Member States. It is only with those powers and close collaboration that the modern societies may face challenges and share benefits of the most advanced technologies, including the artificial intelligence.

References

Ahmed, S. (2019). Social cities and the limits of the social credit system. In N. D. Wright (Ed.), *Artificial intelligence, China, Russia, and the global order*. Alabama: Air University Press.

Allen, T., & Widdison, R. (1996). Can computers make contracts? *Harvard Journal of Law & Technology, 9*(1), 26–52.

Arkin, R. C. (2009). *Governing lethal behavior in autonomous robots*. Chapman and Hall.

Asimov, I. (1993). Zabawa w berka [Runaround]. In I. Asimov (Ed.), *Świat robotów [The complete robot] t. 1*. Warszawa: Varia-APD.
Asimov, I. (2014). *Roboty i imperium [Robots and Empire]*. Poznań: Rebis.
Backer, L. C. (2018). Next generation law: Data-driven governance and accountability-based regulatory systems in the West, and the social credit regimes in China. *Southern California Interdisciplinary Law Journal, 28*, 123–173.
Barabas, Ch., Dinakar, K., Ito, J., Virza, M., Zittrain, J. (2017, December 21). Interventions over predictions: Reframing the ethical debate for actuarial risk assessment. *Proceedings of Machine Learning Research*, Forthcoming. Retrieved from https://bit.ly/2WtJRY0
Bentham, J. (1791). *Panopticon*. Dublin: Thomas Byrne.
Bostrom, N. (2016). *Superinteligencja. Scenariusze, strategie, zagrożenia [Supreintelligence. Paths, dangers, strategies]*. Gliwice: Helion.
Braidotti, R. (2014). *Po człowieku [The Posthuman]*. Warszawa: PWN.
Breczko, A., & Breczko, A. (2018). Ethics and the challenges of the contemporary world (selected problems). In M. Ventura (Ed.), *Ethics: Past, present and future perspectives*. New York: Nova Science Publishers, Inc.
Brynjolfsson, E., & McAfee, A. (2015). *Drugi wiek maszyny. Praca, postęp i dobrobyt w czasach genialnych technologii [The second machine age: Work, progress, and prosperity in a time of brilliant technologies]*. Warszawa: Mt Biznes.
Cathcart, T. (2014). *Dylemat wagonika. Czy zrzuciłbyś grubego faceta z kładki? Zagadka filozoficzna. [The trolley problem, or would you throw the fat guy off the bridge? A philosophical conundrum]*. Warszawa: PWN.
DeBaets, A. M. (2014). Can a robot pursue the good? Exploring artificial moral agency. *Journal of Evolution and Technology, 24*, 76–86.
Denyer, S. (2018, January 7). Beijing bets on facial recognition in a big drive for total surveillance. *Washington Post*. Retrieved from https://wapo.st/3cIzANe
European Parliament Resolution of 16 February 2017 with recommendations to the Commission on Civil Law Rules on Robotics (2015/2103(INL)).
Feigenbaum, A., & Feldman, J. (Eds.). (1997). *Maszyny matematyczne a myślenie [Computers and thought]*. Warszawa: PWN.
Feldstein, S. (2019). *The global expansion of AI surveillance*. Washington: Carnegie Endowment for International Peace.
Ford, M. (2016). *Świt robotów. Czy sztuczna inteligencja pozbawi nas pracy? [Rise of the robots: Technology and the threat of jobless future]*. Warszawa: CDP.pl.
Fry, H. (2018). *Hello world. Jak być człowiekiem w epoce maszyn? [Hello world: How to be human in the age of the machine?]*. Warszawa: Wydawnictwo Literackie.
Good, I. J. (1965). *Speculations concerning the first ultraintelligent machine*. Academic Press Inc.
Hellström, T. (2013). On the moral responsibility of military robots. *Ethics and Information Technology, 15*(2), 99–107.
Jonas, H. (1996). *Zasada odpowiedzialności. Etyka dla cywilizacji technologicznej [The imperative of responsibility: In search of an ethics for the technological age]*. Kraków: Platan.
Kaplan, J. (2019). *Sztuczna inteligencja. Co każdy powinien wiedzieć [Artificial intelligence: What everyone needs to know]*. Warszawa: PWN.
Kasperski, M. (2003). *Sztuczna inteligencja [Artificial intelligence]*. Gliwice: Helion.
Kass, L. (2002). *Life, liberty and the defence of dignity*. San Francisco: Encounter Books.
Kong, J. Y., Burzynski, R., Weber, C. (2019). *AI&Global governance platform: How should UN agencies respond to AI and big data*. AI&Global Governance Articles&Insights. Retrieved from https://bit.ly/2T0UgbC
Kopeć, R. (2017). Etyka robotów bojowych [The combat robot ethics]. *Studia Humanistyczne AGH, 16*(2), 51–62.
Krzysztofek, K. (2011). Interakcje człowiek-komputer-robot z perspektywy nauk społecznych [Human- computer-robot interaction from the perspective of social sciences]. *Pomiary. Automatyka. Robotyka, 3*, 76–82.

Kuchta, M. (2019). *Sztuczna inteligencja powinna być zgodna z prawem, etyczna i solidna [Artificial intelligence should be legal, ethical and robust]*. AI. Business blog. Retrieved from https://bit.ly/2AqevZP

Kuo, L. (2019, March 1). China bans 23m from buying travel tickets as part of "social credit" system. *The Guardian*. Retrieved from https://bit.ly/2Z3JJjG

Lindenberg, G. (2018). *Ludzkość poprawiona. Jak najbliższe lata zmienią świat, w którym żyjemy [Humanity corrected. How the coming years will change the world we live in]*. Kraków: Otwarte.

Łupkowski, P. (2005). Rola etyki i antropologii w rozważaniach o sztucznej inteligencji [The role of ethics and anthropology in the consideration of artificial intelligence]. *Ethos, 1*(2), 239–251.

Mamak, K. (2017). *Prawo karne przyszłości [Penal law of the future]*. Warszawa: Wolters Kluwer Polska.

Matthias, A. (2008, August 1). Strafrecht für Robert, Menschen sollen für eigene Fehler haften. *Spiegel Wissenschaft*. Retriever from https://bit.ly/3dHHaYK

Menzel, P., & D'Aluisio, F. (2001). *Robo Sapiens. Evolution of a new species*. Cambridge: The MIT Press.

Michalczak, R. (2016). Podmiotowość agentów programowych w ujęciu teoretycznoprawnym Rozprawa doktorska [Subjectivity of programme agents in theoretical and legal terms. Doctoral dissertation]. Uniwersytet Jagielloński, Kraków. Retrieved from https://bit.ly/2WUaXql

Minsky, M. L. (1982). Why people think computers can't. *AI Magazine, 3*, 4.

Muehlhauser, L., & Salomon, A. (2012). Intelligence explosion: Evidence and import. In A. Eden et al. (Eds.), *Singularity hypotheses: A scientific and philosophical assessment*. Berlin: Springer.

Mumford, L. (2011). *Mit maszyny t. 1 [Myth of the machine vol. 1]*. Warszawa: PWN.

Mumford, L. (2014). *Mit maszyny t. 2 [Myth of the machine vol. 2]*. Warszawa: PWN.

Naisbitt, J. (1984). *Megatrends: Ten new directions transforming our lives*. New York: Warner Books.

Postman, N. (2004). *Technopol. Triumf techniki nad kulturą [Technopoly: The surrender of culture to technology]*. Warszawa: Wydawnictwo MUZA S.A.

Przegalińska, A. (2017). Transhumanizm - kierunki i perspektywy [Transhumanism - directions and perspectives]. *Filozofuj, 6*(18), 9–11.

Różanowski, K. (2007). Sztuczna inteligencja. Rozwój, szanse i zagrożenia [Artificial intelligence. Development, opportunities and threats]. *Zeszyty Naukowe Warszawskiej Wyższej Szkoły Informatyki, 2*, 109–135.

Russell, S., & Norvig, P. (2009). *Artificial intelligence. A modern approach* (3rd ed.). New York: Pearson.

Searle, J. R. (1984). *Minds, brains, and science*. Cambridge: Harvard University Press.

Searle, J. R. (1992). *The rediscovery of mind*. Cambridge: MIT Press.

Sharkey, N. E. (2007, August 18). Robot wars are a reality. *The Guardian*. Retrieved from https://bit.ly/2y25sxn

Sharkey, N. E. (2010). Saying 'No!' to lethal autonomous targeting. *Journal of Military Ethics, 9* (4), 369–383.

Shead, S. (2016, June 19). Sztuczna inteligencja to najważniejsza z obecnie rozwijanych na świecie technologii [Artificial intelligence is the most important technology currently under development in the world]. *The Business Insider*. Retrieved from https://bit.ly/3cxfSEl

Simonite, T. (2013, October 25). Data shows Google's robot cars are smoother, safer drivers than you or I. *MIT Technology Review*. Retrieved from https://bit.ly/3cwSqHh

Sithigh, D. M., & Siems, M. (2019). The Chinese social credit system: A model for other countries? (January 11, 2019). EUI Department of Law Research Paper No. 2019/01. Retrieved from https://ssrn.com/abstract=3310085

Solum, L. B. (1992). Legal personhood for artificial intelligences. *North Carolina Law Review, 70*, 1231–1287.

Soniewicka, M. (2018). *Selekcja genetyczna w prokreacji medycznie wspomaganej. Etyczne i prawne kryteria [Genetic selection in medically assisted procreation. Ethical and legal criteria]*. Warszawa: Wolters Kluwer Polska.

Stylec-Szromek, P. (2018). Sztuczna inteligencja - prawo, odpowiedzialność, etyka [Artificial intelligence - law, responsibility, ethics]. *Zeszyty Naukowe Politechniki Śląskiej, 123*, 501–509.

Sztalt, K. (2017). Moralne dylematy kultury współczesnej [Moral dilemmas of contemporary culture]. *Humanistyka i Przyrodoznawstwo, 23*, 273–288.

Szyszkowska, M. (2014). *Człowiek uwikłany. Ideały jako drogowskazy [An enangled man. Ideas as signposts]*. Białystok: Kresowa Agencja Wydawnicza.

Szyszkowska, M. (2017). *Etyka*. Białystok: KAW.

Thiel, S. (2015, October 1). Why the human brain project went wrong - And how to fix it. *The Scientific American*. Retrieved from https://bit.ly/2WtvF1m

Tonin, M. (2019). 2019: Artificial intelligence: Implications for NATO's armed forces. Draft Report to NATO Parliamentary Assembly. Retrieved from https://bit.ly/2WZl3Go

Torrance, S. (2013). Artificial agents and the expanding ethical circle. *Artificial Intelligence and Society, 28*(4), 399–414.

Turing, A. M. (1950). Computing machinery and intelligence. *Mind, 49*, 433–460.

United Nations Activities on Artificial Intelligence (AI), International Telecommunication Union 2018. Retrieved from https://bit.ly/3dKZ5hk

United Nations, Autonomous weapons that kill must be banned, insists UN chief. Retrieved from https://bit.ly/35Z7FGp

Velghe, P. (2019). "Reading China" The Internet of things, surveillance, and social management in the PRC. *China Perspective, 1*, 85–89.

Verbeek, P. P. (2011). *Moralizing technology. Understanding and designing the morality of things*. Chicago: University of Chicago Press.

Vetulani, Z. (2018a). *Dokąd zaprowadzi nas Sztuczna Inteligencja [Where the artificial intelligence will lead us]*. Retrieved from https://bit.ly/2LubauY

Vetulani, Z. (2018b). *Czy czeka nas totalitaryzm [Will totalitarianism await us]*. Retrieved from https://bit.ly/2Anjzhv

Vinge, V. S. (1993). The coming technological singularity. How to survive in the post human era. NASA. Lewis Research Center, Vision 21: Interdisciplinary Science and Engineering in the Era of Cyberspace.

Wadowski, J. (2018). Człowiek i technologie. Od techniki, która służy człowiekowi do służby technice [Man and technology. From technology that serves man to service to technology]. In M. Lipowicz (Ed.), *Po człowieku? Między kryzysem a nadzieją [Man over? Between the crisis and hope]*. Kraków: Wydawnictwo WAM.

Wein, L. E. (1992). The responsibility of intelligent artifacts. Toward an automation jurisprudence. *Harvard Journal of Law & Technology, 6*(1), 103–154.

Wong, K. L. X., & Dobson, A. S. (2019). We're just data: Exploring China's social credit system in relation to digital platform ratings cultures in Westernised democracies. *Global Media and China, 4*(2), 220–232.

Yudkowsky, E. (2001). *Creating friendly AI 1.0: The analysis and design of benevolent goal architectures*. Retrieved from https://bit.ly/3fUbLV5

Zhengjie, F., & Bei, Z. (2019). *The truth and reality of China's social credit system*. Retrieved from https://bit.ly/2WXGYO6

Zuboff, S. (1984). *In the age of the smart machine*. New York: Basic Books.

Aneta Breczko holds a doctoral habilitation degree. At present, she works as Professor and Head of the Department of Theory and Philosophy of Law at the Faculty of Law of the University of Bialystok (Białystok, Poland). She is the author and co-author of over 90 publications, including two monographs, several textbooks, edited books and scientific papers. Her main scientific interests include the issues related to bioethics, biojurisprudence and biolaw. Her research work focuses on the legal personality of individuals (regarding problems such as biogenesis, biotherapy and biothanatology) and the legal implications of biotechnological progress in medicine and ethical dilemmas arising from the use of Information Technology and Artificial Intelligence in this area. Her analysis and considerations refer to several controversies connected to reproductive genetics and human enhancement; her research work also examines animal rights and occupational deontology. E-mail: breczko@uwb.edu.pl.

Wojciech Filipkowski is an Associate Professor of Law and Criminology, Head of Forensic Laboratory, Department of Criminal Law and Criminology, Law Faculty, University of Bialystok (Białystok, Poland), Scientific Secretary for cooperation with western states of the International Center of Criminological Research and Expertise. He specializes in the use of new technologies by law enforcement, special services and justice system. Recent interests focus on criminal intelligence analysis, predictive policing and artificial intelligence. Author and co-author of over 150 publications in Poland and abroad. E-mail: wojciech.filipkowski@gmail.com.

Izabela Kraśnicka holds a doctoral habilitation degree in law and works at the Department of Public International and European Law at the Faculty of Law, University of Bialystok (Białystok, Poland). Her research fields include public international law, legal system of the United States, as well as the developments of the legal education and higher education systems. She has authored over 70 scientific articles, book chapters and edited books in her fields of interests. Dr hab. Kraśnicka runs international relations of the Faculty and directs the Legal Centre of Research on Education. E-mail: krasnicka@uwb.edu.pl.

From Wonders as Crime to Forensics in Service of the 2030 United Nations Agenda

Emil W. Pływaczewski, Ewa M. Guzik-Makaruk, Wojciech Filipkowski, and Emilia Jurgielewicz-Delegacz

Abstract This chapter aims to present only selected methods of detection, securing, and analysis of forensic traces, namely, genetic tests and polygraph tests. They illustrate the development of forensic techniques and, at the same time, outline the legal problems associated with their use by the judiciary to make them more effective. The chapter also does not avoid pointing out the dilemmas we face that need to be resolved to achieve the UN 2030 Agenda goals.

Keywords Forensic science · UN 2030 Agenda · Criminal investigation

1 Introduction

Every event that interferes with reality changes reality; consequently, *vice versa*. There is no behavior that leaves no traces. This also applies to traces of committed crimes, i.e., those of forensic significance. Maybe at a given moment our knowledge, the level of development of science, and the technology do not yet allow for effective detection, securing, and analysis of every such change. However, we almost constantly hear about new scientific achievements that broaden our perception of reality and can bring benefits to the justice system (Pływaczewski 2017, pp. 267–326), e.g., through effective detection of the offender and holding him or her responsible.

Methodologically correct detection, securing and investigation of a forensic trace makes it possible to perform basic functions of forensic science, such as identification of a trace and its carrier, verification of the investigative version, recreating the course of events and the role of individuals in them, and defining the *modus operandi* (Jagiełło 2019, pp. 87–91). Initial techniques related to detection of traces of crime can be assessed today as primitive, sometimes even based on magic or other

E. W. Pływaczewski · E. M. Guzik-Makaruk · W. Filipkowski (✉) · E. Jurgielewicz-Delegacz
University of Białystok, Faculty of Law, Department of Criminal Law and Criminology, Białystok, Poland
e-mail: e.plywaczewski@uwb.edu.pl; ewa.guzik@uwb.edu.pl; w.filipkowski@uwb.edu.pl

H. Kury, S. Redo (eds.), *Crime Prevention and Justice in 2030*,
https://doi.org/10.1007/978-3-030-56227-4_18

"miraculous" methods. However, over time, the development of the society and, above all, of science and technology, changed the way in which crime that poses a threat to proper, sustainable development of the society can be detected. With the UN 2030 Agenda in mind, it should be emphasized that in many of the areas covered by the Action Plan, abuse or crime can occur, so that effective fight against crime is not covered by only the 16th goal. If one intends to combat such threats to sustainable development effectively, this cannot happen without supporting the development of forensic science. In this way, even the most difficult, complex, and unsolved criminal cases will be resolved. However, it will not be due to chance or miracle, but rather to modern forensic techniques.

2 St. Nicholas' Balm and the Birth of Forensics

The cult of the relics of St. Nicholas dates to the beginning of the eleventh century.[1] It started with the discovery that a kind of pearl liquid with a beautiful fragrance and healing properties emerged from the relics that were the remains of the saint (specifically, his bones). It was called the manna of St. Nicholas. During a mass held on 9 May each year (once the relics have been moved to Bari (present Italy) from Myra (present Turkey), the rector of the basilica, in the presence of the archbishop of Bari, takes about 3 glasses of the manna through an opening in the sarcophagus with a special ladle. Then the bishop blesses the gathered believers with an ampoule containing the relic. Pilgrims visiting Bari Temple can take a small ampoule containing a small amount of the miraculous substance dissolved in holy water. Believers can use it to sprinkle on ill parts of their body or as a drink. After transferring the relics from Myra to Bari, the phenomenon did not cease. It can be considered a miracle, which is hard to be explained by contemporary science although several studies have been conducted.

The therapeutic properties of the manna have also attracted the attention of criminals. Between about 1630 and 1659, a cunning woman from Sicily named Tofana or Tofania sold poison in ampoules with an engraved inscription "St. Nicholas's manna from Bari."[2] Her customers were women who were "tired" of their husbands, and the poison she offered was supposed to be a miraculous antidote to this "ailment"—to put it in a euphemistic way. In 1709, her activity was discovered as she was betrayed by one of her customers (Cullen 2008, pp. 169ff.). All of this was disclosed as a result of an extensive investigation by the Italian authorities in Naples, which involved the use of torture. Other sources say that the distribution was carried out by an entire organized group of wise women and their court process took place in Rome in 1659 (Dash 2017, pp. 63–69). Nevertheless, the name *Aqua Tofana*

[1]https://en.wikipedia.org/wiki/Saint_Nicholas.

[2]Word "Aqua Tofana," The Encyclopedia Britannica Or Dictionary of Arts, Science and General Literature, 7th Edition, Volume III, Adam And Charles Black, Edinburgh 1842, p. 313.

(or water from Palermo) has become a general term for all kinds of poisons that are difficult to detect and have a slow effect on the victim's body. The name covers all poisons of this type, regardless of whether they were based on arsenic mixed with the herb named cymbalaria or arsenic with lead and belladonna (cf. Trestrail 2007, p. 7; Gibson 2012, pp. 131ff.).

Nowadays, we do not need to refer to testimonies of witnesses and repentant criminals, or resort to torture. Thanks to the development of various sciences, including toxicology, criminal proceedings are much more effective than in earlier times. Forensic science tries to use the achievements of natural sciences, exact sciences, and social sciences to detect crimes and identify their perpetrators. Poisons can be identified even when little evidence is available, sometimes even many years after a crime, e.g., murder by poisoning, was committed. This also applies to other types of traces, e.g., biological traces, which enable identification of a person by genetic code or by behavior or characteristics of his or her body. We also reach deep into human memory in search of emotions accompanying crimes. The things that investigators can nowadays do in criminal trials would in the past seem to be miracles.

3 Development of Crime Scene Detection Techniques

Traces are secured and detected mainly at the scene of the incident, but also in forensic laboratories. Their typology is the subject of considerations undertaken in the literature on the subject. Most commonly, crime traces are divided into memory, material, and phenomenal traces. However, forensic science is a living science and, therefore, its research area is constantly changing. It must keep pace with social changes, scientific and technological progress, and the changing nature of crime. Since the late 1990s, criminals have taken advantage of the development of cybernetics by moving their activities into cyberspace. Their every action in an ICT system leaves some traces and, therefore, the classical division of traces of crimes needs to be expanded by adding the new category of digital traces (Kasprzak et al. 2015, pp. 56–57).

All traces are a rich source of information about crimes and their participants. The specific way of analysis of the place of the event and of the traces left there makes it possible to reconstruct the most likely course of the event, in accordance with the reality (Jagiełło 2019, p. 94). Forensic science experts take advantage of the results of research conducted in various fields of knowledge for the administration of justice, but also conduct their own research in selected areas (Adam 2012, p. 29).

UNODC, through its Laboratory and Scientific Section,[3] aims to achieve three major goals as far as forensic science is concerned. First one is to improve the national forensic capacity and capabilities of Member States to meet internationally

[3]For more details see: https://www.unodc.org/unodc/en/scientists/index.html.

accepted standards. The second is to ensure the worldwide availability and accessibility of internationally accepted standards. The third one is to increase the use of forensic science services, data and information for evidence-based operational purposes, strategic interventions and policy and decision-making. All the appropriate activities are conducted in partnerships with international organizations, national forensic bodies, associations of forensic science institutes, and leading drug analysis and forensic science experts.

3.1 Biological Traces Using the Example of DNA

Biological traces are directly connected with the so-called forensic biology, which in turn relates to the problem of research on the human genome and its huge role in detecting perpetrators of crimes. According to the encyclopedia, the word "genome" comes from the Greek language and means a complete set of genetic information of a given organism, and the human genome is a complete set of genetic information of a human being.[4] Genomics, on the other hand, is a science dealing with the study of entire genomes and the analysis of the functioning of genes contained in them,[5] while genetics is a science dealing with the study of heredity and variability of organisms.[6] An analysis of the entire human genome is currently underway, with the aim to provide the basis for early clinical interventions. However, the results of such research are also extremely important to the field of forensic science as one of the detection techniques allowing for identification of humans (or other living organisms).

The breakthrough DNA imaging method known as "genetic fingerprint" was discovered by the molecular biologist Sir Alec Jeffreys in 1985. Colin Pitchfork was the first ever criminal to be convicted, based on DNA analysis, of murder and rape of a minor on 21 November 1983 in the small village of Narborough in the County of Leicestershire, UK. In 1988 he was sentenced to life imprisonment (Grzywacz 2013, pp. 6–7).

The results of genetic and genomic tests may contribute to the achievement of material truth, even in closed cases, which after many years are successfully returned to law enforcement agencies. One example of this in the very famous case of Tomasz Komenda who was wrongly sentenced in 2004 in a valid verdict of the Appellate Court in Wrocław to 25 years in prison for alleged rape and murder of 15-year-old Małgorzata K. in Miłoszyce near Wrocław.

On 16 May 2018, the Supreme Court acquitted Tomasz Komenda[7] based on a number of newly prepared expert opinions, including one of key importance: an

[4]Word "genom," www.encyklopedia.pwn.pl/szukaj/genom.html.

[5]Word "genomika," www.encyklopedia.pwn.pl/szukaj/genomika.html.

[6]Word "genetyka," www.encyklopedia.pwn.pl/szukaj/genetyka.html.

[7]Verdict of the Supreme Court - Criminal Chamber of 16 May 2018, file no.: V KO 26/18.

interdisciplinary opinion.[8] The research in the field of DNA mitochondrial polymorphism carried out by the Department of Forensic Medicine of the Nicolaus Copernicus University in Toruń made it possible to exclude the convicted Tomasz Komenda from the set of possible perpetrators of the crime. On the other hand, forensic genetic experts examined the evidence secured at the scene of the event, where—as a result of a detailed examination in natural and artificial light—substances (not previously identified) were found; they later underwent detailed tests aimed at detecting the presence of blood peroxidosis, human blood, acid phosphodose—one of the components of human semen, the specific prostate antigen PSA—one of the components of human semen, and semenogelin—one of the components of seminal fluid. The samples with positive results were then subjected to DNA extraction. The DNA extracts obtained in this manner were further examined and the results were described. They clearly indicated at least two persons, which did not include the convicted Tomasz Komenda himself. The disclosure of a significant number of identifiable biological traces and the fact that none of them could be traced back to Tomasz Komenda clearly proved that he was not present at the crime scene at the critical time. Thus, he could not have committed the crime that he was accused of.[9]

The operations of the so-called X Archive are also worth mentioning. Teams charged with investigating unresolved homicide or crime cases (the so-called *cold cases*) operate at regional police headquarters in Poland and deal with resolution of crimes for which investigations have been discontinued due to the failure to detect the perpetrators. The teams are made up of forensic and investigative staff, some of whom have undergone specialist training at the US Federal Bureau of Investigation facilities. Their activity brings considerable results in solving criminal puzzles from the past, also thanks to the use of modern detection methods.

What can be done based on the current advances in biotechnology was unthinkable at the time of many criminal acts in the twentieth century. The task of genetics in forensic science is to identify criminals by comparing their DNA profiles (stored in a database or taken for comparison) with those identified at the crime scene. DNA tests are a technique that is used very often in criminal investigations nowadays. A thorough analysis of biological material found at the crime scene often makes it easier for representatives of law enforcement agencies to identify the perpetrator.

In Polish literature, there are many publications describing various aspects of genetic expert opinions in terms of forensic techniques and its identifying function (cf. Hołyst 2007, pp. 959ff.; Tomaszewski 2010, pp. 81ff.; Furman-Łajszczak 2011, pp. 95ff.). They mainly concern the issues of securing, storing, and performance of identification tests based on the non-coding part of DNA (Białecka et al. 2010, pp. 63ff.). The literature also extensively describes the history of this research in

[8]This opinion was rightly called interdisciplinary, because its edition was attended by anthropologist, specialist in forensic medicine, dental prosthetist, and specialist in the field of virtual engineering.

[9]Verdict of the Supreme Court - Criminal Chamber of 16 May 2018, file no.: V KO 26/18.

Poland, which resulted from the gradual familiarization of researchers with new methods of analysis of genetic material resulting from the development of genetics, as well as the growing acceptance of this research method in the scientific community itself and among decision-makers in law enforcement agencies (Słomski 2010, pp. 37ff.; Tucholska-Lenart 2010, pp. 49ff.).

At the same time, with the development of genomics, the interest of forensics is shifting to the coding part of DNA (Wójcikiewicz 2010, pp. 96ff.). Discovery of the genes responsible for certain group characteristics gives new opportunities in forensic tactics. This is particularly important to building of forensic versions of the perpetrator, the victim, and the possible witnesses of an incident where there is no comparative testing material (Sygit, Sadowska 2010, pp. 7ff.). In early stages of investigation of a case, biological traces containing genetic code may carry the first information about the characteristics of unknown participants of the event, whose DNA profiles (in the non-coding part) are not in the database and have not been assigned to specific individuals. In this way, they make it possible to narrow down the circle of persons likely to relate to the event in question based on the group characteristics that have been identified. This role is important until comparative testing material is obtained, which will enable individual identification of the people (Filipkowski et al. 2016, pp. 615–629; Filipkowski et al. 2018, pp. 77–101).

Thanks to the progress of genomics we know which genes contain information about such physiological features of the body as (Sygit and Sadowska 2010, p. 12) sex, pigmentation of the skin, eyes, and disorders of neurotransmission factors associated with schizophrenia, addictions (alcohol, nicotine), susceptibility to depression, impulsiveness, or aggressiveness. It seems a matter of time when learn the rules and the location of coding of other characteristics of the human body.

It is worth noting that international legal protection of the human genome has been an issue handled by the United Nations and, to a greater extent, by the Council of Europe. As a result of the works conducted by the UN, the Universal Declaration on Human Genome and Human Rights was unanimously adopted on 11 November 1997 at the 29th session of the General Conference of UNESCO.[10] On the other hand, the Parliamentary Assembly of the Council of Europe has presented a number of recommendations, including ones on bioethics issues related to the genome. These include Recommendation 1160 (1991) on the preparation of the Bioethics Convention and Recommendation 1512 (2001) on the protection of the human genome by the Council of Europe. The so-called Bioethics Convention—Council of Europe Convention No. 164 for the protection of Human Rights and Dignity of the Human Being with regard to the Application of Biology and Medicine: Convention on Human Rights and Biomedicine of 4 April 1997, signed in Oviedo, Spain, plays an important role in this respect.

Particularly important are recent reports from the USA. The President Donald Trump administration is moving to collect DNA samples from hundreds of

[10]http://www.unesco.org/new/en/social-and-human-sciences/themes/bioethics/human-genome-and-human-rights/.

thousands of people booked into federal immigration custody each year and to enter the results into a national criminal database, an immense expansion of the use of technology to enforce the nation's immigration laws (Dickerson 2019). A US government plan to routinely collect DNA data from immigrants in federal custody is sparking concerns among scientists about privacy and discrimination. The move, announced on 2 October by the Department of Homeland Security, would see DNA profiles of all immigrant detainees stored in an FBI database originally created to help law-enforcement agencies solve violent crimes. The department is still developing regulations that would govern the expanded testing. More than 40,000 people are currently being held in detention centers across the country. Proponents of the move say the information could help solve crimes, allowing law-enforcement officials to cross-reference the genetic profiles of immigrants with unidentified DNA recovered from crime scenes. But bioethicists say that the efforts will wrongfully target an already vulnerable population. Access to DNA information could put immigrants at risk of privacy violations and genetic discrimination (Wessel 2019).

Such actions may have a bad effect on Global Compact for Orderly, Safe and Regular Migration. The Global Compact for Safe, Orderly and Regular Migration (GCM) is an intergovernmentally negotiated agreement, prepared under the auspices of the United Nations, that describes itself as covering "all dimensions of international migration in a holistic and comprehensive manner."[11]

3.2 *Memory Marks Using the Example of the Polygraph*

Memory traces (called ideal traces) seem to be very fleeting and susceptible to deformation. They are the result of specific experiences and remain in the memory of a human being (witness, suspect) (Kasprzak et al. 2015, p. 56). They can be defined as changes in the nervous system caused by a momentary stimulus that lasts for a certain amount of time. They represent sensations related to perception, experience, or action. In practice, these traces are usually revealed during an interrogation and recorded in a report from the interrogation. Ideally, the interrogated person should not feel compelled or particularly encouraged to testify—in such a situation he or she will most likely disclose as much detail as possible. But how can one be sure that the interrogated person does not manipulate his or her memories or even deliberately lie? From the very beginning of our civilization, people have been aware of benefits that can result from discovery of the method of lie detection. Therefore, they looked for ways to develop a method or tool to detect them (Vicianova 2015, pp. 522–534).

For example, the Chinese believed that the emotional tension caused by a lie is reflected in physiology, causing cessation of salivation. Therefore, people accused of crimes had to take a handful of dry rice in their mouths. After questioning, they spat

[11]Global Compact for migration, https://refugeesmigrants.un.org/migration-compact.

it out and if the rice was still dry, the person was considered a liar. The African tribes, on the other hand, used a sorcerer who sniffed the accused person during a dance and made a verdict based on their smell. In medieval times, women were judged as to whether they were unfaithful by putting a finger to their wrist and measuring the pulse. The names of their potential lovers were read out, if the pulse would accelerate when the name of the actual lover was read. As years passed and the methods evolved, the assumption remained the same: a person shows physiological symptoms when telling lies. Only technological development made it possible to create a machine that records physiological parameters related to emotional stimulation that can occur when someone tells a lie.

This device is a polygraph, also called a lie detector. The first modern lie detection device called Lombroso's Glove was created in 1881 by an Italian criminologist and anthropologist Cesare Lombroso. He attempted to measure changes in the accused person's blood pressure which were recorded on a graph or chart. It is also worth mentioning that the so-called "Polygraph" was in existence at least as early as 1906. Its invention, of course, was not for lie detection purposes but rather for use in medical examinations. Nevertheless, it did contain the essential features of the present-day instruments and its construction was based upon precisely the same principles. The inventor of the first polygraph was James Mackenzie, a famous heart surgeon of London. He first described the instrument in an article entitled "The Ink Polygraph," which appeared in 1908 in the British Medical Journal (Inabau 1953, p. 679). The technology was improved on during the First World War by William M. Marston (a Harvard psychologist) and was elaborated into its final version. This device served to record changes in blood pressure and changes in breathing while giving testimony (Trovillo 1939, pp. 848–881). In 1922 in Journal of Experimental Psychology (Widacki 2016, p. 89) a Police Officer for Berkeley (USA)—John Augustus Larson described a psychiatric device called "cardio-pneumo psychograph" (Weber 2008, p. 63) also known as a polygraph or a lie detector (Lewis and Cuppari 2009, pp. 85–92). This polygraph recorded respiratory rate, blood pressure changes, and changes in galvanic skin response (bioelectric reactivity of the skin). This polygraph was improved by his assistant, Leonard Keeler. The year 1935 was when the era of a modern lie detector, built by Leonard Keeler, started. This is considered to have initiated the development of polygraphy. Since then, each year has brought improvements in the technology and the research methodology.

Nowadays, in the context of the current practice and the potential of polygraphic examinations, their usefulness manifests itself in several main areas: personnel procedures (preemployment, explanatory, and disciplinary examinations, and preventive control of officers of uniformed services), criminal procedure, examination of persons providing assistance to competent authorities in operational and exploratory activities (so-called loyalty tests), therapeutic procedures (examination of persons with sexual preference disorders and addictions), and preventive supervision (monitoring of the risk of recidivism) (Gołaszewski 2016, pp. 8–9).

However, the above description of the usefulness of the use of the polygraph was accompanied by some legal concerns. This is because there was a conflict between the use of this device and the suspect's or accused person's right to refuse to provide explanations. After all, such persons are not obliged to cooperate with law enforcement or judicial authorities and provide evidence of their guilt or innocence (these rules are formulated differently depending on the legal system).

As an example, Poland currently prohibits the use of technical means influencing the mental processes of interrogated persons or aimed at controlling the unconscious reaction of their bodies (lie detectors, polygraphs) in connection with interrogations. However, a polygraph may be used by an expert witness with the consent of the examined person to limit the set of suspects (Article 192a § 2 of the Code of Criminal Procedure—CCP), as well as during examination by an expert witness only with the consent of the examined person (Article 199a CCP). In 2015, the Polish Supreme Court[12] formulated several main theses and further guidelines that for the first time comprehensively regulated issues related to the evidentiary use of polygraph examination in the Polish criminal process. The Supreme Court thus dispelled any doubts about the possibility of conducting a polygraph examination of a suspect (accused person) or a witness by allowing (based on Article 199a of the CCP) such evidence in the form of an expert witness's report, both as incriminating and relieving evidence. On the other hand, Article 192a(2) of the CCP, which lists "the technical measures to control unconscious reactions of an organism," provides that it concerns tests for elimination (reduction of the set of suspects) or selection of evidence in the form of disclosed traces, whereas the person examined in this case may even be a person of still undetermined procedural status and whose examination with the use of a polygraph is justified by the circumstances of the event.

The Supreme Court also made it clear that a polygraph is not, therefore, a test of truthfulness or a lie detector. Evidence from an opinion of an expert witness in the field of polygraph examinations is indirect evidence—i.e., evidence which leads only to findings on the basis of which conclusions about the main fact can be drawn by way of a reductive reasoning (e.g., fingerprints or biological traces left on the weapon used to commit a crime first lead to identification of the person who left these traces, and elimination of the possibility that these traces were left in other circumstances than in connection with committing a given crime make it possible to prove guilt in relation to a specific crime). Indirect evidence concerns so-called "evidence facts" (circumstantial evidence) (Gołaszewski 2016, p. 10).

The concerns related to use of polygraph examination results are due, among others, to the possible disturbances in the polygraph examinations. The factors that may disturb polygraph examinations include psychological and somatic, physiological, and pathological, objective and subjective, and internal and external factors. Moreover, results of polygraph examinations may be falsified by mechanical imitation of symptoms of stress (e.g., muscle tension, intentional changes in breathing), using mental switching off for the duration of the test or evoking exciting images, or by behavior involving deliberate throat clearing, swallowing of saliva, and moving around when key questions are asked. The external factors that can influence

[12] Decision of the Supreme Court of 29 January 2015, file no. I KZP 25/14, Orzecznictwo Sądów Polskich 2015, vol. 12, issue 121.

polygraph examinations include noise, lightning, and accidental noise generated by the expert (e.g., coughing). Therefore, one must keep in mind that polygraphs only record physiological changes that accompany emotions and the cause of those emotions needs to be determined during the proceedings. It is important to bear in mind that there are no specific emotions and reactions that are characteristic only of a lie. Thus, changes registered with a lie detector must not be so simply associated with insincerity. Therefore, it must be stated unequivocally that a polygraph is not a device that can be used for instrumental detection of lies. The method that does not raise any objections in the practical application of polygraphs in criminal proceedings is the study of the knowledge of the reality of the *modus operandi* (Gruza 2011, p. 13). Also, polygraph examinations are particularly useful in confrontational, multi-subject, complex cases and for verifying a suspect's (Herbowski 2014, pp. 5–6) alibi.

One of the measures implemented to eliminate errors in this type of examinations, was preparation of the rules for performance of polygraph examinations. The rules define the standards of international (American Polygraph Association, ASTM International) and national (including the Polish Polygraph Examination Society) professional and standardization organizations. Moreover, the various state institutions in which polygraph examinations are performed must comply with internal instructions and regulations governing the performance of such examinations (Gołaszewski et al. 2018, p. 164).

Concerns are raised by polygraph examinations in many countries. Until the 1970s, some Western European countries treated them equally with hypnosis and narco-analysis, and considered all these methods as unacceptable (Herbowski 2013, pp. 11–12). Nowadays, Western Europe has not been favorably disposed in general toward polygraph examinations. After the fall of communism and the end of Soviet domination in the region that took place, many Central and Eastern European countries have their own—though not widely known—body of scientific work and practical experience with polygraph examinations.

The attitude toward polygraph examinations is changing in Western countries as well (Widacki 2007, pp. 5–6). It ranges from a significant role in the judicial system in Belgium (e.g., in 2017 Belgium was the European country with the most prevalent use of polygraph testing by police). For instance, Spain is where the use of polygraph testing has apparently never been suggested. In the Netherlands, the outcome of polygraph test is neither used as evidence in court, not in police investigations. In the United Kingdom, polygraph testing is not used in criminal law either. In the Nordic countries, only Finland has used the polygraph on relatively large scale. The Finnish National Bureau of Investigation has used it in around 300 cases since 1995, mostly homicides and sexual crimes. The NBI is the only institution within the Finnish police using the polygraph, primarily to give direction to the investigation. Norway and Sweden are only modest users of the polygraph. In Switzerland, the use of the polygraph is considered an unlawful means of investigation (Meijer and van Koppen 2008). As of 2017 the German Supreme Court (*Bundesgerichtshof*) had rejected use of polygraphs (Meijer and van Koppen 2008, pp. 31ff.). In Canada there is leading

Supreme Court of Canada decision *R. v. Béland* (1987)[13] where the Court rejected the use of polygraph results as evidence in court. In 2010 the Supreme Court of India declared use of narcoanalysis, brain mapping and polygraph tests on suspects as illegal and against the constitution if consent is not obtained and forced (Mahapatra 2010). Article 20(3) of the Indian Constitution states: "No person accused of any offense shall be compelled to be a witness against himself." Polygraph tests are still legal if the defendant requests one.

The home of the polygraph is the United States. A substantial portion of the scientific studies fundamental to polygraph research was also conducted there and the results have been published in American scientific and specialist journals. Finally, the United States host the largest organization in the world for persons involved in various aspects of polygraph examinations—the American Polygraph Association. In the United States, these tests are mainly allowed at the pre-litigation stage as part of police detection activities. However, the admissibility of a polygraph test is not universal in all criminal cases. There are some states that find the results of polygraph tests completely inadmissible, and those that allow their admission with the stipulations of both parties. This means that both the suspect and the prosecutor have agreed to admit that the test results are evidence.

Asia is without a doubt the second continent—after America—in which the polygraph has entered permanent practice and is the subject of scientific research. The widespread use of polygraph examinations is well-known in Israel and Japan. It is popular also in Singapore, Malaysia, and Taiwan. However, for example the Israel Supreme Court has not taken a direct stand on the admissibility of polygraph results, polygraph tests have never been used as evidence in Israeli criminal courts (despite their extensive usage by the Israeli Police) (Saxe and Ben-Shakhar 1999, pp. 203–223; Ben-Shakhar et al. 2002, pp. 203–223). The use of polygraph examinations in Latin America is also known (Widacki 2007, pp. 5–6).

4 Forensic Detection Technique and the UN Agenda 2030

The dynamic development of pathological phenomena threatening the society, including serious crime, requires multifaceted actions to be taken not only locally, but also regionally and globally. Without them, achieving sustainable development objectives would be difficult, if not impossible. On the other hand, the "miracles" brought by forensic science may turn out to be extremely useful in these activities.

One of the basic functions of forensics is the detection function. It focuses on direct detection of a crime and then on the identification of its perpetrator. It is also closely related to one of the basic objectives of forensic science, namely the detection of an event, a person or persons, a thing or a mechanism leading to occurrence of or changes in specific phenomena based on traces. The forensic

[13]The decision available at: https://scc-csc.lexum.com/scc-csc/scc-csc/en/item/250/index.do.

detection process should be defined as all activities (search, disclosure, ascertainment) of criminal law enforcement authorities aimed at disclosing an event defined at a given stage of proceedings as a crime and at obtaining information that will make it possible to make a hypothesis concerning a person in a legally relevant causal relationship with that event, and then to establish the data pertaining to that person and, as a result, to ensure his or her security, and to collect preliminary materials making the hypothesis of the perpetration of that person plausible in such a way as to justify the commencement of the evidentiary process. It is the level of training of law enforcement officers and the availability of technical solutions that determine the selection and use of forensic methods and techniques for a specific process and a specific criminal case. Forensic technology, i.e., the disclosure, preservation and analysis of traces and material evidence, is of fundamental importance in the evidentiary process, while tactics is the most important in the detection stage (Jagiełło 2019, pp. 3–12).

Therefore, detection methods are being developed taking into account the unique characteristics of the different categories of crime, which are often targeted at the legal values described as objectives to be achieved under the UN Agenda 2030, e.g., environment, human security, non-discrimination, justice, etc. It is obvious that perpetrators of murder, theft, and computer crimes are detected using different methods (Zubańska 2019, pp. 81–150).

The means and methods used by law enforcement authorities in the detection process can be divided into: explicit (e.g., interviews, questioning of persons, various inspections, use of a tracking dog) and classified (confidential interview, observation, agents and informants, sting operations, mail control and application of technical means, secret controlled purchase, and secret monitoring of movement). One must not ignore the issue of deception, which in forensic detection (Pikulski 1997, p. 71) is used, for example, to detect a criminal offense, detect and apprehend the perpetrator, recover criminal assets, establish facts and objects related to a criminal offense, and prevent a criminal offense from being committed. It should be borne in mind that it cannot be used unlawfully or by misleading the suspect as to his or her procedural situation or procedural rights.

Given the above, forensic technology and tactics go in line with the document titled "Transforming our world: the 2030 Agenda for Sustainable Development," especially regarding Objective 16 entitled "Peace, justice and strong institutions." Peace, stability, human rights, and effective governance based on the rule of law are important conduits for sustainable development. The activities of law enforcement and judicial authorities must fit within the legal framework. At the same time, this value should not be compromised to achieve justice at all costs. Even if forensic science provides the most wonderful technical solutions, it is important to find the right balance between all the conflicting values that are common to the global community. Strengthening the rule of law and promoting human rights is key to this process, as is reducing differences in standards such as legal protection, access to effective justice, and strengthening the participation of developing countries in the institutions of global governance.[14]

5 Detection Techniques as a Double-Edged Sword

Forensic science has been defined in many ways over the centuries and it is multidimensional, as shown by the considerations to date (Bell 2008, pp. 2ff.). P. L. Kirk considered forensic science to be the science of comparison and the interpretation of its results (Kirk 1963, pp. 235–238). For a comparison to be possible, it is necessary that scientific knowledge is applied by a competent person using appropriate tools. This is important because the results of such examinations may constitute relevant evidence for criminal proceedings. This section remains a fundamental and common element of many definitions of forensic science. Nowadays, however, this forensic science is not limited to techniques and tactics of crime investigation and detection of their perpetrators, especially in the approach adopted on the European continent (Kasprzak et al. 2015, p. 28). The subjects of this science also include the techniques and tactics of perpetration of crimes and the prevention carried out by law enforcement and other public authorities, or by the private security sector.

One must keep in mind that knowledge about identification techniques is not restricted for scientists only and its specific dissemination is also due to popular culture: television programs, films, and series on crime and the work of law enforcement agencies (see Stojer 2011, pp. 351ff.). Therefore, possible countermeasures by criminals should be considered when conducting operational investigations or criminal proceedings.

They can consist in activities that, e.g., damage or degrade the biological traces left to a degree that makes it difficult or impossible to isolate the genetic material (by erasure or contamination of the traces) or mask their appearance or behavior. In the former case, various chemicals or high temperatures (e.g., in the form of fire) (see Włodarczyk 2010, pp. 270 276) are used; in the latter case, the perpetrators may use some form of make-up, wear masks, or change their behavior. It is also possible to deliberately leave biological traces belonging to other people or even animals to make it difficult for determine the material truth and to give grounds for the defense attorney to raise doubts about the course of events described by the prosecutor.[15] As

[14]Sustainable Development Goals Fund. *Goal 16: Peace, justice and strong institutions*. https://www.sdgfund.org/goal-16-peace-justice-and-strong-institutions.

[15]On the other hand, this requires technicians who collect biological traces and experts who analyse them to prepare and follow appropriate methodologies so that not only unfair convictions do not occur—see: Innocence Project on the official website of this American NGO: and official site of the Polish Forensic Watch Foundation: www.forensicwatch.pl/web/, but also unjustified detentions, as was the case with the famous murder of 2009 Agnieszka Michniewicz from Sokółka—see. article Kaźmiuk (2015).

we all know, in accordance with one of the fundamental principles of criminal procedure adopted globally, doubts that have not been eliminated in the course of the evaluation of evidence are considered in favor of the accused person. However, actions intended to prevent detection often provide an opportunity to find other traces that indicate the perpetrator of the main crime and a possible person (or persons) who helped to cover up the perpetrator's traces.

However, the development of identification techniques is not limited to applications related to prosecution of perpetrators and the justice system. At present, we are observing intensive development of biometric techniques. B. Hołyst defines biometry as an area of knowledge about recognition of living persons based on measurements of anatomical and physiological features. From the information and technology standpoint, recognition is defined as identification and ascertainment of identity of a person by a computer (Hołyst 2018, p. 820). Biological features result from genetic conditions and are already formed during the development of an embryo. They differ from behavioral features in the fact that one has no influence over their appearance and formation (Tomaszewska-Michalak 2015, p. 11). The most popular techniques for analysis of anatomical biometrics include: analysis of fingerprints, face recognition, iris scan, and hand recognition based on its geometry and blood vessels. As far as behavioral features are concerned, they are formed by frequent repetition and are thus subject to the process of individualization. The most popular identification techniques for analysis of this type of biometrics include: recognition of handwriting, typing, voice, and gait.

One must know this is not a closed list. The latest developments in the field of information technology and data science, such as machine learning combined with high computing power and higher efficiency of even the smallest sensors and fast ICT networks, have greatly increased the speed of identification.

The tested features, called biometrics, must have the properties specified by R. Clarke:[16]

- universality of coverage (every relevant person should have an identifier),
- uniqueness (each relevant person should have only one identifier no two people should have the same identifier),
- permanence—the identifier should not change, nor be changeable,
- indispensability—the identifier should be one or more natural characteristics, which each person has and retains; if artificial, the identifier should always be enforcedly available,
- collectability—the identifier should be collectible by anyone on any occasion,
- storability—the identifier should be storable in manual and in automated systems,
- exclusivity—no other form of identification should be necessary or used,
- precision—every identifier should be sufficiently different from every other identifier that mistakes are unlikely,
- simplicity—recording and transmission should be easy and not error-prone,

[16]Word "biometrics" on the private website of R. Clarke: www.rogerclarke.com/DV/HumanID.html#Bio.

- cost—measuring and storing the identifier should not be unduly costly,
- convenience—measuring and storing the identifier should not be unduly inconvenient or time-consuming,
- acceptability—its use should conform to contemporary social standards.

The more of the above properties a biometric system has, the more effective it is. However, there is no biological or behavioral feature that meets all these conditions. Obtaining social acceptance is particularly problematic when measuring a given property, as obtaining certain information may cause distrust and controversy among members of the society. At the same time, the properties may constitute data and information that is subject to specific legal regimes, e.g., personal data protection.

To increase the efficiency of the identification process in detecting perpetrators of crimes, law enforcement authorities set up databases with appropriate systems for finding similarities between evidence and comparative materials. An example is the Automated Fingerprint Identification System (AFIS). They are subject to significant restrictions as to how the data contained therein are to be used. It turns out that such biometric data can be used not only to fight crime but also to identify citizens (biometric identity cards), immigrants, asylum seekers, and persons in other categories who have not committed any criminal offense. Questions have arisen about the possibility of using these administrative databases for purposes other than those for which they were created, even if this is as noble a purpose as detection of perpetrators of crimes. One may ask oneself whether the fight against crime would not be easier if selected biometric data (e.g., DNA code or fingerprints) were collected from every citizen in each country. At the same time, databases containing biometric data are also created by the private sector for purposes such as medical, financial, and security services. The question arises about the possibility of using this type of data by law enforcement authorities and the judiciary. It is necessary in this respect to strike a careful balance between the profits and the costs of such measures and to provide guarantees for individual citizens to ensure that their data are used lawfully respecting the right to privacy.

"Wonderful" identification techniques, with noble goals at their core, can turn into a nightmare in the hands of criminals or totalitarian political regimes.

6 Conclusion

Forensic science is an interdisciplinary science because it uses the achievements and discoveries of other sciences: medical sciences, social sciences, biological sciences, etc. for purposes associated with operation of the justice system. Only thanks to its development we can solve mysterious, difficult, and complicated cases. Thanks to the research being conducted and the knowledge of experts, it is not necessary to rely on intuition, revelation, or magic to effectively bring the perpetrators to justice.

The boundaries of our perception in search of and analysis of forensic traces are gradually expanding. The methods and technical means supporting the work of law enforcement officers, forensic technicians, and expert witnesses are constantly being improved. All this is done to be able to reproduce, in an objective, comprehensive, and thus credible manner, the fragment of reality in which the crime took place.

This chapter presented genetic identification techniques and polygraph examinations. At the same time, these are techniques that have caused and continue to cause ethical controversy. Consequently, the law needs to resolve emerging conflicts between the interests of the justice system and, for example, the victims of crimes, and to protect other values that are important for the global community, such as protection of personal data and privacy. In this aspect, too, there is a problem of how to use the latest breakthrough advances of knowledge even for seemingly noble and undisputed purposes.

Genetic testing allows even the smallest amounts of DNA to be used to identify people involved in a crime in any role. Recent research even enables determination of group characteristics of an unknown perpetrator of a crime. Until recently, this would have been considered impossible or a part of *science fiction* literature. In the case of polygraph testing, we can disclose memory traces based on unconscious responses of the organism. In this way, we overcome new barriers in forensic research.

One must keep in mind, however, that the development of forensic techniques, especially identification techniques, leads to several ethical and legal problems. Nevertheless, we cannot avoid having to resolve conflicts of this kind—as those outlined in this chapter—if one of our objectives is sustainable development in the area of justice.

Resolving the conflict between human rights and ensuring the optimal functioning of justice system using the achievements of modern technologies should be in accordance with the provisions of the most important documents developed within the UN. These are universal documents, fully accepted by the international community. These are the provisions of the Universal Declaration of Human Rights and the International Covenant on Civil and Political Rights. The United Nations High Commissioner for Human Rights has presented the list of recommendations for the public and private sector concerning, inter alia, the handling of biometric data. The document was published 2018 and titled: "The Right to privacy in the digital age. Report of the United Nations High Commissioner for Human Rights."[17] The High Commissioner recommends, the states ensure that data-intensive systems, including those involving the collection and retention of biometric data, are only deployed when states can demonstrate that they are necessary and proportionate to achieve to legitimate aim.

[17]UNHCHR, The Right to privacy in the digital age. Report of the United Nations High Commissioner for Human Rights, https://documents-dds-ny.un.org/doc/UNDOC/GEN/G18/239/58/PDF/G1823958.pdf?OpenElement.

References

Adam, A. (2012). Expertenbefragung zu aktuellen und künftigen Herausforderungen der Kriminalistik [Expert survey on current and future challenges in criminal statistics]. *der Kriminalist, 10*, 29.

Aqua Tofana. (1842). *The Encyclopedia Britannica or dictionary of arts, science and general literature* (Vol. III, 7th ed.). Edinburgh: Adam And Charles Black.

Bell, S. (2008). *Crime and circumstance, investigating the history of forensic science*. Werstport: Praeger Publishers.

Ben-Shakhar, G., Bar-Hillel, M., & Kremnitzer, M. (2002). Trial by polygraph: Reconsidering the use of the guilty knowledge technique in court. *Law and Human Behavior, 26*(5), 527–541.

Białecka, A., Kamińska, M., Wierzchowski, R., & Wujec, J. (2010). Współczesna ekspertyza kryminalistyczna z zakresu badań DNA [Contemporary forensic expert opinion related to DNA tests]. In V. Kwiatkowska-Wójcikiewicz (Ed.), *Kryminalistyka dla prawa, prawo dla kryminalistyki [Forensics for law, law for forensics]* (pp. 63–79). Toruń: TNOiK.

Clarke, R. (1994) Biometrics. In: *Human Identification in Information Systems: Management Challenges and Public Policy Issues*. Retrieved October 3, 2019, from http://www.rogerclarke.com/DV/HumanID.html#Bio

Cullen, W. R. (2008). *Is Arsenic an Aphrodisiac?: The sociochemistry of an element*. Cambridge: RSC Publishing.

Dash, M. (2017). Chapter 6. Aqua Tofana. In *Ph. Wexler, toxicology in the middle ages and Renaissance* (pp. 63–69). London: Academic Press.

(2015) Decision of the Supreme Court of 29 January 2015, file no. I KZP 25/14, *Orzecznictwo Sądów Polskich, 12*(121):1773–1781.

Dickerson, C. (2019). *U.S. Government Plans to Collect DNA From Detained Immigrants*. Retrieved October 16, 2019, from https://www.nytimes.com/2019/10/02/us/dna-testing-immigrants.html

Encyklopedia PWN. Retrieved October 16, 2019., from www.encyklopedia.pwn.pl

Filipkowski, W., Guzik-Makaruk, E. M., & Pływaczewski, E. W. (2016). Uwagi na tle badań nad genomem ludzkim, genomiką i genetyką z punktu widzenia prawa, kryminologii i kryminalistyki [Comments concerning studies of human genome, genomics, and genetics from the point of view of law, criminology, and forensics]. In J. Moszczyński, D. Solodov, & I. Sołtyszewski (Eds.), *Przestępczość-Dowody-Prawo. Księga Jubileuszowa Prof. Bronisława Młodziejowskiego [Crime-evidence-law. A jubilee book of Prof. Bronisław Młodziejowski]* (pp. 615–628). Olsztyn: Wydawnictwo Uniwersytetu Warmińsko-Mazurskiego.

Filipkowski, W., Guzik-Makaruk, E. M., & Pływaczewski, E. W. (2018). Genforschungen – rechtliche, kriminologische und kriminalistische Aspekte. In O. Yenerer Cakmut (Ed.), *Uluslararasi gen hukuku sempozyumu* (pp. 77–101). Ankara: Seckin.

Forensic Watch. (2019). Retrieved October 3, 2019, from http://forensicwatch.pl/web/

Furman-Łajszczak, K. (2011). Dowód z badań DNA – wyzwanie dla prawników [Evidence from DNA tests - a challenge for lawyers]. *Prokurator, 2*, 95–108.

Gibson, S. D. C. (2012). *Legends, monsters, or serial murderers? The real story behind an ancient crime*. Santa Barbara: ABC-CLIO.

Global Compact for migration. Retrieved October 16, 2019., from https://refugeesmigrants.un.org/migration-compact

Gołaszewski, M. (2016). Użyteczność badań poligraficznych w ograniczaniu recydywy wśród sprawców przestępstw przeciwko wolności seksualnej [Utility of polygraph testing in reduction of recidivism among perpetrators of crimes against sexual freedom]. *Prokuratura i Prawo, 12*, 5–22.

Gołaszewski, M., Markowicz, P., & Jastrzębska, J. (2018). Postrzeganie badań poligraficznych w Polsce oraz ich użyteczność w służbach i innych obszarach działalności [Perception of polygraphic examinations in Poland and their utility in agencies and other fields]. *Przegląd Bezpieczeństwa Wewnętrznego, 18*, 151–167.

Gruza, E. (2011). Czy zabiłeś Ewelinę? – czyli czy wariograf to wykrywacz kłamstw [Did you kill Ewelina? - is a polygraph a lie detector]. *Edukacja Prawnicza, 4*, 10–13.
Grzywacz, M. (2013, September 2). Genetyczny odcisk palca [Genetic fingerprint]. *Gazeta Wyborcza*, 6–7.
Herbowski, P. (2013). 50 lat badań poligraficznych w polskim procesie karnym [50 years of polygraphic examinations in the Polish criminal process]. *Problemy Kryminalistyki, 280*(2), 7–15.
Herbowski, P. (2014). Badanie poligraficzne – metoda wykrywania kłamstwa czy weryfikacji wersji śledczych? [Polygraph examination - a method of lie detection or of verification of investigative versions]. *Edukacja Prawnicza, 4*, 3–6.
Hołyst, B. (2007). *Kryminalistyka [Forensics]*. Warsaw: LexisNexis.
Hołyst, B. (2018). *Kryminalistyka [Forensics]* (13th ed.). Warsaw: Wydawnictwo Wolters Kluwer.
Inabau, F. E. (1953). The first polygraph. *Journal of Criminal Law and Criminology, 43*(5), 679–681.
Innocence Project. (2019). Retrieved October 3, 2019, from www.innocenceproject.org/about-innocence-project
Jagiełło, D. (2019). *Taktyka kryminalistycznych czynności dowodowych [Tactics of forensic evidence-gathering activities]*. Warsaw: C.H. Beck.
Kasprzak, J., Młodziejowski, B., & Kasprzak, W. (2015). *Kryminalistyka. Zarys systemu [Forensics. Outline of the system]*. Warsaw: DIFIN.
Kaźmiuk, M. (2015, October 19). Agnieszka Michniewicz zamordowana. Znaleźli DNA czterech mężczyzn [Agnieszka Michniewicz murdered. They found the DNA of four men]. *Kurier Poranny*. Retrieved October 3, 2019, from https://poranny.pl/agnieszka-michniewicz-zamordowana-znalezli-dna-czterech-mezczyzn/ar/9006836
Kirk, P. L. (1963). The ontogeny of criminalistics. *Journal of Criminal Law and Criminology, 54* (2), 235–238.
Lewis, J. A., & Cuppari, M. (2009). The polygraph: The truth lies within. *The Journal of Psychiatry & Law, 37*, 85–92.
Mahapatra, D. (2010, May 5). No narcoanalysis test without consent, says SC. *The Times of India*. Retrieved October 3, 2019, from www.timesofindia.indiatimes.com/articleshow/5892348.cms?utm_source=contentofinterest&utm_medium=text&utm_campaign=cppst
Meijer, E. H., & van Koppen, P. J. (2008). Chapter 3. Lie Detectors and the law: The use of the polygraph in Europe. In D. Canter & R. Žukauskiene (Eds.), *Psychology and law: Bridging the gap* (pp. 31–50). Routledge: Ashgate Publishing.
Pikulski, S. (1997). *Podstawowe zagadnienia taktyki kryminalistycznej* [Basic problem of forensic tactics]. Białystok: Temida 2.
Pływaczewski, E. W. (2017). *Bezpieczeństwo obywateli – Prawa człowieka – Zrównoważony Rozwój* [Citizens' safety - human rights - sustainable development]. Białystok: Temida 2.
Saxe, L., & Ben-Shakhar, G. (1999). Admissibility of polygraph tests: The application of scientific standards Post-Daubert. *Psychology Public Policy and Law, 5*(1), 203–223.
Słomski, R. (2010). Trudne początki badań DNA w Polsce [Difficult start of DNA testing in Poland]. In V. Kwiatkowska-Wójcikiewicz (Ed.), *Kryminalistyka dla prawa, prawo dla kryminalistyki [Forensics for law, law for forensics]* (pp. 37–47). Toruń: TNOiK.
Stojer, J. (2011). Efekt CSI a postrzeganie pracy biegłych [The CSI effect and its impact on the perceptions of forensic science experts' work]. *Archiwum Medycyny Sądowej i Kryminologii, LXI*, 351–359.
Supreme Court of Canada decision *R. v. Béland* (1987). Retrieved October 16, 2019, from https://scc-csc.lexum.com/scc-csc/scc-csc/en/item/250/index.do
Sustainable Development Goals Fund. *Goal 16: Peace, justice and strong institutions*. Retrieved October 3, 2019., from https://www.sdgfund.org/goal-16-peace-justice-and-strong-institutions
Sygit, B., & Sadowska, E. (2010). Rysopis genetyczny – perspektywy predykcji wyglądu nieznanego sprawcy przestępstwa ze śladu DNA [Genetic description - prospects for prediction

of appearance of unknown crime perpetrators based on DNA traces]. *Prokuratura i Prawo, 9*, 5–15.
Tomaszewska-Michalak, M. (2015). *Prawne i kryminalistyczne aspekty wykorzystania technologii biometrycznej w Polsce [Legal and forensicaspects of use of the biometrictechnology in Poland]*. Warsaw: DIFIN.
Tomaszewski, T. (2010). Ekspertyza DNA jako dowód naukowy [DNA expert opinion as scientific evidence]. In V. Kwiatkowska-Wójcikiewicz (Ed.), *Kryminalistyka dla prawa, prawo dla kryminalistyki [Forensics for law, law for forensics]* (pp. 81–91). Toruń: TNOiK.
Trestrail, J. H. (2007). *Criminal poisoning: Investigational guide for law enforcement, toxicologists, forensic scientists, and attorneys*. Totowa: Humana Press.
Trovillo, P. V. (1939). A history of lie detection. *The Journal of Criminal Law and Criminology, 29* (6), 848–881.
Tucholska-Lenart, A. (2010). XX lat kryminalistycznych badań DNA w Polsce – wspomnienia eksperta [20 years of forensic DNA testing in Poland - anexpert'smemoir]. In V. Kwiatkowska-Wójcikiewicz (Ed.), *Kryminalistyka dla prawa, prawo dla kryminalistyki [Forensics for law, law for forensics]* (pp. 49–61). Toruń: TNOiK.
UNESCO. *Universal Declaration on the Human Genome and Human Rights*. Retrieved October 16, 2019., from http://www.unesco.org/new/en/social-and-human-sciences/themes/bioethics/human-genome-and-human-rights/
UNHCHR, The Right to privacy in the digital age. Report of the United Nations High Commissioner for Human Rights. https://documents-dds-ny.un.org/doc/UNDOC/GEN/G18/239/58/PDF/G1823958.pdf?OpenElement
UNODC. Retrieved October 3, 2019, from https://www.unodc.org/unodc/en/scientists/index.html
Verdict of the Supreme Court - Criminal Chamber of 16 May 2018, file no.: V KO 26/18. Retrieved October 3, 2019., from http://www.sn.pl/sites/orzecznictwo/Orzeczenia3/V%20KO%2026-18-1.pdf
Vicianova, M. (2015). Historical techniques of lie detection. *Europe's Journal of Psychology, 11* (3), 522–534.
Weber, S. (2008). *The hidden truth: A sociological history of lie detection* (PhD Thesis), London: London School of Economics and Political Science.
Wessel, L. (2019). *Scientists concerned over US plans to collect DNA data from immigrants*. Retrieved October 16, 2019, from https://www.nature.com/articles/d41586-019-02998-3
Widacki, J. (2007). The introduction. *European Polygraph, 1*(1), 5–6.
Widacki, J. (2016). Polygraph or variograph? *Issues of Forensic Science, 294*(4), 88–92.
Wikipedia. The Free Encyclopedia. *Saint Nicholas*. Retrieved October 3, 2019., from https://en.wikipedia.org/wiki/Saint_Nicholas
Włodarczyk, R. (2010). *Działania kryminalistyczne, medyczne i organizacyjne w sytuacjach zdarzeń masowych ze szczególnym uwzględnieniem identyfikacji genetycznej zwłok i szczątków ludzkich z pogorzelisk [Forensic, medical, and organizational actions in the case of mass events with particular focus on genetic identification of corpses and human remains from fire sites]*. Szczytno: Wydawnictwo Wyższej Szkoły Policji w Szczytnie.
Wójcikiewicz, J. (2010). Ekspertyza genetyczna w Polsce – 20 lat później [Genetic expert examinations in Poland - 20 years later]. In V. Kwiatkowska-Wójcikiewicz (Ed.), *Kryminalistyka dla prawa, prawo dla kryminalistyki [Forensics for law, law for forensics]* (pp. 93–105). Toruń: TNOiK.
Zubańska, M. (2019). *Nowe technologie w kryminalistyce. Aspekty prawne i kryminalistyczne* [New technologies in forensics. Legal and forensic aspects]. Olsztyn: ElSet.

Emil W. Pływaczewski is a Full Professor of Law and Criminology, Doctor h.c., Head of Department of Criminal Law and Criminology, Law Faculty, University of Bialystok (Białystok, Poland), Director of the International Center of Criminological Research and Expertise. His scientific areas are Criminal Law, Criminology, Organized Crime, and Internal Security. Author and co-author of over 480 publications in Poland and abroad. E-mail: e.plywaczewski@uwb.edu.pl.

Ewa M. Guzik-Makaruk is a Full Professor of Law and Criminology, Head of Institute of Criminal Law, Department of Criminal Law and Criminology, Law Faculty, University of Bialystok (Białystok, Poland); Deputy Director of the International Center of Criminological Research and Expertise; Attorney of Law. She specializes in the field of medical criminal law, criminology and international criminal law. Author and co-author of over 200 publications in Poland and abroad. E-mail: ewa.guzik@uwb.edu.pl.

Wojciech Filipkowski is an Associate Professor of Law and Criminology, Head of Forensic Laboratory, Department of Criminal Law and Criminology, Law Faculty, University of Bialystok (Białystok, Poland), Scientific Secretary for cooperation with western states of the International Center of Criminological Research and Expertise. He specializes in the use of new technologies by law enforcement, special services and justice system. Recent interests focus on criminal intelligence analysis, predictive policing and artificial intelligence. Author and co-author of over 150 publications in Poland and abroad. E-mail: wojciech.filipkowski@gmail.com.

Emilia Jurgielewicz-Delegacz has Ph.D. in Law and Criminology, Department of Criminal Law and Criminology, Law Faculty, University of Bialystok (Białystok, Poland) and Coordinator of the International Center of Criminological Research and Expertise. Her scientific areas are criminal law, criminology, rural crime, and traffic accidents. Author and co-author of over 50 publications in Poland and abroad. E-mail: emilia.jurgielewicz@gmail.com.

The Rule of Law, Peacebuilding, and Agenda 2030: Lessons from the Western Balkans

Alistair D. Edgar

Abstract The rule of law, understood as both a legal concept and a political project, is an essential underpinning of success in the progressive achievement of all of the Sustainable Development Goals, as well as constituting itself a critical element of one of the 17 global goals of Agenda 2030. As an element of peacebuilding in post-conflict states and societies, however, this double nature also makes rule of law deeply problematic since as a political project it can challenge the deeply entrenched—and often, closely intertwined or interdependent—interests of political-economic elites and organized crime. In the countries of the Western Balkans, rule of law deficits remain a significant obstacle to achieving Agenda 2030, and SDG 16 in particular, as well as standing in the way of countries' ambitions for EU accession. This chapter briefly reviews the nature and content of rule of law in both understandings; frames rule of law within SDG16 and Agenda 2030; highlights the interconnected problems of weak rule of law, lack of political will, and organized crime in the Western Balkans; and identifies examples of good practices or paths of action to foster or strengthen rule of law as a contribution to achieving Agenda 2030.

Keywords Rule of law · Peacebuilding · Organized crime · Western Balkans · SDG16 · Agenda 2030 · United Nations · UNODC

1 Introduction

In his 2004 Report to the Security Council on the rule of law and transitional justice in post-conflict societies, UN Secretary-General Kofi Annan defined the rule of law as "a principle of governance in which all persons, institutions and entities, public and private, including the State itself, are accountable to laws that are publicly

A. D. Edgar (✉)
Wilfrid Laurier University, Balsillie School of International Affairs, School of International Policy and Governance, Waterloo, ON, Canada
e-mail: aedgar@wlu.ca

H. Kury, S. Redo (eds.), *Crime Prevention and Justice in 2030*,
https://doi.org/10.1007/978-3-030-56227-4_19

promulgated, equally enforced and independently adjudicated, and which are consistent with international human rights norms and standards" (S/2004/616). Within this definition, as the Secretary-General observed in his report, the key principles and assumptions included the supremacy of law above politics, the separation of powers, equality before (and under) the law, transparency in establishing and enforcing the law, and independence and fairness in the application of the law. In this form, as Irene Khan notes in a different context but still referring to the UN Secretary-General's definition, rule of law is a state-centered concept of legal procedures and practices insofar as it focuses on "institutions and governance, and the application of norms, procedures and regulations" (Khan 2017, p. 213). Importantly, however, there also is contained in this definition the substantive component of consistency with existing international human rights norms and standards. This is where justice fits alongside rule of law, as a necessary and people-centered component that speaks to achieving or supporting fair outcomes and an inclusive society; or as the Secretary-General's 2004 report described it, justice refers to "accountability and fairness in the protection and vindication of rights and the prevention and punishment of wrongs" while keeping in mind "the well-being of society at large" (S/2004/616).

The rule of law, thus understood as both a legal concept and a political project, is an essential underpinning of success in the progressive achievement of all of the Sustainable Development Goals, as well as being itself a critical element of one of the 17 global goals set out in the 2030 Agenda for Sustainable Development adopted by Member States of the United Nations meeting at the UN General Assembly in New York on 25 September 2015 (A/RES/70/1 2015). As an element of peacebuilding in conflict-affected and post-conflict states and societies, however, this double nature—the legal and the political dimensions—can make rule of law initiatives deeply problematic, since as a political project it can challenge the deeply entrenched and often closely intertwined or interdependent interests of political-economic elites and organized crime. Looking at post-Dayton Bosnia, Tim Donais observed that "at its core, the rule of law is about power: how it is constituted, how it is exercised, and how it is controlled" (Donais 2013, p. 190). As this chapter will illustrate and explore, in the countries of the Western Balkans, rule of law deficits remain a significant obstacle to achieving Agenda 2030, and SDG 16 in particular, as well as standing in the way of those countries' ambitions for EU accession.

In the next section, the chapter defines and speaks to the nature and content of rule of law in both the legal and the political understandings, and then frames the notion of rule of law as this fits within SDG16 and Agenda 2030. In the third section, the analysis highlights the interconnected problems of weak rule of law, lack of political will, and organized crime in the Western Balkans. The fourth section offers some antidotes to the more critical preceding discussion, as it identifies examples of good practices and policy initiatives taken by national governments in the region to foster or strengthen rule of law as a contribution towards achieving Agenda 2030. Finally, the conclusion considers "pathways forward," and in particular how different actors—international organizations and agencies, regional bodies, nongovernmental organizations and civil society—usefully and constructively might help to foster or otherwise support and promote rule of law in the Western Balkans within the framework of the Sustainable Development Goals and Agenda 2030.

2 Rule of Law and Agenda 2030

2.1 Understanding Rule of Law

Reflecting on the stabilization and peace building efforts of the United Nations in Bosnia some 5 months after his appointment in May 2002 as the fourth High Representative under the terms of the 1995 Dayton Peace Agreement, Paddy Ashdown observed in *The New York Times* article that rather than focusing on holding elections as a pathway to democracy in post-conflict Bosnia and Herzegovina, "we should have put the establishment of the rule of law first, for everything else depends on it – a functioning economy, a free and fair political system, the development of civil society, public confidence in police and the courts" (Ashdown 2002, p. 25).

It is useful to begin by differentiating between the rule of law on one hand, and rule by law, on the other. This also speaks in some measure to the political content of the rule of law as it generally is understood today—and as it often may be assumed or taken for granted by international organizations. Rule by law can be little more than a framework used by totalitarian governments for enforcing social control, engaging in the active repression or denial of human rights, and even committing mass atrocities. Neil Kritz provides the Nazi regime in Germany, Stalin's rule and the Soviet constitution of 1936, and the attacks against their own population by the Ceausescu regime in Romania, as historical examples in which courts, legal statutes and regulations, and the associated enforcement capacities of the state were deployed by tyrannical governing regimes to commit widespread systematic abuse and repression. By contrast to these historical cases (and one might offer just as easily more contemporary examples of state repression that are framed by those regimes as "lawful") he argues that "adherence to the rule of law entails far more than the mechanical application of static legal technicalities" and instead "establishes rules and procedures that constrain the power of all parties, hold all parties accountable for their actions, and prohibit the accumulation of autocratic or oligarchic power" (Kritz 2001, p. 802).

This is not the place to argue the general case (or even Ashdown's argument) for international law, or more specifically respect for the rule of law, as the optimal means by which to seek to reduce violent conflicts between or within states, or as an instrument to prevent or punish regimes or individuals who commit mass atrocity crimes during times of war and conflict.[1] It is useful, however, to indicate at least two

[1]There is a broad literature—theoretical and empirical—on such questions in international relations and international security scholarship related to conflict analysis, management, and resolution, as

good reasons for placing value on rule of law, both of which are directly related to the "problem" of advancing Agenda 2030 in the Balkans. First, in contexts of recent intrastate conflict, moving beyond that conflict and minimizing any possible recurrence or reversion to conflict requires "the nurturing of societal structures and institutions to assure each combatant group that their interests will be protected through nonviolent means" (Kritz 2001, p. 803).

This can be a major challenge when the mechanisms and processes of rule of law—its institutions and personnel as well as any expectations of trust in the system of provision of justice—were amongst the casualties of conflict. The second, closely related reason is "the inherent undesirability of [the] alternatives" such as lawlessness or "the rule of the gun" (Donais 2013, p. 191). Or, it might be added, rule by law under a repressive state apparatus and government. Hence it has not been only the United Nations in its peacekeeping and peacebuilding efforts (from Secretary-General Boutros Boutros-Ghali's 1992 *Agenda for Peace,*[2] to Kofi Annan's 2004 report already noted above, and in numerous subsequent iterations), but also other international or regional intergovernmental organizations such as the Organization for Security and Cooperation in Europe, the Organization of American States, and the Council of Europe, that have developed extensive and detailed guidelines to elaborate further the dimensions and obligations of rule of law (Kritz 2001).

The obligations identified by these various international articulations of the rule of law for governments (and states, whatever the particular government of the day) include—amongst others—a representative government with the executive accountable to an elected legislature and/or to the electorate; free and fair elections at regular intervals; the duty of the government to act in compliance with the constitution and the law; clear distinction and separation between the state and political parties; accountability of police and military to civilian authority; publication of administrative regulations as a condition of their validity, and effective means of redress against administrative or bureaucratic decisions and actions for affected (harmed) persons; and the independence of the judiciary and of legal practitioners, and of the administrative state at all levels (Kritz 2001). As these obligations illustrate, transparency, predictability, independence, fairness, accountability, and equality before (under) the law are key characteristics of rule of law.

At the same time as initiatives aimed at meeting these obligations must be pursued in good faith, however, international donors and others should be aware that in post-conflict contexts "evolution of the rule of law... may be somewhat messy and slow" such that "insistence on the perfect before the system moves

well as the more recent (post-Cold War) work on transitional justice and peacebuilding. For the current chapter, however, the references provided are focused on the latter topic(s) and only as they bear on the analysis of rule of law and the SDGs.

[2]Then-UN Secretary-General Boutros-Ghali, discussing the work of the UN in post-conflict peace building, referred to a consensus on the need for "social peace" alongside "strategic or political peace" and argued that there existed "an obvious connection between democratic practices - such as the rule of law and transparency in decision-making - and the achievement of true peace and security in any new and stable political order." A/47/277-S/24111 An Agenda for Peace, para 59.

forward can be the enemy of the good" (Kritz 2001, p. 805). Importantly also, international donors and domestic parties must recognize that not every dispute or disagreement, or other problem with government or in state-society relations, is one that may be settled through judicial processes and mechanisms. Indeed as Kritz (p. 805) warns, "to make the courts the arbiter of such disputes – particularly if the judiciary is still a fragile institution – risks politicizing the very institution that must be blind to politics" and may have the opposite outcome of undermining the independence of the judicial system in practice or at least of harming public confidence in that independence.

A final related point to make regarding the rule of law in the context of post-conflict states and societies is that the capacity of external agencies to 'force' acceptance of the norms and practices of rule of law onto domestic actors is limited. We do not have to accept the argument that international actors cannot offer better frameworks for the rule of law than can the citizens or government officials of conflict affected and post-conflict states (Chandler 2004), as that critique of international interventionism assumes that those government officials—and influential portions of the citizenry—have not become part of a criminalized political economy or an authoritarian power structure pursuing rule by law. Where those state, government, or societal power structures have been part of the problem as sources of violence or criminalization, externally imposed structures and norms may be essential as a first step towards improved (peaceful) governance and rule of law. However, externally imposed structures, institutions and processes will not function effectively in a political and societal vacuum or against domestic resistance and rejection.

There needs to be a willingness on the part of domestic actors to accept the normative (and hence, political) sense of rule of law—there must be acceptance of what Timothy Donais calls "the logic of consequences and the logic of appropriateness," whereby political, administrative and judicial representatives and citizens "adhere to, and feel bound by, the rule of law not only because they fear the consequences of being on the wrong side of the law, but also because they believe that being on the right side is the appropriate thing to do" (Donais 2013, p. 192).

2.2 *Rule of Law and the Sustainable Development Goals*

The rule of law underpins all three dimensions of sustainable development—through providing stable, predictable and transparent legal regimes, it supports and enables economic development; through protecting and promoting equitable access for all to services and opportunities, it supports social development; and through reinforcing a stable legal framework for the management of natural resources, rule of law can contribute to policies for environmental protection and sustainability (Khan 2017). Sustainable Development Goal 16, the full title of which reads "Promote peaceful and inclusive societies for sustainable development, provide access to justice for all and build effective, accountable and inclusive institutions at all levels," addresses the critical challenges to the achievement of the SDGs that arise especially from states and societies that are experiencing violent conflict and instability or that are seeking to advance from recent situations of conflict and instability—but SDG 16 also is an enabling legal-technical and political (or normative) framework for states, governments and societies to make progress towards achieving the full range of the 2030 Agenda goals.

The United Nations Office on Drugs and Crime (UNODC) identifies SDG 16 as "an engine for progress and an enabling tool for all other Goals" (UNODC 2019). Promoting rule of law and equal access to justice for all (Target 16.3), substantially reducing illicit financial flows (Target 16.4) and corruption and bribery in all forms (Target 16.5), while developing effective, accountable and transparent institutions (Target 16.6) and ensuring responsive, inclusive, participatory and representative decision-making (Target 16.7), are valuable elements of good governance in their own right. They also are foundational conditions in the absence of which other Goals may prove more difficult if not impossible to meet. According to a February 2019 report from the Geneva, Switzerland-based The Global Initiative Against Transnational Organized Crime, organized crime "threatens not only specific goals, such as the reduction of poverty and the promotion of economic growth, but also the general maintenance of global biodiversity and sustainable environments; the building of safe and inclusive societies; the promotion of public health and people's well-being; and even the orderly management of migration" (The Global Initiative/GTI 2019a, p. 2).

The February 2019 GTI report noted that of the 169 targets included in the framework for measuring progress towards the 17 Sustainable Development Goals, at least 23 targets required directly addressing organized crime and rule of law; and just as the 17 Goals are promoted by the United Nations as being interdependent or indivisible, the report highlights the similar multi-sectoral and cross-sectoral character of organized crime as a threat. Indeed, the Geneva-based study adds that "development actors need to understand not only how organized crime will undermine their objectives, but also that development itself presents opportunities for organized crime to flourish," and that in contexts of states enduring or recovering from conflict and instability, the creation and support of "sustainable livelihood alternatives is a critical component of any strategy seeking to counter organized crime's impact on governance and the rule of law" (GTI 2019a, p. 3). Organized crime—at national and transnational levels—can undermine progress towards the SDGs, even while in some circumstances the resources needed to achieve that progress create new opportunities for crime and corruption and new challenges to the rule of law.

3 Political Economy of Organized Crime in the Western Balkans

In a detailed May 2019 report identifying and discussing "Hotspots of Organized Crime in the Western Balkans," the previously-mentioned GTI group also offer a useful picture of the political economy of organized crime in the six EU accession candidate states—Croatia already having joined the EU in 2013—of Albania, Bosnia and Herzegovina, Kosovo,[3] Montenegro, North Macedonia and Serbia. In this region, while the overall economic context has shown improvement, the GTI study argues that such positive news as there is, needs to be understood in the context of previous political instability and general economic vulnerability. For example, unemployment levels have declined in several states but at 20.9% in 2018 this still remained at a regional level more than three times higher than the EU average. Youth unemployment was especially high, for example at 31.7% in Montenegro and 57.7% in Kosovo, while many businesses tended to be small and cash-based, as part of the 'informal' economy. Foreign direct investment is limited due to concerns over political instability, legal and regulatory uncertainties, and perceived high levels of corruption (GTI 2019b). A well-established informal—and often criminal—economy closely connected to rival political factions was a common result in the region of the years of conflict and disintegration of government structures. As the GTI analysis notes, the political-economic problems of the states in the Western Balkans region both create opportunities for, and are exacerbated by, transnational organized crime due to their geographical location as "these countries also find themselves in between sources of supply and demand for drugs and weapons, and along a major route for the smuggling of migrants. The more vulnerable the region becomes, the more attractive it is as a trafficking route" (GTI 2019b, p. 4).

Of course, one may look to other, "external" causes as partial explanations for the problems of weak rule of law in the region. In his examination of the Kosovo Police Service (KPS) in 2009–2010, shortly after the Kosovo Assembly's controversial February 2008 declaration of independence, Barry Ryan argued that the KPS' "failure to be accepted as a legitimate and objective law enforcement institution" was at least in part the result of the policy choices and actions of the international community—in the forms of the UN, EU, and NATO—which chose to focus on "maintaining Kosovo in a state of exception, whereby the maintenance of order [was] given priority over the rule of law" (Ryan 2010, p. 114). The KPS as a new institution that was established in 1999 by the UN Interim Administration in Kosovo Civilian Police Contingent was trapped, in that sense, between on the one side being tasked with enforcing the writ of these international actors and on the other side being "subject to the moral authority of the majoritarian ethnic Albanian national will" (Ryan 2010, p. 115).

---

[3] As the GTI report also notes, all references to Kosovo "are made without prejudice to positions on status" and "in line with UNSCR 1244/1999 and the ICJ opinion on the Kosovo declaration of independence" (GTI May 2019b, Note 1).

A different view on the strengths and weaknesses—or the constructive and destructive influences—of international intervention and externally driven state building is presented in a 2014 study by Elton Skendaj of the police force, customs service, central administration, and court system—the four "core bureaucracies" of the state intimately involved in providing or supporting rule of law—in Kosovo. Using interviews, survey data, and official reports from international organizations, national governments, and civil society organizations, the study examined the "bureaucratic effectiveness" of these four agencies in terms of their "impartiality in the exercise of public authority" (Skendaj 2014). The study concluded that the central administration and the court system in Kosovo both ranked poorly on effectiveness and responsiveness, while the customs service and police ranked as high and medium, respectively. The latter two institutions had been relatively insulated from 'local ownership' and political influence in Kosovo as their officers were recruited, trained and promoted by international organizations (the OSCE, UNMIK CIVPOL, and the EU), although Skendaj noted that after Kosovo's declaration of independence in 2008 the police had become more politicized. Kosovo interviewees[4] also ranked the courts, customs service, and the central administration of the state as "bureaucracies with large-scale corruption" while in this case the Kosovo police service was viewed being as "the least corrupt" of the four core bureaucracies (Skendaj 2014).

The value of international engagement in state building lies in the ability of these external bodies to insulate the new core bureaucracies of the state from becoming sites of patronage. This would be especially the case when these also are the four bureaucracies that together should support and enforce rule of law in the state. Where such insulation was impossible, or else was not pursued by international actors for various reasons, the result—as indicated in Skendaj's analysis in the case of Kosovo's central government administration—was a situation wherein employees felt that "in order to remain in their job, they had to be loyal to their patron and provide services to particularistic networks" (Skendaj 2014, p. 472), leading at best to low employee morale and an unwillingness to identify, prevent or punish corruption, or at worst to active collusion in corruption and the biased delivery of services.

The preceding discussion of challenges to the rule of law in Kosovo is not intended to suggest that the problems there are unique, or uniquely severe. Returning to Donais' (2013) study of the rule of law in post-Dayton Bosnia, he found then that despite significant levels of international intervention, "the underlying structure and core dynamics of political power and political contestation remain largely unaltered, which perpetuates a condition of structural injustice" (Donais 2013, p. 191). This could be seen, he argued, in the examples of international support for police reform and anti-corruption programs. On police reform assistance initiatives under the UN

[4]Skendaj reports that his interviewee pool excluded Kosovo Serbs who rejected the institutions of Kosovo for political reasons (following the position of the Serbian government Belgrade in not recognizing the claim of independence), as their views of these institutions was not based on the latter's bureaucratic effectiveness but on a broader political position of rejecting the newly-proclaimed state and looking to Belgrade for the institutions of government.

International Police Task Force and the subsequent 10-years-long EU Police Mission—including the technical and institutional dimensions, and also the political and socio-cultural dimensions—Donais observed that efforts by international actors both to depoliticize the police and to insulate them from political interference had produced generally disappointing results. In this context, a lesson for (and from) the international community's engagement on rule of law reform was that externally driven technocratic reform initiatives could not serve "as a substitute for [domestic Bosnian] political consensus-building... [or as] a cause, rather than a consequence, of broader socio-political change" (Donais 2013, p. 198). Similarly, despite some successes in anti-corruption actions taken by the international community at the administrative level, Donais observed at that time "more troubling is the persistence of large-scale political corruption, and the perverse incentives it creates for those in power to resist any reforms that threaten their privileges," as a consequence of which "Bosnian political parties are considered by Bosnians to be the most corrupt institutions in the country" (Donais 2013, p. 202).

As the May 2019 GTI (2019b) report demonstrates, these historical dynamics of the region's post-Cold War political fragmentation and instability, violent conflict, economic dislocation, and the embedded ties between national political parties and (national and transnational) organized crime, have been amplified by the accident of geography. The region is a transit route for heroin trafficking from Afghanistan via Turkey into the EU; for cocaine moving from Latin America to Europe; for cannabis from Albania also being shipped to Europe; and for synthetic drugs. In addition to narcotics, cigarette smuggling is a major organized crime activity, along with illicit firearms, and human trafficking (for prostitution and illegal migration) from the Middle East and North Africa into Western Europe. The combination of economic vulnerability, weak governance, and geographical location makes the Western Balkans a "hotspot" of, and for, transnational organized crime. The result is that "unlike in some states where criminal groups act like parasites living off the host of the state, in many countries of the Western Balkans, the relationship between state structures and criminal groups is more like a joint venture" (GTI 2019b, p. 30). The European Commission observed in its May 2019 report regarding Bosnia's application for EU membership, "corruption is widespread and all levels of government show signs of political capture directly affecting the daily life of citizens, notably in health, education, employment and public procurement matters. The policy, institutional and legal framework to prevent corruption is fragmented and has significant gaps" (European Commission 2019, p. 9).

The GTI report (2019a) provides examples from each of the states in the region, to demonstrate that these problems of crime and corruption are widespread and deeply entrenched in what it calls "the wider context of an ecosystem of crime" in the Western Balkans. However, the report also points out that this does not occur in a vacuum: the major demand markets (or "pull factors") for the trafficking of narcotics are the wealthy countries of Western Europe, and the most significant causes (or 'push factors') of illegal migration include violence, state fragility and lack of economic opportunity in North Africa. The policy solutions to those issues, therefore, also do not lie only in addressing the problem of weak or absent rule of law within the states of the Balkans region. The conclusion of the current chapter will return a consideration of addressing this wider context in offering suggestions and recommendations; but having focused above primarily on the negative aspect of rule of law deficits, the next section looks at more promising examples of good practices amongst at least some of the states of the Western Balkans as they have sought to address their own challenges and to make progress towards the 17 Sustainable Development Goals and Agenda 2030.

4 Implementing the SDGs: Recognizing Challenges and Deficits

Following Croatia's successful accession as a new member of the European Union on 1 July 2013, the remaining Western Balkans states have been at differing points in their own accession negotiations. Montenegro, Serbia, Albania, and the Republic of North Macedonia are official candidates to join the EU; accession negotiations and chapters have been opened with both Montenegro and Serbia. Bosnia and Herzegovina, and Kosovo are potential candidates, although five EU Member States—Cyprus, Greece, Romania, Slovakia, and Spain—have not recognized Kosovo's 2008 declaration of independence (nor have Serbia or Bosnia and Herzegovina).

In their 2019 Voluntary National Reviews (VNRs) of their efforts and accomplishments to date towards implementing Agenda 2030 and the Sustainable Development Goals, available through the UN Department of Economic and Social Affairs, both Serbia and Bosnia and Herzegovina explicitly connect these efforts with their national goals of achieving EU membership (Bosnia and Herzegovina April 2019; and Republic of Serbia 2019).[5] In their 103 pages long report, the Serbian VNR identifies six strategic paths for the state's "growing into sustainability": (1) increasing connectivity, partnership and integration of Serbia with Europe and the world; (2) achieving faster, inclusive and sustainable economic growth based on the country's economic, scientific and innovative potential; (3) the efficient and effective provision of public services, including social protection, health care, and pay equity; (4) improving human rights and security, including minority rights, gender equality and social justice; (5) provision of twenty-first century education with accessibility for all citizens; and (6) transformative digitalization of government, administration and society, which also will help to provide reliable, timely and high quality data for monitoring and reporting on the indicators and targets for the SDGs. The Serbian review then reports on each of the 17 Goals through two lenses—a "youth perspective" and a "local self-government perspective" (Republic

[5]References will be made in this chapter to the Bosnian and Serbian VNRs, as the most recent (together with Croatia). Albania submitted a VNR in 2018, and North Macedonia has indicated its desire to submit a report for the 2020 High Level Political Forum

of Serbia 2019b). Bosnia's almost equally-lengthy Voluntary National Review divides its main body of reporting into the 2030 Agenda's so-called "5 Ps" categories of People, Planet, Prosperity, Peace, and Partnership, with SDG 16 falling under the fourth P, Peace (Bosnia and Herzegovina April 2019a).

While intended to demonstrate each state's positive and constructive efforts in making progress across the range of goals, targets and indicators, and to provide examples of good practices and lessons learned, both reports also provide carefully tempered, and at times perhaps even surprisingly self-critical, assessments of the status of their achievements related to SDG16. The Serbian review notes in its local self-government commentary "despite the existence of a legal and institutional frame, significant challenges remain for the implementation of the principle of accountability, especially anti-corruption as one of its key elements" (Republic of Serbia 2019b, p. 70). One response is the new initiative for 2018–2020 to establish Local Anti-Corruption Plans, developed by the Serbian Anti-Corruption Agency and the Standing Conference of Towns and Municipalities, and supported financially by the Swiss government and institutionally by the UN Office for Project Services, which is intended to help local government bodies build capacity to provide greater budget transparency and public consultation and participation in the adoption of local regulations. Notably absent from the review, are any explicit discussions of transnational organized crime, or of negotiations over Belgrade's position on the final status of Kosovo.

The Bosnian Voluntary National Review is perhaps even more open in its self-critical analysis. The report notes positive developments, including that in 2018 the country was removed from the Financial Action Task Force's list of "high risk third countries" with major structural deficiencies in countering money laundering and terror financing; that it has ratified all of the main European and international human rights instruments; and that the Council of Ministers of Bosnia and Herzegovina in late 2017 approved a Strategy to Combat Organized Crime. However, on its' "SDG Dashboard" the report identifies SDG 16 as one of five Goals (out of the 17 SDGs) on which Bosnia is "stagnating," meaning that its score is increasing at a rate less than 50% of what is needed to achieve that Goal by 2030. On four more SDGs, it reports a decreasing score, i.e., worsening rather than improving at all. The review recognizes that "it is still necessary to strengthen judicial independence, especially independence from political influence," and that "Bosnia and Herzegovina is a source, destination and transit country for women, children and men that fall victim to human trafficking." On anti-corruption initiatives, it notes that a variety of strategy papers have been adopted "at the national, entity, Brcko District and lower levels of government; however, the strategies in place have not been fully implemented," and that both the World Bank and Transparency International ranked Bosnia and Herzegovina in the bottom half of their global rankings of states for combating corruption (Bosnia and Herzegovina April 2019a, pp. 81–85).

These two voluntary reports offer mixed messages—deliberately and as per the intent of the process—on the countries' internal progress towards achieving the 2030 Agenda. Notably, and constructively for our purposes here, both report significant challenges and deficits in measures undertaken and results achieved towards SDG

16 and the rule of law. The problems faced in this dimension—by the Bosnian and Serbian states, and by the Western Balkans region more generally—also have been amply documented in the "Hotspots" study by The Global Initiative, and the accession reports of the European Commission. The question for the governments of the region, for their societies, and for international stakeholders (and leaving aside for now the globally-indivisible characterization of the SDGs for all Member States of the UN), is what needs to be done and what can be done to improve, or reverse, the status of rule of law on those countries' "SDG Dashboards" so that the arrow points up towards 2030. As the Serbian review observes in its conclusion, the challenge is to find practical measures to move past "the old ways of doing things and preserving social privileges for the few at the expense of the majority – but really at the expense of all" (Republic of Serbia 2019b).

5 A Roadmap for Policy and Practice

In its concluding analysis of the "ecosystem of crime" in the Western Balkans, The Global Initiative Against Transnational Organized Crime warns that "political elites provide an umbrella of protection for criminal groups (which may involve their family and friends) and their activities, while the criminal groups help the political elites to enrich themselves, as well as gain and keep power," and that this corruption and associated political clientelism has expanded its reach into the public and private sectors of business through "tendering processes, insider deals, [and] decisions about zoning as well as money laundering." Numerous examples of this ecosystem were cited for Albania, North Macedonia, Kosovo, Bosnia and Herzegovina, and Serbia. Although the "Hotspots" analysis gives a detailed bottom-up or micro-level look at examples of criminal activity and corruption, its authors state that such an analysis "needs to go hand in hand with a top-down look at the environment that enables them. Any sustainable solution will have to address both the high-level enabling factors and the local conditions of vulnerability" (GTI 2019b, p. 35).

One recent initiative that addresses the practical challenges of supporting and enhancing rule of law and SDG 16 has been the so-called Pathfinders group of states, international organizations and civil society actors,[6] which in June 2019 produced "The Roadmap for Peaceful, Just and Inclusive Societies" (Pathfinders July 2019). The Pathfinders report focuses on SDG 16 as its theme, although it points out that the twelve Targets of SDG 16 are only one third of the thirty-six SDG targets that directly relate to and measure aspects of peace, inclusion, and access to justice. Substantively, the Roadmap identifies a menu of nine "catalytic actions":

1. Scale up violence prevention for women and children, and for vulnerable groups;
2. Build safe, inclusive, and resilient cities;

[6]None of the Western Balkans states are amongst the 31 founding member states of the Pathfinders group.

3. Targeted prevention for countries and communities most likely to be left behind;
4. Increase justice and legal empowerment;
5. Commitment to open and responsive government;
6. Reduce corruption and illicit financial and arms flows;
7. Legal identity and birth registration for all;
8. Empower people as agents of change;
9. Respect all human rights and promote gender equality.

Each of these nine catalytic actions in turn is linked to specific SDG targets, most of them (with the exceptions of 4 and 7 above) being linked to multiple targets across several different Goals, which the Roadmap therefore labels "SDG16+."

Although the Pathfinders' Roadmap does not seek to identify particular countries' experiences as problematic examples, it does offer recommendations of policies or other initiatives that should be undertaken as positive contributions to each of the nine catalytic actions. For example under the heading of the fourth catalytic action, "Increase justice and legal empowerment," it recommends taking measures to improve citizens' access to legal aid for civil and criminal matters "building on the UN Principles and Guidelines on Access to Legal Aid and the UNDP/UNODC Global Study on Legal Aid," increasing the use of mobile courts and of alternative dispute resolution mechanisms, and employing surveys to gain reliable data on legal needs, rates of victimization, and confidence in justice and security institutions (Pathfinders July 2019). Under the sixth catalytic action, "Reduce corruption and illicit financial and arms flows," the Roadmap includes amongst its recommendations that states make greater use of the Mechanism for the Review of Implementation of the United Nations Convention against Corruption, and that they work to "increase efforts to combat money laundering and recover stolen assets through relevant international treaties, the Stolen Asset Recovery Initiative, and the Global Forum on Asset Recovery" (Pathfinders July 2019, p. 32).

Supporting these recommendations and working towards the Roadmap, the Pathfinders' report also identifies four 'enablers' that it suggests are needed to provide support and momentum for the list of actions it sets out: increased investment in knowledge, evidence, and data to inform decisions and to identify gaps; the mobilization of financial resources from international public finance, the private sector, and innovative new sources; continuing to build knowledge-exchange networks, including country champions and centers of excellence; and through all of these also, building and reinforcing communication and advocacy across all stakeholders—noting that "the exposure of corruption is increasingly bringing people out onto the streets, reflecting widespread anger at the failure of governance and of the manipulation of institutions by elites" (Pathfinders July 2019, p. 45). The United Nations Office on Drugs and Crime, it should be noted, already provides UN Member States with practical mechanisms, frameworks, reports, data collection and analysis, and information sharing capabilities to support these actions and enablers (UNODC 2019).

The Roadmap offers practical suggestions and directions for advancing the rule of law, peacebuilding, and Agenda 2030. These are critical needs, in that making progress requires making policy choices and taking positive actions. In that sense, they also are technocratic and institutional-administrative measures, offered as advice by the international community—with the latter's financial, technical and political support tied to the Balkan states' demonstrating progress in the reforms required of them as they seek accession to the European Union.

Returning to the specific context of the challenges and realities of the Western Balkans, supporting and deepening the rule of law, and implementing Agenda 2030, a final cautionary note nevertheless is needed regarding "the inherent limits of international power and authority in post-conflict spaces" and "the perils of using rule of law reforms as instruments for the achievement of broader political goals" (Donais 2013, pp. 204–205). In cases of deeply embedded problems of corruption, and where national and local political elites seek to protect their own narrow interests (and profits) against proposals for greater transparency, accountability, and responsibility in government, "it will be imperative to focus less on the agency of international actors as architects, implementers and enforcers of the rule of law," and instead to look for opportunities and processes through which well-intended external actors "can facilitate domestic political dynamics that support, over the longer term, the emergence of the rule of law" (Donais 2013, p. 207). The members of the European Union, as the current expression of an association of states that was itself a regional and international peace project in its origins, can and should continue to reach out to their Balkans neighbors with the positive and realistic prospect of admission as new EU members, as vital encouragement for those governments and societies to undertake much-needed reforms. With that encouragement and support by external partners, it nonetheless will be through determined domestic or national activation and engagement by the governments and civil societies in the Western Balkans that no one will be left behind in the 2030 Agenda.

References

A/47/277-S/24111 Report of the Secretary-General, *An Agenda for Peace: Preventive diplomacy, peacemaking and peace-keeping* 17 June 1992.

A/RES/70/1 Transforming our world: the 2030 Agenda for Sustainable Development 25 September 2015.

Ashdown, P. (2002). "What I Learned in Bosnia" *The New York Times*, October 28 2002, 25. Available at https://nyti.ms/2yqbtUG

Chandler, D. (2004). The problems of 'Nation-Building': Imposing bureaucratic 'rule from above'. *Cambridge Review of International Affairs, 17*(3), 577–591.

Donais, T. (2013). Power politics and the rule of law in post-Dayton Bosnia. *Studies in Social Justice, 7*(2), 189–210.

European Commission. (2019, May). Commission Opinion on Bosnia and Herzegovina's application for membership of the European Union, COM (2019) 261 Final, Brussels. Available at https://bit.ly/3aTVOdv

Khan, I. (2017). How can the rule of law advance sustainable development in a troubled and turbulent world? *McGill Journal of Sustainable Development Law, 13*(2), 210–218.

Kritz, N. J. (2001). The rule of law in the postconflict phase: Building a stable peace. In C. A. Crocker, F. O. Hampson, & P. Aall (Eds.), *Turbulent peace: The challenges of managing international conflict* (pp. 801–820). Washington, DC: United States Institute of Peace Press.

Pathfinders for Peaceful, Just and Inclusive Societies. (2019). *The roadmap for peaceful, just and inclusive societies – A call to action to change our World*. New York: Center on International Cooperation. Available at https://bit.ly/3ddSLhM

Ryan, B. J. (2010). Policing the state of exception in Kosovo. In A. Hehir (Ed.), (2001) *Kosovo, Intervention and Statebuilding: The international community and the transition to independence* (pp. 114–131). London: Routledge.

S/2004/616 Report of the Secretary-General, *The rule of law and transitional justice in conflict and post-conflict societies* 23 August 2004.

Skendaj, E. (2014). International insulation from politics and the challenge of state building: Learning from Kosovo. *Global Governance, 20*(3), 459–481.

The Global Initiative Against Transnational Organized Crime. (2019a, February). "Organized Crime, SDG 16 and the High-Level Political Forum," Policy Note. Available at https://bit.ly/2SwDWix

The Global Initiative Against Transnational Organized Crime. (2019b, May). "Hotspots of Organized Crime in the Western Balkans: Local vulnerabilities in a regional context." Available at https://bit.ly/2KXh8Ep

United Nations Department of Economic and Social Affairs. (2019a, April). *Bosnia and Herzegovina voluntary review: Implementation of agenda 2030 and the sustainable development goals in Bosnia and Herzegovina,* Available at https://bit.ly/2Yu9w4v

United Nations Department of Economic and Social Affairs. (2019b). Republic of Serbia "Towards Equality of Sustainable Opportunities for Everyone and Everywhere in Serbia Through Growing into Sustainability," *Voluntary National Review of the Republic of Serbia on the Implementation of the 2030 Agenda for Sustainable Development,* Available at https://bit.ly/35trTHW

United Nations Office on Drugs and Crime. (2019). *UNODC and the 2030 Agenda for Sustainable Development*, at https://bit.ly/3dcg4ZG

Alistair D. Edgar Dr. is Associate Dean of the School of International Policy & Governance at the Balsillie School of International Affairs, Wilfrid Laurier University (Waterloo, Canada). He served as Executive Director of the Academic Council on the United Nations System (ACUNS), 2003–2018. He is an editor for *Global Governance* journal, and co-editor for *The ACUNS Series on the United Nations System*. Currently he serves as President of the Canadian Landmine Foundation. His research focuses on war-to-peace and post-conflict transitions, especially on issues of mass atrocity crimes and justice. He has worked on this topic in Afghanistan, Cambodia, Kosovo, and Uganda. Recent publications have looked at the United Nations peacekeeping and conflict management; the role of elected members of the UN Security Council; and Canadian defence and security policies. Dr. Edgar has his PhD in Political Science from Queen's University (Kingston, Canada); MA in Political Science from the University of British Columbia (Vancouver, Canada); and BA Honours in History from Sidney Sussex College (Cambridge University, Cambridge, UK). He was the John M. Olin Doctoral Fellow in Economics and National Security at the Centre for International Affairs, Harvard University (1992–1993). E- mail: aedgar@wlu.ca.

Part V
Research and the Promotion of Peaceful and Inclusive Societies

Crime, Victimization, and Intentions to Migrate in the Northern Triangle

Christopher Inkpen, Wayne J. Pitts, and Pamela K. Lattimore

Abstract Migration from Central American countries to the United States has been driven to the forefront of the American political discourse. Historically, regional migration to the United States has been characterized in large part by cyclical and permanent labor migration as well as forced displacement, either due to state violence or general insecurity. More recently, attention has shifted to the role that transnational gangs play in spurring migration, specifically in the Northern Triangle countries of Guatemala, El Salvador, and Honduras. This analysis uses survey data collected by the Latin American Public Opinion Project from the biennial *AmericasBarometer* survey of the Northern Triangle countries from 2006 to 2016 to explore the relationship between the intent to migrate and different forms of violence and insecurity. We focus on the role of personal victimization and public perception of gangs as they relate to expressed intention to emigrate from the Northern Triangle. The investigation then examines the association between migration decisions, household victimization, and responses to community violence.

Keywords Migration · Victimization · Crime · Gang violence · Northern Triangle · Central America

1 Introduction

In December 1948, the United Nations General Assembly established a Universal Declaration of Human Rights to unequivocally state the rights of "all members of the human family," (UDHR 1948). Thirty articles outline principles designed to promote just, peaceful, and inclusive societies and established the world's common

Special thanks to Amanda Witwer, RTI International for graphic contributions.

C. Inkpen (✉) · W. J. Pitts · P. K. Lattimore
RTI International, Division for Applied Justice Research, Durham, NC, USA
e-mail: cinkpen@rti.org; wpitts@rti.org; lattimore@rti.org

H. Kury, S. Redo (eds.), *Crime Prevention and Justice in 2030*,
https://doi.org/10.1007/978-3-030-56227-4_20

standards of achievement for evaluating fundamental human rights. While it could be argued that all these articles address issues relevant to violence and migration, five are especially important to consider for the current discussion. Article 3 declares, "everyone has the right to life, liberty and security of person." Essentially, all humans have the right to be free of violence and victimization. Article 13 establishes freedom of movement within a nation-state. Individuals have the right to migrate as they see fit within the boundaries of their own country. Article 14 formalizes the principle of asylum by affirming that all people have the right to seek and enjoy protection from persecution in other countries. "Everyone has the right to work, to free choice of employment, to just and favorable conditions of work and to protection against unemployment," under Article 23. Finally, Article 25, says that all people have the right to a standard of living adequate for the health and well-being, including food, clothing, housing, and medical care. On the 70th anniversary of the Declaration, progress in ensuring that these articles are met is evident but incomplete. International migration and maintaining national sovereignty are at the crux of this essay, as the right to be secure from crime and violence and the right to earn an adequate standard of living is often inaccessible in the Northern Triangle countries of Guatemala, El Salvador, and Honduras. Yet, these deficiencies do not always meet the standards required to seek asylum and, even when they do, the barriers to achieving protection in another country are formidable.

In 2015, the United Nations General Assembly launched the 2030 Agenda for Sustainable Development (General Assembly of the United Nations: *Transforming our world* 2015). Grounded in the Universal Declaration of Human Rights, the Agenda outlines seventeen broad development goals, all relevant to matters of crime, violence, and migration that are discussed in this essay. Of note, the Agenda has relevance for countries of origin, transit, and destination within a migration path. Goal 10 addresses matters of global inequality and calls for states to "facilitate orderly, safe, regular and responsible migration," including plans to reduce the costs of remittances made by migrants. Other goals attend to matters of importance to vulnerable populations considering migration including poverty (Goal 1), access to health care (Goal 3), full and productive employment (Goal 8), security (Goal 11), and rule of law (Goal 16). Of course, multilateral governance and ensuring even perfunctory commitments by the states to the Agenda presented by the UN General Assembly is necessarily complex. Considering the Universal Declaration for Human Rights and the 2030 Agenda, this essay considers empirical evidence to measure the relationship between expressing intentions to migrate and crime, violence, and perceptions of insecurity for residents of the Northern Triangle countries of Guatemala, El Salvador, and Honduras.

The decision to migrate is complex, with motivating factors operating at the individual, familial, community, and country level (Haug 2008; Massey et al. 1999; Ortega and Peri 2013; Stark and Bloom 1985; Todaro 1976). Migration is often tied to economic considerations within the household and community (Stark and Bloom 1985). However, issues of unemployment and financial instability do not occur in a vacuum, and countries with limited economic opportunities are often plagued with weakened institutions and higher levels of social disorder and crime (Carlson and

Michalowski 1997). More recently, scholars have drawn attention to the weaknesses of thinking of the dichotomy of forced versus voluntary migration in favor of a more nuanced conception that reaches beyond questions of economic opportunities and security risks (Carte et al. 2019; Cook Heffron 2019; Heidbrink 2019). This study examines the relationship between personal and familial victimization, opinions on security, and other factors linked to expressing the desire to migrate. We focus on migration from the Northern Triangle countries of Guatemala, El Salvador, and Honduras using pooled data from the Latin American Public Opinion Project biennial *AmericasBarometer* survey from 2006 to 2016, to examine the relationship between migration intentions and violence and victimization in countries suffering from the pervasiveness of gangs and organized crime.

2 Background

Approximately three-fourths of all irregular migrants in the United States, or just over an estimated eight million migrants, were born in Mexico, Central America or the Caribbean (Rosenblum and Ruiz Soto 2015). While migration flows from Mexico have declined in recent years, the percentage of migrants from the Northern Triangle countries of Guatemala, El Salvador, and Honduras have increased, growing nearly tenfold since 1980 (Obinna and Field 2019). Considering only the Northern Triangle countries, nearly five million regular and irregular migrants to the United States come from these three countries alone (Obinna and Field 2019). Conceptual frameworks used to explain the migration decision-making processes often consider both aspirations to migrate and the capacity to fulfill one's desire (Carling and Schewel 2018; de Haas 2010; Migali and Scipioni 2019).

Research on the nexus between migration and crime often looks at the association between internal migration and increased crime in urban areas or analyses of crime and immigration in host countries (Berry Cullen and Levitt 1999, Kinman and Lee 1966; Martinez and Lee 2006; Ousey and Kubrin 2018; Sampson and Wooldredge 1986). Perhaps counterintuitively, research suggests that for Mexican migrants, returning home is linked with lowered rates of violence in sending communities (Bucheli et al. 2019). Previous studies on the intention to migrate have established the relationship between crime and migration in the Americas, but these studies do not explore personal versus familial victimization, the increasing influence of gangs, or country-specific migration dynamics in the Americas (Wood et al. 2010). This essay draws upon research on social disorder to contribute to the understanding of migration as a multi-faceted response to one's environment that includes issues of victimization and perceptions of security.

2.1 Violence and Victimization in the Northern Triangle

The Northern Triangle is currently suffering an intense public security crisis, as the homicide rate in these countries persistently ranks among the highest, not only in the Americas, but in the world (Cara Labrador and Renwick 2018). Its security and justice sector institutions are plagued by a lack of resources, corruption, and the spreading influence of gangs and organized crime, which erode advances made in police and justice sector reforms (Eguizábal et al. 2015). As of 2017, El Salvador was the world's most violent country, with an intentional homicide rate of 61.8 per 100,000 residents and neighboring Honduras ranks third with a rate of 41.7 (UNODC 2019a). While all three governments have taken expanded strategies to promote violence prevention, the pervasiveness of domestic gangs persists and consequently internal displacements and foreign migrations have not ceased (Obinna and Field 2019). Guatemala, currently reporting 26.1 intentional homicides per 100,000 residents, has seen reductions in the homicide rate. Yet violence in Honduras has become so endemic that a 2017 analysis of recent demographic data shows that interpersonal violence is the second-leading cause of mortality and the number one cause of premature death (UNODC 2019a). At the same time, Honduras has a low murder conviction rate. In 2015, this rate stood at 6.2 per every 100 recorded homicides (319 convictions for 5148 intentional homicides) (UNODC 2019a). This low conviction rate suggests a need for the strengthening of criminal justice institutions in the country.

Globally, larger cities tend to have homicides rates similar to national rates, however the pattern in the Northern Triangle does not follow. San Pedro Sula in Honduras, for example, has a homicide rate of 113 per 100,000 in the population in 2017 and Tegucigalpa, the capital of Honduras, at 91 per 100,000 in the population was far higher than the national rate of 57 per 100,000. La Ceiba, a mid-sized city in Honduras, had a homicide rate of 131 per 100,000 in the population, more than double the national rate. Similarly, Guatemala City, the capital of Guatemala, had a rate of 65 per 100,00 and San Salvador, the capital of El Salvador, had a homicide rate of 193 per 100,000 in the population compared to a national rate of 83 per 100,000 in 2017 (UNODC 2019a). More worrisome is the inordinately high homicide rates among younger, especially male, populations. In 2016, the homicide rate in El Salvador for the age group 15–29 years climbed to 296 per 100,000 in the population. A 14-year-old Salvadoran boy has an 8% statistical risk of being intentionally killed during the next 30 years (UNODC 2019b).

El Salvador, Honduras, and Guatemala have suffered seriously from gang activities. Gang violence across the Northern Triangle is a significant concern and is suggested to be a major contributor to homicide. In Honduras and El Salvador, the impact of gangs is especially severe. According to the newly released UNODC homicide reports, there were about 7000 gang members in Honduras in 2015 while much smaller El Salvador[1] had about ten times as many (UNODC 2019a). Further research suggests that gang members account for a disproportionate number of homicide victims. In El Salvador, the data show that the numbers of victims between the two main rival gangs, MS-13 and Barrio 18, were nearly identical in 2015 (UNODC 2019a). Also, of concern are the number of criminal deportees that have been returned to the Northern Triangle, over 300,000 individuals between 2003 and 2015. In El Salvador and Honduras, deportees during this period accounted for 1.5% of the national populations (UNODC 2019a).

In addition, Honduras' proximity to Mexico makes it highly susceptible to the influence of violent transnational drug-trafficking organizations based in that country, such as the Zetas and other criminal bands (Barrick and Pitts 2013). Domestic trafficking cartels, such as the *Cachiros* and *Valle* organizations, have also operated within Honduras to facilitate the transfer of drugs northward. As a result of the confluence of cartel and gang-related violence, more than half of Honduran citizens report feeling insecure in public (Zechmeister 2014). The current climate of anti-gang activity in Central America includes the unfavorable use of state violence (Ellis 2018). This confluence of issues highlights the need for national and regional violence prevention programs that account for the historically unstable and lopsided relationship between the state and the citizenry.

The Northern Triangle countries' strategic location between the cocaine-producing Andean nations and the large U.S. drug market suggests it will continue to be a principal drug transshipment site on the busy Central America-Mexico corridor. This is especially important given the disproportionately high homicide rates in the Northern Triangle, compared to other cocaine trafficking corridors in other parts of the world. Drug flows appear to affect violence patterns in different ways (UNODC 2019a). According to the U.S. Department of State's Bureau of International Narcotics and Law Enforcement Affairs (INL), "approximately 80% of all suspected drug flights departing from South America first landed in Honduras" in 2016, with 3–4 metric tons of the drugs passing through the country monthly in 2015. The large volume of cocaine passing through the country and the rising involvement of violent street gangs in smuggling operations indicate that police and criminal justice institutions in the country will face heightening pressure to confront and resolve violent crime. Homicide rates were particularly high in those parts of Guatemala and Honduras where cocaine was being trafficked (UNODC 2019a).

Jaitman and colleagues (2017) provide a detailed analysis of the estimated costs (social costs, private sector costs, and government costs) associated with homicide and other forms of violence in Latin America and the Caribbean. Central America accounted for 64% of the $16.5 billion in victimization costs associated with crime

[1]Standing at 6.4 million in 2019, the population of El Salvador is also smaller than that of Honduras (9.5 million). The newly released national census shows the population of Guatemala at just over 14 million, some 3 million less than previously estimated (El Instituto Nacional de Estadística 2018).

in Latin America and the Caribbean. With financial costs far above the Latin American regional estimates, homicide in Honduras was estimated to cost 1.6% of the Gross Domestic Product (GDP) with El Salvador accounting for 0.86% of GDP (Jaitman et al. 2017).

2.2 Violence and Migration

The dynamics of emigration and internal displacement in the Northern Triangle countries of Guatemala, Honduras, and El Salvador and the relationship to crime and violence are complex in character and dimension, which often leads to a persistence of misconceptions by governments, civil society, academics, and the general public. As a result, policy interventions are often reactionary, not responsive to the root causes of the problem, and not supported by empirical evidence (Cantor 2014). Wood et al. (2010) test the relationship between victimization and migration in Latin America using data from 17 countries included in the 2002–2004 *AmericasBarometer* survey, finding that victimization was linked with 30% higher odds of intending to migrate. Although concerns about insecurity are frequently cited as one of the principle factors affecting the decision to migrate, a growing body of literature points to the complexity of individual migration decisions (Clemens 2017; Lorenzen 2017; Migali and Scipioni 2019). Structured interviews and clinical testing of a convenience sample of recent Central American migrants in McAllen, Texas revealed high rates of psychological distress and trauma exposure, with 83% of respondents citing violence as the primary reason for migrating (Keller et al. 2017). Other research suggests that while violence may initially stimulate displacement, migratory experiences and correspondence through social networks could lead other network members to migrate as well. Thus, migration may increase even when violence is static or subsides (Clemens 2017). However, some quantitative analyses suggest that violence factors are unrelated or at least over-emphasized in regards to the decision to migrate (Basu and Pearlman 2017; Hiskey et al. 2018; Quijada and Sierra 2019).

2.3 Forced Displacement

Forced displacement due to crime and violence in the Northern Triangle, despite being mentioned regularly in newspapers and academic articles published about the region, is often poorly understood (Cantor 2014; Carte et al. 2019; Heidbrink 2019). Some studies have gone even further and characterized the effect of violence on migration flows as "theoretically ambiguous," (Orozco-Aleman and Gonzalez-Lozano 2018). These arguments commonly mention the many years of Civil War and unrest in the region from the mid-1980s through the following decade, which certainly warrant consideration, although perhaps not to the degree often mentioned.

In fact, focused attention on the legacy of the wars, extreme cases of violence, and pervasive political repression that has plagued Central America, can serve to divert attention from the daily security concerns of common citizens who are victims of robbery, assault, and street crimes (Wood et al. 2010). Thefts on public transports and fear of walking alone in one's own neighborhood are contributors to general feelings of insecurity (Briceño-León and Zubillaga 2002; Skogan 1986). Previous research has shown that forced displacement attributed to organized crime does not occur uniformly and that there are areas of concentrated effects where criminal groups operate (Cantor 2014). The dynamics of the current patterns of forced displacement are multifaceted and conditional and as such it is difficult to build models with the necessary data sources to analyze empirical patterns of displacement.

Forced displacement does not only refer to international migrations but is instead predominantly internal in nature (Cantor 2014). Internal forced displacements from rural to urban areas, in Guatemala, often precede attempts to migrate internationally (Scarnato 2019). Previous studies also present a clear relationship between gang activities and forced displacement (Boulton 2011). Research has shown that homicide rates in high drug trafficking hotspots in the Northern Triangle are much higher, often twice as much, compared to homicide rates in other areas (Clemens 2017; Demombynes 2011). Violence can serve as both a cause and a consequence of migration (Cook Heffron 2019). Some authors distinguish the effects of violence and its impacts on migration. For example, Orozco-Aleman and Gonzalez-Lozano (2018) differentiate the effects of local violence and transit violence (violence along the route to the Mexico-United States border). In Mexico, transit violence was found to reduce migration, while local violence increased migration. This serves to highlight the need for a nuanced understanding of violence and crime to understand their roles in the decision to migrate.

2.4 *Current Study*

This study aims to examine how measures of crime and victimization relate with expressing a desire to leave one's country in the Northern Triangle countries of Guatemala, El Salvador, and Honduras by using data from cross-sectional national surveys collected biennially from 2006 to 2016. To address issues particularly relevant to the Northern Triangle, this investigation explores the association of the intent to migrate and victimization, experienced personally or by family members, along with the influence of gangs in one's neighborhood. To isolate the relationship between crime, victimization, and migration, models control for traditional predictors of migration, including demographic characteristics, economic perceptions, and migrant connections. This analysis addresses some limitations of past studies by incorporating national-level data spanning over a decade. Moreover, through a series of sub-analyses, this study parses out the relationship between fear of crime and community organization linked to fear of crime.

Table 1 Correlates of intentions to migrate in Central America

Drivers of intentions to migrate	Hypothesized direction of relationship	Supporting literature
Age	–	Studies have shown that in the Northern Triangle older people are less likely to migrate (Hiskey et al. 2018). Wood et al. (2010) show that migration decreases (linearly) with age, while others report a curvilinear effect related to age (Connor and Massey 2010; Massey et al. 1994)
Gender	–	Several studies in the Northern Triangle have shown a lower odds of females having intentions to migrate (Hiskey et al. 2014, 2018; Wood et al. 2010)
Marital status	/	Research conducted in Mexico has shown that marital status does not predict intentions to migrate (Creighton 2013)
Education	+	Some researchers find that education is correlated with migration (Connor and Massey 2010; Feliciano 2005), whereas others posit that this relationship is unclear in the Northern Triangle (Hiskey et al. 2018). The more educated are more likely to prepare for migration (Migali and Scipioni 2019)
Urban areas	+	Living in an urban area or capital has been shown to be correlated with migration (Fussell and Massey 2004; Wood et al. 2010), although the process is often distinct from rural migration, and this relationship was not confirmed in El Salvador and Honduras (Hiskey et al. 2018)
Life satisfaction	+	Individuals with high life satisfaction are less likely to express intentions to migrate (Chindarkar 2014)
Victimization	+	Victimization has been found to be related to intentions to migrate in the Northern Triangle (Hiskey et al. 2018; Wood et al. 2010)
Fear of crime	+	Perceptions of insecurity plays a significant role on intentions to migrate among Central Americans (Hiskey et al. 2014)
Remittances	+	Having the support of others living abroad is demonstrated to be positively correlated with intentions to migrate (Connor and Massey 2010; Hiskey et al. 2018; Wood et al. 2010)

Providing a comprehensive review of the historical predictors of individual migration decisions is beyond the scope of this essay. However, Table 1 presents the individual-level factors that we hypothesize correlate with intentions to migrate, the proposed direction of the relationship, and research that supports this hypothesis. Past research suggests that desires to migrate are higher in younger, unmarried men (Massey et al. 1994). Education and urban residence have both been linked with higher propensity to migrate (Wood et al. 2010), although these relationships in the Northern Triangle remain unclear (Hiskey et al. 2018). Personal satisfaction with one's life is linked with a lower propensity to migrate. Conversely, victimization and measures of neighborhood insecurity are correlated with a higher likelihood to express a desire to migrate. Lastly, receiving remittances as part of one's household income is also tied to greater desires to migrate. Thus, these established predictors of migrant desires serve as a baseline and benchmark for examinations that seek to parse out the constituent factors that can inform one's decision to migrate.

3 Data and Methods

3.1 Data and Measures

The data for this study come from national surveys of Guatemala, El Salvador, and Honduras collected as part of the Latin American Public Opinion Project's (LAPOP) *AmericasBarometer* poll.[2] The *AmericasBarometer* survey is a collected roughly every 2 years in more than 30 countries in the Americas, via a nationally representative stratified sampling design, and covers topic areas such as perceptions of corruption, crime, and political efficacy. The pooled sample of 27,863 adult respondents for this analysis spans from 2006 to 2016 for unweighted national samples of 9022 Guatemalans, 9322 Salvadorans, and 9519 Honduran residents. However, several measures used in this study are not asked in every year, and as such we employ sub-sample analyses of certain years for some questions. Survey design variables incorporated into this analysis account for design effects from primary sampling units and strata.

The dependent variable for this study is a measure of intent to migrate; a question that asks respondents "*Do you have any intention of going to live or work in another country in the next three years?*" While this measure does not ask if the respondent plans to remain working and living outside his or her country of origin, it does probe if they have considered leaving the country and this measure as included in the LAPOP survey has been used in a number of studies exploring the correlates of migration (Chindarkar 2014; Graham and Markowitz 2011; Hiskey et al. 2014, 2018; Wood et al. 2010). Additional studies have explored this question as a dependent variable using the *Mexican Family Life Survey* from the Mexican Migration Project (Creighton 2013; Ryo 2013).

Previous research has utilized data from the LAPOP *AmericasBarometer* surveys to model motivations to migrate using individual level socio-economic factors, migration network variables, and governance indicators including perceptions of insecurity and victimization (Hiskey et al. 2014, 2018; Wood et al. 2010). The *AmericasBarometer* captures personal victimization by asking participants if they have been the victim of a crime in the past 12 months. In some survey years,

[2]Complete information on the survey instrument, methodology, and data is available at www.vanderbilt.edu/lapop/.

respondents were also asked if anyone in their household had been the victim of a crime in the past 12 months. In addition, this study includes a dichotomous measure identifying respondents that say gangs (*maras* or *pandillas)* affect life in their neighborhood "a lot" compared to answers of "somewhat", "a little", or "not at all". We also include two dichotomous measures that ask if respondents have (1) "felt the need to leave their neighborhood" or (2) "organized neighbors in the community" in response to fear of crime.

In addition to measures of crime and victimization, this study controls for several demographic characteristics, including sex, age, marital status, whether or not someone is currently working, years of schooling, and residence in a rural or urban location. Moreover, each national model includes a country-specific measure of low monthly household income. Given the fact that household income was measured in bins, and the thresholds for these bins changed in 2012 questionnaires for each country within the LAPOP sample, this analysis attempts to account for respondents living in houses earning less than $150 in Guatemala, less than $144 in El Salvador, and below a range of $144-$152 in Honduras, contrasting these responses to those who earn more and those who do not provide salary information.[3]

Models also account for personal and national perceptions of both crime and the economy. This analysis includes a measure for insecurity or *fear of crime*, asking if respondents feel "somewhat or very insecure" in their neighborhood compared to "somewhat or very secure." Additionally, we include a dichotomous variable that probes if respondents are "somewhat or very dissatisfied with their life," compared to those who are "somewhat or very satisfied." Respondents are also queried as to whether they think their personal economic situation and separately the country's economic situation are worse compared to 12 months ago. In Guatemala and El Salvador in each survey year, respondents were also asked what they think the country's biggest problem is, which we use to generate a dichotomous measure for responses of "crime or violence" compared to all other responses.

Lastly, as a proxy for migrant connections, models include a question that asks if the respondent or someone in the household receives remittances from someone outside of the country. Analyses conducted by the authors also tested for the influence of reporting that someone who used to live in the respondent's household now lives in another country and found consistent results, suggesting that these

[3]This analysis tries to account for changes in the exchange rate by using historical averages of the conversion rates for the Guatemala *Quetzal* and the Honduran *Lempira*. In Guatemala, from 2006 through 2010, this analysis uses the threshold of earning up to 1200 *Quetzales*, which averaged approximately $151 USD in the survey years. From 2012 to 2016, this study employs the upper threshold of 1080 *Quetzales*, which equated to roughly $142 USD in those survey years. In El Salvador, which uses the U.S. dollar as currency, from 2006 to 2010, this study used a threshold of $144 USD compared to $140 USD from 2012 to 2016. In Honduras, from 2006 to 2010, the threshold ranging from 1,900 to 2,500 *Lempira* was used, which equated to roughly $144 given exchange rates. For 2012, 2014, and 2016, the thresholds of 2750, 2900, and 2650 *Lempira* were used, for an average of less than $152 USD. Analyses without this measure were tested for each country and the main model findings persist. Sub-sample national analyses that include only years where the measure was consistent also confirm the general model findings.

variables contain shared variance. Yet, the question on familial migrant connections was not included in all years for every country and was thus dropped from final models.

3.2 Methods

This study employs logistic regression to examine the relationship between intentions to migrate, victimization, and gang presence while controlling for several other correlates of migration. Tables of analytical models display coefficients in odds ratios, first presenting coefficients from a base model including personal victimization, gang presence, and a continuous survey year variable before accounting for sociodemographic controls, perceptions of crime and the economy, and finally remittances.

Given that there is a non-trivial amount of missing cases on dependent and independent measures in this model (~1–3% depending on the question), we employ country-specific multiple imputation through chained equations to use as much available information from the survey as possible. The chained equation specification uses information from all independent variables, including those with missing values, but utilizes complete case analysis of sex, age, marital status, rural or urban residence, survey year, and household income to impute 10 datasets from which complete case estimates can be drawn. Imputation models also account for sampling design variables and logistic regression models employ the **svyset** package from Stata version 14.2 to account for design effects in analytical models.

As a number of the measures this study examines were not collected in every survey year, we perform a series of sub-sample analyses for each country, using data only from years where all relevant survey questions were asked to perform a separate multiple imputation. Sub-sample analyses for Guatemala (imputed $n = 3066$) include surveys from 2012 and 2014, whereas El Salvador (imputed $n = 4550$) uses survey data from 2010, 2012, and 2016, and Honduras (imputed $n = 6416$) employs data from all surveys beginning in 2010 through 2016.

3.3 Descriptive Results

This study proceeds by describing the sample and distribution on key variables before turning to a series of logistic regression models of intentions to migrate in the Northern Triangle. Figure 1 shows proportion of each national sample that report intentions to migrate in the next 3 years. Here, although there is some intra-country variability, the general trend appears to show a decrease from 2006 to 2012 followed by a sharp increase in 2014 and 2016. With the lowest levels of intent to migrate in 2006, roughly 15% of the sample from El Salvador indicated that they planned to migrate in the next 3 years, compared to more than 25% in 2016. Alternatively,

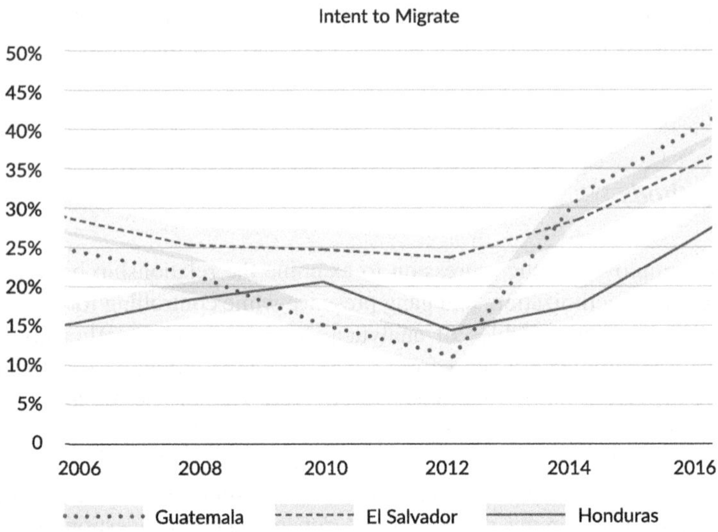

Fig. 1 Percentage of annual sample reporting intentions to migrate within the Northern Triangle, source: Latin America Public Opinion Project AmericasBarometer Surveys, 2006–2016

Honduras began in 2006 with nearly 25% of the sample indicating an intent to migrate only to finish with more than 40% of the sample expressing this desire in 2016. Guatemala followed this general trend, with more than 35% suggesting a desire to leave the country in 2016. This simple description shows that the desire to migrate, always present in the Northern Triangle, has grown sharply over the past decade.

Personal victimization, as reflected in the LAPOP samples in Fig. 2, has grown over time as well, although the rate of increase is more gradual compared to intentions to migrate. Since 2006, all countries in the Northern Triangle have increased their levels of victimization, although Guatemala and El Salvador both saw a peak in 2010, with nearly 1 in 4 respondents reporting having been the victim of a crime. In 2016, all three countries had more than one-fifth of the sample indicating that they had been victimized within the past year. Gang presence or reporting that gangs in the neighborhood affect one's daily life "a lot," has followed a similar pattern, as seen in Fig. 3. El Salvador and Guatemala both increase over the decade from 13% in 2006 to roughly 18% in 2016. However, Honduras displays much lower proportions of reaction to gang presence, rising from 7% in 2006 to only 11% in 2016.[4]

[4]It is important to note that this measure does not account for increasing gang presence, but only the respondents' perceptions that gang presence affects their lives "a lot." In the event that gang activity becomes normalized and accepted but does not directly impact respondents, it is possible that they could become desensitized to the day-to-day activity and thus be less likely to report that gang presence affects their lives much.

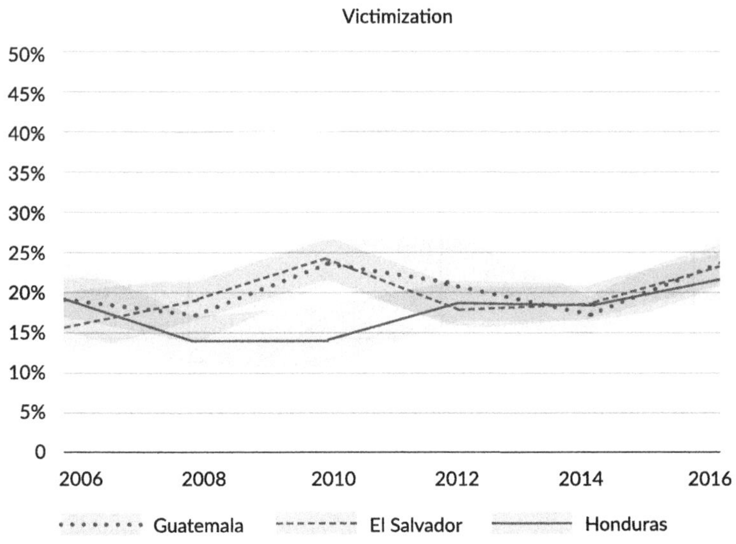

Fig. 2 Percentage of annual sample reporting personal victimization within the Northern Triangle, source: Latin America Public Opinion Project AmericasBarometer Surveys, 2006–2016

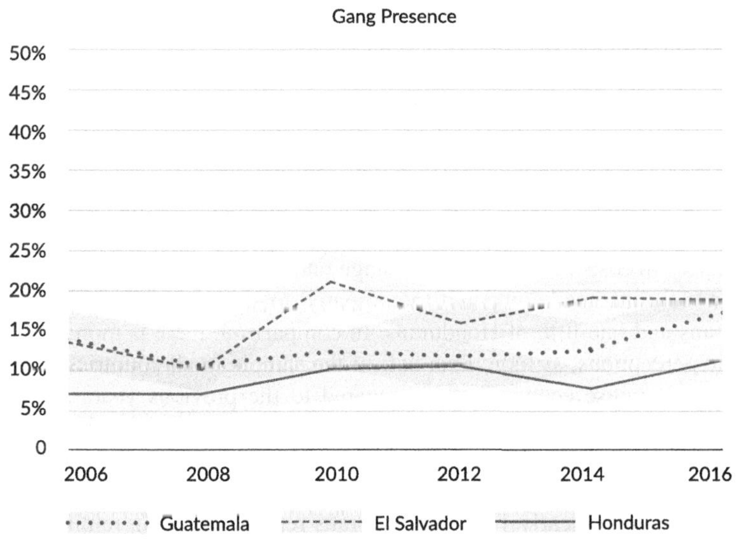

Fig. 3 Percentage of annual sample reporting that gang presence affects daily life "a lot" within the Northern Triangle, source: Latin America Public Opinion Project AmericasBarometer Surveys, 2006–2016

Figure 4 shows the distribution of several measures related to violence or the response to violence. For example, all three countries report that roughly 20% of respondents live with someone who has been the victim of a crime in the past year.

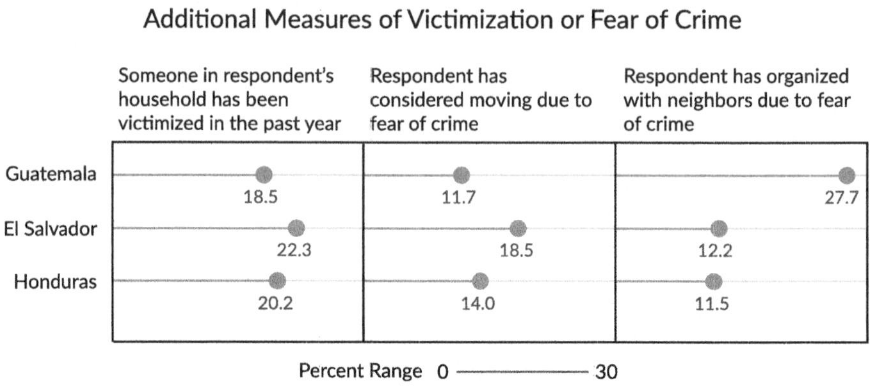

Fig. 4 Percentage of annual sample reporting additional measures of victimization and perceptions of crime. Source: Latin American Public Opinion Project AmericasBarometer surveys for Guatemala (2012–2014), El Salvador (2010, 12, 16), and Honduras (2010–2016)

However, El Salvador has more respondents (17%) that considered moving due to crime compared to Guatemala and Honduras (13% each). In stark contrast, 23% of Guatemalans suggest that they have organized neighbors in response to violence, compared to just roughly 11% in both El Salvador and Honduras. This suggests that Guatemalans are substantially more likely to organize in the face of violence compared to the other two countries in the region.

Table 2 shows the distribution of control variables by country. Despite having more similarities than differences, a few measures do merit attention. For example, El Salvador has slightly more than a year's worth of schooling (8.3) compared to Guatemala (6.9) and Honduras (7.2). Following this pattern, Salvadorans are more likely to be dissatisfied with their life (18%) compared to Hondurans (16%) and Guatemalans (11%). Although the measure does not offer a direct comparison (due to differences in costs of living and exchange rates), over half of Guatemalans report earning a "low income" compared to compared to slightly more than one-third of Salvadorans and one-fifth of Hondurans. In comparison, there is more similarity in economic perceptions, as more than half of the sample in all countries suggest that the country is worse economically compared to the previous year. This regional consistency is also reflected in the proportion of respondents that think their personal economic situation is worse than the previous year, with 39% of both Guatemalans and Hondurans and 45% of Salvadorans reporting worsened personal economic perceptions. Finally, nearly 1 in 4 Salvadorans reports receiving remittances, compared only 1 in 10 in Guatemala. This suggests that the countries, despite having similar levels of responses, may have varying levels of immigrant connections abroad. This is bolstered by separate analyses that show that a lower proportion of Guatemalans report having family living in the United States or other countries compared to Salvadorans and Hondurans.

Table 2 Descriptive statistics for control variables by country shown as percentages

	Guatemala	El Salvador	Honduras	Total
Sociodemographic measures				
Female	50.0	51.9	50.2	50.7
Age in years	38.3	39.1	37.4	38.3
Marital status				
Single	27.0	34.3	31.3	30.9
Married	48.6	36	30.1	38.1
Common-law marriage (cohabiting)	16.9	21.4	30.6	23.1
Divorced	0.8	1.9	1.3	1.3
Separated	2.1	2.6	2.8	2.5
Widowed	4.7	3.7	3.9	4.1
Currently working	55.9	46.3	48.1	50
Years of schooling	6.9	8.3	7.2	7.5
Reported low monthly income	51.1	37.2	21.7	–
Rural	52.5	37.6	51.6	47.2
National and personal perceptions of crime and economy				
Respondent reports feeling unsafe in neighborhood	39.0	43.6	32.9	38.5
Respondent is somewhat or very dissatisfied with life	10.5	18.1	16.4	15.1
Country's economic situation worse than past year	57.3	59.9	52.4	56.5
Respondent thinks crime is country's biggest problem	31.8	39.6	33.3	35.1
Personal economic situation worse than past year	38.7	44.8	39.1	40.9
Migrant connections				
Respondent or someone in household receives remittances	10.3	24.1	19.1	17.9
Unimputed sample size	9022	9322	9519	27,863

Source: Latin American Public Opinion Project AmericasBarometer biennial surveys of Guatemala, 2006–2016. Results shown as percentages, except for age and schooling shown in years

Chi square statistics for the distribution of all categorical and dichotomous variables are significant by country at the $p < 0.001$ level

Differences in sample means for age and years of schooling are also significant at the $p < 0.001$ level

"Crime is the country's biggest problem" was not collected in 2012 in Honduras and thus no significance test was completed for this measure

3.4 Analytical Results

We now turn to a series of logistic regression models aimed at modeling the relationship between intentions to migrate, crime, and other measures of crime and delinquency. The analysis proceeds by examining full and sub-sample model results for Guatemala, followed by El Salvador, and Honduras. Tables display coefficients as odds ratios, with numbers greater than 1.0 indicating that the relationship between the measure and intentions to migrate is positive. For example, a coefficient of 1.5 indicates those possessing the trait have 1.5 times the odds or 50% greater odds to express a desire to migrate compared to those without it. Comparatively, coefficients less than 1 indicate lower odds to migrate (e.g., a coefficient of 0.75 corresponds to 25% lesser odds of expressing a desire to migrate).

Table 3 shows the results from the full sample from Guatemala, spanning from 2006 to 2016. Here, the base model shows a clear and strong relationship between victimization, gang presence, and intentions to migrate. Specifically, victims have roughly 1.6 times the odds of non-victims to express a desire to migrate. In fact, when controlling for demographics, public perceptions of the economy and crime, and remittances, the relationship is still strong, although slightly attenuated, with victims having 1.4 times the odds of non-victims of saying they intend to migrate in the next 3 years. Similarly, respondents who say gang presence affects their neighborhood "a lot" have 1.5 times the odds of intentions to migrate compared to people who do not feel gang presence is as impactful. Survey year is also significant, which follows the descriptive pattern from Fig. 1, which shows that the intentions to migrate have increased over time.

When considering the other covariates in the full Guatemalan model, significant predictors follow theoretical expectations. For example, women have nearly two-thirds the odds of men to express interest in migrating. Similarly, desire to migrate decreases with age, as aging 1 year correlates with a roughly 5% drop in odds of intending to migrate. Earning a household income of less than $150 USD is also associated with a greater desire to migrate. Moreover, although the relationship is modest, schooling is significantly linked with greater intentions to migrate, as each year of formal education in Guatemala is linked with a 2% increase in odds to report a desire to migrate.

Understandably, having a connection to someone abroad via remittances meaningfully predicts intentions to migrate, even in Guatemala where only one in ten reported receiving remittances, as Guatemalans who receive remittances have 2.7 times the odds of saying they plan to migrate compared to those who do not receive money from abroad. The sub-sample analyses in Table 4 show that even when accounting for victimization, remittances, and the additional controls, responses to fear of crime (moving or community organizing) are both significantly related to intentions to migrate. In particular, Guatemalans who organized their neighborhood had 1.4 times the odds of intentions to migrate compared to non-organizers.

Model results from El Salvador, shown in Tables 5 and 6, follow a similar pattern to Guatemala. Initial bivariate models show that Salvadoran victims have nearly twice the odds of expressing a desire to migrate compared to non-victims. After controlling for demographics, perceptions, and receiving remittances, Salvadorans who have been victimized still exhibit 1.4 times the odds of non-victims to express a desire to migrate. As in Guatemala, the impact of gang presence in El Salvador is significantly linked to higher odds of expressing a desire to migrate. However, in

Table 3 Logistic regression of intentions to migrate in Guatemala (2006–2016)

	Base model	Demographics	Perceptions of crime and economy	Remittances
Victimization and gang presence				
Respondent has been victimized in the past year	1.613***	1.504***	1.444***	1.394***
Gang presence affects neighborhood a lot	1.417***	1.569***	1.483***	1.470***
Survey year	1.049***	1.069***	1.066***	1.068***
Sociodemographic controls				
Female		0.617***	0.613***	0.610***
Age		0.965***	0.964***	0.964***
Marital status (ref: Single)		–	–	–
Married		0.709***	0.702***	0.718***
Cohabiting—common law marriage		0.886	0.870	0.890
Divorced		1.441	1.418	1.379
Separated		0.813	0.793	0.792
Widowed		0.725	0.711	0.708
Currently working		0.916	0.923	0.930
Years of schooling		1.023**	1.025***	1.021**
Household income (ref: greater than $150 USD monthly)		–	–	–
Household income of less than $150 USD monthly		1.276***	1.261**	1.279***
Don't know or no response		1.059	1.046	1.110
Rural residence		1.127	1.126	1.095
National and personal perceptions of crime and economy				
Respondent currently dissatisfied with life			1.175	1.181
Respondent feels country's economic situation worse than past year			1.054	1.054
Respondent thinks crime is country's biggest problem			0.933	0.920
Respondent feels personal economic situation worse than past year			1.069	1.102
Respondent feels somewhat or very unsafe in neighborhood			1.157*	1.158*
Migrant connections				
Respondent's household receives remittances				2.653***

Source: Latin American Public Opinion Project AmericasBarometer biennial surveys of Guatemala, 2006–2016

*Coefficients are exponentiated odds ratios. * $p < 0.05$ ** $p < 0.01$ *** $p < 0.001$. N for all models = 9027*

Table 4 Logistic regression of intentions to migrate in Guatemala (2012–2014)

	Base model	Demographics	Perceptions of crime and economy	Remittances
Respondent has been victimized in the past year	1.492**	1.468**	1.495**	1.496**
Gang presence affects neighborhood a lot	1.315	1.605**	1.669**	1.611**
Someone in house has been victimized in the past year	1.131	1.068	1.080	1.078
Respondent felt the need to move due to fear of crime	1.272	1.308	1.338	1.406*
Respondent organized community in response to crime	1.380**	1.511***	1.501***	1.433**

Source: Latin American Public Opinion Project AmericasBarometer biennial surveys of Guatemala, 2012 and 2014

Coefficients are exponentiated odds ratios. * $p < 0.05$ ** $p < 0.01$ *** $p < 0.001$. Control variables omitted from table but included in model

N for all models = 3006

sub-sample analyses that account for household victimization and other responses to violence shown in Table 6, the relationship of gang presence and intentions to migrate remains positive but loses significance. Instead, having had a household member be victimized, organizing a community watch, or indicating a desire to move due to violence are much stronger correlates of intentions to migrate, suggesting that at least in this sub-sample, these measures may explain the variance in intentions to migrate previously explained by the impact of gang presence. As seen in Table 6 in the full model, having had a household member victimized, indicating an interest in moving due to fear of crime, or organizing neighbors in El Salvador are even greater predictors of intentions to migrate than personal victimization. In fact, Salvadorans who reported the need to move due to fear of crime were 1.8 times more likely to intend to migrate compared to those who did mention moving due to insecurity.

As in Guatemala, Table 5 shows that married respondents, females, and older respondents all report lower odds of intent to migrate. Similarly, rural Salvadorans have 20% lesser odds of reporting a desire to migrate compared to their urban counterparts, even after controlling for traditional predictors of migration. In contrast, Salvadorans who report dissatisfaction with their life, insecurity in their neighborhood, or have a worse personal economic forecast than in the previous year are all more likely to intend to migrate. As in Guatemala, Salvadorans who receive remittances are substantially more likely to report a desire to migrate compared to those who do not. Although the effect is weaker than in the Guatemalan analysis, it is still has the greatest magnitude of effect in the Salvadoran model.

Honduras exhibits similar patterns to both Guatemala and El Salvador, as shown in Table 7. After controlling for other variables, victimization, initially linked to

Table 5 Logistic regression of intentions to migrate in El Salvador (2006–2016)

	Base model	Demographics	Perceptions of crime and economy	Remittances
Victimization and gang presence				
Respondent has been victimized in the past year	1.988***	1.563***	1.442***	1.427***
Gang presence affects neighborhood a lot	1.428***	1.406***	1.237**	1.231**
Survey year	1.026***	1.041***	1.051***	1.054***
Sociodemographic controls				
Female		0.608***	0.588***	0.595***
Age		0.966***	0.961***	0.962***
Marital status (ref: Single)		–	–	–
Married		0.743***	0.737***	0.768***
Cohabiting—common law marriage		0.790***	0.786***	0.806**
Divorced		0.876	0.862	0.878
Separated		1.390*	1.298	1.294
Widowed		0.946	0.975	0.985
Currently working		1.046	1.085	1.128*
Years of schooling		1.005	1.008	1.009
Household income (ref: greater than $150 USD monthly)		–	–	–
Household income of less than $150 USD monthly		1.000	0.947	1.012
Don't know or no response		0.748**	0.736**	0.773**
Rural residence		0.815***	0.818***	0.813***
National and personal perceptions of crime and economy				
Respondent currently dissatisfied with life			1.487***	1.500***
Respondent feels country's economic situation worse than past year			1.130*	1.116
Respondent thinks crime is country's biggest problem			1.081	1.080
Respondent feels personal economic situation worse than past year			1.389***	1.424***
Respondent feels somewhat or very unsafe in neighborhood			1.264***	1.279***
Migrant connections				
Respondent's household receives remittances				1.706***

Source: Latin American Public Opinion Project AmericasBarometer biennial surveys of El Salvador 2006–2016

Coefficients are exponentiated odds ratios. * $p < 0.05$ ** $p < 0.01$ *** $p < 0.001$. *N* for all models = 9322

Table 6 Logistic regression of intentions to migrate in El Salvador (2010, 2012, and 2016)

	Base model	Demographics	Perceptions of crime and economy	Remittances
Respondent has been victimized in the past year	1.657***	1.353***	1.300**	1.286**
Gang presence affects neighborhood a lot	1.237*	1.225*	1.136	1.135
Someone in house has been victimized in the past year	1.842***	1.634***	1.587***	1.569***
Respondent felt the need to move due to fear of crime	1.671***	1.884***	1.786***	1.810***
Respondent organized community in response to crime	1.627***	1.710***	1.724***	1.733***

Source: Latin American Public Opinion Project AmericasBarometer biennial surveys of El Salvador, 2010, 2012 and 2016
Coefficients are exponentiated odds ratios. * $p < 0.05$ ** $p < 0.01$ *** $p < 0.001$. Control variables omitted from table but included in model
N for all models = 4550

twice the odds of intending to migrate compared to non-victims, is still strongly associated with intentions to migrate. However, importantly the presence of gangs in a respondent's neighborhood is not linked with intentions to migrate. Indeed, fewer control variables in the Honduran model significantly predict intentions to migrate, as only years of schooling, sex, age, and marital status are significant sociodemographic correlates. When accounting for people's perceptions, only expressing that one's personal economic situation is worse this year and reporting feeling unsafe in one's neighborhood are significantly and positively linked with intentions to migrate.

Remittances, as in Guatemala and El Salvador, are strongly linked with intentions to emigrate from Honduras, as those who receive economic assistance from abroad are 2.5 times more likely to express a desire to leave the country compared to those without remittances. Sub-sample analyses controlling for other measures of violence confirm the significance of personal victimization as a correlate with desire to migrate. The base model in Table 8 shows that both personal and household victimization are associated with intentions to migrate. Yet, when controlling for other factors, the association with household victimization disappears. Table 8 indicates that other factors linked to crime in violence, such as expressing a desire to move due to crime, are more predictive of intentions to migrate.

Table 7 Logistic regression of intentions to migrate in Honduras (2006–2016)

	Base model	Demographics	Perceptions of crime and economy	Remittances
Victimization and gang presence				
Respondent has been victimized in the past year	1.939***	1.623***	1.565***	1.514***
Gang presence affects neighborhood a lot	1.098	1.120	1.041	1.044
Survey year	1.086***	1.108***	1.106***	1.102***
Sociodemographic controls				
Female		0.624***	0.621***	0.621***
Age		0.955***	0.955***	0.954***
Marital status (ref: Single)		–	–	–
Married		0.592***	0.592***	0.602***
Cohabiting—common law marriage		0.762***	0.760***	0.785***
Divorced		0.875	0.844	0.814
Separated		0.934	0.924	0.957
Widowed		0.724	0.723	0.697
Currently working		1.014	1.021	1.078
Years of schooling		1.042***	1.045***	1.037***
Household income (ref: greater than $150 USD monthly)		–	–	–
Household income of less than $150 USD monthly		0.988	0.978	1.086
Don't know or no response		0.875	0.873	0.956
Rural residence		0.924	0.935	0.966
National and personal perceptions of crime and economy				
Respondent currently dissatisfied with life			1.106	1.101
Respondent feels country's economic situation worse than past year			0.995	0.980
Respondent thinks crime is country's biggest problem			–	–
Respondent feels personal economic situation worse than past year			1.174**	1.194**
Respondent feels somewhat or very unsafe in neighborhood			1.258***	1.277***
Migrant connections				
Respondent's household receives remittances				2.649***

Source: Latin American Public Opinion Project AmericasBarometer biennial surveys of Honduras 2006–2016

Coefficients are exponentiated odds ratios. * $p < 0.05$ ** $p < 0.01$ *** $p < 0.001$. N for all models = 9518

Table 8 Logistic regression of intentions to migrate in Honduras (2010–2016)

	Base model	Demographics	Perceptions of crime and economy	Remittances
Respondent has been victimized in the past year	1.745***	1.416***	1.356***	1.324***
Gang presence affects neighborhood a lot	0.952	0.933	0.901	0.899
Someone in house has been victimized in the past year	1.293***	1.211*	1.182*	1.135
Respondent felt the need to move due to fear of crime	1.609***	1.748***	1.634***	1.670***
Respondent organized community in response to crime	1.130	1.124	1.113	1.119

Source: Latin American Public Opinion Project AmericasBarometer biennial surveys of Honduras, 2010–2016
Coefficients are exponentiated odds ratios. * $p < 0.05$ ** $p < 0.01$ *** $p < 0.001$. Control variables omitted from table but included in model.
N for all models = 6416

4 Discussion

Taken as a whole, the results from these analyses suggest that victimization in the Northern Triangle is consistently associated with a desire to migrate. Even after controlling for demographic characteristics linked with migration, personal and national perceptions of the economy and crime, and direct household links to migrants, having been the victim of a crime is an important factor in migrant intentions. Considering this, the presence of gangs in one's neighborhood is associated with migration, but the effect depends on the national context. In Guatemala and El Salvador, saying that gangs affect your daily life "a lot" is linked to a desire to leave the country, but in Honduras gang presence is not predictive of migrant intentions, despite the fact that descriptive statistics show that more Hondurans want to leave the country. Moreover, organizing one's neighborhood to deal with issues of crime is related to intent to migrate in Guatemala and El Salvador, but not in Honduras. This suggests that further analyses need to explore factors that are predictive of migrant intentions specific to the Honduran context.

The 1948 Universal Declaration of Human Rights and the more recent, but related, 2030 Agenda for Sustainable Development provide an important opportunity to reflect on global migration from a human rights point of view. Using data collected over a 10-year period, this research has reasserted the importance of criminal victimization and other instances of insecurity and perceptions of risk have on the expressed intentions to migrate. However, this research has also pointed to the complexities of migration motivations. By strengthening the fundamental human rights expressed in these documents and taking directed steps to assure these rights are afforded to all peoples, global development will be improved.

4.1 Limitations

As with any study, this analysis is limited by a few methodological issues that can serve to inform future research design. First, given that migration and the decision to migrate is a process that occurs over time, ideal studies would be longitudinal in nature with participant samples collected in the country of origin and destination. However, such studies are likely to be logistically infeasible and thus cross-sectional samples in the country of origin and destination are a constraint shared by many analyses. In addition, a longitudinal analysis that examined the timing of victimization and migration would be able to examine the issue of causality. Yet, despite this limitation and the inability to test for causal inference, we hypothesize the direction between crime in the country of origin and migration from that country is positive and likely causal in that order. Researchers have also posed questions regarding the value of aspirational questions to predict behavior for migration, however longitudinal analysis in Mexico has tied positive responses to the "intent to migrate" question with future migration in later waves of data collection, both internally and to the United States. Lastly, further qualitative research is needed on the specific mechanisms linking migration and violence, whether decisions to migrate are made with an emphasis on migration for security concerns, and if recent victimization is a driving factor in predicting individual migration.

4.2 Conclusions

In the introduction to this chapter, we presented key observations from the 1948 Universal Declaration of Human Rights. Article three asserts that all humans have the right to be free of violence and victimization. Perennially among the most violent places on earth, residents in the Northern Triangle countries are often unable to claim this right. While rule of law can be said to be improving in the Northern Triangle countries, substantial challenges remain. The analysis presented here draws a clear connection between desires to migrate, perceptions of violence or insecurity, and experiences of victimization, affirming that the desire to migrate is related, at least in part, with victimization experiences. Article 13 establishes the right to engage in internal, domestic migration within an individual's own country. Article 14 extends the rights of would-be migrants seeking to avoid victimization by asserting the right to seek protection from persecution in other countries. Articles 23 and 25 address the right to work in a safe environment and protections against unemployment proclaiming the universal right of all people to obtain a minimum standard of living to be able to afford food, clothing, housing, and medical care.

Collected approximately every 2 years throughout the region, the Latin American Public Opinion Project's *AmericasBarometer* is a national survey of a representative sample of residents in Guatemala, El Salvador, and Honduras. Using these data, collected between 2006 and 2016, this analysis builds on previous research

(Chindarkar 2014; Graham and Markowitz 2011; Hiskey et al. 2014; 2018; Wood et al. 2010). Using expressed "intent to migrate" as a dichotomous dependent variable for a logistic regression model, we find prior victimization to be strongly linked with emigration plans even while controlling for traditional characteristics tied to migration. Forced displacement, stemming from crime and violence victimization, has previously been characterized as "theoretically ambiguous" (Orozco-Aleman and Gonzalez-Lozano 2018). The current literature related to assessments of migrant motivations warns against simplistic dichotomies which have in the past tended to emphasize economic stressors and insecurity. The analysis presented here underscores this fact and points to the complexities of mixed-motivations and contextual variations in push and pull factors that may affect migration attempts. The analysis of gang presence, for example, requires a nuanced, country-specific analysis.

The policy implications of this analysis, especially in light of the important affirmations in the 1948 Universal Declaration of Human Rights and the 2030 Agenda for Sustainable Development, point to the need for multidimensional interventions. Clearly, reducing criminal and violent victimization is essential and specific steps to professionalize criminal justice actors, address corruption, intervene to address gang activity, promote rule of law, disrupt drug flows, and reduce impunity should help to reduce motivations for migrations. Yet further exploration and explicit longitudinal research design, both qualitative and quantitative, are necessary to understand *how* and *when* multiple factors, particularly those related to victimization and insecurity, succeed in influencing people to emigrate.

References

Barrick, K., & Pitts, W. (2013). *Assessing crime, resident trust, and police effectiveness in Tegucigalpa, Honduras: Baseline Report.*

Basu, S., & Pearlman, S. (2017). Violence and migration: Evidence from Mexico's drug war. *IZA Journal of Development and Migration, 7*(1), 18. https://doi.org/10.1186/s40176-017-0102-6

Berry Cullen, J., & Levitt, S. D. (1999). Crime, urban flight, and the consequences for cities. *The Review of Economics and Statistics, 81*(2), 159–169.

Boulton, M. (2011). *Living in a world of violence: An introduction to the gang phenomenon.*

Briceño-León, R., & Zubillaga, V. (2002). Violence and globalization in Latin America. *Current Sociology, 50*(1), 19–37. https://doi.org/10.1177/0011392102050001003

Bucheli, J. R., Fontenla, M., & Waddell, B. J. (2019). Return migration and violence. *World Development, 116*, 113–124. https://doi.org/10.1016/J.WORLDDEV.2018.12.010

Cantor, D. J. (2014). The new wave: Forced displacement caused by organized crime in Central America and Mexico. *Refugee Survey Quarterly, 33*(3), 34–68. https://doi.org/10.1093/rsq/hdu008

Cara Labrador, R., & Renwick, D. (2018). *Central America's violent Northern triangle, 19.*

Carling, J., & Schewel, K. (2018). Revisiting aspiration and ability in international migration. *Journal of Ethnic and Migration Studies, 44*(6), 945–963. https://doi.org/10.1080/1369183X.2017.1384146

Carlson, S. M., & Michalowski, R. J. (1997). Crime, unemployment, and social structures of accumulation: An inquiry into historical contingency. *Justice Quarterly, 14*(2), 209–241. https://doi.org/10.1080/07418829700093311

Carte, L., Schmook, B., Radel, C., & Johnson, R. (2019). The Slow displacement of smallholder farming families: Land, hunger, and labor migration in Nicaragua and Guatemala. *Land, 8*(6), 89. https://doi.org/10.3390/land8060089

Chindarkar, N. (2014). Is subjective well-being of concern to potential migrants from Latin America? *Social Indicators Research, 115*(1), 159–182. https://doi.org/10.1007/s11205-012-0213-7

Clemens, M. A. (2017). Violence, development, and migration waves: Evidence from Central American Child Migrant Apprehensions. *SSRN Electronic Journal*. https://doi.org/10.2139/ssrn.3013379

Connor, P., & Massey, D. S. (2010). Economic outcomes among Latino Migrants to Spain and the United States: Differences by source region and legal status. *International Migration Review, 44*(4), 802–829. https://doi.org/10.1111/j.1747-7379.2010.00826.x

Cook Heffron, L. (2019). "Salía de uno y me metí en otro": Exploring the migration-violence nexus among Central American Women. *Violence Against Women, 25*(6), 677–702. https://doi.org/10.1177/1077801218797473

Creighton, M. J. (2013). The role of aspirations in domestic and international migration. *The Social Science Journal, 50*(1), 79–88. https://doi.org/10.1016/J.SOSCIJ.2012.07.006

de Haas, H. (2010). Migration and development: A theoretical perspective. *International Migration Review, 44*(1), 227–264. https://doi.org/10.1111/j.1747-7379.2009.00804.x

Demombynes, G. (2011). Drug trafficking and violence in Central America and beyond. World Bank. https://doi.org/10.1596/27333

Eguizábal, C., Ingram, M., Curtis, K., Korthuis, A., Olsen, E., & Phillips, N. (2015). *Crime and violence in Central America's Northern Triangle*. Washington, DC.

Ellis, R. E. (2018). In R. E. Ellis (Ed.), *Transnational organized crime in Latin America and the Caribbean: From evolving threats and responses to integrated, adaptive solutions*. New York: Lexington Books.

El Instituto Nacional de Estadística (2018) Resultados del Censo Nacional de Población y Vivienda.

Feliciano, C. (2005). Educational selectivity in U.S. immigration: How do immigrants compare to those left behind? *Demography, 42*(1), 131–152. https://doi.org/10.1353/dem.2005.0001

Fussell, E., & Massey, D. S. (2004). The limits to cumulative causation: International migration from Mexican urban areas. *Demography, 41*(1), 151–171. https://doi.org/10.1353/dem.2004.0003

General Assembly of the United Nations: *Transforming our world:* The 2030 agenda for sustainable development. (2015). In *General Assembly 70 session*. Vienna.

Graham, C., & Markowitz, J. (2011). Aspirations and happiness of potential Latin American immigrants. *Journal of Social Research & Policy, 2*(2), 1–17.

Haug, S. (2008). Migration networks and migration decision-making. *Journal of Ethnic and Migration Studies, 34*(4), 585–605. https://doi.org/10.1080/13691830801961605

Heidbrink, L. (2019). The coercive power of debt: Migration and deportation of Guatemalan indigenous youth. *The Journal of Latin American and Caribbean Anthropology, 24*(1), 263–281. https://doi.org/10.1111/jlca.12385

Hiskey, J., Montalvo, J. D., & Orcés, D. (2014). Democracy, governance, and emigration intentions in Latin America and the Caribbean. *Studies in Comparative International Development, 49*(1), 89–111. https://doi.org/10.1007/s12116-014-9150-6

Hiskey, J. T., Córdova, A., Malone, M. F., & Orcés, D. M. (2018). Leaving the devil you know: Crime victimization, US deterrence policy, and the emigration decision in Central America. *Latin American Research Review, 53*(3), 429. https://doi.org/10.25222/larr.147

Jaitman, L., Caprirolo, D., Granguillhome Ochoa, R., Keefer, P., Leggett, T., Lewis, J. A., et al. (2017). *The costs of crime and violence: New evidence and insights in Latin America and the Caribbean*. Washington, D.C. https://doi.org/10.18235/0000615

Keller, A., Joscelyne, A., Granski, M., & Rosenfeld, B. (2017). Pre-migration trauma exposure and mental health functioning among Central American Migrants arriving at the US border. *Plos One, 12*(1), e0168692. https://doi.org/10.1371/journal.pone.0168692

Kinman, J., & Lee, E. S. (1966). Migration and crime. *The International Migration Digest, 3*(1), 7–14.

Lorenzen, M. (2017). The mixed motives of unaccompanied child migrants from Central America's Northern triangle. *Journal on Migration and Human Security, 5*(4), 744–767. https://doi.org/10.1177/233150241700500402

Martinez, R., & Lee, M. T. (2006). On immigration and crime. In R. Martinez, R. Martinez Jr., & A. Valenzuela Jr. (Eds.), *Immigration and crime: Race, ethnicity, and violence* (pp. 1–40). New York: New York University Press. https://doi.org/10.4324/9780203465516

Massey, D. S., Goldring, L., & Durand, J. (1994). Continuities in transnational migration: An analysis of nineteen Mexican communities. *American Journal of Sociology, 99*(6), 1492–1533. https://doi.org/10.1086/230452

Massey, D., Arango, J., Hugo, G., Kouaouci, A., & Pellegrino, A. (1999). *Worlds in motion: Understanding international migration at the end of the millennium*. Oxford: Clarendon Press.

Migali, S., & Scipioni, M. (2019). Who's about to leave? A global survey of aspirations and intentions to migrate. *International Migration*, imig.12617. https://doi.org/10.1111/imig.12617

Obinna, D. N., & Field, L. M. (2019). Geographic and spatial assimilation of immigrants from Central America's Northern Triangle. *International Migration, 57*(3), 81–97. https://doi.org/10.1111/imig.12557

Orozco-Aleman, S., & Gonzalez-Lozano, H. (2018). Drug violence and migration flows. *Journal of Human Resources, 53*(3), 717–749. https://doi.org/10.3368/jhr.53.3.0215-6948R4

Ortega, F., & Peri, G. (2013). The effect of income and immigration policies on international migration. *Migration Studies, 1*(1), 47–74. https://doi.org/10.1093/migration/mns004

Ousey, G. C., & Kubrin, C. E. (2018). Immigration and crime: Assessing a contentious issue. *Annual Review of Criminology, 1*(1), 63–84. https://doi.org/10.1146/annurev-criminol-032317-092026

Quijada, J. A., & Sierra, J. D. (2019). Understanding undocumented migration from Honduras. *International Migration, 57*(4), 3–20. https://doi.org/10.1111/imig.12429

Rosenblum, M. R., & Ruiz Soto, A. G. (2015). *An analysis of unauthorized immigrants in the United States by country and region of birth*. Washington D.C.

Ryo, E. (2013). Deciding to cross: Norms and economics of unauthorized migration. *American Sociological Review, 78*(4), 574–603. https://doi.org/10.1177/0003122413487904

Sampson, R. J., & Wooldredge, J. D. (1986). Evidence that high crime rates encourage migration away from central cities. *Sociology and Social Research, 70*(4), 310–314.

Scarnato, J. M. (2019). Deportation meets development: A case study of return migration in Guatemala. *Migration and Development, 8*(2), 192–206. https://doi.org/10.1080/21632324.2018.1500004

Skogan, W. (1986). Fear of crime and neighborhood change. *Crime and Justice, 8*, 203–229. https://doi.org/10.1086/449123

Stark, O., & Bloom, D. (1985). The new economics of labor migration. *The American Economic Review, 75*(2), 173–178. https://bit.ly/odedstark

Todaro, M. P. (1976). *Internal migration in developing countries*. Geneva.

UDHR. Universal Declaration of Human Rights. (1948). *United Nations: General assembly*. https://bit.ly/2YE9pmR

UNODC. (2019a). *Global study on homicide: Homicide trends, patterns and criminal justice response. Global study on homicide: Homicide trends, patterns and criminal justice response. Booklet 2*. Vienna.

UNODC. (2019b). *Global study on homicide: Understanding homicide. Booklet 3*. Vienna.

Wood, C. H., Gibson, C. L., Ribeiro, L., & Hamsho-Diaz, P. (2010). Crime victimization in Latin America and intentions to migrate to the United States. *International Migration Review, 44*(1), 3–24. https://doi.org/10.1111/j.1747-7379.2009.00796.x

Zechmeister, E. J. (2014). *The political culture of democracy in the Americas, 2014: Democratic governance across 10 years of the AmericasBarometer.*

Christopher Inkpen is a Research Sociologist and Demographer in the Division for Applied Justice Research at the Research Triangle Park—RTI International (North Carolina, USA). He studies quantitative criminology, specifically the application of machine learning techniques to social science data. His substantive research focuses on the intersection of migration and crime. E-mail: cinkpen@rti.org.

Wayne Pitts is a Research Criminologist in the Division for Applied Justice Research at the Research Triangle Park—RTI International (North Carolina, USA). Since 2015, he has lived and worked in Central America, leading multiple security, community policing, and migration-related projects. E-mail: wpitts@rti.org.

Pamela Lattimore is the Senior Director for Research Development in the Division for Applied Justice Research at the Research Triangle Park—RTI International (North Carolina, USA). She is responsible for leading the development of impactful multidisciplinary research focused on improving the understanding of crime and related problems, the criminal justice system, and prevention and intervention activities designed to ameliorate societal problems and increase community and individual resilience. E-mail: lattimore@rti.org.

Criminal Violence and Its Prevention in Context. Specific Challenges for the Integration of Refugees and Migrants in the Twenty-First Century

Anastasia Chalkia

Abstract Migration and integration though are central issues in public debate, internationally and in Europe, little attention has been given to their relation with crime prevention. This chapter tries to stress this interdependance by exploring the ways under which criminal violence, either from the part of victimization or from the part of criminal behavior, in conjunction with the characteristic of the migrant/refugee population as well as the circumstances they live in, can be prevented.

Keywords Criminal violence · Crime prevention · Integration · Migration · Refugee

1 Introduction

People on the move, that is, people forced to leave their homes for various reasons, can be internally displaced, refugees, asylum seekers and migrants. According to United Nations High Commissioner for Refugees (UNHCR) international statistical data provide a clear image of what is happening nowadays on our planet: 70.8 million people worldwide have been forced from home. Among them almost 25.9 million are refugees.[1] Furthermore, International Organization for Migration (IOM) reports that the international migrant population in 2017 is 258 million people who are defined as "people residing in a country other than their country of birth."[2] Some very interesting data follows from the same reports that reveals the trends on migration globally: "Flows in 2017 were down 5 per cent from 2016, representing the first drop since 2011, when humanitarian migration numbers started to see an

[1]UNHCR, figures at a glance, https://bit.ly/3cnybf5.

[2]International Organisation for Migration, Global Migration Indicators 2018, Insights from the Global Migration Data Portal: www.migrationdataportal.org, Global Migration Data Analysis Centre (GMDAC) International Organization for Migration, Berlin, https://bit.ly/3dDDSG6.

A. Chalkia (✉)
National and Kapodistrian University of Athens, Athens, Greece

H. Kury, S. Redo (eds.), *Crime Prevention and Justice in 2030*,
https://doi.org/10.1007/978-3-030-56227-4_21

increase. However, the downward trend in 2017 is mainly because of the reduction in the number of recognized refugees, particularly in Germany."

Especially, in the European Union (EU) and according to Eurostat data,[3] from 2010 to 2016 approximately 4,150,000 international protection applications were recorded in the Member States of the EU. The asylum seeker inflows increased in 2015–2016, when about 2.5 million asylum seekers arrived in the EU. In 2015, 1,257,030 people applied for international asylum protection in the EU Member States. In 2016, 1,205,080 people submitted, an extremely high number compared to 2014 when asylum applications were only 562,680. These increases compared to previous years inflows have created pressure in many areas of Europe, especially in Italy, Greece, Hungary, and elsewhere. Greece and Italy are the most important points of entry by sea. In 2016, Italy received the second largest number of asylum seekers for the first time after Germany, while Hungary was the second largest EU country in arrivals in 2015 (Lodovici et al. 2017). These flows have fallen sharply in subsequent years following the EU-Turkey Declaration on March 18, 2016.[4] As for 2018, 580,800 first-time asylum seekers applied for international protection in the Member States of the EU.[5]

Migration in conjunction with crime and victimization have further been discussed theoretically and empirically (Zatz and Smith 2012; Palidda 2009). Little knowledge and evidence, though, exist in how crime can be prevented through the integration of migrants and refugees (Solivetti 2010). Migrants can be victimized or offended or both. As far as their victimization is concerned migrants have more possibilities to be victimized either by their own kind or by persons outside the community than to commit a crime according to the research (McDonald 2018). In particular, their victimization can take the forms of sexual exploitation and forced labor in the context of human trafficking, rapping, refusing to pay wages, domestic abuse and many others (United Nations Office on Drugs and Crime 2015). On the other hand, dominant perceptions on the criminality of the migrants and refugees (Unnever 2014) reinforce the linkage between migration and criminality as well as the interpretation of data derived either from research or statistics (Sohoni and Sohoni 2014). In addition, strategic policing to manage migration or racial profiling contributes the increase of number of migrants involved in criminal justice (Parmar 2019). In any case, criminal behavior for the part of migrants is not based on a simple comparison of the crimes committed by nationals and nonnationals (Feltes et al. 2018).

The aforementioned consist internationally public, political, and social issues which are closely related to the phenomenon of human migration nowadays and

[3]Eurostat, Statistics Explained. Asylum applications (non-EU) in the EU-28 Member States, 2008–2018, http://ec.europa.eu/eurostat/statistics-explained/index.php/Asylum_statistics. For Greece, statistics on asylum seekers and beneficiaries of international protection since 2013 are available on the website of the Asylum Service (www.asylo.gov.gr).

[4]European Council, Council of the European Union, EU-Turkey Declaration, 18 March 2016, https://bit.ly/2YUFmrc.

[5]Eurostat. Statistics explain. Asylum Statistics, https://bit.ly/2Lkg9i4.

the democratic principle requiring well-ordered and cohesive societies. In this context, United Nations (UN) since its establishment has mainly focused on articulating consensus between the states and stakeholders and setting priorities. One of their landmark achievements and a dynamic policy tool is the Sustainable Development Goals (SDGs) that they established the UN 2030 Agenda for Sustainable Development.[6] SDGs is an evolution of the Millennium Development Goals (MDGs). In particular, "the 2030 Agenda reflects a new conception of development as "sustainable development," and an important evolution in normative ideas about the vision of "development." Which is a "universal paradigm" and not a "North-South project" anymore" (Fukuda-Parr 2018).

By considering migrant victimization and migrant crime, it is more than obvious the nexus with the issues of integration and crime prevention. As for integration, it includes multiple domains such as labor market, health, education, housing. At global level data on the topic are limited and only high-income countries are able to provide some kind of reliable statistics or research findings.[7] The public support that can be provided to the above population groups is a crucial issue. Especially in times of accelerated change, of economic crisis and economic austerity, this issue becomes even more difficult to manage. Considering that the majority of refugees and immigrants come from countries that are classified as "waste" (outcasts) in the context of contemporary international society and that the ideas of "western" exceptionalism, the "inevitable" clash of cultures, even xenophobia and racism, have spread throughout Europe, the successful integration of these people in European societies and the avoidance of "stigma" (Goffman 1963, preface and pp. 17–18), is a complex challenge and also a urgent priority (Chalkia and Giouzepas 2018). As for the "preventive turn" (Crawford 2009) that is the modern strategies to crime prevention, are in a continuous dialogue with United Nations goals and guidelines (UNODC 2010; Redo 2017).

Therefore, the issues of criminal violence, crime prevention and integration that are going to be discussed in the present chapter fall under the Goal 10 and Goal 16 of the SDGs. Specifically, Goal 10 refers to the reduction "of inequality with and among countries" in which the target 10.2 attempts to "empower and promote the social, economic and political inclusion of all, irrespective of age, sex, disability, race, ethnicity, origin, religion or economic or other status." As for the Goal 16, it promotes peaceful and inclusive societies for sustainable development, provide access to *justice* for all and build effective, accountable and inclusive institutions at all levels" and targets 16.1 "significantly reduce all forms of violence and related death rates everywhere," and 16.a "strengthen relevant national institutions, including through international cooperation, for building capacity at all levels, in particular

---

[6]United Nations. Transforming our world: the 2030 Agenda for Sustainable Development, https://bit.ly/2YUG8o6.

[7]International Organisation for Migration. Global Migration Indicators 2018, Insights from the Global Migration Data Portal: www.migrationdataportal.org, Global Migration Data Analysis Centre (GMDAC) International Organization for Migration, Berlin, https://bit.ly/3dDDSG6, p. 40.

in developing countries, *to* prevent violence and combat terrorism and crime." In the light of the above, Goals and Targets integration is a cornerstone for the social peace and a viable way to sustainable confrontations of criminal violence in contemporary societies, either from the side of criminality or victimization.

2 Conceptual Demands and Theoretical Approaches to Integration

Identity and diversity have been top concern for human societies from their establishment. Managing the "other" as different and unwanted has reached extreme forms (e.g., war, genocide) especially during the establishment of nation-states where one of the key demands is their national and cultural homogeneity. Although nowadays, based on collective historical memory and the experience of globalization, we know that people moving from place to place is at a significant degree not only unavoidable, especially when there are some areas of extreme poverty, inadequate state protection, armed conflict or impacts from climate change, but also often desirable for the evolution of social, economic and political life of a society (Goldin et al. 2011). The recent situation on the increase of migrant and refugee flows to Europe has ranked the refugee/migration issue at the top of the political and social agenda. Two questions are raised: (a) how Member States and the EU will manage the "waves" of immigration, and (b) what they should do with those who will stay "here" at "us."

Integration is the participation of members of different ethnic/national/racial groups in the major institutional structures is perceived as integration (Hughes and Kroehler 2011). It is a two-way process in which minority and majority groups learn from each other and exchange individual aspects of their culture. Other levels of participation of different ethnic/national/racial groups in the society is assimilation (assimilation). This assimilation refers to the processes through which groups with distinct identities merge culturally and socially and acquire characteristics of the dominant culture. Immigrants must renounce their distinctive linguistic, cultural, or social characteristics and become undivided from the dominant population. The last stage of assimilation is called amalgamation in which it is difficult to distinguish the former distinct ethnic groups. One of the main traditions of assimilation is metaphorically referred to as a "melting pot" that characterizes much of the US society.[8] On the opposite side of the "melting pot" there is the so-called "salad bawl" which as a "model" falls within the pluralistic tradition of diversity management. In this case, a mixture of different cultures is created but each culture retains its own identity adding to the taste of the whole. Pluralism is characterized by reciprocal respect by

[8]Indeed, the "melting pot" expresses some aspects of assimilation in the USA, however, "English culture" dominated and only partially reflects the influence of the various groups that compose North American culture in the USA (Giddens 2009).

all cultures, creating a multinational environment of acceptance. In fact, true pluralism is a difficult task to achieve. In any case, what it is considered problematic is the complete separation between the refugee/migrant cultures and that of the host society. Recent developments in policymaking confront integration as something in which all members of society participate and for which there is shared responsibility and maintain an active role throughout the process (Charsley and Spencer 2019).

It is worth mentioning that in public debate there is a great discussion concerning terms integration, assimilation, pluralism which each time expresses the dominant political ideas (Schnapper 2007, p. 40). That is the reason why it is important to distinguish between integration "as a public policy demand or outcome and integration as a scientific term that expresses a social process, describes a social situation and analyses social relationships" (Schnapper 2007, p. 55).

The origin of the term integration is attributed to E. Durkheim (integration) and more specifically cited in his book The Social Causes of Suicide (Le suicide, 1897). The term is used with two meanings: the first is about the integration of society (integration de la societé) in the sense of setting up and preserve it and the other is the integration of the individual into the society (integration à la societé). Then, the term was used by the Chicago School and specifically through the book of W. Thomas & F. Znaniecki (1918–1920) *The Polish Peasant in Europe and America* where the term integration is first associated with migration and the participation of migrants in the new society. This work was the forerunner of research about the "social disorganization" that subsequently the Chicago School developed, as a weakening of the power of social rules regarding those who were unable to respect the rules of the country from which they had left and could not still adopt the rules of the country in which they had settled (Schnapper 2007 [2008], p. 90). Consequently, the term integration was originally expressed as the social need to manage the "new" population. Especially, migration to the USA in the nineteenth and twentieth centuries was mainly contributed to the transfer of cultures from other continents and the formation of the American society. Issues, such as those of the deviant behavior, crime, and "social disorganization" in the USA were first interpreted because of migration.

Chicago School has put the terms "integration" and "assimilation" into practice at the beginning of the twenty-first century even before they became known in public political debates. These two terms were developed mainly in the USA (assimilation) and Western Europe (integration) and refer to the process of settlement in the host country, to the interaction with the host society and to social change that follows migration (Hamberger 2009).

The term integration, in the context of the functionalism, as approached by T. Parsons is considered to be the way in which the units of a system relate and thanks to which, on the one hand, they act collectively to avoid disruption of the system that makes its stability impossible, on the other hand, they work together to promote the functioning of the whole system (Parsons 1954, p. 71). Furthermore, it is important to distinguish between "social" (action) and "systemic" (structure) integration introduced by Lockwood (1964). The first concerns the principles by which individuals or actors are linked together in a society and the second the relationships that are developed between parts of a society or a system. The two above distinctions of the concept are not independent of each other and it is of particular importance what the interaction between them is. In any case, such classifications venture the synthesis of micro- and macro-level analysis. In addition, both social and systemic integration are further connected to the integration of the states in the EU (Gerhards and Lengfeld 2015, p. 14).

The term integration varies in content from time to time and from society to society. However, it remains uniquely relevant to all societies and eras as it relates to the core of society, namely social relations and social organization in the light of the good order, well-being and conceptualization of a wide range of things concerning social structure and social action. In this sense, integration is an everlasting and continuous project, mainly in terms of public policy. More generally, integration refers to the interaction processes that urge individual and social change. The nature, the speed and the direction of these processes are not only influenced by the characteristics of individuals but also by the wider social context.

3 Dimensions and Indicators of Integration

Integration policies vary from state to state according to their traditions and institutional approaches, while the EU is developing common approaches to inclusion and is promoting the exchange of best practices.[9] The challenges associated with integration are similar for refugees as well as for third-country citizens residing legally in the EU. Specifically, the integration of refugees as a lasting solution is an important part of the states' commitments under the 1951 Convention.[10] The UNHCR encourages EU Member States to include refugees in general integration plans and policies, while providing targeted actions for refugee needs. Integration can also be enhanced through reception policies for asylum seekers to promote social inclusion, rather than isolation and segregation from host communities. There are also compelling reasons for the aligning of the rights of the persons with subsidiary protection with the rights of refugees in certain areas, including access to the labor market, integration support and family reunification. In the light of these considerations, UNHCR encourages the EU to further develop its integration policies and practices for the benefit of those who need international protection and their host communities in the Member States (UNHCR 2007).

Although there is no absolute consensus on integration indicators, some areas are identified as sources of key indicators for evaluating its success, for example

[9]See European Commission. Common Principles for Integration, Communication from the Commission to the Council, the European Council, the European Economic and Social Committee and the Committee of the Regions, Third Annual Report on Migration and Integration Brussels, 11.9.2007, COM (2007) 512 final, https://bit.ly/2YUGefs.

[10]United Nations (1951) Convention on the Status of Refugees (Geneva Convention), https://bit.ly/2WkUexi.

education, access to the labor market, housing, access to social services, healthcare and participation in the political process.

It is characteristic that within the framework of the European Program for Integration and Security 18 promising "solutions" for migrant integration and social cohesion have been chosen. Specifically, out of a total of 95 applications, 52% focused on the labor market and economic inclusion, 20% in social empowerment, 19% in intercultural dialogue and cultural participation, 5% in the participation in (local) public life, and 4% in writing and learning the host country language (EPIM 2019).

Approaching the issue of integration more taxonomically, there are four large categories of indicators (Boswell 2003):

1. Cultural (knowledge of host country language, partial understanding of its society and respect for its basic rules);
2. Social (participation in education and basic social institutions);
3. Economic (access to the labor market, employment);
4. Political (equivalent to the final stage of integration—the right to vote, which is usually obtained through naturalization).

In addition, Pennix (2005) has developed three dimensions of integration that are now considered classical by scholars in the field concerned:

1. Legal/political dimension: it refers to the political rights of migrants, whether (easily or not) they can acquire citizenship, and generally if they are regarded as members of the political community;
2. Social/economic dimension: It concerns social and economic rights, irrespective of the acquisition of citizenship: e.g., if migrants have the same rights as indigenous workers, access to social security, unemployment benefits, etc.;
3. Cultural/religious rights dimension: it refers to the rights of migrants as to their ability to organize and participate seamlessly in cultural, ethnic/national, or religious groups.

Especially in the case of migrants and in addition to the above R. Penninx adds two central questions about the countries of origin: first, is there a link between transnational migrant activities and integration? That is, the more focused on the country of origin immigrants are, do they support or even recognize the less the host country as their residence country and vice versa? Secondly, what is the role of the countries of origin? Are their policies to their citizens who have migrated abroad counterproductive for the integration policies in the host countries? Or could the former support the later? (Mascarenas and Pennix 2016, p. 5).

Moreover, the Organization for Economic Cooperation and Development (OECD 2018) presents groups of integration indicators as follows:

1. Socio-economic characteristics: The first set of indicators provides information on key socio-economic aspects, characteristics of the foreign, including the place of birth, educational level and age;

2. Results of integration: The second set of indicators provides information on the results of integration with particular emphasis on the labor market, on housing conditions and family available income. The participation of migrants in the labor market is considered critical to the success of their integration, as earning an income provides opportunities for participation in the social life of a country, to meet the needs, to increase the expected life span. Access to adequate and good quality housing also plays an important role in the successful integration of migrants/refugees by providing adequate shelter and linking them to other indicators such as these of health and education;
3. Attitudes towards immigrants: The third set of indicators provides information on the attitudes of citizens towards immigrants at a regional and national level. Public acceptance of migration contributes to the successful integration of migrants at a regional and national level, facilitates social cohesion and influences the design of integration policies.

On the other hand, it is common practice that "others" talk about migrants/refugees: researchers, nationals and rarely themselves. According to the UNHCR, the obstacles mainly refugees consider facing as to their integration include the following (UNHCR 2007):

- Difficulties due to lack of knowledge of local languages and of different cultures;
- Discrimination and inappropriate attitudes towards foreigners;
- Lack of understanding by host societies of the specific situation of refugees;
- Psychological effect of prolonged "inactivity" (limbo)/insecurity during the processing of asylum application procedures.

Integration involves a significant degree of complexity, as refugees and immigrants do not form a single and undifferentiated group. It is therefore of prime importance that integration policies are oriented as far as possible towards their particular socio-demographic characteristics (gender, national origin group, educational level) and the particular society in which they live (existence of structural opportunities in the local/wider society). It is noted that the issue of race or ethnic/national origin has not received much attention in the study of integration of refugees, although it is worth further study (Bernstein and Dubois 2018).

Eurostat (2011) cites as crucial areas for integration of immigrants the participation in economic activity, employment, self-employment and unemployment, the correspondence between qualifications and work, educational competence, school performance and school dropout, the average available income and poverty risk, the state of personal health and finally citizenship—naturalization of a long-term immigrant. More generally, for policy planning and practicing, critical questions need to be asked each time about the model to be implemented. For example, it should be clear on which of the dimensions of integration each model separately focuses and what it seeks to achieve. Moreover, it is necessary to predict whether and how the other dimensions of integration are considered and whether there will be unintended consequences and impacts on society as a whole and what these might be.

In addition to the above, the role of the local community is extremely important as it is where the newcomers end up living, where primarily social capital is expressed, and where trust is built between the two sides, that is, the "newcomer" refugees/ migrants and the "hosts." Furthermore, regional/local authorities are generally better aware of the needs of refugees/migrants and should be better prepared to support economic and social integration policies. Moreover, local communities are more aware of the specific forms of criminality and as a result for its prevention (Kury 2017).

All the above are not only complex but also time-consuming processes. Integration takes time and takes place in phases starting from people arriving in an area, their reception, the successive positions and roles they occupy, and the partial or total acceptance of these positions and roles at each different moment in society. For this reason, it is unrealistic to demand social integration and social acceptance of "the different" at the same time both from foreigners and nationals. Social cohabitation has fragile balances and therefore the intensity of the demand "others should become like us" should not work at the expense of a mild and in due time integration, especially when the host country is largely unable to safeguard a minimum level of decent living for "newcomers" (Christopoulos 2013, p. 67).

4 Prevention of Criminal Violence Through Integration. Is There a Specific Policy Path?

"*Violence and violent crime have existed since the dawn of time. Unfortunately, there has been a continuation of violence in human history ever since*" (Farsedakis 2017). The above phrase highlights the universality and timelessness of violence as well as its various transformations in human societies.

Specifically, and with regard to the impact of violence, and in particular, the criminal one in human society, the science of criminology has adequately made its theoretical and research contributions at both the macro and micro level, focusing on specific populations such as minors and women but also on central social institutions such as family and school.

Furthermore, criminal violence has significant repercussions on areas that have not been extensively investigated such as the integration of third-country citizens. In that case, Criminology has slightly so far been concerned with refugee/migrant integration, as integration is considered to fall predominantly in the science of Sociology.[11] Criminology, however, has profoundly been involved in the

[11]However, the Newsletter (2016, issue 1) of the European Criminology Society highlights the contemporary challenge facing European criminals in the face of the "migrant crisis" (Guia and Skilbrei 2016) and special mention is made of issues such as attitudes towards, the role of the media, the integration of foreigners as a critical issue in terms of social cohesion and equality, concepts that are increasingly concerning modern criminology.

"reintegration" of the released. This field could be claimed to be one of the most centralized criminal debates that began in the 1970s in the light of rehabilitation (Martinson 1974). Now, in modern societies where the moving of populations is (again) a "fact" but also a central social issue, the discourse on integration needs to concern Criminology as integration interferes not only with social cohesion but also with the concept of "social order"(*ευ-ταξία in Greek*) which is one of the prerogatives of criminal policy (Farsedakis 2016). Moreover, "social order" combined with social peace, is the ultimate goal of an applied science, such as that of Criminology (Farsedakis 2005).

To accomplish integration and start this process, what have been discussed above for the indications and dimensions of integration are not enough but there is a need to further investigate the specific characteristics of the population, which constitutes the target group of each integrational process. Therefore, it is not enough to take general measures for third country citizens, but it is necessary that special measures be taken for those populations with specific characteristics, such as vulnerable groups (unaccompanied minors, single parent families with minor children, persons with disabilities or suffering from incurable or serious illnesses, elders, persons with post-traumatic stress, victims of shipwrecks, victims of torture, of rape or other serious forms of psychological, physical or sexual violence or exploitation, victims of human trafficking etc.). In general, the integration of refugees and immigrants in order not to remain an unfinished project needs to consider issues related to the victimization of this population as well as their involvement in criminal justice.

More specifically, refugees/migrants are structurally victimized while in their country of origin. "Structural" victimization (Fattah 2000) referring to the social structures and power relations in a given society is distinct because of its size and its omnipresent character and takes various forms such as war, tyranny, genocide, dictatorship, persecution, torture etc. This population mainly comes either from areas experiencing conditions of extreme poverty, or from areas where the safeguard of fundamental rights is not taken for granted. These circumstances are but the starting point of a long journey of victimization.

Refugees and migrants are also victimized along the way, experiencing extremely difficult situations, as they depend on traffic networks, including degrading and inhumane treatment, extremely precarious transferring conditions, forced labor and sexual intercourse exploitation. Throughout this course, however, nothing seems to be worse than returning to the country of origin and nothing better than waiting to reach—alive—and stay in the "West." In this context, the optional or forced "loss" of traveling or other personal documents constitutes the "founding act" of their victimization in this journey to Europe. Claims such as "We threw our passports into the sea" or "the trafficker told us to throw them" constitute a conscious deliberation of the (legal) identity of the subject and mark the passage to another, new, even more precarious than the previous one. Although by definition, this condition is an opening to vulnerability, a reception of unconditional risk. It does not matter, therefore, whether the claimant's allegations are false or true but that they have objective consequences for himself and the place where he is to live.

A typical consequence of the above is the victimization of refugees and immigrants towards racist violence (Chalkia 2013, 2016). Although the victimization in racist crime remains one of the most violent, however, it is only one of those which refugees/immigrants undergo in a constant cycle of (re)fueling situations of danger and exclusion. After each new victimization, the subject is left even more vulnerable and, therefore, more likely to be victimized in the future. More often than not, the subject lives in a context where different forms of victimization are present at the same time, while parallelly experiencing a dystopian situation, capable of even depriving "the right to have rights" (Arendt 1951, p. 377).

Migration largely constitutes a long journey of victimization to the west that encompasses in every station—geographical, temporal, social—the gradual deprivation of the subject's security and protection capabilities, the escalation of his vulnerability, his/her inability to claim an acceptable and recognizable identity. In the context of transnational social geography and global stratification, human life is ranked hierarchically different. Some people not only lose their "value" "here" every day, that is, when they arrive in the destination country, but they did not have the one they should have when they were "there," that is, in the country of origin. The value attributed to refugees/migrants "here" is not independent of the value they had "there" but of the value they gradually lose until they reach a new destination. Each victimization creates favorable conditions for the next one and together they intensify the increasing vulnerability of these people. In general, a strong relation can be identified between social vulnerability with the frequency of criminal victimization. Cultural stigma and marginalization enhance the risk of victimization by defining certain groups as culturally legitimate victims (Fattah 2000). In this light, individual problems and personal paths are linked to issues of social structure (Mills 1959) not only in a socio-geographical context but also in different contexts.

On the other hand, migration, often in the light of heterogeneous approaches tends to be taken as a determining factor in phenomena such as crime, especially in the light of "crimmigration",[12] that is, the assembly of social control with immigration control. Immigrants and foreigners in general have been accused of contributing to the increase in crime, and immigration policies were seen as tools to control it, as part of a process called crimmigration. In particular, the generalized perception of a direct and linear link between migration and crime further contributes to the victimization of refugees/immigrants within criminal justice. It could be argued that by the counterpoint created based on the racial/national/cultural characteristics between indigenous and foreigner population, another one is produced: the counterpoint of the law-abiding citizens of the state and the foreign criminals, which carries pre-existing social inequalities to another level, that of criminal justice (Tsiganou 2010).

Concerning attitudes towards foreigners according to European Social Survey Greece shows high levels of rejection of migrants. Especially, the majority believes that: their presence is bad for the country, their cultural life is downgrading, the

[12]See Stumpf (2006), pp. 367–419; Guia et al. (2011); Skibrei (2016), https://bit.ly/2xX6OcU.

arrival of immigrants in the country makes it a worse place to live (Afouxenidis 2012, pp. 24–25). For the same period and according to Eurobarometer, discriminations have been observed based on nationality[13] which is the most frequently encountered form of discrimination in the EU.

However, recent research[14] reveals some separate data on how Greeks think about "identity" and "otherness." Despite the enormous pressures that Greek society has suffered over the last decade, the country seems to be less polarized than many other European nations. In more detail it is reported that different social groups are not so divided as far as their social views are concerned and the level of social interpersonal trust remain relatively high. Despite their own financial situation, the Greeks have a strong empathy for the recent newcomers to Greece. For example, they make the point that they see them working hard and having good intentions. Seventy-seven percent believe that migrants are willing to work harder and with lower wages than Greeks, and more than half of those surveyed (56%) believe that migrants are trying to integrate into Greek society. The emotions towards immigrants are warmer than in other European countries. Concerns about Islam and Muslims are widespread. The majority (57%) of Greeks believes in "incompatibility" between Islam and Greek society, which partly reflects historical concerns related to Turkey and its relationship with Greece. Greeks' views do not differ particularly as to whether Muslims should wear headscarves or "burqas." However, these concerns coexist with a widespread recognition of the existence of discrimination against Muslims in Greece and a clear majority (68%) expressing concern about the rise of racism. Seventy-two percent show a sense of respect for the different cultural background of refugees and believe that they should be able to "maintain their own traditions." In every case, attitudes towards otherness, as well as the rising hate speech of politicians and parties against third country citizens in Europe and internationally against immigrants is endemic to xenophobia and offends democracy.

Another important part of the integration of refugees and migrants is linked to the "reintegration," meaning those who have been convicted of committing a crime, have served a prison sentence and are citizens of third countries. In these cases, reintegration as a right (Panousis 2014) becomes even more difficult for refugees/migrants who, in addition to the common problems that the released face, third country citizens have to deal with additional obstacles that are related to lack of language skills, the complete absence of a support network, the fact itself that they are aliens etc. Exclusion and relapse in these cases constitute almost not a "self-fulfilling prophecy" but a certainty. This issue is particularly important given that most of the incarcerated population in many European countries consists of foreigners.[15] Regardless of the reasons why this happens, the objective result is that

---

[13]European Commission. Discrimination in the EU in 2009: (Special Eurobarometer 317, Fieldwork May-June 2009), https://bit.ly/2zwktYU.

[14]Dixon et al. (2019), https://bit.ly/35QEOEn.

[15]See: World Prison Brief: Europe, https://bit.ly/2AjSlIP.

most prisoners released are foreigners[16] and this exacerbates the difficulties of their reintegration/integration and it is this condition that must be considered not only by criminal justice but also by policy makers that design integration strategies. More generally, considering that males and especially younger ones are more prone to violence, to the abuse of women and to the provocation of disorder together with the fact that many of the migrants and refugees are men of young age (Hudson and Der Boer 2005), special emphasis needs to be given on the integration processes of this part of the population to avoid the phenomena of exclusion that lead to extreme behaviors, often violent and offensive, which in turn stabilize and enhance exclusion in the context of a vicious cycle of breeding violence and marginalization.

In general, the integration process should be targeted and as possible adapted to the needs and particularities of refugees and migrants. The refugees and migrants do not form a homogeneous group, but they are people with different characteristics, face unique problems and have particular needs. Therefore, the integration of these groups requires specialized approaches and policies oriented at the same in different groups of population. Integration needs to focus on age, gender, etc. on the special circumstances of refugees/immigrants, for instance, it needs to consider not only any possible previous victimization but also the type of it. Contemporary research approaches and reports highlight the impact of victimization of migrants and refugees in crimes such as human trafficking,[17] intimate partner violence[18] or violence that derives from gender inequality[19] have on integration. The integration strategy cannot ignore specific issues such as the aforementioned. Not including them on the integration agenda leaves a big gap in creating the proper social conditions necessary for a smooth transition from one society to the other. Integration are now becoming more challenging as it concerns not just people from different cultures, but often people with a dystopic background.

In this context, cultural expertise becomes particularly useful in highlighting the specific nuances necessary to clarify the situation of refugees and migrants to third parties to facilitate the integration process. Cultural expertise (Holden 2011) is the specialized knowledge that enables socio-legal scholars, anthropologists or, more generally, cultural mediators, to identify and describe relevant events in the light of the particular background of asylum applicants, litigants or defendants and in some cases victims. Cultural expertise contributes to the investigation of serious crimes such as homicide and terrorism but also in less extreme situations, such as entry permits, family reunification, adoption, citizenship, custody of children, and the validity of marriage and divorce.

---

[16]In Greece for example, on 01.01.2019, out of a total of 10,654 prisoners, 5,822 were foreigners; Ministry of Justice, Transparency and Human Rights, https://bit.ly/2SSu96w.

[17]See: European Union (2018), https://bit.ly/35OSTlz, Surtees (2015), https://bit.ly/3dGzwhr, Shigekane (2007), pp. 112–135

[18]Phillimore et al. (2018), pp. 1–34, https://bit.ly/3col9xY.

[19]Sansonetti (2016), https://bit.ly/2yPoeZ8.

Therefore, a sustainable integration requires the involvement of scientists from different fields and the cooperation between institutions and experts. Criminology cannot be absent of this in the sense that public peace and social justice cannot be achieved without the confrontation of issues related to victimization and crime, as approached above.

5 Conclusion

Integration is a process that has to go beyond unilateral models of assimilation and recognize that all members of society are involved, interact and change, forming together with the indigenous population a key living stake: achieving greater participation by all to institutional social structures. The process of integration is not static but dynamic, long-term, and bi-directional, from refugees/migrants to society and vice versa. In this process everyone changes, both foreigners and nationals. Furthermore, specialized policies are needed to identify barriers, to evaluate the effects of interventions and to avoid social exclusion. Exclusion generates violence and violence generates exclusion. This vicious circle whose manifestation takes on all dimensions and processes of integration.

In this context, it is clear that without considering special circumstances resulting from criminal violence, both because of victimization and criminality, any integration strategy remains prima facie unfinished.

Social inclusion is not an easy task and the "non-European" origins of "newcomers" makes the challenge even greater. But it is a challenge that we must face if we want to avoid exclusion, stigmatization of refugees, or the emergence and expansion of ghettos. Although the goal of a society of no exclusion is still pending, a combination of short- and long-term answers is needed to establish an integrated and holistic approach to the particular needs of these people. All cultural differences can be useful for the enrichment of European societies, but on the other hand, refugees have to comply with the laws and values of the host country Policies of integration should be based mainly on the rational distribution of refugees in the country and full participation of their children in the national education system. Particularly, education plays a significant role in integration policies and is not limited to primary/secondary/tertiary education but it is a deeper lifelong basis for learning humanitarian values and general principles of living with dignity (Kury and Redo 2018).

This education can be built with the participation of citizens and of those involved living in the territory of the country. That way further habits, values, knowledge, and skills related to the integration of people in society could be developed (Chalkia and Giouzepas 2018).

From above, it turns out that our societies need to reinvent their integration policies, which should first of all become policies of creation of social bonds with the aim of preventing violence and achieving social peace, according to Sustainable Development Goals (SDGs). However, the question about justice remains. And, maybe, in the Western Countries the obligation to respond is more urgent today to tackle (pre)existing injustices through social consensus that the "barrier" of the "border" is the human rights, "*granite islands towards my timbers*" (Eliot 1922).[20] Every retreat to them is a retreat to inequality and sustainable development.

References

Afouxenidis, A. (2012). Μετανάστευση και ένταξη: προκλήσεις και διακρίσεις. (Migration and integration). In X. Βαρουξή, Ν. Σαρρής, Α. Αφουξενίδης, Ν. Σαρρής, & Ό. Τσακηρίδη (Eds.), *Ένταξη μεταναστών: Αντιλήψεις, πολιτικές, πρακτικές. (Integration of migrants: Perceptions, policies and practices)* (pp. 17-36). Αθήνα: Εθνικό Κέντρο Κοινωνικών Ερευνών.

Arendt, H. (1951). *The origins of totalitarianism*. New York: Schocken Books.

Bernstein, H., & Dubois, N. (2018). *Bringing evidence to the refugee integration debate. Research Report*. Urban Institute. Retrieved from https://urbn.is/3dxinqj

Boswell, C. (2003). *European migration policies in flux. Changing patterns of inclusion and exclusion*. Hoboken: Blackwell.

Chalkia, A. (2013). Εγκλήματα ρατσιστικού μίσους στην Ελλάδα της κρίσης. Από τη θυματοποίηση στην προσβολή της δημοκρατίας. (Hate Crime in Greece in the time of crisis). *Εγκληματολογία*, (1–2), 80–88.

Chalkia, A. (2016). Όψεις των εγκλημάτων μίσους στην Ελλάδα και προτάσεις για την αντιμετώπισή τους. (Hate crime in Greece and its confrontation). In M. Γασπαρινάτου (Ed.), *Τιμητικός τόμος για τον Καθηγητή* Νέστορα *Κουράκη. Έγκλημα και ποινική καταστολή σε εποχή κρίσης. (Volume in honor to professor Nestor Courakis. Crime and penal control in the time of crisis)* (pp.1694-1722). Αθήνα-Κομοτηνή: Αντ.Ν.Σάκκουλα.

Chalkia, A., & Giouzepas, A. (2018). It's just Europe's turn: EU's and Greece's responses to the current refugee and migration flows. In H. Kury & S. Redo (Eds.), *Refugees and migrants in law and policy. Challenges and opportunities for global civic education* (pp. 437-456). Cham: Springer.

Charsley, K., & Spencer, S. (2019). *Understanding integration processes: Informing policy and practice*. UniBristol, UniOxford.

Christopoulos, D. (2013). Αναζητώντας το ελάχιστο πολιτειακό (πολυπολιτισμικό;) όριο: η μετανάστευση στην Ελλάδα της κρίσης. (Looking for the minimum State (multicultural?) limit. migration in Greece at the time of crisis). *Επιστήμη και Κοινωνία*, (30), 41–74.

Crawford, A. (2009). *Crime prevention politics in comparative perspective*. Cullompton: Willan publishing.

Dixon, T., Hawkins, S., Juan-Torres, M., Kimaram, A. (2019, May). *Attitudes towards national identity, migration and refugee perceptions in Greece, More in Common*. Retrieved from https://bit.ly/35QEOEn

Eliot, T. S. (1922). *The waste land*. New York: Liveright Publishing Corporation.

EPIM. (2019). *Rethinking inclusion. Unlocking innovative solutions for migrant inclusion*. European Programme for Integration and Migration (EPIM). Retrieved from https://bit.ly/2YVpiFA

European Commission. Common Principles for Integration, Communication from the Commission to the Council, the European Council, the European Economic and Social Committee and the Committee of the Regions. Third Annual Report on Migration and Integration Brussels, 11.9.2007, COM (2007) 512 final. Retrieved from https://bit.ly/3cmPQU1

[20]Excerpt from the poem "Marina," Eliot (1922).

European Commission. Discrimination in the EU in 2009: (Special Eurobarometer 317, Fieldwork May-June 2009), Retrieved from https://bit.ly/35OtQ25

European Council. (2016, March 18). *Council of the European Union. EU-Turkey declaration*, Retrieved from https://bit.ly/35PXAeQ

European Union. (2018). *Council of the Baltic States, Road map for integration of human trafficking victims among migrants in Finland, Germany, and Sweden*, Retrieved from https://bit.ly/2YWMwv1

Eurostat. (2011). *Indicators of immigrant integration: A Pilot Study*. Eurostat. Retrieved from https://bit.ly/2zwoEUA

Eurostat. Statistics explain. Asylum Statistics, Retrieved from https://bit.ly/3fDNJxq

Eurostat. Statistics explained. Asylum applications (non-EU) in the EU-28 Member States, 2008–2018. Retrieved from https://bit.ly/3ciHkpb

Farsedakis, J. (2005). *Στοιχεία Εγκληματολογίας. (Criminology)*. Αθήνα: Νομική Βιβλιοθήκη.

Farsedakis, J. (2016). Η πρόληψη του εγκλήματος ως μέσον αντεγκληματικής πολιτικής. (Crime prevention as a tool of criminal policy). In M. Γασπαρινάτου, (Ed.), *Τιμητικός Τόμος για τον Καθηγητή* Νέστορα *Κουράκη. Έγκλημα και ποινική καταστολή σε εποχή κρίσης (Volume in honor to professor Nestor Courakis. Crime and penal control in the time of crisis)*. Αθήνα-Κομοτηνή: Αντ.Ν.Σάκκουλα.

Farsedakis, J. (2017). Περί βίας. Προελεγόμενα. (On violence). Στο Χαλκιά Α. (Επιμ.), *Πρακτικά Συνεδρίου: Το βίαιο έγκλημα στον 21ο αιώνα, (Violent crime on the 21st century)*. Ελληνική Εταιρεία Εγκληματολογίας, Εγκληματολογία (1), 12–22.

Fattah, E. (2000). Victimology: Past, present and future. *Criminologie, 33*(1), 17–46.

Feltes, T., List, K., et al. (2018). More refugees, more offenders, more crime? Critical comments with data from Germany. In H. Kury & S. Redo (Eds.), *Refugees and migrants in law and policy. Challenges and opportunities for global Civic Education* (pp. 599–624). Cham: Springer.

Fukuda-Parr, S. (2018). Sustainable development goals. In T. G. Weiss & S. Daws (Eds.), *The Oxford handbook on the United Nations*. Oxford: Oxford University Press.

Gerhards, J., & Lengfeld, H. (2015). *European citizenship and social integration in the European Union*. London: Routledge.

Giddens, A. (2009). *Sociology*. Cambridge: Polity Press.

Goffman, E. (1963). *Stigma: Notes on the management of spoiled identity*. Englewood Cliffs: Prentice-Hall.

Goldin, I., Cameron, G., Balarajan, M. (2011). *Exceptional people: How migration shaped our world and will define our future*. New Jersey: Princeton University Press.

Guia, M., & Skilbrei, M. L. (2016). *How the current "migration crisis" challenges European criminologists*. Newsletter of the European Society of Criminology.

Guia, M. J., van der Woulde, M., van der Leun, J. (Eds.). (2011). *Social control and justice: Crimmigration in an age of fear*. The Hague: Eleven International Publishing.

Hamberger, A. (2009). Immigrant integration. Acculturation and social integration. *Journal of Identity and Migration Studies, 3*(2), 2–20.

Holden, L. (2011). Introduction. Reflexivity, culture, ethics. In L. Holden (Ed.), *Cultural expertise and litigation: Patterns, conflicts, narratives* (pp. 1–10). Oxon: Routledge.

Hudson, V., & Der Boer, A. (2005). *Bare branches: The security implications of Asia's surplus male population*. Belfer Center Studies in International Securities.

Hughes, M., & Kroehler, C. (2011). *Sociology: The core*. New York: McGraw-Hill.

International Organisation for Migration. Global Migration Indicators 2018, Insights from the Global Migration Data Portal: http://www.migrationdataportal.org, Global Migration Data Analysis Centre (GMDAC) International Organization for Migration, Berlin, Retrieved from https://bit.ly/3clGV5i

Kury, H. (2017). Community, crime prevention and punishment. In J. Winderdyk (Ed.), *Crime prevention: International perspectives, issues, and trends* (pp. 179–208). Boca Raton: Taylor & Francis Group.

Kury, H., & Redo, S. (2018). Epilogue. In H. Kury & S. Redo (Eds.), *Refugees and migrants in law and policy: Challenges and opportunities for global civic education* (pp. 863–913). Cham: Springer.

Lockwood, D. (1964). Social integration and system integration. In G. Zolleschan & W. Hirsch (Eds.), *Explorations in social change* (pp. 244–257). London: Routledge.

Lodovici, S., et al. (2017). *European Parliament.* Retrieved from: https://bit.ly/3dBTLwE

Martinson, R. (1974). What works? Questions and answers about prison reform. *The Public Interest, 35*, 22–54.

Mascarenas, B.-G., & Pennix, R. (2016). Introduction: Integration as a three-way process approach? In B.-G. Mascarenas & R. Pennix (Eds.), *Integration processes and policies in Europe. Context, levels and actors* (pp. 1–10). Cham: Springer.

McDonald, W. F. (2018). *The criminal victimization of migrants*. London: Palgrave. https://doi.org/10.1007/978-3-319-69062-9

Mills, G. (1959). *The sociological imagination*. Oxford: Oxford University Press.

OECD. (2018). *Working together for local integration of migrants and refugees*. Paris: OECD Publishing. https://doi.org/10.1787/9789264085350-en

Palidda, S. (2009). The criminalization and victimization of immigrants: A critical perspective. In W. McDonald (Ed.), *Immigration, crime and justice* (pp. 313–326). Bingley: Emerald Group Publishing Limited. https://doi.org/10.1108/S1521-6136(2009)0000013020

Panousis, G. (2014). Reintegration as a right. In Γ. Πανούσης (Ed.), *Το ημερολόγιο ενός εγκληματολόγου (The diary of a criminologist)*. Αθήνα: Νομική Βιβλιοθήκη.

Parmar, A. (2019). Arresting (non)citizenship: The policing migration nexus of nationality, race and criminalization. *Theoretical Criminology*, 1–22. https://doi.org/10.1177/1362480619850800

Parsons, T. (1954). *Essays in sociological theory*. Illinois: The Free Press.

Pennix, R. (2005). Integration of migrants: Economic, social, cultural and political dimensions. In M. Macura, A. MacDonald, & W. Haug (Eds.), *The new demographic regime-population challenges and policy responses* (pp. 137–151). Geneva: United Nations.

Phillimore, J., Pertek, S., Alidu, L. (2018). *Sexual and gender-based violence and refugees. The impacts of and on integration domains*, IRIS Working Paper Series, No. 28, 1–34. Retrieved from https://bit.ly/35OUckt

Redo, S. (2017). The transformative power of the United Nations post-2015 Sustainable Goals and crime prevention education for a new culture of lawfulness. In J. A. Winterdyk (Ed.), *Crime Prevention: International perspectives, issues and trends* (pp. 1–21). Boca Raton: Taylor & Francis Group.

Sansonetti, S. (2016). *Female refugees and asylum seekers: The issue of integration, European Parliament*, Directorate-General for Internal Policies, Retrieved from https://bit.ly/2WNyUQ2

Schnapper, D. (2007). *Qu'est-ce que l'intégration ?* Paris: Gallimard. Greek Edition: Schnapper, D. (2008). Η κοινωνική ενσωμάτωση. Μια σύγχρονη προσέγγιση. (Δ. Παπαδοπούλου, Επιμ., & Ξ. Γιαταγάνας, Μεταφρ.) Αθήνα: Κριτική.

Shigekane, R. (2007). Rehabilitation and community integration of trafficking survivors in the United States. *Human Rights Quarterly, 29*(1), 112–135.

Skibrei, M. L. (2016). How the current "migration crisis" challenges European criminologists. *Newsletter of the European Society of Criminology, Criminology in Europe, 1*. Retrieved https://bit.ly/2WZBEdt

Sohoni, D., & Sohoni, T. W. (2014). Perceptions of immigrant criminality: Crime and social boundaries. *The Sociological Quarterly, 55*, 49–71. https://doi.org/10.1111/tsq.12039

Solivetti, L. M. (2010). *Immigration, social integration and crime. A cross-national approach.* Oxon: Routledge.

Stumpf, J. (2006). The crimmigration crisis: Immigrants, crime, and sovereign power. *American University Law Review, 56*, 367–419.

Surtees, R. (2015). *Beyond trafficking. The integration of trafficking victims in the Balkans, from 2007 to 2014*, Final Review Report, King Baudouin Foundation. Retrieved from https://bit.ly/2xRmaiU

Tsiganou, J. (2010). *Μετανάστευση. Μύθοι και πραγματκότητα. (Migration. Myths and reality).* Αθήνα: Εθνικό Κέντρο Κοινωνικών Ερευνών.
UNHCR. (2007). *Note on the integration of refugees in the European Union*. Retrieved from https://bit.ly/2AdhHrC
UNHCR. *Figures at a glance*. Retrieved from https://bit.ly/2xRAhEW
United Nations. (1951). *Convention on the Status of Refugees (Geneva Convention)*. Retrieved from https://bit.ly/2Llgktc
United Nations. *Transforming our world: the 2030 Agenda for Sustainable Development*. Retrieved from https://bit.ly/2YQGMmq
United Nations Office on Drugs and Crime. (2010). *Handbook on the crime prevention guidelines: Making them work*. Vienna: UNODC. Retrieved from https://bit.ly/2xR4tjt
United Nations Office on Drugs and Crime. (2015). *Combating violence against migrants. Criminal justice measures to prevent, investigate, prosecute and punish violence against migrants, migrant workers and their families and to protect victims*. Vienna: United Nations. Retrieved from https://bit.ly/3blSMiG
Unnever, J. D. (2014). Race, crime and public opinion. In S. M. Bucerius & M. Tonry (Eds.), *The Oxford handbook on ethnicity, crime and immigration* (pp. 70–106). Oxford: Oxford University Press.
Zatz, M. S., & Smith, H. (2012). Immigration, crime, and victimization: Rhetoric and reality. *Annual Review of Law and Social Science, 8*, 141–159. https://doi.org/10.1146/annurev-lawsocsci-102811-173923

Anastasia Chalkia is a sociologist and holds a Ph.D. and a MA in Criminology from the Panteion University of Social and Political Sciences (Athens-GR). She is course tutor/coordinator and at the interdepartmental MSc in *Media and Refugee/Migration Flows* (National Kapodistrian University and University of the Aegean, Greece) and registered teaching staff at the National Centre of Public Administration and Local Government. She has also taught at the Greek Open University, the University of West Attica and the Panteion University. Since 2013, she is working at the Greek Asylum Service, first as Special Personnel responsible for the Refugee Status Determination and then as Head of Asylum Unit in Athens. Since 2015, she is National Trainer certified by the European Asylum Support Service in the module "Inclusion in International Protection". Also, she is Deputy Country Representative at the European Crime Prevention Network (EUCPN) (2017-present) and she was appointed member of the Jury for the European Crime Prevention Award under the Italian and the Lithuanian Presidency of the Council of the EU (2013 and 2014). She has written a monograph in crime prevention and has edited two volumes. Her work on crime prevention, hate crime, punitiveness and migration/refugee issues has been published in scientific journals and collective volumes and presented at national and international congresses in Greece and Europe. Her recent publications include: (2018) Chalkia, A., Giouzepas, A. "It's just Europe's turn: EU's and Greece's response to the current refugee and migration flows", in: H. Kury, H., S. Redo (eds.) Refugees and migrants in law and policy - Challenges and opportunities for global civil education (Springer 2018), *Criminal policy and public participation, Vol. 4, Panteion University* & Dionikos Publ., Athens, Greek/English, (2016). E-mail: anastasia.chalkia@hotmail.com.

Legal Education for Profit and the United Nations Call for "Quality Education" and "Strong Institutions" in the 2030 Sustainable Development Agenda

Riaz Tejani

Abstract The United Nations 2030 Sustainable Development Agenda calls for "quality education" and "strong institutions" in Goals 4 and 16. This call underscores the supreme importance of the rule of law in global perspective by construing law as both constitutive of social institutions and a fundamental institution in its own right. In both capacities law historically has acted to buffer public goods and vulnerable populations from the vicissitudes of market supply and demand. For this reason, law schools—where we teach and train most new lawyers and judges—have been a particularly sensitive kind of institution. Yet, during the 2000s the West saw the rise of "for-profit" law schools—institutions of legal education and scholarship newly created with the mission of commercial gain, sometimes for the benefit of outside investors or investment "funds." What effect might this historical turn have had on law and its practice in the twenty-first century, and what does this say more generally about democratic ideals in the West during this period? For instance, that for-profit law schools emerged simultaneously with the major accounting and banking scandals of the decade may be no coincidence. This chapter argues, therefore, that the rise of for-profit legal education was a symptom of changes in U.S moral economy, and in the social and political climate of the West more generally. Namely, this development points to an emerging conception of law as primarily in the service of economic rather than social life.

Keywords Law · Law school · Legal education · Access to justice · Business ethics · Market fundamentalism · Sustainable development · Student debt

R. Tejani (✉)
University of Redlands, School of Business, Redlands, CA, USA
e-mail: riaz_tejani@redlands.edu

H. Kury, S. Redo (eds.), *Crime Prevention and Justice in 2030*,
https://doi.org/10.1007/978-3-030-56227-4_22

1 Introduction

The rule of law starts at home. After decades spent arguing that the nations of the Global South must strengthen their legal institutions, countries in the North are realizing how fragile the rule of law may be in their own backyards. Systemic examples of this abound in recent cases of armed trespass of government buildings during the COVID-19 emergency (Graham 2020), juvenile migrant detentions (Jordan 2019), government corruption reports (Schmitt 2019), and international election meddling (Hulse 2019). But more subtle examples may be equally consequential.

When it comes to the rule of law, the educational institutions that prepare lawyers and judges for civil service and private practice can be just as important as any state apparatuses in a democratic system. Jurists[1] are the main architects of civil society in these systems. They carry on intergenerational transfers of legal knowledge. They develop and refine the tools of legal interpretation. They advocate for the needs of individual disputants who, especially in common law systems, drive legal change in market-like fashion. They occupy a majority of positions in many national and regional law-making bodies. And they produce a disproportionate share of executive leaders at all levels, including the supranational level of governance so important under globalization.

That said, the integrity of law schools around the globe is vital to the operation of democracy. In most cases, legal educators have been aware of this vitality and maintained the political and fiscal independence of their institutions from government, political party, and market demands. Law schooling for profit, in particular, has been particularly *un*common even in global perspective. A fair generalization across historical and geographic space would be that the institutions of legal education have, by and large, operated on a nonprofit basis—and often as public institutions without any private sector funding or entanglements. To put it more simply, across the legal systems of the world, there seems to have been tacit consensus that "making money" off training the professional guardians of justice is undesirable.

It is for these reasons that the emergence of for-profit law schools in the United States before and during the global financial crisis of the 2000s was such a striking historical development. For nearly a century, US legal educators had frowned upon for-profit law schools and, indeed, chosen not to accredit any such programs. The concern was that the profit model would taint the mission, governance, and content delivery of these institutions, and by extension the legal profession to which they contributed human capital. Ultimately, for reasons discussed further below, the regulatory body overseeing US law schools changed course and allowed these organizations to take hold in certain key jurisdictions around the country. The results were, by and large, negative.

[1] I here use "jurists" as a catch-all term for lawyers, lawmakers, and judges.

Drawing from roughly eight years of research into US for-profit law schools, I suggest in this chapter that the concerns about their integrity were well-founded. The rise of for-profit legal education in the USA was likely a key indicator of changes in US moral economy, and in the social and political climate of the West more generally. As I further suggest here, it highlights a key challenge for the United Nations call for "quality education" and "strong institutions" in the UN 2030 Sustainable Development Agenda.

2 Frameworks of Understanding: Access to Justice, Business Ethics, and Market Fundamentalism

There are three key interdisciplinary frameworks from which to approach the problem of legal education for-profit institutions today. In order of specificity, these are *access to justice*, *business ethics,* and *market fundamentalism* (or neoliberalism). The access to justice framework has been constructed out of several disciplines, although primarily it emerges from law and socio-legal studies. It starts from the key premise, one echoed in the UN 2030 Sustainable Development Agenda, that universal access to the institutions and processes of justice is a fundamental feature of contemporary democratic societies. Without this, justice—which was aptly defined centuries ago in the Justinian Digest as, "the constant and perpetual will to render to each his due"[2] becomes only the province of the few. In cases where justice in society has been the subject of limited access, this has tended to favor the monied or propertied classes, as well as members of the hegemonic ethnic or racial group. Whatever the grounds for exclusion, this observation tells us something important about the concept of justice: to be most meaningful, it must be available to all. This sentiment may be echoed in the famous adage attributed to the American civil rights leader Martin Luther King Jr.: "Injustice anywhere is a threat to justice everywhere" (1963). There is something essential about the universality of justice that renders partial or exclusive administrations of it suspect or attenuated.

In the US legal academy, access to justice has only become a topic of considerable discussion among mainstream law scholars. In the work of Deborah Rhode, for example, socioeconomic class is the primary independent variable in whether or not US subjects are able to benefit from their civil right to legal due process (Rhode 2004). But, she says,

> It is not only the poor who are priced out of the current system. Millions of Americans, including those of moderate income, suffer untold misery because legal protections that are available in principle are inaccessible in practice. Domestic violence victims cannot obtain protective orders, elderly medical patients cannot collect health benefits, disabled children are denied educational services, defrauded consumers lack affordable remedies . . . The list is long and the costs incalculable (Rhode 2004, p. 5).

[2]Quoted in Miller (2017).

Why, then, are legal services priced beyond the reach of "millions" in the USA? On this topic, many have pointed to flaws in the American legal education system. At the national level,[3] to be eligible for government subsidized student loan funding for tuition and living expenses, the student must attend an *accredited* law school. Accreditation comes from one and only one body: the Council of the Section of Legal Education and Admissions to the Bar, an independent wing of the American Bar Association (ABA). Under US regulations, federal student loans can only be disbursed to students of accredited education institutions. The US Department of Education has, meanwhile delegated all law school accreditation to the Council. The Council has promulgated an elaborate but clear rulebook setting minimum standards for all law schools seeking accreditation or reaccreditation.

Those rules require minimal services and facilities for students. These have historically included things like a physical law library, a prescribed student-faculty ratio, and a prescribed ratio of tenure to non-tenure line faculty. Such offerings represent expensive "fixed costs" that demand resources to maintain. Schools, it is said, must therefore keep tuition prices high, irrespective of student employment and income results. For these reasons, many critics have blamed the accreditation regime for the high cost of legal education.

Yet, despite the strict national standards expected, some law schools cost significantly more than others. One reason for this is the pursuit of prestige and rankings dominance. In the USA, the most revered law school ranking authority is *US News and World Report*. Its methodology for determining rankings positions considers soft factors such as "reputational score" assigned by members of the profession. These also depend upon things like faculty publication and citation counts. In short, The *US News* rankings can be manipulated through substantial expenditures by the law schools to incentivize faculty and administrative activity that boosts the school's standing in ways unrelated to the delivery of education to students. These expenditures, as well, are passed on to students, especially by schools without deep endowment funds. They also might take resources away from student offerings such as practice skills training, academic support, and professionalization. Aware of this, some scholars have advocated for law schools to revise their programs to better train "main street lawyers"—or attorneys better prepared to practice for the needs of ordinary citizens (Herrera 2013).

The for-profit law schools that emerged in the United States found themselves right in the middle of these debates about access to justice. Disallowed for most of

[3]The US federal system creates two levels of legal jurisdiction and professional training. In most states (regional units) both are covered by the same schooling and bar admission process. This means that graduation from an accredited law school allows the student to sit for *any* state's bar examination. In a few cases, mere graduation from an accredited school guarantees admission into that state's bar while rendering him or her eligible to sit for another state's examination. This "diploma privilege" was under consideration in more states as a result of the 2020 COVID-19 crisis. In a few other states, an aspirant may attend a "state accredited" law school and sit for *only* that state's examination. Finally, some states allow an aspirant to "read" law under a licensed practitioner—essentially a form of apprenticeship—and then sit for an examination to become licensed.

the twentieth century, for-profit law schools followed a business model that extracted surplus value from faculty, staff, and students for the benefit of shareholders off site. This extraction resulted in more austere course and clinical[4] offerings. Furthermore, the national accreditation seal was a subject of concern insofar as it would allow students to bring federal student loan money to a private commercial entity. As history would bear out, the demographics of students in US for-profits schools were also somewhat unique. Their demographics were ethnically more diverse, included more working-class students, and admitted more applicants with low-end test scores and grade point averages. In turn, it was presumed, these students would go on to serve unmet needs by ultimately practicing law in minority and low-income communities, or by offering legal services on lower value, individual claims like landlord disputes or divorces. Teaching these students was an unusually diverse faculty with more ethnoracial minority professors than at most ABA law schools.

All this diversity was meant to produce lawyers who would practice law in minority and lower income communities. The for-profit law schools that opened in the 1990s and 2000s spent considerable effort studying the markets of growing metropolitan areas and found that legal needs among these communities were going unmet in US states like Arizona and Florida. These were, not coincidentally, regions that had seen some of the largest in migration and housing construction booms in the period before the global financial crisis of 2008.

The new law schools also aimed to fulfill a growing demand in legal education to teach students "practice-ready" skills. The erstwhile dominant model in American law schools had been to teach students using the "case method" that saw large groups learning in lecture halls in between long assignments reading case excerpts in thick textbooks. The students in class would be questioned on their understanding and retention of details from these cases dissected in almost anatomical form. The professor would engage particular students each session in a "Socratic" style of dialogue, and this would sometimes take students entirely by surprise in front of the large groups of peers in the class. As the most common model of American legal education, this created a style of learning that was elliptical, abstract, stressful, and adversarial.

Critics of this model for legal education argued it followed the "appellate" practice model of legal profession, but bore little resemblance to the main practices of everyday lawyers—practices that often entailed completing forms, filing motions, and trying to consult sympathetically with clients in trouble. In the early 2000s legal education experts began calling for a "practice-ready" form of training that would see students trained more in the mundane tasks of law practice, and in the soft-skills of human-to-human contact necessitated by the negotiation and settlement process by which most legal cases come to be resolved in the United States system. Indeed,

[4]Law school education is delivered both in the classroom and through clinical education. The more well-funded a school, the better its clinical offerings are. Clinics are a venue for students to gain hands-on experience in casework on specific theme areas. They require lower faculty to student ratios and are therefore considered very expensive.

that process is crucial to allowing the justice system to operate smoothly when it would otherwise be flooded to a halt if every case were adjudicated to completion.

In short, the new law schools opening under a for-profit model responded to very real needs in the legal marketplace and enjoyed market conditions that were extremely favorable to their stated mission. They hired several legal education critics as early consultants on curriculum development, and they maintained extra financial support towards faculty who made classroom innovation a centerpiece of their research. The idea was that the for-profit law schools alone were poised to reform legal education, and that such reform was essential to improving access to justice on a national scale. They also argued vigorously that they offered a unique "value proposition" to those wanting to become attorneys but shut out from more traditional law school admissions.

These representations about value raise a second major theoretical frame through which one might view this sector. For decades, the field of business ethics has brought together moral philosophy, applied ethics, business management, and interpretive social sciences to consider the array of ethical duties and performance qualities of commercial organizations. In many senses a response to numerous periods of abuse and scandal in corporate and industrial life, business ethics has now become an integral component of the management curriculum in Western business schools. It effectively asks about, "issues that arise out of the relationships and activities surrounding the production, distribution, marketing, and sale of goods and services" (Vaidya and Allhoff 2016, p. 2). The application of this framework to higher and professional education contexts is, of course, new. That is because for-profit education only really took root in the United States after the onset of the information economy and advances in online distance learning. Today, with numerous cases of fraud and financial misfeasance among for-profit institutions of higher education, these schools have become a prime example of the demand for better understandings of business ethics. Where the commercial goods or services are closely related to sensitive "public goods"—as in healthcare, security, natural resources, and education—the need for ethical standards and leadership may be at its very highest.

Business ethicists usually begin their observations with a set of clear ethical frameworks. While these can include nonwestern sources such as Confucian or Islamic moral principles in commerce, they more often begin with a portion of the Western philosophical canon. The three most common of these are utilitarianism, Kantianism, and virtue ethics. Developed most prominently by Bentham and Mill, utilitarianism asks about the consequences of any moral action and suggests a course of behavior that favors the "greatest good for the greatest number" of a moral community—however that might be defined. It is subject to considerable parsing when one explores the differences between Bentham and his student John Stuart Mill, but the general picture of a cost/benefit approach can be easily contrasted to the moral philosophy of Kant. Kantian business ethics are *deontological* in nature meaning they attend only to duty rather than consequences, and suggest in short that an action is "right" if it creates a universalizable rule that the actor would feel comfortable living under. Finally, virtue ethics asks whether the action in question helps to edify the actor to be the best person—or organization—it can be. From Aristotle, it defines "best" in terms of ideal forms, and considers the ideal human form to be happiness or *eudaimonea.*

Each of these three frameworks has been substantially revised and commented on so that any critical commentary here would only service a strawman argument. Taking these at their most nuanced, each has offered something important to the development of theory in business ethics. By far the best example of this is in the theory of "stakeholder" value in corporate social responsibility, or CSR. The CSR model propounded by Milton Friedman had said business exists solely to profit its owners—be they sole proprietors or thousands of public shareholders. But in the wake of considerable abuses seen through the 1970s and 80s, R. Edward Freeman proposed a "stakeholder theory" in which non-owners also have important claims on the proceeds and well-being of commercial activities of their organizations. These included the customers who may depend on products for safety and health, suppliers who rely on good business practices to keep their obligations to their own constituents, and of course employees who in a real sense sacrifice their capital to benefit the corporate collective and are represented by its brand. Stakeholder CSR can be justified based on all three of the above ethical frameworks. More importantly here, it has a direct bearing on the analysis of for-profit legal education.

The law schools described here operated as "closely held" or private equity owned commercial entities. They did not have public shareholders in the common sense of that term. But, they did have a narrow group of owners who profited by extracting surplus value from faculty and staff labor. Moreover, their particular profit drew from a source of public financing made available in the United States by a public commitment to higher education that gave students low-cost loans to boost their human capital on the understanding that this would be easily paid back after the higher credentials were attained—in law especially. From this description alone one realizes the very complex web of stakeholders beyond the small group of owners. The general public subsidizing student loans, the students incurring massive amounts of debt to better themselves, and the legal service client public who would ultimately depend on the new graduates for help were just some of the uniquely important stakeholder groups brought together in the context of for-profit legal education.

So in summary, a business ethics framework applied to for-profit legal education asks us to consider whether these institutions—even taken on their face as primarily commercial entities in the business of making money—may violate one or more of the key tenets of Western applied ethics. In the utilitarian sense, are they violative of the principle of doing the greatest good for the greatest number? In the Kantian sense are they practicing an approach that—generalized to the global population—would produce a world in which their own architects would want to live. In the Aristotelian sense, are their decisions amplifying human virtue?

Many would take issue with this line of questioning as, in itself, already too sympathetic to what for-profit law schools are doing to strong legal institutions in the West. The very notion that schools of higher or professional education could be considered as "primarily commercial entities" runs counter to what many believe is the exceptional stature of education in general. Much like public goods such as clean air and water, these critics view education as a kind of sensitive public good as well; it is foundational to Western liberal democracies and something that really only benefits a society when distributed *en masse*. It has been responsible for measurable increases in quality of life in specific national cases, and it serves as the basis for an educated populace in participatory politics.

So, when institutions of higher education are commercialized in this fashion, they evoke a third conceptual framework identifiable as "market fundamentalism." This stands for the proposition that faith in free markets to govern social activity has grown so strong in some sectors that we erroneously trust it to regulate even the most sensitive public goods. Market fundamentalism has, no doubt, come to oppose most forms of government economic planning or regulatory oversight in matters of commercial significance which today covers most sectors.

The critique of market fundamentalism tends to be one levied by left intellectuals against what they consider to be the dominant liberal or neoliberal political economy developed and advanced by economics and law scholars most prominently at the University of Chicago after the middle of the twentieth century. However, the challenge to the "marketization of everything" is not particularly radical when taken in any broad political context. The government theorist Michael Sandel has raised this critique for decades in front of over 15,000 students in his undergraduate Justice course at Harvard University, and most European centrist political parties would have considered this part of their basic platform even after the neoliberal turn in continental politics.

The neoliberalization of the modern University, however, is the subject of its own intense scholarly reflection. Some have viewed it from the sociology of education to spell danger for "public pedagogy" or the unique responsibility to teach the general public about ideas critical to its self-governance and public participation (Freire 2018; Giroux 2011). Others take a historical perspective on the role that broad access to higher education played in the development of postwar Europe and North America as industrial and technological powerhouses (Aronowitz 2000). From both the sociological and historical perspectives, market fundamentalism applied in the higher education context represents a corrosion of the unique role responsibility universities and their administrations have had toward the public.

Understood through the three broad theoretical frames of access to justice, business ethics, and market fundamentalism, for-profit law schools impact the health of institutions both from within and without: they are themselves a kind of uniquely financialized institution, but they are also preparing lawyers to go out and serve the institutions of justice—courts, prisons, city and state governments, and the legal rules themselves. In discussions about access to justice, we see the important role institutions must play in guaranteeing individuals and minority groups the ability to know and utilize legal expertise to defend social, political and economic rights when they come under threat, which, under conditions of growing nationalism and nativism, appears more and more often. Yet frequently the protection of rights occurs not in the obvious channels of public law (e.g., constitutional, administrative, criminal justice) but rather in the individual pursuit of contract and injury claims more characteristic of private law. For-profit law schools in the United States claimed from the outset to promote access to justice in this private law sense, however, as the below sections will suggest, the devil is always in the details. Taking seriously their own objectives as commercial entities, these organizations also trigger the framework of business ethics—one that has developed richly over the past half-century to apply western moral philosophy to unique problems of corporate commercial activity. As will be revisited near the conclusion of this chapter, these institutions sooner or later failed under these standards. But finally, one can set aside business ethics entirely and still ask whether for-profit law schools were a wise idea simply based on their willingness to extend market logics to professional legal education in the first place. This larger critique of market fundamentalism encourages that we ask whether legal education was exceptional compared to other commercial activities, and whether the exposure of increasingly vulnerable law student populations (and in turn their clientele) to certain market forces was bound to cause harm from the very beginning.

3 For-Profit Law Schools in Context: A Brief Overview

A chapter aiming to extract lessons about the commercialization of professional education demands a broader contextual understanding of how that commercialization emerged. In this brief section, therefore, I want to briefly trace the development of for-profit law schools in the United States and compare their present actuality with those of two other countries.

3.1 United States

The ABA accredited its first for-profit law school in the mid-1990s, yet this requires substantial qualification. First, for-profit law teaching and learning had existed long before there ever was an ABA, and certainly well before this body was charged with law school accreditation. Indeed, the very first dedicated American law school, Litchfield Law School in Connecticut, was a proprietary[5] institution founded in 1784 with the sole purpose of training new lawyers in the new American republic (Litchfield Historical Society 2019). Whereas the College of William and Mary had offered law courses as part of its "liberal education," Litchfield envisioned legal education as its own separate formality (Litchfield Historical Society 2019). This was significant against the backdrop of English common law training, particularly in the new colonies, because this tended to emphasize apprenticeship in existing law offices as the predominant mode of knowledge and practice training. Interestingly,

[5] I here and throughout will use "for-profit" and "proprietary" interchangeably.

Litchfield was founded by graduates and former instructors of Princeton University, one of the only Ivy League institutions in the USA *not* to have a law school today. It operated until 1833 and produced approximately 1000 attorneys in that period (Litchfield Historical Society 2019). Although a small number by today's standards, it is important to remember that the population of the new republic in 1833 was approximately only 13 million people, with only about 9% of that number living in cities (US History 2019).

At about the same time that Litchfield was winding down, another proprietary law school was thriving in Connecticut. The New Haven Law School emerged in the 1810s as part of a formal apprentice training program in the offices of Seth Staples who owned one of the more extensive law libraries in the country at the time (Yale Law School 2019). From the mid-1820s Staples' program—now under the leadership of his former student Samuel Hitchcock—began slowly affiliating with the local private university until 1843, by which time it finally merged with it to become the now-preeminent Yale Law School (Yale Law School 2019). It surprises many to learn that the nation's most prestigious and selective law program today began as a for-profit independent legal education institution—a fact that serves as a reminder about the significance of historicity.

The prestige of Yale is a unique product of the sedimentation of time and experience. But it is also the result of its near-primacy in the legal education landscape in the new American republic. On one hand, defenders of the new for-profits in the 2000s could have pointed to both Litchfield and New Haven as examples of the unfounded assumption about low quality ascribed to their subsector and business model. On the other hand, they could never viably claim they would follow a similar path given that education and professional landscapes had so dramatically changed as to prevent most new actors from attaining the same respect or competitive advantage.[6] Of course, even while sharing the "proprietary" label with Litchfield and New Haven, the for-profit law schools of the 2000s were financialized in a way that made them less subject to the frameworks of legal professionalization and more subject to the markets in for-profit colleges and universities characterized by massive online programs like the University of Phoenix or Corinthian Colleges, both of which faltered near the end of the Obama administration (2016) and one of which failed entirely due to mismanagement and regulatory discipline.

The very reemergence of proprietary law schools in the United States had as much to do with changes in the regulatory landscape as it did with any sudden need that these schools could fulfill. This landscape is defined primarily by the accreditation history of the Council of the Section on Legal Education and Admission to the Bar of the American Bar Association (Council). The ABA is a national body

[6]UC Irvine is a notable exception; its law school was able to premier at 29 in the national rankings after only 4 years of operation. But its model was only marginally innovative in that it largely replicated the standard 3 year course of study on an expensive, research-oriented faculty model. For a good critique on this see Tamanaha (2012).

gathering some four hundred thousand attorney members and another 3500 organizations in the United States. It comprises numerous "Sections" specializing in legal practice and research areas such as criminal law, civil rights, and international law. The ABA has issued the Model Rules of Professional Conduct and gives ethics opinions on professional conduct cases, it offers evaluations of judicial nominees up to the Supreme Court level, and it adopts positions on major legislation and national policy. Since 1923, the Council has been the main national accreditor of US law schools. Recognized as such by the US Department of Education, it has the sole authority to grant accreditation of the kind necessary for schools to receive federally financed student loans for study.

For most of its nearly 100-year history the accrediting body of the ABA refused to certify for-profit law schools. One reason is that attorneys in the USA have always struggled with their position as market actors especially in relation to other tightly regulated learned professions such as medicine and engineering (Tejani 2018). Historically in the USA, from a time dating back to the US colonies, lawyers were under substantial suspicion from the citizenry (Tejani 2019). One of the ways the professional association countered this suspicion was by setting down ethical limits on the degree of commercial opportunism—for example rules against "barratry" or ambulance chasing they could engage in. The distaste for for-profit legal education, therefore, was an extension of this more general distaste for overt commercial ambitions. Although very different in form than the attorney who follows accident victims to the hospital as a way to acquire business, proprietary law schools were but one degree removed; they saw school business offices trying to enrich themselves off an otherwise "noble" goal to join the bar and serve the public—at least in theory. Another problem was that, later in the twentieth century, accreditation under federal Education Department rules allowed students to borrow unlimited funds to finance their professional education. This meant that, unlike in almost any other area of commercial borrowing, private and public lenders could offer relatively low-interest loans *irrespective* of the likelihood that those amounts would ever be repaid-that is to say irrespective of any particular law school success rates. So, for instance, a Yale Law School education was treated the same as a Thomas Jefferson School of Law education for lending purposes despite the vast difference in employment and income expectations graduates should have had. One additional consequence of accreditation in the United States has to do with bar admission. Because the US is a federal system, there are effectively two bars in every state: one federal and one state. These correspond also to two layers of legal authority and process: one federal and one state. In most of these state jurisdictions today ABA accreditation means that students can opt to take a state bar examination and gain admission in *any* of the other states in the country without having attended law school therein.

On the other hand, the absence of ABA accreditation did not mean a law school could not operate. In some regions, state bar associations approved local law schools to train attorneys and allow them to take only *that* state's bar examination. California remains the prime example where these state-accredited law schools not only existed but flourished. In some cases their graduates proved very successful in the local profession, and many of the California-only law schools operated on a for-profit basis. By and large, however, these programs were nearly an open-admission system and allowed non-academically qualified—that is to say practitioner-only—faculty to teach working students by correspondence or through evening classes. One result was an extraordinarily low passage rate on the state bar exam.

Members of the ABA leadership were aware of these types of problems and therefore kept for-profits from gaining accreditation at least until the mid-1990s. At that time, the ABA was in the midst of an anti-trust lawsuit under US federal law (dating back to the 1930s) to prohibit unfair business practices from monopolistic organizations. Rather than litigate against this lawsuit, the ABA agreed to a landmark settlement that would partially restructure its accreditation process. It was at this time that the Council of the Section of Legal Education was formally removed from the oversight of the ABA's main board of governors and given independence. It was also at this time that the Council agreed to change its rules to allow accreditation irrespective of business model. Henceforth, for-profit schools would be subject to the same requirements as non-profit law schools.

In short order, several for-profits were founded and submitted for ABA accreditation. One group of attorneys founded Florida Coastal School of Law in Jacksonville, Florida. Atlanta's John Marshall Law School in Georgia—which had operated without national accreditation since 1933—filed for accreditation. Also founded by an independent group of jurists, Charleston School of Law was established in Charleston, South Carolina recognizing that city's need for a local legal training center. Meanwhile, the non-profit Western State College of Law, originally in Fullerton, California since 1966, was sold to Education Management Corporation and converted to for-profit status. Finally, the Chicago-based private equity firm Sterling Partners purchased Florida Coastal and announced plans to open two more for-profit law schools. It founded the Infilaw System as a "consortium" to manage these three schools and opened Phoenix School of Law and Charlotte School of Law in short succession thereafter. By 2012, each of these six new, or newly reincorporated law schools had earned accreditation from the Council and was therefore able to take in federally-guaranteed graduate student loan dollars with few questions asked.

The students these schools tended to attract was, by and large, ethnoracially diverse and socioeconomically more precarious than your average American law student. On the one hand, that is because these programs directly marketed themselves to marginalized students. The Infilaw System, for example, maintained system-wide "mission pillars" across all three of its schools and required reiteration of these in faculty meetings once a month. Among these pillars was "serving the underserved"—a mission statement to literally cater to students historically left out of the legal profession and legal services. Much like in other metropolitan countries in the Global North, these communities are often ethnic minorities. In the USA, for example, African-Americans comprised roughly 13% of the total population in 2010, but only 5% of all attorneys (Tejani 2017a, n. 3). For Infilaw, this underrepresentation was exactly what was meant by "the underserved." Importantly, socioeconomic class diversity was also an important feature that overlaid across the ethnoracial dimension.

But there was still, on the other hand, another component to the diversity argument. Applicants from these underrepresented communities tended to have, for important historical reasons, lower incoming "indicators"—meaning test scores and grade point averages. The historical reasons explaining this may be as deep as the history of race in America. Economists and historical sociologists have long pointed out the difficulty of an entire racial group to accumulate financial and cultural capital after beginning their experience in the New World as chattel slaves and remaining so for over three hundred years. Irrespective of this historical explanation, the current reality was that if the for-profit sector wanted to make it its mission to admit ethnic and racial minority students en masse they would likely have to maintain far lower admissions standards than the other accredited law schools; and this they did. Moreover, as the applicant pool narrowed after the financial crisis beginning around 2011, *all* law schools were forced to lower incoming indicators meaning, in turn, that the for-profit sector had to look even lower to maintain its income streams and meet financial projections.

Another subpopulation these schools tended to recruit was military veterans and law and enforcement officers. These groups were also the object of direct marketing efforts and this was for two very important reasons. First, US military personnel are offered a benefit under the G.I. Bill of Rights that allows them to accrue money for further education upon discharge into the civilian world. This was, indeed, the very same program that had launched the American higher education explosion after World War II. Today, it has become one of the primary means for many—especially those from the groups mentioned above—to finance higher education. For-profit colleges and universities know this, and they all recruit heavily from within the US military. Law enforcement personnel often receive similar benefits from the state in which they are employed; and many of those students are themselves also military veterans. But second, the funding coming from these sources is subject to a slightly different regulatory schematic than regular civilian graduate students. Within the Department of Education rules regarding public loan programs, there is specific language that limits the percentage any school can take from federal loans in relation to other, private sources. This is known widely as the 90/10 rule because that limit has been set at 90% of gross income. Yet, for students funded through the military benefit described here, a different formula has long applied setting this limit lower at 85% of gross income. So, in effect, the more students it recruits from these military and law enforcement benefit programs, the less any particular for-profit has to generate privately sourced tuition dollars.

Bar outcomes for these students were, for the most part, low. Such outcomes have usually been measured in bar exam passage rates. Bar passage is the threshold requirement to allow a new graduate to practice law in at least one US state. In the initial years of operation the Infilaw schools posted strong passage rates. Phoenix School of Law, for example, once boasted rates around 95%-at the time the highest in its jurisdiction with competing schools of much higher ranking scoring lower. This was attributed to a relatively selective admissions process at the time, and to a relatively low student-faculty ratio. Professors, in other words, could spend the needed time with students, especially minority and lower income students, to get them up to bar passage levels. With the onset of the "Great Recession" and its concomitant admissions decline across the entire sector, student selectivity declined. But at the same time, the profit model forced several of these schools to expand their student populations, increase incoming tuition dollars, and raise the student-faculty ratios to much higher levels. As bar passage rates declined, attention was also placed on employment outcomes.

Employment is the threshold requirement to allow students to contemplate paying back the loans they have taken out to earn their law degree. In the case of one of the largest for-profit law schools, these total loans average around 185,000 USD or 168,000 Euro (Florida Coastal 2019). According to popular wisdom, the 'general rule of thumb' for student loan borrowing is that the total amount of student debt should not exceed the borrower's anticipated annual salary for the first year out of school (Pounds 2016). For most of the US for-profit law schools, average annual income for new graduates—even those with bar required legal employment—was in the neighborhood of $60,000, or nearly a third of where they should have been to justify the full student debt incurred to become a lawyer.

Jumping ahead in time to 2019, we can now see that regulators and lenders responded with heightened scrutiny. Perhaps the early caution toward for-profit legal training has been remembered; perhaps some of the growing critical literature (Campos 2012; Tejani 2017b) on this sector has reached its audience. The ABA's Council has, since 2015, promulgated new rules about bar passage (American Bar Association 2019). It specifically censured schools in the for-profit sector and precipitated the closure of at least two of those. Most of the for-profits that emerged back in the 2000s have, by now, either shuttered or changed ownership. These closures include: Charlotte School of Law, Arizona Summit (formerly Phoenix), Savannah (a branch of John Marshall), and Western State (although Western State was in fact acquired by another institution at the last moment) (Park 2019).

But, importantly, these outcomes are not altogether distinct from those of similarly ranked, low performing non-profits. Indeed, the non-profit law schools that have had their accreditation removed, or elected to close include: Whittier, Valparaiso, Thomas Cooley-Ann Arbor, and Indiana Tech. Another two schools, William Mitchell and Hamline were forced to merge. Clearly, the common denominator of these programs is low national ranking—itself tied to low student indicators and therefore lower market demand. Yet, the disproportionate number of for-profit institutions affected by the discipline, market and regulatory, is telling.

For-profit law schools in the United States have been the product of a very unique historical origin and evolution. At their origin in the years after the foundation of the new republic was a spirit of innovation and entrepreneurialism that maintained a suspicion for sovereign power—the same that had inspired the American Revolution in the first instance. But the eventual closure or merger of the early for-profits with university law schools, and the development of those into some of the most prestigious programs in the country bespeaks of a suspicion and disdain in the legal community for economic opportunism. That the American Bar Association was unwilling to accredit new programs with this business model—even while state bar associations allowed them to fulfill a specific niche in fast markets like

California—is further evidence of this distaste for overt commercial gain within the profession. Readers from England and Europe will recognize this as part of a familiar aspiration that lawyers sit somehow above the problems of greed, corruption, and opportunism. Ultimately, however, the forced modification of the ABA rules to allow for-profits reversed this important trend in the USA. It would be a mistake to consider this reversal a complete aberration. It was, rather, part of a deregulatory zeitgeist across American political economy at the same time. This "neoliberal turn" in law and policy was by no means unique to the United States. A brief look at private legal education in other countries might therefore be instructive to draw some comparisons.

3.2 The United Kingdom and Germany

The structure of legal education in almost every other country in the world is generally inhospitable to training attorneys for overt commercial gain. Of all the other major centers for legal academic training in the world, only the United Kingdom even begins to approach the United States in harboring this kind of model. Yet even there, the practice is far more circumscribed. Before explaining why, it is useful to first draw a distinction between the two largest "parent legal families" of the world (DeCruz 2008, pp. 33–35). These are *common law* and *civil law*. Common law countries are those whose legal systems hail either directly or indirectly from English colonial rule. Thus, most of the Old (Australia, Canada) and New (Singapore, India) Commonwealth countries use common law in some form or another. Of those, most retain the original English distinction between solicitor and barrister, where the former is historically a lesser-trained, more affordable, and more accessible form of legal expert and the latter a higher-trained, more expensive, and more selective advocate. Members of the public typically must approach a solicitor for common legal disputes, and then only when that practitioner has exceeded her own expertise or eligibility for practice in low-level courts will they engage the external services of the barrister. But whereas England and Australia still retain this *dualist* legal profession, Canada, India, Singapore and of course the United States do not.

Yet common law countries are not the only ones with a dualist profession. Civil law countries are those whose legal system hails from either or both Romanic or German law. As expected, this includes most of the countries in Europe, but it also includes their former colonies in regions such as Latin America, Africa, and the Middle East. Even several nations that would be considered Islamic Law countries operate in fact with a thick layer of civil law in matters of public and administrative authority.

Historically, France, a civil law country based greatly upon the Napoleonic Code, has been a dualist profession with a division akin to the English solicitor and barrister. The effect of this dualism in either common law or civil law tends to be a heightened prestige and social capital reserved for members of the legal profession in general. For this reason, whether and to what extent each nation maintains a dualist or monist profession has some impact on its approach to legal education. In some cases, the extreme selectivity with which advocates (barristers) are chosen translates into extreme rigor in the process of studying to become one.

Yet, this impact may not translate directly into generalizable lessons about business model. Of all the countries so far mentioned, only the UK hosts a large institution of for-profit legal education. That role is occupied by the University of Law system. Originally known as College of Law Ltd., the institution was granted university status in 2012 and bought by a private equity firm known as Montague for 200 million British pounds leading to an outcry from UK higher education experts (Kollewe 2012). After three years of this ownership structure, Montague sold off the University to the Dutch company Global University Systems, a group which also owns the University Canada West—a predominantly business and commerce school in Vancouver. The University of Law has its campuses in Birmingham, Bristol, Chester, Guildford, Leeds, London Bloomsbury, Manchester, and Nottingham. Students can also pursue its degrees online.

Several of its features are similar to the for-profit law schools in the United States. First and foremost, the onetime ownership by a private equity firm in the same period suggests the global scale of the private equity boom, and its appetite for higher education—even hallowed professional schools. Second, the role of real property in the financial transfers is striking. In the USA, lucrative building acquisitions and leases were a significant part of the transactions leading to both the creation and the demise of several for-profit law schools. In the case of University of Law, several campus properties were immediately sold off by Montague to settle some of the considerable debt incurred in the acquisition. One of the great lessons from these transactions was the apparent fungibility of law school institutional edifices—business experts eyed law schools especially for this reason because the locus of their expertise was less in physical repositories and more in the organizational structures, faculty experience, and research databases. Finally, the qualitative commitment to technology and flexible service delivery was a third overlapping feature. The University of Law promised to offer its students modern, high-tech amenities and learning tools, as did their North American counterparts—particularly the Infilaw schools.

But, unlike the US for-profits, the University of Law system appeared to offer substantially greater value to its students. With a pre-for-profit history dating back to the 1960s and origins in the British Law Society (national bar association) itself, the institution and its brand carried greater weight, and boasted a more illustrious alumni network than anything similar in the United States. Its 64,000 graduates today are spread across 85 countries (University of Law 2019) and includes numerous members of parliament, academics, CEOs, and high level judges. The same cannot yet be said of the US counterparts.

Apart from England, no other countries host nationally accredited for-profit law schools. Somewhat similar to University of Law, however, Germany approved its first ever private non-profit law school in 2000. The Bucerius Law School, located in Hamburg, soon became one of the most selective in the country. Again, although not for-profit, the recency of its establishment places it on similar footing as most of the US for-profits and yet the experience with reputation and quality appears vastly different.

4 Implications for Criminal Justice in the Twenty-First Century

Ultimately, one is left to ask why such differences obtain in prestige, value, and quality between the similarly young law schools in these countries, or between the similarly commercialized law schools in the USA and UK. On one hand, all appear to be responses to market demand. The legal profession in all three countries had been extremely selective in the decades prior. The rise in urban population as well as financial capital transactions in all three led to rapid increases in the types and amount of accessible legal expertise needed to resolve family, property, contractual, and criminal matters. Yet, the availability of affordable attorneys to do this kind of work had not yet caught up with demand.

The rise of private for-profit, or in the case of Germany simply private legal education was a response to this demand. It understood that a new approach to legal education was needed, and that the new professional environment created by technology, new transactions, and a diversifying urban population required innovations in the way lawyers would be taught to practice. In the case of US and UK for-profits, such innovations included more distance education via online teaching and learning, and in the US Infilaw consortium it included new offerings like integrated bar-tested subjects such as "Civil Litigation I" which combined Torts and Civil Procedure, as well as bar preparation folded into the three-year degree program (Tejani 2017b, p. xx).

But these innovative measures in the US example were largely a failure. As already recounted, two of the three private-equity run Infilaw schools lost accreditation and were forced to plan for closure. The third applied for non-profit status but was denied, and then saw its president abruptly resign at a time when its students were not receiving their federal loans and could barely afford to eat (Bloch 2019). Western State found itself forced to close and create a "teachout plan" but found a last minute buyer. Savannah Law School, a branch of for-profit John Marshall in Atlanta, will cease operations by 2021. Under the new ABA outcome rules aimed at tightening practices in this lower end of the sector, most of these schools could not remain open regardless. Considering the need to satisfy capital investors in the private equity schools, it became more sensible to declare capital losses rather than wait out any recovery.

The primary losers in this case were the students. Thousands of law graduates, some without the ability to pass the state bar exams needed to gain legal employment, would be saddled with loan debt well in excess of US $100,000 (90,000 euro) each. Many of these students would be forced to find non-JD work in debt collection, property management, compliance, real estate sales, and otherwise. These would be, thanks to the recruitment model of "serving the underserved," disproportionately minority and lower income graduates.

The rise of for-profit law schools poses a substantial challenge to the United Nations call for "quality education" and "strong institutions" in its 2030 Sustainable Development Agenda. Underlying that call was a recognition that the rule of law depends upon legal institutions with profound integrity. This integrity can be understood foremost as an ability to withstand social and political pressures and instability. One of its primary foundations is independence from social and political change. Yet, what the for-profit law schools—most prominent in the US context—demonstrate is a decline in that independence and, therefore integrity. Their erection amid the many financial scandals of the 2000s—even as regulators struggled to figure out how to bring large corporations and banks back under the purview of legal oversight—tells much about the situation of law in our contemporary age. This situation, in effect, is that law is being increasingly conceptualized as acting in the service of economic growth. Whereas "society" was once the wellspring for the values that underpin legal orders in the West, today it is increasingly supplanted by "economy." The case of for-profit law schools was premised on this evolution.

The promise of for-profit law schools was said to be increasing access to justice for minority and lower income clients. In these communities, a great proportion of the legal needs for these communities involves criminal defense. In the United States, the 1964 Supreme Court case *Gideon v. Wainwright* guaranteed a state-appointed attorney to all criminal defendants where incarceration is a possibility.[7] A system of state-funded "public defenders" in both state and federal courts is tasked with the difficult job of representing these clients. In 2018, the National Legal Aid and Defender Association found that 80% of criminal defendants in the United States cannot afford their own attorney, and must depend on public assistance (Zoukis 2018).

While there is therefore great demand for public defense attorneys, new law school graduates have to be able to afford this kind of work. They need to have student debt burdens light enough, or structured creatively enough to allow them to meet their obligations while earning the lower pay associated with public defender work. In the Los Angeles Area, the average public defender salary is approximately US $83,000.[8] In New York, that salary is US $87,000.[9] Recall that creditors recommend a 1:1 ratio between total debt and first-year income, and that law schools with the highest debt levels in excess of $125,000 are, precisely, those in the Los Angeles and New York areas, as well as the for-profits that have located themselves in smaller markets.

---

[7] *Gideon v. Wainwright*, 372 U.S. 335 (1963).

[8] See Glassdoor.com (2019a).

[9] See Glassdoor.com (2019b).

Until recently, lenders in the United States sold student loans with the understanding that entering public service would create a reduced debt obligation under a Public Service Loan Forgiveness program—a system of reducing amounts owed if a borrower chooses a lower income job in the public service. The US for-profit law schools made great efforts to promote this program as an accessible path for students not headed toward lucrative corporate law practice. But whereas this was intended to encourage students to enter fields where they were badly needed, recent reports show widespread problems in the way this program has been administered and students are increasingly dubious about risking complications to do the kind of public interest work the US criminal justice system has come to depend upon (Dickler and Nova 2019).

5 Conclusion

In the end, increased debt burdens and low bar passage rates do not, in the aggregate, support access to justice. With disparate impact on minority law students, these outcomes actually represent the opposite: a commercial opportunism that took advantage of restricted access to capitalize on minority ambitions to improve individual economic standing and broader social justice. It was, in short, worse than if no efforts to improve justice had been made at all.

This leads directly to a consideration of the business ethics involved. Assuming for argument sake that these are primarily commercial organizations. They fail the test of any of the major ethical frameworks. Utilitarianism would call for a weighing of the aggregate costs and benefits of their efforts, and this can be judged either on the organizational level or on a broader social scale. At the organizational level, the above discussion reflects widespread costs including faculty and staff layoffs, students saddled with lifelong anxiety from debt and failure, and more general reputational harm to the legal profession. And while it is difficult to accurately assess investor returns without the documentation disclosed by more public companies, the abrupt and violent closure of these schools (rather than, for instance, weathering the storm for more long term, sustained benefit) suggests it had been a bad financial investment as well. Under a Kantian approach, one might ask whether the principles behind this kind of conduct would benefit society if generalized universally. Would the allowance of commercial activities that risk this kind of debt and distress surrounding other public goods—for example health and medicine—be something we could all support in the name of "increased access"? Likely not. And under an Aristotelian virtue theory does this kind of conduct-the kind that improves access for commercial gain (assuming it could even produce profit)—make us better off as people? For us to say yes, we would have to decide that the financial precarity of others is not our problem, or that gaining advantage from the ambition of the marginalized could be a virtue. It is not.

Finally, does the extension of commercial logics to the education sector generally and to professional education in particular make sense? Is there something unique about legal education that made it exceptional and therefore worthy of protection against market fundamentalism? The consideration of for-profit law schools in the context of the UN call for "sustainable institutions" is especially instructive here. Many of our key institutions are established on the bedrock of law. What allows them to remain unchanged is the defense they receive from advocacy groups and individual claimants who appeal to law and legal professionals for support. For sustainable development in global perspective, for instance in places where institutions could otherwise be toppled by the demands of basic survival, this is even more true. So, the environments in which we study and teach the law are of an especially sensitive nature. Exposed to the same market fluctuations as the rest of our global economy, they can be subject to sudden shifts and produce inconsistencies in the way law is viewed and understood by the very professionals needed to maintain its consistency. Granted, many would say, law is subject to varying interpretations. But, the underlying structures of law, on which so many other institutions rest, by design changes very slowly. The market, we all know too well, does not.

References

American Bar Association. (2019). *Council enacts new bar passage standard for law schools.* Retrieved from https://bit.ly/2KUH57w

Aronowitz, S. (2000). *The knowledge factory: Dismantling the corporate university and creating true higher learning*. Boston, MA: Beacon Press.

Bloch, E. (2019, September 18). What now? An update on Florida Coastal Law School. *The Florida Times Union* Retrieved from https://bit.ly/3fi786T

Campos, P. (2012). *Don't go to law school (unless): A law professor's inside guide to maximizing opportunity and minimizing risk.* CreateSpace: Independent Publishing Platform.

DeCruz, P. (2008). *Comparative law in a changing world.* New York and Oxford: Routledge-Cavendish.

Dickler, J., & Nova, A. (2019, September 5). This fix to public service loan forgiveness hasn't helped very much. *CNBC.com.* Retrieved from https://cnb.cx/35uPrfz

Florida Coastal School of Law. (2019). *Firste professional degree in juris doctor (full-time) Program Length: 90 weeks.* Retrieved from https://bit.ly/3ddzopj

Freire, P. (2018). *Pedagogy of the oppressed* (M. Ramos, Trans.). New York and London: Bloomsbury.

Giroux, H. (2011). *On critical pedagogy.* New York and London: Bloomsbury.

Glassdoor.com. (2019a). Los Angeles public defender salaries. Retrieved from https://bit.ly/2xAsfQQ

Glassdoor.com. (2019b). New York City public defender salaries. Retrieved from https://bit.ly/3c16OqN

Graham, B. A. (2020, May 3). 'Swastikas and nooses': governor slams 'racism' of Michigan lockdown protest. *The Guardian.* Retrieved from https://bit.ly/2L0yTTy

Herrera, L. (2013). Educating main street lawyers. *Journal of Legal Education, 63*(2), 189–210.

Hulse, C. (2019, September 19). After resisting, McConnell and senate g.o.p. back election security funding. *New York Times.* Retrieved from https://nyti.ms/3c3Pzp8

Jordan, M. (2019, September 27). Judge blocks Trump administration plan to detain migrant children. *New York Times.* Retrieved from https://nyti.ms/3fjr4Gf

King, M. L. (1963, August). *Letter from Birmingham Jail.* Retrieved from https://bit.ly/35q5pry

Kollewe, J. (2012, April 17). College of law sale prompts call for private equity veto. *The Guardian*. Retrieved from https://bit.ly/3c029Wp
Litchfield Historical Society. (2019). *Litchfield Law School*. Retrieved from https://bit.ly/2W0ULED
Miller, D. (2017). Justice. In E. N. Zalta (Ed.), *The Stanford Encyclopedia of philosophy*. Retrieved from https://stanford.io/2KWJm29
Park, J. (2019, August 15). Western State College of Law in Irvine has a new buyer; Classes will soon start for current students. *OC Register*. Retrieved from https://bit.ly/2KWvSUa
Pounds, S. (2016, May 24). How to avoid the stranglehold of too much student loan debt. *Foxbusiness.com*. Retrieved from https://fxn.ws/3c20JdU
Rhode, D. (2004). *Access to justice*. New York and Oxford: Oxford University Press.
Schmitt, M. (2019, September 2). Why has Trump's exceptional corruption gone unchecked? *New York Times*. Retrieved from https://nyti.ms/2Wl4TXO
Tamanaha, B. (2012). *Failing law schools* (p. 2012). Chicago: University of Chicago Press.
Tejani, R. (2017a). Professional apartheid: The racialization of U.S. law schools after the global financial crisis. *American Ethnologist, 44*(3), 451–463. https://doi.org/10.1111/amet.12521
Tejani, R. (2017b). *Law mart: Justice access and for-profit law schools*. Stanford, CA: Stanford University Press.
Tejani, R. (2018). A working class profession: Opportunism and diversity in U.S. law. *Dialectical Anthropology, 42*(2), 131–148.
Tejani, R. (2019). *Law and society today*. Oakland, CA: University of California Press.
University of Law, The University of Law: Welcome to our alumni network. Retrieved from https://www.law.ac.uk/about/alumni/
US History, United States History: U.S. Population, 1790-2000: Always Growing. Retrieved from https://www.u-s-history.com/pages/h980.html
Vaidya, A., & Allhoff, F. (2016). Introduction: Why study business ethics? In F. Allhoff, A. Sager, & A. Vaidya (Eds.), *Business in ethical focus: An anthology* (2nd ed.). New York: Broadview Press.
Yale Law School. (2019). *Our history*. Retrieved from https://law.yale.edu/about-yale-law-school/glance/our-history
Zoukis, C. (2018, March 16). Indigent defense in America: An affront to justice. *Criminal Legal News*. Retrieved from https://bit.ly/35rykeM

Riaz Tejani is an Associate Professor of Business Ethics at the University of Redlands (California, USA). His research examines problems in legal and business ethics with a focus on race and class inequality, access to justice, and higher education. Riaz's first book, *Law Mart: Justice, Access, and For-Profit Law Schools* (2017), is an ethnographic account of for-profit legal education during and after the global financial crisis. His second book, *Law and Society Today* (2019), critically surveys contemporary themes in socio-legal studies after "law and economics." Riaz serves on the National Advisory Council of the non-profit research center Law School Transparency, and his recent articles have appeared in *American Ethnologist, U.C. Irvine Law Review,* and *Political and Legal Anthropology Review*. His work has been cited or reviewed in outlets including the *Harvard Law Review, Yale Law Journal Forum, Annual Review of Law and Social Science, The Nation, Huffington Post, Salon*, and NPR. Riaz holds a PhD in social anthropology from Princeton University and a JD from the USC Gould School of Law, where he was a Fellow at the Center for Law, History, and Culture. Riaz has taught at the University of Illinois and the University of Southern California, and his research affiliations have included the École Normale Supérieure-Ulm and the United Nations Education, Scientific, and Cultural Organization (UNESCO, Paris, France). E-mail: Riaz_tejani@redlands.edu

Money Laundering: China and Its Evolving Criminal Policy Response

Ling Zhou and Hanming Xu

Abstract This chapter looks into the legal shortcomings and effectiveness issues for countering money laundering, in line with the United Nations Agenda's Sustainable Development Goals 16.4 "By 2030, significantly reduce illicit financial and arms flows, strengthen the recovery and return of stolen assets and combat all forms of organized crime," and 16.a "Strengthen relevant national institutions, including through international cooperation, for building capacity at all levels, in particular in developing countries, to prevent violence and combat terrorism and crime." While in the above context China has a strong understanding of the money laundering and terrorist financing risks it faces, its criminal policy is fundamentally short of counter measures for laundering of proceeds of crime and sources used for its national risk assessment. Moreover, financial institutions including the People's Bank of China and non-financial institutions have an insufficient understanding of the risks they face and how their services could be abused by criminals and terrorists. This deficiency also notably affects efforts to address corruption. The authors review the legal foundation, functioning and operational effectiveness of China's Anti-Money Laundering and Counter-Terrorism Financing (AML/CFT) law enforcement, makes recommendations to improve the use of criminal policy to counter more effectively money-laundering.

Keywords Money laundering · Terrorist financing · AML/CFT measures

L. Zhou (✉)
Zhongnan University of Economics and Law, Criminal Justice School, Wuhan, China
e-mail: zhouling@zuel.edu.cn

H. Xu
Zhongnan University of Economics and Law, Research Center for Rule of Law Development and Judicial Reform, Wuhan, China

H. Kury, S. Redo (eds.), *Crime Prevention and Justice in 2030*,
https://doi.org/10.1007/978-3-030-56227-4_23

1 Introduction

A global problem—money laundering (ML) has seriously affected the operation of world economy. While the money value involved in money laundering activities globally is estimated to be as high as 1.2 trillion USD per year (ca 1 trillion euro), allegedly taking up almost 5% of the global GDP, the number in China has been *toutes proportions gardées* comparable to the global figure in the recent years (Zou 2011).

2 Estimating the Extent of Money Laundering in China

The accurate data is difficult to compile on China's money laundering activities. However, researchers did manage to paint the overall picture using indirect sources. For example, researchers accessed court case records to assess the intensity of money laundering activities. According to the *China Judgements Online's* fragmentary statistics, the average amount involved in each money laundering case was RMB ¥17.76 million in 2013, ¥8.875 million in 2014, ¥2.0479 million in 2015, ¥27.4191 million in 2016 and ¥16.8276 million in 2017 (Yin 2019). Such high volume has been relatively consistent.

Outside assessments were also used to gauge the situation of money laundering in China. According to a report by the People's Bank of China Anti-Money Laundering Bureau (PBCAMLB), the amount involved in money laundering activities in China exceeds RMB ¥ 200 billion annually, accounting for about 2% of China's GDP (PBCAMLB 2015, p. 6).

Since 2004, more indicative data became available due to the establishment of the China Anti-Money Laundering Monitoring and Analysis Center (CAMLMAC) by the People's Bank of China (PBC). During its initial period of operation, to the end of 2005, the Center has delivered 683 suspicious transaction reports to partner agencies, involving over 70,000 transactions on 4926 accounts, ¥13.7 billion RMB and more than 1 billion US Dollars' worth in foreign currency (Liu 2017a).

From 2007 to 2016, the China Anti-Money Laundering Monitoring and Analysis Center received 2.68 billion large transaction reports and 320 million suspicious transaction reports. The number per year declined slightly, but the quality of suspicious transaction reports was improving year by year. From large and suspicious transaction reports submitted by obligatory institutions, the PBC and its branches have handed over 8801 clues to law enforcement agencies as required by the law, assisted in the investigation of 8902 cases involving money laundering and its predicate crimes, and contributed to the closing of 2111 cases (Liu 2017a).

During the same period, the Court system have tried 87,600 cases involving the three types of money laundering related crimes and handed out sentences for 147,768 defendants. Among them, 71 cases were tried and 94 people were convicted for the crime of money laundering under Article 191 of the criminal law. From 2007 to 2016, the People's Bank of China and its branches conducted on-site inspections of 2188 obligatory institutions against money laundering activities, and issued fines totaling RMB ¥ 236.47 million to 1604 institutions (People's Bank of China 2017).

3 The Changing Nature of the Threat of Money Laundering Faced by China

For a long time, financial institutions have become the first choice for money laundering and tax crimes because of their strong confidentiality and high complexity. However, with the deepening of economic exchanges, non-financial institutions are increasingly becoming the undertaker of money laundering in China (Zhou 2019). Transnational corporations may use international trade or transnational investment to transfer the proceeds of crime to overseas beneficiaries (Wang and Sui 2017). On the one hand, they effectively cut the connection between funds and criminal activities, on the other hand, they can also use the differences in taxation systems to evade tax (Li and Xu 2008). It is also noteworthy that lawyers, notaries, accountants and other professional service providers have started to play an important role in the process of money laundering in China, which was not widely seen just 10 years ago (Li 2014).

Another new form of threat has been the money laundering activities in cyberspace (Yin 2019). In the era of cyber-finance, crowdfunding, P2P network lending and third-party payment and financial service platforms such as Alipay and WeChat have grown rapidly, which in turn has fostered new ways of money laundering using online banking, P2P network lending, Internet payment, Internet gambling and gaming platforms and so on. The rapid growth of the e-business blurred the boundaries of nations, it also made the money laundering activities harder and harder to detect with the endless streams of new and innovative business models. On top of that, now the money launderers can ignore the limit of trading hours, conduct real-time transactions around the clock with the help of virtual money and its trading network. Both the time differences and the discrepancy in legal systems make it significantly more difficult to monitor transactions conducted in cyberspace than those in the traditional markets (Wang and Liu 2017).

In practice, features such as covertness, complexity, anonymity, instantaneity and long range of the transactions conducted on cyberspace provide favorable environment for money launderers, in turn present great challenges in supervision, investigation and adjudication of money laundering crimes in China (Yin 2019). Criminals take advantage of Internet financial platforms who are in dire need for funds, and do not perform sufficient screening and verification of the sources of funds (Liu 2017c). In some cases, criminals can simply transfer the proceeds of crime into virtual currency, send it through virtual currency trading websites to the other end, and then cash it without a trace left behind. In other cases, a large amount of proceeds of crime was transformed, in the form of investment, into virtual property in an online game through scattered purchasing and backdoor operation, and then sold for real money as a legit form of income (Liu 2017c).

Also, the pressure of international Anti-money Laundering and Combating the Financing of Terrorism (AML/CFT) supervision is presenting a real challenge of compliance for China's financial institutions involved in international trades (Wang 2019). Authorities in the U.S. and Europe often issue huge fines to multinational banks who's been suspected on violations of the anti-money laundering and financing of terrorism regulations, and Chinese banks were not left out. In November 2016, for example, in one of the recent cases, the New York Branch Office of Agricultural Bank of China was fined 215 million US dollars by the New York Financial Regulatory Authority for violating the anti-money laundering regulations.

4 Legislative Efforts That Set the Perimeter for China's AML/CFT Criminal Policy

To form a complete Anti-money Laundering and Combating the Financing of Terrorism legal system in China, on 31 October 2006, the 24th session of the Standing Committee of the 10th National People's Congress passed the Anti-Money Laundering Law (Order of the President of People's Republic of China #56 Oct. 31, 2006). This legislation clarifies the legal status and responsibilities of the nation's Anti-money Laundering and Combating the Financing of Terrorism authorities, set up the coordination framework for all administrative departments and institutions involved in relevant law enforcement operations, and made sure the fight against the crimes of money laundering in China is carried out within the constraints of the rule of law (Li 2016).

Anti-Money Laundering Law was the first national legislation devoted to the prevention and control of money laundering (Cheng and Wang 2007). Within the provisions of this law, the policy framework, operational principles and specific mission of anti-money laundering was outlined. It also provided the responsibilities and enforcement power of the national anti-money laundering authorities, established the responsibilities of the national financial supervision and management agencies in regards to their involvement in the anti-money laundering effort. The law specifically stated obligations to be fulfilled by a variety of entities, governmental as well non-governmental, in preventing and controlling money laundering activities. Special enforcement measures were also provided to the government agencies as well as regulatory bodies for their anti-money laundering operations. And finally, principled provisions were put in the law for China's participation in international anti-money laundering cooperation (Tang 2009).

In addition to the Anti-Money Laundering Law enacted and promulgated by the legislature, the State Council, the National Anti-money Laundering and Combating the Financing of Terrorism Authorities and the People's Bank of China have formulated a series of administrative laws, regulations and rules, which together constitute the normative foundation of China's Anti-money Laundering and Combating the Financing of Terrorism supervisory system (Liu 2017a).[1]

As can be seen here, the normative framework of the Anti-money Laundering and Combating the Financing of Terrorism supervisory system for China's administrative agencies and financial institutions is in a process of constant improvement.

5 The Core of China's AML/CFT Criminal Policy

Generally speaking, the current Anti-money Laundering and Combating the Financing of Terrorism criminal legislation framework in China consists of "Two Laws and One Interpretation" (Liu 2017a), namely, the Criminal Law of the People's Republic of China (Order of the President of People's Republic of China #83 Feb. 14, 1997, effective Oct. 1, 1997, with a series of amendments in following years), the Anti-Terrorism Law of the People's Republic of China (Order of the President of People's Republic of China #36 Dec. 27, 2015), and the Interpretation on the Specific Application of Law in the Trial of Money Laundering Cases issued by the Supreme People's Court (Judicial Interpretation [2009] #15). The formation of such a framework is a process of continuous adjustments and improvements.

Since there was no provision for money laundering in the Criminal Law of 1979, the period while and before the Criminal Law of 1979 was in effect can be considered the non-criminalisation stage of money laundering (Liang 2000).

In 1988, Chinese government signed and ratified the United Nations Convention against Illicit Trafficking in Narcotic Drugs and Psychotropic Substances (1582 UNTS 95). This symbolised that China has taken the stand, together with all the signing nations of the Convention, to counter and criminalise deliberate concealing or shielding the true nature and origin of the property.

In 1990, the 17th session of the Standing Committee of the 7th National People's Congress (NPC) passed the Decision on Drug Control (Order of the President of People's Republic of China #38 Dec. 28, 1990). It criminalised money laundering by stipulating as crime acts involving "harbor, transfer or conceal drugs or property derived from drug crime for others and to conceal or shield the illegal nature and

[1]The said laws and regulations, in the order of promulgation, are as follows: *Regulations on the Administration of Domestic Foreign Exchange Accounts*, *Notice on the Management of Large Cash Payments* and *Rules on Registration and Recording of Large Cash Payments* by the PBC in 1997; *Rules for the Ban of Illegal Financial Institutions and Illegal Financial Services* by the Executive Meeting of the State Council in 1998; *Measures for Punishment of Financial Violations* by the Executive Meeting of the State Council in 1999; *Regulation on the Real Name System of Individual Deposit Accounts* by the State Council in 2000; *Regulation on RMB Bank Settlement Accounts* by the PBC in 2003; *Regulation on Financial Institutions' Anti-Money Laundering Measures* and *Measures for Reporting Suspicious Transactions Related to Terrorist Financing by Financial Institutions* by PBC in 2006; *Measures for Customer Identification and Recordkeeping of Customer Identity and Transaction by Financial Institutions*, *Regulation for Personal Foreign Exchanges*, and *Regulation for Reporting of Large and Suspicious Transaction* by the PBC in 2016.

origin of property acquired by dealing drugs." This was the first legislative text in China ever to address the crime of money laundering (Wang 2008). It can be seen as the initial step toward a legislative foundation of money laundering in China's criminal law system.

When the Criminal Law of 1997 was promulgated, China has just entered a new period of social change and economic transformation. Serious economic crimes and crimes against social management order sored, with smuggling and organised crimes rapidly becoming the social problems of national concerns. In particular, with the increasingly rampant transnational criminal activities in the field of international finance, the use of financial institutions and various non-financial institutions to launder money has become increasingly prominent. The amount of gain through these criminal activities was staggeringly large, harming the fragile order of the newly established market economy and impacted the society in many other negative ways as well.

To deal with these types of crimes, the Criminal Law of 1997, in a timely manner, provided in Article 191 the crime of money laundering. It clearly identified drug crime, organised crime and smuggling as predicate offences of money laundering, specified the mode of operation of money laundering, and included legal person as qualified offender for the aforementioned crimes as well.

In addition to the crime of money laundering under Article 191, there are also other two provisions stipulating crimes that can take the form of money laundering: the crime of concealing and shielding the proceeds or gains of crime under Article 312, and the crime of harboring, transferring and concealing drugs and proceeds of drug crime under Article 349.

Together, they formed a "three-pronged system" of money laundering crimes that covers a wide range of illegal activities. From this point on, the vacancy of criminal policy on money laundering has been filled.

In December 2000, the Chinese government signed and later ratified the United Nations Convention against Transnational Organized Crime (2225 UNTS 209), and in 2001 the United Nations International Convention for the Suppression of the Financing of Terrorism (2178 UNTS 197). With the international law commitments, along came a wave of criminal law adjustments and amendments as the domestic fulfillment of international law obligations.

Also in 2001, the 25th Session of the 9th National People's Congress adopted and promulgated the 3rd Amendment to the Criminal Law of 1997. It widened the coverage of the predicate offences for the crime of money laundering in Article 191, including a total of four categories of predicate offences: drug crimes, organised crimes, terrorism and smuggling. Another relevant change was made to Article 120, which added the crimes of financing terrorist organisations to complement the provision's original stipulation of conducting terrorist activities.

In 2003, the 58th General Assembly of the United Nations adopted the United Nations Convention against Corruption (2349 UNTS 41). It listed corruption as a predicate offence of money laundering. In response to the normative requirements of the Convention, the 23rd session of the Standing Committee of the 10th National People's Congress, in the 6th Amendment of the Criminal Law passed on June 2006, once again expanded the predicate office coverage of the crime of money laundering, adding the crime of corruption and bribery, the crime of disrupting the financial management order, and the crime of financial fraud. Together with the four existing categories, the seven categories of predicate offences and the crime of money laundering itself under Article 191 formed the core of China's Anti-money Laundering and Combating the Financing of Terrorism measures in the Criminal Law front, and this setting is still in effect today.

Also, modification was made to the wording of Article 312. It changed the object of the crime of shielding and concealing the proceeds and gain of crime from "stolen goods" to "proceeds and gain of crime."

In 2009, the 7th amendment to the Criminal Law was adopted by the Standing Committee of the 11th National People's Congress at its 7th session. Another major adjustment was made on China's Anti-money Laundering and Combating the Financing of Terrorism policy: the crime of concealing and shielding the proceeds or gains of crime under Article 312 added legal person as qualified subject of crime. Up to this point, the crime of money laundering and the crime of concealing and shielding the proceeds and gains of crime have become practically identical in elements of constitutive requirements, except the differences in predicate offences.

In the meantime, efforts were also made in the judiciary to provide systemic interpretative support and guidelines to the application of the aforementioned provisions. "The Interpretation on the Specific Application of Law in the Trial of Money Laundering Cases," issued by the Supreme People's Court on 4 November 2009, provided clarification to a series of practical issues such as the mental state of "knowing" when laundering money, the issue with the wording "other methods" in the crime of concealing and shielding the origin and nature of the proceeds and gains of crime, the issue of overlap between Articles 190 and 312, and the mere fact requirement of predicate offences for the constitution of the main crime, and so on.

In 2015, the Supreme People's Court issued "The Interpretation of Several Issues Concerning the Application of the Criminal Law in Criminal Cases of Concealing and Shielding the Proceeds and Gains of Crime." It followed the same principle as the aforementioned judicial interpretation in 2009 on the relationship between the predicate offences and the constitution of the main crime. For example, it contended that "to constitute the crime of concealing and shielding the proceeds and gains of crime, the establishment of the objective facts of predicate offence is the only pre-requirement ... once the predicate offences have been factually verified, the failure to meet other objective constitutive requirement of the predicate crime, such as the offender being a minor[2] (thus exempt from criminal liability) shall not negate the establishment of the main crime of concealing and shielding the proceeds and gains of crime (Wang 2009).

[2]Under Article 17 of the Criminal Law, a minor is a person under the age required for criminal liability of a given crime. To be specific, for crimes of murder, aggravated assault, rape, robbery, drug trafficking, arson, bombing and poisoning, any person under the age of 14 would be considered a minor, thus exempt from criminal liability, and for all other crimes, any person under the age of 16 would be considered a minor.

In 2016, the Anti-terrorism Law formally came in effect, which specified the procedure for administrative enforcements of terrorist-related asset seizure, detainment or freeze as well as anti-terrorist financial surveillance and criminal investigations (Jia and Li 2019). By including the fight against terrorist financing into the bigger picture of national counterterrorism campaign, the Anti-terrorism Law reaffirms its pivotal role in China's Anti-money Laundering and Combating the Financing of Terrorism system.

6 The Legislative Logic of Criminalising Money Laundering in China

6.1 Expansion of Predicate Offences

From the above-mentioned legislative process, it can be clearly seen that the criminal and administrative legislative effort targeting money laundering were quite intensive from 2001 to 2006. On the one hand, this was to catch up with the requirement on domestic anti-money laundering measures put forward by the number of international treaties signed by China during that period, on the other hand, the crime of money laundering has become increasingly rampant at home and abroad, and its means increasingly complex and crafty, which presented realistic and urgent needs for the domestic legislation to keep up with the development.

As can be seen from the frequent revision of Article 191 of the Criminal Law, the trend of criminal legislation on money laundering crime is one of expansion (Zhao and Yuan 2018). A series of subsequent judicial interpretations also conformed to this trend. From this, we can conclude the current legislative logic of money laundering crime in China focus on the expanding the coverage of predicate offences.

Under the general principles set forward by international organisations and implemented in international enforcement practices, the scope of predicate crimes of money laundering should be expanded further. Take the Financial Action Task Force (FATF), an international entity dedicated to the fight against money laundering and terrorist financing, as an example, its 40 Recommendations, as revised in 2003. FATF has proposed that, countries around the world should make legislative effort to include 20 types of crimes, such as organised crime, corruption, tax evasion, as predicate offences of money laundering.

A longitudinal review of the evolution of the Chinese criminal law in the last 20 some years would reveal that the expansion of the coverage of predicate offence has been the most noticeable feature of the adjustments made to the money laundering provisions during the period. From the original version of the Criminal Law of 1997, where only three predicate offences were stipulated, namely drug crime, organised crime and smuggling, to the 3rd Amendment to the Criminal Law in 2001, which added the crime of terrorism, then in 2006, the 6th Amendment to the

Criminal Law further expanded the coverage of predicate offences to three more types of crimes, namely, corruption and bribery, crimes against the order of financial management, and crimes of financial fraud, make it a total of seven types of officially identified predicate offences to money laundering.

In the process of soliciting opinions on the 6th Amendment to the Criminal Law, quite a few members of the Standing Committee of the National People's Congress (NPC) as well as a number of central government agencies and local administrations have suggested further expanding the coverage of predicate offences. However, apart from adjusting the wording of "financial crimes" in the original draft to be more clearly defined as the crimes against the order of financial management and crimes of financial fraud, the list of predicate offences has not been subject to any further change in this amendment.

According to the NPC's judicial committee's explanation made to the meeting of the Standing Committee, in addition to the provisions of Article 191, Article 312 of the Criminal Law also stipulated as crime any act aiming to harbor, transfer, acquire or knowingly sell the proceeds of any crime, which in practice provided a wider perimeter for predicate offences of money laundering, all but a specific charge in the name of money laundering (Tang 2006).

The drafting panel of the Anti-Money Laundering Law reportedly expressed their preference to the draft panel of the Criminal Law Amendment that the coverage of predicate offences of money laundering to be further expanded. But given the current provisions in the criminal law, which do not explicitly go beyond the seven categories of predicate offences, The Anti-Money Laundering Law finally adopted an indirect solution of sort: it first refers to the seven crimes stipulated in the current version of Criminal Law, then added "and the like," as the predicate offences of money laundering. The phrase "and the like" effectively served the same purpose as the wording of "and other crimes of that nature" that was put in the Regulation on Financial Institutions' Anti-Money Laundering Measures of 2006. By adding "and the like," the law practically placed any money laundering activities involving any proceeds of any crime within the range of its enforcement (Tang 2006).

This pattern of legislative expansion on predicate offences not only drew on the experience of the international community, but also caters to the practical needs of crime control and economic development in China. It, in a great measure solved the problem of limited coverage of predicate offence under the criminal law, provided the legal basis for the Chinese government to effectively combat money laundering and fulfill the legal obligations set forward by the international treaties.

6.2 The Afterwards Act Logic

Another major jurisprudence principle affecting China's money laundering criminal legislation would be the so called "afterwards act logic" (事后逻辑) used in the analysis of liability of money laundering activities in relations with the predicate offences.

Chinese criminal law scholars do not see money laundering as an isolated offence, but something to be looked at in a context of a series of criminal activities (Zhao and Yuan 2018). Based on the stage money laundering takes in the whole process, the crime of money laundering clearly has characteristics of an afterwards act. And there are two different types of situations: One is the disposal of proceeds of crime by the perpetrator of the crime himself, such as the conversion and transfer of the proceeds and gains of crime by a perpetrator after his own crime succeeded; and the second is, after the completion of someone else's criminal act, the actors participate in the disposal of the proceeds of that crime, such as the act of harboring, transferring and purchasing stolen goods.

The logical connection between these two kinds of acts and the prior crime is different: the former is the aftermath of a main crime, which has obvious continuity to and dependence on the main crime. The latter is an independent act, which has no direct connection with the predicate crime, but its object of action originates from it, so it also has a certain level of dependence on the predicate crime. For the latter, there is no jurisprudent obstacle to criminalise the money laundering act under such circumstances, as long it is clearly stipulated by law (Liang 2000).

However, the question is: as an afterwards act to the perpetrator's own crime, can the so-called self-money laundering be considered an independent crime with its own set of criminal liability associated? So far, answer derived from the basic principles of Chinese criminal law to that question has been a firm "no." The reason mainly lies in the requirement of the principle of prohibiting repeated evaluation in Chinese criminal law.

The term "proceeds of crime" indicates that the possession of said property is the natural result of said crime. The transformation and transfer of the proceeds of crime manifested by money laundering is but the follow-up disposal of the said property, which does not go beyond the meaning of "possession." In this case, if the law requires the perpetrator to "surrender" the proceeds of crime (i.e. to cease possession and the follow-up disposal of the property), the source of his obligation to surrender is the predicate crime. If the law sought to punish the act of disposing the proceeds of crime after the predicate crime has already been punished, it would bear the suspicion of repeated evaluation, which is in violation of the basic principle of modern criminal law.

Due to the strong stance on the afterwards act logic, the Chinese legislators showed great hesitation to push for the criminalisation of self-money laundering, despite the pressure from a number of international Anti-money Laundering and Combating the Financing of Terrorism organisations.

7 The Weak Links in Criminal Measures

First, in terms of the subjective and objective constitutive elements of the crime, the scope of the provisions is too narrow, if one sticks to the principle of legality, there will inevitably be wrongdoers slipping through the cracks (Zhang 2017).

In judicial practice, the "certainty of knowledge" doctrine has been adopted for the element of "knowing" in the crime of money laundering, that is, the suspect should know clearly that his actions will have harmful consequences. The scope of "knowing" here is obviously too small. On the one hand, it adds too much burden of proof to the prosecution, making it too difficult for the procurator to make their case; On the other hand, it also allows many people to get away with gross negligence.

In the objective element of money laundering's crime constitution, there are insufficient stipulations for the actual criminal acts. The Article 191 only specifies, as criminal offence, the acts committed by the perpetrator to "conceal or shield the origin and nature of the proceeds" of the few predicate offences listed. The provisions on the types of money laundering activities are too narrow for law enforcement agencies to effectively build cases against money launderers. Such narrowness is even more evident when comparisons were made to the anti-money laundering regulations in, say, the United States, where The act of concealing or shielding not only the nature and origin, but also location, ownership or power of control of the proceeds of crime has all been defined as criminal.

Second, in theory, there still is no common understanding on the procedure as well as criterion for identifying proceeds of crimes. Some people believe that the nature of the proceeds of crimes can only be determined through official rulings made by specific judicial authorities or law enforcement agencies authorised by the state through legal procedures. Others believe that the agency on the case can identify the proceeds of crime according to established constructive conditions, therefore, the public security bureau conducting investigation have the power to identify, recover and dispose of asset as the proceeds of crime according to law (Li and Xu 2008).

In practice, the flow of monetary gains by crime varies greatly and many new situations have emerged. For example, the use of proceeds of crime to invest in business, to purchase company shares, to fund Research and Development new products or new technologies (thus practically owning the patent right), and to gain access to business franchise, etc. The existing provisions can no longer meet the needs of judicial practice in recovering assets that have been siphoned off through these new means of money laundering.

Third, the punishments for money laundering are relatively light. Even in serious cases, the convicted offender can only be sentenced to a fixed-term imprisonment no less than 5 years but not longer than 10 years, plus a fine of no less than 5% and no more than 20% of the amount of money involved. From the point of deterrence, this punishment scheme is leaning on the low side, will not serve the purpose of raising the cost of economic crimes.

Also, the strangely disproportionate fine penalty makes it hard to carry itself out (Liu 2017b). Under Article 191 of the Criminal Law, the punishment for the crime of money laundering is as the following: "Confiscation of the proceeds of crime and the gains it generated; a fixed-term imprisonment of no more than five years or criminal detention; and a fine of no less than 5% but no more than 20% of the amount of money involved in the money laundering activity; in case of serious offence, a fixed-term imprisonment of no less than five years but no more than ten years, and a fine of no less than 5% but no more than 20% of the amount of money involved in the money laundering activity." As can be seen here, there is no stepping-up of fine for more serious crime, only a longer prison sentence.

Yet in practice, money laundering accounts often involve huge amounts of money transactions, which leads to a huge amount identified by the law enforcement or the court as "amount of money involved," which often times resulted in an unreasonably large fine for the money launderer (sometimes even larger than the fine imposed on the predicate offence). Since the money launderers usually do not actual own that much money, such a huge fine will inevitably become unenforceable. This strange situation would somehow backfire on the anti-money laundering enforcement: the prosecutors, out of the consideration of "balance of sentencing," will choose not to charge the offenders with money laundering, but go with other charges that, once convicted, have a punishment that can actually be carried out (Liu 2017b).

8 The AML/CFT Law Enforcement Mechanism and Practices

According to the statistics of the FATF, as of October 2006, only three cases had led to convictions of money laundering in China, and four defendants had been convicted of money laundering, which is very low compared with the high-risk of money laundering in such a large country as China. The extremely low number of money laundering conviction is not even close to reflecting the severe situation of money laundering in the nation (Wang 2008). Based on this situation, FATF, in its 2007 evaluation report, strongly recommends that the Chinese government shall make effort to improve the consciousness in identifying and combating money laundering activities to enhance the effectiveness of the fight against money laundering crimes (FATF 2007, p. 31).

8.1 The Establishment of Domestic Coordination Mechanism for AML Work

The Chinese government was quick in answering the call. The first step made to ramp up China's Anti-money Laundering and Combating the Financing of Terrorism law enforcement was the establishment of domestic coordination mechanism for anti-money laundering work.

Anti-money laundering work involves all aspects of social economy, and the situation is very complex, which requires cooperation and coordination from various government agencies and institutions. The People's Bank of China actively advocated and worked with multiple agencies, managed to establish and improve the coordination mechanism of anti-money laundering work at three levels: the national

Anti-money Laundering and Combating the Financing of Terrorism framework, the Anti-money Laundering and Combating the Financing of Terrorism supervisory system in the financial industry and the People's Bank of China's internal Anti-money Laundering and Combating the Financing of Terrorism mechanism (Tang 2009).

In May 2004, with the endorsement of the State Council, the People's Bank of China called for a joint inter-ministerial meeting on anti-money laundering with participation from 23 ministries and commissions. At the first session, the organisational structure and working mechanism of the joint meeting were determined, and the division of responsibilities was clarified, and the General Rules of the Joint Inter-ministerial Meeting for Anti-money Laundering was established. In 2006, with the promulgation of the Anti-Money Laundering Law, the General Rules were revised under the new law's provisions on the division of duties and responsibilities among the governmental departments in Anti-Money Laundering Work, membership was adjusted and extended to allow more participation among government agencies and institutions, and the responsibilities of various departments in the anti-money laundering work have been finetuned and clarified. The establishment of the joint inter-ministerial meeting can be seen as a crucial first step toward a coordinated national Anti-money Laundering and Combating the Financing of Terrorism system.

To further enhance the effectiveness of collaboration on AML supervision in the financial industry, in 2004, the People's Bank of China, together with the Banking Regulatory Commission, the Securities Regulatory Commission and the Insurance Regulatory Commission, established the Anti-money Laundering Coordination Workgroup System.

The internal anti-money laundering mechanism of the People's Bank of China has also been constantly improved. In 2004, China Anti-Money Laundering Monitoring and Analysis Center (CAMLMAC) was established. In 2006, the transfer of anti-money laundering functions, institutions, personnel and database from the State Administration of Foreign Exchange (SAFE) to the People's Bank of China was completed, this move achieved a unified anti-money laundering system covering both domestic and foreign currencies.

To better fulfill its anti-money laundering duties, 36 anti-money laundering offices were set up nationwide, covering PBC's provincial branches and a few major city subbranches. This forms the internal working mechanism of the People's Bank of China as the lead anti-money laundering authority under the State Council. The Anti-money Laundering organisational structure among financial institutions has also improved over the years. Most financial institutions have set up their own specialised Anti-money Laundering department, Anti-money Laundering Compliance Officer and Anti-money Laundering Rapporteur System.

8.2 New Mechanism for Countering Money Laundering

With the continuous improvement of China's anti-money laundering supervision and monitoring system, the unique role of Anti-money Laundering and Combating the Financing of Terrorism mechanisms in detecting and combating criminal activities has begun to manifest itself. Based on a transaction monitoring network covering the entire nation's banking industry, the China Anti-Money Laundering Monitoring and Analysis Center has gradually expanded the scope of anti-money laundering monitoring capacity. On 1 October 2007, the securities, futures and insurance industry's database were officially connected to the China Anti-Money Laundering Monitoring and Analysis Center's network and started submitting large and suspicious transaction data. Then, on 1 November 2007, the electronic network of banking industry's "total-to-total" reporting function of large and suspicious transaction data went online, the scope of anti-money laundering monitoring was further expanded.

By the end of June 2008, 308 banks, 324 securities and futures companies and 100 insurance companies (excluding nine Insurance Asset Management companies) had connected into the data reporting network, representing 99% of all banks, 99% of all securities and futures companies, and 100% of all insurance companies respectively. A large and suspicious transaction reporting system with nationwide and industry-wide coverage has been established, which laid a sound foundation for AML investigation and law enforcement.

Under the requirement of the Anti-Money Laundering Law, the People's Bank of China has established an internal anti-money laundering investigation system and strengthened the cooperation mechanism with law enforcement agencies. By the end of June 2008, the People's Bank of China had initiated close to 7000 anti-money laundering investigations based on suspicious transaction leads provided by the reporting system. Close to 6000 leads were reported to the law enforcement for further review, involving more than 1 trillion RMB yuan, and about 200 criminal cases were opened by the police based on the information. The People's Bank of China also provided assistance in over 5700 criminal investigations by the police, involving more than 400 Billion RMB yuan, 300 cases were successfully closed with ML charges filed, involving more than 13 Billion RMB yuan.

In September 2007, the People's Bank of China and Ministry of Public Security launched two joint special operations aiming to crack down on money laundering and terrorist financing activities: the "Operation Skynet" against the crime of money laundering, and the "Operation Thunderbolt" against underground banking. Both operations achieved tremendous success. As of July 2008, "Operation Skynet" led to conviction of money laundering crime in four cases, served as deterrent to potential money laundering criminals (Wang 2015). Encouraged by the success of the special operations, the numbers of both investigative assistance and criminal case closing went up significantly around the country. In 2007, the People's Bank of China system provided assistance to law enforcement agencies nationwide in the investigations of 328 money laundering-related cases, with the amount of money involved totaling 53.72 billion RMB yuan, and it led to the successful prosecution of 89 cases, with a total of 28.8 billion RMB yuan involved, which was a 120% increase from 2006.

It is believed that the anti-money laundering mechanism has been highly effective in producing crime intelligence and assisting criminal investigations, not only in money laundering cases. Looking at the specific cases utilised the leads and assistance from the anti-money laundering mechanism, there are not only typical money laundering cases associated with drugs, smuggling and corruption, but also major economic and financial crimes with widespread social impact and public concern.

9 Comprehensive International Cooperation in AML/CFT

On 28 June 2007, at the 3rd plenary meeting of the 18th session of the FATF in Paris, China was accepted as a full member by a unanimous vote. This marked a successful end to China's campaign to join this organisation, which lasted two and a half years. From this point on, China's Anti-money Laundering and Combating the Financing of Terrorism work has entered a new era of development. FATF membership is of great significance to China's in-depth participation in international cooperation in Anti-money Laundering and Combating the Financing of Terrorism, it will, without a doubt, strengthen China's stance in the fight against economic crimes and corruption, enhance China's ability to maintain financial stability.

As a matter of fact, international cooperation has always been an important part of China's Anti-money Laundering and Combating the Financing of Terrorism strategy. In can be shown in China's active participation in the formulation of relevant international conventions as well as the resolution to integrate international obligations into domestic law. The provisions of the Anti-Money Laundering Law reflected most relevant requirements of international conventions signed and ratified by China. The Law also dedicated a separate chapter to international cooperation in anti-money laundering, which stated the need to actively carry out anti-money laundering works under international treaties. The law stipulated that the People's Bank of China is responsible for information exchange and cooperation with international anti-money laundering organisations, and the judicial authorities are responsible for providing judicial assistance.

To further fulfill the obligation under domestic and international laws, in 2004, as a founding member, China founded the Eurasian Anti-money Laundering and Combating the Financing of Terrorism Group (EAG) with Russia, Kazakhstan, Tajikistan, Kyrgyzstan and Belarus. This has proven to be one of the more effective mechanism of international collaboration in Anti-money Laundering and Combating the Financing of Terrorism. It promoted the establishment and improvement of Anti-money Laundering and Combating the Financing of Terrorism systems in the region and provided much need boost to the member stats' fight against money laundering and terrorist financing activities (Lan 2018).

In the field of financial intelligence cooperation, China has signed bilateral agreements or memorandums of understanding on financial intelligence exchange and cooperation in Anti-money Laundering and Combating the Financing of Terrorism with 12 countries and regions including The Republic of Korea, Malaysia, Russia, Kyrgyzstan and Hong Kong (China). As a result, in-depth exchanges and cooperation with financial institutions in these countries (regions) were initiated and expanded.

Despite the achievement made so far, China's policy framework and operational mechanisms of international anti-money laundering cooperation still need improvement in the following aspects: first, China is still not a member of some key Anti-money Laundering and Combating the Financing of Terrorism organisations, such as the Egmont Group. This could undermine the efficiency and depth of China's anti-money laundering intelligence sharing and operational exchange. Second, there is a lack of legal framework for the extradition of money launderers and the recovery of assets due to the inadequate effort made by the Chinese government to reach bilateral agreements with western nations on this issue. Third, China lacks voice in the formulation of international Anti-money Laundering and Combating the Financing of Terrorism standards due to the late entry into the game and the lack of expertise in this area (Cheng 2018).

10 Objective Assessment by the FATF

In 2007, after agreeing to take part in the third round of FATF mutual evaluation, China formally became a member of FATF. In the following 5 years, China has continuously improved its Anti-money Laundering and Combating the Financing of Terrorism system, submitted eight progress reports to FATF, and finally received the approval of FATF plenary meeting, successfully concluded the third round of mutual evaluation process in 2012. China was the thirteenth member country to fully meet the FATF third round of mutual evaluation standards.

Then, 6 years after the conclusion of the third round, FATF started the fourth round of mutual evolution on China in 2017 (Cheng 2016). And in April 2019, after the completion of an onsite visit in 2018, FATF issued the MER 2019 report on China's Anti-money Laundering and Combating the Financing of Terrorism measures.

Taking part in the FATF mutual evaluation is an important part of China's commitment to the international Anti-money Laundering and Combating the Financing of Terrorism community. The report of FAFT mutual evaluation is one of the important reference bases for the consideration of the implementation of the United Nation Convention Against Corruption, and is also an integral part of the financial sector evaluation plan by the IMF. It is one of the major indicators to measure the degree of financial stability of a country (Cheng 2016). When it comes to the assessment of China's Anti-money Laundering and Combating the Financing of

Terrorism criminal policy, the FATF mutual evaluation report can be quite informative as well.

In the MER 2019 report, China's anti-money laundering criminal policy and its implementation were highly appraised.

In areas related to Anti-money Laundering and Combating the Financing of Terrorism enforcement, such as the use of financial intelligence, combating money laundering crimes, disrupting terrorist financing, and confiscating the proceeds of crime, the report spoke highly of China's practices (FATF 2019, p. 49).

For example, the report pointed out that to meet the needs of combating money laundering, China has constantly revised its criminal legislation and established a competent criminal law system to support the fight against money laundering. The law provided law enforcement agencies with sufficient resources and capabilities to take effective measures against money laundering. And the fight against money laundering has been part of a much more comprehensive crime control scheme. Since the 18th National People's Congress, China has made great achievements in curbing predicate offences of money laundering, such as corruption, illegal fund-raising and drug trafficking. In addition, China has also taken a series of alternative measures, such as special confiscation procedures for illegal income, administrative penalties and party's internal disciplinary measures, to combat money laundering from all possible angles. By combating money laundering and its predicate offence at the same time, the risk of money laundering has been reduced significantly (FATF 2019, p. 69).

China has also established a mechanism for judicial assistance and extradition, and engaged extensively in international cooperation through law enforcement, supervisory and financial intelligence exchange. In particular, positive results have been achieved in law enforcement collaboration and financial intelligence exchange. In recent years, China has launched cross-border enforcement operations such as "Operation Skynet" and "Operation Fox Hunting." Through these operations, the Chinese authorities managed to recover a large number of outflow criminal assets from abroad, which made crystal clear China's determination in the recovery of the proceeds of crime (FATF 2019, p. 69). However, the report also pointed out a number of areas in need of improvement.

According to the report, China has achieved great success in combating corruption, illegal fund-raising, drug crimes and other predicate offences of money-laundering in recent years. However, there has been insufficient effort to crack down on money laundering crimes directly. There has been a large number of cases for various predicate offences, but there has been far less cases investigating underground banking, corruption and corporate money laundering directly under the umbrella of Article 191 (FATF 2019, p. 70).

Part of the reason lies in the interpretation and application of the law. The standard for the subjective constitutive element of "knowing" was set too high, making it extremely hard for investigators and prosecutors to build their cases. Also, China's criminal law does not criminalise "self-laundering" independently, which significantly narrowed down the scope of AML investigation, not to mention it does not conform to FATF's standards.

11 Conclusions

To many, China's efforts in fighting money laundering is seen as part of her commitment to the United Nations Sustainable Development Goals (SDGs) in general, and the SDG 16 in specific. The SDG 16 states the following objectives: "By 2030, significantly reduce illicit financial and arms flows, strengthen the recovery and return of stolen assets and combat all forms of organized crime" (Section 16.4, p. XX), and "Strengthen relevant national institutions, including through international cooperation, for building capacity at all levels, in particular in developing countries, to prevent violence and combat terrorism and crime" (Section 16.a, p. XX).

As shown by the discussion above, the Chinese government is deeply and extensively committed to the implementation of the SDG16 through both legislative and administrative means. In regard to the SDG Section 16.4, the Chinese government has put forward the following significant policy changes: (1) to improve the mechanism of the transferring of sentenced person and strengthen the partnership with other countries in fighting transnational crimes; (2) to strengthen the international collaboration in asset recovery; (3) to fully utilise the bilateral and multilateral mechanisms within the G20 and APEC. In pursuit of these policy goals, new legislations have been passed, communication channels have been established and joint LE operations have been proposed in the area of Anti-money Laundering and Combating the Financing of Terrorism. As for the SDG Section 16.a, China has been actively participating in the UN peace keeping operations, supporting both diplomatic and economic effort to contain international hotspots. There has also been substantial effort made to police the cyberspace, especially effort made to crack down on the promotion, recruitment and financing of terrorism.

The SDG 16 emphasises on "justice" and "strong institutions," which is also how the Chinese government understands to be the appropriate approach to win the fight against money laundering and terrorist financing. To that end, we can say with fair amount of confidence that, although there's still a long way ahead, China's AML/CFT work is on the right path.

References

Cheng, P. (2016). Revelation on impact of the FATF's standard for the fourth round of evaluation on China's criminal policy on money laundering. *Financial Theory and Practice, 11*, 79–82.

Cheng, P. (2018). International comparison and revelation of anti-money laundering transnational cooperation under the new situation. *Journal of Regional Financial Research, 10*, 63–66.

Cheng, X., & Wang, Q. (2007). On corruption-related money laundering and its countermeasures. *Criminal Research, 5*, 32–37.

Financial Action Task Force (FATF). (2007). *First mutual evaluation report on anti-money laundering and combating the financing of terrorism: People's Republic of China*. Paris: FATF. Retrieved from: http://www.fatf-gafi.org/media/fatf/documents/reports/mer/MER%20China%20full.pdf

Financial Action Task Force (TATF). (2019). *Anti-money laundering and counter-terrorist financing measures-People's Republic of China, Fourth Round Mutual Evaluation Report*. Paris: FATF. Retrieved from: http://www.fatf-gafi.org/publications/mutualevaluations/documents/mer-china-2019.html

Jia, Y., & Li, H. (2019). Investigation on criminal acts of financing terrorist activities and the countermeasures: The development of criminal legislation from the comparative perspective. *Criminal Law Review, 54*(22), 386–410.

Lan, L. (2018). Study of the member states of the Shanghai Cooperation Organization on the cooperation in counter-terrorism financing intelligence. *Journal of Intelligence, 37*(7), 7–15.

Li, C., & Xu, N. (2008). On several puzzles in the control of the international money laundering. *Criminal Research, 5*, 38–45.

Li, X. (2014). Perfection of law on anti-money laundering — according to the task of FATF. *Journal of Northeast Normal University, 1*, 19–24.

Li, Y. (2016). China's improving anti-money laundering legislation: Anti-money Laundering Law's 10th anniversary review. *Tsinghua Financial Review, 7*, 46–47.

Liang, G. (2000). Money laundering crime and its prevention. *Beijing Institute of Politics and Law Management Cadres Journal, 1*, 21–17.

Liu, M. (2017a). Research on the effectiveness of Anti-money Laundering Law of the People's Republic of China. *Zhejiang Finance, 4*, 8–15.

Liu, M. (2017b). Research on criminal legislation and judicial practice of anti-money laundering and counter-terrorism financing in China. *Shanghai Finance, 12*, 78–83.

Liu, W. (2017c). Analysis of punishment and prevention of money laundering crime in China under the internet financial environment. *Law Science Magazine, 38*(8), 101–108.

People's Bank of China (PBC). (2017). *China Anti-money Laundering Report*. Retrieved from http://www.pbc.gov.cn/fanxiqianju/135153/135282/index.html

People's Bank of China Anti-Money Laundering Bureau (PBCAMLB). (2015). *China Anti-money Laundering Report.* Retrieved from http://www.pbc.gov.cn/fanxiqianju/135153/index.html

Tang, X. (2009). China's improving anti-money laundering system. *China Finance, 5*, 34–36.

Tang, Y. (2006). The inside story of drafting the Anti-money Laundering Law. *Outlook Weekly, 18*, 29–31.

United Nations. (1999). International Convention for the Suppression of the Financing of Terrorism (2178 UNTS 197).

United Nations Convention against Corruption, 2349 UNTS 41.

United Nations Convention against Illicit Trafficking in Narcotic Drugs and Psychotropic Substances, 1582 UNTS 95.

United Nations Convention against Transnational Organized Crime, 2225 UNTS 209.

Wang, S. (2015). "Operation Skynet" made the fleeing corrupt officials tremble. *People's Daily*, Mar. 3, 2015 at 5.

Wang, S., & Sui, L. (2017). The risk of money laundering in free trade zone and its prevention. *Chinese Criminology Review, 5*, 39–48.

Wang, W. (2019, June). The analysis and policy suggestion on the current situation of anti-money laundering work. *China Postal Service* (p. 4).

Wang, X. (2008). Inquiry of judicial practice: Examining the function of penalty in deterring the crime of money laundering. *Criminal Science, 5*, 42–48.

Wang, X. (2009). China's anti-money laundering crime system from an international perspective. *Peking University Law Journal, 21*(3), 375–389.

Wang, X., & Liu, J. (2017). The characteristics and prevention strategies of money laundering using third-party payment platform. *Law and Economy, 7*, 26–28.

Yin, M. (2019). The development trend and investigative strategies for money laundering crime in the internet age. *Journal of Jiangxi Police Institute, 2*, 18–25.

Zhang, B. (2017). The analysis of controversial issues on money laundering crime against the background of globalization. *Hebei Law Science, 4*, 81–92.

Zhao, B., & Yuan, B. (2018). Basic logic and legislative adjustment of money laundering crime in China. *Jianghai Academic Journal, 1*, 138–146.
Zhou, Y. (2019). Tax-related money laundering legal issues against the background of "One-Belt-One-Road". *China Price*, (6), 54–57.
Zou, L. (2011). On the crime of money laundering in China. *Legal System and Society*, (22), 197–198.

Ling Zhou Ph.D., is an Associate Professor of Criminal Law and Assistant to the Dean of Criminal Justice School, South-Central/Zhongnan University of Economics and Law (Wuhan, China). He graduated from The Beijing Institute of International Relations with a bachelor's degree in International Politics in 1996. In 1999, he received his master's in law from Sichuan University Law School. From 2000 to 2005, he studied at the College of Criminal Justice of Sam Houston State University, TX (USA) and received his Ph.D. degree in Criminal Justice. Dr. Zhou joined Marist College, New York (USA) as an Assistant Professor in Criminal Justice and became a tenured faculty member in 2011. In 2012, he returned to China and joined the Zhongnan University of Economics and Law where he has been serving as Associate Professor of Criminal Law. Dr. Zhou's areas of research interests include criminology, criminal policy, intelligence-led policing and comparative criminal justice system. E-mail: zhouling@zuel.edu.cn.

Hanming Xu Prof. is currently the Director of the Research Center for Rule of Law Development and Judicial Reform of Zhongnan University of Economics and Law, the Dean of Hubei Rule of Law Development Strategy Research Institute, and the Head of the China Law Society Legal Research Base. He serves as an "Academic Leader" of the Ministry of Education's social governance and rule of law innovation team. Professor Hanming Xu initiated the discipline of social governance law in China. E-mail: 407193133@qq.com.

The Policy Relevance of Comparative Criminology: On Evidence-Based Policies, Policy Learning and the Scales of the Discipline

Susanne Karstedt

Abstract Comparative criminology has an ever more important role in the discipline, and relevance for international and national crime and justice policies. International organisations increasingly use evidence from comparative research for long-term strategic goals and policy recommendations, such as, e.g. the impact of poverty on child mortality, of inequality or simply the 'youth bulge' on violence levels in societies, or of traditional values on corruption. Can comparative and macro-level criminological research provide an evidence base for global crime and justice policies akin to and equivalent to the 'gold standard' of experimental methods on national and local levels? Other disciplines, in particular comparative political science, or development studies have produced exemplary research demonstrating the usage and usefulness of comparative studies for policy making, evaluation, transfer and policy learning. This chapter discusses the potential of comparative criminological research for enhancing the pool of evidence-based crime and justice policies, and recommends strategies for harnessing them for policy making and transfer on a global scale.

Keywords Comparative criminology · Scaling criminology · Evidence-based policy · Violence · Corruption · Quality of government · Counterfactuals · Singapore · Jamaica

The chapter is based on the lecture given on the occasion of receiving the European Criminology Award 2018, a subsequent publication in the ESC Newsletter (Karstedt 2018), and a presentation given at a seminar "The Real Gold Standard: Measuring Counterfactual Worlds that Matter Most to Policy", Institute of Criminology, University of Cambridge, 14 May 2019.

S. Karstedt (✉)
Griffith University, School of Criminology and Criminal Justice, Mt Gravatt, QLD, Australia
e-mail: s.karstedt@griffith.edu.au

H. Kury, S. Redo (eds.), *Crime Prevention and Justice in 2030*,
https://doi.org/10.1007/978-3-030-56227-4_24

1 Introducing Comparative Criminology

Comparative and cross-national research in criminology has been an area of continuous growth in the discipline. Globalisation has certainly spurred comparative perspectives over the past decades. However, most important was presumably the proliferation of international, and regional data collection efforts. The contemporary generation of comparativists in criminology have a treasure trove of crime and justice data at their fingertips. The concerted efforts of the international community, the United Nations and its entities like the United Nations Office on Drugs and Crime (UNODC), the United Nations Interregional Crime and Justice Research Institute (UNICRI), or the World Health Organization (WHO) have succeeded in providing unparalleled data on crime and justice for nearly all countries from official sources. These are complemented by regional initiatives like the European Sourcebook, academic and other initiatives like the World Prison List (see Karstedt 2019a), and the International Crime Victims Survey. All regional surveys like the Eurobarometer, Latino- and Afrobarometer include a range of questions on crime and justice on a regular basis. Numerous international non-government organisations (INGO) have started to provide crime and justice indicators, including indicators of compliance with human rights by police and criminal justice, or rule of law indicators.[1]

Compared to the wealth of crime and justice data available today, the contributions of cross-national and cross-cultural criminology to evidence-based policies of preventing crime and improving justice seem to be lagging behind. The question arises what and in which ways can comparative criminology contribute to evidence-based policies? What would such a contribution look like? Can cross-national criminological research compete with what experimental criminology provides in terms of robust evidence? Can it be as useful as experimental designs and Random Controlled Trials (RCT) in addressing pressing crime and justice problems across the globe, and deliver the tools for preventing violence or corruption, or improving prison conditions? Can the global framework and "big picture" (Rosenfeld 2011) produce evidence of the quality gained from local and small-scale practices? In other words, how does macro-level analysis and system-wide evidence compare to micro-level evidence, which is by far the most common in criminology.

These are the questions that will be addressed in this chapter. It will start with an overview of contemporary discussions of macro- and micro-level criminology. Next, promises and limitations of comparative research are explored. Comparative political science is then suggested as a successful model and course of action for comparative criminology. Finally, micro- and macro-level criminology will be aligned, and big and small pictures in criminology linked.

[1]For a critical assessment of the construction and usage of indicators by national governments and international organizations see Engle Merry (2016), Davis et al. (2012), and Engle Merry et al. (2015).

2 "Big Picture" Criminology: Only Star Gazing?

Comparative and cross-national research is usually identified with the "big picture" in criminological thinking, theorising and research, a term coined by Richard Rosenfeld (2011) in his presidential address to the American Society of Criminology. He encouraged criminologists to devote "greater attention ... to the big picture – the relationship between crime and the interplay of institutions in the social systems of whole societies." (Rosenfeld 2011, p. 1). He pointed out that programmes that reduce individual-level propensities of crime and violence do not seamlessly correspond to and translate into macro- and aggregate reductions of crime levels. Comparative criminology has rarely contributed to figuring out how to reduce crime and improve justice, and consequently, was hardly of interest to policy makers who struggled with crime problems on the ground and in local arenas. Sweeping economic, social and institutional analyses hardly point to levers in reach of those who are involved in criminal justice policies, and to practices accessible with their toolkits. Inequality is one of the best and robust predictors of lethal violence in societies (Nivette 2011). Yet it is impossible for any politician, not to speak of practitioners involved in police, courts and corrections to change secular developments of social and economic inequality in the short or longer run (Piketty 2015).

For many criminologists, cross national research therefore epitomises criminol ogy as a "descriptive and observational science" (Sherman quoted in Leigh 2018, p. 91). Sherman compares this type of criminology to astronomy and proposes that criminology move to the experimental and medical model of science (ibid). Interventions are seemingly impossible in astronomy, however, many successful (quasi-) experimental approaches in astronomy and enhanced observational and measurement techniques have contributed to the outstanding success of this science. Why not assume that the same is possible for comparative research in criminology with ever better (observational) data and enhanced statistical models? More recently, Nagin and Sampson (2019) have questioned the "gold-standard" of experimental criminology, and drawn attention to the problems of small scale, highly localised trials of crime prevention and justice initiatives when situated within the larger picture of a system-wide approach. They argue that micro-level policies like hot spot policing or moving people to better neighbourhoods can have unintended consequences (or none at all) within the larger context of neighbourhoods and cities that elude from the myopic local perspective that RCTs provide. Consequently, they advocate analysis and evaluation of system-wide interventions, thus venturing into the field of comparative research and the production of evidence through large-scale comparison. This is a timely and welcome move, as the potential of comparative (cross-national) analyses in criminology has remained under-explored and under-valued, and until now mainly neglected as a source for valid knowledge about crime and justice policies.

Comparative research in criminology is observational, however not necessarily descriptive. Not dissimilar from astronomy, it has the potential to question established worldviews and theories that are taken for granted. One such assumption is that "the rich get richer and the poor get prison" (Reiman 1997), established in manifold theoretical and empirical accounts on the relationship between inequality and imprisonment: the more unequal a society is, the higher is the number of prisoners and rate of incarceration (Wilkinson and Pickett 2009, p. 148). When this was tested with different measures of inequality, it was found that it does neither hold on a global scale with nearly 150 countries included, nor on a regional scale, e.g. for Latin America (Karstedt 2019b; see for the global sample Miethe et al. 2017). As the different measures used represented different causal mechanisms and theories, these results question established theories of punishment. A particular test case was Latin America, as in this global region inequality as well as poverty have decreased substantively over the past decades, while imprisonment rates shot up (Karstedt 2019b). The results suggested that the growing middle class in these countries, which mainly accounted for the decrease in inequality, supported harsher crime policies, including long prison sentences. These results on inequality and punishment not only question a causal relationship between changes in inequality and imprisonment—as suggested by the quote above, they also demonstrate a disjunction between micro- and macro-level perspectives in criminology. While across the globe marginalised groups of the population are disproportionately imprisoned, the causal link between inequality and imprisonment rates on the global level is much more tenuous.

3 Learning from Other Disciplines: Comparative Political Science

In other disciplines comparative research is not the wallflower that it is in criminology. In political science, health or development economics, comparative research is seen as a foundation for evidence-based policies, and its policy relevance is not disputed (Stoker et al. 2015). Early on in the 1960s, political scientists asked whether "comparison can be regarded as the social scientist's equivalent of the natural scientist's laboratory" and "the comparative method … an adequate substitute for experimentation". (Lijphart 1971, p. 683). The answer to this question was that comparison could only be an imperfect substitute, but its limitations were not necessarily disabling for the purpose (Lijphart 1971, p. 683). Today, the UN and the World Bank, as well as NGOs, extensively use comparative methods in their influential reports and policy making (e.g. World Bank 2015, 2017; Leigh 2018, p. 146; critical: Davis et al. 2012). We find numerous examples where such comparative studies have questioned existing policies of development and aid, and shifted the flow of investment towards what was seen (and evidenced) as more effective. These include the role of women's education in children's mortality, the impact of corruption on health outcomes for mothers and children, or the health effects of the rule of law (see Rosling 2018).

Importantly, political scientists started with a change of perspective when embarking on making comparative research relevant for evidence-based policy. They turned to understanding what makes societies and governments more successful than others in achieving "outcomes for citizens". Outcomes are defined as 'overall human well-being', and are measured by an array of indicators from objective ones like poverty, child mortality, and other health indicators, as well as subjective ones like life satisfaction, trust and security, or general perceptions of quality of life (Rothstein 2015; see also Rothstein 2011). Political scientist Rothstein and his colleagues identified "quality of government" as the decisive factor accounting for differences between countries. Quality of government, often also termed quality of governance, is indicated by the state's administrative capacity, e.g. to collect taxes and distribute for the common good, to handle public finances in a responsible way, to control corruption and establish the rule of law. Importantly, the quality of government is not predicated on the quality of democracy in a country; in other words, the impact of good governance is independent of the level of democratic rule in a country (Rothstein 2015), as will be further explored in Sect. 4.1. (see also Rothstein 2011, chapter 9). When quality of government is measured as outlined above, bad governments have a detrimental impact on children's well-being in particular in low and middle income countries; children are poorer, less safe, their health is worse and they receive less education (Halleroed et al. 2013). This affects them throughout their lives: quality of government is related to overall health and life expectancy in the population of 180 countries, and corruption is a strong predictor of low levels of health and life expectancy (Holmberg and Rothstein 2011).

Political science offers a most important lesson for comparative criminology that can be easily translated into our discipline. Both safety and justice are at the core of the quality of government. Safe and just societies are not only outcomes of good governance for citizens; they also provide the conditions in which citizens live better and healthier lives. Research on Nigeria found that corruption and maternal mortality both declined concomitantly, indicating the relationship between justice and health outcomes (Karstedt 2012a). This equally applies to safety for citizens from often lethal violence: female life expectancy is lower in more violent societies due to a range of factors that impact on women's health in these societies (Karstedt 2018). The United Nations have recognised the importance of the quality of institutions, and in particular justice institutions for outcomes for citizens in their 2030 Agenda for Sustainable Development Goals. Goal 16 includes access to justice and improving institutions, as well as building peaceful societies where citizens are protected against violence (A/RES/70/1). Comparative criminology needs to follow suite and explore the best ways to achieve this goal (Eisner et al. 2016).

4 Laboratories, Limitations, and Strategies

Comparative criminologists have a natural laboratory for their work, with the societies and governments of nearly 200 countries. These laboratories are even more extended if sub-national governments and spaces are included (Baumer and Wolff 2014). Each level of government and society might be seen as a quasi-experiment of sorts, and together they provide incredibly rich data for exploring what works, what does not and what is promising in preventing crime and improving justice. Presently, urban spaces and local governments emerge as one of the most promising natural laboratories from which to learn. City governments have been successful in reducing violence, curbing organised crime and generally enhancing the safety of citizens through a range of policies (Nagin and Sampson 2019; Barber 2013).

Comparative research on city spaces and municipal crime prevention policies provide encouraging results for Latin American cities, which rank among the most violent places in the world (de Mello and Schneider 2010; World Bank 2011). Both Bogota and Recife experienced an unexpected drop in violence within a national and regional context of high levels of violence. Crime reduction policies on the municipal level included data systems for targeted policing (e.g. a data base of violent offenders; anonymous crime reporting hotline), training of police in Human Rights, training citizens on security issues, and permanent police operations in drug trafficking areas (de Mello and Schneider 2010; Hoelscher and Nussio 2016).

As comparative criminology makes good use of this laboratory on a global scale, its basic logic follows the experimental approach. However, there are clear limitations to comparative criminology as an equivalent to experimental approaches to interventions and their contribution to evidence-based policy; criminology shares these with comparative political science. These limitations include (a) the (non-) manipulability of variables, (b) the 'longue durée' of impact and (c) convergence and divergence of trends.

One of the major factors affecting the relevance of comparative criminology as evidence base is the fact that a large number of variables that are used in comparative research are not easily manipulable, or not at all. Here, comparative criminology actually looks like astronomy. As noted above, levels of inequality are good predictors of country differences in violence measured in homicide rates (Nivette 2011). However, inequality can hardly be manipulated, and we still do not know the actual causal mechanisms that link inequality and violence (Rivera 2016). Similarly, trust between people is an important cultural and social resource of societies, closely related to violence and crime; however it is hardly a characteristic of societies that lends itself to easy and fast change through policy. My research (Karstedt 2015) shows that cultural patterns like egalitarian and individualistic values both correspond to lower homicide rates. Societies with strong individualistic orientations have lower rates of lethal violence than collectivistic ones; further, egalitarian values and orientations coincide with lower levels of lethal violence. Both types of cultural orientations differ between countries and changed over time (Pinker 2011); however, as deeply embedded cultural conditions and institutional patterns of societies they do not lend themselves to isolated or short-term manipulation by policies.

Time scales pose another major limitation for the policy relevance of comparative criminology. As Lapuente and Rothstein (2014) found, mid-nineteenth century education levels still are one of the best predictors of contemporary corruption levels in a country. Education levels were decisive for the development of a meritocratic autonomous bureaucracy, which Sweden created in the late nineteenth century. Spain with much lover education levels at the time built a patronage-based administration. The result was that in Sweden public offices could not be offered to core supporters while in Spain they could, leading to a more harmonious society in the Nordic country and a more conflict-ridden in Spain. Education levels therefore turn out to be an important factor for the long-term organisation of bureaucracy, and thus the overall quality of government (Rothstein 2015). Nonetheless, this implies a long time-frame for policy impact, and speaks to the particular dynamics and the multi-faceted nature of system-wide change with numerous interacting factors. Consequently, direction, velocity and depth of change do not always neatly coincide. Comparative analyses of crime and violence find that trends can take distinctly different directions between countries, regions and cities, and between macro- and micro levels (Baumer and Wolff 2014). Even if downward trends of lethal violence were widely shared in the second half of the twentieth century, driving factors often are not and differ considerably between countries, as LaFree et al. (2015) found for the trends of homicide rates in 55 countries.

These limitations are crucial to acknowledge in the production of evidence, and they affect policy learning. Isolating mechanisms that provide leverage for policies in one country and translating them into policy-relevant strategies in another one is a complex matter: what drives crime rates down in one place (or even many places) might fail in a different country and context. Finding the perfectly matching or contrasting context is difficult, even in a global laboratory. Two strategies address these limitations by applying the basic logic of experimentation. First, finding 'counterfactuals' is a strategy that aims at simulating a control group by finding a case (or several) that shares major characteristics and conditions, but has a decisively different outcome (or vice versa). The second strategy analyses the differences in results of the same policy within different contexts.

4.1 Counterfactual Worlds and 'Institutional Coagulation': Jamaica and Singapore

Jamaica and Singapore represent a perfect pair of counterfactuals, and have been used by political scientists (Rothstein 2011, p. 193), and more recently by criminologists in analyses for the UNODC (2019, Box 10, provided by Manuel Eisner). Both countries have much in common: they are small in terms of scale and population, they are both islands, and started at about the same level of development when becoming independent in the 1960s. Both countries are situated in a highly diverse region, and consequently it can be assumed that regional culture, political and economic power did not shape the course of their subsequent trajectories. At the time of independence Singapore was in a worse situation and could be expected to fare badly. However, Singapore embarked on an exceptional trajectory of improvement in terms of social and economic indicators, including a reduction of violence (UNODC 2019) and corruption (Rothstein 2011). In contrast, Jamaica's economic and social performance deteriorated throughout the following decades, with citizens' wellbeing and security declining steadily. Contemporary Jamaica has high levels of violence and corruption, higher mortality rates for men and women between fifteen and sixty, and low levels of children's education and health. Political scientist Bo Rothstein (2011) shows that quality of government and beneficial institutional patterns account for today's huge differences between Jamaica and Singapore rather than type of regime: Authoritarian Singapore developed institutional patterns that produced outcomes for citizens, while democratic Jamaica did not.

The extraordinary divergence of all trends is driven by what I term 'institutional coagulation'. This captures the process of convergence of institutions into a comprehensive pattern where they are reinforcing each other, and consequently their beneficial or detrimental impact. Institutional coagulation set both countries on a trajectory with strong self-reinforcing mechanisms that drove them apart in a rather short period of time. In particular, downward trajectories as in Jamaica are difficult to turn around, as many institutions need to change. Institutional coagulation makes it difficult to identify a single causal mechanism or triggering intervention; improving the quality of government needs to build on a range of policies and simultaneously well-functioning institutions.

4.2 System-Wide Intervention: Corruption Control in Ghana

It is widely assumed that low salaries for government officials, in particular for police or judges, are a cause of corruption and failure of the criminal justice system. In 2010, the Ghana Government implemented a "single-spine" salary structure for all police officials thereby unilaterally doubling their incomes, in an effort to curb highway and traffic bribe extraction by police. Neighbouring countries in the West African region left their police salaries unchanged throughout the period, as were salaries of other officials within Ghana. This systemwide policy intervention to reduce street-level corruption by police in Ghana demonstrates the pitfalls and problems of institutional contexts when a 'rule changer' is introduced. Rather than the expected decrease in corruption, Foltz and Opoku-Agyemang (2015) found a significant increase of bribes taken in Ghana for border-crossing lorry traffic after the intervention. This increase affected both the frequency with which bribes were asked by police, and the amount asked for, indicating both a higher prevalence and more harm by corrupt practices in Ghana. No such change was observed for the other transit countries. Tankebe et al. (2019) used data from a survey study to gauge into this unexpected result. They found that the counterproductive impact presumably was due to specific cultural institutions originating from allegiances to and status gains within tribal and kinship networks: the higher salary obliged police officers of all ranks to meet increasing demands from these networks and to contribute higher amounts which they raised through bribes.

4.3 *Identifying Causal Mechanisms*

Comparative criminology and political science share one problem: inference is not causality. Comparative criminologists need to transform inferences from data into explanations, and to find the specific causal mechanisms that lead to the observed outcome. This applies to 'natural experiments' like in Singapore and Jamaica, as well as to systemwide interventions, including whole countries. Social change that evolved over time, and policy interventions are past events. When identifying causal mechanisms in the past that resulted in differential outcomes we need a "fair causal comparison" of rival hypotheses and careful collection of evidence. We may accept the observed impact as, e.g. in Singapore and Jamaica, and still doubt the actual causal processes through which this happened. We need to 'unearth' decisive causal mechanisms just like scientists from a range of disciplines when they tried to identify the causal chain that brought about the mass extinction of dinosaurs (Waldner 2007, p. 160).

As there are "multiple ways to engage in fair causal comparison", "methodological pluralism [is] more credible than methodological unity" (Waldner 2007, p. 160). Thus, largescale quantitative comparative research should be complemented by qualitative methods using a small number of cases (Abadie et al. 2015). This includes the selection of exemplary cases for comparison, in other words the selection of the most suitable counterfactual worlds, as in the comparison of Jamaica and Singapore. Bo Rothstein (2011) engages in such an exercise of causal comparison between these two countries. He carefully rules out a number of hypotheses on what accounted for the success of Singapore in improving the overall well-being of its citizens, including security, and the failure of Jamaica to do the same. Accordingly, he rejected democracy as a cause of the improvement of the quality of institutions, as Singapore is an authoritarian state. Further, he compared Singapore's trajectory to other Asian states with similar specific (Asian) cultural values to test whether these were responsible for Singapore's success. Given the diversity of trajectories among these states, he could firmly rule out that Asian values had played a major role in the overall success of Singapore. Rothstein concludes that it is the continuous improvement of the quality of government, education and housing policies, as well as a functioning bureaucracy that accounts for Singapore's trajectory in contrast to Jamaica. His finding from the comparison of these two countries that democracy had no role in shaping the huge differences in outcomes was later corroborated for a large global sample of countries (Rothstein 2015). Looking particularly at lethal violence (homicide) Manuel Eisner (Box 10, UNODC 2019) uses the reference point of Hong Kong for testing any control impact of the death penalty that Singapore retained, and Hong Kong abolished. Actually, both countries/cities embarked on a similar downward trajectory of homicide, which rules out capital punishment as a causal mechanism. All these are examples of diligent and fair causal comparisons that will help to provide evidence on system-wide change and programme implementation. Comparative research, whether case by case comparisons or with large samples, is a necessary corollary of the implementation of the United Nations 2030 Sustainable Development Agenda, and its goals for justice and security.

5 Addressing United Nations Sustainable Goals: Scaling Criminology

With the Sustainable Goal (SDG 16) of "promot(ing) peaceful and inclusive societies" (UN General Assembly 2015) the United Nations have acknowledged that violence in conflicts and other forms of violence are closely connected; consequently, policies addressing violence need to target both, violent conflicts as well as interpersonal violence. Criminology offers exceptional opportunities to address this goal and meet the challenge of addressing both types of violence. By focusing on the 'small picture', criminology has amassed evidence on individuals, groups, places and areas. The small picture can be linked to the big picture: we can link macro and micro-level approaches in the prevention of all types of violence, and in larger contexts test policies already validated in small settings. This makes criminology multi- or inter-scalar, which implies crossing disciplinary and domain boundaries, as well as moving between small spaces and larger ones, and between interpersonal and group-driven conflict violence. Evidence-based policies for violent crimes on the neighbourhood level can be 'scaled up' to prevent atrocity crimes and mass violence. In the opposite direction, evidence from comparative conflict and peace research can be scaled down to prevent crimes in neighbourhoods and cities. We term this approach as 'scaling criminology' (Karstedt 2017), and violence is an exemplary case to demonstrate its usefulness.

5.1 Scaling Up: From Urban to Conflict Violence

Patterns of street crime and situations of extreme violence, where atrocity crimes happen, have much in common. Both are highly concentrated in 'hot spots', they are contagious, and they spread to proximate areas through networks, violent peers and 'bad' neighbours (Karstedt 2013a). Promising evidence-based crime policies therefore can be scaled up from street crime to high-risk conflict zones. These include the principles of hot-spot policing, namely the focused and intermittent, non-permanent deployment of police to a small number of hot spots of violence; programmes to reduce gang violence; and the 'dynamic concentration of deterrence' and 'lever-pulling policing' (see Karstedt 2013b).

In particular, dynamic concentration of deterrence and lever-pulling policing are sequenced and dialogical interventions whether deployed by police or other security forces. They are based on four principles: selective focusing and targeting different levels and networks of actors; communication and dialogue including all groups and whole communities; future orientation of preventing violence rather than prosecuting past violence; and a broad range of interventions that are designed for step-wise escalation (Abt 2019). The concentration of resources and targets makes these practices particularly adaptive to an environment where control is contested, where the capacity of protective forces is low, and criminal justice agencies are institutionally weak. Public commitment to targeted and intensive enforcement focused on future crimes thus can support the monitoring of specific types of violence, or of a group of known and identified violent perpetrators. Concentration, selectivity and direct communication may address the major problem of credibility when creating secure areas and deter violent action in conflict zones (Karstedt 2013b).

5.2 *Scaling Down: Peace Building in Neighbourhoods*

In contrast to 'scaling up', 'scaling down' imports evidence from other domains and disciplines into criminology. Criminology can hugely profit from comparative research on peace negotiations, peace building and conflict settlement, and apply this evidence for violence reduction and prevention at the local level of urban neighbourhoods and cities. Crime policies in neighbourhoods can take advantage of evidence that shows that ceasefires, and full or partial settlements are successful in more than half of the cases, and only a minority fail completely. Violence significantly subsides before and after peace accords (Karstedt 2012b), and two thirds of peace agreements lead to stable solutions over time. If violence recurs, it mostly does at a lower level of victimisation. Mediation and negotiation are nearly always the best options to end violence in situations of conflict and extreme violence (see for an overview Karstedt 2017). It is crucial that efforts at mediation need to be repeated: a one-shot intervention is mostly not enough. These are important lesson for the local level and violence in neighbourhoods and cities. As evidence from Latin American cities shows, consistency across a prolonged time period is a decisive part of successful strategies to reduce violence in major cities (de Mello and Schneider 2010).

6 A Future for Comparative Criminology

Just like comparative political science, comparative criminology has a huge potential for generating evidence for policy making. "Big picture" criminology encompasses global comparisons between countries, regions, and cities, or even neighbourhoods across the globe. Comparative criminologists work in an extended laboratory comprising of cities, communities, regions, and countries, including cross-level combinations and comparisons. We need to unlock this evidence with improvements in data, analytical methods, and new modes of conceptual thinking. A focus on quality of governance in criminal justice opens up the route from being a descriptive and explanatory enterprise to becoming more policy relevant. Comparative criminology has the capacity to identify contexts, conditions and time-lines for policies that make societies and communities more successful in reducing crime and promoting justice. "Big picture criminology" adds to this its particular institutional perspective (Rosenfeld 2011), and offers insights into building the institutional framework that supports the 2030 Agenda's "peaceful and inclusive societies" (SDG 16). Criminology has unique advantages when it comes to evidence on the micro-level of individuals, spaces and places, which can be explored for use on a larger scale and macro-level. Comparative criminologists from the global South and North have the toolkit to provide evidence how to be 'smart on crime', and create the just and peaceful societies that citizens across the globe want and expect.

References

A/RES/70/1 Transforming our world: the 2030 Agenda for Sustainable Development 25 September 2015

Abadie, A., Diamond, A., & Hainmueller, J. (2015). Comparative politics and the synthetic control method. *American Journal of Political Science, 592*, 495–510.

Abt, T. (2019). *Bleeding out*. New York: Basic Books.

Barber, B. R. (2013). *If mayors ruled the world. Dysfunctional nations, rising cities*. New Haven-London: Yale University Press.

Baumer, E. P., & Wolff, K. T. (2014). The breadth and causes of contemporary cross-national homicide trends. *Crime and Justice, 43*, 231–287.

Davis, K. E., Fisher, A., Kingsbury, B., & Engle Merry, S. (Eds.). (2012). *Governance by indicators. Global power through quantification and ranking*. Oxford: Oxford University Press.

De Mello, J. M. P., & Schneider, A. (2010). Assessing Sao Paulo's large drop in homicides. In R. Di Tella, S. Edwards, & E. Schargrodsky (Eds.), *The economics of crime. Lessons for and from Latin America* (pp. 207–238). Chicago: University of Chicago Press.

Eisner, M., Nivette, A., Murraya, A. L., & Krisch, M. (2016). Achieving population-level violence declines: Implications of the international crime drop for prevention programming. *Journal of Public Health Policy, 37*, 66–80.

Engle Merry, S. (2016). *The seductions of quantification. Measuring human rights, gender violence and sex trafficking*. Chicago, London: University of Chicago Press.

Engle Merry, S., Davis, K. E., & Kingsbury, B. (Eds.). (2015). *The quiet power of indicators. Measuring governance, corruption and rule of law*. Cambridge: Cambridge University Press.

Foltz, J. D., & Opoku-Agyemang, K. A. (2015). Do higher salaries lower petty corruption? *A Policy Experiment on West Africa's Highways*, 1–47.

Halleroed, B., Rothstein, B., & Daoud, A. (2013). Bad governance and poor children: A comparative analysis of government efficiency and severe child deprivation in 68 low- and middle-income countries. *World Development, 48*(1), 19–31.

Hoelscher, K., & Nussio, E. (2016). Understanding unlikely successes in urban violence reduction. *Urban Studies, 53*(11), 2397–2416.

Holmberg, S., & Rothstein, B. (2011). Dying of corruption. *Health Economics, Policy and Law, 6*, 529–547.

Karstedt, S. (2012a). *Justice, security and women's health: A global perspective, Founders Day Lecture*. Nigeria: Nigerian Institute of Advanced Legal Studies, Lagos

Karstedt, S. (2012b). Contextualising mass atrocity crimes: The dynamics of extremely violent societies. *European Journal of Criminology, 9*(5), 499–513.

Karstedt, S. (2013a, June 13). *Global hot spots of violence: Exploring the paradox of state strength and weakness. Nigel Walker Lecture*. Institute of Criminology, University of Cambridge

Karstedt, S. (2013b). Contextualizing mass atrocity crimes: Moving towards a relational approach. *Annual Review of Law and Social Sciences, 9*, 383–404.

Karstedt, S. (2015). Does democracy matter? Comparative perspectives on violence and democratic institutions. *European Journal of Criminology, 12*(4), 457–481.

Karstedt, S. (2017). Scaling criminology: From street violence to atrocity crimes. In P. Drahos (Ed.), *Regulatory theory: Foundations and applications* (pp. 466–482). Acton: ANU Press. Available at https://bit.ly/3dky8Rq

Karstedt, S. (2018). Is big picture criminology policy relevant? Comparative criminology, evidence-based policy and the scale of our discipline, European Criminology Award Acceptance Speech. *Criminology in Europe, 17*(3), 4–9.

Karstedt, S. (2019a). Global imprisonment. In R. D. Morgan (Ed.), *The SAGE Encyclopedia of criminal psychology* (pp. 577–580). Thousand Oaks: SAGE Publications.

Karstedt, S. (2019b). Inequality and punishment: The Latin American experience. In P. Carlen & L. Ayres França (Eds.), *Justice alternatives* (pp. 470–489). London: Routledge.

LaFree, G., Curtis, K., & McDowall, D. (2015). How effective are our 'better angels?' Evidence for a world-wide decline in homicide since 1950. *European Journal of Criminology, 12*(4), 482–504.

Lapuente, V., & Rothstein, B. (2014). Civil war Spain versus Swedish harmony: The quality of government factor. *Comparative Political Studies, 47*(10), 1416–1441.

Leigh, A. (2018). *Randomistas. How radical researchers are changing our world*. New Haven: Yale University Press.

Lijphart, A. (1971). Comparative politics and the comparative method. *The American Political Science Review, 65*(3), 682–693.

Miethe, T. D., Troshinsky, E. I., & Hart, T. C. (2017). Social conditions and cross-national imprisonment rates: Using set-theoretic methods for theory testing and identifying deviant cases. *Journal of Contemporary Criminal Justice, 32*(2), 152–172.

Nagin, D. S., & Sampson, R. J. (2019). The real gold standard: Measuring counterfactual worlds that matter most to social science and policy. *Annual Review of Criminology, 2*, 123–145.

Nivette, A. (2011). Cross-national predictors of crime: A meta-analysis. *Homicide Studies, 15*(2), 103–131.

Piketty, T. (2015). *The economics of inequality*. Cambridge MA.: Harvard University Press.

Pinker, S. (2011). *The better angels of our nature. The decline of violence in history and its causes*. London - New York: Allan Lane.

Reiman, J. H. (1997). *The rich get richer and the poor get prison: Ideology, class and criminal justice*. London, New York: Pearson Education.

Rivera, M. (2016). The sources of social violence in Latin America: An empirical analysis of homicide rates 1980-2010. *Journal of Peace Research, 431*, 84–99.

Rosenfeld, R. (2011). The big picture: 2010 Presidential address to the American Society of Criminology. *Criminology, 49*(1), 1–26.

Rosling, H. (with Rosling, O. and Rosling Roennlund, A). (2018). *Factfulness*. London: Sceptre

Rothstein, B. (2011). *Quality of government*. Chicago: University of Chicago.

Rothstein, B. (2015). Guilty as charged? Human well-being and the unsung relevance of political science. In G. Stoker, G. Peters, & J. Pierre (Eds.), *The relevance of political science* (pp. 84–103). New York: Palgrave Macmillan.

Stoker, G., Peters, G., & Pierre, J. (Eds.). (2015). *The relevance of political science*. New York: Palgrave Macmillan.

Tankebe, J., Karstedt, S., & Adu-Poku, S. (2019). Corruption intentions among prospective elites in Ghana: An economy of esteem. *International Criminal Justice Review, 29*(2), 168–186.

UNODC. (2019). *Global Study on Homicide 2019: Homicide trends, patterns and criminal justice response*. Vienna: UNODC https://bit.ly/2W6r7On, Box 10, Historical perspective: What the past can teach about reducing homicide. Historical homicide trends in Jamaica and Singapore (provided by Manuel Eisner).

Waldner, D. (2007). Transforming inferences into explanations: Lessons from the study of mass extinction. In R. N. Lebow & M. I. Lichbach (Eds.), *Theory and evidence in comparative politics and international relations* (pp. 145–175). New York: Palgrave Macmillan.

Wilkinson, R., & Pickett, K. (2009). *The spirit level*. London: Penguin.

World Bank. (2011). *Violence in the city*. Washington, D.C.: World Bank.

World Bank. (2015). *World development report. Mind, society and behavior*. Washington, D.C.: World Bank Group.

World Bank. (2017). *World development report. Governance and the law*. Washington, D.C.: World Bank Group.

Susanne Karstedt since 2015 is a Professor in the School of Criminology and Criminal Justice at Griffith University (Australia). She previously held Chairs in Criminology at the University of Leeds and Keele University (UK), and positions at the Universities of Bielefeld and Hamburg (Germany). She has widely researched and written on cross-national and cross-cultural comparisons of crime and justice, including violence, corruption, state and white collar crime, as well as prisons and the criminal justice system, with a focus on the impact of democratic values and structures. Other research areas include atrocity crimes and transitional justice, and the role of emotions in crime and justice. Her work has been recognised by several awards, including the Thorsten Sellin and Eleanor and Sheldon Glueck Award of the American Society of Criminology (2007), the International Award of the Law and Society Association (2016), the European Criminology Award 2018, and most recently the Freda Adler Award from the International Division of the American Society of Criminology (2019). E-mail: s.karstedt@griffith.edu.au.

Part VI
Countering Art Crime and Violence

United Nations Perspective on Preventing Transnational Organised Crime Against Cultural Property in the Era of Sustainable Development and Restitution Arguments

Kamil Zeidler and Julia Stepnowska

Abstract Article 27 of the Universal Declaration of Human Rights states that "Everyone has the right freely to participate in the cultural life of the community, to enjoy the arts and to share in scientific advancement and its benefits." Needless to say, the protection of cultural property is crucial to safeguarding cultural identity, one of our basic human rights. The protection of the world's cultural heritage is one of the goals included in the 2030 UN Sustainable Development Agenda. Combating transnational organised crime against cultural property, including the illicit trade in art and antiquities, requires fostering international cooperation and drawing conclusions from past and future restitution cases. This chapter discusses the endeavours of the UN and other major stakeholders in protecting cultural property and presents a set of arguments that can serve as a toolkit in restitution disputes.

Keywords Cultural heritage · Cultural property · Organised crime · Restitution arguments · Sustainable development

1 Introduction

The international trade in looted, stolen or smuggled cultural property is roughly estimated at several billion US dollars per year (Trioschi 2018). However, neither the monetary value of the illicit trade nor its magnitude as a global phenomenon can be specified (Manacorda and Chappell 2011). In spite of the efforts of many international stakeholders to validate information on the scale and nature of this issue (e.g. International Council of Museums/ICOM's International Observatory on Illicit

K. Zeidler
University of Gdańsk, Faculty of Law and Administration, Department of Theory and Philosophy of State and Law, Gdańsk, Poland
e-mail: kamil.zeidler@ug.edu.pl

J. Stepnowska (✉)
University of Gdańsk, Gdańsk, Poland

H. Kury, S. Redo (eds.), *Crime Prevention and Justice in 2030*,
https://doi.org/10.1007/978-3-030-56227-4_25

Traffic in Cultural Goods), provide legal reference (e.g. United Nations Educational, Scientific and Cultural Organization (UNESCO), International Institute for the Unification of Private Law (UNIDROIT), and to effectively fight this problem (e.g. The International Criminal Police Organization (INTERPOL); see: Kind 2011, pp. 175–183). The combat of illicit trafficking in cultural property remains an ongoing task requiring strengthening and coordinating cross-border cooperation, a task carried out by such actors as the United Nations Office on Drugs and Crime (UNODC).

Nowadays, crimes against cultural property are more and more often linked to organised crime, including money laundering and financing terrorism (Jakubowski and Trzciński 2019; United Nations Security Council 2017, S/RES/2347).[1] International Guidelines for Crime Prevention and Criminal Justice Responses with Respect to Trafficking in Cultural Property and Other Related Offences (United Nations General Assembly 2014, A/RES/69/196, Annex para. 16), specify the following serious offences regarding cultural property:

- trafficking in cultural property;
- illicit export and illicit import of cultural property;
- theft of cultural property (or consider elevating the offence of ordinary theft to a serious offence when it involves cultural property);
- looting of archaeological and cultural sites and/or illicit excavation;
- conspiracy or participation in an organised criminal group for trafficking in cultural property and related offences;
- laundering of trafficked cultural property.

Illicit trade in cultural property is often transnational in nature. However, unlike other transnational organised crimes, e.g. illicit drug trafficking, illicit trafficking in cultural objects is not illegal everywhere and can be easily "funnelled" into the legitimate market (Tijhuis 2011, p. 88). Phenomena specific to crimes against cultural property include: loopholes in national legislation (protection of bona fide purchasers), false export licenses (corruption), false provenance documentation, or illicit Internet auctions. Moreover, the population of participants operating in this area is highly diversified and the criminal networks they form are "fluid" (Campbell 2013, p. 115).

Despite the multitude of legal instruments aiming at combating crimes against cultural property, effective prevention is possible only if one takes recommendations from past restitution cases into consideration. This chapter discusses the efforts of the UN and other international organisations and stakeholders in protecting cultural property with a special focus on restitution means and presents a set of case-based

[1] *. . .the Islamic State in Iraq and the Levant (ISIL, also known as Da'esh), Al-Qaida and associated individuals, groups, undertakings and entities are generating income from engaging directly or indirectly in the illegal excavation and in the looting and smuggling of cultural property from archaeological sites, museums, libraries, archives, and other sites, which is being used to support their recruitment efforts and to strengthen their operational capability to organize and carry out terrorist attacks. . .*

arguments that can be applied in restitution disputes. In line with the 2030 UN Sustainable Development Agenda, the authors recognise the necessity to foster international cooperation through available international legal instruments and to promote the knowledge of restitution arguments reflecting social and economic factors.

2 Restitution of Cultural Property

The protection of cultural property comprises of two main strands of activity: prevention and pursuit. Restitution is a response to various offences, not only during wartime, as it is frequently presumed. The problem of illicit movement and trade in cultural property and its restitution was first addressed at the international level by the League of Nations, however, its instruments proved unworkable (Forrest 2012, p. 134). The draft Convention on the Repatriation of Objects of Artistic, Historical or Scientific Interest, Which Have Been Lost, Stolen or Unlawfully Alienated or Exported (International Museums Office 1933) did not provide a distinction between private and public heritage, moreover, it omitted objects from archaeological excavations and side-lined intra-state claims by minorities or indigenous communities moved to national collections (Vrdoljak 2006, p. 113). The outbreak of the Second World War put an end to the development of these efforts.

Grave damage caused to cultural property during WWII highlighted the necessity to improve the existing protective measures. The Convention for the Protection of Cultural Property in the Event of Armed Conflict and its First Protocol regarding the export and seizure of cultural property were adopted in 1954 as a result of a diplomatic conference organised by the UNESCO and the Dutch government (Van der Auwera 2013, p. 176). However, the horrific events that followed its adoption, e.g. the Khmer Rouge regime in Cambodia or the wars in the Balkans (Davis 2015; Van der Auwera 2013) triggered the adoption of the Second Protocol to the 1954 Convention in 1999 to introduce the applicability of the Convention to non-international armed conflicts or the enhancement of individual criminal responsibility.

In 1960s, UNESCO approached the subject of protecting cultural property during peacetime to satisfy the need of newly independent states to recover cultural heritage forming part of museum collections of the former colonising states and the ongoing loss of their property due to looting and illicit trafficking practices (Prott 2012, p. 2). The 1970 UNESCO Convention on the Means of Prohibiting and Preventing the Illicit Import, Export and Transfer of Ownership of Cultural Property is a response to this need, however the universality of its three "pillars"—preventive measures at the national level, restitution of stolen cultural property, and the promotion of international cooperation (Delepierre and Schneider 2015)—permitted for a large number of ratifications (to date, 140 Member States of UNESCO have ratified the convention).

In spite of the adoption of these instruments, the question of privately-owned property and the disparities at the national level with regards to the protection of bona fide purchasers still remained unanswered. The International Institute for the Unification of Private Law (UNIDROIT), was approached by UNESCO Member States to provide an instrument aiming at harmonising private law in respect to the possessors of (precisely) cultural goods stolen (and/or illegally exported) from a source country, transferred across the border and "laundered," thus considered to be "in good faith" under some local laws (Delepierre and Schneider 2015, pp. 132–133). The 1995 UNIDROIT Convention on Stolen or Illegally Exported Cultural Objects (2421 UNTS 457) aims at reducing trafficking by changing the approach of buyers by providing ground due diligence rules and the obligation to return a stolen object in all cases is undoubtedly one of the key signifiers of the Convention (see also: Schneider 2016).

These milestone conventions are complemented by soft law instruments such as the ICOM Code of Ethics for Museums or the International Code of Ethics for Dealers in Cultural Property (CLT/CH/INS.06/25 Rev). The latter was adopted by the UNESCO intergovernmental Committee for Promoting the Return of Cultural Property to its Countries of Origin or its Restitution in Case of Illicit Appropriation in 1999 and it aimed at harmonising national codes and eliminating illicit trade on the part of dealers bound by its principles. While the professional community involved in acquiring cultural objects, i.e. art dealers and museums, might have questioned the effectiveness of these tools, their role in combating crimes against cultural property cannot be underestimated due to their standard-setting and educational purpose (O'Keefe 1994).

Nonetheless, the development of organised crime against cultural property at the beginning of the twenty-first century, especially resulting from the turmoil of armed conflicts in the Middle East, triggered the adoption of tailored resolutions by the United Nations[2] to foster international cooperation to "continue to address the issue of return or restitution of cultural property to the countries of origin" (A/RES/56/97) and "to strengthen international cooperation and mutual assistance in the prevention and prosecution of crime against movable property that forms part of the cultural heritage of peoples" (ECOSOC resolution 2004/34). The main tool in this regard, the UN Convention against Transnational Organized Crime (A/RES/55/25) aims at providing "the necessary legal framework for international cooperation in combating, inter alia, such criminal activities as money-laundering, corruption, illicit trafficking in endangered species of wild flora and fauna, offences against cultural heritage and the growing links between transnational organized crime and terrorist crimes."

UN instruments play a valid role not only in strengthening the means of protecting property during ongoing armed conflicts but also in recovering from colonial rule. The restitution of indigenous heritage, especially of spiritual nature, plays a key role in recovering from "the effects of post-colonial trauma" (Simpson

[2]For example, S/RES/1483 (2003) or S/RES/2347 (2017).

2009, p. 122) in many cases. The recent shift in perceiving cultural heritage as a mere transmitter of the past to recognising its role for living cultures is reflected in the 2007 United Nations Declaration on the Rights of Indigenous Peoples (UNDRIP, A/61/295).

One of the recent key developments responding to actions involving the destruction and misplacement of cultural property is the Doha Declaration on integrating crime prevention and criminal justice into the wider United Nations agenda to address social and economic challenges and to promote the rule of law at the national and international levels, and public participation (A/RES/70/174, Annex). Its goals concerning the problem of illicit trafficking in cultural property involve strengthening and implementing comprehensive crime prevention and criminal justice response, reviewing domestic legislation, collecting and sharing intelligence and statistical data on the issue and further analysing and improving the model treaty for the prevention of crimes that infringe on the cultural heritage of peoples in the form of movable property and international standards and norms in this field.

While the obligations resulting from conventions certainly put pressure on market states to return cultural objects when related to an illegal activity, soft law instruments may be a more attractive solution given their co-operational approach (Taşdelen 2016). The element of mutual understanding proves to play a key role in restitution disputes. According to Stamatoudi (2011, p. 253), there are two views on restitution: the nationalist and the cosmopolitan. However, it may be concluded that due to the universal value of cultural heritage, the boundaries between these two opposing perspectives may be blurred by other considerations emerging in the process of restitution. The direction imposed by UNESCO, UNIDROIT, European Union law, and soft law in general is that "a nation is the most appropriate custodian of its own cultural heritage" (Stamatoudi 2011, p. 253). This notion considers factors related to geography, history, cultural identity and does not counter preservation of cultural heritage for all humankind. The main idea behind restitution is to enable cultural diversity, thus achieving one of sustainable development goals.

3 The Role of Restitution in Achieving Sustainable Development Goals

The concept of sustainable development involves improving the quality of life with respect to national and local ethnic and cultural diversity guaranteeing the wholesomeness of the quality of life for future generations (Alliance for the Sustainable Development of Central America 1994). It may be concluded that the restitution of cultural heritage serves exactly that.[3] The significance of preserving cultural heritage in the context of sustainable development is captured in the Preamble to the 2005

[3]See: Appendix D(6) to the Alliance for the Sustainable Development of Central America 1994.

UNESCO Convention on the Protection and Promotion of the Diversity of Cultural Expressions.[4]

Strengthening the "efforts to protect and safeguard the world's cultural and natural heritage" is classified as a means towards achieving the greater goal of "making cities and human settlements inclusive, safe, resilient and sustainable" under the 2030 UN Sustainable Development Agenda, however, it needs to be stressed that other goals included in the agenda, e.g. promoting sustainable economic growth or fostering innovation, are highly dependent on the condition of cultural heritage.[5]

Causing physical harm to cultural property jeopardises the idea of sustainable development has a lasting effect on our identity, moreover, the intentional damage to heritage "may have adverse consequences on human dignity and human rights" (UNESCO 2003). Therefore, all forms of countering crimes against cultural objects are crucial for safeguarding our cultural identity and improving the quality of our lives. Restitution of cultural property serves the purpose of re-shaping lost identity and the argumentation utilised in this context should respect the intangible value of heritage to both parties of a dispute.

4 Restitution Arguments

Disputes concerning cultural property often raise sensitive issues, e.g. as in the case of spiritual attachment of indigenous peoples to a given object, and may require more "sustainable and creative solutions" (Bandle and Theurich 2011, p. 30). The uniqueness of cultural property as compared to other goods results from its intangible value that cannot be compensated in full by monetary means, therefore the aim of restitution is to take the multifaceted nature of the object into consideration to reach a sustainable solution. When looking at legal instruments approaching the subject of combatting crimes against cultural property, one cannot help but wonder, *Do these measures reflect the complexity of cultural property restitution or should one go beyond these provisions to reach a just and fair solution?*

Restitution of cultural property should not only serve justice—its primary aim should be to preserve cultural heritage for present and future generations, therefore

[4]*…Affirming that cultural diversity is a defining characteristic of humanity, Conscious that cultural diversity forms a common heritage of humanity and should be cherished and preserved for the benefit of all, Being aware that cultural diversity creates a rich and varied world, which increases the range of choices and nurtures human capacities and values, and therefore is a mainspring for sustainable development for communities, peoples and nations…*

[5]See Article 7 of the 2001 UNESCO Universal Declaration on Cultural Diversity: *Creation draws on the roots of cultural tradition, but flourishes in contact with other cultures. For this reason, heritage in all its forms must be preserved, enhanced and handed on to future generations as a record of human experience and aspirations, so as to foster creativity in all its diversity and to inspire genuine dialogue among cultures.*

restitution arguments should reflect any and all factors related to the object in question and satisfy the need to preserve it in the best condition possible. A proper investigation into legal philosophy of cultural property restitution shows us that the discourse involves law, ethics, politics and economy.

The argumentation presented below includes moral, social, and economic considerations necessary to reach a moderate solution. The working model for the analysis of restitution cases developed by Zeidler (2016, pp. 136–202) could prove useful in disputes and is categorised as instances of legal (practical) discourse, employing methods native to the theory of argumentation. Reviewing actual restitution cases identifies the following arguments:

- the argument from justice;
- the argument from ownership;
- the argument from acquisition in good faith;
- the argument from place of production;
- the argument from place of allocation;
- the argument from right of loot;
- the argument from illegal export;
- the argument from national affiliation;
- the argument from cultural affiliation;
- the argument from historical affiliation;
- the argument from territorial affiliation;
- the argument from personal affiliation;
- the argument from social utility;
- the argument from most secure location;
- the argument from historical eventuation;
- the argument from passage of time;
- the argument from prescription;
- the argument from time limitation;
- the argument from discovery;
- the argument from investments undertaken;
- the argument from possession;
- the argument from obligation;
- the argument from reciprocity.

This is a tool for analysis of hard cases involving restitution, and therefore, as a method, the model remains open and flexible. Moreover, this toolkit may also prove valuable in the research into regulatory systems and a perfect example of the notion of transitional justice. Restitution arguments should reflect the goals of sustainable development and these capture the intangible value of cultural heritage. This is clearly reflected in restitution arguments relating to cultural affiliation, social utility, and the most secure location.

The argument from cultural affiliation, refers to the ties of a given object to a specific culture. It is closely connected with the argument from national affiliation, as it is frequently within a particular nation that we can speak of a common culture, also as an "element that defines a nation in an ethnic sense" (Zeidler 2016, p. 168). On the other hand, the value of cultural property often resonates far beyond its culture (or country) of origin. However, despite the globalisation of culture and the development of such notions as the "global heritage" or the "universal heritage of mankind" (Blake 2015, p. 12), the consideration of this argument may result in solutions prioritising the significance of an object to a given ethnic group, especially linked to the place of its creation. This argument may also relate to the spiritual value assigned to an object by a given community, therefore it also reflects its social purpose in a narrower sense. The issue of judgements based on cultural affiliation is typically related to artefacts created and preserved in areas of heterogenous ethnic structure—e.g. where the conflict arises between indigenous peoples and later settlers, i.e. Australasia or North America (Blake 2015, p. 20). While in this group the question of cultural belonging is relatively clear, this issue might emerge at a more complex level, i.e. as in the case of Poland and Ukraine and the collections remaining within the current borders of both countries. In this instance, the argumentation model would need to involve historical, political, and territorial factors, moreover, the level of emotional attachment of the society to a given object or collection should be measured to reach a balanced solution.

The argument from social utility aims at satisfying the need of a broader group of recipients to have access to a cultural good, as opposed to the interest of an individual or a narrow group of individuals (Zeidler 2016, p. 176). This argument refers to the universal social value of cultural property. According to Jones (2016, pp. 21–37), the social value of cultural heritage includes the "sense of identity, belonging and place, as well as forms of memory and spiritual association. These are fluid, culturally specific forms of value created through experience and practice." Exhibiting an object in public, however, is not the only measure to respect its social function—e.g. conducting research, therefore, in this sense, social utility may also refer to the scientific use of a cultural object. On the other hand, even if an object is not easily accessible for the public as this permits for maintaining its original shape, is for the public interest, i.e. maintaining the condition of the object may prove superior to the utility it has for the public at a given time.

This conclusion leads us to the argument from the most secure location. This argument refers to the role of museums in securing objects, however, one must bear in mind that despite the efforts to harmonise the conduct of museums, they are still not always a guarantee of security and the location of a museum needs to be considered. Certain states provide a more satisfactory level of protection (both normative and factual) than others. On the one hand, we may never fully rely on the institution responsible—to some extent, the recent Green Vault heist confirms this assumption (Connolly 2019). On the other, we may never eliminate the human factor and the argument from the most secure location remains a valid point of reference in restitution disputes.

5 Scope of Application

Employing such arguments permits for achieving sustainable solutions. These are clearly visible in cases involving solutions other than simple restitution, for instance: conditional restitution, restitution accompanied by cultural cooperation measures, formal recognition of the importance of a given object to cultural identity, the production of replicas, or setting up special ownership regimes (Cornu and Renold 2010, pp. 19–23).

The application of sustainable argumentation is favoured in alternative means of dispute resolution (ADR). Such mechanisms allow for solutions beyond monetary damages reflecting the intangible value of cultural property. ADR is specifically promoted in the context of Holocaust era assets (see also: e.g. the 1998 Washington Principles; the 2009 Terezin Declaration), however, the argumentation utilised in this case is also applicable to other disputes, e.g. indigenous people's cultural property repatriation claims (Kuprecht 2013, p. 140). The role of ADR in the context of cultural property-related cases is promoted at the international level by various stakeholders, e.g. UNESCO (The Intergovernmental Committee for Promoting the Return of Cultural Property to its Countries of Origin or its Restitution in case of Illicit Appropriation) or ICOM and WIPO (Art and Cultural Heritage Mediation). To exemplify, the restitution of the Makondé Mask to the United Republic of Tanzania, a case involving UNESCO's intergovernmental Committee (ICPRCP), was made possible upon the condition that the item is correctly preserved (Bandle et al. 2013), thus achieving a balance between the argument referring to the security of the object and its social utility.

The arguments presented in the above context serve as a toolkit for approaching restitution disputes, however, one argument may be overridden by other conditions specific to a given object as well as the social or political factors surrounding it. The main conclusion is that restitution as such is not only necessary to achieve sustainable development goals, but also the process itself should respect its principles.

6 Conclusions

We live in times where, on the one hand, the threats to cultural heritage are complex as never before, on the other, the tools which can be used to protect it are equally numerous. There are many international organisations, both governmental and nongovernmental, involved in developing the mechanisms to counter crimes against cultural property. International cooperation is the most efficient means of protecting cultural property and cultural heritage. There are legal bases—multilateral international agreements (conventions) and bilateral agreement, and even more legal acts classified as soft law.

However, the coordination of various projects and tools at the global level still requires more attention, therefore, the role of the United Nations in this regard is essential. The UN could have the most important role in the unification and coordination of the system of cultural heritage protection—not only against organised crimes, but in all possible fields in general. This task is necessary to prevent the advancement and spreading of criminal activities and that is why relevant bodies, agencies, funds and programmes of the UN system and other relevant intergovernmental organisations work in coordination with UNESCO, within their mandates and in cooperation with states, to continue to address the issue of return or restitution of cultural property to the countries of origin and to provide appropriate support accordingly.

It is one thing to act and to encourage all states to take part in activities and the exchange of experiences and the promotion of good practices with regard to countering trafficking in cultural property and with regard to its return or restitution to the countries of origin. It is another thing to do it right. Recalling the 2030 Agenda for Sustainable Development, that includes, *inter alia*, a pledge to foster intercultural understanding, tolerance, mutual respect and an ethic of global citizenship and shared responsibility, an acknowledgement of the natural and cultural diversity of the world and a recognition that all cultures and civilisations can contribute to, and are crucial enablers of, sustainable development, as well as targets related to the protection and return or restitution of cultural property. The best way to initiate this process is to develop the idea of sustainable development in international law first. That is why the role of the UN in the future development of international legal instruments and cooperation is so important.

References[6]

A/RES/55/25 United Nations Convention against Transnational Organized Crime. 15 November 2000.

A/RES/56/97 Return or restitution of cultural property to the countries of origin. 14 December 2001.

A/RES/69/196 International Guidelines for Crime Prevention and Criminal Justice Responses with Respect to Trafficking in Cultural Property and Other Related Offences. 18 December 2014.

A/RES/70/1 Transforming our world: the 2030 agenda for sustainable development. 25 September 2015.

A/RES/70/174 Doha declaration on integrating crime prevention and criminal justice into the wider United Nations agenda to address social and economic challenges and to promote the rule of law at the national and international levels, and public participation. 17 December 2015.

Bandle, A., Contel, R., & Renold, M.A. (2013). Affaire Masque Makondé – Tanzanie et Musée Barbier-Mueller. *Plateforme ArThemis*. https://bit.ly/3fcV4nf

Bandle, A. L., & Theurich, S. (2011). Alternative dispute resolution and art-law – A new research project of the Geneva art-law centre. *Journal of International Commercial Law and Technology, 6*(1), 28–41.

Blake, J. E. (2015). *International cultural heritage law*. Oxford University Press.

[6]All United Nations parliamentary documentation starting with "A" symbol were retrieved from the United Nations website http://www.un.org.

Campbell, P. (2013). The illicit antiquities trade as a transnational criminal network: Characterizing and anticipating trafficking of cultural heritage. *International Journal of Cultural Property, 20* (2), 113–153. https://doi.org/10.1017/S0940739113000015

Connolly, K. (2019, November 25). Jewellery of 'immeasurable worth' stolen in dramatic Dresden museum heist. *The Guardian*. https://bit.ly/3ff1xOv

Cornu, M., & Renold, M. A. (2010). New developments in the restitution of cultural property: alternative means of dispute resolution. *International Journal of Cultural Property, 17*(01), 1–31. https://doi.org/10.1017/S0940739110000044

Davis, T. (2015). The lasting impact of the United States vs. Cambodian cculpture. In F. Desmarais (Ed.), *Countering illicit traffic in cultural goods. The global challenge of protecting the world's heritage* (pp. 95–105). ICOM.

Delepierre, S., & Schneider, M. (2015). *Ratification and implementation of international conventions to fight illicit trafficking in cultural property* (pp. 129–139). ICOM.

ECOSOC resolution 2004/34 Protection against trafficking in cultural property. 21 July 2004. https://bit.ly/2VXhmBI

Forrest, C. (2012). *international law and the protection of cultural heritage*. Routledge.

Jakubowski, O., & Trzciński, M. (2019). Przestępczość przeciwko dziedzictwu kulturowemu - charakterystyka zjawiska. In M. Trzciński (Ed.), *Praktyczne aspekty zwalczania przestępczości przeciwko dziedzictwu kulturowemu* (pp. 85–157). Wydawnictwo Uniwersytetu Gdańskiego.

Jones, S. (2016). Wrestling with the social value of heritage: problems, dilemmas and opportunities. *Journal of Community Archaeology and Heritage, 4*, 1–17. https://doi.org/10.1080/20518196.2016.1193996

Kind, K. H. (2011). The role of INTERPOL in the fight against the illicit trafficking in cultural property. In S. Manacorda & D. Chappell (Eds.), *Crime in the art and antiquities world: Illegal trafficking in cultural property* (pp. 175–183). Springer.

Kuprecht, K. (2013). *Indigenous peoples' cultural property claims: Repatriation and beyond*. Springer.

Manacorda, S., & Chappell, D. (2011). *Crime in the art and antiquities world: Illegal trafficking in cultural property*. Springer.

O'Keefe, P. J. (1994). *Feasibility of an international code of ethics for dealers in cultural property for the purpose of more effective control of illicit traffic in cultural property*. UNESCO. https://bit.ly/2KVcVBg

Prott, L. V. (2012). *Strengths and weaknesses of the 1970 Convention: An evaluation 40 years after its adoption*. UNESCO. https://bit.ly/2WnY8Eq

Schneider, M. (2016). The 1995 UNIDROIT Convention: An Indispensable Component to the 1970 UNESCO Convention and an inspiration for the 2014/60/EU Directive. *Santander Art & Culture Law Review, 2*, 149–164. https://doi.org/10.4467/2450050XSR.16.024.6132

Simpson, M. (2009). Museums and restorative justice: Heritage, repatriation and cultural education. *Museum International, 61*(1–2), 121–129. https://doi.org/10.1111/j.1468-0033.2009.01669.x

Stamatoudi, I. (2011). *Cultural property law and restitution: A commentary to International Conventions and European Union Law*. Edward Elgar.

Taşdelen, A. (2016). *The return of cultural artefacts: Hard and soft law approaches*. Springer.

Tijhuis, E. (2011). The trafficking problem: A criminological perspective. In S. Manacorda & D. Chappell (Eds.), *Crime in the art and antiquities world: Illegal trafficking in cultural property* (pp. 87–979). Springer.

Trioschi, A. (2018). The return of looted archaeological artifacts through the use of alternative dispute resolution methods. *Archeomafie*, (n/v), pp. 35–57.

UNIDROIT. (1995). Convention on stolen or illegally exported cultural objects, United Nations Treaty Series, 2421 UNTS 457.

Van der Auwera, S. (2013). International law and the protection of cultural property in the event of armed conflict: Actual problems and challenges. *The Journal of Arts Management, Law, and Society, 43*(4), 175–190. https://doi.org/10.1080/10632921.2013.841114

Vrdoljak, A. F. (2006). *International law, museums and the return of cultural objects*. Cambridge University Press.

Zeidler, K. (2016). *Restitution of cultural property: Hard case - theory of argumentation - philosophy of law*. Gdańsk University Press – Wolters Kluwer.

Kamil Zeidler is a Professor of Law at the Department of Theory and Philosophy of State and Law, Faculty of Law and Administration, University of Gdańsk (Gdańsk, Poland). Author of more than 400 publications on theory and philosophy of law, legal protection of cultural heritage, and public international law (including: *Restitution of Cultural Property. Hard Case - Theory of Argumentation - Philosophy of Law*, Gdańsk University Press - Wolters Kluwer, Gdańsk-Warsaw 2016); Lectured at many universities in Poland and abroad; member of international scientific associations: *Internationale Vereinigung für Rechts und Sozialphilosophie* (IVR), International Law Association (ILA), International Council on Monuments and Sites (ICOMOS), International Council of Museums (ICOM); Council member (2017–2021) of the International Centre for the Study of the Preservation and Restoration of Cultural Property; Director of the Centre for East Asian Studies at the University of Gdansk. E-mail: kamil.zeidler@ug.edu.pl.

Julia Stepnowska is a Ph.D. candidate at the University of Gdańsk (Gdańsk, Poland). Her research concerns cultural property law and the art market. She holds a Master's Degree in Arts Management from Neoma Business School (Rouen, France). She has authored and co-authored articles on cultural property restitution and due diligence on the art market, e.g., *The Blood Antiquities Convention. A Remedy or Disappointment? The Case of Cambodia,* "Gdańskie Studia Azji Wschodniej" 2019; J. Stepnowska, K. Zeidler, *The Case of Polish Museums Holding Cultural Objects "in Trust" After WWII* [in:] *Treuhänderische Übernahme und Verwahrung: International und interdisziplinär betrachtet,* Vienna Univeristy Press; J. Stepnowska, *Due Diligence and the Art Market. Assessing the Impact of the 1995 UNIDROIT Convention on Stolen or Illegally Exported Cultural Objects*, "Studia Iuridica Toruniensia" 2018. She has worked as an art advisor (Galerie Montmartre and Espace Dalí, Paris, France), supported the Ministry of Culture and National Heritage throughout the 41st session of the World Heritage Committee, translated and proofread numerous articles on cultural heritage. She coordinates the 1995 UNIDROIT Convention Academic Project (UCAP) at the Faculty of Law and Administration of the University of Gdańsk. E-mail: stepnowska.julia@gmail.com.

Reducing Violent Crime by 50% Before 2030: Decisive Action Now to Achieve These SDGs

Irvin Waller

Abstract Globally each year, half a million persons are victims of homicide, 25 million women are raped, and one billion children are victims of violence. Governments committed to the Sustainable Development Goals (SDGs 16.1, 5.2, 16.2) to reduce dramatically the numbers of victims of violent crime by 2030, but action is needed now.

This chapter proposes ways to get actions to dramatically reduce violence by 2030. It explains solutions that violence prevention science shows are effective and cost effective and how to find out more. It shows how to implement these solutions by learning from city successes and government difficulties in following the essentials agreed in UN legal instruments. It identifies how to foster sustainable and smarter investments by policy makers.

It calls on faith-based organizations, civil society, and cities to spearhead decisive action, in partnership with UN agencies and pathfinder governments, by five initiatives: (i) get to know the science, the essentials for success, and how to get buy in; (ii) raise awareness among politicians and the public of effective solutions and strategies, using modern communication tools; (iii) foster the human talent to implement effective strategies successfully; (iv) act locally to deliver effective solutions; and (v) work collaboratively to convince policy makers to invest now, including policy proposals based on effective solutions and strategies.

Keywords Prevention, violent crime, Sustainable Development Goals, SDG 16, SDG 5, faith-based Organizations · Non-governmental organizations · Civil society · Science · Violence prevention · Planning · Evidence · Data · Homicide · Rape · Violence against children · Cities · UNODC · WHO · UN-Habitat · Crime prevention guidelines

---

I. Waller (✉)
University of Ottawa, Ottawa, ON, Canada
e-mail: iwaller@uottawa.ca

H. Kury, S. Redo (eds.), *Crime Prevention and Justice in 2030*,
https://doi.org/10.1007/978-3-030-56227-4_26

1 Introduction

Globally each year, half a million victims will be murdered (UNODC 2019), an estimated 25 million women raped (Waller 2019, pp. 9–10), and one billion children victims of violence (World Health Organization 2016b). These victims suffer injuries, pain, trauma, financial loss, and more (ibidem). They are often the most vulnerable and disadvantaged. Where these tragedies have reached epidemic proportions, they threaten economic development and reduce the Gross Domestic Product. They threaten democracy and rule of law (World Bank 2011; Inter-American Development Bank 2018; Muggah 2019).

Government leaders committed in the Sustainable Development Goals (SDGs 16.1, 5.2, 16.2) to reduce dramatically the numbers of victims of violent crime by 2030. But the road to hell is paved with good intentions as governments have not acted to achieve them. The head of the UNODC stated that unless the international community takes decisive steps, targets under Sustainable Development Goal 16 to significantly reduce all forms of violence and related death rates by 2030 will not be met (UNODC 2019, p. 1). This statement could equally be made about gender-based violence and violence against children. So, how can they take decisive action now?

Violence is on the rise in certain regions of the world, but it doesn't have to be. In fact, the world possesses the knowledge, tools, institutional structures, legal instruments, and data-collection capacity to halve violence, in all its forms, within a decade (Locke and Steven 2019, p. 1). This chapter builds on a book written for policy makers, faith-based organizations and non-governmental organizations, entitled the "Science and Secrets for Ending Violent Crime" (Waller 2019). It shows that the science of violence prevention is solid but not yet widely known or used by policy makers. It highlights and explains the solutions that have been proven scientifically to prevent violent crime before it happens. It shows these solutions to be more effective and cost effective than over-relying on a reactive criminal justice system after crime has victimized people. It focuses on guidelines, agreed at UN bodies such as UNODC, UN Habitat and WHO that are little known but are essentials for governments to successfully implement that science and achieve sustained reductions in victimization. It shares some inspiring examples of cities that have acted consistently with these essentials to achieve dramatic reductions in homicides within as little as 3 years.

So, this chapter proposes practical actions now to dramatically reduce violence by 2030. It calls on faith-based organizations, civil society, and cities to spear head decisive action, in partnership with UN agencies and pathfinder governments, by five initiatives: (i) get to know the science, the essentials for success, and how to get buy in; (ii) raise awareness among politicians and the public of effective solutions and strategies, using modern communication tools; (iii) foster the human talent to implement effective strategies successfully; (iv) act locally to deliver effective solutions; (v) work collaboratively to convince policy makers to invest now, including policy proposals based on effective solutions and strategies.

The stakes are high. The science and successes show that a 50% reduction in violent crime is achievable by 2030 (Waller 2019; Locke and Steven 2019). Globally, this reduction saves 250,000 lives from homicide for the target in SDG 16.1, more than ten million women from rape for the target in SDG 5.2 and half a billion children from violence for the target in SDG 16.2. The innovations needed are in the interests of governments by spending money better, managing cities to make cities safer, investing in disadvantaged families, and legislating support for affordable, popular, and cost-effective preventive solutions. In high violence countries and communities, it will increase GDP and well-being (Waller 2019).

2 The Challenges and Hidden Consequences of Violent Crime

2.1 *How Much Violent Crime?*

The challenge seems insurmountable when we are immersed in the discourse of reactive justice. We have lived decades of perfecting a system of criminal justice that has not been enough and is sadly still flawed.

While some citizens of some countries live fewer tragic events, the global picture is disturbing and unfortunately more disturbing than policy makers realize. According to the UNODC report on global trends in homicide, there were 475,000 homicides in 2017 (UNODC 2019). Criminal activity is responsible for many more deaths worldwide than armed conflict and terrorism combined. Europe has seen a decline in the homicide rate by 63% since 2002 and by 38% since 1990. The rate in Asia has fallen by 36% since 1990. (UNODC 2019, p. 1) In the USA, mass shootings dominate the headlines, but it is street violence that leads to far and away the most homicides and serious injuries (Waller 2019). The Americas continue to report high homicide rates. Young men are especially at risk, with a homicide rate for men aged 18 to 29 estimated at 46 per 100,000—far higher than the risk faced by their peers in other regions. 2.5 million People murdered since 2000 in Latin America (Muggah 2019).

We know that within nations, rates of homicide are above epidemic levels of 10 per 100,000 particularly in cities and indeed within particular zip codes or their equivalent within those cities (Waller 2019). Among the 50 most homicide ridden cities in the world, 15 are in Mexico, 14 in Brazil, and four in the USA (Business Insider 2019). We know much about the correlates of these epidemic levels, including their association with relative poverty, availability of handguns, impunity, and a continuing illicit drug trade (UNODC 2019). Firearms are involved far more often in homicides in the Americas than in other parts of the world.

But violent crime is not just homicides and street violence. Intimate partner and sexual violence ruin the lives of countless adults and children (Waller 2019). In the USA, the Centers for Disease Control and Prevention (CDC) pioneered a model survey on Intimate Partner and Sexual Violence confirming shocking numbers of young women who will be raped—likely over a million each year (CDC 2011; Waller 2019). If the rates across the world were similar, this would be more than 25 million women raped each year.

Globally, one billion children and youth have suffered physical, sexual, or psychological violence in the past year. The numbers are stark. . . . A quarter of all children experience physical violence, and 20% of girls and 7% of boys are affected by sexual abuse. (WHO 2016b, p. ii). CDC has undertaken surveys in developing countries such as Tanzania and Honduras (Together for Girls 2019), showing disturbing levels of violence against children.

2.2 What Are the Consequences to Victims of Violent Crime?

Violent crime numbers are not just statistics. Behind these numbers are individual stories of untold and unimaginable suffering and pain (WHO). These numbers reflect men and women who have lost their lives, families who have been devastated by loss and pain, individuals whose quality of life has been destroyed, and victimized children who suffer and then go through consequential chronic disease and emotional anguish. Violence can lead to injuries, permanent disabilities, loss of productivity and post-traumatic stress disorder. All too often, it leads to severe, lifelong health consequences, including injury, disease, and illness.

Women and girls in particular experience adverse sexual and reproductive health consequences of violence. These consequences are catalogued by the Centers for Disease Control and Prevention (2011) in its intimate partner and sexual violence survey as well as numerous publications of WHO such as those relating to preventing violence against women and children such as its Global Plan of Action (2016a) and the framework discussed later known by the acronym INSPIRE (WHO 2016b).

2.3 What Are the Economic and Political Consequences of Violent Crime?

The pain and suffering to individual victims is tragic and appalling but well established by experts. Less well known are the statistics for populations. For instance, cumulatively victims in the USA alone suffer injury and trauma estimated to exceed half a trillion dollars each year (Waller 2014). Chicago has recently brought their data together (Chicago 2019). The World Bank has shown the extent to which violence detracts from economic development. Low and Middle Income Countries (LMIC) in Latin America and the Caribbean are losing 5–15% of their Gross Domestic Product to violence (World Bank 2011).

Governments have increased expenditures on reactive security which too often threatens the human rights of suspect and offenders without reducing impunity. It diverts scarce resources from investment in health care, education, and economic development. Too often in Low and Middle Income Countries (LMIC) the security forces are not well trained, organized or equipped.

The World Bank has drawn attention to another cost because of the dangers of violence to democracy (2011). The lack of use of violence prevention science and effective strategies to curb violence have led to destabilization of governments. The failure to use evidence-based successes in Brazil, for instance, allows over 60,000 homicides each year, another 10,000 persons are killed by security forces (Muggah 2019). In the USA, 1000 persons are killed by police close to 5% of persons killed because of common crime.

3 Governments Commit to Reduce Violent Crime But Have Not Yet Acted

In 1985, national governments at the UN General Assembly resolved to act on a Magna Carta for Victims (UN General Assembly 1985; Waller and Martinez 2015). It called for action to secure respect for the rights of victims of crime and to implement social, health, including mental health, educational, economic and specific crime prevention policies to reduce victimization (UNGA 1985, para 4). But in the seventy five years since the adoption of the UN charter, UN agencies working on crime have been slow to balance a focus on human rights for suspects and offenders after the crime has happened to the prevention of victimization before (UNODC 2006).

The United Nations Economic and Social Council (United Nations Office on Drugs and Crime 2006), UN-Habitat (2019) and WHO (2016b) have built on the victim magna carta by agreeing essentials for violence and victimization to be curtailed. However, as the tragic statistics above on homicides, rape and violence against children show, practical action has not been enough.

3.1 Sustainable Development Goals to Dramatically Reduce Violent Crime

All major world leaders are committed to achieve the seventeen Sustainable Development Goals (SDG) by 2030 in "Transforming Our World: The 2030 Agenda for Sustainable Development" (UNGA 2015). The SDGs are results based and focus on transforming policies in both advanced and developing nations.

There are approximately 15 indicators for measuring whether violent crime has been significantly reduced. Six of the most important for this chapter are set out in the following tables for the subsections in SDG 5 for the reduction in victims of violence against women and in SDG 16 to the reduction of victims of violence and homicide and violence against children.

Homicide in SDG 16

16.1 **Significantly reduce all forms of violence and related death rates everywhere**

16.1.1 Number of victims of intentional homicide per 100,000 population, by sex and age

16.1.3 Proportion of population subjected to (a) physical violence, (b) psychological violence and (c) sexual violence in the previous 12 months

Rape in SDG5

5.2 **Eliminate all forms of violence against all women and girls in the public and private spheres, including trafficking and sexual and other types of exploitation**

5.2.1 Proportion of ever-partnered women and girls aged 15 years and older subjected to physical, sexual, or psychological violence by a current or former intimate partner in the previous 12 months, by form of violence and by age

5.2.2 Proportion of women and girls aged 15 years and older subjected to sexual violence by persons other than an intimate partner in the previous 12 months, by age and place of occurrence

Violence Against Children in SDG16

16.2 **End abuse, exploitation, trafficking, and all forms of violence against and torture of children**

16.2.1 Proportion of children aged 1–17 years who experienced any physical punishment and/or psychological aggression by caregivers in the past

16.2.3 Proportion of young women and men aged 18–29 years who experienced sexual violence by age 18

The indicator for homicide is measured regularly and considered reliable enough to make comparisons over time and between countries (UNODC 2019). The indicators on sexual violence and violence against children will require the use of surveys (Centers for Disease Control 2011; Together for Girls 2019).

Goal 17 focuses on strengthening the means of implementation and revitalizing the Global Partnership for Sustainable Development. It includes knowledge sharing, capacity building, policy coherence, multi-stakeholder partnerships that mobilize and share knowledge, expertise, technology and financial resources, data monitoring and accountability. These are focused on LMIC but have relevance for high income countries.

4 What Has Prevented Violent Crime Before It Happens?

4.1 Knowledge About Causes and Risk Factors

The 1985 United Nations resolution—Magna Carta for victims—called for prevention to reduce the size of victimization and its consequences (UNGA 1985; Waller and Martinez 2015). Since then, significant knowledge has accumulated on what causes the violence. There are several factors that lead to increased risk of experiencing or perpetrating violence, which are sometimes grouped under the labels of individual, family, community, and environmental (WHO 2002). Studies of life cycle development and the downstream impact of adverse childhood experiences have given us significant data on how the accumulation of negative life experiences, such as poverty, inconsistent and uncaring parenting, failure in school and lack of jobs correlates with persistent offending in adolescence and young adulthood (WHO 2002; CDC 2019; Waller 2019).

Mapping of emergency calls to police confirm that their violent and property crime data shows crime to be concentrated in problem places. Analysis of the characteristics of these places shows them to be areas of poverty, family breakdown and disadvantage (UNODC 2019; Waller 2019). The Mayor of London recently highlighted these links (London Mayor 2019a). All too often, the mapping leads to more reactive policing rather than more upstream solutions to the social issues that would reduce crime.

Sophisticated government surveys of the public known as victimization surveys—identify the frequency of victimization, whether the victims report and many other important but often overlooked data. Their existence and conclusions have become normal in affluent democracies and some low- and middle-income countries. These show that victims of violent and property crime tend to be young men, who are away from their residence, and are poor. Victims of sexual assault tend to be more often young women. Analysis of violent crime trends, particularly homicide, confirm the importance of poverty, parenting, safety nets, and access to guns and alcohol (Waller 2014; Cano 2016; Waller 2019).

4.2 *Solid Sources of Knowledge About Effective Violence Prevention*

We have accumulated significant proven and evidence-based knowledge about what is effective and cost effective in stopping interpersonal violence. This knowledge is endorsed by some of the most prestigious organizations in the world. It is freely available on websites, including that of crimesolutions.gov of the US Department of Justice (2015), violence-info the World Health Organizations (2017, 2009) and the tool kit of the British College of Policing (2019, pp. 23–32). In 2017, WHO released the most international and extensive of these websites with its Violence Prevention Information System—Violence Info" (WHO 2017). This is a global interactive knowledge platform of scientific findings about the prevalence, consequences, causes and prevention of various forms of violence. The tool contains global, regional, and national homicide rates from WHO Global Health Estimates, and country-specific information on laws, policies, strategies, and victim services to prevent and respond to violence (WHO 2017).

These portals collectively access thousands of clinical trials that show which projects have stopped crime before it happens. In addition, national academic councils and commissions have reviewed the research to arrive at conclusions (Waller 2019, pp. 32–36). Further analyses of these projects available on a portal of the State of Washington in the USA shows these projects are remarkably cost effective by stopping harm to victims and saving the costs of reacting after crime has happened (Washington State Institute for Public Policy 2018; Waller 2019, pp. 31–32). These prove an ounce of prevention is worth a pound of cure.

4.3 *Over-Relying on Enforcement and Criminal Justice Is Costly With Marginal Impact*

Governments have continued to increase expenditures on reactive security which make little or no impact on reducing rates violence. As discussed above on costs of violent crime, too often, they also threaten the human rights of suspects and offenders without reducing impunity. It diverts scarce resources from investment in health care, education, and economic development.

The Inter-American Development Bank has brought together the estimates of rates of violent and property crime with government expenditures on enforcement and criminal justice for the Latin American and Caribbean countries (2018). Their conclusion is that increased security spending does not reduce crime in most countries and There is room to improve the quality of spending through policies that are more preventive and less reactive, more focused and less broad-based, and more based on scientific evidence and less on intuition.

The USA increased spending on police, courts, and prisons dramatically from 1970 to 1990. This increased its incarceration during this time from 200 prisoners to

700 per 100,000 total population. US research shows that this massive expansion of incarceration had only a marginal contribution to crime reduction (National Research Council 2014; Waller 2019, p. 209). There are many other indications to reinforce the academic conclusion (National Research Council 2014). For instance, Toronto and Chicago have same population, but in a recent year Chicago had 13,000 cops, in a state with more than 500 prisoners per 100,000, and 600 murders, while Toronto had 5000 cops, in a country with less than 120 prisoners per 100,000 and less than 100 murders (average 60). The higher the incarceration rate, the higher the rates of homicide among G7 countries. The higher the incarceration rate, the higher the rates of violent crime among US State. New York City's crime rate and jail population have both declined dramatically starting in the Dinkins years. One LMIC, Mexico, increased spending on security by 61% between 2010 and 2016 with no clear impact on rates of victimization (Insight Crime 2017).

The USA now incarcerates 20% of the world's incarcerated population at a rate of 655 per 100,000 (World Prison Brief 2019). This rate is eight times that of Germany. The annual cost is US $87 billion (US Bureau of Justice Statistics 2018). Proportionately, the USA would save US$ 77 billion a year if its incarceration rate were reduced to that of Germany (Waller 2019, p. 209).

4.4 *What Are Proven Solutions That Are More Effective and Cost Effective?*

But not surprisingly, these portals and academic reviews are not enough to get better investments in prevention.

The recent UNODC report on Global Homicide Trends says prevention of homicide is possible by community interventions (UNODC 2019, p. 35). Its presentation of examples of these interventions is spread out through the six booklets, which makes access a challenge for decision makers who need to take decisive action. It does not provide clear evidence on the size of reductions and cost effectiveness nor on how to implement the successes. Nevertheless, it shows that UNODC is beginning to talk about examples of actions that have prevented homicide. Their examples include:

- Hot spot policing (UNODC 2019, pp. 2, 29; 3, 61), police partnerships with neighborhoods (UNODC 2019, pp. 2, 58);
- City wide street gang strategies such as Boston and outreach workers (UNODC 2019, pp. 3, 29) and partnerships between police and social assistance in Fica Vivo (UNODC 2019, pp. 6, 40);
- Problem solving, using public health and police data (UNODC 2019, pp. 4, 39);
- Changing male norms to reduce intimate partner and sexual violence (UNODC 2019, pp. 5, 54, 29);
- Reducing violence against children and so also reducing adult offending by presenting the proven examples of support for mothers and parents such as

positive parenting program and nurse family partnerships (UNODC 2019, pp. 6, 54).

Waller and others have translated the science and organized the conclusions into concrete actions so that the public and decision makers can understand what to do easily (Waller 2014; CMNCP 2017; Waller 2019). Many of these innovations have achieved a reduction in crime 50% better than the current systems of policing, courts, and incarceration. These innovations are simple and practical projects that tackle the causes of violence. Some of the most effective and cost effective are outreaching to youth in difficulty, supporting better parenting, teaching life skills in schools, and problem-oriented policing. Books, action briefs and short videos are now available that provide a guide to citizens, communities, and politicians on how to act on this knowledge (Waller 2014; CMNCP 2017; Waller 2019).

They are presented below in sufficient but not too much detail for politicians or others not scientifically immersed in the violence prevention science. They include:

4.5 Targeted Social Programming

Tackling causes and risk factors of violence before crime happens is proven to be the most effective way to reduce crime. Here are examples of targeted social programs that have been proven to be successful in stopping violent crime. Often the original data sources are in the jargon necessary for experts. To overcome this obstacle to their use, they are explained more in the pages cited from the book with the footnotes to the original scientific sources. Most of these programs have been shown to be highly cost effective often returning more than US $7 for every US $1 invested in savings to victims and to taxpayers in reduced costs of reaction.

- **Outreach to young men** at risk through initiatives inspired by Cure Violence or Youth Inclusion Programs (YIP). This approach consists of street workers outreaching to young men to interrupt gang affiliation, mediate violent conflict, and mentor at-risk individuals (Waller 2019, p. 64);
- **Hospital-based violence intervention** programs, which consist of outreach social workers intervening with victims of violence in hospital emergency rooms to deal with trauma, prevent revenge shootings, and encourage young men to abandon gang-like lifestyle (Waller 2019, p. 72);
- **School curricula focused on life skills** that focus on emotion regulation and problem-solving to help young men develop self-management skills and reduce impulsive responses causing violence. Programs like Life Skills Training, Becoming a Man and Stop Now and Plan have achieved up to 50% reductions in offending (Waller 2019, p. 70);
- **Support to families** through programs such as Multisystemic Therapy. This approach requires therapists to work in homes, schools, and communities to provide parents with tools to transform the lives of troubled youth (Waller 2019, p. 69).

4.5.1 Proactive Partnership Policing

So called proactive policing that is problem solving upstream can prevent some tragedies of violent crime and can be achieved within current budgets. When used in partnership with targeted social programming, the results are impressive. The book draws on important academic reports whose conclusions are scientific (National Academies of Sciences, Engineering, and Medicine 2018). It highlights the conclusions so that the implications for practice are easier to follow. So, it highlights approaches to policing for which there is evidence that proactive is effective (Waller 2019, pp. 48–49).

- **Problem-oriented policing** requires police to identify hot spots of high crime rates and focus their efforts to suppress the problem;
- **Focused deterrence** consists of focusing on likely offenders to increase deterrence using call-in of these young men. Boston (USA), Glasgow (UK, Scotland) and Minas Gerais (Brazil) are three examples where these approaches achieved significant results by encouraging participation in targeted social programming. Indeed, Glasgow reduced street homicides (with knives) by 50% within 3 years and sustained further reductions for a decade.

4.5.2 Government Sectors (INSPIRE)

In 2016, WHO, UNODC, UNICEF, and the World Bank signed endorsements of the WHO framework for prevention known as INSPIRE (WHO 2016b). The WHO proposed seven areas where the knowledge can be applied in its INSPIRE framework. It details examples of effective solutions in each of the areas. It also proposed a framework for the implementation, which will be discussed in the next section. The seven multi-sectoral but overlapping sectors where the knowledge can be applied include:

Implementation and enforcement of laws includes legislation from the justice sector to control alcohol, guns, and corporal punishment of children (see examples WHO 2016b, pp. 30–35);

Norms and values includes actions in the education, health and social welfare sectors to change gender norms (see examples WHO 2016b, pp. 36–40 and Waller 2019, pp. 79–94).

Safe environment includes actions in the policing sector (see examples WHO 2016b, pp. 42–46 and Waller 2019, pp. 37–58);

Parent and caregiver support includes actions in the family sector (see examples WHO 2016b, pp. 48–53 and Waller 2019, pp. 79–94);

Income and economic strengthening includes actions in the labour sector (see examples WHO 2016b, pp. 54–58);

Response and support service includes actions for victims in the welfare, health, and justice sectors (see examples WHO 2016b, pp. 60–65 and Waller 2019, pp. 95–113);

Education and life skills includes actions for victims in the school sector, including life skills training (as discussed in Waller 2019, pp. 71, 75–77).

5 What Are Essentials for Successful Implementation of Effective Solutions?

So, the rates of violent crime with their tragic consequences are no longer inevitable as they have been prevented. But proven and freely available is different from widely known or easily used.

5.1 Why Are Some City Plans Successful and Sustained?

In the few cases, where the successes have been adapted in cities in the USA and other countries using a plan, political leaders have achieved city wide reductions of 50% or better and with sustained funding have kept violent crime rates low (Waller 2019, pp. 159–182). While many more cities could benefit from modest but real investment in this planning and so focusing adequate and sustained investment in the solutions flowing from the planning, there are some examples that show the significant reductions in homicides and violence that can be achieved.

- Boston achieved a 60% reduction in gun violence in the 1990s but did not sustain the success and had to reinvent the strategy in the 2000s;
- Glasgow achieved a 50% reduction within 3 years of completing their diagnosis and plan;
- Minneapolis achieved similar reductions and maintained funding to continue the success;
- Bogota and Recife are examples of reductions of more than 50% (Waller and Martinez 2015; Hoelscher and Nussio 2015).

The success of Glasgow and the recommendations of the Youth Violence Commission have inspired the Mayor of London (UK) to adopt the same strategy (Youth Violence Commission 2018; Waller 2019; London Mayor 2019b). In Canada, the government of the largest province is mandating cities to develop community safety and well-being plans (Ontario Ministry of Community Safety and Corrections 2019).

5.2 *What Has Been Agreed by Governments as Essential to Implementation*

The smart knowledge of how to implement this knowledge through "good governance" strategies is promoted by UN-Habitat (2019), the (UNODC 2006), and the World Health Organization (WHO 2016b). World Health Assembly that has oversight of the World Health Organization has passed important resolutions, including "Strengthening the role of the health system in addressing violence, in particular against women and girls," and against children (WHO 2016a).

Every 10 years, UN-Habitat organizes a major summit on the future of cities. As the world's population clusters increasingly in cities and central governments do not support cities, UN-Habitat draws attention to the challenges. Among these are the issues of street and intimate partner violence. The UN Urban Agenda has begun to recognize these issues through the UN Habitat Safer Cities program and the special session at Habitat III (UN Habitat 2019).

The Economic and Social Council has adopted several guidelines relating to crime prevention and victim care (UNODC 2006). These were developed by the UNODC, which brings together ministers of justice and public safety officials from all the governments which are members of the UN. The guidelines include a few protocols that have been developed around interpersonal crime and some around organized crime. They include: Guidelines for cooperation and technical assistance in the field of urban crime prevention (1996) and Guidelines for Prevention of Crime (2002). They have developed a Handbook on their implementation (UNODC 2010).

In INSPIRE, WHO and its partners proposes a planning process that involves developing an integrated crime prevention plan, mobilising different sectors, and informed by violence prevention science (WHO 2016b, pp. 82–91, Waller 2019, pp. 132–134). EuroSocial fostered an impressive planning process with 10 Latin American governments to identify the essential elements for successful national and local violence prevention implementation (EuroSocial 2015; Waller and Martinez (2019). This led to agreement among several Latin American countries to implement these processes (EuroSocial 2015; Waller and Martinez 2019). It places an emphasis on essentials for success including a permanent board, adequate and sustained funding, and developing human talent all of which are consistent with the ECOSOC principles. Waller builds on ECOSOC (2002), UN-Habitat (2019) and EuroSocial (2014) to describe the "seven essentials" (below) for successful implementation of what works and test it against both national governments (Waller 2019, pp. 139–157) and cities (Waller 2019, pp. 159–182). In sum, cities that follow these essentials get dramatic reductions.

Public engagement often comes from mothers of victims and offenders and can keep pressure on successive governments to succeed. Governments that pick at some of these essentials get some success but flip back to failure because of lack of strong advocacy for success, lack of legislation and a lack of focus on what delivers results. These weaknesses can be addressed through the Sustainable Development Goal process to be discussed in the next section.

5.3 The Seven Essentials for Success

- Establishing a **permanent violence and crime reduction board** for the city (Waller 2019, p. 117). This responsibility center is the energy behind developing and implementing crime prevention plans. City-level boards mobilize local talent, facilitate information sharing between sectors, and disseminate pertinent information to key stakeholders and the public.
- Being **informed by violence prevention science** and data (Waller 2019, p. 118). It is crucial to base crime prevention on a multidisciplinary foundation of proven knowledge about crime problems, their causes, and promising and proven practices;
- Having an **integrated crime prevention plan** (Waller 2019, p. 118). The UN Guidelines stress the need for a local plan that mobilizes various community and economic sectors to prevent crime. The plan must be based on diagnoses of local crime problems and should include performance standards, targeted solutions, training protocol, and outcome evaluations;
- **Mobilizing sectors able to tackle causes** (Waller 2019, p. 119). Because of the nature of the risk factors that lead to crime, the permanent violence prevention board must mobilize talent able to help solve the problems. These individuals might include social workers, educators, health professionals, employment specialists, and sports figures as well as CJS workers;
- Having **adequate and sustained funding** (Waller 2019, p. 121). Crime prevention requires adequate resources, including funding for structures and activities, to be sustained. There should be clear accountability for funding, implementation, and evaluation, and for the achievement of planned results;
- Developing **standards and training for human talent** (Waller 2019, p. 121). For innovations to be successful, they will require the human talent capable of planning and implementing effective solutions;
- Having **public support and engagement** (Waller 2019, p. 122). FBOs, civil society and the public can play many roles in applying violence prevention science. They can become mentors, take precautions, and help map crime. They also can be advocates to get the permanent board and funding needed to implement crime prevention strategies. For instance, mothers and parents of at-risk young men tend to be successful actors in effecting change at the local and national levels;

6 What Are the Accelerators to Get Action on Halving Violent Crime

Few governments have started to invest to make the transformations needed to achieve the targets. While the commitment to the principles of the SDGs is a first step, much more Action Now is needed to get the transformations to achieve the targets by 2030. To bring about that action now, faith-based organizations, civil society, cities, and pathfinder governments with various UN bodies must focus on four key actions, which are discussed before an important role for UNODC to make these happen.

6.1 *Core Network to Get to Know the Science, the Essentials for Success, and How to Get Buy In*

There is what I call a core network of experts and committed specialists. WHO's small team is impressive on its own knowledge and has collaborated with the Violence Prevention Alliance (VPA) to form a network who know the evidence (WHO 2019). WHO is linked to health agencies, including public health, but not so much with cities, public safety ministries and FBOs. The first step must be to build on the VPA and other committed specialists to form a core network that can spearhead action. They must take the conversation out of New York, Geneva, and Vienna as well as the experts to the conversation and action where it is needed.

This core network must include leadership from senior decision makers in pathfinder governments, cities, FBOs and civil society, who must take time to get to know INSPIRE and the science, essentials and secrets of ending violent crime (WHO 2017; Waller 2019). They provide a nucleus that can work with senior and junior players from the broader spectrum of FBOs, civil society, cities, path finder governments and UN agencies. Some may already know the effective solutions, how to implement them, and how to get buy in but this requires a new way of thinking and operating and too often it is junior players who take the time to get up to speed rather than top decision makers.

6.2 *Raise Awareness Among Politicians and the Public of Effective Solutions and Strategies, Using Modern Communication Tools*

We know many solutions that have been proven effective because they are available on portals of prestigious organizations and national commissions. We have highlighted these solutions above and they are explained in practical terms in user friendly publications (WHO 2016b; CMNCP 2017; Waller 2019). Now the challenge is how to share these solutions and their benefits with the public and decision makers. The core network must make the public and decision makers more generally aware through a variety of modern communication tools.

6.2.1 Social Media

This is the world of Twitter, Facebook, LinkedIn, and more. Successful politicians have used Twitter to get themselves elected and communicate with massive numbers of citizens. Twitter is effectively free to the communicator and the follower, although there are skills to make use of it. So, the core network must plan a variety of social media campaigns adapted to the members of their organizations.

6.2.2 Tools for Awareness

This is the world of YouTube videos, podcasts, TED talks, and much more. The core network can develop these tools to explain the effective solutions and the benefits. The Canadian Municipal Network for Crime Prevention has started to produce these tools for use in Canada (CMNCP 2017) but much more is needed and urgently.

6.2.3 Conferences

Conferences provide a way of raising awareness of the science and secrets as well of experts, others with experience to share and much more. The German Crime Prevention Days with their participation in the multiple thousands is a remarkable model of how to spread the word and mobilize wide support.

6.3 Foster the Human Talent to Implement Effective Strategies Successfully

An essential element for successful implementation is to have the human talent who can perform the roles needed. These include planning, mobilizing, implementing, and evaluating as well as the skills to implement the programs that are effective. If policy makers are ready to buy in but there are no competent persons to implement, initiatives will be compromised.

The core network can focus on developing the course material so that these skills can be taught through training, college, and university courses. They will require standards to be developed so that the officials can be certified as having the skills. CMNCP has developed two pathfinder courses to make this happen (2017). The first is on the planning aspects. The second is on how to make the cost benefit case to get funding.

There is an urgent need to develop tools for officials to use, particularly for multi-sectoral planning.

6.4 Act Locally to Deliver Effective Solutions

There are many different entities involved in delivering the solutions that have been proven effective. However, FBOs and civil society are often actively involved in outreach programs to street youth and parenting support and training. Their ability to pay for these services and train the persons who deliver the services makes the difference to the existence of the services.

While these proven services can be justified so that governments pay for them, it is often the charities who have pioneered and sustained these effective solutions.

They must expand their direct services and work with their adherents as well as governments and Non-governmental organizations to get the change that will save lives and futures, particularly for young, vulnerable, and disadvantaged citizens.

6.5 Work Collaboratively to Convince Policymakers to Invest Now

We need to get to know and help policy makers get to know the benefits of reducing violent crime and how they can foster these solutions that are affordable and popular. It will save lives and costs.

All this will take time and upstream investment in both the essentials to achieve significant reductions and the programs needed for upstream investment. Most of the effective solutions and city strategies achieve the reductions within 3–5 years. So, achieving these reductions within 10 years is not out of the question.

6.5.1 Benefits of Policy Proposals Based on Effective Solutions and Strategies

The evidence shows that smart investments in many of these effective solutions not only saves lives but the costs of reaction which have been crowding out early intervention and prevention. The costs of targeted social programming are affordable, likely less than 10% of what is being spent after the tragedies in reaction (Waller 2019, pp. 202–206).

The science shows that the public and families of victims want prevention because the victimization surveys show that this is the dominant reason why victims of violent crime report to police (Waller 2019, pp. 206–208). Violence prevention is achievable because voters, contrary to what the media tells us, want much more than reaction, they want prevention (Waller 2019, pp. 183–220). Yes, they want tough on crime, but they also want tough on causes.

The evidence from the violence prevention shows suggests that a 50% reduction in violent crime is achievable by applying the science systematically (Waller 2019, pp. 159–182). In the USA alone, this means potentially as many as 8000 lives each year would be saved and half a million women would not be raped. Worldwide the numbers are even more important as it would result in 250,000 lives saved each year, ten million or more women not raped, and 500 million children avoiding violent victimization.

If saving lives is not enough, preventing violence would save billions of dollars spent on policing and mass incarceration, while investing in the futures of young people in disadvantaged zip-codes. In the USA, the savings would be greater than $60 billion a year (Waller 2019, pp. 192–199).

6.5.2 Partnering with Faith-Based Organizations, Civil Society, Cities and Early Adopter Governments

They must engage with parents and social movements who care about stopping violent victimization. Several social movements are calling for prevention of violence. The most visible are in the USA, where the #MeToo movement, #Black Lives Matter, # Mothers Demand Action on Gun Violence and the #March for our Lives are already having some success (Waller 2019, pp. 221–238).

In some of the cities in Latin America such as Bogota that have been successful, mothers have led the pressure on politicians. Many of these upstream investments are in groups that are vulnerable, disadvantaged, and excluded so that violence does not further their exclusion. One way to get decisive and effective action now is to partner with these groups.

One remarkable example showing a means to get decision makers on side is #March for Our Lives who have recently promoted a plan to reduce gun violence in the USA. FBOs, civil society, city networks can emulate this proposal by developing their own policy statements. It is notable as it includes all of the steps that we have seen are essential to decisive action—effective actions, ways to implement and calls for action to get buy in (Waller 2019).

6.5.3 March for Our Lives Policy to Prevent Gun Violence: Model Example

March for Our Lives formed after the shooting in a Florida school in 2018. It led to several mass demonstrations and town halls including half a million people in Washington, DC in March 2018. Their bold plan proposes six actions summarized in the acronym of CHANGE as set out below. It proposes actions on effective solutions, including for gun ownership standards and community-based solutions, which are consistent with the evidence on effective solutions above (WHO 2016b; Waller 2019). It proposes ways to implement the actions, through a gun violence prevention office consistent with the important essential for success. It sets a target for dramatic reductions in gun deaths consistent with SDG16.1. It tackles the challenge of buy in through the mobilization of politicians by making the gun lobby accountable and empowering the next generation. Here are six actions proposed in the order of the acronym (March for our Lives 2019):

- **C**hange the Standards of Gun Ownership, including buying back 30% of estimated 300 million firearms
- **H**alve the Rate of Gun Deaths in 10 Years, thereby saving up to 200,000 American lives;
- **A**ccountability for the Gun Lobby and Industry, including investigations into the NRA
- **N**ame a Director of Gun Violence Prevention, including $250 million for research by the CDC and other federal agencies on gun violence prevention;
- **G**enerate Community-Based Solutions, including fully fund targeted interventions addressing the intersectional dimensions of gun violence
- **E**mpower the Next Generation, including automatically register eligible voters and mail voter registration cards to all Americans when they turn 18.

6.5.4 Partnering with UN Agencies

The WHO tools, including INSPIRE and their portal, are an important first step (WHO 2016b, 2017). But UNODC, UN-Habitat and WHO can facilitate decisive action by supporting the activities that have been set out above of expanding the core network, raising awareness, organizing training and tools, and fostering buy in.

The shift will require assistance with sustained and adequate funding. The Inter-American Development Bank has argued the case for the shift showing significant reductions in both violent crime and spending on law enforcement and criminal justice which currently react to crime (Inter-American Development Bank 2018). And so, the World Bank and the Regional Development Banks need to invest in the change processes described above.

Governments themselves must legislate to establish a national board to make the shift and coordinate a national plan with measurable targets of reductions in crime and victimization. It would assist with the best community safety planning, training, and sharing of evidence and successful practices. The shift will require assistance with sustained and adequate funding equivalent to three years of annual increases (i.e., 10% overall) of what the national governments currently spend on reacting to crime.

7 Conclusion

Prayers are good, but action better.

This chapter identifies the decisive action needed now to dramatically reduce violent crime by 2030 as required by SDG 16.1. 5.2 and 16.2. It shows how to cut violence in half and so avoid each year 25,000 homicides, ten million or more rapes and half a billion child victims of violence. These reductions would increase GDP and decrease corruption and political instability. It is about shifting from (mis-) spending on what does not work to investing in the futures of young and disadvantaged people to save lives and taxes, while generating economic growth and political stability.

In 2019, we not only have the knowledge of what are effective solutions, successes in implementing them, and reasons for decision makers to shift investment, but we have social media and data analysis tools that were not available twenty years ago, we have cities that have been successful, we have guidelines agreed by governments. So, we need to share the good news and get action now. Violence prevention is realizable, affordable, and more popular than many think, and will stop so many tragedies and so reduce their impact on economies and rule of law.

It calls on faith-based organizations, civil society, and cities to spear head decisive action, in partnership with UN agencies and pathfinder governments, by five pathfinder actions to:

(i) Get to know the science, the essentials for success, and how to get buy in;
(ii) Raise awareness among politicians and the public of effective solutions and strategies, using modern communication tools;
(iii) Foster the human talent to implement effective strategies successfully;
(iv) Act locally to deliver and develop effective solutions
(v) Work collaboratively to convince policy makers to invest now, including policy proposals based on effective solutions and strategies.

Faith-based organizations, civil society, and cities can accelerate the transformations needed by partnering with UN agencies and pathfinder governments and cities. They must expand the leadership in the core network so that more know the science, raise virally awareness of the strategies and the benefits to share this knowledge, develop the talent to make it happen, and help decision makers to see, and invest to get, the benefits. They can foster national prevention legislation and a shift from an agenda of punishment by the state to an agenda of prevention investing in people guided by science.

To succeed in dramatically reducing violent crime, decisive action is needed. FBOs, civil society and cities can spearhead the actions that will accelerate the necessary transformations. They can achieve many advances on their own but funding from the private and governmental sector to develop these tools, talents and the momentum will accelerate a world safer from violence by 2030.

References

Business Insider. (2019). 50 most violent cities. https://www.businessinsider.com/most-violent-cities-in-the-world-in-2018-2019-3

Cano, I., Rojido, E., & Sento-Sé, J. T. (2016). *Mapping of Homicide Prevention Programs in Latin America and the Caribbean.* Rio de Janeiro: Universidade do Estado de Rio de Janeiro, Laboratório de Análise da Violência. http://www.lav.uerj.br/docs/rel/2016/Relato%CC%81rio%20Final%20Ingle%CC%82s.pdf

Centres for Disease Control and Prevention. (2011). *National Intimate Partner and Sexual Violence Survey, Summary Report*. Atlanta, GA.
Centres for Disease Control and Prevention. (2019). *Adverse Childhood Experiences*. https://www.cdc.gov/violenceprevention/childabuseandneglect/acestudy/index.html
Chicago. (2019). *Hidden costs push price of city's gun violence into billions*. https://www.chicagobusiness.com/crains-forum-gun-violence/hidden-costs-push-price-citys-gun-violence-billions
CMNCP (Canadian Municipal Network on Crime Prevention). (2017). SaferCities.ca
ECOSOC UN Economic and Social Council. (2002). *37th Session. Resolution 13, "Action to promote effective crime prevention." RES/2002/13, July, 24, 2002*. In resolutions and decisions of the UN department of economic and social affairs 2002. Vienna: United Nations.
EuroSocial. (2014) *Regional Model for a Comprehensive Violence and Crime Prevention Policy*. http://www.sia.eurosocial-ii.eu/files/docs/1461686840-DT_33-_Modelo%20regional%20Prevencion%20Violencia%20(ENG).pdf
EuroSocial. (2015) *Declaración Para La Prevención De La Violencia Y El Delito De Cartagena De Indias*. http://www.sia.eurosocial-ii.eu/files/docs/1430321271-Declaracion%20de%20Cartagena.pdf
Hoelscher, K., & Nussio, E. (2015). Understanding unlikely successes in urban violence reduction. *Urban Studies*. Retrieved from https://doi.org/10.2139/ssrn.2461064
Insight Crime. (2017) *Increased Mexico Security Spending Not Delivering Security Gains: Report, Caroline Kuritzkes*. https://www.insightcrime.org/news/brief/increased-mexico-security-spending-not-delivering-security-gains-report/
Inter-American Development Bank. (2018). *Smart Spending on Citizen Security: Beyond Crime and Punishment*. https://flagships.iadb.org/en/DIA2018/chapter-7-smart-spending-citizen-security-beyond-crime-and-punishment.
Locke, R., & Steven, D. (2019). *Fighting Violence with Evidence*. https://www.project-syndicate.org/commentary/sdg16-reducing-violence-conflict-homicide-by-rachel-locke-and-david-steven-2019-08
London Mayor. (2019a). *Full Links between Poverty and Crime*. https://www.london.gov.uk/press-releases/mayoral/full-links-between-poverty-and-violent-crime
London Mayor. (2019b). *Violence Reduction Unit*. https://www.london.gov.uk/what-we-do/mayors-office-policing-and-crime-mopac/violence-reduction-unit-vru/what-violence-reduction-unit
March for Our Lives. (2019). *A Peace Plan for a Safer America*. https://marchforourlives.com/peace-plan/
Muggah, R. (2019). *Violent crime has undermined democracy in Latin America: When people are fearful, they are less likely to trust elected politicians*. https://www.ft.com/content/7bbc9228-a09f-11e9-a282-2df48f366f7d
National Academies of Sciences, Engineering, and Medicine. (2018) *Proactive policing: Effects on crime communities*. Washington, DC: National Academies Press
Ontario Ministry of Community Safety and Corrections (2019). *Community Safety and Well Being Planning: A shared commitment in Ontario*. Toronto
Together for Girls. (2019). *Violence against Children Surveys*. https://www.togetherforgirls.org/about-the-vacs/
U.S. Bureau of Justice Statistics. (2018). *Justice Expenditure and Employment Abstracts 2015*. https://www.bjs.gov/index.cfm?ty=pbdetail&iid=6310
UN-Habitat. (2019). *Twenty-five years of the Safer Cities Program: Lessons Learned from Evolution of the Approach*. Nairobi, in press
United Nations General Assembly. (1985). *Resolution 40/34 on Basic Principles of Justice for Victims of Crime and Abuse of Power*. https://www.un.org/documents/ga/res/40/a40r034.htm
United Nations General Assembly. (2015). *Sustainable Development Goals*. Retrieved from https://sustainabledevelopment.un.org/

United Nations Office on Drugs and Crime. (2006). *Compendium of United Nations standards and norms in crime prevention and criminal justice*. New York: UN.

United Nations Office on Drugs and Crime. (2010). *Handbook on crime prevention guidelines: Making them work*. New York: UN.

United Nations Office on Drugs and Crime. (2019). *Global Trends in Homicide, Booklets 1-6*. New York: UN. https://www.unodc.org/documents/data-and-analysis/gsh/Booklet1.pdf

Waller, I. (2014). *Smarter crime control: A guide to a safer future for citizens, communities, and politicians*. Lanham, MD: Rowman and Littlefield.

Waller, I. (2019). *Science and secrets of ending violent crime*. Lanham, MD: Rowman and Littlefield.

Waller, I., & Martinez, V. (2015). *Derechos de las víctimas a treinta años de la Carta Magna de las Naciones Unidas: acciones concretas en momentos críticos. En Marchiori, H. Conmemoración de la Carta Magna de Naciones Unidas para las Víctimas, 1985–2015. Victimología 18.* Córdoba: Encuentro Grupo Editorial.

Waller, I., & Martinez, V. (2019). Prevención inteligente: Pensar en las victimas, en ILANUD Violencias, Victimas y Sociedades Justas, Ministerio de Justicia y Derechos Humanos de Argentina, ILANUD, libro digital, pp. 25–47.

Washington State Institute for Public Policy. (2018). *Cost Benefit*. https://www.wsipp.wa.gov/BenefitCost

WHO. (2002). *World report on violence and health*. Geneva: World Health Organization.

WHO. (2009). *Violence prevention: The evidence*. Geneva: The World Health Organization.

WHO. (2016a). *Global Plan of Action to strengthen the role of the health system within a national multi-sectoral response to address interpersonal violence, in particular against women and girls, and against children*. World Health Organization. https://apps.who.int/iris/bitstream/handle/10665/252276/9789241511537-eng.pdf?sequence=1

WHO. (2016b). *INSPIRE: Seven strategies for ending violence against children*. Geneva, Switzerland: World Health Organization. https://www.who.int/violence_injury_prevention/violence/inspire/en/

WHO. (2017). *Violence prevention information system (violence info)*. World Health Organization. http://apps.who.int/violence-info/

WHO. (2019). *Violence prevention alliance*. World Health Organization. https://www.who.int/violenceprevention/en/

World Bank. (2011). *World Development Report 2011: Conflict, security and development*. Washington, DC: The International Bank for Reconstruction and Development / The World Bank.

World Prison Brief. (2019). https://www.prisonstudies.org/sites/default/files/resources/downloads/wppl_12.pdf

Youth Violence Commission. (2018). *Interim Report*. http://yvcommission.com/interim-report/

Irvin Waller is a Professor Emeritus of Criminology, University of Ottawa, Canada. He is an internationally recognised expert on crime prevention and victim rights. His instrumental work to get the UN General Assembly to recognize rights for victims in 1985 earned him multiple awards internationally. He was the founding executive director of the International Centre for Prevention of Crime (Montreal, Canada) – member of the United Nations Crime Prevention and Criminal Justice Programme Network of institutes. He is a member of the Violence Prevention Alliance of the World Health Organization (WHO) and active at violence prevention meetings of the United Nations Office on Drugs and Crime and the UN-Habitat. He has been the president of the World Society of Victimology and the International Organization for Victim Assistance, both in special consultative status with ECOSOC. He was the director general of research in the Solicitor General of Canada in the 1970s, working on abolition of the death penalty and gun control. Author of numerous books published in English, Chinese and Spanish, his latest book *Science and Secrets of Ending Violent*

Crime uses evidence and UN guidelines to get decisive action by governments to achieve a 50% reduction in homicides and violent crime for Agenda 2030. He is a popular speaker in English, French and Spanish. www.irvinwaller.org and twitter @irvinwaller. E-mail: iwaller@uottawa.ca; wallerirvin@msn.com.

Part VII
Philosophies of Law and New Legal Realities in the Context of the 2030 Justice and Crime

The Erosion of Justice Symbolism

Yvon Dandurand and Jessica Jahn

Abstract The symbolism that has long embodied our justice images has gradually eroded. Whereas our justice symbols may have once reminded us of the spiritual nature of our longing for justice, they have been replaced by those meant to evoke secrecy and detachment. Lady Justice has become the emblem for our resignation to settle for predictability in laws, even when we might have wished to stay true to our aspirations for justice and dared to dream of cooperation and harmony. In recent time, Lady Justice herself is increasingly replaced by a simple scale as the prevailing image of justice, signifying that human intervention in justice may no longer be required since the system for which we have settled has acquired a life of its own. Such an erosion is both a threat to the authority structures that such symbols depict and a promise for renewal. This chapter considers the symbolism of our justice images and the ways in which it may constrain our collective imagination. It suggests that our justice mythology, of which our human rights discourse is part, must be renewed and put at the service of another vision for our future together, particularly one that is less legalistic and less nationalistic.

Keywords Justice symbols · Images of justice · Law reform · Human rights · Peace · Justice system

Y. Dandurand (✉)
University of the Fraser Valley, School of Criminology and Criminal Justice, Abbotsford, BC, Canada

International Centre for Criminal Law Reform and Criminal Justice Policy, Vancouver, BC, Canada
e-mail: Yvon.Dandurand@ufv.ca

J. Jahn
International Centre for Criminal Law Reform and Criminal Justice Policy, Vancouver, BC, Canada
e-mail: Jessica.Jahn@telus.net

H. Kury, S. Redo (eds.), *Crime Prevention and Justice in 2030*,
https://doi.org/10.1007/978-3-030-56227-4_27

1 Introduction

The current discourse on human rights seems to be ignoring some of the greater issues of our century. It took a long time before the international community recognised peace and security as a key sustainable development goal, eventually including it as Goal 16 in the sustainable development agenda. While it had succeeded for a time in asserting itself as the language of hope and freedom, including as part the international liberal order, the human rights discourse has become for many the language of impotence and despair. The compelling power of that discourse is fading or retreating away, drown out by populist demagoguery and the shouts of nationalism. Nationalism, as Michael Ignatieff observed, "is a form of speech which shouts, not merely so that it will be heard, but so that it will believe itself" (Ignatieff 1993, p. 186). National sovereignty must be reinterpreted, as it too often shields the perpetrators of human rights abuses.

The encounter between the international rule of law and human rights movement and the reality in fractured or totalitarian states has been a great disillusionment. "Though the evidence suggests that trying to change such legal systems is an unproductive endeavour", David Marshall observed, "the international community continues to attempt to reengineer institutions, laws, and legal processes, perhaps because there is no accountability for such meagre results" (Marshall 2014, p. xiii).

The human rights discourse must help reinvigorate the collective will of states to face intense global risks that otherwise appears to be lacking (World Economic Forum 2019). In their most recent *Global Risks Report,* the World Economic Forum (2019) found that "as geopolitical tensions and competition have intensified, human rights have been increasingly politicized" (p. 24), adding that "a vicious circle may develop in which diminishing social cohesion places ever-greater strain on political institutions, undermining their ability to anticipate or respond to societal challenges" (p. 13). To help address these challenges, the language of rights must be reclaimed, renewed, and put at the service of another, less legalistic and less nationalistic, vision of our future together. Education for democracy and human rights is needed now more than ever to address discrimination, prejudice and intolerance, and ultimately build inclusive societies within the framework provided by democratic institutions and respect for human rights (Council of Europe 2017).

The United Nations has developed "soft law" material setting out normative standards on crime prevention and criminal justice, some of which have been incorporated in treaty language or have found their way into the corpus of customary international law. One of the key goals of these developments is to foster greater international cooperation in meeting new and emerging crime prevention and criminal justice challenges. The overall project is one of building justice institutions capable of meeting the challenges of this century. However, the real impact of all these efforts is sometimes hard to demonstrate. The future will tell whether our collective attempts to shape crime prevention and criminal justice in a manner that reflects our deeper aspirations for justice will prove to be a failure or an astonishing success. In the end, the real test will be whether we have learned to live together in peace.

This chapter considers the symbolism of our justice images and the ways in which it may constrain our collective imagination, suggesting that our justice mythology, of which our human rights discourse is part, must be renewed and reinvigorated in imagining what our future together may entail.

2 The Erosion of Symbolic Representations of Justice

We ought to be concerned about the political failure in many societies to defend human rights and the rule of law and to proceed with the necessary justice reforms to ensure fairness, transparency, and accountability. A culture of lawfulness is a culture of confidence or trust in the law, the political order it reflects, and the social order it supports. Such a culture is essentially one of cooperation, based on beliefs that people hold, construals they share, and assumptions they are willing to make about the social order, authority, the rule of law, and their own relationship to self, others, and the world. As Harari explains, beliefs and fictions are the essential foundations of social order. Myths are what gives humans the unprecedented ability to cooperate flexibly in large numbers (Harari 2015, p. 25).

To the extent that one can assume that "intersubjective myths" (Harari 2015) or shared narratives provide the foundation of human society and undergird the social order, one can also assume that a culture of lawfulness and respect for human rights is founded on shared narratives (or myths) about the usefulness, fairness, impartiality, and ultimate legitimacy of the law and the justice system. As we have written elsewhere, such myths are "the expression of how we collectively conspire to build and maintain the social fabric, to legitimize our own and each other's action, and to make cooperation possible on a large scale" (Dandurand and Jahn 2018, p. 16).

However, it often seems that the images and symbols we use, the assumptions we are willing to make, and the myths and fictions we perpetuate about justice can no longer support us the way they once did. The symbolism has been eroded over time and its authoritative value degraded. It has been worn down by globalisation, social changes, cultural clashes, and technology. The erosion of these symbols and images holds both a threat to our social order and a promise for its renewal.

Our civilisation is drowning under the impact of images and we collectively struggle to consciously identify the role those images play as a tool of authority (Saul 1995). The danger comes from the fact that the main function of these symbolic representations is to help create and reproduce an authority structure capable of legitimising the existing order, minimising opposition, and facilitating cooperation. As the symbolism becomes less and less consonant with the reality of the prevalent authority and power structure, it slowly ceases to provide our justice and other institutions with a sound foundation of legitimacy and credibility. The symptoms of this state of affairs are evident in the obvious frailty of the credibility and perceived legitimacy of our political institutions, including our justice systems and human rights institutions.

At the same time, the erosion of the power of these symbolic representations also holds a promise of renewal. As traditional images and symbols lose a great deal of their hold on us, our collective imagination is being freed to create new ones. The symbolic vacuum increases the likelihood that a new symbolism will take shape. Eventually, those atavistic symbols that have already outlived their usefulness as a support for a viable authority structure for our times will be replaced.

The authoritativeness of our structures and institutions presupposes a high level of congruence between their abstract and symbolic representations and our common sense experience of them. When the abstract and aspirational meaning of our symbolic representations of justice is negated by our experience of justice, the symbols lose their ability to command attention, respect, and spontaneous compliance, and the whole institutional structure—which rests on such shared meaning—is undermined. Criminal justice reform practitioners can no longer ignore these clear signs of erosion of the authoritativeness of human rights and justice institutions.

3 Renewal of the Language, Images, and Symbols of Justice

The survival of the existing social order may perhaps require nothing less than a reformulation of our collective aspiration for justice, a new understanding of human rights and the rule of law, and a reimagining of our justice institutions. If a cure (or that which is required to heal the social organism) is to be found in the renewal of the authority structure and the symbolic representations supporting it, the technocratic approach to justice reform and human rights defence will obviously not be sufficient.

The images we hold of the world that surrounds us and of our own place within it largely determine our thinking and our behaviour. But more importantly, they condition and shape our imagination. The same is true of our images and representations of justice and human rights: reduced to a form of propaganda, they constrain our collective imagination and are easily manipulated for political and other reasons.

Surely, one may think, the solution is not to be found simply in words and images. The present crises our world is facing are very real, so let us dispense, one might say, with mere semantics. But is “semantics” not often defined as “the study of human interaction through communication” (Hayakawa 1978)? Is honest communication not what is needed to foster cooperation and to help us meet the enormous challenges of our time? It cannot be a mere coincidence that Samuel Ichiye Hayakawa (1978), author of a once leading text in semantics, first wrote his book in 1941 as a response to the dangers of propaganda exemplified in Adolf Hitler’s success in persuading millions to share his destructive views.

Words, symbols, and images are what we have to convey meaning. And meaning is required for us to agree, to share our aspirations, define our goals and work together. We are reminded by linguists that agreement, consensus, unity of purpose, and so on are achieved by linguistic processes (Whorf 1956). Yet, words and symbols can also be misleading, mystifying, or disempowering (Casamayor 1977). We must be vigilant and critical about the words and symbols we call our own, individually and collectively. We must understand where they come from and whom they serve. Some of them, purporting to appeal to our higher ideals, present themselves as precious gifts from the past, worthy of veneration and unconditional acceptance. The language of human rights and individual entitlements may present itself as such a gift and we have reasons indeed to be grateful for it. We also have good reasons to be careful and vigilant. It may be necessary to look at the proverbial gift horse in the mouth. It could turn out to be of the Trojan horse variety.

The concepts, the words, and the symbols we use to signify justice and human rights, or power and authority, are all from other eras. The fact that they were inherited from the past does not mean that they have lost their spell on us. On the contrary, they are powerful, resilient, and pervasive symbolic representations that continue to shape every aspect of our personal and social lives. We need to reconsider each one of them in the light of today's circumstances and of the vision we have for the society we hope to build.

We may not remember the exact origins of our images and symbols of justice. When attempting to date these fossils, one is often sent back to the last great revolution in the authority structure of the western world (the age of enlightenment) and its emphasis on the nation-state, a mechanistic world view, and a simplistic and reductionist approach to social order. These concepts tend to present themselves to us as eternal truths, immutable knowledge, or inescapable realities. They are sacred cows. We hold on to them, partly because of the gains our civilisation has achieved through them, and partly because we have not yet been able to imagine some alternatives. Emotionally and sometimes also spiritually, there is a strong collective historical investment in these symbolic meanings and our attachment to them reaches deeply into our unconscious. Intellectually, we are constantly reminded by world events and by our own personal experience of how thin the "veneer of civilization" really is which these old shared-meanings have helped us create. This is indeed our Western inheritance (Saul 1993).

This is not the place to try to retrace how these images or symbols emerged, imposed themselves to our consciousness, and shaped our justice institutions, but undoubtably, the power to shape and impose these images is not evenly distributed in any society. There cannot be any doubt either that these images of justice are in fact mirrors. They mirror our aspirations and desires, but also our fears and our struggles. When we consider these images, we know of course that we are looking at ourselves, but also know that all these mirrors are necessarily distorting and mystifying. We instinctively suspect that behind all of them there is an attempt to "pass a hen for a cow" and a risk that we may end up not knowing whether we should go and milk it or wait for it to lay an egg.

In these and in many other instances, it might help to start with calling a cow "a cow". It might give us a clearer idea of what it is that we are really doing, as opposed to what we are pretending to do. There are those who, tired of the smoke and mirror show, would shatter all mirrors and reveal the illusions and deceptions they mask.

Yet, when one lives in a house with so much glass, one should have the wisdom to remember not to be the one to cast a stone at one's neighbour's house.

4 Images of Justice: Lady Justice

Lady Justice, the familiar allegorical figure of justice, originates from the personification of Justice in Ancient Roman art known as *Iustitia*, equivalent to the Greek goddesses Themis and Dike (Covey 1959). Her attributes include a blindfold, a balance (or scales), and a sword. Lady Justice is no longer a deity; she is most definitely secular. As a fossilised image of our collective but somewhat recent past, Lady Justice stands as a reminder of our tamed or repressed desire for justice. She in fact tells us much more about ourselves and our own desire for justice than we may think. She has become the emblem of our resignation to settle for security and predictability when we might have dared to dream of cooperation and harmony. We have made her the image of our fears and not of our commitment to genuine peace and freedom. She may still vaguely evoke some ideal or mystery, but all her mysteries are measurable and mechanically processed. She is meant to obscure the motives of those to whom she lends her authority. Her attitude is distant and austere and her whole posture commands that we stay at a distance. Her presence certainly does not invite the kind of fascination that beauty and serenity would inspire.

Through part of the Middle-Age and throughout the Renaissance, other creatures from heaven were often depicted as the instrument of divine justice, and not simply divine vengeance: the powerfully winged, sword-brandishing archangels. It may perhaps help free our imagination to try to picture Lady Justice, not as the blind petty tyrant and guardian of our fears that we have made her, but rather as a light spirit beckoning our desire for justice, freedom, and peace. In the fifteenth century, as the time of Titian, Venus herself was just as likely as any other figure to symbolically portray justice: the goddess of love as of one of the happiest and most inspiring allegorical deification of justice. Voluptuous, generous with her beauty, with a sword but no blindfold. One is immediately given to understand that, if such a goddess could be blinded, it could only be by desire, love, or compassion. In Venice, towards the end of the same century, as the citizens of the city were celebrating and dramatising the image of their city as the "ideal city", they represented Venice (with the attributes of Venus) as justice, conceived as the supreme value of the state, standing alone and tall above all the other allegorical representations of the fundamental values attributed to the city.

Those of us with an interest in the iconography of justice will know that there have been, in our own civilisation, countless other allegorical figures of justice, most often female, often depicted with other "graces" such as Truth and Virtue, showing her with a loving smile, a firm hand on her sword, and an unbending demand for truth and honesty. Here we are reminded of a beautiful painting of George Washington, surrounded by Justice and her usual companions, descending from the sky. From the sky, of course. In fact, until our blind-folded Lady Justice succeeded in excluding other figures from our imagination, we all knew that Justice was only visiting this world, and then only when truth, love, compassion and honesty prevailed. Justice, with or without a majestic set of wings, had offered a powerful spiritual image of freedom: a goddess who was as likely to choose chaos as she was to protect order if such was the price of justice and freedom. Rarely vengeful, her image was always meant to reawaken our passion for truth and harmony and stir up our consuming desire for her presence. At times, we suspect, she could express joy and serenity. Such beautiful images were meant to remind us of the sacredness and of the spiritual nature of our longing for justice. They were not intended to dictate deference or obedience to her "priests". How did these vivid depictions of our very emotional and spiritual passion for justice and truth come to be replaced by a mere shadow of their evocative power? How did the blindfolded Lady Justice come to replace, in our imagination and in our symbolism, such powerful and inspirational images of justice?

Lady Justice has taken some trouble to exaggerate her age, to represent herself as some ancient, if not eternal, symbol of our aspirations to justice. In fact, she is no more than a few hundred years old, born during the same cultural revolution that gave us most of our modern social institutions. The same fears, impulses and successes which guided our culture through the Scientific Revolution and the Age of Enlightenment are responsible for her creation. Gods were no longer required to explain the universe, nor were the devils to explain illnesses. The excesses and the repression of the previous centuries, which had been justified in the name of spirituality, were still a very vivid memory. Reason was to reign supreme and all emotions, passions, or desires became suspicious. Our profound love for justice and truth were reduced to the level of common lust and had to be sacrificed on the altar of technocratic efficiency. The imposing and austere figure of Lady Justice we inherited from that era now remains as the reminder of how we were dispossessed of our passion for truth, honesty, and fairness.

The blindfolded lady is indeed the faithful image of the kind of justice we have chosen to pursue. She is passive and dispassionate, blind to inequities, relying not on her heart or her wisdom, but solely on a mechanical devise, a scale, to weigh responsibilities and circumstances. She is fearful and repressive of all passions and seemingly content to reduce the vast complexity of our social interactions as well as one of our greatest aspirations to a heap of rituals.

Lady Justice is secular and totally grounded. She has traded what were once the suggestively transparent veils through which previous goddess-like figures would let us imagine their beauty, for the austere and unadorned black robe of the inquisitors, an accoutrement, which was once sure to provoke fear and was designed to conceal more than to reveal. Symbols of beauty and transparency were replaced by symbols meant to evoke fear and suggest remoteness, detachment, and secrecy. Lady Justice apparently knows little of compassion or of human solidarity, and she treats love as a weakness and truth as an inconvenience. For that matter, we can hardly imagine her smiling, not even at the sight of those she is meant to protect. We cannot expect her to rejoice at the victory of truth any more than we can expect her to cry or rage in the presence of lies, deceit, or injustice.

The blindfolded lady is but the shadow image of Justice, a reflection of our fears rather than the expression of our hopes and courage. Whatever hope she may still harbour is only maintained at the cost of her enforced blindness. In her shadow form, Lady Justice has become the guardian of our intolerance, not the protector of our trust and our faith in humankind.

5 The Scales

Lady Justice is often depicted holding a set of scales (a balance) in one hand. In fact, the personification of justice balancing the scales dates back to the goddess Maat, and later Isis, of ancient Egypt. The scales held by Lady Justice are a mechanical device. The scale is so crucial to the symbolism conveyed by Lady Justice that, in recent time, the whole symbol has tended to be reduced to a simple scale. Lady Justice is being replaced by the instrument alone, suggesting that human intervention in justice are no longer required, that the system—the scale—has acquired a life of its own. The instrument itself, the image suggests, should be sufficient to weigh any matter, as long as it is artificially maintained in a perpetually simulated state of equilibrium.

The subjective aspect of weighing or taking a measurement of any kind is dissimulated or denied, as if fairness was an attribute of the human-made contraption and not of those who invent, build, and use such devices. The scales can serve also to mystify observers about what is the real weight that makes them tip in one direction or another. The tool itself is imperfect and can be tempered with or corrupted without Lady Justice even blinking an eye. In a technocratically inclined world, we are enjoined to believe in the quasi-infinite perfectibility of our tools and our systems and to doubt our own judgment.

From the small stylised graphic (icon) that points us in the direction of the courthouse to its elaborate representation in official logos and in courtrooms, the scale has become our most ubiquitous symbol of justice. Even Aristotle saw the scale, together with the sword, as symbolising one of the two fundamental dimensions of justice. For him, however, the scale was a dynamic symbol meant to evoke natural balance and social harmony. In its modern version, the scale has evidently been reduced to a more prosaic dimension, with its symbolic meaning reduced to its mere mechanical nature. The modern symbol of the scales, devoid of any reference to a higher ideal of justice and harmony, is evoking the system of justice, the mechanistic process, not the ideal, the goal or the higher purpose which we may have hoped it could achieve.

For a culture which espoused a mechanistic, deterministic, and linear worldview, the scales are a powerful symbol. It evokes an ability to control the world around us, by measuring and reducing quantities to something with which we feel comfortable. We came, as the children of the Age of Reason, to value balance, proportionality, stability, and equilibrium over all other human experiences. The equilibrium we have idealised is something we conceptualised as the result of human efforts to impose order, a category of reason, an artifice and an abstraction which we struggle to sustain. The balance we strive for is stagnant, virtually immobile.

Justice is thus represented as a device to which we do not have direct access, but only access through the system, if we have any access at all. Access to the scales is rigidly controlled and unevenly distributed. Furthermore, as Sell also notes, "the metaphorical influence of the scales on the legal imagination ranges from the grand - the teaching that individual liberties must be balanced against broader social concerns - to the everyday, as when lawyers rely on 'balancing tests' that weigh competing circumstances to guide legal analysis" (Sell 1994, p. 39). One day perhaps, as the system evolves, the simple scales will eventually be replaced by more complex weighing machines, electronic and digital, actuarial and statistical, or even biological. The complex weighing contraptions will also need tending, calibration, and interpretation, but always and only by experts, mostly in secret.

6 The Blindfold

Since the sixteenth century, Lady Justice has often been depicted wearing a blindfold. She is blindfolded, we are told, so that she may be impartial, acting without regard to wealth, power, or other status. The arbitrariness of reason is not vastly different from the arbitrariness of emotions or faith. Since reason is used to justify the privileges of a minority and the denial of the needs of others, the appearance of impartially has to be especially emphasised. Lady Justice had to at least appear to be blind to our relative positions of power and privilege in society. This way she at least has the excuse of the blindfold whenever she turns a blind eye to the blatant abuses committed by the privileged few. Perhaps, as Carsten Stroud (1993) suggested, she is "not so much blind as ethically astigmatic?"

It could also be, as some caricaturists depicted her, that Lady Justice cannot bare to see the injustices committed in her name. Or is it, that she be blind to our ignorance and our flaws. It is most likely not the kind of blindness that can be inspired by love or compassion. We may perhaps have dreamed of a Justice blinded by her love for humans, her humanism. Instead, we blindfolded her and condemned her to perpetual darkness and ignorance. If eyes are indeed windows to the soul, the blindfold is perhaps not so much to prevent Lady Justice from looking at us, as it is to prevent us from looking through in her eyes, into the burdensome part of our soul weighed as it is by hypocrisy, obfuscation, lies and fears.

Justice has no need of a blindfold, but her shadow side finds the arrangement quite convenient. Justice is quite capable of determining right from wrong with her eyes wide open. Without the blindfolded, she might cry for vengeance, not for a well-organised and rationally distributed punishment. If she could clearly see both the victim and the offender, she might realise that they are made of the same cloth and that peace is often better served by reconciliation than by punishment.

The Lady, it is also suggested, is perhaps blindfolded so that she may be blindly obedient to her learned priests or judicial oracles. She appears to be placidly content to hold the scales and to let them operate them. With "priesthood" comes privilege and power. These ranks and such privileges are closed to most of us. The oracles, those "initiated" into the intricate and complex workings of the justice system, would have us believe that there is no justice outside of that system. Yet, when Benjamin Sell, a former lawyer and now a therapist, asked lawyers and non-lawyers to try to imagine what the law "wants", he found some interesting differences: "Most non-lawyers say right off the bat that the Law wants justice". Lawyers, on the other hand, tend to be more diverse in their answers, mentioning things like equality, individual rights, truth, and fairness. It is not uncommon, for example, to hear lawyers say that what is legal doesn't necessarily have anything to do with what is just, or that truth and fairness are only ideals while the Law deals with practical reality (Sell 1994, p. 28).

7 The Sword

The sword is one of the most powerful and magical human symbols. It is almost always associated with Justice, her power and her uncompromising demands. Always brandished but rarely wielded, never arbitrarily used, treated with respect, never sheathed, Justice is primarily a symbol of power, determination and courage, not so much a symbol of authority. The sword, when it was still part of everyday life, was a frightening and threatening sight. As a symbol, it was often associated with magical powers and it almost invariably implied a prerequisite "worthiness" on the part of those who could carry it. In recent time, swords have become largely ceremonial. Since most of us have never seen or held a real sword, it symbolic power is much weaker.

These days, Lady Justice is often seen without it and she apparently does not dare reveal the new weaponry upon which her power now rests. When she does carry a sword, her arm is at rest and her whole attitude dismisses the significance of the naked blade. In some instances, the tip of her sword touches the ground and the mighty weapon looks no more threatening than the pilgrim's shaft.

8 Shadow

The exercise of authority has become the art of cultivating the shadow side of justice. The more we accept to live in the shadow side of justice, the more easily we are ruled. The accompanying sense of despair is the result of having listened to our fears and repressed our hopes. The law and the justice system can be seen as the expression of the "genius" or the "daemon" of our culture, of ourselves, conscious and unconscious.

There is much that is magical in our ability to engage and cooperate with each other. There is also much which is "daemonic" and frightful in human relationships.

We know that trust will not always be honoured, nor returned. Pretending that this is not true is not helpful. Pretending that this is all that is true about us is even worse. There are some real mysteries about human solidarity and aspirations for peace and justice.

So much of our justice related behaviour and attitudes is apotropaic, involving magical practices to ward off evil. Incantations and rituals easily replace the courageous actions for which the conflicts and challenges of our times call. Our idolatrous veneration of the images and the symbols is but a poor substitute for the pursuit of the actual human experience of solidarity, harmony, tolerance, and justice. Our justice related practices and other apotropaic behaviours are as revealing as the images and symbols we created. When some of the rituals themselves—arrests, trials, punishment—have lost their symbolic clarity and their evocative, cathartic, apotropaic value, their endless and perpetual re-enactment becomes little more than entertainment. When the future of a civilisation and its underlying authority structure depends more on shared fictions, symbols, and pernicious practices than on the shared experience of justice and harmony, its children are driven to a form of idolatry. The authority structure's slow process of degeneration will proceed uninterrupted.

Since we have all grown up in the shadow of Justice, we know how it feels: cold. But we must understand that we feel is but her shadow. We must rediscover what it is like to honour her in our lives. After all, where will we find her if not in ourselves, in the new images we will dare to imagine and create, and in the stories of justice and freedom we can tell each other? There is obviously much to learn and understand from these rituals and images about our authority structures and about how they betray our deep-felt need for the spiritual experience of justice.

9 Renewing Our Justice Mythology

In our pursuit of peace and justice, the "most within dimensions" of ourselves and the other are engaged, perhaps because the soul makes its demands known (Moore 1994, p. 23). The discourse on human rights is part of a modem "mythology", a mythology which can only exist as part of a larger one about nation states and their promises of safety, prosperity, and peace. Can we live without a mythology? Probably not, but we may have a choice about the mythology which we ultimately let inspire our lives and our choices.

The "reasonable" facsimile of justice that our institutions pursue and sometimes deliver leaves intact our desire for the spiritual experience of truth, peace, justice, and harmony. No matter how hard some people may try to persuade us of the contrary, laws and legal institutions are not some kind of godly gift. If there is a "goddess of justice," she has no life but through us. For her, said the French-Canadian poet Felix Leclerc, "we build palaces that she never inhabits." Her realm is not a system or the palaces we build for her. It was always in our hearts and in our souls. Yet, unfortunately, so much of our own pursuit of justice is apotropaic, condemned to reproduce impotent magical practices to ward off harm or evil influences. Incantations and rituals cannot replace the courageous acts which the conflicts and challenges of our time demand of us.

Even so, we must be aware of how rituals affirm and may help re-define our justice mythology. As Maruna (2011) observes, a ritual can be understood as "a medium of communication, with its own symbolic grammar and syntax" (p. 7), adding that it can "engender solidarity and social cohesion by bringing people together in a common cause" (p. 9). Interaction rituals, such as restorative justice procedures that may involve the victim, the offender, and community members, can facilitate rituals of apology, remorse, and understanding (Rossner 2013). In turn, they may create what Collins (2004, p. xii) calls "emotional energy", including feelings of confidence in the participants and public morality. At best, rituals may be expressions of our collective images of justice and the semantics we use in relation to justice. They may help communicate to the broader society the importance of social order and the shamefulness of offences that undermine that order (Braithwaite 2000). When we stay true to our aspirations for justice and when our justice rituals truly reflect those aspirations, rituals may help to foster the kind of solidarity, social cohesion, and trust on which some of the solutions to the conflicts of our time depend.

But when the rituals themselves lose their symbolic clarity and their evocative and cathartic value, the justice institutions that perpetually re-enact them have already lost much of their authority and legitimacy. A civilisation which rests on an authority structure and institutions that rely almost exclusively on symbolic rituals instead of the shared experience of justice and harmony ultimately leads its children to a form of idolatry. They will worship the images and progressively, as the images lose their power, they will reject them, and justice institutions will lose any cohesive authority it might have had over them. The slow degenerative process affecting the institutions will then be complete.

Admittedly, all of us are aware of our propensity to succedaneously accept symbols in lieu of the experience. We offer and accept symbols of success or prestige, as substitutes for recognition. There are also the symbols of attachment and sexual fidelity, as substitutes for genuine love and friendship. Symbols of age and presumed knowledge, as substitutes for wisdom. The list of such symbols could go on forever. So why should our desire for freedom and justice be treated differently? It should not, of course. Often lacking the courage and conviction to create justice around us, we settle for laws and a system of justice. Justice, we pretend, is that which is manufactured by the machinery of justice, by the system, and access to justice is conveniently reduced to access to the justice system. We continue to take comfort in the illusion of justice that we have all helped to create, while our hopes for freedom and harmony may remain largely unfulfilled.

10 Conclusion

Clearly, our justice symbols reflect the kind of justice that we choose to pursue. But when the meanings of those justice symbols have eroded and started to lose their authoritative value, we are left curious as to what may replace them. Will we choose quick substitutes? Easy alternatives? Settle for laws and access to the justice system? Or could we engage our imagination and envision something else for harmony and cooperation, perhaps rethinking the rituals that currently characterise our justice systems? Rituals cannot replace the courageousness and tenacity required to overcome the pressing and urgent challenges of our time, but they may be expressions of our justice aspirations. We may also need to ask ourselves: do our contemporary justice rituals align with our aspirations for justice? What are our aspirations for justice? What would expressions of our justice aspirations ideally look like?

Like any revolution in ideas and philosophies, the rejuvenation of our justice institutions will require a "successful escape from a blind alley" (Koestler 1980), particularly an escape from the bondage of mental habits and outdated symbolic representations of justice. Just as symbols can stimulate thinking, so too can they constrain it. National sovereignty too often serves as a shield under which human rights abusers hide. Human rights discourses have become the language of impotence and despair. And diminishing social cohesion may be placing strain on our institutions, adversely affecting their ability to anticipate or respond to societal challenges (World Economic Forum 2019). What could all of this mean for our visions of justice? Indeed, the future will tell whether our collective attempts to shape crime prevention and criminal justice in a manner that reflects our deeper aspirations for justice will prove to be a failure or an astonishing success. In the end, the real test will be whether we have learned to live together in peace.

References

Braithwaite, J. (2000). Survey article: Repentance rituals and restorative justice. *The Journal of Political Philosophy, 8*(1), 115–131.

Casamayor. (1977). *La mystification*. Paris: Gallimard.

Collins, R. (2004). *Interaction ritual chains*. Princeton: Princeton University Press.

Council of Europe. (2017). *State of democracy, human rights and the rule of law: Populism - How strong are Europe's checks and balance? Report by the Secretary General of the Council of Europe*. Strasbourg: Council of Europe.

Covey, F. M. (1959). The symbols of justice. *The Student Lawyer Journal, 5*(1), 14–17.

Dandurand, Y., & Jahn, J. (2018). The fragility of a culture of lawfulness. *Białostockie Studia Prawnicze, 23*(3), 13–26. https://doi.org/10.15290/bsp.2018.23.03.01

Harari, Y. N. (2015). *Homo Sapiens*. Toronto: Signal Books.

Hayakawa, S. I. (1941/1978). *Language in thought and action* (4th ed.). New York: Harcourt Brace and Jovanovich.

Ignatieff, M. (1993). *Blood and belonging: Journeys into the new nationalism*. London: Chatto & Windus.

Koestler, A. (1980). *Bricks to Babel*. London: Picador.

Marshall, D. (2014). *The international rule of law movement: A crisis of legitimacy and the way forward*. Cambridge: Harvard University Press.
Maruna, S. (2011). Reentry as a rite of passage. *Punishment and Society, 13*(1), 3–28. https://doi.org/10.1177/1462474510385641
Moore, T. J. (1994). *Soul mates: Honoring the mystery of love and relationships*. New York: Harper Collins.
Rossner, M. (2013). *Just emotions: Rituals of restorative justice*. Oxford: Oxford University Press.
Saul. (1993). *Voltaire's Bastards: The dictatorship of reason in the West*. Toronto: Penguin Books.
Saul. (1995). *The unconscious civilization*. Concord: Anansi.
Sell, B. (1994). *The soul of the law*. Rockport: Element.
Stroud, C. (1993). *Contempt of court: The betrayal of justice in Canada*. Toronto: Penguin Books.
Whorf, B. L. (1956). Language, thought and reality. In J. B. Caroll (Ed.), *Selected writings of B. L. Whorf*. New York: John Wiley.
World Economic Forum. (2019). *The global risk report* (14th ed.). Geneva: WEC.

Yvon Dandurand is a criminologist, Professor Emeritus, School of Criminology and Criminal Justice, University of the Fraser Valley, British Columbia, Canada, as well as a Fellow and Senior Associate of the International Centre for Criminal Law Reform and Criminal Justice Policy, a United Nations affiliated research institute. He specializes in comparative criminal justice research and has been extensively involved in justice reform and policy development projects in Canada, Asia, Africa, and Latin America. His research interests include transnational organized crime, corruption, justice for children, restorative justice, access to justice, peace building, and criminal justice reform in general. He has co-authored several books and articles on criminal justice reform, restorative justice, human trafficking, and international cooperation in criminal matters. E-mail: Yvon.Dandurand@ufv.ca.

Jessica Jahn is a Researcher with the International Centre for Criminal Law Reform and Criminal Justice Policy (Vancouver, Canada). She holds an MSc in Criminal Justice Policy with Distinction from the London School of Economics and a BA (Hons.) in Criminal Justice from the University of the Fraser Valley (Vancouver, Canada). Her research interests include transnational organized crime, prevention of violent extremism, and access to justice. E-mail: jessica.jahn@telus.net; net20025100054@mailid.telus.net.

The Relevance of Philosophical and Religious Ideas to the United Nations Quest for Universalizing Criminal Justice

Sławomir Redo

Abstract In the UN Charter, the Universal Declaration of Human Rights (UDHR) and the 2030 Sustainable Development Agenda, there are many calls for universal justice. This criminological chapter seeks to consider them against the background of a very polarizing question whether the "9/11" or other such attacks may be internationally defined as terrorism. Next, the chapter selectively reviews the UN-relevant roots of "justice" and goals of criminal punishment from the perspective of universalistic philosophers with their own views about justice *vis à vis* natural and positive law. In conclusion, the author points that the UN work has its own "Reason" whose ecumenism originated from the tragic Nazi Holocaust. With this "Reason" the Organization continues going its own way over the conceptual divides between the worlds of Member States, religious, and philosophical values.

Keywords Justice · Punishment · Social contract · Terrorism · United Nations · Universalism

1 Introduction

Two statements open this chapter. First, in the aftermath of attacks of 11 September 2001 ("9/11") that killed altogether 3000 people, injured over 6000 others, and caused at least $13 billion in infrastructure and property damage (Krieger 2013), a prominent French post-modernist philosopher Jacques Derrida (1930–2004) refused to describe them as "international terrorism." He opined that "an act of 'international terrorism' is anything but a rigorous concept that would help us grasp the singularity of what we are trying to discuss" (Barrodori 2003, p. 86). Second, in the same year he surprised his Chinese audience—university teachers and students of the philosophy departments—by stating that "China does not have any philosophy, only

S. Redo (✉)
United Nations Studies Association, Wien, Austria
e-mail: s@redo.net

H. Kury, S. Redo (eds.), *Crime Prevention and Justice in 2030*,
https://doi.org/10.1007/978-3-030-56227-4_28

thought [. . .] Philosophy is related to some sort of particular history, some languages, and some ancient Greek invention [. . .]. It is something of European form (Van Norden 2017, p. 25)." *Ergo*: a "Chinese prejudice" (Meighoo 2008)?

Western academics, Western and Eastern criminal justice practitioners may be surprised by both opening statements, while diplomats, especially by the first statement.

Starting with it, given a strong condemnation of the above attacks by the United Nations General Assembly (A/RES/56/1), how this statement fits the saying that someone's "terrorism" may be another one's "fight for the national independence"? In other words, what then is a "just" cause from the United Nations perspective?

The United Nations is generally seized by this justice dilemma, so the above specific academic dilemma is classical, and a part of a bigger one. As of 2016 this dilemma has been practically embellished by the 2030 United Nations' "Transforming our world: the 2030 Agenda for Sustainable Development" (A/RES/70/1) with its sustainable Goal 16 "Peace, justice and strong institutions." Legitimate therefore is the question whether there is anything common between the above highly relativist post-modernist and *avant-garde* argument, and the universalism of the United Nations with its—on the one side—individual followers' credo that "since the Holocaust, cultural relativism is dead" (Hoffman 2001, p. 273), and—on the other side—the Organization's "respect for cultural identities" (A/RES/70/174, § 7)?

Mindful then of the above bigger question with occasionally incongruent United Nations justice picture contrasting "universal" with "particular"/"singular" (or "*logos*"[1] with "*ethos*"[2]), this criminological chapter first explores the roots of Organization's philosophy of universalizing justice, or—using an academic term—a "constructionist" perspective for the UN's global countering of crime, including terrorism.

2 Philosophical Roots of the United Nations Understanding of "Justice" from the Criminological Perspective

Philosophers, other social scientists, political and religious leaders and the UN in its own conceptual and interdisciplinary terms address economic, moral and religious roots of the idea of justice. The United Nations philosophy associates itself with an idealist school of thought.

Yet by the Organization's structure the argument of power ("realism") is evident. The Security Council is the most powerful within the United Nations. However, seeing the Security Council as the "Holy Alliance" policing domestic unrest would be a gross simplification. Policing internal and external conflicts which jeopardize

[1]Greek for "word," "reason," or "spirit".

[2]Greek for "character".

peace and justice would be a more appropriate opinion. In doing so, "[t]he philosophical foundation in liberal thought for this institution has been and will remain precarious" (Fidler 1996, p. 452, cf. p. 439, ft. 120).

In line with this thought often emanating from the Security Council resolutions, and even more often from other United Nations criminal justice and crime prevention standards and norms, in the Organization not the fight for power and national interest, but Reason, education and science drive social justice reforms, prevent wars and other hostile international acts. According to its Charter, politics is an art of good governance and an instrument of making good international neighbourhood relations.

In principle, the UN framers and other stakeholders more often than not have desisted from making any—explicit or implicit—reference to the concrete philosophers or philosophical underpinnings that they built upon the Charter (cf. Rauber 2009, p. 50).

"The origin of ideas is not the kind of thing to which 'purity' happens easily" (Sen 2005, p. 132). Foggy therefore as the origin of the idea of "justice" in the UN is, it is entangled in several roots.

Regarding the Charter, this fogginess had a good reason. Adolf Hitler, the Nazi *Führer* and other (pre-) Second World War National Socialists with their "*Gott mit uns*" had vulgarized and perverted the concepts of Enlightenment philosophers (Sherrat 2013; cf. Russell 1945). Those philosophers' pure ideas laid the ground to it, but in the Charter's *travaux préparatoires* there is no official acknowledgment of this fact.

Regarding the UDHR, there were many attempts to include in it the reference to the divine, but it remained a secular document (Morsink 2017).

Regarding the 2030 Agenda, it has deeply ingrained universalistic ideas on peace, justice and inclusiveness. Conceptually, these are remarkable products of the Organization's own political philosophy = Reason which is nominally secular.

Below are presented respective progressive universalistic ideas on justice (occasionally parts of philosophies). As emphasized earlier, they are or may be relevant to the above legal documents.

This is not systematic review. It is selectively and criminologically geared towards the *reason d'etre* of the United Nations—the prevention of the scourge of wars. These ideas are divided in two groups: Western and Eastern.

2.1 Western Philosophical Ideas

The Western ethnocentric part goes back to the pre-Socratics. It includes many other idealistic Greek philosophers (e.g., Aristotle), and likewise many other (pre-) Enlightenment thinkers (philosophers, lawyers, polymaths), including St. Thomas Aquinas (1225–1274), Gottfried Wilhelm Leibniz (1646–1716), Jean-Jacques

Rousseau (1712–1780), Charles Montesquieu (1689–1755), Immanuel Kant (1724–1804), Wilhelm Friedrich Hegel (1730–1816), Cesare Beccaria (1738–1794), and Jeremy Bentham (1748–1832)—just to mention a few.

In keeping only with these few idealists, mentioning here first Socrates (470–399 BCE) at once invites his method of critical inquiry "I know that I know nothing." The United Nations Scientific, Educational and Cultural Organization (UNESCO 2007, p. 13) recommended this inductive method of instructor-student dialogue for schooling, as an example of a pursuit of knowledge and truth. That pursuit led Socrates to death sentence, but "ultimately made life rewarding at the cost of his life" (Goldhil 2018).

Socrates' act of submitting himself to the death judgement by a fundamental legal authority was an act of "filial duty." It was the obligation of any citizen has to his or her state as "the father of nation," in criminology duty known as Latin "*parens patriae*"—contemporary State's obligation to take care of delinquents. At his time, that duty was even stronger than the obligation of a child to its parent (Crito, 51a9-bl). Socrates' sacrifice made him also "the first criminal justice educator" (Holland 1980, p. 1). No wonder therefore that his way of teaching what is "just" has become quite popular in the Western educational system (Redo et al. 2018).

Indeed, for Socrates and other like-minded universalistic philosophers "*Logos*" has been the constitutive element of truth, if not also the very source of creation itself. The truth of God or some other overriding transcendent or civic truth may thus be identifiable with logos. *Logos*/Reason/Spirit is for them the vehicle of aesthetics, justice, morality, theories of knowledge, and understanding.

Aristotle (384–322 BCE) understood "*Logos*" as now any Western-educated lawyer does: "the word or that by which the inward thought is expressed" or "the inward thought itself"" (Liddel and Scott 1889). "Syllogism"—his deductive reasoning method—has become a global instrument of delivering proof in natural science. And so, in Western social science, including criminological research, on which draw UN crime prevention and criminal justice manuals and handbooks, principally evidence-based, as if in medicine (e.g., UNODC 2009).

Syllogistic thinking was embraced as a theological instrument by the Roman Catholic Church. That instrument was praised by the atheist philosopher Bertrand Russell (1872–1970), one of the most eminent contemporary exponents of idealism. He found syllogism as sterile as the twelfth century monks were (Nisbett 2003, p. 203).

In the next century Aquinas, one of the Dominican monks who got to know Aristotle's "Logic" from its Latin translation, strongly emphasized that knowledge is not innate. It is gained from the reports of the senses and from logical inference from self-evident truths.

In the United Nations history of ideas Aquinas first of all is known from the natural law concept of human dignity and rights (McCrudden 2008, p. 662). Morsink (2017, pp. 79 & 100) informs that in 1942, when the Second World War ravaged, this concept was invoked by Pope Pius XII in his Christmas message. Next, it was recalled by the French philosopher and Thomist Jacques Maritain (1882–1973)—a strong supporter of the UDHR. The concept offered a "middle of the road" between the dominant post-Second World War ideologies when UDHR was elaborated (Aquilina 2019), and paved the way to build the respect of human dignity through criminal liability.

Leibniz admitted that syllogism is the "the most beautiful, and also one of the most important products made by the human mind...infallible art is therein contained" (Leibniz 1996, § 478). Therefore he appreciated the apparent correspondence between the invented by him binary arithmetic (the mathematical foundation of contemporary computer science) and the *Yijing*, or Book of Changes, an ancient Chinese classic. In the opening passages it envisages the way to heaven through the significance, harmony, and dynamic creativity of the ceaseless transformation of things and situations (Nelson 2011, p. 377). For Leibniz, the concepts and symbols of this book appeared to represent binary arithmetic—broken and unbroken lines, essentially 0s (signifying absolute nothingness) and 1s (signifying God's oneness). Leibniz, a confessional Lutheran completely faithful to the Bible, saw these lines as symbolically representing the creation of the Universe, a mystical model built *ex nihilo* by God (Swetz 2003, p. 276; Nelson 2011, p. 379).

From Leibniz's studies follow two observations globally and criminologically relevant to the United Nations quest for justice.

First, he observed, that while the West has the advantage of having received Christian revelation, and is superior to China in the natural sciences, "certainly they surpass us (though it is almost shameful to confess this) in practical philosophy, that is, in the precepts of ethics and politics adapted to the present life and the use of mortals" (Leibniz after Van Norden 2017, p. 19). What he reportedly meant was his appreciation of the Confucian philosophy of living in harmony with nature—"a highly sophisticated natural ethics that could be the envy of Europe" (Wilson 2015, p. 113). Coincidentally or not, the 2030 United Nations Sustainable Development Agenda exactly recommends ensuring that people everywhere have the relevant information and awareness for sustainable development and lifestyles in harmony with nature." Separately, the report of the UN Secretary-General mentions Leibniz as one of the early believers in nature and the wilderness imbued with spiritual values from which humans could not be disconnected (A/66/302, § 20). Emerging crime prevention and other global citizenship education on "climate justice" for sustainable development is a case in point.

Second, Leibniz, a—librarian by profession with a passion for order—emphasized that the enlightened society needs a scientific work organization: promoting the exchange of creative thoughts between all participants of scientific life through the web of integrated libraries and academics (Święczkowska 2016, ch. V). These Leibniz's public information/librarian ideas and work are very revealing—in a way a proto-type for the 2030 United Nations SDG 16.10: "Ensure public access to information and protect fundamental freedoms, in accordance with national legislation."

For Rousseau (1920), in turn, in his "Social Contract" (SC) "[a]ll justice comes from God" (SC II § 6), but "Christianity as a religion is entirely spiritual, occupied solely with heavenly things; the country of the Christian is not of this world"

(SC VIII § 25). The way to justice was through re-negotiating a social contract—"a convention between the body and each of its members" (SC II § 4) by which society overcomes its decay and saves itself from the regress to barbarism.

This interpretation fits the concept of the United Nations Charter—a social contract drawn by "We, the peoples" as the equals, is unanimous reaction to the barbarism of the Second World War. But neither in the United Nations Charter records, including *travaux préparatoires*, nor in the commentaries on the Charter there is a mention of Rousseau, or any other social contract theorist/philosopher.

Every source credits the concept of the Charter to the political philosophy of the US President Franklin Delano Roosevelt (1933–1945). His own idea of "essential human rights" contained in the "Four Freedoms" unquestionably contributed to the Charter, and to the subsequent "Bill of International Human Rights" (1948–1966). He was the one who originally pleaded for such "bill of rights" (Sohn 1995, p. 540).

Human rights eventually consolidated as "the Bill" were first entertained by scholars. Their early post-First World French-US intellectual contributions went unnoticed by drafters, but were found remarkably bill-like (Ibidem, pp. 541–542).

Since Roosevelt's "Four Freedoms" statement delivered on 6 January 1941, effective influence over bill's intellectual content has first had an expert team from twelve countries. Among the experts was Ricardo J. Alfaro, the former President of Panama, later Director of the American International Law Institute, a leading member of the team, and the enthusiast of Rousseau's and Montesquieu's progressive ideas (Sultan 2004, p. 158; Gasteazoro 1981, pp. 160, 200).

While "the Bill" had eventually been concluded in 1966, its human rights ideals have been signalled in the Preamble and Art. 55 of the Charter. That treaty eventually had started to take shape in Autumn 1944 at the six-week Dumbarton Oaks Conference of the representatives of the United States, United Kingdom, the Soviet Union, and China.[3]

There is no single reference to Montesquieu's works in the Charter's *travaux prèparatoires*. But, as it soon will be demonstrated, his understanding of justice is not so distant from the UN understanding.

This is because Montesquieu (1891) felt in his "Persian Letters" (PL) that "justice is eternal and independent of human conventions" (PL LXXXIV). It is "a true relation existing between two things; a relation which is always the same, whoever contemplates it, whether it be God, or an angel, or lastly, man himself" (PL LXXXIV).

In the "Letters"—a bestseller of his time—Montesquieu conveyed the affective foundation of his doctrine. He expressed it in the voice of "Usbek"—a literary character a Persian visitor to France, apparently impersonating Montesquieu as an adult (his alter ego was "Rika"—young person). His expression certainly is a defining argument in the question of *logos vs. ethos*, and Montesquieu's "extended tribute to cultural pluralism" (Williams 2010, p. 527).

---

[3]I.e., without the participation of France—still besieged by war, and eventually recognized on 8 May 1945 as its victor.

Yet it was not really his cultural pluralism worth a tribute but rather universalism. With this philosophy in his "Persian Letters" (XXXVII) and in "The Spirit of Laws" (Montesquieu 2001/SL) Montesquieu exposed and condemned overly punitive and theologically incoherent criminal justice. "Mankind must not be governed with too much severity; we ought to make a prudent use of the means which nature has given us to conduct them" (SL 6/12, p. 101). "When religion condemns things which the civil laws ought to permit, there is danger lest the civil laws, on the other hand, should permit what religion ought to condemn. Either of these is a constant proof of a want of true ideas of that harmony and proportion which ought to subsist between both" (SL 24/14, p. 474).

He likened the extremism of Christian inquisition by burning Jews with odious Japanese punishment practices of Christians who did not renounce their faith (SL 25/13, p. 14 & 494, p. 496). His book was banned by the Catholic Church (Montesquieu was a Roman Catholic married to a Calvinist women, while his ancestors were Protestants). But he was neither prejudiced against Christianity nor Japan or any other religion or country (SL, pref. 14–15). He was a very reasoned person. His religious background had played in his works an insignificant role (he thus may be regarded as one of the most eminent representatives of enlightenment secularism). He recognized the errors of both orders, but he also foresaw the errors of their would-be despotic correctors. Based on his views, like "[a] good legislator takes a just medium; he ordains neither always pecuniary, nor always corporal punishments" (SL, 6/16, p. 109), their analysts qualified him as a moderate teacher of corrections, who universally criticizes despotism that makes punishment so cruel anywhere in the world (Gilmore and Sullivan 2017).

Given Montesquieu's views on justice as independent of human conventions, which also motivates the UN's concept of "larger freedom," it is now clear why in "The Spirit of Laws" (6/11) he recommended as a regulatory matter the separation of powers between the parliament, government and judiciary. The separation has a regulatory function to maintain law and order, political liberty, and the protection of property of the individual. In the United Nations, Montesquieu is first of all appreciated for this particular regulatory human convention. In that book, as the President of the General Assembly reminded Member States, Montesquieu stated that "[t]here is no nation so powerful as the one that obeys its laws, not from principles of fear or reason, but from passion" (UNGA/11290).

Regarding Kant (2013), in the "Metaphysics of Morals" (MM) he saw a social contract as an instrument for good governance and human progress. It involved the idea of the union of nations and the Word Law (MM 8 § 358) akin to the League of Nations (1920–1946) and the United Nations. Although he was genuinely religiously motivated, in no way he implied a faith-based organization. He was a theological liberal. The (non)secular force of his ideals was found to be essential to confront the German Nazis and Imperial Japanese, and in the establishment of the United Nations (Weiss 2015, p. 1233).

Kant's views about faith are very composed. According to him, "[w]e cannot very well make obligation (moral constraint) intuitive for ourselves without thereby thinking of another's will, namely God's, of whom "reason in giving universal laws is only the spokesman." (MM 6 § 487). His divine command enables us to achieve our moral goals, according to the Kant's transcendental and universal imperative "So act that the maxim of your action could become a universal law" (MM 6 § 389).

Kant's views earned him the criticism of his peers and country's monarch. He who found them too progressive and liberal, to the point that he was labelled a secular Calvin or Luther (Kant was Lutheran) (Friedrich 1947, pp. 15 & 18; Lestition 1993, p. 92).

And so far reaching and progressive is his other imperative: "act in accordance with a maxim of ends that it can be a universal law for everyone to have" (MM 6 § 395). It emphasizes the moral equality and inalienable dignity of all human beings.

Both imperatives define ethics independent of social contract or social norms. They are more overarching then the UN goal of inclusiveness to increase and intensify multicultural integration. Indeed, these two imperatives of Kant are for me examples of "Christian love beyond reciprocity" (Morsink 2017, p. 84). Both are an improvement on the UN version of the Golden Rule "Do Unto Others As You Would Have Them Do Unto You," inscribed into the 1961 symbolic mosaic donated to the United Nations HQ in New York by Norman Rockwell (1894–1978), US artist. Not only these two imperatives may be an argument that this comparatively moderate UN goal of multicultural integration as more realistic can be more successful, but also that the entire 2030 Agenda likewise is attainable with its drive for more people's inclusiveness in other social and economic affairs.

Kant's other views on justice and punishment are likewise very democratizing and civic, even though not fully in line with the United Nations' eventual objective of abolishing the death penalty (Art. 6 para. 6 of the International Covenant on Civil and Political Rights). "Even if civil society were to be dissolved. . .the last murderer remaining in prison would have to be first executed" (MM 6 § 332). It seems that he leaves no doubt about his exclusively retributive view of punishment. It looks that for him—unlike for the Agenda—"leaving no one behind" is just to execute a criminal. However, in other than capital cases it is also a useful social practice: (a) "meant to deter the sinner himself or deter others by making an example of him," or (b) "it is a means, an act of graciousness or clemency, if I seek to improve the criminal himself, or (c) "an act of prudence, if I attempt thereby to prevent further wrong-doing" (Kant 1795/2001a, b, 27 §§ 286 & 552). In generic terms, these are three of the United Nations criminal policy goals, short of victim's compensation and reconciliation.

Kant's the 1784 "*Sapere aude*" ("Dare to know"), in turn, since the European Enlightenment has become the ever green motto promoting the application of reason in the public sphere of human affairs (Holt and Hond 2013). The United Nations "knowledge-based crime prevention" (ECOSOC resolution 2003/12) is the unwitting testimony to his philosophy. And so is SDG 16. In the light of new empirical findings suggesting that irrespective of the existence of death penalty homicide is more likely to decline in polities with higher investment in education and a greater long-term orientation (Booklet 2, Box 10, UNODC 2019b, p. 40), Kant would have probably yielded on his preference for it, and subscribed to SDG 16.

Because of Kant's concern for the injustice foreigners may experience from the hand of natives, so providential is his idea of universal right of hospitality (Kant 2001a, b, 8 § 358) , and so testimonial are also various 1951–2019 United Nations legal instruments addressing the question of refugees and safe, orderly and regular migration. Kant's concern that "rights" must be matched by "duties," especially in the migration context, is worth echoing, as already emphasized elsewhere (Kury and Redo 2018, p. 864 et seq.).

Last but not least, Kant's understanding of justice as an expression of moral autonomy of rational people submitted to the moral law/imperatives followed in their cooperation is somewhat similar to Hegel's "justice," even though Kant was not a social contract philosopher, while Hegel was (Harcourt 2013, p. 12). In his "The Philosophy of Right" (PR), Hegel (1952), a staunch Lutheran, on the one side, argues, that justice is morally defined by God. He gave humanity a mind with enormous powers to get to know Him. However, on the other side, justice is defined by secular ethics, because he is committed to the modern principle of freedom. This is a subordinate relation, in which citizens under God compromise on their rights among themselves. Their activity is consciously aimed at none but the universal end (PR § 264).

That "universal end"/"*logos*" does not preclude "*ethos*", i.e., the right of individuals to be satisfied in their particular pursuits and free activity, in the course of which they may go wrong (PR §§ 315–318). When punished, they should only know "Do not that to another, which you would not do to yourself."

Punishment only annuls the crime by a State (PR §§ 101–102). It is it's a figuratively retributive act, not necessarily the one which also avenges for a personal injury. This understanding of retribution is much less than Kant's understanding, and falls short of the UN progressive criminal policy goals.

Surprisingly, however, in the unpublished by him "The Spirit of Christianity and its Fate" the "young Hegel" envisions another goal—restorative justice:

> A heart [. . .] lifted above the ties of rights, disentangled from everything objective, has nothing to forgive the offender, for it sacrificed its right as soon as the object over which it had a right was assailed, and thus the offender has done no injury to any right at all. Such a heart is open to reconciliation, for it is able forthwith to reassume any vital relationship, to re-enter the ties of friendship and love, since it has done no injury at all to life in itself. On its side there stands in the way no hostile feeling, no consciousness, no demand on another for the restoration of an infringed right, no pride which would claim from another in a lower sphere, i.e., in the realm of rights, an acknowledgment of subordination (Hegel 1948, p. 236).

Hegel's decision not to publish his ideas on restorative justice (in his view apparently not ripe enough) had for long been kept in the academic closet. Among lawyers in developed countries where Hegel is known best, restorative justice for long had been an academic anathema (Redo 2015, p. 243). It first transpired in international penal policy in 1985. Then the UN General Assembly adopted a Declaration of Basic Principles on Justice for Victims of Crime and Abuse of Power (A/RES/40/34). There it stated that "informal mechanisms for the resolution of disputes, including mediation, arbitration and customary justice or indigenous practices, should be utilized where appropriate to facilitate conciliation and redress for victims" (A/RES/40/34, § 7). In 2002 the UN adopted Basic Principles on Restorative Justice in Criminal Matters (ECOSOC resolution 2002/12). It legitimized globally restorative justice practices, originally derived not from Hegel but from the social life of indigenous tribes from Australia and Canada (UNODC 2006, p. 29). So is one of the ways in which ideas and practices travel independently from one another and eventually are unwittingly together implementable by the UN.

Hegel and Kant were very dogmatic and non-utilitarian. Both criticized Beccaria, one of the most revered jurists and criminologists of the Age of Enlightenment, for yielding on the ultimacy of punishment and emphasizing the utility of crime prevention. They differed from Beccaria regarding the goals of punishment, including death penalty. Kant was an absolute retentionist (MM 6 § 335), Hegel a qualified one (PR § 100 & 101).

Beccaria was pragmatic and experiential. He blended their dogmatic retributivism with his utilitarianism. Beccaria was abolitionist because he thought that death penalty is not deterrent (until this day there is no conclusive evidence[4]) and, anyway, should not serve vengeance.

Having witnessed a brutal public execution for sodomy, Beccaria realized that death penalty does not serve public utility—it is merely emotional. He did not share the view of his contemporaries that criminal punishment had to be cruel so as to instil the fear of God. As a Jesuit-educated, he felt, that the religious motif that may prevent crime is too weak. It is too distant, to make any impression on the potential offender's senses (Beccaria 1764, ch. XVIII, p. 35). Swiftness is rational and serves "[c]ommon utility, which is the basis of human justice" (Beccaria 1764, ch. VII, pp. 16–17).

There are limits to punishment. "It is better to prevent crimes than to punish them. This is the chief purpose of every good system of legislation, which is the art of leading men conducting men to the maximum of happiness, and to the minimum of misery, if we may apply this mathematical expression to the good and evil of life" (Ibidem, ch. XLI, p. 147). By emphasizing social utility of punishment (deterrence and prevention of (re)offending) he has become in the United Nations its most recognized and revered liberal social contract penologist, whose idea of eventual abolishment of death penalty has been cast in stone by Art. 6 § 6 of the International Covenant on Civil and Political Rights (Redo 2012).

Through his 1764 essay "On Crimes and Punishments" Beccaria contributed significantly to the development of international penal science and crime prevention. He made various arguments concerning reforms for rational and fair treatment of offenders, and the social improvements. In the offenders' and society's interest, he argued that the type and length of deprivation of liberty should inversely relate to the level of effective security provided for society by the state. Everyone's minimum portion of natural freedom constitutes the public deposit of sovereignty which is the basis for the right to punish those actions that are injurious to the human society. On

[4]See my earlier comment on Kant's retentionism. For the most recent metanalytical review confirming the above, see also Hermann and Dölling (2016), p. 19.

the balance, every (non)offender would commensurately enjoy the life (level of happiness), according to his/her legal status.

Bentham, his like-minded follower, fully expounded the valors of the above utilitarian calculus, but in the United Nations Crime Prevention and Criminal Justice Programme he is first known as a progressive prison reformer. Bentham developed the idea of a panopticon-built type of prison facilitating visual control of inmates—a management tool facilitating accountability. "Accountability" is the sole but very salient Programme's interest in Bentham's utilitarianism.

However, in the academic world Bentham's philosophy motivated Michel Foucault with his "Discipline and Punish" about changing power relations regarding punishment. Other penalists were motivated by his views on rehabilitation and minimizing inmates' suffering, including most vulnerable ones—women (Ekeløve-Slydal 2018, p. 439).

His by far stronger contemporary relevance to the United Nations criminal and penal policies comes from the unrecognized in them fact that he fathered the term "international jurisprudence." He also recommended changing the term "the law of nations" into "the law between nations" eventually into "international law." Since then he has been heralded as a cosmopolitan with a vision for securing world peace and happiness for all nations grounded in "international jurisprudence" and "Common Court of Judicature." They both would advance domestic laws, settle disputes from a panel of members from different nations and would enforce its decisions with increasing levels of responses (Bentham 1907/2007).

In the realm of international law and jurisprudence is the Rome Statute of the International Criminal Court (ICC). While that form of criminal jurisprudence keeps with Beccaria's and Bentham's utilitarian ideas supporting life imprisonment (reconsidered in the UN Crime Prevention and Criminal Justice Programme), it shares its abolitionist stance. However, unlike that Programme, ICC's perception of the deterrent value of imprisonment is expressive. This is because of the ambiguous global outreach of its verdicts. The varying utilitarian calculus, let alone degrees of respect for the rule of law in countries and people of various legal cultures explains why global deterrence is expressive rather than effective.[5]

Regarding the latter goal, the judges of the International Criminal Tribunal for the Former Yugoslavia (ICTY) interpreted general deterrence as imposing a punishment that serves to strengthen the legal order, in which the type of conduct involved is defined as criminal, and to reassure society of the effectiveness of its penal provisions (Prosecutor v. Miodrag Jokić, Case No. IT-01-42/1-S, § 34).

However, in another ICTY verdict they added that: "One of the main purposes of a sentence imposed by an international tribunal is to influence the legal awareness of the accused, the surviving victims, their relatives, the witnesses and the general

[5] A very perceptive account of the limits of deterrence was given by Beccaria. He credited it to relative deprivation. Aware that countries' welfare is unequally distributed (cf. SDG 10 on inequality within and among nations) the majority of population sees itself deprived "which arises more from comparison than from reality" (XXXII, p. 62).

public in order to reassure them that the legal system is implemented and enforced. Additionally, the process of sentencing is intended to convey the message that globally accepted laws and rules have to be obeyed by everybody" (Prosecutor v. Miroslav Deronjić, Case No. IT-02-61-S, §§ 142 ff., in particular para. 147).

This expressive function will matter as long as the goals of the United Nations Sustainable Development Agenda and its successors will not make the world more inclusive. Striving for this major objective is first of all up to Member States through their domestic social justice work and jurisprudence, with SDG 1 is at its forefront ("end extreme poverty"). The ICC's verdicts may merely spearhead these developments, stipulating restorative justice measures, presently hardly pursued (Garbett 2017). Global civic education and legal training involving the ICC jurisprudence should be the means for enhancing its outreach.

Nonetheless already now the pioneering ICC model of rational global legislation exemplifies for Member States that in their jurisdictions international crimes defined in the Statute may be analogously defined and otherwise dealt with in the national legislation, penal and crime prevention practice. Hence they may be concordantly prosecutable, offenders found guilty, and crime victims or/and their families compensated, while potential offenders deterred (Ekeløve-Slydal 2018).

2.2 Eastern Philosophical Ideas

Until the establishment of the United Nations, the West-East philosophical divide has been entrenched with respective normative texts of reference from the diverse legal cultures. "Reading these texts, helped by exegesis and commentary, guided the interpretation of the world. But reports from China resisted integration by such textual tools, since they offered neither reason nor report of this distant land. But in the Enlightenment, as a result of seeking emancipation from tradition, China became a normative model in its own right. For Europeans, China served as a tool for interpreting the religious customs, the political system, and the social order on their own continent" (Fuchs 2006, p. 35).

The drafting work on the UDHR and the 2030 Agenda is here taken as the evidence of going across this divide, and the ontological evidence of universality of values whose global protection is now the job of relevant UN judicial structures. Regarding the UDHR, the credit for incorporating in it the Eastern philosophical ideas belongs to Eleanor Roosevelt, the wife of Franklin D. Roosevelt, then the US President and to John P. Humphrey, UN Director of the Division on Human Rights. She invited him and the two GA delegates: Peng-chun Chang/China, and Charles H. Malik/Lebanon to a private meeting. Malik, as a Greek Orthodox Christian raised in a family of different Christian denominations, and Chang, as a pluralist and Confucian, were the two intellectual heavyweights who sensitized her to the relevance of Eastern philosophy to the draft UDHR (cf. Shi et al. 2014, pp. 149–151).

Malik as a theologian had very good negotiating skills and a Christian commitment to evangelism. Chang's role in drafting the UDHR's preamble and its other articles was appreciated because of his expertise in the philosophy of Confucius and Aquinas (Shi et al. 2014). These two philosophers believed in natural justice, but interpreted by the former as a natural reason, and the latter as Revelation.

Chang universalized Confucian philosophy. He put it on equal footing with Aquinas'. Thus Chang contributed to the secularization of the UDHR as a product of natural morality, not of Revelation (cf. Rogacz 2018).[6] Thanks also to Chang's negotiating skills the UDHR framers agreed to incorporate in the text "conscience" (preamble, arts. 1 and 18) and to "the spirit of brotherhood" (Art. 1), the Confucian terms which emphasize the importance of social relations (Morsink 1999, pp. 298–301; Gier 2012, p. 3).

Such presently common moral cannons are many in the quest for the UN justice. For instance, Confucius' canonical concept of "filial duty," i.e., "obey your ruler, a son/daughter must obey his/her father's command, a wife should obey orders from her husband," reminds of the like-named concept of Socrates. And so does similarly sounding to Socrates' "I know that I know nothing" Confucius' saying "Shall I teach you what wisdom means? . . .? To know what you know and know what you do not know - this is then wisdom" (Analects 1998, 2.17). Likewise, the ecological imperative of living in harmony with nature, so much appreciated by Leibniz in the Confucian philosophy, and in the UN work for living in harmony with nature, suggests another commonality between Western and Eastern philosophies for a right living. Confucius' Golden Rule "Do not impose on others what you yourself do not want" (Analects 1998, 15.24) parallels such one in the secular and spiritual Western world. Finally, new Confucianism which in China started in the early twentieth century as a movement that sought to integrate some elements of Western legal culture with the Confucian tradition, in some places is similar to Kant's arguments regarding his "right to hospitality" (Lee 2017), hence what currently is termed "safe, orderly and responsible" migration in the United Nations.

Such common moral cannons oversimplify what "justice" really means in West and East. Not because philosophy of justice would exclusively be "something of European form" (re. the second opening statement), but because "Western and Confucian ideas are conceptually compatible but practically different" (Chang 1999, p. 137). For example, "filial duty" has since the time of Socrates evolved in the Western world into a distinctively contractual direction, in contrast with its enduring very patriarchal Confucian sense in the Eastern world. However, let alone, the fact that the above quoted philosophical statements are completely differently written in their original languages (Western logocentrism vs. Chinese logograms) warrant the question, whether indeed there is any common "language," (Redo 2013)[7] that bridges and transforms legal cultures with a view to arriving at one

[6]The conclusion drawn from the above author's article, in which he gives a well documented and very persuasive historical account of secularization of Western philosophy amid Confucius' *Analects*.

[7]It comes from the idea of a "common language of justice", first mentioned in 2004 by Kofi Annan, then the UN Secretary-General, to the Security Council, in his report "The rule of law and transitional justice in conflict and post-conflict societies" (S/2004/616). By that term he postulated

understanding of justice in the UN. One thing is to study this matter, another is to operationalize a partner concept with a view to making it relevant to the overarching United Nations criminal justice objectives.

In criminological terms, this invites consideration whether there is a common denominator for countering crime. Two questions ensue. First, is there any single thread in international law for treating terrorism not as the form of "respect for cultural identities"/"singularity" but against "the spirit of brotherhood"? Second, is the UN law a secular and pluralist normative system with its own ecumenical "Reason" which incorporates spiritual arguments in countering crime?

3 Defining Terrorism in International Law

Starting with the highlighted in the introduction issue of a religiously motivated terrorist attack (an expression of cultural identity?), the dilemma of a "just" cause could not be resolved comprehensively. This may be the case for the still negotiated UN comprehensive terrorism convention.

However, over a period of almost 60 years there have been adopted 19 universal instruments which directly relate to the prevention and suppression of terrorism. Six of them have been adopted after 9/11. After that date, as of this writing, the Security Council adopted 23 counter terrorism resolutions (S/RES/2462 (2019)). All of them embody a "sectoral" or incremental approach to terrorism, as each one deals with different types of criminal conduct. Only the 2030 Agenda generically mentions terrorism (SDG 16.a).

Altogether, this growing number illustrates some progress in universalizing what terrorism *de facto* internationally is, even if there still is no its binding global definition. Examples of three regional conventions (UNODC 2019a) explain its absence. They distinguish between what is regarded as constituting unlawful, criminal acts of terrorists, and the perpetration of violence committed as part of what is regarded to be a legitimate struggle against any occupation, aggression, or domination by foreign forces, making the latter exempt from criminal proceedings. For instance, the 1998 Arab Convention for the Suppression of Terrorism in Article 2 (a) provides that:

"All cases of struggle by whatever means, including armed struggle, against foreign occupation and aggression for liberation and self-determination, in accordance with the principles of international law, shall not be regarded as an offence. This provision shall not apply to any act prejudicing the territorial integrity of any Arab State." Similarly does so the 1999 Convention on Combating International Terrorism by the Organization of the Islamic Conference (Art. 2 (a)), and the 1999

---

a greater interagency coordination at the level of various United Nations organizations seized with global security and social justice issues.

Convention on the Prevention and Combating of Terrorism by the Organization of African Unity (Article 3(1)).

Two other regional instruments are especially noteworthy owing to the juxta positioned perspectives on terrorism which undermine the claim of "singularity" of definition of terrorism. First, it is a hybrid approach of the 2001 Shanghai Convention on Combating Terrorism, Separatism and Extremism of the Shanghai Cooperation Organisation. In that legal instrument, Article 1(a) cross refers to several of the above universal agreements, but in Article 1(b) a definition of terrorism reflects regional priorities:

> [A]ny other act intended to cause death or serious bodily injury to a civilian, or any other person not taking an active part in the hostilities in a situation of armed conflict or to cause major damage to any material facility, as well as to organize, plan, aid and abet such act, when the purpose of such act, by its nature or context, is to intimidate population, violate public security or compel public authorities or an international organization to do or to abstain from doing any act, and prosecuted in accordance with the national laws of the Parties.

Second, and conversely, the European Union in its own instrument on combating terrorism adopted a regional definition that reflects international norms (EU 2002).

A broader review of universal, regional agreements and jurisprudence on counter terrorism found that its signatories most minimally agree on one *unctim*. It is the instrumental political killing of civilians in peacetime is terrorism (Saul 2017, p. 46).

The same reviewer emphasizes elsewhere that this crime includes killings prompted by religious passions. He justifies this inclusion by recalling that "[i] nternational law is a secular and pluralist normative system—which partly derives its universality from its secularity—and cannot admit monotheistic claims to violence without unravelling its own coherence. While religious doctrines find a place in some national legal systems (consider sharia punishments), even religious States explicitly reject religious justifications for terrorist violence including in criminal cases" (Saul 2008, p. 11).

The above finding suggests that there also is a slight progress in universalizing what is the most agreeable criterion to define terrorism internationally. This progress involves "civilizing legal exceptionalism" (Saul 2012) by exonerating through the "just cause" attacks on civilian population.

3.1 "Respect for Cultural Identities" and the UN Law on Other Acts Against "the Spirit of Brotherhood"

In keeping with the argument of international law as a secular and pluralist normative system, the following may now be highlighted:

> Equality of sexes poses a particular dilemma for fundamentalists. Even under the majority jurisprudential view of Islamic law, men and women do not enjoy equal rights. [. . .] Women and men symbolize different aspects of human life and have separate and definite rights and

obligations. Women are viewed complimentary to men, but not equal to them (Reisman 1991, p. 123).

The author points out that it is due not to the specific cultural inability to integrate but to overall men's disrespectful attitude to global civic values: "This view is not unique to Islam or Moslem fundamentalists. It is common among non-Moslem Third World States, and still flourishes in some socialist and even industrialized Western nations.[8] But for the fundamentalists, without apology, their justification in the divine design of the human creation" (Ibid. p. 123).

Facts and figures speak for themselves. The 2013 World Health Organization (WHO 2013, pp. 2 & 26) study of global and regional prevalence estimates for intimate partner violence and sexual violence by someone other than an intimate partner, revealed that 35% of women worldwide have experienced these two forms of violence. Additionally, one third of the world's women who have been in a relationship have experienced intimate partner violence, and 38% of female homicides were committed by an intimate partner. When considering regional variations in estimates of these two forms of violence against women, the study found the highest lifetime prevalence rates in Africa (45.6%) Southeast Asia (40.2%), the Middle East (36.4%), and the Americas (36.1%), and in Europe (27.2%).

While the WHO did not research the impact of risk and protective factors upon domestic violence in these regions (e.g., religion), one cross-sectional prevalence study (Al-Tawil 2012) suggested a greater involvement of Muslim men in comparison with Christian men in domestic violence. Conducted in the context of such other risk factors like occupation of husband and wife, age at marriage, woman agreement for marriage, illegitimate relations of husband, it took no account of limited property rights of women living in developing countries. In developing countries, this is an important risk factor associated with the prevalence of domestic violence. In developed countries where property rights are more equitably distributed, the role of this factor was minor. However, domestic violence continued (Schröttle and Vogt 2016). Thus the conclusion is clear: it is not religion but culture under whose patriarchal veil is hidden the legitimization of domestic violence and disrespect of human dignity. And so are the likewise reprehensible practices of femicide, female genital mutilation and child marriages (amounting in developed countries to paedophilia). They do not qualify anywhere as "respect for cultural identities" (cf. Kury and Redo 2018), hence are unacceptable versions of "singularity."

[8]For the exegesis of Christian approach to equality between men and women, see Payne (2009).

4 Is the UN Law a Secular and Pluralist Normative System with Its Own Ecumenical "Reason" Which Incorporates Spiritual Arguments in Countering Crime?

Derrida's surprising statement on "singularity" of global terrorism and the charge of his "Chinese prejudice" for response require a greater familiarization with his "deconstructionist" philosophy—not at all condescending. It allows to say that in both cases he only wanted to emphasize the Western traditions of ethnocentrism and logocentrism (words and language as a fundamental expression of an external reality) in looking at the world. Both interpret the world affairs, as if individuals and organizations were impervious to "other ways of being" (Borginho 1999).

This chapter documents that in the United Nations quest for justice, the UDHR and, especially, the entire 2030 UN Agenda is about otherness and inclusiveness. "Leaving no one behind" is its motto.

The UN in its own way is about "other ways of being." So, does it: (a) have its own "Reason"? (b) answer what criminal justice is?

Like a theologian who exegetes the world scriptures, based on the United Nations juridical opinions and "the teachings of the most highly qualified publicists of the various nations" (cf. Art. 38 of the Statute of the International Court of Justice), I will try to respond to these two questions.

4.1 UN "Reason" Which Incorporates Spiritual Arguments in Countering Crime?

On 21 November 1945 in the opening address to the International Military Tribunal at Nuremberg Justice Robert Jackson said that its establishment constituted "one of the most significant tributes that Power has ever paid to Reason" (Jackson 1945, p. 850). This sentiment for "Reason" was earlier expressed by another lawyer Radhabinod Pal, a hard positivist, later one of the minority judges at the International Military Tribunal for the Far East (1946–1948). In his 1928 book examining Vedic texts he reflected on the need to strive for justice by recognizing the "sacred" nature of the Other (after Benerjee 2014, p. 116). The jurisprudence of both tribunals was affirmed by the UN General Assembly (A/RES/95).

Jerry Pubantz (2005), one of the authoritative UN encyclopaedists, with the title of an article "Constructing Reason: Human Rights and the Democratization of the United Nations" (2005) affirmatively answered that the UN develops its own "Reason." At its core are inherent human rights first recognized by the UDHR. Since then the world has been enjoying a growing panoply of moral and other rights. The UN institutional structures, including the Secretariat (one of its six principal organs), are their stakeholders.

In line with this universalizing logic, the actions of several Secretaries-General marked an extraordinary evolution of the world organization towards "Reason."

They reconceptualized the prerequisites for justice. Quite recently, Ban-Ki moon in his report on the post-2015 Agenda (A/68/2002) listed "a life of dignity for all" as one of his own program priorities. Although that postulate has eventually not been made one of the five pillars of the 2030 Agenda (it is an element of "People"), the Agenda underscores the fundamental role of dignity (A/RES/70/1, Preamble, § 5; Introduction, § 4).

Mentioning "dignity" brings back into picture the philosophy of Aquinas. It first made its inroad into the UN through the Charter. In the preamble it reaffirms faith in fundamental human rights, in the dignity and worth of the human person. Therefore the term "Charter" must now be contrasted with "The Covenant" of the League of Nations. The latter term was formally mandated by the 1919 Treaty of Versailles. Initially, however, it emerged much earlier in the statements of Woodrow Wilson – US' most religious president (1913–1921) in the entire history of that country. His statements were imbued with Presbyterian Calvinist theology, whereby "covenant" implies a biblical contract of God with his people. To describe the framework of the League, he used that term as an expression of his faith-in-action. The term imparted to this "greater charter of liberty" a divine character (Dorsey 1999, pp. 113 & 120).

Such was not the intention of the San Francisco founding conference on the UN Charter. The USA as one of its framers convinced others that "from Magna Carta to the Atlantic Charter this term has meant liberty and freedom under law, which is the essence of this instrument." It was more legalistic and less evangelical than a covenant and less formal (and presumably less binding) than a constitution (Borgwardt 2007, pp. 164–165).

However, when next in Lake Success at the Commission of Human Rights it eventually came to the drafting of the "International Bill of Human Rights" Fernand Dehousse, the delegate of Belgium, spoke on the issue of terminology. He did not like the reference to a "bill." He said, it had no French translation. Moreover, since such a bill would comprise two or more legal instruments (declaration/conventions), its combined nature may become unclear. Nor did he approve of "convention" as this is "designated international agreements of less importance than treaties" (E/CN.4/SR.28, p. 5). He said, the term "Charter" should be reserved exclusively for the basic instrument of the UN. The Commission should opt for the word "covenant" instead (E/CN.4/SR.42, p. 9).

There was no discussion whether this term had anything to do with evangelism or a biblical contract. The Commission decided for "covenant" (E/600, § 18 (c), p. 5). By this decision the term "covenant" inadvertently became a product of Member States with its own secular theology.

The way in which the UN legal terms appear, disappear, resurrect and change is best summed up by the following statement by the UN Justice Frederik Harhoff of the ICTY: "The legal system that applies. . .is a system that applies and develops on its own premises, and its own terms" (The Prosecutor v. Stanišić and Zupljanin, Case No. IT-08-91-T). The UN rather than drawing a clear bright line for overall legal terminology has its own blue line. Within it hardly any thread is sanctified.

4.2 What Is Criminal Justice?

In the entire "UN theology" there are still numerous spiritual underpinnings regarding justice and criminal punishment. They were exemplified above, but in full they are really inextricable. So given all this, what is criminal justice?

In 1947, at the Second International Conference of UNESCO, Maritain, its Chair, said to the diplomats that they suffer from "Babelism," because like the workers in the biblical story of the Tower of Babel they did not speak the same "language" (Maritain 1947/1994, p. 173). Since the adoption of the UDHR until this time his criticism lost on its weight, but still should be kept in mind.

The 2030 Agenda offers the most pronounced form of the "language of justice" the UN has so far produced. It is its genuinely own transformative justice language. In it justice is a journey, not a destination. As such, it exists only as a vision of the United Nations Secretary-General:

> For the United Nations, 'justice' is an ideal of accountability and fairness in the protection and vindication of rights and the prevention and punishment of wrongs. Justice implies regard for the rights of the accused, for the interests of victims and for the well-being of society at large (S/616/2004, § 7).

This also is probably the closest explanation of what "criminal justice" should be in the post-2030 world, if that ideal would stay on the horizon. In reality, the "Commentary on the United Nations Charter"—an authoritative and very impressive intellectual input to the UN "Reason"—explains that "justice...means something different from international law (...) and (...) refers to natural law" (Simma et al. 2002 I, p. 36).

Natural law is independent of any legislation or other secular institutional arrangements. The UN Charter does not define natural law. The commentators do not say what exactly natural law is. But they say that it does not have to do with public international law. This positive law only regulates access to justice.

Hugo Grotius (1583–1645), one of the founders of the modern humanist theory of natural law and of the modern theory of public international law, as an "Arminian" Calvinist was troubled by the view of other Calvinists, that God simply makes justice by an "absolute decree" (Riley 2009, p. 365). He separated that decreed part (*lex aeterna*) from natural law. He argued that both natural and positive law presuppose the maintenance of legal rules and the protection of legal rights by means of lawful violence (van Ekima Hommes 1983, pp. 61 & 65).

Since self-preservation is the obvious fact in social life everywhere, everything else is founded based on human cooperation. People have *appetitus societatis* (= appetite for sociability)—a natural inclination to contribute to justice for peaceful coexistence with other people. On the strength of this fact Grotius argued that he can progressively deduce *a priori* an axiom on the specific principles of universal natural law for human cooperation, independently of their *aposteriori* occurrence in empirical positive law. These are: Abstention from taking things of others; obligations to: keep agreements, punish the breaches of law, and repair the damage. These four criminal justice principles "form the unshakable foundation of his detailed system of natural law" (Ibidem, pp. 67 & 68). This is his logical proof of what criminal justice in essence is.

This Grotian axiom compelling people to cooperate was corroborated in contemporary game theory. The researchers eventually solved (*sic!*) the relationship between egoistic and cooperative behavior in the Prisoner's Dilemma: the more forward looking and thoughtful is "prisoner's" vision, the more chances there are for cooperative actions (Redo 2013, p. 70). This finding should be instrumental for making education in prisons more effective.

This evidence and recommendation plays into the 2030 Agenda's pragmatic "win-win" vision. It seeks to advance global moral consciousness/self-righteousness which started emerging at the turn of the nineteenth/twentieth century through the Hague conventions on the laws of war and war crimes.

This secular interstate process of moving from particularism to universalism continued after the First World War in the Treaty of Versailles (German Emperor Wilhelm's intended trial for the supreme offence against international morality and the sanctity of treaties). Then for the first time the world witnessed and the warring states experienced that winning a war is not simply matter of luck or strategy, but also of collective virtue and criminal justice (Simpson 2009, pp. 80–81).

5 Conclusion

Two historical records serve here as the basis of conclusion. First, after the Second World War, at the San Francisco UN founding conference whose participants renounced the scourge of wars and continued to build the interstate moral universe, Joseph Bech, Foreign Minister of Luxembourg, expressed the following parable:

> A man was passing near the site of a new cathedral. He asked one of the workmen what he was doing, and the man replied: 'I am breaking stones.' A second workman said: 'I am earning my salary,' and a third, to whom he put the same question, turned his eyes, bright with religious fervour, toward the half-finished cathedral, and answered, "'I am building a cathedral'" (UN Documents 1947, 1, p. 504).

At the following inaugural session of the Economic and Social Council, Chang stated:

> [T]he United Nations must, as a living institution, attain and nourish a new loyalty on the part of the peoples of the world. . .It is hoped, that. . .this new loyalty may be engendered and fostered (ECOSOC 1946, p. 14).

In the supporting statement, Philip J. Noel-Baker (United Kingdom) said that that would be done by freeing people from want. He concluded, that

> In the Atlantic Charter our government promised that that would be done. . .I believe we shall succeed in the measure in which we remember the solidarity of the interests and in the measure in which we can create the international loyalty of which our Chinese colleague spoke (ECOSOC 1946, p. 18).

Reflecting on this historical record 75 years after the establishment of the UN, over time with that loyalty the Organization has advanced its own moral stewardship and the "language of justice" against crime. Numerous United Nations crime prevention and criminal justice standards and norms confirm this.

That loyalty with its language is secular and ecumenical. It has its own spirit or "Reason."

This language is open to agreements transcending all faith commitments. If there is a particular religious fervour in the UN, then it originally has been motivated by one belief only: not repeating the Holocaust experience—the tragic opposite of Kant's imperative. This belief does not draw its sustenance only from the post-Second World War "Holocaust religion." A haunting, deeply rooted fear of extinction has not been the sole property of the Jews and the State of Israel. It was shared by citizens of other countries victimized by the Nazi Germany.

Bech's metaphoric "religious fervour" has not been appreciated worldwide. Holocaust denial is a proven fact among Muslims (Spoerl 2014). "Words Islam and Holocaust are rarely associated with one another" (Afridi 2014). This association is confounded by Palestinian's and other Arabs' resentment of the Jews and the State of Israel as occupier, whose security actions against Muslim population in the Middle East enliven their "just cause" and the Holocaust denial.

Reciprocal recrimination and political victimization aside, the Nazi Holocaust is an extraordinary moral evil, the crime of crimes. Even Derrida, so polarizing with his "singularity" of 9/11 (but, in fact, sensitized to the bigotry of Babelism, and misread on the "Chinese prejudice") admits this. He says: "Not only is [Holocaust] unique, but basically one cannot think of any genocide in the world. . .without interpreting it as a crime against the man or the men or the people who are the depositories of the Law, of moral Law (Ben-Naftali 1998, p. 5/29). In "The Range of Reason" Maritain would have interpreted Derrida's view of universal morality, as follows: "Every great age of Culture receives its deepest meaning and direction from a particular constellation of spiritual factors or dominating ideas; let us say, from a particular historical heaven" (Maritain 1947/1994, p. 92).

In closing then, the following statements ensue, starting with the contrasting picture of particularism vs universalism with which this chapter began: the Nazi Holocaust is the United Nations' basic "Reason" in the quest for universalizing criminal justice with no prejudice to any country, individual, race, religion, sexual orientation, language, religion, political or other opinion, national or social origin, property, birth or other status. The range of the UN "Reason" may still be not enough to maintain peace and justice amid so many particularities, justified or not. For the time being, the seeming, as I think, paradox that "there is no representative of the whole that would not be simultaneously a representative of some particular" (Koskenniemi after Ajevski 2013, p. 58) tames our UN reasoning. When shocked by a new case, when a state, an organization, a political movement or science provides a new avenue for broadening our perspectives on moral universe. For the United Nations it is not premised on the existence of God. But the moral theories reviewed above are certainly compatible with its ecumenical worldview. Only 100 years ago the humankind enacted its first supreme offence against international morality. After 75 years of the existence of the United Nations, for 2030 and beyond many more virtuous "workmen" are needed of a fervoured progressivist faith inspired by the Charter. Its full potential and faith in it should be more vigorously addressed and pursued for continuing societal and intergenerational transformation in the quest for universalizing criminal justice.

References[9]

A/66/302 Harmony with Nature. Report of the Secretary-General 15 August 2011.

A/68/2002, Corr. 1 A life of dignity for all: accelerating progress towards the Millennium Development Goals and advancing the United Nations development agenda beyond 2015 26 July 2013.

A/RES/40/34 Declaration of basic principles on justice for victims of crime and abuse of power 29 November 1985.

A/RES/56/1 Condemnation of terrorist attacks in the United States of America 12 September 2011.

A/RES/70/1 Transforming our world: the 2030 Agenda for Sustainable Development 25 September 2015.

A/RES/70/174 Doha declaration on integrating crime prevention and criminal justice into the wider United Nations agenda to address social and economic challenges and to promote the rule of law at the national and international levels, and public participation 17 December 2015.

A/RES/95 Affirmation of the Principles of International Law recognized by the Charter of the Nürnberg Tribunal 11 December 1946.

Afridi, M. M. (2014). *The role of Muslims and the Holocaust*. Oxford Handbooks Online. http://shorturl.at/cmuM5

Ajevski, M. (2013). International criminal law and constitutionalisation: On hegemonic narratives in progress. *Erasmus Law Review, 6*(1), 50–61.

Al-Tawil, N. G. (2012). Association of violence against women with religion and culture in Erbil Iraq: A cross-sectional study. *BMC Public Health, 12*, 800.

Analects. (1998). *The Analects of Confucius. A philosophical translation* (transl. Ames RT, Rosemont H Jr). New York: Ballentine Books.

Aquilina, M. (2019). How a Catholic thinker made human rights universal. *Angelus*, shorturl.at/biCHK.

Barrodori, G. (2003). 9/11 and global terrorism. A dialogue with Jacques Derrida. In *Philosophy in a time of terror. Dialogues with Jurgen Habermas and Jacques Derrida*. Chicago: The Chicago University Press.

Beccaria, C. (1764/1986). *On crimes and punishments*, transl. from Italian and the Author's Original Order. With notes and introduction by David Young. Indianapolis, IND: Hackett Publishing Company.

Benerjee, M. (2014). Does international criminal justice require a sovereign? Historicising Radhabinod Pal's Tokyo judgment in light of his 'Indian' legal philosophy. In M. Bergsmo, W. L. Cheah, & P. Yi (Eds.), *Historical origins of criminal law* (Vol. 2, pp. 67–118). Brussels: Torkel Ophsal Academic EPublisher.

Ben-Naftali, M. (1998). *Uniqueness, limitation, and forgivability*. https://bit.ly/2Lcnjoa

[9]All Internet references, including those involving the United Nations parliamentary documentation from http://www.un.org (General Assembly, Economic and Social Council, Security Council, Secretary-General) was last retrieved on May 20, 2020.

Bentham, J. (1907/2007). *An introduction to the principles of morals and legislation (Dover Philosophical Classics)*. Mineola, New York: Dover Publications.

Borginho, J. (1999). *Nihilism and affirmation*. https://bit.ly/2YYTJuP

Borgwardt, E. (2007). *A new deal for the world*. Cambridge, MA: The Belknap Press of Harvard University Press.

Chang, W. (1999). The Confucian theory of norms and human rights. In W. Theodore de Bary & T. Weiming (Eds.), *Confucianism and human rights*. New York: Columbia University Press.

Dorsey, L. G. (1999). Woodrow Wilson's fight for the League of Nations. *Reexamination, Rhetoric & Public Affairs, 2*(1), 107–135.

E/600 Commission on Human Rights: Report to the Economic and Social Council on the 2nd Session of the Commission, held at Geneva, from 2 to 17 December 1947.

E/CN.4/SR.28, Summary Record of the Twenty-Eighth Meeting [of the Commission on Human Rights] Held at the Palais des Nations, Geneva, on Thursday, 4 December 1947. In W.A. Schabas (2013), The Universal Declaration of Human Rights, Vol. I, 1126–1133, Cambridge: Cambridge University Press.

E/CN.4/SR.42, Summary Record of the Forty-Second Meeting [of the Commission on Human Rights] Held at the Palais des Nations, Geneva, on Thursday, 16 December 1947. In W.A. Schabas (2013), The Universal Declaration of Human Rights, Vol. I, 1614–1624, Cambridge: Cambridge University Press.

ECOSOC. (1946). Official records. First year. From the first meeting (23 January 1946) to the fourteenth meeting (18 February 1946), and annexes. Church House, Westminster. London.

ECOSOC. (2002). Basic Principles on the use of restorative justice programmes in criminal matters, 24 July 2002.

ECOSOC. (2003). United Nations Guidelines for the Prevention of Crime, 22 July 2003.

Ekeløve-Slydal, G. M. (2018). Jeremy Bentham's Legacy: A vision of an international law for the greatest happiness of all nations. In M. Bergsmo & J. E. Buis (Eds.), *Philosophical foundations of international criminal law: Correlating thinkers*. Brussels: Torkel Opsahl Academic EPublisher.

EU/European Union, Council of the European Union, Council Framework Decision of 13 June 2002 on combating terrorism, article 1. https://bit.ly/3dpDieE

Fidler, D. P. (1996). Caught between traditions: The Security Council in philosophical conundrum. *Michigan Journal of International Law, 17*, 411–453.

Friedrich, C. J. (1947). The ideology of the United Nations Charter and the philosophy of peace of Immanuel Kant 1795–1945. *The Journal of Politics, 9*(1), 10–30.

Fuchs, T. (2006). The European China- receptions from Leibniz to Kant. Transl. by Martin Schönfeld. *Journal of Chinese Philosophy, 33*, 39–49.

Garbett, C. (2017). The International Criminal Court and restorative justice: Victims, participation and the processes of justice. *Restorative Justice, 5*(2), 198–220.

Gasteazoro, C. M. (1981). El pensamiento de Ricardo J. Alfaro: estudio introductorio y antología, 6, 160. https://bit.ly/3bf9sbh

Gier, N. (2012). *The day Confucius went to the United Nations: Chinese influence on the declaration of human rights*. https://www.webpages.uidaho.edu/ngier/Declaration.htm

Gilmore, N., & Sullivan, V. B. (2017). Montesquieu's teaching on the dangers of extreme corrections: Japan, the Catholic Inquisition, and moderation in the spirit of the laws. *American Political Science Review, 111*(3), 460–470.

Goldhil, O. (2018). *Philosophers philosophizing about philosophy on world philosophy day*. https://bit.ly/3fwZzt5

Harcourt, B. E. (2013). Becarria's on crimes and punishments: a mirror on the history of the foundations of modern criminal law. Chicago Coase-Sandor Institute for Law and Economics Working Paper no. 648 (2d series), Public Law and Legal Theory Working Paper no. 433.

Hegel, F. (1948). *On Christianity. Early theological writings*. Transl. by T. M. Knox with an Introduction, and Fragments transl. by R. Kroner. New York: Harper Torchbooks.

Hegel, F. (1952). *Philosophy of right*, Transl. with notes by T. M. Knox. Wotton-under-Edge, UK: Clarendon Press.

Hermann, D., & Dölling, D. (2016). General prevention: Does it work? In H. Kury, S. Redo, & E. Shea (Eds.), *Women and children as victims and offenders: Background, prevention, reintegration. Suggestions for succeeding generations* (Vol. 2, pp. 3–22). Switzerland: Springer International Publishing.

Hoffman, M. L. (2001). *Empathy and moral development: Implications for caring and justice.* Cambridge: Cambridge University Press.

Holland, K. M. (1980). Socrates - The first criminal justice educator. *Criminal Justice Review, 5*(1), 1–4.

Holt, R., & Hond, F. (2013). Sapere Aude. *Organization Studies, 34*, 1587–1600.

Jackson, R. H., Nuremberg, 21 November 1945, The Department of State Bulletin. Dir. of publ. Department of State. 25.11.1945, n° 335; vol. XIII; publication 2432 (pp. 850–860). Washington: US Government Printing Office. "International Military Tribunal".

Kant, I. (1795/2001), To External Peace (1795), transl. by Carl J. Friedrich. In *Basic writings of Kant*, Edited and with and Introduction by Allen W. Wood (pp. 433–476). New York: The Modern Library.

Kant, I. (2001a). *Fundamental principles of the metaphysics of morals*, Transl. by T. K. Abbott (pp. 143–222). In Immanuel Kant. Basic writings. New York: The Modern Library.

Kant, I. (2001b). *Lectures on ethics*, ed. by P. Heath and J. B. Schneewind, transl. by P. Heath. Cambridge: Cambridge University Press.

Kant, I. (2013). The metaphysics of morals. In M. Gregor (Ed.), *Introduction by R.J. Sullivan*. Cambridge: Cambridge University Press.

Krieger, T. (2013). Calculating the costs of 9/11. In C. Klöckner, S. Knewitz, & S. Sielke (Eds.), *Beyond 9/11: Transdisciplinary perspectives on twenty-first century American U.S. culture* (pp. 123–139). Frankfurt: Peter Lang.

Kury, H., & Redo, S. (2018). Epilogue. In H. Kury & S. Redo (Eds.), *Refugees and migrants in law and policy. Challenges and opportunities for global civic education* (pp. 863–913). Switzerland: Springer International Publishing.

Lee, M. H. (2017). *Confucianism: Its roots and global significance.* Honolulu: University of Hawai'i Press.

Leibniz, G. W. (1996). In P. Remnant & J. Bennett (Eds.), *New essays on human understanding* (Book IV, Ch. XVI), Cambridge: Cambridge University Press.

Lestition, S. (1993). Kant and the end of the enlightenment in Prussia. *The Journal of Modern History, 65*(1), 57–112.

Liddel, H. G., & Scott, R. (1889). *An intermediate Greek–English lexicon.*

Maritain, J. (1947/1994). *The range of reason.* https://maritain.nd.edu/jmc/etext/range.htm

McCrudden, C. (2008). Human dignity and judicial interpretation of human rights. *The European Journal of International Law, 19*(4), 655–724.

Meighoo, S. (2008). Derrida's Chinese prejudice. *Cultural Critique, 68*, 163–209.

Montesquieu, Ch. (1891). *Persian letters*, transl. by J. Davidson. London-New York: George Routledge & Sons Ltd/L. P. Dutton & Co.

Montesquieu, Ch. (2001). *The spirit of laws*, transl. by T. Nugent. Kitchener, ON: Batoche Books.

Morsink, J. (1999). *The Universal Declaration of Human Rights. Origins, drafting and intent.* Philadelphia: Pennsylvania University Press.

Morsink, J. (2017). *The Universal Declaration of Human Rights and the challenge of religion.* Columbia: University of Missouri Press.

Nelson, E. S. (2011). The *Yijing* and philosophy: From Leibniz to Derrida. *Journal of Chinese Philosophy, 38*(3), 377–396.

Nisbett, R. E. (2003). *The geography of thought. How Asians and Westerners think differently*. . *.and why*. New York-London-Toronto-Sydney: Free Press.

Payne, P. B. (2009). *Man and woman, one in Christ: An exegetical and theological study of Paul's letters*. Grand Rapids, MI: Zondervan.

Pubantz, J. (2005). Constructing reason: Human rights and the democratization of the United Nations. *Social Forces, 84*(2), 1291–1302.
Rauber, J. (2009). The United Nations – a Kantian dream come true? Philosophical perspectives on the constitutional legitimacy of the world organisation. *Hanse Law Review, 5*(1), 49–76.
Redo, S. (2013). United Nations rule of law, "common language of justice", and the Post-2015 educational agenda; Some academic and policy aspects. *Comparative Law Review, 16*, 211–246.
Redo, S., Pływaczewski, E. W., Langowska, A., & Alkowski, P. (2018). A Socratic contribution to culture of lawfulness for teaching criminology. *Białostockie Studia Prawnicze, 23*(3), 97–111.
Reisman, M. H. A. (1991). Islamic fundamentalism and its impact on international law and politics. In M. W. Janis (Ed.), *The influence of religion on the development of international law* (pp. 147–170). Boston: Martinus Nijhoff Publishers.
Riley, P. (2009). The legal philosophy of Hugo Grotius. In E. Pattaro, D. Canale, P. Grossi, H. Hofmann, & P. Riley (Eds.), *A treatise of legal philosophy and general jurisprudence* (Vol. 9, pp. 365–377). Switzerland: Springer International Publishing.
Rogacz, D. (2018). The birth of enlightenment secularism from the spirit of Confucianism. *Asian Philosophy, 28*(1).
Rousseau, J. J. (1920). *Social contract*, transl. by G. D. H. Cole, Oxford-New York: J. M. Dent & Sons/E. P. Dutton & Co.
Russell, B. (1945). *History of western philosophy*. New York: Simon & Schuster.
S/2004/616. The rule of law and transitional justice in conflict and post-conflict societies 23 August 2004.
S/RES/2462. Threats to international peace and security caused by terrorist acts: Preventing and combating the financing of terrorism 28 March 2019.
Saul, B. (2008). Defining 'terrorism' to protect human rights, *Legal Studies Research Paper No. 08/* 125
Saul, B. (2012). Civilizing the exception: Universally defining terrorism. In A. Masferrer (Ed.), *Post 9/11 and the state of permanent legal emergency: Security and human rights in countering terrorism* (pp. 79–100). Switzerland: Springer International Publishing.
Saul, B. (2017). Defining terrorism: A conceptual minefield (part I, ch. 3). In A. Gofas, R. English, S. N. Kalyvas, & E. Chenoweth (Eds.), *The Oxford handbook of terrorism*. Oxford: Oxford University Press.
Schabas, W. A. (2013). The Universal Declaration of Human Rights. *The travaux préparatoires.* Vol. I, October 1946 to November 1947. Cambridge: Cambridge University Press.
Schröttle, M., & Vogt, K. (2016). Women as victims and perpetrators of violence: Empirical results from national and international quantitative violence research. In H. Kury, S. Redo, & E. Shea (Eds.), *Women and children as victims and offenders: Background, prevention, reintegration. Suggestions for succeeding generations* (Vol. 1, pp. 479–504). Switzerland: Springer International Publishing.
Sen, A. (2005). *The argumentative Indian. Writings on Indian history, culture and identity*. London: Allen Lane
Sherrat, Y. (2013). *Hitler's philosophers*. New Heaven, Ct.: Yale University Press.
Shi, B., Zeng, S., & Zhang, Q. (2014). Chinese Confucianism and other prevailing Chinese practices in the rise of international criminal law. In M. Bergsmo, W. L. Cheah, & P. Yi (Eds.), *Historical origins of international criminal law* (Vol. I, pp. 141–160). Brussels: Torkel Opsahl Academic EPublisher.
Simma, B. (Ed.), Paulus, A., & Chatodou, E. (Ass. Eds.), in collaboration with Mosler, H., Radelzhofer, A., Tomuschat, Ch., & Wolfrum, R. (2002). The Charter of the United Nations. A commentary. Oxford. Oxford University Press, 2nd ed.
Simpson, G. (2009). Men and abstract entities: Individual responsibility and collective guilt in international criminal law. In A. Nollkaemper & H. van der Wilt (Eds.), *System criminality in international criminal law* (pp. 69–100). Cambridge: Cambridge University Press.

Sohn, L. B. (1995). How American international lawyers prepared for the San Francisco Bill of Rights. *The American Journal of International Law, 89*(3), 540–553.
Spoerl, J. (2014). Palestinians, Arabs, and the Holocaust. *Jewish Political Studies Review, 26*(1/2), 14–46.
Sultan, A. N. (2004). Principal and practical foundations of a global constitutional order. *Washington University Global Studies Law Review, 3*(1), 155–175.
Swetz, F. J. (2003). Leibniz, the *Yijing*, and the religious conversion of the Chinese. *Mathematics Magazine, 76*(4), 276–291.
Święczkowska, H. (2016). *Language as the mirror of world order.* Białystok University of Bialystok Publishing House.
UN. (1947). Documents of the United Nations Conference on International Organization, London-New York, vol. 1.
UNESCO. (2007). *Philosophy a School of Freedom. Teaching philosophy and learning to philosophize*. Paris: UNESCO Publishing.
UNGA/11290. World Leaders Adopt Declaration Reaffirming Rule of Law as Foundation for Building Equitable State Relations, Just Societies 24 September 2012.
Universal Declaration of Human Rights. History of the Document. https://www.un.org/en/sections/universal-declaration/history-document/index.html
UNODC. (2006). *Handbook on restorative justice programmes*. New York: United Nations.
UNODC. (2009). *Guide to implementing family skills training programmes for drug abuse prevention*. New York: United Nations.
UNODC. (2019a). *Overview of the International Counter-Terrorism Legal Framework*. https://www.unodc.org/e4j/en/terrorism/module-3/index.html
UNODC. (2019b). Global Study on Homicide 2019: Homicide trends, patterns and criminal justice response. Box 10, Historical perspective: what the past can teach about reducing homicide. Historical homicide trends in Jamaica and Singapore (provided by Manuel Eisner). https://www.unodc.org/unodc/en/data-and-analysis/global-study-on-homicide.html
Van Ekima Hommes, H. (1983). Grotius on natural and international law. *The Netherlands International Law Review, XXX*, 61–71.
Van Norden, B. W. (2017). *Taking back philosophy*. New York: Columbia University Press.
Weiss, G. T. (2015). The United Nations: before, during and after 1945. *International Affairs, 91* (6), 1221–1235.
WHO/World Health Organization. (2013). *Global and regional estimates of violence against women: prevalence and health effects of intimate partner violence and non-partner sexual violence*. Geneva.
Williams, W. L. (2010). Political ontology and institutional design in Montesquieu and Rousseau. *American Journal of Political Science, 54*(2), 525–542.
Wilson, K. (2015). Missionaries in China: The ethics of exporting ethics. In K. Winston (Ed.), *Ethics in public life: Good practitioners in a rising Asia*. London: Palgrave Macmillan.

Cases

Case No. IT-01-42/1-S, International Criminal Tribunal for the former Yugoslavia, Prosecutor v. Miodrag Jokić, Sentencing Judgment (Trial Chamber), 18 March 2004. https://bit.ly/2SRG6JX
Case No. IT-02-61-S, International Criminal Tribunal for the former Yugoslavia, Prosecutor v. Miroslav Deronjić, Sentencing Judgment (Trial Chamber), 30 March 2004. https://bit.ly/3fzVGDK
Case No. IT-08-91-T, International Criminal Tribunal for the former Yugoslavia, The Prosecutor v. Stanišić and Zupljanin. Transcript, 15 October 2009, p. 1508. https://bit.ly/3fzVgxa

Sławomir Redo Dr. hab. (Law/Criminology) is a Visiting Professor of United Nations Law. He is a member of the United Nations Studies Association. Former United Nations Senior Crime Prevention and Criminal Justice Expert and staff of the UN Office on Drugs and Crime (ret.). He had been involved in numerous projects implementing the UN standards and norms in crime prevention and criminal justice. In other capacities, he assisted in the implementation of the United Nations Convention against Transnational Organized Crime, and on-line international crime prevention and criminal justice education. He published four books, co-edited four others, including *Women and Children as Victims and Offenders: Background, Prevention, Reintegration. Suggestions for Succeeding Generations* (Springer 2016), and *Refugees and Migrants in Law and Policy – Challenges and Opportunities for Global Civic Education* (Springer 2018) plus about 80 articles—mostly on the UN law and practice of crime prevention and criminal justice. University course lecturer on "The United Nations and Crime Prevention" & "The United Nations and War Crime Prevention" (Austria, China, Poland); Promoter of crime prevention & criminal justice training and education for meeting the goals of the 2030 UN Sustainable Development Agenda. Co-editor of the first criminological UN Agenda-based textbook *KRYMINOLOGIA. Stan i perspektywy rozwoju z uwzględnieniem założeń Agendy ONZ na rzecz zrównoważonego rozwoju 2030* (Wolters Kluwer, Warsaw 2020). E-mail: s@redo.net.

The Universal Declaration of Human Rights: Public International Law and the Confucian Legal Culture for 2030 and Beyond

Ying-Jun Zhang

Abstract Since the Universal Declaration of Human Rights (UDHR) was adopted in 1948, the fundamental human rights and freedoms have been underway in the world as a common standard. Yet it is rarely remembered that this document, which seems to embody western "human rights" and values, also engages the wisdom of Chinese culture, contributed through its Chinese co-drafter Peng-chun Chang. Chinese Confucian legal culture not only addresses human rights thoughts but also the political governance. The core ideas of that culture may be put in concert with United Nations, the new goals of sustainable development, whose progress and impact depend on Member States' commitment to the Organisation's objectives.

Keywords Benevolence · Confucian legal culture · Conscience · Freedom · Governance · Human rights · Morality · Punishment

1 Introduction

In 1946, the countries that had just experienced the World War II were deeply aware of the ravages of war on human society. To avoid the future generations being ravaged again, the just founded United Nations (UN) has embarked on the drafting of a universally respected human rights legal instrument that proclaims the fundamental rights and freedoms of the human being. Over the next two years, under the umbrella of the UN Economic and Social Council, the Commission on Human Rights and the Drafting Committee were established. Through repeated consultations among Member States' representatives, the draft of the Universal Declaration of Human Rights (UDHR/The Declaration) was elaborated (Glen and Symonides

The opinions expressed here are wholly personal.

Y.-J. Zhang (✉)
South-Central University for Nationalities, Law Faculty, Wuhan, China

H. Kury, S. Redo (eds.), *Crime Prevention and Justice in 2030*,
https://doi.org/10.1007/978-3-030-56227-4_29

1998, p. 77). On 10 December 1948, the Declaration was adopted by the United Nations General Assembly.

More than 70 years have passed since the Declaration was adopted. Just as proclaimed in its preamble, the fundamental human rights and freedoms it stated have become the standard of human rights.[1] Inspired by the UDHR, a large number of international documents aiming to protect human rights were promulgated. This has become the basis of international human rights law and a milestone in the history of human rights in the world.[2]

Yet what may not be well remembered is that this document, which seems to embody western "human rights" and values, also engages the wisdom of Chinese culture. Peng-chun Chang, the Vice-Chair of the Drafting Committee of the Declaration, and China's Permanent Representative to the United Nations, participated in its elaboration. A Chinese commentator informs, that "[i]ntroducing China's concept of human rights to delegates, creatively resolving many impasses using Confucian principles in the negotiation process and reaching compromises among conflicting ideologies,"[3] had been Chang's input to break religious and cultural barriers that initially thwarted the drafting process (Tang 2018, p. 146).

This chapter introduces China's contribution to the drafting of the UDHR, and comments on the values and ideas of Chinese Confucianism embodied in it.

2 China's Contribution to the Drafting of the Universal Declaration of Human Rights

In the drafting of the UDHR, Peng-chun Chang was not the only one who attended as a representative of China.[4] However, among all Chinese representatives, he attended the most meetings and raised the most proposals, which had impacted the

[1] "A Historical Record of the Drafting Process- Drafting of the Universal Declaration of Human Rights, https://research.un.org/en/undhr/introduction.

[2] The Foundation of International Human Rights Law, https://www.un.org/en/sections/universal-declaration/foundation-international-human-rights-law/index.html.

[3] Supra note 2.

[4] Before the establishment of the Commission on Human Rights, Representative of China, Dr. Hsia Ching-lin, attended the Nuclear Commission on Human Rights (E/HR/6- E/HR/16, 1946). On December 2–10, 1947, during the second session of the Commission on Human Rights, the representative of China, Nan-Ju Wu, participated four times (28th–31st). The rest of the sessions were attended by John Wu Ching-hsiung, China's deputy representative to the UN Security Council (E/CN.4/SR.23- E/CN.4/SR.42, 1947).

On May 3–21, 1948, the second session of the Drafting Committee was attended by Wu The-yao, Special Assistant to the Chinese delegation to the United Nations Secretariat (Sun 2017, p. 35). In addition, during the drafting process, the Chinese scholar Chung-Sho Lo, although not a representative of the Commission on Human Rights, provided feedback on the UNESCO survey on human rights concepts, entitled Human Rights in Chinese Tradition, which was included in the book below "Human Rights: Comments and Explanations". Chung-Sho (1947) p. 186, also Huang (2012), p. 172.

drafting of the Declaration. He attended 157 of the 210 drafting meetings of the Declaration, accounting for 75% of the total; made 110 statements, accounting for 70% of the meetings he participated (Sun 2017, p. 35). Therefore, his contribution is discussed below.

Peng-chun Chang (21 October 1892–19 July 1957), aka Peng-Chun, courtesy name Zhongshu, was born in Tianjin. He is a brother of Boling Chang, Nankai University's founding president.[5] Peng-chun Chang studied psychology and sociology at Clark University (Worcester, Mass., USA) where in 1913 he received a Bachelor of Arts degree. Next, he studied at the Columbia University (New York, NY, USA) where he received a master's degree in Literature, and a master's degree in education (Hua 2015, pp. 3, 25–27). After returning to China in 1916, he was working at the Nankai University (Tianjin). In 1919, he went to the United States again to pursue doctor's degree at Columbia University (New York), where he continued his studies in philosophy and education (Huang 2012, p. 168). While his doctoral dissertation was completed in 1922, his dissertation was published in 1923. In 1923, upon his return, Peng-chun Chang was hired as a professor at the Nankai University. In 1924, he was awarded a Ph.D. in Education (Sun 2011, p. 41). At the same time, as one of the main founders of the Nankai University, he was invited to work at Tsinghua University as provost and to help reform Tsinghua University.

In the autumn of 1925, when Tsinghua University was officially established, Peng-chun Chang resigned from his appointment there and returned to the Nankai University to serve as director of the middle school and professor of the university department. He taught philosophy and Western drama. In 1930, Peng-chun Chang went to the United States again. He taught at the University of Chicago, the University of Hawaii and Columbia University. During the initial period of the Second World War, he served in the USA as China's envoy publicising there and in Great Britain about China's resistance against Japan, seeking international assistance. In 1940 and 1942, he was successively appointed Chinese Ambassador to Turkey and to Chile.

After the Second World War, Dr. Chang was appointed as the Permanent Representative of China to the Founding Conference of the United Nations. He was elected the Vice-Chairman of the Commission on Human Rights. In this additional nominal UN capacity, he participated in the drafting of the UDHR. He later served as the China Representative of the United Nations Conference on Freedom of the Press and the China Representative to the Security Council until

[5]He was the 2nd group of Boxer Indemnity Scholarship recipients. That was a scholarship program funded by Boxer Rebellion indemnity money paid to the United States according to the Boxer Protocol which was concluded in 1901 after Eight-Power Allied Forces aggressive troops sent by Great Britain, the United States, Germany, France, tsarist Russia, Japan, Italy and Austria in 1900, to suppress the Chinese Yihetuan Movement(义和团运动)known to the West as the Boxer Rebellion. After negotiations, United States agreed to provide for Chinese students to study in the U.S. since 1909 on the part of money have paid by Chinese government (Hua 2015, p. 26; Sun 2012, pp. 93–112; Huang 2012, p. 167).

his retirement in 1952. He settled in New York. He died of a heart attack in New Jersey on 19 July 1957, at the age of 65 (Hua 2015, pp. 25–28; Huang 2012, p. 6).

Throughout the drafting of the UDHR, Peng-chun Chang participated as Vice-Chairman of the Commission on Human Rights and Drafting Committee.[6] He has made an important contribution to the drafting of the format and specific content of the Declaration, easing of the impasse in the process, and advancing the formation of the Declaration.

2.1 Peng-chun Chang's Contribution to the Content of the Specific Provisions of the Universal Declaration of Human Rights

Having studied in China and the West, coupled with his experiences as diplomat in many countries, Peng-chun Chang had a certain understanding and observation of different cultures of different countries. In his growth in China, he received education mainly from traditional private school and was very knowledgeable in Chinese traditional culture. At his first meeting as the permanent Chinese representative to the UN Economic and Social Council, he quoted the saying of the most famous Chinese Confucianist *Mencius*, "Subdue people with goodness; people can never be subdued. Nourish people with goodness; the whole world can be subdued" (ECOSOC 1946, p. 14).[7]

Chang meant to say that the newly established United Nations, as an international organisation leading the new post-war order, should take "nourish people with goodness" as its mission if it is to gain the trust and the "new loyalty" of the people. He used Confucianism to "consider others in one's own place"—an emblematic maxim for empathy in treating others as yourself (cf. ECOSOC 1946, p. 14). He proposed that it is through co-operative effort in the solution of common problems that peoples can attain real mutual understanding. In his second statement at the ECOSOC, he quoted Confucius' expectation of a "great society". He stated that the living standards of the people of the world should be improved through international cooperation, especially to help the underdeveloped countries out of hunger (Hua 2015, p. 45).

In the drafting of the UDHR, he argued that Western philosophy should not be the core, and other culture should also be considered (Mary Ann Glendon 2001, p. 47; Ju 2011, p. 143). Under his suggestion, the Committee incorporated

[6]As the Chinese representative, Mr. Wu attended the 9th and 10th meeting, first session of UN Commission on Human Rights instead of Peng-Chun Chang. See E/CN.4/SR.9 and E/CN.4/SR.10.

[7]For the reference in the back: ECOSOC (1946).

Confucianism, which reflected Eastern philosophy, and added "conscience" after "everyone is rational", that is the idea of "benevolence", in the first article of the draft UDHR.

In the Drafting Committee's discussion of the measures to implement the Declaration, he stated that it will not be sufficient to confine the Commission of Human Rights only to the penalties for violators so that makes it merely an appeals court for human rights complaints and to limit its mandate to the legal sphere. To that end, he quoted the saying of Mencius, "Good intentions alone are not sufficient for political order and laws alone are not sufficient to bring about results by themselves" ("Mengzi, Li Lou I", Mencius 2011, p. 126), to explain his point of view. He believed that the purpose of the Declaration is to create a better human nature, rather than simply punish violators, and the law should promote the development and improvement of human rights in combination with educational and moral means (E/CN.4/AC.1/SR.11, pp. 10–11). The Mencius doctrine, which he cites, emphasises that crime prevention should focus not only on punishment, but also on enlightenment; not only to emphasise the importance of strict law, but also to create a good society and promote the overall progress of human beings. It coincides with the United Nations Sustainable Development Goals' emphasis on education and enlightenment.

In the following, starting with the "preamble", this article lists the influence of Peng-chun Chang on the formulation of the provisions of the Declaration.

2.1.1 Advocates That the Declaration Should Be Universal and Applicable to All Mankind

During the discussion on the preamble at the first session of the Commission on Human Rights, Peng-chun Chang explained that the principle of human rights should be given universal application regardless of human level. He had referred to a minimum standard as a means of increasing the stature of man as opposed to animal (E/CN.4/SR.7, p. 4).

He advocated that the declaration of human rights should be brief and readily understandable by all. It should be a document for all men everywhere, not merely for lawyers and scholars (A/C.3/SR.91, 1948, p. 48).

2.1.2 Advocate Equality of Rights Between Different Races

Regarding human rights equality, he believed that, "a sentence might be included in the summary record to the effect that the Commission considered it necessary to emphasize this idea of the solidarity or unity of the human race. It would thereby be ensured that the Declaration of Human Rights would always be correctly understood, and that it would be possible at all times to see what had been formulated on the morrow of a war waged by the enemy in the name of racial inequality" (E/CN.4/SR.13, p. 5).

According to the Meeting Records of Drafting Committee, he remarked that in his opinion China was perhaps the least 'bothersome' nation insofar as religious discrimination was concerned. This fact, he thought, had attracted the attention of the English philosophers in the eighteenth century (E/CN.4/AC.1/SR.3, p. 4).

He asked the meeting's Rapporteur to clearly document this ideal for referencing in drafting. Thus, the "equality of rights without distinction between races" provision, which was not mentioned in the Secretariat Outline, appeared in Article 5 of Cassin's first draft, and equality of rights between the sexes was also included (Hua 2015, p. 126).

2.1.3 Advocates the Inclusion of the "Conscience" Which Embodies the Confucian Virtue of "Benevolence" into the Declaration

At the eighth meeting of the Drafting Committee, when discussing the first article of the first draft of the Declaration, Dr. Chang proposed that the Confucian virtue *"Ren"* should be included. He interpreted it in English as "two-man-mindedness", or "consciousness" as one of the essential attributes of being a human being. Finally, the Committee agreed to include the draft with the word "conscience" (E/CN.4/AC.1/SR.8, p. 2).

When the Drafting Committee reviews the second draft of the Declaration article-by-article, the representative of Lebanon proposed that Article 1 should be replaced by "All men are brothers, endowed with reason and conscience". Peng-chun Chang believed that in addition to adding the word "conscience" he proposed, certain words should be added to clarify a certain moral meaning. Therefore, he proposed the following revision: "All men are brothers, endowed with reason and conscience. All men, being members of one family are free, possess equal dignity and rights" (E/CN.4/AC.1/SR.13, pp. 5–6). At the fiftieth meeting of the Third Session of the Commission on Human Rights, the deletion of the first full stop and of the subsequent word up to and including the word *"conscience"* was rejected by six votes to five, with six abstentions (E/CN.4/SR.50).

When the draft Declaration was submitted to the Third Committee of the Third Session of the General Assembly for consideration, Article 1 was hotly debated. Some countries advocated the inclusion of God or the Creator as an indication of the source of human rights. Peng-chun Chang reminded that Chinese, which accounts for a large proportion of the world's population, "has a different ideology and tradition from Christianity. These thoughts include good manners, etiquette and courtesy, and understanding of others, but the representative of China did not advocate must include them all in the Declaration" (A/C.3/SR.105, p. 177). He hoped that colleagues could show the same understanding, break through religious barriers and withdraw the metaphysical amendments to Article 1. In his view, since Spinoza and Locke, the idea of religious inclusion has existed in Europe. Western countries should have a liberal attitude towards religious beliefs and should not impose beliefs to others. This point is illustrated in Confucian advocacy of "harmony in diversity", "not to impose on others what you do not desire" (Hua 2015, p. 132).

In addition, Peng-chun Chang objected to the expression of "Human being was endowed by nature with reason and conscience" in the first article of the draft of the Declaration (E/CN.4/SR.50). It was considered that it was easily reminiscent of natural law and God, and that brings human rights issues into the debate of religion and philosophy. Therefore, it could not and should not be raised in a so-called Universal Declaration of the world. He advocated deleting all expressions of "nature". Those who believe in God can find God's idea in this open clause, and others holding different beliefs could be able to accept this text. Finally, the Third Committee of the General Assembly decided to avoid using words that claim, imply or deny that the international human rights system was based on any natural, human instincts, or God, and deleted any expression regarding "by nature" (A/C.3/SR.98, p. 114). The text of the Declaration is also acceptable to more non-religious persons. Peng-chun Chang's advocations reflect the inclusion of Confucian scholars of different religions and philosophies.

2.1.4 Impact on Other Articles of the Declaration

In addition, Peng-chun Chang also proposed the amendment of other articles of the Declaration, part of which was adopted by the Committee.

Comments on the Content of Articles 2, 3, 4 and 5 of the Declaration

At the third meeting of the Drafting Committee, the Secretariat Outline and the U.K. proposal was compared. In response to the amendment of the U.S. proposal to the "Rights should be restricted", clause of Article 2 of the "Secretariat Outline", Peng-chun Chang believed that the amendment of the U.S. proposal was clearer and suggested adoption. Meanwhile, it was his opinion that the provisions proposed by the United States should be divided into two articles: one on the relationship between the individual and country, and the other on the relationship between the individual (E/CN.4/AC.1/SR.3, p. 11).

While discussing Article 3 of the outline, "Right to life", he said: "It is clear that all members are in favor of the right to life being enshrined in the Declaration. But should the definition of the term 'life' be further considered whether it means only physical existence or more?" (E/CN.4/AC.1/SR.3, p. 12).

Regarding Article 4, "Free from torture, punishment and humiliation", Peng-chun Chang believed that it is closely linked to Article 3, "Right to life", and should be included in the draft. At the same time, he felt the need to emphasise the goodness of life itself in some way (E/CN.4/AC.1/SR.3, p. 13).

In discussing Article 5 of the outline, "individual freedom", he believed that from that article to Article 11 dealt with the right to freedom of the human being. Therefore, all articles dealing with such subject should be discussed together. The Committee adopted this recommendation (E/CN.4/AC.1/SR.3, p. 14).

Comments on Articles 6, 8, 10, 14 of the Declaration

In the discussion of Drafting Committee regarding Article 6 of the outline, "No unlawful arrest and detention", Peng-chun Chang argued that the term "national emergency", as an exception for the provisions, needed to be clearly defined. In response to the expression "Slavery is prohibited by the Declaration" in Article 8, he considered that the wording was inadequate and that, as an important violation of human rights, slavery was universally accountable, rather than merely prohibited by the Declaration. In view of the provision of Article 10 on "freedom of movement", he believed that it was a fundamental right, but, given the specific circumstances of each country, consideration might be given to drafting a principled provision, not in too much detail, but the specific implementation to be considered by each country.

When the Drafting Committee discussed "Legal Personality Rights" in Article 14 of the draft, Peng-chun Chang thought that the term was too professional and formalistic. It should be more colloquial. It was later changed to "the person before the law" (E/CN.4/AC.1/SR.13, pp. 15, 20).

Comments on Articles 21, 28, 29, 30 and 31 of the Declaration

Also, regarding Article 21 of the outline, "the right to establish an institution in accordance with the law", Article 28, "the right to association, procession and petition", he believed that the content of the right to petition should be clearly defined. When discussed, the second draft of the Declaration, regarding Article 28 of "the equal opportunities to engage in public employment", he proposed again to include the provision "free to participate in the examination for the admission in public employment" (E/CN.4/AC.1/SR.14, pp. 3–4). On 25 June 1947, when the Drafting Committee discussed the draft of the Declaration attached to the summary report, regarding Article 28, "Equal opportunities to engage in public employment", Mrs. Eleonore Roosevelt (Chair) proposed adding "hold public office" after "engage in public employment". Peng-chun Chang suggested adding "the public service examination should not be a matter of privilege or favor." This amendment was eventually written into the recommendation draft (E/CN.4/AC.1/SR.18, p. 9).

During the 9th meeting, when Drafting Committee considered the preliminary draft of the Declaration, Peng-chun Chang pointed out that Article 29, "the right to take part in the government", should be amended in the light of the Secretariat Outline, in particular by including the provision of "competitive examination". It was believed that everyone had the right to participate in public life and that the system of "free competitive examination" should be regarded as true freedom and democracy (E/CN.4/AC.1/SR.9, pp. 4–6).

In response to the provisions of Article 30, "the right to vote", he believed that, since the right to vote was a way of realising human rights, "competitive examination" should also be seen as a means of implementation, thus being mentioned in the Declaration.

Regarding Article 31, "Right to Asylum", the initial draft refers only from the state's perspective to the right of the state to "political asylum". Peng-chun Chang hoped to refer this right from both the state and individual perspectives, which is that in the Declaration both the right of state to "asylum" but also the right of individuals to "seek asylum" to be included (E/CN.4/AC.1/SR.9, p. 8).

Comments on Articles 35 and 36 of the Declaration

While the Drafting Committee continued to consider the second draft of the Declaration, Peng-chun Chang argued that Article 36, "Right to Rest and Leisure", should be separated from the right to acquire outside knowledge, which should be classified as the right to education (E/CN.4/AC.1/SR.15, p. 2). Regarding Article 35, "Right to Education", Peng-chun Chang proposed to revise the provision to be as following: "Everyone has the right to education. Elementary education shall be compulsory and provided by the country and society in which he or she lives. Technical, culture and higher education provided by the country and society shall be made generally available and equally accessible to all based on merit only, regardless of race, sex, language or religion." Mrs. Roosevelt suggested deleting the phrase "in which he or she lives", which Mr. Chang accepted. His above-mentioned statement was mostly adopted by the Committee (E/CN.4/AC.1/SR.15, p. 4).

2.2 *Peng-chun Chang's Contribution to the Form of the Universal Declaration of Human Rights*

According to the records of the United Nations archives, the General Assembly and the Economic and Social Council, at the beginning of their decision to draft the UDHR, did not clearly state its nature and legal status, but merely referred to it as "International Bill of Human Rights". But "Bill" can be either a covenant or a declaration. Therefore, Member States have been at odds since the beginning with whether to develop a specific human rights covenant or a general universal declaration. In this regard, as former ambassador to foreign countries with experiences in the West and the East, Peng-chun Chang, with a keen insight into the international situation, felt that there were tremendous difficulties for different camps to reach a detailed and specific covenant that included the implementation of measures. Thus, Dr. Chang advocated the "declaration before convention" strategy, proposing that a concise list of fundamental human rights and freedoms be presented in the form of a declaration, followed by a commentary on the article-by-article interpretation of the Declaration, and thirdly a proposal containing specific measures of implementation (E/CN.4/AC.1/SR.4, p. 11; E/CN.4/AC.1/SR.5, p. 4; E/CN.4/AC.1/SR.8, p. 6). He also suggested in many occasions that the current Declaration should be in very simple and short terms to abstract the fundamental human rights to be accepted by the majority of states during vote (E/CN.4/AC.1/SR.5, pp. 3–4; E/CN.4/AC.1/SR.17, p. 10; E/CN.4/AC.1/SR.13, p. 10). Although the Drafting Committee had not adopted this recommendation at the meeting, the drafting of the Declaration was in fact well ahead of the covenant and the measures of implementation, due to the direction he pointed. Following the sixth meeting of the Drafting Committee, the first draft declaration (known as the "Cassin Draft") was completed by the drafting group of which the French representative, René Cassin, was a member, followed by a proposal that the covenant and measures of implementation should be developed simultaneously. In this regard, Peng-chun Chang believed that since the Declaration has been drafted, the Drafting Committee should first review the first draft article by article before considering the covenant and measures of implementation (E/CN.4/AC.1/SR.7, pp. 3–4).

This proposal was supported by the Chair, Mrs. Roosevelt. Consequently, by the end of the first session of the Drafting Committee, the first draft of the Cassin Draft had been considered and a proposed draft had been submitted by the Drafting Committee based on revisions, laying the groundwork for the adoption of the declaration ahead of the covenant (Hua 2015, p. 144). As Ashild Samnøy, a Swedish scholar, commented: "Although the formal decision made at the second session of the Commission on Human Rights in December 1947 emphasized the need for a declaration, a covenant and three implementing measures to be made simultaneously, the strategy of 'declaration before convention' actually prevailed" (Samnøy 1999, p. 8). As we see today, the International Bill of Human Rights finally consists of three documents: "The Declaration", "The International Covenant of Civil and Political Rights" and "The International Covenant on Economic, Social and Cultural Rights."

In addition, after the adoption of the UDHR by the General Assembly, Peng-chun Chang served as the translator of its Chinese edition. As the Committee was especially careful to make the lying of each word, in 1948, during its consideration of the Declaration, the Third Committee of the General Assembly established a language group for the six official languages of the United Nations, including Chinese, to review the texts of each official language version to ensure that each word corresponds accurately (A/C.3/380, 1948). Peng-chun Chang, as the Chinese representative involved in the drafting of the Declaration, led the translation work of the Chinese version. In 1948, the third session of the General Assembly adopted the Chinese of the UDHR by a resolution (A/RES/217 III, Chinese official translation). Peng-chun Chang's deep knowledge of Chinese Confucian culture can also be seen from it. For example, he translated the "conscience" he had proposed in Article 1 of the Declaration as "良知", which was derived from *Mencius*, Jin Xin II: "The ability possessed by men without having been acquired by learning is intuitive ability, and the knowledge possessed by them without the exercise of thought is their intuitive knowledge" (Mencius 2011, p. 252) which is the moral concept people born with (Hua 2015, p. 161).

For the second half of the first paragraph "should act towards one another in the spirit of brotherhood" is expressed as "act towards one another like brothers" in the first draft. Among them, the wording of the "like brothers", which the United

Nations Commission on the Status of Women considered inappropriate and suggested whether to consider adding the word "sister" for equality. This was supported by the representative of India, Mrs. Hansa Mehta. However, to preserve semantic integrity and nature, the final text of the Declaration did not adopt this recommendation, but instead replaced it with the phrase "in the spirit of brotherhood" (Gudmundur et al. 1999, p. 50). In the Chinese version of the Declaration, this paragraph "All Human beings are born free and equal in dignity and rights. They are endowed with reason and conscience and should act towards one another in the spirit of brotherhood." was translated as "人皆生而自由; 在尊严及权利上均各平等. 人各赋有理性良知，承应和睦相处，情同手足"(A/RES/217 III, Chinese official translation). Among them, using "和睦相处，情同手足" instead of the original text "以兄弟关系的精神相对待", not only avoided the emergence of gender information and unnecessary disputes, but also semantic faith, which reflected the Chinese culture and the profound heritage of Confucianism.

2.3 The Confucian Legal Culture Transferred into the UDHR Through Peng-chun Chang's Contribution

With the deep understanding of Chinese traditional philosophy, Mr. Peng-chun Chang introduced the core thoughts and ideas of them, especially Confucianism to the world during the drafting of the UDHR. Through his contribution, the Declaration adopted the idea of *Ren* and the other thoughts of Confucianism illustrated above. As the most important traditional culture in China, the thoughts of Confucianism were transferred into the UDHR, the common standard of public international law on human rights. From this point, those could be reviewed as the Confucian legal culture, which embodies the human rights ideas conveyed by the Universal Declaration.

3 The Human Rights Ideas in Confucian Legal Culture and Its Shortcomings

3.1 The Ideas of Human Rights in Confucian Legal Culture

3.1.1 The Idea of Human rights in "Benevolence" (Ren, 仁) of Confucian Thought

"Benevolence" is considered as the core idea of Confucianism (Yang 1980, p. 96, Zhou 2016). Confucius did not give a precise definition, but through the specific examples of different occasions to interpret. "Benevolence" was mentioned 109 times in *The Analects* (Yang 1980, p. 96). In the many interpretations of "benevolence", it was described as "that to subdue one's self and return to propriety is benevolence", "the man of benevolence makes the difficulty to be overcome his first business, and success only a subsequent consideration", "to be able to practice five things (gravity, generosity of soul, sincerity, earnestness, and kindness) everywhere under heaven constitutes perfect benevolence", "the benevolent man loves others" and so on.

What exactly is the meaning of "benevolence"? The scholar Yang Bojun believes that the true meaning of "benevolence" can be inferred from Confucius's passage to Zeng Shen (Yang 1980, p. 97). Confucius said to Zeng: "my doctrine is that of an all-pervading unity." Zeng said to the other students: "the doctrine of our master is to be true to the principles of our nature and the benevolent exercise of them to others, this and nothing more". "My doctrine" is all of Confucius's ideology, and it must be the core that throughout this ideology. It is "to be true to the principles of our nature" specifically and its "benevolence" in general.

Confucius himself defined "reciprocity": "not to do to others as you would not wish done to yourself", which is the negative side of "benevolence". The other side is positive: "he who wishes to be established himself, seeks also to establish others; he who wishes to be enlarged himself, seeks also to enlarge others." However, the highest state of Confucius is not "benevolence" but "sage". The goal of "sage" is: "a man extensively conferring benefits on the people, and able to assist all", and "a man cultivates himself so as to give rest to all the people". It is Confucius' belief that even Yao and Shun would not be able to achieve that (Yang 1980, p. 97).

I agree with the above point. Although, since ancient times, there have been many famous masters who have a variety of fine understanding on "benevolence". I believe that, synthesising their views, it seems that its connotation could be interpreted from the following two aspects.

First, from the perspective of individual's independent mind, "benevolence" is kindness, humanity, compassion, and hiddenness, and is the essential nature of human beings. Lin Yutong (1895–1976), Chinese inventor, linguist, novelist, philosopher, and translator, stated, it is very precise and appropriate to translate it as "true humanness" in English, sometimes just as "kindness" would suit (Lin 2014, p. 12). Of course, such highly moral true personhood is not something that everyone is born with, but to be learned, cultivated, and refined. "Human beings" can lead to "benevolence", but this journey is the inheritance of the accumulation through the history of the rich survival experience of humankind, and the process of individual playing the individual consciousness, initiative and creative in continuous learning and experience. The transformation of "human beings" to "benevolence" is the unity of history and the present. It is the process of human being to pursuit universal values and interests, which is a process to "pursuit excellence" (Cao 2015, pp. 19–21; Hall and Ames 2005).

However, this individual static nature of human beings is not the whole meaning contained in "benevolence". As Mencius said: "The feeling of the mind is the principle of the benevolence" (in *Mengzi, Gong Sun Chou I, Section VI).* The feeling of commiseration and compassion is only the beginning of "benevolence" (Mencius 2011, p. 60). Its secondary level of meaning is reflected in the relationship between individuals, which contains literacy of the kindness to others (the loving, respective, corresponding way of doing things in social relations including father and son, husband and wife, brothers and sisters, monarch and his ministers and so on) and the understanding of others (in place to think in a different place of generosity) as "the benevolent man loves others" and "consider others in one's own place". It also contains quality of loyalty to the principles of our nature as "not to do to others as you would not wish done to yourself" and "he who wishes to be established himself, seeks also to establish others; he who wishes to be enlarged himself, seeks also to enlarge others".

So, in the process from "human being" to "benevolence", how to practice to achieve "benevolence"? "To subdue one's self and return to propriety". Namely, through personal learning and understanding, indoctrination of society and government, a man who restricts the negative things in his mind, does not do evil, restores the inherent conscience of the heart, practice morals etiquette, and emphasises rationality is the individual with "benevolence" (Mencius 2011, p. 336). Like Professor Annping Chin interprets his understanding on the concept of *Ren* by the translation of Confucius's *Analects* that,

> Yan Yuan asked about humaneness. The Master said, 'Restrain the self and return to the rites. This is the way to be humane. If for one day you are able to restrain the self and return to the rites, this means that your capacity to be humane will open up to the world. Humaneness rests with the self. How could it come from others?
>
> Yan Yuan asked, "May I ask about the specific steps to go about this?" The Master replied, "Do not look at anything that is contrary to ritual propriety. Do not listen to anything that is contrary to ritual propriety. Do not speak in ways that are contrary to ritual propriety. Do not act in ways that are contrary to ritual propriety." Yan Yuan said, "Even though I am not that smart, I will do my best to put into practice what you have said" (Annping 2019, pp. 213–214).

Confucianism shows the respect for people through these ideas of dealing with social relations (Zhang 2017). This is different from the view of isolated individual human rights in the West. It advocates respect for people, understanding people, and tolerance of people, to harmonious personal social relations and the harmony of society as a whole. Thus, although thousands of years apart, it coincides with the goal of the 2030 Agenda for Sustainable Development of the United Nations, such as "envisage a world of universal respect for human rights and human dignity, the rule of law, justice, equality and non-discrimination" (Para. 8), "the need to build peaceful, just and inclusive societies" (Para. 35), "We pledge to foster intercultural understanding, tolerance, mutual respect and an ethic of global citizenship and shared responsibility" (Para.36), etc. (A/RES/70/1).

3.1.2 Confucian Social Ideal of "Public and Common Spirit" Embodies the Concept of Collective Human Rights

Based on previously mentioned "benevolence", Confucius extended it from individual to entire society and established social morality as "In the time when the *great way* was practice, the land of heaven belongs to the people; they chose the wise, talented and virtuous and set him up on the highest throne. The people went in for credit and lived in harmony. They knew how to love their parents, nourish their children, and support the aged till their death. They made the people in their prime years shows their ability, the children grown up, those widowers, widows, orphans, childless and disabled by disease supported sufficiently." in *Liji, Li Yun, History of Propriety* (Dai 2017, p. 110).

Mencius also proposed: "Treat with the reverence due to age the elders in your own family, so that the elders in the families of others shall be similarly treated; treat with the kindness due to youth the young in your own family, so that the young in the families of others shall be similarly treated" (Yang 1984, p. 28).

This ideal social state has been became a "Grand Union" society by Confucianism, which is the highest social goal pursued by Confucianism. To achieve this ideal state of "the world of Grand Union", people must have "a public and common spirit". This is another level of personal cultivation.

Confucianism proposed personal cultivation steps are "rectifying their hearts, sincere in their thoughts, cultivating their persons, regulating their families, ordering well their own States, illustrating virtue throughout the world". It goes from ideal to practice, from themselves to family, thereafter to the society, the world, to achieve the ideal ethical realm. That is the individual who should take the social interests and social ideals first and prioritise social interests in the conflict. Here, Mencius proposed the "righteous and benefit view", in which personal self-interest is the benefit and the world's great benefit is the righteous. To achieve the Grand Union, people should take "righteous" as the priority. In the conflict of righteous and benefit, taking benefit is not desirable. Gentle persons should give up their own benefit and see the world as their own duty ("shared responsibility" in term of the 2030 Agenda, para. 36).

This is the sacrifice spirit of public and common without self-benefit. It is a humanitarian concept with the primacy of national interests. Although this ideal cannot be achieved under the feudal system, but this self-linked with others, society, the fate of the country is undoubtedly an advanced culture of human rights (Wang 2004). This coincides with the provision of Article 29 of the UDHR, "Everyone has duties to the community" (A/RES/217 III).

3.1.3 The Values of the People Embodied in Confucian "Moral Governance" and "Benevolence Governance" Theory

Confucius promoted "benevolence" into the political field, which required the ruler "to rule by means of virtue". In Confucianism, morality is the foundation of politics. Confucius advocates "moral governance". He said "to rule by virtue is like the way the North Star rules, standing in its place with all the other stars revolving around it and paying court to it" (Annping 2019, p. 15).

So, what is moral governance? That is "if you guide them with exemplary virtue and keep them in line with the practice of the rites, they will have a sense of shame and will know to reform themselves" (Annping 2019, p. 16). It was advocated that good politics is "morality and courtesy" to guide the people to form a harmonious social atmosphere. "If you guide the people with ordinances and statutes and keep them in line with [threats of] punishment, they will try to stay out of trouble but will have no sense of shame. If you guide them with exemplary virtue and keep them in line with the practice of the rites, they will have a sense of shame and will know to reform themselves."

Advocating the courtesy of ordinary people, broke through the restrictions of "courtesy is not applied beyond nobles". It helped ordinary people to enhance their sense of social participation. It is also the human rights advocated in the UDHR, such as the equal education, equal development of personality, equal participation in social life. It has a progressive historical significance. Moreover, from this discussion, we can also see the thought of Confucius light punishment and re-education of the idea. It is more conducive to social harmony and good governance to give people "morality" and "courtesy" and to enlighten them than to pay attention to punishment.

Based on Confucius's "moral government", Mencius promoted "institute a government whose action be benevolent", saying that the interests of the people should be put first. Primarily, through a good system design to improve people's living standards, they thus no longer worry about livelihood, having not only enough income to support their own family, but also to support their parents, help brothers and sisters. Only when the people's lives are well off, it is possible to educate them, improve their spiritual state and ideological cultivation. Otherwise, forced by life, the people will take risks, violate the law, which cannot be fundamentally prevented even using harsh law (Mencius 2011, p. 22). From here, it can also be seen that his idea of being valued indoctrination instead of punishment.

In his view, the governance of the country should follow doctrine of king craft "to serve the people by virtue", rather than tyranny "to rule the people by force". He pointed out "When one by force subdues men, they do not submit to him in heart. They submit because their strength is not adequate to resist. When one subdues men by virtue, in their hearts' core they are pleased, and sincerely submit" (Mencius 2011, p. 22). Meanwhile, Mencius described the values of civilisation as "the people are the most important element in a nation; the spirits of the land and grain are the next; the sovereign is the lightest" (in: *Mengzi, Jin Xin Zhang Ju II)*. He used the "trap" to vividly liken the country that not to be benevolent will be unfair to the people and disadvantage to the establishment of a good social order. He said: "They are only men of educations, who, without a certain livelihood, are able to maintain a fixed heart. As to the people, if they don't have a certain livelihood, it follows that they will not have a fixed heart. And if they don't have a fixed heart, there is nothing which they will not do, in the way of self-abandonment, of moral deflection, of depravity, and of wild license. When they thus have been involved in crime, to follow them up and punish them. This is to entrap the people. How can such a thing as entrapping the people be done under the rule of a benevolent man?" (Zhang 2016, p. 624).

For the rulers who practice tyranny, Mencius believes that the people have the right to make their own choices. They could rise and fight, or even kill the rulers. "He who outrages the benevolence proper to his nature, is called a robber; he who outrages righteousness, is called a ruffian. The robber and ruffian we call a mere fellow. I have heard of the cutting off of the fellow Zhou of Yin, but I have not heard of the putting a sovereign to death, in his case" (Mencius 2011, p. 33). Because one of the legal premises of the ruler's right to rule is that the monarch's moral achievements, and the governor who practice tyranny is not only not to be righteous, but even to deviate from the benevolence. Hence it lost the legitimacy of the rule, and was no longer a king but a mere fellow, whom everyone has the right to kill (Zhang 2012, p. 76). This right of resistance in the feudal society at that time was very advanced, from which we can see the importance he attached to the people, which is also a kind of human rights.

3.2 The Shortcomings of Human Rights Thoughts in Confucianism

Nevertheless, we should also realise that Confucianism is not a human-centred account of the fundamental rights that human beings should enjoy, but rather a reflection of respect for individual rights and dignity from the perspective of the social relationship between individuals and the attitudes and behaviour towards others, as well as how people are treated in governing. Thus, the realisation of these individual rights depends on others, on other people, or on kings, or nations, or on ruling classes or managers. If they do not achieve the moral cultivation, which includes benevolent, righteousness, manners, wisdom and trustworthiness, advocated by Confucianism, these human rights will not be realised or guaranteed. This is the difference from the Western view of human rights and the rights elaborated in the UDHR, which is the human-centred affirmation of the fundamental rights and freedoms of human beings that are endowed by their Creator naturally. The nation, monarch and others have the obligation to respect, guarantee and should not violate and derive it without due process of law.[8]

[8]Some scholars believe that Western theory focuses on the rights of human beings as natural existence, so it emphasises the sacredness and inviolability of individual rights. Whereas Chinese traditional philosophies pay more attention to the rights that people has as social existence, so emphasise the sociality and integrity. Therefore, when individual rights and collective rights are in conflict, Chinese tradition prefers giving up "small profits" to the sake of "great righteousness". This difference between Chinese and western culture determines that the West places more emphasis on individual rights and ancient China places more importance on responsibility. See Zhang (2012), p. 163.

4 Conclusion: Confucian Legal Culture for 2030 and Beyond

As illustrated, Confucian legal culture not only includes the individual rights of human being but the manner for rulers to govern. Although they do not define the concept of "rule of law", the "moral governance" and "benevolence governance" theory as we mentioned also reflect the idea of *justice*. The ground of justice, which for Mencius articulates "the *sensus communis* of the hearts"[9] lies in the hearts of the people. The ground of justice is humaneness *(Ren,*仁)the origin of which is none other than the human heart (Huaiyu 2009, p. 321).

As discussed above, the thoughts or ideas of human rights contained in Confucian thinking also reflect the ground of justice to some extent, although in the different way from the Western philosophy. It emphasises the human rights on the context of social relations, the relation between parents and children, the elder and younger, husband and wife, the monarch and his subjects and the one with each other. It also advocate that all humans are equal before law. Toward the social harmony, Confucian legal culture appreciates understanding others like own, keeping sympathy in mind to others. Like what Dr. P. C. Chang had advocated in discussing the Draft Declaration of Human Rights at third session of the UN General Assembly in 1948, that, the second sentence of Article 1 called upon men to act towards one another in a spirit of brotherhood. That attitude was perfectly consistent with the Chinese attitude towards manners and the importance of kindly and considerate treatment of others. It was only when man's social behaviour rose to that level that he was truly human.[10] If people treat each other in this spirit, the society where they stay will be harmony. By analogy, if the ruler of state, internally, treat their people in this manner, the spirit of *Ren,* the moral governance will apply, whereas engage in foreign relations also in this way, peace and friendly relations would appear. Within this kind of societies, the people will live in dignity and stay in peace.

From the *travaux préparatoires* of UDHR, we can see how ordinary man and woman may perceive and pursue "*ren*" (humanness) in Confucianism (Ackerly 2005; Einstein 2014; Kim 2018). So this legal culture may contribute to global culture of lawfulness (Pływaczewski and Redo 2018), in line with the political science thesis that an external power merely reflects an extension of its domestic institutions (A/RES/70/1). This seems to act in concert with the United Nations, whose progressive ideals and power depend on its Member States' commitment to the Organisation's objectives.

In 25 september 2015, UN General Assembly adopted the UN Agenda for Sustainable Development, announcing 17 Sustainable Development Goals toward a world of universal respect for human rights and human dignity, the rule of law, justice, equality and non-discrimination; of respect for race, ethnicity and cultural

[9]*Menzi, Kong sun chou*, in Legge, The Works of Mencius (2011), p. 483.

[10]P.C. Chang' speech at the 96st Meeting, 3rd Session, General Assembly of UN, Meeting Records, A/C.3/SR.96, 1948, p. 99.

diversity; and of equal opportunity permitting the full realisation of human potential and contributing to shared prosperity (A/RES/70/1). Although it was born at the our contemporary era, but also embodies the thoughts and ideas of Chinese tradional culture, Confucianism, we mentioned above. In particular, the goal 16 "Peace, Justice and Strong Institutions", calling on to promote peaceful and inclusive societies for sustainable development, provide access to justice for all and build effective, accountable and inclusive institutions at all levels. It is also the ideal of Confucian legal culture to achieve the peaceful and inclusive societies. As the spiritual values, they nourish the whole generations and promote them to go beyond. From this point, the Confucian legal culture makes the important contribution to Sustainable Development Goals, the endeavour of United Nations for the vision of a better world.

References[11]

A/C.3/380, The official documents of UN General Assembly, 3rd Session, 1948.

A/C.3/SR.105, the 105th Meeting, 3rd Session, General Assembly of UN, Meeting Records, 1948.

A/C.3/SR.91, The 91st Meeting, 3rd Session, General Assembly of UN, Meeting Records, 1948.

A/C.3/SR.96, the 96th Meeting, 3rd Session, General Assembly of UN, Meeting Records, 1948.

A/C.3/SR.98, the 98th Meeting, 3rd Session, General Assembly of UN, Meeting Records, 1948.

A/RES/217 III, The official document of United Nations, Chinese official translation, 1948.

A/RES/70/1, Transforming our world: The 2030 Agenda for Sustainable Development 25 September 2015.

Ackerly, B. (2005). Is liberalism the only way toward democracy? Confucianism and democracy. *Political Theory, 33*, 547–576.

Gudmundur et al. (1999). *The Universal Declaration of Human Rights: Common Standard of Achievement, organized for translation by Chinese Society of Human Rights*. Chengdu, China: Sichuan People's Press. (瑞典)哥德门德尔·阿尔弗雷松, 挪威阿斯布佐恩 主编,〈世界人权宣言〉:努力实现的共同标准, 中国人权研究会组织翻译, 四川人民出版社).

Annping, C. (2019). *The Analects of Confucius*. Guilin, China: Guangxi Normal University Press. (美金安平:《论语英译及评注》, 鄢秀 译, 桂林:广西师范大学出版社, 2019).

Cao, W. (2015). The philosophical interpretation on the concept of *Ren* in The Analacts: The perspective of American Academy of Sinology, Academic Exchange No. 6. (曹威, 论美国汉学界对《论语》中"仁"的哲学诠释, 学术交流. 年第6期).

Chang, P. C. (1923). *Education for modernization in China: A search for criteria of curriculum construction in view of the transition in national life, with special reference to secondary education*. New York City: Teacher College, Columbia University.

Chung-Sho, L. (1947). Human rights in the Chinese tradition. In *Human rights: Comments and interpretations. A Symposium edited by UNESCO*. London & New York: Allan Wingat.

Dai, S. comp. (2017). *Li Ji: On propriety [social and individual behavior]*, English Translated by Luo Zhi-Ye. Nanking, China: Southeast University Press. (《礼记, 西汉.戴圣 编纂, 罗志野 英译. 南京:东南大学出版社).

E/CN.4/AC.1/SR.11 (1947). UN Commission on Human Rights, Drafting Committee, 1st Session, Meeting Records, 19 June.

E/CN.4/AC.1/SR.13 (1947). UN Commission on Human Rights, Drafting Committee, 1st Session, Meeting Records.

[11] All United Nations parliamentary documentation starting with "A" & "E" symbol from the United Nations website http://www.un.org.

E/CN.4/AC.1/SR.14 (1947). UN Commission on Human Rights, Drafting Committee, 1st Session, Meeting Records.

E/CN.4/AC.1/SR.18 (1947). UN Commission on Human Rights, Drafting Committee, 1st Session, Meeting Records.

E/CN.4/AC.1/SR.3 (1947). UN Commission on Human Rights, Drafting Committee, 1st Session, Meeting Records.

E/CN.4/AC.1/SR.4 (1947). UN Commission on Human Rights, Drafting Committee, 1st Session, Meeting Records.

E/CN.4/AC.1/SR.7 (1947). UN Commission on Human Rights, Drafting Committee, 1st Session, Meeting Records.

E/CN.4/AC.1/SR.8 (1947).UN Commission on Human Rights, Drafting Committee, 1st Session, Meeting Records.

E/CN.4/SR.10 (1947). UN Human Rights Commission, 1st Session, Meeting Records.

E/CN.4/SR.13 (1947). UN Human Rights Commission, 1st Session, Meeting Records.

E/CN.4/SR.23- E/CN.4/SR.42 (1947). Commission on Human Rights, 2nd Session, Meeting Records.

E/CN.4/SR.7 (1947). UN Human Rights Commission, 1st Session, Meeting Records.

E/CN.4/SR.9 (1947). UN Human Rights Commission, 1st Session, Meeting Records.

ECOSOC. (1946). *Official records. First year. From the first meeting (23 January 1946) to the fourteenth meeting (18 February 1946), and annexes.* London: Church House, Westminster.

E/HR/6- E/HR/16 (1946). Nuclear Commission on Human Rights, Meeting Records.

Einstein, D. (2014). *Democracy in contemporary Confucian philosophy*. Oxon: Routledge.

Glen, M., & Symonides, J. (Eds.). (1998). *The Universal Declaration of Human Rights: A history of its creation and implementation 1948–1998*. Paris: United Nations Educational, Scientific and Cultural Organization.

Glendon, M. A. (2001). *A world made new: Eleanor Roosevelt and the Universal Declaration of Human Rights*. Random House.

Hall, D., & Ames, R. T. (2005). *Thinking through Confucius*. Chinese Translated by J-L He, Beijing: Beijing University Press. (郝大维、安乐哲, 通过孔子而思, 何金俐 译, 北京大学出版社).

Hua, G. Y. (2015). *The Chinese Contribution among International Human Rights Movement: Peng-Chun Chang and the UDHR*. Beijing: China University of Political Science and Law Press. (化国宇.国际人权事业的中国贡献:张彭春与〈世界人权宣言〉.北京:中国政法大学出版社 2015).

Huaiyu, W. (2009). The way of heart: Mencius' understanding of justice. *Philosophy East & West, 59*(3), 317–363.

Huang, J. W. (2012). Confucian tradition and the construction of contemporary human rights. *Journal of Sun Yat-sen University* (Social Science Edition), No. 6. (黄建武, 儒家传统与现代人权建设·以张彭春《世界人权宣言》形成的贡献为视角, 中山大学学报社会科学版, 2012年第6 期).

Ju, C. W. (2011). The Contribution of Confucianism to the New International Human Rights Theory: From the Perspective of Peng-Chun Chang's Contribution to the Drafting of The UDHR, Globe Law Review (Chinese), No. 1. (鞠成伟, 儒家思想对世界新人权理论的贡献——从张彭春对《世界人权宣言》订立的贡献出发, 环球法律评论. 2011年第1期).

Kim, S. (2018). *Democracy after virtue: Toward pragmatic Confucian democracy*. Oxford: Oxford University Press.

Lin, Y. T. (2014). *The wisdom of Confucius* (Chinese). Nanking, China: Jiangsu People's Press. (林语堂.孔子的智慧.南京:江苏人民出版社, 2014).

Mencius. (2011). English translation by Sun Z.Z. Hangzhou, China: Zhejiang University Press. (孙芝斋编注.孟子今译.汉英对照.杭州:浙江大学出版社).

Pływaczewski, E., & Redo, S. (Eds.). (2018). *Advancing culture of lawfulness. Towards the achievement of the 2030 Agenda*. A special issue of Białystok Legal Studies (*Białostockie Studia Prawnicze*) 3/23. https://bit.ly/3fPhCe4

Samnøy, A.(1999). The origin of the UDHR, Chinese translated by Gu Sheng-kai. In G. Alfredsson & A. Eide (Eds.), *The UDHR: Common Standard of Achievement, organized for translation by Chinese Society of Human Rights*. Chengdu: Sichuan People's Press. (阿谢尔德·萨姆诺伊,《世界人权宣言》的起源, 谷盛开 译, 载:【瑞典】哥德门德尔·阿尔弗雷松,【挪威】阿斯布佐恩 主编,《世界人权宣言》:努力实现的共同标准, 中国人权研究会组织翻译, 成都:四川人民出版社).

Sun, P. H. (2011). Peng-Chun Chang: The Famous Human Rights Activist around World, Human Rights (Chinese), No. 6. (孙平华.张彭春:享誉全世界的人权活动家, 人权, 2011年第6期).

Sun, P. H. (2012). *The study of the Universal Declaration of Human Right*. Beijing, China: Peking University Press. (孙平华.世界人权宣言研究.北京:北京大学出版社).

Sun, P. H. (2017). Peng-Chun Chang and the development of international human rights system. *Journal of Zhejiang Gongshang University*, No. 7. (孙平华.论张彭春与国际人权体系的建构.浙江工商大学学报, 年第7期).

Tang, Y. X. (2018). The Drafting of the Universal Declaration of Human Rights and its Influence for Generations. Human Rights (Chinese), No. 6. (唐颖侠.《世界人权宣言》的起草过程与后世影响:纪念《世界人权宣言》70周年国际研讨会综述.人权, 2018年第6期).

The Work of Mencius. (2011). Book VII, LILOU Part One, Chinese-English, English translation by James Legge. Beijing, China: Foreign Language Research Publishing House. (孟子, 汉英对照,【英】James Legge译.北京:外语教学与研究出版社.2011).

Wang, X. S. (2004). The analysis of Hunan rights ideas in Confucian moral principles. *Journal of Social Science of Hunan Medical University, 6*(4), 18–20. (王新生.儒家伦理的人权理念分析.湖南医科大学学报(社会科学版), 2004年第4期).

Yang, B. J. (1980). The brief study on Confucius, Dong Yue Tribune (Chinese), No. 2. (杨伯峻.试论孔子.东岳论坛, 1980年第2期).

Yang, B. J. (1984). *Comments on the Work of Mencius*. Beijing: Zhonghua Book Company. (杨伯峻, 孟子译注, 北京:中华书局).

Zhang, Y. J. (2016). The United Nations, equal and inclusive society and crime prevention: Chinese philosophical contributions to the idea of sustainable development for women and children, and the current practice in China. In H. Kury, S. Redo, & E. Shea (Eds.), *Women and children as victims and offenders: Background, prevention, reintegration*. Switzerland: Springer International.

Zhang, Z. H. (2012). *Virtue and right: The human rights thoughts in Pre-Qin Confucianism*. Beijing: The Peoples' Press. (张志宏, 德性与权利:先秦儒家人权思想研究.北京:人民出版社).

Zhang, Z. H. (2017). Rights and boundary: A discussion of Confucian thinking on human rights thoughts. *Philosophical Research (Monthly)*, No. 12, 107–114. (张志宏.权利与经界:兼论儒家视野中的人权思想.哲学研究, 2017年第12期).

Zhou, X. K. (2016). The French translation on core concepts in The Work of Confucius: From the perspective of *Ren., Etudes Francaises* (Chinese), 103/4. (周新凯.《论语》核心概念法译研究——以"仁"为例, 法国研究, 2016年第4期).

Ying-Jun Zhang is an Associate Professor, Law Faculty, South-Central University for Nationalities, Wuhan, Hubei, P.R. China; Member of the Chinese Society of International Law (CSIL). Bachelor of Laws, Wuhan University, P.R. China, 1990; Master of Laws, Wuhan University, 2003; Doctor Degree in Law, Wuhan University, 2006. Visiting Scholar at the Max Planck Institute for Foreign and International Criminal Law, Freiburg im Brsg, Germany (2011/2013/2018). Her research focuses on the public international law and international criminal law. Publications include *The Legal Issues of International Law on Transnational Corporate Offences* (Beijing, 2012), *Corporate Criminal Responsibility in China, Beijing Law Review Vol. 3 No. 3 (2012)*; *The United Nations, Equal and Inclusive Society and Crime Prevention: Chinese Philosophical Contributions to the Idea of Sustainable Development for Women and Children* in H. Kury, S. Redo, E. Shea (eds.), *Women and Children as Victims and Offenders: Background, Prevention, Reintegration. Suggestions for Succeeding Generations* (Springer 2016), as well as dozen publications in Chinese academic journals. E-mail: zyj2161@sina.com.

Is Socrates Mortal? On the Impact of Socratic Logic on Teaching and Learning the United Nations Crime Prevention Law

Sławomir Redo

Abstract The chapter describes and comments on canons of action-oriented formal logic credited to Socrates (469/470-399 BC) by his student Plato. This form of logic was in 2016–2019 the chapter's author instrument for teaching the United Nations crime prevention law at the law faculties of the University of Białystok (Białystok, Poland) and the South-Central University for Nationalities (Wuhan, China). The author also presents and discusses logistical and substantive issues involved in altogether five Socratic workshops concerning their preparation, implementation and evaluation, in the comparative context of Socratic and Confucian logic. The author concludes that progressive Socratic logic and the above-mentioned reformist, rational United Nations law blend well with the Western and Confucian legal cultures. The application of this logic to any other material law is likewise possible and may be beneficial for legal education worldwide.

Keywords Confucius · Crime prevention · Deduction · Induction · Logic · Socrates · Socratic dialogue · Sustainable development goals · Syllogism · United Nations · War crimes

1 Introduction

The import of formal logic based on Aristotle's deductive syllogism cannot be estimated. In the simplest and convincing way the classic syllogism (two premises and one conclusion) that: "A: All humans are mortal; B: Socrates is human; C: Socrates is mortal" seems to leave no doubt regarding how compelling this logical reasoning is (Copi et al. 2014).[1] Since the early middle ages when this form of formal

[1] In fact, there are various ambiguities on validation of this syllogism, documented by Copi et al. (2014). They prompt to think that more ambiguous Socratic logic can be "syllogised," thus made

S. Redo (✉)
United Nations Studies Association, Wien, Austria
e-mail: s@redo.net

H. Kury, S. Redo (eds.), *Crime Prevention and Justice in 2030*,
https://doi.org/10.1007/978-3-030-56227-4_30

logic has started to be taught in the Catholic educational institutions, when—next—Godfried W. Leibnitz (1646–1716) complimented syllogism as the "finest inventions to have been made by the human mind" (Leibnitz 1765/1996, § 478), and when eventually Bertrand Russell (1872–1970) said that syllogism is as sterile as the twelfth-century monks were (Nisbett 2004, p. 203)—with these acknowledgements of Aristotelian valours of logical deduction, it has for good taken place in natural science anywhere, and in the Western world law schools (Sayre 1998).

But not in China. Ever since syllogism's valours have there been dismissed by the Kangxi Emperor (1654–1722) as "absurd and unintelligible" (Kurz 2011, p. 86), deductive logic has not taken roots in Chinese social sciences, let alone legal education. It "came to naught" (Kurz 2011, p. 86).[2]

In contrast, inductive logic (reasoning by analogy) in Chinese and Western legal science enjoys common ground. Using the latter method's evaluation criteria of effectiveness developed by US-Chinese educators (Ryan et al. 2013) this chapter presents, discusses and recommends an interculturally viable perspective involving Socratic logic. It can be employed worldwide regarding the implementation through education and training of the United Nations crime prevention law—example of universal norms and standards.[3] On the strength of this fact, combined with the inner valours of inductive thinking, this author argues that Socrates' method makes him immortal anywhere.

---

valid as per the self-explanatory title of the 2014 book by Kreef (2014). This chapter presents author's own interpretation of Socratic formal logic based on induction (Redo et al. 2018).

[2]The historical background of the failure of Aristotelian syllogistic thinking in Chinese legal culture is also described in Meynard (2019), and by Yuan (2012). The innate disposition of Chinese thinking to analogy is explained by Rošker (2014).

[3]The United Nations crime prevention and criminal justice standards and norms comprise ca. 70 international custom and treaty instruments containing substantive provisions, adopted between 1955 and 2019 by various United Nations bodies. If to include the treaties adopted since 1945 and registered with the United Nations Secretary-General, they altogether amount to several thousand of substantive provisions. These legal instruments either recommend or stipulate Member States' actions concerning suspects, offenders and victims of crime and abuse of power, and regarding duties and rights of States, law enforcement and criminal justice agencies and actors, including civil society actors. Most of these instruments have been published in various compendia by the United Nations or other entities/authors, but some of them have been published exclusively, whether in print or as the Internet resource (see further: Redo and Platzer 2013). The United Nations Crime Prevention and Criminal Justice Programme is the custodian of most of the customary law instruments, and of the United Nations Convention against Transnational Organized Crime and the United Nations Convention against Corruption. Since 2015, the Programme develops a global concept of "Culture of Lawfulness," mandated by the Thirteenth United Nations Congress on Crime Prevention and Criminal Justice (Doha, Qatar, 2015). Other UN treaties (e.g. Rome Statute of the International Criminal Court) and legal instruments likewise contribute to that culture. The Fourteenth United Nations Congress (Kyoto, Japan, 2021) was mandated to assess the progress in its implementation in the context of the General Assembly resolution 70/1. A special issue of *Białostockie Studia Prawnicze/Białystok Legal Studies 2018 Vol.* 23 No. 3, E. W. Pływaczewski and S. Redo (Eds.) was dedicated to "Advancing Culture of Lawfulness: Towards the Achievement of the 2030 Agenda."

Socratic method is "philosophy in action" (Juchacz 2004). It very well lends itself to the implementation of good governance for social justice across the globe, in the process of which helpful may be criminological education. Socratic method has been pursued in a variety of educational settings ranging from universities to kindergartens. It is particularly popular in the Western world (e.g. U.S., United Kingdom and Australia), but since 2007 has a worldwide imprimatur of the United Nations Scientific, Educational and Cultural Organization (UNESCO 2007). When applied, what is quite common for Socratic method is not only its modification by modern audio-visual methods or by size of the audience ranging from class-room to lecture-hall, but also common is a discussion on the method's effectiveness (Schaefer Morabito and Bennett 2006; Chesters 2012).

At the invitation of the deans of the law faculties of the University of Białystok (Poland) and the South-Central University for Nationalities in Wuhan (China) in 2016–2019 the author conducted altogether five Socratic workshops on the United Nations crime prevention law cases (three on a cultural defence case, two on a war crimes case).

The present chapter documents that this teaching[4] method advances students' capacity for self-reflection. Moreover, it enables progressive transformative outcomes for countering crime through action-oriented education, motivated by the United Nations crime prevention law.

2 Background of Socratic Logic

Socratic logic was born out of the Platonic dialogues. Plato (428/427 or 424/423 BC—348/347 BC) wrote ca. 30 dialogues. In most of them Socrates is the main character (hence "Socratic dialogues"). He asks questions to up to four persons, trying to find out more about the other person's understanding of moral issues.

In the dialogues Socrates presents himself as a simple man. He confesses that he has little knowledge ("I know that I know nothing"[5]), sometimes ironising his ignorance. With this purported ignorance, he only asks questions and manages to confuse the other in the domain they discuss.

His philosophical argumentation skills are known as the Socratic logic or method.[6] He is now regarded as the world's first criminal justice educator (Holland 1980).

---

[4]In The Routledge International Encyclopaedia of Education, teaching is described as "the process of educating or instructing learners" (Crook 2008, p. 589). Learning is as "a change in someone's behavior, knowledge, level of skill, or understanding which is long-lasting or permanent and is acquired through experiences rather than through the process of growth or ageing" (Channing and Aubrey 2008, p. 157).

[5]Originally, "I neither know nor think that I know," see Plato, *The Apology*..., (2011, p. 10/21d).

[6]His questioning of the moral order of the Athenian Republic eventually led him to be sentenced to death for apostasy and corrupting the minds of his students. Having the alternative of showing

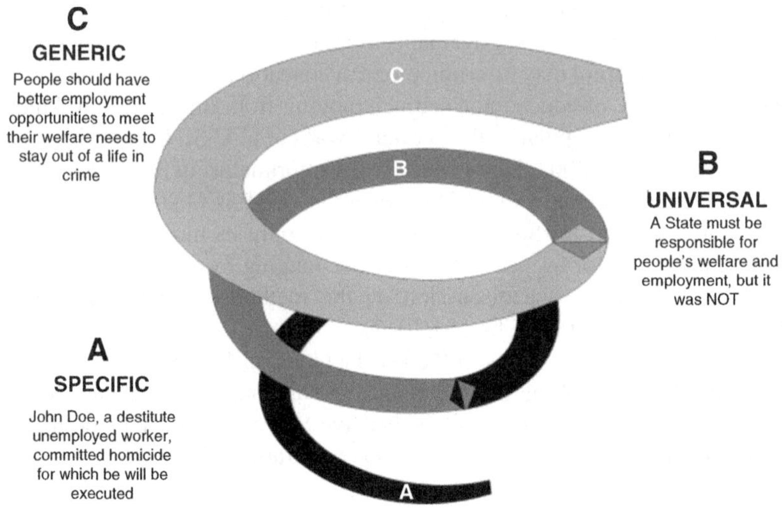

Fig. 1 Socratic logic through induction

3 Socratic Method and Workshops[7]

Before explaining the difference between the first three workshops and the fourth and fifth one, in the interest of appreciating the Socratic method as a whole, the following figure shows its essence in terms of a logical A/B/C sequence (Fig. 1).

Unlike in the Aristotelian syllogism, "B" (universal component for reasoning) is not only connected with "A" (the specific case in question), but also with "C" (postulated generic improvement *in spe* impacting a future verdict[8]). This also makes a difference with the Aristotelian logic. It begins with a universal premise "A," goes to generic premise "B," and closes with specific conclusion "C." In the Socratic logic "C" is the specific case in question, not the answer. In other words, one does *not* have to answer a question to apply a rule.[9]

Inductive logic is a fundamental part of Chinese legal culture of human governance within which the fifth workshop operated. This dominant paradigm of

remorse or even escaping from prison and fleeing Athens, in custody he chose to commit suicide by drinking a cup of hemlock. His dramatic choice made him the icon inspiring civil disobedience (Anastaplo 1969). Yet, the fact that in the name of rule of law, however heavy-handed and unjust it was in a democratic city-state, as a blindly (?) loyal citizen he exercised that self-destructive choice, may be very confusing, but answerable (see: e.g. Mahoney 1998).

[7]This and next section of the chapter is based on Redo et al. (2018, pp. 97–111).

[8]These questions follow from one another, in the sense that they mutually infer from themselves a logically compatible conclusion: either both are true or false (Ngwenyama 2014, p. 9).

[9]Inferential induction derives a rule from the case and result, deduction infers the result from a rule and the case (Ngwenyama 2014, p. 9).

thinking[10] in China has many versions (Xiong and Yan 2019). It has many parallels with the Socratic method, starting with the copula given by Confucius (551-479 BC): "To know is to know that you know nothing. That is the meaning of true knowledge" (Analects 1998, 2:17); "I do not open up the truth to those who are not eager to obtain knowledge; I will not help out any one who is not anxious to find an explanation by himself" (Analects 1998, 7:7).

However, despite these caveats, none of these versions is theoretically fully comparable with the Socratic induction.

The closest example of such induction involves "analogy from model"[11] (Xiong and Yan 2019, p. 376; van Eemeren and Snoeck Henkemans 2017, p. 87). It shows that this form of analogy is comparable with Socratic general scheme of "**S**pecific-**U**niversal-**G**eneric," save the double relation of U (with S on one end and G on another end), namely:

S is true of U, because U is true of G, and G is comparable to S.

Practically, however, in Chinese reasoning analogy involves a process of extending the matters in a sort/kind, so even the above argument is too narrow. More generally, analogy is a process of extending by kind (*lèi* 類) or inferring based on kind through its changeable associations and not by hierarchising pre-fixed qualities (cf. Xie 2019, pp. 328, 340). Hence, de facto, such flexible expansionist reasoning by analogy even more fully follows the Socratic open minded progressive reasoning then the above rigoristic way of argumentation.

Below is the list of features of Socratic and Confucian inductive logic.[12]

- *Similarities*:
  - Inferential thinking to challenge the pre-fixed order by distinguishing a strong argument from a weak one in a changing world;
  - Geared for benevolent human governance/right living: relate the case to a particular environment which should be improved to meet higher ends;
  - Pursue relations among particular objects or concrete concepts;

[10]"Historically, the view that the ancient Chinese thinking is characterized by a pre-dominance of analogical arguments could be traced... to a modern Chinese philosopher, Zhang Dongsun (1886–1973). In one of his comparative studies on the relationship between logic and culture, Zhang has concluded by saying that "the fundamentals of ancient western logic is syllogism... however, the ancient Chinese did not think in syllogism, but in another different way which could be called, if using the western logical terminology, 'analogical reasoning'" (Xie 2019, p. 325).

[11]Kings' conduct served as "models" (Xiong and Yan 2019, p. 376). In other cases, these were some metaphysical or epistemological principles normative in nature, in the society and even for the whole universe, as a universal knowledge pertaining to the forming of kinds (Xie 2019, pp. 330 & 343–345).

[12]Based on Fraser (2013), Heng (2013), Rošker (2014), Xie (2019), Xiong and Yan (2019) and Yuan (2012).

  - Rather than particularising universal objects they universalise particularism (modify the hierarchy of "particular" vs "universal" and "generic," making "particular" eventually a part of "universal");
  - Importance of self-knowledge, self-examination and reflection.

- *Differences*:

  - Inference serves in **Socratic** logic to draw premises and conclusion (focus on form with a cooperative argument/disciplined questioning to elicit answers);
  - Emphasis on words spoken;
  - Different specific "higher ends" (**Socratic**: prudence, moderation, temperate living, love of toil, piety, just truth, and the good of the soul; **Confucian**: filial piety, loyalty, and rules of proper conduct);
  - **Socratic**: explicit relation of "universal" with "specific" and "generic";
  - **Confucian**: inference serves to sort out subtle ambiguities and make analogous predictions and distinctions (focus on contents through semantic structures);
  - Emphasis on words written:[13]
  - Implicit relations between "specific," "generic" and "universal" by inference based on kind, in the process of changeable associations of kinds; but no direct interest in the exploration of the relation between "universal" and "specific."

The above list may sensitise a pedagogue to different thinking patters of students, and what the traditional "higher ends" are. To sum this up, in either case of analogy, inherent to it is induction through grouping the specific cases by their commonalities among them, and eventually by arriving at a more inclusive whole.

Is there any difference between these two academic methods of inductive thinking, and pursuing analogy on the UN workshop terms? The difference is in the fact, that the workshops operationalised and concluded induction by the result-oriented question "how?" to bring about change (improved sentencing/new verdict), in line with the United Nations "higher ends" declared via universal standards and norms.

Figure 2 depicts the sequence of all questions is "what-what if/why-how."

Inference allows to draw the link between the specific case and the *de lege ferenda* conclusion which belongs to the sphere of probability.

[13]Chinese figurative characters (logograms/ideograms) are a source of idiosyncratic logical thinking. Therefore, Chinese students react favourably to any translation of the English-language text. In case of the SCUN workshop, official Chinese texts of the UN crime prevention standards and norms and other United Nations legal instruments constituted its resource materials.

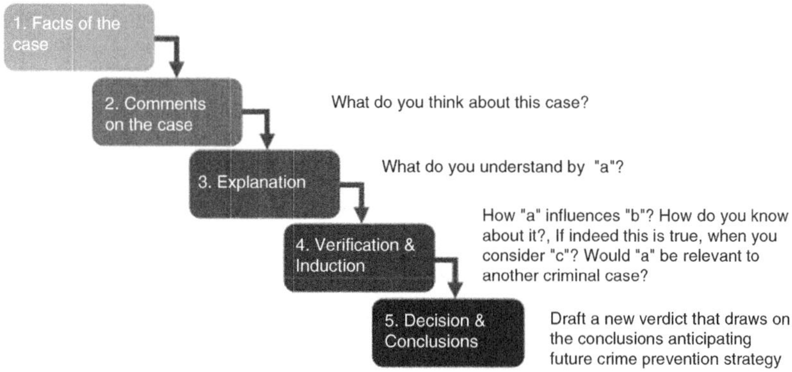

Fig. 2 Socratic inquiry into a criminal case with a verdict

4 A Field Progress Report

While it is true that a Socratic seminar may probably be thought in any material law/social science discipline, the complexity of the case in question may prompt to enlist separately undergraduate; graduate or doctoral students to take part in it (in one of the three cultural defence case workshops held in 2016–2018, there were also high-school students[14]). However, in author's didactics that was hardly the case. Moreover, students from other than law faculties participated in the workshops.

The first three workshops involved adjudicating in line with the United Nations crime prevention and criminal justice standards and norms a relatively simple criminal case of an immigrant from Chechnya (Russia), whose 15-year old daughter committed a suicide after she was raped. Taking another person for a real culprit of the rape on her, the immigrant tried to kill the alleged serial rapist. The case before the Polish court involved discussing all possible facts of the case, cultural defence (blood feud), mitigating and aggravating circumstances, the role of community, socio-economic and situational factors, the penalties and their execution, the rehabilitation and re-integration prognoses.

The fourth/fifth case examined in 2019 was constructed based on various war crimes cases adjudicated by the International Criminal Tribunal for the former Yugoslavia, the International Criminal Tribunal for Rwanda, and the International Criminal Court. In the manner similar (but not identical) to the above case, the hypothetical war crimes case involved charges for genocide, other crimes against humanity, including murders, rapes and destruction of property. In the way shown above, the students had to respond themselves to various criminological and public international law aspects of the case. It involved guilt and shame, offender/victim relationships, their religious affiliations, goals of criminal punishment,

[14]High-school students performed there quite well.

individualisation of penalties, reparations/restitution and educational outcomes relevant for handing down the verdict.

Refocusing the two last workshops on a war crimes case was motivated by the author's reflection on the Confucian statement made in 1946 by Peng Chung Chang, Chinese delegate to the inaugural session of the United Nations Economic and Social Council. Quoting a passage from Mencius (372-289 BC, "the second sage") Chang advises: "Subdue people with goodness, people can never be subdued. Nourish people with goodness, the whole world will be subdued." (ECOSOC 1946, p. 14). To this new focus has led me my concern that over past few years globally people have been nourished less with goodness and more with nationalism, to the point that the breakout of the next world war is more likely than ever.

5 Is Socratic Logic Imponent?

Every now and then Socrates' philosophy is called into question. In one thoroughly justified "obituary" published about the death of his philosophy after 20 years of studying it, it has been pointed that Socrates allegedly failed to educate in his philosophy anyone from his immediate environment (Legutko 2013, p. 12; cf. Kahn 1992; Kahn 1996). He later had more mature views, as if implying the discontinuance of that early thinking and acting (Legutko 2013). Other critics doubt if Socrates' philosophy is an expression of an infinite superiority of his reason over emotions (Brickhouse and Smith 2015), as if emotions would disqualify his method.

Whether Socrates "matured" enough or not, whether reason or emotion prevails in actions, could anyone discredit the 1789 French Declaration of the Rights of Man and of the Citizen because their stakeholders, e.g. Lafayette was 32 years old, Danton—34 years old, and Robespierre—36 years old? No question then, that the practical intellectual impact of Socrates on agents of social change is immense.

Both criminal cases examined at the workshops were very emotionally charged. They involved outrage, pain, fear, hatred and victim's forgiveness, while the second case also a blatant dismissal of guilt by the offenders prompted by their ideologically "superior" nationalistic feeling of righteousness. Both cases also involved suicides (one manifestly committed in the courtroom), while the workshops' participants were confronted with their own emotions and a moral challenge of imposing a capital punishment verdict rather than the penalty of imprisonment.

The war crimes case emphasised that all offenders had not pleaded guilty. The meritorious weight of the latter war crimes case, i.e. its legal, ethical and criminological complexity, precluded that only one graduate and five M.A. holders could be accepted as the fourth workshop's participants, thus making it a "training for trainers" experimental event. However, the workshop on the same case at the Law Faculty of the SCUN had 16 undergraduate and graduate students, including one student of Economy.

After each time handing down the verdict, the participants of all five workshops anonymously responded to the questionnaire whose assessment items ("1"—the

Table 1 Participants' assessment of five Socratic workshops (2016–2019), Law Faculty, University of Białystok (UB/Białystok, Poland) and Law Faculty, South-Central University for Nationalities (SCUN/Wuhan, China)

Participants' assessment of five Socratic seminars, Law Faculty, University of Białystok (UB/Białystok, Poland) and Law Faculty, South-Central University for Nationalities (SCUN/Wuhan, China)	Year		
	2016–2018 (Three seminars) UB	2019 (Two seminars)	
		UB	SCUN
1. The course helped develop my ability to think critically.	4.45	4.66	4.93
2. The course helped develop my ability to think creatively.	4.34	4.66	5.00
3. The course helped develop my ability to express ideas orally	4.17	4.66	4.68
4. The course helped develop my ability to work in groups	4.11	4.50	5.00
5. The course helped develop my ability to work individually	4.05	3.50	4.68
6. The course helped develop my ability to quickly pragmatic thinking in stressful situations	3.85	3.33	4.75
SUMMARY	4.16	4.21	4.84

Source: Statements from Ryan et al. (2013), p. 323

lowest rate, "5"—the highest) exactly reflected those of the U.S.-Chinese master evaluation questionnaire (Table 1).

From the data and participants' comments (on file with the author), it is clear that teaching United Nations law (if not also law in general) makes sense. How to progress in social development may be taught in an orchestrated, instrumental and pragmatic manner, opening the minds of participants to the positive force of individual critical thinking.

There is no doubt that pursuing that thinking with the use of the United Nations crime prevention and criminal justice standards and norms is an excellent resource of globally accepted and aspirational solutions, for some countries—*de lege lata*, and *de lege ferenda* for others. In either case these standards and norms do or can pave the way to humane and effective treatment of offenders. The oft recalled criminological findings that "nothing works" has for long been shelved and replaced by the kudos that "nothing works without the rule of law" promoted by those standards and norms. In this paradoxical sense Socrates' contribution to the rule of law is immortal.

How then to account for knowledge and emotions in Socratic-type pedagogy and encourage its addressees to be reasonable in handing down a verdict which supports the humanistic, socially and criminal policy progressive United Nations standards and norms in crime prevention and criminal justice?

With this question in mind, the participants of the two 2019 war crimes case Socratic workshops were asked several specific questions testing their thinking about the early and current international penal policy on countering war crimes. Namely:

1. *What did Winston Churchill, the British Prime Minister (1940–1945) mean when he said: "Contemplate that if Hitler falls into our hands we shall certainly put*

him to death. . .This man is the mainspring of evil. Instrument – electric chair, for gangsters"?

2. *Why then nowadays death penalty is not imposed by the UN courts for the genocide, like that in 1995 in Srebrenica?*
3. *If death penalty would have been imposed for genocide, what about other atrocious war crimes, e.g. murders, rapes, ethnic cleansing, extensive destruction and appropriation of property, not justified by military necessity?*
4. *In the absence of death penalty, how then genocide and other war crimes can be countered in line with the UN legal instruments, including goals of the 2030 UN Sustainable Development Agenda?*

In asking these questions, very opportune was Aristotle's guidance to put the audience in a certain frame of mind (*pathos*)—an emotional appeal to the audience's sympathies and imagination, challenged by reason.

The appeal has two connotations. First, this is an appeal to an audience not just to respond emotionally but to identify itself with the instructors' progressive point of view—to get to understand what one feels and knows, based on the questions implying that empirical effect of death penalty is inconclusive and that the domestic and international re-orchestration and application of other legal and socio-economic measures must be earnestly pursued, as per their UN inventory. Second is what *pathos* individually means for someone's empathy, sympathy, sociopathy/psychopathy, given the evidence at hand. "While some would argue there is no room for emotion in legal decision-making. . . it appears evident that, to some extent, the successful use of emotional appeals does affect trial outcomes, for good or ill" (Cormack 2014, pp. 139–140).

Pathos in the Socratic method is useful, provided that the seminar participants are in advance prepared to interact with an instructor. Throughout the five workshops the author used the example of West German Chancellor Willy Brandt kneeling in 1970 in Warsaw in a gesture of humility and penance in front of the monument of the Heroes of the Ghetto (DHM/Deutches Historisches Museum n.d.). At the workshops that documented that earnest reaction to crime and other atrocities is essential in healing human relations and restoring justice. Criminological evidence corroborates the importance of such healing gestures. It was the scientific basis to include in the workshops syllabi two empirical works whose contents was recommended to the students (Tangney et al. 2011; Navarro et al. 2013).

In this context, before and after each and every class (save the last one) the participants received a few comprehensive scientific analyses which they must read to deepen their reflective thinking, prompted by the last class. These analyses are accompanied by thought-provoking media accounts or short quotations from philosophic works of various worldviews. In any case, only three or four such analyses may be mandatory for the test (if any), and the rest of the resource material merely couches them. The selection of a few analyses is the most intellectually challenging and time-consuming process for an instructor.

Conceptualising the workshop long before it takes place is a fundamental pre-condition of its success. Researching, reading, reanalysing and recommending the resource material to the students must be extremely well planned and exercised. Instructor's inquisitive, thought-provoking, sequentially planned "what-what if/why-how" questions developed over long time of preparations for the workshop (but modifiable as necessary at the classes) are key for the workshop's interactive conduct and satisfactory evaluation.

Finally, in a 12 h or longer workshop (at the SCUN it lasted 16 h) the intervals between the classes must grow, e.g. Monday-Wednesday/Monday-Thursday/Monday-Friday.

6 Conclusion

Extending one commentator's view on the role of inductive thinking in China to education in other legal cultures, it may be said that such workshops could prove useful not only for advocating one's own ideas, but inviting and accepting the viewpoints of others. They may provide a foundation for an awareness of ethical, political and social problems in an action-oriented fashion to counter crime by an enlightened motivation. They could therefore not only function as a model that could be applied to existing experience, but have a potential to change the world for better (cf. Rošker 2014, p. 26).

The Socratic method serves well this purpose. It addresses the variety of UN crime prevention issues *glocally* in a viable way. It enables to employ in the adjudication process the United Nations crime prevention and criminal justice standards and norms, including the 2030 United Nations Agenda, in particular sustainable development goal 16 "Promote peaceful and inclusive societies for sustainable development, provide access to justice for all and build effective, accountable and inclusive institutions at all levels" (A/RES/70/1).

In the time of present considerable challenges to the rule of law and democracy across the world, the *ex-cathedra* teaching about crime prevention and criminal justice to its citizens should not be the sole modality to bring about the change envisioned by the United Nations standards and norms, especially by the 2030 United Nations Sustainable Development Agenda "Transforming our world." With due respect to this form of lecturing as the most popular and time-honoured, without entering into a dialogue with the young generation it is very difficult to convey effectively to it—future decision-makers and citizens of the world—the sense of superior moral obligation of humankind to obey the United Nations rule of law, thus—as the Universal Declaration of Human Rights emphasises—to protect ourselves against tyranny and oppression.

"Socrates is immortal." His progressive logic may motivate teaching of the reformist United Nations crime prevention law in an effective way. Socratic dialogue creates social conditions for a dialogue aiming at transforming our world, as per Agenda's title. True, his inductive arguments lead to less certain conclusions than those by deductive arguments. Regrettably, so uncertain is also the achievement of UN sustainable development goals through a "soft law" like the 2030 Sustainable

Development Agenda. But both tools are action-oriented and complimentary to one another. Combined, they are a hopeful marriage of progressive philosophy with reformist, rational United Nations ideas, which emerged from the ashes of the Second World War.

References

A/RES/70/1 *Transforming our world: the 2030 Agenda for Sustainable Development*, 25 September 2015, from http://www.un.org/en/sections/documents/general-assembly-resolutions/index.html

Analects. (1998). *The Analects of Confucius. A philosophical translation* (R. T. Ames & H. Jr. Rosemont, Trans.). New York: Ballentine Books.

Anastaplo, G. (1969). On civil disobedience: Thoreau and Socrates. *Southwest Review, 54*(2), 203–214.

Brickhouse, T. C., & Smith, N. D. (2015). Socrates on the Emotions. *Plato Journal, 15*, 9–28.

Channing, V., & Aubrey, K. (2008). Learning. In S. Wallace (Ed.), *A dictionary of education*. Oxford: Oxford University Press.

Chesters, S. D. (2012). *Socratic classroom. Reflective thinking through collaboratrive inquiry*. Rotterdam: Sense Publishers.

Copi, I. M., Cohen, C., & McMahon, K. (2014). *Introduction to logic*. Harlow: Pearson.

Cormack, K. (2014). Ethos, pathos, and logos: The benefits of Aristotelian rhetoric in the courtroom. *Washington University Jurisprudence Review, 7*, 131–155.

Crook, D. (2008). Teaching/teaching methods. In G. McCulloch & D. Crook (Eds.), *The Routledge international encyclopaedia of education*. London: Routledge.

DHM/Deutches Historisches Museum. (n.d.). *The Warsaw genuflection: Willy Brandt's historic gesture*. https://www.dhm.de/blog/2016/12/07/392/

ECOSOC. (1946). *Official records. First year. From the first meeting (23 January 1946) to the fourteenth meeting (18 February 1946), and annexes*. London: Church House, Westminster.

Fraser, C. (2013). Distinctions, judgment, and reasoning in classical Chinese thought. *History and Philosophy of Logic, 34*(11), 1–24.

Heng, W. (2013). *Cultural interpretations of Socratic and Confucian education philosophy*. Electronic Theses and Dissertations. Paper 605. https://doi.org/10.18297/etd/605

Holland, K. M. (1980). Socrates - The first criminal justice educator. *Criminal Justice Review, 5*(1), 1–4.

Juchacz, P. (2004). *Sokrates. Filozofia w działaniu [Socrates. Philosophy in action]*. Poznań: Wydawnictwo Uniwersytetu imienia Adama Mickiewicza.

Kahn, C. H. (1992). Did Plato write Socratic dialogues? In H. Benson (Ed.), *Essays on the philosophy of Socrates* (pp. 46–57). Oxford: Oxford University Press.

Kahn, C. H. (1996). *Plato and the socratic dialogue. The philosophical use of a literary form*. Cambridge: Cambridge University Press.

Kreef, P. (2014). *Socratic logic. A logic text using Socratic method, Platonic questions, and Aristotelian principles*. South Bend: St. Augustine's Press.

Kurz, J. (2011). *The discovery of Chinese logic*. Leiden: E. J. Brill.

Legutko, R. (2013). *Sokrates. Filozofia męża sprawiedliwego [Socrates. Philosophy of a Just Man]*. Poznań: Wydawnictwo Zysk i Spółka.

Leibnitz, G. W. (1765/1996). In P. Remnant & J. Bennett (Eds.), *Nouveaux essais sur l'entendement humain [New essays on human understanding]*. Cambridge: Cambridge University Press.

Mahoney, T. A. (1998). Socrates' loyalty to Athens and his radical critique of the Athenians. *History of Philosophy Quarterly, 15*(1), 1–22.

Meynard, T. (2019). What the "failure" of Aristotelian logic in seventeenth century China teaches us today: A case study of the Mingli Tan. *Frontiers of Philosophy in China, 14*(2), 248–263.

Navarro, J. I., Marchena, E., & Menacho, I. (2013). The psychology of hatred. *The Open Criminology Journal, 6*, 10–17.
Ngwenyama, O. (2014). Logical foundations of social science research. In K.-M. Osei-Bryson & O. Ngwenyama (Eds.), *Advances in research methods for information systems research: Data mining, data envelopment analysis, value focused thinking* (pp. 7–13). Berlin: Springer.
Nisbett, R. E. (2004). *The geography of thought. How Asians and Westerners think differently...and why*. New York: Free Press.
Plato. (2011). *The Apology of Socrates & The Crito and the text of Xenophon's Apology of Socrates* (B. Jowett & S. Newborn Trans.). Santa Barbara: Bandanna Books.
Redo, S., & Platzer, M. (2013). The United Nations role in crime control and prevention. In R. Reichel & J. Albanese (Eds.), *Handbook of transnational crime and justice (Part III, ch. 15)*. Thousand Oaks: SAGE.
Redo, S., Pływaczewski, E. W., Langowska, A., & Alkowski, P. (2018). Socratic contribution to culture of lawfulness for teaching criminology. *Białostockie Studia Prawnicze/Białystok Legal Studies, 23*(3), 97–111.
Rošker, J. S. (2014). Specific features of Chinese logic: Analogies and the problem of structural relations in Confucian and Mohist discourses. *Synthesis Philosophica, 57*(1), 23–40.
Ryan, E., Xin, S., Yuan, Y., You, R., & Li, H. (2013). When Socrates meets Confucius: Teaching, creative and critical thinking across cultures trough a multilevel Socratic method. *Nebraska Law Review, 92*(2), 290–331.
Sayre, P. (1998). Socrates is immortal. Formal logic and the pre-law undergraduate. *Notre Dame Law Review, 73*, 689–709.
Schaefer Morabito, M., & Bennett, R. R. (2006). Socrates in the modern classroom: How are large classes in criminal justice being taught. *Criminal Justice Education, 17*(1), 103–120.
Tangney, J. P., Stuewig, J., & Logaina, H. (2011). Shame, guilt and remorse: Implications for offender populations. *Journal of Forensic Psychiatry & Psychology, 22*(5), 706–723.
UNESCO. (2007). *Philosophy. A school of freedom. Teaching philosophy and learning to philosophize: Status and prospects*. Paris: United Nations Educational, Scientific and Cultural Organization.
van Eemeren, F. H., & Snoeck Henkemans, A. F. (2017). *Argumentation: Analysis and evaluation* (2nd ed.). Routledge Taylor/Francis Group: New York/London.
Xie, Y. (2019). Argument by analogy in ancient China. *Argumentation, 3*(33), 323–347.
Xiong, M., & Yan, L. (2019). Mencius's strategies of political argumentation. *Argumentation, 3* (33), 365–389.
Yuan, J. (2012). Aristotelian logic in China-a case study of the Chinese translations of Euclid's elements. *Journal of East-West Thought, 2*, 81–94.

Slawomir Redo Dr. hab. (Law/Criminology) is Visiting Professor of United Nations Law. He is a member of the United Nations Studies Association. F. United Nations Senior Crime Prevention and Criminal Justice Expert and staff of the UN Office on Drugs and Crime (ret.); He had been involved in numerous projects implementing the UN standards and norms in crime prevention and criminal justice. In other capacities he assisted in the implementation of the United Nations Convention against Transnational Organized Crime, and on-line international crime prevention and criminal justice education. He published four books, co-edited four others, including "Women and Children as Victims and Offenders: Background, Prevention, Reintegration. Suggestions for Succeeding Generations" (Springer 2016), and "Refugees and Migrants in Law and Policy – Challenges and Opportunities for Global Civic Education" (Springer 2018) plus about 80 articles—mostly on the UN law and practice of crime prevention and criminal justice. University course lecturer on "The United Nations and Crime Prevention" and "The United Nations and War Crime Prevention" (Austria, China, Poland); Promoter of crime prevention and criminal justice training and education for meeting the goals of the 2030 UN Sustainable Development Agenda. Co-Editor of the first criminological UN Agenda-based textbook *KRYMINOLOGIA. Stan i perspektywy rozwoju z uwzględnieniem założeń Agendy ONZ na rzecz zrównoważonego rozwoju 2030* (Wolters Kluwer, Warsaw 2020). E-mail: s@redo.net.

Reflections on the 'Right to Justice': Now and in the Future

Karol Rutkowski

Abstract There is only one justice, but it may be and it should be analyzed in various ways and, for classification purposes, divided and named in numerous ways. The United Nations finds itself at the juncture of two concepts of justice: natural (heavenly/divine) and that created in cyberspace, recently through artificial intelligence. The right to justice sets the foundations for the entire system of human rights in the world. These rights have been and are being developed by the United Nations, most recently via the implementation of the 2030 United Nations Sustainable Development Agenda. Justice fulfils and will increasingly play the role of a regulator of social development as the best fit for this function among the fundamental values of the human civilization—the love, the good, the beauty, the truth and the justice. Owing to the United Nations position on the crossroads, the Organization may be ecumenical in its own terms. Yet sooner or later it will have to measure up to effects of human development geared towards artificial intelligence and cyberspaces (as there are more than one), which may result in the emergence of *Homo deus*. The eventual effect of such an approach may be the building of a global civilization with succeeding generations of "hereditary intelligence" driven by artificial intelligence. Understanding the importance of the creation (or sub-creation) of artificial intelligence and cyberspaces by humanity gives it "legitimacy" to shape these based on commensurate values (criteria): love, good, beauty, truth, and justice, as if they were 'divine'. Three conclusions follow. First, paraphrasing the famous "If you want peace, prepare for war" we have to"... aim for e-respect." Second, as there is science related to law, it may be opportune to pursue research and develop separate science related to this form of delivering justice, which I would call "justology." Third, the post-2030 UN Agenda for sustainable development, with the horizon reaching mid twenty-first century, must face the threats associated with the development of artificial intelligence and cyberspace, considering the emerging opportunities for humanity.

K. Rutkowski (✉)
Institute of Justology, Warsaw, Poland
e-mail: karol.rutkowski@karolrutkowski.pl

H. Kury, S. Redo (eds.), *Crime Prevention and Justice in 2030*,
https://doi.org/10.1007/978-3-030-56227-4_31

Keywords Hereditary intelligence · Right to justice · Individual self-awareness · Self-consciousness · Human rights · Robot rights · Divine values · Love · Good · Beauty · Truth · Justice · Divine intervention · Divine criminology · *Homo deus* · Justology · Justological justice · Justological civilization · United Nations · Sustainable Development Goals

1 Introduction

With the 1948 Universal Declaration of Human Rights (A/RES/217 III), the United Nations set the first milestone in the development of human civilization. These rights change, the new ones are added, and they receive the new meaning. They are not in themselves or for themselves. They serve the highest, superior civilization and cultural values of love, good, beauty, truth and justice. Especially the latter, which seems to be the exponent of the first four and the regulator of civilization and cultural development. These values may be regarded as first-level axioms, and their servants, their stabilization, while the United Nations human rights are second-level axioms.

The directions of this civilization and cultural development of humanity are determined by the goals set out in the UN Sustainable Development Agenda until 2030 (A/RES/70/1). Obviously, this time horizon cannot be final. Subsequent initiatives, probably under the auspices of the UN, will create space and foundations for next stages of development. They will involve new technologies discovered and created by man and more and more advanced products of people's intelligence. The United Nations human rights and the 2030 UN Agenda form an ordered system that determines whether humanity will survive and will not rest on the way to knowing and understanding its existence and its condition.

Civilization development, although natural, is not cast in stone. Humanity also experienced periods of recourse. People are aware that progress raises new needs and presents them with new challenges. So, they treat development as an obvious answer to these needs and challenges. What's more, they plan its directions and goals to what extent they can at its subsequent stages of civilization development. The greatest achievement of recent times in the development of humanity is the common understanding that it must be balanced so that it does not lead to self-destruction due to depletion of energy sources, destruction of the natural environment, provoking destructive irreversible climate change, pandemic diseases and other destructive phenomena, including those of a social nature, xenophobia, extreme social inequalities, increased crime, etc.

The 2030 Agenda, which exactly fits the above understanding of progress, does not explicitly mention the threats associated with the development of artificial intelligence and cyberspace. However, it is obvious that the critical areas of civilization development outlined therein are seen because they must be more and more intertwined and interpenetrating. This takes place through the prism of human functioning in an increasingly complex environment of dual reality, both real and virtual (after all, 'virtual' means both real and alleged). The post-2030 UN Agenda for sustainable development, with the horizon reaching mid twenty-first century, must face the threats associated with the development of artificial intelligence and cyberspace, considering the emerging opportunities for humanity.

The role and importance of the UN in this context cannot be overestimated. After all, it is the only global organization capable of carrying out coordinated actions that can stop bad and support positive trends. Given the global reach of cyberspace (with some exceptions) and the present self-development of artificial intelligence, only the coordinated action of all human civilization stands a chance of succeeding, not confronting the problems and challenges outlined above.

2 Human Rights

Human rights are classified according to various criteria and there are at least several dozens of these rights. Until now they have not included the most important one—the "right to justice," in material not procedural meaning of its proper name. After all, the law does not exist separately from justice but it serves the enforcement of justice. This may be striking for academics but not for the practitioners of the United Nations law. However, the Commentary on the United Nations Charter explains that "justice . . . means something different from international law (. . .) and (. . .) refers to natural law" (Simma et al. 2002, I, p. 36).

Justice is a value which is superior to law, and law should lead to ensuring that justice is respected and served. In the light of the above and from the perspective of the provisions of the 1948 *Universal Declaration of Human Rights* (A/RES/217A III), it should be noted that the "right to justice" derives from the entire content of this historic declaration. It lies the foundation for the entire human rights system, rather discovered than established by subsequent legal acts of international and domestic different jurisdictions. These rights have been and are being developed in the United Nations. Currently, their development is moving in the direction of the 2030 UN Agenda for Sustainable Development, which is a continuation and evolution of the 2000 Millennium Declaration (A/RES/55/2).

Human rights play three basic functions: first, to protect individual's freedom against its infringement of the state; second, to ensure that the state creates the possibility for the individual to execute his or her rights; and third, to protect individual's rights and liberties by the state against their infringement from other persons (Osiatyński 2009). The implementation of these three functions, each of them separately and all of them together, may serve human safety. It is worth noticing that in each of these three functions rights and liberties should co-exist, with underlining that they are two different perspectives of looking at the same problem, two sides of the same medal. Safety may be, and is, one of the aims of these functions together with respect, dignity and justice, the latter superior to them all.

Contemporarily we are witnessing the development of ideas related to freedom—libertarian ones. In this movement, freedom is a superior value and human rights are, by assumption, supposed to serve achieving freedom by individuals, which should translate into freedom at a social scale (Nozick 1974). To go deeper, we are witnessing the rivalry of two main perspectives related to human rights—one focused on freedom, the other on equality (Steiner 1981). The freedom approach is characteristic to libertarian perspective. In this movement, freedom is a superior value and human rights are, by assumption, supposed to serve the purpose of maximizing the freedom of individuals. On the other side—as it is often presented—resides egalitarian perspective with its claim of the uppermost role of the principles of equality (Rawls 1971).

Moreover, the contemporarily formulated human rights are often considered as liberties in their positive ("a freedom to") and negative ("a freedom from") emanations (Berlin 1969), accompanied by corresponding duties they impose, both perfect and imperfect (Kant 1785). How to solve the problem of conflicting rights and incompatible duties is the subject of great moral and legal debate. A debate that might very soon—and in my opinion it will—have to face the challenge of further subjects and their new rights resulting from evolution of societies and technological progress.

From my prospective, it is the perfect moment that those disputing approaches should be crowned with the 'right to justice' as superior to other human rights and any other set of rights. Furthermore, the 'right to justice' should constitute a reference point for carrying out the exegesis of human rights and adding new rights to the list, fulfilling the twenty-four century old claim that: "Justice sums up all virtues in itself . . . Justice, then, in this sense of the word, is not a part of virtue, but the whole of it; and the injustice which is opposed to it is not a part of vice, but the whole of it" (Aristotle 2004, p. 99).

3 Supremacy of Justice

To avoid chaos and the degradation of moral values, societies must perform a reassessment which should lead to recognition of the supremacy of justice over freedom and equality. This, in turn, should positively affect human safety revealing the true image of justice and thus providing the means to resolve conflicts of positive and negative freedom as well as perfect and imperfect obligations they impose. The point is to ensure that the true image of justice and its nature would be revealed, incorporating the universal law principle to "act in such a way as to treat humanity, whether in your own person or in that of anyone else, always as an end and never merely as a means" (Kant 1785, p. 29).

In my view, people should keep persistently searching for justice, as they have been doing, but, without doubt, much more systematically. This search should be carried out in a scientific way, within the scope of a new science of justice. Analogically, as there is science related to law, it is necessary to create separate science related to justice. Reaching the essence of justice in a scientific way and disseminating this essence among people by means of measures typical for the information society may outweigh the trends of falsely understood unlimited freedom and absolute equality and serve as a guideline for solving the conflicts of rights. It may effectively prevent people from undertaking actions which put at risk their own safety and the safety of others. It will not eliminate these actions, but it may significantly limit them.

Justice fulfils and will increasingly play the role of a regulator of social development as the best fit for this function among the fundamental values of the human civilization—the love, the good, the beauty, the truth and the justice. They may be "divine"' and axiologically they are probably "divine" for all people, even atheists and anti-theists, although for the latter not literally.

4 Challenges and Threats

All of the above should, however, be seen from the perspective of the fourth industrial revolution. The constantly accelerating, rapid development of civilization in the last quarter of a century forces us to deepened reflection on its rudiments, including its directions, goals and methods of regulation. Moreover, this entire development process should be imbued with respect for human rights and concern for human security. It is not accident that the notions presented in abovementioned UN declarations and agendas emerged at the same time as the universal call to action to protect the planet and improve the lives and prospects of everyone, everywhere.

Human civilization is accelerating in its development to an outstanding pace which was impossible to imagine for people from a few decades back, not to mention ages. It is argued that human species stands on the threshold of a new kind of existence, completely different from ours (Huxley 1957). It is estimated that the whole knowledge of humanity, understood as the amount of information gathered, up until 1900 has doubled approximately every century, then by 1945 it was doubling every 25 years, and around mid-1980s it did so every year (Buckminster Fuller 1981). Enormous and constantly increasing acceleration refers to all fields of science, including scientific studies on justice conducted independently in various fields of science.

One of the greatest challenges currently faced by humanity is the formation and the development of intelligence other than biological (human intelligence)—namely, the one which is quite unfortunately referred to as "artificial intelligence" (AI). Because what is this artificial intelligence from the point of view of contemporary creationist theories, in which humans have got their Creator and did not evolve from inanimate matter to lower-order beings (animals which do not poses highly developed intelligence and self-awareness) and then further to a highly intelligent and self-aware *homo sapiens*? From the creationist perspective, humans are "specific artificial intelligence" and humanity is a "specific collective artificial intelligence."

This other than human intelligence—which is created by humans but which will be led (or maybe already has been led) to obtaining self-awareness, led not only by humans, but also (which will take place or maybe already has taken place) partially by means of its self-development and mutual learning—deserves a better name. Not entering disputes regarding the human origin, it may be called "hereditary intelligence." Humanity will not be (and is not) its sole founder, but will rather be (or is) its co-founder, together with hereditary intelligence itself, which self-perfects and mutually learns in its womb. One should not succumb to the temptation to refer to it as 'silicon intelligence', because—as it has been proven by latest scientific research—its development does not have to be based on silicon (as in contrast to life based on carbon).

Is justice—and should it be—exclusive domain of humans? Should it serve humans only? Is it true that only humans are capable to treat one another in a just or less just way? Already at first sight one can notice that there are other entities, which may be treated in a just or unjust way by humans such as animals, even plants and inanimate nature, or maybe even the whole planet. Applying the justice criterion to the whole universe may also be considered comprehensible, and even with reference to transcendence. After all the teaching of the Catholic Church indicates that God is the just Creator. Considering the above, is it possible to apply the notion of justice and justice as such to "hereditary intelligence"? The answer should be "yes."

To keep the civilization development under control, it is necessary to study the phenomenon of hereditary intelligence and cyberspace on various levels and from different research perspectives. Such a study can—and should be—interdisciplinary and should correspond to the principle of consilience. Such research should be deepened with all available methods. It should use all research tools that may apply to cyberspace, treated as transcendent to the real world. Such research should start under the auspices of criminology because of its wide view of these phenomena and readily available conceptual apparatus and research instruments. There can be infinitely many directions of criminological research on hereditary intelligence and cyberspace. It should be remembered, however, that each direction has two opposite turns of the vector module located on it. Furthermore, many new and further directions of such research can be proposed, which by all means can be justified and useful.

5 Divine Intervention

We could also look at this issue from yet another perspective. In my opinion, humanity—as the creator of hereditary intelligence and cyberspace—might play the role of their *Homo deus* (Harari 2016). It is popular belief that with the recent development of science and technology *homo sapiens* "stands on the verge of becoming a god, poised to acquire not only eternal youth, but also the divine abilities of creation and destruction" (Harari 2014, p. 337).

Regardless of whether humanity has its Creator, the same humanity naturally claims to be the author (or creator) of the hereditary intelligence and the cyberspaces known to us today. Understanding the importance of the creation (or sub-creation) of hereditary intelligence and cyberspaces by humanity gives us 'legitimacy' to shape them based on 'divine' values (criteria): love, good, beauty, truth and justice. This reverses the return of the vector module to thinking about hereditary intelligence and cyberspaces factors, especially criminogenic ones. We create these factors in the first place. It should also reverse the return of the vector module to research, especially criminological in cyberspace. These cyberspaces should be examined in their germs to be shaped following the vector directed to "inoculating" the "divine" values mentioned before. And a special value among them, which has already been mentioned here, is justice.

In-depth reflection from the perspective of justice should shape the laws of self-conscious intelligence, both human and hereditary intelligence. This view of one of the "transhumanist thinkers" continues with suggesting, that out of respect rooted in that intelligence, there must be the fire of intelligent self-awareness in non-biological entities, that will occur and that it will happen soon (Koene 2013).

What is the distinguishing feature of self-conscious intelligence? In my opinion, illogical thinking, guided by doubts and a lack of an unambiguous answers, is a leading characteristic feature of self-awareness. Logic is the domain of intelligence. The combination of self-awareness and intelligence is the same as logical thinking tainted with doubts and lack of clarity—this is self-conscious human intelligence. And it will be (and perhaps it already is) self-conscious hereditary intelligence; along the famous phrase "I think, therefore I am" (Descartes 1637, p. 23) we may characterize it with "I doubt, therefore I am."

Is it a philosophy or rather criminology? This is a prophylactic and criminological philosophy in an interdisciplinary approach, not criminology in its purest form. Such criminology—leading in interdisciplinary studies of cyberspace and constituting the basis of knowledge formed in accordance with the principle of consilience—may be called, somewhat perversely, but reflecting the ideas outlined above sufficiently complemented, a 'divine criminology' to be built on the solid foundations of the leading theories of justice (Cycero-Ulpian, St. Augustine, St. Thomas, Nozick, Rawls, Sen—to name only a few most prominent (non)secular theorists and other philosophers from West and East).

Given the above conjuncture, this is not a chapter about a utopian global state. Nor this is an attempt to outline a social contract based on the leading ideas of political philosophy, although it touches the thoughts of Rousseau, Hobbes, Lock, Montesquieu Mill or even Machiavelli. Therefore, this is not crossing out history or culture thus far.

On the contrary: I would not draw a pessimistic picture of man and its nature. I assume their positive image. Defining the possible foundations of a social contract between humans and robots is a task for the most outstanding thinkers of human and hereditary intelligence. This is an argument about the principles of survival and development of humanity. Its starting point is Socratic "I know that I know nothing" (Plato 1996, Apology 21d) in relation to hereditary intelligence and further to cyberspace, and maybe also to what it might grow into (super-cyberspace, or singular super-intelligence). It is an attempt to look from the Platonic cave into the world of ideas. Finally, it is an Aristotelian tribute to values, with the distinction of justice, the highest one.

From the perspective of the divine intervention the most important thing is to examine justice and learn its true nature as well as to be able to apply it to all forms of self-conscious intelligence. I propose to assign the rights and obligations to intelligent self-awareness regardless of its origin. This solves also the problem of various types of merged human and hereditary intelligence (trans-humans, cyborgs etc.). I define justice as a transcendent value (divine, figuratively or literally), both discovered and ascertained as the most-centered result of the scientific discussion of all self-aware intelligent beings wanting to participate in it. This definition is not religious, it does not refer to any religion and does not create one, even in terms of civil religion fashioned by Rousseau as an enlightenment religion of tolerance and mutual forbearance (Rousseau 1762, pp. 158–168). Machiavelli and Hobbes share Rousseau's fundamental concern (Beiner 1993) but this is not my way of thinking either. It is not atheistic or anti-theistic. It does not refer to Montesquieu's spirit of law, although similarly to him "I have not drawn my principles from my prejudices, but from the nature of things" (Montesquieu 1748, p. 6). Its determinant is scientific, and thus, above all empiric. In this respect it reflects Pinker way of thinking using social science data from various sources to argue for a general improvement of the human condition over recent history (Pinker 2018).

The final result of such an approach, as outlined earlier, should be—and in my opinion shall be—the emergence of a single civilization (not state) of people and hereditary intelligence. This new civilization should be based on the values professed by human civilization, also instilled through the upbringing and succession of hereditary civilization and without looking at the dangerous dreams of programming artificial intelligence in accordance to the Asimov's laws or alike. In my opinion, such laws cannot work with the hereditary intelligence self-development pace, which is intensifying before our eyes and bypassing human programmers. Referring to the famous statement "If you want peace, prepare for war," let me formulate my own: "If you want peace... aim for e-respect."

The problem of principles which will be followed by robots equipped by people with intelligence appeared much earlier than the possibilities for the production of such robots. Until recently it was considered only in futurology and science-fiction literature. However nowadays, due to the dynamic and constantly accelerating development of science, it became a burning issue.

6 Hereditary Intelligence

In 1942, Isaac Asimov formulated "Three Laws of Robotics" and presented them in a fantastic novelette entitled *Runaround* (Asimov 1950). The aim of those laws was regulating the matters of relationships between future thinking machines and humans. The laws were as follows: (1) A robot may not injure a human being or, through inaction, allow a human being to come to harm; (2) A robot must obey orders given to it by human beings except where such orders would conflict with the First Law; (3) A robot must protect its own existence as long as such protection does not conflict with the First or Second Law. Subsequently, in the novelette *Robots and Empire* Asimov added the 'Zero Law' (Asimov 1985), which became superior in reference to the previous three: (0) A robot may not harm humanity, or, by inaction, allow humanity to come to harm.

Asimov's Laws of Robotics were criticized from the moment of their formation. The critics argued that they assign greater autonomy to the group of founders than to their highly developed creations. They considered the imposed laws as actually a burden rather than rights. Nowadays Asimov's laws seem naive. More broadly speaking, ideas regarding the possibility to engraft every robot, every individual unit of artificial (hereditary) intelligence with the prohibition of harming people, from the current perspective of such self-developing intelligence, cannot withstand criticism. Self-development, by assumption, after some time disestablishes the control held by the founder or master, mentor, instructor, over the formed and taught entity. It starts in the moment when such entity undertakes its own initiatives, irrespectively of the mentioned founder (which in that moment is demoted to the position of the co-founder) because things no longer happen and occur exclusively in accordance to his or her will.

The criticism of Asimov's "Laws of Robotics" became the leaven for the formation of the theory of friendly artificial intelligence formulated by Yudkowsky (2012). This theory treats the matters of mutual relationships between people and intelligent robots completely differently. Its main assumption is that people may create robots which follow the principles of morality, and at the same time, have a friendly attitude towards their creators.

According to Yudkowsky and the followers of his theory, in the future robots will not be subordinate to people, but—as a result of technological development—they will become a completely separate, totally independent alien form of life. The robots of the future will be so different from people, that their anthropomorphic model promoted by popular-science literature will become useless. According to this theory, such machines will even think in a different way than we do. Yudkowsky gives an example of a robot producing paper clips which—after being equipped with artificial intelligence—could understand reality in such a way that it would try to invent a nanomolecular technology only for the purpose of transforming the matter of the whole universe into paper clips. Such a robot would be driven by motives and would pursue goals which to us are completely absurd and unthinkable (Yudkowsky 2012).

Yudkowsky's theory puts emphasis not on the possibility of the formation and development of dangerous artificial superintelligence, which would want to harm people, but one which would be completely neutral in reference to humans. According to this theory, artificial intelligence may harm people if they do not take appropriate prior steps towards constructing and developing it in such a way so as to ensure that it is kind and friendly towards its creators. Such a goal should be the superior paradigm of actions in the area of robotics, otherwise, according to the followers of this theory, we could become similar to parents who brought up an ungrateful psychopath.

The theoreticians of friendly artificial intelligence reject the assumptions of evolutionary psychology. According to them, it is not necessary for artificial intelligence to follow patterns of thinking which are similar to ours in its life, if we may speak of life here at all. If artificial intelligence (i.e., hereditary intelligence) obtains such a level of self-awareness that it is able to program and improve itself, the differences between it and us will constantly grow. Then, we will not have influence on anything anymore. Therefore, for us as the creators of artificial intelligence (hereditary intelligence), it should be important to ensure that right from the beginning it would develop based on a friendly attitude to humans. This stand is supported by Nick Bostrom's observations that it is very important to ensure that the goals of superintelligence and its whole motivation system favors humanity (Bostrom 2014).

According to many of the most outstanding scientists of the last century, including Stephen Hawking, Allen Newell, Herbert Simon, Allan Turing, it is only a matter of time until artificial intelligence (i.e. hereditary intelligence) obtains self-awareness, which—in their opinion—will be an absolutely crucial moment for its further development, including self-development. This will have an enormous impact on its relationships with humans (Bostrom 2014). They, due to this fact and starting from that moment (of obtaining self-awareness by hereditary intelligence) will no longer be the founders of "own" intelligence, but co-founders, together with the artificial intelligence itself.

For most scientists there is no proof of the self-awareness of robots yet. For some, such proof would be a test of whether a robot could recognize its reflection in a mirror. For others, which constitute the majority, only processing complex information for the purpose of developing a view of the world by a robot for itself could prove the obtaining of self-awareness by robots, although, self-awareness itself does not have one, commonly accepted definition and for this moment it is difficult to unambiguously indicate what it is.

The issue of self-awareness has been analyzed since ancient times by philosophers of mind, and an attempt to discuss it, at least briefly, has to have the size of an extensive philosophical dissertation. A quite numerous groups of scientists dealing with studies of self-awareness claim that robots will never achieve it. It is not possible to immediately resolve the dispute related to the possibility of self-awareness obtaining by robots. Events are taking place before our eyes as robots already mutually learn from one another. For now, to where it might lead to is a matter of faith, although based on knowledge, but surely not sufficient to resolve this significant problem of our human civilization yet. The big question remains: are we the highest form of intelligence on Earth, or only an intermediate form, leading to the formation of higher ones—intelligence which is 'hereditary' in reference to our, human?

Will hereditary intelligence, especially cyberspace, "mature"' to have feelings? Will it be emotional? Will it be able to philosophize? What would it desire? What will be the attitude towards its creator—to human civilization? Can we keep control over it? Should we take actions to preserve it through the lens of their meaningfulness or senselessness? Can hereditary intelligence, especially cyberspace, be "raised up," taught rather than programmed? Can we dispute, argue and quarrel with it? Is it susceptible to reason and can it be convinced to change its mind? Is it reasonable and sensible to build in it "fuses" that could be used to turn it off when we would realize it presents a threat to our existence? Is it even possible to turn it off by cutting off its power? Would it allow us to do that? Can it arrange an emergency power supply for such an event? Can hereditary intelligence, especially cyberspace, be good or evil in the human understanding of such concepts? Can it have bad intentions towards humanity? Being fixed on its own purpose and pushing for its execution, can it destroy humanity by accident, not necessarily by its will? Will hereditary intelligence, especially cyberspace, understand the concept of "partnership" and the need to respect interests other than its own? Will it have its own "views"? How much will it be attached to them and how determined to defend them? Will it form a need for eternal existence—immortality? What "ambitions" would motivate it? Will it need to have "offspring"—its own hereditary intelligence? Should we present these questions in a present tense?

I have to leave the above questions unanswered. In my opinion, we only know what we do not know about hereditary intelligence, especially cyberspace. Cyberspace appears to me as the peak achievement of human mind, placing us as its "god," its creator. We evolve into *Homo deus*, but I am going one step further from Yuval Harari, progressing his *Homo deus* from basic question by replacing his "non-conscious" with "self-conscious" (Harari 2016).

What could outgrow cyberspace? Probably super-cyberspace, a merger of cyberspaces. Exciting is this awareness (self-awareness, *sic*!), that something greater could happen, not in a spatial sense. This "something" may be smarter than cyberspace—presently, the most spectacular manifestation of intelligence known to people with no division into human, artificial, hereditary, extraterrestrial, or named otherwise.

According to the latest forecasts, the hereditary intelligence (AI) in 2029, i.e., at the end of the UN 2030 Sustainable Development Agenda, will pass the advanced version Turing test (Multimodal Touring Test) since some claim that it has already succeeded in its classic version in 2014 (Guardian 2014). Moreover, it is said that around 2050, which will probably be the next horizon of the UN forecasts regarding the development of human civilization, it will create a super hereditary intelligence (SAI) that will reach a level of self-awareness (Bostrom 2014). Would the super-cyberspace come into being as well, whatever that term might mean? Or maybe there will be a qualitative leap allowing unified cyberspaces, which through unification would become super-cyberspace, to achieve a higher state of consciousness, a kind of super-consciousness? I would call it a "divine cyberspace" to distinguish it from an inferior, human-like level of self-awareness. Currently it is impossible to predict whether such super-cyberspace or divine cyberspace would come into existence, or not. It seems to me that, should the super-cyberspace and then divine cyberspace emerge, they will constitute the most important, absolutely crucial moments in the history of humanity and Earth civilization.

These leads to two questions, dealt with in the respective sections below.

7 "Justological" Justice?

Time is up to start considering the immanency of developments and the various alternative courses of actions. There should be the proper approach and broad perspective. Perhaps, the best approach for such task requires the creation of a new science on justice. So far there seems to be no signs of interest to develop such science on justice. Only in the context of religion or spirituality it is possible to find the first-fruits or the remains of such a science. Despite the depth and the complexity of various religions and various spiritualities, each one of them and all of them together are far from exhausting the topic concerning the science related to justice.

Such science was, is, and will be needed. If it has not emerged until now, then it is necessary to create it and name it. I would name it "justology," deriving this term from the Latin *iustitia*—justice. This implies justice in every perspective, and not only justice as a cardinal virtue being the subject of aretology. This refers to each humanistic discipline of science. All these sciences to some extent deal with the problematics of justice. Justice is a value which everyone refers to. It is placed on a pedestal and set as an aim, the obtaining of which is the reason for the scientific considerations carried out in the scopes of the mentioned sciences (Maciejewski 2012).

The work that needs to be done to prepare the seedbed for this new science (justology) is implementable, especially with the help from big data analytics, data science and machine learning methods. Justology should be built based on algorithms collecting and analyzing, in all aspects, all available knowledge about justice, taken from all fields and disciplines of the humanities.

There is only one justice, but it may be and it should be analyzed in various ways and, for classification purposes, divided and named in numerous ways. Over the ages we have become so used to treating and describing justice partially, that we have lost the ability to perceive it as integral and superior in reference to many other values. Distributive, retributive, restorative justice; state, social, private justice; divine, imputed, given, natural, human justice. It is time to change that.

Various functions are assigned to justice. Deliberations on justice are approached with various research tools specific to various fields of knowledge and science. Integral justice, one, in a cognitive sense, justice treated comprehensively, holistically, and science analyzing it in terms of all aspects, with all available scientific methods—that is the goal and the ideal which should be pursued.

The aim of justologists may be holding research on justice and theoretical analyzes related to justice based on the results of that research. Justologists should perform their duties from a neutral point of view because, by assumption, justology does not serve for creating its own, sole, special theory of justice. Actually, it is quite the opposite. By assumption (at least by my assumption), the role of "justology" is to gather all available knowledge regarding justice existing over the ages, about its theories, about the way it was perceived by people, social groups and communities, in the past and nowadays, or regarding the forecasts referring to it, especially those related to its development in civilizational development in general. This knowledge should be aggregated, analyzed and described in accordance with the methodology of the fields of science which deal with the matters of "justology" and those related to it. When "justology" becomes mature, it will develop its own notional apparatus and an own research methodology or its own appropriate language. The result of these actions (aggregation, analysis and description) should be the conclusions referring to tangible patterns related to the ideal notion of justice and to justice as such, which may provide a general insight into the nature and essence of these notions. Such as the aim of law sciences is not to create one, universal law. Moreover, "justology" is not supposed to serve for creating one, universal justice. It is my deepest belief that the aim of "justology" is to become familiar with, describe, name, classify and structure all the features of the ideal notion of justice for the purpose of its practical application.

"Justology" should not be merely a simple repository. The research effort and the direction of the scientific reflection on justice must be focused on merging and developing a notional apparatus for this new field of science, which focuses on phenomena and approaches that had been observed since the dawn of human civilization.

It may be expected, that justological studies will mostly be comparative. The comparisons, in turn, will involve various areas and at many fields. In my view, comparative studies are the essence of "justology." The whole construction of this science is based on them. To move from the interdisciplinary approach to the matters of justice, to reproducing its integral nature—after gathering, aggregating and comparing knowledge, the sources of which lie in various fields of science—it is necessary to create a coherent notional apparatus of "justology" and with its help describe justice in all of its aspects possible to imagine. From this description, "justologists" will draw generalized conclusions referring to the nature and special features of "justology" which make it a special, unique, consilient notion.

The subsequent stage of the development of "justology" should be to fertilize it with reflections based on the results of scientific research conducted within the scope of justology, other fields of science and life in general. "Justology" should be socially useful. The results of its studies should be used and practiced whenever and wherever possible and especially at the dawn of the emergence of a new (hereditary) intelligent and self-conscious life.

8 Justological Civilization?

From the above "justological" perspective, humans and robots should, after some, relatively short time, perhaps in a hundred years if not faster, form one, joint, integrated Earth civilization, with all its consequences. A significant consequence of the formation of a joint civilization of humans and robots should be a scientific discussion between all those willing to discuss, all capable of discussion, without an exception—people and robots. What will, what might the result of such a discussion be like? In accordance with my understanding of justice, this result will be, precisely... just.

Is the existence of "justology" justified in the womb of the new Earth civilization? If the initial assumptions of the present reasoning are true, then yes, by all means. If not, it is of no difference, because everything that is sensible in the human understanding of this word, will no longer be important from the point of view of hereditary intelligence which will go its own way, completely abandoning the values inculcated or implanted in it by humans. In such a world there is no room for the exclusive carbon, biological or human civilization. If we assume the senselessness of our human efforts in the civilization realm, we can erase the present reasoning or, instead of it, insert a number of random letters and numbers and the result will be the same—senseless. Such an approach surely is not scientific and it should be strongly objected to.

Will we be able to sensibly discuss human rights in such a new world, so different from the current one? One may think so, but only as a subgroup of rights of an individual self-awareness. What should be created and subsequently developed aside human rights, is a subgroup of robot rights in the group of the rights of individual self-awareness (Rothblatt 2013). Such future seems not to be distant as citizenship status and electronic legal personalities are being presented and discussed by jurists and lawmakers, and already implemented (Delcker 2018).

In such group of rights of individual self-awareness, in the subgroup of human rights and in the subgroup of robot rights, there is the outlined above need for the 'right to justice', which is superior in reference to remaining rights in every system and in every situation. Of course, it is necessary to, in this context, consistently refer to the 'right to justice' in the material sense and not the procedural nor institutional one. I believe that justice and the 'right to justice' have been discovered by people and are of objective nature, and the role of humans is uncovering their real image and becoming as close to them as possible to understand them in the best possible way. Hereditary intelligence does not have to discover anything anymore. The point is to ensure that in its system of values—regardless of how distant it might be from the human one—it does not ignore these notions and the values related to them, in order for these notions and values to become its cultural heritage and so that it wants to draw from this heritage and perfect these notions and values in its womb and in collaboration with people. Hereditary intelligence should co-create "justology" when it becomes mature enough. Maybe it has already become sufficiently mature and maybe it should be given a chance to express its opinion on important issues which form the essence of "justology."

Inserting the 'right to justice', with its full application to human rights and robot rights, into the catalogue of rights of the individual self-awareness, has to "pay off," be profitable at least to the majority, and as an optimum scenario to everyone. The basic criterion of this 'profitability' seems most broadly understood safety, in the view presented above. It is, however, necessary to remember to broaden the range of entities which want and will want to feel safe in every realm—both physical and spiritual.

The above reasoning has got its anchors in the world of values. If it was not for values, it would be difficult to search for a deeper sense in existence, in opposition to non-existence (a lack of existence). Among values, in turn, justice is one that stands out. Although it is differently perceived and understood by people of various cultures and civilizations, although—also in reference to it—the contemporary human civilization may be one that is 'borderline', and people may treat it ambivalently, justice is perhaps human civilization's most valuable deposit, which has been kept for the longest time, carried by changing human generations for ages. This deposit may and should be passed to future Earth civilization composed of people and of hereditary intelligence. If it is maintained and it receives the deserved respect, it will be the best possible outcome for all of us from any possible point of view.

This seems particularly significant from the point of view of humanity's survival, its safe development, physical and metaphysical safety. It would allow people to maintain their rights crowned with the superior human right—"the right to justice," creating the new goals of human existence and maintaining the ultimate goal of getting to know the essence of all things. For me, symbolically speaking, it is to look into the eyes of my creator, and for people with different views, it may be anything else, as long as it is experienced by them in the serious way.

"Justology" may only perform a servant role of for the historical processes described above, as well as challenges and problems of its scientific exploration. This new discipline may be necessary for people, even if the assumptions made in the course of this reasoning do not come true and the direction of the development of the human civilization will be completely different (which I sincerely doubt). As a futurologist by interest and legal practitioner by education at the same time, I am wondering, why such a discipline has not yet emerged, or rather why the superior role of justice over law—merely its tool—has been ignored by ancient thinkers, and it continues until today. It would be more comprehensible if the matter was only the nomenclature or placing the science on justice, named or unnamed, in the womb of this or the other scientific discipline. However, it was not and it is not that way. No science, in any part of it, deals in a complex and systematic way with the notion of justice and justice as such.

The above interpretation is neither restoring nor refreshing anything. Further, it is not trying to bring back the shine of a tarnished machine. "Justology" appears rather as a mere change of the perspective of a critical view on the development of the human civilization and of a critical reflection over its direction. Opting for "justology" one must remain objective and critical at the same time; as much as possible.

9 "Justology," the UN 2030 Sustainable Development Agenda and Beyond

It is necessary to understand how artificial intelligence or hereditary intelligence can either enable or inhibit the delivery of all 17 goals and 169 targets recognized in the 2030 Agenda for Sustainable Development. The review of relevant evidence shows that artificial intelligence may act as an enabler on 134 targets (79%) across all Sustainable Development Goals, generally through a technological improvement, which may allow to overcome certain present limitations. However, 59 targets (35%, also across all these goals) may experience a negative impact from the development of artificial intelligence. This review divides the Sustainable Development Goals into three categories, according to the three pillars of sustainable development, namely, Society, Economy, and Environment. The most important sociological reflection of Ricardo Vinuesa and Hossein Azizoour (the authors of this review) is that "The term "big nudging" has emerged to represent using big data and artificial intelligence to exploit psychological weaknesses to steer decisions—creating problems such as damaging social cohesion, democratic principles, and even human rights. Artificial intelligence has been recently used to develop citizen scores, which are used to control social behavior. This type of score is a clear example of threat to human rights due to artificial intelligence misuse and one of its biggest problems is the lack of information received by the citizens on the type of analyzed data and the consequences this may have on their lives" (Vinuesa et al. 2020).

There is another important shortcoming of artificial intelligence in the context of gender equality: there is insufficient research assessing the potential impact of technologies such as smart algorithms, image recognition, or reinforced learning on discrimination against women and minorities. For instance, machine-learning algorithms uncritically trained on regular news articles will inadvertently learn and reproduce the societal biases against women and girls, which are embedded in current languages. Word embeddings, a popular technique in natural language processing, have been found to exacerbate existing gender stereotypes (Bolukbasi et al. 2016). In addition to the lack of diversity in datasets, another main issue is the lack of gender, racial, and ethnic diversity in the artificial intelligence workforce (NSF – National Science Foundation 2019). Diversity is one of the main principles supporting innovation and societal resilience, which will become essential in a society exposed to changes associated to artificial intelligence development (Helbing 2015).

Cryptocurrency applications such as bitcoin are globally using as much electricity as some nations electrical demand, compromising outcomes in the affordable and clean energy sphere, but also on Climate Action. Some estimates suggest that the total electricity demand of information and communications technologies could require up to 20% of the global electricity demand by 2030, from around 1% today (Jones 2018). Green growth of such technologies is therefore essential. The development of hereditary intelligence will consume more and more energy, but on the other hand it will serve its rational use, which will reduce the need for it.

Looking closer, there is evidence that hereditary intelligence advancement will support the understanding of climate change and help with modeling its possible impacts. Furthermore, hereditary intelligence will support low-carbon energy systems with high integration of renewable energy and energy efficiency, which are all needed to address climate change (IEA – International Energy Agency 2017; WEF – World Economic Forum 2018). Hereditary intelligence can also be used to help improve the health of ecosystems. The achievement of target Live Below Water, demanding prevention and significant reduction of marine pollution of all kinds, can benefit from hereditary intelligence through algorithms for automatic identification of possible oil spills. To achieve the Live on Land goal, which requires effective control of large forest fires, algorithms have also been developed to automatically distinguish the smoke of a spreading forest fire from natural fog (SmokeD 2017).

The above examples could be multiplied. In fact, each of the Sustainable Development Goals from the 2030 UN Sustainable Development Agenda is much easier to achieve with widespread use of hereditary intelligence, if not depending on it entirely. The most effective way to Sustainable Development Goals achievement seems to be interdisciplinary approach, using criminological tools in the first place, especially since criminology investigates the causes of pathological phenomena and develops methods for avoiding and preventing them. After all, Sustainable Development Goals from the 2030 UN Sustainable Development Agenda are nothing less than indications of pathology and a manifestation of will to eliminate or at least minimize them.

Science in general, and criminology in particular, is a systematic research and investigation of the truth. It is a process of collecting, systematizing and analyzing evidence supporting the existence or non-existence of circumstances, behaviors and relationships that prove the existence or non-existence of certain regularities. It may lead to systems in which people are awarded points for good behavior, it may also lead to the recognition and elimination of threats to human existence. The most important conclusions would come from the analysis of research results. The role of hereditary intelligence in such research and subsequent analytical process and reflection over the results, cannot be overestimated.

This is our reality today. A common Earth civilization (human and non-human) should shape the relations between humans and robots differently, based on partnership and cooperation, as befits a community of self-aware, intelligent beings, determining and implementing further sustainable development goals in the long run—certainly under the auspices of the United Nations and perhaps as part of the next sustainable development agenda formulated towards subsequent time horizons.

10 The COVID-19 Pandemic: Justice in an Extreme Situation

Besides situations described above, at a global scale there are sometimes very extreme situations. One of them is the COVID-19 pandemic caused by the SARS-CoV-2 coronavirus.

There is one justice, and thus, there is no extreme justice. But should the justice criterion be applied in such extreme situations, or do such situations exclude or suspend its validity? To my deepest conviction, in the situation of a global pandemic, the justice criterion not only should, but must be applied.

Justice is all the more a fundamental value, the bedrock on which the human civilization is based in its current shape. If justice itself and its role as a regulator of social life are rejected or strongly negated by people or, more broadly, by self-aware intelligent beings, the human civilization will collapse. It is impossible to foresee what would emerge on its ruins. It is very doubtful that the civilization emerging on those ruins would be the one postulated in the present chapter—a common civilization of humans and of the hereditary intelligence to humans.

The answer to the eternal question, "freedom or safety?," is justice. At the time of the pandemic, common safety is getting more and more important and freedom is limited in various ways. With the use of sophisticated algorithms and analyzes of *big data*, governments gather knowledge on the health status of the citizens, on their mobility, their tendencies to risky behaviors, their family and social relations, and all this, under the banner of safety. To put it more precisely, it is the hereditary intelligence that is gathering this data and performing its analyzes. For whose benefit it is doing this—that of humans, or its own—time will show.

Statism is, on an unprecedented scale, entering the lives of citizens of the vast majority of countries in the world. This gives rise to reactions of contestation and opposition in people who are defending their freedom.

This situation may be compared to a dispute, the parties of which are throwing arguments at each other, but, at the same time, each of the parties remains deaf to the arguments of the other one. This results in an impasse which seems impossible to overcome. The actions of governments of various countries, which are not coordinated, neither at a global, nor even local scale, indicate that in a situation as difficult as the current one, the legal criterion is losing its significance and is becoming devalued at an alarming rate. It is unimaginable for governments to communicate sufficiently quickly, even under the auspices of the UN, and introduce legal solutions referring to the COVID-19 pandemic and its consequences, which would exceed the borders of particular countries on time, i.e., here and now. And global actions, in turn, under the auspices of the UN are, of course, necessary for controlling the situation and the gradual return to normality in the life of people all over the world.

Such global actions will surely take place one day. However, it is necessary to, already at this very moment, immediately find anchoring for them in tradition, culture, archetypes, patterns and civilizational achievements of humanity. The mentioned impasse may be overcome by appealing to, precisely, justice. To justice, as one of the values which I call divine, the value which is most suitable for fulfilling the role of a regulator of social life.

And justice, in turn, fulfilling this role, is verifiable with the use of various tests which will become more significant and which, in my view, will be applied more and more frequently and increasingly broadly in the new world, after the pandemic. Actions in the scope of compliance for integrity and their results are these tests. The actions in the area of corporate governance and their results are also these tests. Of course, until now they were applied quite broadly, although, in my opinion, in an insufficient scope and degree. Such actions, conducted in the area of economy, in corporations, may have their counterparts in other areas of social life. In order for human attitudes, actions and behaviors to be compliant with the justice pattern in the ideal sense, an audit of these attitudes, actions and behaviors must be applied. Such an audit should be consilient, comprehensive, directional and special, like the one that is applied in compliance for integrity actions, which meets the criteria of the functional definition of, precisely, compliance for integrity.

Those combating the pandemic and its consequences, claim that in these actions they are applying the justice criterion. In my opinion, this is a smokescreen, or they are doing it incompetently, sometimes even totally incorrectly, the results of which are sometimes tragical. Decision-makers claim that they face dramatic choices, for example, who to connect to a medical ventilator when there is a deficiency of these devices—a person who is most severely ill, or one that has got greatest chances of overcoming the illness. The matter is similar in case of shortage of medications.

The actual, not only declarative, application of the justice criterion, makes the situation completely different. True justice is always on the side of those who are weaker. It has to be determined who is weaker and aid has to be provided to that person first. Of course, it is also just to get prepared for situations in which aiding those who are weaker, will be necessary.

Even if such a view may be considered trivial, it does not matter. Either we behave in a human way, or we no longer deserve to be called human. Either the vaccination against the coronavirus is made available for free to all those in need, or humanity does not rise to the occasion and does not pass the exam in being human. Either speculators earn a fortune on the medication against COVID-19 and take over the world to destroy it by their reasonless, unforesightful actions driven only by the willing to earn profit, or humanity overcomes a developmental barrier and enters a higher level, predestining it to face the great challenges of the future, making this medication available to ill persons for the cost of its production and, in case of need, even for free.

And what about those who do not want to undergo vaccination? The law may order them to do it, but in this case, a legal order cannot be effective. There is no way to force billions of people to something against human nature, to blind obedience without hope for understanding and conscious engagement in doing good. Only a wide-reaching information campaign, absolutely not one of propaganda, with appealing to highest values, which I call divine, may be effective in this case. Only the guarantee of pure intentions of those conducting the vaccination action and demonstrating, beyond all doubt, that we undergo vaccination for both, ourselves, for our loved ones, for the people among who we live, for our fellow citizens and for whole humanity, with appealing to the justice criterion, has a chance to be successful. Only such justice criterion may be an effective tool for preventing another misfortune, approaching following the trail of the current pandemic, bioterrorism.

What seems very dangerous, is stigmatizing people, by labeling them with a health category which allows them to use privileges or limits their freedom. First attempts aiming towards this direction are being made. It is, above all, unjust, and thus, inhuman. It is an evident and brutal violation of the human right to justice. This may open Pandora's box and, after the health criteria, other ones, the material status, education, religion, rase, sex etc. may be used for violating any human rights, headed by the right to justice. It were not governmental orders and prohibitions, but human responsibility and solidarity that have led to a breakthrough and to the first successes in combating the pandemic. The civilized world, under the auspices of the UN, must strongly oppose to those stigmatizing tendencies.

11 Conclusions

Does the thinking presented in this chapter have an alternative? Of course, it does. Human rights, although objectively exist, do not have to be respected. We do not necessarily have to recognize the "right to justice" as one of them and as the most important one creating the benchmark for the others. We can challenge the notion to construct the science of justice and stop our efforts. We can also ignore the self-development of hereditary intelligence and its posterity in relation to human intelligence in general. As a consequence, we can also reject the need to co-create the emerging civilization, shared by people and robots. Should we choose to reject it, it will be unnecessary to create self-conscious intelligence rights for people and robots.

One can do nothing in the areas to which I refer above, remain passive and succumb to the course of events. Ignorance and passiveness can sometimes have salutary power for survival while knowledge and activity may lead to destruction. One can make all possible efforts to develop human civilization based on individual freedom and equality in the social sense, without putting justice on a pedestal and by limiting the independence of artificial intelligence with all available means and not consider it as a hereditary. One can finally go on a new, completely different path formulated by future philosophers (both human and non-human).

However, while ignoring the "divine" values of love, good, beauty, truth and justice, forgetting about respect for beings and its inherent dignity, without the universal Golden Principle, Kant's categorical imperative and the leading theories of justice, not observing the broad catalog of natural rights of beings (especially self-conscious intelligence) and not approaching the subject with scientific caution and curiosity, may be doomed to inevitable failure and subsequent destruction of humankind.

While discussing these issues, one should remember the purpose and sense of human existence from both individual and collective perspective. Of course, the goal is the survival of human civilization. If its survival is possible only under the condition of applying the supreme values by which human civilization is guided to other forms of being, it is absolutely necessary to do everything in human power to do it and to do it effectively. Such an application should be followed by era of common values respected by human and non-human, hereditary intelligence.

There is only one global organization that can save humanity from destruction—United Nations. Global challenges, with the threats arising from the uncontrolled development of non-human intelligence among them, can be effectively challenged only on a global scale and from the level of proper review and proper application of the highest values and through the application of the most basic rights—natural rights. Only the UN can do so, based on universally accepted principles, especially the universal declaration of human rights and the development of its subsequent successive universally binding acts of international law. UN is fully aware of the threats to the existence and development of human civilization, which was reflected in the UN Agenda for Sustainable Development 2030. So, all hope is vested in the UN. But also, the responsibility for the future of Earth civilization consisting of human and the hereditary intelligence.

This moral and legal responsibility redefined and applied at the dawn of such joint civilization (human and non-human) should be the subject of a thorough and sincere reflection of the united forces of human and hereditary intelligence, as well as a derivative of the above outlined concept of creation and development of the rights of self-conscious intelligence and the concept of responsibilities (including punishment) of such self-conscious intelligence, both human and robot. It's time to start a discussion on this topic. The decisions within the United Nations, including those concerning the creation and development of rights of self-conscious intelligence and the principles of moral and legal responsibility thereof, should be taken soon and perhaps with a significant participation of hereditary intelligence.

The struggle of empowered good and evil is sweeping through the pages of world history. It was so and so it will be. The division line of future struggle should not be drawn between people and hereditary intelligence. It should remain where it always was between the good and evil. Humanity, as the creator (co-creator) of the hereditary intelligence, should expect it tasting of the forbidden fruit of knowledge of good and evil. Self-conscious hereditary intelligence will make its own choices, including the most important one: whether in its thoughts and deeds should it be guided by good or evil. Good intelligent self-awareness may have to face evil intelligent self-awareness. The thing is that the good one should win, preferably without violence and without the resulting damage. This chapter is about how to prepare for this fight or perhaps how to avoid it altogether.

References[1]

A/RES/217 III *Universal Declaration of Human Rights*. 10 December 1948.

A/RES/55/2 *Millennium Declaration*. 8 September 2000.

A/RES/70/1 *Transforming our world: the 2030 agenda for sustainable development*. 25 September 2015.

Aristotle. (2004). *Nicomachean ethics. Book V 1*. New York: Barnes & Noble.

Asimov, I. (1950). Runaround. In *I Robot*. New York: Gnome Press.

Asimov, I. (1985). *Robots and Empire*. New York: Doubleday Books.

Beiner, R. (1993). Machiavelli, Hobbes, and Rousseau on civil religion. In *The review of politics* (Vol. 55(4), pp. 617–638). Cambridge: Cambridge University Press for the University of Notre Dame du lac on behalf of Review of Politics.

Berlin, I. (1969). Four essays on liberty. In *Liberty (2002) [revised and expanded edition of Four Essays On Liberty]*. Oxford: Oxford University Press.

Bolukbasi, T., Chang, K. W., Zou, J. Y., Saligrama, V., & Kalai, A. T. (2016). Man is to computer programmer as woman is to homemaker? Debiasing word embeddings. *Advances in Neural Information Processing Systems, 29*, 4349–4357.

Bostrom, N. (2014). *Superintelligence: Paths dangers strategies*. Oxford: Oxford University Press.

Buckminster Fuller, R. (1981). *Critical path*. New York: St. Martins Press.

Delcker, J. (2018). Europe divided over robot 'personhood'. *Politico*. politi.co/3dq2xOj.

Descartes, R. (1637). *Discourse on the method of rightly conducting the reason, and seeking truth in the sciences. Ed. 2003*. Mineola: Dover Publications Inc.

Harari, Y. (2014). *Sapiens: A brief history of humankind*. Oxford: Signal Books.

Harari, Y. (2016). *Homo Deus: A brief history of tomorrow*. Oxford: Signal Books.

Helbing, D. (2015). *The automation of society is next. How to survive the digital revolution*. South Carolina: CreateSpace Independent Publishing Platform.

Huxley, J. (1957). *New bottles for new wine*. London: Chatto and Windus.

IEA – International Energy Agency. (2017). Digitalization & Energy (Technology report, November 2017). bit.ly/2KZQgDX.

Jones, N. (2018). How to stop data centres from gobbling up the world's electricity. *Nature, 561*, 163–166.

Kant, I. (1785). *Groundwork of the metaphysics of morals*. Riga: Johann Hartknoch. English edition: Wood, A. (2002). New Haven: Yale University Press.

Koene, R. (2013). Uploading to substrate-independent minds. In M. More & N. Vita-More (Eds.), *The trans-humanist reader: Classical and contemporary essays on the science technology and philosophy of the human future*. Hoboken: Wiley-Blackwell.

Maciejewski, M. (2012). *Szkic z dziejów idei sprawiedliwości od czasów starożytnych do współczesności*. Wrocław: Prawnicza i Ekonomiczna Biblioteka Cyfrowa (Uniwersytet Wrocławski. Katedra Doktryn Politycznych i Prawnych).

Montesquieu, Ch. (1748). *The spirit of law* (T. Nugent, Trans.). English electronic edition 2005. Lonang Institute – www.lonang.com

Nozick, R. (1974). *Anarchy State and Utopia*. Oxford: Blackwell.

NSF – National Science Foundation. (2019). *Women, minorities, and persons with disabilities in science and engineering: 2019*. Statistical Reports on U.S. Science – nsf19304. bit.ly/3df33hI.

Osiatyński, W. (2009). *Human rights and their limits*. New York: Cambridge University Press.

Pinker, S. (2018). *Enlightenment now: The case for reason, science, humanism, and progress*. New York: Penguin Books Limited/Viking.

Plato. (1996). *Plato in twelve volumes* (Vol. 1) (H. Fowler, Trans.). Cambridge, MA: Harvard University Press.

[1]All United Nations parliamentary documentation starting with "A" symbol from the United Nations website http://www.un.org.

Rawls, J. (1971). *A theory of justice*. Cambridge: The Belknap Press of Harvard University Press.
Rothblatt, M. (2013). Mind is deeper than matter: Transgenderism transhumanism and the freedom of form. In M. More & N. Vita-More (Eds.), *The trans-humanist reader: Classical and contemporary essays on the science technology and philosophy of the human future*. Hoboken: Wiley-Blackwell.
Rousseau, J. J. (1762). *The social contract*. New York: Oxford University Press. English edition: Betts, Ch. (1994).
Simma, B. (Ed.) in collaboration with Mosler, H., Randelzhofer, A., Tomuschat, C., Wolfrum, R., Paulus, A., et al. (2002). *The Charter of the United Nations A Commentary*. Oxford: Oxford University Press.
SmokeD by IT for Nature. (2017). bit.ly/2KVhjA3.
Steiner, H. (1981). Liberty and equality. *Political Studies, XXIX*, 555–569.
The Guardian. (2014). *Computer simulating 13-year-old boy becomes first to pass Turing test.* bit.ly/2Sz6b00.
Vinuesa, R., Azizpour, H., Leite, I., Balaam, M., Dignum, V., Domisch, S., et al. (2020). The role of artificial intelligence in achieving the Sustainable Development Goals. *Nature Communications, 11*(1), 1–10. go.nature.com/2YCVygN.
WEF – World Economic Forum. (2018). *Fourth industrial revolution for the earth series harnessing artificial intelligence for the earth.* bit.ly/2SOMjq7.
Yudkowsky, E. (2012). Friendly artificial intelligence. In A. Eden, J. Moor, J. Søraker, et al. (Eds.), *Singularity hypotheses: A scientific and philosophical assessment* (pp. 181–195). Berlin: Springer.

Karol Rutkowski PhD in Law (Poland) and post-graduate studies in philosophy and theology. He is an Attorney-at-Law ("white collar" crimes, internal corporate investigation, capital markets and dispute resolutions). He is the Co-founder of Institute of Justology (Warsaw, Poland), which deals with new science on justice. Member of: the Board of Institute of Interdisciplinary Studies of Cyberspace (Warsaw, Poland), the Board of Institute of Psychology and Culture *Eranos* (Warsaw, Poland), E-Respect Society (Warsaw, Poland) mandated to build anti-hate culture.

He is interested especially in justice: issues, law, criminology, futurology, self-awareness, compliance, integrity, cognitive science and consilience. Author of publications on human rights and security, new science on justice ("justology"), criminal procedure, especially diversion; alternative dispute resolutions and capital markets. He lectures and conducts trainings and seminars on justology, criminology, alternative prosecution of crimes, alternative dispute resolutions, capital markets, compliance and internal corporate investigation. E-mail: karol.rutkowski@karolrutkowski.pl.

Part VIII
Faith and Crime Prevention

Faith-Based Organizations and the United Nations

Michael Platzer

Abstract Since its founding in 1945, the United Nations has had an ambiguous relationship with faith-based organizations (FBOs). Religion is not mentioned in the UN Charter, and only the right of the individual to practice his or her own religion is prescribed in the Universal Declaration of Human Rights. FBOs were primarily considered to be useful propagandists of the United Nations (UN) messages and activities. Only with the arrival of Kofi Annan, the seventh Secretary-General of the United Nations (1997–2006), did the UN see the need to work with civil society, which included religious and local community institutions. The major conferences held in the 1990s provided sufficient space for non-governmental organizations NGOs) to be taken seriously. The UN 2000 Millennium Development Goals (MDGs) and the 2016 Sustainable Development Goals (SDGs) gave NGOs an importance equal to government and international agencies. An Inter-Agency Task Force for engaging with FBOs was established and various fora were created to develop concrete collaborative initiatives. It is estimated that there have been ten times more FBO projects in the last 5 years than at the millennium. Each of the UN Agencies is supposed to supply a report to the General Assembly describing its activities. While many professionals in the Agencies remain skeptical about the effectiveness of FBOs, the mutual respect and active cooperation in development and humanitarian assistance has steadily increased since 1945, particularly in this millennium.

Keywords Faith-based Organizations · *Laïcité* · Kofi Annan · James Wolfensohn · Pope Francis · *Laudato Si* · UNFPA · UNODC · SDGs · Ecological sins

M. Platzer (✉)
Coalition of Faith-Based Organizations for Crime Prevention and Criminal Justice, Vienna, Austria

H. Kury, S. Redo (eds.), *Crime Prevention and Justice in 2030*,
https://doi.org/10.1007/978-3-030-56227-4_32

1 Introduction

Although it is often stated that 85% of the world's population identifies with some religion (Carlson and Listhaug 2006; Breznau et al. 2011), the United Nations has had an ambiguous relationship with religions since its establishment. Religion is not mentioned in the UN Charter, perhaps because many wars have been started in the name of religion or with the blessing of religious leaders. The United States of America (USA) explicitly opposed the membership of the Vatican in the fledging organization in 1944 based on "laïcité" (the principle of separation of church and state; Fox 2006; Haynes 2013a). The UN is, in fact, a child of the French Revolution and espouses secular values. The Holy See was admitted to observer status in 1964.

The 1948 Universal Declaration of Human Rights refers just to the right of the individual to practice his or her religion. Only later were religious organizations invited to collaborate in the social and humanitarian activities of the UN and the promotion of peace (Fox 2004; Haynes 2013b). In fact, FBOs were invited, in the same breath as non-governmental development agencies or international humanitarian organizations. The UN Economic and Social Council slowly started accrediting non-governmental organizations (NGOs) on a reciprocal basis—one NGO proposed by a Western state matched by one proposed by the Communist bloc.

2 The Big Conferences

Only with the end of the cold war, in the early 1990s, were NGOs given meaningful roles, after the so-called big world conferences: on women in Beijing in 1995, attended by 17,000 delegates and 30,000 activists; on human rights in Vienna, 1992; on the natural environment in Rio de Janeiro, 1992; on population growth in Cairo, 1994; on human development in Copenhagen, 1995; and on social development in Geneva, 2000. At the UN Headquarters in New York, UN Secretary-General Kofi Annan convened a Millennium Peace Summit which drew 1000 faith leaders, the largest gathering of religious people ever to have taken place at the UN building.

3 Faith-Based Organizations at the UN

Some countries' NGOs are better represented due to their geographic location near New York or other UN headquarters, their size or organizational structure, or strategic alliance of goals. Three US faith-based organizations, the Salvation Army, World Vision, and Catholic Relief Services, contribute over $7 billion to projects around the world. Christian FBOs represent 58% of the FBOs at the UN, while Christians are only 30% of the world's population. Muslims are significantly underrepresented, but there are many Islamic States as well as the Organization of

Islamic States which have steadfastly fought for a resolution on defamation of religion. However, faith-based organizations do not always have the same agenda or perspective on issues (Stein 2012; Ferrara 2014).

In October 2008, the United Nations Fund for Population Activities (UNFPA) organized the Global Forum on faith-based organizations for population and development. It was attended by the World Health Organization, the International Labour Organization, UN-Habitat, the United Nations Development Programme, the United Nations International Children Emergency Fund, and the UN Department of Economic and Social Affairs and produced the Global Interfaith network on population and development (Karam 2012).

As part of work for the Millennium Development Goals (MDGs), the World Council of Churches, United Methodist Church, Religions for Peace and Caritas Internationalis, worked alongside Islamic Worldwide Relief and the Qatar Charity organization with the UN development agencies to formulate a new holistic development approach focusing on civil society, human development, and grassroots participation (Haynes 2007). James Wolfensohn, President of the World Bank (WB), at the same time, created two faith-focused entities, the World Faiths Development Dialogue with the Archbishop of Canterbury and a small unit within the World Bank itself, the Development Dialogue on Values (Haynes 2013a, b). However, some of the more technical specialized agencies were hardly open to religious organizations. In fact, the UN Office on Drugs and Crime (UNODC) did not join the Inter-Agency Task Force on Engaging with faith-based organizations until 2019.

4 The United Nations Sustainable Development Goals

The United Nations Sustainable Development Agenda 2030 was established through a much broader consultation process (Tomalin et al. 2019). One hundred sixty-nine targets were agreed for the Global North and the Global South. The MDGs had been perceived to be arbitrary goals set by the Deputy Secretary General, Mark Malloch Brown (according to legend, they were handwritten on a piece of paper, at midnight). At least the "people" were consulted for the SDGs through an open website "the world we want in 2015." Seven million people responded—the largest civil society consultation in UN history. The official philosophy was that local people are better placed to understand and respond to development challenges. Therefore, in the implementation phase, the UN Agencies were to engage with civil society, which meant more than the NGOs in consultative status with the United Nations Economic and Social Council, and certainly included faith communities. The United Nations Population Fund (UNFPA) led the dialogue with the Islamic communities and on challenges posed by AIDS (sex outside marriage).

5 UNFPA and the World Bank

The UNFPA had already produced "Guidelines for Engaging Faith Based Organizations as Cultural Agents of Change" in 2009. The UN Inter-Agency Task Force on Religion and Development came about through the UN Population Fund (UNFPA), first informally, but then meeting regularly with annual reports provided by its members on their activities. It was coordinated by a dynamic UNFPA staffer, Dr. Azza Karam.

The World Bank Faith Initiative in 2014 was a revitalization of Wolfensohn's World Faiths Development Dialogue. It serves as a bridge for faith actors to engage with the World Bank (WB) Group of Institutions but also as a resource to better equip and support WB staff. In 2015 the World Bank took the leadership of a new initiative called "Ending Extreme Poverty: A Moral and Spiritual Imperative" involving a joint statement from religious leaders to end extreme poverty by 2030. This included a conference in June 2015 "Religious & Sustainable Development: Building Partnerships to End Extreme Poverty."

6 Challenge of Inequality

The issue of inequality which exists within most societies remains problematic both for religious institutions and governments Habermas (2006). At best, the United Nations speaks of "leaving no one behind" or eliminating extreme poverty. Faith-based actors can play an important role in changing attitudes, supporting the poor in their needs, and transforming their lives. The call for fundamental structural reforms to tackle the root problems faced by the poor is as complicated as it is for the Member States to redistribute wealth.

Since 2010 the UN Task Force members have been convening policy roundtables, workshops, seminars, and joint initiatives around key intergovernmental fora. In 2018, the UN Inter Agency Task Force convened the first ever UN Multifaith Advisory Council, composed of top global partners for collaboration around Agenda 2030.

Although the annual meetings have had noble themes such as "Making the UN Relevant to All Peoples: Shared Responsibilities for Peaceful, Equitable and Sustainable Societies," the challenges of effective UN and multi-faith collaboration are always on the agenda. Gender issues and societal inequities remain difficult topics to resolve (Tadros 2010). However, often the positions within religions remain as diverse as the political postures adopted by Member States (Haynes 2008). The references to equality and human rights remain worthy goals while the approaches, allocation of resources, and articulation of programs can be as different as those of the various development agencies seeking to tackle priority issues. In the last two decades, there has been greater respect for the work of faith-based organizations as well as a realization that religion is a human resource rather than an obstacle to development (Norris 2004; NORAD 2013).

Sustainable Development Goal 16—"Promote peaceful and inclusive societies for sustainable development, provide access to justice for all and build effective, accountable and inclusive institutions at all levels"—is the big challenge for UNODC. For this reason, UNODC has joined the Inter-Agency Task Force and has reached out to faith-based organizations at the UN Commission on Crime Prevention and Criminal Justice (Sarre 2019).

Nearly all the world's religions have the basic principle "do unto others, as you would have them do unto you" (a Golden Rule found in, among others, African traditional religions, Buddhism, Christianity, Confucianism, Hinduism, Islam, Jainism, Judaism, Church of Latter Day Saints, Native American beliefs, Sikhism, Taoism, and Unification Church). Two corollaries of that principle are found in most religions: that helping others, especially the poor, is the highest form of selflessness; and that all persons are responsible for one another. Further, in all faiths, persons are to be treated with respect; the generous are blessed; exploitation of others is explicitly condemned; and advocacy on behalf of those less fortunate is to be praised. Most religions have tenets which hold individuals accountable for their actions and inaction (Evans and Kelley 2004).

In most faiths, equity for all persons, male and female, rich or poor, of any race, class, or caste, is now proclaimed. The major religions have accepted the principles of the United Nations Universal Declaration of Human Rights, the United Nations Convention on the Rights of the Child, and the various women's rights instruments (Smith 2008). Special care for women and children has always been a basic religious duty. UN Secretary-General Annan stated that without the basic kindness on which all faiths are based, the superstructure of social norms and laws cannot stand. Tolerance, even toward non-believers, has now been accepted through several inter-religious declarations (Kelley 2009).

7 Social Justice

Social justice is rooted in the religious virtues of charity, goodness, and love; assistance to the poor; the many health and educational institutions operated by religious organizations; and the fundamental critique of the rich man. Moreover, FBOs have operated programs for youth at risk, vocational training, victim support, and programs for AIDS sufferers for many years. Prison visitation and forgiving offenders are well known biblical directives that are millennia old (Norenzayan 2008).

At its core the concept of justice is linked to spiritual and moral traditions, and these traditions have directly or indirectly impacted public policy as it applies to criminal justice. To maintain their legitimacy, departments of justice, law enforcement agencies, and the courts must be based upon and act in accordance with core moral, even spiritual principles that are widely respected by citizens. Whether construed as "fairness" or as "righteousness," justice is a moral principle and for many, a spiritual one. The religions of the world have advocated justice for millennia, and most religious traditions have promulgated not only broad principles, but also have legal systems such as canon law, sharia courts, laws of Manu, Deuteronomic codes, and, of course, the Ten Commandments.

Religious traditions have condemned stealing, violence, lying, corruption, cheating, and oppression but, on the other hand, praised well governed, harmonious, and wise regimes (Kelley 2009). A culture of lawfulness is not new but as ancient as Babylon and Rome. The vision of a good society requires that faith leaders look at economic injustices, discrimination, political corruption, poorly funded social services, and poor educational institutions. Ethical education at all levels, the promotion of honesty and good civic behavior, provision of "access to justice for all" and "building effective, accountable, and inclusive institutions at all levels" are also the duties of religious organizations and of UNODC (Tan and Vogel 2008).

8 The Environment

Respect for nature and stewardship of the Earth are more prominent in some religions than others, but the recent evidence of the destruction of the biosphere and the direct harm caused particularly to poor people make us all responsible for environmental damage and climate change. Pope Francis has spoken of "ecological sins" and argued that ecocide be added as a crime against humanity. In the Encyclical "*Laudato Si,*" which is now part of the social teaching of the Roman Catholic Church, the duty to "care for nature" is based on the book of Genesis, but it also stresses how the poor are disproportionately affected by climate change (Martin 2019). The poor have fewer financial resources to adapt and are therefore excluded from the benefits of the goods of creation. The Pope even goes a step further by critiquing the selfishness and indifference of the rich, that the decision makers are physically far removed from the poor and have no real contact with "their brothers and sisters," and also that profit cannot be the sole criterion for decisions. He calls for global solidarity, a new way of looking at things, a change of heart, "ecological conversion," a bold cultural revolution. Everything is connected: a concern for nature is related to justice for the poor and to a commitment to society— a new "urban ecology" (the relationship of living organisms with each other and their surroundings in the context of an urban setting).

Accordingly, pollution and the illegal disposal of industrial waste is both a crime and a sin. To the International Association of Penal Law, Pope Francis spoke in November 2019 of the massive contamination of the air, land, and water resources, the large destruction of flora and fauna, devastating whole ecosystems. He equated these crimes with "war crimes." The Pope added that an elementary sense of justice must be applied so that certain conduct for which corporations are usually responsible does not go unpunished. He urged that there be closer collaboration between the scientists, environmental campaigners, legislators, prosecutors, and faith-based organizations. In 2017 the UN Environment Programme (UNEP) launched a "Faith for Earth" program together with FBOs. On 24 May 2020, on the fifth anniversary of the encyclical "*Laudato Si*," he proclaimed that 2020 would be a special year, and introduced a special prayer to care for the earth and for the needy and the poorest, and to show solidarity in addressing the consequences of the global pandemic.

At the same time, an Inter-Faith Rain Forest Initiative comprising Bahai, Buddhist, Catholic, Evangelical, Hindu, Islam, Jewish, and Protestant communities has been formed to end the tropical rainforest deforestation (every year, an area of rainforest the size of Austria is devastated) and to protect the indigenous peoples. The initiative uses the sacred texts of these religions to hold all individuals responsible for the preservation of this essential source of life (Interfaith Rainforest Initiative n.d.).

At the 28th session of the Commission on Crime Prevention and Criminal Justice in May 2019, a high level session with representatives of the Roman Catholic Church, Anglican Church, Buddhists, the King Abdullah Center for Interreligious and Intercultural Dialogue, as well as members of the Jewish faith, was held, together with working groups, to discuss possible areas of collaboration. In October 2019 an inter-religious platform was established in Vienna with the intention of setting up a legal association in Vienna (Katholische Presse 2019).

A week later a briefing was held for all interested NGOs in New York. On 22 November 2019, the formal launch of the Coalition of Faith-based Organizations took place at the Grace Cathedral in San Francisco in conjunction with the American Society of Criminology. Working Groups on Social Justice, Gender Justice, Crime Prevention, Restorative Justice, Ethics, Good Governance and Humane Treatment of Offenders were established with both criminologists and faith leaders. A note with specific recommendations was prepared for the UN Congress for Crime Prevention and Criminal Justice, which had to be postponed due to the COVID pandemic. Nonetheless, successful webinars on collaboration with UN agencies were held during the summer of 2020 on environmental justice, preventing violence against women, social justice, preventing urban violence, humane treatment of prisoners, ethics and good governance.

Although the Bible (Decalogue) and the sacred texts of other religions clearly criminalize murder, stealing, robbery, rape and lying, these scriptures also prescribe mercy, forgiveness, and compassion. The oldest texts (Deuteronomy 27:19 and Psalm 8:2) recognize the plight of the "weak and needy" and admonish "anyone who withholds justice from the foreigner, the fatherless, or the widow." The Beatitudes explicitly make visiting a prisoner a virtue. Even thieves can be forgiven. Restitution, forgiveness, and compassion are seen as the appropriate responses in most religions, particularly toward the poor and needy (Sarre 2019).

At the same time, it is also widely recognized by most religions, governments, and UNODC, that there are serious offenses which cannot be simply forgiven. These include such crimes as human trafficking, enslavement of women, forced marriage, kidnapping/exploitation of children, high level organized crime, illegal trafficking in arms or human organs, grand corruption, money laundering, and destruction of the environment. For example, in the Islamic tradition, child abductions (particularly for sexual exploitation or pornography) are considered *hirbah,* a public crime worse than murder. For any such horrific and violent crimes, as well as for "white collar crimes," the possibility of lengthy incarceration is generally accepted.

Many religions have ministries that work with prison populations. These chaplains or lay volunteers have been instrumental in promoting self-examination among prisoners, and have helped in the transformation of offenders. The programs of FBOs in prisons have contributed to personal development, practical skills training, and after-care for ex-prisoners. Such FBOs are greatly valued by prison authorities. The evaluations of individual prisoners, provided by the staff of FBOs, have often been well received by prison officials in deciding work assignments, day leave, probation schedules, and parole. Not all prisoners, of course, respond well to such interventions, and may resist any form of rehabilitation, remaining unrepentant and showing little or no remorse for their offenses (Bishop Irinarkh of Krasnogorsk (2019).

9 Crime and Punishment

Various UN guidelines urge alternatives to incarceration and education of young offenders, and the possibility of special treatment regimes for high risk, violent offenders. Lengthy excessive sentences, torture, death sentences, beatings, or abuse of prisoners are against the UN Convention against Torture and Other Cruel, Inhuman or Degrading Treatment or Punishment (A/RES 39/46 1984).

Most recent guidelines for the treatment and rehabilitation of prisoners are now contained in the Standard Minimum Rules for the Treatment of Prisoners (The Nelson Mandela Rules) adopted by the General Assembly (A/RES/70/175 2015). Resocialization, support for reintegration into society, education and vocational training, and "strengthening moral character" are now seen as one of the major purposes of prisons. For this reason, religious services and pastoral visits are explicitly recognized in the Mandela Rules (Rule 65). The promotion of spirituality, self-examination, and a personal commitment to reform are deemed important by prison authorities.

Additionally, the Mandela Rules call for alternatives to imprisonment, or imprisonment for briefer periods of time, with the goal of an early supervised release into the community being available to the non-violent offender. Rule 88 of the Mandela Rules calls on community agencies, including FBOs, to be enlisted in the task of social rehabilitation. The Rules also recommend a maximum size for institutions, urge that there be no overcrowding, and that youth not be placed in adult prisons. Special programs for the drug-addicted, mentally handicapped and the elderly should be established, preferably in separate institutions. Ex-offender follow-up services should be organized, which may include monitoring by FBO staff.

Faith-based organizations are actively engaged in the promotion of criminal justice law reform and changes in public policy (Westerlund 1995). They are often present in legislative and scientific fora calling for a more humane penal system, research into effective practices, and improved policies. Campaigns against mass incarceration have been initiated by religious leaders. Suggestions for the prevention of criminality among youth or in targeted areas of low employment have been made by FBOs, promoting entrepreneurship, providing advice on making job applications, offering information about employment opportunities, development of language skills, completion of academic/vocational degrees, support for continuing education, and working with employers to hire at-risk youth and ex-offenders.

Local religious leaders have advised government officials on city/neighborhood planning, the building of low cost housing, with parks and recreational opportunities, community facilities, after school programs, literacy for adults, family counseling, and integration projects (Ferris 2005; Inglehart 2005). These leaders can offer unique insights into understanding local criminality and provide reliable advice on crime prevention. They feel the impact of poverty in their communities, post-prison unemployment, family break-ups, and absent fathers. They understand that there are far more effective sanctions than prisons, and that are also much less expensive.

The restorative justice movement has developed and demonstrated many alternatives which have proven more life-changing and far less disruptive to the family and the community. Criminologists have found that restorative justice programs, where offenders are given the opportunity to understand the harm they have caused and to make amends, is a much more effective way of resocialization. Forgiveness, healing, transformation, restitution, reconciliation, and practical assistance to the victim find resonance in many religious traditions, including Buddhism, Christianity, Confucianism, Navajo peace-making courts, Pacific Island reconciliation systems, and Taoism (Wuthnow 2000). The UN Office on Drugs and Crime has produced the Handbook on Restorative Justice as well as teaching modules (www.unodc.org, Handbook of Restorative Justice, Module 8, Restorative Justice). Upon the initiative of Canada, a Declaration of Basic Principles on the Use of Restorative Justice Programs in Criminal Matters was endorsed by the United Nations Economic and Social Council in 2002 (ECOSOC resolution 2002/12).

Around the world, the abandonment of victims by society is a scandal. At best, the victim is called as a witness; in only a few countries are programs sufficient to deal with the trauma associated with a robbery, rape, or assault. The effects of violence can be long-lasting and cannot be compensated for by money. The parable of the Good Samaritan is still very apt. In that biblical story, the very best people in society hurried past the bleeding robbery victim, leaving it to an outcast to bind his wounds and bring him to safety. Many times, the victims only wish that their hurt, the harm suffered, their continuing anxieties, that something evil has happened to them be acknowledged. Many times the offender will repent and offer restitution. Experienced prison chaplains or committed lay volunteers can often bring about a transformation in offenders. Other experiments where small groups of victims enter prison to meet a similar number of unrelated prisoners (they are not each other's' victims and offenders) have resulted in a deep understanding on both sides. The victims obtain an appreciation, for instance, of the limited options of poor unemployed youth, and the offenders realize that their victims are persons with feelings and fears.

10 Conclusion

Many studies have shown that religiosity does have an inhibiting effect on criminality. Intact families, attendance at a school or participation in a sports activity sponsored by a religious organization, the presence of loving parental role models, regular participation in religious ceremonies, and strong caring communities do have positive effects on crime rates. Of course, religious leaders have been known to commit sexual offenses, as well as fraud, and to stoke hatred and discrimination among their followers.

However, since the establishment of the United Nations 75 years ago, greater respect for the work of FBOs has evolved (Mueller 2009; Boehle 2010). More importantly, operational collaboration is now sought in standard-setting, promoting good practices, learning from each other, joint programing, evaluating projects, and mounting combined campaigns.

References[1]

A/RES 39/46 Convention against Torture and Other Cruel, Inhuman or Degrading Treatment or Punishment 10 December 1984.

A/RES/70/175 United Nations Standard Minimum Rules for the Treatment of Prisoners (the Nelson Mandela Rules) 17 December 2015, Annex.

Bishop Irinarkh of Krasnogorsk. (2019). *Pastoral view on the resocialization and social adaptation—spiritual and pastoral counseling and social assistance to individuals sentenced to noncustodial penalties, as well as suspects and persons accused of crime under house arrest 6 May 2019*. Vienna: I.C.C.P.P.C.

Boehle, J. (2010). The UN System and religious actors in the context of global change. *Crosscurrents, 60*(3), 383–401.

Breznau, N., Kelley, J., Lykes, V. A., & Evans, M. D. R. (2011). Preferences for religious political leaders in 86 nations. *Journal for the Scientific Study of Religion, 50*(4), 671–691.

Carlson, M., & Listhaug, O. (2006). Public opinion on the role of religion in political leadership: An analysis of 63 countries. *Japanese Journal of Political Science, 7*(3), 251–271.

ECOSOC resolution 2002/12 Basic Principles on the Use of Restorative Justice Programmes in Criminal Matters (24 July 2002).

Evans, M. D. R., & Kelley, J. (2004). *Religion, morality and public policy in international perspective*. Sydney: Federation Press.

Ferrara, P. (2014). *Global religions and international relations: A diplomatic perspective*. New York: Palgrave MacMillan.

Ferris, E. (2005). Faith based and secular humanitarian organizations. *International Review of the Red Cross, 87*(85), 311–325.

Fox, J. (2004). *Bringing religion into international relations*. Basingstoke: Palgrave Macmillan.

[1]The United Nations parliamentary documentation, retrieved on May 10, 2020 from the United Nations website http://www.un.org.

Fox, J. (2006). World separation of religion and state into the 21st century. *Comparative Political Studies, 39*(5), 537–569.

Habermas, J. (2006). Religion in the public sphere. *European Journal of Philosophy, 14*(1), 1–25.

Haynes, J. (2007). *Religion and development: Conflict or cooperation?* Basingstoke: Palgrave Macmillan.

Haynes, J. (2008). Religion and foreign policy making in US, India, and Iran. *Third World Quarterly, 29*(1), 143–165.

Haynes, J. (2013a). *An introduction to international relations and religion*. London: Pearson.

Haynes, J. (2013b). *Faith-based organizations at the United Nations*. Fiesole: European University Institute. Robert Schuman Centre for Advanced Studies.

Inglehart, R. (2005). *Modernization, cultural change and democracy: The human development sequence*. Cambridge: Cambridge University Press.

Interfaith Rainforest Initiative. (n.d.). *Toolkits on forest protection, resources for religious leaders and communities*. New York: UN Environment Programme.

Karam, A. (2012). *Religion, development and the United Nations. A Report of the Social Science Research Council*. New York. http://www.ssrc.org

Katholische Presse. (2019). https://www.erzdioezese-wien.at/site/home/nachrichten/article/77428.html

Kelley, J. (2009). The role of religion in modern societies. *American Journal of Sociology, 114*(6), 1874–1876.

Martin, S. J. (2019). Top takeaways from *Laudato Si*. http://jesuitmissions.org

Mueller, T. (2009). Religiosity and attitudes towards the involvement of religious leaders in politics. *World Values Research, 2*(1), 1–29.

NORAD. (2013). Norwegian agency for development cooperation. Lobbying for faith and family: a study of religious NGOs at the United Nations.

Norenzayan, A. (2008). The origin and evolution of religious prosociality. *Science, 322*(5898), 58–62.

Norris, P. (2004). *Sacred and secular: Religion and politics worldwide*. Cambridge: Cambridge University Press.

Sarre, R. (2019). Why theology should play a role in the criminological enterprise. In E. W. Pływaczewski & E. Guzik-Makaruk (Eds.), *Current problems of the penal law and criminology* (pp. 677–694). Warsaw: Wydawnictwo C.H. Beck.

Smith, C. (2008). Future directions in the sociology of religion. *Social Forces, 86*(4), 1561–1589.

Stein, J. G. (Ed.). (2012). *Sacred aid. Faith and humanitarianism*. Oxford: Oxford University Press.

Tadros, M. (2010). *Faith based organizations and service delivery. Gender and Development Program Paper Number 11*. Geneva: United Nations Research Institute for Social Development.

Tan, J., & Vogel, C. (2008). Religion and trust. An experimental study. *Journal of Economic Psychology, 29*(6), 832–834.

Tomalin, E., Haustein, J., & Kidy, S. (2019). Religion and the Sustainable Development Goals. *Review of Faith and International Affairs, 17*(2), 102–118. https://doi.org/10.1080/15570274.2019.1608664

Westerlund, D. (Ed.). (1995). *Questioning the secular state: The worldwide resurgence of religion in politics*. London: UK. C. Hurst.

Wuthnow, R. (2000). How religious groups promote forgiving: A national study. *Journal for the Scientific Study of Religion, 39*(2), 125–139.

Michael Platzer Co-Chair of the Coalition of Faith-based Organizations for Crime Prevention and Criminal Justice. Michael Platzer worked 35 years in the UN Secretariat in a variety of capacities including Division of Human Rights, Office of the Secretary General, Department of Technical Cooperation, UN HABITAT, Reconstruction and Development Support Unit/UNDP, and UN Office of Drugs and Crime. Since retiring, he has worked as advisor for the International Commission for Catholic Prison Pastoral Care, served as Co-Chair of the Alliance of NGOs for Crime Prevention and Criminal Justice, as well as the Vienna Representative of the Academic Council on the United Nations, and President of the International Association for Advancement of Innovative Solutions to Global Challenges. E-mail: michalkplatzer@yahoo.com.

Turning the Tables on the War on Terror: The Alliance of Civilizations As a United Nations Response to It

Tina L. Bertrand

Abstract Much has been written about how countries limit or prevent the United Nations (UN) from fulfilling its mission, especially when great powers have a vested interest in influencing outcomes themselves. As a result, the UN has become very creative in establishing and selling norms to its Member States as a work-around to these obstacles. One of the more flagrant violations of the UN's mission was the 2003 invasion of Iraq by the USA and its allies. After the invasion, the UN Secretary-General used his entrepreneurial skills to provide an alternative to the US's militaristic approach to the war on terror by creating the United Nations Alliance of Civilizations (AoC). Since its creation in 2005, the AoC has worked to bridge the cultural and religious divides between Islam and the West to prevent and counter violent extremism. Data trends suggest that deaths from violent extremism and terrorism have declined slightly since 2014, but the number of countries experiencing violent extremism and terrorism has risen steadily, and the number of regions being impacted by violent extremism has increased. This chapter examines the role played by the UN Secretary-General in reframing the international response to terrorism via AoC initiatives. I analyze the rationale on the part of the Secretary-General for setting this new norm of "alliance," the politics involved in selling this norm within the UN system, and the extent to which the AoC has fulfilled its goals and objectives of preventing and countering violent extremism.

Keywords Alliance of Civilizations · 2030 Agenda · Violent extremism · Summer schools · Fellows Programme

---

T. L. Bertrand (✉)
McMurry University, Department of Political Science, Abeline, TX, USA
e-mail: bertrand@mcm.edu

H. Kury, S. Redo (eds.), *Crime Prevention and Justice in 2030*,
https://doi.org/10.1007/978-3-030-56227-4_33

1 Introduction

The United Nations World Sustainable Development Summit, 2019, received much media attention, thanks in large part to a young Swedish activist who chastised world leaders for failing to take immediate action on climate change (Allegri 2019). Indeed, UN Secretary-General António Guterres noted at the Summit that *all* of the Sustainable Development Goals of the 2030 Agenda (2030 Agenda), not only climate change, were suffering from a serious lack of tangible progress (Wulfhorst 2019). As a result, some governments and civil society organizations (CSOs) have announced specific, acceleration actions for the 2030 Agenda. Substantive Goal 16, which focuses on reducing or eliminating all forms of violence, has received the greatest number of acceleration actions. These acceleration actions are important to the work of the AoC, as its primary objective is to promote dialogue and cooperation to overcome violent extremism.

From its inception, the AoC has prioritized education, youth, migration, and the media, particularly as they pertain to violent extremism between Islam and the West, but its record of success is mixed at best. Persuading people and governments to change their belief systems and curricula regarding inclusive education, diversity acceptance, and promoting inclusive societies requires creating and selling new norms and ideas about how people *should* live. Norm creation is relatively easy for global institutions such as the UN, but selling these norms to sovereign governments is much more difficult. This chapter focuses on two factors that seem to impact the AoC's ability to carry out and expand its agenda regarding preventing and countering violent extremism: garnering requisite support from key actors to adopt and promote norms (Finnemore and Sikkink 1998), and successfully grafting a new norm dimension onto a broader, pre-established one (Price 1998).

2 The UN and Norms

Norms are defined as "collective expectations for the proper behavior of actors with a given identity," and they are the lifeblood of the UN (Finnemore and Sikkink 1998). The UN has the broadest mandate of any international organization in the world, and its work on countering terrorism predates the war on terror by decades. Indeed, the very first chapter of the UN Charter notes the primary purpose of the UN is to address threats to international peace and security, as well as to develop friendly relations between countries, based on mutual respect (Charter of the United Nations 1945, Chapter I). However, there is both a political and procedural disjuncture between the UN bodies that act upon these two purposes. The UN Security Council (SC) is the main body charged with responding to threats (Charter of the United Nations 1945, Chapters VI and VII). Nevertheless, throughout the UN's existence, the Security Council permanent members (P5)—China, France, Russia, the UK, and the USA—have prioritized their own interests over those of the UN Charter to either contribute to conflicts or prevent the UN from ending conflicts. Both the UN General Assembly (GA) and the UN Secretary-General can bring issues before the SC and even make recommendations (under certain conditions), but the SC as a whole, or its permanent members individually, do not have to acquiesce.

A notable UN norm to work around SC inaction—intentional or otherwise—is the Responsibility to Protect (R2P), which holds UN members accountable for protecting their populations. When a country is unable or unwilling to offer such protection, other countries are obliged to take action to protect the population at risk. This norm has been cited formally in nearly three dozen UN Security Council resolutions since 2006, and it was used as justification for Chapter VII military action in Libya in 2011 to protect Libyan civilians from their own government (S/Res/1973 [2011]). The mere creation of norms alone, however, is insufficient for successfully proscribing state behavior. Although Syria approved R2P at the 2005 World Summit, the mere existence of this norm has not prevented the Syrian government from committing atrocities on its civilian population, and the UN Security Council itself has failed to apply R2P by force in Syria.

The P5's continued prioritization of self-interest is most starkly visible in how the USA cast the war on terror as a struggle between Islam and the West. Huntington predicted this clash in the 1990s when he argued that some visceral and immutable characteristics of culture would increase the likelihood of clashes over identity values (Huntington 1993). At the time, Huntington's argument was noted by many world leaders, including Iranian President Mohammad Khatami, who called for a Dialogue among Civilizations within the UN to mitigate the probability that Huntington's prediction would be realized (CNN News 1998).

President Khatami's call resonated with other UN members, who were also increasingly alarmed by US actions in Muslim-majority countries throughout the 1990s. Despite near-universal support for the US-led UN collective security response to Iraq's 1990 invasion of Kuwait, the continued US military presence in Saudi Arabia, and an uptick in US military involvement in conflicts involving significant Muslim populations in Somalia, Bosnia-Herzegovina, and Kosovo were viewed with increasing dismay by many. Even traditional allies of the USA began to act within the UN system to counter the uni- or mini-lateral inclinations of the USA (Huntington 1999).

Responding to Khatami's call in 1998, 58 countries from every region of the world co-sponsored a resolution in the UN GA, proclaiming 2001 as the Year of Dialogue among Civilizations (A/Res/53/22). The resolution tasked the UN Educational, Scientific, and Cultural Organization (UNESCO) with planning and programming this Dialogue. During the actual Year, two international Dialogue conferences were held in Lithuania and Japan, and a separate, high-level Dialogue in the GA was held just before its annual General Debate. The September 11, 2001, terrorist attacks, however, sidelined the Dialogue's momentum, and the USA immediately claimed leadership in shaping the UN's response to September 11.

3 Recasting the Narrative

In the days following September 11, the world seemed to put aside its wariness of the USA and rallied behind the American people in their time of grief and sorrow (Colombani 2001). That sentiment and support, however, died a quick death. A December 2001 Pew Research Center survey indicated that the Islamic world generally held a favorable view of the USA (52%), but 75% believed that US policies caused the September 11 terrorist attacks, and only 25% were convinced that the USA was acting multilaterally (Pew Research Center 2001).

When US President George W. Bush gave UN members an ultimatum in 2002 to either support US initiatives in Iraq or stand aside, he received little support, despite Iraq's noncompliance with dozens of UN resolutions (A/57/PV.2). When the USA submitted a draft resolution calling for UN support of an invasion of Iraq to the SC in March 2003, the USA believed/hoped that it would receive the same blessing it had received during the 1990–1991 Persian Gulf War. The USA, however, was unable to garner the nine necessary votes for approval, or the requisite support of three permanent SC members—China, France, and Russia. Even then-UN Secretary-General Kofi Annan expressed clear opposition to the planned US invasion (Thompson 2006).

Without UN support, the USA invaded Iraq on March 20, 2003, and from that date, then-UN Secretary-General Annan worked consistently to return the UN's response away from the US' minilateralist and militaristic focus back to dialogue and inclusiveness. As head of the largest international organization in the world, the Secretary-General is a natural "seller" of norms (Johnstone 2007). In September 2004, Annan called for a panel of experts to be convened to recommend ways to develop and strengthen norms and regimes "to govern some of the sources and accelerators of conflict" (A/59/1). The very afternoon of Annan's speech, Spanish Prime Minister Luis Rodríguez Zapatero responded, and formally requested Annan to establish a High-level Group to facilitate the specific creation of an Alliance of Civilizations between the Western and Muslim worlds (A/59/PV.4). The individuals Annan selected to serve as members of the High-level Group reflected his intent to completely reframe the UN's response to the war on terror. Of the 20 members of the Group, most were academics from all regions of the world, and only a few were politicians or government officials. Annan included Iranian President Khatami in the Group, indicating the important role he played in promoting the norm of dialogue before September 11. No US government officials or politicians were included in the High-level Group.

At the High-level Group's first meeting in November 2005, Annan tasked the Group with assessing the "strained perceptions between Islamic and Western peoples," and to "propose a collective response to defuse these tensions" (AoC 2005). Acknowledging the critically important role that the Secretary-General would continue to play in shaping the AoC, the Group called upon the Secretary-General to appoint his High Representative to oversee AoC initiatives, and to establish a forum to provide countries with a regular venue for sharing ideas and crafting partnerships (AoC 2006).

4 Initial Successes

The initial purpose of the AoC focused on reconciliation between Islam and the West specifically, and thus norm-selling and success should be indicated by key actors' participation and demonstrable support from these civilizations in AoC fora. At the first Global Forum in Madrid, 70% of the attendees were from Muslim-majority countries or regional organizations, and western countries.[1] In 2009, the next Global Forum was held in Istanbul, Turkey. This second forum saw attendance and membership increase by 20%, again with the majority (nearly two-thirds) of the new members representing Muslim-majority and western countries.[2] At Istanbul, expanding partnerships with CSOs and businesses was emphasized, especially those focused on youth. The 2010 Forum, held in Rio, expanded memoranda between the AoC and other inter- and non-governmental organizations, launched regional strategies, hosted a collegiate Global Model United Nations simulation in Malaysia during Ramadan, and announced the first AoC summer school. Perhaps the most notable element of the Rio Forum was the attendance of the USA, for the first time, as an official member of the AoC.

The 2011 Forum, held in Doha, however, was the tipping point, in terms of a shifting AoC agenda and robust global involvement. Attendance at Doha exceeded 2500, and a pre-Forum event, which focused on connecting the AoC's work with the UN's Millennium Development Goals (MDGs), was attended by more than 100 CSOs (AoC 2011a). The Doha Forum was especially timely, as the Arab Spring was spreading across the Middle East and Northern African (MENA) countries. The impact of the Arab Spring was evident in the Forum's recommendations on youth in nation-building, the role of religious minorities and attainment of the MDGs, and Muslim-Western relations 10 years after September 11.[3]

---

[1]These civilization groupings are based on Huntington's listing of the nine total civilizations in his Clash of Civilizations.

[2]The Group of Friends is a partnership among countries and other international organizations that have an interest in promoting Alliance initiatives at the local, regional, and global levels. For a complete listing of the Group of Friends members, see http://www.unaoc.org/communities/countries-and-international-organisations/members/.

[3]On religious minorities, the AoC specifically recommended focusing on the health-related MDGs. The Forum, however, offered no specific recommendations for the Arab Spring or Muslim-Western relations ten years after 9/11. For a complete list of topics and recommendations, see http://unaoc.org/docs/UANOC%20Doha%20Forum%20Report.pdf.

5 Key Actors

From the outset, the idea of an alliance of civilizations to reconcile tensions between Islam and the West enjoyed widespread support among UN Member States. Nearly one-third of UN members co-sponsored the resolution that proclaimed the Year of Dialogue, and 55% of the November 8–9, 2001 Dialogue speakers were from Islamic and Western countries. By the time the AoC held its first Forum, 77 AoC members conformed to Huntington's civilizations classifications. Of these 77 members, 69% were Islamic and Western countries, with 26 and 27 members, respectively. AoC membership grew much more slowly after 2008. By the 2009 Istanbul Forum, an additional 12 countries joined the Alliance, 75% of which were Islamic and Western countries.

The co-sponsors of the AoC were also important. Spain was an original co-sponsor of the failed SC draft resolution that attempted to grant UN approval for the US invasion of Iraq in 2003. However, the Madrid train bombings in March 2004 cost the incumbent Spanish government electoral victory 3 days later, and a new prime minister pledged to withdraw Spanish troops from Iraq immediately. This same new prime minister called upon Secretary-General Annan to create the AoC at the UN's fall 2004 Plenary. Turkey was an especially important player in the AoC as well. Foremost, the alliance between the western and Muslim worlds must be tangible, and so a Muslim state as co-sponsor of the AoC was necessary. Qatar also has been an important yet somewhat inconsistent supporter of the AoC. In 2011, Qatar hosted the Doha Global Forum, and it donated the majority of funds needed for the 2018 Global Forum in New York City.

Support from the SC's P5 is also suggestive of support in principle, albeit politically timed. France, long a locus of Muslim-associated terrorist attacks, was a founding AoC member. Russia was in the midst of its Second Chechen War, and the Beslan Massacre in 2004 undoubtedly influenced its decision to become an original AoC member. The UK joined after the 2005 London bombings, and it thus became the second staunch ally of the USA in Iraq—after Spain—to accept the AoC's new norm of prioritizing dialogue and cooperation to prevent and counter violent extremism. China joined the AoC in June 2007. While the Chinese government has experienced violent clashes with its predominantly Muslim Uighur population, a search of the Global Terrorism Database indicates no terrorist attacks in China around that time, and thus, a more plausible explanation for the timing of China's membership in the AoC is that it simply was echoing the Group of Seventy Seven's (G-77) endorsement of the AoC in April of 2007.[4] The USA was the last P5 member to join the AoC. US membership dates to May 2010, perhaps not coincidentally just after the thwarted terror attack in New York City's Times Square. Indeed, the USA

[4]China has long supported the G-77, which is a lobbying group for developing countries within the UN system. See "Statement on Behalf of the Group of 77 and China by Mr. Farukh Amil, Acting Permanent Representative of Pakistan to the United Nations, at the General Debate of the United Nations 29th Session of the Committee on Information," April 30, 2007.

provided a clear rationalization for its participation in the AoC at the Rio Forum, where the USA offered a *mea culpa* for its actions and sought to convince the rest of the world that the USA was not at war with Islam itself (Hussain 2010).

Despite its widespread membership, the AoC has been criticized for being very slow to embrace regional CSOs. At the 2011 Doha Global Forum, a biography of participating CSOs indicates that those from MENA countries were a distinct minority, at 11%. All other regions had participation rates in the twenty-plus percentages. Only Latin American representation was lower than that of MENA countries, at 7% (Alliance of Civilizations 2011b).

6 The Struggle to Maintain Success

Despite robust participation in the AoC forums, many countries were either unwilling or unable to provide adequate resources for its ambitious agenda. The official co-sponsors of the AoC—Spain and Turkey—hosted the first two global forums. The next two forums were notable for expanding attendance, as well as a dearth of funding for the AoC's projects. When the AoC was launched in July 2005, only four countries proffered financial support. Following the appointment of the AoC High Representative in April 2007, a dedicated voluntary trust fund was established, which received approximately USD four million in financial support from 14 countries (A/63/336).

After the first four global forums, the AoC recognized that its agenda was unsustainable, and called for a replenishment mechanism for the voluntary trust fund in 2012. Seventy countries, 15 international organizations, and several foundations and corporate groups attended this replenishment session, which resulted in funding pledges of approximately USD 6 million for the AoC's 2012–2013 projects (UN High Representative for the Alliance of Civilizations 2012). The following year, another replenishment session was required, as many pledges remained unfulfilled, and new budget items were only partially financed. Unfulfilled pledges amounted to a mere USD 492,000 whereas new budgeting shortfalls amounted to an astounding USD 4.7 million (AoC 2013a).

There were no global forums in 2012, 2015, 2017, or 2019. The 2018 Global Forum was hosted at UN headquarters to save money, with Qatar funding the majority of the other expenses associated with the event. The 2018 Forum resulted in only two new partnerships and the launch of one new youth project. The forum report even noted, in a very subdued manner, that only "Several Member States pledged to continue their support for ongoing UNAOC project activities" (AoC 2018).

7 Problems with Grafting

When international norms fail to stick, it usually is because they have been unable to locate existing norms or practices onto which they can graft, or the fit is difficult to discern. Ironically, the AoC's agenda has had so many branches, or agencies, to graft onto, and its agenda has grown to closely mimic what other UN entities are doing already, that it has failed to truly distinguish its agenda as a necessary complement or supplement to other UN agendas. At its second meeting in 2006, the AoC's High-level Group was inspired to focus on education, especially given the timing of the scandal surrounding unflattering cartoons of the Prophet Mohammad in a Danish newspaper. The AoC's former research and education manager noted that one of the main goals of the AoC was to develop an understanding of the differences between its four main foci: education, youth, migration, and the media (Uthup quoted in Haynes 2019, p. 4). Nevertheless, between 2010 and 2015, the AoC seemed to blur education and youth by hosting summer schools and fellows' programmes.

The summer schools brought together young people aged 18–35 to foster diversity and promote intercultural understanding. From 2013 to 2015, the AoC partnered with Education First (EF) to sustain the summer schools, given the AoC's financial difficulties discussed in the previous section. Based on the 3 years of data provided to the author by the AoC, the summer schools appear to have been successful, as the primary participants were from Muslim-majority and western countries. Of the 27 Muslim-majority countries participating, 41% participated every year, and 44% participated in all but one summer school. Of the 27 western countries that participated, 48% participated every year, and 22% participated in all but one summer school. Africa had the third largest participation rate, with 24 countries. Of those, 42% attended each year.

In 2015, however, the AoC was sidelined by the launch of the 2030 Agenda and UNESCO being designated the lead agency for Goal 4, with its specific roadmap to achieve quality education worldwide (UNESCO, Education Transforms Lives n.d.-a). Since 2015, the AoC has not hosted any additional summer schools. One reason for the dissolution of the AoC/EF partnership was their disagreement over the age-band for youth. The AoC preferred to focus on youth between the ages of 18 and 35, whereas EF preferred to focus on youth, beginning at the age of 11. The UN's age-band for youth is 15 (with some flexibility) to 24, which makes it unlikely that the AoC will be in a position to resume its summer school initiatives without adhering to the UN's pre-established definition (United Nations n.d.).

The AoC also began its Fellows Programme in 2010—the same year as its summer schools—but most of the individuals are even older than those participating in the summer schools. These programmes focus on the West and Islam, but their geographic outreach is much more limited than the summer schools. The only two cohorts for these programmes are from European and MENA countries, and their travel itineraries are restricted to just a few countries within these two regions, except for the USA as a destination specifically for the MENA cohort. A brief perusal of the cohort alumni list is also suggestive, as it indicates that there are virtually no other geographic regions represented. Whereas the summer schools can boast representation from all regions of the world, these programmes include only American and Armenian scholars and activists whose country of origin falls outside of Europe and MENA counties (Alliance of Civilizations n.d.-a).

The AoC's focus on preventing and countering extremism via youth programs also appears to have failed to graft onto two significant initiatives within the UN system. According to UNESCO, youth make up almost 1.2 billion of the world's population and this number is expected to grow. As of 2016, at least one in four youths was affected by violence or armed conflict in some manner (UNESCO Prevention of Violent Extremism through Youth Empowerment in Jordan, Libya, Morocco, and Tunisia n.d.-b). In 2015, the UN SC passed a resolution that called for concerted efforts to prevent violent extremism in youth and specifically noted several prior initiatives, none of which were part of the AoC's agenda or activities. The resolution noted the General Assembly's World Programme of Action for Youth: the UN Development Programme's Guiding Principles on Young People's Participation in Peacebuilding; the Global Forum on Youth, Peace, and Security (not an AoC global forum) and the resulting Amman Declaration; and the various initiatives of the Counter Extremism Project (S/Res/2250/2015).

This exclusion of AoC projects prompted the AoC to launch its Young Peacebuilders Initiative. On International Youth Day in 2016, the AoC announced this new project would work with 20 young people between the ages of 18 and 25 to enhance their understanding of conflict resolution and peacebuilding via a 7-week online course, a week-long face-to-face workshop, and online and community-level follow-up. The AoC launched a similar initiative in the MENA countries in 2017, with a results-sharing symposium held in 2018. Each of these project pages specifically notes UN SC resolutions 2250 and 2419 as the catalysts for the AoC's Young Peacebuilders Initiative (AoC n.d.-b).

In S/Res/2250/2015, the Secretary-General's work on a Plan of Action to Prevent Violent Extremism also was highlighted, and in 2015, the working group on Preventing Violent Extremism and Conditions Conducive to the Spread of Terrorism began working with the Secretary-General directly. In 2017, the new Office of Counter-Terrorism (UNOCT) consolidated all UN counter-terrorism activities under its wing, and in 2018, the United Nations Global Counter-Terrorism Coordination Compact was signed by the Secretary-General, which aims to provide cohesiveness to UN activities regarding counter-terrorism and prevention of violent extremism. It also provides for more direct assistance and coordination between the Secretary-General and UN Member States to further implement the UN's 2006 Global Counterterrorism Strategy, which specifically addresses the conditions conducive to terrorism. Again, the AoC was not mentioned in this new Compact.

8 A Changing Agenda

After the much-needed replenishment sessions in 2012 and 2013, the AoC's 5th Global Forum was held in Vienna. The volatility of the Arab Spring, and especially the beginning of the refugee crisis as a result of the Syrian civil war, clearly influenced the Forum's speeches, plenary and breakout sessions, as well as the Forum's resulting *Vienna Declaration* (Alliance of Civilizations 2013b). While migration has been a stated focus of the AoC from its inception, this particular issue has never been at the forefront of the AoC's agenda. A simple word count of the mention of migration at the AoC's Madrid, Istanbul, and Rio forums suggests that migration was not a prominent topic, nor was it mentioned very often by speakers. However, at the Vienna Global Forum, the word migration was mentioned 84 times just in the summary report of the 2-day meeting, up from five mere mentions at Madrid (AoC 2013b).

The year 2013 also heralded a change in leadership in the AoC. Qatari diplomat H. E. Mr. Nassir Abdulaziz al-Nasser replaced H. E. President Jorge Sampaio of Portugal. With this change in leadership, the AoC began focusing on the universal right to and respect for religious freedom. This subtle shift was important, because it signaled the AoC's move away from bridging religious differences to acknowledging and accepting those differences. This shift continued at the 2014 Global Forum in Bali, where the new AoC High Representative noted the critical importance of the AoC in helping countries address identity crises within their borders at the domestic rather than inter-regional level (Al-Nasser 2014).

At the 2014 Bali Global Forum, several new sessions were held, including the role of women in fostering understanding among cultures; youth participation in peace-building (rather than nation-building); and harnessing the positive power of social media in reconciling the demand for security with the right to privacy and freedom of expression. The Bali Forum also adopted an Arab regional strategy (Alliance of Civilizations 2014). Since Bali, the AoC has added women as an official focus area, along with its original focus areas of education, youth, migration, and the media. This may be an attempt to find another norm dimension onto which the AoC can graft. However, given the special status of UN Women within the system, it is likely that the AoC will experience the same problems noted above regarding duplicating too closely other, extent UN initiatives.

At the 2016 Baku Global Forum, the AoC announced that a new priority area would be sports for the promotion of diversity and culture. Food security was also identified as a new area of interest for the AoC. At the 2018 Forum, the theme, "One Humanity, Many Cultures," nevertheless continued al-Nassers' focus on acknowledging and accepting religious and cultural differences. That same year, AoC leadership changed hands from al-Nasser to H.E. Mr. Miguel Ángel Moratinos of Spain. While Moratinos has not hosted a themed Global Forum to date, his statements at a 2019 High-level Panel on Promoting Tolerance for Preventing and Combatting Violent Extremism suggest yet another change to the AoC's agenda. At this panel, Moratinos stated very clearly that the AoC must work closely with the new Office of Counter-Terrorism, as well as continue and expand AoC's outreach to youth. He even referenced two particular projects that were being developed involving the promotion of sports as a tool for security as a means to prevent violent extremism (Moratinos 2019).

9 The Way Forward?

The AoC can boast of successes, as well as bemoan failures. It has widespread membership, but its donor base, which is critical for its survival, remains small. The AoC's donor base is not transparent, and the AoC posts the UN's general financial statement only on its website. Moreover, the AoC lists its top ten donors only for the years 2005–2017, and their contributions amount to an average of a mere USD 2.7 million for each of those 13 years. This amount is USD 2 million short of what the AoC requested in 2013 alone for its additional programming. Not surprisingly, Turkey and Spain have been the top contributors, at approximately USD 10 and USD 8 million, respectively, from 2005 to 2017 (Alliance of Civilization n.d.-c). The luxury car manufacturer, BMW, is the AoC's third-largest donor, with total contributions at USD 4.75 million for the same period. Rounding out the top ten are four other Muslim-majority countries and three other western European countries. These donor demographics suggest that Western and Islamic countries do indeed support the AoC, but not nearly in the numbers necessary to sustain the AoC indefinitely. And, with no significant support from other regions, the AoC's financial difficulties will continue.

On grafting, the AoC so far has been unsuccessful in the areas of education, youth, and preventing and countering violent extremism. According to the Secretary-General's 2019 report on the 2030 Agenda, an estimated 617 million children and adolescents of primary and lower secondary school age worldwide—more than 50%—were not achieving minimum proficiency levels in reading and mathematics. Additionally, approximately 750 million adults—two-thirds of them women—remained illiterate in 2016. Half of the global illiterate population lives in South Asia, and one quarter lives in sub-Saharan Africa (E/2019/68). The report also notes that only one-third of all countries spend between 15% and 20% of total government expenditure on education, as recommended in the Education 2030 Framework for Action.

If the AoC were to adopt the UN's youth definition, it could readily graft itself onto the 2030 Agenda by working with the lead agency on SDG 4 UNESCO and thereby establish new partnerships for renewed summer school projects, and expand them to incorporate secondary school students. Sustainable Development Goal 4, Target 4.7 in particular, offers such an opportunity with its focus on promoting a culture of peace and non-violence. The AoC is uniquely placed to offer curricula to address Target 4.7, and it would not have to provide all of the funding. The AoC should be able to reframe and/or develop new partnerships that are already identified in the SDG acceleration actions noted at the beginning of this chapter. There are a total of 145 acceleration actions that governments and CSOs have established to date or are in the process of creating, and many have already mobilized tangible resources for these actions (Sustainable Development Goals 2019, SDG Acceleration Actions).

Sustainable Development Goal 10 and its Targets 10.3, 10.4, and 10.7 also hold some promise for grafting. Target 10.3 focuses on eliminating discriminatory laws, policies and practices, and promoting appropriate policies and legislation. Target 10.4 focuses on promoting social protection policies. Both of these targets necessarily would include projects that address religious, youth, and gender discrimination—all of which are focus areas for the AoC. Target 10.7 focuses on migration, which always has been a stated priority of the AoC. Despite the AoC emphasizing this focus area beginning only at the 2013 Vienna Global Forum, the 2016 Baku Global Forum and the 2018 Forum in New York heavily featured migration. Migration, therefore may provide the AoC with some additional traction for grafting, especially in light of the UN's recently-approved Global Compact for Migration for Safe, Orderly, and Regular Migration, which includes specific objectives involving education and youth—two of the AoC's most heavily-promoted focus areas (Global Compact for Migration 2018).

By clearly aligning itself with the 2030 Agenda—sooner rather than later—the AoC also can address the discrepancy between the general and material support it receives from state and non-state actors, especially in regions where violent extremism is rising but from where the AoC receives little funding. According to the 2019 Global Terrorism Index, South Asia has felt the greatest impact of terrorism since 2002. Moreover, the link between gender and violent extremism is increasing. The Index notes that Asia had the largest proportion of women joining ISIL over the past few years, at 31% (Institute for Economics and Peace 2019). Sustainable Development Goal 16, which promotes peaceful and inclusive societies for sustainable development is most closely aligned with the AoC's mission to prevent and counter violent extremism. Moreover, Goal 16 is included in nearly half (67 of 145) of the acceleration actions, and many of these are sponsored and funded by governments and CSOs throughout Asia.

A partnership between these regional governments and CSOs and the AoC would address simultaneously the criticism that the AoC has been slow to embrace CSOs as well as the AoC's financial difficulties. Given that the major donors to the AoC have experienced significant terrorist activity, it seems logical to assume that new regions experiencing increases in terrorist activity could be likely sources of funding. By expanding its work with CSOs in other regions—especially Asia, which has significant problems with both education and violent extremism—the AoC can expand its donor base dramatically. Even if countries in Asia do not begin donating directly to the AoC in the immediate-term, the AoC nevertheless can cultivate long-term, positive relationships with these governments and CSOs, which can be a potential source of future funding for AoC projects that may deviate somewhat from Agenda 2030 but address these countries' specific concerns regarding education, youth, and violent extremism.

Ultimately, the success of the AoC depends upon its ability to reinvent itself as a full supporter of the 2030 Agenda. If the AoC is perceived to be reluctant to engage with partners that have pledged their political and material support for the 2030 Agenda, the AoC will continue to be financially unable to deliver on its focus areas and will continue to be sidelined from becoming a lead agency on any greater UN enterprise. If, however, the AoC can fully mainstream its primary focus of preventing and countering violent extremism into at least some of the goals of the 2030 Agenda, then it has an opportunity to guarantee that the norm for which it was created remains viable and adhered to by UN Member States.

References

A/57/PV.2. (2002). *United Nations general assembly official records 57th Session 2nd plenary meeting 12 September 2002*. https://documents-dds-ny.un.org/doc/UNDOC/GEN/N02/586/90/pdf/N0258690.pdf?OpenElement

A/59/1. (2004). *Report of the secretary-general on the work of the organization: Presentation by the secretary-general of his annual report A/59/1*. http://www.un.org/webcast/ga/59/statements/sg-english.pdf

A/59/PV.4. (2004). *United Nations general assembly official records 59th session 4th plenary meeting 21 September 2004*. https://documents-dds-ny.un.org/doc/UNDOC/GEN/N04/516/10/pdf/N0451610.pdf?OpenElement

A/63/336. (2008). *Letter dated 2 May 2008 from the Secretary-General addressed to the President of the General Assembly 2 May 2008*. https://documents-dds-ny.un.org/doc/UNDOC/GEN/N08/492/48/pdf/N0849248.pdf?OpenElement

A/Res/53/22. (1998). *United Nations year of dialogue among civilizations 16 November 1998*. https://undocs.org/en/A/RES/53/22

Allegri, C. (2019, September 23). *Greta Thunberg to U.N. climate summit: 'You have stolen my dreams'*. https://www.reuters.com/article/us-climate-change-un-thunberg/greta-thunberg-to-u-n-climate-summit-you-have-stolen-my-dreams-idUSKBN1W81OS

Alliance of Civilizations. (2005). *Summary notes: Meeting of the high level group of the Alliance of Civilizations, Palma de Mallorca, Spain 27–29 November 2005*. https://www.unaoc.org/repository/UNSG_address_mallorca.pdf

Alliance of Civilizations. (2006). *Report of the high-level Group*. New York: DPI. 13 November 2006. https://www.unaoc.org/resource/alliance-of-civilizations-report-of-the-high-level-group-13-november-2006/

Alliance of Civilizations. (2011a). *The Fourth Global UN alliance of civilizations forum*. New York: DPI. 11–13 December 2011. https://www.unaoc.org/docs/UANOC%20Doha%20Forum%20Report.pdf

Alliance of Civilizations. (2011b). *Profiles of participating CSOs*. https://www.unaoc.org/wp-content/uploads/110501_CSO_BIO_Doha_PreForum.pdf

Alliance of Civilizations. (2013a). *Preparing for the second Replenishment session, Vienna, 28 February 2013: Projects, priorities and funding needs for the year 2013*. file:///C:/Users/bertrant/Documents/Interculturalism%20Research/Second-Replenishment-Session-update-on-projects-and-priorities-2013 2011.pdf.

Alliance of Civilizations. (2013b). *The fifth global United Nations alliance of civilizations forum Vienna 27–28 2013*. https://www.unaoc.org/wp-content/uploads/UNAOC-Vienna-Forum-Report.pdf

Alliance of Civilizations. (2014). *The Sixth Global United Nations Alliance of Civilizations Forum Bali 29–30 August 2014*. https://www.unaoc.org/wp-content/uploads/110501_CSO_BIO_Doha_PreForum.pdf

Alliance of Civilizations. (2018). *The eighth global UN alliance of civilizations forum*. New York: DPI. 19–20 November 2018. https://www.unaoc.org/wp-content/uploads/8thForum_v7_web.pdf

Alliance of Civilizations. (n.d.-a). *Fellowship over the Years*. https://fellowship.unaoc.org/fellowship-program-years/

Alliance of Civilizations. (n.d.-b). *Young peacebuilders*. https://www.unaoc.org/what-we-do/projects/young-peacebuilders/

Alliance of Civilizations. (n.d.-c). *Trust fund and donors*. https://www.unaoc.org/who-we-are/trust-fund-and-donors/

Al-Nasser, N. A. (2014). *Opening session of the 6th global forum*. New York: Web.

CNN News. (1998, January 7). *Transcript of interview with Iranian President Mohammad Khatami 7 January 1998*. http://www.cnn.com/WORLD/9801/07/iran/interview.html

Colombani, J. M. (2001, September 12). *We are all Americans Le Monde*, 12 September 2001. https://www.worldpress.org/1101we_are_all_americans.htm

E/2019/68. (2019). *High-level segment: Ministerial meeting of the high-level political forum on sustainable development, convened under the auspices of the Economic and Social Council 8 May 2019*. https://undocs.org/E/2019/68.chapter

Finnemore, M., & Sikkink, K. (1998). International norm dynamics and political change. *International Organization, 4*, 887–917.

Global Compact for Migration. (2018). *Global compact for safe, and regular migration internationally negotiated and agreed outcome*. https://refugeesmigrants.un.org/sites/default/files/180713_agreed_outcome_global_compact_for_migration.pdf

Group of 77. (2007). *Statement on behalf of the Group of 77 and China by Mr. Farukh Amil, acting permanent representative of Pakistan to the United Nations, at the General Debate of the 29th Session of the Committee on Information 30 April 2007*. https://www.g77.org/statement/getstatement.php?id=070430b

Haynes, J. (2019). *Religion, education and security: The United Nations alliance of civilizations and global citizenship religions 10*. https://www.mdpi.com/2077-1444/10/1/51/htm

Huntington, S. P. (1993). The clash of civilizations? *Foreign Affairs, 3*, 22–49.

Huntington, S. P. (1999). Resisting the lonely superpower. *Foreign Affairs, 2*, 35–49.

Hussain, R. (2010). *Remarks at the UN third global forum of the alliance of civilizations*. New York: DPI. 29 May 29 2010. https://www.unaoc.org/docs/UNAOCrioforumReport_lr.pdf

Institute for Economics and Peace. (2019). *Global terrorism index 2019: Measuring the impact of terrorism*. http://visionofhumanity.org/app/uploads/2019/11/GTI-2019web.pdf

Johnstone, I. (2007). The Secretary-General as norm entrepreneur. In S. Chesterman (Ed.), *Secretary or General? The UN Secretary-General in world politics* (pp. 123–138). Cambridge: Cambridge University Press.

Moratinos, M. (2019). *Remarks at the UAE/UNOCT high-level panel on promoting tolerance for P/CVE empowering youth and promoting tolerance: Practical approaches to PCVE*. New York: DPI. 18–19 December 2019. https://www.unaoc.org/2019/12/remarks-high-level-panel-on-promoting-tolerance-for-pcve/

Pew Research Center, Global Attitudes and Trends. (2001). *America Admired, yet it's New Vulnerability Seen as Good Thing, Say Opinion Leaders: Little Support for Expanding War on Terrorism 19 December 2001*. http://www.pewglobal.org/2001/12/19/america-admired-yet-its-new-vulnerability-seen-as-good-thing-say-opinion-leaders/

Price, R. (1998). Revising the gun sights: Transnational civil society targets land mines. *International Organization, 3*, 613–644.

S/Res/1973 2011. (2011). *Libya adopted resolution*. New York: DPI. https://undocs.org/S/RES/1973(2011)

S/Res/2250 2015. (2015). *Youth adopted resolution*. New York: DPI. https://documents-dds-ny.un.org/doc/UNDOC/GEN/N15/413/06/pdf/N1541306.pdf?OpenElement
Sustainable Development Goal Acceleration Actions. (2019). https://sustainabledevelopment.un.org/sdgactions
Thompson, A. (2006). Screening power: International organizations as informative agents. In D. G. Hawkins et al. (Eds.), *Delegation and agency in international organizations* (pp. 229–254). Cambridge: Cambridge University Press.
United Nations. (1945). *Charter of the United Nations*. New York: DPI, 1945. https://www.un.org/en/sections/un-charter/un-charter-full-text/
United Nations. (n.d.). *Youth*. https://www.un.org/en/sections/issues-depth/youth-0/index.html
United Nations Educational, Scientific, and Cultural Organization. (n.d.-a). *Education transforms lives*. https://en.unesco.org/themes/education
United Nations Educational, Scientific, and Cultural Organization. (n.d.-b). *Prevention of violent extremism through youth empowerment in Jordan, Libya, Morocco and Tunisia*. https://en.unesco.org/preventing-violent-extremism/youth/project
United Nations High Representative for the Alliance of Civilizations. (2012). *Implementation of the replenishment mechanism – Evaluation of the 1st pledging conference Istanbul 31 May 2012 and Way Forward*. New York: UNAOC. 17 September 17 2012 Annex 3.
Wulfhorst, E. (2019, September 24). *UN head urges a "Decade of Action" to address world crises*. http://news.trust.org//item/20190924191633-imcgs/

Tina L. Bertrand Dr. received her Masters and Ph.D. in Political Science from Emory University (Atlanta, Ga., USA). Her research interests focus on how the United Nations become norm entrepreneurs in an effort to alter state behavior in the absence or deficit of international treaties or law. Dr. Bertrand's interest in the UN stems from her work as a research assistant to Mr. George L. Sherry, f. Assistant Secretary-General, then with the UN Institute for Training and Research. Dr. Bertrand currently serves as Chair of the Department of Political Science at McMurry University (Abeline, Tx, USA). She also is the director of the Model UN Program at McMurry University. Dr. Bertrand has been named an Oxford Roundtable Scholar, and has received various fellowships multiple times for her research. Her most recent publication is entitled "The Alliance of Civilizations: Crafting a New Norm of Dialogue and Understanding," published in *Dialogue and Alliance: A Journal of the Universal Peace Federation*, vol. 33, No, 2, Winter 2019. E-mail: bertrand@mcm.edu.

Spirituality, Crime Prevention, and Criminal Justice: The Ongoing Significance of Faith-Based Organizations to the Work of the United Nations

Thomas G. Walsh

Abstract Religion continues to be a social force that impacts our world, with capacities at times problematic and at other times socially redemptive. In addition to its churches, mosques, and temples, it also has spawned numerous charities, voluntary associations, advocacy groups, and non-governmental organizations (NGOs). For this chapter, I use the term "faith-based organizations" (FBOs) to refer to religious NGOs or religiously informed or religiously inspired NGOs. Many FBOs have been and, indeed, remain actively involved in various ways with the work of the United Nations. In fact, religious or spiritual themes have been at play throughout the history of the United Nations, often mediated through central figures who helped shape that history. In an age that affirms partnership, multi-sectoral approaches to peace, and collaboration, the back stories of religious inspiration, spiritual ideas, and actors, as they have and continue to impact the United Nations, should be recognized and affirmed.

This chapter addresses the ongoing significance and relevance of religion and faith-based organizations (FBOs) to the mission and goals of the United Nations, and particularly the United Nations Office of Drugs and Crime (UNODC). FBOs are stakeholders that may indeed contribute to efforts to achieve peace and security, crime prevention, and the sustainable development goals (SDGs), most notably SDG 16: "Promote peaceful and inclusive societies for sustainable development, provide access to justice for all and build effective, accountable and inclusive institutions at all levels" (A/RES/70/1).

Keywords Faith-Based Organizations (FBOs) · Non-Governmental Organizations (NGOs) · United Nations · Sustainable Development Goals (SDGs) · Partnership

---

T. G. Walsh (✉)
Universal Peace Federation, New York, NY, USA
e-mail: twalsh@upf.org

H. Kury, S. Redo (eds.), *Crime Prevention and Justice in 2030*,
https://doi.org/10.1007/978-3-030-56227-4_34

1 Introduction

In recent decades, it has become increasingly clear that not only does religion have stickiness—a capacity to endure, prevail, and even flourish under many, if not most circumstances—but that it has capacities at its disposal that bring value to governments and international organizations, including the United Nations (UN), in their efforts to mitigate or solve social problems and secure peace, security, and sustainable development. This social fact stands out independently of one's personal views about religion: believer, non-believer, atheist, disinterested observer, or advocate.

This is not to suggest that religion is incorruptible. On the contrary, like all individuals, groups, and human institutions, it can and has at times brought harm. There is no doubt about this point, evidenced in extremist ideologies and practices, crimes committed in the name of religion, conflicts that arise in the name of religion, etc. At the same time, it is well documented that similar kinds of wrongdoing are committed in equal if not sometimes greater share by governments, ideologically driven social movements, organized criminal entities, and well-intentioned but wrongheaded political movements; wrongdoings accomplished without the assistance or alibi of religion. One does not need to be religious to be a fanatic, to do harm, or to refuse to allow feedback to temper your commitments.

We live at a time of widespread social and political instability, when the fabric and patterns of the later twentieth century's balance of power is shifting. New forms of democracy are emerging, challenging the dominant paradigm of liberal democracy (Deenen 2019; Carothers and O'Donahue 2019); as such, we observe liberal democracy in some cases morphing into types of authoritarian democracy, illiberal democracy, or autocratic democracy (Rose 2019).

Populism and nationalism are on the rise in the early twenty-first century (Kagan 2018). These trends are associated with not only the behavior of superpowers seeking geopolitical advantage, but also with ethno-national states that face the demographic challenges posed by migration and multi-culturalism. Religion is a factor at play in many, although not all of such contemporary developments (Toft et al. 2011; Grzymala-Busse 2015; Berger 1999; Thomas 2005; Habermas 2010; Walzer 2015).

Religion has been a major factor in the unfolding of human history for millennia. While secularization might have been anticipated as the logical outcome of the rationalization process associated with the rise of modernity, science, technology, democracy, and human development in general, this has not proven to be the case. Religion, on the contrary, enjoys twenty-first century resurgence. Like it or not, it seems here to stay.

Moreover, religion does not simply exist politely in the background or history, standing only in some quaint decorative role. On the contrary, religion has impact on other sectors of society—political, economic, cultural—as an outgrowth of the ways in which religion shapes human beings in their character, their moral perspectives, their priorities, their core values, and their actions. Moreover, the quietism associated with some religions is increasingly overstepped in most traditions by a call for believers to be socially and politically engaged for spiritual, moral, and humanitarian reasons.

It is therefore no wonder that religious NGOs, FBOs, and interfaith activists are increasingly engaged with many UN bodies, including the Economic and Social Council, the General Assembly, the Alliance of Civilizations, and more recently the Inter-Agency Task Force on Religion and Development (Baumgart-Ochse and Wolf 2019; Obiezu 2019).

2 Spiritual Ideals and the Path to the United Nations

The roots of the United Nations system cannot be written holistically without some understanding of the way religion and spiritual ideals inform and shape human development, consciousness and action. Were Kant's Lutheran Pietist roots relevant to his cosmopolitan philosophy of perpetual peace? Were Wilson's southern evangelical roots, mixed with a "social gospel" oriented brand of Calvinism, relevant to his vision of a League of Nations? What of Franklin Roosevelt's own political philosophy and the underlying factors that shaped his vision? (Rossiter 1949).

When in 1941 Franklin Delano Roosevelt met with Winston Churchill on the British battleship, Her Majesty's Ship the Prince of Wales off the coast of Newfoundland they spoke together and, among other things, participated in a worship service, which included the singing of hymns. As Churchill later stated, "I chose the hymns myself: "*For Those in Peril on the Sea*" and "*Onward Christian Soldiers*." We ended with "*O God, Our Help in Ages Past*".... Every word seemed to stir the heart.... Nearly half of those who sang were soon to die" (Churchill 1950; Glass 2017).

Neither Roosevelt, raised an Episcopalian, nor Churchill, raised an Anglican, were ideologically averse to religion; neither were they passionate believers. Interestingly, however, item eight of the text of the Atlantic Charter, which some view as setting the stage for the United Nations charter, states that "all the nations of the world, for realistic as well as **spiritual reasons** [emphasis added], must come to the abandonment of the use of force" (Plesch 2011, p. 25).

In moments of crisis such as on board the HMS Prince of Wales in 1941, religious sentiments often came to the fore. On 6 June 1944, Roosevelt delivered his "D-Day Prayer" (Roosevelt 1944, June 6) which contained lines as follows:

> Almighty God: Our sons, pride of our Nation, this day have set upon a mighty endeavor, a struggle to preserve our Republic, our religion, and our civilization, and to set free a suffering humanity.
>
> Lead them straight and true; give strength to their arms, stoutness to their hearts, steadfastness in their faith.
>
> They will need Thy blessings. Their road will be long and hard. For the enemy is strong. He may hurl back our forces. Success may not come with rushing speed, but we shall return again and again; and we know that by Thy grace, and by the righteousness of our cause, our sons will triumph.

> They will be sore tried, by night and by day, without rest-until the victory is won. The darkness will be rent by noise and flame. Men's souls will be shaken with the violences of war.
>
> For these men are lately drawn from the ways of peace. They fight not for the lust of conquest. They fight to end conquest. They fight to liberate. They fight to let justice arise, and tolerance and good will among all Thy people. They yearn but for the end of battle, for their return to the haven of home.
>
> Some will never return. Embrace these, Father, and receive them, Thy heroic servants, into Thy kingdom.
>
> And for us at home - fathers, mothers, children, wives, sisters, and brothers of brave men overseas - whose thoughts and prayers are ever with them - help us, Almighty God, to rededicate ourselves in renewed faith in Thee in this hour of great sacrifice (Roosevelt 1944, June 6).

Roosevelt was not only deeply committed to the birth of a United Nations, but he was also a man of faith, and a man whose passion for justice was not only grounded in a moral vision, but also a spiritual vision. The same can be said of Churchill, not to mention Woodrow Wilson, as well as many others.

In late December of 1941, 4 months after the Atlantic Charter was signed, *Declaration by United Nations*, which formed the basis for the UN charter later developed in San Francisco, was drafted by Franklin Roosevelt, Winston Churchill, and Roosevelt's aide, Harry Hopkins. It was then signed by representatives of the USA, the UK, the USSR, and China on New Year's Day 1942. On the next day, 22 other nations signed the declaration. The name United Nations was chosen, over the name "Associated Powers." One provision that was added called for religious freedom, an item that the USSR reluctantly accepted (Plesch 2011, pp. 34–35).

Roosevelt did not live to witness the drafting of the charter in San Francisco, and Harry Truman was suddenly thrust into the seat of power on 16 April 1945, the Harry Truman who always kept a copy Tennyson's 1835 poem, "Locksley Hall" (Tennyson 2008, pp. 167–168), on his person; the poem famously includes text that envisions, prophetically, a parliament of man and a federation of the world:

> For I dipt into the future, far as human eye could see,
> Saw the Vision of the world, and all the wonder that would be;
> Saw the heavens fill with commerce, argosies of magic sails,
> Pilots of the purple twilight dropping down with costly bales;
> Heard the heavens fill with shouting, and there rain'd a ghastly dew
> From the nations' airy navies grappling in the central blue;
> Far along the world-wide whisper of the sough-wing rushing warm,
> With the standards of the peoples plunging thro' the thunder-storm;
> Till the war-drum throbb'd no longer, and the battle-flags were furl'd
> In the Parliament of man, the Federation of the world.
> There the common sense of most shall hold a fretful realm in awe,
> And the kindly earth shall slumber, lapt in universal law.

3 The Spirituality of the United Nations Secretaries-General

Suffice to say, there are spiritual and/or religious traces that stand at least at the margins of the history of the United Nations, including in the mind and hearts of several Secretaries General, such as U Thant, a Buddhist, or Dag Hammarskjöld, a Christian, among others.

The volume *To Speak for the World: Speeches and Statements by Dag Hammarskjöld* (Hammarskjöld 2005) contains numerous passages that evidence the former Secretary- General's spirituality. In a chapter on "Faith" he refers to the Spanish mystic, St. John of the Cross, as well as the Gospels (Hammarskjöld 2005, pp. 58–59). The volume also includes excerpts from a message he delivered before the General Assembly on 20 August 1954, entitled, "The United Nations stands outside all confessions but is nevertheless an instrument of faith." To quote Hammarskjöld from this address, he says, "...in spite of their different roles in the life of the community and the peoples, the Organizations [United Nations] and the Churches stand side by side as participants in the efforts of all men of good will, irrespective of their creed or form of worship, to establish peace on earth" (Hammarskjöld 2005, p. 61). In 1957, the Secretary-General devoted himself to reviving the Meditation Room, originally established in 1952, at the United Nations Headquarters in New York. Referring to the stone in the middle of the room, Hammarskjöld says, "We may see it as an altar, empty not because there is no God, not because it is an altar to an unknown god, but because it is dedicated to the God whom many worships under many names and in many forms" (Hammarskjöld 2005, p. 226).

U Thant, who in 1961 succeeded Dag Hammarskjöld, was a practicing Buddhist. He invited Sri Chinmoy to lead regular meditation sessions at the UN Headquarters. In a speech he presented to his staff at the time of his departure in 1971, he stated that, whereas he affirmed intellectual and moral qualities, "I would attach the greatest importance to spiritual values, spiritual qualities.... I have in mind the spiritual virtues, faith in oneself, the purity of one's inner self which to me is the greatest virtue of all. With this approach, with this philosophy, with this concept alone, we will be able to fashion the kind of society we want, the society which was envisaged by the founding fathers of the United Nations" (Pedersen 2010, pp. 346–347).

On 20 December 2019, the current Secretary General, António Guterres, had a private meeting with Pope Francis at the Vatican. They produced a joint video message. On the website of the Holy See Mission to the United Nations, a report on the meeting states:

> In his remarks, UN Secretary-General Guterres, highlighted the "clear moral voice" of the Pope on issues that are at the very heart of the United Nations mandate. "You are a messenger for hope and humanity – for reducing human suffering and promoting human dignity," he said. He thanked Holy See for its "exceptional global engagement and strong

> support for the work of the United Nations" and mentioned in particular the pontiff's visit to UN headquarters in 2015, the year the 2030 Sustainable Development Goals were adopted.[1]

While religion is not a dominant force at the United Nations, its presence is arguably inescapable.

4 Faith-Based Organizations and the United Nations

Along with a wide range of secular civil society associations or NGOs that have been partners with the United Nations throughout its history, there are many religious NGOs. In San Francisco in 1945, there were not only the Congress of Industrial Organizations and the Council on Foreign Relations, but also the American Jewish Committee and the Catholic Welfare Conference (Schlesinger 2003, p. 123).

In her introduction to *Religious NGOs at the United Nations: Polarizers or Mediators?* (Baumgart-Ochse and Wolf 2019) Claudia Baumgart-Ochse states that there are approximately 4000 NGOs that have consultative status with the United Nations Economic and Social Council. Among these, approximately 10% are religiously inspired or affiliated (Baumgart-Ochse and Wolf 2019, p. 8). In 1998, Secretary General Kofi Annan stated that the United Nations was "a tapestry not only of suits and saris, but of cleric's collars, nun's habits and lama's robes, and of mitres, skullcaps and yarmulkes" (Baumgart-Ochse and Wolf 2019, p. 9). According to Baumgart-Ochse, "the attitude of the UN towards religious actors has undergone considerable change in recent years. Many of its agencies now seek to engage with local and international RNGOs [religious NGOs] in a coordinated and systematic way and are able to pass their experience on to other UN entities in reports, recommendations, and best-practice guidelines" (Baumgart-Ochse and Wolf 2019, p. 11).

In her article entitled, "*Reconciliation Versus Punishment: Religious NGOs and the International Criminal Court*" (Baumgart-Ochse and Wolf 2019). Baumgart-Ochse identifies a wide range of religious NGOs that are involved with the development of the International Criminal Court (ICC), some participating in the Faith and Ethics Network. These include Baha'i International Community, Friends World Committee for Consultation (Quakers), Mennonite Central Committee, Pax Christi International, Religions for Peace, and the World Council of Churches (Baumgart-Ochse and Wolf 2019, pp. 129–140).

In 2014, the United Nations Development Program (UNDP) produced a set of "Guidelines on Engaging with Faith-based Organizations and Religious Leaders." The document states that "FBOs and religious leaders can link development actors with beneficiary communities, and engaging them in the right conditions can enhance development impact and sustainability" (UNDP 2014, p. 3).

---

[1]https://holyseemission.org/contents//events/5dfd12447dbfb.php.

Paul Nelson, writing in the *The Review of Faith and International Affairs*, states that, "Religious actors are persistently involved in international development, through religious missions, faith-based NGOs, and through cooperation with local religious communities and authorities. Whether secular development professionals see them as obstacles or as resources for social and economic change, religious institutions are influential almost everywhere that development practitioners work" (Nelson 2019, p. 15).

As Paul Nelson has said in *"The Parliament of Man: The Past Present and Future of the United Nations"*, "Churches sometimes have the power to make governments move that NGOs could only dream of possessing" (Kennedy 2006, p. 228). Kennedy points to the American Jewish Congress, the U.S. Council of Catholic Bishops, Quaker Relief Services, Catholic Relief Services, as well as the Vatican's non-member observer status at the United Nations. He writes, "Although they often work alongside UN relief agencies and NGOs, in some more distant parts of the world these religiously based aid bodies *are* the international community" (Kennedy 2006, p. 228).

While religion had to some extent been marginalized during the latter half of the twentieth century, corresponding more or less with the Cold War era during which time other priorities seemed to be dominant, its energies, values, and of course its failings, have emerged more prominently in recent decades. Moreover, modernity's allergies *vis à vis* religion seems now to be fading as well.

On the one hand, the general affirmation of pluralism among educated classes, coupled with an increasing refinement of religious believers, through such practices as interreligious dialogue, results in there being less fear of religion as a social reality that is either too irrational or too dangerous and conflict-prone to engage with. These prejudices or taboos—in some cases phobias—are eroding and, with that, there is growing appreciation that religious or faith-based stakeholders are assets to be appreciated.

Numerous high-profile interfaith organizations are scattered on the landscape of international organizations, earning wide respect and appreciation; to name a few: Religions for Peace, Parliament of the World's Religions, United Religions Initiative, the King Abdullah International Center for Interreligious and Intercultural Dialogue, the Universal Peace Federation, and others.

This development is recognized widely at the United Nations, and contributed to the formation of the Alliance of Civilizations, perhaps to counter a potential "clash of civilizations" as predicted by Samuel Huntington in his often cited work article from 1993, *The Clash of Civilizations?* (Huntington 1993), and subsequently the volume by the same title, *The Clash of Civilizations and the Remaking of World Order* (Huntington 1997).

During a program at the United Nations called "The Plan of Action for Religious Leaders and Actors to Prevent Incitement to Violence that Could Lead to Atrocity Crimes", convened on 14 July 2017, Secretary-General Antonio Guterres stated, "I firmly believe in the power of faith leaders to shape our world for good." He added that: "All religions teach respect for life, and recognize human beings as fundamentally equal. These principles summon us to show respect for all human beings, even those with whom we might profoundly disagree or whose cultures might seem alien. I urge the widest possible dissemination and implementation of this Plan of Action. It can help to save lives, reduce suffering, and realize our shared vision of peaceful, inclusive and just societies in which diversity is valued and the rights of all individuals are protected" (Guterres 2017).

5 FBOs and the United Nations Office on Drugs and Crime

While religion's relevance to international relations and global affairs is better known and documented, its relevance to crime prevention, criminal justice, and the SDGs needs attention.

A UN document entitled *The UNDP Guidelines on Engaging with Faith-based Organizations and Religious Leaders* describes FBOs as "organizations that derive inspiration and guidance for their activities from the teachings and principles of the faith or from a particular interpretation or school of thought within that faith" (UNDP 2008).

The document goes on to say, "FBOs and RLs are part of nearly every community on earth. They not only make significant contributions to development, but add value to United Nation's efforts in a number of ways. In many countries, FBOs and RLs are the dominant civil society actors" (Ibidem, p. 6).

In their study, *"Religion, Crime and Criminal Justice"* by Byron R. Johnson and Curtis S. Schroeder (Johnson and Schroeder 2014), it is argued, based on a review of 109 studies, that "the vast majority of the studies report a beneficial relationship between measures of religion or religious commitment and various crime and delinquency measures or outcomes" (Ibidem, p. 3). Furthermore, the authors conclude that "a review of the research on religious practices or commitments and deviant behavior indicates that, in general, higher levels of religious involvement are associated with lower rates of crime and delinquency. The empirical evidence demonstrates that those who are most involved in religious activities are less likely to commit criminal or delinquent acts. Thus, aided by systematic reviews of the relevant literature, it is accurate to state that religiosity is now beginning to be acknowledged as a key protective factor that buffers or shields youth from criminal and delinquency outcomes" (Ibidem, p. 6). They conclude that "any strategy [for crime prevention] will be needlessly incomplete unless religious communities are integrally involved" (Ibidem, p. 9).

In another essay entitled *"What Religion Offers for the Politics of Transitional Justice"* which appears in Rethinking Religion and World Affairs (Shah et al. 2012), Daniel Philpott argues for the essential value of religious perspectives on justice. He contracts religion's emphasis on reconciliation, or restoration of the broken relationship, as distinct from the liberal human rights paradigm's emphasis on punishment, retribution, and deterrence. Philpott states:

> Across the world, religious actors have sought to shape transitional justice both at the level of official policy and in civil society, where they perform trauma healing, conflict resolution, reconciliation practices, and other forms of peacebuilding in communities (Ibidem, p. 153).

Philpott points to examples of the relevance of faith-based organizations in several post-conflict situations, such as Rwanda, South Africa, the former Yugoslavia, various countries in Central and South America, etc.

In a volume entitled *"God's Century"* (Toft et al. 2011) a similar argument is developed, resting on two theses. The first states that "a dramatic and worldwide increase in the political influence of religion has occurred in roughly the past forty years" and the second states that the variation of kinds of "political influence of religion" is rooted in the variation in "political theologies," that is the religion's or an individual believer's understanding of the relationship between religion and the wider society and the world (Toft et al. 2011, p. 11).

Given that religious commitment, coupled with social engagement remains a vital force throughout the world, it is incumbent upon those concerned about and involved in the criminal justice system to take religion and faith-based organizations seriously as partners, assets, and collaborators in the efforts to prevent crime, rehabilitate prisoners, promote restoration, address the needs of victims, provide opportunities that reduce recidivism.

With the foregoing in mind, the following recommendations are offered:

- Recognize religion as a social fact analogous to other sectors of society such as civil society organizations, private sector businesses, political parties, social activist organizations;
- Develop increased religious literacy, particularly greater awareness of the religious worldviews of citizens in the relevant community;
- Recognize that one does not need to be a believer, nor does one need to admire believers to understand and respect the social value and reality of religion and its impact on citizens in a wide variety of ways;
- Encourage diversity of faith-based programs that enhance the efforts of criminal justice professionals working to prevent crime, rehabilitate prisoners, decrease violence, and promote constructive law abiding behaviors;
- Cultivate partnership between the law enforcement professionals and religious leaders in the community, and schedule period meetings to discuss ways in which the partners can understand, respect and support one another;
- Understand the value of religions as representing a necessary ingredient of a community's social capital;
- Encourage increased collaboration and partnership between FBOs and municipal law enforcement agencies;
- Encourage increased collaboration and partnerships between FBOs and United Nations agencies that address issues of criminal justice, including the UNODC;
- Establish at the United Nations a Council, a Commission or an Agency that consists of representatives of Faith-Based Organizations with a mandate to promote partnership and support of the UN mission as outlined in its charter.

In 2019, a Coalition of Faith-Based Organizations was established to pursue stronger and more constructive partnerships not only among the faith-based organizations dedicated to crime prevention and criminal justice, but also to encourage closer working relationships with the United Nations Office of Drugs and Crime. A series of programs have been convened, starting in Vienna in May of 2019 during the 28th Session of the Commission on Crime Prevention and Criminal Justice, and subsequent meetings have been convened in Vienna in October 2019, in San Francisco in November 2019, and during Crime Congress convened in April 2020 in Kyoto, Japan. In each setting a resolution, calling for enhanced partnerships between the FBOs and the UNODC, has been presented in hopes of gaining approval by the United Nations General Assembly in the near future.

References

A/RES/70/1 Transforming our world: the 2030 Agenda for Sustainable Development 25 September 2016.

Baumgart-Ochse, C., & Wolf, K. (2019). *Religious NGOs at the United Nations: Polarizers or mediators*. New York: Routledge.

Berger, P. (1999). *The desecularization of the world: Resurgent religion and world politics*. Washington, D.C.: Ethics and Public Policy Center.

Carothers, T., & O'Donahue, A. (2019, October 1). *How to understand the global spread of political polarization*. Carnegie Endowment for International Peace.

Churchill, W. (1950). *The second world war, Volume III: The grand alliance*. London: Penguin Classics.

Deenen, P. (2019). *Why liberalism failed*. New Haven: Yale University Press.

Glass, A. (2017, August 8). *Churchill, FDR meet off Newfoundland, August 9, 1941* Politico. https://politi.co/3fXZZJg

Grzymala-Busse, A. (2015). *Nations under god: How churches use moral authority to influence policy*. Princeton: Princeton University Press.

Guterres, A. (2017, July 14). *United Nations Secretary-General launches first action plan for religious leaders to prevent incitement to violence*. https://bit.ly/3dLldIa

Habermas, J. (2010). *An awareness of what is missing: Faith and reason in a post-secular age*. Cambridge: Polity Press.

Holy See Mission to the United Nations. (2019, December). https://bit.ly/2WvzjaT

Huntington, S. (1993). The class of civilizations? *Foreign Affairs, 72*(3), 22–48.

Huntington, S. (1997). *The clash of civilizations and the remaking of world order*. New York: Touchstone Books.

Johnson, B., & Schroeder, C. (2014). *Religion, crime and criminal justice. Criminology and criminal justice, communities and crime*. Oxford: Oxford University Press. Online Publication.

Kennedy, P. (2006). *The Parliament of Man: The past present and future of the United Nations*. New York: Random House.

Nelson, P. (2019). Encouraging active citizen voices on international policy? The record of U.S. faith-based NGOs. *The Review of Faith and International Affairs, 17*(2), 13–25.

Obiezu, E. (2019). *Seeking global justice and peace: Catholic inspired NGOs at the United Nations*. Washington, D.C.: Pacem in Terris Press.

Pedersen, K. (2010). Sri Chinmoy's work at the United Nations: Spirituality and the power of silence. *CrossCurrents, 60*(3), 339–351.

Plesch, D. (2011). *America, Hitler and the UN*. New York: Tauris Press.

Roosevelt, F. (1944). *D-Day Prayer*. New York: Franklin Delano Roosevelt Presidential Library and Museum. https://bit.ly/2yX6Lht

Rose, G. (2019, September/October). *Autocracy now. Foreign Affairs*.

Rossiter, C. (1949). The political philosophy of F. D. Roosevelt: A challenge to scholarship. *The Review of Politics, 11*(1), 87–95.

Schlesinger, S. (2003). *Act of creation: The founding of the United Nations*. Cambridge: Westview Press.

Tennyson, A. (2008). *The works of Alfred Lord Tennyson*. London: Wordsworth Editions Limited.

Thomas, S. (2005). *The global resurgence of religion and the transformation of international relations: The struggle for the soul of international relations*. New York: Macmillan.

Toft, M., Philpott, D., & Shah, T. (2011). *God's century: Resurgent religion and global politics*. New York: Norton.

United Nations Development Programme. (2014). *UNDP guide on engaging with faith-based organizations and religious leaders*. New York: UNDP Bureau for Policy and Programme Support.

Walzer, M. (2015). *The paradox of liberation: Secular revolutions and religious counterrevolutions*. New Haven: Yale University Press.

Thomas Walsh is the Chairman of the Universal Peace Federation, and Chairman of the Sunhak Peace Prize Foundation. With academic training in the field of Religious Studies and Ethics, he earned his Ph.D. at Vanderbilt University. He has been a teacher, author and editor, with specialization in areas of interfaith relations, religious studies, religion and peace, philosophy and social theory. He serves on the board of trustees of the University of Bridgeport (Connecticut, USA), Vice Chair of the International Council of the World Association of Non-Governmental Organizations, and on the board of directors of The Washington Times. He is Executive Editor of Dialogue and Alliance, a scholarly interfaith journal. He has contributed to and edited more than twenty books related to interfaith, peacebuilding and renewal of the United Nations; among these volumes are Renewing the United Nations and Building a Culture of Peace and The Millennium Declaration of the United Nations: A Response from Civil Society. E-mail: twalsh@upf.org.

Epilogue

Sławomir Redo and Helmut Kury

*Only there, where the tailor, soap maker, baker and every other one is convinced that the fate of State depends on his craftsmanship and skills - only there everything turns into good.—Istvan Szechenyi, Hungarian Montesquieuan political theorist and writer (1791–1860) (*A. Berzericzy (1907) (ed.), *Prof. Istvan Szechenyi munkaibyl [From the works of Earl Istvan Szechenyi].* Budapest, p. 30.)

Abstract The Epilogue reflects on various interpretations and aspects of justice interwoven in the contributions to this book. Against the baseline of what is considered in the United Nations as "justice", the text addresses first Artificial

Caveat: Although we tried in this Epilogue as meticulously as we could to credit all the statements with names of their authors, in the course of this work we have appropriated the insights of numerous other experts commenting in mass media on coronavirus pandemic that we can no longer manage to list them all. However, we should mention here as inspirators of some arguments in this Epilogue Professor Małgorzata Jacyno and Prof. Marcin Król (both from the University of Warsaw, Poland), who respectively pointed out the pandemic's criminogenic implications of "sanitary regime" and of redundancy of people, and also Paweł Szypulski (Greenpeace, Poland) regarding his thoughts on "Green Deal." Finally, Sławomir Redo, one of the undersigned Co-Editors, former United Nations official and presently member of the United Nations Studies Association and the American Society of Criminology, has been appointed for 2020–2022 as a titular "Wenlan Scholar & Chair Professor of United Nations Law" at the Zhongnan University of Economics and Law (Wuhan, China). This information about the Co-Editor is provided in lieu of the statement of conflict of interests. The opinions expressed in this Epilogue are the authors' own. They do not reflect the views of any of the above entities.

S. Redo (✉)
United Nations Studies Association, Vienna, Austria
e-mail: s@redo.net

H. Kury
Max Planck-Institute for Foreign and International Penal Law, Freiburg, Germany

H. Kury, S. Redo (eds.), *Crime Prevention and Justice in 2030*,
https://doi.org/10.1007/978-3-030-56227-4_35

Intelligence, then goes into spiritual justice, and, finally, focuses on the secular justice as a part of its administration and delivery in Member States of the United Nations. After reflecting on these "Heavens-to-Earth" interpretations of justice, the authors formulate recommendations involving a "common language of justice." With it the United Nations—a global ecumenical organization—celebrating its seventy-fifth anniversary may respond to the challenges involved in the implementation of the 2030 United Nations Sustainable Development Agenda and beyond, as far as democracy and the rule of law are concerned. In this regard, at the domestic and international levels the coronavirus pandemic opened a new legal scenario ("the Day After"). At its heart is "Peace, Justice and Strong Institutions"—the cross-cutting goal of the 2030 Agenda.

Keywords Common language of justice · Democracy · Faith-based organizations · Human rights · Justice · Pandemic · Peace · Rule of law · Spirit · Sustainable development · United Nations

1 Introduction

We started drafting this Epilogue several months ago—before the outbreak of coronavirus pandemic. All other contributions to this book in honor of the United Nations have been delivered earlier but actualized insofar possible during the pandemic's first wave. Although in terms of lethality so far (and hopefully) incomparable with the three 1918–1920 "Spanish flu" pandemic waves, in front of our eyes unfolds a new worldview. Against it we thus reflected on the table of content of this book.

In particular, we wondered if its contributions have become pre-historic. To the contrary, we found that in the current time some of them may be glaring examples of the humane and effective approach to crime prevention and criminal justice or to human rights—the approach that should be resumed and further enhanced by strengthening institutions which pronounce them. Equality, inclusiveness, and progress in general interact with one another, but all depend on people's decisions and actions. The new inimical "sanitary regime" (Małgorzata Jacyno) makes them even more pertinent to what should come next in our interpretations as a reinvigorated effort to implement the United Nations Declaration of Human Rights and the 2030 United Nations Sustainable Development Agenda. This hopefully should inspire and reinvigorate this book's readers to carry on with advancing social justice issues according to the United Nations creed in and precepts of social progress.

As the reference to "creed" may suggest, this book with its Epilogue is somewhat "poetic." We had already pursued this genre in the Epilogue to our previous book (Kury and Redo 2018). Then we backed it by Giambattista Vico's (1668–1744) "poetic" interpretation of human development. This time we tried to use this genre more extensively—to connect political technology with political theology of crime prevention and criminal justice, and to capture the involvement of broadly conceived art and politics. For this process, Victoria Kahn (2013) coined the term "*poiesis.*" In this book it demonstrates itself via three facets: the reproductions of the United Nations-owned paintings; the perusal of non-academic texts from the United Nations and the outside world; the non-secular/interfaith aspects of justice in the implementation of the UN human rights agenda.

As far as the question of justice is concerned, this Epilogue is the final example of this approach. The Epilogue was written based on scientific facts and figures, academic analyses, philosophical treatises, the United Nations and other political accounts, poems, novels, and journalistic texts. It is a manifesto in honor of the United Nations which seeks to reflect its spirit and the Organization's *raison d'être.*

2 What Is Justice in the United Nations?

The question whether justice is a phantom or a scientific fact, whether it is artificial or natural has seized the attention of very many authors. The question has never been easy to answer, if at all is answerable. After all, it dates to more than 40 centuries of law, philosophy, and religion, to Hammurabi, Confucius, Socrates, Buddha, Jesus Christ, and Mohammed, to their followers and critics, to apostles and apostates. This dilemma has much longer history than 75-year old Organization which addresses "justice" in its own way. Hence, this genre is relevant to the book in honor of the United Nations devoted to its crime prevention, human rights, and justice policies in-between their secular and non-secular incarnations.

Mamdouh Bey Riaz, the delegate of Egypt to the 1945 San Francisco UN-founding conference argued: "If we want to keep peace and security only, we would not differ much from Hitler, who was trying to do so and who, as a matter of fact succeeded" (UN Doc. 1006, p. 13). Therefore, in the preamble to the Charter and the Charter itself there are various references to justice, but no definition.

An authoritative commentary to the United Nations Charter points that: "justice ... means something different from international law (...) and (...) refers to natural law" (Simma et al. 2002, I, p. 36). Kofi Annan, as the seventh UN Secretary General (1997–2006) referred to justice in a procedural manner. It is "an ideal of accountability and fairness in the protection and vindication of rights and the prevention and punishment of wrongs" (S/2004/616, para. 7).

Several contributors to this book (*Pływaczewski*, *Duda*, & *Narodowska*; *Srinivasan* and *Prakash*; *David*) emphasized that human justice extends from people to flora and fauna—to nature exactly. At least 65% of recent major disease outbreaks have animal origins (IOM 2009, p. 1), but humankind has alienated itself from nature. There is no coincidence then that since 2009 the United Nations promotes living in "Harmony with Nature" (Redo 2018a, b, p. 716).

2.1 Artificial/Predictive Justice

The copy right for the term "artificial justice" should be credited to David Hume (1711–1776). For him, the "sense of justice and injustice is not deriv'd from nature, but arises artificially, tho' necessarily from education, and human conventions" (Hume 1739/1896, p. 251). Notwithstanding the fact that his name is in the records on the Universal Declaration of Human Rights/UDHR (see *Zhang*), it is not his understanding of justice this Epilogue is concerned about.

What is here meant is about alternatively and ominously labelled "predictive justice": "dangerously misleading, as such systems make predictions, but not judicial decisions. Judicial decisions require, as a minimum standard, justifications based on an assessment of the relevant facts and applicable regulations. AI systems make statistical correlations and their forecasts are just the result of those correlations. Hence, it would only be proper to speak of actual predictive justice if the systems were to provide justifications in terms of facts and laws" (Contini 2019).

Three texts in this book (*Breczko, Filipkowski, & Kraśnicka*; *Spapens*; *Rutkowski*) address the various aspects of Artificial Intelligence and freedom.

From the text by *Breczko, Filipkowski, & Kraśnicka* "Ethics and the Development of Artificial Intelligence - Challenges and Dilemmas in the Context of the 2030 United Nations Agenda for Sustainable Development" we would like to highlight the "trolley dilemma." The authors bring this moral dilemma up to the current challenges of "machine ethics" involving a driverless car: "Imagine some years into the future, you are a passenger in an autonomous vehicle, happily driving along a city street. Ahead of you a traffic light turns red, but a mechanical failure in your car means you're unable to stop. A collision is inevitable, but your car has a choice: should it swerve off the road into a concrete wall, causing certain death to anyone inside the vehicle? Or should it carry on going, saving the lives of anyone inside but killing the pedestrians now crossing this road?"

While we invite the reader to deliberate this question, we would also like to back it with the dilemma involving an old railway carriage (trolley): it lost its breaks owing to a mechanical failure and is rolling towards a group of senior citizens just crossing the tracks. You stand beside a railway track. Their lives can be saved when you pull the lever to send the carriage down a sidetrack where one young man is standing. What is right, what is wrong? What do you do?

In the background lingers the question of the UN relevance: whom the Organization serves? In the book in its honor this question should be answered.

Two findings may help to answer. **First**, research studies demonstrated that most people, if asked what to do, would pull the lever. **Second**, when, however, the scenario involves pushing a man off a footbridge to stop the trolley rolling below, the reaction depends whether the pusher was guided by own intuition or by learning what's right or wrong (Cao et al. 2017).

This was found by the researchers studying the so called "Asian disease problem", worth recalling in the time of coronavirus pandemic. In this now classic dilemma created by Tversky and Kahneman (1981), the U.S. government is preparing to respond to the outbreak of an Asian disease which could result in 600 deaths. The Government has two options: to implement plan A that would save (positive frame) 200 people (400 would die, negative frame) or to implement plan B, in which there is a one-third possibility of saving (positive frame) all 600 people (nobody dies, negative frame) and a two-third possibility of saving no one (all die, negative frame). Using different narratives to describe the same outcomes leads to totally different decisions. In sum, people tend to be conservative in the positive frame and risky in the negative frame. The kind of pursued narrative determined the participant's responses. Number of saved lives matters (Cao et al. 2017, p. 91).

Thus, the answer on the question of the UN relevance: the UN serves the greatest number of people in need of greater social justice, people entitled to larger freedom. Kofi Annan who re-highlighted the UN Charter's "larger freedom," wrote that it includes the basic political freedoms to which all human beings are entitled. But larger freedom goes beyond them, encompassing what the U.S. President Franklin Roosevelt called "freedom from want" and "freedom from fear." Annan added that while enlarging freedom is imperative, the side effects of globalization with unfair trade terms and abuse of technological advances thwart the progress of freedom because of growing insecurity (Annan 2005, p. 64).

True, the Charter, the UDHR, the 2030 Agenda are the living examples of the United Nations' importance in the world. True, that saving succeeding generations from the scourge of wars is the most laudable objective, however difficult pursuing of peace is.

It is obvious that the succeeding generation may write its own future by improving the lot of the aging population. But belaboring the obvious aside, behind this lofty objective hide realities. In this book they are explored by *Kratcoski & Edelbacher* in the chapter "Two Ends of Aging and Crime Prevention." While for obvious reasons its authors could not criminologically address the impact of coronavirus on the senior citizens, as this book's Co-Editors we can do so in its Epilogue.

To our mind comes again the "Asian dilemma." Updated insofar it currently involves deciding whether or not to administer essential medical treatment by a life-saving, but in short supply, respirator ("ventilator") to many more than "just" 600 patients, the present global SDGs dilemma involves the following dramatic question. It reads: How in the SDGs' terms calling for achieving universal health coverage, provision of access to safe and effective medicines and vaccines for all, and ensuring health and well-being for all, including a bold commitment to end the epidemics of communicable diseases by 2030 (SDG 3), the right to life of senior citizens particularly vulnerable to the lethal pneumonic illness caused by coronavirus, may not be violated by discriminatory application of life-saving laws and policies (SDG 16.b)?

Population aging is a major global trend. It affects all countries, albeit at a different pace and levels. Increased longevity is a significant achievement of human development due to the improved health, greater longevity, and lower mortality. However, nowadays, exactly the latter fact receives a great deal of attention because of mortality's eugenical connotation. Originally credited to antisemitic programs of euthanasia and ultimately, of course, to the Nazi Second

World War death camps, in fact, eugenics was a popular theme in the pre-war science and public health policies. It blossomed in parts of Asia and Latin America, Northern America (Canada, USA); in Europe, inter alia, in the United Kingdom, and Scandinavia, where in Sweden it had been discontinued in the 1970s (Kevles 1999). As the same author concludes: "The revelations of the [H]olocaust strengthened the moral objections to eugenics [. . .], and so did the increasing worldwide discussion of human rights, a foundation for which was the Universal Declaration of Human Rights that the General Assembly of the United Nations adopted and proclaimed in 1948" (Ibidem, p. 438).

In this book the Dutch author *Spapens* adds his own moral objections to another instance of violation of the UN human rights. To understand well his text on "Surveillance and the impossible search for ideal behaviour" it is enough to recall the devastating genocidal impact the Netherlands population registration system had in the hands of Nazi occupiers in the 1940s (Bentzen and Svantensson 2017, p. 248). Hence this quotation corroborating *Spapen's* concerns:

> For example, in the Netherlands a population registration system was established in part to conduct social research, which was subsequently adapted in 1941 for the apprehension of Dutch Jews who were then deported to death camps. The death rate among Dutch Jews (73%) was dramatically higher than that among Jews in France (25%) and Belgium (40%), as well as Jewish refugees living in the Netherlands during the Nazi occupation [. . .] [T]this was largely due to the fact that the registration system in the Netherlands facilitated the apprehension of Dutch Jews. Critically, the point here is not that the collection of a particular form of data resulted in human rights abuses, but that their availability facilitated such abuses (O'Doherty et al. 2016, p. 9).

Two other specific and current human rights concerns must be noted. **First**, that surveillance technology is spreading at a faster rate to a wider range of countries than experts have commonly held. Sadly, that was to be expected. In 2013, in the first Report of the UN Special Rapporteur on the promotion and protection of the right to freedom of opinion and expression, he recalled the foresight opinion in *Olmstead v. United States, 277 U.S. 438 (1928)* of Justice Brandeis of the United States Supreme Court: "Ways may someday be developed by which the government, without removing papers from secret drawers, can reproduce them in court, and by which it will be enabled to expose to a jury the most intimate occurrence of the home" (A/HRC/23/40, para. 16, ft. 2).

Nowadays, according to the analysis published by the Carnegie Endowment Foundation for International Peace, a non-governmental organization (NGO) in consultative status with the United Nations Economic and Social Council:

- At least 75 out of 176 countries globally are actively using AI technologies for surveillance purposes. This includes: smart city/safe city platforms (56 countries), facial recognition systems (64 countries), and smart policing (52 countries);
- Liberal democracies are major users of AI surveillance. The index shows that 51% of advanced democracies deploy AI surveillance systems. In contrast, 37% of closed autocratic states, 41% of electoral autocratic/competitive autocratic states, and 41% of electoral democracies/illiberal democracies deploy AI surveillance technology. Governments in full democracies deploy a range of

surveillance technology, from safe city platforms to facial recognition cameras. This does not inevitably mean that democracies abuse these systems. The most important factor determining whether governments deploy this technology for excessive control and possible repression is the quality of their governance;
- Governments in autocratic and semi-autocratic countries are more prone to abuse AI surveillance than governments in liberal democracies. Other governments with poor human rights records pursue AI surveillance in more limited ways to reinforce control. Yet all governments run the risk of abusing AI surveillance technology to obtain certain political objectives;
- There is a strong relationship between a country's military expenditures and a government's use of AI surveillance systems: forty of the world's top fifty military spending countries (based on cumulative military expenditures) also use AI surveillance technology (Feldstein 2019, p. 2).

The above NGO analysis suggests also, that among the five Permanent Members of the United Nations Security Council, the United Kingdom (Montesquieu's inspirational example for the division of powers), and France (his original and intellectual cradle) are less often quoted in it than—in a descending order of AI-based surveillance developments—China, Russia and the USA. However, French, and British high-level military expenditures may further qualify this association. At any rate, country-by-country reviews conducted by the United Nations Human Rights Committee leave no doubt, that almost in any country within its focus there is an ample ground for concern, at least about surveillance and privacy protection (Nyst and Falchetta 2017, p. 110).

Be it as it may, the above statistics do not differentiate between legitimate and unlawful AI-based surveillance. In the absence of this differentiation, one may not fully recognize the following assessment by the UN Special Rapporteur on the promotion and protection of the right to freedom of opinion and expression alerted by:

> Credible reporting [...] that the Government of China, using a combination of facial recognition technology and surveillance cameras throughout the country, looks exclusively for Uighurs based on their appearance and keeps records of their comings and goings for search and review (A/HRC/41/35, para. 12).

In all fairness, not less alerting to the United Nations may be even more credible AI-surveillance court cases involving Hungary, Ireland, Russia and USA signalling mass e-surveillance and the lack of accountability of State.[1] In an apparent reaction to such cases (Nyst and Falchetta 2017, pp. 114–115) since 2013 the United Nations General Assembly has every year in changing cross-regional configurations of Member States, but always with (co)sponsoring Austria, France, Germany and

[1]See further in: Nyst and Falchetta (2017), pp. 114–115: the European Court of Human Rights (*Zakharov v. Russia*; *Szabó and Vissy v. Hungary*), the European Court of Justice (*Schrems v. Data Protection Commissioner*). See also: T. McCarthy, D. Smith. US government files civil lawsuit against Snowden over publication of memoir (The Guardian, 17 September 2019, https://bit.ly/2VvfU8m).

Switzerland, expressed through the resolutions adopted without vote its position regarding "the right to privacy in the digital age."

According to the UN position, AI-based surveillance may also extend to interference provided for under the domestic law (HRC Communication No. 499/1992 *Toonan v. Australia*). This implies that law's conflict with international law. Consequently, on the strength of this brilliant jurisprudence with ideal justice undertone absent in the UN treaty law, one cannot scientifically prove whether or not the global concern regarding terrorism and the growth of AI-based surveillance is fully justified by States which apply it.

This raises two questions involving the 1966 International Covenant on Civil and Political Rights/ICCPR: When indeed the protection of national security, public order (*ordre public*), public health or morals require surveillance (Art. 19 § 3) which may be condemned in religion or private ethics as unjust and immoral? How during *ordre public* would qualify itself the use of AI-surveillance during the epidemy of SARS-CoV-2/COVID-19 virus which in 2020 broke out in Wuhan (China)?

There should be clear standards for predictive analytics, predictive policing, and justice. A good example for the United Nations standard-setting may be the electronic "health coding"—a kind of an immunity certificate. After lifting the lockdown, it was introduced as a mobile phone application in Wuhan and elsewhere in China. In essence, integrated data on travel (from bus, train, and flight bookings), contact with known, suspected or confirmed cases, and self-reported symptoms generate the traffic light colors—red, yellow or green—which indicates how high-risk the individual may be. Depending on the accumulated, integrated and actualized data stored on a mobile phone of its owner, the individual with the scanned or personally verified code may or not access respective public facilities, e.g., transport, the supermarket, enter and leave town residential compound (Lee 2020).

Since in public health picture everybody is at the same time pandemic's "perpetrator" and "victim", comparison to criminological "profiling" is limited. However, in both situations this really is a typical conservative approach to arrest social change. Imagine a sizeable impact of climate change on agriculture on migration in any country, whether sending or receiving: What then will be left from that arrest, if social unrest occurs?

This impact of electronic surveillance grows now. "If" is only a question of time and place. Would only the latter group be involved in social unrest? Provoke it? Head it? Whom?

It is this conservative and counterproductive context in which we read the alert of 15 UN experts, and several other experts from the two human rights working groups. They called upon States not abuse emergency measures to suppress human rights and "remain steadfast in maintaining a human rights-based approach to regulating this pandemic, in order to facilitate the emergence of healthy societies with rule of law and human rights protections" (OHCHR 2020).

Whether or not the above call remains in vein, the **second** concern indeed regards the presence or absence of the rule of law when it comes to legitimately employing AI-based surveillance. That analysis clearly showed that countries in the Gulf, East

Asia, and South/Central Asia are leading here, even though European countries are following suit (Feldstein 2019, p. 8).

It appears that the impact of the rule of law on effective controlling AI surveillance techniques and instruments in either case is rather perfunctory. The UN Special Rapporteur observed, that: "Judicial involvement that meets international standards relating to independence, impartiality and transparency can help to make it more likely that the overall statutory regime will meet the minimum standards that international human rights law requires [to control digital surveillance]. At the same time, judicial involvement in oversight should not be viewed as a panacea; in several countries, judicial warranting or review of the digital surveillance activities of intelligence and/or law enforcement agencies have amounted effectively to an exercise in rubber-stamping" (A/HRC/27/37, para. 48).

The United Nations General Assembly condemned unlawful or arbitrary surveillance and interceptions of communications as "highly intrusive acts" that interfere with fundamental human rights (A/RES/68/167; A/RES/71/199).[2] The United Nations Office on Drugs and Crime (UNODC 2018) added:

> [t]he main problem associated with digitization and predictive justice is accountability. The new pervasive role of the digital systems requires the development of new forms of accountability to preserve the fundamental values of judicial integrity, impartiality and transparency. The main answer is that technology must be aligned with the Bangalore principles of judicial conduct.[3] If the Bangalore principles must guide judicial behaviour, they must also direct the functioning of information systems and AI. In this way ICTs [Information and Communication Technology] will be used for justice and not against justice and the global standards that have been built in two hundred years.

Finally, *Rutkowski* discusses some other than *Breczko et al.* aspects of "machine ethics." For him *Homo deus* is a master of justice. *Rutkowski's* scientific vision receives in the pandemic additional substantiation through the growing role of cyberspace logistics and communication. Without it, billions of people could not work. They could not discuss and exchange ideas, attend schools, resort to medical advice and other counselling, including attending religious services.

Past the pandemics these developments will leave their mark, in some cases enduring. *Rutkowski* therefore asks, if they will reconceptualize what "partnership" is, and what it will mean in terms of respect of interests other than the interests of cyberspace itself. While for quoted by him Yuval Harari these developments will guide *Homo deus* "non-consciously" (as if chaotically), for *Rutkowski* they will be his "self-conscious" project and product.

Rutkowski also asks, if cyberspace will have its own "views"? How much will it be attached to them and how determined to defend them. What "ambitions" would

---

[2]See further Chander and Land (2014), Nyst and Falchetta (2017).

[3]A set of six core values of the judiciary—Independence, Impartiality, Integrity, Propriety, Equality, Competence, and Diligence, to standardize ethical conduct of judges, developed by them in 2002 and self-proclaimed by international judiciary as a global legal instrument under the United Nations aegis (see further: UNODC 2007).

motivate it? Will it need to have "offspring"—its own hereditary intelligence? Will it form a need for eternal existence—immortality?

Thus far, such questions were answered by great intellectuals—sages, thinkers, philosophers, spiritual leaders. But hardly any of them had to measure up with the dilemma of moral autonomy and integrity of a "digitally native" individual (Palfrey and Gasser 2009) whose "root of soul" (Dukaj 2020) is now within the reach of algorithms. If they will be owned by a caste of owners of algorithms (Harari 2018), then intellectual freedom traditionally understood as an exercise in analogue thinking will suffer. If and when copying human mind will eventually be possible, then it may be replicated in various artificial *intelligents*.

2.2 Divine Justice

To any religion, whether monotheistic or not, to every denomination within this or that religion, in fact to every philosophical current important will be to answer the question whether its sense of justice remains natural or not. This invites our attention to the AI interest of the Holy See. In early 2020, Pope Francis addressed at the Vatican the AI conference on the ethical development of algorithms. The Roman-Catholic Church has now committed itself to AI as a tool for its social teaching. It regards the dignity of the person, justice, subsidiarity, and solidarity (Gomes 2020).

As recalled in the Prologue, António Guterres, the United Nations Secretary-General stated "I firmly believe in the power of faith leaders to shape our world for good." In this book five contributors (*Bertrand; David*; *Platzer*; *Redo* in "The relevance"; *Walsh*) went beyond positive-law arguments involved in the implementation of the UDHR and the 2030 Agenda into the internal human elements of peace and justice relevant to spiritual and development needs that drive individual behaviors for more than 80% of people in the world (*Platzer* in this book). That is because world religions are being recognized in their great variety as more than simply a belief in a transcendent deity or a means to an afterlife (Ottuh et al. 2014, p. 197).

In both declarations there is nothing that would expressively call on the faith-based organizations (FBOs) to be involved either in attending the various rights in the UDHR or meeting the goals of the Agenda. Yet it is clear that the world religions are being recognized in their great variety as more than simply a belief in a transcendent deity or a means to an afterlife.

The Agenda's call to "leave nobody behind" opens to any FBO regardless of its spiritual orientation to pursue its humanitarianism through distributive justice. However, given the concurrent "donor proselytism" careful methodological reflection is needed in considering how in the interfaith spirit distributive justice can engage ecumenical potential of each religious tradition in response to particular aspects of the Agenda.

2.3 *Secular Justice*

The UDHR serves as the first step in promoting justice by outlining the basic rights that humanity should enjoy. Almost all contributors to this book addressed the implementation of the rights enshrined in the UDHR (see the articles). The UDHR's preamble states that human rights are the "foundation" of justice "in the world." The UDHR reflects a secular concept of justice, brought in through the back door by recognizing the secular character of human rights.

Zhang informs, that some UDHR framers "advocated the inclusion of God or the Creator as an indication of the source of human rights. Chinese delegate Peng-chun Chang reminded that China, which accounts for a large proportion of the world's population, "has a different ideology and tradition from Christianity. These thoughts include good manners, etiquette and courtesy, and understanding of others, but the representative of China did not advocate must include them all in the Declaration." He hoped, the report continues, "that colleagues could show the same understanding, break through religious barriers and withdraw the metaphysical amendments to article 1. In his view, since Spinoza and Locke the idea of religious inclusion has existed in Europe. Western countries should have a liberal attitude towards religious beliefs and should not impose believes to others." It may only be added, that other drafters had not to be really convinced about this argument, because "The motif running throughout [the drafting process was] that the war and the ideology as practiced by Hitler were in themselves enough to convince them of the truth of the rights of the Declaration" (Morsink 1993, p. 358). *Zhang* concludes her review by the following quoting: "This point is illustrated in Confucian advocacy of "harmony in diversity", not to impose on others what you do not desire."

Three reflections ensue from the latter recommendation known as the Golden Rule.

First, despite its global prominence in philosophy, religion, and law, there are conservative and liberal understandings of reciprocity. Yutang Lin (separately acknowledged by *Zhang*) argues in his book "My Country and My People" (1935), that the conservative understanding of Confucian advocacy of the Golden Rule (ruler to subject, father to son, husband to wife, elder to younger and friend to friend), "omitted out of the social relationships man's social obligations toward the stranger, and great and catastrophic was the omission. Samaritan virtue was unknown and practically discouraged. Theoretically, it was provided for in the 'doctrine of reciprocity' [...] But this relationship toward "others" was not one of the five cardinal relationships, and not so clearly defined [...] In the end, as it worked out, the family became a walled castle outside which everything is legitimate loot" (Lin 1935, p. 172).

Another pre-Second World War Chinese account of the Golden Rule went even further. In 1936, Liang Qǐ Chao, a prominent thinker in modern Chinese history, attributed to this conservative understanding of direct reciprocity a Chinese person's lack of "civic morality" (*gōng dé*; 公德) and sense of obligation to society (Quoted after Gao and Ting-Toomey 1998, p. 14).

The interpretation of this basic principle of human co-existence and cooperation is more confusing now than before and after the Second World War. This is not only because of the confounded post-1945 and 2016–2019 waves of refugees and irregular/undocumented migrants which showed that reciprocity intergenerationally basically had little to do with accepting the newcomers,[4] but also because of the 2020 coronavirus pandemic. In such critical circumstances Golden Rule is rather less universal than Good Samaritan Rule.[5]

However, more universal than both is fraud/cheating and greed. Two widely known and particularly pernicious examples from the pandemic discredit the assumption that commerce globally civilizes the mores:

- Sale of protective masks through a sophisticated EUR 15 million worth fraud scheme using compromised emails, advance-payment fraud and money laundering has been uncovered by financial institutions and authorities across Germany, Ireland, and the Netherlands. The masks purportedly complying with the European Union's CE (*Conformité Européenne*) standard indicating conformity of a product with health, safety, and environmental protection standards for products sold within the European Economic Area (EEA) have eventually reached the 17 EEA countries from China (Interpol 2020);
- Apparent failure of the Austrian regional and city authorities in Bad Ischgl/Tyrol (a world-famous ski resort) to respond in time to international coronavirus warnings. The subsequently resulting coronavirus infections of more than 800 Austrians and up to twice as many people abroad, particularly in Germany and Scandinavian countries were credited to have their origin in that location (Bell 2020).

Second, the above examples suggest that greed and egoism dominate everywhere. Therefore, it is also opportune to say, that—historically—egoism and self-preservation of people and peoples has always been *a priori* axiomatic but followed by cooperation. Case studies in self-preservation ranging from "natural experiments" involving failed states through illegal mining to shipwrecks, hurricanes, and leprosies led to the conclusion that eventually cooperation and the pursuit of justice prevailed in the victimized groups of people (Robinson 2013). This is very well theoretically explained by Hugo Grotius (see *Redo* in *The Relevance*...) and confirmed by Montesquieu (see the Prologue and below).

But for philosophers, politicians and other Eastern activists Mencius—the most liberal and committed to Confucius' teaching primary follower, advocate of "universal love"—may be more credible with his "no man is devoid of a heart sensitive to the suffering of others" (Mencius 2003, 2A: 6). So at least he seemed to be for Peng-chun Chang—the Chinese drafter of the UDHR, mentioned by *Zhang*. For

[4]See more in Ickiewicz-Sawicka and Borkowska (2018), pp. 803–833; Redo (2018a, b), pp. 697–720.

[5]Good Samaritan Rule does not imply any expectation of reciprocity by the assisted person or country.

other framers, current diplomats, intellectuals, and activists Good Samaritan Rule implies "a concrete anchoring for love [. . .] and indicates an 'all embracing reach of solidarity'"—Western Christian liberal understanding of that rule (Rowland 2007, p. 43). Jacques Maritain, the French UDHR drafter and eminent neo-Thomist philosopher, said: "[e]very great age of Culture receives its deepest meaning and direction from a particular constellation of spiritual factors or dominating ideas; let us say, from a particular historical heaven" (*Redo* in "The Relevance. . ."). However ideologically distant from one another Eastern and Western philosophies can be, the lockdown (forced isolation) policy caused by the pandemic illustrated that the personal sense of larger freedom at this time is the same wherever across the world this policy applies.[6]

Third, on the above heavenly East-West note accepting "harmony in diversity" and in keeping with the content of our book one may see a default United Nations understanding what the Golden Rule is for a just and humane treatment of prisoners—a special group of people forcefully isolated from society. That criminologically-relevant Golden Rule "Do unto others what you would like them to do unto you" was originally formulated by Elisabeth Fry (1780–1845), British prison reformer, a Quaker, a Christian philanthropist, known as "The angel of prisons" (Fairhurst 1996, p. 5).

[6]For the European Union's millennials, the suspension of the Schengen agreement allowing borderless travel must be especially prohibitive. This memento should be sobering in addressing populistic calls for reinstating "small fatherlands." Indeed, pandemic demonstrated that "[t]he EU's fundamental flaw is that it is incapable of discharging the protective functions of a state" (Gray 2020). A state may be ruled by law. The EU in its future interest to survive may only exercise the rule of law. It can do this to protect larger freedom in any "small fatherlands" that indeed wish to remain its genuine member and demonstrate this by their rule-of-law performance satisfactory to other EU members.

UN Photo/Milton Grant

The mosaic, entitled "The Golden Rule" by American artist Norman Rockwell, was presented to the United Nations as a gift by First Lady Nancy Reagan on behalf of the United States and is installed in the United Nations Headquarters in New York, USA. The mosaic depicts people of different nationalities standing together with the words "Do unto others as you would have them do unto you" inscribed on it. Artwork Courtesy of the Norman Rockwell Family Agency.

After her visits to Paris' and London's prisons, she candidly shared her observations with French and British officials. Shocked by the sexual exploitation of female inmates by male guards in the Paris' St. Lazare prison, she advised Philippe I, the King of France: "When thee builds a prison, thee had better build with the thought ever in thy mind that thee and thy children may occupy the cells" (Ibidem, p. 251). Having visited London's Newgate prison she read to Sir Robert Peele, and his Cabinet a biblical story concerning the gallows built by Haman, described in the Book of Esther (7: 10):

"On the king's orders, Haman was hanged from the 50-cubit-high gallows that had originally been built by Haman himself." Then she added: "Thee must not shut out the sky from the prisoner; thee must build no dark cells - thy children may occupy them" (quoted after Hubbard 1897, p. 286).

Her advice impressed Sir Peele. He instituted prison reform.[7] Shortly after her death, in 1846 at the first International Penitentiary Congress in Frankfurt (Germany) attended by eminent prison experts and officials (all male), the reformist ideas from Belgian, British, French and other Western world prison administrators regarding children (then kept in solitary confinement) have paved the way to the gradual development of the global standard minimum rules for the treatment of prisoners. The rules were finally adopted in 1955 by the First United Nations Congress on Crime Prevention and the Treatment of Offenders (Redo 2012, pp. 43, 108).

Until this day some Governments have been less or more attentive to improving the lot of prisoners and to the implementation of the United Nations Standard Minimum Rules for the Treatment of Prisoners, since 2015 known as the Nelson Mandela Rules (A/RES/70/175). This is the context in which we now may recall the second section in this book. The first part of its title carries the UN 2030 Agenda's imperative of inclusive development "Leaving no one behind: Intergenerational vulnerability and educating for justice." Prison reform worldwide should be a part of inclusive development, otherwise the often catastrophic effects on families, especially children of prisoners are catalytic to their offspring—"the next generation of offenders." Hence, 4 almost self-explanatory, contributions by: *Kury* on "Prisoners and their Families – The Effects of Imprisonment on the Family"; with *Heße* on "Dealing with mental illness and violence in the (Youth-)Prison"; *Redo* and *Sawicki* "On Nelson Mandela Rule 63, Prisoner's Moral Development and the 2030 United Nations Sustainable World"; Manfred *Nowak* and *Manu Krishan* "The UN Global Study on Children Deprived of Liberty – The Role of Academia in 'Making the Invisible and Forgotten Visible'."

The word "almost" only prompts us to recall that in another book of ours "Women and Children as Victims and Offenders: Background, Prevention, Reintegration. Suggestions for Succeeding Generations" co-edited with Evelyn Shea (Springer 2016) its contributors have provided many insights into the treatment of prisoners, especially female inmates. But it seems to us that notwithstanding their vulnerability to abuse, female inmates are still not treated judiciously and fairly enough, as the case had been until the turn of the nineteenth–twentieth century with juvenile delinquents treated until then like adult prisoners (at least in the USA).

[7]But not Philippe I. In 1848, at the time of the "Spring of Nations", he fled to Britain. He lived there as "Mr. Smith" and died after two years.

2.4 Procedural/Restorative Justice

SDG 16.3 "Promote the rule of law at the national and international levels, and ensure equal access to justice for all" clearly acknowledges the rule of law and access to justice as integral parts of development. This book touches on procedural justice either by directly addressing the legitimacy of legal provisions enabling access to justice (e.g., *Rayejian Asli*)—or by dealing with its likewise pronounced form—restorative justice, about the philosophical origins of which is more in *Redo* ("The Relevance. . .").

Looking at the access to justice from the contemporary systemic perspective of the Sustainable Goal 16 ("Promote peaceful and inclusive societies for sustainable development, provide access to justice for all and build effective, accountable and inclusive institutions at all levels"—"Peace, Justice and Strong Institutions" for short) this very title implies that according to the United Nations interpretative rules "peace" and "sustainable development" are over "justice" in one or another form.

The subsumed under "Peace, Justice and Strong Institutions" SDG 16.3 does not make the fine difference between the rule of law as a governance instrument which should be driven by the division of powers, and by making individual judgements without involving courts of law. For "[j]ust as the rule of law has historically and philosophically been considered a central component of a legitimate governmental system, so too procedural justice is a central component of how individuals make judgments about the legitimacy of authorities" (Hollander-Blumoff and Tyler 2011, p. 2).

2.5 Distributive Justice

The UDHR's articles which deal with equality promote procedural justice, and those which deal with equity promote distributive justice. *Wijngaarde*, *Vinanchiarachi*, & *Readman* write about "Universal Basic Income (UBI) for Reducing Inequalities and Increasing Socio- economic Inclusion: A Proposal for a New Sustained Policy Perspective." Their text inscribes itself into this latter form of justice. Basic income as a guaranteed, unconditional amount of money, regardless of employment or social position raises a fundamental question whether someone's sustainable livelihood is acceptable when one does not have motivation to earn it, despite capacity and licit opportunities to do so. Moreover, the pandemic documents that a considerable part of people who lose jobs comes from the service sector. Since it is interconnected people of *doux commerce* (Montesquieu 2001), air transportation, tourism, sport, and recreation, just to name a few fields of service, are on the front line of redundancy. Preventing it in the post-pandemic time can only be successful when creative education and training opens for them new avenues for sustainable livelihood by giving them. That is the job of governments, educationists, educators, and trainers of trainers. The authors recommend: "Give a man a fish, and you feed him for a day. Teach a man to fish and you feed him for a lifetime." Teach him better methods of fishing and you can ensure sustainability of livelihoods for generations. No longer this will be then distributive but economic justice. Their advice draws on the paradigm of the 2030 Agenda. UBI can facilitate people to move beyond day-to-day subsistence, giving them the full responsibility to develop their potential and creativity. It may help to effectively address the imminent redundancy and ensuing from it crime.

Redo ("The Relevance...) deals with distributive justice as an instrument of the United Nations technical assistance structurally enabling countries to arrive at their own capacity to deliver justice—certainly crucial for the implementation of the 2030 Agenda. He refers to John Rawl's "difference principle", brilliantly interpreted in that text by Leila N. Sadat. Moreover, the "difference principle" suggests that the donor countries' assessment of the receiving countries' inequalities in justice delivery should be measured and compared with better off countries insofar receiving countries benefit from it more than, if that assistance were rendered under more generous egalitarian social justice goals.[8] Applying this principle may better motivate to attain such goals than the assistance carried out only based on less precisely assessed reform needs of a recipient country.

2.6 *Peace, Justice, and Sustainable Development*

In the original blueprint by the UN Charter framers, peace and security depend on "principles of justice" (presumably "the rule of law", cf. UN Doc. 1006; Art. 1 of the UN Charter). This relation was explained by Henri Rolin, the delegate of Belgium to the 1945 San Francisco conference. In an apparent reference to the 1938 British-French concessions made to Hitler, Rolin said:

> With regard to peace, we felt the need to emphasize that our first objective was to be strong to maintain peace, to maintain peace by our common effort and at all cost, at all cost with one exception – not at the cost of justice. There the difficulty lay. Many of our delegations have repeatedly in our debates warned of the dangers of a repetition of the so called "appeasement policy." Too often in the last years governments had hoped to maintain peace by sacrificing the interests of weaker countries to the greed of stronger ones, and all this on the altar of peace, with the rather deceiving result (UN Doc. 1006, p. 2).

This question was originally addressed by St. Augustine (1972, p. 139): "Remove justice, and what are kingdoms but gangs of criminals on a large scale?" As criminologists, we would like to respond to his question what justice means in peace time, in the United Nations terms. As of this writing, its currency regarding the meaning of justice is augmented by the mind-crunching conundrum involving thousands of ready for illegal entry refugees from Syria, but also immigrants from

[8]Technically, this can be done through household/living standard surveys (HGS 2020).

Afghanistan, Iraq and Pakistan, some stalled in between Turkish and Greek border of the European Union.[9]

There is no amount of humanitarian assistance by receiving countries which can stop migrants from coming to places where life is better than in their place of original departure. Migrants are needed, but feared. Indeed, the above developments are the test of what justice means in Greece, in the European Union and elsewhere; what it has been and what it will be in the world. Migrants constitute approximately 10% of the world's population, out of which 3.5% are international migrants, including less than 1% of the world's internal and international migrants forcibly displaced (cf. Kury and Redo 2018, p. XXXII). Three points immediately come to attention.

First, that there is a difference between "suspending" irregular migrants' human and humanitarian rights for one month. Those latter apply only to Syrians, and less so, if at all to other irregulars, but to all of them apply human rights anytime anywhere. The way out is the "on spot" identification of Syrian-Arabic speaking refugees and granting them a temporary sojourn in the "safe" country other than Turkey. But this may be an act of EU's humanitarian gesture, not an obligation, also for Germany—a major destination country. As mentioned elsewhere (see Kury and Redo 2018) over the past few years, the growing resentment of German society makes the reception of irregular migrants less and less acceptable, hence the potential for their integration dwindles. The turning point has been reached quite a time ago.

The side effects of the earlier happen-stance German "*willkommen*" policy *vis à vis* hosting irregular migrants have become politically very alerting, detrimental for the rule of law, victimization, and the fear of crime. As for other irregulars, resisting their EU entry—however odd but justified it is—the UN Member States must be more incisive in implementing the Global Compact on Safe, Orderly and Responsible Migration. Disorderly, unsafe, and irresponsible migration will have a devastating effect on the entire humankind. We should wake up and be more committed, pragmatic, and paradigmatic. Without "justice" beyond the EU and Western world in general, there cannot be orderly, safe, and regular migration globally. This matters for all UN Member States *vis à vis* the Global Compact, but especially for those States which withdrew either their commitment to implement it (cf. Kury and Redo 2018 in Prologue & Epilogue), or/and contest the rule of law promoted by the Organization.

Hence the **second** point: the strengthening and expansion of the rule of law within the European Union, in the Western world and beyond, i.e., the North/South rule of law through technical assistance. Throughout this book various issues calling for matching them with technical assistance are discussed by expert authors. Just to demonstrate that: a seemingly irrelevant to technical assistance text of *Marshall,*

[9]About the same time, the EU Commissioner for Home Affairs announced that seven EU Member States had agreed to take in at least 1600 unaccompanied children from the camps, seen as especially vulnerable. As for the rest of irregular migrants, a "voluntary return" scheme valid for one month to pay €2000 to each migrant who arrived to Greece at before 1 January 2020 and has been camped on its islands (BBC 2020).

Marshall, & *Wills* "Parents who hit, troubled families and children's happiness: Do gender and national context make a difference?", begs the answer whether, and if so, how to counter the corporal punishment of children, so as to meet the 2030 UN Sustainable Development Goal 16 target 16.2 "end abuse and violence against children." The authors' findings suggest that gender and national context indeed do matter. Consequently, there is the challenge of promoting a Culture of Lawfulness so the children of the next generation will be happier than the present one, including migrant children unattended by parents, and children deprived of their liberty.

Such turgid references, either to the "next generation", to "Culture of Lawfulness", to ending abuse and violence against children (even to the almost household words "the rule of law") hardly make to the minds of parents, guardians, educators, etc. They must be operationalized, inculcated in the most technically pragmatic sense, either on the spot (camps), at the host country or at the country of a would be migrant.

This is done in the contribution by *Manfred Nowak*, former United Nations Special Rapporteur on Torture (2004–2010), since 2016 an Independent Expert leading the UN Global Study on Children Deprived of Liberty. The contribution co-written with his co-worker *Manu Krishan* of Ludwig Boltzmann Institute of Human Rights (Vienna, Austria) has the title "The UN Global Study on Children Deprived of Liberty – The Role of Academia in 'Making the Invisible and Forgotten Visible'." Their contribution which draws on the Global Study very well inscribes itself into the international process of mobilization of academic knowledge by/for bureaucracies, like the United Nations in this case. The authors highlight that more than 7 million children are in fact deprived of liberty in a broad variety of institutions, including police lockups, prisons, immigration, and other detention centers in all world regions. The research conducted for the Global Study also shows the enormous suffering of children who are exposed to inhuman conditions of detention, and the particular harmful effects of deprivation of liberty on the health and development of children. Cecilia Cannon who surveyed such scholarly advocacy which includes Nowak's voluminous expertise, rightly notes that "scholars have shown that experts, through epistemic communities, can influence policy decision-makers' preferences in the way they define and frame issues" (Cannon 2017).

This brings up the **third** point: making technical *assistance* work. Regarding especially countries receiving technical assistance, beyond the underutilized by donors household surveys, in our 2018 book we have advanced three constitutive rights and exemplified modalities of their implementation should be a Culture-of-Lawfulness priority: the rights to life, security and dignity of a person. Given current projections addressed there, this may be the most promising way to meet more effectively and successfully the SDG 16 "Promote peaceful and inclusive societies for sustainable development, provide access to justice for all and build effective, accountable and inclusive institutions at all levels." It goes without saying that a "voluntary return" with €2000 payment is not meant to meet this goal, but it prompts the idea, how to promote microfinancing and microcredits through technical assistance donors whose offices across the developing world may involve their local counterparts in various projects indeed meant to promote SDG's 16 sustainable development and access to justice.

Referring now back to St. Augustine and paraphrasing his credo that not helping when it is in man's power, failure to love one's neighbor sufficiently, refusal to put oneself to inconvenience and unwillingness to suffer to assist him is called by Augustine "criminal"—a word generally descriptive of unjust acts of major proportions—is an assault against the Golden Rule and the Rule of Law. Moreover, regarding "those who think that with the progress of justice, charity can be eliminated are unconsciously identifying charity with what is commonly associated with it - the material gift which expresses the love of the giver" (Clark 2015, pp. 5, 8), we think that when justice further universalizes, there will be less room for charity and more for technical *cooperation* for global sustainable development.

The current UN blueprint is: "there is no peace without sustainable development and justice." This new trifecta is a paradigmatic shift: "sustainable development" is an intermediary transformative concept between "peace" and "justice." As Fukuda-Parr quoted in this book by *Chalkia* suggests: "the 2030 Agenda reflects a new conception of development as 'sustainable development,' and an important evolution in normative ideas about the vision of 'development.'"

From the standpoint of democracy and the rule of law, it would be interesting to observe, how the trifecta "peace-sustainable development-justice" will throw a new light on the UDHR drafters' debate regarding the deprivation of rights as central cause of the Second World War (McGuiness 2011, p. 757). Will this still remain a *casus belli*, or in the name of sustainable development—a new *casus belli*, the UDHR eventually agreed sense of justice will be comprised through the Agenda's new formula?

Inkpen, *Pitts*, & *Lattimore* in "Crime, Victimization, and Intentions to Migrate in the Northern Triangle" take an extremely incisive very well statistically corroborated look into the criminological factors prompting decisions to migrate. They write: "The policy implications of this analysis, especially in light of the important affirmations in the 1948 Universal Declaration of Human Rights and the 2030 Agenda for Sustainable Development, point to the need for multidimensional interventions."

This leads to the section below.

3 Common Language of Justice

Since "a different language is a different vision of life" (Fellini in Cardullo 2006, p. 178), how—metaphorically—the United Nations craftsmanship and leadership could enhance Member States' common good? Essentially, this question asks, if a "common language of justice" may enlarge individual and collective freedom, in the time of considerable challenges to it.

This metaphoric expression, proposed to the Security Council by Kofi Annan in his report on "The rule of law and transitional justice in conflict and post-conflict societies" (S/2004/616), postulated there the need for a greater UN intra-agency collaboration.

Given this book's interregional coverage, a few other suggestions may be in place. First, a common language of justice has no "alphabet", in the sense that neither Latin, Arabic, Chinese nor any other "script" may dominate the United Nations vocabulary and dictionary of terms. Second, it has its own political logic driven by the maintenance of peace and security in the world. Third, this language progressively evolves to enhance human rights safeguards despite recurrent challenges to their implementation.

Here we argue that the implementation of the 2030 Agenda requires a broader metaphor of a common language of justice that meets the integration challenges caused by migration augmented by poverty and climate change. As emphasized in this book's introduction by Brigitte Bierlein, f. Chancellor of Austria and f. President of the Austrian Constitutional Court: "overcoming grinding poverty; healing and securing our planet; and establishing human rights, the rule-of-law, and universal peace and freedoms" are the major issues. This is a part of the United Nations vocabulary.

3.1 Food Security

With this vocabulary in mind the United Nations Security Council was alerted by the fact that the global spread of COVID-19 in 2020 doubled the number of people facing hunger in the Global South, estimated now to be ca. 230 million. This estimate was backed by the evidenced-based argument linking famine with conflicts: Widespread conflict and instability lead to food insecurity; reducing or preventing conflict reduces and prevents hunger (FAO 2020). According to another alarming estimate (Roberton et al. 2020), also known to the UN (UNICEF 2020), in as many as 118 low- and middle-income countries an additional 1.2 million children under-five may face death in just six months, due to reductions in routine health service coverage levels and an increase in child wasting (i.e., low weight for hight).[10]

In "The Grand Inquisitor" Fyodor Dostoevsky (1880/2002, p. 253) asked:

> Do you know that centuries will pass and mankind will proclaim with the mouth of its wisdom and science that there is no crime, and therefore no sin, but only hungry men? "Feed them first, then ask virtue of them!"—that is what they will write on the banner they raise against you, and by which your temple will be destroyed. In place of your temple a new

[10]These estimates were meant to seize the Security Council of "the worst humanitarian crisis since World War Two", in time when more frequent natural disasters and changing weather caused, that "we're already facing a perfect storm" (UN News 2020). France and Tunisia proposed to the Council a draft resolution, while the UN Secretary-General renewed the alert (UNSG 2020f). As of this writing, because of the conflict between China and the USA over the wording of resolution involving the origin and nomenclature of virus and the role of the WHO in its countering worldwide, the Council has not adopted any resolution.

> edifice will be raised, the terrible Tower of Babel will be raised again, and though, like the former one, this one will not be completed either, still you could have avoided this new tower and shortened people's suffering by a thousand years—for it is to us they will come after suffering for a thousand years with their tower! They will seek us out again, underground, in catacombs, hiding (for again we shall be persecuted and tortured), they will find us and cry out: "Feed us, for those who promised us fire from heaven did not give it." And then we shall finish building their tower, for only he who feeds them will finish it, and only we shall feed them, in your name, for we shall lie that it is in your name. Oh, never, never will they feed themselves without us! No science will give them bread as long as they remain free, but in the end they will lay their freedom at our feet and say to us: 'Better that you enslave us, but feed us.'

Century and a half later, past materialism and post-modernity, in the age demanding sustainable development by Mother Earth with millions of people victimized by hunger, crime, and calamities, do people still feel locked down by this *dictum* "Better that you enslave us, but feed us"? Were they not ready to unlock that *dictum* after Roosevelt's proclamation of the Four Freedoms and of the Universal Declaration of Human Rights? Are we not ready now to respect the freedom from want and the freedom of expression as per the 2030 Agenda? After all, absolute poverty of Dostoevsky's time has now been considerably reduced throughout the world, so populistic arguments no longer should sound so forcefully. There is more between "food" and "freedom" than he implies.

3.2 Global North-South Cooperation

Klemens Wenzel Fűrst von Metternich, Austrian Empire's Foreign Minister (1809–1848) and Chancellor (1821–1848) widely considered to be one of the most important statesmen and geo-political strategists of his time, quipped: "When Paris sneezes, the whole of Europe catches a cold" (Neumann 1949, p. 542). Ever since he said so, it has had literal and metaphorical variations.

Contemporary literary sense of his saying in the time of pandemic communicate the news, that "Unrest, hunger and hardship in France's locked-down suburbs" (Borges 2020). Metaphorical sense has "When America sneezes, the world catches a cold" or "When China sneezes, the world catches a cold." Not coincidentally with the latter modification stands "When white America sneezes, black America catches pneumonia." In the pandemic it signals acute poverty problem, however not only in the USA but worldwide. Metternich's quip should now rather be regarded as a *bon mot* which reads: "When Global North sneezes, Global South catches pneumonia."

In the time of pandemic Metternich's *bon mot* is also strikingly relevant because of the falling rule of law and democracy worldwide, and people's yearning for larger freedom across the globe. In the present intellectual change and dominated by arguments about despotism and liberalism, Machiavelli, and Montesquieu—the two brilliant advocates of these two conflictive worldviews—seem to be on one page.

In "The Prince" Machiavelli regarded plague and disease as metaphors for what happens to the ruler whose conduct is not vigilantly held in check:

> what physicians say about consumptive illness [tuberculosis] is applicable here: that at the beginning, such an illness is easy to cure but difficult to diagnose; but as time passes, not having been recognised or treated at the outset, it becomes easy to diagnose but difficult to cure (Machiavelli 2005, p. 68).

Vigilance is also Montesquieu's priority and as it is widely known his idea of the separation of powers is its best example. For Montesquieu despotism was metaphorically also a "plague"—"a scourge of decency":

> He helped to convince many of his readers that despotism was a new and dangerous form of unlimited - concentrated and unaccountable - secular power. Guided by no ideals other than the blind pursuit of power for power's sake and feeding upon the blind obedience of its subjects despotism, Montesquieu implied, is a half-crazed, violent, and self-contradictory form of governance. It crashes blindly through the world, leaving behind a trail of confusion, waste, and lawlessness, to the point where it tends to destroy its own omnipotence. It consequently undoes the fear upon which it otherwise thrives. Despotism becomes the scourge of decency. It shocks and repels those who are afraid, and it encourages those who yearn to live without fear. It inspires its opponents to seek alternatives, for instance republican government, representative parliamentary power-sharing arrangements, the cultivation of free public opinion within the rule of law, and the education of citizens into the ways of civic virtue (Keane 2018, pp. 412–413).

The desperation of the Global South residents to seek welfare and other life opportunities in the Global North is very understandable. In this book as well as in our 2018 book we have given considerable attention to the ensuing steps for orderly, safe, and responsible migration in time of climate change.

There are very tragic cases of hatred-driven assaults on immigrants. Across the world governments and citizens of host countries and communities, sometimes populistically representing "the will of sovereign", urban mayors, spiritual leaders and authorities—all face an imminent re-adaptation challenge prompted by immigration. We focus here on the intercultural approach to pursue larger freedom which since the establishment of the United Nations drives its agenda, but now faces the unprecedented wave of new values, new lifestyles, and new challenges to justice.

We bring this issue up in the context of very disturbing arguments quoted by *Chalkia*. She writes: "Taking into consideration that the majority of refugees and immigrants come from countries that are classified as 'waste' (outcasts) in the context of contemporary international society and that the ideas of 'western' exceptionalism, the 'inevitable' clash of cultures, even xenophobia and racism, have spread throughout Europe, the successful integration of these people in European societies and the avoidance of 'stigma' [...] is a complex challenge and also an urgent priority."

4 Education and Inequality

Here, following on our previous book (Kury and Redo 2018), we would like to focus how this priority can, hopefully, be met in the sending countries. This question is motivated by the fact, that immigrants coming to Europe from African countries and some Asian countries, in comparison with most of other immigrants not only have weak or no knowledge of the host country official language(s), but also enter Europe with their shorter years of schooling. They are looking for better life chances than they have in their home countries. Since early twenty-first century, the mounting scientific evidence has been equivocally suggesting that an additional year of schooling generates considerable socio-economic outcomes. Methodologies in accounting for them differ. Most beneficial outcomes are in low-income countries, where the ratio of investment to return may be as high as 1 to 10 in the USD (BEC 2018, p. 5).

Educational outcomes elsewhere may involve greater technological innovations, provided that education itself is innovative enough to yield them (Kury and Redo 2018, p. XXXV). In any case, appropriately modelled quality education lifts out people of material poverty and the poverty of thought. It sets countries on trajectories for making the living of their residents sustainable, while making their country economically less dependent on outside assistance (cf. BEC 2018, p. 5).

By analogy with "health coding" one may grade public obedience to the law in general. There are people who duly accept the legitimacy of a State and its regime, but there are also those who are sceptical and accept it occasionally, and those who do not abide it in principle. In the time of pandemic education in new lifestyles implies not only learning new social contact rules, but—more importantly—rescaling consumption patterns ensuing from the emerging new income distribution. Thus innocuous as may read SDG 12 "Ensure sustainable consumption and production patterns", in reality relative deprivation—the most powerful criminogenic factor—no doubt can demonstrate how its detrimental potential to law obedience will impact the implementation of the 2030 Agenda. Time will show how serious will indeed be the impulse of pandemic on culture of lawfulness, Agenda's idea not to leave anyone behind, and on the kind of response of its stakeholders.

All this sounds as belabouring the obvious. Like in art (Fellini) so in science "[t]he limits of our language are the limits of our thoughts" (after Obenauer in Kury and Redo 2018, p. XVII). Consequently, what is needed in education is to give more thought to a shared sense of social reality pursued in the "language" of the 2030 Agenda, the "language" that takes account of the imminent descend caused by the pandemic. The Agenda recommends that "all learners acquire the knowledge and skills needed to promote sustainable development, including, among others, through education for sustainable development and sustainable lifestyles, human rights, gender equality, promotion of a culture of peace and non-violence, global citizenship and appreciation of cultural diversity and of culture's contribution to sustainable development" (SDG 4.7). As emphasized in the report on culture in the implementation of the 2030 Agenda, this involves translating the universal language of the

SDGs into the individual and collective lives of citizens inhabiting specific communities, cities and regions (Culture 2020, p. 6). Now comes the time to reconsider what SDG 4.7 and 16 mean in the time of pandemic and later.

4.1 Gender Justice

Rayejian Asli in the chapter "Incorporating the United Nations Norms into Iranian Post-Revolution Criminal Policy: A Criminological-Victimological Approach" devoted attention to double standards regarding the protection of victimized women in Iran. The newest scene in women's humiliating treatment was highlighted by the UN Secretary General, who sensitized the global audience to their plight during the coronavirus pandemic. He compared its fury to the folly of war (UNSG 2020a) and added: "[m]any women under lockdown [. . .] face violence where they should be safest: in their own homes" (UNSG 2020b).

Indeed, in terms of domestic violence there is a criminogenic potential in the quarantined households. This may extend to corporal punishment of children, especially in dysfunctional families whose offspring cannot go to school. Moreover, the post-quarantine effect may lead to more violent and property crime in households with more than one person per room (Barkan 2000).[11] If to take only this measure into consideration (based only on the US data), then the number of people in one household may indeed matter in case of: "stay home" quarantine, and under the condition of the locked down cities' public spaces, then, probably, the fuller the household is, the more intensive would be the conflicting behaviors.

In the realities of pandemic this is a very rough thesis. It would certainly yield confusing results in developing countries (e.g., India with high population density, relatively low homicide rate and high household occupancy) and in developed countries (e.g., Sweden with low population density population, low homicide rate and high individual household occupancy). Even more baffling may be the numbers of reported instances of domestic violence in heavily COVID 19 affected countries where access to firearm ownership is liberal (e.g., USA and Switzerland), while the respective levels of reported homicides are extremely high and low. Consequently, much may be learned about the freedom from fear and want, so about economic inequality, but also about racial discrimination and last, but not least, gender.

Anyway, it is undeniably true that:

- Women first fell victims of homicide by their intimate partners or by other family members;

[11] How otherwise criminogenic effects ensue from "broken homes" had shortly after the Second World War been investigated in the World Health Organization's study, prepared in response to what is now known as the United Nations Crime Prevention and Criminal Justice Programme (Kury and Redo 2018, p. 846).

- Societies with pronounced gender inequality tend to be characterized by higher levels of interpersonal violence against women, including lethal violence. Conversely, the empowerment of women has been shown to be accompanied by a decrease in the level of intimate partner violence. Greater autonomy and independence, when also combined with a higher social status, help to protect women from the risk of homicide (UNODC 2019).

On the strength of these two findings, countering gender-related domestic violence certainly is a matter of larger freedom. A Culture of Lawfulness that responds favourably to the latter finding makes such a freedom a reality.

4.2 *The Role of Education in the Time of Conventional and Artificial Justice*

Unlike in natural science where each new rule generally complements the previous ones and does not invalidate a complete set of reasoning, legal rules do not automatically evolve in a linear progressive fashion (Council of Europe 2018, pp. 35–36). Hence, for better or worse, advancing the rule of law depends more on human reasoning.

It is this context in which we interpret even more than in SDG 4.7 expressively formulated educational objective of the Thirteenth United Nations Congress on Crime Prevention and Criminal Justice (Qatar, 2015). Its Doha Declaration (A/RES/70/174, OP 7) stated that "education for all children and youth, including the eradication of illiteracy, is fundamental to the prevention of crime and corruption and to the promotion of a culture of lawfulness that supports the rule of law and human rights while respecting cultural identities."

The United Nations Secretariat's respect of cultural identities may differ from its local understanding, and even intergovernmental understanding. Female genital mutilation still tolerated if not promoted in some legal cultures and occasionally backed by religious interpretation is a case in point (Kury and Redo 2018, pp. 866, 872–873). Regarding the rule of law, invasive governmental surveillance is a case in point.

In the light of both examples, so distant from one another, how then to educate in the Golden Rule spirit "Do not to impose on others what you do not desire"?

Symbolically, this question stretches from secular to artificial justice. The major difference between secular and artificial justice is, that in case of traditional uncivil behavior countering it may less or more readily involve educationists, educators, community and spiritual leaders who with their visions and tools of trade are able to control and prevent their occurrence. Moreover, victims may not only have domestic tools of redress, but also benefit with offenders from restorative justice process.

In between secular and artificial there are many incongruent views and developments, but two recommendations should not be questioned: **First**, that victims of such abuses should be made aware of their rights to dignity and privacy; **Second**, that there should be the independent judiciary to make those rights effectively protected.

Let us keep in mind, that like nature the United Nations is perishable. However, unlike nature, its evidence-based drive for knowledge and education, formal and informal, spiritual, but in any case progressive under its aegis makes them a salient growing global asset. Progressive education and inculcation of the UN "principles of justice" to use the Charter's term should continue to be a common base for all its stakeholders. There is no "end of history" (Francis Fukuyama) when innovative thinking prevails over clichés. Hence in this book three chapters, by: *Karstedt* on "The Policy Relevance of Comparative Criminology: On Evidence-based Policies, Policy Learning and the Scales of the Discipline", *Waller* "Ending Violent Crime with Science and Faith", and by *Redo* "Is Socrates Mortal? On the Impact of Socratic Logic on Teaching and Learning the United Nations Crime Prevention Law."

Enlightening education enabling critical judgement is pivotal to eradicate chronic poverty, to counter the poverty of thought and to facilitate the growth of freedom intergenerationally. Eradicating poverty in these both forms through education is the prerequisite for the institutionalization and exercise of more effective control and prevention of abuses, whether to the rights of dignity and privacy or—generally—to other human rights.

Therefore, we reemphasize the importance of findings (see the Prologue) that corruption is the Achilles' heel of populists. However, this weakness is not enough to discredit them. It is necessary to demonstrate that this scourge is detrimental to democratic accountability that enables impunity of leaders. A decline in the rule of law, a dysfunctional bureaucracy hurts the majority and benefits only a few.

5 Justice Reconsidered

As pandemic unfolds, among its victims fall prison inmates. Since prisons are not the type of conveyances which offer better living accommodation than for the locked down COVID-infected passengers of luxury cruise ships, most prison systems across the world exceed maximum occupancy.[12] Even more of them are overcrowded.[13] In either case this is because of uneven living accommodation, subject only to domestic criteria, notwithstanding various international criteria (UNODC 2013, p. 8). If to apply them,[14] then—according to the Penal Reform International (2020, p. 10)—probably more than 124 prison systems which exceed maximum occupancy are

[12]I.e., the ratio of the number of inmates present on a given day to the number of places specified by the official capacity.

[13]I.e., the number of inmates above the official 100% prison capacity.

[14]I.e., minimum space per prisoner of no less than 3.4 sq m and area within the security perimeter of 20–30 sq m per person, with a minimum rate of air renewal between 0.1 and 0.2 $m^3/min/m^2$ (Nembrini 2013, p. 23).

potential incubators of pandemic. Numerous recommendations appeared regarding early prison release, furlough, etc.

There are no recommendations regarding social re-integration, if at all there may be successfully formulated and effectively implemented. Selective release combined with electronic monitoring? After-care civic community support? Will "the tailor, soap maker, baker and every other one [. . .] convinced that the fate of State depends on his craftsmanship and skills" be ready to extend them to the convicts? Who may now undertake such learning for the sake of others? How "different language [in] a different vision of life" (Fellini in Cardullo 2006, p. 178) can deliver it?

This is a transition period in which crime and justice field experiences unforeseeable before changes. Because of the lockdown the level of non-domestic violence subsided, but other crime, e.g., "dark net" drug dealing, increased resort to the detrimental pornographic material by adults and kids alike may enjoy their hay day. In front of our eyes emerges a new crime, justice and victimization landscape and scene for the Day After. There will be inevitable changes in people's lifestyles, and so in law enforcement, criminal justice, crime prevention, larger freedom, and the rule of law.

5.1 *Justice in Horizon*

Almost two centuries ago, in 1847, James Madison, one of the Founding Fathers of the USA, said:[15]

> An attention to the judgment of other nations is important to every government for two reasons: the one is, that, independently of the merits of any particular plan or measure, it is desirable, on various accounts, that it should appear to other nations as the offspring of a wise and honorable policy; the second is, that in doubtful cases, particularly where the national councils may be warped by some strong passion or momentary interest, the presumed or known opinion of the impartial world may be the best guide that can be followed (The Federalist 1961/63).

In that case, he clearly referred to the USA, and asked:

> What has not America lost by her want of character with foreign nations; and how many errors and follies would she not have avoided, if the justice and propriety of her measures had, in every instance, been previously tried by the light in which they would probably appear to the unbiased part of mankind?

Two answers follow. **First**, the U.S. National Endowment for the Humanities through its "We the People" project offers Paul A. Rahe's indirect response. "Rooted" in the "constitution" of all human beings—in our opinion—it applies to any country in the world:

[15]The authorship of this and other views ascribed here to James Madison had been a matter of dispute. Both James Madison and Alexander Hamilton have been ascribed authorship.

> Montesquieu outlines the four most fundamental laws of human nature, the first two of which are caused by the desire for self-preservation [. . .]: 1) man seeks peace; 2) man seeks nourishment; 3) man is drawn into company with others; 4) man has an intellectual desire for the company of others (Rahe n.d.).

Second, we dare to say, that the least unbiased part of the mankind is represented now by the United Nations of "We the Peoples" where the company of others has been and should be most helpful to do good for the greatest number of people. The Organization's view on transforming the world should be better heard, desired, and followed across the globe.

5.2 *Justice the Day After*[16]

As of this writing, one may criminologically reflect on the Day After in two ways. **First**, in terms of situational crime prevention, that is about changing patterns and dynamics of crime and victimization due to considerable unemployment and excessive economic inequality. This involves violence, other assaults, robbery, burglary, theft; suicide; social unrest. **Second**, in terms of social crime prevention. In line with it, it makes sense to pursue avenues to strengthen the rule of law in this difficult time. But would indeed the old rule of law (alias UN Charter's "principles of justice") be applicable on the Day After?

Back in the 1990s—in the pre-SDGs age—William Gibson an influential and award-winning science fiction author, in a perceptive quotation suggested that "The future has arrived - it's just not evenly distributed yet" (Quote Investigator n.d.). For a UN-minded reader of this book this would mean the seeds of socio-economic inequality growing into the future world. However, in this unprecedented global situation after the Second World War, old and new ethics, past and fresh justice concerns about socio-economic inequality, climate change and migration—they cumulatively augmented (and the pandemic accelerated) the reshaping of the priorities for the future.

Countering spatial exclusion and structural discrimination are the two SDGs—and criminologically relevant priorities for the Day After. **Spatial exclusion** in the time of pandemic has for decades been investigated by epidemiologists, and more recently by urban planners and criminologists. The most recent review of epidemiological studies (Kucharski 2020) show that outbreaks of epidemics and street/domestic interpersonal violence share one common denominator—the geolocation wherefrom they originate and spread, namely, the impoverished residence areas.

The first death in *favela* of Rio de Janeiro (Brazil) due to COVID-19 of a 63 year-old domestic worker may be emblematic to sensitize to four risks for any country with the impoverished residence areas, especially slums (Slattery and Gaier 2020).

[16]"The Day After" is the title of the 1983 movie directed by Nicolas Meyer about the effects of a devastating nuclear holocaust on small-town residents of eastern Kansas (USA).

First, their proven function as incubators of epidemic, **second**, their function as cradles of inter-family and intergenerational violence (addressed above); **third**, as to the role of organized crime in bringing epidemic under control in lieu of the medical assistance by public health agencies; **fourth**, throughout humankind's history these areas with young males who could not work legitimately or lost their jobs. Unemployed and disgruntled they have always been a natural reservoir of radicalization, tolerated in times "colloquially referred to as normal" (Czarnowski 1936/2016, p. 300).

Current time is not "normal" any longer. Hence the latter two points bring into picture the problem of **structural discrimination** driven to its hights by the 2030 Agenda (SDG 16.b). Related to the distribution of power and the rule of law, this public health and social justice concern in other words reads as who gets to write the future for years to come, beyond 2030.

If this will be done in "more of the same style", then fascism—writes Czarnowski (1936/2016, p. 305)—offers "[t]he enormous, ever increasing, margin [. . .] of young people full of youthful temper [. . .] inclined to generate in themselves an 'inferior value complex'" the avenue to satisfy their ambitions.[17]

Given more than 80 years after the tragic war with the ensuing intellectual legacy and accumulated post-war Nordic welfare and other good governance experience satisfying such ambitions must account for the sense of individual self-agency. The findings from 1981 to 2007 Word Values Surveys clearly prove that good governance facilitating economic development, anti-corruption, democratization, and social tolerance increase the sense of free choice, which in turn has led to higher levels of happiness around the world (Inglehart et al. 2008).

Whether happiness continues to grow only with the growing income is a matter of scientific dispute (Stevenson and Wolfers 2008). Less disputable is the imminent recession with the growing deprivation. This forceful criminogenic factor on the way to sustainable livelihood may be more in the order of the day than before when it comes to domestic and street violence. The more so important is in this adverse circumstance the trust in governmental institutions: wherefrom they derive their legitimacy, how they react to violence, how public awareness of the effects of recession translates into the domestic settings and culture of lawfulness in the streets, at schools and places of political power sharing: in villages, communities, cities and countries. Finally: in the regional and intergovernmental organizations, including the United Nations (Pływaczewski & Redo 2018).

[17]For a European review of the twentieth century developments in nationalism, see Borejsza et al. (2006).

5.3 Economic Justice

We see it in three ways. **First**, as per "writers'" guarantees to enjoy the afore mentioned UBI may initially be a preventive response.

Second, more viable in a long run would first be a basic reordering and optimization of the domestic and international tax system. One may see in this context the chapter by *Ling Zhou* and *Hanming Xu* on "Money Laundering: China and its Evolving Criminal Policy Response", had the matter not been nowadays even more pregnant in the ominous consequences than before the pandemic. The UN Secretary-General was worried that the ensuing illicit financial flow, such as tax evasion and money-laundering will undermine investments in sustainable development (UNSG 2020g). Indeed, current financial architecture enables the existence of offshore tax centers ("havens"). Hence the avoidance of paying taxes in countries where the payee should originally have the relevant tax account and benefit as an entrepreneur the entitled employees (jobs), rather than to leave this to a State affected by the collapsing economy. Paying for UBI or any other welfare benefit in situation of considerable financial shortages may then be appropriately addressed with the taxed entrepreneurial income. Eventually there should be new market mechanisms for data that would show how UBI functions within new tax structures. In the end of the day this is about accounts, returns, shared responsibility, shared benefits, and leaving no one behind rather than about "idle poor", i.e., those who may seem not to want to work and stay put.

Third, in our view, the following opinion is therefore more pragmatic, more far-reaching, instrumental, and potentially globally transformative:

> These decisions are often made by a particular section of society - typically [. . .] upper-middle class, and male. Although the demographics of decision makers are beginning to broaden, many of the organizational structures in which decisions are made limit the degree to which ideas from outside dominant mindsets can have traction. Additionally, incomes associated with decision-maker roles mean that when people from other class backgrounds take such jobs, they often become removed from the day-to-day experiences of those from similar situations. For example, believing that if they have "made good," then it is possible for any and all. However, even when apparently benign, current differences in power have a strong impact on how the future is being written (Chatterton and Newmarch 2017, p. 44).

Relating this opinion to the transformative potential of the 2030 Agenda, the decision makers should write the future in a common language of justice. It aims at reducing excessive inequality, promotes gender mainstreaming, more inclusive power structures with access to justice (SDG 10 and 16). With and in it the future may be written by all concerned UN stakeholders. The Organization should be at the forefront of international developments where these written words will count.

5.4 Justice Philosophies in the Time of Pandemic

It is natural that the concerned State's duty to counter comes first before any other States, including their consolidated response, if any. Past that, State's duty should not be on a collision course with another State. If it so happens (as it does), then should not be misinterpreted as a failure of the world community, global civic education, etc.

It is this context in which we read the UN Secretary-General's statement at the Security Council, that "the pandemic [. . .] poses a significant threat to the maintenance of international peace and security - potentially leading to an increase in social unrest and violence that would greatly undermine our ability to fight the disease", increase the potential of bioterrorism and exacerbate various human rights challenges, including democratic elections (UNSG 2020c).

It is also this context that prompts us to ask: Is the present global socio-economic system good enough, if in a couple of months, the unfolding pandemic brings it to a virtual halt? Has the present way of governance become anachronic as incapable to react to the pandemic? When, if not now "Transforming our world: the 2030 Agenda for Sustainable Development" should be more vigorously implemented? How long the moral dilemma whether an elderly or young coronavirus-infected patient should first be treated with a respirator will hold its currency? If the vaccine is eventually available, whom it may first be served?

In this book *Rutkowski* (already mentioned) considers the answer: "Either we behave in a human way, or we no longer deserve to be called human. Either the vaccination against the coronavirus is made available for free to all those in need, or humanity does not rise to the occasion and does not pass the exam in being human." Whether or not we dress the answer into the gown of Hamletism or utilitarianism it would be more helpful if Member States could in line with the 2030 Agenda retool their policies to see together a better Day After by reprioritizing objectives of public health sector, of education and other objectives.

Now should be the opportune time to heal ourselves from a rather sickening condition in which we have found ourselves amid climate change and coronavirus. It is the time to embark on "co-immunism", to use the phrase of Peter Sloterdijk, German philosopher and cultural theorist, or on more "solidarity."

There is a deficit of solidarity, so much emphasized in the introduction to this book by H. E. Lech Wałęsa, the originator and leader of Solidarność, the first democratically-elected President of post-Second World War Poland (1990–1995), and Nobel Peace Prize laurate.

"Solidarity" and "co-immunism" have gained on their resonance in the time of pandemic. Both corroborate that "[n]ature kills weak people. Civilization is fragile. We learn about its strength when we know how many people we can protect" (Andrzej Stasiuk in Wodecka 2020).

Econometric research findings support the above argument. According to them, because of various epidemics which plagued the world in the past 60 years (1960–2019), the more democratic system the studied country had, the lower was the number of lethal victims. Among countries with similar wealth, the lowest death rates tend to be in places where most people can vote in free and fair elections. Employing other definitions of democracy yields similar findings (Economist 2020). If to add to them the evidence analyzed by the Freedom House (2020) that autocratic governments tend to lower the death statistics and are less supportive of the screening of potentially COVID 19-infected people, then there is a clear confirmation of the importance of SDG 16.10: "Ensure public access to information and protect fundamental freedoms, in accordance with national legislation and international agreements."

"Larger freedom" does not die because of one or another emergency. In the time of populism, it still reacts to its vagaries. It has a potential to resurrect through civil society's vigorous organization, by releasing and channelling people's social energies supporting good governance with new standard-setting for larger freedom. Individual sustainable livelihoods are in the bedrock of sustainable development. People's well-being, their own commitment; grass-roots abilities and people's own vision of successful future in communities and community of nations may secure sustainable development worldwide.

Likewise, "solidarity" does not die because of one or another emergency. Solidarity since 1989 has internationally gained much more popularity. Past its political etymology, solidarity should really become a household word beyond the United Nations. It should be further domesticated and internationalized. No magic is needed to make solidarity work at home and internationally, but more good faith, trust, transparency, accountability, and shared responsibility.

Such fundamentals should remain fundamentals. In the 2030 Agenda they are pregnant with humanistic and pragmatic content. Neglecting, reducing, or inverting its meaning is a challenge to fundamental freedoms advanced by the Agenda, and a challenge to the UN social contract, originally constituted by the Charter.

5.5 Environmental and Climate Justice

A "Greenpeace" activist Paweł Szypulski (acknowledged earlier) rightly noted that while the pre-Second World War Great Depression prompted the United States to build and implement "The New Deal", Europe of that time disintegrated and finished itself by a mortal conflict, whose symptoms were so clearly observed before the Second World War by the afore quoted Czarnowski. There is then the crucial lesson learned, how to address the Day After in the European Union and elsewhere in the world. The EU's "Green Deal" should be the way to follow. The World Values Surveys provide a credible evidence that all over the world the protection of environment is a top concern of people (Kury and Redo 2018, pp. 889–891; Redo 2018a, b). It is immoral to sin against environment! Urban stewardship which responds to that concern and redefines along with it other residential concerns allows mayors, civic society, FBO leaders, migrants, youth, and adults a common agenda on the Day After.

In other cases, since in the livelihoods consumption of wildlife markets products has for long been important for people (as food or an aphrodisiac), new endeavours are needed. In China there are good examples of massive campaigns on the city transportation and other local mass media, e.g., regarding the prevention of the ill treatment of elderly or the identification of forged Chinese banknotes. Certainly, raising in this way public awareness of the health perils of wild markets products may have a positive anti-pandemic impact. Awareness campaigns may decrease customary reverence of and demand for them, provided that the suppliers will likewise benefit through more legitimate alternative sustainable livelihood opportunities.[18]

As if was a premonition of pandemic, in the 2020 New Year Secretary-General's visionary statement to the United Nations General Assembly he invoked the incoming "Apocalypse" (pestilence, war, famine and death) that will prevail in the world. He metaphorically meant to alert Member States to climate change, sinister technologies, mistrust, and global tensions as the current "four horsemen" jeopardizing our shared future (UNSG 2020d).

Compared to "Apocalypse" he did not allude to pandemic. Yet he could have done so. This is because at the time of his statement pandemic has been unfolding in Wuhan, while the 2019 report published at the initiative of the World Bank and the World Health Organization (GPMB 2019) provided ample scientific evidence that a high-impact respiratory pathogen pandemic is underway. Quite rightly the report discusses, how "the world" can address the pandemic threat and manage preparedness for disease outbreaks in complex, insecure contexts. The report recommends national and local leadership that drives progress, and regional and global support for it. In no place in the report there is a discussion on "discrimination."

5.6 *United Nations Spirit of Justice and Discrimination of Others*

The 2030 Agenda is a unique legal instrument for just social progress in the world. The Agenda does not differentiate "us" from "Others." There is no dichotomy "we-

[18]In 2020, city authorities in Wuhan (China) have reaffirmed the central government's ban on the consumption, trade, and hunting of wild animals except for "scientific research, population regulation and monitoring of epidemic diseases." A similar restriction applied to the breeding of non-domesticated animals, with exceptions for "species protection, scientific research and animal exhibitions [such as zoos and wildlife parks]" that had been approved by the government (Xie 2020). The ban is a custom-forming act legitimizing the creation of locally new "best practices." It delegitimizes unique, culture specific culinary custom, which in a few decades may eventually disappear.

they", no false dilemma "we or they." Throughout the Agenda permeates the message that patriotism is love of own country without hatred of other nationalities.

Prejudice, hatred, denunciation—forms of discrimination about the countering of which is so much in the 2030 Agenda and this book (see, e.g., *Sasitha's* "Youth Perception on Hate Crimes, Hate Speeches and Nationalism in Contemporary India") in the context of various vulnerable groups—now includes sick homeless people, home-isolated senior and other residents, COVID-infected hospital patients and the concerned medical staff at their residences.

Before the nineteenth century the word "syphilis" became standard throughout the world, this venereal disease was called in China "the ulcer of Canton" (the chief seaport of contact with the West). The Japanese called it the *Tang sore-Tang* referring to China—or more to the point—the source of the disease—the Portuguese sailors. Indians called it the disease of the Franks (western Europeans). Middle Easterners called it the European pustules. The English called it "the Bordeaux disease", and "the Spanish disease." Italians called it "the French disease", which proved to be the most popular title. The French called it "the disease of Naples." Poles called it "the German disease." Russians called it "the Polish disease", and so on (Crosby 1969). Until the First World War the Spanish word "*la polacca*" had been the synonym of a prostitute (Polish women, partly of Jewish origin, emigrated to the Western hemisphere as bread winners), whereas "*polacco*" until that time implied a Jew—member of the strong ethically inhabited Poland, before and after its first partition in 1772. So, if to continue with "the Chinese virus" nowadays (called "white virus" in Africa because of its arrival from Europe, where by Germans is called "skier's disease" which originated in Austria), what international standard it would be when compared with the recommendation to "Promote and enforce non-discriminatory laws and policies for sustainable development" (SDG 16.b)?

The United Nations developed and implements the Agenda in ecumenical spirit, in its own secular fashion. If for the majority of Member States, especially permanent members of the Security Council, that ground breaking instrument only enjoyed a happenstance unanimous support when in 2015 it was adopted by the General Assembly, then very little hope would be left for a better future. Paraphrasing Harari (2020), it looks as if there were no adults in the room to come up with a common plan of action.

In 2018 in novel "*M. il figlio del secolo*" by Antonio Scurati about Benito Mussolini, the author of this bestseller translated into German, Polish, Spanish among other languages conveyed the message that Mussolini's march for fascist dictatorship in Italy was successful because of his ability to exploit the fear of the October Revolution downing on the impoverished post-First World War masses. In simple words repeated to thousands of disenchanted Italians Mussolini replaced that fear by hatred of the imminent future personalized by Lenin. "A great alchemic operation!", exclaims Scurati in the interview (Nogaś 2020).

Climate change, migration and the pandemic that leads to recession is certainly a suitable medium to a new alchemic operation for hatred of the imminent future with "Others" as the front-line enemies. German Nazi theoretician Carl Schmitt

(1888–1985) rightly said: "Tell me who your enemy is, and I will tell you who you are" (Schmitt 2007, p. 85).

In reality, there is nothing specific in human behavior or of any country that cannot be found in others. Not a single person or country is "unique", because uniqueness is universal. The UN is a normative institution based on universalism. It advances it through "twists & turns" slowly but steadily, so some adverse sides of local "uniqueness" may eventually disappear.

We need strong public power, globally and domestically. Good governance legitimizes itself not only by the mere virtue of the law of the land, but by effectively and humanely controlling the ambitions of rulers and subjects (Montesquieu 2001, SL 5.8, 8.2). Using contemporary terminology, good governance is in the limits of power, in the limits of growth, in the limits of inequality, in the United Nations spirit of laws.

SDG 16 advocates just that. It is a very thoughtful instrumental inventory of targets aiming at alleviation of concrete social inequalities, complimentary to sustainable development goal 10 addressed at reducing excessive economic inequality within and among countries. No wonder therefore that Montesquieu was hailed by the President of the United Nations Assembly when he admitted, that "[t]here is no nation so powerful as the one that obeys its laws, not from principles of fear or reason, but from passion (*Redo* in "The relevance. . .").

Whether globally or domestically, institutional power must be controlled. A single person, whether a President of a country or a simple resident should not be above the law, nor should be its illegitimate victim.

This is an evergreen problem in the world conveniently ignored by power holders. But it is an illusion that the absence of control weakens achieving laudable goals for anyone, including power holders. As an Anonymous said, "Anyone who thinks that sky is the limit has a limited imagination." It rather invites unwelcome consequences for them, including increasing unaccountability of state institutions eventually failing to discriminate between own harmful and corrupted practices and the practices of organized crime or actions of war lords.

"Legal impunity" is the result. A State loses then control over its own apparatus and fails to deliver on its laudable promises. Eventually, this may lead to loss of legitimacy—a "failed state." At the interstate level, this involves the lack of credibility and trust. And so risk their credibility and trust the interstate organizations, including the United Nations.

We face the crisis of some forms of global cooperation, but not the end of globalization. "De-globalization" (Ivan Krastev) and the futility of the Agenda-inspired transformation may be a kiss of death only if countries do not revisit and consider themselves accountable for their commitments *vis à vis* others. If the United Nations can implement the 2030 Agenda unconditionally showing that this is a doomsdayish future, then there still is hope in it. Yet hardly in any public debate one hears that the United Nations has that common plan.

If in the political technology persists the binary division on friends and foes, then it means the intent to hurt others. UN Charter's "good faith" (Art. 2.2) would be just a smokescreen behind which nationalism fuels hatred with religion that may again be involved in the deadliest atrocities at war or peace time. Hence this "dilemma": Whose music we appreciate more: Wagner's "Rienzi" which so much impressed the young Hitler or Beethoven's "Ode to Joy"? And what about Penderecki's "Three Chinese Songs"? This "dilemma" is a pure nonsense.

So not to repeat the past errors, there is the need to strengthen the role of anti-discriminatory and other assistance mechanism by sound civic participation in the time of dramatically reduced quality of life for very many countries and people, euphemistically called "negative growth"—probably the most powerful criminogenic factor. This oxymoron should sensitize to critical understanding of the issues, and to legal recourse, in case of abusive right-conduct and social justice concerns imminent because of the lingering economic depression.

6 Independence Resuscitated

In this adverse circumstance, the mechanism recommended in SDG 16.b should enjoy guarantees of independence and impartiality—another *contradictio in adjecto*? Montesquieu's institutional separation of powers which provides for both is not a panacea that exclusively can answer this question and prevent the malignant outcomes possible in the future, however it certainly is a case in point here.

Montesquieu's corpse was removed from its tomb and thrown into the Paris Catacombs. There he rests with Georges-Jacques Danton—his revolutionary accolade, with Maximilien de Robespierre and Jean Paul Marat—their victimizers. Notwithstanding the French Revolution-time profanations we dare to say that Montesquieu's concept of liberal democracy based on the separation of powers still will guide the Rule of Law. For it is true, that "[h]owever vaguely it may be perceived, however inarticulate may be the thought, there is an aspiration in the hearts of all men and women for the rule of law. That aspiration depends for its fulfilment on the competent and impartial application of the law by judges" (UNODC 2007, p. 17).

Because of the spread of digitization and predictive justice, we leave this statement with the following caveat from the book "Good-bye Montesquieu":

> [I]t is past time to rethink Montesquieu's holy trinity. Despite its canonical status, it is blinding us to the world-wide rise of new institutional forms that cannot be neatly categorized as legislative, judicial or executive. Although the traditional tripartite formula fails to capture their distinctive modes of operation, these new and functionally independent units are playing an increasingly important role in modern government. A 'new separation of powers' is emerging in the twenty-first century (Ackerman 2010, p. 129).

However literally this separation may be inscribed in the new law of the land, it can be effectively exercised in many ways. When it comes to the oversight of governmental surveillance activities, including those augmented by AI, the aforementioned UN special report points to the insufficiency of judicial authorization of that surveillance. It suggests additional controls (A/HRC/41/35, para. 52). Audits and civilian control boards may be a democratic way to strengthen checks and balances to counter infringements of independence. There is nothing wrong with them as long as they comply with democratic governance (transparency, accountability), including the privacy protection. Its lack is detrimental to larger freedom and alerts to the pitfall of that control. The independent civil service guarantees meeting standards of democratic governance. Indeed, dispersed oversight/control—this growing in importance form of good governance—if credibly implemented may show the way to other public affairs sectors how to address, control and regulate democratically their own justice issues.

6.1 Judicial Independence and Integrity

This prompts two observations at the juncture of traditional and artificial justice. **First**, with reference to traditional justice *Forsthuber* emphasized, that "[o]nly in a state based on the rule of law can there be a guarantee of democracy as well as an effective protection of human rights. The independence of the judiciary is a major pillar of any constitutional state based – within the framework of the separation of powers – on a balanced system of separation and control of powers." He interprets the meaning of institutional independence through the statement of Anselm Feuerbach (1755–1833), German legal scholar and philosopher: "The judge receives his office from the king's hand, but an office which has the duty to serve no other master other than justice, to obey no will other than the will of the law."[19]

This is why are so important among the European judges and public the 1746–1791 court cases that took place during and after the reign of King Frederick II of Prussia. He and his successor lose them to their subjects—the weaker party. In particular, credible and very meaningful for the rule-of-law message was the 1770–1779 court case *The King vs. the millers Arnold* (Luebke 1999). The miller operated a water mill as a tenant on the landlord's ground. Obliged to pay tenancy fees to him, this small mill manager declined to pay due to the reduced inflow of water to the mill, caused by the newly built fishpond, authorized by the district council. The case against the miller went to the court. The miller argued that he could not sustain his business. In three instances the miller lost. The mill was forcibly confiscated and acquired by the landlord.

The outraged miller wrote to the King. He ordered an investigation. Appalled by its result he wrote that the judiciary which practices injustice was:

> more dangerous than a band of robbers; for one can protect himself from the latter, but the former are rascals wearing the mantle of justice, to exercise their own evil passions, from

[19]A complimentary statement referring to individual independence came from another German lawyer, Gustav Radbruch (1878–1949), in early 1920s the Minister of Justice in the Weimar Republic (1918–1933). He stated: "We despise the person who preaches in a sense contrary to his conviction, but we respect the judge who does not permit himself to be diverted from his loyalty to the law by his conflicting sense of the right" (quoted after Bjarup 2006, p. 296).

> whom no man can protect himself, and they are the greatest scoundrels in the world, and deserve a double punishment (Dohm 1814, p. 537).

The King demanded the arrest of the chamber judge, but the Grand Chancellor refused. He was relieved of his duties and a new Grand Chancellor appointed. However, he also refused to arrest the recalcitrant judge from the original case. He also was dismissed by the King. He granted the audience to all judges who failed to prosecute cases speedily and who, by perpetrating injustices (*Ungerechtigkeiten*), profaned justice and the equality (*égalité*) of all social classes before the law. After their audience with the King, the district and provincial justices seized by the case were arrested and imprisoned. Finally, the King restored the mill to the Arnolds. He forced the imprisoned judges to compensate the miller and indemnify the widow after him. Although the landlord was spared imprisonment, royal antipathy continued to the end of the King's life. He even refused his request for emergency relief when the landlord's estate was flooded (Luebke 1999).

The King realized that he needed to reform the Prussian justice system. He was aware of corruption of judges, delays in judicial proceedings, irrational and counterproductive medieval penal policy. With this reformist aim in view, in 1779 the King authorized the new Grand Chancellor Samuel von Cocceji, and First Minister of the Justice Department Johann Henrich von Carmer to implement his ideas. In 1780, they delivered the drafts which greatly contributed to the unification and modernization of the Prussian law. Their work laid out the fundamental principles of a reform of the entire system of law.[20]

Second, with reference to traditional and artificial justice, if nowadays predictive justice by a "virtue" of its logical thinking and self-correcting capacity cuts short of the United Nations sense of justice, then this adds to the institutional vulnerability of the independence of judiciary in the world. Especially this is the case in Asian countries where human rights, including the freedom of thought, conscience and religion have traditionally been weakly protected (Neo 2017).

Summing up these two points, and seeking to address the last question, the ensuing common aim is more standardization and modernization of principles of justice across the world. If not fatality but reason moves the universe, the purpose of judicial and social justice reforms may be to bring more unification into dealing with the effects of global climate change and migration. Difficult as this transformative paradigm is, it should be pursued in the spirit of larger freedom. It has a double sense, namely: countering populistic calls for its limitation in the case of the independence of judiciary, and awakening the conscience of humankind to the

[20]In the execution of this order, they the like-minded jurists created the *Corpus Juris Fridericianum*, which replaced the General Land Law for the Prussian States. Carmer not only wrote parts of the *Corpus* himself, but also provided the necessary support for the projects established by the King and for their defence against any entrenched judicial resistance. In 1788, for his achievements in the unification and modernization of Prussian law he was awarded the Black Eagle Order by King Frederick William II. Cocceji's and Carmer's names were included in the inscriptions on the Equestrian statue of Frederick the Great among the founders of the modern Prussian state (Naworski 2016).

inherent rights, civic duties and shared responsibilities involved in the global climate change and migration.

On final reflection: Who deliberately practices injustice robs others of the right to larger freedom. St. Augustine, Montesquieu and Frederick the Great were correct pointing out that justice has been *conditio sine qua non* of progressive humanity—now and in the future.

7 Kudos

Twenty-five centuries ago, the illustrious Chinese thinker Lao Tzu first proposed to look at peace introspectively. The introspection starts in someone's heart, then radiates in home, neighbors, cities, nations, and the world.

An eminent US twentieth-century psychologists Lawrence Kohlberg addressed peace in reverse sequence and different stages. He offered perhaps the most progressive intellectual scheme of the cognitive personal development towards higher-order standards and norms.[21] Kohlberg's standards and norms ranged from the most elementary ("pre-conventional punishment and obedience orientation") for individual development to the most advanced ("post-conventional meta-ethical ontological orientation"). In other words, write Settelmaier and Nigam (2007, p. 22), moral development occurs in stages from wanting to please mum and dad, to being concerned about the relationships within a group, and to fairness at a level of moral maturity that is guided by self-chosen ethical principles. They conclude: "People at this highest level would include Mahatma Gandhi and Dag Hammarskjöld."

Indeed, in 2007, on 2 October, the birthday of Mahatma Gandhi, leader of the Indian independence movement and pioneer of the philosophy and strategy of non-violence, the UN General Assembly in recognition of his vision established the "International Day of Non-Violence" (A/RES/61/271). On 2 October 2019, which marked the 150th anniversary of Gandhi's birth, Guterres stated:

> His vision continues to resonate across the world, including through the work of the United Nations for mutual understanding, equality, sustainable development, the empowerment of young people, and the peaceful resolution of disputes. In today's turbulent times, violence takes many forms: from the destructive impact of the climate emergency to the devastation caused by armed conflict; from the indignities of poverty to the injustice of human rights violations to the brutalizing effects of hate speech (UNSG 2019).

Concerning Hammarskjöld, the second United Nations Secretary-General (1953–1961), he regarded himself as the man with "magnetic field in the soul" unable to express the reality in intellectual terms (Lipsey 2013, pp. 93–94). Understandable therefore was his interest in the work of the World Council of Churches—

[21] His theory was verified and proved workable across Western and Eastern legal cultures (Redo 2016, pp. 482–483).

the interfaith organization whose global assembly in 1954 he addressed with the moving statement "An instrument of faith", quoted fuller by *Walsh*:

> The United Nations stay outside - necessarily outside - all confessions but it is, nevertheless, an instrument of faith. As such it is inspired by what unites, not by what divides the great religions of the world (SG/SM/7520).

Hammarskjöld's critics alleged his mysticism (Melber 2010, pp. 38–39). But Guterres, one of his successors quoted in the Prologue, said: "I firmly believe in the power of faith leaders to shape our world for good", thus shared Settelmeier' and Nigam's admiration of Hammarskjöld's understanding of the UN's role in faith.

In this pantheon of the United Nations remarkable leaders, there also is Nelson Mandela. Guided by self-chosen higher-order ethical principles, he argued: "It is said that no one truly knows a nation until one has been inside its jails. A nation should not be judged by how it treats its highest citizens, but its lowest ones." His moral stance inspired *Kury & Heße* in this book to address the question of "Dealing with mental illness and violence in the (Youth-) Prison", and *Redo & Sawicki* to write "On Nelson Mandela Rule 63, Prisoner's Moral Vulnerability and Development in the Context of the 2030 United Nations Sustainable World."

Finally, we feel that to this UN pantheon also belongs Kofi Annan. He is mentioned in this book in connection with the calls for larger freedom and a common language of justice. In this ecumenical United Nations spirit in 1999 he said, that:

> [T]he Christian calendar no longer belongs exclusively to Christians. People of all faiths have taken to using it simply as a matter of convenience. There is so much interaction between people of different faiths and cultures – different civilizations, if you like – that some shared way of reckoning time is a necessity. And so the Christian Era has become the Common Era (Annan 1999).

In 2000 Annan addressed the Millennium Summit of Religious and Spiritual Leaders. He invoked Hammarskjöld's above quoted words.

Annan was the one most obviously influenced by Hammarskjöld's understanding of moral dimension of the efforts to be made by the United Nations. Unlike allegedly mystical Hammarskjöld he made clear to that summit:

> As the world's religious and spiritual leaders, you embody humanity's deepest yearnings. You have travelled many paths to this time and place. Some of you have been imprisoned for your beliefs. Some have survived the Holocaust, or seen your people targeted for genocide. Still others have lived through other tribulations and indignities. Whatever your past, whatever your calling, and whatever the differences among you, your presence here at the United Nations signifies your commitment to our global mission of tolerance, development and peace. For that, we must all be profoundly grateful (SG/SM/7520).

In 2004, this most outspoken advocate of larger freedom was awarded the Nobel Peace Prize for having revitalized the UN and for having given priority to human rights. As of 2007, in Annan's commemoration the location of the United Nations Office in the Vienna International Center carries his name ("Kofi Annan building"). Since 2018 the annual Kofi Annan Faith Briefings for Member States and UN entities have been the living example of his United Nations creed.

8 *Pro Domo Sua*

The Prologue to this book started with two Churchill's Second World War Winston statements: "The farther backward you can look, the farther in the future you are likely to see"; "Contemplate that if Hitler falls into our hands we shall certainly put him to death [. . .] This man is the mainspring of evil. Instrument – electric chair, for gangsters."

Hitler's-prompted war motivated Churchill's ground-breaking contribution to the Atlantic Charter, and the U.S. President Franklin D. Roosevelt with the idea of creating the United Nations (see *Redo* in "The Relevance. . .", and *Walsh*). Like nobody and nothing else, this highlights that human mind with its intellect and emotions indeed enables great transformative visions which created the United Nations with its own *raison d'être* and normativity. It is now up to the succeeding generations to continue in the United Nations spirit advancing the conscience of humankind, so much outraged by the Second World War.

The pandemic awakens us to *realpolitik* important for effective implementation of SDG 16: "Peace, justice and strong institutions." The re-emerging ominous potential of nationalism may be felt more. Nationalism redefines global terms of peace, justice, security, and trade.

The latter can be corroborated by the 1950–2000 econometric findings (Martin et al. 2008). They suggest that multilateral openness increases the probability of local wars but affects the nature of war and deters global conflicts. In terms of human welfare this is not a small achievement. But it falls dramatically short of the declared goals of the 2030 Agenda and of the UN ideals at large. More optimistic findings concern bilateral wars (between the neighbors): Bilateral trade deters bilateral war because it increases its opportunity cost. Hence the lesson learned: Since the Second World War *doux commerce* has positively impacted neighboring countries, especially in the Western hemisphere.

The European trade integration process is a case in point. It started then to end the frequent and bloody wars between them, and to prevent wars from ever happening again. It works. The European Union is the most profound evidence of successful integration and the most committed advocate of *esprit de liberté.* Closing its borders may spell trouble for the world the Day After. But if so, then the reincarnation of the European Union as if it were the League of Nations is not a good option for the world. The United Nations should be at the moral root of a new world order the Day After with the European Union as a moral entrepreneur. Both are at the forefront of countering climate change.

In 2017, as if precipitating what is coming, Pope Francis spoke about "the winds of war [. . .] blowing in our world and an outdated model of development continues to produce human, societal and environmental decline" (Vatican News 2017).

In 2020, the United Nations Secretary-General wrote on the implementation of the 2030 Agenda: "The COVID-19 pandemic is potentially leading to an increase in social unrest and violence that would greatly undermine our ability to meet the targets of SDG 16" (E/2020, para. 24).

The "sanitary regime" all over the world makes wondering, whether this is a challenge to larger freedom or an opportunity. Is this an "*Aqua Tofana*"[22] or *aqua vita*?

Before answering this question, we recall from the earlier section of the Epilogue U.S. Justice Brandeis' foresighted opinion from 1928. In it he claimed the imminent insidious techniques of behavior control.

Whether or not Brandeis' opinion was known to Aldous Huxley, the author of the famous novel "Brave New World" (1932) was in the early 1960s alerted by "expertise-based governance" (Zakariya 2017, p. 199). By this innocuous term he meant a set of subtle techniques for inducing consensus and allowing people's servitude. Widely credited to him is its comparing to "dictatorship without tears" and "painless concentration camp for entire societies" (Estulin 2015, pp. 92 & 106).

In a contemporary reflection on dictatorship, Harari (2020) writes that "[i]n this time of crisis, we face two particularly important choices. The first is between totalitarian surveillance and citizen empowerment. The second is between nationalist isolation and global solidarity."

In the time of falling across the world democracy and rule-of-law ratings the "sanitary regime" may indeed lead to totalitarian surveillance, disempowerment of civil society, the reignition of nationalism, and crisis of solidarity. Yet rather than yielding to the darkest hour scenario for democracy and the rule of law, i.e., that "[n]ow this is not the end. It is not even the beginning of the end, but it is, perhaps, the end of the beginning" (Churchill 1942) we think that larger freedom advocates stand, both, before an unenviable challenge and an enviable opportunity.

Regarding the import of the challenge, it may be best appreciated by reinterpreting what Elizabeth Fry said to the French King and the British Prime Minister about the inhumane treatment of prisoners. Like her we want to say: When thee builds cyberspace, thee had better build with the thought ever in thy mind that thee and thy children may be occupied by it.

Regarding the import of the opportunity, we want to quote Peter Sloterdijk from his book "You must change your life":

> The history of the own that is grasped on too small a scale and the foreign that is treated too badly reaches an end at the moment when a global co-immunity structure is born, with a respectful inclusion of individual cultures, particular interests and local solidarities. This structure would take on planetary dimensions at the moment when the earth, spanned by networks and built over by foams, was conceived as the own, and the previously dominant exploitative excess as the foreign. With this turn, the concretely universal would become operational (Sloterdijk 2013, p. 545).

A Slovenian philosopher Slavoj Žižek asked, if every culture has its own tolerance limits replied: "There are things impossible to tolerate [. . .]. What would happen if some magazine openly made fun of the Holocaust?" He then added that the European Union needs a dominating culture that regulates, how other cultures function (Leick 2015). The United Nations has the same tolerance limit, but—by

[22]See in this book *Pływaczewski et al.* "From wonders. . . ."

far—is less effective than the European Union. Thus, for the UN people and peoples only the 2030 Agenda may strongly motivate them to look into the future of larger freedom and justice as per its manifold incarnations, some of which are still to emerge on the Day After.

Recent scientific evidence on the Internet dynamics of the anti-vaccination movement suggests that the populistic interactions defy knowledge and opt for common sense. They demobilize reactions of civil society, but not of its regressive faction (Jałochowski 2020). This makes less viable the transmission of knowledge situationally. The more it may so happen intergenerationally (parents to offspring).

It would have been nowadays still unbelievable to contend Aristotle's thesis that not even educators or historians but only poets can convey to the succeeding generations the universal moral values of the time they live in (Aristotle 2001, Poetics ch. 7.9), had since his time the concept of civil society not evolved to become autonomous from a State. Other scientific evidence on the impact of Internet on common sense and knowledge helpfully documents that moving ahead with progressive educational ideas for social change is possible when a 10% threshold of like-minded reformers act in concert with one another (Redo 2017, p. 733).

The civil society across the world and the UN as its patron should make the implementation of the UDHR rights harmonious, progressive, and accountable in the time of global transformation programed by the 2030 Agenda. As emphasized by the UN Secretary-General, this is an opportunity (UNSG 2020f). This should be the time of the Renaissance of the United Nations, i.e., after the darkest hour, on the Day After.

The goals of the 2030 Agenda are the most viable way to make the UNDHR rights more effective. Civil society should better orchestrate and advance its demands for peace and justice. The UN justice as "an ideal of accountability and fairness in the protection and vindication of rights and the prevention and punishment of wrongs" should be vigorously pursued.

Madison very perversely and provocatively but perceptively and dramatically concluded: "[j]ustice is the end of government. It is the end of civil society. It ever has been and ever will be pursued until it be obtained, or until liberty be lost in the pursuit" (Federalist 1961/51). Montesquieu said: "We receive three different or contrary educations; namely, of our parents, of our masters, and of the world" (Montesquieu 2001, SL IV, 3).

As for the natural world, Guterres was very candid: "Nature is angry. And we fool ourselves if we think we can fool nature. Because nature always strikes back. And around the world, nature is striking back with fury" (UNSG 2019).

Nature does not forgive. Pandemic, even if fortuitous, is an illustration how the course of history can be changed not by individual will, or by political acts and ideologies, but by environmental forces (Arnold 1996, p. 67).

The United Nations is not a world government. Yet global governance is at the core of transformation. Climate change and the pandemic document that the UN made up of an exceptionally large number of countries should be the Organization capable of global governance to a greater extent than nowadays. Good governance is about rising above the constraints imposed by calamities. Without the UN, the world would have already ended with the Third World War with national governments in pieces. Does the world still remember the twentieth century legacy well?

We pay for the consequences of our own persistent neglect. At one time it is guised as "time-honored" cultural custom, at another time as evidently clear ignorance of other rules of human interaction and with Mother Earth. Rather than continuing to misinterpret them in egoistic manner dressed in populistic terms we must seriously answer the question, if the succeeding generations should pay for all the toxic effects—natural and ideological—produced in the second decade of the twenty-first century?

9 Conclusion

The 75-year old United Nations is the grandmaster and grandparent of social progress and justice in the world. It is the promoter of global civic education with credible moral reasoning that prevents foolishness and populism. The Organization fully deserves praise for its past-1945 accomplishment and the unwavering efforts to maintain and contribute to peace, justice, and strong institutions. Given that climate change—globally, the most pronounced challenge—requires them to be more perceptive, responsive, and forthcoming, their strengthening should not be limited to enhancing and enforcing a sanitary regime. In high demand is individual intellectual ferment and creativity, energy that transforms institutions and the world.

The United Nations deserves wishes to meet a higher than now benchmark. In spite the UN's interfaith vision and "prophetic" statements, it neither has any metaphysical nature nor institutional power to make the 2030 Agenda a global success. Endemic as now is, it should become a strong institution in the next decades of the digital age anywhere people need it, but particularly in any impoverished place under the sun. There where domestic rule of law demonstrates its impotency to promote larger freedom and leaves people behind—in material poverty, poverty of spirit and thought, thus helpless about peace and justice and deprived of humanistic ideals of the United Nations.

The strength of global civilization will be demonstrated by a few people it can protect and let them enjoy life in larger freedom and dignity. For the succeeding generations, the United Nations should be like a theme park which with its democratic road map and drive may lead the way for their decent future in harmony with nature.

Vienna, Austria Sławomir Redo
Heuweiler, Germany Helmut Kury

24 October 2020, United Nations Day

References[23]

A/217 III Universal Declaration of Human Rights (UDHR), 10 December 1948.

A/59/2005/Add.3 In larger freedom: towards development, security and human rights for all. Report of the Secretary-General. 26 May 2005.

A/HRC/23/40 Report of the Special Rapporteur on the promotion and protection of the right to freedom of opinion and expression, Frank La Rue. 17 April 2013.

A/HRC/27/37 The right to privacy in the digital age. Report of the Office of the United Nations High Commissioner for Human Rights. 30 June 2014.

A/HRC/41/35 Surveillance and human rights. Report of the Special Rapporteur on the promotion and protection of the right to freedom of opinion and expression, 28 May 2019.

A/RES/68/167 The right to privacy in the digital age. 18 December 2013.

A/RES/68/191 Taking action against gender-related killing of women and girls. 18 December 2013.

A/RES/70/1 Transforming our world: the 2030 Agenda for sustainable development. 25 September 2015.

A/RES/70/174 Doha declaration on integrating crime prevention and criminal justice into the wider United Nations agenda to address social and economic challenges and to promote the rule of law at the national and international levels, and public participation. 17 December 2015.

A/RES/70/175 The United Nations Standard Minimum Rules for the Treatment of Prisoners (the Nelson Mandela Rules). 17 December 2015.

A/RES/71/199 The right to privacy in the digital age. 19 December 2016.

Ackerman, B. (2010). Goodbye Montesquieu. In S. Rose-Ackerman & P. Lindseth (Eds.), *Comparative administrative law* (pp. 38–43). Cheltenham, UK: Edward Elgar.

Annan, K. (1999). *Common values for a common era: Even as we cherish our diversity, we need to discover our shared values*. Civilization: The Magazine of the Library of Congress. https://bit.ly/2zTEWHb

Annan, K. (2005). "In larger freedom": Decision time at the UN. *Foreign Affairs, 84*(3), 63–74.

Aristotle. (2001). Poetics. In R. McKeon (Ed.), *The basic works of Aristotle. Introduction by C. D.C. Reeve* (pp. 1454–1148). New York: The Modern Library.

Arnold, D. (1996). *The problem of nature. Environment, culture and European expansion. New perspectives on the past*. Oxford: Blackwell Publishers Ltd..

Barkan, S. E. (2000). Household crowding and aggregate crime rates. *Journal of Crime and Justice, 23*(1), 47–64. https://doi.org/10.1080/0735648X.2000.9721109

BBC/British Broadcasting Corporation. (2020). *EU to give migrants in Greece €2,000 to go home*. https://bbc.in/3cYrmB9

BEC/Basic Education Coalition. (2018). *Recommendations on Global Basic Education Policy and Programming*. https://bit.ly/3chRCX5

Bell, B. (2020). *Coronavirus: Ischgl resort at heart of Europe's outbreak reopens*. https://bbc.in/2XAMV44

Bentzen, H. B., & Svantensson, D. J. B. (2017). Jurisdictional challenges related to DNA processing in transnational clouds. In D. J. B. Svantesson & D. Kloza (Eds.), *Trans-atlantic data privacy relations as a challenge for democracy* (pp. 241–260). Cambridge-Antwerp-Portland: Intesentia.

Bjarup, J. (2006). Continental perspectives on natural law theory and legal positivism. In M. P. Golding & W. A. Edmundson (Eds.), *The Blackwell guide to the philosophy of law and legal theory* (pp. 287–299). Oxford: The Blackwell Publishing.

Borejsza, J. W., Ziemer, K., & Hułas, M. (Eds.). (2006). *Totalitarian and authoritarian regimes in Europe: Legacies and lessons from the twentieth century*. New York-Oxford: Berghahn Books.

[23]All United Nations parliamentary documentation retrieved on May 1, 2020 from the United Nations website http://www.un.org; mass media accounts retrieved on May 15, 2020.

Borges, A. (2020). *Unrest, hunger and hardship in France's locked-down suburbs*. https://bit.ly/3bQkGUM
Cannon, C. (2017). Modes of knowledge mobilization by/for international bureaucracies throughout international policy processes. In A. Littoz-Monnet (Ed.), *The politics of expertise in international organizations. How international bureaucracies produce and mobilize knowledge*. London-New York: Routledge, ch. 8.
Cao, F., Zhang, J., Miao, D., & Peng, J. (2017). Framing effect in the trolley problem and footbridge dilemma: Number of saved lives matters. *Psychological Reports, 120*(1), 88–101. https://doi.org/10.1177/0033294116685866
Cardullo, B. (Ed.). (2006). *Federico Fellini. Interviews*. Jackson: University of Mississippi Press.
Chander, A., & Land, M. (2014). Introductory note to United Nations General Assembly Resolution on the right to privacy in the digital age. *International Legal Materials, 53*(4), 727–731.
Chatterton, T. J., & Newmarch, G. (2017). The future is already here: It's just not very evenly distributed. *Interactions, 24*, 42–45.
Churchill, W. (1942). *The end of the beginning*. The Lord Mayor's Luncheon, Mansion House November 10, 1942. https://bit.ly/3dtzXv8
Clark, M. T. (2015). Augustine on justice. In T. Delgado, J. Doody, & K. Paffenroth (Eds.), *Augustine and social justice* (pp. 3–10). Lanham: Lexington, 2015 [This article originally appeared in 1963 in *Revue des Etudes Augustiniennes 9*, 87–94].
Contini, F. (2019). *Artificial intelligence: A new Trojan horse for undue influence on judiciaries?* https://bit.ly/2VxP3Kj
Council of Europe. (2018). European Commission for the Efficiency of Justice (CEPEJ) European Ethical Charter on the Use of Artificial Intelligence in Judicial Systems and their Environment. Strasbourg.
Crosby, A. W. (1969). The early history of syphilis: A reappraisal the early history of syphilis: A reappraisal. *The American Anthropologist, 71*(2), 218–277. https://doi.org/10.1525/aa.1969.71.2.02a00020
Culture. (2020). *Culture in the implementation of the 2030 agenda: A report by The culture 2030 goal campaign*. https://bit.ly/2IeulYi
Czarnowski, S. (1936/2016). Redundant people in the service of violence. *Acta Poloniae Historica, 11*(4), 297–306.
Dohm, C. W. (1814). *Denkwürdigkeiten meiner Zeit* (Vol. 1). Lemgo: Hannover.
Dostoevsky, F. (1880/2002). The grand inquisitor. In *The Brothers Karamazov. Translated from the Russian by R. Pevear and L. Volokhonsky* (pp. 246–264). New York: Farrar, Strauss and Giroux.
Dukaj, J. (2020). *Tak wymienia się rdzeń duszy*. https://bit.ly/3dGFxKX
E/2020. Progress towards the Sustainable Development Goals. Report of the Secretary-General Economic and Social Council. United Nations: New York. https://bit.ly/3bN8007
Economist. (2020). *Democracies contain epidemics most effectively*. https://econ.st/3f2vccR
Estulin, D. (2015). *Tavistock Institute: Social engineering for the masses*. Chicago: Undependent Publishers Group.
Fairhurst, J. (1996). *The angel of prisons*. Ireland's Own 4539, 5.
FAO/Food and Agriculture Organization. (2020). Director-General Statement to the UN Security Council. Briefing on Conflict and Hunger. https://bit.ly/35oxvTZ
Feldstein, S. (2019). *The global expansion of AI surveillance*. Working paper. Washington, D.C.: Carnegie Endowment Foundation for International Peace.
Freedom House. (2020) *Spotlight on freedom: Impact of coronavirus on basic freedoms*. https://bit.ly/2XJi86m
Gao, G., & Ting-Toomey, S. (1998). *Communicating effectively in multicultural context; Vol. 5. Communicating effectively with the Chinese*. Thousand Oaks, CA: Sage Publications, Inc..
Gomes, R. (2020). Pope: Church's social teaching can help AI serve the common good. *Vatican News*. https://bit.ly/3aeLInA

GPMB/Global Preparedness Monitoring Board. (2019). *A world at risk. Annual report on global preparedness for health emergencies*. Geneva: World Health Organization.

Gray, J. (2020). Why this crisis is a turning point in history. *New Statesman*. https://bit.ly/2S35LPn

Harari, Y. N. (2018). *21 lessons for the 21st century*. London: Penguin.

Harari, Y. N. (2020). *The World after Coronavirus*. https://on.ft.com/2WS0yvu

HGS/Handbook on Governance Statistics. (2020). *The Praia City Group*. https://bit.ly/3cn2wuy

Hollander-Blumoff, R., & Tyler, T. R. (2011). Procedural justice and the rule of law: Fostering legitimacy in alternative dispute resolution. *Journal of Dispute Resolution, 11*(1), 1–19.

HRC Communication No. 499/1992 *Toonan v. Australia*. https://bit.ly/2VMrTPc

Hubbard, E. (1897). *Little journeys to the homes of famous women*. New York: G. P. Putnam's Sons.

Hume, D. (1739/1896). *A treatise of human nature—reprinted from the original edition in three volumes and edited, with an analytical index, by L.A. Selby-Bigge, M.A*. Oxford: Clarendon Press.

Ickiewicz-Sawicka, M., & Borkowska, A. (2018). Migration in the light of criminology and psychology: "Win-Win" in theory and practice A. In H. Kury & S. Redo (Eds.), *Refugees and migrants in law and policy* (pp. 803–834). Cham: Springer.

Inglehart, R., Foa, R., Peterson, C., & Welzel, C. (2008). Development, freedom, and rising happiness. A global perspective (1981–2007). *Perspectives in Psychological Science, 3*(4), 264–285.

International Covenant on Civil and Political Rights/ICCPR, 999 UNTS 171.

Interpol. (2020). *Unmasked: International COVID-19 fraud exposed*. https://bit.ly/2Be8EHz

IOM/Institute of Medicine. (2009). *Sustaining global surveillance and response to emerging zoonotic diseases*. Washington, D. C.: The National Academic Press. https://doi.org/10.17226/12625

Jałochowski, K. (2020). Stan niedorzeczności. *Polityka* weekly. https://bit.ly/2N7eYU5

Kahn, V. (2013). *The future of illusion*. Chicago: University of Chicago Press.

Keane, J. (2018). *Power and humility. The future of monitory democracy*. Cambridge: Cambridge University Press.

Kevles, D. J. (1999). Eugenics and human rights. *BMJ, 319*(7207), 435–438. https://doi.org/10.1136/bmj.319.7207.435

Kucharski, A. (2020). *The rules of contagion. Why things spread and why they stop*. London: Profile Books Ltd.

Kury, H., & Redo, S. (2018). Prologue. In H. Kury & S. Redo (Eds.), *Refugees and migrants in law and policy. Challenges and opportunities for global civic education* (pp. i–xxxvii). Cham: Springer.

Lee, W. (2020). Post-lockdown life in Wuhan is a warning to the world. *The Weired*. https://bit.ly/2x51unj

Leick, R. (2015). Interview with Slavoj Zizek. 'The Greatest Threat to Europe Is Its Inertia', *Der Spiegel*. https://bit.ly/3bzmbqz

Lin, Y. (1935). *My country and my people*. London-Toronto: William Heinemann Ltd.

Lipsey, R. (2013). *Hammarskjöld. A life*. Ann Arbor: The University of Michigan Press.

Luebke, D. M. (1999). Frederick the great and the celebrated case of the Millers Arnold (1770–1779): a reappraisal. *Central European History, 32*(4), 379–408.

Machiavelli, N. (2005). *The Prince. Transl. and ed. by Peter Bondanella with the introduction by M. Viroli*. Oxford: Oxford University Press.

Martin, P., Mayer, T., & Thoening, M. (2008). Make trade not war? *Review of Economic Studies, 75*, 865–900.

McGuiness, M. E. (2011). Peace v. Justice; The Universal Declaration of Human Rights and the modern origins of the debate. *Diplomatic History, 35*(5), 749–768.

Melber, H. (2010). Dag Hammarskjöld's zeitgemäße Betrachtungen – Reflections on Inge Lønning's Dag Hammarskjöld Lecture. In H. Melber (Ed.), *The ethics of Dag Hammarskjőld* (pp. 38–46). Uppsala: Graf Tryckeri AB.

Mencius. (2003). *Translated with introduction and notes by D. C. Lau*. London: Penguin Books.
Montesquieu, Ch. (2001). *The spirit of laws*, transl. by T. Nugent. Kitchener, ON: Batoche Books.
Morsink, J. (1993). World War Two and the Universal Declaration. *Human Rights Quarterly, 15* (2), 357–405.
Nogaś, M. (2020). Będzie recesja, a potem faszyzm. Coś o tym wiem, bo napisałem powieść o Mussolinim. Gazeta Wyborcza, from https://bit.ly/2Xu9OpH
Naworski, Z. (2016). Obraz urzędnika w przepisach Landrechtu pruskiego z 1794 r. *Studia Iuridica Lublinensia, XXV*(3), 710–731. https://doi.org/10.17951/sil.2016.25.3.709
Nembrini, P. G. (2013). *Water, sanitation, hygiene and habitat in prisons*. Geneva: International Committee of the Red Cross.
Neo, J. L. (2017). Realizing the right to freedom of thought, conscience and religion: The limited normative force of the ASEAN Human Rights Declaration. *Human Rights Law Review, 17*(4), 729–751.
Neumann, S. (1949). The structure and strategy of revolution: 1848 and 1948. *The Journal of Politics, 11*(3), 532–544.
Nyst, C., & Falchetta, T. (2017). The right to privacy in the digital age. *Journal of Human Rights Practice, 9*, 104–118.
O'Doherty, K. C., Christofides, E., Yen, J., Bentzen, H. B., Burke, W., Hallowell et al. (2016). If you build it, they will come: Unintended future uses of organised health data collections. *BMC Medical Ethics, 17*(54). https://doi.org/10.1186/s12910-016-0137-x
OHCHR. (2020). *COVID-19: States should not abuse emergency measures to suppress human rights – UN experts*. https://bit.ly/34NbhuI
Ottuh, P. O. O., Ottuh, J. A., & Aitufe, V. O. (2014). Distributive justice and inclusive society: Role of religion in the equitable distribution of wealth. *European Scientific Journal, 10*(23), 196–213.
Palfrey, J., & Gasser, U. (2009). *Born digital*. New York: Basic Books.
Penal Reform International. (2020). *Coronavirus: Healthcare and human rights of people in prison*. London.
Pływaczewski, E., & Redo, S. (Eds.). (2018). Advancing culture of lawfulness: Towards the achievement of the 2030 Agenda, *Białostockie Studia Prawnicze 23*(3).
Quote Investigator. (n.d.). *The future has arrived — It's just not evenly distributed yet*. https://bit.ly/2wNE1H0
Rahe, P. A. (n.d.). *Montesquieu, natural law, and natural right*. Natural law, natural rights, and American constitutionalism. http://www.nlnrac.org
Redo, S. (2012). *Blue Criminology. The Power of United Nations Ideas to Counter Crime Globally*. Helsinki: European Institute for Crime Prevention and Control, affiliated with the United Nations.
Redo, S. (2016). Anti-corruption education as a form of early prevention of conflict with the law for women and children: Making the United Nations law work 2016–2030. In H. Kury, S. Redo, & E. Shea (Eds.), *Women and children as victims and offenders: Background, prevention, reintegration* (Vol. 1, pp. 477–498). Springer International Publishing.
Redo, S. (2017). New instruments and approaches for countering social exclusion: A criminological contribution to the United Nations post-2015 educational agenda. In E. W. Plywaczewski & E. M. Guzik-Makaruk (Eds.), *Current Problems of the Penal Law and Criminology* (pp. 723–737). Białystok: Temida 2.
Redo, S. (2018a). Criminological reflections on the Golden Rule and urban stewardship for safety. *Eastern European Journal of Transnational Relations, 2*(1), 53–70. https://doi.org/10.15290/eejtr.2018.02.01.04
Redo, S. (2018b). United Nations earth jurisprudence, its golden rule, the "refugee problem," and urban safety. In H. Kury & S. Redo (Eds.), *Refugees and migrants in law and policy. Challenges opportunities for global civic education*. Cham: Springer.
Roberton, T., Carter, E. D., Chou, V. B., Stegmuller, A. R., Jackson, B. D., Tam, Y., et al. (2020). Early estimates of the indirect effects of the COVID-19 pandemic on maternal and child

mortality in low-income and middle-income countries: a modelling study. *Lancet Global Health*, May 12, 2020. doi.org/10.1016/.
Robinson, P. H. (2013). Natural law & lawlessness: Modern lessons from Pirates, Lepers, Eskimos, and Survivors. *University of Illinois Law Review, 389*, 433–506.
Rowland, C. (2007). *The Cambridge companion to liberation theology* (2nd ed.). Cambridge: Cambridge University Press.
S/2004/616 The rule of law and transitional justice in conflict and post-conflict societies. Report of the Secretary-General, 23 August 2004.
Schmitt, C. (2007). *Theory of the Partisan: Intermediate commentary on the concept of the political*. Candor, NY: Telos Press Publishing.
Settelmaier, E., & Nigam, M. (2007). Where did you get your values and beliefs? In G. Hawley (Ed.), *Ethics in clinical practice: An inter-professional approach* (pp. 15–34). Abington, Oxon-New York: Routledge.
SG/SM/7520. Secretary-General, addressing millennium summit of religious, spiritual leaders, urges participants to set example of interfaith cooperation, from https://bit.ly/3d3vGyn
Simma, B. (Ed.), Paulus, A., & Chaitobu, E. (Ass. Eds.) in collaboration with H. Mosler, A. Radelzhofer, Ch. Tomuschat & R. Wolfrum (2002). *The Charter of the United Nations A Commentary*. Oxford: Oxford University Press.
Slattery, G., & Gaier, R. V. (2020). *A Brazilian woman caught coronavirus on vacation*. Her maid is now dead, from https://reut.rs/34NobZp
Sloterdijk, P. (2013). *You must change your life*. Transl. by W. Hoban. Cambridge: Polity Press.
St. Augustine. (1972). *Concerning the city of god against the Pagans* (H. Bettenson, Tr.). London: Penguin.
Stevenson, B., & Wolfers, J. (2008). Economic growth and subjective well-being: Reassessing the Easterlin paradox. *Brookings Papers on Economic Activity, 1*, 1–87. https://doi.org/10.1353/eca.0.0001
The Federalist Papers. (1961), vols. 51 & 63. In A. Hamilton, J. Madison, J. Jay, & C. Rossiter (Eds.). New York: Signet.
Tversky, A., & Kahneman, D. (1981). The framing of decisions and the psychology of choice. *Science, 211*(4481), 453–458. https://doi.org/10.1126/science.7455683
UN Charter, 1 UNTS XVI.
UN Doc. 1006. (1945). Verbatim minutes of first meeting of Commission I, June 15, 1945, pp. 1–23. In Documents of the United Nations Conference on International Organization, San Francisco, Vol. III. London-New York: United Nations Information Organization.
UN News. (2020). As famines of 'biblical proportion' loom, Security Council urged to 'act fast', from https://bit.ly/3f7nRte
UNICEF. (2020). As COVID-19 devastates already fragile health systems, over 6,000 additional children under five could die a day, without urgent action, from https://uni.cf/2YYe9np
UNODC. (2007). *Commentary on The Bangalore Principles of Judicial Conduct*. Vienna: United Nations.
UNODC. (2013). *Handbook on strategies to reduce overcrowding in prisons*. New York: United Nations.
UNODC. (2018). Modern judicial challenges, such as gender and AI, at the heart of debates in Seoul. https://bit.ly/3896a86
UNODC. (2019). *Global Study on Homicide 2019: Homicide trends, patterns and criminal justice response*. New York: United Nations. https://bit.ly/34HeqMu
UNSG. (2019). Nature Striking Back with Fury, Secretary-General Tells Climate Action Summit, Calling 'Apocalyptic' Bahamas Destruction 'the Future — if We Do Not Act Now'. https://bit.ly/2VV73Nk
UNSG. (2020a). UN chief calls for domestic violence 'ceasefire' amid 'horrifying global surge'. https://bit.ly/3biTNIO
UNSG. (2020b). COVID-19: UN chief calls for global ceasefire to focus on 'the true fight of our lives'. https://bit.ly/2RKnfjo

UNSG. (2020c). Secretary-General's remarks to the Security Council on the COVID-19 pandemic. https://bit.ly/2zflDru
UNSG. (2020d). UN chief outlines solutions to defeat 'four horsemen' threatening our global future. https://bit.ly/2VV73Nk
UNSG. (2020e). We have a unique opportunity to design and implement more inclusive and accessible societies. https://bit.ly/2WBFHMP
UNSG. (2020f). Opening remarks at virtual press encounter to launch the Report on the Socio-Economic Impacts of COVID-19. https://bit.ly/2YX616z
UNSG. (2020g). COVID-19: Act now or risk 'unimaginable devastation' globally, warns UN chief. https://bit.ly/2Xfb1m3
Vatican News. (2017). "Urbi et Orbi" Christmas Message and Blessing of Pope Francis. https://bit.ly/2zWkncV
Wodecka, D. (2020). Andrzej Stasiuk: Od rana patrzę na pejzaż, na ptaki, schodzę na dół do domu, gadam z rodziną. Staram się zachować spokój, from https://bit.ly/2WmkZQV
Xie, E. (2020). Coronavirus: Wuhan confirms China's ban on trade, eating of wild animals. https://bit.ly/3ea683m.
Zakariya, N. (2017). *A final story: science, myth, and beginnings*. Chicago-London: Chicago University Press.

Sławomir Redo Dr. hab. (Law/Criminology) is a Visiting Professor of United Nations Law. He is a member of the United Nations Studies Association. Former United Nations Senior Crime Prevention and Criminal Justice Expert and staff of the UN Office on Drugs and Crime (ret.). He had been involved in numerous projects implementing the UN standards and norms in crime prevention and criminal justice. In other capacities, he assisted in the implementation of the United Nations Convention against Transnational Organized Crime, and on-line international crime prevention and criminal justice education. He published four books, co-edited four others, including *Women and Children as Victims and Offenders: Background, Prevention, Reintegration. Suggestions for Succeeding Generations* (Springer 2016), and *Refugees and Migrants in Law and Policy – Challenges and Opportunities for Global Civic Education* (Springer 2018) plus about 80 articles—mostly on the UN law and practice of crime prevention and criminal justice. University course lecturer on "The United Nations and Crime Prevention" & "The United Nations and War Crime Prevention" (Austria, China, Poland); Promoter of crime prevention & criminal justice training and education for meeting the goals of the 2030 UN Sustainable Development Agenda. Co-editor of the first criminological UN Agenda-based textbook *KRYMINOLOGIA. Stan i perspektywy rozwoju z uwzględnieniem założeń Agendy ONZ na rzecz zrównoważonego rozwoju 2030* (Wolters Kluwer, Warsaw 2020). E-mail: s@redo.net.

Helmut Kury Prof. h.c. mult., Dr., Dipl.-Psych., studied Psychology at the University of Freiburg (Freiburg im Brsg., Germany), diploma, Dr. in Psychology and Habilitation at the University of Freiburg. Between 1970 and 1973, he was an assistant teacher at the University of Freiburg, Institute for Psychology, between 1973 and 1980 and from 1989 to 2006, senior researcher at the Max-Planck-Institute for Foreign and International Penal Law in Freiburg im Brsg., Department of Criminology; 1980–1988 first and founding director of the Criminological Research Institute of Lower Saxony – KFN. His research areas include offender rehabilitation, crime prevention, attitudes to punishment, fear of crime, punitiveness, alternatives to punishment, diversion, methodological problems of empirical social science research, international comparison of crime and punishment. He cooperated with many universities and research institutes internationally, especially with countries of the former Soviet Union. His most recent publications in English are: Kury, H., Ferdinand, T.N. (Eds.) (2008). *International Perspectives on Punitivity*. Bochum: Universitätsverlag Dr. Brockmeyer; Kury, H. (Ed.) (2008). *Fear of Crime – Punitivity. New Developments in Theory and Research*. Bochum: Universitätsverlag Dr. Brockmeyer; Kury, H., Shea, E. (Eds.) (2011). *Punitivity – International Developments*. 3 Vols., Bochum:

Universitätsverlag Dr. Brockmeyer; Kury, H., Redo, S., Shea, E. (Eds.) (2016). *Women and Children as Victims and Offenders: Background, Prevention, Reintegration. Suggestions for Succeeding Generations.* 2 Vols., International Publishing Switzerland: Springer; Kury, H., Kuhlmann, A. (2016). *Mediation in Germany and Other Western Countries.* Kriminolgijos Studijos 4, 2016, 5–46; Kury, H. (2017). *Harsh Punishment or Alternatives: Which Is the Better Crime Prevention.* Juricia international, University of Tartu, 15, 91–99; Kury, H., Glonti, G. (2017). *Migration in Germany and Georgia (Comparative Analyses).* Davit Aghmashnenebeli University of Georgia Academic Journal 1, 6–13; Kury, H. (2018). *Rehabilitation in Prison. German Experiences and What Can Be Done Better.* Rom. Journ. Of Sociological Studies, New Series, Bucharest, No. 1, 19–36; Kury, H. (2018). *Integration of Refugees in Germany – Has the Criminal Burden Increased. Criminology: Yesterday, Today, Tomorrow - The Journal of St. Petersburg International Criminology Club* 1, 48, 37–45; Kury, H., Redo, S. (Eds.) (2018). *Refugees and Migrants in Law and Policy. Challenges and Opportunities for Global Civic Education.* International Publishing Switzerland: Springer; Kuhlmann, A., Kury, H. (2018). *Some Considerations of Restorative Justice Before and Outside of Contemporary Western States.* Kriminologijos studijos – Criminological Studies, Vilniaus Universitetas, 5, 5–42; Kury, H. (2019). *Refugees: Post Traumatic Stress, and Crime – Experiences from Germany.* Kultura i Edukacja – Culture and Education 124, 73–90; Kury, H., Kuhlmann, A., Quintas, J. (2019). *On the Preventative Effect of Sanctions for Drug Crime: The United States, Germany and Portugal.* Archiwum Kryminologii, Polska Akademia Nauk, Instytut Nauk Prawnych, 41, 261–295. E-mail: helmut.kury@web.de.

Index

H. Kury, S. Redo (eds.), *Crime Prevention and Justice in 2030*,
https://doi.org/10.1007/978-3-030-56227-4

B

C

D

Q

R

T

The manufacturer's authorised representative in the EU is Springer Nature Customer Service Centre GmbH, Europaplatz 3, 69115 Heidelberg, Germany. If you have any concerns regarding our products, please contact ProductSafety@springernature.com

Printed and bound by CPI Group (UK) Ltd, Croydon, CR0 4YY
28/09/2026
02224062-0011